Get started with your **Connected Casebook**

Redeem your code below to access the **e-book** with search, highlighting, and note-taking capabilities; a **study center** complete with practice questions, explanations, and videos; **case briefing** and **outlining** tools to support efficient learning; and more.

1. Go to www.casebookconnect.com
2. Enter your access code in the box and click **Register**
3. Follow the steps to complete your registration and verify your email address

If you have already registered at CasebookConnect.com, simply log into your account and redeem additional access codes from your Dashboard.

ACCESS CODE:
Scratch off with care.

STXT43828191657

Is this a used casebook? Access code already redeemed? Purchase a digital version at **CasebookConnect.com/catalog**.

If you purchased a digital bundle with additional components, your additional access codes will appear below.

"I liked being able to search quickly while in class."

"Being able to highlight and easily create case briefs was a fantastic resource and time saver for me!"

"I loved the practice exercises and study questions; they really helped me learn the material!"

For technical support, please visit http://support.wklegaledu.com.

10052186-0002

THE REGULATORY STATE

ASPEN CASEBOOK SERIES

THE REGULATORY STATE

Third Edition

Lisa Schultz Bressman
David Daniels Allen Distinguished Chair in Law
Vanderbilt University Law School

Edward L. Rubin
University Professor of Law and Political Science
Vanderbilt University Law School

Kevin M. Stack
Lee S. and Charles A. Speir Chair in Law
Director of Graduate Studies
Professor of Law
Vanderbilt University Law School

 Wolters Kluwer

Published by Wolters Kluwer in New York.

Wolters Kluwer Legal & Regulatory U.S. serves customers worldwide with CCH, Aspen Publishers, and Kluwer Law International products. (www.WKLegaledu.com)

To contact Customer Service, e-mail customer.service@wolterskluwer.com,
call 1-800-234-1660, fax 1-800-901-9075, or mail correspondence to:

Wolters Kluwer
Attn: Order Department
PO Box 990
Frederick, MD 21705

Printed in the United States of America.

1 2 3 4 5 6 7 8 9 0

ISBN: 978-1-4548-7879-7

Library of Congress Cataloging-in-Publication Data

Names: Bressman, Lisa Schultz, author. | Rubin, Edward L., 1948- author. |
    Stack, Kevin M., author.
Title: The regulatory state / Lisa Schultz Bressman, David Daniels Allen
    Distinguished Chair in Law, Vanderbilt University Law School; Edward L. Rubin,
    University Professor of Law and Political Science, Vanderbilt
    University Law School; Kevin M. Stack, Lee S. and Charles A. Speir Chair
    in Law, Vanderbilt University Law School.
Description: Third edition. | New York : Wolters Kluwer, 2020. | Series:
    Aspen casebook series | Includes bibliographical references and index. |
    Summary: "Law school text in the regulatory state course for upper-year
    law school students"—Provided by publisher.
Identifiers: LCCN 2019027593 (print) | LCCN 2019027594 (ebook) | ISBN
    9781454878797 (hardcover) | ISBN 9781543815979 (ebook)
Subjects: LCSH: Administrative agencies—United States. | LCGFT: Casebooks
    (Law)
Classification: LCC KF5407 .B74 2020 (print) | LCC KF5407 (ebook) | DDC
    342.73/064—dc23
LC record available at https://lccn.loc.gov/2019027593
LC ebook record available at https://lccn.loc.gov/2019027594

About Wolters Kluwer Legal & Regulatory U.S.

Wolters Kluwer Legal & Regulatory U.S. delivers expert content and solutions in the areas of law, corporate compliance, health compliance, reimbursement, and legal education. Its practical solutions help customers successfully navigate the demands of a changing environment to drive their daily activities, enhance decision quality and inspire confident outcomes.

Serving customers worldwide, its legal and regulatory portfolio includes products under the Aspen Publishers, CCH Incorporated, Kluwer Law International, ftwilliam.com and MediRegs names. They are regarded as exceptional and trusted resources for general legal and practice-specific knowledge, compliance and risk management, dynamic workflow solutions, and expert commentary.

For my husband, Michael, and my children,
Zachary, Jacob, and Zoe

L.S.B.

For my parents, Sabina and George

E.L.R.

For my children, Isabel, Sarah, and Henry

K.M.S.

Summary of Contents

Preface   *xxiii*
Acknowledgments   *xxvii*

Chapter 1   From Common Law to Regulation   1
Chapter 2   Legislation   45
Chapter 3   Statutory Interpretation by Courts   145
Chapter 4   Policy Making by Rule: A Case Study   359
Chapter 5   Statutory Implementation by Agencies   435
Chapter 6   Control of Agency Action   645

Appendix A   Selected Provisions of the Constitution of the
              United States of America   949
Appendix B   Selected Provisions of the Administrative
              Procedure Act   971
Appendix C   Presidential Administrations and Secretaries
              of Department of Transportation, 1967-87   995

Table of Cases   *999*
Index   *1003*

Contents

Preface   *xxiii*
Acknowledgments   *xxvii*

Chapter 1
From Common Law to Regulation   1

A. The Limitations of Tort Law   **3**
      MacPherson v. Buick Motor Co.   6
      Notes and Questions   9
      Rotche v. Buick Motor Co.   10
      Notes and Questions   13
      The Law and Economics Perspective   15
      Ford Motor Co., Fatalities Associated with Crash
          Induced Fuel Leakage and Fires   17
      Grimshaw v. Ford Motor Co.   18
      Notes and Questions   23
      Note on the Limitations of Common Law Adjudication
          More Generally   24
B. The Limitations of Contract Law   **27**
      Notes and Questions   28
C. The Justifications for Regulation   **30**
    1. Economic Justifications for Regulation   31
      OMB, Circular A-4, To the Heads of Executive Agencies
          and Establishments, Subject: Regulatory Analysis   31
      Notes and Questions   33
    2. Social Justifications for Regulation   35
      Cass Sunstein, After the Rights Revolution: Reconceiving
          the Regulatory State   35
      Notes and Questions   38
      From Justification to Legislation: A Note on the Role of
          Politics   39
D. What is an Agency?   **40**
    1. Agencies in General   41

Chapter 2
Legislation   45

A. The Legislative Process   **45**
    1. A General Description   46
      Nelson Polsby, Congress and the Presidency   46
      Abbe R. Gluck, Anne J. O'Connell, and Rosa Po,
          Unorthodox Lawmaking, Unorthodox Rulemaking   53
      Notes and Questions   56

Notes on Theories of the Legislative Process   57

B. Legislative Drafting   **60**

  1. The Basic Steps of Legislative Drafting   60

Legislative Drafting Manual, Office of the Legislative
Counsel, U.S. Senate   61

House Legislative Counsel's Manual on Drafting Style,
Office of the Legislative Counsel, U.S. House of
Representatives   62

Notes and Questions   65

  2. The Political Realities of Legislative Drafting   65

Victoria F. Nourse & Jane S. Schacter, The Politics of
Legislative Drafting: A Congressional Case Study   65

Notes and Questions   74

C. A Statute: The 1966 Motor Vehicle Safety Act   **76**

  1. The Story of Auto Safety Legislation   76

Notes and Questions   80

  2. The National Traffic and Motor Vehicle Safety Act of 1966   82

The National Traffic and Motor Vehicle
Safety Act of 1966   82

Notes and Questions   98

Senate Report (Commerce Committee)
[To accompany S. 3005]   99

Notes and Questions   106

D. The Structure of a Modern Statute   **106**

Note on the Relationship Between Operative and
Implementation Provisions   110

Note on Preemption Provisions, Savings Clauses, and
Federalism Issues   111

Notes and Questions   112

The Sherman Antitrust Act   112

The Truth in Lending Act   113

The Clean Air Act   113

The Telephone Consumer Protection Act   114

The Dodd-Frank Wall Street Reform and Consumer
Protection Act   115

The Dodd-Frank Wall Street Reform and Consumer
Protection Act   118

E. Specificity and Delegation   **122**

  1. The Constitutional Limits of Delegation   123

Whitman v. American Trucking Associations, Inc.   124

Notes and Questions   129

  2. Political Reasons for Delegation   130

David Epstein & Sharyn O'Halloran, The Nondelegation
Doctrine and the Separation of Powers: A Political
Science Approach   130

Notes and Questions   134

  3. The Normative Implications of Delegation   135

David Schoenbrod, Power Without Responsibility: How
Congress Abuses the People Through Delegation   136

Jerry L. Mashaw, *Greed, Chaos & Governance:*
    Using Public Choice to Improve Public Law   138
Lisa Schultz Bressman, *Schechter Poultry at the Millennium:*
    A Delegation Doctrine for the Administrative State   139
Edward L. Rubin, *Law and Legislation in the*
    Administrative State   141
    Notes and Questions   142

Chapter 3
Statutory Interpretation by Courts   145

A. A Classic of Statutory Interpretation   **146**
    Church of the Holy Trinity v. United States   147
    Notes and Questions   152
B. Text-Based Tools   **159**
  1. Ordinary Meaning vs. Technical Meaning   160
    Nix v. Hedden   161
    Notes and Questions   163
    Barber v. Gonzales   163
    Notes and Questions   165
    Muscarello v. United States   166
    Notes and Questions   173
  2. Textual Canons of Construction   174
    a. A Classic Example of Textual Canons   175
      Babbitt v. Sweet Home Chapter of Communities for a
        Great Oregon   175
      Notes and Questions   188
    b. Linguistic Canons   189
      i. *Ejusdem generis*   189
      ii. *Noscitur a sociis*   191
      iii. *Expressio unius est exclusio alterius*   194
      iv. Other Linguistic Canons   194
        (1) Punctuation   194
        (2) The Last Antecedent Rule   196
        (3) Conjunctive vs. Disjunctive   198
        (4) May vs. Shall   199
        (5) The Dictionary Act, 1 U.S.C. §§1-8   200
        Notes and Questions   202
    c. Whole Act Canons   203
      i. The Whole Act Rule   203
        (1) Identical Words—Consistent Meaning   204
        (2) Avoiding Redundancy and Surplusage   206
      ii. Titles and Provisos   207
        (1) Titles   207
        (2) Provisos   208
    d. Whole Code Canons   208
      i. *In pari materia*   209
      ii. Inferences Across Statutes   211
      iii. Repeals by Implication   213

e.	The Court's Most Recent Word on Text	215
	King v. Burwell	215
	Notes and Questions	229
3.	Substantive Canons	230
a.	The Rule of Lenity	231
	United States v. Santos	231
	Notes and Questions	241
	Note on the Remedial Purposes Canon	241
b.	The Constitutional Avoidance Canon	242
	Zadvydas v. Davis	243
	Almendarez-Torres v. United States	248
	Notes and Questions	254
c.	The Federalism Clear Statement Rule	255
	Gregory v. Ashcroft	255
	Notes and Questions	264
d.	The Presumption Against Preemption	265
e.	The Presumption Against Retroactivity	266
f.	The Presumption Against Extraterritorial Application	268
4.	Scrivener's Errors and Absurd Results	268
	United States v. Locke	269
	Notes and Questions	271
5.	Criticisms of Canons of Construction	272
	Karl N. Llewellyn, Remarks on the Theory of Appellate Decision and the Rules or Canons About How Statutes Are to Be Construed	272
	Notes and Questions	276
	Abbe R. Gluck & Lisa Schultz Bressman, Statutory Interpretation from the Inside—An Empirical Study of Congressional Drafting, Delegation, and the Canons: Part I	277
	Nina A. Mendelson, Change, Creation, and Unpredictabillity in Statutory Interpretation: Interpretive Canon Use in the Roberts Court's First Decade	279
	Notes and Questions	284
C.	**Intent and Purpose-Based Tools**	**285**
1.	Forms of Legislative History	285
2.	Judicial Reliance on Legislative History	289
	Moore v. Harris	289
	Notes and Questions	298
3.	Principles for Reliance on Legislative History	302
	Victoria F. Nourse, A Decision Theory of Statutory Interpretation: Legislative History by the Rules	303
	Notes and Questions	309
D.	**Tools for Considering Changed Circumstances**	**309**
	Bob Jones University v. United States	310
	Notes and Questions	322
E.	**Theories of Statutory Interpretation**	**322**
1.	Intentionalism	324
a.	What Does Intent Mean?	324

b. Whose Intent Is Relevant?   325
c. Is Collective Intent Coherent?   325
d. Does Intent Reflect More Than Legislative Self-Interest?   327
e. Does Intent Constitute Law?   328
f. May Intent Trump Text?   328
2. Purposivism and Legal Process Purposivism   328
    Henry M. Hart, Jr. & Albert M. Sacks,
        The Legal Process: Basic Problems in the
        Making and Application of the Law   330
    Notes and Questions   332
3. Imaginative Reconstruction   333
    Richard A. Posner, Statutory Interpretation in the
        Classroom and in the Courtroom   334
    Notes and Questions   337
4. Textualism and New Textualism   337
a. Is Textualism Constitutionally Compelled?   339
b. Is Textualism More Constraining?   340
c. Is Textualism Distinctive?   341
d. Is Textualism Internally Consistent?   341
e. Is Legislative History an Impermissible Interpretive Tool?   342
    Antonin Scalia, A Matter of Interpretation: Federal
        Courts and the Law   343
    Notes and Questions   347
5. Dynamic Interpretation   350
    T. Alexander Aleinikoff, Updating Statutory
        Interpretation   350
    Notes and Questions   356

Chapter 4
Policy Making by Rule: A Case Study   **359**

A. NHTSA Gets Organized   **361**
    Michael R. Lemov, Car Safety Wars: One Hundred
        Years of Technology, Politics, and Death   361
    Notes and Questions   363
B. Standard 208 Takes Shape: 1967 to 1971   **364**
    NHTSA, Title 23—Highways and Vehicles   364
    Notes and Questions   366
    NHTSA, Occupant Crash Protection in Passenger
        Cars, Multipurpose Passenger Vehicles, Trucks,
        and Buses   368
    Notes and Questions   371
C. Standard 208 Hits a Wall: 1971 to 1976   **373**
    Transcript of Public Record; Conversation 488-15,
        Nixon Presidential Library and Museum, National
        Archives   375
    Transcript of Public Record, Nixon Presidential
        Library and Museum, National Archives   377
    Notes and Questions   380

Chrysler Corp. v. Department of Transportation   381
Notes and Questions   393
NHTSA, Motor Vehicle and School Bus Safety
    Amendments of 1974   394
Gerald R. Ford, Statement on Signing the Motor
    Vehicle and School Bus Safety Amendments of 1974   396
Notes and Questions   397
NHTSA, Notice, Seat Belt Interlock Option (1974)   399
Notes and Questions   399

D. Standard 208's Death and Resurrection: 1976 to 1989   **400**
NHTSA, Final Rule, Occupant Restraint Systems (1981)   400
Notes and Questions   402
Motor Vehicle Manufacturers Ass'n of the United States,
    Inc. v. State Farm Mutual Automobile Insurance Co.   403
Notes and Questions   415
Kathryn A. Watts, Proposing a Place for Politics in
    Arbitrary an Capricious Review   418
NHTSA, NPRM, Occupant Crash Protection   419
Notes and Questions   422
NHTSA, Final Rule, Occupant Crash Protection   424
Notes and Questions   427
Concluding Question   428
Jody Freeman, Collaborative Governance in the
    Administrative State   432

Chapter 5
Statutory Implementation by Agencies   **435**

A. The Notice-and-Comment Rulemaking Process   **436**
Notes and Questions   440
B. An Example of Notice and Comment
Rulemaking: NHTSA Standard 208   **440**
NHTSA, Notice, Occupant Crash Protection (1981)   444
Notes and Questions   449
NHTSA, Final Rule, Occupant Crash Protection (1981)   449
Notes and Questions   465
C. The Standard Form of Regulations   **466**
Note on the Formalization of the Agency Explanation   468
D. The Tools of Statutory Implementation   **469**
  1. Statutory Analysis   471
    a. Two Examples of Statutory Analysis   472
NHTSA, Denial of Petitions for Rulemaking,
    Passenger Automobile Average Fuel Economy
    Standards (1988)   472
Notes and Questions   476
NHTSA, Notice of Proposed Rulemaking, Civil Penalty
    Procedures and Factors   476
Notes and Questions   477
    b. The "Discovery" of Agency Interpretation: *Chevron* 478
Chevron U.S.A. Inc. v. Natural Resources Defense
    Council, Inc.   479
Notes and Questions   481

c. The Practice of Agency Interpretation   484
       Jerry L. Mashaw, Agency Statutory Interpretation   485
       Notes and Questions   488
       Jerry L. Mashaw, Agency Statutory Interpretation   490
       Notes and Questions   493
       Kevin M. Stack, Purposivism in the Executive Branch:
           How Agencies Interpret Statutes   494
       Notes and Questions   496
2. Scientific Analysis   497
    a. Two Examples of Scientific Analysis   498
       NHTSA, Final Rule, Occupant Crash Protection (2000)   498
       Notes and Questions   501
       NHTSA, Interim Final Rule, Bumper Standard   501
       Notes and Questions   503
    b. The Use of Science   504
       Thomas O. McGarity, The Internal Structure of EPA
           Rulemaking   504
       Sidney Shapiro, Elizabeth Fisher & Wendy Wagner, The
           Enlightenment of Administrative Law: Looking
           Inside the Agency for Legitimacy   506
    c. Assessing Risk   508
       David Ropeik & George Gray, Risk!   511
       Notes and Questions   514
    d. The Misuse and Abuse of Science   516
       Wendy E. Wagner, The Science Charade in Toxic Risk
           Regulation   516
       Notes and Questions   523
3. Economic Analysis   525
    a. An Example of Cost-Benefit Analysis   526
       OIRA, Return Letter   527
       Notes and Questions   536
       NHTSA, Final Rule (Part Two)   536
       Notes and Questions   543
    b. The Mechanics of Cost-Benefit Analysis   544
       W. Kip Viscusi, Fatal Tradeoffs   544
       Notes and Questions   546
       Further Note on Monetization   546
       Cass R. Sunstein, Cost-Benefit Default Principles   550
       Notes and Questions   552
       NHTSA, Final Rule, Average Fuel Economy Standards for
           Light Trucks Model Years 2008-2011 (2006)   553
       Notes and Questions   555
       OMB, Circular A-4   555
       Notes and Questions   556
    c. The Controversy over Cost-Benefit Analysis   557
       Cass R. Sunstein, Cost-Benefit Default Principles   557
       Frank Ackerman & Lisa Heinzerling, Pricing the
           Priceless: Cost-Benefit Analysis of Environmental
           Protection   562
       Notes and Questions   564
    d. Statutory Variations in Economic Analysis   566

Cass R. Sunstein, Cost-Benefit Default Principles | 567
Notes and Questions | 569
4. Political Analysis | 570
EPA, Notice of Denial of Petition for Rulemaking, Control of Emissions From New Highway Vehicles and Engines (2003) | 571
Notes and Questions | 573
EPA, Notice of Denial of Petition for Rulemaking, Control of Emissions From New Highway Vehicles and Engines (2003) | 574
Notes and Questions | 576
E. Other Policymaking Formats | **576**
1. Adjudication | 576
  a. Formal Adjudication | 578
Boston Medical Center Corporation and House Officers' Association/Committee of Interns and Residents, Petitioner | 579
Notes and Questions | 589
  b. "Informal" Adjudication | 590
Notes and Questions | 600
Statement of David Friedman, Acting Administrator, NHTSA, Before the Subcommittee on Consumer Protection, Product Safety and Insurance of the Senate Committee on Commerce, Science and Transportation | 602
Office of Inspector General, Audit Report: Inadequate Data and Analysis Undermine NHTSA's Efforts to Identify and Investigate Vehicle Safety Concerns | 606
Notes and Questions | 617
2. Guidance | 618
NHTSA, Laws & Regulations: Guidance Documents | 619
FDA, §10.115 Good Guidance Practices | 620
Notes and Questions | 624
Nina Mendelson, Regulatory Beneficiaries and Informal Agency Policymaking | 625
Notes and Questions | 637
NHTSA's Interpretation Files Search | 638
Paul Hemmersbaugh, NHTSA Chief Counsel, to Brian Latour, Exec. Director of Global Safety and Field Investigations, General Motors Corp. | 639
Notes and Questions | 643

Chapter 6
Control of Agency Action | **645**

A. Presidential Control of Agency Action | **645**
1. The Constitutionality of Independent Agencies and Presidential Control Thereof | 647
Myers v. United States | 648
Humphrey's Executor v. United States | 652

Morrison v. Olson	657
Notes and Questions	665
Free Enterprise Fund v. Public Company Accounting Oversight Board	669
Notes and Questions	677
2. Control of Agency Personnel	679
3. Control of Appropriations	681
Eloise Pasachoff, OMB's Resource Management Offices and Agency Policy Control	682
Notes and Questions	684
4. Regulatory Planning and Review	685
Executive Order No. 12,866, Regulatory Planning and Review	686
Notes and Questions	700
a. Return and Prompt Letters	701
b. The Debate About Regulatory Planning and Review	710
Notes and Questions	714
5. Presidential Directives	714
6. Other White House and Agency Involvement	715
B. Congressional Control of Agency Action	**717**
1. New Legislation	719
2. Appropriations Legislation	720
3. Oversight Hearings	723
Brian D. Feinstein, Congress in the Administrative State	723
4. Fire Alarms	727
5. Legislative Vetoes	728
Immigration & Naturalization Service v. Chadha	730
Notes and Questions	743
6. Congressional Review Act	745
Notes and Questions	749
7. Congressional Control of Agency Officials	750
Bowsher v. Synar	750
Notes and Questions	761
C. Judicial Control of Agency Action	**762**
1. Judicial Control of Agency Statutory Interpretation	762
a. Before *Chevron: Skidmore*	763
Skidmore v. Swift & Co.	763
Notes and Questions	766
b. *Chevron*	767
Chevron U.S.A. Inc. v. Natural Resources Defense Council, Inc.	767
Notes and Questions	776
i. Step One: Clear Statutory Meaning	778
MCI Telecommunications Corp. v. American Telephone & Telegraph Co.	779
Notes and Questions	787
Food & Drug Administration v. Brown & Williamson Tobacco Corp.	787
Notes and Questions	800

King v. Burwell	802
Notes and Questions	803
ii. Step Two: Unreasonable Agency Interpretations	803
c. After *Chevron: Mead* and *Barnhart*	804
United States v. Mead Corp.	805
Notes and Questions	815
Barnhart v. Walton	817
Notes and Questions	819
d. The Debate Over *Chevron*	820
2. Judicial Control of Agency Regulatory Interpretation	823
Auer v. Robbins	825
Kisor v. Wilkie, Secretary of Veterans Affairs	829
Notes and Questions	836
Note on the Interpretation of Regulations	837
Notes and Questions	840
3. Empirical Evidence on Deference Frameworks	841
Kent Barnett & Christopher J. Walker, *Chevron* in the Circuits	841
Notes and Questions	844
4. Judicial Control of Agency Statutory Implementation	845
a. Review of Agency Policy	846
Citizens to Preserve Overton Park, Inc. v. Volpe	847
Notes and Questions	851
Motor Vehicle Manufacturers Ass'n of the United States, Inc. v. State Farm Mutual Automobile Insurance Co.	852
Notes and Questions	853
FCC v. Fox Television Stations, Inc.	855
Notes and Questions	872
b. Empirical Evidence on Judicial Control of Agency Policymaking	872
Cass R. Sunstein & Thomas J. Miles, Depoliticizing Administrative Law	872
c. Judicial Control of Agency Procedure	874
Vermont Yankee Nuclear Power Corp. v. Natural Resources Defense Council, Inc.	877
Notes and Questions	884
Perez v. Mortgage Bankers Assn.	886
Notes and Questions	891
United States v. Nova Scotia Food Products, Inc.	891
Notes and Questions	895
Home Box Office v. FCC	897
Notes and Questions	900
d. Judicial Control of Agency Fact-Finding	903
Universal Camera v. National Labor Relations Board	903
Notes and Questions	909
Allentown Mack Sales and Service, Inc. v. NLRB	909
Notes and Questions	920

3. Availability of Judicial Review   920
   a. Standing   920
            Massachusetts v. EPA   921
            Notes and Questions   932
   b. Reviewability   934
            Heckler v. Chaney   934
            Notes and Questions   945
   c. Timing   945

Appendix A   Selected Provisions of the Constitution of the
                United States of America   949
Appendix B   Selected Provisions of the Administrative
                Procedure Act   971
Appendix C   Presidential Administrations and Secretaries
                of Department of Transportation, 1967-87   995

Table of Cases   *999*
Index   *1003*

Preface

This book provides an introduction to the modern regulatory state, the system of federal laws and institutions that determine the major part of our nation's social and economic policy today. This system is a relatively new one. Prior to the modern era, federal regulatory efforts were haphazard. Social and economic policy were largely determined by the forces of supply and demand—in other words, the market—and common law, developed mainly by state judges in the process of deciding cases, provided most of the rules governing private conduct. But during the past century and a half, this regime has been largely displaced by statutes and regulations. Statutes are laws enacted by legislatures, such as Congress, and regulations are laws issued by administrative agencies, such the Department of Transportation, the Environmental Protection Agency, or the Federal Communications Commission. Statutes and regulations are paramount in this book because they are principal sources of law in our modern state. We examine judicial decisions as well, but they play more of a supporting role in this course, as they do in our contemporary legal system.

Many law school courses involve statutes and regulations, legislatures, and agencies, but they do not routinely step back to consider the fundamental questions about these laws and institutions. How are statutes enacted or regulations issued? What tools do lawyers use to influence their content and development? Who makes decisions within regulatory agencies? How do statutes and regulations relate to one another, and how do the various institutions of government interact to produce them? What institutions or actors outside those agencies most directly influence their actions, and how do they do so? Even courses that have a significant statutory or regulatory component—such as tax, securities regulation, or environmental law—do not focus these foundational questions. Other courses, including administrative law, constitutional law, and legislation, deal with them, but not in a manner designed to provide students with a vision of the basic and essential skills that lawyers use to navigate the regulatory state.

The overarching purpose of this book is to provide that vision. In addition, we offer information and ideas for evaluating the regulatory state. But the principle goal is practical: to provide an introduction to the laws and institutions that lawyers confront on a daily basis. It may come as a surprise, but we are referring to *all* lawyers. Of course, government lawyers must deal regularly with such laws and institutions. Yet they are far from the only ones. When lawyers give legal advice to private clients, they must often base that advice on legal rules established by statutes and regulations. When lawyers litigate on behalf of their clients, their arguments often center on the meaning of a statute or regulation. When lawyers negotiate contracts on their clients' behalf, they must be aware, in almost every field, of the rules established by statutes and regulations. To think like a lawyer, it is necessary to learn how to do so in the context of the regulatory state.

Chapter 1 begins by addressing the limitations of the common law as a regulatory regime. As we mentioned, judge-made rules were once the primary mechanism for governing private conduct. We explore justifications for this reliance and explanations for why the government has turned to statutes and administrative agencies as primary regulators of private action.

Chapter 1 then provides brief consideration of the way in which modern government is structured. By modern government, we mean modern *federal* government, as contrasted with state or local government, although many of the lessons may translate into those contexts. The standard approach to learning about our government is largely conventional, focusing on the three branches enumerated in the Constitution: the legislative, the executive, and the judicial. This picture does not fully describe the government that we actually possess. In particular, it does not describe the units of government that actually exercise power over our day-to-day lives: administrative agencies. We bring those agencies into the picture.

Chapter 2 concerns legislation. It describes the process for generating statutes—the legislative process. We then present actual statutes, describing their basic components and demonstrating that they have predictable features. We also set out the basic steps of legislative drafting. Understanding how statutes are put together is a crucial step toward understanding what they mean and how they function.

Chapter 3 introduces judicial interpretation of statutes. Statutes are not always easy to read or understand. But even the most straightforward require an act of interpretation, because words really have no meaning until they are interpreted by someone. We explore the tools and theories that courts have developed for interpreting statutes. This chapter focuses on courts because courts have been interpreting statutes for many centuries, well before the advent of the regulatory state, and the tools and theories they have developed are well-established and familiar features of our legal system.

Chapter 4, new to this edition, presents a case study of the regulatory process. It is intended to capture a fuller picture of the institutions and laws that we discuss throughout this book as they come together to solve a particular social problem. This example demonstrates that the various actors do not operate in isolation but are responsive to one another and that there may be more to a regulatory story than meets the eye.

Chapter 5 turns to agency implementation of statutes. Statutes often grant agencies the power to make them work in practice, and agencies often issue regulations for that purpose. Like statutes, regulations are generated by a process—the notice-and-comment rulemaking process. We describe that process and present examples of actual regulations. We show that regulations, like statutes, have predictable components. We then consider in some detail the tools and modes of analysis that agencies use in deciding how to implement their statutes. We also introduce some other ways in which agencies implement their statutes, including trial-type hearings called formal adjudication, and advice to outside parties, often called administrative guidance.

Chapter 6 discusses political and judicial control of agency action. In implementing their statutes, agencies are subject to control by all of the three constitutionally enumerated branches. For example, the President has both formal and informal means for maintaining ongoing involvement in agency action. Congress also monitors agency action through various means, including oversight hearings as well as less visible and more continuous contacts. Courts are routinely asked to review agency action once it is final, and they are subject to particular standards and doctrines of judicial review. Because agencies are subject to these influences in making their decisions, the operation of regulatory governance cannot be fully described without discussing them.

Before we begin, we offer some general notes that cut across this book. We have chosen to focus throughout on one particular statute and one particular regulation. Both concern the issue of auto safety. We have selected this issue to make the material accessible. We could have chosen a statute and a regulation dealing with the production of natural gas, or the control of the money supply, but you are likely less familiar with those matters than you are with the safety features of a car. The problems that agencies handle often are technical and complex, making them difficult to understand. The focus on auto safety will allow you to rely a bit on your own personal experience in your efforts to digest some of the more challenging aspects of the regulatory process. The familiarity of the auto safety example is also meant to show you how statutes and regulations can and do affect our daily lives, in ways that you now take for granted, such as by requiring seatbelts and airbags in your car. At the same time, the point of the course is *not* to teach you about auto safety. It is to teach you how to understand any federal statute or regulation, regardless of its content.

For ease of reading, we have edited the cases, statutes, and other primary material that we present, as well as the secondary sources that we present. We have also renumbered the footnotes in the cases and secondary sources so that they run sequentially. We have generally not indicated when these changes have been made.

As you may already gather, this material raises points of connection between politics and law. What our regulatory state looks like—who makes decisions and what decisions emerge—depends on who is in control of the relevant decisionmakers and decisions. This is often a matter of politics. In this respect, politics is an important part of this book. Lawyers cannot navigate the regulatory state without an appreciation of the relationship between politics and law.

Lisa Schultz Bressman
Edward L. Rubin
Kevin M. Stack

Nashville, Tennessee
June 2019

Acknowledgments

In preparation of this third edition, we owe our greatest debt to our colleague and friend, Peter Strauss, whose comments on the first edition and a draft version of the second edition have improved it immeasurably. We are also grateful to Nicholas Bagley, Rachel Barkow, Anuj Desai, Michael Herz, Eloise Pasachoff, and Ganesh Sitaraman for comments and corrections in response to teaching earlier editions.

We remain grateful to those who made substantive contributions to the first edition. For comments and conversations, we thank Bill Eskridge, John Goldberg, Jeff Hirsch, Sally Katzen, David Lewis, Preston Stein, and Michael Vandenbergh, as well as several anonymous reviewers. We are thankful for the excellent research assistance of Alec Denton, Matthew Downer, Andrew Gould, Joel Heller, Joshua Hoyt, Sarah Parker, Kyle Robisch, Joshua Ruby, Amy Sanders, Lauren Solberg, Lauren Winter, and members of the Vanderbilt University Law School Library. We thank Brandy Drinnon for her extraordinary dedication and administrative assistance in preparing the original manuscript. Finally, we thank our colleagues at Vanderbilt University Law School for their enthusiastic support of this book and the first-year Regulatory State course.

We gratefully acknowledge the following authors and publishers who granted us permission to reprint copyrighted material:

American Broadcasting Companies, for the use of the photograph of the *Schoolhouse Rocks!* picture of "I'm Just a Bill" with the little boy on the steps of the U.S. Capitol Building, Copyright © 1975 American Broadcasting Companies. Reprinted with permission from American Broadcasting Companies. All rights reserved.

Cambridge University Press, for excerpts from David Epstein, Sharyn O'Halloran (1999), Copyright © 1999 Cambridge University Press. Reprinted with permission of Cambridge University Press.

Cornell Law Review, Chris Guthrie, Jeffrey J. Rachlinski, & Andrew J. Wistrich for excerpts from Chris Guthrie, Jeffrey J. Rachlinski, & Andrew J. Wistrich, *Blinking on the Bench: How Judges Decide Cases*, 93 CORNELL L. REV. 1 (2007), Copyright © 2007 Cornell Law Review. Reprinted with permission of Cornell Law Review, Chris Guthrie, Jeffrey J. Rachlinski, and Andrew J. Wistrich.

Harvard University Press, for excerpts from "Typical Justifications for Regulation," reprinted by permission of the publisher from REGULATION AND ITS REFORM BY STEPHEN BREYER, pp.16-34, Cambridge, Mass.: Harvard University Press, Copyright © 1982 by the President and Fellows of Harvard College; and for excerpts from "The Functions of Regulatory

Statutes," reprinted by permission of the publisher from AFTER THE RIGHTS REVOLUTION: RECONCEIVING THE REGULATORY STATE by CASS SUNSTEIN, pp.57-69, Cambridge, Mass.: Harvard University Press, Copyright © 1990 by the President and Fellows of Harvard College.

Morton International, Inc. (Morton Salt Division), for the use of the photograph of a Morton Salt canister featuring the 1914 Morton Salt Girl and slogan "When it Rains, It Pours," Copyright © Morton International, Inc. Reprinted with permission from Morton International, Inc.

New York University Law Review, for excerpts from Victoria F. Nourse & Jane S. Schacter, *The Politics of Legislative Drafting: A Congressional Case Study*, 77 N.Y.U. L. REV. 575 (2002), Copyright © 2002 New York University Law Review. Reprinted with permission from New York University Law Review.

Penguin Group (USA), for excerpts from RALPH NADER, UNSAFE AT ANY SPEED (1965), Copyright © 1965, 1972 by Ralph Nader. Used by permission of Viking Penguin, a division of Penguin Group (USA).

Polsby, *Congress and Presidency*, 3rd Ed., ©1986. Reprinted by permission of Pearson Education, Inc., New York, New York.

University of Chicago Press, for excerpts from DANIEL A. FARBER & PHILIP P. FRICKEY, LAW AND PUBLIC CHOICE: A CRITICAL INTRODUCTION (1991), Copyright © 1991 University of Chicago Press. Reprinted with permission of University of Chicago Press.

Vanderbilt Law Review, *The Consequences of Congress's Choice of Delegate: Judicial and Agency Interpretations of Title VII*, 63 VAND. L. REV. 363, 365 (2010). Copyright ©2010 Vanderbilt Law Review. Reprinted with permission from Vanderbilt Law Review.

Martha Wright, Scott Paul Wines, for the use of their photograph of the Uneeda Biscuit Building mural in New Orleans, LA, Copyright © Martha Wright. Reprinted by courtesy of Martha Wright, Scott Paul Wines.

Yale Law Journal, for excerpts from Lisa Schultz Bressman, Schechter Poultry *at the Millennium: A Delegation Doctrine for the Administrative State*, 109 YALE L.J. 1399 (2000), Copyright © 2000, Yale Law Journal. Reproduced with permission from Yale Law Journal.

Yale University Press, for excerpts from DAVID SCHOENBROD, POWER WITHOUT RESPONSIBILITY: HOW CONGRESS ABUSES THE PEOPLE THROUGH DELEGATION (1993), Copyright © 1993 Yale University Press. Reproduced with permission from Yale University Press; and for excerpts from JERRY L. MASHAW, GREED, CHAOS, & GOVERNANCE: USING PUBLIC CHOICE TO IMPROVE PUBLIC LAW (1997), Copyright © 1997 Yale University Press. Reproduced with permission from Yale University Press.

THE REGULATORY STATE

1

From Common Law to Regulation

Legend has it that a famous law professor, now a judge, began his first-year torts course each year with the following hypothetical:

> Extraterrestrials come to the United States and offer the American people a wonderful gift. The gift is the sort that will improve the efficiency of the society, the wealth of the society, and the happiness of the society. "Please accept our gift," implore the extraterrestrials. But here's the catch. "In exchange," the extraterrestrials continue, "your country must send us 45,000 people a year — men, women, and children — and they never will be seen or heard from again." What is the gift?

This hypothetical nicely presents the problem of auto safety. Motor vehicles are a wonderful gift. At the same time, they pose real risks to human life and health. The safety risks posed by the introduction of this technology provide a classic example of the social and economic issues that arise every day.

A familiar option for addressing the problem of auto safety is legislation and regulation, whether enacted at the federal or state level. It is within the constitutional power of Congress to enact a statute mandating that auto manufacturers install certain kinds of safety equipment, such as anti-lock brakes, on new motor vehicles. Auto safety requirements, whether detailed in the statute or later developed by an agency through the issuance of regulations, might decrease the likelihood of auto accidents or mitigate their harmful effects.

Although such instances of government intervention are prevalent today, the law can respond in other ways to activities that generate risks to human safety and the like. Indeed, until the turn of the twentieth century, two other bodies of law — contract and tort — functioned as the primary mechanisms for addressing risks to human safety. Today, these bodies of law maintain an uneasy co-existence with statutes and regulations designed for that purpose.

Contract and tort law are part of the common law. The common law is a mode of government action — in other words, a regulatory regime. This may seem obvious, but law school courses tend to present the common law as the law itself, rather than as one source of law. In fact, the common law is nothing more than the particular set of legally binding rules that are made and implemented by judges in the course of resolving formal disputes between contesting parties.

How did the common law handle the problem of auto safety or the safety of any other product? We can start with contract law, which generally empowers individuals and entities to enter into legally binding agreements with one another. Prospective buyers of cars are always free to seek from sellers various safety features. Of course, the sellers may not be able to provide those safety features or may not offer them even if available. Likewise, consumers may not always have meaningful choices as to safety features if all the members of the auto industry basically offer the same features. Still, consumers usually have at least some degree of choice. For example, a person more concerned with auto safety than, say, fuel efficiency, can buy a larger car that is better able to withstand a crash than a smaller one. Similarly, consumers can choose to purchase special safety features such as side airbags or "crumple zones." These sorts of choices are legally enforceable in a particular way. If the safety feature fails to deliver a promised safety benefit, the buyer can sue the seller under contract law for breach of actual or implied warranty. A judge would determine whether the plaintiff was entitled to relief by considering whether a warranty was made, whether it was breached, and whether that breach caused the buyer to suffer a loss. In resolving contractual disputes, judges developed a set of rules that allocate the risk of harm between consumer and manufacturer.

For as long as there have been motorized vehicles (and, for that matter, horse-drawn wagons), Americans have also had the ability to bring a suit under tort law for harms caused by unsafe vehicles. Generally speaking, tort law, in contrast to contract law, imposes obligations independently of whether the person on whom the obligation is being imposed made any sort of promise or warranty to the person bringing the suit. For example, the buyer of a car whose steering mechanism fails while he is driving the car, resulting in an accident that injures him, could sue the manufacturer for the tort of negligence, regardless of whether the seller made any promise or warranty as to the soundness of the steering mechanism. If a judge or jury determined that the seller was at fault for the failure of the mechanism, then the court would order the seller to compensate the victim for his injuries. In this case-by-case manner, judges developed tort rules for what does and does not count as faulty conduct. In turn, these rules generated incentives for all auto manufacturers to design and build their vehicles in different ways to avoid future damages awards.

The current legal system still relies on contract and tort law but to a much lesser extent, in part because those bodies of law have been supplemented and, in some respects, superseded by statutes and regulations. *See* Barbara L. Atwell, *Products Liability and Preemption: A Judicial Framework*, 39 BUFF. L. REV. 181 (1991). This chapter examines the shift from the common law to statutes and regulations. It begins by discussing the limitations of tort law for addressing safety risks, such as those from motor vehicles. It then discusses the limitations of markets and, indirectly, the limitations of contract law for addressing safety risks. The discussion of so-called market failures is part of a broader one about economic justifications for government regulation. The chapter then presents social justifications for government regulation. At times, society demands more for itself as a whole than any one individual would for herself. The chapter concludes by providing a brief introduction to administrative agencies.

A. THE LIMITATIONS OF TORT LAW

In the early history of our legal system, tort law did not impose significant obligations on product manufacturers to take precautions against injury to the users of their products. From at least 1842 through 1916, the individuals who brought suit against manufacturers for injuries caused by a faulty product were mainly those who had bought products directly from those manufacturers. Consumers did not always buy products directly from the manufacturer, even though they were the intended users. As a result, they often could not bring suit. Many courts took the famous English decision of Winterbottom v. Wright, 152 Eng. Rep. 402 (1842), as authority for this regime.

In *Winterbottom v. Wright*, Wright had manufactured and maintained carriages and had a contract to provide the Postmaster-General with mail coaches. Under that contract, Wright agreed to keep these mail coaches in a safe condition for their use. The Postmaster-General, in turn, had a contract with another party, Nathaniel Atkinson, to convey these coaches along particular routes, providing both horses and coachmen for those purposes. One of the coachmen hired by Atkinson, Winterbottom, suffered a severe injury to his leg when the wheel of one of Wright's coaches collapsed. Because Winterbottom was an employee of the company that had a contract to provide coaches to the Postmaster-General, he did not have a direct contractual relationship with either the Postmaster-General or with Wright.

Winterbottom sued Wright alleging that Wright had "improperly and negligently conducted himself" by failing to satisfy his duty to furnish mail coaches in a safe condition, free of "latent defects," and that as a result, Winterbottom suffered severe injury. The judges of the English Exchequer's court forcefully rejected Winterbottom's theory of liability. The chief judge, Lord Abinger, reasoned as follows:

> We ought not to permit a doubt to rest upon this subject, for our doing so might be the means of letting in upon us an infinity of actions. . . . There is no privity of contract between these parties; and if the plaintiff can sue, every passenger, or even any person passing along the road, who was injured by the upsetting of the coach, might bring a similar action. Unless we confine the operation of such contracts as this to the parties who entered into them, the most absurd and outrageous consequences,

to which I can see no limit, would ensue. Where a party becomes responsible to the public, by undertaking a public duty, he is liable, though the injury may have arisen from the negligence of his servant or agent. . . . The plaintiff in this case could not have brought an action on the contract; if he could have done so, what would have been his situation, supposing the Postmaster-General had released the defendant? That would, at all events, have defeated his claim altogether. By permitting this action, we should be working this injustice, that after the defendant had done everything to the satisfaction of his employer, and after all matters between them had been adjusted, and all accounts settled on the footing of their contract, we should subject them to be ripped open by this action of tort being brought against him.

Id. at 405-06.

 Winterbottom stood for the proposition that manufacturers cannot be held liable to consumers or other users of their products if those consumers or users are not in contractual "privity" with the manufacturer. The idea of privity made sense prior to the modern era. To buy a chair, you went to a carpenter, who built it for you out of raw wood from the lumber mill; your fancy clothes were made to order by a tailor or a dressmaker from cloth delivered to his shop in large rolls, or bolts; bread came from the baker who made it from raw flour. In these circumstances, the customer was generally in privity with the person most responsible for producing the purchased item. If there was something wrong with your purchase, it was most likely the seller's fault, and if the raw material the seller used was defective, well then, that was his or her responsibility. How could the owner of the lumber mill or a flour mill know where the materials they produced were being used? It was from the artisan who used the materials to produce a finished product that the ultimate consumer bought.

 These circumstances began to change in the nineteenth century when factories began producing finished products that bore the name of

their manufacturer, like Wedgwood china, Singer sewing machines, and Brewster carriages. (As late as the 1930s, Cole Porter could still write, in his famous song "*You're the top! You're a Ritz hot toddy. You're the top! You're a Brewster body.*") Items were completed by the manufacturer and sold to the public by retail stores that had no role in their manufacture. Department stores, carrying a variety of finished products, evolved in the United States during the mid- to late nineteenth century. Many items continued to be sold in bulk; if you wanted to buy crackers, for example, you went to the general store, and the store keeper would scoop the desired quantity out of the proverbial cracker barrel. In 1898, the National Biscuit Company introduced Uneeda Biscuits, the first pre-packaged food product sold directly from a manufacturer to the public. The original purpose of marketing the product in this way was to protect it against moisture, and the product's symbol, a boy in a raincoat, was designed to advertise that virtue. The Morton Salt girl, a symbol that dates from the same era and is still in use, emphasized the same virtue for pre-packaged salt.

The fact that the crackers and salt had a symbol in the first place was groundbreaking because the symbol was specifically designed to market the product to the general public. Note also that the crackers did not bear the name of the manufacturer, but a made-up name generated by an advertising slogan ("Lest you forget, we say it yet, *you need a* biscuit."). In fact, advertising signs for Uneeda Biscuits appeared on the sides of buildings all across America. The surviving ones are often designated as landmarks.

As a result of these developments, the merchants with whom individuals regularly dealt were no longer the people who made the product or even

packaged it for sale. They were mere intermediaries, transferring a product that was produced, packaged, and labeled by remote manufacturers. These manufacturers, moreover, were now advertising their products directly to the public through newspaper and magazine ads, signs on buildings, and, as the twentieth century progressed, radio and motion picture ads. Their ads necessarily contained various assertions and promises about the use, performance, and quality of the product being advertised.

In this new situation, what was the rationale for the doctrine of privity? Consider the famous decision printed below, which returns the discussion to auto safety.

MacPherson v. Buick Motor Co.

111 N.E. 1050 (N.Y. 1916)

Cardozo, J.

The defendant is a manufacturer of automobiles. It sold an automobile to a retail dealer. The retail dealer resold to the plaintiff. While the plaintiff was in the car, it suddenly collapsed. He was thrown out and injured. One of the wheels was made of defective wood, and its spokes crumbled into fragments. The wheel was not made by the defendant; it was bought from another manufacturer. There is evidence, however, that its defects could have been discovered by reasonable inspection, and that inspection was omitted. There is no claim that the defendant knew of the defect and willfully concealed it. The charge is one, not of fraud, but of negligence. The question to be determined is whether the defendant owed a duty of care and vigilance to any one but the immediate purchaser.

The foundations of this branch of the law, at least in this state, were laid in *Thomas v. Winchester* (6 N.Y. 397). A poison was falsely labeled. The sale was made to a druggist, who in turn sold to a customer. The customer recovered damages from the seller who affixed the label. "The defendant's negligence," it was said, "put human life in imminent danger." A poison falsely labeled is likely to injure any one who gets it. Because the danger is to be foreseen, there is a duty to avoid the injury. Cases were cited by way of illustration in which manufacturers were not subject to any duty irrespective of contract. The distinction was said to be that their conduct, though negligent, was not likely to result in injury to any one except the purchaser. We are not required to say whether the chance of injury was always as remote as the distinction assumes. Some of the illustrations might be rejected to-day. The principle of the distinction is for present purposes the important thing.

Thomas v. Winchester became quickly a landmark of the law. In the application of its principle there may at times have been uncertainty or even error. There has never in this state been doubt or disavowal of the principle itself. The chief cases are well known, yet to recall some of them will be helpful. *Loop v. Litchfield* (42 N.Y. 351) is the earliest. It was the case of a defect in a small balance wheel used on a circular saw. The manufacturer pointed out the defect to the buyer, who wished a cheap article and was ready to assume the risk. The risk can hardly have been an imminent one, for the wheel lasted five years before it broke. In the meanwhile, the buyer had made a lease of the machinery. It was held that the manufacturer was not answerable to the lessee. *Loop v. Litchfield* was followed in *Losee v. Clute* (51 N.Y. 494), the case of the explosion of a steam boiler. That decision has been criticized; but it must be confined to its special facts. It was put upon the ground that the risk of injury was too remote. The buyer in that case had not only accepted the boiler, but had tested it. The manufacturer knew that his own test was not the final one. The finality of the test has a bearing on the measure of diligence owing to persons other than the purchaser.

These early cases suggest a narrow construction of the rule. Later cases, however, evince a more liberal spirit. First in importance is *Devlin v. Smith* (89 N.Y. 470). The defendant, a contractor, built a scaffold for a painter. The painter's servants were injured. The contractor was held liable. He knew that the scaffold, if improperly constructed, was a most dangerous trap. He knew that it was to be used by the workmen. He was building it for that very purpose. Building it for their use, he owed them a duty, irrespective of his contract with their master, to build it with care.

From *Devlin v. Smith* we pass over intermediate cases and turn to the latest case in this court in which *Thomas v. Winchester* was followed. That case is *Statler v. Ray Mfg. Co.* (195 N.Y. 478, 480). The defendant manufactured a large coffee urn. It was installed in a restaurant. When heated, the urn exploded and injured the plaintiff. We held that the manufacturer was liable. We said that the urn "was of such a character inherently that, when applied to the purposes for which it was designed, it was liable to become a source of great danger to many people if not carefully and properly constructed."

It may be that *Devlin v. Smith* and *Statler v. Ray Mfg. Co.* have extended the rule of *Thomas v. Winchester*. If so, this court is committed to the extension. The defendant argues that things imminently dangerous to life are poisons, explosives, deadly weapons — things whose normal function it is to injure or destroy. But whatever the rule in *Thomas v. Winchester* may once have been, it has no longer that restricted meaning. A scaffold is not inherently a destructive instrument. It becomes destructive only if imperfectly constructed. A large coffee urn may have within itself, if negligently made, the potency of danger, yet no one thinks of it as an implement whose normal function is destruction. . . .

Devlin v. Smith was decided in 1882. A year later a very similar case came before the Court of Appeal in England (*Heaven v. Pender*, L. R. [11 Q. B. D.] 503). We find in the opinion of [Lord Esher], the same conception of a duty, irrespective of contract, imposed upon the manufacturer by the law itself: "Whenever one person supplies goods, or machinery, or the like, for the purpose of their being used by another person under such circumstances that every one of ordinary sense would, if he thought, recognize at once that unless he used ordinary care and skill with regard to the condition of the thing supplied or the mode of supplying it, there will be danger of injury to the person or property of him for whose use the thing is supplied, and who is to use it, a duty arises to use ordinary care and skill as to the condition or manner of supplying such thing." He then points out that for a neglect of such ordinary care or skill whereby injury happens, the appropriate remedy is an action for negligence. The right to enforce this liability is not to be confined to the immediate buyer. The right extends to the persons or class of persons for whose use the thing is supplied. It is enough that the goods "would in all probability be used at once . . . before a reasonable opportunity for discovering any defect which might exist," and that the thing supplied is of such a nature "that a neglect of ordinary care or skill as to its condition or the manner of supplying it would probably cause danger to the person or property of the person for whose use it was supplied, and who was about to use it." On the other hand, he would exclude a case "in which the goods are supplied under circumstances in which it would be a chance by whom they would be used or whether they would be used or not, or whether they would be used before there would probably be means of observing any defect," or where the goods are of such a nature that "a want of care or skill as to their condition or the manner of supplying them would not probably produce danger of injury to person or property." . . .

We hold, then, that the principle of *Thomas v. Winchester* is not limited to poisons, explosives, and things of like nature, to things which in their normal operation are implements of destruction. If the nature of a thing is such that it is reasonably certain to place life and limb in peril when negligently made, it is then a thing of danger. Its nature gives warning of the consequences to be expected. If to the element of danger there is added knowledge that the thing will be used by persons other than the purchaser, and used without new tests, then, irrespective of contract, the manufacturer of this thing of danger is under a duty to make it carefully. That is as far as we are required to go for the decision of this case. There must be knowledge of a danger, not merely possible, but probable. It is *possible* to use almost anything in a way that will make it dangerous if defective. That is not enough to charge the manufacturer with a duty independent of his contract. Whether a given thing is dangerous may be sometimes a question for the court and sometimes a question for the jury. There must also be knowledge that in the usual course of events the danger will be shared by others than the buyer. Such knowledge may often be inferred from the nature of the transaction. But it is possible that even knowledge of the danger and of the use will not always be enough. The proximity or remoteness of the relation is a factor to be considered. We are dealing now with the liability of the manufacturer of the finished product, who puts it on the market to be used without inspection by his customers. If he is negligent, where danger is to be foreseen, a liability will follow. We are not required at this time to say that it is legitimate to go back of the manufacturer of the finished product and hold the manufacturers of the component parts. To make their negligence a cause of imminent danger, an independent cause must often intervene; the manufacturer of the finished product must also fail in *his* duty of inspection. It may be that in those circumstances the negligence of the earlier members of the series is too remote to constitute, as to the ultimate user, an actionable wrong. We leave that question open. . . .

From this survey of the decisions, there thus emerges a definition of the duty of a manufacturer which enables us to measure this defendant's liability. Beyond all question, the nature of an automobile gives warning of probable danger if its construction is defective. This automobile was designed to go fifty miles an hour. Unless its wheels were sound and strong, injury was almost certain. It was as much a thing of danger as a defective engine for a railroad. The defendant knew the danger. It knew also that the car would be used by persons other than the buyer. This was apparent from its size; there were seats for three persons. It was apparent also from the fact that the buyer was a dealer in cars, who bought to resell. The maker of this car supplied it for the use of purchasers from the dealer just as plainly as the contractor in *Devlin v. Smith* supplied the scaffold for use by the servants of the owner. The dealer was indeed the one person of whom it might be said with some approach to certainty that by him the car would not be used. Yet the defendant would have us say that he was the one person whom it was under a legal duty to protect. The law does not lead us to so inconsequent a conclusion. Precedents drawn from the days of travel by stage coach do not fit the conditions of travel to-day. The principle that the danger must be imminent does not change, but the things subject to the principle do change. They are whatever the needs of life in a developing civilization require them to be. . . .

We think the defendant was not absolved from a duty of inspection because it bought the wheels from a reputable manufacturer. It was not merely a dealer in automobiles. It was a manufacturer of automobiles. It was responsible for the finished product. It was not at liberty to put the finished product on the market without subjecting the component parts to ordinary and simple tests. The obligation to inspect must vary with the nature of the thing to be inspected. The more probable the danger, the greater the need of caution. . . .

The judgment should be affirmed with costs.

Notes and Questions

1. Cardozo, who was subsequently appointed to the U.S. Supreme Court, is considered one of the greatest jurists in American history. Consider Cardozo's decision in light of the brief description we gave you above about changes in marketing practices at this time. Can you identify the sentences in the decision that take cognizance of these changes? What does Cardozo conclude from them? Why didn't he say so more explicitly?

2. How does Cardozo justify his decision? Are you convinced that the decision is simply an extension of prior cases? Why does Cardozo work so hard to show that it is?

3. Did Cardozo change the law, or did he simply generalize it? How do we justify judicial lawmaking? If we can't, how do we justify the common law, which, as described above, is a system of judge-made rules?

To the extent that *MacPherson* jettisoned or modified the privity rule, it held the potential to alter the future conduct of automakers. Under the privity rule, tort law had little effect on the future conduct of automakers because they faced no prospect of liability to buyers for negligently manufacturing an unsafe product. In response to *MacPherson*, do you suppose that Buick improved its inspection practices? Consider the following decision.

Rotche v. Buick Motor Co.

193 N.E. 529 (Ill. 1934)

Per Curiam.

Nathan Rotche brought an action. . . against the Buick Motor Company and the Cicero Buick Sales Company, both corporations, to recover damages for personal injuries. The jury found the defendants guilty and assessed the plaintiff's damages at $20,000. . . . The Buick Motor Company applied to this court for a writ of certiorari, the writ was issued, and the record of the cause is submitted for a further review.

On August 13, 1929, Nathan Rotche, forty years of age, employed as a train guard on an elevated railway in the city of Chicago, bought a five-passenger Buick automobile from the Cicero Sales Company. Twenty-six days later, on September 8, 1929, accompanied by his son, he drove the automobile over a highway known as "Rand road." At a point about a mile northwest of the village of Des Plaines, the automobile, while running at a speed of thirty miles an hour, left the roadway, struck and damaged a concrete culvert, crossed a ditch adjoining the roadway, and came to a stop in a ploughed field at a point about twenty feet beyond the ditch. At rest, the automobile lay on its right side with the front of the car to the northwest. The right front tire and left front wheel were destroyed, the rear axle was bent, the top and sides of the body were damaged, and a clevis connecting a cable with the left front wheel-brake was missing. The automobile was first towed to a garage in the village of Des Plaines. About two weeks later the car was removed to another garage in Chicago. Rotche, the defendant in error, suffered injuries necessitating an operation upon his left leg and foot. As a result the leg is shortened and the foot turned outward. . . .

The garage owner who towed the automobile to Des Plaines made no particular examination of it at the time. Three or four weeks later, pursuant to a request made in behalf of the defendant in error, he examined the automobile in the garage in Chicago to which it had been removed. He then found that a clevis and two cotter pins were missing. Certain cotter pins on the left equalizer apparently had not been spread and could readily be removed.

The proprietor of the garage in Chicago made an examination of the car in Des Plaines on September 21, 1929, and found a loose cable. After the car had been taken to his garage, the left front wheel was removed. A clevis was missing. The cotter pins on the right side of the brake mechanism were properly clinched, while the free ends of some on the opposite side were not separated. Nothing in the mechanism underneath the left front fender was broken. . . .

Evidence was introduced showing the inspections to which Buick automobiles are subjected during the course of their construction. With respect to the brakes on these cars, two men at or near the end of a conveyor inspect all the parts as well as the adjustments. The brake inspectors examine every cotter key or pin to ascertain whether it is properly clinched to hold in place the clevis through which it extends. When any part of an automobile is found missing or defective, the car is tagged and excluded from the conveyor. No record is kept of the automobiles inspected except those found defective and therefore rejected. There was no record that the automobile in question was rejected for any defect in the construction or adjustment of the brakes or for any other defect.

The Buick Motor Company ships its automobiles to be sold to dealers in and about Chicago to its plant in the southwest part of that city. Two employees at this plant inspect the brakes of all automobiles received from the factory at Flint, Mich. They examine the pins and cotter keys in the brake connections and inspect the steering mechanism. Any defect found is reported to the superintendent. After inspection each automobile is tagged and kept for two weeks. The automobile concerning which the present controversy arises was sold and delivered to the Cicero Buick Sales Company on August 5, 1929.

The sales company also maintains a system of inspection. After a new automobile is sold, it is prepared for delivery to the purchaser and this process requires four and one-half or five hours. The inspection includes, among other things, the removal of the wheels, the greasing of the bearings, the oiling of brake connections, and the testing of the brakes by driving the car at a speed of thirty-five miles an hour. A mechanic employed by the sales company who inspected the car in question testified that the brake rods, cables, clevises, and cotter pins were in place and correctly adjusted and that the brakes were in perfect condition. The card which he filled out upon the completion of his inspection was introduced in evidence and showed that he had checked various items among which were the adjustments of the clutch, the pedals, and the brakes. He had an independent recollection of his inspection of the particular car because he permitted it to leave the possession of the sales company without a sufficient supply of gasoline.

Another employee of the sales company also inspected the car. He testified that he found all the cotter pins in place and properly spread or clinched; that the brakes were in the same condition when the car was sold to the defendant in error as when it was received from the manufacturer; that the cotter pin which witnesses called by the defendant in error testified was missing, he actually saw in its proper place; that it held the clevis; and that the ends of the cotter pin were spread or separated. . . .

The contentions of the plaintiff in error are that, even if, at the time the defendant in error bought the automobile from the sales company it was defective in the respect claimed by him, the defect charged was a patent one and would not subject the manufacturer of the automobile to liability to a third person for injuries suffered as the result of the defect; that, in any event, no competent evidence was adduced by the defendant in error to prove that the automobile was defective at the time it was delivered to the dealer or later when the accident occurred; and that, for either of the foregoing reasons, the motion to direct a verdict should have been granted.

The defendant in error seeks to trace the accident which gave rise to this case to an unspread cotter pin in the brake mechanism of his automobile. The plaintiff in error insists that such a defect or omission, if assumed, is a patent one, open and visible to every person and readily adjusted or corrected, and cannot, in the event personal injury or property damage ensues, charge the manufacturer with liability therefore. . . . Some cases hold that, since an automobile is not a dangerous instrumentality per se, a manufacturer owes no duty to third persons, irrespective of contractual relations, to use reasonable care in its manufacture and, consequently, is not liable to such persons for injuries caused by negligence in construction. On the other hand, courts have declared in later cases that a manufacturer who places in trade and commerce a manufactured article, such as an automobile, which is not inherently dangerous to life or limb, or which may become so, because of its negligent construction, is liable to one who sustains injury by reason of such negligent construction. *MacPherson v. Buick Motor Co.*, 217 N.Y. 382. . . .

Ordinary care in the building of an automobile requires that the free ends of a cotter pin used to hold a clevis in place be clinched or separated. It follows that a manufacturer will be liable to a purchaser from a dealer where the competent evidence shows that a cotter pin was not spread when the automobile left the factory and, in consequence, the pin fell from a clevis, the clevis worked out of place, and a cable was released so that, upon the application of sufficient pressure, the brake failed to operate and an accident and injuries to the purchaser resulted.

The plaintiff in error contends, however, that even if the cause of action alleged is maintainable, the defendant in error introduced no evidence to prove one of its essential elements, namely, that the automobile was negligently constructed, and, consequently, the motion to direct a verdict for the plaintiff in error should have been granted. . . .

The mere fact that an accident resulting in an injury to a person or in damage to property has occurred does not authorize a presumption or inference that the defendant was negligent. The burden was upon the defendant in error to prove by competent evidence, direct or circumstantial, that the plaintiff in error was guilty of negligence in the manufacture or assemblage of the automobile in question. Testimony concerning the condition of cotter pins in the brake mechanism several weeks after the accident occurred without proof that the condition of the pins remained unchanged was inadmissible and should have been excluded. Such testimony was not responsive to the allegations of the declaration and could not subject the plaintiff in error to liability. . . .

Defendant in error had driven the car about six hundred miles; he testified that, prior to the accident, the brakes had given him no trouble, and that, by their application, he could stop the car, when running at a speed of twenty-five miles an hour, within six or eight feet. The tire marks on the earth embankment made just before the automobile struck the concrete culvert showed that the brakes had been applied and apparently operated effectively. The uncontradicted evidence shows that the automobile was subjected to several inspections before it was delivered to the defendant in error. At the factory two men stationed at a conveyor inspected the parts and adjustments of the car. They examined every cotter pin to determine whether it was properly clinched. No car with a part missing or defective in any respect passed this inspection. At the manufacturer's plant in Chicago, two employees inspected the brakes, the cotter keys in the brake connections and the steering mechanism of all cars. The sales company caused further inspections to be made. One of its mechanics inspected the particular car and found the brake rods, cobles, clevises and cotter pins in place and correctly adjusted. Another employee of the same company found every cotter pin in place and clinched.

Whether there was negligence in the assembly of the parts of the automobile owned by the defendant in error, as a result of which the accident occurred, depends almost wholly upon the condition of the cotter pins previous to the sale of the car. With the incompetent testimony excluded, the competent evidence is not sufficiently definite to justify the conclusion that the automobile remained in the same condition from the time of the accident until it was examined by persons who testified that some of the cotter pins were unspread two weeks or more after the accident occurred.

The judgments of the Appellate and superior courts are reversed, and the cause is remanded to the superior court.

Reversed and remanded.

Notes and Questions

1. If *Rotche* is an indication, what changes did Buick make to its inspection practices by 1934? Automakers had begun inspecting all wheels using multiple tests by 1920, just four years after *MacPherson* was decided. By the time that *Rotche* was decided, wasn't it clear that the common law worked to reduce the risk of auto accidents and corresponding harms?

2. The common law worked, but to what extent? More specifically, to what extent did *MacPherson* prompt automakers to address the problem of auto safety beyond making changes to its inspection practices? If you were legal counsel to Buick or similar automakers, what other changes would you recommend that they make following *MacPherson*? Would they all involve safety improvements? Consider the following sorts of changes, drawn from CORNELIUS W. GILLAM, PRODUCTS LIABILITY IN THE AUTOMOBILE INDUSTRY: A STUDY IN STRICT LIABILITY AND SOCIAL CONTROL (1960), and Sally H. Clarke, *Unmanageable Risks:* MacPherson v. Buick *and the Emergence of a Mass Consumer Market,* 23 LAW & HIST. REV. 1 (2005).

    a. *Advertising.* In the aftermath of *MacPherson*, automakers made their safety claims more realistic and cautious. For example, they changed their claims of "shatterproof glass" to claims of "safety glass." (After *MacPherson*, other lawsuits specifically and successfully challenged the claim of "shatterproof glass," see, e.g., Baxter v. Ford Motor Co., 168 Wash. 456 (1932).)

    b. *Customer Service.* Automakers routinely began providing repair service not required by the terms of warranties to ensure customer satisfaction. But their generosity typically ended when drivers filed lawsuits. Indeed, automakers were quick to invoke disclaimers as bars against tort claims.

    c. *Business Organization.* Some automakers reorganized their businesses in complex ways to frustrate tort plaintiffs. McLean v. Goodyear Tire & Rubber Co., 85 F.2d 150 (5th Cir. 1936), provides a dramatic illustration. Goodyear manufactured tires in Ohio but transferred distribution to a Delaware corporation with the same name. A Texas plaintiff sued the Delaware distributor for injuries resulting from a blown tire. The Delaware distributor argued that it did not manufacture the tires and was therefore not liable. When the plaintiff moved to amend his complaint to include the Ohio manufacturer, the court held it had no jurisdiction over the Ohio corporation, which had no business in Texas. (Note that now the court would have jurisdiction over the Ohio corporation in Texas.)

    d. *Disclaimers and Limited Warranties.* Automakers limited their liability as much as possible using limited warranties and disclaimers. Although a warranty is a promise of quality that, in principle, ought to work to the advantage of the buyer, warranties were often drafted with significant limitations that actually left consumers at a disadvantage. For example, an auto manufacturer might provide a warranty that lasted only for a few months. Or, it might limit recourse to replacement of the defective product or component part, rather than damages for the injuries suffered by the consumer in the accident.

    e. *Products Liability Insurance.* Some automakers acquired greater products liability insurance throughout the early age of auto insurance, but many did not. Instead, these automakers chose to accept the risk of accidents. After all, they could extensively reduce their liability through warranties and disclaimers. They could also spread the costs of liability by increasing the price of new cars.

3. The common law worked in part to address the problem of auto safety, but how well did it work for MacPherson himself? MacPherson testified that he was driving carefully at only eight miles per hour when his left rear wheel collapsed and his car flipped over, breaking his wrist and gouging out his right eye. *See* Clarke, *supra*, at 2. For the injured party, does tort law provide too little too late? This is often a shortcoming of tort law as a regulatory device. But here is another account: MacPherson recovered despite only a shred of evidence as to negligence because of a sympathetic jury. *See* James A. Henderson, Jr., MacPherson v. Buick Motor Co.: *Simplifying the Facts While Reshaping the Law, in* TORT STORIES (Robert Rabin & Steven D. Sugarman eds., 2003). Although Cardozo was not required to take MacPherson's account as true, it is at least arguable that for *this* injured party, tort law provided too much recovery. Isn't this also a flaw of tort law as a regulatory device?

4. Now focus on Buick. What advice do you suppose its lawyers provided before *MacPherson* was decided? Jeremy Bentham once disparagingly referred to the common law as "dog law" — that is, akin to the practice of imposing a punishment on a pet who did not and could not have known that what he was doing was wrong until he was smacked on the nose for misbehaving. *MacPherson* put Buick in the doghouse in more ways than one, right?

5. In other contexts, tort law has additional limitations for regulating future conduct and preventing future harm. For example, how well does tort law work to prevent harm from airborne pollutants in the workplace when the health risk is obvious but the actual injury is latent — that is, when the adverse effects may not materialize for years, or when the full extent is unknown? How well does it work to prevent harms from airborne pollutants to the environment or the public at large? Did you ever read Dr. Seuss's *The Lorax* when you were a child, which is a parable about environmental degradation? Some might ask, who speaks for the trees?

The Law and Economics Perspective

Common law's ability to provide consumers with protection in the age of factory-made products and mass marketing has been reassessed by law and economics scholarship, a mode of analysis that uses microeconomics to determine the effect of legal rules. In tort law, its central insight is that liability rules induce those who are potentially liable to exercise precaution. An economically efficient result will be obtained if liability is assigned to the party who can exercise precaution at the lowest cost. Law and economics scholars have argued that this result has often been achieved by common law courts through incremental decision making. The careless driver (the notorious "nut behind the wheel") should not have a cause of action against the manufacturer because he is in the best position to take precaution against his careless behavior. According to this view, it would be excessively expensive to design a car that prevented such a driver from injuring himself; doing so would unfairly impose costs on all the people who drive carefully. But the manufacturer should be liable for producing defective cars, since it is obviously in the best position to exercise precaution against such defects.

The next question that law and economics analysis addresses is how much precaution we want the potentially liable party to take. When the party involved is an individual, the answer can be built into the definition of legal terms. The law defines "careless" as the type of behavior that we want the person to avoid. The tired driver who suddenly swerves into an adjoining lane on the freeway and hits another car is deemed careless and held liable; that means that we do not want people to drive when they are overly tired, and we do not want them swerving. The driver of the other car could have avoided the accident if she had been driving on the freeway at 30 miles per hour, but we do not define that as careless behavior (it might be on a hilly side street) and we do not impose any liability on her.

For a manufacturer, the level of precaution is more difficult to define because we cannot rely on norms of expected behavior. But law and economics analysis offers an answer: the proper level of precaution is one where the benefits exceed the costs. Later in this course, you will see the way the federal government has used this principle to determine whether to enact regulatory measures. In that setting, the calculation involves the cost and benefit to American society. Here the issue is more limited, being concerned with the effects of the product that the manufacturer is marketing. Suppose the question is whether to add a particular safety feature to a car. In a competitive market, the cost of the safety feature must be passed on to the consumer, and can thus be measured by the increase in the price of the product. The benefit consists of the cost of all the injuries and property damage that the device prevents. To compare these benefits to the costs, they need to be stated in monetary terms, but those are not quite so readily measured because different people assess the cost of injuries quite differently.

Does this sort of calculation lead to the socially desirable outcome? In other words, is this the behavior that we want manufacturers to adopt, or do we want them to take a greater level of precaution? Consider the famous case of the Ford Pinto. The Pinto was one of the attempts by American car manufacturers in the 1960s and '70s to produce a low-cost compact car that could compete with the foreign-made compacts (most notably from Japan) that were taking over both foreign and domestic markets. The problem was that the American manufacturers, for a variety of interesting reasons that will be also be discussed later, were not particularly good at designing these types of cars. Their general quality was substantially lower, and they tended to have serious safety problems because they were rushed into production. The Chevy Corvair had a tendency to spin out of control or roll over on a curve, a problem that played a central role in the events we will discuss later on. The Pinto had an unfortunate tendency to burst into flames when rear-ended by another car.

Here is an internal memo from Ford about the way the company should address this problem.

Fatalities Associated with Crash Induced
Fuel Leakage and Fires

Ford Motor Co., 1977

. . . Benefits

The appropriateness of the estimate of 700 burn deaths each year resulting from motor vehicle crashes has been discussed in the main text of this, study. Data from both the Calspan fire study (3) and the Oklahoma analysis (1) of a New York State fire study (5) suggest that when occupants are burned, the injuries tend to be quite serious, and about half of the casualties sustain fatal injuries. Thus the 700 fatalities should be complemented by another 700 non-fatally (though seriously) injured occupants. Given the NSC estimate (2) of 10,000 yearly crash induced vehicle fires, about 8,500 of these fire crashes occur with no resultant occupant burns each year. Benefits from FMVSS 301 compliance based on these numbers represent an overestimate, since some undetermined number of these instances relate to large trucks not covered by the proposed Standard. . . .

The proportion of fuel leaks which occur in rollovers is indicated in Table 2 to be slightly less than one-fourth. If this proportion is applied to the fire numbers themselves, the consequences of fire in rollovers can be estimated as 180 deaths, 180 non-fatal injuries, and 2,100 other fire crashes. These values are predicated upon two postulations: rollover fuel leaks result in fire just as often as other fuel leaks, and rollover fires are just as likely to result in burns as other fires.

This analysis assumes that all these fires and the resultant casualties can be eliminated entirely through compliance with the rollover requirement. In addition, it is assumed that vehicle modification designed to ensure compliance with non-rollover portions of the Standard will not reduce at all the number of rollover fires. The extent to which either of these assumptions is not completely accurate represents a measure of the extent to which benefits derived here are overestimates of the true values.

To compare the benefits of eliminating the consequences of these rollover fires with the requisite costs, the benefits and costs must be expressed in terms of some common measure. The measure typically chosen is dollars; this requires, then, converting the casualty losses to this metric. The casualty to dollars conversion factors used in this study were the societal cost values prepared by the NHTSA (6). These values are generally higher than similarly-defined costs from other sources, and their use does not signify that Ford accepts or concurs in the values. Rather, the NHTSA figures are used only to be consistent with the attempt not to understate the relevant benefits.

The NHTSA has calculated a value of $200,000 for each fatality. While the major portion of this amount relates to lost future wages, the total also includes some consideration for property damage. The NHTSA average loss for all injuries was about $7,000. Burn injuries which do occur tend to be quite serious, however, as discussed above. Thus a higher value $67,000, which is the NHTSA estimate of partial disability injuries, was used for each of the 180 non-fatal burn injuries. The $700 property damage per vehicle is the NHTSA estimate of vehicle property damage costs in non-disabling injury crashes.

COSTS

The Retail Price Equivalent (the customer sticker price with no provision for Ford profit) of vehicle modifications necessary to assure compliance with the static rollover portion of the proposed Standard has been determined by Ford to be an average of $11 per passenger car and $11 per light truck. While these are Ford costs, they have been applied across the industry in this analysis. Total yearly sales estimates of 11 million passenger cars and 1.5 million light trucks (under 6,000 lbs. GVW) were used in conjunction with the unit cost determinations.

BENEFIT AND COST COMPARISON

The total benefit is shown in Table 3 to be just under $50 million, while the associated coat is $137 million. Thus the cost is almost three times the benefits, even using a number of highly favorable benefit assumptions. As better estimates of the parameters used in the benefit analysis become available, they could be inserted into the general analysis framework. It does not appear likely, however, that such alternate estimates could lead to the substantial benefit estimate increase which would be required to make compliance with the rollover requirement cost effective. . . .

After one of these Pintos exploded, an injured passenger and the heirs of the dead driver brought suit in California state court. The memo was discovered during the course of the litigation and lead to a punitive damage award of $125 million, the largest-ever award to that point. Ford appealed. Although California had enacted a legal code (the famous Field Code), tort cases were generally decided on a common law basis.

Grimshaw v. Ford Motor Co.

119 Cal. App. 3d 757, 174 Cal. Rptr. 348 (1981)

TAMURA, Acting P.J.

A 1972 Ford Pinto hatchback automobile unexpectedly stalled on a freeway, erupting into flames when it was rear ended by a car proceeding in the same direction. Mrs. Lilly Gray, the driver of the Pinto, suffered fatal burns and 13-year-old Richard Grimshaw, a passenger in the Pinto, suffered severe and permanently disfiguring burns on his face and entire body. Grimshaw and the heirs of Mrs. Gray (Grays) sued Ford Motor Company and others. Following a six-month jury trial, verdicts were returned in favor of plaintiffs against Ford Motor Company. Grimshaw was awarded $2,516,000 compensatory damages and $125 million punitive damages. On Ford's motion for a new trial, Grimshaw was required to remit all but $3.5 million of the punitive award as a condition of denial of the motion. . . .

Ford contends that the evidence was insufficient to support a finding of malice or corporate responsibility for malice. . . .

In 1968, Ford began designing a new subcompact automobile which ultimately became the Pinto. Mr. Iacocca, then a Ford vice president, conceived the project and was its moving force. Ford's objective was to build a car at or below 2,000 pounds to sell for no more than $2,000.

Ordinarily marketing surveys and preliminary engineering studies precede the styling of a new automobile line. Pinto, however, was a rush project, so that styling preceded engineering and dictated engineering design to a greater degree than usual. Among the engineering decisions dictated by styling was the placement of the fuel tank. It was then the preferred practice in Europe and Japan to locate the gas tank over the rear axle in subcompacts because a small vehicle has less "crush space" between the rear axle and the bumper than larger cars. The Pinto's styling, however, required the tank to be placed behind the rear axle leaving only 9 or 10 inches of "crush space"—far less than in any other American automobile or Ford overseas subcompact. . . .

The crash tests revealed that the Pinto's fuel system as designed could not meet the 20-mile-per-hour proposed standard. Mechanical prototypes struck from the rear with a moving barrier at 21 miles per hour caused the fuel tank to be driven forward and to be punctured, causing fuel leakage in excess of the standard prescribed by the proposed regulation. . . .

When a prototype failed the fuel system integrity test, the standard of care for engineers in the industry was to redesign and retest it. The vulnerability of the production Pinto's fuel tank at speeds of 20- and 30-miles-per-hour fixed barrier tests could have been remedied by inexpensive "fixes," but Ford produced and sold the Pinto to the public without doing anything to remedy the defects. . . .

Ford contends that Grimshaw's counsel committed prejudicial misconduct in referring to Ford's executives meeting in the "glass house" and deciding to approve the Pinto's fuel tank design with knowledge that it was unsafe and would result in the loss of many lives. Ford argues that although there was evidence that the corporate headquarters of Ford was referred to as the "glass house" there was no evidence of management meetings held there in connection with the Pinto design. The record contains substantial evidence from which it reasonably may be inferred that Ford's management knew that the Pinto was unsafe but nevertheless decided not to alleviate the problem because of cost considerations, and thus that those decisions were made in Ford's corporate headquarters. . . .

Some two weeks before this case went to the jury, the Supreme Court in *Barker v. Lull Engineering Co.*, (1978) 20 Cal.3d 413, [143 Cal. Rptr. 225, 573 P.2d 443,] formulated the following "two-pronged" definition of design defect, embodying the "consumer expectation" standard and "risk-benefit" test: "First, a product may be found defective in design if the plaintiff establishes that the product failed to perform as safely as an ordinary consumer would expect when used in an intended or reasonably foreseeable manner. Second, a product may alternatively be found defective in design if the plaintiff demonstrates that the product's design proximately caused his injury and the defendant fails to establish, in light of the relevant factors, that, on balance, the benefits of the challenged design outweigh the risk of danger inherent in such design." The "relevant factors" which a jury may consider in applying the *Barker* "risk-benefit" standard include "the gravity of the danger posed by the challenged design, the likelihood that such danger would occur, the mechanical feasibility of a safer alternative design, the financial cost of an improved design, and the adverse consequences to the product and to the consumer that would result from an alternative design." Under the risk-benefit test, once the plaintiff makes a prima facie showing that the injury was proximately caused by the product's design, the burden shifts "to the defendant to prove, in light of the relevant factors, that the product is not defective."

Ford requested two instructions purporting to set out the *Barker* tests for design defect, but the court gave only the following instruction: "A product is defective in design if the product has failed to perform as safely as an ordinary consumer would expect when used in an intended or reasonably foreseeable manner." Ford complains that the failure to give the balance of the other requested instruction constituted prejudicial error. For the reasons set out below, we conclude that the contention lacks merit.

. . . [T]he risk-benefit test was formulated primarily to aid injured persons. The instant case was submitted solely on the consumer expectation standard because the trial had been virtually completed before the *Barker* decision was rendered in which our high court for the first time articulated the risk-benefit standard of design defect. . . .

[E]ven had it been proper to instruct on the risk-benefit test, Ford's requested version of the standard was defective in two important respects. First it omitted the crucial element of the manufacturer's burden of proof in the risk-benefit posture. Nor did Ford offer a separate instruction covering the subject of the burden of proof. Second, the proposed instruction erroneously included among the "relevant factors," "the extent to which its [Pinto's] design and manufacture matched the average quality of other automobiles and the extent to which its design and manufacture deviated from the norm for automobiles designed and manufactured at the same point in time." In a strict products liability case, industry custom or usage is irrelevant to the issue of defect. . . . The *Barker* court's enumeration of factors which may be considered under the risk-benefit test not only fails to mention custom or usage in the industry, the court otherwise makes clear by implication that they are inappropriate considerations. *Barker* contrasts the risk-benefit strict liability test with a negligent design action, stating that "the jury's focus is properly directed to the condition of the product itself, and not to the reasonableness of the manufacturer's conduct. Thus, [the court explains] "the fact that the manufacturer took reasonable precautions in an attempt to design a safe product or otherwise acted as a reasonably prudent manufacturer would have under the circumstances, while perhaps absolving the manufacturer of liability under a negligence theory, will not preclude the imposition of liability under strict liability principles if, upon hindsight, the trier of fact concludes that the product's design is unsafe to consumers, users, or bystanders. . . .

The concept of punitive damages is rooted in the English common law and is a settled principle of the common law of this country. (Owen, Punitive Damages in Products Liability Litigation (1976) 74 Mich. L. Rev. 1258, 1262-1263; Mallor & Roberts, Punitive Damages: Towards a Principled Approach (1980) 31 Hastings L.J. 639, 642-643.) . . .

Ford argues that "malice" as used in section 3294 and as interpreted by our Supreme Court in *Davis v. Hearst* (1911) 160 Cal. 143 [116 P. 530], requires animus malus or evil motive—an intention to injure the person harmed—and that the term is therefore conceptually incompatible with an unintentional tort such as the manufacture and marketing of a defectively designed product. This contention runs counter to our decisional law. . . .

The interpretation of the word "malice" as used in section 3294 to encompass conduct evincing callous and conscious disregard of public safety by those who manufacture and market mass produced articles is consonant with and furthers the objectives of punitive damages. The primary purposes of punitive damages are punishment and deterrence of like conduct by the wrongdoer and others. . . .

Ford's argument that there can be no liability for punitive damages because there was no evidence of corporate ratification of malicious misconduct is equally without merit. California follows the Restatement rule that punitive damages can be awarded against a principal because of an action of an agent if, but only if, "'(a) the principal authorized the doing and the manner of the act, or (b) the agent was unfit and the principal was reckless in employing him, or (c) the agent was employed in a managerial capacity and was acting in the scope of employment, or (d) the principal or a managerial agent of the principal ratified or approved the act.' (Rest.2d Torts (Tent. Draft No. 19, 1973) §909.)" . . .

There is substantial evidence that management was aware of the crash tests showing the vulnerability of the Pinto's fuel tank to rupture at low speed rear impacts with consequent significant risk of injury or death of the occupants by fire. . . .

On appeal, Ford contends that the phrase "conscious disregard of its possible results" used in the two instructions would permit a plaintiff to impugn almost every design decision as made in conscious disregard of some perceivable risk because safer alternative designs are almost always a possibility. Ford argues that to instruct the jury so that they might find "malice" if any such "possibility" existed was erroneous; it maintains that an instruction on "malice" in products liability must contain the phrase "conscious disregard of [the probability/a high probability] of injury to others," in order to preclude prejudicial error. . . .

"But 'intent,' in the law of torts, denotes not only those results the actor desires, but also those consequences which he knows are substantially certain to result from his conduct. (Rest.2d Torts, §8a; Prosser, Torts (4th ed. 1971) pp. 31-32.) The jury in the present case could reasonably infer that defendants acted in callous disregard of plaintiffs' rights, knowing that their conduct was substantially certain to vex, annoy, and injure plaintiffs. Such behavior justifies the award of punitive damages. . . .

The jury was instructed that Ford was not required under the law to produce either the safest possible vehicle or one which was incapable of producing injury. The instructions on malice manifestly referred to conduct constituting conscious and callous disregard of a substantial likelihood of injury to others and not to innocent conduct by the manufacturer. . . .

Ford's final contention is that the amount of punitive damages awarded, even as reduced by the trial court, was so excessive that a new trial on that issue must be granted. Ford argues that its conduct was less reprehensible than those for which punitive damages have been awarded in California in the past; that the $3½ million award is many times over the highest award for such damages ever upheld in California; and that the award exceeds maximum civil penalties that may be enforced under federal or state statutes against a manufacturer for marketing a defective automobile. We are unpersuaded. . . .

In assessing the propriety of a punitive damage award, as in assessing the propriety of any other judicial ruling based upon factual determinations, the evidence must be viewed in the light most favorable to the judgment. . . . Viewing the record thusly in the instant case, the conduct of Ford's management was reprehensible in the extreme. It exhibited a conscious and callous disregard of public safety in order to maximize corporate profits. Ford's self-evaluation of its conduct is based on a review of the evidence most favorable to it instead of on the basis of the evidence most favorable to the judgment. Unlike malicious conduct directed toward a single specific individual, Ford's tortious conduct endangered the lives of thousands of Pinto purchasers. Weighed against the factor of reprehensibility, the punitive damage award as reduced by the trial judge was not excessive.

Nor was the reduced award excessive taking into account defendant's wealth and the size of the compensatory award. Ford's net worth was $7.7 billion and its income after taxes for 1976 was over $983 million. The punitive award was approximately .005 percent of Ford's net worth and approximately .03 percent of its 1976 net income. Nor was the size of the award excessive in light of its deterrent purpose. An award which is so small that it can be simply written off as a part of the cost of doing business would have no deterrent effect. An award which affects the company's pricing of its product and thereby affects its competitive advantage would serve as a deterrent. The award in question was far from excessive as a deterrent against future wrongful conduct by Ford and others.

Notes and Questions

1. Obviously, the Ford memo was a defendant's nightmare, guaranteed to elicit rage from the jury when it considered the dead and injured occupants of the vehicle. But was it truly as evil as the case made it appear? Isn't Ford correct in saying that in a competitive market, each additional safety precaution adds to the cost of the vehicle? How should the manufacturer determine the safety features of the vehicle if not by balancing the costs and benefits? A large car with a heavy metal frame is certainly safer than a thin-framed compact, but it will cost much more. Aren't consumers who buy the smaller car in effect deciding that they are willing to accept a somewhat greater level of risk in order to get a car they can afford?

2. Ford was willing to pay compensatory damages, was it not? Of course, its lawyers would contest liability in any case they thought that they could win, but the company assumed that it would lose a certain number of cases and pay the required damages. Punitive damages of the sort that were awarded in *Grimshaw* would obviously require the company to remedy the problem, and it would produce a consequent increase in the price of the vehicle. Does this seem like a good way to determine the safety features that cars should have?

3. Perhaps the real precaution that the *Grimshaw* decision will produce is that manufacturers will avoid documenting their economically based decisions and thereby prevent plaintiffs from throwing stones at their glass houses. Recall the difficulties facing consumers who bring common law suits against manufacturers, even after outmoded legal impediments have been cleared away by decisions such as *McPherson*. Does common law lead to a situation where a small number of plaintiffs are lucky enough to find some dramatic piece of evidence such as the Pinto memo or a whistleblowing employee. Where does that leave all the other plaintiffs who must prove facts that would require a massive investigation to reveal?

4. Does a common law decision making approach inevitably lead to the conundrums described in the preceding notes? The "risk-benefit" standard of the *Barker* decision seems to recognize the problem and attempt to articulate a common law standard that resolves it. Clearly, it reflects the microeconomic approach to tort liability for producers of consumer products. How different is it from the alternative "consumer expectation" test that the trial court relied on in framing its instructions to the jury? Does it represent an effort to dress up an outmoded means of regulation with the finery (or fig leaf) of modern economic analysis?

5. Another way to resolve the situation may be to focus on the issue that seems to have been the most persuasive in the Pinto case, and that constitutes one of the factors in the *Barker* standard. This is the idea that Ford could have resolved the problem with an equally inexpensive but safer design, and that it failed to do so from sheer callousness or laziness. But doesn't this require the sort of comparative inquiry that the court claims is irrelevant in a strict liability case? Even (or perhaps especially) if comparison is avoided, doesn't this solution require a detailed inquiry into the practices of the company and a profound knowledge of automotive engineering? And that brings us back again to the basic problem with the common law as a means of dealing with the realities of the modern economy.

Note on the Limitations of Common Law Adjudication More Generally

Common law is often regarded in our system as unique and occupying some sort of special status. It is treated as an in-dwelling set of principles distinctive to Anglo-American culture, so much so that the American revolutionaries, who condemned the king and killed or expelled his appointees, never seriously considered replacing English common law as the applicable law to be applied by the judiciary of the new republic. As you have certainly noticed, it continues to dominate the first-year law school curriculum. Given the aura that is attached to common law, we need to step back and think about its actual origins and operation. The term, of course refers to law that is declared by judges and developed incrementally, always with attention (although not necessarily with obedience) to precedent. But why is it called common law?

In early medieval England, even after the reorganization of the kingdom by William the Conqueror, leading noblemen ran their own courts and administered their own sets of laws. When King Henry I, William's son, died without a male heir, a civil war broke out between the two claimants to the throne, his nephew, Stephen, and his daughter, Matilda. After nearly twenty years of war (the period is known as the Anarchy), a settlement was reached that brought Matilda's son to the throne as Henry II. The problem Henry faced was that Stephen and Matilda had issued overlapping and conflicting land grants, this being the way to obtain or reward supporters at the time.

To resolve the problem, Henry enacted several statutes (called assizes) that established a group of royal judges who would ride circuit (that is why we still refer to federal appellate courts as circuit courts) and administer a *common law* for the entire realm. But Henry did not specify the rules by which his new judges were to resolve the conflicting grants. He didn't care which grant prevailed; his only concern was that the conflicts were definitively resolved and order was restored to his kingdom. Therefore, he left the development of the applicable rules to the new judges he had created.

Thus common law originated as a statutory authorization by the ruling authority that created an institution staffed by government officials, defined its authority, and then gave it discretion to develop the rules that it would enforce. Does this sound familiar? It is precisely what happens now when Congress enacts a regulatory statute. If it is an organic statute, it creates an institution staffed by government officials (NTSA), defines its authority (motor vehicle safety), and gives it discretion to develop the rules that it enforces (motor vehicle safety standards).

One difference is that the courts that were authorized to create a common law were not granted rulemaking authority; they could only develop rules by adjudication. Modern agencies can do so as well (the NLRB relies exclusively on this approach), but they also have authority to make rules in the manner of a legislature. A second difference is that the common law courts lacked prosecutorial authority. Civil cases (and most criminal cases until the eighteenth century) had to be initiated by private parties. As a result, these courts, although well suited to resolving concrete disputes, suffered from serious limitations when dealing with the complexities of industrial society.

Consider the following dimensions:

Retrospective vs. Prospective: When a court announces a new rule, it applies that rule to prior conduct — which is to say, the conduct of the parties in the case. As a result, the parties may receive something of an unfair penalty or windfall. We were getting at this issue when asking what advice Buick's lawyers provided before *MacPherson* was decided, as compared to the advice they provided after the case was decided. Statutes typically apply to conduct that occurs after enactment, so they are typically not retroactive in the sense that common law judicial decisions can be.

Reactive vs. Proactive: A court can only address an issue when a party brings a case. A party can only bring a case if she suffers an injury. Thus, courts cannot reach out to prevent an injury, at least not all of them. We raised this issue when we asked whether tort law provided MacPherson himself too little too late. Legislatures and agencies can take action at any time. They need not await an injury.

Uncertainty: Courts often introduce uncertainty in the common law through a practice that Professor Melvin Eisenberg calls "transforming" prior precedent. MELVIN ARON EISENBERG, THE NATURE OF THE COMMON LAW 4-7, 58-60, 132-34 (1988). Courts do not forthrightly acknowledge that they are changing the law by overruling past decisions. Rather, courts recast those decisions in terms consistent with the present one. This practice leaves future parties and courts without a clear sense whether or to what extent the law has changed. As we asked above after *MacPherson*, did Judge Cardozo engage in transforming? Why would courts do this? Courts introduce other types of uncertainty in the common law. Even when courts acknowledge a change and other courts follow (courts are only bound by precedent in their own jurisdictions), they tend to approach broad legal questions from a narrow perspective. More specifically, they resolve such questions based on the facts of the case and only as necessary to decide the case. The resulting narrowness of judicial rules can decrease predictability for parties. Privity is no longer necessary for car purchasers to sue automakers, but exactly where else is it no longer necessary? Legislatures and agencies do not typically suffer from these sorts of uncertainty. First, federal statutes apply in all jurisdictions across the nation. Second, legislatures and agencies typically create rules of general application and future effect.

Institutional Competence: Courts are suited to resolve concrete disputes among parties. They are not well suited to redesign cars or other defective products. More generally, they lack the technical or specialized skill to craft the rules that govern risk-generating conduct. And while courts are well suited to award damages or issue injunctions, they are not well suited to set phase-in schedules for new requirements, which are often necessary to give regulated entities adequate time to change their conduct. Courts also lack the information gathering and processing capability that is necessary to craft and implement rules. In our civil system, courts do not initiate their own fact gathering. They are dependent on the parties for information, which means that information relevant to risk-related rules may be presented in a certain light or not at all. Even when courts have access to information, they are limited in the capacity to process it. No matter how intelligent or sophisticated, judges are generalists. They ordinarily lack the time let alone the experience to become experts in any given area. (The U.S. Court of Appeals for the D.C. Circuit is often said to be an expert in administrative law because so many cases involve such law, but the judges are still not experts in auto safety.) Legislatures and agencies have their own fact-gathering apparatuses. Legislatures often hold hearings regarding bills that are being considered for enactment; in the context of these hearings, they can call witnesses and obtain documents. They can also talk to just about anyone they choose. Agencies are even better off in this respect. They have research staffs and continuous contacts with industry leaders, interest groups, and others with relevant information. They also house many specialists — lawyers, scientists, economists, and policymakers — and these specialists make agencies superior even to Congress for processing information.

Political Accountability: Judges, at least in the federal courts, are insulated from democratic politics. A federal judge cannot be voted off the bench no matter how much the people dislike her decisions. As a result, judges are less responsive to public preferences than elected officials. This political insulation is a deliberate constitutional choice, beneficial especially when judges are resolving disputes over unpopular rights. But when setting risk-related rules, it can be seen as somewhat less so. Such rules often involve complex political tradeoffs that elected officials or their agents are better suited to make. *See* Albert C. Lin, *Beyond Tort: Compensating Victims of Environmental Toxic Injury*, 78 S. CAL. L. REV. 1439, 1465-66 (2005).

Parties vs. Interested Participants: Adjudication before a court (as opposed to courts or judges themselves) is less pluralist in a different sense. It is restricted to the parties in the case, with some limited participation by others with a specific interest in the outcome. By contrast, the legislative process is open to anyone who can garner legislative attention. The administrative process is even more accessible; as you will see in Chapter 5, agencies have an obligation to solicit and consider the views of all interested parties.

Collective Action Problems: Adjudication before a court is dependent on private initiative, which not only requires an injury (see above) and a legal cause of action but the wherewithal to bring a lawsuit. Pursuing a lawsuit is notoriously expensive. Individuals have little incentive to bring lawsuits where the cost of litigation is likely to exceed the value of their recovery. Even when the value of recovery is likely to be greater than the cost of litigation, the inconvenience, not to mention the stress, may discourage individuals from bringing the suit. Note that certain litigation devices have helped by "collectivizing" similarly situated individuals and effectively spreading the costs among them. For example, the class action lawsuit provides a way of making litigation of many small-value claims practicable by effectively joining them together. But these and other devices do not completely eliminate the obstacles to addressing risk-generating conduct through adjudication. *See* Caroline Vaile Wright & Louise F. Fitzgerald, *Correlates of Joining a Sexual Harassment Class Action*, 33 LAW & HUM. BEHAV. 265 (2009).

B. THE LIMITATIONS OF CONTRACT LAW

If tort law has limitations for regulating risks, what about market mechanisms? For instance, why can't consumers simply demand enhanced safety features when buying new cars? In turn, why won't automakers, seeing a market opportunity, compete with each other by offering safer cars at increasingly affordable prices? In short, why doesn't the market provide the right amount of auto safety—which is to say, as much as consumers demand? Note that the market is assisted by contract law in these scenarios. If a consumer purchases a safety feature and it fails to perform as promised, she can sue the automaker for breach of actual or implied warranty.

Why can't you just ask for what you want?

One reason concerns information. To make choices about auto safety or any other issue for that matter, people not only need access to information but the ability to make sense of it. The more technical the information, the harder it is to process. The less sophisticated the consumer of the information (contrast the typical car buyer to a car engineer), the greater it is still. To put this problem in a concrete context, search online for information concerning new car safety options. The Internet unquestionably has improved access to information, and websites offer help digesting information. Isn't that good enough?

Below is a select list of features to consider when buying a new car. They appear here in alphabetical order. Almost all are "passive" or automatic like airbags, in the sense that they operate without driver assistance. Some are also like original ignition interlocks and current seatbelt warnings because they emit an audible warning (often along with providing a visual warning). Which of these features are most important and worth your money? If you consult online resources, the recommendations differ. At least one resource, the one on which we relied in compiling this list, presents some of them "convenience" features rather than safety features. *See* Must-Have Features to Get in Your New Car, https://www.consumerreports.org/automotive-technology/must-have-features-to-get-in-next-new-car/ (Jon Linkov, Mar. 11, 2019). In other words, they are nice to have but not integral to auto safety. Do you agree? Are you uncertain?

360-degree surround-view camera: Provides an aerial view from above your car to detect things all around your car (including children and animals).

Android Auto and Apple SmartPlay: Integrates your Android phone or iPhone into your car's head unit screen to facilitate hands-free driving, reduce distractions, and promote better attention to the road.

Automatic dimming mirrors: Dims your mirrors when bright lights appear in them from a vehicle behind your car.

Automatic emergency braking: Brakes when another vehicle is your immediate path. Some systems detect pedestrians, and others do not.

Automatic high beams: Turns on high beams when there are no oncoming vehicles, and turns them off when oncoming vehicles become visible.

Blind spot warning: Gives a visual and/or audible warning when a vehicle is in your blind spot.

Forward collision warning: Gives a visual and/or audible warning when your car is in danger of an imminent collision.

Head-up display: Projects your car's information on the driver's side windshield to make it easier to keep your eyes on the road.

Knobs for audio and temperature controls: Provides old-fashioned knobs instead of touch-screen functionality to make, for example adjusting the sound-system volume and the air conditioning level, easier and thereby allowing you to keep your eyes on the road.

Lane keeping assist: Steers or brakes when a vehicle in front of your car moves into your lane without signaling.

Rear cross traffic warning: Sends a visual and/or audible warning when your car is in reverse and something (including a child or animal) may be in a blind spot.

Notes and Questions

1. Suppose you were buying a new car. Which safety features would you demand? How could you be certain that these features would satisfy your safety preferences? What sources of information would you consult? The dealer? *Consumer Reports*? Web sites? What are the limitations of relying on consumer preferences to determine the level of safety in vehicles? Does anyone besides the purchaser of the vehicle have an interest in the choice?

2. What if people are limited in their capacity to process information not by the technical nature of that information but by external influences, such as advertising? People may want to have safe, efficient, inexpensive cars (their actual preferences), but they buy unsafe and more expensive cars (their revealed preferences) because advertising portrays these cars as desirable. In such a case, there is an argument that regulation is necessary to realize the actual preferences of the public. Are you convinced? How does the government distinguish actual preferences from revealed preferences? And why should the government favor one over the other? Why not allow people to maximize image even at the expense of safety? Put differently, what is the argument for paternalism regarding adults? It is one thing for a parent to advocate for a child's best interests — by refusing to buy the sugary cereal marketed to kids with cute animals and fabulous prizes rather than the nutritious one. But governments and grownups?

3. What if people are limited in their information processing capacity by internal forces often called cognitive biases? Psychologists and sociologists have determined that people systematically undervalue or overvalue certain risks. For example, they discount low probability events against current conveniences. They discount risks within their control — like risks of driving — and overestimate risks beyond their control — like risks of airline travel. They overvalue risks to children. They overvalue risks that they can visualize through an example: the so-called availability heuristic. *See* Amos Tversky & Daniel Kahneman, *Judgment Under Uncertainty: Heuristics and Biases*, 185 SCIENCE 1124 (1974). These errors in judgment suggest that there are certain situations where people find it difficult to honor their own preferences. Thus, even if we are willing to trust their judgment as a general matter, we may want the government to step in on particular issues. But do we? There is a further issue: what is to say that government officials do not suffer from precisely the same cognitive biases as the rest of us?

4. Information does not necessarily guarantee choice. For example, you could not have purchased an airbag for your new car regardless of how much you knew until it was included as optional equipment in mass-produced cars. Either the manufacturers must decide on their own to install safety features and offer them to the public, or a substantial number of people must know what you do and communicate their preferences to the manufacturers. This is a collective action problem on the contracts side. Will coordination among like-minded individuals occur? How long will it take? How many people will be killed or injured in the interim?

5. Information asymmetries likely played a role in supporting auto safety legislation, which came on the scene in 1966. *See* National Traffic and Motor Vehicle Safety Act of 1966, Pub. L. No. 89-563, 80 Stat. 718. We will introduce you to that legislation in Chapter 2. Think here about the possible market-related justifications. Were there other market failures? It was not monopoly — there were three big American manufacturers, and they competed vigorously with one another, as well as with a variety of foreign companies. It certainly was not the existence of rents or public goods. What about externalities? In his book *Unsafe at Any Speed* (1965), Ralph Nader, the most vocal advocate for auto safety legislation in the 1960s, discussed some obvious externalities. For example, he pointed out that the fins and jutting metal ornaments on American cars often injured pedestrians in ways that would not have occurred with a differently designed car. But the differential cannot be particularly great; a pedestrian hit by a car is going to get hurt, regardless of the car's design, the biggest variable being the speed at which the car is traveling. Most of the injuries Nader wrote about were to drivers or passengers in the car, and that is the issue to which his title refers. Do drivers impose externalities on others when they refuse to take adequate safety precautions themselves, such as wearing a manual seatbelt? Who is hurt by such behavior?

C. THE JUSTIFICATIONS FOR REGULATION

Broadly speaking, two different types of justifications for regulation have emerged. The first is rooted in economic theory. It reflects the notion of market failures: sometimes the market, reinforced by the common law, will not supply consumers with their preferred option. The other is rooted in democratic theory. It reflects the idea of social justice or welfare: sometimes people will demand more for society than any individual will seek for herself as a consumer.

We set forth both types of justifications below. They are important for three reasons. First, they help to pinpoint the weaknesses in the old regime that created room for the rise of a new order. Second, they are useful, as a practical matter, for understanding the statutes that Congress has enacted over time. For example, Congress has used both economic and social justifications to support its statutes, such as auto safety legislation. Third, much federal regulation must be explicitly justified based on these rationales (as required by Executive Order No. 12866, which is addressed in detail in Chapter 6). Lawyers can use such justifications as lenses through which to view statutes and regulation when interpreting or applying them. These justifications can also be used more abstractly to defend government intervention against claims that the market would better handle a problem. By presenting the justifications here, we are not asking *you* to accept any of them. Rather, we are asking you to appreciate them as all lawyers must to serve their clients well.

1. Economic Justifications for Regulation

Economic justifications date back to the earliest regulatory statutes from the progressive era and the New Deal. During this period, a "policing model" of regulation triumphed. *See* Robert L. Rabin, *Federal Regulation in Historical Perspective*, 38 STAN. L. REV. 1189, 1192 (1986). This model emphasized "the limited responsibility of government for economic well-being," premised on the view that the individuals and corporations were best able to safeguard their well-being through market transactions. *Id.* But even with that basic commitment, certain "market failures" still occurred, with grave economic and social consequences. In some conditions, for instance, the market generated incentives to set discriminatory pricing or excessive rates. *See id.* A railroad, with a monopoly on routes, might charge shippers an arbitrary or exorbitant amount. The railroad shipper had little power to bargain for a lower rate. Addressing such a market failure provided a justification for regulation beyond the relatively ad hoc approach of adjudication. (For example, a shipper could sue a railroad, arguing that the rate was "unreasonable.") This logic provides a basis for many early regulatory statutes, including those intended to stabilize the ailing domestic economy in the wake of the Great Depression.

The Office of Management and Budget (OMB) has issued a document addressed to executive agencies stating the basic economic rationales for regulation, rationales these agencies must considering when acting.

OMB, Circular A-4, To the Heads of Executive Agencies and Establishments, Subject: Regulatory Analysis

Sept. 17, 2003

THE NEED FOR FEDERAL REGULATORY ACTION

. . . Executive Order 12866 states that "Federal agencies should promulgate only such regulations as are required by law, are necessary to interpret the law, or are made necessary by compelling need, such as material failures of private markets to protect or improve the health and safety of the public, the environment, or the well being of the American people. . . ."

Executive Order 12866 also states that "Each agency shall identify the problem that it intends to address (including, where applicable, the failures of private markets or public institutions that warrant new agency action) as well as assess the significance of that problem." Thus, you should try to explain whether the action is intended to address a significant market failure or to meet some other compelling public need such as improving governmental processes or promoting intangible values such as distributional fairness or privacy. . . .

Market Failure or Other Social Purpose

The major types of market failure include: externality, market power, and inadequate or asymmetric information. Correcting market failures is a reason for regulation, but it is not the only reason. Other possible justifications include improving the functioning of government, removing distributional unfairness, or promoting privacy and personal freedom.

1. Externality, Common Property Resource and Public Good

An externality occurs when one party's actions impose uncompensated benefits or costs on another party. Environmental problems are a classic case of externality. For example, the smoke from a factory may adversely affect the health of local residents while soiling the property in nearby neighborhoods. If bargaining were costless and all property rights were well defined, people would eliminate externalities through bargaining without the need for government regulation.[3] From this perspective, externalities arise from high transactions costs and/or poorly defined property rights that prevent people from reaching efficient outcomes through market transactions.

Resources that may become congested or overused, such as fisheries or the broadcast spectrum, represent common property resources. "Public goods," such as defense or basic scientific research, are goods where provision of the good to some individuals cannot occur without providing the same level of benefits free of charge to other individuals.

2. Market Power

Firms exercise market power when they reduce output below what would be offered in a competitive industry in order to obtain higher prices. They may exercise market power collectively or unilaterally. Government action can be a source of market power, such as when regulatory actions exclude low-cost imports. Generally, regulations that increase market power for selected entities should be avoided. However, there are some circumstances in which government may choose to validate a monopoly. If a market can be served at lowest cost only when production is limited to a single producer B local gas and electricity distribution services, for example B a natural monopoly is said to exist. In such cases, the government may choose to approve the monopoly and to regulate its prices and/or production decisions. Nevertheless, you should keep in mind that technological advances often affect economies of scale. This can, in turn, transform what was once considered a natural monopoly into a market where competition can flourish.

3. Inadequate or Asymmetric Information

Market failures may also result from inadequate or asymmetric information. Because information, like other goods, is costly to produce and disseminate, your evaluation will need to do more than demonstrate the possible existence of incomplete or asymmetric information. Even though the market may supply less than the full amount of information, the amount it does supply may be reasonably adequate and therefore not require government regulation. Sellers have an incentive to provide information through advertising that can increase sales by highlighting distinctive characteristics of their products. Buyers may also obtain reasonably adequate information about product characteristics through other channels, such as a seller offering a warranty or a third party providing information.

Even when adequate information is available, people can make mistakes by processing it poorly. Poor information-processing often occurs in cases of low probability, high-consequence events, but it is not limited to such situations. For instance, people sometimes rely on mental rules-of-thumb that produce errors. If they have a clear mental image of an incident which makes it cognitively "available," they might overstate the probability that it will occur. Individuals sometimes process information in a biased manner, by being too optimistic or pessimistic, without taking sufficient account of the fact that the outcome is exceedingly unlikely to occur. When mistakes in information processing occur, markets may overreact. When it is time-consuming or costly for consumers to evaluate complex information about products or services (e.g., medical therapies), they may expect government to ensure that minimum quality standards are met. However, the mere possibility of poor information processing is not enough to justify regulation. If you think there is a problem of information processing that needs to be addressed, it should be carefully documented.

4. Other Social Purposes

There are justifications for regulations in addition to correcting market failures. A regulation may be appropriate when you have a clearly identified measure that can make government operate more efficiently. In addition, Congress establishes some regulatory programs to redistribute resources to select groups. Such regulations should be examined to ensure that they are both effective and cost-effective. Congress also authorizes some regulations to prohibit discrimination that conflicts with generally accepted norms within our society. Rulemaking may also be appropriate to protect privacy, permit more personal freedom or promote other democratic aspirations.

Notes and Questions

1. The concept of market failures helps to explain why citizens cannot always protect themselves through the forces of supply and demand, backed by the common law. Arguments over whether government intervention is a proper response typically center on whether the market will "clear" the failure and how soon. For example:

   a. *Monopoly*. If a monopolist is making exceptional profits, other entrepreneurs will be motivated to enter the market. The question then turns on whether there are "barriers to entry" and how high these barriers may be. In this era of globalization, foreign firms as well as domestic firms can serve as potential competitors (think of the U.S. auto industry).

b. *Externalities.* Perhaps externalities can be overcome by affected individuals or groups getting together and bargaining for a solution in which the externalities they experience are "internalized" by the entity producing those spillover costs. If people near a factory are bothered by pollution, can't they convince the factory owner to install a pollution control system—or even contribute to the costs of paying for one? This solution is rarely simple because it requires collective action: residents may continue to suffer the effects of pollution because it is too difficult to organize. Collective action almost always imposes transaction costs, and as the number of individuals affected increases, communication and bargaining becomes more difficult. A legal default rule often is necessary to overcome these transaction costs by allocating responsibility for the harm to one party (i.e., the factory) rather than the other (i.e., the residents). Is the common law a candidate for solving the problem? For example, an expansion of nuisance law might grant people near a factory the right to sue the factory in tort; the factory owner would then need to compensate them for their damages or bargain with them to accept some contractual payment. Now we are back to the limitations of tort law.

c. *Information Asymmetries.* Competitors have an incentive to provide information in areas where their product has a market advantage. They want consumers to know why their product is the best. Will this incentive solve the problem and how soon?

2. Circular A-4 notes that creating or protecting public goods is an economic justification for regulation. Here is a description of the problem of protecting public goods from ROBERT COOTER & THOMAS ULEN, LAW & ECONOMICS 45-46 (5th ed. 2008):

> A public good is a commodity with two very closely related characteristics:
>
> a. *nonrivalrous consumption:* consumption of a public good by one person does not leave less for any other consumer, and
> b. *nonexcludability:* the costs of excluding nonpaying beneficiaries who consume the good are so high that no private profit-maximizing firm is willing to supply the good.

Consider national defense. Suppose, for the purposes of illustration, that national defense was provided by competing private companies. For an annual fee a company would sell protection to its customers against loss from foreign invasion by air, land, or sea. Only those customers who purchase some company's services would be protected against foreign invasion. Perhaps these customers could be identified by special garments, and their property denoted by a large white "X" painted on the roof of their homes. Who will purchase the services of these private national defense companies?

Some will, but many will not. Many of the nonpurchasers will reason that if their neighbor purchases a protection policy from a private national defense company, then they, too, will be protected: it will prove virtually impossible for the private company to protect the property and person of the neighbor without also providing security to the nearby nonpurchaser. Thus, the consumption of national defense is nonrivalrous: consumption by one person does not leave less for any other consumer. For that reason, there is a strong inducement for consumers of the privately provided public good to try to be *free riders*: they hope to benefit at no cost to themselves from the payment of others. How can public policy correct the market failure in the provision of public goods? There are two general correctives. First, the government may undertake to *subsidize* the private provision of the public good, either directly or indirectly through the tax system. An example might be research on basic science. Second, the government may undertake to provide the public good itself and to pay the costs of providing the service through the revenues raised by compulsory taxation. This is, in fact, how national defense is supplied.

2. Social Justifications for Regulation

Much government regulation stems from the recognition that, as a society, we may aspire to certain norms of conduct for their own sake. The 1960s and 1970s produced many statutes that fit this mold. Legislation exploded on the scene in diverse areas such as employment discrimination, environmental quality, consumer protection, and occupational safety. The 1966 auto safety statute is part of this wave of legislation. This statute may have addressed market failures, but that was not its only or sometimes even primary aim. So large was the wave of legislation that one scholar termed this period the Public Interest Era, *see* Robert L. Rabin, *Legitimacy, Discretion, and the Concept of Rights*, 92 YALE L.J. 1174 (1983), and another (see below) called it the Rights Revolution. As you read the excerpt from Professor Sunstein below, consider the ways in which the social justifications for government regulation that he discusses interact with the economic justifications for such regulation.

Cass Sunstein, After the Rights Revolution: Reconceiving the Regulatory State

57-69 (1990)

COLLECTIVE DESIRES AND ASPIRATIONS

Some statutes . . . might be described as collective desires, including aspirations, "preferences about preferences," or considered judgments on the part of significant segments of society. Laws of this sort are a product of deliberative processes on the part of citizens and representatives. They cannot be understood as an attempt to aggregate or trade off private preferences. This understanding of politics recalls Madison's belief in deliberative democracy.

Frequently, political choices cannot easily be understood as a process of aggregating prepolitical desires. Some people may, for example, want nonentertainment broadcasting on television, even though their own consumption patterns favor situation comedies; they may seek stringent environmental laws even though they do not use the public parks; they may approve of laws calling for social security and welfare even though they do not save or give to the poor; they may support antidiscrimination laws even though their own behavior is hardly race- or gender-neutral. The choices people make as political participants are different from those they make as consumers. Democracy thus calls for an intrusion on markets. The widespread disjunction between political and consumption choices presents something of a puzzle. Indeed, it sometimes leads to the view that market ordering is undemocratic and that choices made through the political process are a preferable basis for social ordering.

A generalization of this sort would be far too broad in light of the multiple breakdowns of the political process and the advantages of market ordering in many arenas. But it would also be a mistake to suggest, as some do, that markets always reflect individual choice more reliably than politics, or that political choices differ from consumption outcomes only because of confusion, as voters fail to realize that they must ultimately bear the costs of the programs they favor. Undoubtedly consumer behavior is sometimes a better or more realistic reflection of actual preferences than is political behavior. But since preferences depend on context, the very notion of a "better reflection" of "actual" preferences is a confused one. Moreover, the difference might be explained by the fact that political behavior reflects a variety of influences that are distinctive to the context of politics.

These include four closely related phenomena. First, citizens may seek to fulfill individual and collective aspirations in political behavior, not in private consumption. As citizens, people may seek the aid of the law to bring about a social state in some sense higher than what emerges from market ordering. Second, people may, in their capacity as political actors, attempt to satisfy altruistic or other-regarding desires, which diverge from the self-interested preferences characteristic of markets. Third, political decisions might vindicate what might be called meta-preferences or second-order preferences. A law protecting environmental diversity and opposing consumption behaviors is an example. People have wishes about their wishes; and sometimes they try to vindicate those second-order wishes, or considered judgments about what is best, through law. Fourth, people may precommit themselves, with regulation, to a course of action that they consider to be in the general interest; the story of Ulysses and the Sirens is the model here. The adoption of a Constitution is itself an example of a precommitment strategy.

For all these reasons people seem to favor regulation designed to secure high-quality broadcasting even though their consumption patterns favor situation comedies — a phenomenon that helps justify certain controversial regulatory decisions by the Federal Communications Commission requiring nonentertainment broadcasting and presentations on issues of public importance. The same category of aspirations or public spiritedness includes measures designed to protect endangered species and natural preserves in the face of individual behavior that reflects little solicitude for them. . . .

These general considerations suggest that statutes are sometimes a response to a considered judgment on the part of the electorate that the choices reflected in consumption patterns ought to be overcome. A related but more narrow justification is that statutes safeguard noncommodity values that an unregulated market protects inadequately. Social ordering through markets may have long-term, world-transforming effects that reflect a kind of collective myopia in the form of an emphasis on short-term considerations at the expense of the future. Here regulation is a natural response. Examples include promoting high-quality programming in broadcasting, supporting the arts, and ensuring diversity through protection of the environment and of endangered species. In all of these respects, political choices are not made by consulting given or private desires, but instead reflect a deliberative process designed to shape and reflect values. . . .

SOCIAL SUBORDINATION

Some regulatory statutes attempt not simply to redistribute resources, but to eliminate or reduce the social subordination of various social groups. Much of antidiscrimination law is designed as an attack on practices and beliefs that have adverse consequences for members of disadvantaged groups. Discriminatory attitudes and practices result in the social subordination of blacks, women, the handicapped, and gays and lesbians. Statutes designed to eliminate discrimination attempt to change both practices and attitudes. The motivating idea here is that differences that are irrelevant from the moral point of view ought not to be turned into social disadvantages, and they certainly should not be permitted to do so if the disadvantage is systemic. In all of these cases, social practices turn differences into systemic harms for the relevant group. Such measures as the Equal Pay Act, the Civil Rights Act of 1964, and the Developmentally Disabled Assistance and Bill of Rights Act attempt to supply correctives. . . .

One goal of the advocates of antisubordination is to restructure market arrangements so as to put disadvantaged groups on a plane of equality—not by helping them to be "like" members of advantaged groups, but by changing the criteria themselves. A law cannot make it up to someone for being deaf or requiring a wheelchair; but it can aggravate or diminish the social consequences of deafness and lameness. Regulation requiring sign language and wheelchair ramps ensures that a difference is not turned into a systemic disadvantage. Here the conventional test of discrimination law—is the member of the disadvantaged group "similarly situated" to the member of the advantaged group?—itself reflects inequality, since it takes the norms and practices of the advantaged group as the baseline against which to measure inequality.

Statutes protecting the handicapped are the best example here. To say this is not to suggest the nature or degree of appropriate restructuring of the market—a difficult question in light of the sometimes enormous costs of adaptation to the norms and practices of disadvantaged groups. But it is to say that markets are far from a sufficient protection against social subordination. . . .

IRREVERSIBILITY, FUTURE GENERATIONS, ANIMALS, AND NATURE

Some statutes are a response to the problem of irreversibility—the fact that a certain course of conduct, if continued, will lead to an outcome from which current and future generations will be able to recover not at all, or only at very high cost. Since markets reflect the preferences of current consumers, they do not take account of the effect of transactions on future generations. The consequences of reliance on market ordering will sometimes be an irretrievable loss. The protection of endangered species stems in part from this fear. Much of the impetus behind laws protecting natural areas is that environmental degradation is sometimes final or extraordinarily expensive to repair. Protection of cultural relics stems from a similar rationale.

To a large degree, social and economic regulation of this sort is produced by a belief in obligations owed by the present to future generations. Current practices may produce losses that might be acceptable if no one else were affected, but that are intolerable in light of their consequences for those who will follow. Effects on future generations thus amount to a kind of externality. Such externalities might include limitations in the available range of experiences or the elimination of potential sources of medicines and pesticides; consider the Endangered Species Act.

. . . Sometimes the invocation of the rights of nonhuman creatures and objects can best be understood as a rhetorical device designed to inculcate social norms that will overcome collective action problems in preserving the environment—problems that are ultimately harmful to human beings. In many hands, however, the argument, sounding in what is sometimes called "deep ecology," does not even refer to human desires. The idea here is that animals, species as such, and perhaps even natural objects warrant respect for their own sake, and quite apart from their interactions with human beings. Sometimes such arguments posit general rights held by living creatures (and natural objects) against human depredations. In especially powerful forms, these arguments are utilitarian in character, stressing the often extreme and unnecessary suffering of animals who are hurt or killed. The Animal Welfare Act reflects these concerns.

Notes and Questions

1. As Sunstein explains, sometimes our "preferences about preferences" are entitled to more weight than the preferences that we act upon in our daily lives. If the government gives effect to our aspirations, how is this

different from paternalism? In name only? Paternalism is often viewed as a poor justification for intervention. Is it always?

2. One way to view government intervention on the basis of public aspirations is leadership — that is, the government is acting on our behalf with the expectation that we will catch up. When is the government entitled to lead? Is the government on firmer footing when a significant minority is already "with the program"? If so, where might we see such leadership today?

3. Consider anti-discrimination norms. Sunstein offers four reasons why market pressures are insufficient to counter social subordination. Where might we see the reasons persist or materialize today?

4. In other parts of his book, Sunstein emphasizes a more general concern about the market as a natural, fixed baseline: "[M]arket outcomes — including prices and wages pursuant to a system of freedom of contract — are affected by a wide range of factors that are morally arbitrary. They include, for example, supply and demand at any particular place and time, unequally distributed opportunities before people become traders at all, existing tastes, the sheer number of purchasers and sellers, and even the unequal distribution of skills. There is no good reason for government to take these factors as natural or fixed, or to allow them to be turned into social and legal advantages, when it is deciding on the proper scope of regulation." SUNSTEIN, AFTER THE RIGHTS REVOLUTION 39. Thus, Sunstein argues that the market is a human creation and subject to evaluation on the same grounds as any other human creation, such as regulation. It need not only "fail" to be replaced, but can be rejected if another system is preferable. In a similar vein, Professor Neil Komesar proposes that we regard the market as just another means of regulation, which we can use or not depending on the results we want to achieve. *See* IMPERFECT ALTERNATIVES: CHOOSING INSTITUTIONS IN LAW, ECONOMICS, AND PUBLIC POLICY (1997). Do you see why arguments such as these are important?

5. We mentioned that auto safety legislation came on the scene in 1966 during the Rights Revolution. To what extent do social justifications support such legislation? Auto safety might be viewed as a societal right, along with other "rights" like workplace safety or environmental quality or employment equality: every citizen is entitled to protection in their own vehicles, and the government can play a role in guaranteeing it. We were entering an age when technology could put a man on the moon; why not take the small steps necessary to make new cars safer for all?

From Justification to Legislation: A Note on the Role of Politics

Economic and social justifications for government regulation may play a role in the shift from the common law to the regulatory state, in general and in the auto safety context. They are also central to the public discourse about legislation. Specifically, they help courts, agencies, lawyers, and citizens understand what regulatory statutes mean and how they apply. But do these justifications explain why Congress enacts regulatory statutes?

Leading political scientists argue that they do not. Instead, they contend that Congress is motivated to enact a statute whenever that statute serves the self-interest of a majority of legislators. This claim is based on public choice theory, which holds that legislators, no different than any other rational actors, take actions that serve their self interest. *See, e.g.,* DENNIS C. MUELLER, PUBLIC CHOICE III (2003); DANIEL A. FARBER & PHILIP P. FRICKEY, LAW AND PUBLIC CHOICE: A CRITICAL INTRODUCTION (1991). For many legislators, this self-interest is reelection. Above all else, they want to keep their jobs for their own sakes. But even legislators who intend to pursue other, more public-minded goals must hold office to accomplish those goals. The consequence, by and large, is that legislators will cater to the preferences of wealthy and organized constituent groups because these groups fund reelection campaigns. Sometimes legislators are motivated by a different sort of self-interest, such as creating their own legacy, however long in office. They will take actions consistent with this goal. Note that political scientists are not making a normative claim; they are not contending that Congress *should* act this way or that statutes are justified on the basis of such legislative behavior. They are making a positive or descriptive claim: Congress *does* act in conformance with the self-interest of its members.

As we will see in the chapters that follow, there is a complex relationship between the justifications for government regulation and the political explanations for it. Consider, for instance, the question of statutory interpretation. When a court interprets a statute, is it the political explanation or the justification for the statute that matters? Theories of statutory interpretation diverge on that point. Some theories are based on the assumption that statutes reflect nothing more than legislative self-interest: the words are what it took to obtain legislative consensus and "do the deal" on behalf of powerful constituents, and, therefore, the words of the statute are all that should be subject to interpretation. Others posit that it is the justification for the statute — its purpose — that should guide statutory interpretation. The same questions arise as to how an agency should implement a statute. For now, the important point is seeing that both explanations and justifications for government regulation matter.

D. WHAT IS AN AGENCY?

The transition from common law to legislation and regulation requires an introduction to administrative agencies, which play a significant role in the shift. In this section, we describe the basics of agency structure. Our aim is exceedingly practical: to provide just enough information for you to understand what agencies look like. We do not consider in depth here the variations among agencies or their place in the constitutional structure.

1. Agencies in General

An agency is a unit of government created by statute. It owes its existence, form, and power to legislation. In this book, we are primarily concerned with *federal* agencies, which are established through *federal* legislation. Although the President occasionally will establish an agency by executive order, Congress usually follows by enacting a statute establishing the agency and delegating authority to it. The Environmental Protection Agency and the Department of Homeland Security are the most well-known examples of agencies that were first established by executive order and then delegated authority by statute. By and large, statutes create and specify the powers of agencies.

Agencies play a prominent role in public law for the simple reason that they possess considerable power. Many agencies possess the power to act with the force of law, just as Congress or a court does. They exercise this power by issuing rules (sometimes called regulations), which are analogous to statutes, and by issuing orders, after conducting an adjudication that is similar to a judicial, trial-type hearing. Agencies have power to do many other things short of issuing legally binding statements — conduct research, provide public information, produce guidance documents, issue opinion letters, write internal office manuals, inspect premises, and more. Indeed, people in regulated industries often find themselves immersed in fairly continuous interactions with the relevant regulator.

Even focusing only on rules or regulations, it becomes immediately clear why agencies are paramount. As a matter of sheer volume, the number of regulations issued by agencies far exceeds the number of statutes issued by Congress. For instance, in 2011, there were considerably fewer statutes than regulations:

- 80 statutes[1]
- 3,807 regulations[2]

In 2008, there were more statutes (and more regulations) but still considerably fewer statutes than regulations:

- 284 statutes[3]
- 3,955 regulations[4]

But these numbers only tell a small part of the story. As we will examine in depth, statutes frequently delegate to agencies many of the most significant decisions of social and economic policy. The startling contrast between the number of regulations and statutes likely understates how much authority

---

1. Pub. L. No. 112-1 (signed January 31, 2011) through Pub. L. No. 112-81 (signed December 31, 2011).

2. This data comes from the Office of the Federal Register.

3. Pub. L. No. 110-176 (signed January 4, 2008) through Pub. L. No. 110-460 (signed December 23, 2008).

4. This data comes from the Office of the Federal Register.

agencies have in establishing rules that govern society. Agencies also adjudicate more cases than the entire federal judiciary.

Another window on agency authority concerns the costs of compliance with regulations. Although the estimates vary, the federal government itself estimates that the cost of compliance with regulations is one-tenth of the gross domestic product. *See* COUNCIL OF ECONOMIC ADVISORS, ECONOMIC REPORT OF THE PRESIDENT 296 (Feb. 2004), available at *www.gpoaccess.gov/eop/ index.html.* With such great social and economic implications, it is no wonder that regulations play so large a role in public and corporate life — not to mention lawyer workload.

A final consideration is the sheer size of the federal bureaucracy. It is difficult for private parties to engage in any commercial or professional endeavor without encountering an agency. When you apply for a school loan or pick up your snail mail, you are encountering an agency. The regulatory state is comprised of 15 cabinet departments and their sub-cabinet agencies, along with a large number of other "alphabet soup" agencies. Here is a list of the cabinet departments and other agencies:

Cabinet Departments

Department of Agriculture (USDA)	Department of Commerce	Department of Defense (DOD)
Department of Education (ED)	Department of Energy (DOE)	Department of Health and Human Services (HHS)
Department of Homeland Security	Department of Housing and Urban Development (HUD)	Department of the Interior
Department of Justice (DOJ)	Department of Labor (DOL)	Department of State
Department of Transportation (DOT)	Department of the Treasury	Department of Veterans Affairs

Other Agencies

Central Intelligence Agency (CIA)	Commodity Futures Trading Commission (CFTC)	Consumer Product Safety Commission (CPSC)
Defense Nuclear Facilities Safety Board (DNFSB)	Environmental Protection Agency (EPA)	Equal Employment Opportunity Commission (EEOC)
Export-Import Bank of the United States	Farm Credit Administration	Federal Communications Commission (FCC)
Federal Deposit Insurance Corporation (FDIC)	Federal Election Commission (FEC)	Federal Housing Finance Board
Federal Labor Relations Authority	Federal Maritime Commission	Federal Mine Safety and Health Review Commission
Federal Reserve System (FRS)	Federal Trade Commission (FTC)	General Services Administration (GSA)

Merit Systems Protection Board (MSPB)	National Aeronautics and Space Administration (NASA)	National Archives and Records Administration (NARA)
National Capital Planning Commission	National Credit Union Administration (NCUA)	National Foundation on the Arts and the Humanities
National Labor Relations Board (NLRB)	National Mediation Board	National Railroad Passenger Corporation (Amtrak)
National Science Foundation (NSF)	National Transportation Safety Board	Nuclear Regulatory Commission (NRC)
Occupational Safety and Health Review Commission (OSHRC)	Office of Government Ethics	Office of Personnel Management (OPM)
Office of Special Counsel (OSC)	Peace Corps	Pension Benefit Guaranty Corporation
Postal Rate Commission	Railroad Retirement Board	Securities and Exchange Commission (SEC)
Selective Service System	Social Security Administration (SSA)	Small Business Administration (SBA)
Tennessee Valley Authority	United States Agency for International Development (USAID)	United States Trade and Development Agency
United States Commission on Civil Rights	United States International Trade Commission (USITC)	United States Postal Service

For a comprehensive description of federal agencies, *see* DAVID E. LEWIS & JENNIFER L. SELIN, SOURCEBOOK OF UNITED STATES EXECUTIVE AGENCIES (Administrative Conference of the United States 2012).

The federal government employs over 2.5 million workers and more than 1,100 full- and part-time Senate-confirmed political appointees, as well as presidential appointees, career civil servants, and other non-political government workers. Anne Joseph O'Connell, *Vacant Offices: Delays in Staffing Top Agency Positions*, 82 S. CAL. L. REV. 913 (2009); *see also* David E. Lewis, THE POLITICS OF PRESIDENTIAL APPOINTMENTS 20-30 (2008) (describing the types of employees and officers that make up the federal government). Given the place that agencies occupy in our federal system, there is a continual quest for control of their decisions by the President, Congress, regulated parties, public interest groups, and even the courts. We focus on these issues later in the book.

2

Legislation

The rise of the regulatory state is in part a story of the rise of legislation. Legislation is the legal basis of much modern social and economic policy. As a result, lawyers who operate in the regulatory state (which is to say nearly all lawyers) need to have an understanding of legislation. This chapter describes the basic aspects of the legislative process, the standard features of statutory design, and the main components of legislative drafting. Of course, every statute has its own particular history; we aim to capture the principal commonalities among them. By providing a view of the forces that shape statutes and the elements that they contain, we hope to provide a baseline for understanding the body of law that Congress enacts.

A. THE LEGISLATIVE PROCESS

We begin our discussion of legislation with a snapshot of the process that generates it. Thus, we trace the path from bill to law, in a bit more detail

than *Schoolhouse Rock!* (pictured here). We then provide some theories of how the legislative process actually works and a specific example in the context of auto safety.

1. A General Description

When describing the legislative process, the place to start is with the Constitution. For a bill to become a law, the Constitution requires a majority vote of both houses of Congress (bicameralism) and a presidential signature (presentment), or a two-thirds majority vote of both houses of Congress to override a presidential veto. U.S. CONST. art. 1, §7. Note how onerous these requirements are; few bills will survive them to become laws. The Framers of the Constitution seemed to have this very result in mind, as a formal check against the tyranny of the majority. *See* THE FEDERALIST No. 73 (Hamilton, viewing the requirements of bicameralism and presentment as an "an additional security against [the production] of improper laws"); THE FEDERALIST No. 63 (Madison, viewing the legislative process as "suspend[ing] the blow mediated by the people themselves, until reason, justice, and truth can regain their authority over the public mind").

As onerous as the constitutional requirements are, most bills never make it to that stage. The modern legislative process is considerably more complicated. Both the House and the Senate maintain rules of procedure that allow smaller groups to derail a bill along the way. Thus, most bills actually "die in committee." Consider the following account.

Nelson Polsby, Congress and the Presidency

138-57 (1986)

The task of the student of Congress and the Presidency would be greatly simplified if there were a typical process by which a bill becomes a law, that is to say, a process typical in some sense other than the narrowly formalistic. But most bills do not become laws; they are introduced, referred to committees, and there languish and die. So even to speak of a bill's actually becoming a law is to speak of an atypical event. . . .

Furthermore, bills have all shapes and sizes. Some propose to authorize the expenditure of billions of dollars; others tinker with existing laws, expanding or contracting the powers of executive agencies; still others provide for the relief of individual citizens. . . .

THE ORIGIN OF BILLS

Bills begin their formal existence by being dropped into a hopper, a mahogany box that sits on a clerk's desk, by a representative in the house and by being sent to the clerk's desk by a senator in the Senate. The process is separate for the House of Representatives and the Senate, but since no bill can become law without being passed in identical form by both houses, some coordination is necessary. This can take place in a variety of ways. Perhaps

FIGURE 2.1
The Standard Legislative Process for a Major Bill

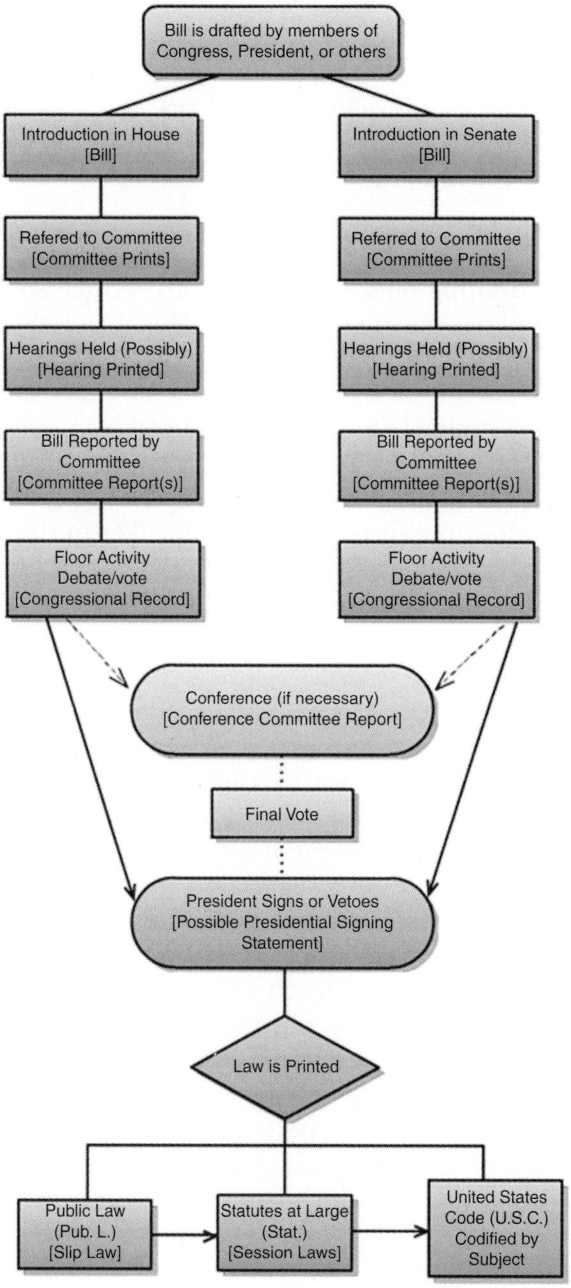

```
                   ┌─────────────────────────────┐
                   │  Bill is drafted by members of │
                   │  Congress, President, or others │
                   └─────────────────────────────┘
                    ╱                           ╲
      ┌──────────────────────┐        ┌──────────────────────┐
      │ Introduction in House │        │ Introduction in Senate│
      │         [Bill]        │        │         [Bill]        │
      └──────────────────────┘        └──────────────────────┘

      ┌──────────────────────┐        ┌──────────────────────┐
      │ Refered to Committee  │        │ Referred to Committee │
      │  [Committee Prints]   │        │  [Committee Prints]   │
      └──────────────────────┘        └──────────────────────┘

      ┌──────────────────────┐        ┌──────────────────────┐
      │Hearings Held (Possibly)│       │Hearings Held (Possibly)│
      │   [Hearing Printed]   │        │   [Hearing Printed]   │
      └──────────────────────┘        └──────────────────────┘

      ┌──────────────────────┐        ┌──────────────────────┐
      │   Bill Reported by    │        │   Bill Reported by    │
      │      Committee        │        │      Committee        │
      │ [Committee Report(s)] │        │ [Committee Report(s)] │
      └──────────────────────┘        └──────────────────────┘

      ┌──────────────────────┐        ┌──────────────────────┐
      │    Floor Activity     │        │    Floor Activity     │
      │     Debate/vote       │        │     Debate/vote       │
      │[Congressional Record] │        │[Congressional Record] │
      └──────────────────────┘        └──────────────────────┘
                    ╲                           ╱
              ┌───────────────────────────────────┐
              │      Conference (if necessary)     │
              │   [Conference Committee Report]    │
              └───────────────────────────────────┘

                       ┌──────────────┐
                       │  Final Vote  │
                       └──────────────┘

              ┌───────────────────────────────────┐
              │     President Signs or Vetoes      │
              │  [Possible Presidential Signing    │
              │            Statement]              │
              └───────────────────────────────────┘

                       ◆ Law is Printed ◆

      ┌────────────┐   ┌──────────────┐   ┌──────────────┐
      │Public Law  │   │Statutes at   │   │United States │
      │(Pub. L.)   │→  │Large (Stat.) │→  │Code (U.S.C.) │
      │[Slip Law]  │   │[Session Laws]│   │Codified by   │
      │            │   │              │   │   Subject    │
      └────────────┘   └──────────────┘   └──────────────┘
```

the most usual is for identical bills to be introduced at about the same time in each house of Congress, for their provisions to be remolded in somewhat divergent ways in the separate houses, and then for their differences to be reconciled for joint action at the last stage, in the conference committee.

Where to bills come from? The President's preeminence as legislative leader is more obvious in this first stage of the process . . . Friendly senior congressman and senators from the various committees, usually the chairmen, are consulted and asked to introduce in their respective houses bills prepared by the executive agencies. These bills are referred in a semiautomatic process to the appropriate committees for study.

Not all bills introduced in Congress are inspired by the executive departments or included in the presidential program. Some embody a congressman's or a senator's own ideas, and some are offered at the request of an interest group or a constituent.

REFERENCE TO COMMITTEES

There is an art to drafting bills. In part, bills are written so as to be sent to committees that will act on them favorably. This is not always as easy as it sounds, however. . . .

Strategic maneuvering designed to keep a bill alive begins while it is being written and certainly before it is introduced. Sometimes it is possible to word bills ambiguously and hope for a favorable referral. But the committees guard their jurisdictions; the parliamentarians (who do the actual referring of bills under the direction of the Speaker in the House and the Majority Leader in the Senate) know the precedents, and only a case of genuine ambiguity gives the Speaker or the Majority Leader any real option in referral. . . .

IN COMMITTEE

Once bills are in committee, automatic processes carry them no farther. From this point onward they must be carefully and assiduously nurtured or they die. Needless to say, those bills in which the committee chairman is personally interested are given the most prompt attention, but even for a chairman it is futile to promote legislation that cannot command widespread support, at least from the leadership of his own party or from a vast majority of his colleagues on the floor.

In every session of Congress each committee has a great many bills referred to it, more bills than it can possibly attend to. The committee chairmen play a strategic role in selecting the bills that committees will take up, but in this decision the party leaders weigh heavily. Chairmen pride themselves on their success in obtaining passage of legislation reported favorably out of their committees. The chances of success are enormously enhanced if the full weight of the party leadership is behind a measure. If party leaders are indifferent, the entire burden of assembling a majority on the floor falls on the chairman; if party leaders are opposed, it will probably be very difficult to build this majority.

Chairmen who oppose White House measures may delay taking up the offending bill or may seek to water it down or substitute legislation on the same subject more satisfactory to themselves. A firm and intense majority on the committee may oppose a chairman who wishes to do this, and some committees conscientiously enforce rules which require chairmen to refer bills to an appropriate subcommittee by a specified time. Such majorities are rare, however. . . .

HEARINGS

Hearings serve a variety of functions. Ideally, they are an effective research device, a way of focusing the attention of congressman on the substantive merits of a proposed bill and its possible pitfalls. In an ideal world, of course, issues are raised *de novo*, and legislators' minds are clean slates. In the real world, however, the subjects of major legislative proposals are familiar to committee members long before they reach the stage of hearings. Sometimes these proposals have been the subject of protracted partisan debate, and interest groups often exist on all sides of the issue. Therefore it is not uncommon for hearing to become rather perfunctory, with spokesmen for the various points of view coming before the committee and delivering speeches that the members have heard many times before. As one congressman said, "I get so bored with those repetitious hearings. We've been listening to the same witnesses saying the same things the same way for ten years." Still, all this is necessary- to make a record, to demonstrate good faith to leaders and members of the House and Senate, to provide a background of demonstrated need for the bill, to show how experts anticipate that the bill's provisions will operate, to allay fears, and to gather support from the wavering. Not only does it tell congressman what the technical arguments for and against a bill are, but, even more important, it tells them who, which interest and which groups, are for and against bills and how strongly they feel about them.

The committee staff at the direction of the chairman can manipulate the roster of witnesses before the committee and can ask witnesses unfriendly to the bill to file statements rather than appearing in person. . . Committee chairmen do often play scrupulously fair with all interested parties and allow everyone to speak his piece. The timing and length of hearings are of course strategically important. . . .

The format for the hearing varies with the committee and the circumstances. At each hearing the ground rules may change ever so slightly, but in general it works as follows: Witnesses from the executive agencies, first of all, are invited to appear in order to describe how they anticipate the bill will operate and in order to record their support for the bill. After the government witnesses and interested congressman and senators appear, it is customary for witnesses from interest groups to testify for and against the bill. Usually each witness makes a prepared statement and then is questioned by members of the committee in order of seniority, starting with the chairman, then the ranking minority member, and so on, alternating back and forth between the parties. Ordinarily, time is limited and so it is quite unusual for all members of the committee on either side to get a chance to question witnesses on the record in any great detail. . . .

THE MARK-UP

At the conclusion of hearings, the subcommittee may meet and consider the bill. The bill will be read line by line, and the various members will voice their approval or objections to its provisions. It is at this point, the mark-up, where the bill is amended and rewritten so as to gather the necessary support in the committee to make it possible for the bill to survive its subsequent trip through the Congress. If the bill can be written here so as to receive substantial support, its chances of survival later are immensely improved. If, on the other hand, the provisions of the bill are such as to divide the committee, the chances of the bill's survival are much less. . . .

After a suitable amount of bargaining, the subcommittee may take a vote on the bill and report to the full committee. In some cases, the full committee provides on a perfunctory review of subcommittee action. In other cases, however, amendments that failed to be adopted in the sub-committee may be in order in the full committee, if their proponents wish to bring them forward. On some committees, doing this is regarded as bad form, but on an increasing number it is regarded as perfectly acceptable to sustain subcommittee conflict within the full committee.

Customarily, by this time the chairman has instructed the staff to prepare a report. The report is an explanation of the bill from both a substantive and political standpoint. The purpose of the report is to explain the bill and its contemplated effects to members of Congress and also, on occasion, to the courts, who later, in the course of litigation, may look at reports to ascertain legislative intent. The report may include minority views. It is a point of pride with committee chairmen to bring their minority along with them as much as possible. In committee, at any rate, the process is very similar to that in the subcommittee. Once the bill is marked up and the report written, it may be voted out of committee. It then goes on the calendars of the respective houses.[*]

THE CALENDARS

In the Senate there are only two legislative calendars; from them the Majority Leader, in consultation with the Minority Leader, the legislative liaison from the President, committee chairmen, and interested senators, selects bills for floor action. The method and timing of introduction may be manipulated at the discretion of the Majority Leader to his strategic advantage.

In the House there are five calendars. One is the consent calendar. A second calendar is for bills introduced for the relief or benefit of named individuals or groups. A third, rarely used, is the calendar for bills discharged

[*][Eds.: Over the course of the past two decades, the number of bills passed by Congress in each session (the 106th to the 115th) has varied from 284 to 603, with an average of 417 per session. The success rate for introduced bills has varied from 2% to 6%. Resolutions (some of which are perfunctory) have varied from 663 to 1,464 with a success rate from 6% to 11%. Presidential vetoes are rare, ranging from 0 to 9 during this period. As might be expected, the number of bills introduced is greatest early in the session and quickly declines, while the number of enactments rises slowly and peaks near the end].

by petition from committees. The other two calendars are for the public bills of some importance; bills are listed on them on a first-come (from any committee), first-served basis. This method of setting priorities has been found to be unacceptable, and so these calendars are never called. Rather, substitute methods for placing bills on the agenda are used. Some committees are granted privileged use of the floor, most notably the Appropriations Committee, which can bring its bills to the floor whenever it is ready to report them and suitable arrangements for their consideration can be made with the Speaker and Majority Leader. The Rules Committee is also privileged to bring to the floor special orders making it possible for the House to consider specific bills. These special orders are voted by the Rules Committee and brought to the floor at the request of leaders of the various committees of the House. Thus, normally when a bill is voted out of a House committee and is entered on a calendar, the next step is for the chairman to ask the Rules Committee for a special order taking the bill from the calendar and placing it before the House. The Rules Committee chairman may be quick or slow in responding to this request. Normally, however, he will respond with reasonable promptness and schedule a hearing at which the managers of the bill from the substantive committee and its opponents can appear before the Rules Committee and state the case for and against the granting of a special order. . . .

The business of the committee itself is to determine the structure of debate on all major issues, the order in which amendments are to be offered, and the time allocated to each subject. This ability is highly significant in organizing the legislative process in the House, but the Rules Committee does not operate as autonomously in this sphere as it once did. The power of the Speaker to appoint committee members is more than adequate to keep the Rules Committee cooperative over the long run.

At the conclusion of hearings before this committee, the committee votes whether or not to grant a special rulemaking in order floor debate on the bill that has just come before them. If the vote is affirmative, the chairman and the ranking minority member each appoints a member of the committee from his side of the table to take the rule to the floor.

FLOOR ACTION IN THE HOUSE

When a special order is granted by the Rules Committee, this fact is rapidly communicated to the House leadership, the Speaker and the Majority Leader, who schedule the bill for debate. They have some flexibility in this process and may wait for strategic reasons or reasons of convenience. On the scheduled day two members of the Rules Committee, one each from the majority and the minority, appear on the floor of the House and ask that the committee resolution setting the terms of debate on the bill be given immediate consideration. This resolution is itself debatable, and sometimes debate on the resolution provides a hint of the controversy that will ensue when a bill is debated directly. Only in rare instances is the resolution from the Rules Committee not adopted; when it is, the House resolves itself into the Committee of the Whole.

The membership of the Committee of the Whole House is identical to that of the House of Representatives itself, but parliamentary rules in the committee are somewhat relaxed. Proponents and opponents of the bill from the substantive committee-customarily senior members from the majority and minority sides- move up to long tables on either side of the center aisle in the house. They will manage the time for debate, make split-section decisions whether to support or oppose amendments, and keep a weather eye on the attendance of friends, waverers, and foes. . . .

At the conclusion of debate in the Committee of the Whole, the committee rises and reports the bill back to the whole House with such amendments as may have been agreed to. At that point the Speaker asks if a separate vote is demanded on any amendment reported favorably. Any member may demand such a vote. After all such votes the title is read a third time. A motion to recommit may be offered, and then a vote is taken on final passage. If the bill is passed, it is sent to the Speaker for his signature. It is then sent to the Senate.

FLOOR ACTION IN THE SENATE

The Senate may or may not have been waiting for the House bill. It is not uncommon for Senate committees to undertake hearings on their own bill on a subject. Senate committees hear bills and mark them up in a process very similar to that in the House. However, these committees are much smaller than House committees; thus individual senators have greater opportunities to question witnesses and participate in the mark-up. On the other hand, senators have many more committee assignments than representatives, so unless the bill is within a senator's area of special interest or attracts his attention for some reason, he is likely to depend heavily on staff members. . . .

Senate debate is less restricted than debate in the House as to both time and substance. In the House there is a strict rule of germaneness, but in the Senate germaneness is required only for short periods of time.

A famous feature of senatorial debate is the filibuster. This refers to the occasions when senators, by prolonging their talk, tie up the Senate for days (sometimes weeks) at a time a thus stall the legislative machinery so as to win concessions on the substance of the legislation being debated. A filibuster, which can be halted only by a vote of three-fifths of the membership of the Senate, may be undertaken for a variety of purposes. Proponents claim that this is a valid way of bringing sharply to the attention of the country the imminent passage of laws that they feel are unjust or unwise. Opponents regard filibusters as inimical to the rule of the majority. . . .

If a bill evades the severe controversy implied by the filibuster, it can be debated and voted on promptly in the Senate. Normally, however, the Senate and the House pass bills that are not identical in every particular.

Therefore either house may ask for a conference in which their differences are resolved.

THE CONFERENCE

Conference committees are appointed, for the House by the Speaker, and for the Senate by the vice president, on the recommendation of the chairmen of the substantive committees handling the legislation. The conference committees normally consist of senior members from the substantive committees or subcommittees that had the most to do with the managing the bill, with the majority usually outnumbering the minority in a ratio that reflects the party ration on the full committee. The entire delegation from each house votes as a unit in conference committees. Occasionally it is possible to pack a delegation by varying its size, but this normally requires cooperation between the committee chairman and the presiding officer of his house. These *ad hoc* committees meet and attempt to reconcile the differences between the House and the Senate bills. They are generally given great latitude in reporting a consolidated bill back to their respective houses.

Sophisticated members take advantage of ideological differences between the two houses when they occur. . . .

Close observers have often noted differences between House and Senate members of conference committees. Conference committee behavior often reflects greater degrees of technical specialization by House members and preoccupation with matters other than the business at hand by senators. . . .

When the conference report returns to the House and Senate floors for a vote, no amendments are in order, and the opponents of some of the bill's provisions can only vote yes or no on the whole package. On issues where there is an overwhelming consensus that *some* legislation is necessary, opponents of the conference report are a great disadvantage.

Abbe R. Gluck, Anne J. O'Connell, and Rosa Po, Unorthodox Lawmaking, Unorthodox Rulemaking

115 Colum. L. Rev. 1789 (2015)

[T]he *Schoolhouse Rock!* cartoon version of the conventional legislative process is dead. It may never have accurately described the lawmaking process in the first place. This is not news to anyone in the halls of Congress or the executive branch. . . . "Unorthodox lawmaking" was first brought to the attention of the academy by political scientist Barbara Sinclair, in her eponymous book, [UNORTHODOX LAWMAKING: NEW LEGISLATIVE PROCESSES IN THE U.S. CONGRESS (1st ed. 1997)]. . . . Lest there be any doubt about the importance of the subject matter, a few descriptive statistics should suffice to document the prevalence of the phenomenon. . . .

Table 1:   Empirical Snapshot of Unorthodox Practices

• *Legislative bundling* through *omnibus vehicles* has increased dramatically, both for substantive legislation and for appropriations. In recent Congresses, omnibus packages have made up about 12% of major legislation.
• *Overlapping delegations* to multiple agencies and *joint rulemaking* have risen in recent years.
• *Process deviations* are prevalent. As one example, in the first year of the 112th Congress, fewer than 10% of enacted laws proceeded through the "textbook" legislative process (first passing through committees on each side, then moving to debate and vote in each chamber, followed by conference between the chambers, and concluding with a final vote by both chambers before passage). More than 40% of enacted statutes did not go through the committee process in *either* chamber, but proceeded directly from the floor or were shepherded through by party leadership or the White House. Although variable by year, legislation bypassed committees much more in the 1990s and 2000s than in the preceding decades. . . .
• New *unorthodox delegations* outside of traditional federal actors to states, private, and quasi-private actors have been widely observed by scholars. Other measures support these conclusions, including a more-than-tenfold rise in federal grants-in-aid to states; a dramatic tripling, to 18 million, in the total number of state and local government employees, while the size of the federal civil service has remained roughly constant at 2 million; and an increase in private outsourcing. As one example, DHS at times has used more contract employees than federal employees. [Peter] Strauss has tracked another example—the increase in private standards in rulemaking, which nearly doubled between 2011 and 2012 alone. . . .
The prevalence of these practices seems clear—as does their variety, the subject to which we now turn. . . .

1. *Omnibus Legislation.* —There is no single definition of omnibus legislation, but there is consensus that legislation that "packages together several measures into one or combines diverse subjects into a single bill" fits the label, as do so-called "money bills," including omnibus appropriations bills and budget bills. Some experts, including Sinclair, add to this definition legislation that is "usually highly complex and long" and that takes on numerous issues, even within a single subject area—for example the 800-page Clean Air Act and the 2,700-page health reform statute, the ACA. Omnibus legislation has "proliferated" since the 1970s.

Omnibus bills that bring together many different subjects depart from conventional process in multiple ways. Omnibus legislation often comprises "mini-bills"—separate pieces of legislation, or at least separate topics within a single subject, drafted by different committees and linked together. Some parts of an omnibus bill might have been drafted years earlier. The 2008 financial bailout legislation, for example, included the Paul Wellstone and Pete Domenici Mental Health Parity and Addiction Equity

Act of 2008, which was originally introduced but failed to make it through Congress in 2007. Even omnibus bills that are drafted all at once and deal with a single subject can have a wide array of authors. The 1990 Clean Air Act was initially drafted by the Bush I Administration and ultimately included the work of at least nine different congressional committees.

Omnibus vehicles also sometimes mask transparency for certain objectives. The 2008 bailout, for instance, had a variety of individual goodies attached to it, ranging from subsidies for wooden arrow makers to those for racetrack owners. Omnibus bills also sometimes quietly *reverse* both legislation and delegation. The latest omnibus spending bill undid a controversial Dodd-Frank mandate. With respect to undoing delegation, omnibus bills often contain appropriations riders, which prevent agencies from using funding to carry out previously delegated authority. As another example from the spending bill, a rider prohibited the Secretary of the Interior from using congressional appropriations to "issue further rules to place sage-grouse on the Endangered Species List."

From a statutory interpretation standpoint, omnibus bills pose particular challenges for common doctrinal assumptions of legislative perfection: these are often long and messy bills. They may have errors or linguistic inconsistencies that statutory interpretation doctrine does not usually tolerate. Legislative history for omnibus bills also is often outdated, because parts of such bills often are drafted years before — as part of earlier, failed bills that later are bundled into an omnibus package as part of a bigger deal. Sometimes omnibus legislative history is simply nonexistent, because many omnibus bills bypass the committee stage, where reports are typically produced. . . .

[2.] *Emergency Legislation.* — Like omnibus bills, emergency legislation often bypasses conventional process, including committee deliberation and report writing. The AUMF, for example, passed Congress just three days after the September 11 attacks, without going through the foreign relations committees in the House and Senate. Instead, the majority and minority leaders of both chambers conducted the negotiations, and the AUMF was drafted jointly by White House and congressional lawyers beginning just hours after the attacks. As a result, there is no formal legislative history for the AUMF that can be found in committee reports or conference reports, and there was minimal floor debate.

The Hurricane Katrina Relief legislation came on September 2, 2005, just four days after the hurricane hit land, under circumstances so rushed there was not even a quorum of senators present for the vote. The Troubled Asset Relief Program (TARP) — the "bailout" legislation responding to the financial crisis — was a 450-page bill that was drafted first by the Secretary of the Treasury as a three-page, $700 billion request, then given to Congress to flesh out the details, and brought to a vote just fourteen days after Lehman Brothers filed for bankruptcy. The initial version did not pass the House, but a revised version — sweetened with additional pieces of legislation, including the Wellstone Mental Health Parity Act and provisions for rural schools — passed just four days later. After watching the Dow Jones industrial average drop more than 700 points after the bill's failure to pass the

House the first time, the House moved quickly on the second turn. In the 113th Congress, many of the bills that were enacted in less than a month were appropriations bills. . . .

[3.] *"Automatic" Lawmaking as a Legislative Workaround.* —Congress has increasingly resorted to what might be called *automatic lawmaking processes.* Automatic lawmaking processes establish procedures that effectively make law without Congress having to do anything other than set up the initial framework. These procedures both overcome the structural vetogates that Congress has created for itself to intentionally slow down lawmaking in most instances—vetogates such as the multistage legislative process or special-ized debate and amendment rules—and also allow legislators to avoid hav-ing to engage with particularly controversial issues.

The Base Realignment and Closure Commissions (BRAC) of the 1990s are common examples; the ACA's Medicare-cutting board, the Independent Payment Advisory Board (IPAB), is a more recent one. In both cases, Congress enacted a statute that charges an outside board to decide an extremely dif-ficult question—no member would agree to closing a naval base in her own state and cutting Medicare is similarly a political third rail. The recom-mendations of the board take effect automatically unless Congress adopts a joint resolution of disapproval, in the case of BRAC, or a substitute provision to reduce Medicare spending, in the case of IPAB. This mechanism conve-niently prevents any legislator from having to say that he or she voted *for* the unpopular policy decision.

On the one hand, these devices allow members of Congress to com-mit credibly to particular policy goals, without being tempted by political concerns. On the other, they intentionally allow members to avoid account-ability for any actual vote on the controversial issue. . . . "Fast track"-type rules—such as the special rules for the budget process and fast-track trade deals—are related unorthodox workarounds. Congress has created expe-dited procedures for both areas to prevent common legislative bottlenecks, including filibusters. But here, the expedited procedures seem motivated less by the hot politics of the topic and more by a normative judgment that certain types of special policymaking (including budgets and trade deals) must happen in a timely fashion. Earlier this year, Congress approved con-troversial fast-track legislation giving the President the power to submit trade deals to Congress for an up-or-down vote without amendments.

Notes and Questions

1. You can now appreciate the steps of the legislative process, many of which can also be described as hurdles or obstacles. Indeed, political scien-tists have used the concept of "vetogates" to describe the junctures in the legislative process where a proposed bill can be derailed by a relatively small number of individuals. *See* Mathew McCubbins, Roger Noll & Barry Weingast, *Legislative Intent, The Use of Positive Political Theory in Statutory Interpretation,* 57

LAW & CONTEMP. PROBS. 3 (1994). How many vetogates can you identify from the foregoing description of the process? Are they worrisome?

2. How can vetogates work in practice to the advantage of your client? Suppose your law firm represents companies that produce artificial honey through a chemical process. These companies think that their business will be destroyed by a bill that is about to be introduced into Congress, which will require them to list a series of disclosures on their product describing the way it was produced. They have hired you to go to Washington, D.C. and prevent the bill from being enacted into law. At which point in the legislative process do you think intervention would be most effective? Who would you contact? What would you say?

3. Can you identify the key moments in the legislative process when documents or statements other than the text of the bill are produced? These documents or statements form a part of the legislative history of the statute to which they relate. Whose views do these documents and statements reflect? Are there any that reflect the views of the majority of Congress? Which are most likely to be read by a majority of Congress? Which pieces are likely to capture the views of the minority or a dissenting legislator?

4. What effect do changes in the legislative process, such as omnibus bills, have the control over legislation? Without committee consideration, can you trace moments when legislative history is formed? Can you anticipate what implications these unorthodox practices have for statutory intepretation?

Notes on Theories of the Legislative Process

Over time, different theories have arisen to describe how the legislative process actually works. Although a full discussion of theories is best left to a course on legislation, we provide you with a brief introduction to some of the more important and influential ones:

Public Choice Theory and the Role of Interest Groups. What is the role of interest groups in the legislative process? In *The Logic of Collective Action* (1965), economist Mancur Olson asserted that it is more difficult to organize large groups with diffuse interests than small groups with common interests. Extending this logic, it is possible to see that small groups will have a disproportionate share of influence in the legislative process. The result is that "actual political choices [will be] determined by the efforts of individuals and groups to further their own interests." Gary Becker, *A Theory of Competition Among Pressure Groups for Political Influence*, 98 Q.J. ECON. 371, 372 (1983). Consistent with this theory, if you think that statutes reflect "the will of the people," think again. Statutes reflect the self-interest of the well-organized groups that prevail upon Congress to enact them. Why would Congress respond to interest groups in this fashion? The answer comes from public choice theory. Members of Congress are inclined to pursue their own self-interest, which is generally taken to be an interest in reelection. And well-organized, small interest groups can often promise members of Congress what they seek, while the diffuse public cannot. As Professors Daniel Farber and Philip Frickey have written:

> The core of the economic models is a jaundiced view of legislative motivation. In place of their prior assumption that legislators voted to promote their view of the public interest, economists now postulate that legislators are motivated solely by self-interest. In particular, legislators must maximize their likelihood of reelection. A legislator who is not reelected loses all the other possible benefits flowing from office.
>
> The question, then, is what do legislators have to do to get reelected? In other words, what determines the outcomes of elections? Economic models can be classified into two groups, depending on how they answer this question.
>
> Models in the first group assume that legislators attempt to maximize their appeal to their constituents. These constituents, in turn, vote according to their own economic self-interest. Thus, those models suggest that legislative votes can be easily predicted from the economic interests of constituents.
>
> Models in the second group give a greater role to special interest groups. Because voters don't know much about a legislator's conduct, elections may turn on financial backing, publicity, and endorsements. These forms of support, as well as other possible benefits including outright bribes, are likely to be provided by organized interest groups, which thereby acquire the ability to affect legislative action.
>
> The economic theory of interest groups can be traced to Mancur Olson's theory of collective action. Olson pointed out that political action generally benefits large groups. For example, everyone presumably benefits from improved national security. But any single person's efforts to protect national security normally can have only an infinitesimal effect. Hence, a rational person will try to "free ride" on the efforts of others, contributing nothing to the national defense while benefiting from other people's actions.
>
> This "free rider" problem suggests that it should be nearly impossible to organize large groups of individuals to seek broadly dispersed public goods. Instead, political activity should be dominated by small groups of individuals seeking to benefit themselves, usually at the public expense. The easiest groups to organize would presumably consist of a few individuals or firms seeking government benefits for themselves, which will be financed by the general public. Thus, if Olson is correct, politics should be dominated by "rent-seeking" special interest groups.

DANIEL A. FARBER & PHILIP P. FRICKEY, LAW AND PUBLIC CHOICE: A CRITICAL INTRODUCTION 22-23 (1991). On this theory, would Congress ever respond to the interests of the general public? It might if it believed that the public could be energized enough by a particular issue to vote on that basis. *See* R. DOUGLAS ARNOLD, THE LOGIC OF CONGRESSIONAL ACTION (1990).

Social Choice Theory and the Problem of Cycling. How does a multi-member body such as Congress ever agree on the details of legislation when confronted with multiple options? In *Social Choice and Individual Values* (2d ed. 1963), Kenneth Arrow demonstrated that a multi-member body with three or more options will engage in "cycling" if the options are voted on in pairs. (Social choice theory is similar to public choice theory; both rely on the economic, "rational actor" model of legislative behavior, which sees members of Congress as pursuing their own self-interest.) To see the point about cycling, assume a committee of three individuals (Alan, Betty, and Carol) is asked to award a contract to one of three states (Florida, Illinois, and Texas). The individuals on the committee each rank their preferences among the three states as follows, with the most preferred state at the top and the least preferred state at the bottom of each list:

Alan	*Betty*	*Carol*
Texas	Illinois	Florida
Illinois	Florida	Texas
Florida	Texas	Illinois

As between Texas and Illinois, which has majority support (two out of three votes)? The answer is Texas because both Alan and Carol prefer Texas to Illinois. But there's still another option: Florida. Maybe Florida has stronger support than Texas. As between Florida and Texas, which has majority support? The answer is Florida because both Betty and Carol prefer Florida to Texas. But neither Alan nor Betty prefer Florida over Illinois, so let's continue the contest for a third round. As between Illinois (which Alan and Betty prefer to Florida) and Texas, Texas wins. We get a different winner in each two-state comparison. But we're back to the beginning. According to Arrow's theorem, the only way to arrive at a choice is to end the cycling. In the legislative process, that result can be accomplished if one person, such as the chair of the committee, is given power to end the cycling by limiting the number of rounds. For discussion along these lines, see Kenenth Shepsle, *Congress Is a "They," Not an "It": Legislative Intent as Oxymoron*, 12 Int'l Rev. L. & Econ. 239 (1992); Richard Pildes & Elizabeth Anderson, *Slinging Arrow's at Democracy: Public Choice Theory, Value Pluralism, and Democratic Politics*, 90 Colum. L. Rev. 2121 (1990). How is the result different if Betty discovers information about the preferences of her cohorts and changes her vote strategically to avoid her least favorite option?

Positive Political Theory and the Role of Institutions. Positive political theory provides a different window on the legislative process. Also growing out of economics, it turns the focus toward game theory. Individual legislators seek to ensure that legislation reflects their preferences, knowing that they are not the only players in the game. *See* William N. Eskridge, Jr. & John Ferejohn, *The Article I, Section 7 Game*, 80 Geo. L.J. 523 (1992); on positive political theory more generally, *see* Daniel Rodriguez & Barry Weingast, *The Positive Political Theory of Legislative History: New Perspectives on the 1964 Civil Rights Act and Its Interpretation*, 151 U. Pa. L. Rev. 1417 (2003); Mathew McCubbins, Roger Noll & Barry Weingast, *Legislative Intent: The Use of Positive Political Theory in Statutory Interpretation*, 57 Law & Contemp. Probs. 3 (1994). As a result, individual legislators develop statutes not only taking account of their own preferences but the reaction of others who participate in the process — for example, the median legislator and the President. The term "median legislator" refers to the legislator in the middle necessary to secure majority support for legislation. The political players must even anticipate the likely reaction of the Supreme Court, which may review the statute if subjected to judicial challenge. The situation is more complicated still if Congress selects an agency to implement the statute; then the players must anticipate the likely preferences of the agency. *See* Jonathan R. Macey, *Separated Powers and Positive Political Theory: The Tug of War over Administrative Agencies*, 80 GEO. L.J. 671 (1992).

What do you think of the legislative process now? These theories of the legislative process begin to give you an idea of how the sausage is made, or, the metaphor that we prefer, what goes on underneath the hood. Such information is important not only in its own right but when considering how statutes are interpreted and applied. Keep it in mind as we go along.

B. LEGISLATIVE DRAFTING

Lawyers need to know how to draft statutes, and not only those lawyers who work on a legislative staff or for other government offices. Private parties, including interest groups and lobbies, often ask their lawyers to draft statutes for them. Once those parties have a draft, they will seek members of the legislature to introduce and sponsor the legislation on their behalf. But even if your client does not ask you to draft legislation, you might want to recommend such legislation as an alternative to filing a lawsuit under existing law. Depending on the scope of the issues at stake, drafting and submitting a bill may be cheaper and more effective than bringing litigation. It is easy to miss this fact if only focusing on litigation.

It is useful to study statutory drafting for a separate reason: you will inevitably need to read and apply statutes in law school and thereafter. Thinking about statutes from the perspective of creating them will help you understand the statute from the perspective of those subject to them. This is a familiar phenomenon. People who have themselves played a sport are generally more knowledgeable spectators of that sport than those who have not; people who play a musical instrument are in a better position to appreciate the virtuosity of a performer. Even if you are only a consumer of statutes, you will be a better one for having learned the strategies and techniques for drafting them.

1. The Basic Steps of Legislative Drafting

Given the importance of the drafting process, there is surprisingly little written about the steps of that process. The reason may be that many regard the process as pure politics. Political forces are obviously crucial for the basic policy embodied in the statute. But "when the shouting and the tumult dies, the captains and the kings depart," lawyers are often called to perform the job of writing the actual language of the statutory provisions. We include excerpts from the current style manuals of the Senate Office of Legislative Counsel and the House Office of Legislative Counsel. They describe what these offices, the nonpartisan professional drafting offices in Congress, see as the basic steps of legislative drafting.

Legislative Drafting Manual, Office of the Legislative Counsel, U.S. Senate

February 1997

TITLE I — GENERAL DRAFTING PRINCIPLES

Subtitle A — Fundamental Rules

Sec. 101. Organization of a Draft.

A draft bill or amendment to a bill should be well organized. Always keep the organization of a draft in mind when working with its individual provisions.

Sec. 102. Brevity.

Use short, simple sentences rather than complex or compound sentences. If a shorter term is as good as a longer term, use the shorter term.

Sec. 103. Verbs.

(a) TENSE. — Always use the present tense unless the provision addresses only the past, the future, or a sequence of events that requires use of a different tense. A legislative provision speaks as of any date on which it is read (rather than as of when drafted, enacted, or put into effect).

(b) VOICE. —

(1) IN GENERAL. — Avoid using the passive voice unless the actor cannot be identified.

(2) FORM. — The use of the passive in "appropriate actions shall be taken to carry out the program" obscures who bears responsibility for taking the action. The correct form is as follows: "The Secretary shall take appropriate actions to carry out the program."

Sec. 104. Nouns.

(a) NUMBER. — A subject, direct object, or other noun should be expressed in the singular. The singular includes the plural (see section 1 of title 1, United States Code).

(b) APPLICABILITY. —

(1) IN GENERAL. — A legislative provision speaks to each individual or entity subject to the provision. Generally, "a" or "an" should precede a noun (if an indefinite article is needed at all).

(2) EACH AND ANY. — If there is any possibility that a provision could be read to apply to fewer than all of the members of the class of individuals or entities described in the provision, in place of the indefinite article —

(A) use "each" with "shall"; and

(B) use "any" with "may".

(3) RATIONALE. — Use of the singular eliminates an unnecessary layer of possible relationships. "Any employee who . . ." works the same as "Employees who . . .", yet it avoids any misreading (A) an implicit

precondition exists that 2 employees must be involved before either gets covered; or (B) the statement applies only to a group of employees, as such.
(c) PRONOUNS. —

      (1) IN GENERAL. — Avoid pronouns, especially pronouns in the possessive.

      (2) GENDER. — Use gender-neutral terms. The preferred method is to repeat the noun rather than use a personal pronoun (or "he/she" or "his/her").

Sec. 105. Word Choice.

      (a) CONSISTENT USAGE. — Do not use different words in a single bill or statute to refer to the same thing. A court presumes that different words have different meanings. Similarly, do not use the same word in 2 different senses in the same bill or statute.

      (b) SURPLUSAGE. — In interpreting a statute, a court presumes that every word is there for a reason. If a provision would have the same meaning if a word were deleted, delete the word.

      (c) ENGLISH RATHER THAN LATIN. — Use English rather than Latin.

Sec. 106. Defined Terms.

      (a) IN GENERAL. — The use of defined terms promotes clarity, brevity, and consistency. If a term expressing a concept is used in a sense other than the sense in which the term is commonly understood and the term is used more than once or twice in the draft, choose a term to describe the concept and define the term in accordance with section 125.

      (b) STATUTORILY DEFINED WORDS. — Be aware of the rules contained in chapter 1 of title 1, United States Code, regarding terminology. Especially useful is the definition of the term "person".

Sec. 107. Focus on Reader.

A draft must be understandable to the reader. The rules in this manual should be applied in a manner that makes the draft clearer and easier to understand.

House Legislative Counsel's Manual on Drafting Style, Office of the Legislative Counsel, U.S. House of Representatives

November 1995

TITLE I — DRAFTING PRINCIPLES UNDERLYING THE HOUSE LEGISLATIVE COUNSEL'S OFFICE STYLE

Sec. 101. Start.

This manual assumes that the attorney assigned to draft legislation already has (or is in the process of learning) the 4 basic drafting skills:

(1) Find out what the client *really* wants to do.

(2) Analyze the legal and other problems in doing that.

(3) Help the client come up with solutions to these problems that will—

    (A) be administrable and enforceable; and

    (B) keep hassles and litigation to a minimum.

(4) Convince the client that the drafter is the best to come down the pike since Solomon.

Sec. 102. Main Message.

    (a) ORGANIZATION.—

        (1) EVERY DRAFT SHOULD BE ORGANIZED.—Every draft should be organized.

        (2) ORGANIZATION SHOULD FIT THE MESSAGE.—The organization should be appropriate for the message the client wants to get across.

        (3) START WITH MOST IMPORTANT THOUGHTS.—Usually the most important thoughts should come first, and the thoughts should dwindle in importance from there down.

    (b) USE SHORT SIMPLE SENTENCES.—

        (1) IN GENERAL.—Use short simple sentences.

        (2) ELABORATION.—A listener survey was conducted recently. The median listener tunes out after the 12th word.

        (3) BREAK UP COMPLEX AND COMPOUND SENTENCES.—Most complex and compound sentences should be broken into 2 or more sentences. Often the offending sentence contains—

        (A) an unresolved policy issue; or

        (B) both a general rule and 1 or more exceptions and special rules.

    (c) STAY IN THE PRESENT.—Whenever possible, use the present tense (rather than the past or future). Your draft should be a movable feast—that is, it speaks as of whatever time it is being read (rather than as of when drafted, enacted, or put into effect).

    (d) CHOOSE WORDS CAREFULLY.—

        (1) IN GENERAL.—Choose each word as if it were an integral part of the Taj Mahal you are building. There is 1 best word to get across each thought. To find that word, use the dictionary and bounce words and drafts off any member of the office who will listen. What a word means to you may not be what it means to the next person.

        (2) USE ENGLISH RATHER THAN LATIN.—If you have a choice, use the English word rather than the Latin. Those few people who have had Latin in school can't agree on pronunciation.

        (3) USE PUNCHY WORDS.—Seek out words that suggest action. For this, verbs are usually better than nouns and adjectives.

        (4) USE SAME WORD OVER AND OVER.—If you have found the right word, don't be afraid to use it again and again. In other words, don't show your pedantry by an ostentatious parade of synonyms. Your English teacher may be disappointed, but the courts and others who are straining to find your meaning will bless you.

(5) AVOID UTRAQUISTIC SUBTERFUGES. — Do not use the same word in 2 different ways in the same draft (unless you give the reader clear warning).

(6) CAST OUT IDLE WORDS. — If any word is idle, cast it out.

(e) DEFINE YOUR TERMS. —

(1) IN GENERAL. — Check to see if the use of 1 or more defined terms will improve the draft. Often a skillful use of definitions will promote clarity, brevity, and consistency.

(2) FEAR NOT INVENTING WORDS. — If there is no right word, or if the available words carry with them too much baggage, invent a word or term and define it.

(f) PART OF YOUR JOB IS TO GET THE MESSAGE ACROSS. —

(1) IN GENERAL. — Your client comes to you because of wanting to send a message to 1 or more of the following:

    (A) The world.

    (B) The American people.

    (C) Fellow legislators.

    (D) Legislative staff.

    (E) Administrators.

    (F) Courts.

    (G) Constituents.

    (H) The media.

    (I) Others.

(2) IDENTIFY THE AUDIENCE. — Decide who is supposed to get the message.

(3) DRAFT SHOULD BE READABLE AND UNDERSTANDABLE. — In almost all cases, the message has a better chance of accomplishing your client's goal if it is readable and understandable. It should be written in English for real people.

(4) USE READABILITY AIDS. — Use the following with enthusiasm whenever they will increase readability and understandability:

    (A) Headings.

    (B) Cut-ins.

    (C) Numbered lists of items.

    (D) Tables.

    (E) Mathematical formulas.

    (F) Diagrams.

(5) DOWN-PLAY THE LESS IMPORTANT. —

    (A) SUBORDINATING. — Often the draft can be improved by subordinating the less important.

    (B) SUBORDINATING TECHNIQUES TO BE CONSIDERED. — Among the techniques for subordinating to be considered are the following:

        (i) Consolidate or eliminate the less important.

        (ii) Place lesser rules in a special rule section or subsection.

        (iii) Weave the lesser rules into the main body by a series of inserts set off by parentheses.

        (iv) Merely state that the rules that apply to "X" also apply to "Y".

Notes and Questions

1. The full treatments contain more specific steps of legislative drafting, from other rules of grammar to the technical form of complex subject bills and amendments. These excerpts capture some guidance and reflect an "attitude" toward legislative drafting. Based on this reading, what is the proper attitude for legislative drafting? Did the humor, particularly in the House manual, surprise you? You've already begun to experience the difference between reading a statute, with all those dry words, and reading a judicial decision, with all those interesting facts and arguments. Perhaps those who write statutes feel it, too.

2. Most of you probably could not chew gum in your elementary school classroom. Try drafting a statutory provision that establishes that prohibition.

3. Every time you go to class in law school, you take a seat. Draft statutory provisions that instruct the students in a class of 60 to take seats on the basis of a seating chart that they filled out on the first day of class. Now draft provisions that instruct the students to take seats in alphabetical order.

4. The student-edited law review at Regulatory State Law School has decided to switch from selecting students on the basis of their first-year grades to selecting them on the basis of a writing competition. The Editorial Board of Review met and decided that the competition should consist of the students writing a short, closed-universe note (that is, a note based on materials provided to the students in a packet). The note must be between 3,000 and 4,000 words, plus footnotes documenting all the major points. Notes are to be submitted anonymously and will be evaluated by three law review editors, who will provide independent evaluations. Twenty-five students will be accepted onto the Review each year, based solely on this evaluation. Draft the rules for the writing competition. These rules have to tell both the students competing for the Review and the students evaluating their submissions what to do.

2. The Political Realities of Legislative Drafting

The preceding discussion should not mislead you: legislative drafting is not merely a technical act. Because the legislative process is so difficult, legislation ends up looking a certain way as members of Congress make compromises to enact it. The drafting process itself reflects much of the strategic and political maneuvering of the legislative process. Consider the following.

Victoria F. Nourse & Jane S. Schacter,
The Politics of Legislative Drafting:
A Congressional Case Study

77 N.Y.U. L. Rev. 575, 576-77, 583-97, 610-11 (2002)

Articles about statutory interpretation fill the pages of law reviews, but the vast majority of this scholarship focuses on courts. If the scholarship looks at legislatures at all, it does so from an external perspective, looking at Congress through a judicial lens. Little has been written from the legislative end of the telescope. How does the legislative drafting process proceed? What do its participants believe about how courts interpret the bills that they write? To what extent are legislative drafters affected by judicial rules of interpretation, knowledge of which routinely is imputed to legislators by courts?

In this Article, we make a first step toward filling this gap in the literature with a case study of drafting in the Senate Judiciary Committee. Our interviews with staffers responsible for drafting bills provided us with a useful vantage point from which to view the assumptions and priorities of existing judicial accounts of the legislative process. Our aim in conducting these interviews was twofold. First, we sought to paint a more textured picture of the drafting process than is currently available, beginning with a close look at the work of one influential legislative committee. Second, we sought to begin empirical scrutiny of what might be called the judicial story of how laws are written — that is, the legislative drafting process as told by federal courts in the judicial opinions that interpret ambiguous statutory provisions. In these opinions, courts characteristically impute to Congress highly specific and sophisticated knowledge about both the rules of statutory interpretation and the substantive area of law into which a new statute will fit. . . .

A. Complexity and Variability in Legislative Drafting

The first strong theme to emerge from our interviews is that respondents repeatedly — and emphatically — rejected the notion of a monolithic drafting process and described in some detail the ways in which the drafting process can vary. This diversity begins at the very inception of a bill. Respondents told us, for example, that ideas for new legislation came from a broad array of sources — newspapers and court cases, lobbyists and the White House, Sunday-school teachers and law-review articles, to name a few. More pertinent for our purposes, the drafting process itself can look very different in different contexts, and our interviews made clear the rich array of contexts in which drafting takes place. . . .

1. Multiple Drafters

To gain a better understanding of the drafting process, we asked staffers about the role of various potential participants in the drafting process. We specifically asked about staffers themselves, senators, professional drafters from the Legislative Counsel's office, and lobbyists. Because we did not observe any drafting ourselves, what we report, of course, can reflect only the staffers' perceptions of the roles that these parties play.

In pressing this line of inquiry, we had in mind that the Supreme Court, for example, routinely has referred to legislators as the drafters of federal law. Sometimes the Court refers simply to "Congress" as the drafter, but frequently the justices specify "legislators" as drafters. It may well be that the justices do not actually believe this to be true; they may be invoking a fiction or using a simple proxy for a process they know to be more complex. Nevertheless, Supreme Court opinions typically place the legislator in the role of drafter.

a. Staffers

Perhaps unsurprisingly, our staff respondents saw themselves as centrally involved in bill drafting efforts. They also richly described the role of others in drafting but consistently described staffers as having principal responsibility for producing bill drafts. The precise nature of their roles in drafting varied widely according to the bill. Some of this variability, of course, flows from the diversity of subject-matter areas under the Judiciary Committee's jurisdiction. When asked to describe their most recent drafting effort, for example, respondents covered a lot of substantive territory, including gun control, juvenile crime, bankruptcy, intellectual property, victims' rights, Y2K liability, employment discrimination, antitrust law, and more. Subject-matter area, in turn, influenced staffers' roles relative to other players. For instance, in the crime area, staffers saw themselves as more important because of a relative lack of lobbying interests, while in areas like intellectual property, there was a consensus that lobbyists had a significant role.

b. Senators

. . . All in all, only a minority of staffers reported that their respective senators engaged in any substantial drafting of language for a bill. Three staffers said that their senators did draft at least some language on amendments or bills. But even these staffers tended to characterize drafting by a senator as unusual. Two of these three staffers said that involvement with words was not typical for their particular senators or for most senators. Overall, eleven of twelve responding staffers said that senators, as a general rule, do not draft text as an original matter. . . .

Although staffers placed themselves at the center of the drafting process, they also insisted that they sought to implement the policies of their senators, not to impose their own views. They saw themselves as faithful agents in the drafting process. As one put it: "It's a member's power, not the staffer's." Another considered it "laughable" to believe that staffers routinely act outside the parameters of their bosses' positions on legislative matters. Some staffers emphasized that senators reviewed staff work carefully and that staffers had strong incentives — including keeping their jobs — to ensure that their drafting efforts did not diverge from their bosses' positions and remained loyal to their senators' missions.

c. Lobbyists

Every staffer we interviewed told us that lobbyists regularly were involved in drafting bills. Staffers seemed to use a broad concept of lobbyist, one that included any group — profit or nonprofit — that had an interest in influencing legislation and either had information relevant to the issue or potentially would be affected by the legislation. Thus, the term "lobbyist" sometimes included administrative agencies, the White House, the Justice Department, or even federal judges, as well as church groups, universities, and homeless shelters. When a bill touched on a substantive area in the committee's jurisdiction that was heavily lobbied, staffers indicated that it was highly likely that lobbyists would offer up draft language, be asked to do so by staff, or receive from staff proposed language for the lobbyists' comments. Intellectual property, bankruptcy, and "hot button" issues like gun control, abortion, and pornography were areas in which staffers indicated there was extensive lobbyist involvement. Lobbyists were active even in areas that lacked strong financial interests, for example, matters affecting children's interests. The only area in which we heard that paid lobbyists had a limited role was standard criminal law issues, where there is no real lobby but where the Department of Justice is a regular player. . . .

d. Legislative Counsel

The Legislative Counsel's office is specifically constituted to assist the Senate in drafting legislation. In our interviews, we discussed Legislative Counsel's role in the drafting process with both staffers and with two Legislative Counsel attorneys with extensive experience with the Judiciary Committee. Unlike the practice in some states, no law or rule requires that Senate legislation be drafted by Legislative Counsel attorneys. Legislative Counsel attorneys told us that, because of the nonmandatory nature of their role, their involvement in writing any particular bill is "strictly up to the client" (i.e., the senator or the committee). Legislative Counsel attorneys, therefore, "live on [their] reputation and good relationships."

i. Legislative Counsel from the Perspective of Committee Staffers

Every respondent said that Legislative Counsel attorneys had some role in the drafting process. Respondents differed, however, in how they described the nature and importance of that role. Many staffers told us that the role of the Legislative Counsel's office varied from bill to bill. On some occasions, the staffer would send a memo describing what the proposed legislation would do and then would receive back a first draft from the Legislative Counsel's office. More typically, however, a staffer would prepare a first draft and then forward it to Legislative Counsel attorneys for what was repeatedly characterized as "stylistic" or "technical" input. . . .

Comments by some staffers suggested an inverse relationship between how long a staffer had been on the job and the use of Legislative Counsel attorneys. As one put it, "especially because many staffers have not been here that long," the Legislative Counsel's office "has an important role." One staffer explained that he works with the Legislative Counsel's office, but that its role for him has changed as he has become more experienced:

> Early on, [Legislative Counsel] would draft the bill. Now, I do the first draft and give it to them to tighten and polish. They will take out extra words, see certain aspects of the big picture for drafting when [I am] lost in the details of one subsection, etc.

Several staffers emphasized the importance of political and institutional context in shaping Legislative Counsel's role. One staffer, for example, generally asks the Legislative Counsel's office to draft bills but not if particular language in the bill is politically sensitive and requires special attention. Similarly, if language is being drafted on the floor or in conference, then input from Legislative Counsel attorneys might not be available.

Most staffers praised the Legislative Counsel's office. One staffer, however, reported working for a senator who was wary of Legislative Counsel's drafting on the grounds that "they add more words." Another staffer noted the frequent usage of Legislative Counsel services but observed that there was "a tension with the Judiciary Committee because there are so many lawyers here." This staffer opined that the Legislative Counsel attorneys see themselves as professional drafters and fear that they are being treated by staffers as mere "typists."

ii. Legislative Counsel from the Perspective of Legislative Counsel Attorneys

Legislative Counsel attorneys reported that they receive work from the Judiciary Committee in a variety of ways. This can range from receiving the most amorphous "specs" for a bill (e.g., "We want to make the tax code more fair") to reviewing a comprehensive first draft of a bill written by someone other than a Legislative Counsel attorney. When Legislative Counsel attorneys receive bills written by others, it is usually a staffer, a lobbyist, or an administrator who has drafted the bill.

Legislative Counsel attorneys see their principal objective as to produce a clear, well-sequenced statute. Legislative Counsel's style favors certain elements, such as setting out general rules and exceptions, making liberal use of definitions, including an effective date, and providing coordination rules. When called upon to improve a bill drafted by someone else, Legislative Counsel attorneys say that they frequently encounter problems like a lack of definitions, inconsistent usage of statutory terms, poor organization, or ambiguity in identifying the statutory actors or statutory exceptions.

Despite the considerable variability in the sources and content of assignments given to the Legislative Counsel's office, one near-constant is that the request for assistance comes from committee staffers rather than senators themselves. Legislative Counsel attorneys strongly assert their nonpartisan nature and emphasize that they stand in an attorney-client relationship with senators and staffers. "We are lawyers first," one told us. Because of this attorney-client relationship, Legislative Counsel attorneys do not communicate with any outside groups, except in the presence of a staffer. Legislative Counsel attorneys sometimes do observe the role of lobbyists or others in the drafting process, but only in the presence of staffers. More often, their knowledge of the role played by any outside group is both limited and filtered through staffers.

2. Multiple Drafting Processes

The picture of the drafting process that emerged from our interviews is one of striking variability. There was widespread agreement among staffers that different drafting processes are engaged for different kinds of bills. Sometimes more than one process is applied to the same bill, and the use of one drafting process at a later time (for example, drafting on the floor or in conference) can wipe out the results of an earlier process. We describe below several versions of the drafting process that emerged in our interviews.

a. The Extended Drafting Process

The most thorough drafting process that staffers told us about was described by one in these terms:

> We [the staffers] will come up with an idea, make a list of points to cover. Legislative Counsel will then draft or revise the draft written by staff. We might consult with the [full committee] staff before sending it to Legislative Counsel or other . . . offices to reach some kind of consensus. We might vet language with lobbyists whose clients would be affected by the bill or would be concerned about the bill. [The] final layer [might involve a] check with the [presidential] administration.

This general outline suggests that thorough, time-consuming drafting of this sort is staff driven and that the process involves more negotiation and consultation than exacting word choice. This description was consistent with several stories we heard about various pieces of major legislation. In describing work on drafting a large bankruptcy bill, for example, one staffer said:

> We began with [staff] meetings asking [about] the goal of the [party] caucus. We met with consumer groups, credit card companies, and banks, looking at what would be feasible. After a first draft [by the staff], we sent it to Legislative Counsel and then vetted it with groups and others in the Senate.

Another staffer, who worked on the same bill in a different office, also indicated that the process had begun with a staff draft prepared after consulting with various affected entities and other members' staffs. Because this was to be a high-profile bill, the process was quite extensive; staffers had worked on the bill, met, consulted, and researched for as much as a year:

> A lot was anticipated in advance, input was widely sought, multiple drafts were generated before introduction. Our subcommittee used academics, people who had been involved in the '78 reform bill [the last big bankruptcy bill], [and] Legislative Counsel, along with [our] subcommittee's own ideas. . . . There was about one year of drafting and a hearing.

The staffer contrasted this process with the process that generated the House companion bill, which the staffer characterized as having been negotiated and drafted by lobbyists and introduced with only "minor changes."

b. Consensus Drafting

In a variant of this extended process, staffers told us that some bills were drafted jointly by staffers working for several senators. Language would be negotiated jointly in order to achieve consensus in a committee markup.

Sometimes, staff of members who supported and opposed a bill would meet before the markup, and a bill would be hammered out by the principal interests in a "committee substitute." Staffers provided two examples of this alternative. The first pertained to an internet bill. In that instance, the minority leader in the committee (or "ranking member") thought the bill raised a number of substantive issues; in committee, a number of these issues were addressed by offering a substitute that had been agreed upon by the ranking member and the chair. In this way, the drafting process produced a committee consensus. The second example was of an antidrug bill in which the original mandatory minimum penalties section was amended to include provisions for prevention, research, and training. Once again, a compromise was reached by staff before the committee markup.

Staffers noted, however, sharp limits on this kind of consensus-oriented drafting process. On some issues there was no room for compromise. Abortion and pornography were cited by one staffer as the kind of "edgy" partisan issues as to which accommodation was unlikely. In other cases, compromise did not represent consensus-driven decisionmaking but, instead, was forced by powerful decisionmakers on the committee when, for example, a member "needed" to have a bill for reelection purposes and the committee chair was willing to push the issue.

c. Drafting on the Floor

A strikingly different kind of drafting process was "doing a bill on the floor." In the Senate, where there are virtually no rules, it is possible that senators will choose to construct a bill during debate. Indeed, at least a part of every major bill is so constructed in the form of "managers' amendments," which are typically provisions deemed acceptable to both political parties and included in one omnibus attachment. If this is where a bill is drafted, then the normal processes of drafting change. As one staffer put it, "There is no chance to do legal research here. . . . There is no 'adult supervision.' We do a quick read and correct it on the fly."

Several staff members complained about the dangers of drafting bills on the floor, as this increased the risks of the process becoming "ugly," haphazard, and driven by political imperative. Staffers expressed concern about last-minute drafting without a lot of public scrutiny. Specific fears included provisions being "slipped in," people losing track of whether one provision squared with another, or a provision being added to satisfy the needs of a senator in trouble for reelection. Staffers expressed the dangers of rapidly drafted bills in pointed terms. . . .

d. Drafting in Conference

Several staffers identified, as another venue for drafting, the House-Senate conferences that legislators use to reconcile differences in bills that are passed by both bodies. Like drafting on the floor, drafting in conference was described by staffers with a significant measure of concern. Several staffers thought that pressures of time, and the political imperative to get a bill "done," bred ambiguity. Indeed, one staffer emphasized that while it was well and good to draft a bill clearly, there was no guarantee that the clear language would be passed by the House or make it through conference. Staffers noted that in House-Senate conferences:

> "They can do behind closed doors what can't be done on the floor."

> "[T]here are deals cut with four people in the room, deals on the floor are dropped, nobody knows what's in the bill. There is a big incentive for people to be in conference because it is a big site of action. You can draft carefully and then it gets dropped in conference, and they put in something from the House that you never saw."

> "You work hard, and someone in the House will want to put their fingerprints on something and will mess it up at the end."

B. INSTITUTIONAL DIFFERENCES: DIVERGENT DRAFTING VIRTUES

The second strong theme to emerge from our interviews is an intriguing contrast between how our respondents saw the production of legislative language and what courts identify as important in writing statutory text. We found that the institutional imperatives governing congressional action suggested a different and sometimes conflicting set of legislative drafting virtues.

1. The Virtue of Clarity

Perhaps the single most significant judicial drafting virtue is clarity, the simple idea that legislative language should be written to be as unambiguous as possible. Staffers did not disagree with that fundamental proposition. All agreed that language should be as clear as it can be under the circumstances. Whether simply as the common sense of drafting or as a matter of getting a bill passed, staffers recognized the need for clarity in statutory language:

> "People do use words carefully. Everyone is a lawyer, everyone is careful."

> "Congress has an obligation to the reader of statutes to try to make them as clear as possible."

> "We do try to think of what a court will do with certain language. In [one bill], we thought about how a court might look at the term 'clear and conspicuous disclosure.'"

While sharing the general notion that clarity is a drafting virtue, many staffers were sensitive to dynamics that undermine the ideal of statutory clarity. They tended to see these dynamics as an intrinsic part of the legislative process, rather than as some sort of aberration requiring apology or rationalization. Staffers regularly cited two clarity-undermining dynamics: the lack of sufficient time and the phenomenon of deliberate ambiguity. Here, our findings tend to confirm assertions in the scholarly literature on statutory interpretation about both time pressures and deliberate ambiguity as factors in the lawmaking process. Both of these dynamics were attributed by staff to what might be seen as a conflicting set of legislative drafting virtues: action and agreement (e.g., "we had to get a bill"; "there was no other way to achieve agreement"). Staffers viewed deliberate ambiguity and timing pressures as justified by the felt need for action or the perceived threat that inflexible political positions would thwart passage of any bill at all. . . .

Deliberate ambiguity was seen by staffers as a second, equally powerful force working against statutory clarity. With virtual unanimity, staffers confirmed this phenomenon. One circumstance frequently cited as likely to produce a willful lack of clarity was the absence of consensus on a particular point in a bill:

> "Why [deliberate ambiguity]? To get a bill passed where there is a distinct difference of opinion."

> "[A]mbiguity was essential, in some cases, to get a bill passed."

> "It is all compromise."

> "Politics drives the ambiguity. . . . The decision is made to kick the can."

> "We know that if we answer a certain question, we will lose one side or the other."

As these comments reflect, staffers felt constrained in their quest for clarity by conflicting legislative imperatives and the fact that consensual ambiguity on one point could be essential to getting action on a bill. Staffers repeatedly insisted that having something done could be better than nothing. One staffer, for example, cited the Violence Against Women Act and claimed that the committee chair and the ranking member had decidedly different views about a single key phrase, but since both wanted a bill, they agreed to let it go. Another said that "[p]eople want a bill, and therefore they want to come away with different interpretations." As one staffer summed it up: "This is not a law school process, it is a political process. Sometimes one cannot allow the perfect to be the enemy of the good."

On the whole, staffers seemed quite aware that the principal effect of deliberate ambiguity was to leave it to the courts to decide. Indeed, this course was sometimes chosen precisely for this reason: "You can't get someone to agree to it your way, and you hope that the courts will give you the victory." Staffers also realized that statutory ambiguity created an opportunity to let an agency, as opposed to a court, resolve the issue, and sometimes they specifically desired this result as well. . . .

D. LOBBYISTS AS DRAFTERS

We asked specific questions about the role of lobbyists in the drafting process. . . . Our interest in this issue was piqued by the reaction that followed a story published several years ago revealing that industry lobbyists had assisted Republican members of Congress in drafting a bill relating to environmental law. In light of the firestorm created by that story, we wondered whether staffers thought that lobbyist involvement in drafting was really as rare as the reaction to that news story might have suggested. As we discussed above, one argument against the use of legislative history by courts is that lobbyists frequently draft it. We wondered, therefore, about staffers' views on the prevalence and particulars of lobbyists drafting legislative history and whether staffers saw lobbyists as equally involved in the drafting of statutes as well.

Every staffer we talked to said that lobbyists were involved in at least some drafting of statutory language. As we have noted above, staffers were quick to define "lobbyist" in the broadest terms possible, including everyone from the White House to the local church group to the silk-suited K-Street telecommunications lawyer. The "average person," one staffer told us, does not understand the "broad spectrum" of interests offering their views, like universities who lobby on everything from immigration to healthcare reform. But with that caveat, the sentiment was uniform that lobbyists can have a strong influence on statutory text and that this was not a rare event but, instead, a normal part of the drafting process:

"Lobbyists serve an important and useful role."

"[Lobbyists add] expertise, legal research, information to the process. . . ."

"The good ones have a lot of information and you can turn to them for information."

"As experienced and trained as we are, outsiders have the practical experience — they know the problems in the area and the law in detail."

One staffer confessed that he had changed his mind: Before moving to the Senate, he had been skeptical about lobbyists and had been supportive of lobbying reforms. Now, he said, he had a "more nuanced view of what's appropriate," given the scarcity of time and resources available to staffers. Over time, this staffer has come to ask for proposed language or other help from outsiders. "I have concerns about the power of interest groups," he said, "but the alternative might be worse — i.e., to write the bill without the necessary knowledge." Another staffer saw lobbyist drafts as a "form of free assistance" that staffers can take or leave, noting that some outside interests have a "cadre of lawyers" available for information and drafting attempts.

Staffers repeatedly sought to justify the use of lobbyists in terms of the legislative drafting virtues — as essential to effective action. They said that outsiders were the ones who could give them the necessary information about how the legislation would "affect the world." Lobbyists are the closest to the people who will be affected by the bill, explained one staffer. Another said that lobbyists are a part of "open government," and that they "aren't so sinister as the public image . . . but [instead provide] a way to know how the bill will affect those with a stake." Others suggested that the point of lobbyist involvement was actually a form of deliberation and participation. . . .

Notes and Questions

1. Lobbyists are often regarded as unwelcome or unfortunate intruders into the process of democratic legislation. Should we worry that the lobbyists represent special interests rather than the views of the general public? On the one hand, of course we should. On the other hand, if we consider weighted preferences, the situation isn't quite so unbalanced. Suppose we assign a weight of 1 to 100 based on how much each particular person cares

about an issue and multiply that by the number of people at each preference level. The status of lobbyists might then look quite different, as a matter of democratic theory. Take an ill-considered proposal to regulate an attorney's ability to represent unpopular clients. Suppose this is favored by a majority of voters in the country, let's say by 60 percent of the eligible voters. But they do not care about the proposal very much, so we can assign an average preference rating of 2 to their level of intensity. The opponents do not care much either, so they get a 2 as well. But lawyers care a great deal, and they are overwhelmingly opposed, so let's set their average intensity level at 90. If we multiply the 60 percent of the country's 200 million eligible voters who favor the proposal by two, and subtract the 40 percent of the voters who oppose the proposal times two, we get 40 million times two, or 80 million preference-level votes for the proposal. But now consider that 90 percent of the lawyers, about 1 million people, oppose the proposal at an intensity level of 90. That is now 90 million preference-level votes against the proposal. A legislator considering this proposal would certainly be subject to lobbying by lawyers' groups, but maybe that "special interest" pressure in fact reflects popular sentiment when the weight of the people's preferences are taken into account.

Review the discussion of lobbying in the Nourse-Schacter article from this perspective. Is it truly a problem for the democratic process, or is it part of the democratic process? What problems does it create, even if the limitations on elections and the weightings of preferences are taken into account?

2. With respect to the role of Legislative Counsel, do you think that too much of the legislative process is controlled by amateurs (the legislators) as opposed to legal specialists?

3. How can you tell whether an ambiguity in a statute is deliberate or inadvertent? What significance might this have for how the statute is later interpreted?

4. An empirical study by Abbe Gluck and Lisa Bressman has confirmed many of the Nourse/Schacter findings about legislative drafting and offered much more. *See* Abbe R. Gluck & Lisa Schultz Bressman, *Statutory Interpretation from the Inside— An Empirical Study of Congressional Drafting, Delegation and the Canons: Part I*, 65 STAN. L. REV. 901 (2013). That study contains the result of interviews with 137 congressional counsels, divided roughly equally between the House and the Senate and between the two major political parties, from 26 different committees as well from the House and Senate Offices of Legislative Counsel. The interviews revealed several key influences on legislative drafting. For example, staffers indicated that whether more than one committee participated in drafting a bill can shape the way that a bill is drafted. Staffers also stated that the type of bill (i.e., whether it is a single-subject bill or a multi-subject, omnibus bill) can shape the way that it is drafted. Other factors include the path of the bill (i.e., whether it goes through committee or is moved by party leadership); the role of Legislative Counsel (i.e., whether and how they are involved, either as drafters or editors); and the personal reputation, experience, and job description of the staffer drafting (e.g., whether the staffer is a committee staffer, tending to be more experienced as well as legally trained, or a personal staffer, tending to be less so); and the reputation and history of the agency and agency head implementing the statute (i.e., whether reputation or past conduct indicates that the agency can be trusted with implementing the statute or not). As to ambiguity, the study confirmed that staffers are deliberately ambiguous in statutes for a variety of reasons, and importantly suggested that drafters view agencies as playing a primary role in interpreting statutes. But, in some tension with the Nourse-Schacter study, these respondents did not view courts as playing a primary role in interpreting statutes; rather, courts were seen as a second-best or a last resort. Furthermore, the respondents in the Gluck-Bressman study did not intend for agencies or courts to have authority to resolve the biggest sort of questions — those that involve major policy questions or questions of major political or economic significance — indicating that drafters bear responsibility to resolve such questions themselves.

5. Legislative drafting is a much more complicated endeavor than a series of textbook steps. Appreciating the complexities is essential for those (both inside and outside of Congress) involved in legislative drafting. For example, if you are a lobbyist, you might benefit from knowing that multiple committees are responsible for drafting a particular bill. The complexities might also inform our rules and theories of statutory interpretation. What if you knew that the Legislative Counsel was heavily involved in drafting a statute? Would you argue for a more precise, "legalistic" interpretation of the text? What do you make of theories of statutory interpretation that view courts as having the primary role in interpreting statutes rather than agencies? Now is not the time to answer these questions definitely; you need to know more about the rules and theories of statutory interpretation, which we take up in the next chapter.

C. A STATUTE: THE 1966 MOTOR VEHICLE SAFETY ACT

1. The Story of Auto Safety Legislation

With this description of the legislative process as background, it should be clear that every statute has a history, from introduction and floor debate to ultimate signature by the President. Not every statute follows the same "orthodox" path: some are fast-tracked, escape committee assignment, go forward without debate, and so on. But each statute has a story.

In a moment, we will introduce the National Traffic and Motor Vehicle Safety Act of 1966 to continue our study of legislation. This statute was the first piece of comprehensive federal auto safety legislation. What was its story? Who were the important players in Congress? Which committees were responsible for its passage? What were the key factors in avoiding a veto-gate? We draw the following account from several leading sources, including

RALPH NADER, UNSAFE AT ANY SPEED (1965), and JERRY L. MASHAW & DAVID L. HARFST, THE STRUGGLE FOR AUTO SAFETY (1990).

Early efforts begin.   With the enormous growth of the American auto industry in the 1950s and 1960s, the number of casualties from motor vehicle accidents kept rising. By the mid-1960s, Detroit expected to sell eight million cars in an average year and ten million in a good year. Although the rates of death and injury per passenger mile remained relatively flat, the dramatic increase in miles driven led to an increased toll on the roads. The number of deaths by the mid-1960s exceeded 50,000 per year. Government officials began to look with a more critical eye at the existing system of hands-off motor vehicle safety regulation.

The first efforts occurred at the state level. As Governor of Connecticut between 1955 and 1961, Abraham Ribicoff earned himself the nickname "Mr. Safety" for his dedication to and public focus on traffic safety issues. The New York State Legislature, under the leadership of State Senator Edward Speno, compelled auto manufacturers to install anchorage units for front seat belts in all cars sold in New York. State authorities did not reserve all their regulatory muscle for the auto manufacturers. Sen. Speno's committee, for example, took aim at the tire industry for its lack of safety performance standards. But this and other state initiatives were spotty and uncoordinated. Moreover, the auto industry often blocked state regulatory efforts by citing the difficulty of complying with a patchwork of different rules and implying that one state's stringent regulations might threaten the availability of cars in that state. By the mid-1960s, several states enacted laws mandating installation of manual seat belts in all cars sold within their borders; the auto industry had succeeded in delaying and limiting these efforts for years. All evidence indicated that the industry could continue to stall and convince legislatures in nearly every state to defer implementing any meaningful regulatory scheme.

Congress gets involved.   Congress held its first auto safety hearings in 1956. A proposal to set and enforce brake fluid performance standards went nowhere, leading Congressman Kenneth Roberts of Alabama, who chaired the hearings, to exclaim, "I am getting tired of introducing bills and holding hearings on safety matters. This is certainly not a far-reaching bill. But it is a bill that can save a lot of lives." The other stakeholders seemed content to leave the old order in place.

Neither Congress generally nor the Eisenhower administration shared Rep. Roberts' interest in making motor vehicle designs safer. But Rep. Roberts did compile an impressive investigative record that lay the groundwork for future legislation. More importantly, he managed to get the executive branch into the business of setting auto safety standards, albeit through the back door. Using a new authority that Rep. Roberts pushed through the House, the federal General Services Administration (GSA), the executive branch's procurement department, began to set minimum safety parameters for the cars it purchased for the government's fleet. Because the federal fleet represented a substantial part of Detroit's sales in any given year, the GSA's standards induced manufacturers to comply so that they could keep their government contracts. However, the fundamental regulatory scheme did not change; the federal government merely exercised its power in the marketplace. Despite some effort to mandate federal regulation, the common law remained the primary source of legal rules regarding motor vehicle safety.

Senator Ribicoff takes the lead. In mid-1965, Abraham Ribicoff, by this time senator from Connecticut and chair of the Senate Government Operations Committee's Subcommittee on Executive Reorganization, convened a new, comprehensive set of auto safety hearings. The Subcommittee heard impassioned testimony from Daniel Patrick Moynihan, then a Labor Department official, championing the citizen's right to safer cars, and citing the dramatic promise of the new science of accident prevention and mitigation. Waxing futuristic, he even envisioned a day when people would drive a vehicle that would automatically obey traffic laws and prevent accidents. But a parade of other administration officials testified approvingly of auto manufacturers' safety efforts and of the existing balance between federal and state regulation. Sen. Ribicoff adjourned his committee in the summer without producing any new legislative proposals.

Ralph Nader takes the spotlight. Late that fall, a new actor burst on the scene and changed the terms of the debate. Ralph Nader, a lawyer and among the first of what we now call consumer advocates, published *Unsafe at Any Speed*. Here is an excerpt from that book:

> The American automobile is produced exclusively to the standards which the manufacturer decides to establish. It comes into the marketplace unchecked. When a car becomes involved in an accident, the entire investigatory, enforcement and claims apparatus that makes up the post-accident response looks almost invariably to driver failure as the cause. The need to clear the highways rapidly after collisions contributes to further burying the vehicle's role. Should vehicle failure be obvious in some accidents, responsibility is seen in terms of inadequate maintenance by the motorist. Accommodated by superficial standards of accident investigation, the car manufacturers exude presumptions of engineering excellence and reliability, and this reputation is acceptable by unknowing motorists. . . .
>
> Today almost every [traffic safety] program is aimed at the driver—at educating him, exhorting him, watching him, judging him, punishing him, compiling records about his driving violations, and organizing him in citizen support activities. Resources and energy are directed into programs of enforcement, traffic laws, driver education, driver licensing, traffic courts, and vehicle inspection. The reasoning behind this philosophy of safety can be summarized in this way: Most accidents are in the class of driver fault; driver fault is in the class of violated traffic laws; therefore, observance of traffic laws by drivers would eliminate most accidents.
>
> The prevailing view of traffic safety is much more a political strategy to defend special interests than it is an empirical program to save lives and prevent injuries. For "traffic safety" is not just an abstract value to which lip service is paid. In the automobile industry, safety could represent an investment in research, a priority in production design and manufacturing, and a theme of marketing policy. But under existing business values potential safety advances are subordinated to other investments, priorities, preferences, and themes designed to maximize profit. Industry insists on maintaining

the freedom to rank safety anywhere it pleases on its list of commercial considerations. In the protection of these considerations the industry supports and fosters the traffic safety policy focused on driver behavior; through lobbying and other close relations with state and municipal administrators the efforts of the automobile manufacturers have resulted not only in the perpetuation of that policy but also in some side effects which help the industry preserve its exclusive control over vehicle design.

RALPH NADER, UNSAFE AT ANY SPEED 42-43, 235-36 (1965). Meanwhile, most of the book exposed in detail the deadly designs that auto manufacturers knowingly set on the roads. By pitting the underdog consumer against the biggest symbol of American corporate power, Nader could not have set up a morality play with greater clarity.

Rearmed by Nader, Sen. Ribicoff reopened his hearings when Congress reconvened for the 1966 session. This time, the Subcommittee had much greater visibility and a new tide of public opinion. Even a noted proponent of state, as opposed to federal, regulation testified in front of the committee that the problem required strong action.

Other political actors take an interest. With the new visibility also came new political actors looking for a share of the national spotlight and a hand in setting policy. President Johnson embraced the issue of auto safety as part of his wider call for centralized transportation policy under the umbrella of a new Department of Transportation. He said that a great transportation system was the mark of a great nation and that the United States was the only major nation in the world lacking such a system. On March 2, 1966, he delivered a Message on Transportation to Congress, proposing a far-reaching bill. *See* The American Presidency Project, *Lyndon B. Johnson: Special Message to the Congress on Transportation,* http://www.presidency.ucsb.edu/ws/index.php?pid=28114.

After that, different groups competed to be the first to take significant action on auto safety. The Senate Commerce Committee, chaired by Warren Magnuson of Washington, proceeded to hold hearings on the administration's bill. Sen. Magnuson was eager to take public responsibility for the issue and claim credit with his constituents. Meanwhile, many, including members of Congress and Nader, complained in hearings that the administration's bill was too weak. The race was on in Congress to propose a stronger alternative.

But Sen. Ribicoff was the one who arguably tipped the balance in favor of regulation. Sen. Ribicoff called Nader to testify before his committee about General Motors. The substance of the hearings did not concern the design choices of the automaker, but its actions to discredit Nader himself in response to the momentum that his book had produced. The hearing revealed that GM had hired private detectives to dig up dirt about Nader's past and hired prostitutes to create new dirt about Nader's character. The man who had conducted the investigation on GM's behalf described his mission as: "They [GM] want to get something, somewhere, on this guy to get him out of their hair and to shut him up." Shortly after Congress enacted the statute you are about to read, it enacted legislation that established the

Department of Transportation and transferred responsibility for automobile safety to a National Highway Traffic Safety Administration operating within the Department. You may be interested in acquainting yourself with NHTSA's website, http.//www.nhtsa.gov.

A statute is enacted.   This revelation confirmed Nader's portrayal of auto manufacturers as callous peddlers of a dangerous product, and from that point, new auto safety legislation was all but inevitable. *Time* magazine, in those days a barometer of the nation's political center of gravity, soon ran a piece titled *Why Cars Must — and Can — Be Made Safer.* Congress faced continuous pressure to add new provisions to the bill that was pending before the Commerce Committee: new authority to federally supervise and publicize recalls, tougher compliance provisions, and independent research capacity quickly found their way into the legislation. The Senate soon passed its version of the auto safety bill virtually without opposition. Its ultimate report on the legislation concluded that "[t]he promotion of motor vehicle safety through voluntary standards has largely failed. The unconditional imposition of mandatory standards at the earliest practicable date is the only course commensurate with the highway death and injury toll."

The House, which many had expected to offer resistance, or at least some substantive changes, fell into line. Before the House Commerce Committee, even the auto manufacturers dropped their resistance to the legislation. After a perfunctory conference process that quickly reconciled the minor differences between the two bills, both houses passed the legislation by overwhelming margins. In early September, President Johnson signed it into law and officially created the federal auto safety regulatory scheme. When signing the legislation, he stated:

> For years, we have spent millions of dollars to understand polio and fight other childhood diseases. Yet until now we have tolerated a raging epidemic of highway death which has killed more of our youth than all other diseases combined. Through the Highway Safety Act, we are going to find out more about highway disease — and we aim to cure it.
>
> In this age of space, we are getting plenty of information about how to send men into space and how to bring them home. Yet we don't know for certain whether more auto accidents are caused by faulty brakes, or by soft shoulders, or by drunk drivers, or by deer crossing the highway. . . . [Auto safety] is no luxury item, no optional extra: it must be a normal cost of doing business.

Notes and Questions

1. According to the story above, how did auto safety first get the attention of Congress? What role, if any, did the following play: (a) individual members of Congress; (b) political entrepreneurs outside of Congress; (c) the President; (d) interest groups; and (e) public attitudes, perhaps in response to a crisis or series of events?

2. Once auto safety became a priority for Congress, was the path through the legislative process a fairly typical or "orthodox" one? Can you map parts of the story onto the general description of the legislative process provided above? As you compare the two, is there anything unusual or missing?

3. From the story above, we might gather a sense for the political motivations of certain actors, like Senator Ribicoff. What was in it for him? Does public choice theory help? As we mentioned above, public choice theory suggests that members of Congress enact statutes when doing so is in their own self-interest, which is mainly taken to be an interest in reelection. But, consistent with public choice theory, legislators can also have an interest in their own status or legacy. *See* RICHARD FENNO, CONGRESSMEN IN COMMITTEES (1973). If this is too cynical a view, what else might have motivated Senator Ribicoff?

4. Considering the role of interest groups from a public choice perspective, the 1966 Motor Vehicle Safety Act was not a strong candidate for enactment. On the one hand, a small and economically powerful group of manufacturers were to be burdened by the Act. At the time, the Big Three automakers — General Motors, Ford, and Chrysler — were the first, second, and fifth largest companies in the nation. MASHAW & HARFST. Congress often seeks to please such groups because they can promise the most campaign funding and support. On the other hand, the potential beneficiaries of the Act were as numerous as automobile purchasers themselves. Diffuse groups such as these often face difficulty organizing to make their voice heard, and so Congress might fail to listen. What do you suppose happened in 1966 to belie this prediction? Professors Jerry Mashaw and David Harfst, who wrote the leading account of the politics surrounding the legislation, report that, by 1966, the auto industry lobby was "nearing collapse." *Id.* at 57. Because motor vehicle production had never been federally regulated, the lobby had never developed strong connections to the corporate officials in Detroit and failed to keep them apprised as political momentum built. Moreover, the corporate officials themselves were "not in touch with large areas of social and political reality." *Id.* The corporate culture kept senior managers focused on their own business activities and professional circles rather than the world around them. Badly stung by this experience, where do you suppose the auto industry lobby focused its attention after Congress enacted the Act?

5. Can any theory of legislative behavior fully account for auto safety legislation? Mashaw and Harfst think not: "If the *Nader-General Motors* morality play was the spark that ignited the tinder, and congressman and reporters had personal and institutional interests in fanning the flame," the tinder itself was the ideological context of the moment. MASHAW & HARFST, *id.* at 59. Consider that this legislation came about at the same time as the Civil Rights Act, the Clean Air Act, and many other right-based statutes. It also came about during a time of intense love for science and space, as President Johnson's statement makes clear. As Mashaw and Harfst describe the explanation for the legislation, it was "somewhere at the intersection of the civil rights movement and the space program — a wedding in the mid-1960's of egalitarian ethical judgment, scientific enthusiasm, and activist national politics." *Id.* Note how, in the Mashaw-Harfst description, the justifications for government regulation coincide with political explanations and even work with them.

6. A short postscript: After testifying about GM's behavior to Congress, Nader sued the automaker on a variety of legal claims. The case reached the New York Court of Appeals, which decided in his favor. *See* Nader v. General Motors Corp., 255 N.E.2d 765 (N.Y. 1970). The court's decision articulated a new legal rule by creating the tort of "overzealous surveillance." (The common law lives!) Nader ultimately received $284,000 from GM, which he used to fund further regulatory efforts.

2. The National Traffic and Motor Vehicle Safety Act of 1966

We now present the actual statute that will facilitate our study of legislation. Below is the National Traffic and Motor Vehicle Safety Act of 1966 (which we will often refer to as the "1966 Motor Vehicle Safety Act"). It is reprinted in full, without any editing whatsoever.

The National Traffic and Motor Vehicle Safety Act of 1966

Pub. L. No. 89-563, 80 Stat. 718 (Sept. 9, 1966)

AN ACT

To provide for a coordinated national safety program and establishment of safety standards for motor vehicles in interstate commerce to reduce accidents involving motor vehicles and to reduce the deaths and injuries occurring in such accidents.

Be it enacted by the Senate and House of Representatives of the United States of America in Congress assembled, That Congress hereby declares that the purpose of this Act is to reduce traffic accidents and deaths and injuries to persons resulting from traffic accidents. Therefore, Congress determines that it is necessary to establish motor vehicle safety standards for motor vehicles and equipment in interstate commerce; to undertake and support necessary safety research and development; and to expand the national driver register.

TITLE I — MOTOR VEHICLE SAFETY STANDARDS

SEC. 101. This Act may be cited as the "National Traffic and Motor Vehicle Safety Act of 1966."

SEC. 102. As used in this title —

(1) "Motor vehicle safety" means the performance of motor vehicles or motor vehicle equipment in such a manner that the public is protected against unreasonable risk of accidents occurring as a result of

the design, construction or performance of motor vehicles and is also protected against unreasonable risk of death or injury to persons in the event accidents do occur, and includes nonoperational safety of such vehicles.

(2) "Motor vehicle safety standards" means a minimum standard for motor vehicle performance, or motor vehicle equipment performance, which is practicable, which meets the need for motor vehicle safety and which provides objective criteria.

(3) "Motor vehicle" means any vehicle driven or drawn by mechanical power manufactured primarily for use on the public street, roads, and highways, except any vehicle operated exclusively on a rail or rails.

(4) "Motor vehicle equipment" means any system, part, or component of a motor vehicle as originally manufactured or any similar part or component manufactured or sold for replacement or improvement of such system, part, or component or as an accessory, or addition to the motor vehicle.

(5) "Manufacturer" means any person engaged in the manufacturing or assembling of motor vehicles or motor vehicle equipment, including any person importing motor vehicles or motor vehicle equipment for resale.

(6) "Distributor" means any person primarily engaged in the sale and distribution of motor vehicles or motor vehicle equipment for resale.

(7) "Dealer" means any person who is engaged in the sale and distribution of new motor vehicles or motor vehicle equipment primarily to purchasers who in good faith purchase any such vehicle or equipment for purposes other than resale.

(8) "State" includes each of the several States, the District of Columbia, the Commonwealth of Puerto Rico, Guam, the Virgin Islands, the Canal Zone, and American Samoa.

(9) "Interstate commerce" means commerce between any place in a State and any place in another State, or between places in the same State through another State.

(10) "Secretary" means Secretary of Commerce.

(11) "Defect" includes any defect in performance, construction, components, or materials in motor vehicles or motor vehicle equipment.

(12) "United States district courts" means the Federal district courts of the United States and the United States courts of the Commonwealth of Puerto Rico, Guam, the Virgin Islands, the Canal Zone, and American Samoa.

(13) "Vehicle Equipment Safety Commission" means the Commission established pursuant to the joint resolution of the Congress relating to highway traffic safety, approved August 20, 1958 (72 Stat. 635), or as it may be hereafter reconstituted by law.

SEC. 103. (a) The Secretary shall establish by order appropriate Federal motor vehicle safety standards. Each such Federal motor vehicle safety standard shall be practicable, shall meet the need for motor vehicle safety, and shall be stated in objective terms.

(b) The Administrative Procedure Act shall apply to all orders establishing, amending, or revoking a Federal motor vehicle safety standard under this title.

(c) Each order establishing a Federal motor vehicle safety standard shall specify the date such standard is to take effect which shall not be sooner than one hundred and eighty days or later than one year from the date such order is issued, unless the Secretary finds, for good cause shown, that an earlier or later effective date is in the public interest, and publishes his reasons for such finding.

(d) Whenever a Federal motor vehicle safety standard established under this title is in effect, no State or political subdivision of a State shall have any authority either to establish, or to continue in effect, with respect to any motor vehicle or item of motor vehicle equipment any safety standard applicable to the same aspect of performance of such vehicle or item of equipment which is not identical to the Federal standard. Nothing in this section shall be construed to prevent the Federal Government or the government of any State or political subdivision thereof from establishing a safety requirement applicable to motor vehicles or motor vehicle equipment procured for its own use if such requirement imposes a higher standard of performance than that required to comply with the otherwise applicable Federal standard.

(e) The Secretary may by order amend or revoke any Federal motor vehicle safety standard established under this section. Such order shall specify the date on which such amendment or revocation is to take effect which shall not be sooner than one hundred and eighty days or later than one year from the date the order is issued, unless the Secretary finds, for good cause shown, that an earlier or later effective date is in the public interest, and publishes his reasons for such finding.

(f) In prescribing standards under this section, the Secretary shall—

(1) consider relevant available motor vehicle safety data, including the results of research, development, testing and evaluation activities conducted pursuant to this Act;

(2) consult with the Vehicle Equipment Safety Commission, and such other State or interstate agencies (including legislative committees) as he deems appropriate;

(3) consider whether any such proposed standard is reasonable, practicable and appropriate for the particular type of motor vehicle or item of motor vehicle equipment for which it is prescribed; and

(4) consider the extent to which such standards will contribute to carrying out the purposes of this Act.

(g) In prescribing safety regulations covering motor vehicles subject to part II of the Interstate Commerce Act, as amended (49 U.S.C. 301 et seq.), or the Transportation of Explosives Act, as amended (18 U.S.C.

831-835), the Interstate Commerce Commission shall not adopt or continue in effect any safety regulation which differs from a motor vehicle safety standard issued by the Secretary under this title, except that nothing in this subsection shall be deemed to prohibit the Interstate Commerce Commission from prescribing for any motor vehicle operated by a carrier subject to regulation under either or both of such Acts, a safety regulation which imposes a higher standard of performance subsequent to its manufacture than that required to comply with the applicable Federal standard at the time of manufacture.

(h) The Secretary shall issue initial Federal motor vehicle safety standards based upon existing safety standards on or before January 31, 1967. On or before January 31, 1968, the Secretary shall issue new and revised Federal motor vehicle safety standards under this title.

SEC. 104. (a) The Secretary shall establish a National Motor Vehicle Safety Advisory Council, a majority of which shall be representatives of the general public, including representatives of State and local governments, and the remainder shall include representatives of motor vehicle manufacturers, motor vehicle equipment manufacturers, and motor vehicle dealers.

(b) The Secretary shall consult with the Advisory Council on motor vehicle safety standards under this Act.

(c) Members of the National Motor Vehicle Safety Advisory Council may be compensated at a rate not to exceed $100 per diem (including travel time) when engaged in the actual duties of the Advisory Council. Such members, while away from their homes or regular places of business, may be allowed travel expenses, including per diem in lieu of subsistence as authorized by section 5 of the Administrative Expenses Act of 1946 (5 U.S.C 73b-2), for persons in the Government service employed intermittently. Payments under this section shall not render members of the Advisory Council employees or officials of the United States for any purpose.

SEC. 105. (a) (1) In a case of actual controversy as to the validity of any order under section 103, any person who will be adversely affected by such order when it is effective may at any time prior to the sixtieth day after such order is issued file a petition with the United States court of appeals for the circuit wherein such person resides or has his principal place of business, for a judicial review of such order. A copy of the petition shall be forthwith transmitted by the clerk of the court to the Secretary or other officer designated by him for that purpose. The Secretary thereupon shall file in the court the record of the proceedings on which the Secretary based his order, as provided in section 2112 of title 28 of the United States Code.

(2) If the petitioner applies to the court for leave to adduce additional evidence, and shows to the satisfaction of the court that such additional evidence is material and that there were reasonable grounds

for the failure to adduce such evidence in the proceeding before the Secretary, the court may order such additional evidence (and evidence in rebuttal thereof) to be taken before the Secretary, and to be adduced upon the hearing, in such manner and upon such terms and conditions as to the court may seem proper. The Secretary may modify his findings as to the facts, or make new findings, by reason of the additional evidence so taken, and he shall file such modified or new findings, and his recommendation, if any, for the modification or setting aside of his original order, with the return of such additional evidence.

(3) Upon the filing of the petition referred to in paragraph (1) of this subsection, the court shall have jurisdiction to review the order in accordance with section 10 of the Administrative Procedure Act (5 U.S.C. 1009) and to grant appropriate relief as provided in such section.

(4) The judgment of the court affirming or setting aside, in whole or in part, any such order of the Secretary shall be final, subject to review by the Supreme Court of the United States upon certiorari or certification as provided in section 1254 of title 28 of the United States Code.

(5) Any action instituted under this subsection shall survive, notwithstanding any change in the person occupying the office of Secretary of any vacancy in such office.

(6) The remedies provided for in this subsection shall be in addition to and not in substitution for any other remedies provided by law.

(b) A certified copy of the transcript of the record and proceedings under this section shall be furnished by the Secretary to any interested party at his request, and payment of the costs thereof, and shall be admissible in any criminal, exclusion of imports, or other proceeding arising under or in respect of this title, irrespective of whether proceedings with respect to the order have previously been initiated or become final under subsection (a).

SEC. 106. (a) The Secretary shall conduct research, testing, development, and training necessary to carry out the purposes of this title, including, but not limited to —

(1) collecting data from any source for the purpose of determining the relationship between motor vehicle or motor vehicle equipment performance characteristics and (A) accidents involving motor vehicles, and (B) the occurrence of death, or personal injury resulting from such accidents;

(2) procuring (by negotiation or otherwise) experimental and other motor vehicles or motor vehicle equipment for research and testing purposes;

(3) selling or otherwise disposing of test motor vehicles and motor vehicle equipment and reimbursing the proceeds of such sale or disposal into the current appropriation available for the purpose of carrying out this title.

(b) The Secretary is authorized to conduct research, testing, development, and training as authorized to be carried out by subsection (a) of this section by making grants for the conduct of such research, testing, development, and training to States, interstate agencies, and nonprofit institutions.

(c) Whenever the Federal contribution for any research or development activity authorized by this Act encouraging motor vehicle safety is more than minimal, the Secretary shall include in any contract, grant, or other arrangement for such research or development activity, provisions effective to insure that all information, uses, processes, patents, and other developments resulting from that activity will be made freely and fully available to the general public. Nothing herein shall be construed to deprive the owner of any background patent or any right which he may have thereunder.

SEC. 107. The Secretary is authorized to advise, assist, and cooperate with, other Federal departments and agencies, and State and other interested public and private agencies, in the planning and development of—

(1) motor vehicle safety standards;

(2) methods for inspecting and testing to determine compliance with motor vehicle safety standards.

SEC. 108. (a) No person shall—

(1) manufacture for sale, sell, offer for sale, or introduce or deliver for introduction in interstate commerce, or import into the United States, any motor vehicle or item of motor vehicle equipment manufactured on or after the date any applicable Federal motor vehicle safety standard takes effect under this title unless it is in conformity with such standard except as provided in subsection (b) of this section;

(2) fail or refuse access to or copying of records, or fail to make reports or provide information, or fail or refuse to permit entry or inspection, as required under section 112;

(3) fail to issue a certificate required by section 114, or issue a certificate to the effect that a motor vehicle or item of motor vehicle equipment conforms to all applicable Federal motor vehicle safety standards, if such person in the exercise of due care has reason to know that such certificate is false or misleading in a material respect;

(4) fail to furnish notification of any defect as required by section 113.

(b) (1) Paragraph (1) of subsection (a) shall not apply to the sale, the offer for sale, or the introduction or delivery for introduction in interstate commerce of any motor vehicle or motor vehicle equipment after the first purchase of it in good faith for purposes other than resale. In order to assure a continuing and effective national traffic safety program, it is the policy of Congress to encourage and strengthen the enforcement of State inspection of used motor vehicles. Therefore to that end the Secretary shall conduct a thorough study and investigation to determine the adequacy of motor vehicle safety standards and motor vehicle inspection requirements and procedures applicable to used motor vehicles in each State, and the effect of programs authorized by this title upon such standards, requirements, and procedures for used motor vehicles, and as soon as practicable but not later than one year after the date of enactment of this title, the results of such study, and recommendations for such additional legislation as he deems necessary to carry out the purposes of this Act. As soon as practicable after the submission of such report, but no later than one year from the date of submission of such report, the Secretary, after consultation with the Council and such interested public and private agencies and groups as he deems advisable, shall establish uniform Federal motor vehicle safety standards applicable to all used motor vehicles. Such standards shall be expressed in terms of motor vehicle safety performance. The Secretary is authorized to amend or revoke such standards pursuant to this Act.

(2) Paragraph (1) of subsection (a) shall not apply to any person who establishes that he did not have reason to know in the exercise of due care that such vehicle or item of motor vehicle equipment is not in conformity with applicable Federal motor vehicle safety standards, or to any person who, prior to such first purchase, holds a certificate issued by the manufacturer or importer of such motor vehicle or motor vehicle equipment, to the effect that such vehicle or equipment conforms to all applicable Federal motor vehicle safety standards, unless such person knows that such vehicle or equipment does not so conform.

(3) A motor vehicle or item of motor vehicle equipment offered for importation in violation of paragraph (1) of subsection (a) shall be refused admission into the United States under joint regulations issued by the Secretary of the Treasury and the Secretary; except that the Secretary of the Treasury and the Secretary may, by such regulations, provide for authorizing the importation of such motor vehicle or item of motor vehicle equipment into the United States upon such terms and conditions (including the furnishing of a bond) as may appear to them appropriate to insure that any such motor vehicle or item of motor vehicle equipment will be brought into conformity with any applicable Federal motor vehicle safety standard prescribed under this title, or will be exported or abandoned to the United States.

(4) The Secretary of the Treasury and the Secretary may, by joint regulations, permit the temporary importation of any motor vehicle or item of motor vehicle equipment after the first purchase of it in good faith for purposes other than resale.

(5) Paragraph (1) of subsection (a) shall not apply in the case of a motor vehicle or item of motor vehicle equipment intended solely for export, and so labeled or tagged on the vehicle or item itself and on the outside of the container, if any, which is exported.

(c) Compliance with any Federal motor vehicle safety standard issued under this title does not exempt any person from any liability under common law.

SEC. 109. (a) Whoever violates any provision of section 108, or any regulation issued thereunder, shall be subject to a civil penalty of not to exceed $1,000 for each such violation. Such violation of a provision of section 108, or regulations issued thereunder, shall constitute a separate violation with respect to each motor vehicle or item of motor vehicle equipment or with respect to each failure or refusal to allow or perform an act required thereby, except that the maximum civil penalty shall not exceed $400,000 for any related series of violations.

(b) Any such civil penalty may be compromised by the Secretary. In determining the amount of such penalty, or the amount agreed upon in compromise, the appropriateness of such penalty to the size of the business of the person charged and the gravity of the violation shall be considered. The amount of such penalty, when finally determined, or the amount agreed upon in compromise, may be deducted from any sums owing by the United States to the person charged.

SEC. 110. (a) The United States district courts shall have jurisdiction, for cause shown and subject to the provisions of rule 65(a) and (b) of the Federal Rules of Civil Procedure, to restrain violations of this title, or to restrain the sale, offer for sale, or the introduction or delivery for introduction, in interstate commerce, or the importation into the United States, of any motor vehicle or item of motor vehicle equipment which is determined, prior to the first purchase of such vehicle in good faith for purposes other than resale, not to conform to applicable Federal motor vehicle safety standards prescribed pursuant to this title, upon petition by the appropriate United States attorney or the Attorney General on behalf of the United States. Whenever practicable, the Secretary shall give notice to any person against whom an action for injunctive relief is contemplated and afford him an opportunity to present his views, and, except in the case of a knowing and willful violation, shall afford him reasonable opportunity to achieve compliance. The failure to give such notice and afford such opportunity shall not preclude the granting of appropriate relief.

(b) In any proceeding for criminal contempt for violation of an injunction or restraining order issued under this section, which violation also constitutes a violation of this title, trial shall be by the court or, upon demand of the accused, by a jury. Such trial shall be conducted in accordance with the practice and procedure applicable in the case of proceedings subject to the provisions of rule 42(b) of the Federal Rules of Criminal Procedure.

(c) Actions under subsection (a) of this section and section 109(a) of this title may be brought in the district wherein any act or transaction constituting the violation occurred, or in the district wherein the defendant is found or is an inhabitant or transacts business, and process in such cases may be served in any other district of which the defendant is an inhabitant or wherever the defendant may be found.

(d) In any actions brought under subsection (a) of this section and section 109(a) of this title, subpoenas for witnesses who are required to attend a United States district court may run into any other district.

(e) It shall be the duty of every manufacturer offering a motor vehicle or item of motor vehicle equipment for importation into the United States to designate in writing an agent upon whom service of all administrative and judicial processes, notices, orders, decisions and requirements may be made for and on behalf of said manufacturer, and to file such designation with the Secretary, which designation may from time to time be changed by like writing, similarly filed. Service of all administrative and judicial processes, notices, orders, decisions and requirements may be made upon said manufacturer by service upon such designated agent at his office or usual place of residence with like effect as if made personally upon said manufacturer, and in default of such designation of such agent, service of process, notice, order, requirement or decision in any proceeding before the Secretary or in any judicial proceeding for enforcement of this title or any standards prescribed pursuant to this title may be made by posting such process, notice, order, requirement or decision in the Office of the Secretary.

SEC. 111. (a) If any motor vehicle or item of motor vehicle equipment is determined not to conform to applicable Federal motor vehicle safety standards, or contains a defect which relates to motor vehicle safety, after the sale of such vehicle or item of equipment by a manufacturer or a distributor to a distributor or a dealer and prior to the sale of such vehicle or item of equipment by such distributor or dealer:

(1) The manufacturer or distributor, as the case may be, shall immediately repurchase such vehicle or item of motor vehicle equipment from such distributor or dealer at the price paid by such distributor or dealer, plus all transportation charges involved and a reasonable reimbursement of not less than 1 per centum per month of such price paid prorated from the date of notice of such nonconformance to the date of repurchase by the manufacturer or distributor; or

(2) In the case of motor vehicles, the manufacturer or distributor, as the case may be, at his own expense, shall immediately furnish the purchasing distributor or dealer the required conforming part or parts or equipment for installation by the distributor

or dealer on or in such vehicle and for the installation involved the manufacturer shall reimburse such distributor or dealer for the reasonable value of such installation plus a reasonable reimbursement of not less than 1 per centum per month of the manufacturer's or distributor's selling price prorated from the date of notice of such nonconformance to the date such vehicle is brought into conformance, with applicable Federal standards: Provided, however, that the distributor or dealer proceeds with reasonable diligence with the installation after the required part, parts or equipment are received.

(b) In the event any manufacturer or distributor shall refuse to comply with the requirements of paragraphs (1) and (2) of subsection (a), then the distributor or dealer, as the case may be, to whom such nonconforming vehicle or equipment has been sold may bring suit against such manufacturer or distributor in any district court of the United States in the district in which said manufacturer or distributor resides, or is found, or has an agent, without respect to the amount in controversy, and shall recover the damage by him sustained, as well as all court costs plus reasonable attorneys' fees. Any action brought pursuant to this section shall be forever barred unless commenced within three years after the cause of action shall have accrued.

(c) The value of such installations and such reasonable reimbursements as specified in subsection (a) of this section shall be fixed by mutual agreement of the parties, or failing such agreement, by the court pursuant to the provisions of subsection (b) of this section.

SEC. 112. (a) The Secretary is authorized to conduct such inspection and investigation as may be necessary to enforce Federal vehicle safety standards established under this title. He shall furnish the Attorney General and, when appropriate, the Secretary of the Treasury any information obtained indicating noncompliance with such standards, for appropriate action.

(b) For purposes of enforcement of this title, officers or employees duly designated by the Secretary, upon presenting appropriate credentials and a written notice to the owner, operator, or agent in charge, are authorized (1) to enter, at reasonable times, any factory, warehouse, or establishment in which motor vehicles or items of motor vehicle equipment are manufactured, or held for introduction into interstate commerce or are held for sale after such introduction; and (2) to inspect, at reasonable times and within reasonable limits and in a reasonable manner, such factory, warehouse, or establishment. Each such inspection shall be commenced and completed with reasonable promptness.

(c) Every manufacturer of motor vehicles and motor vehicle equipment shall establish and maintain such records, make such reports, and provide such information as the Secretary may reasonably require to enable him to determine whether such manufacturer has acted or is acting in compliance with this title and motor vehicle safety standards prescribed pursuant to this title and shall, upon request of an officer or employee duly designated by the Secretary, permit such officer or employee to inspect appropriate books, papers, records, and documents relevant to determining whether such manufacturer has acted or is acting in compliance with this title and motor vehicle safety standards prescribed pursuant to this title.

(d) Every manufacturer of motor vehicles and motor vehicle equipment shall provide to the Secretary such performance data and other technical data related to performance and safety as may be required to carry out the purposes of this Act. The Secretary is authorized to require the manufacturer to give such notification of such performance and technical data at the time of original purchase to the first person who purchases a motor vehicle or item of equipment for purposes other than resale, as he determines necessary to carry out the purposes of this Act.

(e) All information reported to or otherwise obtained by the Secretary or his representative pursuant to subsection (b) or (c) which information contains or relates to a trade secret or other matter referred to in section 1905 of title 18 of the United States Code, shall be considered confidential for the purpose of that section, except that such information may be disclosed to other officers or employees concerned with carrying out this title or when relevant in any proceeding under this title. Nothing in this section shall authorize the withholding of information by the Secretary or any officer or employee under his control, from the duly authorized committees of the Congress.

SEC. 113. (a) Every manufacturer of motor vehicles shall furnish notification of any defect in any motor vehicle or motor vehicle equipment produced by such manufacturer which he determines, in good faith, relates to motor vehicle safety, to the purchaser (where known to the manufacturer) of such motor vehicle or motor vehicle equipment, within a reasonable time after such manufacturer has discovered such defect.

(b) The notification required by subsection (a) shall be accomplished —

(1) by certified mail to the first purchaser (not including any dealer of such manufacturer) of the motor vehicle or motor vehicle equipment containing such a defect, and to any subsequent purchaser to whom has been transferred any warranty on such motor vehicle or motor vehicle equipment; and

(2) by certified mail or other more expeditious means to the dealer or dealers of such manufacturer to whom such motor vehicle or equipment was delivered.

(c) The notification required by subsection (a) shall contain a clear description or such defect, an evaluation of the risk to traffic safety reasonably related to such defect, and a statement or the measures to be taken to repair such defect.

(d) Every manufacturer of motor vehicles shall furnish to the Secretary a true or representative copy of all notices, bulletins, and other communications to the dealers of such manufacturer or purchasers of motor vehicles or motor vehicle equipment of such manufacturer regarding any defect in such vehicle or equipment sold or serviced by such dealer. The Secretary shall disclose so much of the information contained in such notice or other information obtained under section 112(a) to the public as he deems will assist in carrying out the purposes of this Act, but he shall not disclose any information which contains or relates to a trade secret or other matter referred to in section 1905 of title 18 of the United States Code unless he determines that it is necessary to carry out the purposes of this Act.

(e) If through testing, inspection, investigation, or research carried out pursuant to this title, or examination of reports pursuant to subsection (d) of this section, or otherwise, the Secretary determines that any motor vehicle or item of motor vehicle equipment—

> (1) does not comply with an applicable Federal motor vehicle safety standard prescribed pursuant to section 103; or
>
> (2) contains a defect which relates to motor vehicle safety;
>
> then he shall immediately notify the manufacturer of such motor vehicle or item of motor vehicle equipment of such defect or failure to comply. The notice shall contain the findings of the Secretary and shall include all information upon which the findings are based. The Secretary shall afford such manufacturer an opportunity to present his views and evidence in support thereof, to establish that there is no failure of compliance or that the alleged defect does not affect motor vehicle safety. If after such presentation by the manufacturer the Secretary determines that such vehicle or item of equipment does not comply with applicable Federal motor vehicle safety standards, or contains a defect which relates to motor vehicle safety, the Secretary shall direct the manufacturer to furnish the notification specified in subsection (c) of this section to the purchaser of such motor vehicle or item of motor vehicle equipment as provided in subsections (a) and (b) of this section.

Sec. 114. Every manufacturer or distributor of a motor vehicle or motor vehicle equipment shall furnish to the distributor or dealer at the time of delivery of such vehicle or equipment by such manufacturer or distributor the certification that each such vehicle or item of motor vehicle equipment conforms to all applicable Federal motor vehicle safety standards. In the case of an item of motor vehicle equipment such certification may be in the form of a label or tag on such item or on the outside of a container in which such item is delivered. In the case of an item of motor vehicle equipment such certification shall be in the form of a label or tag permanently affixed to such motor vehicle.

SEC. 115. The Secretary shall carry out the provisions of this Act through a National Traffic Safety Agency (hereinafter referred to as the "Agency"), which he shall establish in the Department of Commerce. The Agency shall be headed by a Traffic Safety Administrator who shall be appointed by the President, by and with the advice and consent of the Senate, and shall be compensated at the rate prescribed for level V of the Federal Executive Salary Schedule established by the Federal Executive Salary Act of 1964. The Administrator shall be a citizen of the United States, and shall be appointed with due regard for his fitness to discharge efficiently the powers and the duties delegated to him pursuant to this Act. The Administrator shall perform such duties as are delegated to him by the Secretary.

SEC. 116. Nothing contained herein shall be deemed to exempt from the antitrust laws of the United States any conduct that would otherwise be unlawful under such laws, or to prohibit under the antitrust laws of the United States any conduct that would be lawful under such laws.

SEC. 117. (a) The Act entitled "An Act to provide that hydraulic brake fluid sold or shipped in commerce for use in motor vehicles shall meet certain specifications prescribed by the Secretary of Commerce", approved September 5, 1962 (76 Stat. 437; Public Law 87-637), and the Act entitled "An Act to provide that seat belts sold or shipped in interstate commerce for use in motor vehicles shall meet certain safety standards", approved December 13, 1963 (77 Stat. 361; Public Law 88-201), are hereby repealed.

(b) Whoever, prior to the date of enactment of this section, knowingly and willfully violates any provision of law repealed by subsection (a) of this section, shall be punished in accordance with the provisions of such laws as in effect on the date such violation occurred.

(c) All standards issued under authority of the laws repealed by subsection (a) of this section which are in effect at the time this section takes effect, shall continue in effect as if they had been effectively issued under section 103 until amended or revoked by the Secretary, or a court of competent jurisdiction by operation of law.

(d) Any proceeding relating to any provision of law repealed by subsection (a) of this section which is pending at the time this section takes effect shall be continued by the Secretary as if this section had not been enacted, and orders issued in any such proceeding shall continue in effect as if they had been effectively issued under section 103 until amended or revoked by the Secretary in accordance with this title, or by operation of law.

(e) The repeals made by subsection (a) of this section shall not affect any suit, action, or other proceeding lawfully commenced prior to the date this section takes effect, and all such suits, actions, and proceedings, shall be continued, proceedings therein had, appeals therein taken, and judgments therein rendered, in the same manner and with the same effect as if this section had not been enacted. No suit, action, or other proceeding lawfully commenced by or against any agency or officer of the United States in relation to the discharge of official duties under any provision of law repealed by subsection (a) of this section shall abate by reason of such repeal, but the court, upon motion or supplemental petition filed at any time within 12 months after the date of enactment of this section showing the necessity for the survival of such suit, action, or other proceeding to obtain a settlement of the questions involved, may allow the same to be maintained.

SEC. 118. The Secretary, in exercising the authority under this title, shall utilize the services, research and testing facilities of public agencies to the maximum extent practicable in order to avoid duplication.

SEC. 119. The Secretary is authorized to issue, amend, and revoke such rules and regulations as he deems necessary to carry out this title.

SEC. 120. (a) The Secretary shall prepare and submit to the President for transmittal to the Congress on March 1 of each year a comprehensive report on the administration of this Act for the preceding calendar year. Such report shall include but not be restricted to (1) a thorough statistical compilation of the accidents and injuries occurring in such year; (2) a list of Federal motor vehicle safety standards prescribed or in effect in such year; (3) the degree of observance of applicable Federal motor vehicle standards; (4) a summary of all current research grants and contracts together with a description of the problems to be considered by such grants and contracts; (5) an analysis and evaluation, including relevant policy recommendations, of research activities completed and technological progress achieved during such year; and (6) the extent to which technical information was disseminated to the scientific community and consumer-oriented information was made available to the motoring public.

(b) The report required by subsection (a) of this section shall contain such recommendations for additional legislation as the Secretary deems necessary to promote cooperation among the several States in the improvement of traffic safety and to strengthen the national traffic safety program.

SEC. 121. (a) There is authorized to be appropriated for the purpose of carrying out the provisions of this title, other than those related to tire safety, not to exceed $11,000,000 for fiscal year 1967, $17,000,000 for fiscal year 1968, and $23,000,000 for the fiscal year 1969.

(b) There is authorized to be appropriated for the purpose of carrying out the provisions of this title related to tire safety and title II, not to exceed $2,900,000 for fiscal year 1967, and $1,450,000 per fiscal year for the fiscal years 1968 and 1969.

SEC. 122. The provisions of this title for certification of motor vehicles and items of motor vehicle equipment shall take effect on the effective date of the first standard actually issued under section 103 of this title.

TITLE: II — TIRE SAFETY

SEC. 201. In all standards for pneumatic tires established under title I of this Act, the Secretary shall require that tires subject thereto be permanently and conspicuously labeled with such safety information as he determines to be necessary to carry out the purposes of this Act. Such labeling shall include —

(1) suitable identification of the manufacturer, or in the case of a retreaded tire suitable identification of the retreader, unless the tire contains a brand name other than the name of the manufacturer in which case it shall also contain a code mark which would permit the seller of such tire to identify the manufacturer thereof to the purchaser upon his request.

(2) the composition of the material used in the ply of the tire.

(3) the actual number of plies in the tire.

(4) the maximum permissible load for the tire.

(5) a recital that the tire conforms to Federal minimum safe performance standards, except that in lieu of such recital the Secretary may prescribe an appropriate mark or symbol for use by those manufacturers or retreaders who comply with such standards. The Secretary may require that additional safety related information be disclosed to the purchaser of a tire at the time of sale of the tire.

SEC. 202. In standards established under title I of this Act the Secretary shall require that each motor vehicle be equipped by the manufacturer or by the purchaser thereof at the time of the first purchase thereof in good faith for purposes other than resale with tires which meet the maximum permissible load standards when such vehicle is fully loaded with the maximum number of passengers it is designed to carry and a reasonable amount of luggage.

SEC. 203. In order to assist the consumer to make an informed choice in the purchase of motor vehicle tires, within two years after the enactment of this title, the Secretary shall, through standards established under title I of this Act, prescribe by order, and publish in the Federal Register, a uniform quality grading system for motor vehicle tires. Such order shall specify the date such system is to take effect which shall not be sooner than one hundred and eighty days or later than one year from the date such order is issued, unless the Secretary finds, for good cause shown, that an earlier or later effective date is in the public interest, and publishes his reasons for such finding. The Secretary shall also cooperate with industry and the Federal Trade Commission to the maximum extent practicable in efforts to eliminate deceptive and confusing tire nomenclature and marketing practices.

SEC. 204. (a) No person shall sell, offer for sale, or introduce for sale or deliver for introduction in interstate commerce, any tire or motor vehicle equipped with any tire which has been regrooved, except that the Secretary may by order permit the sale of regrooved tires and motor vehicles equipped with regrooved tires which he finds are designed and constructed in a manner consistent with the purposes of this Act.

(b) Violations of this section shall be subject to civil penalties and injunction in accordance with sections 109 and 110 of this Act.

(c) For the purposes of this section the term "regrooved tire" means a tire on which a new tread has been produced by cutting into the tread of a worn tire.

SEC. 205. In the event of any conflict between the requirements of orders or regulations issued by the Secretary under this title and title I of this Act applicable to motor vehicle tires and orders or administrative interpretations issued by the Federal Trade Commission, the provisions of orders or regulations issued by the Secretary shall prevail.

TITLE III — ACCIDENT AND INJURY RESEARCH AND TEST FACILITY

SEC. 301. The Secretary of Commerce is hereby authorized to make a complete investigation and study of the need for a facility or facilities to conduct research, development, and testing in traffic safety (including but not limited to motor vehicle and highway safety) authorized by law, and research, development, and testing relating to the safety of machinery used on highways or in connection with the maintenance of highways (with particular emphasis on tractor safety) as he deems appropriate and necessary.

SEC. 302. The Secretary shall report the results of his investigation and study to Congress not later than December 31, 1967. Such report shall include but not be limited to (1) an inventory of existing capabilities, equipment, and facilities, either publicly or privately owned or operated, which could be made available for use by the Secretary in carrying out the safety research, development, and testing referred to in section 301, (2) recommendations as to the site or sites for any recommended facility or facilities, (3) preliminary plans, specifications, and drawings for such recommended facility or facilities (including major research, development, and testing equipment), and (4) the estimated cost of the recommended sites, facilities, and equipment.

SEC. 303. There is hereby authorized to be appropriated not to exceed $3,000,000 for the investigation, study, and report authorized by this title. Any funds so appropriated shall remain available until expended.

Title IV — National Driver Register

Sec. 401. The Act entitled "An Act to provide for a register in the Department of Commerce in which shall be listed the names of certain persons who have had their motor vehicle operator's licenses revoked," approved July 14, 1960, as amended (74 Stat. 526; 23 U.S.C. 313 note), is hereby amended to read as follows: "That the Secretary of Commerce shall establish and maintain a register identifying each individual reported to him by a State, or political subdivision thereof, as an individual with respect to whom such State or political subdivision has denied, terminated, or temporarily withdrawn (except a withdrawal for less than six months based on a series of nonmoving violations) an individual's license or privilege to operate a motor vehicle.

"Sec. 2. Only at the request of a State, a political subdivision thereof, or a Federal department or agency, shall the Secretary furnish information contained in the register established under the first section of this Act, and such information shall be furnished only to the requesting party and only with respect to an individual applicant for a motor vehicle operator's license or permit.

"Sec. 3. As used in this Act, the term 'State' includes each of the several States, the Commonwealth of Puerto Rico, the District of Columbia, Guam, the Virgin Islands, the Canal Zone, and American Samoa."

Approved September 9, 1966, 1:10 p.m.

Notes and Questions

1. Reproduce in outline form the structure of the 1966 Motor Vehicle Safety Act. In other words, copy the number or letter of each section, and the subject matter of that section. Be sure to include every numbered or lettered section. This task is more difficult than it might seem because the structure of the statute is quite complex and indeed counter-intuitive at certain points. It is also more useful than it might seem because it will help you understand how to read and apply the statute, which is the ultimate goal of our study.

2. Identify the language in the 1966 Motor Vehicle Safety Act that corresponds to each component of a statute, as just described. Summarize what each provision actually does.

3. Take a look at the preemption provision and the savings clause in the 1966 Motor Vehicle Safety Act, also discussed in the Senate Report. What do you think Congress was trying to accomplish with these provisions? What sorts of state laws are preempted and what sorts are saved? *See* Geier v. American Honda Motor Co., 529 U.S. 861 (2000).

You have seen the text of the 1966 Motor Vehicle Safety Act; now consider a major piece of its legislative history. We will discuss the use of legislative history by courts in Chapter 3 and agencies in Chapters 4 and 5. For now, we want you to see what one piece looks like and ask whether you find it helpful in understanding the basic structure of the statute that you just read. Here is an excerpt from the Report of the Senate Commerce Committee regarding the bill that subsequently became the 1966 Motor Vehicle Safety Act. Note that some section numbers in the version of the bill that the Report discusses differ from those in the final Act (e.g., the definition of "defect" is referred to as sec. 101(1) in the Report and sec. 102(11) in the Act; the provision for federal motor vehicle safety standards is sec. 104 in the Report and sec. 103 in the Act).

Senate Report (Commerce Committee)
[To accompany S. 3005]

S. Rep. No. 1301, 89th Cong., 2d Sess. (1966)

PURPOSE AND NEED

The legislation which the Commerce Committee unanimously reports today reflects the conviction of the committee that the soaring rate of death and debilitation on the Nation's highways is not inexorable. This legislation also reflects the committee's judgment that the Federal Government has a major responsibility to meet in assuring safer performance of private passenger cars which it has not yet met. Finally, this legislation reflects the faith that the restrained and responsible exercise of Federal authority can channel the creative energies and vast technology of the automobile industry into a vigorous and competitive effort to improve the safety of vehicles.

It should not be necessary to call again the grim roll of Americans lost and maimed on the Nation's highways. Yet the compelling need for the strong automobile safety legislation which the Commerce Committee is today reporting lies embodied in those statistics: 1.6 million dead since the coming of the automobile; over 50,000 to die this year. And unless the accelerating spiral of death is arrested, 100,000 Americans will die as a result of their cars in 1975.

On March 2 of this year, President Johnson delivered to Congress his message on transportation and traffic safety, together with the proposed Traffic Safety Act of 1966. In this message, the President urged that the Secretary of Commerce ". . . be given the authority to determine the necessary safety performance criteria for all vehicles and their components." In addition, he called for the dynamic expansion of Federal traffic research programs, including the development of a national highway safety research and test center.

It was the committee's task to determine the extent to which Federal automobile safety standards could contribute to the reduction of traffic deaths and injuries on the highways. To that end, the committee held 7 days of hearings, calling upon distinguished witnesses, encompassing the widest range of expertise in the automotive safety field.

The American automotive industry has been for many years one of the most dynamic factors in the entire national economy. One out of every six Americans is employed in the industry or in the provision of automotive components or the service of automotive vehicles. The industry's growth and productivity have been outstanding. And American cars — whatever their shortcomings — are among the world's safest.

Moreover, the hearings produced evidence that the automobile industry has made commendable progress in many aspects of automotive safety. With respect to such critical components as lights, brakes, and suspension systems, the automobile of 1966 demonstrates marked improvement over its predecessors.

But the committee met with disturbing evidence of the automobile industry's chronic subordination of safe design to promotional styling, and of an overriding stress on power, acceleration, speed, and "ride" to the relative neglect of safe performance or collision protection. The committee cannot judge the truth of the conviction that "safety doesn't sell," but it is a conviction widely held in industry which has plainly resulted in the inadequate allocation of resources to safety engineering.

Until the industry had been subjected to the prod of heightened public interest and governmental concern, new models showed little improvement in safe design or in the incorporation of safety devices. Such elemental safe design features as safety door latches made their appearance as standard equipment only a decade after their desirability and feasibility had been established.

As late as 1959, in testimony before a committee of Congress, the chairman of the Automotive Manufacturer's Association's Engineering Advisory Committee was still resisting the suggestion that seat belt fittings be made standard equipment on all automobiles.

The committee hearings also documented past laxity in furnishing adequate notification to car owners of latent defects which had crept into the manufacturing process — defects frequently related to safety. Equally disturbing was evidence that the manufacturers have not always taken effective steps to insure the speedy and efficient repair of such defects. Although current industry defect-curing practices now appear to be improved, the committee concluded that Federal oversight of defect notification and correction is essential.

For too many years, the public's proper concern over the safe driving habits and capacity of the driver (the "nut behind the wheel") was permitted to overshadow the role of the car itself. The "second collision" — the impact of the individual within the vehicle against the steering wheel, dashboard, windshield, etc. has been largely neglected. The committee was greatly impressed by the critical distinction between the causes of the accident itself and causes of the resulting death or injury. Here, the design of the vehicle as well as the public willingness to use safety devices, such as seat belts, are the critical factors. Recessed dashboard instruments and the use of seat belts can mean the difference between a bruised forehead and a fractured skull.

The committee heard compelling testimony that passenger cars can be designed and constructed so as to afford substantial protection against the "second collision" for both driver and passenger; further, that some of these design changes can be achieved at little or no additional manufacturing cost.

Yet the committee was presented with graphic evidence that the interior design of many 1966 model cars reveal interiors bristling with rigid tubes, angles, knobs, sharp instruments, and heavy metal of small radius of curvature. While such objects are sometimes placed and shaped as they are for the convenience of driver and passenger, substantial safety improvement could be achieved without inconvenience to the car occupants. . . .

Out of the committee's hearings there emerged a clear outline of the basic needs to be served by Federal legislation:

1. The promotion of motor vehicle safety through voluntary standards has largely failed. The unconditional imposition of mandatory standards at the earliest practicable date is the only course commensurate with the highway death and injury toll.

2. While the contribution of the several States to automobile safety has been significant, and justifies securing to the States a consultative role in the setting of standards, the primary responsibility for regulating the national automotive manufacturing industry must fall squarely upon the Federal Government. . . .

6. The individual in the marketplace, upon whom the free market economy normally relies to choose the superior among competing products, is incapable of evaluating the comparative safety of competing model cars. The public which has lately become increasingly interested in safety still has no means of satisfying that interest. Both industry and Government share the responsibility for supplying adequate consumer information of automobile safety.

It is to the credit of the automotive industry that industry leaders have come to recognize the gravity of the problem and have joined in support of a law establishing binding Federal vehicle safety standards.

The committee also recognizes that the broad powers conferred upon the Secretary, while essential to achieve improved traffic safety, could be abused in such a manner as to have serious adverse effects on the automotive manufacturing industry. The committee is not empowering the Secretary to take over the design and manufacturing functions of private industry. The committee expects that the Secretary will act responsibly and in such a way as to achieve a substantial improvement in the safety characteristics of vehicles.

It is the committee's judgment that enactment of this legislation can further industry efforts to produce motor vehicles which are, in the first instance, not unduly accident prone; and perhaps, even more significantly, vehicles which, when involved in accidents, will prove crash-worthy enough to enable their occupants to survive with minimal injuries.

SCOPE OF THE BILL

The critical definitions which delimit the scope of the bill are those of "motor vehicle" and "motor vehicle safety."

"Motor vehicle" for purposes of coverage of the act is defined as "any vehicle driven or drawn by mechanical power primarily for use on the public roads, streets, and highways . . ." (sec. 101(c)). The act thus covers not only passenger cars but buses, trucks, and motorcycles. . . .

"Motor vehicle safety" is defined as "the performance of motor vehicles or motor vehicle equipment in such a manner that the public is protected against unreasonable risk of accident occurring as the result of the design or construction of motor vehicles; and is also protected against unreasonable risk of death or injury to persons in the event accidents do occur, and includes nonoperational safety of such vehicles" (sec. 101(a)).

Thus the bill is intended to reach not only the safety of driver, passenger, and pedestrian, but the safety of those who must work with or otherwise come in contact with the vehicle while it is not operating.

INTERIM AND REVISED STANDARDS

. . . Subsequently, on or before January 31, 1968, and thereafter at least once every 2 years, as Federal safety research and development matures, the Secretary is directed to issue new and revised standards (sec. 103(a)). Unlike the General Services Administration's procurement standards, which are primarily design specifications, both the interim standards and the new and revised standards are expected to be performance standards, specifying the required minimum safe performance of vehicles but not the manner in which the manufacturer is to achieve the specified performance (sec. 101(b)). Manufacturers and parts suppliers will thus be free to compete in developing and selecting devices and structures that can meet or surpass the performance standard.

The Secretary would thus be concerned with the measurable performance of a braking system, but not its design details. Such standards will be analogous to a building code which specifies the minimum load-carrying characteristics of the structural members of a building wall, but leaves the builder free to choose his own materials and design. Such safe performance standards are thus not intended or likely to stifle innovation in automotive design.

In promulgating any standard, the Secretary is required to consider whether such standard is reasonable, practicable and appropriate for the particular type of motor vehicle or item of motor vehicle equipment for which it is prescribed, and consider, also, the extent to which such standard would contribute to carrying out the purposes of the act (secs. 102(c) and 103(c)). The Secretary is not expected to issue a standard covering every component and function of a motor vehicle, but only for those vehicle characteristics that have a significant bearing on safety.

The General Counsel of the Commerce Department stated in a letter to the committee:

> The tests of reasonableness of cost, feasibility and adequate lead time should be included among those factors which the Secretary could consider in making his total judgment.

The committee intends that safety shall be the overriding consideration in the issuance of standards under this bill. The committee recognizes, as the Commerce Department letter indicates, that the Secretary will necessarily consider reasonableness of cost, feasibility and adequate lead time.

In determining whether any proposed standard is "appropriate" for the particular type of motor-vehicle equipment or item of motor-vehicle equipment for which it is prescribed, the committee intends that the Secretary will consider the desirability of affording consumers continued wide range of choices in the selection of motor vehicles. Thus it is not intended that standards will be set which will eliminate or necessarily be the same for small cars or such widely accepted models as convertibles and sports cars, so long as all motor vehicles meet basic minimum standards. Such differences, of course, would be based on the type of vehicle rather than its place of origin or any special circumstances of its manufacturer. . . .

NOTIFICATION

In order to insure the uniform notification of car owners as to any safety-related defects and to facilitate the prompt curing of such defects, the bill provides that every manufacturer of motor vehicles notify the purchaser of any vehicle which the manufacturer determines, in good faith, contains a safety-related defect (sec. 116).

A "defect" is defined to include any defect in design, construction, components or materials in motor vehicles or motor vehicle equipment (sec. 101(l)). The term "defect" is used in the sense of an error or mistake in design, manufacture or assembly.

Such notification must be accomplished within a reasonable time (sec. 116(a)) after the manufacturer has discovered the defect and formulated the corrective procedure (sec. 116(c)) and must be made by certified mail to the first purchaser and by certified mail or more expeditious means to the manufacturer's dealer (sec. 116(b)). Moreover, the notification must contain a clear disclosure of the defect, an evaluation of the risks to traffic safety reasonably related to the defect and a statement of the measures to be taken to repair the defect (sec. 116(c)).

In addition, every manufacturer is required to furnish the Secretary copies of all communications with his dealers relating to any defect, whether or not safety-related (sec. 116(d)).

The Secretary is directed to notify the manufacturer of any failure to conform to safety standards or any other safety-related defect which he determines to exist on the basis of evidence that comes to his attention through reports from manufacturers, Government research and testing, complaints or other sources, and to require that the manufacturer furnish the purchaser and dealer appropriate notification (sec. 116(e)).

This process would be in addition to and not in place of, nor a condition upon, taking any other enforcement action under the provisions of the act. The Secretary could elect to impose a civil penalty (sec. 110) for a violation and require notification of defects of non-compliance with a safety standard (sec. 116). The Attorney General could also seek an injunction to stop the sale of a noncomplying vehicle (sec. 111). These and all alternative enforcement techniques should be exercised within the administrative discretion of the responsible officials.

The Secretary is also authorized to make public information concerning safety-related defects or noncompliance with standards where necessary for the public safety (sec. 116(d)).

The committee expects that the Secretary would use this power to publish defect information as a last resort. It is the committee's expectation that the Secretary would promptly review the matter with the manufacturer and give the manufacturer an opportunity to accomplish the required notification and correction through the manufacturer's own procedures. Publicity would be invoked only if the Secretary concluded that the manufacturer's own actions would fail or had failed to provide car owners with adequate and prompt notice on the existence and safety significance of the defect and the procedure for correction.

The committee also expects that the Secretary will act with extreme caution to avoid premature publicity of unevaluated reports as to suspected defects, before the suspicions have been evaluated. Premature publicity of this type, of course, can cause undue public alarm, with a damaging and unwarranted effect on vehicle sales even though the suspicions may ultimately prove to be without foundation. . . .

PENALTIES AND INJUNCTION

The bill imposes a civil penalty not to exceed $1,000 for each prohibited act (sec. 110(a)). The maximum civil penalty is limited to $400,000 for any related series of violations (sec. 110(a)). For example, if a manufacturer produces several thousand substandard vehicles or items of equipment as the result of the same error in design or construction, or the use of the same defective component, the maximum penalty to be imposed upon any one person for those violations would be limited to $400,000.

The Secretary is authorized to compromise any civil penalty and, in determining the amount of the penalty, the Secretary or court is directed to consider the appropriateness of the proposed penalty to the size of the business of the person charged and the gravity of the violation (sec. 110(b)).

The Attorney General is also authorized to seek injunctions against the performance of any prohibited act and to enjoin the sale of any vehicle which fails to conform to applicable standards under the act (sec. 111).

INSPECTION, RECORDS, AND REPORTS

The Secretary is authorized to conduct such testing, inspection, and investigations as he deems necessary to aid in the enforcement of standards prescribed under the act (sec. 114(a)). He is given express authority to conduct on-site inspection in factories, warehouses, or sales offices (sec. 114(b)). Manufacturers are required to maintain records, make reports, and provide the information reasonably required by the Secretary (sec. 114(c)).

The committee bill provides that the records, reports, and information the Secretary may reasonably require shall be limited to those relevant to determining whether the manufacturer has acted or is acting in compliance with title I and motor vehicle safety standards issued thereunder (sec. 114(c)). For example, the relevant records, reports, and information would include data relating to design, manufacturing procedures, quality control, and shipping records for currently manufactured vehicles, and would not include such closely held competitive trade secrets as financial, price, or cost data (sec. 114(d)).

EFFECT ON STATE LAW

The centralized, mass production, high volume character of the motor vehicle manufacturing industry in the United States requires that motor vehicle safety standards be not only strong and adequately enforced, but that they be uniform throughout the country. At the same time, the committee believes that the States should be free to adopt standards identical to the Federal standards, which apply only to the first sale of a new vehicle, so that the States may play a significant role in the vehicle safety field by applying and enforcing standards over the life of the car. Accordingly, State standards are preempted only if they differ from Federal standards applicable to the particular aspect of the vehicle or item of vehicle equipment (sec. 104).

The States are also permitted to set more stringent requirements for purposes of their own procurement. Moreover, the Federal minimum safety standards need not be interpreted as restricting State common law standards of care. Compliance with such standards would thus not necessarily shield any person from product liability at common law.

Notes and Questions

1. Is the Report helpful in determining the basic structure of the statute? With the help of the Senate Report, make a list of the different implementation and enforcement mechanisms that the 1966 Motor Vehicle Safety Act employs to obtain compliance with its provisions.

2. Can you go further in light of the Senate Report? For example, are you better able to understand the main purpose of the 1966 Motor Vehicle Safety Act? The first section of the Report ("Purpose and Need") can be regarded as an expansion of the Act's purpose section ("An Act to . . ."). How does the Report justify a statute that is, in the final analysis, a rather extensive intrusion into the marketplace? What is the model of corporate behavior that the Report reflects? What is the model of consumer behavior that it reflects?

3. Most of the Report's sections relate to particular sections of the statute. For example, the Report's second section ("The Scope of the Bill") expands on two of the statute's most important definitions. How helpful is this explanation? How about the explanation of the term "defect" in the "Notification" section? Note that the definition of "defect" changed from the Senate Commerce Committee bill to the final Act—did you pick up the change, and how significant might it be? *See* Geier v. American Honda Motor Co., 529 U.S. 861 (2000) (addressing the question whether the Act preempts state tort law for a certain sort of defect).

4. Have you identified anything in the Report that might provide insight on why some judges are reluctant to rely too heavily on legislative history in determining the purpose of the statute or the meaning of particular statutory words or phrases?

D. THE STRUCTURE OF A MODERN STATUTE

The 1966 Motor Vehicle Safety Act might seem like a unique creature, and in some ways it is. No statute is constructed exactly like it or accomplishes exactly what it does. But many statutes actually contain the same basic structure. Here is the list of standard statutory provisions from a leading treatise on statutory drafting, F. Reed Dickerson's *Legislative Drafting* (1954), which we have elaborated:

- **Title ("*An Act to* . . ."):** The formal title states the basic purpose or function of the statute.
- **Enacting clause:** The enacting clause is meant to proclaim the fact that the statute has become law, but it often repeats the basic purpose and function of the statute.

- **Short title:** Statutes often have long titles and therefore need a shorter designation for the sake of reference. Often, the long title reduces to a clever acronym. Consider the statute entitled "Uniting and Strengthening America by Providing Appropriate Tools Required to Intercept and Obstruct Terrorism" Act. The fourteen words of this long title are thirteen more than were needed to name an anti-terrorism act, but they abbreviate to USA PATRIOT. We like VISTA for the Volunteers in Service to America statute because it sounds natural.

  The short title of a statute is also its Popular Name. In the old days, the Popular Name of a statute was typically the name of its primary sponsor or sponsors — the Sherman Act, the Mann Act, the Glass-Steagall Act — or the name of the agency it created — the Federal Trade Commission Act, the Federal Reserve Act. The first snazzy nick-name was the Truth in Lending Act, which was originally called the Consumer Credit Labeling Act. The Popular Name can be an acronym.

  Popular Names are important because they are easy to find. The United States Code Annotated, which is the standard compilation of federal statutes, includes a Popular Name Index. The Popular Name is often the best way to find the text of a statute on the Internet.

- **Statement of purpose, preamble, and findings:** A statute may include a more elaborate statement of purpose than the ones in the formal title or enacting clause. In addition, it may have a preamble, which contains introductory information about the statute. Some statutes also add findings, which may simply restate the purpose of the law ("Congress finds that occupational retraining programs in the food industry are unsatisfactory"), but may include factual material that served as background for the statute ("Congress has found that the unemployment rate among food service workers who are dismissed from their position is 2.4 times the national average").

- **Definitions:** Typically, but not always, definitions appear at the beginning of the statute. Although definitions are an optional component, they constitute operative language when they do appear. When defined terms are capitalized in the definitions section, they are usually capitalized each time they are used in the body of the statute. Very roughly, statutory definitions can serve three purposes:

  a. *Shorthand references to organizations.* These may be acronyms, short forms, or substituted terms. It would be awkward to refer to the National Oceanographic and Atmospheric Administration over and over again, so a statute might begin by defining the term "NOAA" and then use that designation thereafter. The statute might define the Department for Air and Water Quality Control and Industrial Employment Protection as "the Department," or the Committee on Scientific Integrity in Environmental Policymaking as "the Committee."

  b. *Shorthand references to repeated provisions.* Suppose a statute establishes a bidding process for awarding government contracts in a variety of different fields, and the process in each field is to issue a request for bids, consult with potential bidders in specified ways, receive bids on a special form, open them in a specified way, and then announce the awards at a given time after the bids are opened. It would clearly be awkward to repeat the entire description for each field, so the description can be provided once, in the definitions section, and then be referred to as "the Bidding Process" each time it appears in the subsequent statutory provisions.

c. *Increased precision.* Statutes often use words in a particular sense, and that specialized meaning can be established in the definitions section. For example, the Endangered Species Act defines "plant" as "any member of the plant kingdom, including seeds, roots and other parts thereof." 16 U.S.C. §1532(14). Thus, it includes seeds, which we may not consider a plant, and excludes a factory or a spy, both of which are sometimes called "plants" in ordinary language. Some statutes also define terms more expansively than ordinary language would suggest. The Endangered Species Act prohibits people from "taking" certain animals, 16 U.S.C. §1538(a)(1), and states in its definitions section that "take" "means to harass, harm, pursue, hunt, shoot, wound, kill, trap, capture, or collect, or to attempt to engage in any such conduct." 16 U.S.C. §1532(19). By doing so, the drafters made sure that their prohibition applied to wounding an endangered animal as well as killing or capturing it, something that may not seem apparent from ordinary language.

Do not assume that a definition in a statute will eliminate all ambiguity about the meaning of a word. Drafters often reintroduce ambiguity, whether intentionally or unintentionally. In the government contracting example above, it seems perfectly reasonable to define the entire process as the "Bidding Process," but how can the drafter then refer to that element of the process when the actual bid is submitted without creating ambiguity? And if an ordinary word such as "take" is defined, what happens if the drafter uses that term in its ordinary sense? Having defined "take" in ways that the Endangered Species Act does, the drafters would be ill advised to say: "Visitors to wildlife areas where endangered species are present will have part of their entrance fees remitted if they take their children."

- **Principal operative provisions:** Such provisions are the heart and soul of the statute. They contain the result that the statute is trying to achieve or the state of the world that it is designed to create. Some operative provisions impose prohibitions on private conduct—for example, prohibiting private contracts "in restraint of trade," as does the Sherman Antitrust Act, which is reprinted below. Others impose requirements on private conduct—for example, requiring auto manufacturers to comply with auto safety standards for new vehicles. Operative provisions can also seek to encourage or discourage certain conduct rather than requiring or prohibiting it outright — for example, they can provide industrial sources with "offsets" or credits for carbon emissions that can be sold if not used. Operative provisions can also transfer resources — for example, by imposing taxes or providing benefits. Note that some operative provisions are directed to government conduct rather than private conduct. And some are directed to both, as when a statute authorizes an agency to determine the prohibitions or set the requirements to which private actors are subject. We will have more to say about this sort of provision in a moment.

- **Subordinate operative provisions and exceptions:** A statute may contain other operative provisions that are separate from the principal operative provision. These provisions have an effect on the world but they are supportive of or secondary to the main objective. A statute may also contain exceptions to its principal operative provision in a separate section (e.g., "Nothing in this section shall be construed to prevent the importation or migration of foreigners and aliens under contract or agreement to perform as professional actors, artists, lecturers, or singers"). But a statute may also include exceptions, if any, in the principal operative provision.

- **Implementation provisions:** If the principal operative provisions are the heart and soul of a regulatory statute, the implementation provisions are its legs and arms. They enable the statute to do what it purports to do. All statutes require implementation, unless they are merely symbolic, but they do so in different ways. Criminal statutes impose criminal sanctions (for example, imprisonment) to enforce their operative provisions. Civil statutes impose other penalties (for example, monetary fines). Regulatory statutes do many things other than impose penalties, whether criminal or civil, to achieve their goals. They tend to contain rather distinctive implementation provisions, involving an agency in taking action to make a statute work. Implementation provisions are not always separate from operative provisions. As we noted above, an operative provision might direct an agency to establish requirements or prohibitions for private conduct. We will discuss the relationship between operative and implementation provisions in more detail below.

- **Specific repeals and related amendments:** If a statute either repeals or amends a preexisting statute, it may contain a statement to that effect. Thus, a federal statute that repeals or amends another federal statute will generally contain a provision to that effect. Statutes can also repeal or amend prior statutes without expressly so stating, although repeals *by implication* are disfavored.

- **Preemption provision:** A preemption provision in a federal statute bars the application of state law. The Supremacy Clause of the U.S Constitution establishes the Constitution, federal statutes, and U.S. treaties as "the supreme law of the land," U.S. CONST. art. VI,

§2, and therefore gives Congress the power to preempt any state law. But the scope of the preemption is not always clear. Does the federal statute preempt all state law, including state common law, state regulations, and state statutes, or only particular sources? Does it preempt any state law that is not identical to federal law or only those that are inconsistent with or less stringent than federal law? You must read these provisions carefully. Note that a statute can preempt state law *implicitly,* which means in the absence of an express preemption provision. We discuss this issue below.

- **Savings clause:** A savings clause preserves the application of state law in some respect. It may save a particular type of law, notwithstanding preemption of other types of law. It may provide information concerning the relationship between federal law and state law — for example, it may state that compliance with federal law is not a defense to liability in a state tort suit. Such a provision preserves state tort despite its overlap with the federal statute. As with preemption, you must read these provisions carefully. We also address this issue below.

- **Temporary provisions (if any):** Sometimes a statute will contain a provision that has only a limited duration, while the rest of the statute remains in effect until repealed or amended.

- **Expiration date:** A statute may contain a provision indicating that it will expire or "sunset" on a date specified. This is the exception, not the rule. Typically, statutes are conceived as continuing in perpetuity unless, of course, they are repealed or amended by a subsequent legislature.

- **Effective date (if different from date of enactment):** A statute may contain a provision indicating that it becomes effective on a specific date, generally later than the date of enactment. Statutes that apply to conduct that occurred before the date of enactment are said to apply "retroactively," and they are relatively uncommon.[1]

Note on the Relationship Between Operative and Implementation Provisions

Statutes do not always contain separate operative and implementation provisions. Thus, a statute might read, in part, as follows: "Sec. 3. No vehicle may be taken into the park." "Sec. 5. The Parks Department shall have the authority to enforce the prohibition in Section 3 by confiscating any vehicle in the park." But a statute may also read: "Sec. 4. The Parks Department may confiscate any vehicle that is taken into the park." Are these two provisions exactly the same? It is worth noting that, for some legal thinkers, they are

---

1. The Constitution actually forbids Congress from enacting retroactive criminal statutes, which are called ex post facto laws. *See* U.S. CONST. art. I, §9. Thus, Congress cannot criminalize conduct that was legal when committed. While we are on the subject of constitutional limitations on criminal statutes, Congress also cannot enact bills of attainder, which impose criminal penalties on a specific person or group without a trial. *See* U.S. CONST. art. I, §9. Congress can enact a private bill, which also singles out a specific person or group, but not for criminal punishment.

not. This seemingly arcane point has been one of the central controversies of modern jurisprudence. *Compare* HANS KELSEN, GENERAL THEORY OF LAW AND THE STATE (1945) (defending the view that laws are of the second sort, stating a negative consequence the state would impose for a particular action), *with* H.L.A. HART, THE CONCEPT OF LAW (1961) (taking the view that the two are distinct and arguing that laws are general provisions that establish a norm of behavior government wants people to follow and impose sanctions in the case of disobedience). Similarly, there is a debate about whether a particular implementation provision is simply a price ("you can do X, but we will charge you Y for doing so") or a sanction ("we don't want you to do X, and we will impose a penalty of Y to deter you from doing so"). *See* Robert Cooter, *Prices and Sanctions*, 84 COLUM. L. REV. 1523 (1984). For our purposes, it is enough to note that statutes sometimes combine implementation and operative provisions and sometimes separate them.

Note on Preemption Provisions, Savings Clauses, and Federalism Issues

Congress often enacts regulatory statutes in areas where the states also have regulatory statutes and agencies. The interaction between federal and state regulatory efforts ranges from cooperative to competitive and every possible combination in between. On the cooperative end of the spectrum, federal statutes often enlist or authorize the federal agency to enlist state agencies to implement the statute or its regulations. Examples can be found in diverse areas such as environmental protection, consumer protection, and occupational safety. The Clean Air Act, reprinted below, is one. On the competitive side, federal statutes preclude state agencies from exercising any control over an area. Examples can be found in areas such as broadcasting, commercial aviation, and pharmaceutical licensing. There are many situations that fall somewhere in the middle. For example, the Occupational Safety and Health Administration (OSHA) will defer to equivalent state agencies, but only if the "state OSHA" meets federal requirements. 29 U.S.C. §667. The Food and Drug Administration asserts comprehensive control over drug licensing, 21 U.S.C. §355, but state tort law may provide remedies against a drug company that mislabels its product, even if that product has been approved by the FDA. *See* Riegel v. Medtronic, Inc., 552 U.S. 312 (2008).

The legal basis for displacing or preempting state law is the Constitution's Supremacy Clause, which makes any federal enactment the "supreme Law of the Land." U.S. CONST. art. VI, §2, cl. 2. Although preemption is a constitutionally grounded doctrine, judicial determinations of preemption rarely turn on interpretation of the Constitution's language, because the typical question is not whether Congress can preempt state law (it can), but whether Congress intended to exercise this power in the particular statute under consideration. As we mentioned above, statutes may contain express preemption provisions, as well as express savings clauses. These typically require interpretation as to what sorts of state laws—state constitutional provisions, statutes, regulations, common law claims—they preempt or save. Note that, even in the absence

of an express preemption provision, courts consider the issue of implied preemption, which occurs when compliance with both state law and federal law is
impossible, or a state statute or regulation frustrates the operation of a federal
one. *See* Freightliner Corp. v. Myrick, 514 U.S. 280 (1995); Florida Lime &
Avocado Growers, Inc. v. Paul, 373 U.S. 132, 142-43 (1963). Courts are generally reluctant to find implied preemption because of the important federalism
values at stake. For example, in Wyeth v. Levine, 555 U.S. 555 (2009), the
Supreme Court held that the Food, Drug, and Cosmetic Act did not preempt
a state law failure-to-warn claim against a drug manufacturer that failed to
adequately warn of dangers from administering an antihistamine through an
IV-push rather than an IV-drip method. Preemption cases often pose some of
the most challenging statutory interpretation issues that the courts confront.
We will have a bit more to say on this subject in Chapter 4.

Notes and Questions

1. Most provisions in the list above concern the internal functioning of
the statute at issue. But some provisions concern the relationship between
the statute at issue and other laws. We have already discussed preemption
provisions and savings clauses. Which other provisions listed above fall into
this latter category?

2. Identify the language in the 1966 Motor Vehicle Safety Act that corresponds to each component of a statute, as just described. Summarize what
each provision actually does.

3. Take a look at the preemption provision and the savings clause in
the 1966 Motor Vehicle Safety Act, also discussed in the Senate Report.
What do you think Congress was trying to accomplish with these provisions?
What sorts of state laws are preempted and what sorts are saved? *See* Geier
v. American Honda Motor Co., 529 U.S. 861 (2000).

Consider the five provisions reprinted below, each of which is part of
a broader statute: the Sherman Antitrust Act, the Truth in Lending Act,
the Clean Air Act, the Telephone Consumer Protection Act, and the Dodd-
Frank Act. See if you can identify the basic "structural" function that each
performs in its statute.

The Sherman Antitrust Act (1890)

Ch. 647, §1, 26 Stat. 209, 209
(codified as amended at 15 U.S.C. §1)

Every contract, combination in the form of trust or otherwise, or conspiracy,
in restraint of trade or commerce among the several States, or with foreign
nations, is declared to be illegal. Every person who shall make any contract
or engage in any combination or conspiracy hereby declared to be illegal

shall be deemed guilty of a felony, and, on conviction thereof, shall be punished by fine not exceeding $100,000,000 if a corporation, or, if any other person, $1,000,000, or by imprisonment not exceeding ten years, or by both said punishments, in the discretion of the court.

The Truth in Lending Act (1968)

Pub. L. No. 90-321, §103, 82 Stat. 146, 147
(provision below codified as amended at 15 U.S.C. §1602)

The term "creditor" refers only to a person who both
   (1) regularly extends, whether in connection with loans, sales of property or services, or otherwise, consumer credit which is payable by agreement in more than four installments or for which the payment of a finance charge is or may be required, and
   (2) is the person to whom the debt arising from the consumer credit transaction is initially payable on the face of the evidence of indebtedness or, if there is no such evidence of indebtedness, by agreement. Notwithstanding the preceding sentence, in the case of an open-end credit plan involving a credit card, the card issuer and any person who honors the credit card and offers a discount which is a finance charge are creditors. For the purpose of the requirements imposed under part D of this subchapter and sections 1637(a)(5), 1637(a)(6), 1637(a)(7), 1637(b)(1), 1637(b)(2), 1637(b)(3), 1637(b)(8), and 1637(b)(10) of this title, the term "creditor" shall also include card issuers whether or not the amount due is payable by agreement in more than four installments or the payment of a finance charge is or may be required, and the Board shall, by regulation, apply these requirements to such card issuers, to the extent appropriate, even though the requirements are by their terms applicable only to creditors offering open-end credit plans. Any person who originates 2 or more mortgages referred to in subsection (aa) of this section in any 12-month period or any person who originates 1 or more such mortgages through a mortgage broker shall be considered to be a creditor for purposes of this subchapter.

The Clean Air Act (1970)

§107 (provision below codified as amended at 42 U.S.C. §7407)

   (a) Responsibility of each State for air quality; submission of implementation plan
   Each State shall have the primary responsibility for assuring air quality within the entire geographic area comprising such State by submitting an implementation plan for such State which will specify the manner in which national primary and secondary ambient air quality standards will be achieved and maintained within each air quality control region in such State.
   (b) Designated regions
   For purposes of developing and carrying out implementation plans under section 7410 of this title—

(1) an air quality control region designated under this section before December 31, 1970, or a region designated after such date under subsection (c) of this section, shall be an air quality control region; and

(2) the portion of such State which is not part of any such designated region shall be an air quality control region, but such portion may be subdivided by the State into two or more air quality control regions with the approval of the Administrator.

(c) Authority of Administrator to designate regions; notification of Governors of affected States

The Administrator shall, within 90 days after December 31, 1970, after consultation with appropriate State and local authorities, designate as an air quality control region any interstate area or major intrastate area which he deems necessary or appropriate for the attainment and maintenance of ambient air quality standards. The Administrator shall immediately notify the Governors of the affected States of any designation made under this subsection.

(d) Designations

(1) Designations generally

(A) Submission by Governors of initial designations following promulgation of new or revised standards

By such date as the Administrator may reasonably require, but not later than 1 year after promulgation of a new or revised national ambient air quality standard for any pollutant under section 7409 of this title, the Governor of each State shall (and at any other time the Governor of a State deems appropriate the Governor may) submit to the Administrator a list of all areas (or portions thereof) in the State, designating as—

(i) nonattainment, any area that does not meet (or that contributes to ambient air quality in a nearby area that does not meet) the national primary or secondary ambient air quality standard for the pollutant,

(ii) attainment, any area (other than an area identified in clause (i)) that meets the national primary or secondary ambient air quality standard for the pollutant, or

(iii) unclassifiable, any area that cannot be classified on the basis of available information as meeting or not meeting the national primary or secondary ambient air quality standard for the pollutant.

The Administrator may not require the Governor to submit the required list sooner than 120 days after promulgating a new or revised national ambient air quality standard.

The Telephone Consumer Protection Act (1991)

Pub. L. No. 102-243, §3, 105 Stat. 2394, 2397 (provision below codified as amended at 47 U.S.C. §227)

(c) Protection of subscriber privacy rights

(1) Rulemaking proceeding required

Within 120 days after December 20, 1991, the Commission shall initiate a rulemaking proceeding concerning the need to protect residential telephone subscribers' privacy rights to avoid receiving telephone solicitations to which they object. The proceeding shall—

(A) compare and evaluate alternative methods and procedures (including the use of electronic databases, telephone network technologies, special directory markings, industry-based or company-specific "do not call" systems, and any other alternatives, individually or in combination) for their effectiveness in protecting such privacy rights, and in terms of their cost and other advantages and disadvantages;

(B) evaluate the categories of public and private entities that would have the capacity to establish and administer such methods and procedures;

(C) consider whether different methods and procedures may apply for local telephone solicitations, such as local telephone solicitations of small businesses or holders of second class mail permits;

(D) consider whether there is a need for additional Commission authority to further restrict telephone solicitations, including those calls exempted under subsection (a)(3) of this section, and, if such a finding is made and supported by the record, propose specific restrictions to the Congress; and

(E) develop proposed regulations to implement the methods and procedures that the Commission determines are most effective and efficient to accomplish the purposes of this section.

(2) Regulations

Not later than 9 months after December 20, 1991, the Commission shall conclude the rulemaking proceeding initiated under paragraph (1) and shall prescribe regulations to implement methods and procedures for protecting the privacy rights described in such paragraph in an efficient, effective, and economic manner and without the imposition of any additional charge to telephone subscribers.

The Dodd-Frank Wall Street Reform and Consumer Protection Act (2010)

Pub. L. No. 111-203, §§111, 112, 124 Stat. 1376, 1392
(provisions below codified at 12 U.S.C. §§5321, 5322)

Sec. 111. Financial Stability Oversight Council Established.

(a) ESTABLISHMENT. Effective on the date of enactment of this Act, there is established the Financial Stability Oversight Council.

(b) MEMBERSHIP. The Council shall consist of the following members:

(1) VOTING MEMBERS. The voting members, who shall each have 1 vote on the Council shall be —

(A) the Secretary of the Treasury, who shall serve as Chairperson of the Council;

(B) the Chairman of the Board of Governors;

(C) the Comptroller of the Currency;

(D) the Director of the Bureau;

(E) the Chairman of the [Securities and Exchange] Commission;

(F) the Chairperson of the [Federal Deposit Insurance] Corporation;

(G) the Chairperson of the Commodity Futures Trading Commission;

(H) the Director of the Federal Housing Finance Agency;

(I) the Chairman of the National Credit Union Administration Board; and

(J) an independent member appointed by the President, by and with the advice and consent of the Senate, having insurance expertise.

(2) NONVOTING MEMBERS. The nonvoting members, who shall serve in an advisory capacity as a nonvoting member of the Council, shall be —

(A) the Director of the Office of Financial Research;

(B) the Director of the Federal Insurance Office;

(C) a State insurance commissioner, to be designated by a selection process determined by the State insurance commissioners;

(D) a State banking supervisor, to be designated by a selection process determined by the State banking supervisors; and

(E) a State securities commissioner (or an officer performing like functions), to be designated by a selection process determined by such State securities commissioners.

(3) NONVOTING MEMBER PARTICIPATION. The nonvoting members of the Council shall not be excluded from any of the proceedings, meetings, discussions, or deliberations of the Council, except that the Chairperson may, upon an affirmative vote of the member agencies, exclude the nonvoting members from any of the proceedings, meetings, discussions, or deliberations of the Council when necessary to safeguard and promote the free exchange of confidential supervisory information.

(c) TERMS; VACANCY.

(1) TERMS. The independent member of the Council shall serve for a term of 6 years, and each nonvoting member described in subparagraphs (C), (D), and (E) of subsection (b)(2) shall serve for a term of 2 years.

(2) VACANCY. Any vacancy on the Council shall be filled in the manner in which the original appointment was made.

(3) ACTING OFFICIALS MAY SERVE. In the event of a vacancy in the office of the head of a member agency or department, and pending the appointment of a successor, or during the absence or disability of the head of a member agency or department, the acting head of the member agency or department shall serve as a member of the Council in the place of that agency or department head. . . .

Sec. 112. Council Authority.

(a) PURPOSES AND DUTIES OF THE COUNCIL.

(1) IN GENERAL. The purposes of the Council are —

(A) to identify risks to the financial stability of the United States that could arise from the material financial distress or failure, or ongoing activities, of large, interconnected bank holding companies or nonbank financial companies, or that could arise outside the financial services marketplace;

(B) to promote market discipline, by eliminating expectations on the part of shareholders, creditors, and counterparties of such companies that the Government will shield them from losses in the event of failure; and

(C) to respond to emerging threats to the stability of the United States financial system.

(2) DUTIES. The Council shall, in accordance with this subchapter —

(A) collect information from member agencies, other Federal and State financial regulatory agencies, the Federal Insurance Office and, if necessary to assess risks to the United States financial system, direct the Office of Financial Research to collect information from bank holding companies and nonbank financial companies;

(B) provide direction to, and request data and analyses from, the Office of Financial Research to support the work of the Council;

(C) monitor the financial services marketplace in order to identify potential threats to the financial stability of the United States;

(D) to monitor domestic and international financial regulatory proposals and developments, including insurance and accounting issues, and to advise Congress and make recommendations in such areas that will enhance the integrity, efficiency, competitiveness, and stability of the U.S. financial markets;

(E) facilitate information sharing and coordination among the member agencies and other Federal and State agencies regarding domestic financial services policy development, rulemaking, examinations, reporting requirements, and enforcement actions;

(F) recommend to the member agencies general supervisory priorities and principles reflecting the outcome of discussions among the member agencies;

(G) identify gaps in regulation that could pose risks to the financial stability of the United States;

(H) require supervision by the Board of Governors for nonbank financial companies that may pose risks to the financial stability of the United States in the event of their material financial distress or failure, or because of their activities pursuant to section 113;

(I) make recommendations to the Board of Governors concerning the establishment of heightened prudential standards for risk-based capital, leverage, liquidity, contingent capital, resolution plans and credit exposure reports, concentration limits, enhanced public disclosures, and overall risk management for nonbank financial companies and large, interconnected bank holding companies supervised by the Board of Governors;

(J) identify systemically important financial market utilities and payment, clearing, and settlement activities (as that term is defined in title VIII);

(K) make recommendations to primary financial regulatory agencies to apply new or heightened standards and safeguards for financial activities or practices that could create or increase risks of significant liquidity, credit, or other problems spreading among bank holding companies, nonbank financial companies, and United States financial markets;

(L) review and, as appropriate, may submit comments to the Commission and any standard-setting body with respect to an existing or proposed accounting principle, standard, or procedure;

(M) provide a forum for —

(i) discussion and analysis of emerging market developments and financial regulatory issues; and

(ii) resolution of jurisdictional disputes among the members of the Council; and

(N) annually report to and testify before Congress on —

(i) the activities of the Council;

(ii) significant financial market and regulatory developments, including insurance and accounting regulations and standards, along with an assessment of those developments on the stability of the financial system;

(iii) potential emerging threats to the financial stability of the United States;

(iv) all determinations made under section 113 or title VIII, and the basis for such determinations;

(v) all recommendations made under section 119 and the result of such recommendations; and

(vi) recommendations —

(I) to enhance the integrity, efficiency, competitiveness, and stability of United States financial markets;

(II) to promote market discipline; and

(III) to maintain investor confidence.

The Dodd-Frank Wall Street Reform and Consumer Protection Act (2010)

Pub. L. No. 111-203, §§1011, 1021, 1022, 1023 124 Stat. 1376, 1964 (provisions below codified at 12 U.S.C. §§5491, 5501, 5502, 5503)

Sec. 1011. Establishment of the Bureau of Consumer Financial Protection.

(a) BUREAU ESTABLISHED. There is established in the Federal Reserve System, an independent bureau to be known as the "Bureau of Consumer Financial Protection," which shall regulate the offering and provision of consumer financial products or services under the Federal consumer financial laws. The Bureau shall be considered an Executive agency, as defined in section 105 of title 5, United States Code. Except as otherwise provided expressly by law, all Federal laws dealing with public or Federal contracts, property, works, officers, employees, budgets, or funds, including the provisions of chapters 5 and 7 of title 5, shall apply to the exercise of the powers of the Bureau.

(b) DIRECTOR AND DEPUTY DIRECTOR.

(1) IN GENERAL. There is established the position of the Director, who shall serve as the head of the Bureau.

(2) APPOINTMENT. Subject to paragraph (3), the Director shall be appointed by the President, by and with the advice and consent of the Senate.

(3) QUALIFICATION. The President shall nominate the Director from among individuals who are citizens of the United States.

(4) COMPENSATION. The Director shall be compensated at the rate prescribed for level II of the Executive Schedule under section 5313 of title 5, United States Code.

(5) DEPUTY DIRECTOR. There is established the position of Deputy Director, who shall —

(A) be appointed by the Director; and

(B) serve as acting Director in the absence or unavailability of the Director.

(c) TERM.

(1) IN GENERAL. The Director shall serve for a term of 5 years.

(2) EXPIRATION OF TERM. An individual may serve as Director after the expiration of the term for which appointed, until a successor has been appointed and qualified.

(3) REMOVAL FOR CAUSE. The President may remove the Director for inefficiency, neglect of duty, or malfeasance in office.

(d) SERVICE RESTRICTION. No Director or Deputy Director may hold any office, position, or employment in any Federal reserve bank, Federal home loan bank, covered person, or service provider during the period of service of such person as Director or Deputy Director.

(e) OFFICES. The principal office of the Bureau shall be in the District of Columbia. The Director may establish regional offices of the Bureau, including in cities in which the Federal reserve banks, or branches of such banks, are located, in order to carry out the responsibilities assigned to the Bureau under the Federal consumer financial laws.

Sec. 1021. Purpose, Objectives, and Functions.

(a) PURPOSE. The Bureau shall seek to implement and, where applicable, enforce Federal consumer financial law consistently for the purpose of ensuring that all consumers have access to markets for consumer financial products and services and that markets for consumer financial products and services are fair, transparent, and competitive.

(b) OBJECTIVES. The Bureau is authorized to exercise its authorities under Federal consumer financial law for the purposes of ensuring that, with respect to consumer financial products and services —

(1) consumers are provided with timely and understandable information to make responsible decisions about financial transactions;

(2) consumers are protected from unfair, deceptive, or abusive acts and practices and from discrimination;

(3) outdated, unnecessary, or unduly burdensome regulations are regularly identified and addressed in order to reduce unwarranted regulatory burdens;

(4) Federal consumer financial law is enforced consistently, without regard to the status of a person as a depository institution, in order to promote fair competition; and

(5) markets for consumer financial products and services operate transparently and efficiently to facilitate access and innovation.

(c) FUNCTIONS. The primary functions of the Bureau are—

(1) conducting financial education programs;

(2) collecting, investigating, and responding to consumer complaints;

(3) collecting, researching, monitoring, and publishing information relevant to the functioning of markets for consumer financial products and services to identify risks to consumers and the proper functioning of such markets;

(4) subject to sections 1024 through 1026, supervising covered persons for compliance with Federal consumer financial law, and taking appropriate enforcement action to address violations of Federal consumer financial law;

(5) issuing rules, orders, and guidance implementing Federal consumer financial law; and

(6) performing such support activities as may be necessary or useful to facilitate the other functions of the Bureau.

Sec. 1022. Rulemaking Authority.

(a) IN GENERAL. The Bureau is authorized to exercise its authorities under Federal consumer financial law to administer, enforce, and otherwise implement the provisions of Federal consumer financial law.

(b) RULEMAKING, ORDERS, AND GUIDANCE.

(1) GENERAL AUTHORITY. The Director may prescribe rules and issue orders and guidance, as may be necessary or appropriate to enable the Bureau to administer and carry out the purposes and objectives of the Federal consumer financial laws, and to prevent evasions thereof.

(2) STANDARDS FOR RULEMAKING. In prescribing a rule under the Federal consumer financial laws—

(A) the Bureau shall consider—

(i) the potential benefits and costs to consumers and covered persons, including the potential reduction of access by consumers to consumer financial products or services resulting from such rule; and

(ii) the impact of proposed rules on covered persons, as described in section 1026, and the impact on consumers in rural areas;

(B) the Bureau shall consult with the appropriate prudential regulators or other Federal agencies prior to proposing a rule and during the comment process regarding consistency with prudential, market, or systemic objectives administered by such agencies; and

(C) if, during the consultation process described in subparagraph (B), a prudential regulator provides the Bureau with a written objection to the proposed rule of the Bureau or a portion thereof, the Bureau shall include in the adopting release a description of the objection and the basis for the Bureau decision, if any, regarding such objection, except that nothing in this clause shall be construed as altering or limiting the procedures under section 1023 that may apply to any rule prescribed by the Bureau. . . .

(4) EXCLUSIVE RULEMAKING AUTHORITY.

(A) IN GENERAL. Notwithstanding any other provisions of Federal law and except as provided in section 1061(b)(5), to the extent that a provision of Federal consumer financial law authorizes the Bureau and another Federal agency to issue regulations under that provision of law for purposes of assuring compliance with Federal consumer financial law and any regulations thereunder, the Bureau shall have the exclusive authority to prescribe rules subject to those provisions of law.

(B) DEFERENCE. Notwithstanding any power granted to any Federal agency or to the Council under this title, and subject to section 1061(b)(5)(E), the deference that a court affords to the Bureau with respect to a determination by the Bureau regarding the meaning or interpretation of any provision of a Federal consumer financial law shall be applied as if the Bureau were the only agency authorized to apply, enforce, interpret, or administer the provisions of such Federal consumer financial law. . . .

Sec. 1023. Review of Bureau Regulations.

(a) REVIEW OF BUREAU REGULATONS. On the petition of a member agency of [the Financial Stability Oversight] Council, the Council may set aside a final regulation prescribed by the Bureau, or any provision thereof, if the Council decides, in accordance with subsection (c), that the regulation or provision would put the safety and soundness of the United States banking system or the stability of the financial system of the United States at risk.

(b) PETITION.

(1) PROCEDURE. An agency represented by a member of the Council may petition the Council, in writing, and in accordance with rules prescribed pursuant to subsection (f), to stay the effectiveness of, or set aside, a regulation if the member agency filing the petition —

(A) has in good faith attempted to work with the Bureau to resolve concerns regarding the effect of the rule on the safety and soundness of the United States banking system or the stability of the financial system of the United States; and

(B) files the petition with the Council not later than 10 days after the date on which the regulation has been published in the Federal Register.

(2) PUBLICATION. Any petition filed with the Council under this section shall be published in the Federal Register and transmitted contemporaneously with filing to the Committee on Banking, Housing, and Urban Affairs of the Senate and the Committee on Financial Services of the House Of Representatives.

(c) STAYS AND SET ASIDES.

(1) STAY.

(A) IN GENERAL. Upon the request of any member agency, the Chairperson of the Council may stay the effectiveness of a regulation for the purpose of allowing appropriate consideration of the petition by the Council. . . .

(4) DECISIONS TO SET ASIDE.

(A) EFFECT OF DECISION. A decision by the Council to set aside a regulation prescribed by the Bureau, or provision thereof, shall render such regulation, or provision thereof, unenforceable. . . .

(7) RULEMAKING PROCEDURES INAPPLICABLE. The notice and comment procedures under section 553 of title 5, United States Code, shall not apply to any decision under this section of the Council to issue a stay of, or set aside, a regulation.

(8) JUDICIAL REVIEW OF DECISIONS BY THE COUNCIL. A decision by the Council to set aside a regulation prescribed by the Bureau, or provision thereof, shall be subject to review under chapter 7 of title 5, United States Code. . . .

You have now begun in earnest the study of legislation. This chapter has provided information about how statutes are enacted, structured, and drafted. The next step is addressing how they are implemented. We have told you that both courts and agencies implement statutes, though they do so differently. We will address courts in the following chapter and agencies in Chapters 4 and 5.

E. SPECIFICITY AND DELEGATION

When Congress writes a statute, it must decide whether to resolve the problems that the statute addresses with a greater or lesser degree of specificity. This decision is crucial for the regulatory state because it determines how much authority Congress delegates to the implementing institution. For example, Congress can write a statute that seeks to promote auto safety by specifically requiring that automakers install airbags in new vehicles. NHTSA would merely ensure that automakers comply with the requirement. Or Congress can write a statute that seeks to promote motor vehicle safety by "reducing the occurrence of accidents by x percent of vehicles sold per year, and the occurrence of injuries or deaths by y percent of vehicles sold per year." NHTSA would determine the means for accomplishing this goal, as well as ensuring automaker compliance with those means. The 1966 Motor Vehicle Safety Act actually requires NHTSA to issue auto safety standards that are "practicable" and meet "the need for motor vehicle safety," §103, and defines "motor vehicle safety" as preventing an "unreasonable risk of accidents occurring . . . and an unreasonable risk of death or injury to persons in the event accidents do occur." §102(1). This is the broadest formulation of the three, granting NHTSA the greatest degree of authority to set auto safety standards. Note that a statute may be relatively specific or general whether it is implemented by an agency or a court. For example, the Sherman Antitrust Act, reprinted above, prohibits certain private contracts, combinations, and conspiracies "in restraint of trade." This language is relatively general, and courts determine how it applies in particular cases.

When Congress forgoes specificity, the result is a delegation of authority, but not every delegation is explicit in the statute. Look at the Sherman Antitrust Act: the provision does not expressly grant courts authority to determine which contracts, etc., are "in restraint of trade." The delegation is implicit, as are all delegations to courts. In fact, we may not even acknowledge legislation effectively delegates to courts. *See* Margaret H. Lemos, *The Consequences of Congress's Choice of Delegate: Judicial and Agency Interpretations of Title VII*, 63 VAND. L. REV. 363, 365 (2010). This may reflect the view that courts find law rather than make it. Regardless, vague language leaves courts, like agencies, substantial discretion. *See id.* As one of us has noted, a statute that applies directly to citizens and that a court implements can be called "transitive," which is distinct from those that do not and which can be called "intransitive." *See* Edward L. Rubin, *Law and Legislation in the Administrative State*, 89 COLUM. L. REV. 369, 381-85 (1989).

With regard to agencies, the delegation of authority from Congress is often explicit in the statute. The 1966 Motor Vehicle Safety Act contains a good example. The Act directs NHTSA to issue regulations determining the actual safety requirements that auto manufacturers have to meet, providing only broad guidance on the content. Congress also makes implicit delegations to agencies by the very act of writing ambiguous language—or at least the Supreme Court has so stated in a famous case that we will study called *Chevron U.S.A., Inc. v. Natural Resources Defense Council.* When Congress leaves a term or phrase imprecise, it typically intends for agencies to determine the meaning.

For the most part, Congress does not write very specific regulatory statutes but shifts crucial policy choices to agencies. Thus, as between specificity and delegation, Congress frequently chooses delegation. Many might describe delegation as the defining characteristic of modern government. Because delegation is central to the issues that we consider in this book, we pause to examine several aspects of it.

1. The Constitutional Limits of Delegation

One persistent question about the delegation of authority from Congress to agencies is whether it is constitutionally permissible. The constitutional argument against such delegation is that Congress is vested with legislative power and cannot delegate that power to other institutions. The Supreme Court has considered this argument on many occasions, but it has only enforced the so-called nondelegation doctrine in two 1935 decisions. Those decisions involved different provisions of the same unusually sweeping statute, the National Industrial Recovery Act (NIRA). *See* Panama Refining Co. v. Ryan, 293 U.S. 388 (1935); A.L.A. Schechter Poultry Corp. v. United States, 295 U.S. 495 (1935). The NIRA was intended to stem the economic effects of the Great Depression. It granted the President authority to approve codes that ensured "fair competition" across virtually every aspect of the economy—from employment wages and hours to the price and quality of livestock. Thus, the statute was broad along two dimensions: it contained a general license to improve economic conditions, rather than a specific directive, and it reached almost every aspect of the economy, not a particular problem or industry. Furthermore, individual codes were actually set by members of the industry to which they applied; the President merely rubber-stamped them. The Court had little hesitation in striking down the delegation of authority, which was not only "unconfined and vagrant" but effectively placed government power in private hands. *Schechter Poultry*, 295 U.S. at 537, 551 (Cardozo, J., concurring).

With the exception of these two early decisions, the Court has gone out of its way to uphold broad delegating statutes as long as they contain an "intelligible principle" to constrain the agency.[2] An "intelligible principle" is language in an operative provision (sometimes together with language in the definition section) of a statute that provides the agency some guidance on its mission. Few intelligible principles provide any more guidance than the vague instruction to the Secretary in the 1966 Motor Vehicle Safety Act to issue regulations that are "practicable" and "meet the need for auto safety" (§103(a)) or that avoid an "unreasonable risk" of injury or death (§102(1)). Nevertheless, the Court has been clear that language such as this satisfies the intelligible principle requirement.

Whitman v. American Trucking Associations, Inc.

531 U.S. 457 (2001)

I

Section 109(a) of the [Clean Air Act (CAA) . . . requires the Administrator of the EPA to promulgate [National Ambient Air Quality Standards (NAAQS)] for each air pollutant for which "air quality criteria" have been issued under [statute]. Once a NAAQS has been promulgated, the Administrator must review the standard (and the criteria on which it is based) "at five-year intervals" and make "such revisions . . . as may be appropriate." CAA §109(d)(1), 42 U.S.C. §7409(d)(1). These cases arose when, on July 18, 1997, the Administrator revised the NAAQS for particulate matter and ozone . . . American Trucking Associations, Inc., and its co-respondents in . . . challenged the new standards in the Court of Appeals for the District of Columbia Circuit. . . . [Challenger alleges, among other things, that the CAA violates the nondelegation doctrine.]

The District of Columbia Circuit . . . agreed with respondents . . . that §109(b)(1) delegated legislative power to the Administrator in contravention

---

2. The "intelligible principle" formulation actually came from a pre-1935 case. *See* J.W. Hampton, Jr. & Co. v. United States, 276 U.S. 394, 409 (1928).

of the United States Constitution, Art. I, §1, because it found that the EPA had interpreted the statute to provide no "intelligible principle" to guide the agency's exercise of authority. *American Trucking Assns., Inc. v. EPA,* 175 F.3d 1027, 1034 (C.A.D.C.1999). The court thought, however, that the EPA could perhaps avoid the unconstitutional delegation by adopting a restrictive construction of §109(b)(1), so instead of declaring the section unconstitutional the court remanded the NAAQS to the agency. . . .

III

Section 109(b)(1) of the CAA instructs the EPA to set "ambient air quality standards the attainment and maintenance of which in the judgment of the Administrator, based on [the] criteria [documents of §108] and allowing an adequate margin of safety, are requisite to protect the public health." 42 U.S.C. §7409(b)(1). The Court of Appeals held that this section as interpreted by the Administrator did not provide an "intelligible principle" to guide the EPA's exercise of authority in setting NAAQS. "[The] EPA," it said, "lack[ed] any determinate criteria for drawing lines. It has failed to state intelligibly how much is too much." 175 F.3d, at 1034. The court hence found that the EPA's interpretation (but not the statute itself) violated the nondelegation doctrine. *Id.,* at 1038. We disagree.

In a delegation challenge, the constitutional question is whether the statute has delegated legislative power to the agency. Article I, §1, of the Constitution vests "[a]ll legislative Powers herein granted . . . in a Congress of the United States." This text permits no delegation of those powers, *Loving v. United States,* 517 U.S. 748, 771, 116 S. Ct. 1737, 135 L. Ed. 2d 36 (1996); see *id.,* at 776-777 (Scalia, J., concurring in part and concurring in judgment), and so we repeatedly have said that when Congress confers decisionmaking authority upon agencies *Congress* must "lay down by legislative act an intelligible principle to which the person or body authorized to [act] is directed to conform." *J.W. Hampton, Jr., & Co. v. United States,* 276 U.S. 394, 409, 48 S. Ct. 348, 72 L. Ed. 624 (1928). We have never suggested that an agency can cure an unlawful delegation of legislative power by adopting in its discretion a limiting construction of the statute. . . . The idea that an agency can cure an unconstitutionally standardless delegation of power by declining to exercise some of that power seems to us internally contradictory. The very choice of which portion of the power to exercise — that is to say, the prescription of the standard that Congress had omitted — would *itself* be an exercise of the forbidden legislative authority. Whether the statute delegates legislative power is a question for the courts, and an agency's voluntary self-denial has no bearing upon the answer.

We agree with the Solicitor General that the text of §109(b)(1) of the CAA at a minimum requires that "[f]or a discrete set of pollutants and based on published air quality criteria that reflect the latest scientific knowledge, [the] EPA must establish uniform national standards at a level that is requisite to protect public health from the adverse effects of the pollutant in the ambient air." Tr. of Oral Arg. in No. 99-1257, p. 5. Requisite, in turn, "mean[s] sufficient, but not more than necessary." *Id.,* at 7. These limits on the EPA's discretion are strikingly similar to the ones we approved in *Touby v. United States,* 500 U.S. 160 (1991), which permitted the Attorney General to designate a drug as a controlled substance for purposes of criminal drug enforcement if doing so was " 'necessary to avoid an imminent hazard to the public safety.' " *Id.,* at 163. They also resemble the Occupational Safety and Health Act of 1970 provision requiring the agency to " 'set the standard which most adequately assures, to the extent feasible, on the basis of the best available evidence, that no employee will suffer any impairment of health' " — which the Court upheld in *Industrial Union Dept., AFL-CIO v. American Petroleum Institute,* 448 U.S. 607, 646 (1980), and which even then-Justice REHNQUIST, who alone in that case thought the statute violated the nondelegation doctrine, see *id.,* at 671 (opinion concurring in judgment), would have upheld if, like the statute here, it did not permit economic costs to be considered. See *American Textile Mfrs. Institute, Inc. v. Donovan,* 452 U.S. 490, 545 (1981) (Rehnquist, J., dissenting).

The scope of discretion §109(b)(1) allows is in fact well within the outer limits of our nondelegation precedents. In the history of the Court we have found the requisite "intelligible principle" lacking in only two statutes, one of which provided literally no guidance for the exercise of discretion, and the other of which conferred authority to regulate the entire economy on the basis of no more precise a standard than stimulating the economy by assuring "fair competition." See *Panama Refining Co. v. Ryan,* 293 U.S. 388 (1935); *A.L.A. Schechter Poultry Corp. v. United States,* 295 U.S. 495 (1935). We have, on the other hand, upheld the validity of §11(b)(2) of the Public Utility Holding Company Act of 1935, 49 Stat. 821, which gave the Securities and Exchange Commission authority to modify the structure of holding company systems so as to ensure that they are not "unduly or unnecessarily complicate[d]" and do not "unfairly or inequitably distribute voting power among security holders." *American Power & Light Co. v. SEC,* 329 U.S. 90, 104 (1946). We have approved the wartime conferral of agency power to fix the prices of commodities at a level that " 'will be generally fair and equitable and will effectuate the [in some respects conflicting] purposes of th[e] Act.' " *Yakus v. United States,* 321 U.S. 414, 420, 423-426, (1944). And we have found an "intelligible principle" in various statutes authorizing regulation in the "public interest." See, *e.g., National Broadcasting Co. v. United States,* 319 U.S. 190, 225-226 (1943) (Federal Communications Commission's power to regulate airwaves); *New York Central Securities Corp. v. United States,* 287 U.S. 12, 24-25, 53 S. Ct. 45, 77 L. Ed. 138 (1932) (Interstate Commerce Commission's power to approve railroad consolidations). In short, we have "almost never felt qualified to second-guess Congress regarding the permissible degree of policy judgment that can be left to those executing or applying the law." *Mistretta v. United States,* 488 U.S. 361, 416 (1989) (Scalia, J., dissenting); see *id.,* at 373, 109 S. Ct. 647 (majority opinion).

It is true enough that the degree of agency discretion that is acceptable varies according to the scope of the power congressionally conferred. See *Loving v. United States,* 517 U.S., at 772-773; *United States v. Mazurie,* 419 U.S. 544, 556-557 (1975). While Congress need not provide any direction to the EPA regarding the manner in which it is to define "country elevators," which are to be exempt from new-stationary-source regulations governing grain elevators, see 42 U.S.C. §7411(i), it must provide substantial guidance on setting air standards that affect the entire national economy. But even in sweeping regulatory schemes we have never demanded, as the Court of Appeals did here, that statutes provide a "determinate criterion" for saying "how much [of the regulated harm] is too much." 175 F.3d, at 1034. In *Touby,* for example, we did not require the statute to decree how "imminent" was too imminent, or how "necessary" was necessary enough, or even—most relevant here—how "hazardous" was too hazardous. 500 U.S., at 165-167. Similarly, the statute at issue in *Lichter* authorized agencies to recoup "excess profits" paid under wartime Government contracts, yet we did not insist that Congress specify how much profit was too much. 334 U.S., at 783-786. It is therefore not conclusive for delegation purposes that, as respondents argue, ozone and particulate matter are "nonthreshold" pollutants that inflict a continuum of adverse health effects at any airborne concentration greater than zero, and hence require the EPA to make judgments of degree. "[A] certain degree of discretion, and thus of lawmaking, inheres in most executive or judicial action." *Mistretta v. United States, supra,* at 417 (Scalia, J., dissenting) (emphasis deleted); see 488 U.S., at 378-379 (majority opinion). Section 109(b)(1) of the CAA, which to repeat we interpret as requiring the EPA to set air quality standards at the level that is "requisite" that is, not lower or higher than is necessary—to protect the public health with an adequate margin of safety, fits comfortably within the scope of discretion permitted by our precedent.

We therefore reverse the judgment of the Court of Appeals remanding for reinterpretation that would avoid a supposed delegation of legislative power. It will remain for the Court of Appeals—on the remand that we direct for other reasons—to dispose of any other preserved challenge to the NAAQS under the judicial-review provisions contained in 42 U.S.C. §7607(d)(9)....

Justice THOMAS, concurring.

I agree with the majority that §109's directive to the agency is no less an "intelligible principle" than a host of other directives that we have approved. I also agree that the Court of Appeals' remand to the agency to make its own corrective interpretation does not accord with our understanding of the delegation issue. I write separately, however, to express my concern that there may nevertheless be a genuine constitutional problem with §109, a problem which the parties did not address.

The parties to these cases who briefed the constitutional issue wrangled over constitutional doctrine with barely a nod to the text of the Constitution. Although this Court since 1928 has treated the "intelligible principle" requirement as the only constitutional limit on congressional grants of power to administrative agencies, see *J.W. Hampton, Jr., & Co. v. United States,* 276 U.S. 394, 409 (1928), the Constitution does not speak of "intelligible principles." Rather, it speaks in much simpler terms: "*All* legislative Powers herein granted shall be vested in a Congress." U.S. Const., Art. 1, §1 (emphasis added). I am not convinced that the intelligible principle doctrine serves to prevent all cessions of legislative power. I believe that there are cases in which the principle is intelligible and yet the significance of the delegated decision is simply too great for the decision to be called anything other than "legislative."

As it is, none of the parties to these cases has examined the text of the Constitution or asked us to reconsider our precedents on cessions of legislative power. On a future day, however, I would be willing to address the question whether our delegation jurisprudence has strayed too far from our Founders' understanding of separation of powers.

Justice STEVENS, with whom Justice SOUTER joins, concurring in part and concurring in the judgment.

Section 109(b)(1) delegates to the Administrator of the Environmental Protection Agency (EPA) the authority to promulgate national ambient air quality standards (NAAQS). In Part III of its opinion, the Court convincingly explains why the Court of Appeals erred when it concluded that §109 effected "an unconstitutional delegation of legislative power." *American Trucking Assns., Inc. v. EPA,* 175 F.3d 1027, 1033 (C.A.D.C.1999) *(per curiam).* I wholeheartedly endorse the Court's result and endorse its explanation of its reasons, albeit with the following caveat.

The Court has two choices. We could choose to articulate our ultimate disposition of this issue by frankly acknowledging that the power delegated to the EPA is "legislative" but nevertheless conclude that the delegation is constitutional because adequately limited by the terms of the authorizing statute. Alternatively, we could pretend, as the Court does, that the authority delegated to the EPA is somehow not "legislative power." Despite the fact that there is language in our opinions that supports the Court's articulation of our holding, I am persuaded that it would be both wiser and more faithful to what we have actually done in delegation cases to admit that agency rulemaking authority is "legislative power."

The proper characterization of governmental power should generally depend on the nature of the power, not on the identity of the person exercising it. See Black's Law Dictionary 899 (6th ed.1990) (defining "legislation" as, *inter alia,* "[f]ormulation of rule[s] for the future"); 1 K. Davis & R. Pierce, Administrative Law Treatise §2.3, p. 37 (3d ed. 1994) ("If legislative power means the power to make rules of conduct that bind everyone based on resolution of major policy issues, scores of agencies exercise legislative power routinely by promulgating what are candidly called 'legislative rules'"). If the NAAQS that the EPA promulgated had been prescribed by Congress, everyone would agree that those rules would be the product of an exercise of "legislative power." The same characterization is appropriate when an agency exercises rulemaking authority pursuant to a permissible delegation from Congress.

My view is not only more faithful to normal English usage, but is also fully consistent with the text of the Constitution. In Article I, the Framers vested "All legislative Powers" in the Congress, Art. I, §1, just as in Article II they vested the "executive Power" in the President, Art. II, §1. Those provisions do not purport to limit the authority of either recipient of power to delegate authority to others. . . .

It seems clear that an executive agency's exercise of rulemaking authority pursuant to a valid delegation from Congress is "legislative." As long as the delegation provides a sufficiently intelligible principle, there is nothing inherently unconstitutional about it. Accordingly, while I join Parts I, II, and IV of the Court's opinion, and agree with almost everything said in Part III, I would hold that when Congress enacted §109, it effected a constitutional delegation of legislative power to the EPA.

[Justice Breyer's opinion, concurring in part and concurring in the judgment, is omitted.]

Notes and Questions

1. In *Whitman* and other decisions, the Court has justified this permissive approach in pragmatic terms: some delegation is unavoidable given the demands on modern government, and once the Court allows some delegation, it has no basis for distinguishing constitutional from unconstitutional ones. In Justice Scalia's words, "the debate over unconstitutional delegation becomes a debate not over a point of principle but over a question of degree." *Mistretta*, 488 U.S. at 415 (Scalia, J., dissenting). Because this determination requires consideration of facts "both multifarious and (in the nonpartisan sense) highly political," he continued, the Court has "almost never felt qualified to second-guess Congress regarding the permissible degree of policy judgment that be left to those executing or applying the law." *Id.* at 416 (Scalia, J., dissenting). How distinctive are delegation issues in this regard?

2. What is at stake in the debate between the majority and Justice Stevens? Is this just a matter of vocabulary?

3. Although the Court has shown an unwillingness to invalidate broad delegations on constitutional nondelegation grounds, it has continued to raise concerns about broad delegations and address those concerns through a non-constitutional route: statutory interpretation. Thus, the Court has interpreted statutes narrowly in some instances to deprive an agency of what it plainly considers to be overbroad authority. *See, e.g.*, Industrial Union Dep't, AFL-CIO v. American Petroleum Inst., 448 U.S. 607 (1980).

4. As this edition of the casebook is going to print, the Supreme Court rejected a nondelegation doctrine challenge to a federal criminal statute in Gundy v. U.S., 588 U.S. ___ (2019), without a majority opinion. With four Justices ready to or interested in reconsidering the doctrine, and Justice Kavanaugh not participating, the near-term status of the doctrine would seem to fall to Justice Kavanaugh. What is the doctrine as you read this?

2. Political Reasons for Delegation

Assuming that Congress has the constitutional ability to delegate, a practical political question is why Congress delegates so much authority to agencies. If it has the choice, why does it forgo resolving an issue itself in favor of delegating that issue to an agency? Political scientists working in public choice and positive political theory have attempted to identify the circumstances that are conducive to delegation. Consider the following:

David Epstein & Sharyn O'Halloran,
The Nondelegation Doctrine and the Separation of
Powers: A Political Science Approach

20 Cardozo L. Rev. 947, 960-67 (1999)

II. THEORY: THE POLITICAL LOGIC OF DELEGATION

We now juxtapose the legislative organization literature with the delegation literature to address our central questions of how much authority Congress delegates to the executive branch, and why Congress delegates more authority in some policy areas than in others. . . .

Here, we wish to explain delegation from the legislative to the executive branch and the impact of this delegation on public policy. The key actors in this situation are legislators, the President, and executive agencies. We assume the preferences of legislators and the President to be, first and foremost, reelection. They may have other concerns as well, such as the desire for power, rewarding friends, and good government, but to satisfy any of the above they must first retain public office. The preferences of bureaucrats are more difficult to specify, as they lack any direct electoral motivation. The bureaucracy literature suggests that they may be controlled by their political superiors, driven by the desire to expand their budgets, seek to protect their professional reputation, or angle for lucrative post-agency positions. We will concentrate here on the former motivation — control by other political actors — as it is the most sensitive to variation in external political conditions.

We further assume that political actors who seek reelection will, on any given policy, attempt to bring final outcomes as close as possible to the median voter in their politically relevant constituency. Note that legislators will not necessarily take into account the preferences of all voters in their district if only a subset are mobilized on a particular issue, hence the possibility for special interest politics. On some issues, though, such as Social Security, minimum wage, and health care, a large proportion of the electorate will be mobilized, in which case the legislator will try to satisfy this broader constituency. Furthermore, we assume that actors' preferences over policy outcomes differ because they respond to different constituents. For instance, the fact that presidents have a national constituency usually means that they will be less susceptible to the demands of any one special interest, as opposed to House members who represent more narrowly defined geographical bases.

A. Choosing How to Decide

Our institutional analysis begins with the observation that there are two alternative modes for specifying the details of public policy. Policy can be made through the typical legislative process, in which a committee considers a bill and reports it to the floor of the chamber, and then a majority of the floor members must agree on a policy to enact. Alternatively, Congress can pass a law that delegates authority to regulatory agencies, allowing them to fill in some or all of the details of policy. The key is that, given a fixed amount of policy details to be specified, these two modes of policymaking are substitutes for each other. To the degree that one is used more, the other will perforce be used less.

Note also that it is Congress who chooses where policy is made. Legislators can either write detailed, exacting laws, in which case the executive branch will have little or no substantive input into policy, they can delegate the details to agencies, thereby giving the executive branch a substantial role in the policymaking process, or they can pick any point in between. Since legislators' primary goal is reelection, it follows that policy will be made so as to maximize legislators' reelection chances. Thus, delegation will follow the natural fault lines of legislators' political advantage.

In making this institutional choice, legislators face costs either way. Making explicit laws requires legislative time and energy that might be profitably spent on more electorally productive activities. After all, one of the reasons bureaucracies are created is for agencies to implement policies in areas where Congress has neither the time nor expertise to micromanage policy decisions, and by restricting flexibility, Congress would be limiting agencies' ability to adjust to changing circumstances. This tradeoff is captured well by Terry Moe in his discussion of regulatory structure:

> The most direct way [to control agencies] is for today's authorities to specify, in excruciating detail, precisely what the agency is to do and how it is to do it, leaving as little as possible to the discretionary judgment of bureaucrats — and thus as little as possible for future authorities to exercise control over, short of passing new legislation. . . . Obviously, this is not a formula for creating effective organizations. In the interests of public protection, agencies are knowingly burdened with cumbersome, complicated, technically inappropriate structures that undermine their capacity to perform their jobs well.

Where oversight and monitoring problems do not exist, legislators would readily delegate authority to the executive branch, taking advantage of agency expertise, conserving scarce resources of time, staff, and energy, and avoiding the logrolls, delays, and informational inefficiencies associated with the committee system.

Consider, for example, the issue of airline safety, which is characterized on the one hand by the need for technical expertise, and on the other hand by an almost complete absence of potential political benefits. That is, policymakers will receive little credit if airlines run well and no disasters occur, but they will have to withstand intense scrutiny if something goes wrong. Furthermore, legislative and executive preferences on this issue would tend to be almost perfectly aligned — have fewer accidents as long as the costs to airlines are not prohibitive. The set of individuals receiving benefits, the public who use the airlines, is diffused and ill organized, while those paying the costs of regulation, the airline companies, are well-organized and politically active. Furthermore, keeping in mind that deficiencies in the system are easily detectable, delegated power is relatively simple to monitor. For all these reasons, even if legislators had unlimited time and resources of their own (which they do not), delegation to the executive branch would be the preferred mode of policymaking.

However, delegation implies surrendering at least some control over policy, and legislators will be loathe to relinquish authority in politically sensitive policy areas where they cannot be assured that the executive branch will carry out their intent. To the extent that legislators delegate to the executive branch, they face principal-agent problems of oversight and control since agencies will be influenced by the President, by interest groups, by the courts, and by the bureaucrats themselves. If agencies are so influenced, they may abuse their discretionary authority and enact policies with which Congress is likely to disagree.

Take, by way of illustration, the issue of tax policy, where Congress uses considerable resources to write detailed legislation that leaves the executive branch with little or no leeway in interpretation. The political advantages of controlling tax policy do not come from the duty of setting overall rates, which taxpayers tend to resent, but from the possibility of granting corporations and other well-organized lobby groups special tax breaks, so-called corporate welfare. If designed correctly, these benefits can target a specific industry or group and are paid for by the general public, either through taxes paid into general revenues or by the decrease in revenue stemming from the tax break. Such political benefits are not lightly foregone, and they would be difficult to replicate through a delegation scheme with open-ended mandates. Thus, Congress continues to make tax policy itself, despite the demands of time and expertise that this entails.

So, when deciding where policy will be made, legislators will trade off the internal costs of policymaking in committees against the external costs of delegating authority to regulatory agencies. We can think of Congress's decision of where to make policy as equivalent to a firm's make-or-buy decision-legislators can either produce policy internally, or they can subcontract it out (delegate) to the Executive. In making this decision, legislators face a continuum of possibilities: Congress can do everything itself by writing specific legislation and leave nothing to the Executive; it can give everything to the Executive by writing very general laws and do nothing itself; or it can choose any alternative in between. So, Congress will choose the point along this continuum — how much discretionary authority to delegate — that balances these two types of costs at the margin.

As a result, Congress delegates to the Executive in those areas which it handles least efficiently, where the committee system is most prone to over-logrolling and/or the under-provision of expertise. Conversely, it retains control over those areas where the political disadvantages of delegation — loss of control due to the principal-agent problem — outweigh the advantages. Just as companies subcontract out the jobs that they perform less efficiently than the market, legislators subcontract out the details of policy that they produce at a greater political cost than executive agencies. . . .

C. Empirical Predictions

If this theory aptly describes legislators' preferences over delegation, then what patterns should we expect to see in executive discretion from law to law? To begin with, legislators should be more willing to delegate authority to executive branch actors who share their preferences than to those who do not, as such actors are less likely to use their discretion in the pursuit of policy goals contrary to legislators' desires. To the extent that partisan affiliation can serve as a proxy for preferences, and to the extent that the President can control agency actions through appointment powers, we should expect to see Congress delegate more authority to Presidents of their own party than to Presidents of the opposite party.

In a similar vein, legislators should be more apt to rely on committees whose membership mirrors that of the floor, and to distrust outlying committees. The legislative organization literature reviewed above emphasizes that committees whose preferences differ from those of the floor will not receive procedural benefits such as closed rules and deference in the policymaking process. If our theory is correct, then these should also be the committees that lose authority to their executive branch counterparts.

A third prediction arising from our approach concerns the informational as opposed to distributive nature of policymaking. As policy becomes more complex, Congress will rationally rely more on the executive branch to fill in policy details. This occurs for two reasons. The first and most obvious reason is that the executive branch is filled (or can be filled) with policy experts who can run tests and experiments, gather data, and otherwise determine the wisest course of policy, much more so than can 535 members of Congress and their staff. The second, less obvious reason has to do with the fact that expertise garnered in legislative committees cannot be transformed directly into policy outcomes. Rather, it must first pass through the floor, which may decide to make some alterations to the committee's proposals. The existence of the floor as a policy middle-man gives committees less incentive to gather information in the first place. Executive agencies, on the other hand, are not hampered by the need to obtain congressional approval; their rulings become law directly. Therefore, even purely policy-motivated executive agencies will be more informationally efficient than will be congressional committees.

Bringing together these statements, we predict that Congress would delegate more authority to the Executive:

1. The closer are the preferences of the Executive to the median floor voter, so that divided government leads to less discretion;
2. The higher the level of conflict between the committee and the median floor voter, so that committee outliers lead Congress to delegate less authority; and
3. The more complex is a policy area.

Note that our theory, if correct, contradicts the key predictions of the nondelegation forces. Rather than portraying Congress as delegating ever-increasing authority to executive actors, we assert that levels of delegation will rise and fall over time in response to changing external factors. Instead of assuming that legislators have no interest in monitoring delegated authority, we assert that they will empower interest groups, the courts, and other actors to challenge agency actions through administrative procedures as well as direct oversight. Finally, a revitalized nondelegation doctrine would have the effect of shifting back to Congress precisely those policy areas, such as the reduction of pork barrel benefits, that it handles poorly relative to the Executive, so limits on delegation would only tend to diminish the efficacy of the political process. . . .

Notes and Questions

1. The first section of the Epstein and O'Halloran article states the behavioral assumptions of public choice theory. Recall that public choice theory begins from the premise that people, as rational actors, try to maximize their material self-interest. In the case of legislators, this is generally taken to be an interest in reelection. Take a moment to consider whether this explanation is satisfying. Is it too cynical? Note that even those legislators who are motivated to serve the public must hold and maintain their jobs to do so.

2. Epstein and O'Halloran assert that Congress must balance the benefits and costs of delegation. What are the benefits and costs that they identify?

In which circumstances is Congress more likely to delegate? In which circumstances is it less likely to delegate?

3. What if an issue is complex—militating toward delegation—but the opposite political party holds the White House—increasing monitoring costs and militating against delegation? Can you think of strategies for Congress to maintain the benefits without incurring the costs of delegation? Here are Epstein and O'Halloran again:

> One method by which delegated authority is circumscribed lies in the administrative procedures that constrain executive branch actions. . . . But structural choices also include the particular actors to whom authority is delegated: cabinet departments, independent agencies, or state-level actors. Legislators must first decide whether to give authority to the executive or to the states—this is the *federalism* question. And if the authority will be located in the executive branch, Congress must choose the type of executive actor to receive the delegated authority—this is the *locational* question.

DAVID EPSTEIN & SHARYN O'HALLORAN, DELEGATING POWERS: A TRANSACTION COST APPROACH TO POLICY MAKING UNDER SEPARATE POWERS 153 (1999).

4. When Congress expressly delegates authority to an agency, it typically chooses one agency. But recent scholarship has shown that Congress sometimes involves more than one agency in issuing rules or taking other actions. *See* Eric Biber, *The More the Merrier: Multiple Agencies and the Future of Administrative Law Scholarship*, 125 HARV. L. REV. 78, 82-83 (2012); Keith Bradley, *The Design of Agency Interactions*, 111 COLUM. L. REV. 745, 750-56 (2011); Jody Freeman & Jim Rossi, *Agency Coordination in Shared Regulatory Space*, 125 HARV. L. REV. 1131 (2012); Jacob E. Gersen, *Overlapping and Underlapping Jurisdiction in Administrative Law*, 2006 SUP. CT. REV. 201, 212; Jason Marisam, *Duplicative Delegations*, 63 ADMIN. L. REV. 181, 187-90 (2011); DANIEL A. CRANE, THE INSTITUTIONAL STRUCTURE OF ANTITRUST ENFORCEMENT 27-48 (2011) (examining the overlapping enforcement authority of the FTC and the Department of Justice over antitrust). An important example is the Dodd-Frank Act, the major financial legislation intended to promote market stability, which assigns rulemaking to four separate agencies and directs them to work together in issuing regulations, see *Freeman & Rossi, supra*—a collaborative form of rulemaking that is different from the paradigm that we will study in this book. As we move forward, keep in mind the variations among agencies that might complicate the creation and implementation of legislation.

3. The Normative Implications of Delegation

Although Congress may choose to delegate for strategic reasons, that choice has normative implications. What exactly are the normative advantages and disadvantages of delegation? This question has divided legal scholars for some time. Consider the following positions, which are somewhat representative but by no means exhaustive.

David Schoenbrod, Power Without Responsibility: How Congress Abuses the People Through Delegation

10-12 (1993)

Congress and the president delegate for much the same reason that they continue to run budget deficits. With deficit spending, they can claim credit for the benefits of their expenditures yet escape blame for the costs. The public must pay ultimately of course, but through taxes levied at some future time by some other officials. The point is not that deficits always have bad economic consequences, but that they have the political consequence of allowing officials to duck responsibility for costs.

Likewise, delegation allows legislators to claim credit for the benefits which a regulatory statute promises yet escape the blame for the burdens it will impose, because they do not issue the laws needed to achieve those benefits. The public inevitably must suffer regulatory burdens to realize regulatory benefits, but the laws will come from an agency that legislators can then criticize for imposing excessive burdens on their constituents. Just as deficit spending allows legislators to appear to deliver money to some people without taking it from others, delegation allows them to appear to deliver regulatory benefits without imposing regulatory costs. It provides "a handy set of mirrors — so useful in Washington — by which a politician can appear to kiss both sides of the apple."

Politicians understand that delegation helps them to avoid blame. For example, in 1988 legislators used delegation to try to give themselves a 50-percent pay raise without losing votes in the next election. They enacted a statute that delegated to a commission the power to set pay for themselves and other top officials whose pay they linked to their own. Under the statute, if the commission grants a pay increase, another statute passed before (but not after) the increase goes into effect could cancel it. When the commission recommended the 50-percent increase, some legislators introduced bills to cancel it. But that action was part of a plan in which the congressional leadership would prevent a vote on the bills until it was too late to stop the increase. Legislators could then tell their constituents that they would have voted against the increase if given a chance. Thus they could get the pay raise and also credit for opposing it. However, the size of the increase, in an atmosphere of antipathy to Congress, provoked such a storm of protest and publicity that the public came to see through the charade. Embarrassed, the House leadership conducted a secret ballot among members to determine whether to hold a roll-call vote on the pay increase. Fifty-seven percent of the members who responded opposed a roll call, although 95 percent of the House members surveyed by the Public Citizen group claimed that they had supported it. After public opposition to the pay increase rose to an extraordinary 88 percent, Congress passed a bill to cancel it.

The pay raise controversy illustrates the willingness of Congress to use delegation to manipulate voters' perceptions of its activities. In this instance the manipulation failed — indeed backfired — because the public came to see it for what it was. Yet such manipulation is usually successful because routine government action is neither so readily understood nor so pregnant with symbolic value as the pay raise was, and so eludes the sustained attention of the press and the public.

So far, I have suggested that delegation as well as budget deficits help lawmakers escape blame for the direct costs of federal regulation, such as the higher grocery prices caused by marketing orders. Both budget deficits and delegation also impose important indirect costs on the public. Budget deficits require interest payments on the new debt, increase inflation, and raise interest rates. Delegation has indirect costs of even greater consequence, as illustrated by the environmental statutes that I tried to make work in my own career.

In those statutes, Congress and the president generally did not resolve the key conflicts between business and environmental groups but instead promised to satisfy each side and instructed the Environmental Protection Agency (EPA) to make the laws accordingly. Subsequently, when EPA attempted to issue a law that industry did not like, legislators — sometimes even those who took the strongest environmental positions on the floor of Congress — would tell EPA to back off. And, on the other hand, should EPA fail to satisfy environmentalists, legislators — sometimes even those with close ties to industry — would strike environmentalist poses. To camouflage the statute's lack of substance, our elected lawmakers had included all the decisions on procedures that any constituent might want — for example, the agency shall issue a law to protect the public from pollutant x by deadline y, but not before preparing an analysis of the impact on industry z although they knew that the agency could never come close to discharging these duties with the time, resources, and political power given to it.

This experience . . . illustrates the profound indirect costs of delegation:

- It undercuts the government's capacity to resolve disputes through compromise by allowing the only officials with authoritative power to impose compromises to instead claim to be all things to all interests.
- It allows disputes to be prolonged and keeps standards of conduct murky, because pressure from legislators and the complicated procedures imposed upon agencies turn lawmaking into an excruciatingly slow process. Agencies typically report that they have issued only a small fraction of the laws that their longstanding statutory mandates require. Competing interests devote large sums of money and many of their best minds to this seemingly interminable process. Meanwhile, those potentially subject to regulation have no reliable way to plan their activities, as they do not know what the law eventually will be.

The public is unprotected during these struggles: a statute that delegates provides no law until an agency makes one.

In the very act of allowing our elected lawmakers to shape laws that make themselves look like heroes, delegation renders them less responsible to the people and less responsive to their interests.

Jerry L. Mashaw, Greed, Chaos & Governance: Using Public Choice to Improve Public Law
146-47, 152-55 (1997)

. . . I do not believe that failure to reach consensus on detail should disable legislators from legislating because I see no reason to believe that it has negative consequences either for public welfare or for political accountability. A decision to go forward notwithstanding continuing ambiguity or disagreement about the details of implementation is a decision that the polity is better off legislating generally than maintaining the status quo. Citizens may disagree, but they can also hold legislators accountable for their choice. If citizens want more specific statutes, or fear that legislating without serious agreement on implementing details is dangerous, they can, after all, throw the bums out.

To be sure, it may be argued that this requires a significant level of sophistication on the part of voters. But that is precisely the problem with the suggestion that broad delegations of authority in legislation enhance the ability of representatives either to dissemble or to be inconsistent, by comparison with more specific legislative action. The sad truth is that legislators can as easily convey information selectively or take up inconsistent positions in specific statutes as in more general ones.

The Clean Air Act that Schoenbrod uses as an example for his view as easily supports mine. There are indeed some critical gaps in this statute and its many amendments that leave substantial policy discretion to administrators. On the other hand, the statute goes on for hundreds of pages, many of them containing hyper technical provisions that few citizens could possibly understand. Moreover, to the extent that the Clean Air Act and its amendments do things that dramatically depart from citizens' expectation, I would suggest that they are largely in the detailed provisions, not in the broad aspirational sections. Voters do not read bills and would have little chance of understanding most of them if they did. Hence, legislators can selectively convey information about legislation whether they legislate specifically or generally.

Nor does specificity help voters police for inconsistency in legislators' ideological positions. Indeed, it would seem to me much easier for a voter to detect the inconsistency in a legislator's statement that he or she intended "to protect the public health through strict air quality regulation while avoiding any serious economic dislocation" than by attempting to figure out that the specific provisions of a bill were indeed trading off these values and in precisely what ways.

Consider a different, but now well-known, example: The most specific legislation that comes out of the Congress these days is perhaps the gargantuan and mind-numbingly detailed legislation drafted by the Budget, Appropriations, and Finance Committees. But an Omnibus Budget Reconciliation Act can hardly be carried, much less read. And perhaps nowhere in American politics do legislators make better use of selective information and creative incoherence than in explaining to the American people what has been done in constructing the federal budget. . . .

Lisa Schultz Bressman, *Schechter Poultry* at the Millennium: A Delegation Doctrine for the Administrative State

109 Yale L.J. 1399, 1415-16, 1422-26 (2000)

[Consider a new] delegation doctrine [that] requires administrative agencies to issue rules containing reasonable limits on their discretion in exchange for broad grants of regulatory authority. Thus, the new delegation doctrine upholds the congressional transfer of lawmaking authority to administrative agencies, but imposes restraints on the exercise of that authority. Instead of demanding intelligible principles from Congress, it permits agencies to select their own standards, consistent with the broad purposes of the statutory scheme. (Administrative limiting standards are distinct from congressional intelligible principles because the former are not discernible from the statute itself, but rather are chosen by the agency in accordance with the broad purposes of the statute. Both serve, however, to define the parameters of permissible administrative action.) These administrative limiting standards, once promulgated, function no differently than if Congress had written them into the original statute — that is, they bind agencies in implementing the statutory provision to which they apply. In this way, the standards serve to limit administrative discretion and prevent arbitrary administrative decisionmaking. . . .

The current scholarly debate might have difficulty making sense of the new delegation doctrine in terms of democracy. Schoenbrod's side of the debate might find that the administrative-standards requirement perpetuates the general abdication of democratic values in this area because it fails to ensure that Congress makes the hard choices. On the other side, Mashaw . . . might conclude that the administrative-standards requirement arbitrarily intrudes on democratic values because it interferes with the legitimate exercise of administrative lawmaking authority. Put simply, one side might claim that the administrative-standards requirement does too little, and the other side might contend that it does too much.

Whatever the merits of each side's argument, the entire debate falls short of addressing the particular conception of democracy reinforced by the new delegation doctrine and its administrative-standards requirement. The new delegation doctrine does not focus on the proper locus of lawmaking authority, which is the issue that has seemed to dominate at least one side of the current scholarly debate. Rather, it accepts Congress's assignment of power and consequent relinquishment of policy control. But it does not thereby abdicate responsibility for promoting and protecting democracy. Nor does it arbitrarily interfere with legitimate delegations. Instead, it restrains the exercise of delegated authority by invoking a principle — an obligation to provide limiting standards — that reflects classic democratic values in precisely those cases that raise familiar concerns about democracy.

This principle can be understood to advance democracy in several ways. For example, it may increase congressional accountability by improving congressional oversight of agency action. Administrative limiting standards may enhance congressional oversight by providing an additional piece of information for Congress to consider in evaluating a controversial agency proposal. Moreover, that piece of information is particularly useful to Congress in formulating a legislative response because it provides insight not only into the agency's rationale but also into its overarching regulatory theory.

Administrative limiting standards also may spur calls for oversight hearings. Traditionally, Congress has used such hearings sparingly and for matters of some prominence. Interest groups may increase the pressure for congressional review of agency standards they dislike, either before or after those standards are promulgated. Or interest groups, fearing unfavorable administrative standards, may push for more precise and protective standards in the initial statute. To the extent that this occurs, the new delegation doctrine may force Congress to make more basic choices up front — the result that Schoenbrod seeks to achieve through use of the original nondelegation doctrine. . . .

Perhaps more significantly and intuitively, the new delegation doctrine promotes the rule of law. As Jerry Mashaw succinctly explains,

> A consistent strain of our constitutional politics asserts that legitimacy flows from "the rule of law." By that is meant a system of objective and accessible commands, law which can be seen to flow from collective agreement rather than from the exercise of discretion or preference by those persons who happen to be in positions of authority. By reducing discretion, and thereby the possibility for the exercise of the individual preferences of officials, specific rules reinforce the rule of law.

The rule-of-law rationale for delegation review is hardly new. It has always been present in the Court's intelligible-principle requirement. Although the Court has primarily understood this requirement to preserve separation of powers, it has made it clear that the requirement also serves an important role in controlling administrative discretion. Thus, the rule of law has always supplied a partial doctrinal basis for the nondelegation principle.

Moreover, the rule of law has furnished a major theoretical underpinning of delegation review for some time. In his 1978 treatise, Kenneth Culp Davis stated:

> The purpose [of a nondelegation doctrine] should be to do what can be done through such a doctrine to protect private parties against injustice on account of unnecessary and uncontrolled discretionary power.
>
> Instead of saying that delegations are unlawful or that delegations are unlawful unless accompanied by meaningful standards, the courts should affirmatively assert that delegations are lawful and desirable, as long as the broad legislative purpose is discernible and as long as protections against arbitrary power are provided. . . .
>
> The change in the basic purpose is essential because the underlying problem is broader than control of delegation; the problem is to provide effective protection against administrative arbitrariness. . . .
>
> . . . The courts should continue their requirement of meaningful standards, except that when the legislative body fails to prescribe the required standards for discretionary action in particular cases, the administrators should be allowed to satisfy the requirement by prescribing them within a reasonable time.

Thus, Davis understood the purpose of delegation review as advancing rule-of-law values and further recognized that administrative, as well as congressional, standards could serve those values. Davis certainly was not alone on this point. As Judge Leventhal recognized in the important case of *Amalgamated Meat Cutters v. Connally*, an administrative-standards requirement "means that however broad the discretion of the Executive at the outset, the standards once developed limit the latitude of subsequent executive action."

Edward L. Rubin, Law and Legislation in the Administrative State

89 Colum. L. Rev. 369, 388-92 (1984)

In doctrinal terms, delegation has very little relevance to modern legislation. A proper use of the term in our contemporary context shows that Congress has virtually never delegated any of its power. The entire concept was born from a misunderstanding of the administrative state and from an image of modern legislation restricted to transitive rules.

When the legislature directs an agency to implement a program of some sort, the legislature is exercising its power, not giving that power away. The "legislative power" does not consist of a monopoly on the enactment of a certain set of preexisting rules. Rather, it is the power to issue directives that allocate resources among citizens and government agencies, form public and private organizations, and authorize regulatory action by administrative agencies. When the legislature takes such actions, when it creates an agency, allocates resources to it, or authorizes it to act, the legislature is simply carrying out its basic task: it is exercising the legislative power it possesses.

A legislature could conceivably delegate its power, that is, give away the legislative power itself. It could do so by authorizing some other body to enact and repeal a broad range, or perhaps all, of the statutes that lie within the legislature's jurisdiction. But the enactment of a particular statute hardly represents such a delegation. Rather, it represents the mode of legislative action demanded by the separation of powers doctrine, the very doctrine from which delegation itself is derived. A central feature of this doctrine is that the legislature may not enforce its legislation or engage in similar operational activities. Such activities are reserved to implementation mechanisms—agencies and courts—belonging to the executive and judicial branches. Thus, the separation of powers doctrine obligates the legislature to act by granting power. Whether a particular statute is broadly or narrowly worded, it represents an exercise of the legislative power, not a delegation of it.

The reason why modern legislation is often regarded as a delegation of the legislative power is that it grants to an implementation mechanism the power to make rules. According to this view, while the power to adjudicate is separate from the legislative process, the power to make rules is the power of the legislature itself, and a grant of this power represents at least a partial surrender of the legislature's own prerogatives. But rule-making power cannot be equated with legislation in a modern administrative state. Such power must be exercised by other governmental units, and the legislature must act in ways that do not involve rule making. As has frequently been pointed out, rule making is an intrinsic and unavoidable part of the process by which administrative agencies implement statutes. An agency that exercises any degree of planning or any prosecutorial or inspection function, that operates an institution, or that makes any positive effort to secure compliance, must engage in rule making of some sort. At the same time, a modern legislature must engage in many activities that cannot be described as rule making, such as creating administrative agencies and allocating resources to them.

Notes and Questions

1. How does the Schoenbrod argument against delegation fit in with the Epstein and O'Halloran account of delegation? Is the desire to escape blame a reelection strategy that favors delegation?

2. Schoenbrod assumes that the Supreme Court, by reinvigorating the nondelegation doctrine, can help to reform the legislative process. Is this a proper role for the Court? What would Rubin say? Is delegation a legislative failure, or the essence of modern legislation?

3. Will reinvigorating the nondelegation doctrine work to reform the legislative process? Or will it, as Mashaw suggests, simply shut down modern government? Is the risk worth running if Congress can escape blame anyway through specific legislation?

4. Does your answer change if Congress truly cannot provide detailed rules in some area that it nonetheless wants to regulate? For example, some rules may require information that can only be obtained through the regulatory process itself; this was arguably the case with the 1966 Motor Vehicle Safety Act. Take a look at the Act again and see if you can identify some areas where Congress expected the regulatory process to generate relevant information.

5. Does accountability argue for locating policy decisions in a single elected legislature rather than in administrative agencies headed by political appointees and supervised by the President? This is one point of disagreement between Schoenbrod and Mashaw.

6. Given the choice, Schoenbrod would have courts invalidate broad delegations and Mashaw would have courts uphold them. Is there a middle ground? As we briefly mentioned above, in certain circumstances, a court can interpret a statute narrowly rather than invalidate or approve it wholesale. *See, e.g.,* Cass R. Sunstein, *Nondelegation Canons*, 67 U. Chi. L. Rev. 315 (2000). This approach is widely used, though not without limits. Bressman suggests another possibility: courts can prod agencies to issue "limiting standards," which would function no differently than standards that Congress itself might supply in the statute. A different approach is for courts to interpret regulatory statutes as requiring the agency to state reasons for its actions. *See* SEC v. Chenery Corp., 318 U.S. 80, 87 (1943) (a court may uphold an agency's action only for reasons stated by the agency at the time it acted). *See* Kevin M. Stack, *The Constitutional Foundations of* Chenery, 116 Yale L.J. 952, 958 (2007). What is gained and lost through approaches such as these?

3

Statutory Interpretation by Courts

Statutes are a pervasive part of contemporary law and understanding how to interpret statutes is a crucial skill for virtually all lawyers. Litigators often handle disputes that turn on the meaning of statutes. But even lawyers who never set foot in a courtroom encounter questions about the meaning of statutes. When lawyers advise clients concerning the legality of proposed actions, they often must consider the relevance of various statutes ranging from anti-discrimination, labor relations, and retirement security to environmental law. If they structure business deals, they are likely to confront issues concerning the application of statutes governing antitrust, securities, and tax. Lawyers who work for the government or handle cases involving the government face problems involving the interpretation of statutes at almost every turn.

This chapter examines how *courts* interpret statutes. It makes sense to devote considerable attention to this subject. Courts have a long, well-defined practice of statutory interpretation. And because courts can have the last word on the interpretation of a statute, other institutions pay attention to how they interpret statutes.

Before launching into this overview of judicial statutory interpretation, it is worth noting that courts are not the only (or even the primary) institutions that interpret statutes; agencies and other government officials also do so. Consider, for instance, the provision of the Motor Vehicle Safety Act that authorizes NHTSA to set minimum performance standards for new motor vehicles and provides that all standards "shall be practicable, shall meet the need for motor vehicle safety, and shall be stated in objective terms." §103. In order to adopt standards, the agency will have to determine whether its standards are "practicable" and stated in "objective terms." Suppose NHTSA issued a standard that forced manufacturers to develop new technology in order to meet its safety requirements (say, a tire-pressure detection method that has not yet been developed). To do so, NHTSA had to interpret the statute and, more specifically, decide that a technology-forcing rule was "practicable." This interpretation could end up in court—for example, if auto manufacturers challenge the standard in court arguing that it was not "practicable" because it depends on technology not currently in use. A complex framework applies when courts review the statutory interpretations that agencies issue, as discussed in later chapters. But for our purposes here, it is enough to highlight that even when courts are not the first (or even the primary) interpreters of a statute, they are often involved in some respect.

To understand how courts interpret statutes, we make a distinction between the tools and theories of statutory interpretation. A *tool of statutory interpretation* is an instrument for ascertaining the meaning of a statute. For example, a dictionary is a tool of statutory interpretation because it can assist a court in understanding the ordinary meaning of a contested word. Legislative history, like a Senate Committee Report, is also a tool of statutory interpretation because it can assist a court in determining the intent of the legislature or the purpose of the statute. When you read a judicial opinion, you will see courts using these and other tools to interpret statutes. As a lawyer, you will use these tools and others when making statutory arguments to courts.

A *theory of statutory interpretation* is a normative view of how courts should interpret statutes. Theories of statutory interpretation thus concern the role of courts in our governance system. There are many different theories of statutory interpretation, and legal academics and judges have engaged in a longstanding debate about which is best. As you will see, a particular theory of statutory interpretation may lead a court to exclude or deemphasize particular tools. For example, *textualism* permits courts to rely on dictionaries as a source of statutory meaning but prohibits them from relying on indications of legislative intent in legislative history. By contrast, *intentionalism* instructs courts to implement legislative intent, even when that intent is not clear from the plain meaning of the statutory text and discernible only through other sources. These theories are helpful to lawyers because they provide insight into how particular judges will interpret statutes — for example, Justice Scalia was a textualist, while now-retired Justice Stevens is an intentionalist. In addition, theories of statutory interpretation are useful for evaluating the tools of statutory interpretation. Textualism offers a biting critique of legislative history, intentionalism of plain meaning, and so on. But, as you will see, judges rarely expressly or consistently rely on any particular theory when interpreting a statute; they do, however, rely on the tools of statutory interpretation.

In this chapter, we first present the tools of statutory interpretation and then the theories of statutory interpretation. We follow with some positive descriptions of judicial behavior. Do courts really interpret statutes by applying whichever tools or theories of statutory interpretation they believe are best? Do they favor an approach that is more pragmatic, or political, or intuitive? These questions should interest lawyers who want to understand actual judicial behavior.

A. A CLASSIC OF STATUTORY INTERPRETATION

Before we turn to the tools and theories of statutory interpretation, we present a concrete example of statutory interpretation for you to keep in mind as you read this chapter. We could have chosen an auto safety example, to pick up on the theme that runs through most of this book. Instead, we begin with a famous decision: *Church of the Holy Trinity v. United States.* Over time, this decision has attracted more criticism than praise. Whatever your view, it is a classic illustration of the major tools and theories of statutory interpretation. As you read this opinion, see if you can identify the different interpretive "moves" that the Supreme Court makes.

Church of the Holy Trinity v. United States

143 U.S. 457 (1892)

Justice BREWER delivered the opinion of the Court.

Plaintiff in error is a corporation duly organized and incorporated as a religious society under the laws of the state of New York. E. Walpole Warren was, prior to September, 1887, an alien residing in England. In that month the plaintiff in error made a contract with him, by which he was to remove to the city of New York, and enter into its service as rector and pastor; and, in pursuance of such contract, Warren did so remove and enter upon such service. It is claimed by the United States that this contract on the part of the plaintiff in error was forbidden by [an act of February 26, 1885, chapter 164] . . .; and an action was commenced to recover the penalty prescribed by that act. The circuit court held that the contract was within the prohibition of the statute, and rendered judgment accordingly, and the single question presented for our determination is whether it erred in that conclusion.

The first section describes the act forbidden, and is in these words:

> "*Be it enacted by the senate and house of representatives of the United States of America, in congress assembled,* that from and after the passage of this act it shall be unlawful for any person, company, partnership, or corporation, in any manner whatsoever, to prepay the transportation, or in any way assist or encourage the importation or migration, of any alien or aliens, any foreigner or foreigners, into the United States, its territories, or the District of Columbia, under contract or agreement, parol or special, express or implied, made previous to the importation or migration of such alien or aliens, foreigner or foreigners, to perform labor or service of any kind in the United States, its territories, or the District of Columbia."

It must be conceded that the act of the corporation is within the letter of this section, for the relation of rector to his church is one of service, and implies labor on the one side with compensation on the other. Not only are the general words "labor" and "service" both used, but also, as it were to guard against any narrow interpretation and emphasize a breadth of meaning, to them is added "of any kind"; and, further, as noticed by the circuit judge in his opinion, the fifth section, which makes specific exceptions, among them professional actors, artists, lecturers, singers, and domestic servants, strengthens the idea that every other kind of labor and service was intended to be reached by the first section.* While there is great force to this reasoning, we cannot think Congress intended to denounce with penalties a transaction like that in the present case. It is a familiar rule that a thing may be within the letter of the statute and yet not within the statute, because not within its spirit nor within the intention of its makers. This has been often asserted, and the Reports are full of cases illustrating its application. This is not the substitution of the will of the judge for that of the legislator; for frequently words of general meaning are used in a statute, words broad enough to include an act in question, and yet a consideration of the whole legislation, or of the circumstances surrounding its enactment, or of the absurd results which follow from giving such broad meaning to the words, makes it unreasonable to believe that the legislator intended to include the particular act. . . .

[As the Court noted in United States. v. Kirby, 7 Wall. 482, 486:] "All laws should receive a sensible construction. General terms should be so limited in their application as not to lead to injustice, oppression, or an absurd consequence. It will always, therefore, be presumed that the legislature intended exceptions to its language which would avoid results of this character. The reason of the law in such cases should prevail over its letter. The common sense of man approves the judgment mentioned by Puffendorf, that the Bolognian law which enacted 'that whoever drew blood in the streets should be punished with the utmost severity,' did not extend to the surgeon who opened the vein of a person that fell down in the street in a fit. The same common sense accepts the ruling, cited by Plowden, that the statute of 1 Edw. II., which enacts that a prisoner who breaks prison shall be guilty of felony, does not extend to a prisoner who breaks out when the prison is on fire, 'for he is not to be hanged because he would not stay to be burnt.' And we think that a like common sense will sanction the ruling we make, that the act of congress which punishes the obstruction or retarding of the passage of the mail, or of its carrier, does not apply to a case of temporary detention of the mail caused by the arrest of the carrier upon an indictment for murder."

Among other things which may be considered in determining the intent of the legislature is the title of the act. We do not mean that it may be used to add to or take from the body of the statute, but it may help to interpret its meaning. [United States v. Palmer, 3 Wheat 610, raised the question whether the statutory words "any person or persons" in an anti-piracy statute extended to foreign citizens engaged in acts of piracy on the high seas

---

*[Section 5 provides in relevant part:

[N]or shall the provisions of this act apply to professional actors, artists, lecturers or singers, nor to persons employed strictly as personal or domestic servants: Provided, That nothing in this act shall be construed as prohibiting any individual from assisting any member of his family or any relative or personal friend, to migrate from any foreign country to the United States, for purposes of settlement here.—EDS.]

against a foreign ship. Chief Justice Marshall reasoned that] . . . [t]he title of this act is, "An act for the punishment of certain crimes against the United States." It would seem that offenses against the United States, not offenses against the human race, were the crimes which the legislature intended by this law to punish.

It will be seen that words as general as those used in the first section of this act were by that decision limited, and the intent of congress with respect to the act was gathered partially, at least, from its title. Now, the title of this act is, "An act to prohibit the importation and migration of foreigners and aliens under contract or agreement to perform labor in the United States, its territories, and the District of Columbia." Obviously the thought expressed in this reaches only to the work of the manual laborer, as distinguished from that of the professional man. No one reading such a title would suppose that congress had in its mind any purpose of staying the coming into this country of ministers of the gospel, or, indeed, of any class whose toil is that of the brain. The common understanding of the terms "labor" and "laborers" does not include preaching and preachers, and it is to be assumed that words and phrases are used in their ordinary meaning. So whatever of light is thrown upon the statute by the language of the title indicates an exclusion from its penal provisions of all contracts for the employment of ministers, rectors, and pastors.

Again, another guide to the meaning of a statute is found in the evil which it is designed to remedy; and for this the court properly looks at contemporaneous events, the situation as it existed, and as it was pressed upon the attention of the legislative body. The situation which called for this statute was briefly but fully stated by Mr. Justice Brown when, as district judge, he decided the case of *U.S. v. Craig*, 28 Fed. Rep. 795, 798: "The motives and history of the act are matters of common knowledge. It had become the practice for large capitalists in this country to contract with their agents abroad for the shipment of great numbers of an ignorant and servile class of foreign laborers, under contracts by which the employer agreed, upon the one hand, to prepay their passage, while, upon the other hand, the laborers agreed to work after their arrival for a certain time at a low rate of wages. The effect of this was to break down the labor market, and to reduce other laborers engaged in like occupations to the level of the assisted immigrant. The evil finally became so flagrant that an appeal was made to congress for relief by the passage of the act in question, the design of which was to raise the standard of foreign immigrants, and to discountenance the migration of those who had not sufficient means in their own hands, or those of their friends, to pay their passage."

It appears, also, from the petitions, and in the testimony presented before the committees of congress, that it was this cheap, unskilled labor which was making the trouble, and the influx of which congress sought to prevent. It was never suggested that we had in this country a surplus of brain toilers, and, least of all, that the market for the services of Christian ministers was depressed by foreign competition. Those were matters to which the attention of congress, or of the people, was not directed. So far, then, as the evil which was sought to be remedied interprets the statute, it also guides to an exclusion of this contract from the penalties of the act.

A singular circumstance, throwing light upon the intent of congress, is found in this extract from the report of the senate committee on education and labor, recommending the passage of the bill: "The general facts and considerations which induce the committee to recommend the passage of this bill are set forth in the report of the committee of the house. The committee report the bill back without amendment, although there are certain features thereof which might well be changed or modified, in the hope that the bill may not fail of passage during the present session. Especially would the committee have otherwise recommended amendments, substituting for the expression, 'labor and service,' whenever it occurs in the body of the bill, the words 'manual labor' or 'manual service,' as sufficiently broad to accomplish the purposes of the bill, and that such amendments would remove objections which a sharp and perhaps unfriendly criticism may urge to the proposed legislation. The committee, however, believing that the bill in its present form will be construed as including only those whose labor or service is manual in character, and being very desirous that the bill become a law before the adjournment, have reported the bill without change." Page 6059, Congressional Record, 48th Cong. And, referring back to the report of the committee of the house, there appears this language: "It seeks to restrain and prohibit the immigration or importation of laborers who would have never seen our shores but for the inducements and allurements of men whose only object is to obtain labor at the lowest possible rate, regardless of the social and material well-being of our own citizens, and regardless of the evil consequences which result to American laborers from such immigration. This class of immigrants care nothing about our institutions, and in many instances never even heard of them. They are men whose passage is paid by the importers. They come here under contract to labor for a certain number of years. They are ignorant of our social condition, and, that they may remain so, they are isolated and prevented from coming into contact with Americans. They are generally from the lowest social stratum, and live upon the coarsest food, and in hovels of a character before unknown to American workmen. They, as a rule, do not become citizens, and are certainly not a desirable acquisition to the body politic. The inevitable tendency of their presence among us is to degrade American labor, and to reduce it to the level of the imported pauper labor." Page 5359, Congressional Record, 48th Cong.

We find, therefore, that the title of the act, the evil which was intended to be remedied, the circumstances surrounding the appeal to congress, the reports of the committee of each house, all concur in affirming that the intent of congress was simply to stay the influx of this cheap, unskilled labor.

But, beyond all these matters, no purpose of action against religion can be imputed to any legislation, state or national, because this is a religious people. This is historically true. From the discovery of this continent to the present hour, there is a single voice making this affirmation. The commission to Christopher Columbus, prior to his sail westward, is from "Ferdinand and Isabella, by the grace of God, king and queen of Castile," etc., and recites that "it is hoped that by God's assistance some of the continents and islands in the ocean will be discovered," etc. The first colonial grant, that made to Sir Walter Raleigh in 1584, was from "Elizabeth, by the grace of God, of England, France and Ireland, queen, defender of the faith," etc.; and the grant authorizing him to enact statutes of the government of the proposed colony provided that "they be not against the true Christian faith nowe professed in the Church of England." . . .

The first charter of Virginia, granted by King James I in 1606, after reciting the application of certain parties for a charter, commenced the grant in these words: "We, greatly commending, and graciously accepting of, their Desires for the Furtherance of so noble a Work, which may, by the Providence of Almighty God, hereafter tend to the Glory of his Divine Majesty, in propagating of Christian Religion to such People." . . .

If we examine the constitutions of the various states, we find in them a constant recognition of religious obligations. Every constitution of every one of the 44 states contains language which, either directly or by clear implication, recognizes a profound reverence for religion, and an assumption that its influence in all human affairs is essential to the well-being of the community. This recognition may be in the preamble, such as is found in the constitution of Illinois, 1870: "We, the people of the state of Illinois, grateful to Almighty God for the civil, political, and religious liberty which He hath so long permitted us to enjoy, and looking to Him for a blessing upon our endeavors to secure and transmit the same unimpaired to succeeding generations," etc.

It may be only in the familiar requisition that all officers shall take an oath closing with the declaration, "so help me God." It may be in clauses like that of the constitution of Indiana, 1816, art. 11, §4: "The manner of administering an oath or affirmation shall be such as is most consistent with the conscience of the deponent, and shall be esteemed the most solemn appeal to God. . . ."

Even the constitution of the United States, which is supposed to have little touch upon the private life of the individual, contains in the first amendment a declaration common to the constitutions of all the states, as follows: "Congress shall make no law respecting an establishment of religion, or prohibiting the free exercise thereof," etc., and also provides in article 1, §7, (a provision common to many constitutions,) that the executive shall have 10 days (Sundays excepted) within which to determine whether he will approve or veto a bill. . . .

If we pass beyond these matters to a view of American life, as expressed by its laws, its business, its customs, and its society, we find everywhere a clear recognition of the same truth. Among other matters note the following: The form of oath universally prevailing, concluding with an appeal to the Almighty; the custom of opening sessions of all deliberative bodies and most conventions with prayer; the prefatory words of all wills, "In the name of God, amen"; the laws respecting the observance of the Sabbath, with the general cessation of all secular business, and the closing of courts, legislatures, and other similar public assemblies on that day; the churches and church organizations which abound in every city, town, and hamlet; the multitude of charitable organizations existing everywhere under Christian auspices; the gigantic missionary associations, with general support, and aiming to establish Christian missions in every quarter of the globe. These, and many other matters which might be noticed, add a volume of unofficial declarations to the mass of organic utterances that this is a Christian nation. In the face of all these, shall it be believed that a congress of the United States intended to make it a misdemeanor for a church of this country to contract for the services of a Christian minister residing in another nation? . . .

The judgment will be reversed, and the case remanded for further proceedings in accordance with this opinion.

Notes and Questions

1. *A Preview of Interpretive Tools. Holy Trinity* illustrates many of the tools of statutory interpretation that we will study in this chapter.

> **a.** *Text.* The Court begins with the concession that the Church's act is "within the letter of this section" prohibiting the payment for aliens to enter the country. In what sense is the importation of the pastor within the letter of the provision at issue? That provision reads in relevant part:

>> [I]t shall be unlawful for any person, company, partnership, or corporation, in any manner whatsoever, to prepay the transportation, or in any way assist or encourage the importation or migration, of any alien or aliens, any foreigner or foreigners, into the United States, its territories, or the District of Columbia, under contract or agreement, parol or special, express or implied, made previous to the importation or migration of such alien or aliens, foreigner or foreigners, to perform labor or service of any kind in the United States, its territories, or the District of Columbia.

Holy Trinity, 143 U.S. at 457 (citing statute). Make the argument that the pastor falls within the letter of this provision. Can you make the opposite argument?

> **b.** *Title.* In making the argument that the statute did not apply to the Church's action, the Court relies on the title of the statute. The title was "An act to prohibit the importation and migration of foreigners and aliens under contract or agreement to perform labor in the United States, its territories, and the District of Columbia." What

conclusions does the Court draw from this language? Should the title play such an important role in interpreting provisions of a statute? It is part of the law that Congress enacted and the President signed. What arguments are there that the title (or section headings) should control or function as a strong guide for interpreting provisions of a statute? What are the arguments that the title should *not* have controlled here?

c. *Statutory Purpose and Statutory Context.* The Court does not stop at the text of the statute to determine its meaning. Rather, it invokes the purpose of the Act to guide its interpretation. In particular, the Court states that the purpose of the Act was to prevent the influx of "cheap, unskilled labor," which was viewed as harming the labor market in the United States. Because the problem of unskilled labor was the "evil" that Congress sought to address, the statute had no application to "brain toilers," such as the pastor in the case. Why did the Court cite the purpose of the Act rather than simply relying on the text? How did the Court determine that the purpose of the Act was to prevent the influx of cheap labor? Was this purpose in the actual minds of the legislators who wrote the Act or did the Court glean it from the circumstances surrounding the statute — which is to say, the statutory context?

d. *Legislative Intent and Legislative History.* To interpret the statute, the Court also relies upon the proceedings and reports surrounding the passage of the Act. These proceedings and reports are part of the legislative history of the statute. The Court quotes extensively from Senate and House Committee Reports recommending passage of the bill. The Senate Report specifically noted that the Senate Committee would have preferred substituting "manual labor" or "manual service" for the phrase "labor and service" to remove objections. The Senate Committee, however, did not recommend making that change. Preferring passage of the bill prior to Congress's adjournment, the committee nonetheless suggested "labor and service" provisions "will be construed as including only those whose labor or service is manual in character." What inferences does the Court in *Holy Trinity* draw from this report? Do those inferences appear to be strong or weak ones?

What happens when the legislative history conflicts with the statutory text? Which should control? Many read *Holy Trinity* as permitting the legislative history to trump the statutory text and thus have condemned the decision for this result. Justice Scalia reflects this view in his dissenting opinion in Zuni Public School Dist. No. 89 v. Department of Education, 550 U.S. 81, 108 (2007) (Scalia, J., dissenting): "[T]oday, *Church of the Holy Trinity* arises, Phoenix-like, from the ashes. The Court's contrary assertions aside, today's decision is nothing other than the elevation of judge-supposed legislative intent over clear statutory text." What does Justice Scalia mean by "judge-supposed legislative intent"?

In this regard, consider Professor Adrian Vermeule's evaluation of the legislative history of the statute in *Holy Trinity*. Vermeule showed that the legislative history as a whole (rather than the select parts on which the Court relied) supports the view that Congress sought the Act to apply to "any employee, manual or professional, except those specifically exempted." Adrian Vermeule, *Legislative History and the Limits of Judicial Competence: The Untold Story of* Holy Trinity Church, 50 STAN. L. REV. 1833, 1845 (1998). Vermeule focused on the exceptions for "professional actors, singers and lecturers," suggesting that, absent these exceptions, the Act would apply to these "brain toilers." *Id.* at 1846. According to Vermeule, members of the House viewed the bill as including "brain toilers" and accordingly argued for broader exceptions to protect these categories. Meanwhile, activities in the Senate demonstrated an understanding that the bill did not apply only to manual laborers, despite the claim to the contrary in the Senate Report and in the floor debate by Senator Blair—a committee member and floor manager of the bill. *Id.* at 1850. Does Vermeule's version of the legislative history affect your view of the Court's decision? Does it carry a more general warning for courts about placing great weight on legislative history? Professor Carol Chomsky offers a contrary view of the broad history of the Act and a defense of the use of legislative history. Carol Chomsky, *Unlocking the Mysteries of* Holy Trinity: *Spirit, Letter, and History in Statutory Interpretation,* 100 COLUM. L. REV. 901 (2000) (describing the legislative and political history of the Act and arguing that "*Holy Trinity Church* establishes the importance of recourse to legislative history and affords a better foundation for non-textualist approaches to statutory interpretation than its critics have acknowledged"). Confused about what to think? We will examine the arguments for and against the use of legislative history in detail.

2. *A Preview of Interpretive Theories.* When courts interpret statutes, they often reveal an underlying theory of statutory interpretation—that is, a general sense for how statutes should be interpreted as a normative matter. Courts rarely refer to theories of interpretation by name in written opinions. Indeed, when *Holy Trinity* was decided, neither courts nor academics devoted much time to describing or debating interpretive theories. That phenomenon began in the twentieth century. Nevertheless, the Court in *Holy Trinity* has something to offer on this score. For example, it stated that its ultimate aim in interpreting the statute was to determine the way in which "Congress intended" the statute to be applied.

In this respect, *Holy Trinity* reflects a widely shared assumption that the primary role for courts is to serve as "faithful agents" of Congress in interpreting statutes, that is, to "identify and enforce the legal directives that an appropriately informed interpreter would conclude the enacting legislature meant to establish." Caleb Nelson, *What Is Textualism?*, 91 VA. L. REV. 347, 353-54 (2005). Most theories of statutory interpretation rest on this assumption (or some version of it). It reflects the view that law should be made by Congress not courts, which has roots in notions of legislative supremacy and judicial restraint. But some depart from it, viewing courts more as partners

with Congress rather than as faithful agents of Congress at the time the statute was enacted.

The following subsections provide a brief chronological description of
the basic theories of statutory interpretation, using *Holy Trinity* as the jump-
ing off point for each. The description is intended to be detailed enough
for you to begin to develop a working vocabulary of the theories, which are
discussed at greater length in section E of this chapter.

a. *Intentionalism.* Under one of the earliest approaches to statutory interpretation, courts looked to find the actual or specific
meaning that Congress meant for a particular word or phrase to
carry. Intentionalists interpret statutory provisions by relying on
sources that most directly bear on actual legislative intent, including the text of the statute, its legislative history, and the conditions
at the time of enactment. Where do you see intentionalism at work
in *Holy Trinity*? What did Congress intend when it wrote the word
"labor"?

b. *Purposivism.* In the 1930s, the realist movement cast doubt on
the quest for an actual, discernible legislative intent. At best, legal
realists asserted, legislative intent is difficult to reconstruct given
the complexities of the legislative process. How can a court know
with confidence what Congress actually intended a particular word
or phrase to mean? At worst, legislative intent is incoherent. No
group as large and diverse as Congress can share a unified intent.
Collective legislative intent simply does not exist. In response, courts
began to shift their focus away from the actual intent of Congress to
the broad purposes of the statute. They still examined the same sort
of sources: text, legislative history, and circumstances at the time
of enactment. But the inquiry concerning what Congress intended
to accomplish was no longer at the level of the specific meaning of
words but rather at the overall aims of the statute. Even in earlier
cases such as *Holy Trinity*, you can see purposivism at work. What
was the purpose of the statute, and how does that purpose affect the
meaning of the words of the statute, including "labor"?

c. *Legal Process Purposivism.* In the 1940s and 1950s, a group
of scholars refined purposivism to make it a more objective theory. The most prominent Legal Process thinkers, Henry Hart and
Albert Sacks, posited that law, including statutory law, should be
viewed as having a rational, purposive character. "Law is a doing
of something," Hart and Sacks write, "a purposive activity, a continuous striving to solve the basic problems of social living," of
maintaining social order and "maximizing the total satisfactions of
valid human wants." HENRY M. HART, JR. & ALBERT SACKS, THE LEGAL
PROCESS: BASIC PROBLEMS IN THE MAKING AND APPLICATION OF LAW
104-148 (William N. Eskridge, Jr. & Philip P. Frickey eds., 1994).
Based on that premise, when there is ambiguity in a statute, the
court should determine what a reasonable legislature would have

sought to achieve in the circumstances. When faced with ambiguity, the courts should interpret statutes assuming that the legislature was "made up of reasonable persons pursuing reasonable purposes reasonably." HART & SACKS, *supra*, at 1378. The Legal Process approach asked courts to construct an objective, reasonable purpose or purposes of statutes based on the available evidence, including the text, legislative history, and policy context.

Can you see any foreshadowing of Legal Process purposivism in *Holy Trinity*? What do you make of the religious discussion? There the Court stated that a purpose against religion would not be attributed to the legislature. Was the Court saying it would not have been reasonable for Congress, if acting reasonably, to have applied the statute to religious workers given that the United States at that time was a "Christian nation"? (This is not to say that Legal Process scholars would endorse the religious discussion in the opinion.)

d. *Imaginative Reconstruction.* A modern variant of intentionalism applies when Congress has not foreseen or considered a particular problem. Judge Posner is the leading proponent of this theory, which is called imaginative reconstruction. It does not purport to uncover the actual intent of Congress; indeed, it applies when Congress failed to appreciate an issue and therefore cannot be understood as having an intention as to that issue. Imaginative reconstruction asks the court to stand in the shoes of Congress, asking how the enacting legislature would have resolved the issue if it had envisioned it.

Do you see any seeds of this theory in *Holy Trinity*? Is this a better understanding of the religious discussion? (Again, that is not to say that proponents of imaginative reconstruction would endorse this religious discussion in the Court's opinion.) Was the Court conceding that Congress probably had not thought about whether the statute applies to pastors, reasoning instead that Congress would not have applied the statute to pastors if it had thought about the issue?

e. *Textualism and New Textualism.* In the late 1980s and 1990s, textualism began to ascend as a prominent theory of statutory interpretation, and it remains so today. Judges always have looked to the text of statutes to see if it reveals a meaning. But textualists set themselves apart by refusing to consult sources like legislative history in search of legislative intent or statutory purpose. Textualists are committed to the view that the text should be the sole tool of interpretation, though they believe that the text should be interpreted in its statutory context rather than in isolation. This view has both constitutional and pragmatic underpinnings. Textualists argue that intent- and purpose-based analyses do not comport with constitutional or rule-of-law values because only the text is enacted into law. Furthermore, textualists join ranks with realists in believing that the legislature has no intent or purpose other than to forge compromises in the chaotic and messy environment of the legislative process. The text manifests those compromises. Textualists also find support in the law-and-economics movement, which views legislators as writing statutes to deliver benefits to powerful interest groups. By sticking to the text, courts can confine such groups to the deals that they extracted rather than allowing them to find more generous interpretations in the legislative history.

In *Holy Trinity*, the Court looked well beyond the text in support of its interpretation (even though the Court was quite formalistic in other decisions, as you will see when you read the next case in the book, *Nix v. Heddon*). Here you see the Court employing textual tools when it construes the words of the provision first on their own and then in the context of the broader statute, including the title. But there is a great difference between textual analysis and textualist theory.

f. *Dynamic Interpretation.* There is another theory that is not really reflected in *Holy Trinity*: dynamic interpretation. Dynamic interpretation sees courts more as partners with Congress than as faithful agents of the enacting Congress in developing the meaning of statutes. Partly, this theory is based on the reality of the judicial process. When courts interpret statutes, they generally act as if they are not imposing their own background understandings and core values but are simply recovering the intent of the legislature, the purpose of the statute, or the meaning of the text. In truth, dynamic theorists claim, courts are applying their own understandings and values in order to interpret statutes. Because such an approach is inevitable, particularly as statutes age, courts ought to be honest about their method of interpretation. There is something to this, right? Just from reading *Holy Trinity*, you have a sense that text-, intent-, and purpose-based approaches do not always point in the same direction or yield a single, objective result. Perhaps the results vary more with judicial understandings and core values than courts are willing to acknowledge.

Dynamic theorists also argue that their partnership or pragmatic approach is normatively desirable. Some suggest that the courts should approach statutes as they approach the common law, construing them in light of legal and social developments that have occurred over time. Others argue that courts should take particular note of current legislative preferences because these preferences determine whether a statute or an interpretation could be enacted today, and therefore are more objective than picking and choosing among original meanings. Overall, these theorists view courts as (a) producing the best interpretations of statutes, and (b) best serving Congress when taking account of social and legal developments.

3. Following *Holy Trinity*, how would you advise Grace Church, also located in Manhattan, if it sought to enter a contract to pay a group of bricklayers from Italy to come and build an extension to its chapel, including the carving of several new gargoyles? Following *Holy Trinity*, how would you advise a mosque if it sought to enter into a contract with an Egyptian muezzin, by which the mosque would pay for the muezzin's transportation to New York City and the muezzin, in return, would begin service for the mosque?

4. Return to the Motor Vehicle Safety Act and the provision that authorizes NHTSA to set minimum performance standards for new motor vehicles and provides that all standards "shall be practicable, shall meet the need for motor vehicle safety, and shall be stated in objective terms." §103. Is a standard "practicable" if it depends on technology not currently in use? Consider the potential sources for determining the meaning of "practicable":

The provision itself.

Webster's Third New International Dictionary defines "practicable" as "possible or practical to perform," "capable of being put into practice, done or accomplished," and "feasible."

Other provisions of the same statute.

The express purpose of the Act is "to reduce traffic accidents and deaths and injuries to persons resulting from traffic accidents." 15 U.S.C. §1381.

The Act establishes a research and development section within the agency itself. *See* 15 U.S.C. §1395.

The Act permits the Secretary to extend the effective date beyond the usual statutory maximum of one year from the date of issuance. 15 U.S.C. §1392(c).

The legislative history of the statute.

The Senate Committee Report, in a section entitled "Purpose and Need," states: "[T]his legislation reflects the faith that the restrained and responsible exercise of Federal authority can channel the creative energies and vast technology of the automobile industry into a vigorous and competitive effort to improve the safety of vehicles." S. REP. 1301, 89th Cong., 2d Sess. 2 U.S.C.C.A.N. 2709 (1966).

The same report adds: "While the bill reported by the committee authorizes the Secretary to make grants or award contracts for research in certain cases, a principal aim is to encourage the auto industry itself to engage in greater auto safety and safety-related research." *Id.* at 2718.

The report, explaining the effective date provision, states: "The power to specify a later effective date is needed because it may be a practical economic and engineering impossibility, as well as a source of great hardship and unnecessary additional cost, to require that all vehicle changes required by any new safety standard, whatever its scope or subject matter, be accomplished by all manufacturers on all their vehicles within 1 year." *Id.* at 2714.

The House Committee Report states: "In establishing standards the Secretary must conform to the requirement that the standard is practicable. This would include consideration of all relevant factors, including technological ability to achieve the goal of a particular standard as well as consideration of economic factors." H.R. REP. 1776, p. 16.

The Automobile Manufacturers Association transmitted to the House Committee several amendments to HR 13228 (the House Bill) proposing a requirement that: ". . . the Secretary, in proposing and issuing orders establishing, amending, or withdrawing Federal motor vehicle safety standards under this section, shall be guided so far as practicable by the following criteria, and the Secretary shall include in each such order findings of fact with respect thereto: . . . (2) The standard shall be consistent with the continuation or adoption by motor vehicle manufacturers of efficient designing, engineering, and manufacturing practices, and with innovation, progressiveness, and customary model changes in the automotive industry. (3) The standard, the means of complying with the standard, and the methods of testing for compliance should embody feasible devices and techniques that are available or can be made available in a reasonable time and at costs commensurate with the benefit to be achieved. . . . (5) The standard should be made effective so as to allow adequate time for compliance, taking into account the time required for designing, engineering, tooling and production. . . ." Hearings Before the Committee on Interstate and Foreign Commerce, U.S. House of Representatives, 89th Cong., 2d Sess., on H.R. 13228, "Part 2, Traffic Safety," p. 1203.

If you were a lawyer for NHTSA, which sources would you emphasize and which arguments would you make in your brief defending the agency's technology-forcing standard as "practicable" under the 1966 Act? Alternatively, if you were a lawyer for the automakers, which sources would you stress and which arguments would you make? How might either the lawyer for NHTSA or the automaker use *Holy Trinity*? Finally, if you were a judge, how would you rule and why? Suppose that one of your judicial colleagues refused to consult the legislative history. How would that refusal influence the interpretation of the word "practicable"?

B. TEXT-BASED TOOLS

The tools of statutory interpretation are instruments for ascertaining the meaning of statutory words or phrases. We group them according to whether they ascertain meaning based on (a) text; (b) other indicia of legislative intent and statutory purpose; or (c) changed circumstances. Although we do not include every tool upon which courts rely, we cover the most popular.

We begin with the tools for ascertaining meaning based on text because that is generally where courts begin. As the Supreme Court has stated, "[t]he starting point in every case involving construction of a statute is the language itself." Watt v. Alaska, 451 U.S. 259 (1981). The "plain meaning rule" directs courts to give effect to the text if it has a plain meaning—that is, the text is not only a starting point but the stopping point. Not all courts follow this rule when the plain meaning is at odds with other evidence of legislative intent or statutory purpose. But all agree that the place to begin in interpreting a statute is with the text.

In many instances, the text of a statute has an evident meaning. The reason is not because the terms used in the statute require no interpretation but because there happens to be agreement on that interpretation. If the text has no evident meaning and courts are interested in the literal or ordinary meaning of a statutory term, they might look it up in the dictionary, just as you might do. Sometimes a dictionary is helpful, but sometimes the dictionary contains many alternative definitions. The statute that serves as our running example in this book, the Motor Vehicle Safety Act, conjures up H.L.A. Hart's famous example in the *Concept of Law* of a statute that provides, "No vehicle may be taken into the park." We know that the statute forbids people from driving their cars in the park because we have a general sense for what the statute is about. Can you also get this meaning from the dictionary? If your answer is yes, then do you think that the statute also forbids an organization from showing movies in the park? How about an artist painting a picture in the park? How about a clinic dispensing medicine in the park? Check the dictionary. It defines "vehicle" in a way that can cover movies, paint, and medicine.

Apart from dictionaries, courts consult other tools in pursuit of text-based meaning. They look for usage in the relevant industry or expert community, particularly if the term is technical. Courts can also consult canons of construction, which are judicially created principles for understanding statutory text. There are very many such canons, and, for that reason, they occupy a considerable amount of the discussion in this chapter. We take each type of text-based tool in turn.

1. Ordinary Meaning vs. Technical Meaning

Courts must determine whether to interpret a statutory text according to its ordinary meaning (sometimes called common meaning) or to accord it a form of technical meaning, such as a legal meaning or trade meaning. As a matter of longstanding doctrine, courts approach statutes assuming that their terms will be interpreted in accordance with "the ordinary meaning of the words used," American Tobacco Co. v. Patterson, 456 U.S. 63, 68 (1982), but that presumption can be overcome by indications that the words were intended to have or acquired a technical meaning. To see these issues in operation, consider the following decision, now a classic, involving the question of whether a tomato is a "vegetable." As you read, note the different sources and types of meaning that the Supreme Court identifies.

Nix v. Hedden

149 U.S. 304 (1893)

Justice GREY delivered the opinion of the Court.

This was an action brought February 4, 1887, against the collector of the port of New York to recover back duties paid under protest on tomatoes imported by the plaintiff from the West Indies in the spring of 1886, which the collector assessed under "Schedule G. Provisions," of the tariff act of March 3, 1883, (chapter 121) imposing a duty on "vegetables in their natural state, or in salt or brine, not specially enumerated or provided for in this act, ten per centum ad valorem"; and which the plaintiffs contended came within the clause in the free list of the same act, "Fruits, green, ripe, or dried, not specially enumerated or provided for in this act." 22 Stat. 504, 519.

At the trial the plaintiff's counsel, after reading in evidence definitions of the words "fruit" and "vegetables" from Webster's Dictionary, Worcester's Dictionary, and the Imperial Dictionary, called two witnesses, who had been for 30 years in the business of selling fruit and vegetables, and asked them, after hearing these definitions, to say whether these words had "any special meaning in trade or commerce, different from those read."

One of the witnesses answered as follows: "Well, it does not classify all things there, but they are correct as far as they go. It does not take all kinds of fruit or vegetables; it takes a portion of them. I think the words 'fruit' and 'vegetable' have the same meaning in trade to-day that they had on March 1, 1883. I understand that the term 'fruit' is applied in trade only to such plants or parts of plants as contain the seeds. There are more vegetables than those in the enumeration given in Webster's Dictionary under the term 'vegetable,' as 'cabbage, cauliflower, turnips, potatoes, peas, beans, and the like,' probably covered by the words 'and the like.' "

The other witness testified: "I don't think the term 'fruit' or the term 'vegetables' had, in March 1883, and prior thereto, any special meaning in trade and commerce in this country different from that which I have read here from the dictionaries."

The plaintiff's counsel then read in evidence from the same dictionaries the definitions of the word "tomato."

The defendant's counsel then read in evidence from Webster's Dictionary the definitions of the words "pea," "egg plant," "cucumber," "squash," and "pepper."

The plaintiff then read in evidence from Webster's and Worcester's dictionaries the definitions of "potato," "turnip," "parsnip," "cauliflower," "cabbage," "carrot," and "bean."

No other evidence was offered by either party. The court, upon the defendant's motion, directed a verdict for him, which was returned, and judgment rendered thereon. The plaintiffs duly excepted to the instruction, and sued out this writ of error.

The single question in this case is whether tomatoes, considered as provisions, are to be classed as "vegetables" or as "fruit," within the meaning of the tariff act of 1883.

The only witnesses called at the trial testified that neither "vegetables" nor "fruit" had any special meaning in trade or commerce different from that given in the dictionaries, and that they had the same meaning in trade to-day that they had in March, 1883.

The passages cited from the dictionaries define the word "fruit" as the seed of plants, or that part of plants which contains the seed, and especially the juicy, pulpy products of certain plants, covering and containing the seed. These definitions have no tendency to show that tomatoes are "fruit," as distinguished from "vegetables," in common speech, or within the meaning of the tariff act.

There being no evidence that the words "fruit" and "vegetables" have acquired any special meaning in trade or commerce, they must receive their ordinary meaning. Of that meaning the court is bound to take judicial notice, as it does in regard to all words in our own tongue; and upon such a question dictionaries are admitted, not as evidence, but only as aids to the memory and understanding of the court.

Botanically speaking, tomatoes are the fruit of a vine, just as are cucumbers, squashes, beans, and peas. But in the common language of the people, whether sellers or consumers of provisions, all these are vegetables which are grown in kitchen gardens, and which, whether eaten cooked or raw, are, like potatoes, carrots, parsnips, turnips, beets, cauliflower, cabbage, celery, and lettuce, usually served at dinner in, with, or after the soup, fish, or meats which constitute the principal part of the repast, and not, like fruits generally, as dessert.

The attempt to class tomatoes as fruit is not unlike a recent attempt to class beans as seeds, of which Mr. Justice Bradley, speaking for this court, said: "We do not see why they should be classified as seeds, any more than walnuts should be so classified. Both are seeds, in the language of botany or natural history, but not in commerce nor in common parlance. On the other hand in speaking generally of provisions, beans may well be included under the term 'vegetables.' As an article of food on our tables, whether baked or boiled, or forming the basis of soup, they are used as a vegetable, as well when ripe as when green. This is the principal use to which they are put. Beyond the common knowledge which we have on this subject, very little evidence is necessary, or can be produced."

Notes and Questions

1. When ordinary and technical meanings differ, litigants will have a lot at stake in urging the court to adopt their preferred interpretation. For instance, it would have made all the difference in the *Nix* case had the Court adopted the technical, botanical meaning of tomato as opposed to the ordinary one. Why didn't the Court adopt the botanical meaning?

2. Industry custom is another potential source of technical meaning. Why didn't the Court follow industry custom rather than relying on the ordinary meaning?

3. In determining the ordinary meaning of a term, courts often rely on dictionary definitions. In *Nix*, the Court relied on a commonsense judgment about tomatoes. It was confident that tomatoes are usually served with dinner and therefore are vegetables. Although it viewed the dictionary definition of vegetables as supporting its conclusion, that definition seems almost peripheral. Why was the Court so confident? Are you persuaded? (And if you are, you now have the answer to the perennial dinnertime question: is ketchup a vegetable?)

4. The Court makes virtually no reference to why Congress actually intended to tax vegetables but not fruit. Suppose that the differential tax treatment was designed to protect American farmers, who mainly grow vegetables and not fruit. By taxing imported vegetables, the statute raises their prices and thus increases demand for lower-priced domestic vegetables. How might this information be useful?

On the question of how a court determines whether to adopt the ordinary as opposed to the technical meaning of a term, consider the following decision.

Barber v. Gonzales

347 U.S. 637 (1954)

Mr. Chief Justice WARREN delivered the opinion of the Court.

Respondent was born in the Philippine Islands in 1913 and came therefrom to the continental United States in 1930. He has lived here ever since. In 1941, he was convicted in the State of California of assault with a deadly weapon and was sentenced to imprisonment for one year in the Alameda County jail. In 1950, he was convicted in the State of Washington of second degree burglary and was sentenced under the indeterminate sentence law of that State to a minimum term of two years in the state penitentiary. In 1951, after an administrative hearing, he was ordered deported to the Philippine Islands under §19(a) of the Immigration Act of 1917 as an alien who "after entry" had been sentenced more than once to imprisonment for terms of one year or more for crimes involving moral turpitude. . . .

After respondent was taken into custody, he filed a petition for a writ of habeas corpus in the United States District Court for the Northern District of California. The petition attacked the validity of the deportation order on the ground, among others, that he was not subject to deportation under §19(a) since he had not made an "entry" within the meaning of that section. The District Court dismissed the petition. On appeal, the Court of Appeals for the Ninth Circuit, with one judge dissenting, reversed the District Court's judgment and remanded the case with directions to order respondent's release from custody. We granted certiorari.

The sole question presented is whether respondent—who was born a national of the United States in the Philippine Islands, who came to the continental United States as a national prior to the Philippine Independence Act of 1934, and who was sentenced to imprisonment in 1941 and 1950 for crimes involving moral turpitude—may now be deported under §19(a) of the Immigration Act of 1917.

It is conceded that respondent was born a national of the United States; that as such he owed permanent allegiance to the United States, including the obligation of military service; that he retained this status when he came to the continental United States in 1930 and hence was not then subject to the Immigration Act of 1917 or any other federal statute relating to the exclusion or deportation of aliens. . . .

Section 19(a) provides:

> ". . . except as hereinafter provided, any alien who is hereafter sentenced to imprisonment for a term of one year or more because of conviction in this country of a crime involving moral turpitude, committed within five years after the entry of the alien to the United States, or who is hereafter sentenced more than once to such a term of imprisonment because of conviction in this country of any crime involving moral turpitude, committed at any time after entry . . . shall, upon the warrant of the Attorney General, be taken into custody and deported . . . ."

The Court of Appeals sustained respondent's contention that he had never made the requisite "entry." With this conclusion, we agree.

The Government would have us interpret "entry" in §19(a) in its "ordinary, everyday sense" of a "coming into the United States." Under this view, respondent's "coming into the United States" from the Philippine Islands in 1930 would satisfy the "entry" requirement. While it is true that statutory language should be interpreted whenever possible according to common usage, some terms acquire a special technical meaning by a process of judicial construction. So it is with the word 'entry' in §19(a). . . . In *United States ex rel. Claussen v. Day*, 279 U.S. 398, 401, this Court stated the applicable rule:

> "The word 'entry' (in §19(a)) by its own force implies a coming from outside. The extent shows that in order that there be an entry within the meaning of the act there must be an arrival from some foreign port or place. There is no such entry where one goes to sea on board an American vessel from a port of the United States and returns to the same or another port of this country without having been in any foreign port or place."

This concept of "entry" was codified by Congress in the Immigration and Nationality Act of 1952.[1]

At the time respondent came to the continental United States, he was not arriving "from some foreign port or place." On the contrary, he was a United States national moving from one of our insular possessions to the mainland. It was not until the 1934 Philippine Independence Act that the Philippines could be regarded as "foreign" for immigration purposes. Having made no "entry," respondent is not deportable under §19(a) as an alien who "after entry" committed crimes involving moral turpitude. The Government warns that this conclusion is inconsistent with a broad congressional purpose to terminate the United States residence of alien criminals. But we believe a different conclusion would not be permissible in view of the well-settled meaning of "entry" in §19(a). Although not penal in character, deportation statutes as a practical matter may inflict "the equivalent of banishment or exile," *Fong Haw Tan v. Phelan*, 333 U.S. 6, and should be strictly construed. See *Delgadillo v. Carmichael*, 332 U.S. 388, 391. In the absence of explicit language showing a contrary congressional intent, we must give technical words in deportation statutes their usual technical meaning.

The judgment of the Court of Appeals is affirmed.

[The dissenting opinion of Mr. Justice MINTON, with whom Mr. Justice REED and Mr. Justice BURTON join, is omitted.]

Notes and Questions

1. What justified the Court's decision in *Barber* to adopt a technical meaning? When determining whether to adopt the ordinary meaning as opposed to a technical meaning, there is no single grand theory but rather a collection of factors that courts consider. As *Barber* shows, statutory definitions of terms also establish a technical meaning of the term defined. A term that has an established meaning at common law will generally be interpreted according to that established legal meaning. Put differently, courts will "presume that Congress incorporates the common-law meaning of the terms it uses if those 'terms . . . have accumulated settled meaning under . . . the common law'" and "'the statute [does not] otherwise dictat[e].'" United States v. Wells, 519 U.S. 482, 491 (1997). Other factors that courts consider are the audience to which the statute is addressed, whether there is an industry understanding, and whether the term appears in a technical context. *See* Zuni Public School Dist. No. 89 v. Department of Education, 550 U.S. 81,

---

1. Section 101(a)(13) of the 1952 Act, 66 Stat. 167, 8 U.S.C. § 1101(a)(13), provides in pertinent part: "The term 'entry' means any coming of an alien into the United States, from a foreign port or place or from an outlying possession . . . ." Section 101(a)(29), 66 Stat. 170, 8 U.S.C. § 1101(a)(29), defines "outlying possessions" as American Samoa and Swains Island.

93-94 (2007). For instance, penal statutes are addressed to the public and state proscriptions for which the public is assumed to have knowledge. As a result, courts generally interpret penal statutes according to ordinary meaning or usage. In contrast, regulatory statutes are often addressed to policymakers, granting authority to such policymakers as opposed to directly binding the public, and frequently deal with complex technical matters. A court might find that these factors weigh in favor of technical meaning. How would a court interpret a provision in a complex regulatory statute — say involving the disposal of toxic waste — that imposes criminal penalties on violators?

Even when the decision to use ordinary meaning (as opposed to technical meaning) seems straightforward, application issues may arise. For example, a term or phrase may have more than one ordinary meaning. Consider the following case, paying particular attention to the sources on which the justices in the majority and the dissent rely in determining the ordinary meaning of the language at issue.

Muscarello v. United States

524 U.S. 125 (1998)

Justice BREYER delivered the opinion of the Court.

A provision in the firearms chapter of the federal criminal code imposes a 5-year mandatory prison term upon a person who "uses or carries a firearm" "during and in relation to" a "drug trafficking crime." 18 U.S.C. §924(c)(1). The question before us is whether the phrase "carries a firearm" is limited to the carrying of firearms on the person. We hold that it is not so limited. Rather, it also applies to a person who knowingly possesses and conveys firearms in a vehicle, including in the locked glove compartment or trunk of a car, which the person accompanies.

I

The question arises in two cases, which we have consolidated for argument. Petitioner in the first case, Frank J. Muscarello, unlawfully sold marijuana, which he carried in his truck to the place of sale. Police officers found a handgun locked in the truck's glove compartment. During plea proceedings, Muscarello admitted that he had "carried" the gun "for protection in relation" to the drug offense, though he later claimed to the contrary, and added that, in any event, his "carr[ying]" of the gun in the glove compartment did not fall within the scope of the statutory word "carries."

Petitioners in the second case, Donald Cleveland and Enrique Gray-Santana, placed several guns in a bag, put the bag in the trunk of a car, and then traveled by car to a proposed drug-sale point, where they intended to steal drugs from the sellers. Federal agents at the scene stopped them, searched the cars, found the guns and drugs, and arrested them.

In both cases the Courts of Appeals found that petitioners had "carrie[d]" the guns during and in relation to a drug trafficking offense.

106 F.3d 636, 639 (C.A.5 1997). We granted certiorari to determine whether the fact that the guns were found in the locked glove compartment, or the trunk, of a car precludes application of §924(c)(1). We conclude that it does not.

II

A

We begin with the statute's language. The parties vigorously contest the ordinary English meaning of the phrase "carries a firearm." Because they essentially agree that Congress intended the phrase to convey its ordinary, and not some special legal, meaning, and because they argue the linguistic point at length, we too have looked into the matter in more than usual depth. Although the word "carry" has many different meanings, only two are relevant here. When one uses the word in the first, or primary, meaning, one can, as a matter of ordinary English, "carry firearms" in a wagon, car, truck, or other vehicle that one accompanies. When one uses the word in a different, rather special, way, to mean, for example, "bearing" or (in slang) "packing" (as in "packing a gun"), the matter is less clear. But, for reasons we shall set out below, we believe Congress intended to use the word in its primary sense and not in this latter, special way.

Consider first the word's primary meaning. The Oxford English Dictionary gives as its *first* definition "convey, originally by cart or wagon, hence in any vehicle, by ship, on horseback, etc." 2 Oxford English Dictionary 919 (2d ed. 1989); *see also* Webster's Third New International Dictionary 343 (1986) (*first* definition: "move while supporting (*as in a vehicle* or in one's hands or arms)"); Random House Dictionary of the English Language Unabridged 319 (2d ed. 1987) (*first* definition: "to take or support from one place to another; convey; transport").

The origin of the word "carries" explains why the first, or basic, meaning of the word "carry" includes conveyance in a vehicle. *See* Barnhart Dictionary of Etymology 146 (1988) (tracing the word from Latin "carum," which means "car" or "cart"); 2 Oxford English Dictionary, at 919 (tracing the word from Old French "carier" and the late Latin "carricare," which meant to "convey in a car"); Oxford Dictionary of English Etymology 148 (C. Onions ed. 1966) (same); Barnhart Dictionary of Etymology, at 143 (explaining that the term "car" has been used to refer to the automobile since 1896).

The greatest of writers have used the word with this meaning. *See, e.g.,* The King James Bible, 2 *Kings* 9:28 ("[H]is servants carried him in a chariot to Jerusalem"); *id., Isaiah* 30:6 ("[T]hey will carry their riches upon the shoulders of young asses"). Robinson Crusoe says, "[w]ith my boat, I carry'd away every Thing." D. Defoe, Robinson Crusoe 174 (J. Crowley ed. 1972). And the owners of Queequeg's ship, Melville writes, "had lent him a [wheelbarrow], in which to carry his heavy chest to his boarding-house." H. Melville, Moby Dick 43 (U. Chicago 1952). This Court, too, has spoken of the "carrying" of drugs in a car or in its "trunk." *California v. Acevedo,* 500 U.S. 565, 572-573 (1991); *Florida v. Jimeno,* 500 U.S. 248, 249 (1991).

These examples do not speak directly about carrying guns. But there is nothing linguistically special about the fact that weapons, rather than drugs, are being carried. Robinson Crusoe might have carried a gun in his boat; Queequeg might have borrowed a wheelbarrow in which to carry not a chest, but a harpoon. And, to make certain that there is no special ordinary English restriction (unmentioned in dictionaries) upon the use of "carry" in respect to guns, we have surveyed modern press usage, albeit crudely, by searching computerized newspaper databases — both the New York Times data base [sic] in Lexis/Nexis, and the "US News" data base in Westlaw. We looked for sentences in which the words "carry," "vehicle," and "weapon" (or variations thereof) all appear. We found thousands of such sentences, and random sampling suggests that many, perhaps more than one-third, are sentences used to convey the meaning at issue here, *i.e.,* the carrying of guns in a car.

The New York Times, for example, writes about "an ex-con" who "arrives home driving a stolen car and carrying a load of handguns," Mar. 21, 1992, section 1, p. 18, col. 1, and an "official peace officer who carries a shotgun in his boat," June 19, 1988, section 12WC, p. 2, col. 1; *cf.* The New York Times Manual of Style and Usage, a Desk Book of Guidelines for Writers and Editors, foreword (L. Jordan rev. ed. 1976) (restricting Times journalists and editors to the use of proper English). The Boston Globe refers to the arrest of a professional baseball player "for carrying a semiloaded automatic weapon in his car." Dec. 10, 1994, p. 75, col. 5. The Colorado Springs Gazette Telegraph speaks of one "Russell" who "carries a gun hidden in his car." May 2, 1993, p. B1, col. 2. The Arkansas Gazette refers to a "house" that was "searched" in an effort to find "items that could be carried in a car, such as . . . guns." Mar. 10, 1991, p. A1, col. 2. The San Diego Union-Tribune asks, "What, do they carry guns aboard these boats now?" Feb. 18, 1992, p. D2, col. 5.

Now consider a different, somewhat special meaning of the word "carry" — a meaning upon which the linguistic arguments of petitioners and the dissent must rest. The Oxford English Dictionary's *twenty-sixth* definition of "carry" is "bear, wear, hold up, or sustain, as one moves about; habitually to bear about with one." 2 Oxford English Dictionary, at 921. Webster's defines "carry" as "to move while supporting," not just in a vehicle, but also "in one's hands or arms." Webster's Third New International Dictionary, at 343. And Black's Law Dictionary defines the entire phrase "carry arms or weapons" as "To wear, bear or carry them upon the person or in the clothing or in a pocket, for the purpose of use, or for the purpose of being armed and ready for offensive or defensive action in case of a conflict with another person." Black's Law Dictionary 214 (6th ed. 1990).

These special definitions, however, do not purport to *limit* the "carrying of arms" to the circumstances they describe. No one doubts that one who bears arms on his person "carries a weapon." But to say that is not to deny that one may *also* "carry a weapon" tied to the saddle of a horse or placed in a bag in a car.

Nor is there any linguistic reason to think that Congress intended to limit the word "carries" in the statute to any of these special definitions. To the contrary, all these special definitions embody a form of an important, but secondary, meaning of "carry," a meaning that suggests support rather than movement or transportation, as when, for example, a column "carries" the weight of an arch. 2 Oxford English Dictionary, at 919, 921. In this sense a gangster might "carry" a gun (in colloquial language, he might "pack a gun") even though he does not move from his chair. It is difficult to believe, however, that Congress intended to limit the statutory word to this definition-imposing special punishment upon the comatose gangster while ignoring drug lords who drive to a sale carrying an arsenal of weapons in their van.

We recognize, as the dissent emphasizes, that the word "carry" has other meanings as well. But those other meanings (*e.g.*, "carry all he knew," "carries no colours") are not relevant here. And the fact that speakers often do *not* add to the phrase "carry a gun" the words "in a car" is of no greater relevance here than the fact that millions of Americans did *not* see Muscarello carry a gun in his truck. The relevant linguistic facts are that the word "carry" in its ordinary sense includes carrying in a car and that the word, used in its ordinary sense, keeps the same meaning whether one carries a gun, a suitcase, or a banana.

B

We now explore more deeply the purely legal question of whether Congress intended to use the word "carry" in its ordinary sense, or whether it intended to limit the scope of the phrase to instances in which a gun is carried "on the person." We conclude that neither the statute's basic purpose nor its legislative history support circumscribing the scope of the word "carry" by applying an "on the person" limitation. . . .

This Court has described the statute's basic purpose broadly, as an effort to combat the "dangerous combination" of "drugs and guns." *Smith v. United States,* 508 U.S. 223, 240 (1993). And the provision's chief legislative sponsor has said that the provision seeks "to persuade the man who is tempted to commit a Federal felony to leave his gun at home." 114 Cong. Rec. 22231 (1968) (Rep. Poff).

From the perspective of any such purpose (persuading a criminal "to leave his gun at home"), what sense would it make for this statute to penalize one who walks with a gun in a bag to the site of a drug sale, but to ignore a similar individual who, like defendant Gray-Santana, travels to a similar site with a similar gun in a similar bag, but instead of walking, drives there with the gun in his car? How persuasive is a punishment that is without effect until a drug dealer who has brought his gun to a sale (indeed has it available for use) actually takes it from the trunk (or unlocks the glove compartment) of his car? It is difficult to say that, considered as a class, those who prepare, say, to sell drugs by placing guns in their cars are less dangerous, or less deserving of punishment, than those who carry handguns on their person.

We have found no significant indication elsewhere in the legislative history of any more narrowly focused relevant purpose. We have found an instance in which a legislator referred to the statute as applicable when an individual "has a firearm on his person," *ibid.* (Rep. Meskill); an instance in which a legislator speaks of "a criminal who takes a gun in his hand," *id.,* at 22239 (Rep. Pucinski); and a reference in the Senate Report to a "gun carried in a pocket," S. Rep. No. 98-225, p. 314, n.10 (1983); *see also* 114 Cong. Rec. 21788, 21789 (1968) (references to gun "carrying" without more). But in these instances no one purports to define the scope of the term "carries"; and the examples of guns carried on the person are not used to illustrate the reach of the term "carries" but to illustrate, or to criticize, a different aspect of the statute.

Regardless, in other instances, legislators suggest that the word "carries" has a broader scope. One legislator indicates that the statute responds in part to the concerns of law enforcement personnel, who had urged that "carrying short firearms in motor vehicles be classified as carrying such weapons concealed." *Id.,* at 22242 (Rep. May). Another criticizes a version of the proposed statute by suggesting it might apply to drunken driving, and gives as an example a drunken driver who has a "gun in his car." *Id.,* at 21792 (Rep. Yates). Others describe the statute as criminalizing gun "possession" a term that could stretch beyond both the "use" of a gun and the carrying of a gun on the person. *See id.,* at 21793 (Rep. Casey); *id.,* at 22236 (Rep. Meskill); *id.,* at 30584 (Rep. Collier); *id.,* at 30585 (Rep. Skubitz).

We are not convinced by petitioners' remaining arguments to the contrary. . . .

Finally, petitioners and the dissent invoke the "rule of lenity." The simple existence of some statutory ambiguity, however, is not sufficient to warrant application of that rule, for most statutes are ambiguous to some degree. *Cf. Smith,* 508 U.S., at 239 ("The mere possibility of articulating a narrower construction . . . does not by itself make the rule of lenity applicable"). "The rule of lenity applies only if, after seizing everything from which aid can be derived," . . . we can make "no more than a guess as to what Congress intended." *United States v. Wells,* 519 U.S. 482, 499 (1997). To invoke the rule, we must conclude that there is a "grievous ambiguity or uncertainty" in the statute." *Staples v. United States,* 511 U.S. 600, 619 n.17 (1994). Certainly, our decision today is based on much more than a "guess as to what Congress intended," and there is no "grievous ambiguity" here. The problem of statutory interpretation in these cases is indeed no different from that in many of the criminal cases that confront us. Yet, this Court has never held that the rule of lenity automatically permits a defendant to win.

In sum, the "generally accepted contemporary meaning" of the word "carry" includes the carrying of a firearm in a vehicle. The purpose of this statute warrants its application in such circumstances. The limiting phrase "during and in relation to" should prevent misuse of the statute to penalize those whose conduct does not create the risks of harm at which the statute aims. For these reasons, we conclude that petitioners' conduct falls within the scope of the phrase "carries a firearm."

Justice GINSBURG, with whom THE CHIEF JUSTICE, Justice SCALIA, and Justice SOUTER join, dissenting.

. . . Without doubt, "carries" is a word of many meanings, definable to mean or include carting about in a vehicle. But that encompassing definition is not a ubiquitously necessary one. Nor, in my judgment, is it a proper construction of "carries" as the term appears in §924(c)(1). In line with *Bailey* and the principle of lenity the Court has long followed, I would confine "carries a firearm," for §924(c)(1) purposes, to the undoubted meaning of that expression in the relevant context. I would read the words to indicate not merely keeping arms on one's premises or in one's vehicle, but bearing them in such manner as to be ready for use as a weapon.

Unlike the Court, I do not think dictionaries,[1] surveys of press reports,[2] or the Bible[3] tell us, dispositively, what "carries" means embedded in §924(c)(1). On definitions, "carry" in legal formulations could mean, *inter alia*, transport, possess, have in stock, prolong (carry over), be infectious, or wear or bear on one's person.[4] At issue here is not "carries" at large but "carries a firearm." The Court's computer search of newspapers is revealing in this light. Carrying guns in a car showed up as the meaning "perhaps more than one-third" of the time. One is left to wonder what meaning showed up some two-thirds of the time. Surely a most familiar meaning is, as the Constitution's Second Amendment ("keep and *bear* Arms") (emphasis added) and Black's Law Dictionary, at 214, indicate: "wear, bear, or carry . . . upon the person or in the clothing or in a pocket, for the purpose . . . of being armed and ready for offensive or defensive action in a case of conflict with another person."

On lessons from literature, a scan of Bartlett's and other quotation collections shows how highly selective the Court's choices are. If "[t]he greatest of

---

1. I note, however, that the only legal dictionary the Court cites, Black's Law Dictionary, defines "carry arms or weapons" restrictively.

2. Many newspapers, the New York Times among them, have published stories using "transport," rather than "carry," to describe gun placements resembling petitioners'. *See, e.g.*, Atlanta Constitution, Feb. 27, 1998, p. 9D, col. 2 ("House members last week expanded gun laws by allowing weapons to be *carried into restaurants or transported anywhere in cars*."); Chicago Tribune, June 12, 1997, sports section, p. 13 ("Disabled hunters with permission to hunt from a standing vehicle would be able to *transport a shotgun in an all-terrain vehicle* as long as the gun is unloaded and the breech is open."); Colorado Springs Gazette Telegraph, Aug. 4, 1996, p. C10 (British gun laws require "locked steel cases bolted onto a car for *transporting guns from home to shooting range*."); Detroit News, Oct. 26, 1997, p. D14 ("It is unlawful to *carry afield or transport a rifle* . . . or shotgun if you have buckshot, slug, ball loads, or cut shells in possession except while traveling directly to deer camp or target range with firearm not readily available to vehicle occupants."); N.Y. Times, July 4, 1993, p. A21, col. 2 ("[T]he gun is supposed to be *transported unloaded*, in a locked box in the trunk."); Santa Rosa Press Democrat, Sept. 28, 1996, p. B1 ("Police and volunteers ask that participants . . . *transport* [*their guns*] *to the fairgrounds* in the trunks of their cars."); Worcester Telegram & Gazette, July 16, 1996, p. B3 ("Only one gun can be turned in per person. *Guns transported in a vehicle* should be locked in the trunk.") (emphasis added in all quotations).

3. The translator of the Good Book, it appears, bore responsibility for determining whether the servants of Ahaziah "carried" his corpse to Jerusalem. Compare [majority citations] with, *e.g.,* The New English Bible, 2 *Kings* 9:28 ("His servants *conveyed* his body to Jerusalem."); Saint Joseph Edition of the New American Bible ("His servants *brought* him in a chariot to Jerusalem."); Tanakh: The Holy Scriptures ("His servants *conveyed* him in a chariot to Jerusalem."); *see also id., Isaiah* 30:6 ("They *convey* their wealth on the backs of asses."); The New Jerusalem Bible ("[T]hey *bear* their riches on donkeys' backs.") (emphasis added in all quotations).

4. The dictionary to which this Court referred in *Bailey v. United States*, 516 U.S. 137, 145 (1995), contains 32 discrete definitions of "carry," including "[t]o make good or valid," "to bear the aspect of," and even "[t]o bear (a hawk) on the fist." *See* Webster's New International Dictionary 412 (2d ed. 1949).

writers" have used "carry" to mean convey or transport in a vehicle, so have they used the hydra-headed word to mean, *inter alia,* carry in one's hand, arms, head, heart, or soul, sans vehicle. Consider, among countless examples:

> "[H]e shall gather the lambs with his arm, and carry them in his bosom."
>
> The King James Bible, Isaiah 40:11.
>
> "And still they gaz'd, and still the wonder grew,
> That one small head could carry all he knew."
>
> O. Goldsmith, The Deserted Village, ll. 215-216, in The Poetical Works of Oliver Goldsmith 30 (A. Dobson ed. 1949).
>
> "There's a Legion that never was 'listed,
> That carries no colours or crest."
>
> R. Kipling, The Lost Legion, st. 1, in Rudyard Kipling's Verse, 1885-1918, p. 222 (1920).
>
> "There is a homely adage which runs, 'Speak softly and carry a big stick; you will go far.'"
>
> T. Roosevelt, Speech at Minnesota State Fair, Sept. 2, 1901, in J. Bartlett, Familiar Quotations 575:16 (J. Kaplan ed. 1992).[5]

These and the Court's lexicological sources demonstrate vividly that "carry" is a word commonly used to convey various messages. Such references, given their variety, are not reliable indicators of what Congress meant, in §924(c)(1), by "carries a firearm." . . .

[Moreover, r]eading "carries" in §924(c)(1) to mean "on or about [one's] person" is fully compatible with these and other "Firearms" statutes. For example, under §925(a)(2)(B), one could carry his gun to a car, transport it to the shooting competition, and use it to shoot targets. Under the conditions of §926A, one could transport her gun in a car, but under no circumstances could the gun be readily accessible while she travels in the car. "[C]ourts normally try to read language in different, but related, statutes, so as best to reconcile those statutes, in light of their purposes and of common sense." . . . So reading the "Firearms" statutes, I would not extend the word "carries" in §924(c)(1) to mean transports out of hand's reach in a vehicle.[6]

---

5. Popular films and television productions provide corroborative illustrations. In "The Magnificent Seven," for example, O'Reilly (played by Charles Bronson) says: "You think I am brave because I carry a gun; well, your fathers are much braver because they carry responsibility, for you, your brothers, your sisters, and your mothers." *See* http://us.imdb.com/M/search_quotes?for=carry. And in the television series "M*A*S*H," Hawkeye Pierce (played by Alan Alda) presciently proclaims: "I will not carry a gun. . . . I'll carry your books, I'll carry a torch, I'll carry a tune, I'll carry on, carry over, carry forward, Cary Grant, cash and carry, carry me back to Old Virginia, I'll even 'hari-kari' if you show me how, but I will not carry a gun!" *See* http://www.geocities.com/Hollywood/8915/mashquotes.html.

6. The Court places undue reliance on Representative Poff's statement that §924(c)(1) seeks "'to persuade the man who is tempted to commit a Federal felony to leave his gun at home.'" As the Government argued in its brief to this Court in *Bailey*: "In making that statement, Representative Poff was not referring to the 'carries' prong of the original Section 924(c). As originally enacted, the 'carries' prong of the statute prohibited only the 'unlawful' carrying of a firearm while committing an offense.

II

Section 924(c)(1), as the foregoing discussion details, is not decisively clear one way or another. The sharp division in the Court on the proper reading of the measure confirms, "[a]t the very least, . . . that the issue is subject to some doubt. Under these circumstances, we adhere to the familiar rule that, 'where there is ambiguity in a criminal statute, doubts are resolved in favor of the defendant.' " *Adamo Wrecking Co. v. United States,* 434 U.S. 275, 284-285 (1978) (citation omitted); *see United States v. Granderson,* 511 U.S. 39, 54 (1994) ("[W]here text, structure, and history fail to establish that the Government's position is unambiguously correct we apply the rule of lenity and resolve the ambiguity in [the defendant's] favor."). "Carry" bears many meanings, as the Court and the "Firearms" statutes demonstrate. The narrower "on or about [one's] person" interpretation is hardly implausible nor at odds with an accepted meaning of "carries a firearm."

Notably in view of the Legislature's capacity to speak plainly, and of overriding concern, the Court's inquiry pays scant attention to a core reason for the rule of lenity: "[B]ecause of the seriousness of criminal penalties, and because criminal punishment usually represents the moral condemnation of the community, legislatures and not courts should define criminal activity. This policy embodies 'the instinctive distaste against men languishing in prison unless the lawmaker has clearly said they should.' " *United States v. Bass,* 404 U.S. 336, 348 (1971) (quoting H. Friendly, Mr. Justice Frankfurter and the Reading of Statutes, in Benchmarks 196, 209 (1967)).

. . . [G]iven two readings of a penal provision, both consistent with the statutory text, we do not choose the harsher construction. The Court, in my view, should leave it to Congress to speak "in language that is clear and definite" if the Legislature wishes to impose the sterner penalty. *Bass,* 404 U.S. at 347.

Notes and Questions

1. The criminal provision at issue, 18 U.S.C. §924(c), provides that "whoever, during and in relation to any crime of violence or drug trafficking crime . . . uses or carries a firearm, shall, in addition to the punishment provided for such crime . . . be sentenced to imprisonment for five years." This provision subjects a defendant to a "mandatory minimum" sentence of five years in prison. The majority and dissenting justices invoke a wide array

---

The statute would thus not have applied to an individual who, for instance, had a permit for carrying a gun and carried it with him when committing an offense, and it would have had no force in 'persuading' such an individual 'to leave his gun at home.' Instead, Representative Poff was referring to the 'uses' prong of the original Secion 924(c)." Brief for United States in *Bailey v. United States,* O.T. 1995, Nos. 94-7448 and 94-7492, p. 28. Representative Poff's next sentence confirms that he was speaking of "uses," not "carries": "Any person should understand that if he *uses* his gun and is caught and convicted, he is going to jail." 114 Cong. Rec., at 22231 (emphasis added).

of sources, all with the aim of discerning the ordinary English meaning of the phrase "carries a firearm." Which sources are most persuasive in determining the meaning of a criminal statute: (1) the *Oxford English Dictionary*, (2) the *Barnhart Dictionary of Etymology*, (3) the Bible, (4) use in classic literature, such as *Moby Dick*, (5) use by the *New York Times*, or (6) *Black's Law Dictionary*?

2. If the Court was most interested in the "generally accepted *contemporary* meaning," would other sources be relevant? For example, what role would surveys about how the public understands "carrying a firearm" play? Would it matter if half the public did not think that "carrying a firearm" includes stowing a firearm in one's car?

3. One issue that divides the justices is whether to apply the rule of lenity, which is a substantive canon of construction. The rule of lenity directs courts to resolve "doubts" or ambiguities in criminal statutes in favor of criminal defendants. *See* Adamo Wrecking Co. v. United States, 434 U.S. 275, 284-85 (1978). We address the rule of lenity in the next section but want to flag a point here. If a statutory phrase has two possible "ordinary meanings," isn't it ambiguous enough for the rule of lenity to apply? How would the majority respond? Does it believe that the phrase is ambiguous?

4. In 1998, Congress amended §924(c)(1), making it an offense to "use or carry" a firearm "during and in relation to" a violent or drug offense, or to "posses[s]" a firearm "in furtherance of" such an offense. Congress also added further sentencing enhancements if a defendant actively uses the firearm, either by "brandish[ing]" or "discharg[ing]" it. The amendment was a response to Bailey v. United States, 516 U.S. 137 (1995), in which the Court held that a defendant must "actively employed the firearm during and in relation to the predicate crime" in order to "sustain a conviction under the 'use' prong" of the statute. *Id.* at 150. Congress has not amended the statute since. Does this amendment suggest that the Court interpreted "carry" correctly in *Muscarello*? What result under the amended version of the statute if the defendant accidentally "discharges" his firearm in the course of a violent crime, such as bank robbery? *See* Dean v. United States, 556 U.S. 558 (2009). What if a bank guard grabs the gun from the defendant and "discharges" it?

2. Textual Canons of Construction

The idea of consulting a dictionary or technical resource to ascertain the meaning of a word may seem familiar — it is a practice in which any reader might engage when confronted with an unknown word in a book or other document. But there are specific tools for statutes. Courts have developed a series of rules, principles, and presumptions for interpreting statutes collectively referred to "canons of construction." (Note that nothing magical turns on the classification of a particular tool as a "canon of construction"; that phrase is meant to cover any established tool for interpreting statutes.) Canons of construction can be divided into three broad categories: textual canons, substantive canons, and other canons (absurd results and scrivener's errors). This section addresses *textual canons*. Textual canons, which themselves fall into three subgroups, help courts to interpret statutory language based on surrounding text. First, *linguistic canons*, sometimes called grammar canons or syntactic canons, are rules or presumptions about how words fit together within a particular provision. If you are making an argument about the meaning of a term based on the grammar, punctuation, or associated words in a particular provision, you are invoking a linguistic canon. Second, *whole act canons* are presumptions or rules about the meaning of a term in relation to other terms, phrases, or provisions in the same statute. If you are comparing the text in one provision to the text in other provisions of the same statute, you are invoking a whole act canon. Third, *whole code canons* seek to make sense of a word in light of other statutes in the U.S. Code. If you are seeking to reconcile the text of one statute with the text of another statute or statutes, you are invoking a whole code canon. You can think of textual canons together as a sort of a global positioning system (GPS) for statutory text. Linguistic canons locate the meaning of a term or phrase by reference to its street, whole act canons by reference to its city, and whole code canons by reference to its state. Courts generally move from narrow to broad when applying these canons.

a. A Classic Example of Textual Canons

Before we examine particular textual canons, we want to give you a general feel for how they function. The following Supreme Court decision is a classic illustration of many of them. As you read this decision, try to identify canons in both the majority and dissenting opinions, and note how the canons interact with one another. In addition, note the ways in which the canons interact with other textual tools, such as dictionaries, in both the majority and dissenting opinions. Many describe this case as involving the "battle of the dictionaries" and the "battle of the canons." The case also involves judicial review of agency action; the Court is considering whether to uphold an interpretation that the Secretary of the Interior provided of the relevant statutory language. We will have much more to say about that aspect of the case in Chapters 5 and 6. For now, set aside that feature and concentrate on how the Court approaches the relevant statutory language.

Babbitt v. Sweet Home Chapter of Communities for a Great Oregon

515 U.S. 687 (1995)

Justice STEVENS delivered the opinion of the Court.

The Endangered Species Act of 1973 (ESA or Act), 16 U.S.C. §1531, contains a variety of protections designed to save from extinction species that the Secretary of the Interior designates as endangered or threatened. Section 9 of the Act makes it unlawful for any person to "take" any endangered or threatened species. The Secretary has promulgated a regulation that defines the statute's prohibition on takings to include "significant habitat modification or degradation where it actually kills or injures wild-life." This case presents the question whether the Secretary exceeded his authority under the Act by promulgating that regulation.

I

Section 9(a)(1) of the Act provides the following protection for endangered species:

> [No person shall] . . .
>
> "(B) take any such species within the United States or the territorial sea of the United States." 16 U.S.C. §1538(a)(1).

Section 3(19) of the Act defines the statutory term "take":

> "The term 'take' means to harass, harm, pursue, hunt, shoot, wound, kill, trap, capture, or collect, or to attempt to engage in any such conduct." 16 U.S.C. §1532(19).

The Act does not further define the terms it uses to define "take." The Interior Department regulations that implement the statute, however, define the statutory term "harm":

> "*Harm* in the definition of 'take' in the Act means an act which actually kills or injures wildlife. Such act may include significant habitat modification or degradation where it actually kills or injures wildlife by significantly impairing essential behavioral patterns, including breeding, feeding, or sheltering." 50 CFR §17.3 (1994).

This regulation has been in place since 1975.

A limitation on the §9 "take" prohibition appears in §10(a)(1)(B) of the Act, which Congress added by amendment in 1982. That section authorizes the Secretary to grant a permit for any taking otherwise prohibited by §9(a)(1)(B) "if such taking is incidental to, and not the purpose of, the carrying out of an otherwise lawful activity." 16 U.S.C. §1539(a)(1)(B).

In addition to the prohibition on takings, the Act provides several other protections for endangered species. Section 4, 16 U.S.C. §1533, commands the Secretary to identify species of fish or wildlife that are in danger of extinction and to publish from time to time lists of all species he determines to be endangered or threatened. Section 5, 16 U.S.C. §1534, authorizes the Secretary, in cooperation with the States, *see* §1535, to acquire land to aid in preserving such species. Section 7 requires federal agencies to ensure that none of their activities, including the granting of licenses and permits, will jeopardize the continued existence of endangered species "or result in the destruction or adverse modification of habitat of such species which is determined by the Secretary . . . to be critical." 16 U.S.C. §1536(a)(2).

Respondents in this action are small landowners, logging companies, and families dependent on the forest products industries in the Pacific Northwest and in the Southeast, and organizations that represent their interests. They brought this declaratory judgment action against petitioners, the Secretary of the Interior and the Director of the Fish and Wildlife Service, in the United States District Court for the District of Columbia to challenge the statutory validity of the Secretary's regulation defining "harm," particularly the inclusion of habitat modification and degradation in the definition. Respondents challenged the regulation on its face. Their complaint alleged that application of the "harm" regulation to the red-cockaded woodpecker, an endangered species, and the northern spotted owl, a threatened species, had injured them economically. . . .

II

. . . The text of the Act provides three reasons for concluding that the Secretary's interpretation is reasonable. First, an ordinary understanding of the word "harm" supports it. The dictionary definition of the verb form of "harm" is "to cause hurt or damage to: injure." Webster's Third New International Dictionary 1034 (1966). In the context of the ESA, that definition naturally encompasses habitat modification that results in actual injury or death to members of an endangered or threatened species.

Respondents argue that the Secretary should have limited the purview of "harm" to direct applications of force against protected species, but the dictionary definition does not include the word "directly" or suggest in any way that only direct or willful action that leads to injury constitutes "harm."[1] Moreover, unless the statutory term "harm" encompasses indirect as well as direct injuries, the word has no meaning that does not duplicate the meaning of other words that §3 uses to define "take." A reluctance to treat statutory terms as surplusage supports the reasonableness of the Secretary's interpretation. *See, e.g., Mackey v. Lanier Collection Agency & Service, Inc.*, 486 U.S. 825, 837, and n.11 (1988).[2]

Second, the broad purpose of the ESA supports the Secretary's decision to extend protection against activities that cause the precise harms Congress enacted the statute to avoid. In *TVA v. Hill*, 437 U.S. 153 (1978), we described the Act as "the most comprehensive legislation for the preservation of endangered species ever enacted by any nation." *Id.*, at 180. Whereas

---

1. Respondents and the dissent emphasize what they portray as the "established meaning" of "take" in the sense of a "wildlife take," a meaning respondents argue extends only to "the effort to exercise dominion over some creature, and the concrete effect of [*sic*] that creature." This limitation ill serves the statutory text, which forbids not taking "some creature" but "tak[ing] any [endangered] *species*" — a formidable task for even the most rapacious feudal lord. More importantly, Congress explicitly defined the operative term "take" in the ESA, no matter how much the dissent wishes otherwise, thereby obviating the need for us to probe its meaning as we must probe the meaning of the undefined subsidiary term "harm." Finally, Congress' definition of "take" includes several words — most obviously "harass," "pursue," and "wound," in addition to "harm" itself — that fit respondents' and the dissent's definition of "take" no better than does "significant habitat modification or degradation."

2. In contrast, if the statutory term "harm" encompasses such indirect means of killing and injuring wildlife as habitat modification, the other terms listed in §3 — "harass," "pursue," "hunt," "shoot," "wound," "kill," "trap," "capture," and "collect" — generally retain independent meanings. Most of those terms refer to deliberate actions more frequently than does "harm," and they therefore do not duplicate the sense of indirect causation that "harm" adds to the statute. In addition, most of the other words in the definition describe either actions from which habitat modification does not usually result (*e.g.*, "pursue," "harass") or effects to which activities that modify habitat do not usually lead (*e.g.*, "trap," "collect"). To the extent the Secretary's definition of "harm" may have applications that overlap with other words in the definition, that overlap reflects the broad purpose of the Act. *See infra.*

predecessor statutes enacted in 1966 and 1969 had not contained any sweeping prohibition against the taking of endangered species except on federal lands, *see id.*, at 175, the 1973 Act applied to all land in the United States and to the Nation's territorial seas. As stated in §2 of the Act, among its central purposes is "to provide a means whereby the ecosystems upon which endangered species and threatened species depend may be conserved. . . ." 16 U.S.C. §1531(b).

In *Hill*, we construed §7 as precluding the completion of the Tellico Dam because of its predicted impact on the survival of the snail darter. *See* 437 U.S., at 193. Both our holding and the language in our opinion stressed the importance of the statutory policy. "The plain intent of Congress in enacting this statute," we recognized, "was to halt and reverse the trend toward species extinction, whatever the cost. This is reflected not only in the stated policies of the Act, but in literally every section of the statute." *Id.*, at 184. Although the §9 "take" prohibition was not at issue in *Hill*, we took note of that prohibition, placing particular emphasis on the Secretary's inclusion of habitat modification in his definition of "harm." In light of that provision for habitat protection, we could "not understand how TVA intends to operate Tellico Dam without 'harming' the snail darter." *Id.*, at 184, n.30. Congress' intent to provide comprehensive protection for endangered and threatened species supports the permissibility of the Secretary's "harm" regulation.

Third, the fact that Congress in 1982 authorized the Secretary to issue permits for takings that §9(a)(1)(B) would otherwise prohibit, "if such taking is incidental to, and not the purpose of, the carrying out of an otherwise lawful activity," 16 U.S.C. §1539(a)(1)(B), strongly suggests that Congress understood §9(a)(1)(B) to prohibit indirect as well as deliberate takings. The permit process requires the applicant to prepare a "conservation plan" that specifies how he intends to "minimize and mitigate" the "impact" of his activity on endangered and threatened species, 16 U.S.C. §1539(a)(2)(A), making clear that Congress had in mind foreseeable rather than merely accidental effects on listed species. No one could seriously request an "incidental" take permit to avert §9 liability for direct, deliberate action against a member of an endangered or threatened species, but respondents would read "harm" so narrowly that the permit procedure would have little more than that absurd purpose. "When Congress acts to amend a statute, we presume it intends its amendment to have real and substantial effect." *Stone v. INS*, 514 U.S. 386, 397 (1995). Congress' addition of the §10 permit provision supports the Secretary's conclusion that activities not intended to harm an endangered species, such as habitat modification, may constitute unlawful takings under the ESA unless the Secretary permits them.

The Court of Appeals made three errors in asserting that "harm" must refer to a direct application of force because the words around it do. First, the court's premise was flawed. Several of the words that accompany "harm" in the §3 definition of "take," especially "harass," "pursue," "wound," and "kill," refer to actions or effects that do not require direct applications of force. Second, to the extent the court read a requirement of intent or purpose into the words used to define "take," it ignored §11's express provision that a "knowin[g]" action is enough to violate the Act. Third, the court employed *noscitur a sociis* to give "harm" essentially the same function as other words in the definition, thereby denying it independent meaning. The canon, to the contrary, counsels that a word "gathers meaning from the words around it." *Jarecki v. G.D. Searle & Co.*, 367 U.S. 303, 307 (1961). The statutory context of "harm" suggests that Congress meant that term to serve a particular function in the ESA, consistent with, but distinct from, the functions of the other verbs used to define "take." The Secretary's interpretation of "harm" to include indirectly injuring endangered animals through habitat modification permissibly interprets "harm" to have "a character of its own not to be submerged by its association." *Russell Motor Car Co. v. United States*, 261 U.S. 514, 519 (1923).

Nor does the Act's inclusion of the §5 land acquisition authority and the §7 directive to federal agencies to avoid destruction or adverse modification of critical habitat alter our conclusion. Respondents' argument that the Government lacks any incentive to purchase land under §5 when it can simply prohibit takings under §9 ignores the practical considerations that attend enforcement of the ESA. Purchasing habitat lands may well cost the Government less in many circumstances than pursuing civil or criminal penalties. In addition, the §5 procedure allows for protection of habitat before the seller's activity has harmed any endangered animal, whereas the Government cannot enforce the §9 prohibition until an animal has actually been killed or injured. The Secretary may also find the §5 authority useful for preventing modification of land that is not yet but may in the future become habitat for an endangered or threatened species. The §7 directive applies only to the Federal Government, whereas the §9 prohibition applies to "any person." Section 7 imposes a broad, affirmative duty to avoid adverse habitat modifications that §9 does not replicate, and §7 does not limit its admonition to habitat modification that "actually kills or injures wildlife." Conversely, §7 contains limitations that §9 does not, applying only to actions "likely to jeopardize the continued existence of any endangered species or threatened species," 16 U.S.C. §1536(a)(2), and to modifications of habitat that has been designated "critical" pursuant to §4, 16 U.S.C. §1533(b)(2). Any overlap that §5 or §7 may have with §9 in particular cases is unexceptional, and simply reflects the broad purpose of the Act set out in §2 and acknowledged in *TVA v. Hill.* . . .

III

Our conclusion that the Secretary's definition of "harm" rests on a permissible construction of the ESA gains further support from the legislative history of the statute. The Committee Reports accompanying the bills that became the ESA do not specifically discuss the meaning of "harm," but they make clear that Congress intended "take" to apply broadly to cover indirect as well as purposeful actions. The Senate Report stressed that "'[t]ake' is defined . . . in the broadest possible manner to include every conceivable

way in which a person can 'take' or attempt to 'take' any fish or wildlife."
S. Rep. No. 93-307, p. 7 (1973). The House Report stated that "the broadest
possible terms" were used to define restrictions on takings. H.R. Rep. No.
93-412, p. 15 (1973). The House Report underscored the breadth of the
"take" definition by noting that it included "harassment, *whether intentional
or not." Id.,* at 11 (emphasis added). The Report explained that the definition "would allow, for example, the Secretary to regulate or prohibit the
activities of birdwatchers where the effect of those activities might disturb
the birds and make it difficult for them to hatch or raise their young." *Ibid.*
These comments, ignored in the dissent's welcome but selective foray into
legislative history, support the Secretary's interpretation that the term "take"
in §9 reached far more than the deliberate actions of hunters and trappers.

Two endangered species bills, S. 1592 and S. 1983, were introduced in
the Senate and referred to the Commerce Committee. Neither bill included
the word "harm" in its definition of "take," although the definitions otherwise closely resembled the one that appeared in the bill as ultimately
enacted. *See* Hearings on S. 1592 and S. 1983 before the Subcommittee on
Environment of the Senate Committee on Commerce, 93d Cong., 1st Sess.,
pp. 7, 27 (1973) (hereinafter Hearings). Senator Tunney, the floor manager of the bill in the Senate, subsequently introduced a floor amendment
that added "harm" to the definition, noting that this and accompanying
amendments would "help to achieve the purposes of the bill." 119 Cong.
Rec. 25683 (1973). Respondents argue that the lack of debate about the
amendment that added "harm" counsels in favor of a narrow interpretation.
We disagree. An obviously broad word that the Senate went out of its way to
add to an important statutory definition is precisely the sort of provision that
deserves a respectful reading.

The definition of "take" that originally appeared in S. 1983 differed
from the definition as ultimately enacted in one other significant respect: It
included "the destruction, modification, or curtailment of [the] habitat or
range" of fish and wildlife. Hearings, at 27. Respondents make much of the
fact that the Commerce Committee removed this phrase from the "take"
definition before S. 1983 went to the floor. *See* 119 Cong. Rec. 25663 (1973).
We do not find that fact especially significant. The legislative materials contain no indication why the habitat protection provision was deleted. That
provision differed greatly from the regulation at issue today. Most notably,
the habitat protection provision in S. 1983 would have applied far more
broadly than the regulation does because it made adverse habitat modification a categorical violation of the "take" prohibition, unbounded by the
regulation's limitation to habitat modifications that actually kill or injure
wildlife. The S. 1983 language also failed to qualify "modification" with the
regulation's limiting adjective "significant." We do not believe the Senate's
unelaborated disavowal of the provision in S. 1983 undermines the reasonableness of the more moderate habitat protection in the Secretary's "harm"
regulation. . . .

The judgment of the Court of Appeals is reversed.

It is so ordered.

Justice SCALIA, with whom THE CHIEF JUSTICE and Justice THOMAS join, dissenting.

I think it unmistakably clear that the legislation at issue here (1) forbade the hunting and killing of endangered animals, and (2) provided federal lands and federal funds *for the acquisition of private lands,* to preserve the habitat of endangered animals. The Court's holding that the hunting and killing prohibition incidentally preserves habitat on private lands imposes unfairness to the point of financial ruin not just upon the rich, but upon the simplest farmer who finds his land conscripted to national zoological use. I respectfully dissent. . . .

If "take" were not elsewhere defined in the Act, none could dispute what it means, for the term is as old as the law itself. To "take," when applied to wild animals, means to reduce those animals, by killing or capturing, to human control. *See, e.g.,* 11 Oxford English Dictionary (1933) ("Take . . . To catch, capture (a wild beast, bird, fish, etc.)"); Webster's New International Dictionary of the English Language (2d ed. 1949) (take defined as "to catch or capture by trapping, snaring, etc., or as prey"); *Geer v. Connecticut,* 161 U.S. 519, 523 (1896) (" '[A]ll the animals which can be taken upon the earth, in the sea, or in the air, that is to say, wild animals, belong to those who take them' ") (quoting the Digest of Justinian); 2 W. Blackstone, Commentaries 411 (1766) ("Every man . . . has an equal right of pursuing and taking to his own use all such creatures as are *ferae naturae*"). This is just the sense in which "take" is used elsewhere in federal legislation and treaty. *See, e.g.,* Migratory Bird Treaty Act, 16 U.S.C. §703 (no person may "pursue, hunt, take, capture, kill, [or] attempt to take, capture, or kill" any migratory bird); Agreement on the Conservation of Polar Bears, Nov. 15, 1973, Art. I, 27 U.S.T. 3918, 3921, T.I.A.S. No. 8409 (defining "taking" as "hunting, killing and capturing"). And that meaning fits neatly with the rest of §1538(a)(1), which makes it unlawful not only to take protected species, but also to import or export them, §1538(a)(1)(A); to possess, sell, deliver, carry, transport, or ship any taken species, §1538(a)(1)(D); and to transport, sell, or offer to sell them in interstate or foreign commerce, §§1538(a)(1)(E), (F). The taking prohibition, in other words, is only part of the regulatory plan of §1538(a)(1), which covers all the stages of the process by which protected wildlife is reduced to man's dominion and made the object of profit. It is obvious that "take" in this sense a term of art deeply embedded in the statutory and common law concerning wildlife describes a class of acts (not omissions) done directly and intentionally (not indirectly and by accident) to particular animals (not populations of animals).

The Act's definition of "take" does expand the word slightly (and not unusually), so as to make clear that it includes not just a completed taking, but the process of taking, and all of the acts that are customarily identified with or accompany that process ("to harass, harm, pursue, hunt, shoot, wound, kill, trap, capture, or collect"); and so as to include attempts. §1532(19). The tempting fallacy which the Court commits with abandon is to assume that *once defined*, "take" loses any significance, and it is only the definition that matters. The Court treats the statute as though Congress had directly enacted the §1532(19) definition as a self-executing prohibition, and had not enacted §1538(a)(1)(B) at all. But §1538(a)(1)(B) *is* there, and if the terms contained in the definitional section are susceptible of two readings, one of which comports with the standard meaning of "take" as used in application to wildlife, and one of which does not, an agency regulation that adopts the latter reading is necessarily unreasonable, for it reads the defined term "take" — the only operative term — out of the statute altogether.[3]

That is what has occurred here. The verb "harm" has a *range* of meaning: "to cause injury" at its broadest, "to do hurt or damage" in a narrower and more direct sense. *See, e.g.,* 1 N. Webster, An American Dictionary of the English Language (1828) ("Harm, *v.t.* To hurt; to injure; to damage; *to impair soundness of body, either animal* or vegetable") (emphasis added); American College Dictionary 551 (1970) ("harm . . . *n.* injury; damage; hurt: *to do him bodily harm*"). In fact the more directed sense of "harm" is a somewhat more common and preferred usage; "*harm* has in it a little of the idea of specially focused hurt or injury, as if a personal injury has been anticipated and intended." J. Opdycke, Mark My Words: A Guide to Modern Usage and Expression 330 (1949). *See also* American Heritage Dictionary 662 (1985) ("*Injure* has the widest range. . . . *Harm* and *hurt* refer principally to what causes physical or mental distress to living things"). To define "harm" as an act or omission that, however remotely, "actually kills or injures" a population of wildlife through habitat modification is to choose a meaning that makes nonsense of the word that "harm" defines requiring us to accept that a farmer who tills his field and causes erosion that makes silt run into a nearby river which depletes oxygen and thereby "impairs [the] breeding" of protected fish has "taken" or "attempted to take" the fish. It should take the strongest evidence to make us believe that Congress has defined a term in a manner repugnant to its ordinary and traditional sense.

Here the evidence shows the opposite. "Harm" is merely one of 10 prohibitory words in §1532(19), and the other 9 fit the ordinary meaning of "take" perfectly. To "harass, pursue, hunt, shoot, wound, kill, trap, capture, or collect" are all affirmative acts (the provision itself describes them as "conduct," *see* §1532(19)) which are directed immediately and intentionally against a particular animal not acts or omissions that indirectly and

---

3. The Court suggests halfheartedly that "take" cannot refer to the taking of particular animals, because §1538(a)(1)(B) prohibits "tak[ing] any [endangered] *species*." The suggestion is halfhearted because that reading obviously contradicts the statutory intent. It would mean no violation in the intentional shooting of a single bald eagle—or, for that matter, the intentional shooting of 1,000 bald eagles out of the extant 1,001. The phrasing of §1538(a)(1)(B), as the Court recognizes elsewhere, is shorthand for "take any *member of* an endangered] species."

accidentally cause injury to a population of animals. The Court points out that several of the words ("harass," "pursue," "wound," and "kill") "refer to actions or effects that do not require direct *applications of force.*" (emphasis added). That is true enough, but force is not the point. Even "taking" activities in the narrowest sense, activities traditionally engaged in by hunters and trappers, do not all consist of direct applications of force; pursuit and harassment are part of the business of "taking" the prey even before it has been touched. What the nine other words in §1532(19) have in common and share with the narrower meaning of "harm" described above, but not with the Secretary's ruthless dilation of the word is the sense of affirmative conduct intentionally directed against a particular animal or animals.

I am not the first to notice this fact, or to draw the conclusion that it compels. In 1981 the Solicitor of the Fish and Wildlife Service delivered a legal opinion on §1532(19) that is in complete agreement with my reading:

> "The Act's definition of 'take' contains a list of actions that illustrate the intended scope of the term. . . . With the possible exception of 'harm,' these terms all represent forms of conduct that are directed against and likely to injure or kill *individual* wildlife. Under the principle of statutory construction, *ejusdem generis,* . . . the term 'harm' should be interpreted to include only those actions that are directed against, and likely to injure or kill, individual wildlife." Memorandum of Apr. 17, reprinted in 46 Fed. Reg. 29490, 29491 (1981) (emphasis in original).

I would call it *noscitur a sociis,* but the principle is much the same: The fact that "several items in a list share an attribute counsels in favor of interpreting the other items as possessing that attribute as well," *Beecham v. United States,* 511 U.S. 368, 371 (1994). The Court contends that the canon cannot be applied to deprive a word of all its "independent meaning." That proposition is questionable to begin with, especially as applied to long lawyers' listings such as this. If it were true, we ought to give the word "trap" in the definition its rare meaning of "to clothe" (whence "trappings") since otherwise it adds nothing to the word "capture." *See Moskal v. United States,* 498 U.S. 103, 120 (1990) (Scalia, J., dissenting). In any event, the Court's contention that "harm" in the narrow sense adds nothing to the other words underestimates the ingenuity of our own species in a way that Congress did not. To feed an animal poison, to spray it with mace, to chop down the very tree in which it is nesting, or even to destroy its entire habitat in order to take it (as by draining a pond to get at a turtle), might neither wound nor kill, but would directly and intentionally harm. . . .

So far I have discussed only the immediate statutory text bearing on the regulation. But the definition of "take" in §1532(19) applies "[f]or the purposes of this chapter," that is, it governs the meaning of the word *as used everywhere in the Act.* Thus, the Secretary's interpretation of "harm" is wrong if it does not fit with the use of "take" throughout the Act. And it does not. In §1540(e)(4)(B), for example, Congress provided for the forfeiture of "[a]ll guns, traps, nets, and other equipment . . . used to aid the taking, possessing, selling, [etc.]" of protected animals. This listing plainly relates to "taking" in the ordinary sense. If environmental modification were part (and necessarily a major part) of taking, as the Secretary maintains, one would have expected the list to include "plows, bulldozers, and backhoes." As another example, §1539(e)(1) exempts "the taking of any endangered species" by Alaskan Indians and Eskimos "if such taking is primarily for subsistence purposes"; and provides that "[n]on-edible byproducts of species taken pursuant to this section may be sold . . . when made into authentic native articles of handicrafts and clothing." Surely these provisions apply to taking only in the ordinary sense, and are meaningless as applied to species injured by environmental modification. The Act is full of like examples. *See, e.g.,* §1538(a)(1)(D) (prohibiting possession, sale, and transport of "species taken in violation" of the Act). "[I]f the Act is to be interpreted as a symmetrical and coherent regulatory scheme, one in which the operative words have a consistent meaning throughout," *Gustafson v. Alloyd Co.,* 513 U.S. 561, 569 (1995), the regulation must fall.

The broader structure of the Act confirms the unreasonableness of the regulation. Section 1536 provides:

> "Each Federal agency shall . . . insure that any action authorized, funded, or carried out by such agency . . . is not likely to jeopardize the continued existence of any endangered species or threatened species or *result in the destruction or adverse modification of habitat* of such species which is determined by the Secretary . . . to be critical." 16 U.S.C. §1536(a)(2) (emphasis added).

The Act defines "critical habitat" as habitat that is "essential to the conservation of the species," §§1532(5)(A)(i), (A)(ii), with "conservation" in turn defined as the use of methods necessary to bring listed species "to the point at which the measures provided pursuant to this chapter are no longer necessary," §1532(3).

These provisions have a double significance. Even if §§1536(a)(2) and 1538(a)(1)(B) were totally independent prohibitions the former applying only to federal agencies and their licensees, the latter only to private parties Congress's explicit prohibition of habitat modification in the one section would bar the inference of an implicit prohibition of habitat modification in the other section. "[W]here Congress includes particular language in one section of a statute but omits it in another . . . , it is generally presumed that Congress acts intentionally and purposely in the disparate inclusion or exclusion." *Keene Corp. v. United States,* 508 U.S. 200, 208 (1993). And that presumption against implicit prohibition would be even stronger where the one section which uses the language carefully defines and limits its application. That is to say, it would be passing strange for Congress carefully to define "critical habitat" as used in §1536(a)(2), but leave it to the Secretary to evaluate, willy-nilly, impermissible "habitat modification" (under the guise of "harm") in §1538(a)(1)(B).

In fact, however, §§1536(a)(2) and 1538(a)(1)(B) do *not* operate in separate realms; federal agencies are subject to *both,* because the "person[s]" forbidden to take protected species under §1538 include agencies and departments of the Federal Government. *See* §1532(13). This means that the "harm" regulation also contradicts another principle of interpretation: that statutes should be read so far as possible to give independent effect to all their provisions. *See Ratzlaf v. United States,* 510 U.S. 135, 140-141 (1994). By defining "harm" in the definition of "take" in §1538(a)(1)(B) to include significant habitat modification that injures populations of wildlife, the regulation makes the habitat-modification restriction in §1536(a)(2) almost wholly superfluous. As "critical habitat" is habitat "essential to the conservation of the species," adverse modification of "critical" habitat by a federal agency would also constitute habitat modification that injures a population of wildlife. . . .

The Court maintains that the legislative history of the 1973 Act supports the Secretary's definition. Even if legislative history were a legitimate and reliable tool of interpretation (which I shall assume in order to rebut the Court's claim); and even if it could appropriately be resorted to when the enacted text is as clear as this, but see *Chicago v. Environmental Defense Fund,* 511 U.S. 328, 337 (1994); here it shows quite the opposite of what the Court says. I shall not pause to discuss the Court's reliance on such statements in the Committee Reports as " '[t]ake' is defined . . . in the broadest possible manner to include every conceivable way in which a person can 'take' or attempt to 'take' any fish or wildlife.' " S. Rep. No. 93-307, p. 7 (1973) U.S. Code Cong. & Admin. News 1973, pg. 2995. This sort of empty flourish — to the effect that "this statute means what it means all the way" — counts for little even when enacted into the law itself. See *Reves v. Ernst & Young,* 507 U.S. 170, 183-184 (1993).

Much of the Court's discussion of legislative history is devoted to two items: first, the Senate floor manager's introduction of an amendment that added the word "harm" to the definition of "take," with the observation that (along with other amendments) it would " 'help to achieve the purposes of the bill' "; second, the relevant Committee's removal from the definition of a provision stating that "take" includes " 'the destruction, modification or curtailment of [the] habitat or range' " of fish and wildlife. The Court inflates the first and belittles the second, even though the second is on its face far more pertinent. But this elaborate inference from various pre-enactment actions and inactions is quite unnecessary, since we have *direct* evidence of what those who brought the legislation to the floor thought it meant — evidence as solid as any ever to be found in legislative history, but which the Court banishes to a footnote.

Both the Senate and House floor managers of the bill explained it in terms which leave no doubt that the problem of habitat destruction on private lands was to be solved principally by the land acquisition program of §1534, while §1538 solved a different problem altogether — the problem of takings. Senator Tunney stated:

> "*Through [the] land acquisition provisions, we will be able to conserve habitats necessary to protect fish and wildlife from further destruction.*
>
> "Although most endangered species are threatened primarily by the destruction of their natural habitats, a significant portion of these animals are subject to *predation by man for commercial, sport, consumption, or other purposes.* The provisions of [the bill] would

prohibit the commerce in or the importation, exportation, or taking of endangered species. . . ." 119 Cong. Rec. 25669 (1973) (emphasis added).

The House floor manager, Representative Sullivan, put the same thought in this way:

> "[T]he principal threat to animals stems from destruction of their habitat. . . . [*The bill*] *will meet this problem by providing funds for acquisition of critical habitat.* . . . It will also enable the Department of Agriculture to cooperate with willing landowners who desire to assist in the protection of endangered species, *but who are understandably unwilling to do so at excessive cost to themselves.*
>
> "Another hazard to endangered species arises from those who would *capture or kill them for pleasure or profit.* There is no way that the Congress can make it less pleasurable for a person to take an animal, but we can certainly make it less profitable for them to do so." *Id.,* at 30162 (emphasis added).

Habitat modification and takings, in other words, were viewed as different problems, addressed by different provisions of the Act. The Court really has no explanation for these statements. All it can say is that "[n]either statement even suggested that [the habitat acquisition funding provision in §1534] would be the Act's exclusive remedy for habitat modification by private landowners or that habitat modification by private landowners stood outside the ambit of [§1538]." That is to say, the statements are not as bad as they might have been. Little in life is. They are, however, quite bad enough to destroy the Court's legislative-history case, since they display the clear understanding (1) that habitat modification is separate from "taking," and (2) that habitat destruction on private lands is to be remedied by public acquisition, and *not* by making particular unlucky landowners incur "excessive cost to themselves." The Court points out triumphantly that they do not display the understanding (3) that the land acquisition program is "the [Act's] only response to habitat modification." *Ibid.* Of course not, since that is not so (all *public* lands are subject to habitat-modification restrictions); but (1) and (2) are quite enough to exclude the Court's interpretation. They identify the land acquisition program as the Act's only response to habitat modification *by private landowners,* and thus do not in the least "contradic[t]," the fact that §1536 prohibits habitat modification *by federal agencies.* . . .

[T]he Court seeks support from a provision that was added to the Act in 1982, the year after the Secretary promulgated the current regulation. The provision states:

> "[T]he Secretary may permit, under such terms and conditions as he shall prescribe—
>
> . . .
>
> "any taking otherwise prohibited by section 1538(a)(1)(B) . . . if such taking is incidental to, and not the purpose of, the carrying out of an otherwise lawful activity." 16 U.S.C. §1539(a)(1)(B).

This provision does not, of course, implicate our doctrine that reenactment of a statutory provision ratifies an extant judicial or administrative interpretation, for neither the taking prohibition in §1538(a)(1)(B) nor the definition in §1532(19) was reenacted. See *Central Bank of Denver, N.A. v. First*

Interstate Bank of Denver, N.A., 511 U.S. 164, 185 (1994). The Court claims, however, that the provision "strongly suggests that Congress understood [§1538(a)(1)(B)] to prohibit indirect as well as deliberate takings." That would be a valid inference if habitat modification were the only substantial "otherwise lawful activity" that might incidentally and nonpurposefully cause a prohibited "taking." Of course it is not. This provision applies to the many otherwise lawful takings that incidentally take a protected species — as when fishing for unprotected salmon also takes an endangered species of salmon, see *Pacific Northwest Generating Cooperative v. Brown*, 38 F.3d 1058, 1067 (CA9 1994). Congress has referred to such "incidental takings" in other statutes as well — for example, a statute referring to "the incidental taking of . . . sea turtles in the course of . . . harvesting [shrimp]" and to the "rate of incidental taking of sea turtles by United States vessels in the course of such harvesting," 103 Stat. 1038, §609(b)(2), note following 16 U.S.C. §1537 (1988 ed., Supp. V); and a statute referring to "the incidental taking of marine mammals in the course of commercial fishing operations," 108 Stat. 546, §118(a). The Court shows that it misunderstands the question when it says that "[n]o one could seriously request an 'incidental' take permit to avert . . . liability for direct, deliberate action *against a member of an endangered or threatened species.*" (emphasis added). That is not an *incidental* take at all.

This is enough to show, in my view, that the 1982 permit provision does not support the regulation. I must acknowledge that the Senate Committee Report on this provision, and the House Conference Committee Report, clearly contemplate that it will enable the Secretary to permit environmental modification. See S. Rep. No. 97-418, p. 10 (1982); H.R. Conf. Rep. No. 97-835, pp. 30-32 (1982). But the *text* of the amendment cannot possibly bear that asserted meaning, when placed within the context of an Act that must be interpreted (as we have seen) not to prohibit private environmental modification. The neutral language of the amendment cannot possibly alter that interpretation, nor can its legislative history be summoned forth to contradict, rather than clarify, what is in its totality an unambiguous statutory text. See *Chicago v. Environmental Defense Fund*, 511 U.S. 328 302 (1994). There is little fear, of course, that giving no effect to the relevant portions of the Committee Reports will frustrate the real-life expectations of a majority of the Members of Congress. If they read and relied on such tedious detail on such an obscure point (it was not, after all, presented as a revision of the statute's prohibitory scope, but as a discretionary-waiver provision) the Republic would be in grave peril. . . .

The Endangered Species Act is a carefully considered piece of legislation that forbids all persons to hunt or harm endangered animals, but places upon the public at large, rather than upon fortuitously accountable individual landowners, the cost of preserving the habitat of endangered species. There is neither textual support for, nor even evidence of congressional consideration of, the radically different disposition contained in the regulation that the Court sustains. For these reasons, I respectfully dissent.

Notes and Questions

1. Are you clear on the statutory provisions at issue in *Sweet Home?* The case involves two provisions — an operative provision (no person shall "take any such species within the United States or the territorial sea of the United States," 16 U.S.C. §1538(a)(1)) and a definition ("The term 'take' means to harass, harm, pursue, hunt, shoot, wound, kill, trap, capture, or collect, or to attempt to engage in any such conduct." 16 U.S.C. §1532(19)). The agency responsible for implementing the statute had issued a regulation further defining "harm" to include "significant habitat modification or degradation where it actually kills or injures wildlife by significantly impairing essential behavioral patterns, including breeding, feeding, or sheltering." 50 C.F.R. §17.3 (1994). Thus, the question in the case is whether "take," defined to include "harm," can include "significant habitat modification or degradation where it actually kills or injures wildlife by significantly impairing essential behavioral patterns, including breeding, feeding, or sheltering."

2. After reading the decision, you can see why *Sweet Home* is regarded as involving a battle of the dictionaries and the canons. The majority and dissenting opinions show that the same tools of statutory interpretation — dictionaries and canons — can be deployed to reach different results. In the end, how helpful were the dictionary definitions of "harm" to either the majority or the dissent? Did they resolve the dispute?

3. Now let's focus on the canons. Because "harm" appears in a list of terms, it is a prime candidate for one of the linguistic canons. Justice Stevens, writing for the majority, says that if "harm" does not extend to indirect harms, then the word is mere surplusage. Are you convinced? The other words in the provision besides "harm" are "harass, pursue, hunt, shoot, wound, kill, trap, capture, or collect." Those terms seem to refer to deliberate actions, so "harm" must have added indirect actions. Can you imagine a direct action that harm might add?

4. Justice Stevens also applies the whole act rule in support of his interpretation, reconciling his interpretation of §9 with several other provisions of the statute. He consults the purpose provision, which suggests that the Act extends to all activities that cause harm. He argues that §10 would not require a permit for "incidental" takings if such takings were already lawful. He rejects an argument that §5, which authorizes the Government to buy private land to prevent habitat destruction, is the exclusive means of preventing habitat destruction. Rather, he states that §5 provides an alternative means of preventing habitat destruction when the Government deems it cheaper or easier to acquire habitat land than to enforce §9.

5. Justice Scalia, in his dissenting opinion, chooses a linguistic canon that supports a narrow definition of the words "take" and "harm." He relies on *noscitur a sociis*, which directs courts to construe words in a list to have a common meaning. Thus, "harm" takes shape by the company it keeps. Because all the other words in the list concern direct actions, "harm" also concerns direct actions. Are you convinced? Is direct action the only way to link the terms?

6. Justice Scalia also employs the whole act rule but reaches the opposite conclusion from Justice Stevens. He finds that the word "take" is used to mean direct actions in other parts of the statute. He notes that the statute expressly prohibits the government from modifying a habitat, and he therefore refuses to imply that it prohibits private parties from modifying a habitat. This is especially true because the statute defines "critical habitat" destruction for purposes of §7 but not §9, which would leave the Secretary free to define habitat destruction by private parties "willy-nilly." Which argument is more persuasive?

7. Although we mean to focus you on textual canons, consider for a moment which side has the better view of the legislative history. After Justice Scalia has his say, does the legislative history strike you as helpful to Justice Stevens or harmful (pun intended)? We will have much more to say about the use of legislative history later in this chapter.

8. A brief note about the role of the agency interpretation in this case. The bottom line is that the Court actually decided less about the Endangered Species Act than it might seem. The Court decided that the Act *permits* the interpretation that the Secretary picked but does not actually *require* that interpretation. In other words, the agency interpretation was reasonable and therefore entitled to deference. Again, we merely want to raise this issue for later. Our principal reason for studying *Sweet Home* here is to appreciate the operation of the canons.

b. Linguistic Canons

With *Sweet Home* as background, we now examine the principal textual canons and their (overlapping) applications. We begin with linguistic canons. Linguistic canons are useful for interpreting words in the narrowest context in which they appear: within a provision of a statute. Thus, they are useful for determining how a word fits with other words in the same provision. They are also useful for assessing the effect of grammar and punctuation.

The three most prominent of these canons are known by Latin phrases: *ejusdem generis* ("of the same kind"), *noscitur a sociis* ("a thing is known by its companions"), and *expressio unius est exclusio alterius* ("the mention of one thing is the exclusion of another"). They are rules of association among words in a phrase or provision.

i. Ejusdem generis

According to *ejusdem generis*, "when a statute sets out a series of specific items ending with a general term, that general term is confined to covering subjects comparable to the specifics it follows." Hall Street Associates, L.L.C. v. Mattel, Inc., 552 U.S. 576, 586 (2008); *see also* E.A. Driedger, On the Construction of Statutes 135 (3d ed. 1995) ("Where general words are found, following an enumeration of persons or things all susceptible of being regarded as specimens of a single genus or category, but not exhaustive thereof, their construction should be restricted to things of that class or category.").

In Yates v. United States, 135 S. Ct. 1074, 1086-87 (2015), the Court confronted a question concerning a provision in 18 U.S.C. §1519 that made it a crime to destroy or conceal "any record, document, or tangible object" to obstruct a federal investigation. The Court held that the term "tangible object" does not include a fish. Instead, it only encompasses objects that compile information. The Court reasoned:

> [E]*jusdem generis*, counsels: "Where general words follow specific words in a statutory enumeration, the general words are [usually] construed to embrace only objects similar in nature to those objects enumerated by the preceding specific words." *Washington State Dept. of Social and Health Servs. v. Guardianship Estate of Keffeler*, 537 U.S. 371, 384 (2003) (internal quotation marks omitted). In *Begay v. United States*, 553 U.S. 137, 142-143 (2008), for example, we relied on this principle to determine what crimes were covered by the statutory phrase "any crime . . . that . . . is burglary, arson, or extortion, involves use of explosives, or otherwise involves conduct that presents a serious potential risk of physical injury to another," 18 U.S.C. § 924(e)(2)(B)(ii). The enumeration of specific crimes, we explained, indicates that the "otherwise involves" provision covers "only *similar* crimes, rather than *every* crime that 'presents a serious potential risk of physical injury to another.'" 553 U.S., at 142. Had Congress intended the latter "all encompassing" meaning, we observed, "it is hard to see why it would have needed to include the examples at all." Ibid. See also *CSX Transp., Inc. v. Alabama Dept. of Revenue*, 562 U.S. 277, __, 131 S. Ct. 1101, 1113, (2011) ("We typically use *ejusdem generis* to ensure that a general word will not render specific words meaningless."). Just so here. Had Congress intended "tangible object" in §1519 to be interpreted so generically as to capture physical objects as dissimilar as documents and fish, Congress would have had no reason to refer specifically to "record" or "document." The Government's unbounded reading of "tangible object" would render those words misleading surplusage.

The Court also held that *noscitur a sociis* compels the same conclusion. After you read more about that canon below, ask if you can see why.

As you can see from the cases described in *Yates*, *ejusdem generis* is often useful when specific items are followed by a general phrase that begins with "otherwise." It is also helpful when specific items are followed by a general term that begins with "or other." In addition, you can see that *ejusdem generis* cannot be used to obscure the clear meaning of specific words. In United States v. Alpers, 338 U.S. 680, 682-83 (2015), the Court stated:

> When properly applied, the rule of ejusdem generis is a useful canon of construction. But it is to be resorted to not to obscure and defeat the intent and purpose of Congress, but to elucidate its words and effectuate its intent. It cannot be employed to render general words meaningless. *Mason v. United States*, 260 U.S. 545, 554. What is or is not a proper case for application of the rule was discussed in *Gooch v. United States*, 297 U.S. 124. In that case a bandit and a companion had kidnaped two police officers for the purpose of avoiding arrest and had transported them across a state line. The defendant was convicted of kidnaping under a federal statute which made it an offense to transport across state lines any person who had been kidnaped "and held for ransom or reward or otherwise." The police officers had been held not for ransom or reward but for protection, and it was contended that the words "or otherwise" did not cover the defendant's conduct, since under the rule of ejusdem generis, the general phrase was limited in meaning to some kind of monetary reward. This Court rejected

such limiting application of the rule, saying: "The rule of ejusdem generis, while firmly established, is only an instrumentality for ascertaining the correct meaning of words when there is uncertainty. Ordinarily, it limits general terms which follow specific ones to matters similar to those specified; but it may not be used to defeat the obvious purpose of legislation. And, while penal statutes are narrowly construed, this does not require rejection of that sense of the words which best harmonizes with the context and the end in view." 297 U.S. at page 128, 56 S. Ct. at page 397.

We think that to apply the rule of ejusdem generis to the present case would be "to defeat the obvious purpose of legislation."

ii. Noscitur a sociis

Under the canon of *noscitur a sociis,* "a word is known by the company it keeps." Jarecki v. G.D. Searle & Co., 367 U.S. 303, 307 (1961). This canon aims to ensure that a term is interpreted consistently with surrounding words so as not to unduly expand statutes beyond their reasonable reach. *Noscitur a sociis* is a close cousin of *ejusdem generis,* even a specific application of it. As a result, the two are often used interchangeably.

In Dolan v. United States Postal Service, 546 U.S. 481, 485 (2006), the plaintiff tripped over an item that the postal carrier had negligently left on his porch. He sued the Postal Service, which pointed to a statutory provision barring claims arising from "loss, miscarriage, or negligent transmission of letters or postal matter," 28 U.S.C. §2680(b). The Court had to decide whether this language precluded the plaintiff's claim. To do so, it relied on *noscitur a sociis*:

> The definition of words in isolation, however, is not necessarily controlling in statutory construction. A word in a statute may or may not extend to the outer limits of its definitional possibilities. Interpretation of a word or phrase depends upon reading the whole statutory text, considering the purpose and context of the statute, and consulting any precedents or authorities that inform the analysis. Here, we conclude both context and precedent require a narrower reading, so that "negligent transmission" does not go beyond negligence causing mail to be lost or to arrive late, in damaged condition, or at the wrong address. . . . The phrase does not comprehend all negligence occurring in the course of mail delivery.
>
> Starting with context, the words "negligent transmission" in §2680(b) follow two other terms, "loss" and "miscarriage." Those terms, we think, limit the reach of "transmission." "[A] word is known by the company it keeps" a rule that "is often wisely applied where a word is capable of many meanings in order to avoid the giving of unintended breadth to the Acts of Congress." *Jarecki v. G.D. Searle & Co.,* 367 U.S. 303, 307 (1961); *see also Dole v. Steelworkers,* 494 U.S. 26, 36 (1990) ("[W]ords grouped in a list should be given related meaning" (internal quotation marks and citations omitted)). Here, as both parties acknowledge, mail is "lost" if it is destroyed or misplaced and "miscarried" if it goes to the wrong address. Since both those terms refer to failings in the postal obligation to deliver mail in a timely manner to the right address, it would be odd if "negligent transmission" swept far more broadly to include injuries like those alleged here — injuries that happen to be caused by postal employees but involve neither failure to transmit mail nor damage to its contents.

Id. at 486-87.

In United States v. Williams, 553 U.S. 285, 294 (2008), the Supreme Court employed *noscitur a sociis* in determining whether a child pornography criminal statute was overbroad under the First Amendment (that is, prohibits a substantial amount of constitutionally protected speech). The statute subjected to criminal penalties anyone who knowingly "advertises, promotes, presents, distributes, or solicits" through the mail or other sources child pornography. 18 U.S.C. §2252A. The Court read "promotes" and "presents" in view of the accompanying words:

> "[T]he statute's string of operative verbs — 'advertises, promotes, presents, distributes, or solicits' — is reasonably read to have a transactional connotation. That is to say, the statute penalizes speech that accompanies or seeks to induce a transfer of child pornography — via reproduction or physical delivery — from one person to another. For three of the verbs, this is obvious: advertising, distributing, and soliciting are steps taken in the course of an actual or proposed transfer of a product, typically but not exclusively in a commercial market. When taken in isolation, the two remaining verbs — 'promotes' and 'presents' — are susceptible of multiple and wide-ranging meanings. In context, however, those meanings are narrowed by the commonsense canon of *noscitur a sociis* — which counsels that a word is given more precise content by the neighboring words with which it is associated. *See Jarecki v. G.D. Searle & Co.,* 367 U.S. 303, 307 (1961); 2A N. Singer & J. Singer, Sutherland Statutes and Statutory Construction §47.16 (7th ed. 2007). 'Promotes,' in a list that includes 'solicits,' 'distributes,' and 'advertises,' is most sensibly read to mean the act of recommending purported child pornography to another person for his acquisition. *See* American Heritage Dictionary 1403 (4th ed. 2000) (def. 4: 'To attempt to sell or popularize by advertising or publicity'). Similarly, 'presents,' in the context of the other verbs with which it is associated, means showing or offering the child pornography to another person with a view to his acquisition. *See id.,* at 1388 (def. 3a: 'To make a gift or award of')."

Id. at 294-95. *See also* Gustafson v. Alloyd Co., 513 U.S. 561, 575-76 (1995) (relying on *noscitur a sociis*).

Lagos v. United States, 138 S. Ct. 1684, 1687-89 (2018), provides an example involving the Mandatory Victims Restitution Act, which requires defendants convicted of "crime[s] of violence" and "offense[s] against property" to pay their victims restitution. 18 U.S.C. §3663A(c)(1)(A). In the case of property offenses, it requires return of the property taken or its value, §3663A(b)(1); in the case of bodily injury, it requires the payment of medical expenses and lost income, §3663A(b)(1); in the case of death, it requires the payment of funeral expenses, §3663A(b)(3); and, in all cases, it requires "reimburse[ment]" to "the victim for lost income and necessary child care, transportation, and other expenses incurred during participation i*n the investigation or prosecution of the offense or attendance at proceedings related to the offense.*" §3663A(b)(4) (emphasis added).

> We here consider the meaning of that italicized phrase. Specifically, we ask whether the scope of the words "investigation" and "proceedings" is limited to government investigations and criminal proceedings, or whether it includes private investigations and civil or bankruptcy litigation. We conclude that those words are limited to government investigations and criminal proceedings.
>
> Our conclusion rests in large part upon the statute's wording, both its individual words and the text taken as a whole. The individual words suggest (though they do not demand) our limited interpretation. The word "investigation" is directly linked by the word "or" to the word "prosecution," with which it shares the article "the." This suggests that the "investigation[s]" and "prosecution[s]" that the statute refers to are of

the same general type. And the word "prosecution" must refer to a government's criminal prosecution, which suggests that the word "investigation" may refer to a government's criminal investigation. A similar line of reasoning suggests that the immediately following reference to "proceedings" also refers to criminal proceedings in particular, rather than to "proceedings" of any sort.

Furthermore, there would be an awkwardness about the statute's use of the word "participation" to refer to a victim's role in its own private investigation, and the word "attendance" to refer to a victim's role as a party in noncriminal court proceedings. A victim opting to pursue a private investigation of an offense would be more naturally said to "provide for" or "conduct" the private investigation (in which he may, or may not, actively "participate"). And a victim who pursues civil or bankruptcy litigation does not merely "atten[d]" such other "proceedings related to the offense" but instead "participates" in them as a party. In contrast, there is no awkwardness, indeed it seems perfectly natural, to say that a victim "participat[es] in the investigation" or "attend[s] . . . proceedings related to the offense" if the investigation at issue is a government's criminal investigation, and if the proceedings at issue are criminal proceedings conducted by a government.

Moreover, to consider the statutory phrase as a whole strengthens these linguistic points considerably. The phrase lists three specific items that must be reimbursed, namely, lost income, child care, and transportation; and it then adds the words, "and other expenses." §3663A(b)(4). Lost income, child care expenses, and transportation expenses are precisely the kind of expenses that a victim would be likely to incur when he or she (or, for a corporate victim like GE, its employees) misses work and travels to talk to government investigators, to participate in a government criminal investigation, or to testify before a grand jury or attend a criminal trial. At the same time, the statute says nothing about the kinds of expenses a victim would often incur when private investigations, or, say, bankruptcy proceedings are at issue, namely, the costs of hiring private investigators, attorneys, or accountants. Thus, if we look to noscitur a sociis, the well-worn Latin phrase that tells us that statutory words are often known by the company they keep, we find here both the presence of company that suggests limitation and the absence of company that suggests breadth. See, e.g., *Yates v. United States*, 574 U.S. ___, 135 S. Ct. 1074, 1085, 191 L. Ed. 2d 64 (2015).

Both *ejusdem generis* and *noscitur a sociis* rely on our ability to recognize categories. Courts often treat this ability as natural or obvious, but psychologists, anthropologists, and others who have studied categorization recognize it as an extremely complex, culturally dependent process. Jorge Luis Borges makes this same point in what is perhaps the most famous passage in modern literature about categorization:

> On those remote pages it is written that animals are divided into (a) those that belong to the Emperor, (b) embalmed ones, (c) those that are trained, (d) suckling pigs, (e) mermaids, (f) fabulous ones, (g) stray dogs, (h) those that tremble as if they were mad, (j) innumerable ones, (k) those drawn with a very fine camel's hair brush, (l) others, (m) those that have just broken the flower pot, (n) those that resemble flies from a distance.

OTHER INQUISITIONS 106 (1966). Can you apply *ejusdem generis* or *noscitur a sociis* to this list? See if you can identify the features of Borges' list that prevent you from doing so.

George Lakoff quotes this passage in his important study of categorization, *Women, Fire, and Dangerous Things* (1987). The title may seem similar to Borges' list, but in fact it represents items in a real categorization used by the Dyirbal people of Australia. They would immediately recognize these items as being of the same kind and could apply *ejusdem generis* or *noscitur a sociis* to include other items that belong to this category, including fireflies, water, and the sun.

iii. Expressio unius est exclusio alterius

Expressio unius est exclusio alterius literally means "the mention of one thing is the exclusion of another." Courts apply the canon when they can infer from the inclusion of one term that the omission of another term was intentional. That negative inference is justified only where the terms themselves have a commonality. "As we have held repeatedly," the Supreme Court has explained, "the canon *expressio unius est exclusio alterius* does not apply to every statutory listing or grouping; it has force only when the items expressed are members of an 'associated group or series,' justifying the inference that items not mentioned were excluded by deliberate choice, not inadvertence." Barnhart v. Peabody Coal Co., 537 U.S. 149, 168 (2003); see also Chevron U.S.A. Inc. v. Echazabal, 536 U.S. 73, 81 (2002) ("The canon depends on identifying a series of two or more terms or things that should be understood to go hand in hand, which is abridged in circumstances supporting a sensible inference that the term left out must have been meant to be excluded.").

The Supreme Court has broken down *expressio unius* into several more specific rules for certain types of provisions. Thus, the Court has stated that "[w]here Congress explicitly enumerates certain exceptions to a general prohibition, additional exceptions are not to be implied, in the absence of evidence of a contrary legislative intent." Andrus v. Glover Construction Co., 446 U.S. 608, 616-17 (1980). In a similar vein, the Court has stated that "[w]hen a statute limits a thing to be done in a particular mode, it includes a negative of any other mode." Christensen v. Harris County, 529 U.S. 576, 583 (2000) (quoting Raleigh & Gaston R. Co. v. Reid, 13 Wall. 269, 270 (1872)). The Court has also particularized a rule for preemption provisions: "When Congress has considered the issue of pre-emption and has included in the enacted legislation a provision explicitly addressing that issue, and when that provision provides a 'reliable indicium of congressional intent with respect to state authority,' . . . 'there is no need to infer congressional intent to pre-empt state laws from the substantive provisions' of the legislation." Cipollone v. Liggett Group, Inc., 505 U.S. 504, 517 (1992).

iv. Other Linguistic Canons

There are a number of canons that concern other linguistic elements of a provision. Below is a description of the most important ones.

(1) Punctuation

Courts may consider the punctuation of a phrase to confirm an interpretation, but punctuation alone is rarely sufficient to sustain or contradict an interpretation. *See* United States National Bank of Oregon v. Independent

Insurance Agents of America Inc., 508 U.S. 439, 454 (1993) ("[A] purported plain-meaning analysis based only on punctuation is necessarily incomplete and runs the risk of distorting a statute's true meaning."). Thus, arguments based on punctuation are less strong than those based on other tools or canons.

Some punctuation issues are recurring. Courts are often asked to decide whether a word separated by a comma modifies a subsequent phrase. Consider the following statute. 18 U.S.C. §2252 provides in part that

> (a) Any person who (1) knowingly transports or ships in interstate or foreign commerce by any means including by computer or mails, any visual depiction, if (A) the producing of such visual depiction involves the use of a minor engaging in sexually explicit conduct; and (B) such visual depiction is of such conduct . . . shall be punished as provided in subsection (b) of this section.

Does the word "knowingly" modify the phrase "use of a minor"? What if the transporter or shipper had no knowledge of the age of the performer? The Supreme Court held that the term "knowingly" in §2252 "extends both to the sexually explicit nature of the material and to the age of the performers." *See* United States v. X-Citement Video, Inc., 513 U.S. 64, 77 (1994). It acknowledged that the "most natural grammatical reading . . . suggests that the term knowingly modifies only the surrounding verbs: transports, ships, receives, distributes, or reproduces." *Id.* at 68. But the Court rejected this understanding "both because of anomalies which result from this construction, and because of the respective presumptions that some form of scienter [proof of knowledge or intent of wrongdoing] is to be implied in a criminal statute even if not expressed, and that a statute is to be construed where fairly possible so as to avoid substantial constitutional questions." *Id.* at 68-69. Unless "knowingly" modifies other terms in the provision, the Court raised concern that the statute would cover FedEx couriers and others without knowledge of the contents of the material. *Id.* at 69-70. The Court also worried that the statute would impose criminal liability without the requisite criminal intent, which cuts against other interpretive "presumptions." The scienter canon is specific to criminal statutes or penalties. *See id.* at 70 (describing "our cases interpreting criminal statutes to include broadly applicable scienter requirements, even where the statute by its terms does not contain them"). We address the canon of avoiding constitutional questions, which applies to all statutes, later in this chapter.

The most famous comma controversy in Anglo-American law involved the trial of Sir Roger Casement, the Irish patriot and crusader for the rights of the Congolese people against King Leopold of Belgium's "rubber terror." During World War I, Casement was accused of violating the Treason Act of 1351, whose crucial clause read (in translation from its Norman-French original) as follows: "If a man be adherent to the king's enemies in his realm giving to them aid or comfort in the realm or elsewhere. . . ." Casement's defense was that the actions of which he was accused were carried out overseas, not in the realm. The court held that the proper interpretation of the statute however, was to read the phrase "giving to them aid or comfort in the realm" as set off by commas, such that giving aid to the king's enemies "elsewhere" was still being adherent to the king's enemies. Newspapers sympathetic to Casement claimed that he was "hanged by a comma."

Parentheticals raise their own distinctive issues. Courts have held that language inside a parenthetical is entitled to less weight than language outside a parenthetical. *See, e.g.,* Cabell Huntington Hosp., Inc. v. Shalala, 101 F.3d 984, 990 (4th Cir. 1996) ("A parenthetical is, after all, a parenthetical, and it cannot be used to overcome the operative terms of the statute."). Consider the following example from Chicasaw Nation v. United States, 534 U.S. 84 (2001). The Indian Gaming Regulatory Act (IGRA), 25 U.S.C. §§2701-2721, exempts tribes from paying certain gambling-related taxes. Specifically, it provides: "The provisions of [the Internal Revenue Code of 1986] (including sections 1441, 3402(q), 6041, and 6050I, and chapter 35 of such [Code]) concerning the reporting and withholding of taxes with respect to the winnings from gaming or wagering operations shall apply to Indian gaming operations conducted pursuant to this chapter, or under a Tribal-State compact entered into under section 2710(d)(3) of this title that is in effect, in the same manner as such provisions apply to State gaming and wagering operations." *Id.* §2719(d)(1). Two Indian tribes argued that this provision exempted them from paying gambling-related taxes imposed under chapter 35 that state casinos do not have to pay. The Court rejected this argument, arguing that the IGRA provision only applies to the *reporting or withholding* of taxes, not the *imposition or payment* of taxes, and that chapter 35 concerns those later issues. Thus, the Court refused to give the parenthetical reference to chapter 35 more weight than the "reporting and withholding" language outside the parenthetical. It stated that the parenthetical is best read as an illustrative list, and "'chapter 35' is simply a bad example — an example that Congress included inadvertently." *Id.* at 533. Justice O'Connor disagreed, stating in her dissenting opinion that "I am aware of no generally accepted canon of statutory construction favoring language outside of parentheses to language within them . . . nor do I think it wise for the Court to adopt one today." *Id.* at 537 (O'Connor, J., dissenting). Indeed, Justice O'Connor reasoned that illustrative language is arguably entitled to more weight because of the canon that the "specific governs the general," which is closely related to *ejusdem generis. Id.* at 537.

(2) The Last Antecedent Rule

Under the last antecedent rule, "a limiting clause or phrase . . . should ordinarily be read as modifying only the noun or phrase that it immediately follows." Barnhart v. Thomas, 540 U.S. 20, 26 (2003). In *Thomas,* the Court applied the last antecedent rule to a provision of the Social Security Act concerning disability benefits. The Act defines "disability" as the "inability to engage in any substantial gainful activity by reason of any medically determinable physical or mental impairment which can be expected to result in death or which has lasted or can be expected to last for a continuous period of not less than 12 months." 42 U.S.C. §423(d)(1)(A). It further provides that: "An individual shall be determined to be under a disability only if his physical or mental impairment or impairments are of such severity that *he is not only unable to do his previous work but cannot,* considering his age, education, and work experience, *engage in any other kind of substantial gainful work which exists in the national economy. . . .*" §423(d)(2)(A) (emphases added). The claimant argued that she was entitled to benefits even though she was able to do her previous work as an elevator operator because such work no longer existed in the national economy. The Court rejected this argument. Invoking the last antecedent rule, it stated that the phrase concerning work in the national economy only modifies the clause that immediately precedes it: "[engaging] in any other kind of substantial gainful work." Therefore, the Court found the claimant was not entitled to benefits because she was able to perform her previous work, regardless of whether that work still existed in the national economy. To illustrate the grammatical problem with the claimant's argument, the Court stated:

> Consider, for example, the case of parents who, before leaving their teenage son alone in the house for the weekend, warn him, "You will be punished if you throw a party or engage in any other activity that damages the house." If the son nevertheless throws a party and is caught, he should hardly be able to avoid punishment by arguing that the house was not damaged. The parents proscribed (1) a party, and (2) any other activity that damages the house. As far as appears from what they said, their reasons for prohibiting the home-alone party may have had nothing to do with damage to the house for instance, the risk that underage drinking or sexual activity would occur. And even if their only concern was to prevent damage, it does not follow from the fact that the same interest underlay both the specific and the general prohibition that proof of impairment of that interest is required for both. The parents, foreseeing that assessment of whether an activity had in fact "damaged" the house could be disputed by their son, might have wished to preclude all argument by specifying and categorically prohibiting the one activity hosting a party that was most likely to cause damage and most likely to occur.

Thomas, 540 U.S. at 27-28.

The last antecedent rule, like any canon of construction, may be overcome by other indicia of meaning. Consider United States v. Hayes, 555 U.S. 415 (2009). Section 922(g)(9) of the federal criminal code makes it "unlawful for any person . . . who has been convicted in any court of a misdemeanor crime of domestic violence . . . [to] possess in or affecting commerce, any firearm or ammunition." 18 U.S.C. §922(g)(9). Section 921(a)(33)(A) defines "misdemeanor crime of domestic violence" as follows:

> [T]he term "misdemeanor crime of domestic violence" means an offense that
>
> (i) is a misdemeanor under Federal, State, or Tribal law; and
> (ii) has, as an element, the use or attempted use of physical force, or the threatened use of a deadly weapon, committed by a current or former spouse, parent, or guardian of the victim, by a person with whom the victim shares a child in common, by a person who is cohabiting with or has cohabitated with the victim as a spouse, parent, or guardian, or by a person similarly situated to a spouse, parent, or guardian of the victim (footnotes omitted).

As the Court nicely summarized:

> This definition, all agree, imposes two requirements: First, a "misdemeanor crime of domestic violence" must have, "as an element, the use or attempted use of physical force, or the threatened use of a deadly weapon." Second, it must be "committed by" a person who has a specified domestic relationship with the victim. The question here is whether the language of §921(a)(33)(A) calls for a further limitation: Must the statute describing the predicate offense include, as a discrete element, the existence of a domestic relationship between offender and victim? In line with the large majority of the Courts of Appeals, we conclude that §921(a)(33)(A) does not require a predicate-offense statute of that specificity. Instead, in a §922(g)(9) prosecution, it suffices for the Government to charge and prove a prior conviction that was, in fact, for "an offense . . . committed by" the defendant against a spouse or other domestic victim.

Hayes, 555 U.S. at 421. In so holding, the Court rejected the application of the last antecedent rule. Under that rule, the words "committed by" could be read as modifying the use-of-force language, making both the specified domestic relationship and the use of force required elements. (Is this a strict application of the rule?) The Court stated:

> Applying the rule of the last antecedent here would require us to accept two unlikely premises: that Congress employed the singular "element" to encompass two distinct concepts, and that it adopted the awkward construction "commi[t]" a "use." Moreover, as the dissent acknowledges . . . , the last antecedent rule would render the word "committed" superfluous: Congress could have conveyed the same meaning by referring simply to "the use . . . of physical force . . . by a current or former spouse. . . ." "Committed" retains its operative meaning only if it is read to modify "offense."
>
> Most sensibly read, then, §921(a)(33)(A) defines "misdemeanor crime of domestic violence" as a misdemeanor offense that (1) "has, as an element, the use [of force]," and (2) is committed by a person who has a specified domestic relationship with the victim. To obtain a conviction in a §922(g)(9) prosecution, the Government must prove beyond a reasonable doubt that the victim of the predicate offense was the defendant's current or former spouse or was related to the defendant in another specified way. But that relationship, while it must be established, need not be denominated an element of the predicate offense.

Id. at 1086-87.

(3) Conjunctive vs. Disjunctive

The Court has recognized that "terms connected by a disjunctive [should] be given separate meanings, unless the context dictates otherwise." Reiter v. Sonotone Corp., 442 U.S. 330, 339 (1979). In *Reiter*, the Court applied this rule in interpreting §4 of the Clayton Act, which provides:

> Any person who shall be injured in his business *or property* by reason of anything forbidden in the antitrust laws may sue therefore in any district court of the United States . . . without respect to the amount in controversy, and shall recover threefold the damages by him sustained, and the cost of suit, including a reasonable attorney's fee. 15 U.S.C. §15 (emphasis added).

The Court read the word "property" to include money, rejecting the argument that "property" refers only to property used in business activity.

Reiter, 442 U.S. at 339. It reasoned that "Congress' use of the word 'or' makes plain that 'business' was not intended to modify 'property,' nor was 'property' intended to modify 'business.' " *Id.* Although a person engaged in a commercial enterprise suffers injury to both "business" and "property" when suffering a monetary loss, the words retain independent significance in other contexts. (What canon is the Court applying here? See below for the description of the rule against redundancy or surplusage). "[A] consumer not engaged in a 'business' enterprise, but rather acquiring goods or services for personal use, is injured in 'property' when the price of those goods or services is artificially inflated by reason of the anticompetitive conduct complained of." *Id.* at 339.

By the same token, the Court has recognized that "the word 'or' is often used as a careless substitute for the word 'and'; that is, it is often used in phrases where 'and' would express the thought with greater clarity." De Sylva v. Ballentine, 351 U.S. 570, 573 (1956). This canon dates backs to some of the earliest cases of statutory interpretation. *See, e.g.,* Kerlin's Lessee v. Bull, 1 U.S. 175 (1786); United States v. Fisk, 70 U.S. 445 (1865). These cases are a reminder that for the conjunctive/disjunctive canon, as for all canons, context matters. When a court senses a "careless usage," it may substitute "or" for "and" and vice versa. In *De Sylva,* the Court provided an illustration from the Copyright Act, which enables an author's executors to renew a copyright if "if such author, widow, widower *or* children be not living." 17 U.S.C. §24 (emphasis added).

> If the italicized "or" in that clause is read disjunctively, then the author's executors would be entitled to renew the copyright if any one of the persons named "be not living." It is clear, however, that the executors do not succeed to the renewal interest unless all of the named persons are dead, since from the preceding clause it is at least made explicit that the "widow, widower, or children of the author" all come before the executors, after the author's death. The clause would be more accurate, therefore, were it to read "author, widow or widower, and children." It is argued with some force, then, that if in the succeeding clause the "or" is to be read as meaning "and" in the same word grouping as is involved in the clause in question, it should be read that way in this clause as well. If this is done, it is then an easy step to read "widow" and "children" as succeeding to the renewal interest as a class, as the Court of Appeals held they did.

De Sylva, 350 U.S. at 573-74.

(4)   May vs. Shall

Remember this one from elementary school? The Court's approach is the same as your teacher's approach. The word "may" connotes a permissive or discretionary action, whereas the word "shall" connotes a mandatory one. *See* Lopez v. Davis, 531 U.S. 230, 241 (2001) (noting Congress's "use of a mandatory 'shall' . . . to impose discretionless obligations"); Lexecon Inc. v. Milberg Weiss Bershad Hynes & Lerach, 523 U.S. 26, 35 (1998) ("[T]he mandatory 'shall' . . . normally creates an obligation impervious to judicial discretion"). In National Association of Homebuilders v. Defenders of Wildlife, 551 U.S. 644 (2007), the Court applied the may/shall canon in interpreting §402(b) of the Clean Water Act, which provides that the EPA "shall approve" an application from a state to exercise permitting authority unless the agency determines that the state lacks adequate authority to perform the nine permitting functions specified in the section. 33 U.S.C. §1342(b). The Court held that the statute says what it means and means what it says: "By its terms, the statutory language is mandatory and the list exclusive; if the nine specified criteria are satisfied, the EPA does not have the discretion to deny a transfer application." *Id.* at 661-62.

The Court seems especially likely to apply the may/shall canon when a statute uses the words "may" and "shall" in "contraposition" to one another. *See* Jama v. Immigration & Customs Enforcement, 543 U.S. 335, 346 (2005). For example, the Court construed the two words literally in section 1231(b)(2) of the Immigration and Nationality Act, 8 U.S.C. §1231(b)(2), which provides that "the Attorney General 'shall remove' an alien to the designated country, except that the Attorney General 'may' disregard the designation if any one of four potentially countervailing circumstances arises." *Id; see also* Lopez v. Davis, 531 U.S. 230, 241 (2001) ("Congress' use of the permissive 'may' in §3621(e)(2)(B) contrasts with the legislators' use of a mandatory 'shall' in the very same section.").

In other decisions, the Court has acknowledged that the word "shall" can convey an element of discretion and can even have the same meaning as "may." *See* Gutierrez de Martinez v. Lamagno, 515 U.S. 417, 432-33 n.9, (1995) ("Though 'shall' generally means 'must,' legal writers sometimes use, or misuse, 'shall' to mean 'should,' 'will,' or even 'may.' " *See* D. Mellinkoff, Mellinkoff's Dictionary of American Legal Usage 402-03 (1992) ("shall" and "may" are "frequently treated as synonyms" and their meaning depends on context); B. Garner, Dictionary of Modern Legal Usage 939 (2d ed. 1995) ("Courts in virtually every English-speaking jurisdiction have held by necessity that shall means may in some contexts, and vice versa.")). These citations are reminders that no canon is absolute; context matters.

(5)   The Dictionary Act, 1 U.S.C. §§1-8

Congress enacted the Dictionary Act in 1871 "to supply rules of construction for all legislation." Inyo County, Cal. v. Paiute-Shoshone Indians of the Bishop Community of the Bishop County, 538 U.S. 701, 713 n.1 (2003) (Stevens, J., concurring). By its terms, the Act applies "in determining the meaning of any Act of Congress, unless the context indicates otherwise." 1 U.S.C. §1. Thus, it does not relieve courts of the obligation to determine whether "the context" of a particular statute "indicates" that a different interpretation should apply. In Rowland v. California Men's

Colony, Unit II Men's Advisory Council, 506 U.S. 194, 199-201 (1993), the Court stated that courts have a fair degree of leeway to determine when another interpretation is appropriate. In other words, courts are largely free to disregard the Dictionary Act—and they often do. Here are the major rules:

SECTION 1:
In determining the meaning of any Act of Congress, unless the context indicates otherwise—
words importing the singular include and apply to several persons, parties, or things;
words importing the plural include the singular;
words importing the masculine gender include the feminine as well;
words used in the present tense include the future as well as the present;
the words "insane" and "insane person" and "lunatic" shall include every idiot, lunatic, insane person, and person non compos mentis;
the words "person" and "whoever" include corporations, companies, associations, firms, partnerships, societies, and joint stock companies, as well as individuals;
"officer" includes any person authorized by law to perform the duties of the office;
"signature" or "subscription" includes a mark when the person making the same intended it as such;
"oath" includes affirmation, and "sworn" includes affirmed;
"writing" includes printing and typewriting and reproductions of visual symbols by photographing, multigraphing, mimeographing, manifolding, or otherwise.

SECTION 2:
The word "county" includes a parish, or any other equivalent subdivision of a State or Territory of the United States.

SECTION 3:
The word "vessel" includes every description of watercraft or other artificial contrivance used, or capable of being used, as a means of transportation on water.

SECTION 4:
The word "vehicle" includes every description of carriage or other artificial contrivance used, or capable of being used, as a means of transportation on land.

SECTION 5:
The word "company" or "association," when used in reference to a corporation, shall be deemed to embrace the words "successors and assigns of such company or association," in like manner as if these last-named words, or words of similar import, were expressed.

SECTION 6:
Wherever, in the statutes of the United States or in the rulings, regulations, or interpretations of various administrative bureaus and agencies of the United States there appears or may appear the term "products of American fisheries" said term shall not include fresh or frozen fish fillets, fresh or frozen fish steaks, or fresh or frozen slices of fish substantially free of bone (including any of the foregoing divided into sections), produced in a foreign country or its territorial waters, in whole or in part with the use of the labor of persons who are not residents of the United States.

SECTION 7:

In determining the meaning of any Act of Congress, or of any ruling, regulation, or interpretation of the various administrative bureaus and agencies of the United States, the word "marriage" means only a legal union between one man and one woman as husband and wife, and the word "spouse" refers only to a person of the opposite sex who is a husband or a wife.

SECTION 8:

(a)   In determining the meaning of any Act of Congress, or of any ruling, regulation, or interpretation of the various administrative bureaus and agencies of the United States, the words "person," "human being," "child," and "individual," shall include every infant member of the species homo sapiens who is born alive at any stage of development.

(b)   As used in this section, the term "born alive," with respect to a member of the species homo sapiens, means the complete expulsion or extraction from his or her mother of that member, at any stage of development, who after such expulsion or extraction breathes or has a beating heart, pulsation of the umbilical cord, or definite movement of voluntary muscles, regardless of whether the umbilical cord has been cut, and regardless of whether the expulsion or extraction occurs as a result of natural or induced labor, cesarean section, or induced abortion.

(c)   Nothing in this section shall be construed to affirm, deny, expand, or contract any legal status or legal right applicable to any member of the species homo sapiens at any point prior to being "born alive" as defined in this section.

Notes and Questions

1. An occupancy tax applies to businesses renting rooms if the operator of the business is a "retailer." Under the statute, "[o]perators of hotels, motels, tourist homes, tourist camps, and similar types of business . . . are considered retailers." The taxing authority has sued an online travel company arguing that it should be able to tax the room rate charged by an online travel company that arranges for consumers to let hotel rooms, arguing that the online travel company qualifies as a retailer under the statute. What canons would you invoke to argue that the online retailer was not a "retailer" under the Act?

2. Under federal law, a convicted felon is required to make restitution to the victim, including to "reimburse the victim for lost income and necessary child care, transportation, and other expenses incurred during participation in the investigation or prosecution of the offense or attendance at proceedings related to the offense." 18 U.S.C. §3663A(c)(1)(A)(ii). Is a convicted felon required to reimburse the victim for attorney fees incurred by the victim during the defendant's criminal proceedings? (*Hint*: Does *ejusdem generis* apply?)

3. Suppose a statute authorized insurance companies to exclude coverage for damage caused by "flood, surface water, waves, tidal water or tidal waves, overflow of streams or other bodies of water, or spray from any of the foregoing, all whether driven by wind or not." Insurance companies routinely excluded coverage in the same terms for such damage from the policies that they sold. After the levees broke in New Orleans in the midst of Hurricane Katrina, policyholders sued their insurance companies seeking coverage for damage. The policyholders argued that "flood" is limited to natural events, not rising waters due to the collapse of man-made structures. Are plaintiffs' claims excluded from coverage under the statute? (*Hint*: Does *noscitur a sociis* apply?)

4. The Federal Claims Act provides that "[n]o court shall have jurisdiction over an action under this section based upon the public disclosure of allegations or transactions in a criminal, civil, or administrative hearing, in a congressional, administrative, or Government Accounting Office report, hearing, audit, or investigation, or from the news media. . . ." 31 U.S.C. §3730(e)(4)(A). If state and local administrative reports are "public disclosures" under the provision, then suits arising out of them would be barred from private enforcement. Are state and local administrative reports "public disclosures" under the Act?

5. How would you argue that the definition of "vehicle" in the Dictionary Act should not apply to the Motor Vehicle Safety Act?

6. A conventional justification for many canons of construction is that they rest on assumptions about how Congress drafts statutes. It is worth considering this assumption based on some recent empirical evidence. Of 137 committee staffers who were interviewed, more than 70 percent indicated that they draft in line with *ejusdem* and *noscitur*. (Very few recognized these canons by Latin name.) *See* Abbe R. Gluck & Lisa Schultz Bressman, *Statutory Interpretation from the Inside—An Empirical Study of Congressional Drafting, Delegation, and the Canons: Part I*, 65 STAN. L. REV. 901 (2013). Although only 33 percent stated that they draft in line with *expressio unius*, more articulated a more specific rule—namely, that they use the word "including" or a broad catch-all term when they want to create a non-exclusive list. If Congress does draft in line with these canons, does that make them a more acceptable part of statutory interpretation? If Congress uses special conventions—such as "including" to indicate a non-exclusive list—should courts incorporate that signal into their practice?

c. Whole Act Canons

In many cases, courts interpreting a statutory word or phrase look not only at the immediate provision in which it appears but to the rest of the statute. When they do so, they are applying whole act canons. These canons fall into two groups: (1) the whole act rule and its corollaries, and (2) rules related to specific parts of statutes, such as titles and provisos.

i. The Whole Act Rule

The whole act rule instructs courts to view statutory terms as a part of the entire legislation in which they were enacted. As the Supreme Court has repeatedly stated, "[i]n reading a statute we must not 'look merely to a particular clause,' but consider it 'in connection with it the whole statute.' "

Dada v. Mukasey, 554 U.S. 1, 16 (2008) (quoting Kokoszka v. Belford, 417 U.S. 642, 650 (1974)); *see also* Gozlon-Peretz v. United States, 498 U.S. 395, 407 (1991) ("'In determining the meaning of the statute, we look not only to the particular statutory language, but to the design of the statute as a whole and to its object and policy'" (quoting Crandon v. United States, 494 U.S. 152, 158 (1990)). The whole act rule presumes that Congress views each statute as a whole, intending words to have the same meaning throughout and individual provisions to work together, thus creating coherence and avoiding redundancy. Stop and ask yourself to what extent that presumption is a viable one, given the complexities of the legislative process.

Whenever a court is interpreting statutory language by reference to other parts of the same statute, it is applying the whole act rule. But the Court has offered several more concrete principles, which we describe as follows:

(1) Identical Words — Consistent Meaning

"A standard principle of statutory construction provides that identical words and phrases within the same statute should normally be given the same meaning." Powerex Corp. v. Reliant Energy Services, Inc., 551 U.S. 224, 231 (2007). This canon is a fundamental aspect of the whole act rule, though — like all canons — it is far from absolute. As the Court has explained, the "'natural presumption that identical words used in different parts of the same act are intended to have the same meaning . . . is not rigid and readily yields whenever there is such variation in the connection in which the words are used as reasonably to warrant the conclusion that they were employed in different parts of the act with different intent.'" Environmental Defense v. Duke Energy Corp., 549 U.S. 561, 574 (2007) (internal citation omitted). Consequently, "[a] given term in the same statute may take on distinct characters from association with distinct statutory objects calling for different implementation strategies." *Id.*

"[A] classic case" applying the identical words canon is Commissioner of Internal Revenue v. Lundy, 516 U.S. 235, 249-50 (1996). The Court considered whether "a claim" under 26 U.S.C. §6512(b)(3) meant "a claim filed on a return." It found that the use of "claim" in a neighboring provision of the same act illuminated the meaning of this term:

> Perhaps the most compelling evidence that Congress did not intend the term "claim" in §6512 to mean a "claim filed on a return" is the parallel use of the term "claim" in §6511(a). Section 6511(a) indicates that a claim for refund is timely if it is "filed by the taxpayer within 3 years from the time the return was filed," and it plainly contemplates that a claim can be filed even "if no return was filed." If a claim could *only* be filed with a return, as Lundy contends, these provisions of the statute would be senseless, *cf.* 26 U.S.C. §6696 (separately defining "claim for refund" and "return"), and we have been given no reason to believe that Congress meant the term "claim" to mean one thing in §6511 but to mean something else altogether in the very next section of the statute. The interrelationship and close proximity of these provisions of the statute "presents a classic case for application of the 'normal rule of statutory construction that identical

words used in different parts of the same act are intended to have the same meaning."' *Sullivan v. Stroop,* 496 U.S. 478, 484 (1990) (quoting *Sorenson v. Secretary of Treasury,* 475 U.S. 851, 860 (1986) (internal quotation and citation omitted)).

Id. at 249-50. Under certain circumstances, a court may have reason to believe that Congress used the same term in two different senses. In General Dynamics Land Systems, Inc. v. Cline, 540 U.S. 581 (2004), the Court confronted the question whether the Age Discrimination in Employment Act of 1967, 29 U.S.C. §§621 *et seq.,* prohibits employers from favoring older employees over younger employees, and vice versa. The plaintiffs argued that the word "age" in the ADEA should be given the same meaning throughout the statute, and, as a result, "discrimina[tion] . . . because of [an] individual's age," 29 U.S.C. §623(a)(1), could ban favoring older employees. The Court disagreed:

> The [plaintiffs'] first response to our reading is the dictionary argument that "age" means the length of a person's life, with the phrase "because of such individual's age" stating a simple test of causation: "discriminat[ion] . . . because of [an] individual's age" is treatment that would not have occurred if the individual's span of years had been longer or shorter. The case for this reading calls attention to the other instances of "age" in the ADEA that are not limited to old age, such as 29 U.S.C. §623(f), which gives an employer a defense to charges of age discrimination when "age is a bona fide occupational qualification." Cline and the EEOC argue that if "age" meant old age, §623(f) would then provide a defense (old age is a bona fide qualification) only for an employer's action that on our reading would never clash with the statute (because preferring the older is not forbidden).
>
> The argument rests on two mistakes. First, it assumes that the word "age" has the same meaning wherever the ADEA uses it. But this is not so, and Cline simply mis-employs the "presumption that identical words used in different parts of the same act are intended to have the same meaning." *Atlantic Cleaners & Dyers, Inc. v. United States,* 286 U.S. 427, 433 (1932). Cline forgets that "the presumption is not rigid and readily yields whenever there is such variation in the connection in which the words are used as reasonably to warrant the conclusion that they were employed in different parts of the act with different intent." *Ibid.; see also United States v. Cleveland Indians Baseball Co.,* 532 U.S. 200, 213 (2001) (phrase "wages paid" has different meanings in different parts of Title 26 U.S.C.); *Robinson v. Shell Oil Co.,* 519 U.S. 337, 343-344 (1997) (term "employee" has different meanings in different parts of Title VII). The presumption of uniform usage thus relents when a word used has several commonly understood meanings among which a speaker can alternate in the course of an ordinary conversation, without being confused or getting confusing.
>
> "Age" is that kind of word. As Justice Thomas agrees, the word "age" standing alone can be readily understood either as pointing to any number of years lived, or as common shorthand for the longer span and concurrent aches that make youth look good. Which alternative was probably intended is a matter of context; we understand the different choices of meaning that lie behind a sentence like "Age can be shown by a driver's license," and the statement, "Age has left him a shut-in." So it is easy to understand that Congress chose different meanings at different places in the ADEA, as the different settings readily show. Hence the second flaw in Cline's argument for uniform usage: it ignores the cardinal rule that "[s]tatutory language must be read in context [since] a phrase 'gathers meaning from the words around it.' " *Jones v. United States,* 527 U.S. 373, 389 (1999). . . . The point here is that we are not asking an abstract question about the meaning of "age"; we are seeking the meaning of the whole phrase "discriminate . . . because of such individual's age," where it occurs in the ADEA, 29 U.S.C. §623(a)(1). As we have said, social history emphatically reveals an understanding of age discrimination as aimed against the old, and the statutory

reference to age discrimination in this idiomatic sense is confirmed by legislative history. For the very reason that reference to context shows that "age" means "old age" when teamed with "discrimination," the provision of an affirmative defense when age is a bona fide occupational qualification readily shows that "age" as a qualification means comparative youth. As context tells us that "age" means one thing in §623(a)(1) and another in §623(f), so it also tells us that the presumption of uniformity cannot sensibly operate here.

Cline, 540 U.S. at 594-97. For another instance in which the Court found that the same word carried two different meanings in a single statute, see Watson v. United States, 552 U.S. 74, 82 (2007) ("Subsections (d)(1) and (c)(1)(A) as we read them are not at odds over the verb 'use'; the point is merely that in the two subsections the common verb speaks to different issues in different voices and at different levels of specificity. The provisions do distinct jobs, but we do not make them guilty of employing the common verb inconsistently.").

(2) Avoiding Redundancy and Surplusage

"It is 'a cardinal principle of statutory construction' that 'a statute ought, upon the whole, to be so construed that, if it can be prevented, no clause, sentence, or word shall be superfluous, void, or insignificant.' " TRW Inc. v. Andrews, 534 U.S. 19, 31 (2001) (citation omitted). Under this principle, a court will avoid an interpretation of a provision that renders any other provision of the same act redundant or "surplusage." Like the other canons of construction, this principle is not absolute but merely a guide. As the Court has stated, "our hesitancy to construe statutes to render language superfluous does not require us to avoid surplusage at all costs. It is appropriate to tolerate a degree of surplusage rather than adopt a textually dubious construction that threatens to render the entire provision a nullity." United States v. Atlantic Research Corp., 551 U.S. 128, 137 (2007); *see also* Lamie v. U.S. Trustee, 540 U.S. 526, 536 (2004) (declining to apply rule against surplusage where it would create statutory ambiguity).

Note that the rule against redundancy or surplusage can be applied not only to a provision within a statute but words within a provision. For example, the Court has found that when Congress includes a list of words in a provision, it intends for each word in that list to have independent legal significance. *See, e.g.*, Babbitt v. Sweet Home Chapter of Communities for a Great Oregon, 515 U.S. 687, 697-98 n.10 (1995). This provision-specific application of the rule against surplusage is no more absolute than the whole act variant. Consistent with *noscitur a sociis*, a court may find that Congress intended words in a list to have a shared, overlapping meaning. *See id.* at 717-18 (Scalia, J., dissenting).

Note also that canons often work together. For example, the rule against redundancy (whether applied at the provision or whole act level) can interact with *ejusdem generis*. Circuit City Stores, Inc. v. Adams, 532 U.S. 105

(2001), provides a nice illustration. There, the Court addressed the question of whether the Federal Arbitration Act applies to employment contracts. Section 1 of the Act excludes from its coverage "contracts of employment of seamen, railroad employees, or any other class of workers engaged in foreign or interstate commerce." 9 U.S.C. §1. The Court construed the exclusion for contracts of "any other class of workers engaged in foreign or interstate commerce" as applying only to contracts of transportation workers, reversing the Ninth Circuit's conclusion that it applied to all employment contracts:

> Respondent, endorsing the reasoning of the Court of Appeals for the Ninth Circuit that the provision excludes all employment contracts, relies on the asserted breadth of the words "contracts of employment of . . . any other class of workers engaged in . . . commerce." . . . This reading of §1, however, runs into an immediate and, in our view, insurmountable textual obstacle. . . . [T]he words "any other class of workers engaged in . . . commerce" constitute a residual phrase, following, in the same sentence, explicit reference to "seamen" and "railroad employees." Construing the residual phrase to exclude all employment contracts fails to give independent effect to the statute's enumeration of the specific categories of workers which precedes it; there would be no need for Congress to use the phrases "seamen" and "railroad employees" if those same classes of workers were subsumed within the meaning of the "engaged in . . . commerce" residual clause. The wording of §1 calls for the application of the maxim *ejusdem generis,* the statutory canon that "[w]here general words follow specific words in a statutory enumeration, the general words are construed to embrace only objects similar in nature to those objects enumerated by the preceding specific words." N. Singer, Sutherland on Statutes and Statutory Construction §47.17 (1991); *see also Norfolk & Western R. Co. v. Train Dispatchers,* 499 U.S. 117, 129 (1991). Under this rule of construction the residual clause should be read to give effect to the terms "seamen" and "railroad employees," and should itself be controlled and defined by reference to the enumerated categories of workers which are recited just before it; the interpretation of the clause pressed by respondent fails to produce these results.

Circuit City, 532 U.S. at 114-15.

ii. Titles and Provisos

In interpreting a provision, courts occasionally make reference to titles and provisos found elsewhere in the statute. Courts generally do not give any of these sources "controlling" weight. That is, courts neither use them on par with other textual tools to give meaning to a word or phrase nor use them to contradict an interpretation reached through other means. Rather, courts tend to use them to confirm an interpretation reached through other means.

(1) Titles

In *Holy Trinity,* the Court invoked the title of the statute to support its conclusion that the statute did not apply to contracts for the transportation of clergymen. Courts occasionally refer to titles but again mainly to confirm interpretations reached through other sources. The Court has repeatedly emphasized that "a title alone is not controlling." INS v. St. Cyr, 533 U.S. 289, 308 (2001) (citing Pennsylvania Dep't of Corrections v. Yeskey, 524 U.S. 206, 212 (1998) ("'[T]he title of a statute . . . cannot limit the plain meaning of the text. For interpretive purposes, [it is] of use only when [it] shed[s] light on some ambiguous word or phrase.'" (quoting Trainmen v. Baltimore & Ohio R. Co., 331 U.S. 519, 528-29 (1947)))). Was the *Holy Trinity* Court's use of the title consistent with this contemporary statement? Or did the Court use the title to "control" the meaning of the statutory language?

Sometimes the title of a statute is useful to a court where the other sources reveal no clear meaning. In United States v. Villanueva-Sotelo, 515 F.3d 1234, 1243-47 (D.C. Cir. 2008), after concluding that the language of a criminal statute was ambiguous, the D.C. Circuit relied upon the title of a criminal statute — "[a]ggravated identity theft," 18 U.S.C. §1028A — as a consideration supporting its conclusion that the statute did not encompass a forged alien registration number that the defendant picked out the air. *See id.* at 1243. "As that title demonstrates, the statute concerns 'theft,' i.e., 'the felonious taking and removing of personal property with intent to deprive the rightful owner of it.' . . . Yet Villanueva-Sotelo, having no idea that his forged alien registration belonged to anyone at all, couldn't possibly have had the intent to deprive another of his or her identity." *Id.*

(2) Provisos

Provisos are clauses that state exceptions to or limitations on the application of a statute — for example, "provided that. . . ." One issue that arises is whether the proviso applies only to matters that were included by the immediately preceding clause, or whether it applies more broadly. *See* Alaska v. United States, 545 U.S. 75, 106 (2005) ("Though it may be customary to use a proviso to refer only to things covered by a preceding clause, it is also possible to use a proviso to state a general, independent rule."); McDonald v. United States, 279 U.S. 12, 21 (1929) ("[A] proviso is not always limited in its effect to the part of the enactment with which it is immediately associated; it may apply generally to all cases within the meaning of the language used."). In *Alaska v. United States*, the Court held that a proviso governing transfer of land was not limited to lands that fell within the preceding clause. *See* 545 U.S. at 108-09.

d. Whole Code Canons

Once enacted, a federal statute takes its place alongside other federal statutes in the U.S. Code. The whole code rule directs courts to construe language in one statute by looking to language in other statutes. Like the whole act rule, the whole code rule has more specific sub-rules.

i. **In pari materia**

Under the "*in pari materia* canon of statutory construction, statutes addressing the same subject matter generally should be read 'as if they were one law.' " Wachovia Bank v. Schmidt, 546 U.S. 303, 315-16 (2006) (quoting Erlenbaugh v. United States, 409 U.S. 239, 243 (1972) (internal citation omitted)). *In pari materia*, like inferences from other parts of the same statute, is entitled to "great weight in resolving any ambiguities and doubts." *See Erlenbaugh*, 409 U.S. at 244; United States v. Stewart, 311 U.S. 60, 64 (1940).

In pari materia "is but a logical extension of the principle that individual sections of a single statute should be construed together." *Erlenbaugh*, 409 U.S. at 244. As traditionally justified, construing statutes *in pari materia* "is a reflection of practical experience in the interpretation of statute: a legislative body generally uses a particular word with a consistent meaning in a given context." *Id.* at 243-44. Under this canon, "a 'later act can be . . . regarded as a legislative interpretation of [an] earlier act. . . . in the sense that it aids in ascertaining the meaning of words used in their contemporary setting.' " *Id.* at 243-44. Because *in pari materia* assumes that "whenever Congress passes a new statute, it acts aware of all previous statutes on the same subject," it applies with greatest force "when the statutes were enacted by the same legislative body at the same time." *Id.* at 244. But it can also apply to statutes enacted by different Congresses at different times.

Courts applying *in pari materia*, therefore, must determine which statutes concern the same subject matter and therefore should be read together. Consider a classic example, United States v. Stewart, 311 U.S. 60 (1940). The question was whether the taxpayer was entitled to a refund on taxes on capital gains on farm bonds issued under the Federal Farm Loan Act. To resolve that question, the Supreme Court had to consider two different statutes, the Revenue Act of 1928, 45 Stat. 791, and the Farm Loan Act, 39 Stat. 360 (July 17, 1916). The relevant provisions of these Acts are as follows:

Revenue Act

> Section 22(a) includes as gross income "gains, profits and income derived from . . . sales, or dealings in property, whether real or personal."
> Section 22(b)(4) excepts from taxation "[i]nterest upon securities issues under the provisions of the Federal Farm Loan Act, or under the provisions of such Act as amended."

Farm Loan Act

> Section 26 provides that "farm loan bonds issued under the provisions of this Act (chapter), shall be deemed and held to be instrumentalities of the Government of the United States, and as such they and the income derived therefrom shall be exempt from Federal, State, municipal, and local taxation."

The taxpayer argued that the capital gains were "income derived therefrom" under the Farm Loan Act, and therefore should be exempted from taxation. The government took the position that capital gains were "income" under §22(a) of the Revenue Act and thus not exempted by §22(b)(4), which only excludes "interest." *Stewart*, 11 U.S. at 64. The Court concluded that the Acts should be read *in pari materia*, in part because the relevant terms of the Revenue Act of 1928 replicated the terms of the Revenue Act of 1916, and the Revenue Act of 1916 was enacted during the same congressional session as the Farm Act:

> The Revenue Act of 1916, 39 Stat. 756, was enacted shortly after the Farm Loan Act by the same Congress and at the same session. Sec. 2 of that Act, like §22(a) of the 1928 Act, included in taxable income "gains, profits, and income derived from . . . sales, or dealings in property." And §4 of that Act, like §22(b)(4) of the 1928 Act, exempted from taxation "interest upon . . . securities issued under the provisions of the Federal Farm Loan Act." It is clear that "all acts in pari materia are to be taken together, as if they were one law." *United States v. Freeman*, 3 How. 556, 564 (1845). That these two acts are in pari materia is plain. Both deal with precisely the same subject matter, *viz.*, the scope of the tax exemption afforded farm loan bonds. The later act can therefore be regarded as a legislative interpretation of the earlier act (*Cope v. Cope*, 137 U.S. 682, 688; *Cf. Stockdale v. Atlantic Insurance Company*, 20 Wall. 323, 331, 332 (1873), in the sense that it aids in ascertaining the meaning of the words as used in their contemporary setting. . . . It is therefore entitled to great weight in resolving any ambiguities and doubts. *Cf. United States v. Stafoff*, 260 U.S. 477, 480 (1922). In that view the express exemption of interest alone makes tolerably clear that capital gains are not exempt.

Id. at 64-65. Because the same Congress enacted the Farm Loan Act and the Revenue Act, the exemption in the latter concerning taxation on interest, which did not mention capital gains, should be understood to confine the potentially broader exemption in the former. What other canons could the Court have invoked to justify its conclusion?

For a point of contrast, consider Erlenbaugh v. United States, 409 U.S. 239 (1972), a decision that involved exceptions in two statutes enacted close in time. The defendants were convicted of violating 18 U.S.C. §1952, which makes it unlawful to use a facility of interstate commerce in furtherance of certain criminal activity. The defendants, who had circulated a gaming publication across state lines, challenged their convictions on the basis of an exception in a different statute, 18 U.S.C. §1953, enacted in the same section of the criminal code on the same day as §1952. In relevant part, these provisions read:

> Section 1952(a) makes it unlawful for anyone who "uses any facility in interstate . . . commerce . . . with the intent to . . . promote, manage, establish, carry on, or facilitate the promotion, management, establishment, or carrying on, of any unlawful activity, and thereafter performs or attempts to perform any of [these] acts. . . ."
>
> Section 1953(a) makes it unlawful for anyone to "carr[y] or [to send] in interstate . . . commerce any . . . paraphernalia; . . . paper, writing, or other device used, or to be used . . . in (a) bookmaking; or (b) wagering pools. . . ." Section 1953(b)(3), however, makes the section inapplicable to "the carriage of transportation in interstate commerce of any newspaper or similar publication."

The defendants argued that their activities fell within §1953(b)(3)'s exception because they circulated newspapers and, as a result, they could not be convicted under §1952. The Supreme Court, after careful consideration, rejected reading these two sections *in pari materia*:

Petitioners' argument starts from the premise that they could not have been prosecuted under 1953(a) because the Illinois Sports News falls within the newspaper exception contained in §1953(b)(3).[1] Petitioners recognize that §1952 contains no express exception for newspapers comparable to §1953(b)(3), but contend that §1952 and §1953 are *in pari materia* that is, pertain to the same subject and, under settled principles of statutory construction, should therefore be construed "as if they were one law," *United States v. Freeman*, 3 How. 556, 564 (1845). . . . Thus, petitioners would have us read the exception contained in §1953(b)(3) as applicable to not only §1953(a) but also §1952(a), thereby barring their prosecution under the latter as well as the former. This we cannot do.

The rule of *in pari materia* like any canon of statutory construction is a reflection of practical experience in the interpretation of statutes: a legislative body generally uses a particular word with a consistent meaning in a given context. Thus, for example, a "later act can . . . be regarded as a legislative interpretation of [an] earlier act . . . in the sense that it aids in ascertaining the meaning of the words as used in their contemporary setting," and "is therefore entitled to great weight in resolving any ambiguities and doubts." *United States v. Stewart*, 311 U.S. at 64-65. . . .

True, §1952 and §1953 were both parts of a comprehensive federal legislative effort to assist local authorities in dealing with organized criminal activity which, in many instances, had assumed interstate proportions and which in all cases was materially assisted in its operations by the availability of facilities of interstate commerce. The two statutes, however, play different roles in achieving these broad, common goals.

Section 1953 has a narrow, specific function. It erects a substantial barrier to the distribution of certain materials used in the conduct of various forms of illegal gambling. By interdicting the flow of these materials to and between illegal gambling businesses, the statute purposefully seeks to impede the operation of such businesses.

Section 1952, by contrast, does not apply just to illegal gambling; rather, it is concerned with a broad spectrum of "unlawful activity," illegal gambling businesses being only one element. Moreover, the statute does not focus upon any particular materials, but upon the use of the facilities of interstate commerce with the intent of furthering an unlawful "business enterprise." It is, in short, an effort to deny individuals who act for such a criminal purpose access to the channels of commerce. Thus, while §1952 ultimately seeks, like §1953, to inhibit organized criminal activity, it takes a very different approach to doing so. To introduce into §1952 an exception based upon the nature of the material transported in interstate commerce would carve a substantial slice from the intended coverage of the statute. This we will not do without an affirmative indication which is lacking here that Congress so intended.

Id. at 243-47. Can you distinguish the treatment of *in pari materia* in *Stewart* and *Erlenbaugh*?

ii. Inferences Across Statutes

Courts have interpreted statutes together, even when the statutes are insufficiently related to construe them *in pari materia*. In such cases, courts are drawing an inference about the language in one statute from similar language in another statute. Thus, the Supreme Court has stated that "when

---

1. Representative Celler, who introduced the statute in the House, described its purposes as follows: "The primary purpose is to prevent the transportation in interstate commerce of wagering material. The purpose actually is to (cut off) and (shut off) gambling supplies, in reality to prevent these lotteries and kindred illegal diversions." 107 Cong. Rec. 16537. *See also* S. Rep. No. 589, 87th Cong., 1st Sess., 2 (1961); H.R. Rep. No. 968, 87th Cong., 1st Sess., 2 (1961).

Congress uses the same language in two statutes having similar purposes, particularly when one is enacted shortly after the other, it is appropriate to presume that Congress intended that text to have the same meaning in both statutes." Smith v. City of Jackson, 544 U.S. 228, 233 (2005). The Court has also recognized that when "judicial interpretations have settled the meaning of an existing statutory provision, repetition of the same language in a new statute indicates, as a general matter, the intent to incorporate its . . . judicial interpretations as well." Merrill Lynch, Pierce, Fenner & Smith Inc. v. Dabit, 547 U.S. 71, 85-86 (2006). For another example of statutory interpretation relying on a cross-statutory inference, see National Federation of Federal Employees, Local 1309 v. Dep't of Interior, 526 U.S. 86, 105-06 (1999) (O'Connor, J., dissenting) (concluding that the relevant language of the Federal Labor Statute is unambiguous in part based upon a comparison to the language of the National Labor Relations Act).

Sometimes courts draw an *expressio unius*-type inference from other statutes — that is, they read the inclusion of language in one statute to preclude the inference of such language in another. Or they apply a rule against surplusage, rejecting a reading of one statute that would make specific words in another statute superfluous or redundant. A classic and controversial example is West Virginia University Hospitals, Inc. v. Casey, 499 U.S. 83 (1991). In that case, the question was whether 42 U.S.C. §1988, which authorizes shifting "a reasonable attorney's fee" to the losing party in civil rights litigation, includes an expert witness's fee. The Court, with Justice Scalia writing, held that it did not, citing numerous statutes in which Congress had specifically allowed for shifting of expert witness fees:

> The record of statutory usage demonstrates convincingly that attorney's fees and expert fees are regarded as separate elements of litigation cost. While some fee-shifting provisions, like §1988, refer only to "attorney's fees," *see, e.g.*, Civil Rights Act of 1964, 42 U.S.C. §2000e-5(k), many others explicitly shift expert witness fees *as well as* attorney's fees. In 1976, just over a week prior to the enactment of §1988, Congress passed those provisions of the Toxic Substances Control Act, 15 U.S.C. §§2618(d), 2619(c)(2), which provide that a prevailing party may recover "the costs of suit and reasonable fees for attorneys *and expert witnesses.*" (Emphasis added.) Also in 1976, Congress amended the Consumer Product Safety Act, 15 U.S.C. §§2060(c), 2072(a), 2073, which as originally enacted in 1972 shifted to the losing party "cost[s] of suit, including a reasonable attorney's fee," *see* 86 Stat. 1226. In the 1976 amendment, Congress altered the fee-shifting provisions to their present form by adding a phrase shifting expert witness fees *in addition to* attorney's fees. *See* Pub. L. 94-284, §10, 90 Stat. 506, 507. Two other significant Acts passed in 1976 contain similar phrasing: the Resource Conservation and Recovery Act of 1976, 42 U.S.C. §6972(e) ("costs of litigation (including reasonable attorney and expert witness fees)"), and the Natural Gas Pipeline Safety Act Amendments of 1976, 49 U.S.C. App. §1686(e) ("costs of suit, including reasonable attorney's fees and reasonable expert witnesses fees").
>
> Congress enacted similarly phrased fee-shifting provisions in numerous statutes both before 1976, *see, e.g.*, Endangered Species Act of 1973, 16 U.S.C. §1540(g)(4) ("costs of litigation (including reasonable attorney and expert witness fees)"), and afterwards, see, *e.g.*, Public Utility Regulatory Policies Act of 1978, 16 U.S.C. §2632(a)(1) ("reasonable attorneys' fees, expert witness fees, and other reasonable costs incurred in preparation and advocacy of [the litigant's] position"). These statutes encompass diverse categories of legislation, including tax, administrative procedure, environmental

protection, consumer protection, admiralty and navigation, utilities regulation, and, significantly, civil rights: The Equal Access to Justice Act (EAJA), the counterpart to §1988 for violation of federal rights by federal employees, states that " 'fees and other expenses' [as shifted by §2412(d)(1)(A)] includes the reasonable expenses of expert witnesses . . . and reasonable attorney fees." 28 U.S.C. §2412(d)(2)(A). At least 34 statutes in 10 different titles of the United States Code explicitly shift attorney's fees *and* expert witness fees. . . .

The laws that refer to fees for nontestimonial expert services are less common, but they establish a similar usage both before and after 1976: Such fees are referred to *in addition to* attorney's fees when a shift is intended. A provision of the Criminal Justice Act of 1964, 18 U.S.C. §3006A(e), directs the court to reimburse appointed counsel for expert fees necessary to the defense of indigent criminal defendants — even though the immediately preceding provision, §3006A(d), already directs that appointed defense counsel be paid a designated hourly rate plus "expenses reasonably incurred." WVUH's position must be that expert fees billed to a client through an attorney are "attorney's fees" because they are to be treated as part of the expenses of the attorney; but if this were normal usage, they would have been reimbursable under the Criminal Justice Act as "expenses reasonably incurred" and subsection 3006A(e) would add nothing to the recoverable amount. The very heading of that subsection, "Services *other than* counsel" (emphasis added), acknowledges a distinction between services provided by the attorney himself and those provided to the attorney (or the client) by a nonlegal expert. . . .

We think this statutory usage shows beyond question that attorney's fees and expert fees are distinct items of expense. If, as WVUH argues, the one includes the other, dozens of statutes referring to the two separately become an inexplicable exercise in redundancy.

Id. at 88-92.

Justice Stevens dissented, arguing that comparison to other statutes was irrelevant because Congress has enacted *this* fee-shifting provision to overrule a Supreme Court decision that prohibited courts from making the prevailing party whole. *See id.* at 108 (Stevens, J., dissenting).

iii.   Repeals by Implication

What happens when the interpretation of a statute would implicitly repeal another statute? The Supreme Court has stated that "repeals by implication are not favored and will not be presumed unless the intention of the legislature to repeal [is] clear and manifest." National Ass'n of Home Builders v. Defenders of Wildlife, 551 U.S. 644, 662 (2007) (internal quotation marks omitted). More specifically, the Court has stated:

We will not infer a statutory repeal "unless the later statute 'expressly contradict[s] the original act' " or unless such a construction "is absolutely necessary . . . in order that [the] words [of the later statute] shall have any meaning at all." *Traynor v. Turnage*, 485 U.S. 535, 548 (1988) (quoting *Radzanower v. Touche Ross & Co.*, 426 U.S. 148, 153 (1976), in turn quoting T. Sedgwick, The Interpretation and Construction of Statutory and Constitutional Law 98 (2d ed. 1874)); *see also Branch v. Smith*, 538 U.S. 254, 273 (2003) ("An implied repeal will only be found where provisions in two statutes are in 'irreconcilable conflict,' or where the latter Act covers the whole subject of the earlier one and 'is clearly intended as a substitute' "); *Posadas v. National City Bank*, 296 U.S. 497, 503 (1936) ("[T]he intention of the legislature to repeal must be clear and manifest").

Id.

The presumption against repeals by implication is, in some sense, the inverse of a whole code or coherence rule. Rather than presuming that Congress intends the whole code as one, it views statutes as confined to their own domains, particularly when later-enacted statutes are more general than earlier-enacted statutes. Thus, the Court has stated, "a statute dealing with a narrow, precise, and specific subject is not submerged by a later enacted statute covering a more generalized spectrum." *Radzanower*, 426 U.S. at 153.

But the presumption against repeals by implication is also different from the other canons that we have seen because it can be overcome only by clear language to the contrary—that is, an explicit provision repealing an earlier statute or provision. We discussed repeal provisions briefly in Chapter 3 when discussing the structural components of statutes. Unless a statute contains an express repeal provision, it will not likely be interpreted to have that effect.

There are many examples in which the Court has applied the presumption against repeals by implication, finding no clear language sufficient to overcome it. In *National Ass'n of Home Builders*, the Court refused to read a provision of the Endangered Species Act as implicitly repealing a provision of the Clean Water Act. *See* 551 U.S. at 662-64. The issue was complicated. Section 402(b) of the Clean Water Act provides that EPA "shall" transfer its authority to issue pollution permits to a state that applies for such a transfer and meets nine statutory criteria. 33 U.S.C. §1342(b). Section 7(a)(2) of the Endangered Species Act provides that "[e]ach Federal agency shall, in consultation with and with the assistance of the Secretary [of the Interior], insure that any action authorized, funded, or carried out by such agency . . . is not likely to jeopardize" endangered or threatened species or their habitats. 16 U.S.C. §1536(a)(2). The question was whether EPA had to consult with the Secretary of Interior before transferring its permitting authority to a state under the Clean Water Act. The Court declined to read the Endangered Species Act as effectively engrafting a tenth criterion on the Clean Water Act. It reasoned that the Clean Water Act clearly established nine criteria: "The provision operates as a ceiling as well as a floor." *Id.* at 662. Interpreting §7(a)(2) to raise that floor would alter or partially repeal §402(b)'s statutory mandate (i.e., the part that says only nine criteria), as well as the statutory mandates of other federal laws. *Id.*

In Hawaii v. Office of Hawaiian Affairs, 556 U.S. 163, 175-76 (2009), the Court applied this canon to interpret a joint resolution that Congress passed in 1993 to apologize for the role that the United States played in overthrowing the Hawaiian monarchy in the late nineteenth century. The issue was whether this joint resolution effectively amended or repealed Hawaii's rights and obligations under the Admission Act, which Congress enacted in 1959 to admit Hawaii to the Union. The Court held that it did not. The Court stated that "[t]he Apology Resolution reveals no indication—much less a 'clear and manifest' one—that Congress intended to amend or repeal the State's rights and obligations under [the] Admission Act (or any other federal law); nor does the Apology Resolution reveal any evidence that Congress intended *sub silentio* to 'cloud' the title that the United States held in 'absolute fee' and transferred to the State in 1959." *Id.* at 175-176. The joint resolution, the Court concluded, does nothing more than offer an apology. *Id.* For Congress to amend or repeal preexisting statutes, it must use express language.

Now you have a sense for the basic textual canons of construction. As we have noted, courts often apply more than one canon when interpreting statutory language. Furthermore, courts do not always refer to canons by name or use the same formulation to describe them. Thus, when you read a judicial opinion, you may have to look for clues, such as canonical language introducing the rule — "It is well settled that . . . ," "A foundational principle is . . . ," or "As we have long recognized, . . ." — and a citation or two following the rule. And remember, even the label "canon," which sometimes appears in an opinion, has little special significance. Any interpretive rule or principle can be considered a canon of construction.

e. The Court's Most Recent Word on Text

In the second case regarding the Affordable Care Act (ACA) to reach the Supreme Court, the Court relied heavily on whole act inferences, the statute's findings and purposes, and context to give the ACA a construction that the Court conceded was not, at first glance, the most natural one. The case, *King v. Burwell*, shows the power of cross-textual inferences in discerning the meaning of particular provisions.

King v. Burwell

135 S. Ct. 2480 (2015)

Chief Justice ROBERTS delivered the opinion of the Court.

The Patient Protection and Affordable Care Act adopts a series of interlocking reforms designed to expand coverage in the individual health insurance market. First, the Act bars insurers from taking a person's health into account when deciding whether to sell health insurance or how much to charge. Second, the Act generally requires each person to maintain insurance coverage or make a payment to the Internal Revenue Service. And third, the Act gives tax credits to certain people to make insurance more affordable.

In addition to those reforms, the Act requires the creation of an "Exchange" in each State—basically, a marketplace that allows people to compare and purchase insurance plans. The Act gives each State the opportunity to establish its own Exchange, but provides that the Federal Government will establish the Exchange if the State does not.

This case is about whether the Act's interlocking reforms apply equally in each State no matter who establishes the State's Exchange. Specifically, the question presented is whether the Act's tax credits are available in States that have a Federal Exchange.

I

A

The Patient Protection and Affordable Care Act, 124 Stat. 119, grew out of a long history of failed health insurance reform. In the 1990s, several States began experimenting with ways to expand people's access to coverage. One common approach was to impose a pair of insurance market regulations—a "guaranteed issue" requirement, which barred insurers from denying coverage to any person because of his health, and a "community rating" requirement, which barred insurers from charging a person higher premiums for the same reason. Together, those requirements were designed to ensure that anyone who wanted to buy health insurance could do so.

The guaranteed issue and community rating requirements achieved that goal, but they had an unintended consequence: They encouraged people to wait until they got sick to buy insurance. Why buy insurance coverage when you are healthy, if you can buy the same coverage for the same price when you become ill? This consequence—known as "adverse selection"—led to a second: Insurers were forced to increase premiums to account for the fact that, more and more, it was the sick rather than the healthy who were buying insurance. And that consequence fed back into the first: As the cost of insurance rose, even more people waited until they became ill to buy it.

This led to an economic "death spiral." As premiums rose higher and higher, and the number of people buying insurance sank lower and lower, insurers began to leave the market entirely. As a result, the number of people without insurance increased dramatically.

This cycle happened repeatedly during the 1990s. For example, in 1993, the State of Washington reformed its individual insurance market by adopting the guaranteed issue and community rating requirements. Over the next three years, premiums rose by 78 percent and the number of people enrolled fell by 25 percent. By 1999, 17 of the State's 19 private insurers had left the market, and the remaining two had announced their intention to do so. . . .

In 1996, Massachusetts adopted the guaranteed issue and community rating requirements and experienced similar results. But in 2006, Massachusetts added two more reforms: The Commonwealth required individuals to buy insurance or pay a penalty, and it gave tax credits to certain individuals to ensure that they could afford the insurance they were required to buy. . . . The combination of these three reforms—insurance market regulations, a coverage mandate, and tax credits—reduced the uninsured rate in Massachusetts to 2.6 percent, by far the lowest in the Nation. Hearing on Examining Individual State Experiences with Health Care Reform Coverage Initiatives in the Context of National Reform before the Senate Committee on Health, Education, Labor, and Pensions, 111th Cong., 1st Sess., 9 (2009).

B

The Affordable Care Act adopts a version of the three key reforms that made the Massachusetts system successful. First, the Act adopts the guaranteed issue and community rating requirements. The Act provides that "each health insurance issuer that offers health insurance coverage in the individual . . . market in a State must accept every . . . individual in the State that applies for such coverage." 42 U.S.C. §300gg-1(a). The Act also bars insurers from charging higher premiums on the basis of a person's health. §300gg.

Second, the Act generally requires individuals to maintain health insurance coverage or make a payment to the IRS. 26 U.S.C. §5000A. Congress recognized that, without an incentive, "many individuals would wait to purchase health insurance until they needed care." 42 U.S.C. §18091(2)(I).[2] So Congress adopted a coverage requirement to "minimize this adverse selection and broaden the health insurance risk pool to include healthy individuals, which will lower health insurance premiums." *Ibid.* In Congress's view, that coverage requirement was "essential to creating effective health insurance markets." *Ibid.* Congress also provided an exemption from the coverage requirement for anyone who has to spend more than eight percent of his income on health insurance. 26 U.S.C. §§5000A(e)(1)(A), (e)(1)(B)(ii).

Third, the Act seeks to make insurance more affordable by giving refundable tax credits to individuals with household incomes between 100 percent and 400 percent of the federal poverty line. §36B. Individuals who meet the Act's requirements may purchase insurance with the tax credits, which are provided in advance directly to the individual's insurer. 42 U.S.C. §§18081, 18082.

These three reforms are closely intertwined. As noted, Congress found that the guaranteed issue and community rating requirements would not work without the coverage requirement. §18091(2)(I). And the coverage requirement would not work without the tax credits. The reason is that, without the tax credits, the cost of buying insurance would exceed eight percent of income for a large number of individuals, which would exempt them from the coverage requirement. Given the relationship between these three reforms, the Act provided that they should take effect on the same day—January 1, 2014. See Affordable Care Act, §1253, redesignated §1255, 124 Stat. 162, 895; §§1401(e), 1501(d), *id.,* at 220, 249.

C

In addition to those three reforms, the Act requires the creation of an "Exchange" in each State where people can shop for insurance, usually online. 42 U.S.C. §18031(b)(1). An Exchange may be created in one of

---

2. [The Court cites here to an enacted statement of findings.—Eds.]

two ways. First, the Act provides that "[e]ach State shall . . . establish an American Health Benefit Exchange . . . for the State." *Ibid.* Second, if a State nonetheless chooses not to establish its own Exchange, the Act provides that the Secretary of Health and Human Services "shall . . . establish and operate such Exchange within the State." §18041(c)(1).

The issue in this case is whether the Act's tax credits are available in States that have a Federal Exchange rather than a State Exchange. The Act initially provides that tax credits "shall be allowed" for any "applicable taxpayer." 26 U.S.C. §36B(a). The Act then provides that the amount of the tax credit depends in part on whether the taxpayer has enrolled in an insurance plan through "an Exchange *established by the State* under section 1311 of the Patient Protection and Affordable Care Act [hereinafter 42 U.S.C. §18031]." 26 U.S.C. §§36B(b)-(c) (emphasis added).

The IRS addressed the availability of tax credits by promulgating a rule that made them available on both State and Federal Exchanges. 77 Fed. Reg. 30378 (2012). As relevant here, the IRS Rule provides that a taxpayer is eligible for a tax credit if he enrolled in an insurance plan through "an Exchange," 26 CFR §1.36B-2 (2013), which is defined as "an Exchange serving the individual market . . . regardless of whether the Exchange is established and operated by a State . . . or by HHS," 45 CFR §155.20 (2014). At this point, 16 States and the District of Columbia have established their own Exchanges; the other 34 States have elected to have HHS do so.

D

Petitioners are four individuals who live in Virginia, which has a Federal Exchange. They do not wish to purchase health insurance. In their view, Virginia's Exchange does not qualify as "an Exchange established by the State under [42 U.S.C. §18031]," so they should not receive any tax credits. That would make the cost of buying insurance more than eight percent of their income, which would exempt them from the Act's coverage requirement. 26 U.S.C. §5000A(e)(1).

Under the IRS Rule, however, Virginia's Exchange *would* qualify as "an Exchange established by the State under [42 U.S.C. §18031]," so petitioners would receive tax credits. That would make the cost of buying insurance *less* than eight percent of petitioners' income, which would subject them to the Act's coverage requirement. The IRS Rule therefore requires petitioners to either buy health insurance they do not want, or make a payment to the IRS.

Petitioners challenged the IRS Rule in Federal District Court. The District Court dismissed the suit, holding that the Act unambiguously made tax credits available to individuals enrolled through a Federal Exchange. *King v. Sebelius*, 997 F. Supp. 2d 415 (ED Va. 2014). The Court of Appeals for the Fourth Circuit affirmed. 759 F.3d 358 (2014). The Fourth Circuit viewed the Act as "ambiguous and subject to at least two different interpretations." *Id.*, at 372. The court therefore deferred to the IRS's interpretation under *Chevron U.S.A. Inc. v. Natural Resources Defense Council, Inc.*, 467 U.S. 837 (1984). 759 F.3d, at 376.

The same day that the Fourth Circuit issued its decision, the Court of Appeals for the District of Columbia Circuit vacated the IRS Rule in a different case, holding that the Act "unambiguously restricts" the tax credits to State Exchanges. *Halbig v. Burwell*, 758 F.3d 390, 394 (2014). We granted certiorari in the present case.

II

[The Court addressed whether the IRS's interpretation of the ACA should be accorded deference under Chevron U.S.A. Inc. v. Natural Resources Defense Council, Inc., 467 U.S. 837 (1984), as the Fourth Circuit had held. The Court held that it declined to apply *Chevron* deference, holding that the issue at stake was too important to presume that Congress would have implicitly delegated it to an agency, and especially to the IRS, without apparent expertise in health care policy.]

It is instead our task to determine the correct reading of Section 36B. If the statutory language is plain, we must enforce it according to its terms. *Hardt v. Reliance Standard Life Ins.* Co., 560 U.S. 242, 251 (2010). But oftentimes the "meaning—or ambiguity—of certain words or phrases may only become evident when placed in context." [*FDA v. Brown & Williamson*, 529 U.S. 120-132 (2000).] So when deciding whether the language is plain, we must read the words "in their context and with a view to their place in the overall statutory scheme." *Id.,* at 133 (internal quotation marks omitted). Our duty, after all, is "to construe statutes, not isolated provisions." *Graham County Soil and Water Conservation Dist. v. United States ex rel. Wilson*, 559 U.S. 280, 290 (2010) (internal quotation marks omitted).

A

We begin with the text of Section 36B. As relevant here, Section 36B allows an individual to receive tax credits only if the individual enrolls in an insurance plan through "an Exchange established by the State under [42 U.S.C. §18031]." In other words, three things must be true: First, the individual must enroll in an insurance plan through "an Exchange." Second, that Exchange must be "established by the State." And third, that Exchange must be established "under [42 U.S.C. §18031]." We address each requirement in turn.

First, all parties agree that a Federal Exchange qualifies as "an Exchange" for purposes of Section 36B. . . . Section 18031 provides that "[e]ach State shall . . . establish an American Health Benefit Exchange . . . for the State." §18031(b)(1). Although phrased as a requirement, the Act gives the States "flexibility" by allowing them to "elect" whether they want to establish an Exchange. §18041(b). If the State chooses not to do so, Section 18041 provides that the Secretary "shall . . . establish and operate *such Exchange* within the State." §18041(c)(1) (emphasis added).

By using the phrase "such Exchange," Section 18041 instructs the Secretary to establish and operate the *same* Exchange that the State was directed to establish under Section 18031. See Black's Law Dictionary 1661 (10th ed. 2014) (defining "such" as "That or those; having just been mentioned"). In other words, State Exchanges and Federal Exchanges are equivalent—they must meet the same requirements, perform the same functions, and serve the same purposes. Although State and Federal Exchanges are established by different sovereigns, Sections 18031 and 18041 do not suggest that they differ in any meaningful way. A Federal Exchange therefore counts as "an Exchange" under Section 36B.

Second, we must determine whether a Federal Exchange is "established by the State" for purposes of Section 36B. At the outset, it might seem that a Federal Exchange cannot fulfill this requirement. After all, the Act defines "State" to mean "each of the 50 States and the District of Columbia"—a definition that does not include the Federal Government. 42 U.S.C. §18024(d). But when read in context, "with a view to [its] place in the overall statutory scheme," the meaning of the phrase "established by the State" is not so clear. *Brown & Williamson*, 529 U.S., at 133 (internal quotation marks omitted).

After telling each State to establish an Exchange, Section 18031 provides that all Exchanges "shall make available qualified health plans to qualified individuals." 42 U.S.C. §18031(d)(2)(A). Section 18032 then defines the term "qualified individual" in part as an individual who "resides in the State that established the Exchange." §18032(f)(1)(A). And that's a problem: If we give the phrase "the State that established the Exchange" its most natural meaning, there would be *no* "qualified individuals" on Federal Exchanges. But the Act clearly contemplates that there will be qualified individuals on *every* Exchange. As we just mentioned, the Act requires all Exchanges to "make available qualified health plans to qualified individuals"—something an Exchange could not do if there were no such individuals. §18031(d)(2)(A). And the Act tells the Exchange, in deciding which health plans to offer, to consider "the interests of qualified individuals . . . in the State or States in which such Exchange operates"—again, something the Exchange could not do if qualified individuals did not exist. §18031(e)(1)(B). This problem arises repeatedly throughout the Act. See, *e.g.*, §18031(b)(2) (allowing a State to create "one Exchange . . . for providing . . . services to both qualified individuals and qualified small employers," rather than creating separate Exchanges for those two groups).[1]

These provisions suggest that the Act may not always use the phrase "established by the State" in its most natural sense. Thus, the meaning of that phrase may not be as clear as it appears when read out of context.

Third, we must determine whether a Federal Exchange is established "under [42 U.S.C. §18031]." This too might seem a requirement that a Federal Exchange cannot fulfill, because it is Section 18041 that tells the

---

1. The dissent argues that one would "naturally read instructions about qualified individuals to be inapplicable to the extent a particular Exchange has no such individuals." *Post*, at 10-11 (Scalia, J., dissenting). But the fact that the dissent's interpretation would make so many parts of the Act "inapplicable" to Federal Exchanges is precisely what creates the problem. It would be odd indeed for Congress to write such detailed instructions about customers on a State Exchange, while having nothing to say about those on a Federal Exchange.

Secretary when to "establish and operate such Exchange." But here again, the way different provisions in the statute interact suggests otherwise.

The Act defines the term "Exchange" to mean "an American Health Benefit Exchange established under section 18031." §300gg-91(d)(21). If we import that definition into Section 18041, the Act tells the Secretary to "establish and operate such 'American Health Benefit Exchange established under section 18031.'" That suggests that Section 18041 authorizes the Secretary to establish an Exchange under Section 18031, not (or not only) under Section 18041. Otherwise, the Federal Exchange, by definition, would not be an "Exchange" at all. See *Halbig*, 758 F.3d, at 399-400 (acknowledging that the Secretary establishes Federal Exchanges under Section 18031).

This interpretation of "under [42 U.S.C. §18031]" fits best with the statutory context. All of the requirements that an Exchange must meet are in Section 18031, so it is sensible to regard all Exchanges as established under that provision. In addition, every time the Act uses the word "Exchange," the definitional provision requires that we substitute the phrase "Exchange established under section 18031." If Federal Exchanges were not established under Section 18031, therefore, literally none of the Act's requirements would apply to them. Finally, the Act repeatedly uses the phrase "established under [42 U.S.C. §18031]" in situations where it would make no sense to distinguish between State and Federal Exchanges. See, *e.g.*, 26 U.S.C. §125(f)(3)(A) (2012 ed., Supp. I) ("The term 'qualified benefit' shall not include any qualified health plan . . . offered through an Exchange established under [42 U.S.C. §18031]"); 26 U.S.C. §6055(b)(1)(B)(iii)(I) (2012 ed.) (requiring insurers to report whether each insurance plan they provided "is a qualified health plan offered through an Exchange established under [42 U.S.C. §18031]"). A Federal Exchange may therefore be considered one established "under [42 U.S.C. §18031]."

The upshot of all this is that the phrase "an Exchange established by the State under [42 U.S.C. §18031]" is properly viewed as ambiguous. The phrase may be limited in its reach to State Exchanges. But it is also possible that the phrase refers to *all* Exchanges—both State and Federal—at least for purposes of the tax credits. If a State chooses not to follow the directive in Section 18031 that it establish an Exchange, the Act tells the Secretary to establish "such Exchange." §18041. And by using the words "such Exchange," the Act indicates that State and Federal Exchanges should be the same. But State and Federal Exchanges would differ in a fundamental way if tax credits were available only on State Exchanges—one type of Exchange would help make insurance more affordable by providing billions of dollars to the States' citizens; the other type of Exchange would not. . . .[2]

---

2. The dissent argues that the phrase "such Exchange" does not suggest that State and Federal Exchanges "are in all respects equivalent." *Post*, at 8. In support, it quotes the Constitution's Elections Clause, which makes the state legislature primarily responsible for prescribing election regulations, but allows Congress to "make or alter such Regulations." Art. I, §4, cl. 1. No one would say that state and

Petitioners and the dissent respond that the words "established by the State" would be unnecessary if Congress meant to extend tax credits to both State and Federal Exchanges. . . . But "our preference for avoiding surplusage constructions is not absolute." *Lamie v. United States Trustee*, 540 U.S. 526, 536 (2004); see also *Marx v. General Revenue Corp.*, 568 U.S. __ (2013) ("The canon against surplusage is not an absolute rule"). And specifically with respect to this Act, rigorous application of the canon does not seem a particularly useful guide to a fair construction of the statute.

The Affordable Care Act contains more than a few examples of inartful drafting. (To cite just one, the Act creates three separate Section 1563s. See 124 Stat. 270, 911, 912.) Several features of the Act's passage contributed to that unfortunate reality. Congress wrote key parts of the Act behind closed doors, rather than through "the traditional legislative process." . . . And Congress passed much of the Act using a complicated budgetary procedure known as "reconciliation," which limited opportunities for debate and amendment, and bypassed the Senate's normal 60-vote filibuster requirement. . . . As a result, the Act does not reflect the type of care and deliberation that one might expect of such significant legislation.

Anyway, we "must do our best, bearing in mind the fundamental canon of statutory construction that the words of a statute must be read in their context and with a view to their place in the overall statutory scheme." *Utility Air Regulatory Group*, 573 U.S., at __ (slip op., at 15) (internal quotation marks omitted). After reading Section 36B along with other related provisions in the Act, we cannot conclude that the phrase "an Exchange established by the State under [Section 18031]" is unambiguous.

B

Given that the text is ambiguous, we must turn to the broader structure of the Act to determine the meaning of Section 36B. "A provision that may seem ambiguous in isolation is often clarified by the remainder of the statutory scheme . . . because only one of the permissible meanings produces a substantive effect that is compatible with the rest of the law." *United Sav. Assn. of Tex. v. Timbers of Inwood Forest Associates, Ltd.*, 484 U.S. 365, 371 (1988). Here, the statutory scheme compels us to reject petitioners' interpretation because it would destabilize the individual insurance market in any State with a Federal Exchange, and likely create the very "death spirals" that Congress designed the Act to avoid. See *New York State Dept. of Social Servs. v. Dublino*, 413 U.S. 405-420 (1973) ("We cannot interpret federal statutes to negate their own stated purposes.").[3]

---

federal election regulations are in all respects equivalent, the dissent contends, so we should not say that State and Federal Exchanges are. But the Elections Clause does not precisely define what an election regulation must look like, so Congress can prescribe regulations that differ from what the State would prescribe. The Affordable Care Act *does* precisely define what an Exchange must look like, however, so a Federal Exchange cannot differ from a State Exchange.

3. The dissent notes that several other provisions in the Act use the phrase "established by the State," and argues that our holding applies to each of those provisions. *Post*, at 5-6. But "the presumption

As discussed above, Congress based the Affordable Care Act on three major reforms: first, the guaranteed issue and community rating requirements; second, a requirement that individuals maintain health insurance coverage or make a payment to the IRS; and third, the tax credits for individuals with household incomes between 100 percent and 400 percent of the federal poverty line. In a State that establishes its own Exchange, these three reforms work together to expand insurance coverage. The guaranteed issue and community rating requirements ensure that anyone can buy insurance; the coverage requirement creates an incentive for people to do so before they get sick; and the tax credits—it is hoped—make insurance more affordable. Together, those reforms "minimize . . . adverse selection and broaden the health insurance risk pool to include healthy individuals, which will lower health insurance premiums." 42 U.S.C. §18091(2)(I).

Under petitioners' reading, however, the Act would operate quite differently in a State with a Federal Exchange. As they see it, one of the Act's three major reforms—the tax credits—would not apply. And a second major reform—the coverage requirement—would not apply in a meaningful way. As explained earlier, the coverage requirement applies only when the cost of buying health insurance (minus the amount of the tax credits) is less than eight percent of an individual's income. 26 U.S.C. §§5000A(e)(1)(A), (e)(1)(B)(ii). So without the tax credits, the coverage requirement would apply to fewer individuals. And it would be a *lot* fewer. In 2014, approximately 87 percent of people who bought insurance on a Federal Exchange did so with tax credits, and virtually all of those people would become exempt. . .

The combination of no tax credits and an ineffective coverage requirement could well push a State's individual insurance market into a death spiral. One study predicts that premiums would increase by 47 percent and enrollment would decrease by 70 percent. . . . Another study predicts that premiums would increase by 35 percent and enrollment would decrease by 69 percent. . . . And those effects would not be limited to individuals who purchase insurance on the Exchanges. Because the Act requires insurers to treat the entire individual market as a single risk pool, 42 U.S.C. §18032(c)(1), premiums outside the Exchange would rise along with those inside the Exchange. . . .

It is implausible that Congress meant the Act to operate in this manner. See *National Federation of Independent Business v. Sebelius*, 567 U.S. ___, ___ (2012) (Scalia, Kennedy, Thomas, and Alito, JJ., dissenting) (slip op., at 60) ("Without the federal subsidies . . . the exchanges would not operate as Congress intended and may not operate at all."). Congress made the guaranteed issue and community rating requirements applicable in every

---

of consistent usage readily yields to context," and a statutory term may mean different things in different places. *Utility Air Regulatory Group v. EPA*, 573 U.S. ___, ___ (2014) (slip op., at 15) (internal quotation marks omitted). That is particularly true when, as here, "the Act is far from a *chef d'oeuvre* of legislative draftsmanship." *Ibid.* Because the other provisions cited by the dissent are not at issue here, we do not address them.

State in the Nation. But those requirements only work when combined with the coverage requirement and the tax credits. So it stands to reason that Congress meant for those provisions to apply in every State as well.[4]

Petitioners respond that Congress was not worried about the effects of withholding tax credits from States with Federal Exchanges because "Congress evidently believed it was offering states a deal they would not refuse." . . . Congress may have been wrong about the States' willingness to establish their own Exchanges, petitioners continue, but that does not allow this Court to rewrite the Act to fix that problem. That is particularly true, petitioners conclude, because the States likely *would* have created their own Exchanges in the absence of the IRS Rule, which eliminated any incentive that the States had to do so. *Id.,* at 36-38.

Section 18041 refutes the argument that Congress believed it was offering the States a deal they would not refuse. That section provides that, if a State elects not to establish an Exchange, the Secretary "shall . . . establish and operate such Exchange within the State." 42 U.S.C. §18041(c)(1)(A). The whole point of that provision is to create a federal fallback in case a State chooses not to establish its own Exchange. Contrary to petitioners' argument, Congress did not believe it was offering States a deal they would not refuse — it expressly addressed what would happen if a State *did* refuse the deal. . . .

D

Petitioners' arguments about the plain meaning of Section 36B are strong. But while the meaning of the phrase "an Exchange established by the State under [42 U.S.C. §18031]" may seem plain "when viewed in isolation," such a reading turns out to be "untenable in light of [the statute] as a whole." *Department of Revenue of Ore. v. ACF Industries, Inc.,* 510 U.S. 332, 343 (1994). In this instance, the context and structure of the Act compel us to depart from what would otherwise be the most natural reading of the pertinent statutory phrase.

Reliance on context and structure in statutory interpretation is a "subtle business, calling for great wariness lest what professes to be mere rendering becomes creation and attempted interpretation of legislation becomes legislation itself." Palmer v. *Massachusetts,* 308 U.S. 79, 83 (1939). For the reasons we have given, however, such reliance is appropriate in this case, and leads us to conclude that Section 36B allows tax credits for insurance purchased

---

4. The dissent argues that our analysis "show[s] only that the statutory scheme contains a flaw," one "that appeared as well in other parts of the Act." *Post,* at 14. For support, the dissent notes that the guaranteed issue and community rating requirements might apply in the federal territories, even though the coverage requirement does not. *Id.,* at 14-15. The confusion arises from the fact that the guaranteed issue and community rating requirements were added as amendments to the Public Health Service Act, which contains a definition of the word "State" that includes the territories, 42 U.S.C. §201(f), while the later-enacted Affordable Care Act contains a definition of the word "State" that excludes the territories, §18024(d). The predicate for the dissent's point is therefore uncertain at best.

on any Exchange created under the Act. Those credits are necessary for the Federal Exchanges to function like their State Exchange counterparts, and to avoid the type of calamitous result that Congress plainly meant to avoid.

In a democracy, the power to make the law rests with those chosen by the people. Our role is more confined—"to say what the law is." *Marbury v. Madison*, 1 Cranch 137, 177 (1803). That is easier in some cases than in others. But in every case we must respect the role of the Legislature, and take care not to undo what it has done. A fair reading of legislation demands a fair understanding of the legislative plan.

Congress passed the Affordable Care Act to improve health insurance markets, not to destroy them. If at all possible, we must interpret the Act in a way that is consistent with the former, and avoids the latter. Section 36B can fairly be read consistent with what we see as Congress's plan, and that is the reading we adopt.

The judgment of the United States Court of Appeals for the Fourth Circuit is

Affirmed.

Justice SCALIA, with whom Justice THOMAS and Justice ALITO join, dissenting.

The Court holds that when the Patient Protection and Affordable Care Act says "Exchange established by the State" it means "Exchange established by the State or the Federal Government." That is of course quite absurd, and the Court's 21 pages of explanation make it no less so.

I

. . . This case requires us to decide whether someone who buys insurance on an Exchange established by the Secretary gets tax credits. You would think the answer would be obvious—so obvious there would hardly be a need for the Supreme Court to hear a case about it. In order to receive any money under §36B, an individual must enroll in an insurance plan through an "Exchange established by the State." The Secretary of Health and Human Services is not a State. So an Exchange established by the Secretary is not an Exchange established by the State—which means people who buy health insurance through such an Exchange get no money under §36B.

Words no longer have meaning if an Exchange that is *not* established by a State is "established by the State." It is hard to come up with a clearer way to limit tax credits to state Exchanges than to use the words "established by the State." And it is hard to come up with a reason to include the words "by the State" other than the purpose of limiting credits to state Exchanges. "[T]he plain, obvious, and rational meaning of a statute is always to be preferred to any curious, narrow, hidden sense that nothing but the exigency of a hard case and the ingenuity and study of an acute and powerful intellect would discover." *Lynch v. Alworth-Stephens Co.*, 267 U.S. 364, 370 (1925) (internal quotation marks omitted). Under all the usual rules of interpretation, in short, the Government should lose this case. But normal rules of interpretation seem always to yield to the overriding principle of the present Court: The Affordable Care Act must be saved.

II

. . . I wholeheartedly agree with the Court that sound interpretation requires paying attention to the whole law, not homing in on isolated words or even isolated sections. Context always matters. Let us not forget, however, *why* context matters: It is a tool for understanding the terms of the law, not an excuse for rewriting them.

Any effort to understand rather than to rewrite a law must accept and apply the presumption that lawmakers use words in "their natural and ordinary signification." *Pensacola Telegraph Co. v. Western Union Telegraph Co.*, 96 U.S. 1, 12 (1878). Ordinary connotation does not always prevail, but the more unnatural the proposed interpretation of a law, the more compelling the contextual evidence must be to show that it is correct. . . .

Far from offering the overwhelming evidence of meaning needed to justify the Court's interpretation, other contextual clues undermine it at every turn. To begin with, other parts of the Act sharply distinguish between the establishment of an Exchange by a State and the establishment of an Exchange by the Federal Government. The States' authority to set up Exchanges comes from one provision, §18031(b); the Secretary's authority comes from an entirely different provision, §18041(c). Funding for States to establish Exchanges comes from one part of the law, §18031(a); funding for the Secretary to establish Exchanges comes from an entirely different part of the law, §18121. States generally run state-created Exchanges; the Secretary generally runs federally created Exchanges. §18041(b)-(c). And the Secretary's authority to set up an Exchange in a State depends upon the State's "*[f]ailure* to establish [an] Exchange." §18041(c) (emphasis added). Provisions such as these destroy any pretense that a federal Exchange is in some sense also established by a State.

Reading the rest of the Act also confirms that, as relevant here, there are *only* two ways to set up an Exchange in a State: establishment by a State and establishment by the Secretary. §§18031(b), 18041(c). So saying that an Exchange established by the Federal Government is "established by the State" goes beyond giving words bizarre meanings; it leaves the limiting phrase "by the State" with no operative effect at all. That is a stark violation of the elementary principle that requires an interpreter "to give effect, if possible, to every clause and word of a statute." *Montclair v. Ramsdell*, 107 U.S. 147, 152 (1883). In weighing this argument, it is well to remember the difference between giving a term a meaning that duplicates another part of the law, and giving a term no meaning at all. Lawmakers sometimes repeat themselves—whether out of a desire to add emphasis, a sense of belt-and-suspenders caution, or a lawyerly penchant for doublets (aid and abet, cease and desist, null and void). Lawmakers do not, however, tend to use terms that "have no operation at all." *Marbury v. Madison*, 1 Cranch 137, 174

(1803). So while the rule against treating a term as a redundancy is far from categorical, the rule against treating it as a nullity is as close to absolute as interpretive principles get. The Court's reading does not merely give "by the State" a duplicative effect; it causes the phrase to have no effect whatever. . . .

III

For its next defense of the indefensible, the Court turns to the Affordable Care Act's design and purposes. . . . The Court reasons that Congress intended [the Act's] three reforms to "work together to expand insurance coverage"; and because the first two apply in every State, so must the third.

This reasoning suffers from no shortage of flaws. To begin with, "even the most formidable argument concerning the statute's purposes could not overcome the clarity [of] the statute's text." *Kloeckner v. Solis*, 568 U.S. ___, n.4 (2012). Statutory design and purpose matter only to the extent they help clarify an otherwise ambiguous provision. Could anyone maintain with a straight face that §36B is unclear? . . .

Having gone wrong in consulting statutory purpose at all, the Court goes wrong again in analyzing it. The purposes of a law must be "collected chiefly from its words," not "from extrinsic circumstances." *Sturges v. Crowninshield*, 4 Wheat. 122, 202 (1819) (Marshall, C.J.). Only by concentrating on the law's terms can a judge hope to uncover the scheme *of the statute*, rather than some other scheme that the judge thinks desirable. Like it or not, the express terms of the Affordable Care Act make only two of the three reforms mentioned by the Court applicable in States that do not establish Exchanges. It is perfectly possible for them to operate independently of tax credits. The guaranteed-issue and community-rating requirements continue to ensure that insurance companies treat all customers the same no matter their health, and the individual mandate continues to encourage people to maintain coverage, lest they be "taxed."

IV

Perhaps sensing the dismal failure of its efforts to show that "established by the State" means "established by the State or the Federal Government," the Court tries to palm off the pertinent statutory phrase as "inartful drafting." *Ante*, at 14. This Court, however, has no free-floating power "to rescue Congress from its drafting errors." *Lamie v. United States Trustee*, 540 U.S. 526, 542 (2004) (internal quotation marks omitted). Only when it is patently obvious to a reasonable reader that a drafting mistake has occurred may a court correct the mistake. The occurrence of a misprint may be apparent from the face of the law, as it is where the Affordable Care Act "creates three separate Section 1563s." *Ante*, at 14. But the Court does not pretend that there is any such indication of a drafting error on the face of §36B. The occurrence of a misprint may also be apparent because a provision decrees an absurd result—a consequence "so monstrous, that all mankind would, without hesitation, unite in rejecting the application." *Sturges*, 4

Wheat., at 203. But §36B does not come remotely close to satisfying that demanding standard. It is entirely plausible that tax credits were restricted to state Exchanges deliberately—for example, in order to encourage States to establish their own Exchanges. We therefore have no authority to dismiss the terms of the law as a drafting fumble. . . .

V

The Court's decision reflects the philosophy that judges should endure whatever interpretive distortions it takes in order to correct a supposed flaw in the statutory machinery. That philosophy ignores the American people's decision to give *Congress* "[a]ll legislative Powers" enumerated in the Constitution. Art. I, §1. They made Congress, not this Court, responsible for both making laws and mending them. This Court holds only the judicial power—the power to pronounce the law as Congress has enacted it. We lack the prerogative to repair laws that do not work out in practice, just as the people lack the ability to throw us out of office if they dislike the solutions we concoct. We must always remember, therefore, that "[o]ur task is to apply the text, not to improve upon it." *Pavelic & LeFlore v. Marvel Entertainment Group, Div. of Cadence Industries Corp.*, 493 U.S. 120, 126 (1989).

. . .

Rather than rewriting the law under the pretense of interpreting it, the Court should have left it to Congress to decide what to do about the Act's limitation of tax credits to state Exchanges. If Congress values above everything else the Act's applicability across the country, it could make tax credits available in every Exchange. If it prizes state involvement in the Act's implementation, it could continue to limit tax credits to state Exchanges while taking other steps to mitigate the economic consequences predicted by the Court. If Congress wants to accommodate both goals, it could make tax credits available everywhere while offering new incentives for States to set up their own Exchanges. And if Congress thinks that the present design of the Act works well enough, it could do nothing. Congress could also do something else altogether, entirely abandoning the structure of the Affordable Care Act. The Court's insistence on making a choice that should be made by Congress both aggrandizes judicial power and encourages congressional lassitude. . . .

Today's opinion changes the usual rules of statutory interpretation for the sake of the Affordable Care Act. That, alas, is not a novelty. In *National Federation of Independent Business v. Sebelius*, this Court revised major components of the statute in order to save them from unconstitutionality. The Act that Congress passed provides that every individual "shall" maintain insurance or else pay a "penalty." 26 U.S.C. §5000A. This Court, however, saw that the Commerce Clause does not authorize a federal mandate to buy health insurance. So it rewrote the mandate-cum-penalty as a tax. The Act that Congress passed also requires every State to accept an expansion of its Medicaid program, or else risk losing *all* Medicaid funding. 42 U.S.C. §1396c. This Court, however, saw that the Spending Clause does not authorize this coercive condition. So it rewrote the law to withhold only the *incremental* funds associated with the Medicaid expansion. Having transformed two major parts of the law, the Court today has turned its attention to a third. The Act that Congress passed makes tax credits available only on an "Exchange established by the State." This Court, however, concludes that this limitation would prevent the rest of the Act from working as well as hoped. So it rewrites the law to make tax credits available everywhere. We should start calling this law SCOTUScare.

Perhaps the Patient Protection and Affordable Care Act will attain the enduring status of the Social Security Act or the Taft-Hartley Act; perhaps not. But this Court's two decisions on the Act will surely be remembered through the years. The somersaults of statutory interpretation they have performed ("penalty" means tax, "further [Medicaid] payments to the State" means only incremental Medicaid payments to the State, "established by the State" means not established by the State) will be cited by litigants endlessly, to the confusion of honest jurisprudence. And the cases will publish forever the discouraging truth that the Supreme Court of the United States favors some laws over others, and is prepared to do whatever it takes to uphold and assist its favorites.

I dissent.

Notes and Questions

1. The *King v. Burwell* decision begins with a very extensive treatment of the background leading to the statute and the "interlocking" elements of the statutory scheme. Why do you think the Court gave that background such prominence, and established, at the outset, the critical features of the statutory scheme?

2. On what grounds did court conclude that the phrase "an Exchange established by the State" was ambiguous at least as to whether it included Exchanges established by the federal government? The Court says that it reaches this conclusion based on textual sources alone. To what extent does the Court's characterization of the statute's design and intent play a role in that determination? In other words, is the Court's ambiguity interpretation simply an operation of whole act evaluation or does it also involve relying on what the Act was intended to do?

3. Why did the Court read a determination that the Act was ambiguous? Having decided that the question was not delegated to the agency the Court could simply have reasoned to what it thought the best construction of the statute was, without necessarily concluding that it was ambiguous. After the Court concludes that the statute is ambiguous, it expressly invokes the statute's purpose. Does that help explain why it made an ambiguity determination?

4. How does the Court treat the surplusage canon here? To what extent does the Court's view that the statute involves "more than a few examples of inartful drafting" support its willingness to disregard the surplusage arguments?

5. In what ways does the Court grant "context" as having a bearing on the meaning of statutory terms? What context is most relevant to the Court?

6. Once the Court finds the statute ambiguous, it then relies on the principle that it "cannot interpret federal statutes to negate their own stated purposes" to conclude that the ACA is best read to make tax credits available on federal Exchanges. In what sense would the alternative construction "negate" the purposes of the Act? What kind of principle or canon is this? If the purposes are enacted, this appears to be a type of whole act canon stating that the Act should not be construed to thwart the enacted purposes or aims. But it also has a substantive element, requiring the interpretation to remain consistent with the Act's purposes. Do enacted purpose provisions merit special weight, given their prominence? Does the decision rely on these purposes being enacted? Would it matter if within the enacted text the Court relies upon, part of the enacted findings was drafted by interest groups? For an examination of the scope of this principle in interpretation, see Kevin M. Stack, *The Enacted Purposes Canon*, 105 IOWA L. REV. (2019).

3. Substantive Canons

The canons of construction that we have discussed thus far (provision, act, and code canons) are rules about how language is read. By contrast, *substantive canons* are rules about how the law should look. They expressly protect or reflect substantive values. For example, the rule of lenity instructs courts to construe ambiguities in criminal statutes leniently toward criminal defendants. It does so based on a longstanding principle of providing fair notice to those confronting criminal penalties. It is possible to relate substantive canons to Congress, now that they have been in place for some time. Congress might enact statutes in reliance on substantive canons like the rule of lenity — that is, with the expectation that courts will continue to invoke them.

There are many different substantive canons. Among the most well-established are: (a) the rule of lenity, (b) the canon of constitutional avoidance, (c) the federalism clear statement rule, (d) the presumption against preemption, (e) the presumption against retroactivity, and (f) the presumption against extra-territorial application. As you can see from this list, substantive canons go by different names, among them rule, canon, clear statement rule, and presumption. Furthermore, many have slightly different functions or applications. We'd like to alert you upfront to some of those differences.

The rule of lenity effectively functions as a tie-breaker in the event that a word or provision has more than one possible interpretation. It provides a reason to pick the interpretation that is more favorable toward criminal defendants. The canon of constitutional avoidance also fits this description. That canon says, in the event of a statutory ambiguity, a court should adopt the interpretation that will spare it from having to resolve a question about the constitutionality of the statute. But the constitutional avoidance canon is also a bit different from the rule of lenity because it has an extra step. To apply it, the court must determine whether choosing a particular interpretation would very likely render the statute (or part thereof) unconstitutional. So, the court has more work to do than simply identifying a statutory ambiguity and tipping the balance in favor of a well-established normative value (e.g., criminal leniency).

The federalism clear statement rule prohibits a court from construing a statute to interfere with state sovereignty absent express language indicating that Congress intended that result. For a clear statement rule, it is not ambiguity per se, but the absence of express language that opens up the possibility for its application. A court will not adopt a particular interpretation — say, one that impinges states' rights — unless the statute plainly requires that result. Presumptions function very similarly to clear statement rules, though they are somewhat weaker, at least in theory. They state a default as to how a statute should be construed (say, not to apply retroactively or extra-territorially) that can be overcome based on clear language or other strong evidence that Congress intended otherwise.

a. The Rule of Lenity

Under the rule of lenity, "ambiguity concerning the ambit of criminal statutes should be resolved in favor of lenity," Huddleston v. United States, 415 U.S. 814, 830-31 (1974), that is, in favor of the defendant. *See also* United States v. Gradwell, 243 U.S. 476, 485 (1917); McBoyle v. United States, 283 U.S. 25, 27 (1931); United States v. Bass, 404 U.S. 336, 347-49 (1971). The justification for the rule of lenity is well-established: this "rule of narrow construction is rooted in the concern of the law for individual rights, and in the belief that fair warning should be accorded as to what conduct is criminal and punishable by deprivation of liberty or property." *Huddleston*, 415 U.S. at 831.

The rule of lenity applies when criminal statutes are ambiguous, as determined through application of other tools of statutory interpretation. As the Supreme Court, with Justice Ginsburg writing, emphasized in United States v. Hayes, 555 U.S. 415, 429 (2009): " '[T]he touchstone of the rule of lenity is statutory ambiguity.' " Bifulco v. United States, 447 U.S. 381, 387 (1980). We apply the rule " 'only when, after consulting traditional canons of statutory construction, we are left with an ambiguous statute.' " *Id.* (citing United States v. Shabani, 513 U.S. 10, 17 (1994)).

In particular cases, judges can disagree on whether a statutory provision is sufficiently ambiguous to warrant application of the rule of lenity. Consider the exchange between the justices in *United States v. Santos*:

United States v. Santos

553 U.S. 507 (2008)

Justice SCALIA announced the judgment of the Court and delivered an opinion, in which Justice SOUTER and Justice GINSBURG join, and in which Justice THOMAS joins as to all but Part IV.

We consider whether the term "proceeds" in the federal money-laundering statute, 18 U.S.C. §1956(a)(1), means "receipts" or "profits."

I

From the 1970's until 1994, respondent Santos operated a lottery in Indiana that was illegal under state law. . . . Santos employed a number of helpers to run the lottery. At bars and restaurants, Santos's runners gathered bets from gamblers, kept a portion of the bets (between 15% and 25%) as their commissions, and delivered the rest to Santos's collectors. Collectors, one of whom was respondent Diaz, then delivered the money to Santos, who used some of it to pay the salaries of collectors (including Diaz) and to pay the winners. . . .

II

The federal money-laundering statute prohibits a number of activities involving criminal "proceeds." Most relevant to this case is 18 U.S.C. §1956(a)(1)(A)(i), which criminalizes transactions to promote criminal activity.[1] This provision uses the term "proceeds" in describing two elements of the offense: The Government must prove that a charged transaction "in fact involve[d] the proceeds of specified unlawful activity" (the proceeds element), and it also must prove that a defendant knew "that the property involved in" the charged transaction "represent[ed] the proceeds of some form of unlawful activity" (the knowledge element). §1956(a)(1).

The federal money-laundering statute does not define "proceeds." When a term is undefined, we give it its ordinary meaning. *Asgrow Seed Co. v. Winterboer*, 513 U.S. 179, 187 (1995). "Proceeds" can mean either "receipts" or "profits." Both meanings are accepted, and have long been accepted, in ordinary usage. *See, e.g.,* 12 Oxford English Dictionary 544 (2d ed. 1989); Random House Dictionary of the English Language 1542 (2d ed. 1987); Webster's New International Dictionary 1972 (2d ed. 1957) (hereinafter Webster's 2d). The Government contends that dictionaries generally prefer the "receipts" definition over the "profits" definition, but any preference is too slight for us to conclude that "receipts" is the primary meaning of "proceeds."

"Proceeds," moreover, has not acquired a common meaning in the provisions of the Federal Criminal Code. Most leave the term undefined. *See, e.g.,* 18 U.S.C. §1963; 21 U.S.C. §853. Recognizing the word's inherent ambiguity, Congress has defined "proceeds" in various criminal provisions, but sometimes

---

1. Section 1956(a)(1) reads as follows:

"Whoever, knowing that the property involved in a financial transaction represents the proceeds of some form of unlawful activity, conducts or attempts to conduct such a financial transaction which in fact involves the proceeds of specified unlawful activity . . . (A)(i) with the intent to promote the carrying on of specified unlawful activity . . . shall be sentenced to a fine of not more than $500,000 or twice the value of the property involved in the transaction, whichever is greater, or imprisonment for not more than twenty years, or both."

has defined it to mean "receipts" and sometimes "profits." Compare 18 U.S.C. §2339C(e)(3) (2000 ed., Supp. V) (receipts), §981(a)(2)(A) (2000 ed.) (same), with §981(a)(2)(B) (profits).

Since context gives meaning, we cannot say the money-laundering statute is truly ambiguous until we consider "proceeds" not in isolation but as it is used in the federal money-laundering statute. *See United Sav. Assn. of Tex. v. Timbers of Inwood Forest Associates, Ltd.*, 484 U.S. 365, 371 (1988). The word appears repeatedly throughout the statute, but all of those appearances leave the ambiguity intact. Section 1956(a)(1) itself, for instance, makes sense under either definition: one can engage in a financial transaction with either receipts or profits of a crime; one can intend to promote the carrying on of a crime with either its receipts or its profits; and one can try to conceal the nature, location, etc., of either receipts or profits. The same is true of all the other provisions of this legislation in which the term "proceeds" is used. They make sense under either definition. See, for example, §1956(a)(2)(B), which speaks of "proceeds" represented by a "monetary instrument or funds."

Justice Alito's dissent (the principal dissent) makes much of the fact that 14 States that use and define the word "proceeds" in their money-laundering statutes, the Model Money Laundering Act, and an international treaty on the subject, all define the term to include gross receipts. . . . We do not think this evidence shows that the drafters of the federal money-laundering statute used "proceeds" as a term of art for "receipts." Most of the state laws cited by the dissent, the Model Act, and the treaty postdate the 1986 federal money-laundering statute by several years, so Congress was not acting against the backdrop of those definitions when it enacted the federal statute. If anything, they show that "proceeds" is ambiguous and that others who believed that money-laundering statutes ought to include gross receipts sought to clarify the ambiguity that Congress created when it left the term undefined.[2]

Under either of the word's ordinary definitions, all provisions of the federal money-laundering statute are coherent; no provisions are redundant; and the statute is not rendered utterly absurd. From the face of the statute, there is no more reason to think that "proceeds" means "receipts" than there is to think that "proceeds" means "profits." Under a long line of our decisions, the tie must go to the defendant. The rule of lenity requires ambiguous criminal laws to be interpreted in favor of the defendants subjected to them. *See United States v. Gradwell*, 243 U.S. 476, 485 (1917); *McBoyle v. United States*, 283 U.S. 25, 27 (1931); *United States v. Bass*, 404 U.S. 336,

---

2. The principal dissent also suggests that Congress thought "proceeds" meant "receipts" because the House of Representatives (but not the Senate) had passed a money-laundering bill that did not use the word "proceeds" but rather used and defined a term ("criminally derived property") that, perhaps, included receipts. Putting aside the question of whether resorting to legislative history is ever appropriate when interpreting a criminal statute, compare *United States v. R.L.C.*, 503 U.S. 291, 306, n.6 (1992), with *id.*, at 307 (Scalia, J., concurring in part and concurring in judgment), that bit of it is totally unenlightening because we do not know why the earlier House terminology was rejected—because "proceeds" captured the same meaning, or because "proceeds" carried a narrower meaning?

347-349 (1971). This venerable rule not only vindicates the fundamental principle that no citizen should be held accountable for a violation of a statute whose commands are uncertain, or subjected to punishment that is not clearly prescribed. It also places the weight of inertia upon the party that can best induce Congress to speak more clearly and keeps courts from making criminal law in Congress's stead. Because the "profits" definition of "proceeds" is always more defendant-friendly than the "receipts" definition, the rule of lenity dictates that it should be adopted.

III

Stopping short of calling the "profits" interpretation absurd, the Government contends that the interpretation should nonetheless be rejected because it fails to give the federal money-laundering statute its proper scope and because it hinders effective enforcement of the law. Neither contention overcomes the rule of lenity.

A

According to the Government, if we do not read "proceeds" to mean "receipts," we will disserve the purpose of the federal money-laundering statute, which is, the Government says, to penalize criminals who conceal or promote their illegal activities. On the Government's view, "[t]he gross receipts of a crime accurately reflect the scale of the criminal activity, because the illegal activity generated all of the funds."

When interpreting a criminal statute, we do not play the part of a mind reader. In our seminal rule-of-lenity decision, Chief Justice Marshall rejected the impulse to speculate regarding a dubious congressional intent. "[P]robability is not a guide which a court, in construing a penal statute, can safely take." *United States v. Wiltberger*, 5 Wheat. 76, 105 (1820). And Justice Frankfurter, writing for the Court in another case, said the following: "When Congress leaves to the Judiciary the task of imputing to Congress an undeclared will, the ambiguity should be resolved in favor of lenity." *Bell v. United States*, 349 U.S. 81, 83 (1955).

The statutory purpose advanced by the Government to construe "proceeds" is a textbook example of begging the question. To be sure, if "proceeds" meant "receipts," one could say that the statute was aimed at the dangers of concealment and promotion. But whether "proceeds" means "receipts" is the very issue in the case. If "proceeds" means "profits," one could say that the statute is aimed at the distinctive danger that arises from leaving in criminal hands the yield of a crime. A rational Congress could surely have decided that the risk of leveraging one criminal activity into the next poses a greater threat to society than the mere payment of crime-related expenses and justifies the money-laundering statute's harsh penalties.

If we accepted the Government's invitation to speculate about congressional purpose, we would also have to confront and explain the strange consequence of the "receipts" interpretation, which respondents have described as a "merger problem." If "proceeds" meant "receipts," nearly every violation of the illegal-lottery statute would also be a violation of the money-laundering statute, because paying a winning bettor is a transaction involving receipts that the defendant intends to promote the carrying on of the lottery. Since few lotteries, if any, will not pay their winners, the statute criminalizing illegal lotteries, 18 U.S.C. §1955, would "merge" with the money-laundering statute. Congress evidently decided that lottery operators ordinarily deserve up to 5 years of imprisonment, §1955(a), but as a result of merger they would face an additional 20 years, §1956(a)(1). Prosecutors, of course, would acquire the discretion to charge the lesser lottery offense, the greater money-laundering offense, or both which would predictably be used to induce a plea bargain to the lesser charge.

The merger problem is not limited to lottery operators. For a host of predicate crimes, merger would depend on the manner and timing of payment for the expenses associated with the commission of the crime. Few crimes are entirely free of cost, and costs are not always paid in advance. Anyone who pays for the costs of a crime with its proceeds for example, the felon who uses the stolen money to pay for the rented getaway car would violate the money-laundering statute. . . .

V

The money-laundering charges brought against Santos were based on his payments to the lottery winners and his employees, and the money-laundering charge brought against Diaz was based on his receipt of payments as an employee. Neither type of transaction can fairly be characterized as involving the lottery's profits. Indeed, the Government did not try to prove, and respondents have not admitted, that they laundered criminal profits. We accordingly affirm the judgment of the Court of Appeals.

It is so ordered.

[Justice STEVENS' concurring opinion is omitted.]

Justice BREYER, dissenting.

I join Justice Alito's dissent while adding the following observations about what has been referred to as the "'merger problem.'" Like the plurality, I doubt that Congress intended the money laundering statute automatically to cover financial transactions that constitute an essential part of a different underlying crime. Operating an illegal gambling business, for example, inevitably involves investment in overhead as well as payments to employees and winning customers; a drug offense normally involves payment for drugs; and bank robbery may well require the distribution of stolen cash to confederates. If the money laundering statute applies to this kind of transaction (*i.e.*, if the transaction is automatically a "financial transaction" that "involves the proceeds of specified unlawful activity" made "with the intent to promote the carrying on of specified unlawful activity"), then the

Government can seek a heavier money laundering penalty (say, 20 years), even though the only conduct at issue is conduct that warranted a lighter penalty (say, 5 years for illegal gambling). 18 U.S.C. §1956(a)(1).

It is difficult to understand why Congress would have intended the Government to possess this punishment-transforming power. Perhaps for this reason, the Tenth Circuit has written that "Congress aimed the crime of money laundering at conduct that follows in time the underlying crime rather than to afford an alternative means of punishing the prior 'specified unlawful activity.'" *United States v. Edgmon*, 952 F.2d 1206, 1214 (1991). And, in 1997, the United States Sentencing Commission told Congress that it agreed with the Department of Justice that "money laundering cannot properly be charged for 'merged' transactions that are part of the underlying crime." Report to Congress: Sentencing Policy for Money Laundering Offenses, including Comments on a Dept. of Justice Report, p. 16 (Sept. 1997).

Thus, like the plurality, I see a "merger" problem. But, unlike the plurality, I do not believe that we should look to the word "proceeds" for a solution. For one thing, the plurality's interpretation of that word creates the serious logical and practical difficulties that Justice Alito describes. For another thing, there are other, more legally felicitous places to look for a solution. The Tenth Circuit, for example, has simply held that the money laundering offense and the underlying offense that generated the money to be laundered must be distinct in order to be separately punishable. *Edgmon*, at 1214. Alternatively the money laundering statute's phrase "with the intent *to promote* the carrying on of specified unlawful activity" may not apply where, for example, only one instance of that underlying activity is at issue. (The Seventh Circuit on a prior appeal in this case rejected that argument, and thus we do not consider it here. See *United States v. Febus*, 218 F.3d 784, 789 (2000).)

Finally, if the "merger" problem is essentially a problem of fairness in sentencing, the Sentencing Commission has adequate authority to address it. Congress has instructed the Commission to "avoi[d] unwarranted sentencing disparities" among those "found guilty of *similar criminal conduct*." 28 U.S.C. §991(b)(1)(B) (emphasis added); see also §994(f) (instructing the Commission to pay particular attention to those disparities). The current money laundering Guideline, United States Sentencing Commission, Guidelines Manual §2S1.1 (Nov. 2007) (USSG), by making no exception for a situation where *nothing but a single instance of the underlying crime has taken place*, would seem to create a serious and unwarranted disparity among defendants who have engaged in identical conduct. My hope is that the Commission's past efforts to tie more closely the offense level for money laundering to the offense level of the underlying crime, see *id.*, Supp. to App. C, Amdt. 634 (Nov. 2001), suggest a willingness to consider directly this kind of disparity. Such an approach could solve the "merger" problem without resort to creating complex interpretations of the statute's language. And any such solution could be applied retroactively. See 28 U.S.C. §994(u).

Justice ALITO, with whom THE CHIEF JUSTICE, Justice KENNEDY, and Justice BREYER join, dissenting.

Fairly read, the term "proceeds," as used in the principal federal money laundering statute, 18 U.S.C. §1956(a), means "the total amount brought in," the primary dictionary definition. Webster's Third New International Dictionary 1807 (1976) (hereinafter Webster's 3d). *See also* Random House Dictionary of the English Language 1542 (2d ed. 1987) ("the total sum derived from a sale or other transaction"). The plurality opinion, however, makes no serious effort to interpret this important statutory term. Ignoring the context in which the term is used, the problems that the money laundering statute was enacted to address, and the obvious practical considerations that those responsible for drafting the statute almost certainly had in mind, that opinion is quick to pronounce the term hopelessly ambiguous and thus to invoke the rule of lenity. Concluding that "proceeds" means "profits," the plurality opinion's interpretation would frustrate Congress' intent and maim a statute that was enacted as an important defense against organized criminal enterprises. . . .

I

A

While the primary definition of the term "proceeds" is "the total amount brought in," I recognize that the term may also be used to mean "net profit," Webster's 3d 1807, and I do not suggest that the question presented in this case can be answered simply by opening a dictionary. When a word has more than one meaning, the meaning that is intended is often made clear by the context in which the word is used, and thus in this case, upon finding that the term "proceeds" may mean both "the total amount brought in" and "net profit," the appropriate next step is not to abandon any effort at interpretation and summon in the rule of lenity. Rather, the next thing to do is to ask what the term "proceeds" customarily means in the context that is relevant here a money laundering statute.

The federal money laundering statute is not the only money laundering provision that uses the term "proceeds." On the contrary, the term is a staple of money laundering laws, and it is instructive that in every single one of these provisions in which the term "proceeds" is defined and there are many the law specifies that "proceeds" means "the total amount brought in."

The leading treaty on international money laundering, the United Nations Convention Against Transnational Organized Crime (Convention), Nov. 15, 2000, 2225 U.N.T.S. 209 (Treaty No. I-39574), which has been adopted by the United States and 146 other countries, is instructive. This treaty contains a provision that is very similar to §1956(a)(1)(B)(i). . . . The Convention defines the term "proceeds" to mean "any property derived from or obtained, directly or indirectly, through the commission of an offence." *Id.*, at 275 (Art. 2(e)). The money laundering provision of the Convention thus covers gross receipts.

The term "proceeds" is given a similarly broad scope in the Model Money Laundering Act (Model Act). . . . Section 5(a)(1) of the Model Act criminalizes transactions involving property that is "the proceeds of some form of unlawful activity," and the Model Act defines "proceeds" as "property acquired or derived directly or indirectly from, produced through, realized through, or caused by an act or omission . . . includ[ing] any property of any kind," §4(a).

Fourteen States have money laundering statutes that define the term "proceeds," and in every one of these laws the term is defined in a way that encompasses gross receipts. . . .

This pattern of usage is revealing. It strongly suggests that when lawmakers, knowledgeable about the nature and problem of money laundering, use the term "proceeds" in a money laundering provision, they customarily mean for the term to reach all receipts and not just profits.

B

There is a very good reason for this uniform pattern of usage. Money laundering provisions serve two chief ends. First, they provide deterrence by preventing drug traffickers and other criminals who amass large quantities of cash from using these funds "to support a luxurious lifestyle" or otherwise to enjoy the fruits of their crimes. Model Act, Policy Statement, p. C-105. . . . Second, they inhibit the growth of criminal enterprises by preventing the use of dirty money to promote the enterprise's growth. [Citing statutes.]

Both of these objectives are frustrated if a money laundering statute is limited to profits. Dirty money may be used to support "a luxurious lifestyle" and to grow an illegal enterprise whenever the enterprise possesses large amounts of illegally obtained cash. And illegal enterprises may acquire such cash while engaging in unlawful activity that is unprofitable. . . .

It is certainly true that Congress, in enacting the federal money laundering statute, was primarily concerned about criminal enterprises that realize profits. A criminal operation that consistently loses money will not last very long and thus presents a lesser danger than a profitable operation. But narrowing a money laundering statute so that it reaches only profits produces two perverse results that Congress cannot have wanted. First, it immunizes successful criminal enterprises during those periods when they are operating temporarily in the red. Second, and more important, it introduces pointless and difficult problems of proof. Because the dangers presented by money laundering are present whenever criminals have large stores of illegally derived funds on their hands, there is little reason to require proof which may be harder to assemble than the plurality opinion acknowledges that the funds represent profits. . . .

C

. . . A net income interpretation would risk hamstringing . . . prosecutions. To violate 18 U.S.C. §1956(a), a defendant must "kno[w] the property involved in a financial transaction represents the proceeds of some form of unlawful activity." A professional money launderer is not likely to know (or perhaps even to care) whether the enterprise is operating in the black when the funds in question were acquired. Therefore, under a net income interpretation, financial specialists and others who are hired to launder funds would generally be beyond the reach of the statute, something that Congress almost certainly did not intend. . . .

D

. . . The plurality opinion suggests that the application of a profits interpretation will be easy in cases in which the financial transactions are payments of "expenses." But it may be no small matter to determine whether particular payments are for "expenses." When the manager of a gambling operation distributes cash to those who work in the operation, the manager may be paying them the rough equivalent of a salary; that is, the recipients may expect to receive a certain amount for their services whether or not the operation is profitable. On the other hand, those who work in the operation may have the expectation of receiving a certain percentage of the gross revenue (perhaps even in addition to a salary), in which case their distribution may include profits. Such was the case in Santos' lottery, where the runners were paid a percentage of gross revenue. *See* Indictment 5; 16 Tr. 1399 (Oct. 9, 1997).

The plurality opinion cites 18 U.S.C. §1963(a) and 21 U.S.C. §853(a), for the proposition that Congress has "elsewhere" imposed the burden of proving that illegally obtained funds represent profits, but the plurality opinion's examples are inapposite. Neither of these provisions, however, requires a determination of net income. Both provisions permit a fine in the amount of "not more than twice the gross profits or other proceeds." 18 U.S.C. §1963(a). Thus, the term "proceeds" as used in these provisions is not limited to profits. . . .

For all these reasons, I am convinced that the term "proceeds" in the money laundering statute means gross receipts, not net income. . . .

II

A

It is apparent that a chief reason for interpreting the term "proceeds" to mean net income in all money laundering cases (the approach taken in the plurality opinion) . . . is the desire to avoid a "merger" problem in gambling cases that is, to avoid an interpretation that would mean that every violation of §1955 (conducting an illegal gambling business) would also constitute a violation of the money laundering statute, which carries a much higher maximum penalty (20 as opposed to 5 years' imprisonment). This concern is misplaced and provides no justification for hobbling a statute that applies to more than 250 predicate offenses and not just running an illegal gambling business.

First, the so-called merger problem is fundamentally a sentencing problem, and the proper remedy is a sentencing remedy. While it is true that the money laundering statute has a higher maximum sentence than the gambling business statute, neither statute has a mandatory minimum. Thus, these statutes do not require a judge to increase a defendant's sentence simply because the defendant was convicted of money laundering as well as running a gambling business. When the respondents were convicted, their money laundering convictions resulted in higher sentences only because of the money laundering Sentencing Guideline, United States Sentencing Commission, Guidelines Manual §2S1.1 (Nov. 1997) (USSG). . . .

Second, the merger problem that the plurality opinion . . . seek[s] to avoid assumes the correctness of the interpretation of the promotion prong of the money laundering statute that the Seventh Circuit adopted in Santos' direct appeal, i.e., that a defendant "promotes" an illegal gambling business by doing those things, such as paying employees and winning bettors, that are needed merely to keep the business running. As Santos' brief puts it, the merger problem arises when the interpretation of "proceeds" as gross receipts is "[c]ombined with the Government's broad application of the 'promotion' prong of the money laundering statute." But the meaning of the element of promotion is not before us in this case, and it would not make sense to allow our interpretation of "proceeds" to be dictated by an unreviewed interpretation of another statutory element.

Third, even if there is a merger problem, it occurs in only a subset of money laundering cases. The money laundering statute reaches financial transactions that are intended to promote more than 250 other crimes, as well as transactions that are intended to conceal or disguise the nature, location, source, ownership, or control of illegally obtained funds. *See* 18 U.S.C. §1956(a). The meaning of the term "proceeds" cannot vary from one money laundering case to the next. . . .

B

The plurality opinion defends its interpretation by invoking the rule of lenity, but the rule of lenity does not require us to put aside the usual tools of statutory interpretation or to adopt the narrowest possible dictionary definition of the terms in a criminal statute. On the contrary, "[b]ecause the meaning of language is inherently contextual, we have declined to deem a statute 'ambiguous' for purposes of lenity merely because it was possible to articulate a construction more narrow than that urged by the Government." *Moskal v. United States*, 498 U.S. 103, 108 (1990) (citing *McElroy v. United States*, 455 U.S. 642, 657-658 (1982)). As I have explained above, the meaning of "proceeds" in the money laundering statute emerges with reasonable clarity when the term is viewed in context, making the rule of lenity inapplicable.

Notes and Questions

1. In this case, we see an intense disagreement between Justice Scalia, the author of the plurality opinion, and Justice Alito, the author of the principal dissent, on whether the provision at issue is ambiguous enough to warrant application of the rule of lenity. In Justice Scalia's view, the criminal statute is sufficiently ambiguous to trigger application of the rule of lenity. In Justice Alito's view, the statute is clear and therefore ineligible for the rule of lenity. Do these two justices reach different conclusion because they invoke different tools of statutory interpretation, apply the same tools differently, or have a different threshold for the level of ambiguity necessary to invoke the rule of lenity?

2. Do you find yourself thinking that Justice Scalia and Justice Alito each offered plausible interpretations of the statutory provision at issue? If so, why not allow the rule of lenity to serve as a tiebreaker for the pro-defendant interpretation? Is that a good description of how Justice Scalia employs the rule? What are the advantages of this approach? What counsels in favor of Justice Alito's view? Recall that he will not resort to the rule of lenity "merely because it was possible to articulate a construction more narrow than that urged by the Government."

3. According to Justice Breyer, what is this case really about? Why was the Justice Department's position abandoned here?

4. In 2009, Congress amended 18 U.S.C. §1956(c) now to provide that "the term 'proceeds' means any property derived from or obtained or retained, directly or indirectly, through some form of unlawful activity, including the gross receipts of such activity." What do you make of this fact?

5. Return to the rule of lenity. Suppose committee staffers who worked on criminal legislation did not widely recognize the rule of lenity, let alone apply it. *See* Abbe R. Gluck & Lisa Schultz Bressman, *Statutory Interpretation from the Inside—An Empirical Study of Congressional Drafting, Delegation, and the Canons: Part I*, 65 STAN. L. REV. 901 (2013). Should that matter, or is the argument in favor of the rule of lenity more pointedly about securing important normative values? In other words, should courts apply the rule of lenity regardless of what Congress knows or does?

Note on the Remedial Purposes Canon

As we have described it, the rule of lenity effectively functions as a tiebreaker when a criminal statute is ambiguous. Another canon of construction that works in a similar fashion provides that "remedial legislation should be construed broadly to effectuate its purposes." Tcherepnin v. Knight, 389 U.S. 332, 336 (1967). How does a court determine whether a statute is remedial? As you might expect, the statute has to be directed at remedying a prior problem. But most statutes can be characterized this way, right? Some examples of qualifying remedial statutes are helpful. The Securities and Exchange Act of 1933 has been held to be remedial because it was the "product of a lengthy and highly publicized investigation by the Senate Committee on Banking and Currency into stock market practices and the reasons for the stock market crash of October 1929." *Id.* at 336 n.10. Anti-discrimination statutes have been declared to be remedial. *See, e.g.*, Dudley v. Hannaford Bros. Co., 333 F.3d 299, 307 (1st Cir. 2003) (holding that the Americans with Disabilities Act, 42 U.S.C. §§12101-12213, is remedial because it aims to eliminate discrimination). Reform statutes have been declared remedial as well. *See, e.g.*, In re Carter, 553 F.3d 979, 985 n.5 (6th Cir. 2009) (holding that the Real Estate Settlement Procedures Act of 1974, 12 U.S.C. §2607, is remedial because it was enacted to reform real estate settlements). Once a court determines that a statute is remedial, it then construes that statute broadly in order to effectuate its purposes. Although the remedial canon has a long pedigree, the Supreme Court has not often invoked it in recent decades. Can you think of why?

b. The Constitutional Avoidance Canon

The constitutional avoidance canon is part of a doctrine tracing its origins to one of the earliest cases in constitutional law concerning the proper role of courts: Marbury v. Madison, 5 U.S. (1 Cranch) 137 (1803). This doctrine requires a court to avoid interpretations of statutes that render them unconstitutional or raise serious doubts about their constitutionality, at least when other interpretation of the statute are permissible. There are two primary formulations of the doctrine.

First, in its most traditional formulation, the doctrine provides that "as between two possible interpretations of a statute, by one of which it would be unconstitutional and by the other valid, [the court's] plain duty is to adopt the one which will save the Act." Rust v. Sullivan, 500 U.S. 173, 190 (1991) (quoting Bloggett v. Holden, 275 U.S. 142 (1927)). This rule is a "categorical" one, meaning that "every reasonable construction must be resorted to, in order to save a statute from unconstitutionality." *Id.* (citing Hooper v. California, 155 U.S. 648, 657 (1895)). This rule is generally known as the "unconstitutionality canon." It is premised on the notion that Congress intends to enact statutes that are constitutional, and that courts accordingly ought to pick the interpretation that renders them constitutional.

Second, in its more modern variant, the doctrine requires that "[a] statute must be construed, if fairly possible, so as to avoid not only the conclusion that it is unconstitutional but also grave doubts upon that score." Rust v. Sullivan, 500 U.S. at 191 (quoting United States v. Jin Fuey Moy, 241 U.S. 394, 401 (1916)). Under this second formulation, courts should avoid interpretations that raise a serious question as to the constitutionality of a statute. This rule is the "constitutional avoidance" canon. It also assumes that Congress "legislates in light of constitutional limitations." *Id.* This canon arises more often than the unconstitutionality canon (can you think of why?). Consider this question in light of the next two decisions.

Zadvydas v. Davis

533 U.S. 678 (2001)

Justice BREYER delivered the opinion of the Court.

When an alien has been found to be unlawfully present in the United States and a final order of removal has been entered, the Government ordinarily secures the alien's removal during a subsequent 90-day statutory "removal period," during which time the alien normally is held in custody.

A special statute authorizes further detention if the Government fails to remove the alien during those 90 days. It says:

> "An alien ordered removed [1] who is inadmissible . . . [2] [or] removable [as a result of violations of status requirements or entry conditions, violations of criminal law, or reasons of security or foreign policy] or [3] who has been determined by the Attorney General to be a risk to the community or unlikely to comply with the order of removal, may be detained beyond the removal period and, if released, shall be subject to [certain] terms of supervision. . . ." 8 U.S.C. §1231(a)(6) (1994 ed., Supp. V).

In these cases, we must decide whether this post-removal-period statute authorizes the Attorney General to detain a removable alien *indefinitely* beyond the removal period or only for a period *reasonably necessary* to secure the alien's removal. We deal here with aliens who were admitted to the United States but subsequently ordered removed. Aliens who have not yet gained initial admission to this country would present a very different question. . . . Based on our conclusion that indefinite detention of aliens in the former category would raise serious constitutional concerns, we construe the statute to contain an implicit "reasonable time" limitation, the application of which is subject to federal-court review. . . .

III

The post-removal-period detention statute applies to certain categories of aliens who have been ordered removed, namely, inadmissible aliens, criminal aliens, aliens who have violated their nonimmigrant status conditions, and aliens removable for certain national security or foreign relations reasons, as well as any alien "who has been determined by the Attorney General to be a risk to the community or unlikely to comply with the order of removal." 8 U.S.C. §1231(a)(6) (1994 ed., Supp. V). It says that an alien who falls into one of these categories "may be detained beyond the removal period and, if released, shall be subject to [certain] terms of supervision." 8 U.S.C. §1231(a)(6) (1994 ed., Supp. V).

The Government argues that the statute means what it literally says. It sets no "limit on the length of time beyond the removal period that an alien who falls within one of the Section 1231(a)(6) categories may be detained." Hence, "whether to continue to detain such an alien and, if so, in what circumstances and for how long" is up to the Attorney General, not up to the courts. "[I]t is a cardinal principle" of statutory interpretation, however, that when an Act of Congress raises "a serious doubt" as to its constitutionality, "this Court will first ascertain whether a construction of the statute is fairly possible by which the question may be avoided." *Crowell v. Benson,* 285 U.S. 22 (1932); *see also United States v. X-Citement Video, Inc.,* 513 U.S. 64, 78 (1994); *cf. Almendarez-Torres v. United States,* 523 U.S. 224, 238 (1998) (construction of statute that avoids invalidation best reflects congressional will). We have read significant limitations into other immigration statutes in order to avoid their constitutional invalidation. *See United States v. Witkovich,* 353 U.S. 194, 195, 202 (1957) (construing a grant of authority to the Attorney General to ask aliens whatever questions he "deem[s] fit and proper" as limited to questions "reasonably calculated to keep the Attorney General advised regarding the continued availability for departure of aliens whose deportation is overdue"). For similar reasons, we read an implicit limitation into the statute before us. In our view, the statute, read in light of the Constitution's demands, limits an alien's post-removal-period detention to a period reasonably necessary to bring about that alien's removal from the United States. It does not permit indefinite detention.

A

A statute permitting indefinite detention of an alien would raise a serious constitutional problem. The Fifth Amendment's Due Process Clause forbids the Government to "depriv[e]" any "person . . . of . . . liberty . . . without due process of law." Freedom from imprisonment from government custody, detention, or other forms of physical restraint lies at the heart of the liberty that Clause protects. *See Foucha v. Louisiana,* 504 U.S. 71, 80 (1992). And this Court has said that government detention violates that Clause unless the detention is ordered in a *criminal* proceeding with adequate procedural protections, *see United States v. Salerno,* 481 U.S. 739, 746 (1987), or, in certain special and "narrow" nonpunitive "circumstances," *Foucha,* at 80, where a special justification, such as harm-threatening mental illness, outweighs the "individual's constitutionally protected interest in avoiding physical restraint." *Kansas v. Hendricks,* 521 U.S. 346, 356 (1997). . . .

B

Despite this constitutional problem, if "Congress has made its intent" in the statute "clear, 'we must give effect to that intent.' " *Miller v. French,* 530 U.S. 327, 336 (2000) (quoting *Sinclair Refining Co. v. Atkinson,* 370 U.S. 195, 215 (1962)). We cannot find here, however, any clear indication of congressional intent to grant the Attorney General the power to hold indefinitely in confinement an alien ordered removed. And that is so whether protecting the community from dangerous aliens is a primary or (as we believe) secondary statutory purpose. . . . After all, the provision is part of a statute that has as its basic purpose effectuating an alien's removal. Why should we assume that Congress saw the alien's dangerousness as unrelated to this purpose?

The Government points to the statute's word "may." But while "may" suggests discretion, it does not necessarily suggest unlimited discretion. In that respect the word "may" is ambiguous. Indeed, if Congress had meant to authorize long-term detention of unremovable aliens, it certainly could have spoken in clearer terms. *Cf.* 8 U.S.C. §1537(b)(2)(C) (1994 ed., Supp. V) ("If no country is willing to receive" a terrorist alien ordered removed, "the Attorney General may, notwithstanding any other provision of law, retain the alien in custody" and must review the detention determination every six months).

. . . The Government also points to the statute's history. . . . We have found nothing in the history of these statutes that clearly demonstrates a congressional intent to authorize indefinite, perhaps permanent, detention. Consequently, interpreting the statute to avoid a serious constitutional threat, we conclude that, once removal is no longer reasonably foreseeable, continued detention is no longer authorized by statute. *See* 1 E. Coke, Institutes 70b (*"Cessante ratione legis cessat ipse lex"*) (the rationale of a legal rule no longer being applicable, that rule itself no longer applies). . . .

While an argument can be made for confining any presumption to 90 days, we doubt that when Congress shortened the removal period to 90 days in 1996 it believed that all reasonably foreseeable removals could be accomplished in that time. We do have reason to believe, however, that Congress previously doubted the constitutionality of detention for more than six months. *See* Juris. Statement in *United States v. Witkovich,* O.T. 1956, No. 295, pp. 8-9. Consequently, for the sake of uniform administration in the federal courts, we recognize that period. After this 6-month period, once the alien provides good reason to believe that there is no significant likelihood of removal in the reasonably foreseeable future, the Government must respond with evidence sufficient to rebut that showing. And for detention to remain reasonable, as the period of prior postremoval confinement grows, what counts as the "reasonably foreseeable future" conversely would have to shrink. This 6-month presumption, of course, does not mean that every alien not removed must be released after six months. To the contrary, an alien may be held in confinement until it has been determined that there is no significant likelihood of removal in the reasonably foreseeable future.

V

. . . [W]e vacate the judgments below and remand both cases for further proceedings consistent with this opinion.

It is so ordered.

[The dissenting opinion of Justice SCALIA, joined by Justice THOMAS, is omitted.]

Justice KENNEDY, with whom THE CHIEF JUSTICE joins, and with whom Justice SCALIA and Justice THOMAS join as to Part I, dissenting.

The Court says its duty is to avoid a constitutional question. It deems the duty performed by interpreting a statute in obvious disregard of congressional intent; curing the resulting gap by writing a statutory amendment of its own; committing its own grave constitutional error by arrogating to the Judicial Branch the power to summon high officers of the Executive to

assess their progress in conducting some of the Nation's most sensitive negotiations with foreign powers; and then likely releasing into our general population at least hundreds of removable or inadmissible aliens who have been
found by fair procedures to be flight risks, dangers to the community, or
both. Far from avoiding a constitutional question, the Court's ruling causes
systemic dislocation in the balance of powers, thus raising serious constitutional concerns not just for the cases at hand but for the Court's own view
of its proper authority. . . . In the guise of judicial restraint the Court ought
not to intrude upon the other branches. The constitutional question the
statute presents, it must be acknowledged, may be a significant one in some
later case; but it ought not to drive us to an incorrect interpretation of the
statute. The Court having reached the wrong result for the wrong reason,
this respectful dissent is required.

I

The Immigration and Nationality Act (INA), 8 U.S.C. §1101 *et seq.* (1994 ed.
and Supp. V), is straightforward enough. It provides:

> "An alien ordered removed who is inadmissible under section 1182 of this title, remov-
> able under section 1227(a)(1)(C), 1227(a)(2), or 1227(a)(4) of this title or who has
> been determined by the Attorney General to be a risk to the community or unlikely to
> comply with the order of removal, may be detained beyond the removal period and,
> if released, shall be subject to the terms of supervision in paragraph (3)." 8 U.S.C.
> §1231(a)(6). (1994 ed., Supp. V).

By this statute, Congress confers upon the Attorney General discretion
to detain an alien ordered removed. It gives express authorization to detain
"beyond the removal period." *Ibid.* The class of removed aliens detainable
under the section includes aliens who were inadmissible and aliens subject
to final orders of removal, provided they are a risk to the community or likely
to flee. The issue to be determined is whether the authorization to detain
beyond the removal period is subject to the implied, nontextual limitation
that the detention be no longer than reasonably necessary to effect removal
to another country. The majority invokes the canon of constitutional doubt
to read that implied term into the statute. One can accept the premise that
a substantial constitutional question is presented by the prospect of lengthy,
even unending, detention in some instances; but the statutory construction
the Court adopts should be rejected in any event. The interpretation has
no basis in the language or structure of the INA and in fact contradicts and
defeats the purpose set forth in the express terms of the statutory text.

The Court, it is submitted, misunderstands the principle of constitutional avoidance which it seeks to invoke. The majority gives a brief bow
to the rule that courts must respect the intention of Congress, but then
waltzes away from any analysis of the language, structure, or purpose of the
statute. Its analysis is not consistent with our precedents explaining the limits of the constitutional doubt rule. The rule allows courts to choose among
constructions which are "fairly possible," *Crowell v. Benson,* 285 U.S. 22, 62
(1932), not to "'press statutory construction to the point of disingenuous

evasion even to avoid a constitutional question.' ". . . Were a court to find two interpretations of equal plausibility, it should choose the construction that avoids confronting a constitutional question. The majority's reading of the statutory authorization to "detai[n] beyond the removal period," however, is not plausible. An interpretation which defeats the stated congressional purpose does not suffice to invoke the constitutional doubt rule, for it is "plainly contrary to the intent of Congress." *United States v. X-Citement Video, Inc.*, 513 U.S. 64, 78 (1994). The majority announces it will reject the Government's argument "that the statute means what it literally says," but then declines to offer any other acceptable textual interpretation. The majority does not demonstrate an ambiguity in the delegation of the detention power to the Attorney General. It simply amends the statute to impose a time limit tied to the progress of negotiations to effect the aliens' removal. The statute cannot be so construed. The requirement the majority reads into the law simply bears no relation to the text; and in fact it defeats the statutory purpose and design.

Other provisions in §1231 itself do link the requirement of a reasonable time period to the removal process. *See, e.g.*, §1231(C)(1)(A) (providing that an alien who arrives at a port of entry "shall be removed immediately on a vessel or aircraft" unless "it is impracticable" to do so "within a *reasonable time*" (emphasis added)); §1231(c)(3)(A)(ii)(II) (requiring the "owner of a vessel or aircraft bringing an alien to the United States [to] pay the costs of detaining and maintaining the alien . . . for the period of time *reasonably necessary* for the owner to arrange for repatriation" (emphasis added)). That Congress chose to impose the limitation in these sections and not in §1231(a)(6) is evidence of its intent to measure the detention period by other standards. . . .

The 6-month period invented by the Court, even when modified by its sliding standard of reasonableness for certain repatriation negotiations, makes the statutory purpose to protect the community ineffective. . . . The risk to the community posed by a removable alien is a function of a variety of circumstances, circumstances that do not diminish just because the alien cannot be deported within some foreseeable time. Those circumstances include the seriousness of the alien's past offenses, his or her efforts at rehabilitation, and some indication from the alien that, given the real prospect of detention, the alien will conform his or her conduct. This is the purpose for the periodic review of detention status provided for by the regulations. . . . The Court's amendment of the statute reads out of the provision the congressional decision that dangerousness alone is a sufficient basis for detention (citing 1 E. Coke, Institutes 70b), and reads out as well any meaningful structure for supervised release. . . .

II

The aliens' claims are substantial; their plight is real. They face continued detention, perhaps for life, unless it is shown they no longer present a flight risk or a danger to the community. In a later case the specific circumstances of a detention may present a substantial constitutional question. That is not a reason, however, for framing a rule which ignores the law governing alien status. . . .

For these reasons, the Court should reverse the judgment of the Court of Appeals for the Ninth Circuit and affirm the judgment of the Court of Appeals for the Fifth Circuit.

I dissent.

Almendarez-Torres v. United States

523 U.S. 224 (1998)

Justice BREYER delivered the opinion of the Court.

Subsection (a) of 8 U.S.C. §1326 defines a crime. It forbids an alien who once was deported to return to the United States without special permission, and it authorizes a prison term of up to, but no more than, two years. Subsection (b)(2) of the same section authorizes a prison term of up to, but no more than, 20 years for "any alien described" in subsection (a), if the initial "deportation was subsequent to a conviction for commission of an aggravated felony." The question before us is whether this latter provision defines a separate crime or simply authorizes an enhanced penalty. If the former, *i.e.*, if it constitutes a separate crime, then the Government must write an indictment that mentions the additional element, namely, a prior aggravated felony conviction. If the latter, *i.e.*, if the provision simply authorizes an enhanced sentence when an offender also has an earlier conviction, then the indictment need not mention that fact, for the fact of an earlier conviction is not an element of the present crime.

We conclude that the subsection is a penalty provision, which simply authorizes a court to increase the sentence for a recidivist. It does not define a separate crime. Consequently, neither the statute nor the Constitution requires the Government to charge the factor that it mentions, an earlier conviction, in the indictment. . . .

II

An indictment must set forth each element of the crime that it charges. *Hamling v. United States*, 418 U.S. 87, 117 (1974). But it need not set forth factors relevant only to the sentencing of an offender found guilty of the charged crime. Within limits, *see McMillan v. Pennsylvania*, 477 U.S. 79, 84-91 (1986), the question of which factors are which is normally a matter for Congress. *See Staples v. United States*, 511 U.S. 600, 604 (1994) (definition of a criminal offense entrusted to the legislature, "'particularly in the case of federal crimes, which are solely creatures of statute'"). . . . We therefore look to the statute before us and ask what Congress intended. Did it intend the factor that the statute mentions, the prior aggravated felony conviction, to help define a separate crime? Or did it intend the presence of an earlier conviction as a sentencing factor, a factor that a sentencing court might use to increase punishment? In answering this question, we look to the statute's language, structure, subject matter, context, and history — factors that typically help courts determine a statute's objectives and thereby illuminate its text. *See, e.g., United States v. Wells,* 519 U.S. 482, 490-492 (1997). . . .

The directly relevant portions of the statute as it existed at the time of petitioner's conviction included subsection (a), which Congress had enacted in 1952, and subsection (b), which Congress added in 1988. . . . We print those portions of text below:

> "§1326. Reentry of deported alien; criminal penalties for reentry of certain deported aliens.
>
> "(a) Subject to subsection (b) of this section, any alien who—
>
> "(1) has been . . . deported . . . , and thereafter
>
> "(2) enters . . . , or is at any time found in, the United States [without the Attorney General's consent or the legal equivalent],
>
> "shall be fined under title 18, or imprisoned not more than 2 years, or both.
>
> "(b) Notwithstanding subsection (a) of this section, in the case of any alien described in such subsection—
>
> "(1) whose deportation was subsequent to a conviction for commission of [certain misdemeanors], or a felony (other than an aggravated felony), such alien shall be fined under title 18, imprisoned not more than 10 years, or both; or
>
> "(2) whose deportation was subsequent to a conviction for commission of an aggravated felony, such alien shall be fined under such title, imprisoned not more than 20 years, or both." 8 U.S.C. §1326.

A

Although the statute's language forces a close reading of the text, as well as consideration of other interpretive circumstances, *see Wells,* we believe that the answer to the question presented — whether Congress intended subsection (b)(2) to set forth a sentencing factor or a separate crime — is reasonably clear. . . .

In essence, subsection (a) says that "any alien" once "deported," who reappears in the United States without appropriate permission, shall be fined or "imprisoned not more than 2 years." Subsection (b) says that "any alien described in" subsection (a), "whose deportation was subsequent to a conviction" for a minor, or for a major, crime, may be subject to a much longer prison term.

The statute includes the words "subject to subsection (b)" at the beginning of subsection (a), and the words "[n]otwithstanding subsection (a)" at the beginning of subsection (b). If Congress intended subsection (b) to set forth substantive crimes, in respect to which subsection (a) would define a lesser included offense, *see Blockburger v. United States,* 284 U.S. 299, 304 (1932), what are those words doing there? The dissent believes that the words mean that the substantive crime defined by "subsection (a) is inapplicable to an alien covered by subsection (b)," hence the words represent an effort to say that a defendant cannot be punished for both substantive crimes. But that is not what the words say. Nor has Congress ever (to our knowledge) used these or similar words anywhere else in the federal criminal code for such a purpose. *See, e.g.,* 18 U.S.C. §113 (aggravated and simple assault); §§1111, 1112 (murder and manslaughter); §2113 (bank robbery and incidental crimes); §§2241, 2242 (aggravated and simple sexual abuse). And this should come as no surprise since, for at least 60 years, the federal courts have presumed that Congress does *not* intend for a defendant to be cumulatively punished for two crimes where one crime is a lesser included offense of the other. *See Whalen v. United States,* 445 U.S. 684, 691-693 (1980).

If, however, Congress intended subsection (b) to provide additional penalties, the mystery disappears. The words "subject to subsection (b)" and "[n]otwithstanding subsection (a)" then are neither obscure nor pointless. They say, without obscurity, that the crime set forth in subsection (a), which both defines a crime and sets forth a penalty, is "subject to" subsection (b)'s different penalties (where the alien is also a felon or aggravated felon). And (b)'s higher maximum penalties may apply to an offender who violates (a) "notwithstanding" the fact that (a) sets forth a lesser penalty for one who has committed the same substantive crime. Nor is it pointless to specify that (b)'s punishments, not (a)'s punishment, apply whenever an offender commits (a)'s offense in a manner set forth by (b). . . .

We also note that "the title of a statute and the heading of a section" are "tools available for the resolution of a doubt" about the meaning of a statute. *Trainmen v. Baltimore & Ohio R. Co.,* 331 U.S. 519, 528-529 (1947). . . . The title of the 1988 amendment is "Criminal *penalties* for reentry of certain deported aliens." §7345, 102 Stat. 4471 (emphasis added). A title that contains the word "penalties" more often, but certainly not always, signals a provision that deals with penalties for a substantive crime.

In this instance the amendment's title does not reflect careless, or mistaken, drafting, for the title is reinforced by a legislative history that speaks about, and only about, the creation of new penalties. *See* S. 973, 100th Cong., 1st Sess. (1987), 133 Cong. Rec. 8771 (1987) (original bill titled, "A bill to provide for additional criminal penalties for deported aliens who reenter the United States, and for other purposes"). . . . The history, to our knowledge, contains no language at all that indicates Congress intended to create a new substantive crime.

Finally, the contrary interpretation — a substantive criminal offense — risks unfairness. If subsection (b)(2) sets forth a separate crime, the Government would be required to prove to the jury that the defendant was previously deported "subsequent to a conviction for commission of an aggravated felony." As this Court has long recognized, the introduction of evidence of a defendant's prior crimes risks significant prejudice. *See, e.g., Spencer v. Texas,* 385 U.S. 554, 560 (1967) (evidence of prior crimes "is generally recognized to have potentiality for prejudice"). . . .

In sum, we believe that Congress intended to set forth a sentencing factor in subsection (b)(2) and not a separate criminal offense.

B

. . . [P]etitioner and the dissent argue that the doctrine of "constitutional doubt" requires us to interpret subsection (b)(2) as setting forth a separate crime. As Justice Holmes said long ago: "A statute must be construed, if fairly possible, so as to avoid not only the conclusion that it is unconstitutional but also grave doubts upon that score." *United States v. Jin Fuey Moy,* 241 U.S. 394, 401 (1916) . . . *see also Ashwander v. TVA,* 297 U.S. 288, 348 (1936) (Brandeis, J., concurring). "This canon is followed out of respect for Congress, which we assume legislates in the light of constitutional limitations." *Rust v. Sullivan,* 500 U.S. 173, 191 (1991); *see also FTC v. American Tobacco Co.,* 264 U.S. 298, 305-307 (1924). The doctrine seeks in part to minimize disagreement between the branches by preserving congressional enactments that might otherwise founder on constitutional objections. It is not designed to aggravate that friction by creating (through the power of precedent) statutes foreign to those Congress intended, simply through fear of a constitutional difficulty that, upon analysis, will evaporate. Thus, those who invoke the doctrine must believe that the alternative is a serious likelihood that the statute will be held unconstitutional. Only then will the doctrine serve its basic democratic function of maintaining a set of statutes that reflect, rather than distort, the policy choices that elected representatives have made. For similar reasons, the statute must be genuinely susceptible to two constructions after, and not before, its complexities are unraveled. Only then is the statutory construction that avoids the constitutional question a "fair" one.

Unlike the dissent, we do not believe these conditions are met in the present case. The statutory language is somewhat complex. But after considering the matter in context, we believe the interpretative circumstances point significantly in one direction. More important, even if we were to assume that petitioner's construction of the statute is "fairly possible," *Jin Fuey Moy,* at 401, the constitutional questions he raises, while requiring discussion, simply do *not* lead us to doubt gravely that Congress may authorize courts to impose longer sentences upon recidivists who commit a particular crime. The fact that we, unlike the dissent, do not gravely doubt the statute's constitutionality in this respect is a crucial point. That is because the "constitutional doubt" doctrine does not apply mechanically whenever there arises a significant constitutional question the answer to which is not obvious. And precedent makes clear that the Court need not apply (for it has not always applied) the doctrine in circumstances similar to those here where a constitutional question, while lacking an obvious answer, does not lead a majority gravely to doubt that the statute is constitutional. *See, e.g., Rust,* 500 U.S., at 190-191 (declining to apply doctrine although petitioner's constitutional claims not "without some force"). . . .

[The Court held that Congress's decision to treat recidivism merely as a sentencing factor did not exceed due process or other constitutional limitations on Congress's power to define elements of a crime.]

The judgment of the Court of Appeals is affirmed.

Justice SCALIA, with whom Justices STEVENS, SOUTER, and GINSBURG join, dissenting.

Because Hugo Roman Almendarez-Torres illegally re-entered the United States after having been convicted of an aggravated felony, he was subject to a maximum possible sentence of 20 years' imprisonment. *See* 8 U.S.C. §1326(b)(2). Had he not been convicted of that felony, he would have been subject to a maximum of only two years. *See* 8 U.S.C. §1326(a). The Court today holds that §1326(b)(2) does not set forth a separate offense, and that conviction of a prior felony is merely a sentencing enhancement for the offense set forth in §1326(a). This causes the Court to confront the difficult question whether the Constitution requires a fact which substantially increases the maximum permissible punishment for a crime to be treated as an element of that crime to be charged in the indictment, and found beyond a reasonable doubt by a jury. Until the Court said so, it was far from obvious that the answer to this question was no; on the basis of our prior law, in fact, the answer was considerably doubtful. . . .

"[W]here a statute is susceptible of two constructions, by one of which grave and doubtful constitutional questions arise and by the other of which such questions are avoided, our duty is to adopt the latter." *United States ex rel. Attorney General v. Delaware & Hudson Co.*, 213 U.S. 366, 408 (1909). This "cardinal principle," which "has for so long been applied by this Court that it is beyond debate," *Edward J. DeBartolo Corp. v. Florida Gulf Coast Building & Constr. Trades Council*, 485 U.S. 568, 575 (1988), requires merely a determination of serious constitutional *doubt,* and not a determination of *unconstitutionality.* That must be so, of course, for otherwise the rule would "mea[n] that our duty is to first decide that a statute is unconstitutional and then proceed to hold that such ruling was unnecessary because the statute is susceptible of a meaning, which causes it not to be repugnant to the Constitution." *United States ex rel. Attorney General v. Delaware & Hudson Co., supra*, at 408. The Court contends that neither of the two conditions for application of this rule is present here: that the constitutional question is not doubtful, and that the statute is not susceptible of a construction that will avoid it. I shall address the former point first.[1]

[Justice Scalia argued that there is genuine doubt whether the Constitution permits a judge, rather than a jury, to determine by a preponderance of the evidence, as opposed to by a reasonable doubt, a fact that increases the maximum penalty to which a criminal defendant is subject.] . . .

---

1. The Court asserts that we have declined to apply the doctrine "in circumstances similar to those here—where a constitutional question, while lacking an obvious answer, does not lead a majority gravely to doubt that the statute is constitutional." The cases it cites, however, do not support this contention. In *Rust v. Sullivan,* 500 U.S. 173 (1991), the Court believed that "[t]here [was] *no question* but that the statutory prohibition . . . [was] constitutional," *id.,* at 192 (emphasis added). And in *United States v. Locke,* 471 U.S. 84 (1985), the Court found the doctrine inapplicable not because of lack of constitutional doubt, but because the statutory language did not permit an interpretation that would "avoid a constitutional question," *id.,* at 96. Similarly, in *United States v. Monsanto,* 491 U.S. 600 (1989), "the language of [the statute was] plain and unambiguous," *id.,* at 606.

The Court contends that the doctrine of constitutional doubt is also inapplicable because §1326 is not fairly susceptible of the construction which avoids the constitutional problem *i.e.,* the construction whereby subsection (b)(2) sets forth a separate criminal offense. . . .

The *relevant* question for present purposes is not whether prior felony conviction is "typically" used as a sentencing factor, but rather whether, in statutes that provide higher maximum sentences for crimes committed by convicted felons, prior conviction is "typically" treated as a mere sentence enhancement or rather as an element of a separate offense. The answer to that question is the latter. That was the rule at common law, and was the near-uniform practice among the States at the time of the most recent study I am aware of. . . . At common law, the fact of prior convictions *had* to be charged in the same indictment charging the underlying crime, and submitted to the jury for determination along with that crime. *See, e.g., Spencer v. Texas,* at 566. . . . While several States later altered this procedure by providing a separate proceeding for the determination of prior convictions, at least as late as 1965 all but eight retained the defendant's right to a jury determination on this issue. *See* Note, 40 N.Y.U. L. REV., at 333-334, 347. I am at a loss to explain the Court's assertion that it has "found no statute that clearly makes recidivism an offense element" added to another crime. There are many such. . . .

[L]et me turn now to the statute at issue §1326 as it stood when petitioner was convicted. The author of today's opinion for the Court once agreed that the "language and structure" of this enactment "are subject to two plausible readings," one of them being that recidivism constitutes a separate offense. *United States v. Forbes,* 16 F.3d 1294, 1298 (C.A.1 1994) (opinion of Coffin, J., joined by Breyer, C.J.). This would surely be enough to satisfy the requirement expressed by Justice Holmes, *see United States v. Jin Fuey Moy,* 241 U.S. 394, 401 (1916), and approved by the Court, that the constitutional-doubt-avoiding construction be "fairly possible." Today, however, the Court relegates statutory language and structure to merely two of five "factors" that "help courts determine a statute's objectives and thereby illuminate its text". . . .

In sum, I find none of the four nontextual factors relied upon by the Court to support its interpretation ("typicality" of recidivism as a sentencing factor; titles; legislative history; and risk of unfairness) persuasive. What does seem to me significant, however, is a related statutory provision, introduced by a 1996 amendment, which explicitly refers to subsection (b)(2) as setting forth "offenses." *See* §334, 110 Stat. 3009-635 (instructing United States Sentencing Commission to amend sentencing guidelines "for offenses under . . . 1326(b)"). This later amendment can of course not cause subsection (b)(2) to have meant, at the time of petitioner's conviction, something different from what it then said. But Congress's expressed understanding that subsection (b) creates separate offenses is surely evidence that it is "fairly possible" to read the provision that way. . . .

For the foregoing reasons, I think we must interpret the statute before us here as establishing a separate offense rather than a sentence enhancement. It can be argued that, once the constitutional doubts that require this course have been resolved, statutes no less ambiguous than the one before us here will be interpretable as sentence enhancements, so that not much will have been achieved. That begs the question, of course, as to how the constitutional doubt will be resolved. Moreover, where the doctrine of constitutional doubt does not apply, the same result may be dictated by the rule of lenity, which would preserve rather than destroy the criminal defendant's right to jury findings beyond a reasonable doubt. . . . Whichever doctrine is applied for the purpose, it seems to me a sound principle that whenever Congress wishes a fact to increase the maximum sentence without altering the substantive offense, it must make that intention unambiguously clear. Accordingly, I would find that §1326(b)(2) establishes a separate offense, and would reverse the judgment below.

Notes and Questions

1. In *Zadvydas v. Davis*, Justice Breyer, writing for the Court, reads the statutory provision narrowly to avoid the constitutional doubt that a broader interpretation would raise. In *Almendarez-Torres v. United States*, Justice Breyer, again writing for the Court, refuses to apply the constitutional avoidance canon. Is Justice Breyer's position consistent? What factors best explain the different outcomes in the cases?

2. The constitutional avoidance canon is only available when a statutory provision is ambiguous. If there is no question as to the meaning of a provision, then a court has no choice but to determine whether the provision violates the Constitution. If the court determines that the provision does violate the Constitution, it will next determine whether the provision can be severed from the statute or whether the whole statute must be invalidated. (The touchstone for severability is whether Congress would have enacted the statute without the unconstitutional section. *See* Leavitt v. Jane L., 518 U.S. 137, 139 (1996).)

3. Even if a provision is ambiguous, the constitutional avoidance canon only applies in the face of a "grave" constitutional doubt. When is a doubt serious enough? When it seems nearly certain that the interpretation will fail constitutional muster? Highly likely? More likely than not? If you were a judge, which understanding would you favor? Think about the question in a different way: Would you seek to apply the avoidance canon more often or less often? Why?

4. What purposes does the constitutional avoidance canon serve? Think about this question from two perspectives: Congress and the Court. We have said that the canon is based on the notion that Congress legislates in light of constitutional limits. Why might the Court be eager to select the interpretation that avoids a grave risk of unconstitutionality? In answering this question, consider that, in a recent empirical study, more than 69 percent of the 137 committee staffers surveyed indicated that how they expected courts to rule on the constitutionality of their statutes played a significant role in drafting. *See* Abbe R. Gluck & Lisa Schultz Bressman, *Statutory Interpretation from the Inside — An Empirical Study of Congressional Drafting, Delegation, and the Canons: Part I*, 65 STAN. L. REV. 901 (2013).

5. In *Almendarez-Torres*, the majority and the dissent disagree on the inference to draw from the words "notwithstanding" and "subject to" in the provisions at issue. Is Justice Breyer using a "super-ordinating/subordinating" canon, which would direct courts to interpret subsections in a statutory provision that contain these terms as each limiting the application of the other? Is there any general position on what those qualifiers signify? Which side has the better reading?

c. The Federalism Clear Statement Rule

Courts often express substantive canons as "clear statement" or "plain statement" rules. Such rules are different from other substantive canons because they prohibit certain interpretations absent express language in the statute authorizing the interpretations. Put differently, clear statement rules require Congress to use specific language when affecting certain substantive interests. Mere ambiguity is not enough for a court to adopt an interpretation affecting such interests. In this sense, clear statement rules are different from other substantive canons because they have an institutional dimension — shifting interpretive responsibility from courts to Congress. The following case provides an example of the leading clear statement rule, which protects federalism interests.

Gregory v. Ashcroft

501 U.S. 452 (1991)

Justice O'CONNOR delivered the opinion of the Court.

Article V, §26, of the Missouri Constitution provides that "[a]ll judges other than municipal judges shall retire at the age of seventy years." We consider whether this mandatory retirement provision violates the federal Age Discrimination in Employment Act of 1967 (ADEA or Act), 81 Stat. 602, as amended, 29 U.S.C. §§621-634, and whether it comports with the federal constitutional prescription of equal protection of the laws.

I

Petitioners are Missouri state judges. Judge Ellis Gregory, Jr., is an associate circuit judge for the Twenty-first Judicial Circuit. Judge Anthony P. Nugent, Jr., is a judge of the Missouri Court of Appeals, Western District. Both are subject to the §26 mandatory retirement provision. Petitioners were appointed to office by the Governor of Missouri, pursuant to the Missouri Non-Partisan Court

Plan, Mo. Const., Art. V, §§25(a)-25(g). Each has, since his appointment, been retained in office by means of a retention election in which the judge ran unopposed, subject only to a "yes or no" vote. *See* Mo. Const., Art. V, §25(c)(1).

Petitioners and two other state judges filed suit against John D. Ashcroft, the Governor of Missouri, in the United States District Court for the Eastern District of Missouri, challenging the validity of the mandatory retirement provision. The judges alleged that the provision violated both the ADEA and the Equal Protection Clause of the Fourteenth Amendment to the United States Constitution. The Governor filed a motion to dismiss.

The District Court granted the motion, holding that Missouri's appointed judges are not protected by the ADEA because they are "appointees . . . 'on a policymaking level' " and therefore are excluded from the Act's definition of "employee." The court held also that the mandatory retirement provision does not violate the Equal Protection Clause because there is a rational basis for the distinction between judges and other state officials to whom no mandatory retirement age applies.

The United States Court of Appeals for the Eighth Circuit affirmed the dismissal. 898 F.2d 598 (1990). That court also held that appointed judges are " 'appointee[s] on the policymaking level,' " and are therefore not covered under the ADEA. *Id.*, at 604. The Court of Appeals held as well that Missouri had a rational basis for distinguishing judges who had reached the age of 70 from those who had not. *Id.*, at 606.

We granted certiorari on both the ADEA and equal protection questions, 498 U.S. 979 (1990), and now affirm.

II

The ADEA makes it unlawful for an "employer" "to discharge any individual" who is at least 40 years old "because of such individual's age." 29 U.S.C. §§623(a), 631(a). The term "employer" is defined to include "a State or political subdivision of a State." §630(b)(2). Petitioners work for the State of Missouri. They contend that the Missouri mandatory retirement requirement for judges violates the ADEA.

A

As every schoolchild learns, our Constitution establishes a system of dual sovereignty between the States and the Federal Government. This Court also has recognized this fundamental principle. In *Tafflin v. Levitt*, 493 U.S. 455, 458 (1990), "[w]e beg[a]n with the axiom that, under our federal system, the States possess sovereignty concurrent with that of the Federal Government, subject only to limitations imposed by the Supremacy Clause." . . .

The Constitution created a Federal Government of limited powers. "The powers not delegated to the United States by the Constitution, nor prohibited by it to the States, are reserved to the States respectively, or to the people." U.S. Const., Amdt. 10. The States thus retain substantial sovereign authority under our constitutional system. . . .

This federalist structure of joint sovereigns preserves to the people numerous advantages. It assures a decentralized government that will be more sensitive to the diverse needs of a heterogenous society; it increases opportunity for citizen involvement in democratic processes; it allows for more innovation and experimentation in government; and it makes government more responsive by putting the States in competition for a mobile citizenry. . . .

Perhaps the principal benefit of the federalist system is a check on abuses of government power. "The 'constitutionally mandated balance of power' between the States and the Federal Government was adopted by the Framers to ensure the protection of 'our fundamental liberties.' " *Atascadero State Hospital v. Scanlon,* 473 U.S. 234, 242 (1985), quoting *Garcia v. San Antonio Metropolitan Transit Authority,* 469 U.S. 528, 572 (1985) (Powell, J., dissenting). Just as the separation and independence of the coordinate branches of the Federal Government serve to prevent the accumulation of excessive power in any one branch, a healthy balance of power between the States and the Federal Government will reduce the risk of tyranny and abuse from either front.

The Federal Government holds a decided advantage in this delicate balance: the Supremacy Clause. U.S. Const., Art. VI, cl. 2. As long as it is acting within the powers granted it under the Constitution, Congress may impose its will on the States. Congress may legislate in areas traditionally regulated by the States. This is an extraordinary power in a federalist system. It is a power that we must assume Congress does not exercise lightly.

The present case concerns a state constitutional provision through which the people of Missouri establish a qualification for those who sit as their judges. This provision goes beyond an area traditionally regulated by the States; it is a decision of the most fundamental sort for a sovereign entity. Through the structure of its government, and the character of those who exercise government authority, a State defines itself as a sovereign. "It is obviously essential to the independence of the States, and to their peace and tranquility, that their power to prescribe the qualifications of their own officers . . . should be exclusive, and free from external interference, except so far as plainly provided by the Constitution of the United States." *Taylor v. Beckham,* 178 U.S. 548, 570-571 (1900). . . .

Congressional interference with this decision of the people of Missouri, defining their constitutional officers, would upset the usual constitutional balance of federal and state powers. For this reason, "it is incumbent upon the federal courts to be certain of Congress' intent before finding that federal law overrides" this balance. *Atascadero,* 473 U.S., at 243. We explained recently:

> "[I]f Congress intends to alter the 'usual constitutional balance between the States and the Federal Government,' it must make its intention to do so 'unmistakably clear in the language of the statute.' *Atascadero State Hospital v. Scanlon,* 473 U.S. 234, 242 (1985). *Atascadero* was an Eleventh Amendment case, but a similar approach is applied in other contexts. Congress should make its intention 'clear and manifest' if it intends

to pre-empt the historic powers of the States, *Rice v. Santa Fe Elevator Corp.*, 331 U.S. 218, 230 (1947). . . . 'In traditionally sensitive areas, such as legislation affecting the federal balance, the requirement of clear statement assures that the legislature has in fact faced, and intended to bring into issue, the critical matters involved in the judicial decision.' *United States v. Bass,* 404 U.S. 336, 349 (1971)." *Will v. Michigan Dept. of State Police,* 491 U.S. 58, 65 (1989).

This plain statement rule is nothing more than an acknowledgment that the States retain substantial sovereign powers under our constitutional scheme, powers with which Congress does not readily interfere. . . .

[Past] cases stand in recognition of the authority of the people of the States to determine the qualifications of their most important government officials. It is an authority that lies at " 'the heart of representative government.' " *Ibid.* It is a power reserved to the States under the Tenth Amendment and guaranteed them by that provision of the Constitution under which the United States "guarantee[s] to every State in this Union a Republican Form of Government." U.S. Const., Art. IV, §4. . . .

The authority of the people of the States to determine the qualifications of their government officials is, of course, not without limit. Other constitutional provisions, most notably the Fourteenth Amendment, proscribe certain qualifications; our review of citizenship requirements under the political function exception is less exacting, but it is not absent. Here, we must decide what Congress did in extending the ADEA to the States, pursuant to its powers under the Commerce Clause. *See EEOC v. Wyoming,* 460 U.S. 226 (1983) (the extension of the ADEA to employment by state and local governments was a valid exercise of Congress' powers under the Commerce Clause). As against Congress' powers "[t]o regulate Commerce . . . among the several States," U.S. Const., Art. I, §8, cl. 3, the authority of the people of the States to determine the qualifications of their government officials may be inviolate.

We are constrained in our ability to consider the limits that the state-federal balance places on Congress' powers under the Commerce Clause. *See Garcia v. San Antonio Metropolitan Transit Authority,* 469 U.S. 528 (1985) (declining to review limitations placed on Congress' Commerce Clause powers by our federal system). But there is no need to do so if we hold that the ADEA does not apply to state judges. Application of the plain statement rule thus may avoid a potential constitutional problem. Indeed, inasmuch as this Court in *Garcia* has left primarily to the political process the protection of the States against intrusive exercises of Congress' Commerce Clause powers, we must be absolutely certain that Congress intended such an exercise. "[T]o give the state-displacing weight of federal law to mere congressional *ambiguity* would evade the very procedure for lawmaking on which *Garcia* relied to protect states' interests." L. Tribe, American Constitutional Law §6-25, p. 480 (2d ed. 1988).

B

In 1974, Congress extended the substantive provisions of the ADEA to include the States as employers. Pub. L. 93-259, §28(a), 88 Stat. 74, 29

U.S.C. §630(b)(2). At the same time, Congress amended the definition of "employee" to exclude all elected and most high-ranking government officials. Under the Act, as amended:

> "The term 'employee' means an individual employed by any employer except that the term 'employee' shall not include any person elected to public office in any State or political subdivision of any State by the qualified voters thereof, or any person chosen by such officer to be on such officer's personal staff, or an appointee on the policymaking level or an immediate adviser with respect to the exercise of the constitutional or legal powers of the office." 29 U.S.C. §630(f).

Governor Ashcroft contends that the §630(f) exclusion of certain public officials also excludes judges, like petitioners, who are appointed to office by the Governor and are then subject to retention election. The Governor points to two passages in §630(f). First, he argues, these judges are selected by an elected official and, because they make policy, are "appointee[s] on the policymaking level."

Petitioners counter that judges merely resolve factual disputes and decide questions of law; they do not make policy. Moreover, petitioners point out that the policymaking-level exception is part of a trilogy, tied closely to the elected-official exception. Thus, the Act excepts elected officials and: (1) "any person chosen by such officer to be on such officer's personal staff"; (2) "an appointee on the policymaking level"; and (3) "an immediate advisor with respect to the exercise of the constitutional or legal powers of the office." Applying the maxim of statutory construction *noscitur a sociis* that a word is known by the company it keeps petitioners argue that since (1) and (3) refer only to those in close working relationships with elected officials, so too must (2). Even if it can be said that judges may make policy, petitioners contend, they do not do so at the behest of an elected official.

Governor Ashcroft relies on the plain language of the statute: It exempts persons appointed "at the policymaking level." The Governor argues that state judges, in fashioning and applying the common law, make policy. Missouri is a common law state. *See* Mo. Rev. Stat. §1.010 (1986) (adopting "[t]he common law of England" consistent with federal and state law). The common law, unlike a constitution or statute, provides no definitive text; it is to be derived from the interstices of prior opinions and a well-considered judgment of what is best for the community. As Justice Holmes put it:

> "The very considerations which judges most rarely mention, and always with an apology, are the secret root from which the law draws all the juices of life. I mean, of course, considerations of what is expedient for the community concerned. Every important principle which is developed by litigation is in fact and at bottom the result of more or less definitely understood views of public policy; most generally, to be sure, under our practice and traditions, the unconscious result of instinctive preferences and inarticulate convictions, but nonetheless traceable to views of public policy in the last analysis." O. Holmes, The Common Law 35-36 (1881).

Governor Ashcroft contends that Missouri judges make policy in other ways as well. The Missouri Supreme Court and Courts of Appeals have supervisory authority over inferior courts. Mo. Const., Art. V, §4. The Missouri

Supreme Court has the constitutional duty to establish rules of practice and procedure for the Missouri court system, and inferior courts exercise policy judgment in establishing local rules of practice. *See* Mo. Const., Art. V, §5. The state courts have supervisory powers over the state bar, with the Missouri Supreme Court given the authority to develop disciplinary rules. *See* Mo. Rev. Stat. §§484.040, 484.200-484.270 (1986); Rules Governing the Missouri Bar and the Judiciary (1991).

The Governor stresses judges' policymaking responsibilities, but it is far from plain that the statutory exception requires that judges actually make policy. The statute refers to appointees "on the policymaking level," not to appointees "who make policy." It may be sufficient that the appointee is in a position requiring the exercise of discretion concerning issues of public importance. This certainly describes the bench, regardless of whether judges might be considered policymakers in the same sense as the executive or legislature.

Nonetheless, "appointee at the policymaking level," particularly in the context of the other exceptions that surround it, is an odd way for Congress to exclude judges; a plain statement that judges are not "employees" would seem the most efficient phrasing. But in this case we are not looking for a plain statement that judges are excluded. We will not read the ADEA to cover state judges unless Congress has made it clear that judges are *included*. This does not mean that the Act must mention judges explicitly, though it does not. *Cf. Dellmuth v. Muth,* 491 U.S. 223, 233 (1989) (Scalia, J., concurring). Rather, it must be plain to anyone reading the Act that it covers judges. In the context of a statute that plainly excludes most important state public officials, "appointee on the policymaking level" is sufficiently broad that we cannot conclude that the statute plainly covers appointed state judges. Therefore, it does not.

The ADEA plainly covers all state employees except those excluded by one of the exceptions. Where it is unambiguous that an employee does not fall within one of the exceptions, the Act states plainly and unequivocally that the employee is included. It is at least ambiguous whether a state judge is an "appointee on the policymaking level." . . .

In *Pennhurst State School & Hosp. v. Halderman,* 451 U.S. 1 (1981), we adopted a rule fully cognizant of the traditional power of the States: "Because such legislation imposes congressional policy on a State involuntarily, and because it often intrudes on traditional state authority, we should not quickly attribute to Congress an unstated intent to act under its authority to enforce the Fourteenth Amendment." . . . Because Congress nowhere stated its intent to impose mandatory obligations on the States under its §5 powers, we concluded that Congress did not do so. *Ibid.*

The *Pennhurst* rule looks much like the plain statement rule we apply today. In *EEOC v. Wyoming,* the Court explained that *Pennhurst* established a rule of statutory construction to be applied where statutory intent is ambiguous. 460 U.S., at 244, n.18. In light of the ADEA's clear exclusion of most important public officials, it is at least ambiguous whether Congress intended that appointed judges nonetheless be included. In the face of such ambiguity, we will not attribute to Congress an intent to intrude on state governmental functions regardless of whether Congress acted pursuant to its Commerce Clause powers or §5 of the Fourteenth Amendment.

Affirmed.

Justice WHITE, with whom Justice STEVENS joins, concurring in part, dissenting in part, and concurring in the judgment. . . .

I

. . . [The majority] holds that whether or not the ADEA can fairly be read to exclude state judges from its scope, "[w]e will not read the ADEA to cover state judges unless Congress has made it clear that judges are *included*." I cannot agree with this "plain statement" rule because it is unsupported by the decisions upon which the majority relies, contrary to our Tenth Amendment jurisprudence, and fundamentally unsound. . . .

The dispute in this case therefore is not whether Congress has outlawed age discrimination by the States. It clearly has. The only question is whether petitioners fall within the definition of "employee" in the Act, §630(f), which contains exceptions for elected officials and certain appointed officials. If petitioners *are* "employee[s]," Missouri's mandatory retirement provision clearly conflicts with the antidiscrimination provisions of the ADEA. . . . Pre-emption therefore is automatic, since "state law is pre-empted to the extent that it actually conflicts with federal law." *Pacific Gas & Elec. Co. v. State Energy Resources Conservation and Development Comm'n*, 461 U.S. 190, 204 (1983). The majority's federalism concerns are irrelevant to such "actual conflict" pre-emption. . . .

While acknowledging this principle of federal legislative supremacy, the majority nevertheless imposes upon Congress a "plain statement" requirement. The majority claims to derive this requirement from the plain statement approach developed in our Eleventh Amendment cases, *see, e.g., Atascadero State Hospital v. Scanlon*, 473 U.S. 234, 243 (1985), and applied two Terms ago in *Will v. Michigan Dept. of State Police*, 491 U.S. 58, 65 (1989). The issue in those cases, however, was whether Congress intended a particular statute to extend to the States *at all*. . . . In the present case, by contrast, Congress has expressly extended the coverage of the ADEA to the States and their employees. Its intention to regulate age discrimination by States is thus "unmistakably clear in the language of the statute." *Atascadero*, 473 U.S., at 242. The only dispute is over the precise details of the statute's application. We have never extended the plain statement approach that far, and the majority offers no compelling reason for doing so. . . .

The majority's approach is also unsound because it will serve only to confuse the law. First, the majority fails to explain the scope of its rule. Is the rule limited to federal regulation of the qualifications of state officials? Or does it apply more broadly to the regulation of any "state governmental functions"? Second, the majority does not explain its requirement that Congress' intent to regulate a particular state activity be "plain to anyone reading [the federal statute]." Does that mean that it is now improper to look to the purpose or history of a federal statute in determining the scope of the statute's limitations on state activities? If so, the majority's rule is completely inconsistent with our pre-emption jurisprudence. *See, e.g., Hillsborough County v. Automated Medical Laboratories, Inc.,* 471 U.S. 707, 715 (1985) (pre-emption will be found where there is a " 'clear and manifest *purpose*' " to displace state law) (emphasis added). The vagueness of the majority's rule undoubtedly will lead States to assert that various federal statutes no longer apply to a wide variety of state activities if Congress has not expressly referred to those activities in the statute. Congress, in turn, will be forced to draft long and detailed lists of which particular state functions it meant to regulate.

The imposition of such a burden on Congress is particularly out of place in the context of the ADEA. Congress already has stated that all "individual[s] employed by any employer" are protected by the ADEA unless they are expressly excluded by one of the exceptions in the definition of "employee." *See* 29 U.S.C. §630(f). The majority, however, turns the statute on its head, holding that state judges are not protected by the ADEA because "Congress has [not] made it clear that judges are *included*." *Cf. EEOC v. Wyoming,* 460 U.S. 226 (1983), where we held that state game wardens are covered by the ADEA, even though such employees are not expressly included within the ADEA's scope.

The majority asserts that its plain statement rule is helpful in avoiding a "potential constitutional problem." It is far from clear, however, why there would be a constitutional problem if the ADEA applied to state judges, in light of our decisions in *Garcia* and *Baker,* discussed above. As long as "the national political *process* did not operate in a defective manner, the Tenth Amendment is not implicated. *Baker,* 485 U.S., at 513. There is no claim in this case that the political process by which the ADEA was extended to state employees was inadequate to protect the States from being "unduly burden[ed]" by the Federal Government. *See Garcia,* 469 U.S., at 556. In any event, as discussed below, a straightforward analysis of the ADEA's definition of "employee" reveals that the ADEA does not apply here. . . .

The majority's departures from established precedent are even more disturbing when it is realized, as discussed below, that this case can be affirmed based on simple statutory construction.

II

The statute at issue in this case is the ADEA's definition of "employee," which provides:

> "The term 'employee' means an individual employed by any employer except that the term 'employee' shall not include any person elected to public office in any State or political subdivision of any State by the qualified voters thereof, or any person chosen by such officer to be on such officer's personal staff, or an appointee on the policymaking level or an immediate adviser with respect to the exercise of the constitutional or legal powers of the office. The exemption set forth in the preceding sentence shall not

include employees subject to the civil service laws of a State government, governmental agency, or political subdivision." 29 U.S.C. §630(f).

A parsing of that definition reveals that it excludes from the definition of "employee" (and thus the coverage of the ADEA) four types of (noncivil service) state and local employees: (1) persons elected to public office; (2) the personal staff of elected officials; (3) persons appointed by elected officials to be on the policymaking level; and (4) the immediate advisers of elected officials with respect to the constitutional or legal powers of the officials' offices.

The question before us is whether petitioners fall within the third exception. Like the Court of Appeals, I assume that petitioners, who were initially appointed to their positions by the Governor of Missouri, are "appointed" rather than "elected" within the meaning of the ADEA. For the reasons below, I also conclude that petitioners are "on the policymaking level."

"Policy" is defined as "a definite course or method of action selected (as by a government, institution, group, or individual) from among alternatives and in the light of given conditions to guide and usu[ally] determine present and future decisions." Webster's Third New International Dictionary 1754 (1976). Applying that definition, it is clear that the decisionmaking engaged in by common-law judges, such as petitioners, places them "on the policymaking level." In resolving disputes, although judges do not operate with unconstrained discretion, they do choose "from among alternatives" and elaborate their choices in order "to guide and . . . determine present and future decisions." The quotation from Justice Holmes in the majority's opinion, is an eloquent description of the policymaking nature of the judicial function. Justice Cardozo also stated it well:

> "Each [common-law judge] indeed is legislating within the limits of his competence. No doubt the limits for the judge are narrower. He legislates only between gaps. He fills the open spaces in the law. . . . [W]ithin the confines of these open spaces and those of precedent and tradition, choice moves with a freedom which stamps its action as creative. The law which is the resulting product is not found, but made." B. Cardozo, The Nature of the Judicial Process 113-115 (1921).

Moreover, it should be remembered that the statutory exception refers to appointees "on the policymaking level," not "policymaking employees." Thus, whether or not judges actually *make* policy, they certainly are on the same *level* as policymaking officials in other branches of government and therefore are covered by the exception. The degree of responsibility vested in judges, for example, is comparable to that of other officials that have been found by the lower courts to be on the policymaking level. *See, e.g., EEOC v. Reno,* 758 F.2d 581 (C.A.11 1985) (assistant state attorney); *EEOC v. Board of Trustees of Wayne Cty. Community College,* 723 F.2d 509 (C.A.6 1983) (president of community college).

Petitioners argue that the "appointee[s] on the policymaking level" exception should be construed to apply "only to persons who advise or work closely with the elected official that chose the appointee." In support of that claim, petitioners point out that the exception is "sandwiched" between the "personal staff" and "immediate adviser" exceptions in §630(f), and thus should be read as covering only similar employees.

Petitioners' premise, however, does not prove their conclusion. It is true that the placement of the "appointee" exception between the "personal staff" and "immediate adviser" exceptions suggests a similarity among the three. But the most obvious similarity is simply that each of the three sets of employees are connected in some way with elected officials: The first and third sets have a certain working relationship with elected officials, while the second is *appointed* by elected officials. There is no textual support for concluding that the second set must *also* have a close working relationship with elected officials. Indeed, such a reading would tend to make the "appointee" exception superfluous since the "personal staff" and "immediate adviser" exceptions would seem to cover most appointees who are in a close working relationship with elected officials. . . .

For these reasons, I would hold that petitioners are excluded from the coverage of the ADEA because they are "appointee[s] on the policymaking level" under 29 U.S.C. §630(f).

I join Parts I and III of the Court's opinion and concur in its judgment.

[The dissenting opinion of Justice BLACKMUN is omitted.]

Notes and Questions

1. The rule in *Gregory* is not a mere tie-breaker in a close case, tipping the balance in favor of states' interests. Another substantive canon — the federalism canon — serves this function. The clear statement rule establishes a principle of legislative drafting: whenever Congress intends to alter the federal-state balance, it must do so expressly in the statute. Thus, the clear statement rule forces Congress to make the hard policy choices in the statute. What are the justifications for so doing?

2. In *Gregory,* the federalism clear statement rule also served another purpose — it assisted the Court in avoiding the constitutional question of whether Congress has the constitutional authority to apply the ADEA to state judges. Why didn't the Court use the constitutional avoidance canon instead? Was there a greater advantage in requiring a clear statement? Was there a problem in raising a constitutional question? Consider that on the same day as the Court decided *Gregory*, it also decided Chisom v. Roemer, 501 U.S. 380 (1991). In that case, the Court held that Congress has power under §5 to apply the Voting Rights Act to the election of state judges. Given this holding, was the ADEA likely unconstitutional as applied to state judges? Likewise, was the statute ambiguous enough to apply the constitutional avoidance canon?

3. Why didn't the Court declare, as Justice White would have, that state judges come within the exception to the statute for appointees on the policymaking level? Was there a danger in saying so that Justice White did not adequately appreciate?

4. Clear statement rules are not the only canons that shift interpretive responsibility away from the courts to another institution. The most famous administrative law case, Chevron U.S.A. Inc. v. Natural Resources Defense Council, Inc., 467 U.S. 837 (1984), is another. In that decision, the Court stated that courts should defer to agencies that have issued reasonable interpretations of ambiguities in the statutes that those agencies are charged with administering. In this way, agencies should be allowed to make the policy choices that Congress left open in their statutes. We will study *Chevron* in some detail in the following chapters. Based on what you have read so far, can you speculate on the justifications for this principle?

5. What if there was evidence that Congress is not even aware of the federal clear statement rule? Does it lose its central justification? Although staffers who were interviewed know of and rely on the federalism canon (as well as *Chevron*) in drafting, most were not aware of clear statement rules of any variety. *See* Abbe R. Gluck & Lisa Schultz Bressman, *Statutory Interpretation from the Inside — An Empirical Study of Congressional Drafting, Delegation, and the Canons: Part I*, 65 STAN. L. REV. 901 (2013).

d. The Presumption Against Preemption

Gregory v. Ashcroft involved the question whether a federal statute preempted a state constitutional provision. Questions often arise as to whether a federal statute preempts other state laws, including state statutes, regulations, and common law rules. In such cases, courts often apply a presumption against preemption. That presumption rests on the notion that "the historic police powers of the States [a]re not to be superseded . . . unless that was the clear and manifest purpose of Congress." Rice v. Santa Fe Elevator Corp., 331 U.S. 218, 230 (1947). The presumption against preemption "provides assurance that 'the federal-state balance' will not be disturbed unintentionally by Congress or unnecessarily by the courts." Jones v. Rath Packing Co., 430 U.S. 519, 525 (1977) (citation omitted). The logic is quite similar to the federalism clear statement rule, although the canon itself functions in a slightly weaker fashion. The presumption against preemption states a default as to how a statute should be construed (i.e., so as not to preempt state law) that can be overcome based on clear language or other strong evidence that Congress intended otherwise.

The presumption against preemption can apply in two circumstances: (a) when a federal statute contains an express preemption provision, and (b) when it does not. *See* Bates v. Dow Agrosciences LLC, 544 U.S. 431, 449 (2005). When a statute contains an express preemption provision, courts can construe the provision narrowly to preempt some state laws but not others. As Justice Ginsburg has written,

> Federal laws containing a preemption clause do not automatically escape the presumption against preemption. A preemption clause tells us that Congress intended to supersede or modify state law to some extent. In the absence of legislative precision,

however, courts may face the task of determining the substance and scope of Congress' displacement of state law. Where the text of a preemption clause is open to more than one plausible reading, courts ordinarily "accept the reading that disfavors preemption." *Bates,* 544 U.S., at 449.

Riegel v. Medtronic, Inc., 552 U.S. 312, 334-35 (2008) (Ginsburg, J., dissenting).

Even when a statute contains no preemption provision, courts can still imply preemption if state laws frustrate the federal scheme or compliance with both federal and state laws is impossible. *See* Freightliner Corp. v. Myrick, 514 U.S. 280, 282 (1995); Florida Lime & Avocado Growers, Inc. v. Paul, 373 U.S. 132, 142-43 (1963). But, consistent with the presumption against preemption, they can imply preemption narrowly. For example, courts can imply preemption only as necessary to avoid a direct conflict between the statute and state law. *See* Wyeth v. Levine, 555 U.S. 555, 565 (2009).

Although the presumption against preemption is an important textual tool, many scholars have noted that it is a mess. The Court has been inconsistent in its application of the canon, particularly when a case involves the conflict between an agency regulation and a state law. We flag this issue so that you will not be surprised if you encounter it in your legal career. If you are interested in more on this issue now, see Stuart Minor Benjamin & Ernest A. Young, *Tennis with the Net Down: Administrative Federalism Without Congress,* 57 Duke L.J. 2111 (2008); Brian Galle & Mark Seidenfeld, *Administrative Law's Federalism: Preemption, Delegation, and Agencies at the Edge of Federal Power,* 57 Duke L.J. 1933 (2008); Gillian E. Metzger, *Administrative Law as the New Federalism,* 57 Duke L.J. 2023 (2008); Caleb Nelson, *Preemption,* 86 Va. L. Rev. 225 (2000); and Catherine M. Sharkey, *Products Liability Preemption: An Institutional Approach,* 76 Geo. Wash. L. Rev. 449, 450 (2008). A recent empirical study of legislative drafting suggests that the presumption against preemption is a well-recognized canon of construction. *See* Abbe R. Gluck & Lisa Schultz Bressman, *Statutory Interpretation from the Inside — An Empirical Study of Congressional Drafting, Delegation, and the Canons: Part I,* 65 Stan. L. Rev. 901 (2013). About 80 percent of staffers who participated in the survey were familiar with either the presumption against preemption or the federalism canon (the non-clear statement version, which says that ambiguous statutes should be construed in favor of state law) and about 50 percent were familiar with both. Here is an interesting finding: although most staffers know the canons, they do not seem to regard the canons in the same way that courts do. Specifically, they do not seem to regard the canons as a "thumb on the scale" or tie-breaker that tips the interpretation of ambiguous statutes in favor of state law. Rather, the canons serve to focus legislative drafters on the importance of state interests. Should these findings affect how courts apply the canons?

e. The Presumption Against Retroactivity

Courts applying a presumption against retroactivity "decline[] to give retroactive effect to statutes burdening private rights unless Congress had made clear its intent." Landgraf v. USI Film Prods., 511 U.S. 244, 270 (1994). What does it mean for a statute to have retroactive effect? The established formulation is that a statute operates retroactively if "the new provision attaches new legal consequences to events completed before its enactment." *Id.* at 270.

The presumption against retroactivity has deep roots. As the Court explained in *Landgraf*:

> Elementary considerations of fairness dictate that individuals should have an opportunity to know what the law is and to conform their conduct accordingly; settled expectations should not be lightly disrupted. For that reason, the "principle that the legal effect of conduct should ordinarily be assessed under the law that existed when the conduct took place has timeless and universal appeal." *Kaiser Aluminum & Chemical Corp. v. Bonjorno*, 494 U.S. 827, 855 (1990) (Scalia, J., concurring). In a free, dynamic society, creativity in both commercial and artistic endeavors is fostered by a rule of law that gives people confidence about the legal consequences of their actions.

Id. at 265-66.

The presumption against retroactivity can be defeated if Congress has clearly authorized retroactive application of a statute. Thus, this presumption operates akin to a clear statement rule, requiring Congress to expressly authorize the interpretation in question. The Court has found that Congress has authorized retroactive effect only when the statutory language is "so clear that it could sustain only one interpretation." *See* Lindh v. Murphy, 521 U.S. 320, 328 n.4 (1997) (citing cases including Graham v. Goodcell, 282 U.S. 409, 416-20 (1931) (concluding that a statutory provision "was manifestly intended to operate retroactively according to its terms" where the tax statute specified the circumstances that defined the applicable claims and where the alternative interpretation was absurd)); Automobile Club of Mich. v. Commissioner, 353 U.S. 180, 184 (1957) (finding a clear statement authorizing the Commissioner of Internal Revenue to correct tax rulings and regulations "retroactively" where the statutory authorization for the Commissioner's action spoke explicitly in terms of "retroactivity").

The presumption against retroactivity frequently conflicts with other substantive canons, including the canon that a remedial statute should be construed broadly, as well as the principle that a court "should 'apply the law in effect at the time it renders its decision.' " *Landgraf*, 511 U.S. at 273. The Court has held that the presumption against retroactivity generally trumps the remedial canon. Put differently, the fact that retroactive application of a remedial statute will almost always give broader effect to that statute is insufficient to "rebut the presumption against retroactivity." *Id.* at 285-86. The presumption against retroactivity also tends to trump the principle that a court should apply the law in effect at the time of its decision. More precisely, the Court has treated the presumption against retroactivity as an exception to the general principle that a court should apply the law in effect at the time of its decision. *See, e.g., Landgraf,* 511 U.S. at 280.

f. The Presumption Against Extraterritorial Application

"It is a longstanding principle of American law that legislation of Congress, unless a contrary intent appears, is meant to apply only within the territorial jurisdiction of the United States." EEOC v. Arabian American Oil Co., 499 U.S. 244, 248 (1991). Under this doctrine, Congress is assumed to "legislate[] against the backdrop of the presumption against extraterritoriality." *Id.* The presumption against extraterritorial application is based on the "commonsense notion that Congress generally legislates with domestic concerns in mind." Smith v. United States, 507 U.S. 197, 204 n.5 (1933).

Applying this presumption, the Court had held that numerous statutes do not apply outside the territorial boundaries of the United States. *See, e.g., id.* (holding that the Federal Tort Claims Act does not apply to claims arising in Antarctica); *Arabian American Oil*, 499 U.S. at 249 (holding that Title VII of Civil Rights Act of 1964 does not apply to employment practices of U.S. firms abroad); Foley Bros., Inc. v. Filardo, 336 U.S. 281, 285-86 (1949) (labor statute does not apply to work of private contractor with the United States done in foreign country). Like other presumptions, the presumption against extraterritorial application of federal law operates like a clear statement rule, essentially requiring Congress to make clear its intention for a particular statute to have effect beyond the territorial borders of the United States.

4. Scrivener's Errors and Absurd Results

Two interpretive principles sit on the line between textual and substantive canons. They are not merely textual, but they are not entirely substantive. The first principle directs courts to correct legislative drafting mistakes, or so-called scrivener's errors. Statutes, which are a human product, reflect such mistakes or errors no less often than other written documents. For example, statutes can omit necessary words, include extraneous words, or simply contain a phrase that makes little sense in context. Courts will correct "scrivener's errors" to effectuate what Congress really meant to say or what otherwise makes sense of the statute. *See* United States National Bank of Oregon v. Independent Ins. Agents of America, Inc., 508 U.S. 439, 462 (1993). The second principle directs courts to avoid statutory interpretations that produce absurd results. Courts apply this principle on the assumption that Congress intends statutes to have sensible effects or that statutes should have sensible effects, as a normative matter. *See* United States v. Wilson, 503 U.S. 329, 334 (1992).

These principles are sensible enough, but courts often have difficulty determining when a statute contains a legislative mistake or produces an absurd result. Courts are not at liberty to simply rewrite statutes to improve their clarity or minimize their harsh effects. How often would you expect courts to apply these principles? Consider the following case, in which the Supreme Court refused to apply either.

United States v. Locke

471 U.S. 84 (1985)

Justice MARSHALL delivered the opinion of the Court.

Claimants, whose mining claims were extinguished under the Federal Land Policy and Management Act for failure to make a timely annual filing, brought suit against the Government. Congress in 1976 enacted the FLPMA, 43 U.S.C. §1701 *et seq.* Section 314 of the Act establishes a federal recording system that is designed both to rid federal lands of stale mining claims and to provide federal land managers with up-to-date information that allows them to make informed land management decisions. For claims located before FLPMA's enactment, the federal recording system imposes two general requirements. First, the claims must initially be registered with the BLM by filing, within three years of FLPMA's enactment, a copy of the official record of the notice or certificate of location. 43 U.S.C. §1744(b). Second, in the year of the initial recording, and "prior to December 31" of every year after that, the claimant must file with state officials and with BLM a notice of intention to hold the claim, an affidavit of assessment work performed on the claim, or a detailed reporting form. 43 U.S.C. §1744(a). Section 314(c) of the Act provides that failure to comply with either of these requirements "shall be deemed conclusively to constitute an abandonment of the mining claim . . . by the owner." 43 U.S.C. §1744(c).

The second of these requirements — the annual filing obligation — has created the dispute underlying this appeal. Appellees, four individuals engaged "in the business of operating mining properties in Nevada," purchased in 1960 and 1966 10 unpatented mining claims on public lands near Ely, Nevada. These claims were major sources of gravel and building material: the claims are valued at several million dollars, and, in the 1979-1980 assessment year alone, appellees' gross income totaled more than $1 million. Throughout the period during which they owned the claims, appellees complied with annual state-law filing and assessment work requirements. In addition, appellees satisfied FLPMA's initial recording requirement by properly filing with BLM a notice of location, thereby putting their claims on record for purposes of FLPMA.

At the end of 1980, however, appellees failed to meet on time their first annual obligation to file with the Federal Government. After allegedly receiving misleading information from a BLM employee, appellees waited until December 31 to submit to BLM the annual notice of intent to hold or proof of assessment work performed required under §314(a) of FLPMA, 43 U.S.C. §1744(a). As noted above, that section requires these documents to be filed annually "prior to December 31." Had appellees checked, they further would have discovered that BLM regulations made quite clear that claimants were required to make the annual filings in the proper BLM office "on or before December 30 of each calendar year." 43 CFR §3833.2-1(a)

(1980) (current version at 43 CFR §3833.2-1(b)(1) (1984)). Thus, appellees' filing was one day too late.

This fact was brought painfully home to appellees when they received a letter from the BLM Nevada State Office informing them that their claims had been declared abandoned and void due to their tardy filing. In many cases, loss of a claim in this way would have minimal practical effect; the claimant could simply locate the same claim again and then rerecord it with BLM. In this case, however, relocation of appellees' claims, which were initially located by appellees' predecessors in 1952 and 1954, was prohibited by the Common Varieties Act of 1955, 30 U.S.C. §611; that Act prospectively barred location of the sort of minerals yielded by appellees' claims. Appellees' mineral deposits thus escheated to the Government.

Before the District Court, appellees asserted that the §314(a) requirement of a filing "prior to December 31 of each year" should be construed to require a filing "on or before December 31." Thus, appellees argued, their December 31 filing had in fact complied with the statute, and the BLM had acted ultra vires in voiding their claims.

It is clear to us that the plain language of the statute simply cannot sustain the gloss appellees would put on it. As even counsel for appellees conceded at oral argument, §314(a) "is a statement that Congress wanted it filed by December 30th. I think that is a clear statement. . . ." Tr. of Oral Arg. 27. While we will not allow a literal reading of a statute to produce a result demonstrably at odds with the intentions of its drafters, with respect to filing deadlines a literal reading of Congress' words is generally the only proper reading of those words. To attempt to decide whether some date other than the one set out in the statute is the date actually "intended" by Congress is to set sail on an aimless journey, for the purpose of a filing deadline would be just as well served by nearly any date a court might choose as by the date Congress has in fact set out in the statute. Actual purpose is sometimes unknown, and such is the case with filing deadlines; as might be expected, nothing in the legislative history suggests why Congress chose December 30 over December 31, or over September 1 (the end of the assessment year for mining claims, 30 U.S.C. §28), as the last day on which the required filings could be made. But deadlines are inherently arbitrary, while fixed dates are often essential to accomplish necessary results. Faced with the inherent arbitrariness of filing deadlines, we must, at least in a civil case, apply by its terms the date fixed by the statute.

In so saying, we are not insensitive to the problems posed by congressional reliance on the words "prior to December 31." But the fact that Congress might have acted with greater clarity or foresight does not give courts a *carte blanche* to redraft statutes in an effort to achieve that which Congress is perceived to have failed to do. There is a basic difference between filling a gap left by Congress' silence and rewriting rules that Congress has affirmatively and specifically enacted. Nor is the Judiciary licensed to attempt to soften the clear import of Congress' chosen words whenever a court believes those words lead to a harsh result. On the contrary, deference to the supremacy of the Legislature, as well as recognition that Congressmen typically vote on the language of a bill, generally requires us to assume that the legislative purpose is expressed by the ordinary meaning of the words used. Going behind the plain language of a statute in search of a possibly contrary congressional intent is 'a step to be taken cautiously' even under the best of circumstances." When even after taking this step nothing in the legislative history remotely suggests a congressional intent contrary to Congress' chosen words, and neither appellees nor the dissenters have pointed to anything that so suggests, any further steps take the courts out of the realm of interpretation and place them in the domain of legislation. The phrase "prior to" may be clumsy, but its meaning is clear. Under these circumstances, we are obligated to apply the "prior to December 31" language by its terms.

Notes and Questions

1. For adherents of the plain meaning rule, this case is an easy one. The Act requires the filing of a mining claim "prior to December 31." Otherwise, the claim is forfeited. The claimants filed on December 31. Why wasn't that the end of the matter?

2. The result in this case was troubling because it imposed harsh penalties on the claimants. In addition, those claimants had sought advice from the government concerning the filing date, relying on that mistaken advice to their detriment. Why wasn't this case one of absurd results?

3. At times, the Supreme Court has offered a broad formulation of the absurd results doctrine. Consider this excerpt from Chapman v. United States, 500 U.S. 453, 476-77 (1991):

> In the past, we have recognized that "frequently words of general meaning are used in a statute, words broad enough to include an act in question, and yet a consideration of . . . the absurd results which follow from giving such broad meaning to the words, makes it unreasonable to believe that the legislator intended to include the particular act." *Church of the Holy Trinity v. United States*, 143 U.S. 457, 459 (1892). These words guided our construction of the statute at issue in *Public Citizen v. Department of Justice*, 491 U.S. 440, 454 (1989), when we also noted that "[l]ooking beyond the naked text for guidance is perfectly proper when the result it apparently decrees is difficult to fathom or where it seems inconsistent with Congress' intention. . . ." *Id.*, at 455.

In United States v. X-Citement Video, Inc., 513 U.S. 64, 69-70 (1994), the Court questioned subjecting to criminal liability a person who "knowingly transports or ships in interstate or foreign commerce . . . any visual depiction, if . . . the producing of such visual depiction involves the use of a minor engaging in sexually explicit conduct," without knowing that the depiction involves the use of a minor:

> Some applications of respondents' position would produce results that were not merely odd, but positively absurd. If we were to conclude that "knowingly" only modifies the relevant verbs in §2252 [i.e., "transports" or "ships"], we would sweep within the ambit of the statute actors who had no idea that they were even dealing with sexually explicit material.

> For instance, a retail druggist who returns an uninspected roll of developed film to a customer "knowingly distributes" a visual depiction and would be criminally liable if it were later discovered that the visual depiction contained images of children engaged in sexually explicit conduct. Or, a new resident of an apartment might receive mail for the prior resident and store the mail unopened. If the prior tenant had requested delivery of materials covered by §2252, his residential successor could be prosecuted for "knowing receipt" of such materials. Similarly, a Federal Express courier who delivers a box in which the shipper has declared the contents to be "film" "knowingly transports" such film. We do not assume that Congress, in passing laws, intended such results.

X-Citement Video, 513 U.S. at 69-70.

4. Should the Court have found that the filing deadline contained a scrivener's error? Why would Congress create such a trap for the unwary, omitting just one filing day from the calendar year? Surely any reasonable legislator would have written "prior to the close of business on December 31," or "on or before December 31." Can you think of any reason for Congress to write the statute as is? What if the statute had said "prior to November 31"?

5. Should the Court have examined the legislative history to determine whether the language contained a scrivener's error? Why or why not?

5. Criticisms of Canons of Construction

For decades, scholars and courts have criticized canons of construction. Perhaps the most widely cited criticism of canons of construction was set out in an early article by the iconic Karl Llewellyn. Llewellyn produced a chart that he claimed showed that for every canon, one could locate an opposing canon that supported the contrary result:

Karl N. Llewellyn, Remarks on the Theory of Appellate Decision and the Rules or Canons About How Statutes Are to Be Construed

3 Vand. L. Rev. 395, 401-06 (1950)

When it comes to presenting a proposed construction in court, there is an accepted conventional vocabulary. As in argument over points of case-law, the accepted convention still, unhappily requires discussion as if only one single correct meaning could exist. Hence there are two opposing canons on almost every point. An arranged selection is appended. Every lawyer must be familiar with them all: they are still needed tools of argument. At least as early as Fortescue the general picture was clear, on this, to any eye which would see.

Plainly, to make any canon take hold in a particular instance, the construction contended for must be sold, essentially, by means other than the use of the canon: The good sense of the situation and a simple construction of the available language to achieve that sense, by tenable means, out of the statutory language.

Statutory interpretation still speaks a diplomatic tongue. Here is some of the technical framework for maneuver.

Thrust	But	Parry
1. A statute cannot go beyond its text.		1. To effect its purpose statute may be implemented beyond its text.
2. Statutes in derogation of the common law will not be extended by construction.		2. Such acts will be liberally construed if their nature is remedial.
3. Statutes are to be read in the light of the common law and a statute affirming a common law rule is to be construed in accordance with the common law.		3. The common law gives way to a statute which is inconsistent with it and when a statute is designed as a revision of a whole body of law applicable to a given subject it supersedes the common law.
4. Where a foreign statute which has received construction has been adopted, previous construction is adopted too.		4. It may be rejected where there is conflict with the obvious meaning of the statute or where the foreign decisions are unsatisfactory in reasoning or where the foreign interpretation is not in harmony with the spirit or policy of the laws of the adopting state.
5. Where various states have already adopted the statute, the parent state is followed.		5. Where interpretations of other states are inharmonious, there is no such restraint.
6. Statutes *in pari materia* must be construed together.		6. A statute is not *in pari materia* if its scope and aim are distinct or where a legislative design to depart from the general purpose or policy or previous enactments may be apparent
7. A statute imposing a new penalty or forfeiture, or a new liability or disability, or creating a new right of action will not be construed as having a retroactive effect.		7. Remedial statutes are to be liberally construed and if a retroactive interpretation will promote the ends of justice, they should receive such construction.

Thrust	But	Parry
8. Where design has been distinctly stated no place is left for construction.		8. Courts have the power to inquire into real—as distinct from ostensible—purpose.
9. Definitions and rules of construction contained in an interpretation clause are part of the law and binding.		9. Definitions and rules of construction in a statute will not be extended beyond their necessary import nor allowed to defeat intention otherwise manifested.
10. A statutory provision requiring liberal construction does not mean disregard of unequivocal requirements of the statute.		10. Where a rule of construction is provided within the statute itself the rule should be applied.
11. Titles do not control meaning; preambles do not expand scope; section headings do not change language.		11. The title may be consulted as a guide when there is doubt or obscurity in the body; preambles may be consulted to determine rationale, and thus the true construction of terms; section headings may be looked upon as part of the statute itself.
12. If language is plain and unambiguous it must be given effect.		12. Not when literal interpretation would lead to absurd or mischievous consequences or thwart manifest purpose.
13. Words and phrases which have received judicial construction before enactment to be understood according to that construction.		13. Not if the statute clearly requires them to have a different meaning.
14. After enactment, judicial decision upon interpretation of particular terms and phrases controls.		14. Practical construction by executive officers is strong evidence of true meaning.

Thrust	But	Parry
15. Words are taken in their ordinary meaning unless they are technical terms or words or art.		15. Popular words may bear a technical meaning and technical words may have a popular signification and they should be so construed as to agree with evident information or to make the statute operative.
16. Every word and clause must be given effect.		16. If inadvertently inserted or if repugnant to the rest of the statute, they may be rejected as surplusage.
17. The same language used repeatedly in the same connection is presumed to bear the same meaning throughout the statute.		17. This presumption will be disregarded where it is necessary to assign different meanings to make the statute consistent.
18. Words are to be interpreted according to the proper grammatical effect of their arrangement within the statute.		18. Rules of grammar will be disregarded where strict adherence would defeat purpose.
19. Exceptions not made cannot be read.		19. The letter is only the "bark." Whatever is within the reason of the law is within the law itself.
20. Expression of one thing excludes another.		20. The language may fairly comprehend many different cases where some only are expressly mentioned by way of example.
21. General terms are to receive a general construction.		21. They may be limited by specific terms with which they are associated or by the scope and purpose of the statute.
22. It is a general rule of construction that where general words follow an enumeration they are to be held as applying only to persons and things of the same general kind or class specifically mentioned (ejusdem generis).		22. General words must operate on something. Further, *ejusdem generis* is only an aid in getting the meaning and does not warrant confining the operations of statute within narrower limits than were intended.

Thrust	But	Parry
23. Qualifying or limiting words or clauses are to be referred to the next preceding antecedent.		23. Not when evident sense and meaning require a different construction.
24. Punctuation will govern when a statute is open to two constructions.		24. Punctuation marks will not control the plain and evident meaning of language.
25. It must be assumed that language has been chosen with due regard to grammatical propriety and is not interchangeable on mere conjecture.		25. "And" and "or" may be read interchangeably whenever the change is necessary to give the statute sense and effect.
26. There is a distinction between words of permission and mandatory words.		26. Words imparting permission may be read as mandatory and words imparting command may be read as permissive when such construction is made necessary by evident intention or by the rights of the public.
27. A proviso qualifies the provision immediately preceding.		27. It may be clearly be intended to have a wider scope.
28. When the enacting clause is general, a proviso is construed strictly.		28. Not when it is necessary to extend the proviso to persons or cases which comes within its equity.

Notes and Questions

1. Llewellyn belonged to a school of thought called legal realism, which flourished in the period between 1920 and 1940. Like the legal realists who attacked legislative intent as undiscoverable and incoherent, Llewellyn criticized linguistic canons of construction as essentially useless. More recent scholars might add that they allow courts to mask judicial judgment with legal-sounding analysis. Thus, they are not only useless but obscuring and dangerous. Llewellyn's harsh criticisms have not gone without response. Justice Scalia, for instance, argues that Llewellyn's list of "thrust[s]" and "parr[ies]" includes some maxims that are not canons at all, and otherwise overstates the case that all canons are useless:

> [I]f one examines the list, it becomes apparent that there really are not two opposite canons on "almost every point" — unless one enshrines as a canon whatever vapid statement

has ever been made by a willful, law-bending judge. For example, the first canon Llewellyn lists under "Thrust," supported by a citation to Sutherland, is "A statute cannot go beyond its text." Hooray for that. He shows as a "Parry," with no citation of either Sutherland or Black (his principal authorities throughout), the following: "To effect its purpose a statute may be implemented beyond its text." That is *not* a generally accepted canon, though I am sure some willful judges have used it — the judges in *Church of the Holy Trinity*, for example. And even if it were used more than rarely, why not bring to the canons the same discernment that Llewellyn brought to the study of common-law decisions? . . .

Mostly, however, Llewellyn's "Parries" do not contract the corresponding canon but rather merely show that it is not absolute. For example, Thrust No. 13: "Words and phrases which have received judicial construction before enactment are to be understood according to that construction." Parry: "Not if the statute clearly requires them to have a different meaning." Well, certainly. Every canon is simply *one indication* of meaning; and if there are more contrary indications (perhaps supported by other canons), it must yield. But that does not render the entire enterprise a fraud — not, at least, unless the judge wishes to make it so.

ANTONIN SCALIA, A MATTER OF INTERPRETATION 26-27 (1997). Does Justice Scalia offer a satisfying defense of canons? Put another way, how does Justice Scalia imagine that the canons function, at least the textual ones?

2. As you consider the role of canons for Justice Scalia and other textualists, consider also how Professors Henry Hart and Albert Sacks viewed the role of canons. *See* HENRY M. HART, JR. & ALBERT M. SACKS, THE LEGAL PROCESS: BASIC PROBLEMS IN THE MAKING AND APPLICATION OF LAW 1190-91 (William N. Eskridge, Jr. & Philip P. Frickey eds., 2004). They argued that neither dictionaries nor canons of construction "should . . . be treated . . . as saying what meaning a word or group of words *must* have in a given context." *Id.* The assessment of linguistic meaning operates as a negative to rule out interpretations and works "almost wholly to *prevent* rather than to *compel* expansion of the scope of statutes." *Id.* at 1367. Do courts treat canons (or dictionaries) as Hart and Sacks suggest they should, that is, merely to identify the range of linguistic possibilities, rather than to determine what a statutory phrase must mean? Should they?

3. The debate over canons of interpretation has been augmented with empirical investigations both of how much knowledge congressional drafters have of the canons of interpretation and how they are actually used in the Supreme Court. Consider the following two studies.

Abbe R. Gluck & Lisa Schultz Bressman, Statutory Interpretation from the Inside— An Empirical Study of Congressional Drafting, Delegation, and the Canons: Part I

65 Stan. L. Rev. 901 (2013)

[Professors Lisa Bressman and Abbe Gluck surveyed 137 congressional staffers, largely committee counsels with drafting responsibility, drawn from both the House and the Senate. They asked about their knowledge of a wide variety of canons of interpretation, and how frequently they relied upon them in their own work drafting legislation. The following figures report some of the central results of their study.]

FIGURE 1

Empirical Survey of 137 Congressional Staffers 2011-2012:
Do Legislative Drafters Know the Canons of Statutory Interpretation by Name?

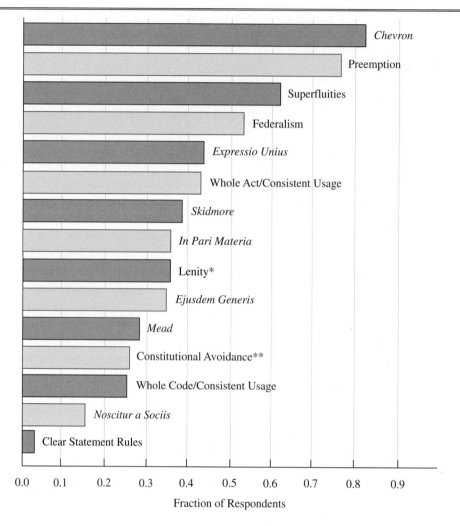

Sources: Q17; Q20; Q30; Q32a; Q35 (comment code); Q45a-g.

    * Out of the 65 respondents who participated in drafting criminal legislation.

    ** Out of the 67 respondents asked.

Nina A. Mendelson,
Change, Creation, and Unpredictabillity
in Statutory Interpretation: Interpretive Canon Use
in the Roberts Court's First Decade

117 Mich. L. Rev. 71 (2018)

[Professor Mendelson studied the use of canons in statutory interpretation during the first decade of the Roberts Court, from the October Term 2005 through the October Term 2015, including tracing 36 textual and substantive canons in 838 majority, concurring, and dissenting opinions.]

The principal findings are these. First, the Court relies extensively on canons, both textual and substantive. Second, rather than stability, it is *change* that characterizes the Roberts Court's current collection of interpretive canons. Some traditionally recognized canons, such as the punctuation canon and the remedial purposes canon, are used rarely and may soon evaporate altogether. Meanwhile, the Court continues to create new canons. This Article discusses several new textual and substantive canons, including a location of codification canon, a jurisdictional rules canon, and a veterans' benefits canon, as well as new modifications to existing canons.

Second, the data suggest that canon critics are right to worry about judges using canons unpredictably. Karl Llewellyn's famous point was that for every canon, there was an "opposing" canon that could overcome it. [Judge Richard] Posner and [Abbe] Gluck also have argued that the Court appears to deploy no hierarchy for canon use, enabling judges freely to choose among them. This study's findings confirm Llewellyn's implication that one indeed cannot predict which of two conflicting canons the Court will apply.

But [there are] two additional ways in which canon use goes beyond the unpredictability Llewellyn anticipated. First, when canons are discussed, the justices very often decline to apply them, even if there is no other canon present. The most frequently considered and applied canons are still not applied at least 20-30% of the time they are discussed—and numerous canons are applied even less reliably. The common presence of multiple potentially applicable canons simply makes canon use even less predictable. Second, and at least as critically, the reasons the justices have invoked for *not* using canons are a slippery group, extraordinarily difficult to anticipate or even to define.

In other words, although this study is not (and could not be) a controlled study, the findings strongly suggest that canon use is of dubious value to interpretive predictability and in turn to judicial constraint or a stable interpretive background for Congress. As currently used, then, canons seem hard to justify on these "second-order" grounds. Considerable reform would be required for canon use to positively contribute to interpretive predictability.

Finally, returning to the first-order arguments that canons could approximate congressional practices, this Article's findings reveal a striking mismatch between the top canons in current use in the Roberts Court and Gluck and Bressman's findings. Three, and possibly four, of the five most frequently applied canons in the Roberts Court were identified by Gluck and Bressman as canons outright "rejected" by congressional staff—and as to the fifth, the evidence of congressional staff acceptance is equivocal. In short, the most used canons seem the least defensible on first-order grounds. Meanwhile, the canons seemingly most accepted by congressional staff were used by the Roberts Court only fitfully. . . .

III. Selected Findings

Majority opinions considered (though did not necessarily apply) at least one canon in roughly 70% of contested statutory issues. Opinions overall considered at least one canon in about two-thirds of contested issues. Both substantive and textual canons were regularly engaged. Opinions overall considered at least one textual canon in 48% of contested statutory issues and applied at least one textual canon with approval to help resolve 40% of contested statutory issues. Opinions overall considered substantive canons in 37% of issues—applying at least one with approval to help resolve the issue in 27% of issues, not counting agency deference canons. Canon use outstripped that of dictionaries, though dictionary use was greater than any individual canon. Including agency deference canons, opinions overall considered substantive canons in 45% of issues and applied at least one with approval in 32% of issues. Opinions overall cited at least one dictionary in 20.3% of contested statutory issues; majority opinions cited dictionaries in 24.2% of contested statutory issues. . . .

[Professor Mendelson provides reports not only the percentage of statutory decisions in which a canon was discussed, but also the "approval rate," meaning the "percentage of times a discussed canon was actually applied to help resolve a contested statutory issue."]

Table 1. Rates of Engagement, All Tracked Canons, All Opinions

Canon	Percentage of Issues in Which Canon Was Discussed (any opinion type)	Approval Rate (percentage of times canon discussed in which it was ultimately applied with approval to resolve statutory issue)
More Frequently Considered Canons		
Expressio Unius	18.6%	75%
Whole Act Rule	15.2%	76%
Rule Against Surplusage	13.2%	70%
Whole Code Rule	11.5%	75%
Agency Deference Canons (*Chevron/Skidmore*)	11.9%	53%
Harmonious Reading Canon	11.8%	75%
Statutes in Derogation of the Common Law Shall Be Strictly Construed or "Common Law Canon"	11.6%	72%
Rule Against Absurdity	7.4%	67%
Constitutional Avoidance Canon	6.8%	57%
Legislative Acquiescence	5.9%	71%
Less Frequently Considered Canons		
Federalism Canon	5.1%	62%
In Pari Materia	4.6%	63%
Rule of Lenity	3.3%	55%
Noscitur a Sociis	3.0%	79%
May/Shall Rule	2.9%	85%
Presumption Against Preemption	2.5%	48%
Titles Canon	2.3%	67%
Specific Rules Govern over General Ones	2.3%	67%
No Elephants in Mouseholes	1.9%	89%
Presumption Against Implied Repeal	1.7%	69%
Ejusdem Generis	1.6%	73%
Presumption Against Retroactivity	1.3%	33%
Presumption Against Waiver of Sovereign Immunity	1.2%	45%
And/Or Rule	1.1%	90%
Rule of Last Antecedent	1.0%	56%
Jurisdictional Rules Canon	0.9%	100%
Presumption Against Extraterritorial Application	0.8%	71%
Remedial Statutes Shall Be Liberally Construed	0.6%	50%
Whole Session Laws Rule	0.5%	80%
Punctuation Canon	0.3%	33%
Major Question Canon	0.3%	100%
Native American/Indian Canon	0.2%	100%

Professor Mendelson also reports a high percentage of decisions in which the Court considered more than one canon. Specifically, in 66.9 percent of the cases in which the majority opinion considered one canon, the majority opinion considered two or more canons, and in 37.9 percent of that group, the opinion considered three or more canons. Professor Mendelson documents these results, as well as the rate of applications of those canons in the following table.

Table 5. Rate of Canon Usage with Approval When Multiple Canons Considered

Number of Canons Discussed (Both Textual/Syntax Canons and Substantive Canons)	Statutory Issues in Majority Opinions		Statutory Issues in All Opinions	
	Mean Number of Canons Applied with Approval	Percentage Applied (Mean Number of Canons Applied with Approval divided by Number of Canons Discussed)	Mean Number of Canons Applied with Approval	Percentage Applied (Mean Number of Canons Applied with Approval divided by Number of Canons Discussed)
0	N/A		N/A	
1	0.76	76.3%	0.75	75.0%
2	1.36	68.0%	1.38	69.2%
3	2.03	67.7%	1.99	66.3%
4	2.92	73.0%	2.95	73.8%
5	3.15	63.0%	3.13	62.7%
6	3.89	64.8%	4.07	67.8%
7	7.00	100.0%	4.75	67.9%
8	3.00	37.5%	4.00	50.0%
9	N/A		6.00	66.7%

Professor Mendelson compared the result of the use of canons by the Roberts Court with Professors Bressman and Gluck's study of congressional knowledge of these canons, yielding some interesting results, reported in the following table:

Table 4

High approval rate canons also identified in Gluck and Bressman findings as "approximating" congressional preferences[335]	Top-scoring canons in Roberts Court (frequently applied, high approval rate) "rejected" in Gluck and Bressman findings
• *Ejusdem generis* (73% approval rate; discussed in 1.6% of issues) • *Noscitur a sociis* (79% approval rate; discussed in 3.0% of issues)	• Rule against surplusage (70% approval rate; discussed in 13.2% of issues) • Whole act rule (76% approval rate; discussed in 15.2% of issues) • Whole code rule (75% approval rate; discussed in 11.5% of issues)
Top-scoring canons with equivocal or unknown status in Gluck and Bressman study • *Expressio unius* (75% approval rate; discussed in 18.6% of issues) (Approximates congressional practices in drafting statutory lists; unknown in other settings) • Common law canon (72% approval rate; discussed in 11.6% of issues) (Unknown status) • Rule against absurdity (67% approval rate; discussed in 7.4% of cases) (Unknown status) • Harmonious reading canon (75% approval rate; discussed in 11.8% of issues) (Possibly rejected asvariant of rule against surplusage)	**Low approval rate canons identified as "approximating" congressional preferences or driving congressional drafting in Gluck and Bressman findings** • Agency deference canons (53% approval rate; discussed in 11.9% of issues) • Presumption against preemption (48% approval rate; discussed in 2.5% of issues) • Federalism canons (62% approval rate; discussed in 5.1% of issues).

. . .

IV. IMPLICATIONS FOR PREDICTABILTY AND STABILITY

Even if impressionistic, this Article's findings nonetheless raise significant questions about whether canons improve interpretive predictability, constrain judicial discretion, or supply a stable interpretive background for

Congress. First, interpretive canons, as a group, are in flux. The Roberts Court has added to the list of canons in use, modified existing ones, and apparently withdrawn others. There is no "closed set" of canons. . . .

Also in sharp tension with the claim that canons are rule-like: the unpredictable and seemingly limitless catalogue of reasons *not* to apply canons. Opinions declined to apply canons because their conditions were not met, but also owing to context, other canons, and an assortment of other reasons that are hard to wrestle to the ground. . . . Opinions were also vague regarding how *strong* such a countervailing reason must be to defeat a canon. For example, sometimes *expressio unius*'s implications were sufficient to defeat the rule against surplusage and sometimes not. Cases came out both ways. . . .

Moreover, some canons lack clear criteria for application, making them inherently more standard-like than rule-like. . . . Even superficially rule-like canons lose their rule-like quality when the conditions that trigger them are indistinct: how ambiguous a statute must be to trigger the rule of lenity; how clear a statute must be to overcome a clear statement rule; and so on. . . .

So, can we consider any of this objectively "predictable"? Certainly not a purported rule with poorly specified conditions for application—or a canon with an approval rate hovering between 45% and 60%. A 75% approval rate might strike some as predictable—but we should deem it predictable only if such a canon is the sole potential interpretive tool in a case and if the reason for not applying it was that its conditions were unmet, a prospect that the data calls into question.

Cases with multiple canons fare even worse. Scholars have already sharply criticized the lack of explicit hierarchy among the canons. And interpretive canon use in the Roberts Court has given us few, if any, hierarchy hints. For example, in some majority opinions considering both the federalism canon and rule against surplusage, the federalism canon was applied with approval and the rule against surplusage was disregarded, and in other opinions, it was the opposite. As noted, sometimes the rule against surplusage was applied in preference to *expressio unius*, and sometimes the reverse. . . . And the vast majority of Roberts Court opinions that considered multiple canons did not apply at least one of those canons. . . .

If canons cannot be systematically justified on these second-order grounds, as rule-like methods that increase interpretive predictability or constraint, what then? Is there any hope of redeeming canons on other grounds?

Conceivably, an individual canon deployed in a streamlined regime could still be justified on first-order grounds—as connected to congressional preferences or another defensible value. Perhaps a canon defender still could meet the burden of demonstrating that a particular canon is indeed an "entrenched generalization" of congressional preferences or actual drafting practices, that it supplies an assurance that readers will have notice of legal requirements, or that it serves some other appropriate goal. Or if the defense is that a canon serves as a "higher-order rule[]" of some sort, such as bringing an extrastatutory value to bear in interpretation, further work is needed on this as well. Of course, the canon must also function in a genuinely rule-like fashion; it must be well-defined, including limiting the conditions under which the canon will not apply and specifying its relationship to other interpretive tools. And it must be consistently applied.

Notes and Questions

1. Professor Mendelson distinguishes between "first-order" and "second-order" justifications for canons. First-order justifications include "approximating congressional preferences," whereas the most typical second-order justifications represent "clear interpretive rules that can coordinate and constrain judicial decisionmaking and render interpretation more predictable." Based on Professors Bressman and Gluck's findings, which canons have the best first-order justifications? Which of Professor Mendelson's findings most undermines the second-order justifications for the use of canons?

2. Suppose the federal judiciary chose one canon from each of Llewellyn's pairs and applied it as comprehensively and as inflexibly as they possibly could. Wouldn't that be helpful to Congress? Its members would then know how their statutory language would be read, and they could adjust that language to produce the results that they desired. One might even regard this as a selfless or self-sacrificial approach on the part of the judiciary. The judges would be imposing rigid rules on themselves, and often writing opinions that they themselves didn't particularly like, for the sake of making Congress more effective. What defects do you see in this modest proposal? Note that Bressman and Gluck found that 81 percent of staffers who participated in a recent empirical study of legislative drafting reported that it would affect the way that they draft if they knew that the Court applied certain interpretive principles consistently. Do Mendelson's finding undermine this possibility?

3. A specific criticism of substantive canons is that they are not as well justified as they appear. *See* Cass R. Sunstein, After the Rights Revolution 158 (1990) (noting that substantive canon must be justified on normative and institutional grounds). What prevents a court from adding new canons, as Mendelson observes? Do the established substantive canons reflect the substantive values that courts would or should choose?

4. Perhaps it does not matter which canon a court chooses because Congress can always enact a new statute if the court applies the wrong one. Indeed, one purpose of clear statement rules might be to force Congress to enact a new statute if it prefers a different interpretation than a court has announced. What if Congress fails to enact a new statute even when it might prefer a different interpretation and the Supreme Court in fact has called for a clear statement? *See* Note, *New Evidence on Presumption Against Preemption: An Empirical Study of Congressional Responses to Supreme Court Preemption Decisions*, 120 Harv. L. Rev. 1604 (2007) (examining congressional responses to Supreme Court preemption decisions from the 1993 to the 2003 Terms and concluding that Congress almost never responds). What do you think of canons now?

C. INTENT AND PURPOSE-BASED TOOLS

Although all courts start with the text of a statute, most do not stop there. They look to see whether their reading of the text comports with other sources of legislative intent or statutory purpose. For example, a court can look at the context in which the statute was enacted and ask whether that context sheds light on what Congress intended the words to mean or the statute to accomplish. It can also consult congressional policies, executive actions, and judicial decisions in the area for the same purpose. But perhaps the most prominent source of information about legislative intent and statutory purpose apart from the text is the legislative history of the statute. The legislative history, as we have mentioned before and describe in detail below, includes the full record that accompanies a statute. These sources have the potential to shed light on the intent of the enacting Congress concerning a particular word, phrase, or provision in a statute, and they can reveal the purpose of the statute as a whole or the purpose of a provision within the statute. In this section, we focus on legislative history.

1. Forms of Legislative History

The legislative history consists of the full record concerning the debate and passage of a statute. Legislation textbooks include the following:

1. Floor debate
2. Planned colloquy
3. Prepared statements on submission of a bill, in committee hearings and at the time of floor debates
4. Revised and amended statements
5. Statements in committees by the relevant executive-branch administrators
6. Committee reports
7. Transcripts of discussions at committee hearings
8. Statements and submissions by interested persons, both local and state government, and private parties
9. Committee debates on "mark-up" of bills
10. Conference committee reports
11. Analysis of bills by legislative counsel
12. Analysis of bills by relevant executive departments
13. Amendments, accepted or rejected
14. Actions on and discussions about separate bills on the same topic, offered by each house, or in contrast to a similar composite bill
15. Executive-branch messages and proposals whether from the President, cabinet secretaries, or independent agencies

16. Prior relevant administrative action of judicial decisions, with or without congressional acknowledgment
17. Other subsequent or prior legislation, especially conflicting acts
18. Recorded votes
19. The status of the person speaking, that is, sponsor, committee chairman, floor leader, etc.
20. Actions taken and reports, hearing and debates on prior related legislation.[5]

You have already seen in this chapter that courts frequently consult the legislative history of a statute when interpreting it. What you may not have detected is that courts do not view all forms of legislative history as equally probative of legislative intent or statutory purpose. Here is an overview of the relative weight of the pieces on which courts most often rely.

Committee Reports. Committee Reports occupy the highest position in the hierarchy of legislative history. They are written by those who are charged with responsibility for a bill and who are best informed about that bill. They circulate with the bill to the whole chamber (or whole Congress in the case of Conference Committee Reports) and are read by legislative staff and members of Congress perhaps even more widely than the bill itself because, as you have seen, they contain a fairly plain language account of the legislation. Judges and lawyers also read them because they are readily accessible and relatively easy to understand. But committee reports are not always reliable indications of legislative intent. Even if widely read and relied upon, they are not subject to a vote by a full chamber of Congress. They cannot be amended and therefore do not reflect disagreements that arise once the bill has left committee but is still under consideration by Congress. This objection does not apply to Conference Committee Reports, which emerge after reconciliation of bills from the House and the Senate; remember, though, that Conference Committee Reports are generally less comprehensive because they only address areas of disagreement between the chambers. Furthermore, any given Committee Report may be unhelpful or misleading. It may replicate ambiguities in the bill rather than clarifying them. It may leave out important details of the bill. It may even be deliberately "doctored" in anticipation of use by courts. For these reasons, courts consider the reliability of Committee Reports — and all pieces of legislative history — not only in the abstract but on the basis of their content and context. For the most part, they do so implicitly. That is, you do not usually see discussion in a judicial decision of the reliability of a particular piece of legislative history.

---

5. *See* Otto Hetzel, Michael Libonati & Robert Williams, Legislative Law and Process 438 (2d ed. 1993); and William N. Eskridge, Jr., Philip Frickey & Elizabeth Garrett, Legislation 937 (3d ed. 2001) (citing Hetzel et al.).

But there are exceptions. See Montana Wilderness Ass'n v. U.S. Forest Serv., 192 F.3d 1132 (9th Cir. 1998).

Author or Sponsor Statements.   The statement of an author or sponsor is often treated as a reliable indication of legislative intent because it is prepared by an individual knowledgeable about the bill. It therefore occupies a relatively high position in the hierarchy of legislative history, though lower than a committee report. A sponsor statement still reflects only one voice rather than the views of the whole chamber or even the responsible committee. That voice may reflect an idiosyncratic understanding of the bill, despite a genuine effort to reflect the sentiments of the whole. This concern arises with respect to any isolated statement, no matter the speaker. Furthermore, any particular statement may reflect a strategic attempt to convey a unique message — to gain public support for the speaker or to influence judicial interpretation of the bill. For example, it may be the product of hearings that are stacked with witnesses who favor the bill. It may be laden with "sales talk." Likewise, it can be amended or supplemented with remarks after the bill is enacted in response to a problem or in anticipation of litigation.

Member Statements.   Remarks of other members of Congress fall below author and sponsor statements but still may contain relevant information. A member may make it her business to become informed about a particular bill, even if not the sponsor, or author, or member of the relevant committee; after all, staying informed about legislation *is* her job. Note that if the member is on the "losing side" of a particular provision or statute — that is, the majority rejected her view about how the statute should have been written or whether the statute should have been enacted — her statement will not receive much weight. Can you think of a reason that it would be entitled to any weight at all? What if she discussed the various positions that were on the table? Might her statement be relevant as to the presence of disagreement or ambiguity on the meaning of a particular word or phrase? Might she have nonetheless accurately captured the purpose of the statute? Keep in mind that courts might rely on pieces of legislative history for reasons other than locating the precise meaning of a particular word or phrase.

Hearing Records.   The committees that draft and debate bills in both the House and Senate frequently hold hearings on the bills. The records of those hearings include oral testimony, written submission of reports, as well as comments and questions from the members themselves. A court may examine the record at a hearing to gain a better understanding of the information before the committee responsible for the legislation or to discern the awareness of that committee of issues raised in the legislation. In a sense, the hearing record provides a repository of information that the committee members are likely to have considered (or a least heard) during the evaluation of the bill. At the same time, it would be a strain to impute knowledge of every aspect of testimony to the committee. Moreover, hearings are attended just by the committee members, not the entire Congress. You will see the court in *Moore v. Harris*, the next decision below, use hearing records to support its analysis.

Other Legislative Statements. What about statements that do not come from members of the enacting Congress? The legislative history of other statutes, both past and future, might serve as guides to the meaning of a word, provision, or the purpose of a statute, particularly if written close in time and treat the same subject. The use of legislative history from subsequent statutes or amendments to an earlier statute relies upon similar assumptions as the whole code canons addressed in the discussion of textual tools. The court is making an assumption that the legislative history of one statute can support an inference about what Congress meant or said with regard to another. Those inferences can be stronger or weaker depending on many factors, including closeness in time and similarity of subject matter. Of course, the legislative history of other statutes is still subject to the general critiques of legislative history (e.g., ambiguous, incomplete, idiosyncratic, strategic, and so on). Note that sometimes a court will refer to subsequent statutes themselves (as opposed to the legislative history of those subsequent statutes) as part of the "subsequent legislative history" of a statute. *See, e.g.*, FDA v. Brown & Williamson Tobacco Corp., 529 U.S. 120, 137-39, 160-61 (2001). Although such statutes are subject to the questions about whole code assumptions (are they too remote or dissimilar to support valid inferences?), note that they are enacted laws.

Presidential and Agency Statements. What about statements from the President or agency officials, which do not even emanate from the legislative branch? Why should they be considered reliable indications of legislative intent? Consider that Presidential signing statements come from an actor with a constitutional role in enacting legislation: the President signed the bill into law. The President is therefore presumed to have read the bill. In addition, the President may have proposed or drafted the original version of the bill and provided key support through the process. Similarly, agency officials often participate in the drafting of legislation. Furthermore, they often advise the President on the content of those bills. They are also frequently delegated responsibility for interpreting legislation in the course of implementing it. But, again, the particulars matter: the President and agency officials may hold interpretations that depart from those of Congress. They may offer those interpretations strategically in part to influence a court.

In sum, different pieces of legislative history have different weights relative to one another. Furthermore, each piece is only as good as the inferences it supports. Perhaps a Committee Report, though in general a reliable indication of legislative intent, contains no helpful discussion of a particular provision or is just as ambiguous as the text itself. Or there may be evidence that an item of legislative history was "manufactured" for strategic reasons, to please the public, or to persuade a court.

One final note: sometimes silence speaks louder than words. Courts can find it significant when the legislative history contains no mention of a particularly dramatic interpretation—for example, one that expands the scope of the statute in an unusual direction. Would Congress have intended such a dramatic interpretation without saying anything about it in the Committee Report, during the debates, or somewhere along the way? In this way, legislative silence itself can be relevant in determining whether an interpretation reflects legislative intent. What are the concerns about relying too heavily on legislative silence? See Montana Wilderness Ass'n v. U.S. Forest Serv., 192 F.3d 1132 (9th Cir. 1998).

2. Judicial Reliance on Legislative History

Although you have seen courts rely on legislative history in some of the decisions that you have already read, we now want to focus specifically on the practice. As you read the following decision, consider the forms of legislative history on which the court relies, and the character of the inferences that it draws from them. Also consider whether the court relies on the legislative history to establish legislative intent or statutory purpose (or both).

Moore v. Harris

623 F.2d 908 (4th Cir. 1980)

MURNAGHAN, Circuit Judge:

In 1971 Charles H. Moore, appellant, sought black lung benefits under the Black Lung Benefits Title of the Federal Coal Mine Health and Safety Act of 1969 ("Black Lung Benefits Act"). The claim was denied by the Secretary of Health, Education and Welfare, now the Secretary of Health and Human Services ("the Secretary"), whose action was sustained by the district court as supported by substantial evidence.

The problem which confronts us is whether nearly a decade of activity as a miner while Moore was self-employed in a family mine or employed by a close corporation of which he was a principal shareholder should be considered for purposes of certain favorable presumptions established by statute to determine eligibility. We hold that it should be so considered and reverse. Considering those years of self-employment gives Moore over fifteen years of coal mine employment, as against the less than ten years allowed by the Secretary for periods when Moore's mining activities took place while he was the employee of mine operators other than himself and his close corporation.

I

The Statute

The case is governed by the provisions of the act as they existed prior to amendment in 1978. Under those provisions, benefits shall be paid with respect to the disability of a person if four requirements are satisfied:

1. The person must be a miner, which the statute defines as "any individual who is or was employed in a coal mine."
2. The person must be totally disabled as determined by regulations prescribed by the Secretary.
3. The total disability must be due to pneumoconiosis, "a chronic dust disease of the lung."
4. It must be shown that the disease is one "arising out of employment in a coal mine."

To facilitate the administration of the act and to ease the inherent difficulties of proving the existence and the causation of the disease, the statute makes available several presumptions to help establish requirements 2, 3, and 4 above. . . . "[I]f a miner was employed for fifteen years or more in one or more underground coal mines, and if [a chest X-ray fails to yield specified medical symptoms], and if other evidence demonstrates the existence of a totally disabling respiratory or pulmonary impairment, then there shall be a rebuttable presumption that such miner is totally disabled due to pneumoconiosis . . ." ("the fifteen-year presumption"). That is, requirements 2, 3, and 4 may be deemed satisfied.

Finally, "if a miner who is suffering or suffered from pneumoconiosis was employed for ten years or more in one or more coal mines there shall be a rebuttable presumption that his pneumoconiosis arose out of such employment" ("the ten-year presumption"). That is, requirement 4 may be deemed satisfied.

The Regulation

By regulation the Secretary has attempted to modify and restrict the statutory definition of "miner." Where the statute speaks of an "individual who is or was employed in a coal mine," the Secretary has substantially altered the phraseology to an "individual who is working or has worked as an *employee.*" 20 C.F.R. §410.110(j) (1979) (emphasis added). Having introduced the word "employee," which nowhere appears in the relevant portion of the statute, the Secretary has also prescribed that it refers to a "legal relationship . . . under the usual common-law rules."

The Facts

The findings of the administrative law judge ("ALJ") were adopted by the Secretary. The ALJ determined that claimant had 7¼ years of work as a coal-mine employee, at least 7¼ years of work in an unincorporated family coal mine of which he was part owner, and approximately 2 years of work in that mine after its incorporation. Thus, even if the work for the close corporation is treated as that of an employee under usual common law rules, of Moore's conceded sixteen or more years of work in coal mines, less than ten years were as an employee as defined by the Secretary's regulation. The ALJ, applying the definition contained in the regulation, refused Moore the benefit of any of the statutory presumptions. . . . [The district court affirmed.]

Moore claims that for purposes of the ten- and fifteen-year presumptions, Congress did not authorize a distinction between self-employment in one's own coal mine and wage labor in someone else's coal mine, that "employment in a coal mine" or being "employed in a coal mine" were intended by Congress to refer simply to miners' occupations and customary activities, not to who was the entrepreneur.

II

The regulation on its face accomplishes a change in the statutory language. As a simple matter of customary usage, one who is "employed" is not automatically or predominantly an employee. Since the regulation immediately generates a doubt as to whether it truly interprets the statute, our first task is to determine what Congress intended when it enacted the statute before us.

Although the isolated language of the presumptions and of the definition of "miner" may be susceptible both to the Secretary's interpretation and to the interpretation which Moore urges, the legislative history and statutory purpose of the provisions make abundantly clear that Congress intended to benefit all persons those employed by third parties and self-employed persons alike who had contracted a chronic dust disease of the lung as a result of their work in the nation's coal mines.[1]

The Statutory Language

The ease with which the statutory language supports the meaning which Moore urges is shown by the construction of the current version of the statute. In 1978, Congress amended the definition of "miner"[2] and made unmistakable its intent that self-employed miners be eligible for black lung benefits. The Secretary fully accepts that, under the current language of the Black Lung Benefits Act, self-employment in a coal mine counts toward

---

1. Congress saw the benefits not as charity but as the nation's repayment of a debt to the families whose sacrifices in the production of coal were making possible the economic success and the high standard of living enjoyed by the nation as a whole. *See, e.g.,* 115 Cong. Rec. 39714 (1969) (remarks of Rep. Saylor):

> [This bill] is a little effort to square accounts for what the country did not do before. Heretofore, Mr. Speaker, we followed the practice of getting the most out of our miners and our coal get it out. . . .
>
> Mr. Speaker, it is our privilege to sit here in the Halls of the Congress tonight. The lights are bright, not only here in the Halls of Congress, on Capitol Hill, but throughout Washington and throughout our land, not cognizant of the fact that about 80 percent of those lights are generated by coal. Whether you folks realize it or not, this country is today short 15,000 coal miners. If we expect to have the kind of economy that we have developed, and if we expect to have electricity throughout the length and breadth of our land; if we expect to have the good things of this country and our world, then we had better pass this conference report.

2. *See* Black Lung Benefits Reform Act of 1977, Pub. L. No. 95-239, §2(b), 92 Stat. 95 (1978):

> The term "miner" means any individual who works or has worked in or around a coal mine or coal preparation facility in the extraction or preparation of coal. Such term also includes an individual who works or has worked in coal mine construction or transportation in or around a coal mine, to the extent such individual was exposed to coal dust as a result of such employment.

the definitions of "miner" and "pneumoconiosis" and toward the presumptions. That is, Moore's suggested reading of the statute is accepted today notwithstanding that a miner's work is referred to as "such employment," 30 U.S.C.A. §902(d) (West Supp. 1979), that pneumoconiosis still must arise out of "coal mine employment," *id.* §902(b), and that the rebuttable presumptions are still based on the miner's having been "employed for (at least some period of time) in one or more" coal mines. *Id.* §921(c)(1), (2), (4).

The expected reply of the Secretary, of course, is that self-employment now falls within those sections only because other evidence shows that the 1978 amendments were intended to make benefits available to qualifying self-employed miners. But implicit in that approach is the assumption that, before 1978, other evidence equally clearly established the opposite, namely that self-employment was not to count for purposes of qualifying for black lung benefits. Yet there is overwhelming evidence that in 1969 and 1972 Congress intended to benefit all persons who were totally disabled by pneumoconiosis as a result of coal mine work. Those constructions of "employed in" and "employment" which are correct to effect Congress' 1978 wishes are also correct in light of, and are required by, earlier congressional intent as well.

The Secretary's only evidence that "employed in" and "employment" as used in the statute referred to an employer-employee relation is very indirect and the argument is forced. For the other titles of the Federal Coal Mine Health and Safety Act of 1969 the definition of "miner" was "any individual working in a coal mine." An individual engaged in coal mine activity works there as much if self-employed as he does if employed by another. The rebuttable presumption of formal consistency states that use of different language creates the inference that Congress meant different things.[3] So the Secretary's contention is that "employed in" must mean something other than "working in."

However, where the statutory purpose and legislative history establish that no difference was in fact intended, the presumption is rebutted. Inadvertent statutory usage of synonyms in parallel sections does not require us to conjure up a distinction which would violate the statute's raison d'être.[4]

Statutory Purpose and the Legislative History

The act's remedial purpose was to recognize the widespread incidence of pneumoconiosis among American coal miners and to provide, on a national basis, alleviating compensation. A federal program was needed because in most instances workers' compensation programs of the several states did not provide benefits. That consideration would, of course, be stronger, not weaker, in the case of the self-employed than in the case of those in a

3. *See* R. DICKERSON, THE INTERPRETATION AND APPLICATION OF STATUTES 224 (1975).
4. *See id.* at 215 ("[I]f the context of a statute shows a legislative purpose that is broader than the literal import of the words used, the meaning of the statute is correspondingly broadened, but only so far as the words have enough semantic leeway to carry the broadened meaning.").

traditional common law employer-employee relationship.[5] Nowhere in the legislative history is there any suggestion that a distinction should be drawn between miners in a formal employer-employee relationship to coal mine operators and the individual miner/operators of small mines whose working conditions were comparable to those of miners hired by larger mines. The legislative history contains no suggestion that the American enthusiasm for the sturdy, independent sole proprietor was waning to the point where he would be treated in a disadvantageous manner as compared with miners hired to work by larger operators. The difference between the definition of "miner" in the Black Lung Benefits Title and that applicable to the rest of the 1969 Act arose from the legislative decision to limit black lung benefits to those who actually had been engaged in underground coal mining activities and from the need for a definition which would cover retired as well as active miners.[6] Thus the special definition was inserted for purposes altogether independent of, and unrelated to, a distinction between "self-employed" and "employed by another."

The members of Congress as the legislation made its way from introduction to enactment appeared to use interchangeably the phrases "was employed in a mine" and "worked in a mine." For example, a frequently used[7] summary of the conference committee's version of the 1969 bill described one of the presumptions as follows: "If a miner worked ten years in (an underground coal) mine and died of a respirable disease, there will be a rebuttable presumption that his death was due to pneumoconiosis." The statute, however, happened to use "was employed . . . in" for this presumption. The "worked in" language for the presumption was also employed during debates by Representative Carl D. Perkins, one of the House conferees and the chairman of the House Committee on Education and Labor, and by Representative John H. Dent, another of the conferees and the chairman of that committee's General Subcommittee on Labor.

Even more to the point is the way the two phrases were indiscriminately used by those who created the fifteen-year presumption in 1972. The presumption was added to the House Bill, H.R. 9212, by the Senate Committee

5. *See* 115 Cong. Rec. 39998 (1969) (remarks of Sen. Javits):

[The Black Lung Benefits Title is] a step to insure that the victims of this tragic occupational disease receive some bare minimum of compensation, with the cost to be borne by the Federal Government, insofar as workers for whom no employer liability can be established under traditional workmen's compensation criteria, and by the employers insofar as their responsibility can be established under such traditional criteria.

6. Neither the Senate bill nor the House bill which was substituted for it contained a special-purpose definition of "miner." *See* S. 2917, 91st Cong., 1st Sess., §§501-502, 115 Cong. Rec. 28243 (1969); H.R. 13950, 91st Cong., 1st Sess. §110(b), 115 Cong. Rec. 32061 (1969). H.R. 13950 did, however, have a special definition of "coal mine" in §110(b)(7)(A), which restricted the term to underground mines. Despite the latitude possessed by a conference committee when one house substitutes an entire bill for that passed by the other house, *see* 8 Cannon's Precedents of the House of Representatives of the United States §§3265-3268, at 750-54 (1936), the conference bill, which was enacted, was unlikely to have introduced a restriction on benefits that was not present in either of the constituent bills.

7. *See* 115 Cong. Rec. 39709, 39718, 39983-84 (1969).

on Labor and Public Welfare and was then accepted by the full Senate and finally by the House. Although the presumption itself used "employed in" and "employment," the Senate committee report tended to use "worked in" and "work":

> The bill . . . establishes a rebuttable presumption that a totally disabled coal miner who *worked* in an underground mine for 15 years or a surface miner who was *employed* under environmental conditions similar to those experienced by underground miners, is totally disabled by pneumoconiosis if he has a totally disabling respiratory or pulmonary impairment, even if he has an X-ray which cannot be interpreted as positive for complicated pneumoconiosis. The Secretary of Health, Education and Welfare may rebut the presumption if . . . he establishes . . . that the miner's disability did not arise out of, or in connection with, his *work* in a coal mine. . . .
>
> The Committee intends that the burden will be placed on the claimant to prove the existence of pneumoconiosis in cases where the miner worked fewer than fifteen years in a coal mine, but that judgment will be allowed to be exercised in determining the validity of claims in such cases, including the determination that the miner's disability is not due to pneumoconiosis or that it is not related to his employment in a coal mine. A miner's work history reflecting many years of mining work, though short of fifteen, and the severity of his impairment, shall also be considered. . . .
>
> It must be made clear by the Committee, however, that it expects and intends that miners with fewer than fifteen years in the mines who are totally disabled and who have X-ray evidence of pneumoconiosis other than complicated pneumoconiosis, who are now eligible for benefits, will remain so under the Committee amendments. [Citing Senate Committee Report.]

Such random alternation is not the mark of legislators who intend to deny disability benefits on the basis of the distinction between "worked in" and "was employed in."

The legislators who created the statute believed that it covered all individuals suffering from lung problems contracted in the coal mines.[8] Opponents of the benefits program attacked it as discriminatory because it provided neither for miners disabled by other maladies nor for workers disabled by occupational lung diseases in other industries, but none of the opponents suggested that the program differentiated among victims of black lung disease itself on the basis of "self-employment" versus "employment by another."

---

8. *See, e.g.*, 115 Cong. Rec. 27623-24 (1969) (remarks of Sen. Williams) ("[T]here is another 'forgotten man' in this industry who also cries for help. He is the inactive miner who was unfortunate enough to have breathed the coal dust wh(en) he toiled in the mines and who now is totally disabled from a disease that he can hardly pronounce pneumoconiosis but [t]hat he can feel."); *id.* at 31607 (remarks of Rep. Flood) ("[This bill] recognize[s] financial responsibility on the part of the Federal Government to those individuals disabled as a result of pneumoconiosis and anthracosilicosis which was contracted in the coal mining industry and who are not entitled to compensation under existing workmen's compensation laws."); *id.* at 31610 (remarks of Rep. Saylor) ("Whether we can call it the original name of miners' cough or pneumoconiosis, it is the same dreadful disease that strikes some of the men who work in the mines. . . . What this bill does is to give these people who have had this mining experience and [are] suffering from the disease, a one-shot operation to be taken care of."); . . . *id.* at 39998 (remarks of Sen. Javits) ("[W]e can ensure that those unfortunate miners who have been totally disabled by black lung receive some minimal amount of benefits which would enable them and their widows and children to live with some small amount of economic security. That, in essence, is what has been done in this [conference] report.").

In considering the target population for the benefit program, members of Congress frequently estimated that there were 100,000 victims of pneumoconiosis, of whom 50,000 were disabled. One hundred thousand was the figure given by the Surgeon General as the total incidence of black lung in the United States.[9] The Secretary's predecessor contributed to Congress' belief that all afflicted individuals were covered by the legislation in question. In 1972, nearly two years after the regulations we are considering had been promulgated, the Secretary's predecessor wrote to the chairman of the Senate Committee on Labor and Public Welfare, "'Employment in underground coal mines' has been interpreted as work in an underground coal mine, whether below the surface performing functions in extracting the coal or above the surface at the mine preparing the coal so extracted."[10] The Secretary stated that he favored continuation of the provisions restricting the program to underground miners. He characterized removing that restriction removal which, despite the Secretary's opposition, was effected in 1972, retroactive to 1969 as "extension of Federal black lung benefits to all coal miners."

In oral argument, counsel for the Secretary tried to explain why Congress might have restricted benefits to miners employed by others. He suggested that perhaps Congress erroneously believed that all black lung sufferers had been employees. If Congress had had that mistaken belief and if *in haec verba* it had restricted benefits to "employees," then perhaps only Congress could rectify the error. The error is highly unlikely, however, for Senators and Representatives from coal-mining states would surely have known their constituents well enough to appreciate that not all who mined coal did so wearing another's collar. Congress had the manifest purpose of covering all victims, and where it used language which, without strained construction, extends to all victims, we find no justification for an alternate, improbable construction which would rely on a hypothesized congressional mistake and would substantially frustrate the statutory purpose.

Thus, a foundation was altogether lacking for the modification by the Secretary of the statutory language through insertion of the concept represented by the words "by another" after the word "employed." . . .

---

9. 2 Coal Mine Health & Safety: Hearings on S. 355, S. 467, S. 1094, S. 1178, S. 1300, S. 1907, S. 2118, and S. 2284 Before the Subcomm. on Labor of the Senate Comm. on Labor & Public Welfare, 91st Cong., 1st Sess. 729-30 (1969) (statement of Dr. William H. Stewart, Surgeon General, Public Health Service) ("I have used the figure 100,000 as an estimate of pneumoconiosis that was based on the prevalence rates we found in our study of both active miners and inactive miners. . . . In addition we know from other data . . . that you can come up with a figure close to 100,000 for the total of coal miners pneumoconiosis cases.").

10. Letter from Elliot L. Richardson, Secretary of Health, Education & Welfare, to Senator Harrison A. Williams, Jr., at 9 (Feb. 15, 1972), reprinted in Black Lung Legislation, 1971-72: Hearings on S. 2675, S. 2289 & H.R. 9212 Before the Subcomm. on Labor of the Senate Comm. on Labor and Public Welfare, 92d Cong., 1st & 2d Sess. 22, 30 (1971-1972).

III

Despite the clear indications of congressional intent in 1969 and 1972 to cover all victims of black lung, the Secretary, to justify the unduly restrictive definition of miner for purposes of eligibility for black lung benefits, points to events since 1969 which, she says, contradict the intent and which, therefore, should bar us from giving effect to the intent. The events may be grouped as administrative, judicial, and legislative interpretations of the act. . . .

[The administrative argument is the argument that the statute gave the Secretary authority to specify the meaning of the term. The judicial argument is that courts had already relied and upheld the Secretary's regulation as consistent with the language of the Act.]

Legislative Interpretation

Finally, the Secretary relies on congressional action in 1972 and 1978 as confirming the accuracy of her perception of the 1969 legislative intent. In 1972, distressed by the rate at which the Secretary was denying benefits under the 1969 act,[11] Congress liberalized many provisions of the act and made the liberalized provisions retroactive to December 30, 1969. Among the 1972 changes were the introduction of the fifteen-year presumption and an amendment to the definition of "miner" in 30 U.S.C. §902(d) which substituted "a coal mine" for "an underground coal mine." Since in 1970 her predecessor had promulgated the regulation with the requirement that "miners" be "employees," the Secretary may point to the 1972 action by Congress as a statutory reenactment which adopted the extant administrative interpretation.

Although reenactment may be "persuasive evidence that the [administrative] interpretation is the one intended by Congress," *NLRB v. Bell Aerospace Co.*, 416 U.S. 267, 275 (1974), that evidence is subject to rebuttal. As Professor Davis put it, "[T]he committees or subcommittees of Congress may or may not know of outstanding interpretations when they are considering reenactment; they do not in fact approve what they know nothing about."

Moreover, the Supreme Court has stated, "Where the law is plain the subsequent reenactment of a statute does not constitute adoption of its administrative construction." *Biddle v. Commissioner*, 302 U.S. 573, 582 (1938). . . .

In the instant case, when the Secretary's predecessor sent his letter dated February 15, 1972, to the chairman of the Senate Committee on Labor and Public Welfare, the letter may have misled Congress about the substance of the extant administrative interpretation. The letter discussed both the pre-1972 law and the proposed amendment as if there were no employee-status requirement. Although Senator Randolph during a committee hearing

---

11. *See* S. Rep. No. 92-743, at 3 ("Not only have the number of claims far exceeded those earlier expectations of Congress, . . . but also the rate of denials . . . suggests strongly that the solution has not been nearly as complete as Congress believed and expected it would be.").

once mentioned the Secretary's requirement, no other legislator or witness even alluded to that requirement, either during committee hearings[12] or on the floor of either house of Congress.[13] It is at least as likely as not, therefore, that the action of Congress in reenacting the language to which the Secretary's interpretation attached was in part the result of reliance on the Secretary's misleading communication. . . .[14]

As her last shot, the Secretary puts forth the contention that, in 1978, when Congress clearly included self-employed miners among the beneficiaries of the act,[15] the Committee reports treated that inclusion as an expansion of the act's coverage, rather than as a correction of a prior administrative misinterpretation.[16]

This, of the Secretary's three interpretation arguments, is the one with the most force. While a later Congress cannot dictate what was meant by an earlier Congress, its understanding as to what was meant should be accorded substantial deference by the courts. But it is the intent of the earlier Congress, which enacted the statute, that controls. In the instant case, we regard the committees' subsequent interpretation of the 1969 act as inconsistent with the clear 1969 statutory purpose and history. To the extent a later Congress erred, the error was induced by the Secretary's regulatory definition and by some courts' uncritical application of the definition. The main purpose of Congress in 1978 was to insure that benefits would no longer be denied because part or all of a miner's activities had been in "self"-employment. It was interested in curing a situation for the future and not in apportioning blame by ascertaining whether the situation arose as a result of misinterpretation of the earlier statute or as a result of inadequacy of the earlier statute. The clear meaning of the 1969 statute itself suffices to outweigh anything a congressional committee could have said in later years.

12. *See* Black Lung Benefits: Hearing on H.R. 18, H.R. 42, H.R. 43, & H.R. 5702 Before the Gen'l Subcomm. on Labor of the House Comm. on Education & Labor, 92d Cong., 1st Sess. (1971); Black Lung Legislation, 1971-72: Hearings on S. 2675, S. 2289, & H.R. 9212 Before the Subcomm. on Labor of the Senate Comm. on Labor & Public Welfare, 92d Cong., 1st & 2d Sess. (1971-1972).

13. *See* 117 Cong. Rec. 36494-507, 40428-58 (1971); 118 *id.* at 12662-63, 12877-905, 15974-80, 16577-87, 18683-86 (1972).

14. *Cf., e.g.,* 118 Cong. Rec. 18684 (1972) (remarks of Rep. Dent immediately after the enactment of the Black Lung Benefits Act of 1972) ("Every living, nonworking miner who has not made a claim, and has at least 15 years of mining experience . . . , should make a claim now.").

15. Black Lung Benefits Reform Act of 1977, Pub. L. No. 95-239, §2(b), 92 Stat. 95 (1978). Under the new definition, the term " 'miner' means any individual who works or has worked in or around a coal mine or coal preparation facility in the extraction or preparation of coal." 30 U.S.C.A. §902(d) (West Supp. 1979). We note that standing alone, the present language, no less than the prior language, could permit the insertion by the Secretary of the concept "for another" after "works" and "worked." Congress, however, made clear in the legislative history that its objective was to insure coverage of self-employed miners. [Citing H. Conf. Rep. & S. Rep.]

16. For instance, the conference committee report described the change as one which "modified the definition." H.R. Conf. Rep. 95-864. The Senate committee report stated, "The term is expanded in the Committee bill to include additional workers. . . . The expanded definition in the Committee bill includes those managers or owners of very small mining operations who themselves work or have worked in the extraction of coal." S. Rep. 95-209. The report also sets out certain items under the heading "Clarifications of Legislative Intent" but does not list in that category the Secretary's introduction of the requirement of employment by another. *Id.* at 22-23.

For this court, on the other hand, the question of the origin of the exclusion of self-employment is the crucial one. With all deference to the Ninety-Fifth Congress, we adhere to our conclusion that the 1969 statute enacted by the Ninety-First Congress was misinterpreted, first administratively, then judicially, and finally legislatively.

IV

Accordingly, we reverse and remand with instructions that the district court order the Secretary to make her findings giving the claimant the benefit of presumptions deriving from over fifteen years of coal mine employment.

REVERSED AND REMANDED.

K. K. HALL, Circuit Judge, dissenting:

As much as I would like to concur in the majority opinion, I cannot. The majority concludes, despite the Secretary's regulation to the contrary, 20 C.F.R. §410.110(j), that the Federal Coal Mine Health and Safety Act of 1969, and its 1972 amendment, provides benefits to self-employed miners. The bare language of the 1969 Act is subject to the majority's interpretation, but I think that interpretation is foreclosed by the legislature's explicit response to the dilemma of the self-employed miner and by our own precedents, which have already developed a body of case law implementing the regulation which the majority now strikes down as unreasonable. . . .

Notes and Questions

1. *Moore* involved the question whether the Black Lung Benefits Act excludes self-employed miners from the category of "miners," which is defined as "any individual who is or was employed in a coal mine." The Secretary of Health Education and Welfare had issued a regulation in 1970, shortly after the Act's enactment, interpreting the Act this way. Thus, the question for the court in the case was actually whether the agency was entitled to interpret the Act as it did. As we have mentioned before and discuss later, judicial review of agency action raises distinct issues; for now, however, focus just on how the court uses legislative history to support its conclusion that Congress, from 1969 forward, did not intend to exclude self-employed miners from the Act.

2. In *Moore*, the court relies on many pieces of legislative history and draws many different inferences from them in support of its conclusion about legislative intent and statutory purposes. Consider the following:

> **a.** What pieces of legislative history does the court rely on to directly support its ultimate conclusion that Congress intended the Act to cover self-employed miners? Take a look at footnote 8. Do these members' statements explicitly assert that self-employed miners are covered by the Act, or something short of that? Most of these statements reflect the members' view that the bill was aimed to apply

to *all* miners who are victims of black lung disease. From that proposition, the court infers that the Act includes self-employed miners. How would you challenge the court's reasoning? Would you focus on the sources on which the court relies or the inferences it makes from them?

b. The court devotes considerable attention to establishing that the members of Congress who debated the bill in 1969 used "employed in a mine" interchangeably with "worked in a mine." What was the point of this discussion? What chain of inferences is necessary to move from that usage to the meaning of the Act in 1969?

c. Interestingly, the court also relies upon the fact the Congress in 1972 used "employed in" and "worked in" interchangeably when amending the Act. What inferences are needed to connect the 1972 Congress's usage of these terms to the meaning of the terms in the 1969 Act? You might compare the inferences the court makes to those discussed in connection with "whole code canons," above. Whole code canons involve making inferences from one statute's use of a phrase or term to the meaning of the phrase or term in another statute. One premise underlying these whole-code inferences is that Congress should be presumed to know about its prior use of similar terms. Is the inference from the 1972 committee's usage to the 1969 committee (or Congress) in *Moore* similar? Is it stronger or weaker than an inference from statutory text in different statutes? Is this inference stronger than the one made in West Virginia University Hospitals, Inc. v. Casey, 499 U.S. 83 (1991)? See below.

d. What pieces of legislative history does the court rely on to rebut the argument that Congress may have *mistakenly* believed that all coal miners were employed by others (and therefore a legislative amendment would be required to cover them)? In particular, what do you make of the court's statement that "Senators and Representatives from coal-mining states would surely have known their constituents well enough to appreciate that not all whom mined coal did so wearing another's collar"? Is this a fair reliance on the constructive knowledge of the members of Congress likely to be most interested in the legislation?

e. Congress amended the 1969 Act in 1972 after the Secretary had issued the regulation defining "miners" as "employees" without changing the definition of "miners" from the 1969 Act. As a result, the court needed to rebut the argument whether Congress in 1972 effectively ratified the Secretary's earlier restrictive interpretation. The court did so by relying upon a letter from the Secretary to the Senate Committee that did not assert there was an "employee-status" requirement that was part of the law. What set of inferences are need to link the Secretary's letter to the aim of the 1972 Act? In particular, the court appears to prioritize the Senate Committee's knowledge of the Secretary's letter over knowledge of the Secretary's regulations. Is that a realistic assumption (and, if it is, what does it say about Congress's capacities)?

f. Was the court consistent in what inferences it drew about the 1969 Congress from the actions of a subsequent Congress? Consider that by the time of the 1978 amendment, Congress redefined "miner," and the accompanying Committee report claimed this new definition as an expansion of the Act's coverage. The court did not conclude this offered persuasive evidence of the 1969 Congress's aim, writing "[t]he clear meaning of the 1969 state itself suffices to outweigh anything a congressional committee could have said in later years." Is that consistent with the court's reliance on the 1972 Congress, and in particular the 1972 Congress's interchangeable usage of "worked in" and "employed in?" See note 2(c) above.

g. Even if the court was open to criticism on a piece-by-piece basis for its handling of the legislative history, do you think that the legislative history overall led the court to the right conclusion about self-employed miners? Why?

Here are two additional examples of judicial reliance on legislative history from cases that you have seen before. When discussing inferences across statutes, we introduced West Virginia University Hospitals, Inc. v. Casey, 499 U.S. 83 (1991). In that case, Justice Scalia held that an attorney's fees shifting statute, 42 U.S.C. §1988, did not include expert witness fees. He compared the text of §1988 to other fee-shifting statutes in the U.S. Code, concluding that Congress treated attorney's fees and expert witness fees as distinct items, and therefore a provision for recovery of attorney's fees should be construed to include expert fees. Justice Stevens dissented, relying on the legislative history to show that Congress intended to cover expert witness fees in §1988, regardless of what it had done in other statutes:

> This Court's determination today that petitioner must assume the cost of $104,133 in expert witness fees is at war with the congressional purpose of making the prevailing party whole. As we said in *Hensley v. Eckerhart*, 461 U.S. 424, 435 (1983), petitioner's recovery should be "fully compensatory," or, as we expressed in *Jenkins*, petitioner's recovery should be "comparable to what 'is traditional with attorneys compensated by a fee-paying client.'" S. Rep. No. 94-1011, p. 6 (1976). . . .
>
> In recent years the Court has vacillated between a purely literal approach to the task of statutory interpretation and an approach that seeks guidance from historical context, legislative history, and prior cases identifying the purpose that motivated the legislation. Thus, for example, in *Christiansburg Garment Co. v. EEOC*, 434 U.S. 412 (1978), we rejected a "mechanical construction," *id.*, at 418, of the fee-shifting provision in §706(k) of Title VII of the Civil Rights Act of 1964 that the prevailing defendant had urged upon us. Although the text of the statute drew no distinction between different kinds of "prevailing parties," we held that awards to prevailing plaintiffs are governed by a more liberal standard than awards to prevailing defendants. That holding

rested entirely on our evaluation of the relevant congressional policy and found no support within the four corners of the statutory text. Nevertheless, the holding was unanimous and, to the best of my knowledge, evoked no adverse criticism or response in Congress. . . .

On those occasions, however, when the Court has put on its thick grammarian's spectacles and ignored the available evidence of congressional purpose and the teaching of prior cases construing a statute, the congressional response has been dramatically different. It is no coincidence that the Court's literal reading of Title VII, which led to the conclusion that disparate treatment of pregnant and nonpregnant persons was not discrimination on the basis of sex, *see General Electric Co. v. Gilbert,* 429 U.S. 125 (1976), was repudiated by the 95th Congress; that its literal reading of the "continuous physical presence" requirement in §244(a)(1) of the Immigration and Nationality Act, which led to the view that the statute did not permit even temporary or inadvertent absences from this country, *see INS v. Phinpathya,* 464 U.S. 183 (1984), was rebuffed by the 99th Congress; that its literal reading of the word "program" in Title IX of the Education Amendments of 1972, which led to the Court's gratuitous limit on the scope of the antidiscrimination provisions of Title IX, *see Grove City College v. Bell,* 465 U.S. 555 (1984), was rejected by the 100th Congress; or that its refusal to accept the teaching of earlier decisions in *Wards Cove Packing Co. v. Atonio,* 490 U.S. 642 (1989) (reformulating order of proof and weight of parties' burdens in disparate-impact cases), and *Patterson v. McLean Credit Union,* 491 U.S. 164 (1989) (limiting scope of 42 U.S.C. §1981 to the making and enforcement of contracts), was overwhelmingly rejected by the 101st Congress, and its refusal to accept the widely held view of lower courts about the scope of fraud, *see McNally v. United States,* 483 U.S. 350 (1987) (limiting mail fraud to protection of property), was quickly corrected by the 100th Congress.

Id. at 111-13 (Stevens, J., dissenting). Note how Justice Stevens deploys legislative history: he uses it, along with the historical context of the statute and the "teaching of prior cases," to uncover the purpose of the statute. On which piece(s) of legislative history does he rely? What inferences does he draw? What does he claim has happened in the past when the Court refused to consider such sources of statutory purpose and instead took a "purely literal approach," as the majority did in the case?

Another case you have seen is Gregory v. Ashcroft, 501 U.S. 452 (1991). In that case, the Court held that the Age Discrimination in Employment Act (ADEA), 29 U.S.C. §§621-634, did not apply to state judges because the statute lacked a "clear statement" including them as "employee[s]." Justice White dissented from that section of the opinion, refusing to require a clear statement as to the status of state judges given that the ADEA unquestionably applied to the states. But he concurred in the judgment (i.e., reached the same result) because he thought that state judges fell within the express exemption to the statute for "appointee[s] on the policymaking level." Petitioners challenged this reading, relying on the legislative history of the ADEA. Here is what Justice White had to say in response:

Petitioners seek to rely on legislative history, but it does not help their position. There is little legislative history discussing the definition of "employee" in the ADEA, so petitioners point to the legislative history of the identical definition in Title VII of the Civil Rights Act of 1964, 42 U.S.C. §2000e(f). If anything, that history tends to confirm that the "appointee[s] on the policymaking level" exception was designed to exclude from the coverage of the ADEA all high-level appointments throughout state government structures, including judicial appointments.

For example, during the debates concerning the proposed extension of Title VII to the States, Senator Ervin repeatedly expressed his concern that the (unamended) definition of "employee" would be construed to reach those "persons who exercise the legislative, executive, *and judicial* powers of the States and political subdivisions of the States." 118 Cong. Rec. 1838 (1972) (emphasis added). Indeed, he expressly complained that "[t]here is not even an exception in the [unamended] bill to the effect that the EEOC will not have jurisdiction over . . . State judges, whether they are elected or appointed to office." *Id.,* at 1677. Also relevant is Senator Taft's comment that, in order to respond to Senator Ervin's concerns, he was willing to agree to an exception not only for elected officials, but also for "those at the top decisionmaking levels in the executive and judicial branch as well." *Id.,* at 1838.

The definition of "employee" subsequently was modified to exclude the four categories of employees discussed above. The Conference Committee that added the "appointee[s] on the policymaking level" exception made clear the separate nature of that exception:

"It is the intention of the conferees to exempt elected officials and members of their personal staffs, and persons appointed by such elected officials as advisors *or* to policymaking positions at *the highest levels* of the departments or agencies of State or local governments, such as cabinet officers, and persons with comparable responsibilities at the local level." H.R. Conf. Rep. No. 92-899, pp. 15-16 (1972) (emphasis added).

The italicized "or" in that statement indicates, contrary to petitioners' argument, that appointed officials need not be advisers to be covered by the exception. Rather, it appears that "Congress intended two categories: policymakers, who need not be advisers; and advisers, who need not be policymakers." *EEOC v. Massachusetts,* 858 F.2d 52, 56 (C.A.1 1988). This reading is confirmed by a statement by one of the House Managers, Representative Erlenborn, who explained that "[i]n the conference, an additional qualification was added, exempting those people appointed by officials at the State and local level in policymaking positions." 118 Cong. Rec., at 7567.

In addition, the phrase "the highest levels" in the Conference Report suggests that Congress' intent was to limit the exception "down the chain of command, and not so much across agencies or departments." *EEOC v. Massachusetts,* 858 F.2d, at 56. I also agree with the First Circuit's conclusion that even lower court judges fall within the exception because "each judge, as a separate and independent judicial officer, is at the very top of his particular 'policymaking' chain of command, responding . . . only to a higher appellate court." *Ibid.*

Id. at 483-85. Note that Justice White is using legislative history not to uncover the purpose of the statute but to uncover the meaning of particular words and phrases (i.e., "employee" and "appointee on the policymaking level"). If there is "little legislative history," why does Justice White spend so much time considering it? On which pieces of legislative history does he rely? What inferences does he draw?

3. Principles for Reliance on Legislative History

Professor Victoria Nourse argues that legislative history cannot be intelligibly used without knowing Congress's own rules.

Victoria F. Nourse, A Decision Theory of Statutory Interpretation: Legislative History by the Rules

122 Yale L.J. 70 (2012)

. . .

II. SIMPLE PRINCIPLES FOR READING LEGISLATIVE HISTORY

. . . Legislative history is at its best when understood within Congress's own rules. Just as no one would try to understand the meaning of a trial transcript without understanding the rules of evidence or civil procedure, no one should try to understand legislative history without understanding Congress's own rules. . . At its most minimal, my claim is for one simple, but powerful, canon of construction: just as Congress is presumed to know and follow the "surrounding body of law," there should be an even stronger presumption that Congress knows and follows its own rules.

A. First Principle: Never Read Legislative History Without Knowing Congress's Own Rules

Consider an easy example based on an apparently hard case. *Public Citizen v. U.S. Department of Justice* involved the American Bar Association's recommendations to the President on judicial nominations. The question raised was whether the ABA had to satisfy the Federal Advisory Committee Act (FACA), which requires certain governmental entities "established or utilized" by the President to open their meetings, balance their membership, and release public reports.

Today, *Public Citizen* is taught as a controversial case. For textualists, the majority opinion commits judicial surgery, cutting the word "utilized" from the statute. . . . Among textualists, the majority opinion raises eyebrows not only for its apparent judicial surgery, but also for its use of the much-debated absurdity canon and constitutional avoidance.

There was an easier way to resolve *Public Citizen*, although this road was taken neither by the majority opinion (which performed the apparent surgery) nor by the concurrence (which concluded the statute could not be constitutionally applied to the President). The answer lies in understanding when Congress added the term "utilize" to the statute. No lengthy legislative history is necessary to find the answer. The term "utilize" first appears in the conference committee report resolving House and Senate differences on FACA. Conference reports are moments when Congress must resolve disagreements between texts; more specifically, between the House and Senate versions of a bill. This was certainly true in *Public Citizen*. The Senate bill going to conference covered committees "established or organized" by the President; the House bill used the term "establish." In other words, the votes in both the House and the Senate prior to the conference were for "establish" and at the most "established or organized." The term "utilize" was nowhere in sight. Indeed, "utilize" was added in the conference committee, contrary to the bills passed in both House and Senate.

That "utilize" first appears in the conference report should raise a red flag for anyone knowledgeable about Congress's rules. Conference committees cannot—repeat, cannot—change the text of a bill where both houses have agreed to the same language. Both House and Senate rules bar such changes. These rules limit opportunism by conference committees' members and ex post control by drafting committees, since drafters are typically appointed as conferees and thus get another shot at legislation they themselves drafted. . . .

In *Public Citizen*, the conference report was simple, strong, and proximate legislative history. It was the last act on the precise statutory term at issue—"utilize." Viewed within the Principles outlined above, a court should defer to the meaning demanded by Congress's own rules. According to congressional rules, the conferees had no power to change the text in any significant way and therefore a judge should interpret "utilize" precisely as a member of Congress would interpret it—as making no significant change to "established or organized." Ironically, this is precisely the result the Court reached, albeit in ways that seem highly strained and controversial. . . .

B. Second Principle: Later Textual Decisions Trump Earlier Ones

Historians worry about using the present to interpret the past. Precisely the opposite presumption should apply in reading legislative debates. The very notion of legislative "history" should be treated as a misnomer. In legislative debates, sequence is important. Later textual decisions trump earlier ones. Put in the simplest terms, legislative history should be read in reverse. The last act may occur in a debate on a post-cloture amendment or in a conference report or in committee, but one should always start by looking for the last textual decisionmaking point. The aim should not be to imagine that one is actually writing a history, but to look for the last textual decision on the interpretive question.

This Principle of reverse sequential consideration explains the value of conference committee reports. It is the conventional and correct wisdom that, of all legislative history "apart from the statute itself, [conference committee reports are] the most reliable evidence of congressional" decisions. This is not necessarily because of deliberative quality: at the end of a bill, particularly a long-debated bill, much may be assumed and rushed. This is the moment when the rules narrow the decisions available to the negotiators. However, conference reports are not the only key moments of decision; often, the cloture process in the Senate makes the pre-filibuster compromise text a very important point of textual decision. . . .

C. Third Principle: The Best Legislative History Is Not Identified by Type, but by Specificity to the Interpretive Question and Proximity to the Textual Decision

It is often asserted that some kinds of legislative history are inherently better than others: committee reports are better than author statements, and author statements are better than the statements of hearing witnesses. Some scholars have asserted a de facto hierarchy of reliability when it comes to legislative history. . . . The standard hierarchy is not only under-theorized, it is wrong as far as its judgments about reliability. The best legislative history should not be defined by essentialist category, such as the category of all committee reports or all floor statements. Instead, the best legislative history is the last, most specific decision related to the interpretive question prior to the textual decision. Note that this Principle is not simply a repetition of the Second Principle, which privileges later decisions over earlier legislative history, all other things being equal. Specificity and proximity need not be conjoined; for example, there may be cases where the most specific legislative history on the issue appears earlier rather than later in the process, as, for example, when a committee report speaks directly to the question being litigated.

That the best legislative history is the history most proximate to text, rather than a particular type of report or statement, might seem banal. Others have noted this phenomenon, for example, in canonical cases such as *Church of the Holy Trinity v. United States.* The question was whether alien-labor legislation governing "labor or service of any kind" applied to a rector from England. Reviewing the legislative history, Professor [Adrian] Vermeule is clearly right in concluding that an early report cannot be "authoritative history." Professor Vermeule is clearly right in concluding that such a report cannot be "authoritative" history because no decision was in fact made. The committee report on which Justice Brewer relied was simply too far in advance of the ultimate debate. Bills change dramatically over time, and in fact the Alien Contract Labor Act was amended after that report was issued. One should always be cautious in asserting that committee reports are necessarily better than author statements or amendment debate. Of course, if the committee report refers to a decision on the particular matter, and is roughly contemporaneous in time, then that may be the relatively best legislative history available.

A proximity and specificity rule not only helps to ensure reliability, but it may also whittle down vast amounts of legislative history . . . Reading legislative history in reverse, coupled with a specificity rule, may make even the longest debates manageable if, for example, the change was made in an amendment on the floor, either in the House or Senate.

D. Fourth Principle: Never Cite Legislative History Without Knowing Who Won and Who Lost the Textual Debate

In Congress, winning and losing matter. Yet scholars and judges feel free to rifle through the debates, picking and choosing quotations supporting their interpretive positions. There is nothing partisan in this: so-called liberal and conservative judges rely on losers' history and both are wrong in doing so despite rather ancient and well-known pronouncements against the use of such history. This point has become far more important recently, however, because of the ubiquity of the filibuster. The point of statutory interpretation cannot be to look for the position of a filibustering minority. There has been an enormous hue and cry against judicial activism in the use of legislative history, but one of the more significant problems is using it improperly. It should be far clearer that it is "activist" to use losers' history. Positive political theorists are correct that losers are likely to exaggerate the limits of a bill, just as winners are likely to exaggerate the advantages of the bill. But losers' history should generate far more caution: surely the job of judges is not to aid legislative obstructionists. At the very least, students of the legislative process must be taught to distinguish between winners' and losers' history.

Positive political theorists have urged that winners' history cannot be enough and that compromise positions must be taken into account. This is surely true, but it is also true that one cannot find such compromises without looking at the legislative history and the rules governing it: chunks of text do not come with an attached footnote saying, "this was a compromise." Perhaps more importantly, Congress's own rules are the only way to identify significant decisionmaking points when compromise is essential. The rules tell us, for example, that conference committees and cloture motions are places where important compromises must be made for a bill to move forward. Positive political theorists know these rules and apply them; they have simply forgotten that the average lawyer and judge do not know the rules.

To say that those opposed to the bill should be cited with great caution is not to say that their statements are irrelevant. Costly concessions, as the political scientists say, are important: after all, it was the great opponent of the bill [at issue in *Holy Trinity*], Senator Morgan, who argued that "lecturers" on religious topics were excluded from the Act. It is to say that there is a great risk in picking out losers' history as authoritative history without determining whether it is simply a reflection of a superminority's opposition. . . .

In *Holy Trinity*, it means that those who reject the Court's outcome based on Senator Morgan's statements about the broad scope of the bill risk becoming judicial activists in favor of a congressional minority. No lawyer would last long at a law firm if he or she cited the Supreme Court's dissenting opinions as if they were majority opinions, but this is precisely the risk when lawyers and scholars cite legislative history without regard to legislative winners and losers. Both intentionalism and purposivism tend to exacerbate this problem because they appear to assume that there will be a unanimous intention when, as Congress's procedures make clear, the majority (or in most cases today, a supermajority) prevails. . . .

An important caveat to this Principle remains: to say that losers' history should not be outcome-determinative or authoritative is not to say that it should be ignored. Minorities' views may be essential to understanding changes in textual meaning to provide context in legislative changes, or when their arguments in effect "win."

E. Fifth Principle: Structure-Induced Misunderstandings: Congress's Rules May Create Ambiguity for Courts but Not for Congress

We have come to a far more nuanced appreciation of the ways in which Congress's rules may defy lawyerly expectations. Let me call these "structure-induced misunderstandings": cases in which faithful legislators following the rules may operate under rule-based expectations that contradict what a court might expect if it looked solely to the text and not the structural context of Congress's decision.

. . .

"Structure-induced" misunderstandings do not arise only around conference reports. . . . The cloture rules give an incentive for bill opponents to revisit issues agreed to in the substitute. Today, Senate Rule XXII actually encourages this by requiring that post-cloture amendments be introduced prior to cloture. Given the incentives produced by the rules, proponents of the underlying bill will always suspect that amendments offered in opposition are efforts to obtain benefits lost in the major substitute negotiations. Nevertheless, proponents will want to see the already-filibustered bill move forward, which will give them an incentive to agree to redundant language. Redundant language raises no immediate electoral costs to the proponents or opponents, but may be the subject of very serious inquiry by judges who apply canons of construction, particularly the canon against surplusage. In such a case, the rules of the Senate create incentives to create surplusage likely to offend judges' canonically induced preference for parsimony.

Consider, finally, another type of rule likely to create "structure-induced misunderstandings"—those governing appropriations bills. . . .

The congressional bar against legislating on appropriations "is derived from House and Senate rules." The basic principle of the rule keeps textual authorizing language out of appropriations bills, which may be a list of numbers. Authorizing committees are separate from appropriating committees. Authorize all you want, but the ultimate monetary decision will be made by the appropriating committees. This rule is followed every day in the Senate and the House, as authorizing committees pursue their part of the division of labor while appropriating committees pursue theirs. The division of labor between the committees is preserved against encroachment by committee structure and sequential referral, but violations are subject to a point of order or floor objection to the completed bill. However well known are Congress's attempts to violate this rule, it remains embedded in the structure of Congress's committees and the rules governing floor debate on appropriations bills.

The Supreme Court's opinion in *TVA v. Hill* fails to appreciate both the structure and rules governing appropriations and authorizations. The Court applied a judicial canon against "repeal by implication," which effectively reversed members' presumption that appropriations trump legislation. Elsewhere, the canon against repeal by implication may be both wise and important, but, in this particular case, it reversed the assumptions of those within the legislative process. . . . What judges see as ambiguity and lack of deliberation in appropriations matters is quite the opposite for those within Congress. Experts believe that members have every incentive to and do actively participate in the appropriations process and that these bills are among the most important and actively deliberated of all bills Congress passes.

In the end, there was no way for the appropriators or authorizers alone to provide the textual clarity the Supreme Court sought. The Supreme Court wrote, "There is nothing in the appropriations measures, as passed, which states that the Tellico Project was to be completed irrespective of the requirements of the Endangered Species Act." But under House Rule XXI(2) and Senate Rule XVI(4) (rules that the Court itself cites), neither the Committee nor the full House could have added legislative text to the appropriations bill, for that would have been legislating on appropriations, subjecting the bill to a point of order. An appropriations committee cannot change authorizing legislation — it cannot call up the Endangered Species Act and amend it, for that is outside the appropriations committee's jurisdiction; it would have to go to the authorizing committee to do that. The Court ruled that the appropriations "Committee[] Report[]" language discussing the dam was insufficient, even though there was nowhere else where the appropriating committees could express their understanding (short of passing an entirely new bill outside their jurisdiction).

The Supreme Court seemed to think that making a clear exception in the text was simple, but under Congress's rules, it may not have been easy at all. The appropriators could not put legislating text in their appropriations bill, and they could not amend the authorizing legislation. The same was true of the authorizing committee: it could not amend the appropriations bill with legislation, and it had no jurisdiction over the appropriations bill. Functionally speaking, it is as if the Supreme Court was asking Nebraska to pass a law for Louisiana or vice versa. One might simply say that the Court was forcing the House committees to compromise, but it was also risking the possibility that, even if the House committees cooperated, no final legislation would be passed because of the ever-present risk of a Senate filibuster. Resolving the situation in *TVA* was not a matter of a small textual fix but required complex congressional negotiations because of a structural conflict between two committees' plans.

Notes and Questions

1. Perhaps the biggest departure from how courts and scholars often think about legislative history is Nourse's Third Principle, which shifts focus from the type of legislative history (e.g., committee report or author statement) to the "last, most specific decision related to the interpretive question." Might that depend on whether a court is consulting legislative history for mention of the specific interpretive question or the general purpose of the statute? Would the traditional hierarchy of legislative history produce more reliable indications of general purpose?

2. If we follow Nourse's lead, should we consider adding another principle: "Know the Audience to Whom Legislative History Is Addressed?" Courts and scholars often assume that legislative history is produced to educate courts or members of Congress about the contents of a bill. What if instead legislative history is a means of communicating with the agency that will implement the legislation? As you will see in Chapter 5, agencies may take legislative history, particularly committee reports, more seriously than courts do precisely because it may contain instructions to or guidance for them.

3. Is Nourse's overall point to encourage consideration of the actual legislative process that accompanies a bill rather than relying on generalizations about that process in assessing the reliability of legislative history? This move seems wise, especially as the legislative process becomes more unorthodox. But is it as easy for courts to do as Nourse suggests? Which of Nourse's principles are most difficult and which are easiest for courts to employ?

D. TOOLS FOR CONSIDERING CHANGED CIRCUMSTANCES

So far, we have been discussing statutes as static — their meaning is fixed at the time of enactment. The tools that we have examined are used to ascertain that fixed meaning. But societies change, governments change, and technology changes. Courts sometimes factor in such changes when interpreting statutes. The decision below is a famous example, involving an interpretation of a statute that upheld an agency's changed reading of the statute it was enforcing. We present only one such decision in the interest of space, but there are many other examples, and their multiplicity raises several questions worth noting, such as whether some statutes are more amenable to updating than others, and how courts measure changed circumstances. There is another, larger point that is equally worth noting. Although we are examining questions about how courts take account of changed circumstances when interpreting statutes, there are also questions about why they do, whether they should, and whether they can avoid doing so. We will examine the theories of statutory interpretation that justify this practice later in the chapter.

Bob Jones University v. United States

461 U.S. 574 (1983)

CHIEF JUSTICE BURGER delivered the opinion of the Court.

We granted certiorari to decide whether petitioners, nonprofit private schools that prescribe and enforce racially discriminatory admissions standards on the basis of religious doctrine, qualify as tax-exempt organizations under §501(c)(3) of the Internal Revenue Code of 1954.

I

A

Until 1970, the Internal Revenue Service granted tax-exempt status to private schools, without regard to their racial admissions policies, under §501(c)(3) of the Internal Revenue Code, 26 U.S.C. §501(c)(3),[1] and granted charitable deductions for contributions to such schools under §170 of the Code, 26 U.S.C. §170.[2]

On January 12, 1970, a three-judge District Court for the District of Columbia issued a preliminary injunction prohibiting the IRS from according tax-exempt status to private schools in Mississippi that discriminated as to admissions on the basis of race. . . . Thereafter, in July 1970, the IRS concluded that it could "no longer legally justify allowing tax-exempt status [under §501(c)(3)] to private schools which practice racial discrimination." IRS News Release (7/10/70). At the same time, the IRS announced that it could not "treat gifts to such schools as charitable deductions for income tax purposes [under §170]." *Ibid.* By letter dated November 30, 1970, the IRS formally notified private schools, including those involved in this case, of this change in policy, "applicable to all private schools in the United States at all levels of education." *See id.*

On June 30, 1971, the three-judge District Court issued its opinion on the merits of the Mississippi challenge. *Green v. Connally*, 330 F. Supp. 1150 (D.D.C.), *aff'd sub nom. Coit v. Green*, 404 U.S. 997 (1971) (*per curiam*). . . . The court permanently enjoined the Commissioner of Internal Revenue from

---

1. Section 501(c)(3) lists the following organizations, which, pursuant to §501(a), are exempt from taxation unless denied tax exemptions under other specified sections of the Code:

"Corporations, and any community chest, fund, or foundation, *organized and operated exclusively for religious, charitable,* scientific, testing for public safety, literary, *or educational purposes,* or to foster national or international amateur sports competition (but only if no part of its activities involve the provision of athletic facilities or equipment), or for the prevention of cruelty to children or animals, no part of the net earnings of which inures to the benefit of any private shareholder or individual, no substantial part of the activities of which is carrying on propaganda, or otherwise

2. Section 170(a) allows deductions for certain "charitable contributions." Section 170(c)(2)(B) includes within the definition of "charitable contribution" a contribution or gift to or for the use of a corporation "organized and operated exclusively for religious, charitable, scientific, literary, or educational purposes. . . ."

approving tax-exempt status for any school in Mississippi that did not publicly maintain a policy of nondiscrimination.

The revised policy on discrimination was formalized in Revenue Ruling
71-447, 1971-2 Cum. Bull. 230:

> "Both the courts and the Internal Revenue Service have long recognized that the stat-
> utory requirement of being 'organized and operated exclusively for religious, char-
> itable, . . . or educational purposes' was intended to express the basic common law
> concept [of 'charity']. . . . All charitable trusts, educational or otherwise, are subject to
> the requirement that the purpose of the trust may not be illegal or contrary to public
> policy." *Id.,* at 230.

Based on the "national policy to discourage racial discrimination in
education," the IRS ruled that "a private school not having a racially nondiscriminatory policy as to students is not 'charitable' within the common law concepts reflected in sections 170 and 501(c)(3) of the Code."
Id., at 231.

The application of the IRS construction of these provisions to petitioners, two private schools with racially discriminatory admissions policies, is
now before us. . . . attempting, to influence legislation . . . , and which does
not participate in, or intervene in (including the publishing or distributing
of statements), any political campaign on behalf of any candidate for public
office." (Emphasis added.)

II

A

In Revenue Ruling 71-447, the IRS formalized the policy first announced in
1970, that §170 and §501(c)(3) embrace the common law "charity" concept.
Under that view, to qualify for a tax exemption pursuant to §501(c)(3), an
institution must show, first, that it falls within one of the eight categories
expressly set forth in that section, and second, that its activity is not contrary
to settled public policy.

Section 501(c)(3) provides that "[c]orporations . . . organized and operated exclusively for religious, charitable . . . or educational purposes" are
entitled to tax exemption. Petitioners argue that the plain language of the
statute guarantees them tax-exempt status. They emphasize the absence of
any language in the statute expressly requiring all exempt organizations to
be "charitable" in the common law sense, and they contend that the disjunctive "or" separating the categories in §501(c)(3) precludes such a reading.
Instead, they argue that if an institution falls within one or more of the
specified categories it is automatically entitled to exemption, without regard
to whether it also qualifies as "charitable." The Court of Appeals rejected
that contention and concluded that petitioners' interpretation of the statute
"tears Section 501(c)(3) from its roots." *United States v. Bob Jones University,*
639 F.2d, at 151.

It is a well-established canon of statutory construction that a court should go beyond the literal language of a statute if reliance on that language would defeat the plain purpose of the statute:

> "The general words used in the clause . . . , taken by themselves, and literally construed, without regard to the object in view, would seem to sanction the claim of the plaintiff. But this mode of expounding a statute has never been adopted by any enlightened tribunal because it is evident that in many cases it would defeat the object which the Legislature intended to accomplish. And it is well settled that, in interpreting a statute, the court will not look merely to a particular clause in which general words may be used, *but will take in connection with it the whole statute . . . and the objects and policy of the law. . . .*" *Brown v. Duchesne,* 19 How. 183, 194 (1857) (emphasis added).

Section 501(c)(3) therefore must be analyzed and construed within the framework of the Internal Revenue Code and against the background of the Congressional purposes. Such an examination reveals unmistakable evidence that, underlying all relevant parts of the Code, is the intent that entitlement to tax exemption depends on meeting certain common law standards of charity namely, that an institution seeking tax-exempt status must serve a public purpose and not be contrary to established public policy. . . .

This "charitable" concept appears explicitly in §170 of the Code. That section contains a list of organizations virtually identical to that contained in §501(c)(3). It is apparent that Congress intended that list to have the same meaning in both sections. In §170, Congress used the list of organizations in defining the term "charitable contributions." On its face, therefore, §170 reveals that Congress' intention was to provide tax benefits to organizations serving charitable purposes. The form of §170 simply makes plain what common sense and history tell us: in enacting both §170 and §501(c)(3), Congress sought to provide tax benefits to charitable organizations, to encourage the development of private institutions that serve a useful public purpose or supplement or take the place of public institutions of the same kind.

Tax exemptions for certain institutions thought beneficial to the social order of the country as a whole, or to a particular community, are deeply rooted in our history, as in that of England. The origins of such exemptions lie in the special privileges that have long been extended to charitable trusts.[3]

More than a century ago, this Court announced the caveat that is critical in this case:

> "[I]t has now become an established principle of American law, that courts of chancery will sustain and protect . . . a gift . . . to public charitable uses, *provided the same*

---

3. The form and history of the charitable exemption and deduction sections of the various income tax acts reveal that Congress was guided by the common law of charitable trusts. *See* Simon, *The Tax-Exempt Status of Racially Discriminatory Religious Schools,* 36 Tax L. Rev. 477, 485-489 (1981) (hereinafter Simon). Congress acknowledged as much in 1969. The House Report on the Tax Reform Act of 1969, Pub. L. 91-172, 83 Stat. 487, stated that the §501(c)(3) exemption was available only to institutions that served "the specified charitable purposes," H.R. Rep. No. 413 (Part 1), 91st Cong., 1st Sess. 35 (1969), and described "charitable" as "a term that has been used in the law of trusts for hundreds of years." *Id.,* at 43. We need not consider whether Congress intended to incorporate into the Internal Revenue Code any aspects of charitable trust law other than the requirements of public benefit and a valid public purpose.

is consistent with local laws and public policy. . . ." Perin v. Carey, 24 How. 465, 501 (1861) (emphasis added).

Soon after that, in 1878, the Court commented:

"A charitable use, *where neither law nor public policy forbids,* may be applied to almost any thing *that tends to promote the well-doing and well-being of social man." Ould v. Washington Hospital for Foundlings,* 95 U.S. 303, 311 (1878) (emphasis added). . . .

These statements clearly reveal the legal background against which Congress enacted the first charitable exemption statute in 1894: charities were to be given preferential treatment because they provide a benefit to society.

What little floor debate occurred on the charitable exemption provision of the 1894 Act and similar sections of later statutes leaves no doubt that Congress deemed the specified organizations entitled to tax benefits because they served desirable public purposes. *See, e.g.,* 26 Cong. Rec. 585-586 (1894); *id.,* at 1727. In floor debate on a similar provision in 1917, for example, Senator Hollis articulated the rationale:

"For every dollar that a man contributes to these public charities, educational, scientific, or otherwise, the public gets 100 percent." *Id.,* at 6728 (1917). *See also, e.g., id.,* at 4150 (1909); *id.,* at 1305-1306 (1913). . . .

In enacting the Revenue Act of 1938, ch. 289, 52 Stat. 447 (1938), Congress expressly reconfirmed this view with respect to the charitable deduction provision:

"The exemption from taxation of money and property devoted to charitable and other purposes is based on the theory that the Government is compensated for the loss of revenue by its relief from financial burdens which would otherwise have to be met by appropriations from other public funds, and by the benefits resulting from the promotion of the general welfare." H.R. Rep. No. 1860, 75th Cong., 3d Sess. 19 (1938).

A corollary to the public benefit principle is the requirement, long recognized in the law of trusts, that the purpose of a charitable trust may not be illegal or violate established public policy. In 1861, this Court stated that a public charitable use must be "consistent with local laws and public policy," *Perin v. Carey,* 24 How., at 501. Modern commentators and courts have echoed that view. *See, e.g.,* Restatement (Second) of Trusts, §377, comment c (1959); 4 Scott §377, and cases cited therein; Bogert §378, at 191-192.

When the Government grants exemptions or allows deductions all taxpayers are affected; the very fact of the exemption or deduction for the donor means that other taxpayers can be said to be indirect and vicarious "donors." Charitable exemptions are justified on the basis that the exempt entity confers a public benefit, a benefit which the society or the community may not itself choose or be able to provide, or which supplements and advances the work of public institutions already supported by tax revenues. History buttresses logic to make clear that, to warrant exemption under §501(c)(3), an institution must fall within a category specified in that section and must demonstrably serve and be in harmony with the public interest.

The institution's purpose must not be so at odds with the common community conscience as to undermine any public benefit that might otherwise be conferred.

B

We are bound to approach these questions with full awareness that determinations of public benefit and public policy are sensitive matters with serious implications for the institutions affected; a declaration that a given institution is not "charitable" should be made only where there can be no doubt that the activity involved is contrary to a fundamental public policy. But there can no longer be any doubt that racial discrimination in education violates deeply and widely accepted views of elementary justice. Prior to 1954, public education in many places still was conducted under the pall of *Plessy v. Ferguson*, 163 U.S. 537 (1896); racial segregation in primary and secondary education prevailed in many parts of the country. This Court's decision in *Brown v. Board of Education*, 347 U.S. 483 (1954), signaled an end to that era. Over the past quarter of a century, every pronouncement of this Court and myriad Acts of Congress and Executive Orders attest a firm national policy to prohibit racial segregation and discrimination in public education.

An unbroken line of cases following *Brown v. Board of Education* establishes beyond doubt this Court's view that racial discrimination in education violates a most fundamental national public policy, as well as rights of individuals.

"The right of a student not to be segregated on racial grounds in schools . . . is indeed so fundamental and pervasive that it is embraced in the concept of due process of law." *Cooper v. Aaron*, 358 U.S. 1, 19 (1958). . . .

Congress, in Titles IV and VI of the Civil Rights Act of 1964, Pub. L. 88-352, 78 Stat. 241, 42 U.S.C. §§2000c *et seq.*, 2000c-6, 2000-d *et seq.*, clearly expressed its agreement that racial discrimination in education violates a fundamental public policy. Other sections of that Act, and numerous enactments since then, testify to the public policy against racial discrimination. See, *e.g.*, the Voting Rights Act of 1965 . . . ; Title VIII of the Civil Rights Act of 1968 . . . ; the Emergency School Aid Act of 1972. . . .

The Executive Branch has consistently placed its support behind eradication of racial discrimination. Several years before this Court's decision in *Brown v. Board of Education*, President Truman issued Executive Orders prohibiting racial discrimination in federal employment decisions, Exec. Order No. 9980, 3 CFR 720 (1943-1948 Comp.), and in classifications for the Selective Service, Exec. Order No. 9988, *id.* 726, 729. In 1957, President Eisenhower employed military forces to ensure compliance with federal standards in school desegregation programs. Exec. Order No. 10730, 3 CFR 389 (1954-1958 Comp.). And in 1962, President Kennedy announced:

"[T]he granting of federal assistance for . . . housing and related facilities from which Americans are excluded because of their race, color, creed, or national origin is unfair, unjust, and inconsistent with the public policy of the United States as manifested in its Constitution and laws." Exec. Order No. 11063, 3 CFR 652 (1959-1963 Comp.).

These are but a few of numerous Executive Orders over the past three decades demonstrating the commitment of the Executive Branch to the fundamental policy of eliminating racial discrimination.

Few social or political issues in our history have been more vigorously debated and more extensively ventilated than the issue of racial discrimination, particularly in education. Given the stress and anguish of the history of efforts to escape from the shackles of the "separate but equal" doctrine of *Plessy v. Ferguson,* it cannot be said that educational institutions that, for whatever reasons, practice racial discrimination, are institutions exercising "beneficial and stabilizing influences in community life," *Walz v. Tax Comm'n,* 397 U.S. 664, 673 (1970), or should be encouraged by having all taxpayers share in their support by way of special tax status.

There can thus be no question that the interpretation of §170 and §501(c)(3) announced by the IRS in 1970 was correct. That it may be seen as belated does not undermine its soundness. It would be wholly incompatible with the concepts underlying tax exemption to grant the benefit of tax-exempt status to racially discriminatory educational entities, which "exer[t] a pervasive influence on the entire educational process." *Norwood v. Harrison,* 413 U.S., at 469. Whatever may be the rationale for such private schools' policies, and however sincere the rationale may be, racial discrimination in education is contrary to public policy. Racially discriminatory educational institutions cannot be viewed as conferring a public benefit within the "charitable" concept discussed earlier, or within the Congressional intent underlying §170 and §501(c)(3).

II

C

Petitioners contend that, regardless of whether the IRS properly concluded that racially discriminatory private schools violate public policy, only Congress can alter the scope of §170 and §501(c)(3). Petitioners accordingly argue that the IRS overstepped its lawful bounds in issuing its 1970 and 1971 rulings.

Yet ever since the inception of the tax code, Congress has seen fit to vest in those administering the tax laws very broad authority to interpret those laws. In an area as complex as the tax system, the agency Congress vests with administrative responsibility must be able to exercise its authority to meet changing conditions and new problems. . . . [T]his Court has long recognized the primary authority of the IRS and its predecessors in construing the Internal Revenue Code, *see, e.g., Commissioner v. Portland Cement Co.,* 450 U.S. 156, 169 (1981); *United States v. Correll,* 389 U.S. 299, 306-307 (1967); *Boske v. Comingore,* 177 U.S. 459, 469-470 (1900).

On the record before us, there can be no doubt as to the national policy. In 1970, when the IRS first issued the ruling challenged here, the position of all three branches of the Federal Government was unmistakably clear. The correctness of the Commissioner's conclusion that a racially discriminatory private school "is not 'charitable' within the common law concepts reflected in . . . the Code," Rev. Rul. 71-447, is wholly consistent with what Congress, the Executive and the courts had repeatedly declared before 1970. Indeed, it would be anomalous for the Executive, Legislative and Judicial Branches to reach conclusions that add up to a firm public policy on racial discrimination, and at the same time have the IRS blissfully ignore what all three branches of the Federal Government had declared. . . .

D

The actions of Congress since 1970 leave no doubt that the IRS reached the correct conclusion in exercising its authority. It is, of course, not unknown for independent agencies or the Executive Branch to misconstrue the intent of a statute; Congress can and often does correct such misconceptions, if the courts have not done so. . . .

Ordinarily, and quite appropriately, courts are slow to attribute significance to the failure of Congress to act on particular legislation. *See, e.g., Aaron v. SEC,* 446 U.S. 680, 694 n.11 (1980). We have observed that "unsuccessful attempts at legislation are not the best of guides to legislative intent," *Red Lion Broadcasting Co. v. FCC,* 395 U.S. 367, 381-382 n.11 (1969). Here, however, we do not have an ordinary claim of legislative acquiescence. Only one month after the IRS announced its position in 1970, Congress held its first hearings on this precise issue. *Equal Educational Opportunity: Hearings Before the Senate Select Comm. on Equal Educational Opportunity,* 91st Cong., 2d Sess. 1991 (1970). Exhaustive hearings have been held on the issue at various times since then. These include hearings in February 1982, after we granted review in this case. *Administration's Change in Federal Policy Regarding the Tax Status of Racially Discriminatory Private Schools: Hearing Before the House Comm. on Ways and Means,* 97th Cong., 2d Sess. (1982).

Non-action by Congress is not often a useful guide, but the non-action here is significant. During the past 12 years there have been no fewer than 13 bills introduced to overturn the IRS interpretation of §501(c)(3). Not one of these bills has emerged from any committee, although Congress has enacted numerous other amendments to §501 during this same period, including an amendment to §501(c)(3) itself. Tax Reform Act of 1976, Pub. L. 94-455, §1313(a), 90 Stat. 1520, 1730 (1976). It is hardly conceivable that Congress and in this setting, any Member of Congress was not abundantly aware of what was going on. In view of its prolonged and acute awareness of so important an issue, Congress' failure to act on the bills proposed on this subject provides added support for concluding that Congress acquiesced in the IRS rulings of 1970 and 1971.

The evidence of Congressional approval of the policy embodied in Revenue Ruling 71-447 goes well beyond the failure of Congress to act on legislative proposals. Congress affirmatively manifested its acquiescence in the IRS policy when it enacted the present §501(i) of the Code, Act of October 20, 1976, Pub. L. 94-568 (1976). That provision denies tax-exempt status to social clubs whose charters or policy statements provide for "discrimination against any person on the basis of race, color, or religion." Both the House and Senate committee reports on that bill articulated the national policy against granting tax exemptions to racially discriminatory private clubs. S. Rep. No. 1318, 94th Cong., 2d Sess., 8 (1976); H.R. Rep. No. 1353, 94th Cong., 2d Sess., 8 (1976).

Even more significant is the fact that both reports focus on this Court's affirmance of *Green v. Connally,* as having established that "discrimination on account of race is inconsistent with an *educational institution's* tax exempt status." S. Rep. No. 1318, *supra,* at 7-8 and n.5; H.R. Rep. No. 1353, at 8 and n.5 (emphasis added). These references in Congressional committee reports on an enactment denying tax exemptions to racially discriminatory private social clubs cannot be read other than as indicating approval of the standards applied to racially discriminatory private schools by the IRS subsequent to 1970, and specifically of Revenue Ruling 71-447.

[In Part III, Chief Justice Burger rejected the argument that the IRS policy violated the Free Exercise Clause of the Constitution as applied to religious institutions. In Part IV, he rejected the argument that the policy was improperly applied to Bob Jones University because it did not actually engage in racial discrimination.]

[The concurring opinion of Justice POWELL is omitted.]

Justice REHNQUIST, dissenting.

The Court points out that there is a strong national policy in this country against racial discrimination. To the extent that the Court states that Congress in furtherance of this policy could deny tax-exempt status to educational institutions that promote racial discrimination, I readily agree. But, unlike the Court, I am convinced that Congress simply has failed to take this action and, as this Court has said over and over again, regardless of our view on the propriety of Congress' failure to legislate we are not constitutionally empowered to act for them.

In approaching this statutory construction question the Court quite adeptly avoids the statute it is construing. This I am sure is no accident, for there is nothing in the language of §501(c)(3) that supports the result obtained by the Court. Section 501(c)(3) provides tax-exempt status for:

> "Corporations, and any community chest, fund, or foundation, organized and operated exclusively for religious, charitable, scientific, testing for public safety, literary, or educational purposes, or to foster national or international amateur sports competition (but only if no part of its activities involve the provision of athletic facilities

or equipment), or for the prevention of cruelty to children or animals, no part of the net earnings of which inures to the benefit of any private shareholder or individual, no substantial part of the activities of which is carrying on propaganda, or otherwise attempting, to influence legislation (except as otherwise provided in subsection (h)), and which does not participate in, or intervene in (including the publishing or distributing of statements), any political campaign on behalf of any candidate for public office." 26 U.S.C. §501(c)(3).

With undeniable clarity, Congress has explicitly defined the requirements for §501(c)(3) status. An entity must be (1) a corporation, or community chest, fund, or foundation, (2) organized for one of the eight enumerated purposes, (3) operated on a nonprofit basis, and (4) free from involvement in lobbying activities and political campaigns. Nowhere is there to be found some additional, undefined public policy requirement.

The Court first seeks refuge from the obvious reading of §501(c)(3) by turning to §170 of the Internal Revenue Code which provides a tax deduction for contributions made to §501(c)(3) organizations. In setting forth the general rule, §170 states:

> "There shall be allowed as a deduction any charitable contribution (as defined in subsection (c)) payment of which is made within the taxable year. A charitable contribution shall be allowable as a deduction only if verified under regulations prescribed by the Secretary." 26 U.S.C. §170(a)(1).

The Court seizes the words "charitable contribution" and with little discussion concludes that "[o]n its face, therefore, §170 reveals that Congress' intention was to provide tax benefits to organizations serving charitable purposes," intimating that this implies some unspecified common law charitable trust requirement.

The Court would have been well advised to look to subsection (c) where, as §170(a)(1) indicates, Congress has defined a "charitable contribution":

> "For purposes of this section, the term 'charitable contribution' means a contribution or gift to or for the use of . . . [a] corporation, trust, or community chest, fund, or foundation . . . organized and operated exclusively for religious, charitable, scientific, literary, or educational purposes, or to foster national or international amateur sports competition (but only if no part of its activities involve the provision of athletic facilities or equipment), or for the prevention of cruelty to children or animals; . . . no part of the net earnings of which inures to the benefit of any private shareholder or individual; and . . . which is not disqualified for tax exemption under Section 501(c)(3) by reason of attempting to influence legislation, and which does not participate in, or intervene in (including the publishing or distributing of statements), any political campaign on behalf of any candidate for public office." 26 U.S.C. §170(c).

Plainly, §170(c) simply tracks the requirements set forth in §501(c)(3). Since §170 is no more than a mirror of §501(c)(3) and, as the Court points out, §170 followed §501(c)(3) by more than two decades, it is at best of little usefulness in finding the meaning of §501(c)(3).

Making a more fruitful inquiry, the Court next turns to the legislative history of §501(c)(3) and finds that Congress intended in that statute to offer a tax benefit to organizations that Congress believed were providing a public benefit. I certainly agree. But then the Court leaps to the conclusion that this history is proof Congress intended that an organization seeking §501(c)(3) status "must fall within a category specified in that section *and must demonstrably serve and be in harmony with the public interest.*" (emphasis added). To the contrary, I think that the legislative history of §501(c)(3) unmistakably makes clear that *Congress has decided* what organizations are serving a public purpose and providing a public benefit within the meaning of §501(c)(3) and has clearly set forth in §501(c)(3) the characteristics of such organizations. In fact, there are few examples which better illustrate Congress' effort to define and redefine the requirements of a legislative act.

The first general income tax law was passed by Congress in the form of the Tariff Act of 1894. A provision of that Act provided an exemption for "corporations, companies, or associations organized and conducted solely for charitable, religious, or educational purposes." Ch. 349, §32, 28 Stat. 509, 556 (1894). The income tax portion of the 1894 Act was held unconstitutional by this Court, *see Pollock v. Farmers' Loan & Trust Co.,* 158 U.S. 601 (1895), but a similar exemption appeared in the Tariff Act of 1909 which imposed a tax on corporate income. The 1909 Act provided an exemption for "any corporation or association organized and operated exclusively for religious, charitable, or educational purposes, no part of the net income of which inures to the benefit of any private stockholder or individual." Ch. 6, §38, 36 Stat. 11, 113 (1909).

With the ratification of the Sixteenth Amendment, Congress again turned its attention to an individual income tax with the Tariff Act of 1913. And again, in the direct predecessor of §501(c)(3), a tax exemption was provided for "any corporation or association organized and operated exclusively for religious, charitable, scientific, or educational purposes, no part of the net income of which inures to the benefit of any private stockholder or individual." Ch. 16, §II(G)(a), 38 Stat. 114, 172 (1913). In subsequent acts Congress continued to broaden the list of exempt purposes. . . . Again, the exemption was left unchanged by the Revenue Acts of 1936 and 1938.

The tax laws were overhauled by the Internal Revenue Code of 1939, but this exemption was left unchanged. . . .

One way to read the opinion handed down by the Court today leads to the conclusion that this long and arduous refining process of §501(c)(3) was certainly a waste of time, for when enacting the original 1894 statute Congress intended to adopt a common law term of art, and intended that this term of art carry with it all of the common law baggage which defines it. Such a view, however, leads also to the unsupportable idea that Congress has spent almost a century adding illustrations simply to clarify an already defined common law term.

Another way to read the Court's opinion leads to the conclusion that even though Congress has set forth *some* of the requirements of a §501(c)(3) organization, it intended that the IRS additionally require that organizations meet a higher standard of public interest, not stated by Congress, but to be determined and defined by the IRS and the courts. This view I find equally unsupportable. Almost a century of statutory history proves that Congress itself intended to decide what §501(c)(3) requires. Congress has expressed its decision in the plainest of terms in §501(c)(3) by providing that tax-exempt status is to be given to any corporation, or community chest, fund, or foundation that is organized for one of the eight enumerated purposes, operated on a nonprofit basis, and uninvolved in lobbying activities or political campaigns. The IRS certainly is empowered to adopt regulations for the enforcement of these specified requirements, and the courts have authority to resolve challenges to the IRS's exercise of this power, but Congress has left it to neither the IRS nor the courts to select or add to the requirements of §501(c)(3). . . .

Perhaps recognizing the lack of support in the statute itself, or in its history, for the 1970 IRS change in interpretation, the Court finds that "[t]he actions of Congress since 1970 leave no doubt that the IRS reached the correct conclusion in exercising its authority," concluding that there is "an unusually strong case of legislative acquiescence in and ratification by implication of the 1970 and 1971 rulings." The Court relies first on several bills introduced to overturn the IRS interpretation of §501(c)(3). But we have said before, and it is equally applicable here, that this type of congressional inaction is of virtually no weight in determining legislative intent. *United States v. Wise,* 370 U.S. 405, 411 (1962); *Waterman Steamship Corp. v. United States,* 381 U.S. 252, 269 (1965). These bills and related hearings indicate little more than that a vigorous debate has existed in Congress concerning the new IRS position.

The Court next asserts that "Congress affirmatively manifested its acquiescence in the IRS policy when it enacted the present §501(i) of the Code," a provision that "denies tax exempt status to social clubs whose charters or policy statements provide for" racial discrimination. Quite to the contrary, it seems to me that in §501(i) Congress showed that when it wants to add a requirement prohibiting racial discrimination to one of the tax-benefit provisions, it is fully aware of how to do it.

The Court intimates that the Ashbrook and Dornan Amendments also reflect an intent by Congress to acquiesce in the new IRS position. The amendments were passed to limit certain enforcement procedures proposed by the IRS in 1978 and 1979 for determining whether a school operated in a racially nondiscriminatory fashion. The Court points out that in proposing his amendment, Congressman Ashbrook stated: "My amendment very clearly indicates on its face that all the regulations in existence as of August 22, 1978, would not be touched." The Court fails to note that Congressman Ashbrook also said:

"The IRS has no authority to create public policy. . . . So long as the Congress has not acted to set forth a national policy respecting denial of tax exemptions to private schools, it is improper for the IRS or any other branch of the Federal Government to seek denial of tax-exempt status. . . . There exists but a single responsibility which is proper for the Internal Revenue Service: To serve as tax collector." 125 Cong. Rec. H5879-80 (daily ed. July 13, 1979).

In the same debate, Congressman Grassley asserted: "Nobody argues that racial discrimination should receive preferred tax status in the United States. However, the IRS should not be making these decisions on the agency's own discretion. Congress should make these decisions." *Id.*, at 5884. The same debates are filled with other similar statements. While on the whole these debates do not show conclusively that Congress believed the IRS had exceeded its authority with the 1970 change in position, they likewise are far less than a showing of acquiescence in and ratification of the new position.

This Court continuously has been hesitant to find ratification through inaction. *See United States v. Wise.* This is especially true where such a finding "would result in a construction of the statute which not only is at odds with the language of the section in question and the pattern of the statute taken as a whole, but also is extremely far reaching in terms of the virtually untrammeled and unreviewable power it would vest in a regulatory agency." *SEC v. Sloan*, 436 U.S. 103, 121 (1978). Few cases would call for more caution in finding ratification by acquiescence than the present one. The new IRS interpretation is not only far less than a long standing administrative policy, it is at odds with a position maintained by the IRS, and unquestioned by Congress, for several decades prior to 1970. The interpretation is unsupported by the statutory language, it is unsupported by legislative history, the interpretation has led to considerable controversy in and out of Congress, and the interpretation gives to the IRS a broad power which until now Congress had kept for itself. Where in addition to these circumstances Congress has shown time and time again that it is ready to enact positive legislation to change the tax code when it desires, this Court has no business finding that Congress has adopted the new IRS position by failing to enact legislation to reverse it.

I have no disagreement with the Court's finding that there is a strong national policy in this country opposed to racial discrimination. I agree with the Court that Congress has the power to further this policy by denying §501(c)(3) status to organizations that practice racial discrimination. But as of yet Congress has failed to do so. Whatever the reasons for the failure, this Court should not legislate for Congress.

Petitioners are each organized for the "instruction or training of the individual for the purpose of improving or developing his capabilities," 26 CFR §1.501(c)(3)-1(d)(3), and thus are organized for "educational purposes" within the meaning of §501(c)(3). Petitioners' nonprofit status is uncontested. There is no indication that either petitioner has been involved in lobbying activities or political campaigns. Therefore, it is my view that unless and until Congress affirmatively amends §501(c)(3) to require more, the IRS is without authority to deny petitioners §501(c)(3) status. For this reason, I would reverse the Court of Appeals.

Notes and Questions

1. Are you clear on the statutory provisions at issue? Section 501(c)(3) of the U.S. Tax Code provides tax exempt status for corporations organized for "charitable" (or "educational") purposes. Section 170 authorizes individual tax deductions for "charitable contributions" to such corporations. Where in these provisions is the requirement that a charitable corporation act in a fashion that comports with established public policy?

2. The Court found that Bob Jones University failed to comport with established public policy because the school maintained a racially discriminatory admissions policy. It therefore upheld the IRS's decision to deny tax-exempt status to the University. Were racially discriminatory admissions policies contrary to public policy when Congress enacted §501(c)(3)? Why wasn't that the relevant consideration?

3. The Court found that public policy had evolved since the Tax Code was enacted. What evidence did the Court consider of legal and social change? Does similar evidence exist today against discrimination on basis of gender, age, disability, or sexual preference?

4. What is the role of time? In order for a court to "update" a statute in light of changed circumstances, how old must a statute be?

5. If circumstances really had changed, why not wait for Congress to amend the statute? This question really goes to why courts interpret statutes in light of changed circumstances, not how they do so — a theory question as opposed to a tool question. We will address the theory question in the next section of the chapter.

E. THEORIES OF STATUTORY INTERPRETATION

What is the proper aim of statutory interpretation? The decisions that you have read in this chapter suggest several possibilities. Courts should discern the meaning of a statute based solely on the text. Courts should ascertain the meaning of a statute based on the intent of the legislature or purpose of the statute, as reflected not only in the text but also other sources such as legislative history or statutory context. Courts should interpret statutes in light of changed circumstances.

These aims are associated with different theories of statutory interpretation. Theories of statutory interpretation reflect views of how courts should interpret statutes. The different theories rest on different conceptions of judicial process, the legislative process, and even the constitutional structure. The theories also require courts to consider or exclude different tools of statutory interpretation. For example, if the aim of statutory interpretation is to discern the meaning of the statute based on its text alone, then other evidence of legislative intent will have no relevance.

As you can gather, the Supreme Court has not settled on a single theory of statutory interpretation. Some justices have been vocal advocates of certain theories, and some provide clues as to their preferred method in particular cases. But there is no unifying theory of statutory interpretation at the Court or among lower courts. Nor do legal scholars agree. The academic debate over the best theory of statutory interpretation is as alive today as ever.

Lawyers benefit from understanding the theories of statutory interpretation, although few opportunities arise to expressly invoke a theory in brief writing or oral argument. In general, the theories provide a "behind-the-scenes" view of statutory interpretation by courts. Most judges will consider all of the tools, roughly in the order that we have presented them, but not all are equally persuasive to every judge. If you know which theory a particular judge espouses, you can predict which arguments are most likely to persuade that judge.

For a quick illustration of the different theories, presented roughly in the order in which they appeared historically, consider the following:

> I say to you, "Go to Starbucks and get me some coffee." You are now standing in front of the barista who asks for your order. Your eyes dilate as you picture the combinations for following my instructions: Did I want regular coffee? If so, mild or bold? Room for milk? Which size? What if I wanted something altogether different: An espresso, a latte, a macchiato? Iced coffee?

Intentionalism: *The intent of the legislature.* What did I mean by "coffee?" What do I normally order when I go to Starbucks at this time of day?

Purposivism: *The problem that the legislature sought to address.* For what purpose did I actually want coffee? To start my morning or in place of an afternoon sweet?

Legal Process Purposivism: *The purpose that a reasonable legislature would reasonably pursue.* Why would a reasonable person reasonably want coffee under the circumstances?

Imaginative Reconstruction: *The intent of the legislature with respect to an issue or aspect that it did not consider.* As it happens, Starbucks has no coffee available when you reach the counter because one of its machines is down and the other is still brewing. What else would I want? Hot tea? Ice water? A cookie? Nothing?

Textualism: *The ordinary meaning of words.* What does "coffee" typically mean? In this complex world, does an unadorned request for "coffee" still mean a cup of Joe?[3]

Dynamic Interpretation: *The meaning in light of changed circumstances.* Assume that this is a standing order, but suddenly coffee prices skyrocket to new levels because fair trade negotiations with the bean growers break down. Do I still want coffee?

---

3. The origin of this phrase is contested, but perhaps the most prominent is: "Josephus Daniels (1862-1948) was appointed Secretary of the U.S. Navy by President Woodrow Wilson in 1913. Among his numerous reforms of the Navy was the abolition of the officers' wine mess. From that time on, the strongest drink aboard navy ships was coffee and over the years, a cup of coffee became known as 'a cup of Joe.'" *See* http://www.answerbag.com/q_view/15444.

1. Intentionalism

Professor William Eskridge provides a classic formulation of intentionalism:

> Intentionalism . . . directs the interpreter to discover or replicate the legislature's orig-
> inal intent as the answer to an interpretive question. Anglo-American scholars from
> early modern times to the present have argued that original intent is and should be
> the cornerstone of statutory interpretation. Intentionalism is in some respects a natural
> way to view statutory interpretation in a representative democracy. If the legislature is
> the primary lawmaker and interpreters are its agents, then requiring interpreters to
> follow the legislature's intentions constrains their choices and advances democracy by
> carrying out the will of the elected legislators.

WILLIAM N. ESKRIDGE, JR., DYNAMIC STATUTORY INTERPRETATION 14 (1994). To
reiterate the important points, intentionalism directs courts to ascertain
statutory meaning by looking at "the legislature's original intent," and the
normative justification for intentionalism is legislative supremacy or democracy itself: courts should act as faithful agents of Congress because Congress
is the primary lawmaker in a representative democracy.

Intentionalism has many proponents among scholars and judges.
Eskridge describes the academic pedigree. But courts, with too many
instances to cite, routinely refer to legislative intent as the touchstone of
statutory interpretation. Perhaps the best-known contemporary proponent
is now-retired Justice Stevens.

We have shown you how courts ascertain legislative intent in our tools
section. As a reminder, the text of a statute is often the best indication of legislative intent: Congress wrote what it meant. In some cases, Congress may
have spoken imprecisely, as a result of inadvertence or carelessness. Words
often introduce ambiguities, even when the author thinks she is expressing
herself clearly. Intentionalists, therefore, will look to the context and the
legislative history of the statute for assistance or confirmation. The hardest
cases arise when the legislative history contradicts a literal reading of the
text. Under such circumstances, the intentionalist must determine which
she thinks best reflects legislative intent.

Intentionalism has been subject to many critiques. To the extent intentionalism directs courts to rely upon legislative history, it has run headlong
into all the critiques of that practice. For example, as we have discussed
judges can find support for their preferred interpretation in the various
legislative statements surrounding a statute. Judicial reliance on legislative
history is subject to a host of other critiques, which are mainly associated
with textualism. We discuss those critiques along with that theory later in
this chapter. Here we focus on the more broad-based theoretical critiques
of intentionalism.

a. What Does Intent Mean?

What kind of mental plans, aims, or expectations matter? Is it the expectation about how the law will specifically apply or an intention as to the
achievement of a general goal? Even this apparently subtle distinction can

make an important difference in how intentionalism operates. If intentionalism aims to implement the enacting legislature's expectations as to the specific application of a statute, then, for instance, a law enacted to prohibit "discrimination" in employment might be read to prohibit only racial discrimination — not gender discrimination — if the enacting legislature's own expectations were that the statute would apply only to racial discrimination. By contrast, if intentionalism aims to implement the general aim or principle of the legislation, then the same statute might also be read to prohibit gender discrimination in employment. Which sort of intention should matter? For an elaboration of this distinction, see, for example, RONALD DWORKIN, LAW'S EMPIRE 321-24 (1986). Perhaps purposivism, which we describe below, answers these questions by saying that implementing the general aim rather than the specific application should be the focus of statutory interpretation. But then how do we choose between intentionalism and purposivism, either in general or in a particular case?

b. Whose Intent Is Relevant?

Few statutes are enacted with unanimous approval. Does the "intent of Congress" refer to the intent of all those voting in favor of the legislation, the majority necessary for the approval of the legislation, the majority plus the President, the legislation's sponsors, the sponsoring committee, or some other set of individuals? What about the views of the citizens supporting its passage? The group to whom a court looks to discern legislative intent would likely make a large difference to what the court ends up finding. Thinking back to the Motor Vehicle Safety Act, how might a court find a different legislative intent depending on whose intent counted? To the extent that intentionalism aims to be a theory grounded in the actual intent of a body, it requires taking some view on whose intent counts.

c. Is Collective Intent Coherent?

Consider the following classic challenge to intentionalism by Max Radin:

It has frequently been declared that the most approved method is to discover the intent of the legislator. Did the legislator in establishing this determinable have a series of pictures in mind, one of which was this particular determinate? On this transparent and absurd fiction it ought not to be necessary to dwell.

It is clearly enough an illegitimate transference to law of concepts proper enough in literature and theology. The least reflection makes clear that the law maker . . . does not exist, and only worse confusion follows when in his place there are substituted the members of the legislature as a body. A legislature certainly has no intention whatever in connection with words which some two or three men drafted, which a considerable number rejected, and in regard to which many of the approving majority might have had, and often demonstrably did have, different ideas and beliefs.

That the intention of the legislature is undiscoverable in any real sense is almost an immediate inference from a statement of the proposition. The chances that of several hundred men each will have exactly the same determinate situations in mind as possible reductions of a given determinable, are infinitesimally small. The chance is still smaller that a given determinate, the litigated issue, will not only be within the minds of all these men but will be certain to be selected by all of them as the present limit to which the determinable should be narrowed. In an extreme case, it might be that we could learn all that was in the mind of the draftsman, or of a committee of half a dozen men who completely approved of every word. But when this draft is submitted to the legislature and at once accepted without a dissentient voice and without debate, what have we then learned of the intentions of the four or five hundred approvers? Even if the contents of the minds of the legislature were uniform, we have no means of knowing that content except by the external utterances or behavior of these hundreds of men, and in almost every case the only external act is the extremely ambiguous one of acquiescence, which may be motivated in literally hundreds of ways, and which by itself indicates little or nothing of the pictures which the statutory descriptions imply. It is not impossible that this knowledge could be obtained. But how probable it is, even venturesome mathematicians will scarcely undertake to compute.

Max Radin, *Statutory Interpretation*, 43 HARV. L. REV. 863, 870-71 (1930).

Social choice theory gives Radin's critique a modern cast. Arrow's theorem, which we introduced in Chapter 3, demonstrates the point through the concept of vote cycling. Rather than reflecting a collective intent, statutes reflect the sequence in which multi-member groups consider multiple alternatives — and in particular, the point at which the cycling is artificially stopped. How deeply do the results of Arrow's theorem undermine the basis for examining legislative intent?

Professor Andrei Marmor offers perhaps the most sophisticated contemporary defense of intentionalism. He responds to the claim that a collective intent is incoherent:

It is sometimes embarrassingly difficult to answer the question of just whose intentions count. In such cases . . . the appropriate conclusion should be that the legislature had no particular intention with respect to the issues bearing on the case before the court. But it would be a great distortion to maintain that this is always the case. Suggesting that there are never, or almost never, cases where the majority of legislators share a certain intention vis-à-vis a law they enacted would render the phenomenon of legislation a rather mysterious achievement. After all, legislation is a complex political action which strives to bring about a certain change in the normative fabric of the law. It is the kind of action which is done with a purpose in sight, striving to achieve something. The fact that legislation in legislative assemblies is a complex and concerted action involving elaborate procedures does not undermine this simple fact. On the contrary: Unless we assume that the legislators have a pretty good sense of what it is they strive to achieve by enacting a law, it would be very difficult to understand how they manage to achieve legislation at all.

ANDREI MARMOR, INTERPRETATION AND LEGAL THEORY 126 (2d ed. 2005). Marmor also points out that we frequently ascribe a shared intention to a group. For instance, "'The 'Red Sox' are desperate to win tomorrow's game.'; 'The Palestinians want to have a state of their own.'; 'The Dada movement strove to challenge some of the most established conventions of European art.', etc. In such cases, what we basically say is that a certain intention or aspiration or such is shared by all, or perhaps most, members of a certain group of people." *Id.* at 124. *See also* Robert A. Katzmann, *Statutes*, 87

N.Y.U. L. REV. 637, 667 (2012) ("Just as intentions are attributed to other large entities—such as local governments, trade associations, and businesses—so too do linguistic protocols, every day mores, and context facilitate an inquiry into what Congress intended to do when statutory text is vague or ambiguous.").

Do you think this mounts a sufficient defense of the coherence of a collective (in the sense of shared) intention? Is "intention or aspiration" better regarded as "purpose"? *See* Stephen G. Breyer, *On the Uses of Legislative History*, 65 S. CAL. L. REV. 845, 865 (1992) (describing the shared intention of the legislature as purpose). We will have more to say below on the relationship between intent and purpose.

d. Does Intent Reflect More Than Legislative Self-Interest?

Public choice theory, which we also described in Chapter 3, suggests that legislators have no intent apart from the desire to get reelected. Thus, statutes are "sold" to the highest bidder—the group that promises to best support the reelection efforts of legislators, through campaign contributions or votes. *See, e.g.*, DANIEL A. FARBER & PHILIP P. FRICKEY, LAW AND PUBLIC CHOICE: A CRITICAL INTRODUCTION (1991). Because the words of the statute reflect the minimum necessary to get the "deal" done, some argue that they should be read for what they say and no more. *See* Frank H. Easterbrook, *Statutes' Domains*, 50 U. CHI. L. REV. 533, 547-48 (1983). Others simply have argued that the search for a meaningful or public-interested intent is fruitless.

What can be said of this view of the legislative process? Former Chief Judge Mikva of the U.S. Court of Appeals for the District of Columbia Circuit, who before that served as a member of Congress and after that as White House Counsel, is often cited as reflecting an alternative perspective:

> The politicians and other people I have known in public life just do not fit the "rent-seeking" egoist model that the public choice theorists offer. . . . Not even my five terms in the Illinois state legislature—that last vestige of democracy in the "raw"—nor my five terms in the United States Congress, prepared me for the villains of the public choice literature.

Abner J. Mikva, *Foreword*, 74 VA. L. REV. 167, 167 (1988).

Justice Breyer, who early in his career was a staffer to Senator Edward M. Kennedy, echoed this sentiment and added:

> [O]ne should recall that legislative history is a *judicial* tool, one judges use to resolve difficult problems of judicial interpretation. It can be justified, at least in part, by its ability to help judges interpret statutes, in a manner that makes sense and that will produce a workable set of laws. If judicial use of legislative history achieves this kind of result, courts might use it as part of their overarching interpretive task of producing a coherent and relatively consistent body of statutory law, even were the "rational member of Congress" a pure fiction, made up out of whole cloth.

Stephen G. Breyer, *On the Uses of Legislative History in Interpreting Statutes*, 65 S. CAL. L. REV. 845, 867 (1992). Which view is more accurate?

e. Does Intent Constitute Law?

Another conventional challenge is that intentionalism confuses the intentions of the lawmaker with the law itself. Max Radin writes that even if the intention of the legislature were discoverable,

> [i]t would be powerless to bind us. What gives the intention of the legislature obligating force? . . . [B]ut in law, the specific individuals who make up the legislature are men to whom a specialized function has been temporarily assigned. That function is not to impose their will even within limits on their fellow-citizens, but to "pass statutes," which is a fairly precise operation. That is, they make statements in general terms of undesirable and desirable situations, from which flow certain results. As a rule, the statements must be made in the words of a specified language. . . . A statute which presented a photograph of two automobiles and printed the legend beneath it that drivers who get into the situation pictured above would be prosecuted would not be a statute, although intention would be no less easily, and perhaps more easily, discoverable in this way than in set words. When the legislature has uttered the words of a statute, it is *functus officio,* not because of the Montesquieuan separation of powers, but because that is what legislating means.

Radin, *Statutory Interpretation,* 43 HARV. L. REV. at 871.

Does intentionalism have a response to this charge that it is premised on a fundamental category error? Does intentionalism actually treat intent as law?

f. May Intent Trump Text?

The *Holy Trinity* case, which you read at the beginning of this chapter, is infamous in part because the Supreme Court has been understood as elevating legislative intent over plain meaning. As you may recall, the Court conceded that the importation of ministers was within the "letter" of the statute that prohibited the importation of laborers. Yet the Court rejected the plain meaning argument as inconsistent with the "spirit" of the statute as found in other provisions of the statute and the legislative history. It's easy to be an intentionalist when all indications of legislative intent point in the same direction. But intentionalists really show their mettle when they disregard plain meaning in favor of a more contextual analysis. Is intentionalism legitimate only when the statutory language has no plain meaning as determined solely through application of textual tools, such as canons of construction? What about to demonstrate that the language *is* ambiguous — that is, the meaning is not as "plain" as it seems?

2. Purposivism and Legal Process Purposivism

Purposivism directs courts to ascertain the meaning of a statute by examining the evil that the legislature sought to address. The early variants of purposivism developed as a specification or outgrowth of intentionalism.

While intentionalism asks "what specifically did Congress mean when it used this language?," purposivism asks "what generally was Congress seeking to accomplish when it used this language?" *See* Michael Herz, *Purposivism and Institutional Competence in Statutory Interpretation*, 2009 MICH. ST. L. REV. 89, 93. In some cases, the intentionalist and purposivist inquiries are difficult to distinguish. It may be helpful to think about intentionalism and purposivism as operating at different levels of generality. Rather than directing courts to search for the intent of the legislature as to the specific meaning of a word or phrase, it instructs courts to interpret a word or phrase in line with the general purpose of the statute or a provision within a statute. Courts consult the same tools of statutory interpretation under both theories. As a result, purposivism is subject to many of the same critiques as intentionalism. Is judicial reliance on legislative history problematic? Is the notion of a single purpose or even a single set of purposes discernible and coherent and separate from legislative self-interest?

In the 1950s, Henry Hart and Albert Sacks, in their famous materials entitled *The Legal Process*, reformulated purposivism to address some of these concerns. As reconceived by Hart and Sacks, the purposive approach to statutory interpretation has four basic elements: the court is to (1) "[d]ecide what purpose ought to be attributed to the statute and any subordinate provision of it," (2) "[i]nterpret the words of the statute immediately in question so as to carry out [that] purpose as best it can," making sure (3) not to give the words "a meaning they will not bear," and finally, (4) not to "violate any established policy of clear statement." HENRY M. HART, JR. & ALBERT M. SACKS, THE LEGAL PROCESS: BASIC PROBLEMS IN THE MAKING AND APPLICATION OF THE LAW 1374 (William N. Eskridge, Jr. & Philip P. Frickey eds., 1994). In this multi-step interpretive process, the aim of the interpretation is to construe the statute to carry out its purpose or purposes as best as possible. In this process, the text of the statute serves a dual role. The text of the statute is a primary ground for attributing purpose to the statute in this first interpretive step. But it also plays a role in the third step; the prospective construction must be checked against the text to ensure that it does not ascribe meaning to the words that is not linguistically permissible. Finally, the court must check the interpretation against established background policies, such as criminalizing conduct not thought to be morally blameworthy or impinging on constitutionally protected values. *See id.* at 1376-77. If the interpretation is not consistent with such a policy, the legislation must, according to Hart and Sacks, "speak with more than [the] ordinary clearness" on the issue. *Id.*

Hart and Sacks readily acknowledge that the most important and controversial element of their approach to statutory interpretation is the first step, specifying how a court is to attribute purpose to a statute or particular provisions within it. Here is Hart and Sacks' classic summary of their guidance on "attributing purpose."

Henry M. Hart, Jr. & Albert M. Sacks, The Legal Process: Basic Problems in the Making and Application of the Law

1374-80 (William N. Eskridge, Jr. & Philip P. Frickey eds., 1994)

THE ATTRIBUTION OF PURPOSE

1. Enacted statements of purpose

A formally enacted statement of purpose in a statute should be accepted by the court if it appears to have been designed to serve as a guide to interpretation, is consistent with the words and context of the statute, and is relevant to the question of meaning at issue.

In all other situations, the purpose of a statute has in some degree to be inferred.

2. Inferring purpose: the nature of the problem

In drawing such inferences the court needs to be aware that the concept of purpose is not simple.

(a) Purposes may be shaped with differing degrees of definiteness.

The definiteness may be such that resolution of a doubt about purpose resolves, without more, a question of specific application. . . .

Or a purpose may be deliberately formulated with great generality, openly contemplating the exercise of further judgment by the interpreter even after he has fully grasped the legislature's thought. *E.g.*, the direction to the Federal Trade Commission to prevent, in certain ways, "unfair methods of competition in commerce."

(b) Purposes, moreover, may exist in hierarchies or constellations. *E.g.* (to give a very simple illustration), to do *this* only so far as possible without doing *that*.

(c) One form of such a constellation or relationship is invariable in the law and of immense importance. The purpose of a statute must always be treated as including not only an immediate purpose or group of related purposes but a larger and subtler purpose as to how the particular statute is to be fitted into the legal system as a whole.

. . .

3. Inferring purpose: the technique

In determining the more immediate purpose which ought to be attributed to a statute, and to any subordinate provision of it which may be involved, a court should try to put itself in imagination in the position of the legislature which enacted the measure.

The court, however, should not do this in the mood of a cynical political observer, taking account of all the short-run currents of political expedience that swirl around any legislative session.

It should assume, unless the contrary unmistakably appears, that the legislature was made up of reasonable persons pursuing reasonable purposes reasonably.

It should presume conclusively that these persons, whether or not entertaining concepts of reasonableness shared by the court, were trying responsibly and in good faith to discharge their constitutional powers and duties.

The court should then proceed to do, in substance, just what Lord Coke said it should do in *Heydon's Case* [Exchequer, 1584, 76 Eng. Rep. 637]. The gist of this approach is to infer purpose by comparing the new law with the old. Why would reasonable men, confronted with the law as it was, have enacted this new law to replace it? Answering this question, as Lord Coke said, calls for a close look at the "mischief" thought to inhere in the old law and at "the true reason of the remedy" provided by the statute for it.

The most reliable guides to an answer will be found in the instances of unquestioned application of the statute. Even in the case of a new statute there almost invariably *are* such instances, in which, because of the perfect fit of words and context, the meaning seems unmistakable.

Once these points of reference are established, they throw a double light. The purposes necessarily implied in them illuminate facets of the general purpose. At the same time they provide a basis for reasoning by analogy to the disputed application in hand. *E.g.,* why would the legislature distinguish, for purposes of punishment, between an escaper serving only a single sentence and one serving the first of several? What is crucial here is the realization that law is being made, and that law is not supposed to be irrational.

4. Inferring purpose: aids from the context

The whole context of a statute may be examined in aid of its interpretation, and should be whenever substantial doubt about its meaning exists in the interpreter's mind, or is suggested by him.

Not only the state of the law immediately before enactment but the course of its prior development is relevant.

The court may draw on general public knowledge of what was considered to be the mischief that needed remedying.

Formal public announcements of those concerned with the preparation or advocacy of the measure may be freely consulted. *E.g.,* messages of the chief executive, reports of commissions, and the like.

The internal legislative history of the measure (that is, its history from the filing of the bill to enactment) may be examined, if this was reduced to writing officially and contemporaneously. But in the use which is made of this material two closely related limitations should be scrupulously observed.

First.   The history should be examined for the light it throws on *general purpose*. Evidence of specific intention with respect to particular applications is competent only to the extent that the particular applications illuminate the general purpose and are consistent with other evidence of it.

Second.   Effect should not be given to evidence from the internal legislative history if the result would be to contradict a purpose otherwise indicated and to yield an interpretation disadvantageous to private persons who had no reasonable means of access to the history.

5. Inferring purpose: post-enactment aids

The judicial, administrative, and popular construction of a statute, subsequent to its enactment, are all relevant in attributing a purpose to it.

The court's own prior interpretations of a statute in related applications should be accepted, on the principle of *stare decisis*, unless they are manifestly out of accord with other indications of purpose. Once these applications are treated as fixed, they serve as points of reference for juristic thinking in the same fashion as verbally clear applications in the case of a new statute.

An administrative or popular construction is relevant for different reasons. Such a construction affords weighty evidence that the words *may* bear the meaning involved. In the absence of reasons of self-interest or the like for discounting the construction, it is persuasive evidence that the meaning is a natural one. Considerations of the stability of transactions and of existing understandings counsel in favor of its acceptance, if possible. In cases where the construction has been widely accepted and consistently adhered, it may be said to fix the meaning — to *be* the meaning which experience has demonstrated the words to bear.

6. Inferring purpose: presumptions

The court's last resort, when doubt about the immediate purpose of a statute remains, is resort to an appropriate presumption drawn from some general policy of the law.

This is likely to be its only resort when the question concerns more nearly ultimate policy, or the mode of fitting the statute into the general fabric of the law.

Reflection about these presumptions is the most important task in the development of a workable and working theory of statutory interpretation.

Notes and Questions

1. What are the primary tools that Hart and Sacks direct courts to use when attributing purpose or purposes to a statute? Will the enacted text of the statute ever be the primary or even near-exclusive basis for attributing purpose? (Consider, for instance, Hart and Sacks' comments on enacted statements of purpose.) More generally, how does the text figure into discerning the statute's purpose or purposes?

2. Try to list all the sources other than enacted statutory text from which the court is to infer purpose. Some pertain to the context at the time of the statute's enactment, like legislative history and the prior law. But they also include post-enactment sources, such as established interpretations of the statutes by courts or agencies. Given that the sources for inferring purpose include the post-enactment sources, how would you characterize the difference between Hart and Sacks' approach and intentionalism (or even more intentionalist versions of purposivism)? What is the aim of interpretation for Hart and Sacks? How might their approach lead to different results than intentionalism? In that regard, compare Hart and Sacks' comment on the use of legislative history to the use of legislative history for intentionalism.

3. You will notice above that under "3. Inferring purpose: the technique," Hart and Sacks counsel that in inferring purpose, the court "should assume, unless evidence to the contrary unmistakably appears, that the legislature was made up of reasonable persons pursuing reasonable purposes reasonably." This advice is the most famous language from their expansive book. Critics have sometimes taken this as shorthand for their entire approach to statutory interpretation. Is that accurate? Critics also challenge Hart and Sacks' theory as based on an unrealistic or naïve view of the legislature. The legislature, these critics assert, pursues its "rational" interests, brokering deals that benefit its constituents or powerful interest groups. Do Hart and Sacks believe that the reasonable legislature accurately describes the legislature, or do they have different reasons for suggesting that courts "treat" the legislatures as public-regarding and reasonable?

4. Others argue that there simply are no knowable purposes behind much legislation. In this vein, Richard Posner writes that "the spectrum of respectable opinion on political and social questions has widened so enormously that even if we could assume that legislators intended to bring about reasonable results in all cases, the assumption would not generate specific legal concepts." Richard A. Posner, *Legal Formalism, Legal Realism, and the Interpretation of Statutes and the Constitution*, 37 CASE W. RES. L. REV. 179, 193 (1986). Some critics extend the point further, arguing that Hart and Sacks' approach is so demanding on judges — it requires them to make numerous synthetic judgments from a variety of sources, ranging from text, the policy context at the time of enactment, background values, and policies — that it creates a systematic risk of error, or worse makes it all the harder for even a judge operating in good faith to tell the line between her own policy positions and those enforced by the law. Is Legal Process purposivism any less constraining than other theories? How could we tell? Toward the end of the chapter, we present an empirical analysis of the constraints that interpretive methods impose of judicial ideology. *See* FRANK B. CROSS, THE THEORY AND PRACTICE OF STATUTORY INTERPRETATION (2009).

3. Imaginative Reconstruction

Imaginative reconstruction is a theory of statutory interpretation that Judge Richard Posner on the U.S. Court of Appeals for the Seventh Circuit has brought to the fore. In his view, it is often best to admit that Congress did not even think about a particular issue. Take *Holy Trinity* as an example. In that case, the enacting Congress likely did not consider whether the statute addressing the importation of laborers applied to pastors. Under such circumstances, what is gained by acting as though an actual intent or purpose can resolve the question? Why not simply inquire how Congress would have treated pastors, given its proclivities on issues that the statute does address? Imaginative reconstruction asks courts to place themselves in the shoes of the enacting Congress.

Richard A. Posner, Statutory Interpretation in the Classroom and in the Courtroom

50 U. Chi. L. Rev. 800, 817-22 (1983)

I offer not a substitute algorithm but only an attitude, or maybe a slogan, and leave it to the reader to choose between what seems to me to be the delusive rigor of the canons and the guidance offered by my suggested approach. I suggest that the task for the judge called upon to interpret a statute is best described as one of imaginative reconstruction. The judge should try to think his way as best he can into the minds of the enacting legislators and imagine how they would have wanted the statute applied to the case at bar.

Now it is easy to ridicule this approach by saying that judges do not have the requisite imagination and that what they will do in practice is assume that the legislators were people just like themselves, so that statutory construction will consist of the judge's voting his own preferences and ascribing them to the statute's draftsmen. But the irresponsible judge will twist any approach to yield the outcomes that he desires and the stupid judge will do the same thing unconsciously. If you assume a judge who will try with the aid of a reasonable intelligence to put himself in the place of the enacting legislators, then I believe he will do better if he follows my suggested approach than if he tries to apply the canons.

The judge who follows this approach will be looking at the usual things that the intelligent literature on statutory construction tells him to look at such as the language and apparent purpose of the statute, its background and structure, its legislative history (especially the committee reports and the floor statements of the sponsors), and the bearing of related statutes. But he will also be looking at two slightly less obvious factors. One is the values and attitudes, so far as they are known today, of the period in which the legislation was enacted. It would be foolish to ascribe to legislators of the 1930's or the 1960's and early 1970's the skepticism regarding the size of government and the efficacy of regulation that is widespread today, or to impute to the Congress of the 1920's the current conception of conflicts of interest. It is not the judge's job to keep a statute up to date in the sense of making it reflect contemporary values; it is his job to imagine as best he can how the legislators who enacted the statute would have wanted it applied to situations that they did not foresee.

Second, and in some tension with the first point, the judge will be alert to any sign of legislative intent regarding the freedom with which he should exercise his interpretive function. Sometimes a statute will state whether it is to be broadly or narrowly construed; more often the structure and language of the statute will supply a clue. If the legislature enacts into statute law a common law concept, as Congress did when it forbade agreements in "restraint of trade" in the Sherman Act, that is a clue that the courts are to interpret the statute with the freedom with which they would construe and apply a common law principle in which event the values of the framers may not be controlling after all.

The opposite extreme is a statute that sets out its requirements with some specificity, especially against a background of dissatisfaction with judicial handling of the same subject under a previous statute or the common law (much federal labor and regulatory legislation is of this character). Here it is probable that the legislature does not want the courts to paint with a broad brush in adapting the legislation to the unforeseeable future. The Constitution contains several such provisions — for example, the provision that the President must be thirty-five years old. This provision does not invite construction; it does not invite a court to recast the provision so that it reads, "the President must be either thirty-five or mature." There is nothing the court could point to that would justify such an interpretation as consistent with the framers' intent. It is not that the words are plain; it is that the words, read in context as words must always be read in order to yield meaning, do not authorize any interpretation except the obvious one.

The approach I have sketched a word used advisedly in this part of the paper has obvious affinities with the "attribution of purpose" approach of Hart and Sacks, the antecedents of which go back almost 400 years. But I should like to stress one difference between my approach and theirs. They say that in construing a statute a court "should assume, unless the contrary unmistakably appears, that the legislature was made up of reasonable persons pursuing reasonable purposes reasonably." Coupled with their earlier statement that in trying to divine the legislative will the court should ignore "short-run currents of political expedience," Hart and Sacks appear to be suggesting that the judge should ignore interest groups, popular ignorance and prejudices, and other things that deflect legislators from the single-minded pursuit of the public interest as the judge would conceive it. But to ignore these things runs the risk of attributing to legislation not the purposes reasonably inferable from the legislation itself, but the judge's own conceptions of the public interest. Hart and Sacks were writing in the wake of the New Deal, when the legislative process was widely regarded as progressive and public spirited. There is less agreement today that the motives behind most legislation are benign. That should be of no significance to the judge except to make him wary about too easily assuming a congruence between his concept of the public interest and the latent purposes of the statutes he is called on to interpret. He must not automatically assume that the legislators had the same purpose that he thinks he would have had if he had been in their shoes.

A related characteristic of the passages I have quoted from Hart and Sacks is a reluctance to recognize that many statutes are the product of compromise between opposing groups and that a compromise is quite likely not to embody a single consistent purpose. Of course there are difficulties for the judge, limited as he is to the formal materials of the legislative process the statutory text, committee reports, hearings, floor debates, earlier bills, and so forth in identifying compromise. A court should not just assume that a statute's apparent purpose is not its real purpose. But where the lines of compromise are discernible, the judge's duty is to follow them, to implement not the purposes of one group of legislators, but the compromise itself.

But what if the lines of compromise are not clear? More fundamentally, what if the judge's scrupulous search for the legislative will turns up nothing? There are of course such cases, and they have to be decided some way. It is inevitable, and therefore legitimate, for the judge in such a case to be moved by considerations that cannot be referred back to legislative purpose. These might be considerations of judicial administrability what interpretation of the statute will provide greater predictability, require less judicial factfinding, and otherwise reduce the cost and frequency of litigation under the statute or considerations drawn from some broadly based conception of the public interest. It is always possible, of course, to refer these considerations back to Congress to say that Congress would have wanted the courts, in cases where they could not figure out what interpretation would advance the substantive objectives of the statute, to adopt the "better" one, or to say à la Hart and Sacks that congressmen ought to be presumed reasonable until shown otherwise. But these methods of imputing congressional intent are artificial; and as I argued earlier, it is not healthy for the judge to conceal from himself that he is being creative when he is, as sometimes he has to be even when applying statutes. . . .

[C]ontrary to a widespread impression, strict that is, narrow construction, if perhaps a useful antidote to the school of no construction, is not a formula for ensuring fidelity to legislative intent. It is almost the opposite. It is the lineal descendant of the canon that statutes in derogation of the common law are to be strictly construed and, like that canon, was used in nineteenth-century England to emasculate social welfare legislation.

To construe a statute strictly is to limit its scope and its life span to make Congress work twice as hard to produce the same effect. The letter killeth but the spirit giveth life.

There is a story of a Vermont justice of the peace before whom a suit was brought by one farmer against another for breaking a churn. The justice took time to consider, and then said that he had looked through the statutes and could find nothing about churns, and gave judgment to the defendant.

It is not an accident that most "loose constructionists" are political liberals and most "strict constructionists" are political conservatives. The former think that modern legislation does not go far enough, the latter that it goes too far. Each school has developed interpretive techniques appropriate to its political ends. But as I said earlier, I know of no principled, nonpolitical basis for a court to adopt the view that Congress is legislating too much and ought therefore to be reined in by having its statutes construed strictly. I add now that such a view would be a form of judicial activism because it would cut down the power of the legislative branch; and at this moment in history, we do not need more judicial activism.

Notes and Questions

1. When Congress has not considered an issue, would Judge Posner say that reliance on intentionalism or purposivism is disingenuous? Is it also damaging? To answer this question, consider the practical differences between imaginative reconstruction and intentionalism or purposivism — that is, in terms of the tools upon which courts rely. Given these differences, would relying on imaginative reconstruction make a difference in certain cases?

2. Judge Posner acknowledges that imaginative reconstruction shares "affinities" with Legal Process purposivism. What are the differences as a theoretical matter? Do these differences make imaginative reconstruction preferable to Legal Process purposivism?

3. How well does imaginative reconstruction constrain judges from creating their preferred intent and reaching their preferred interpretation? How can courts be confident what Congress would have intended when drawing information about legislative intent from unrelated issues?

4. Again we ask: once we are departing from actual intent, why not allow courts to consider other factors, such as the practical consequences or real world effects of an interpretation, rather than attempting to imaginatively reconstruct legislative intent?

5. In short order, we will introduce you to dynamic interpretation. Dynamic interpretation and imaginative reconstruction are similar in that both attempt to address circumstances that Congress did not address. But they part company in a significant respect. Imaginative reconstruction, as we understand it, applies to circumstances that Congress failed to address but could have addressed at the time of enactment — for example, the importation of pastors, as in *Holy Trinity*. Dynamic interpretation applies to circumstances that have changed since the time of enactment — for example, the sea change in attitudes and laws concerning racial discrimination in education. Congress could not have fully appreciated the change when enacting §501(c)(3) of the tax code in 1954 because it was still unfolding. A court cannot fairly determine what Congress would have intended if doing so would require replacing all the core beliefs of its members. Dynamic interpretation, therefore, asks courts how best to interpret the statute in light of changed circumstances.

4. Textualism and New Textualism

Textualism directs courts to discern the ordinary meaning of the text in context. The "ordinary meaning" is the meaning that a reasonable reader would discern for the text, and "in context" requires viewing the text as part of the whole body of law rather than in isolation. Textualists find the ordinary meaning of statutory text through application of the textual tools that we described above, including dictionaries and canons. Textualists can recognize a technical meaning when industry customs or reference books establish one, though they may have a preference for the literal meaning. *See, e.g.*, Zuni Public School Dist. No. 89 v. Department of Education, 550 U.S. 81, 112-14 (2007) (Scalia, J., dissenting).

The defining feature of textualism is that, in its strongest form, it directs courts to stop with the text of the statute. Thus, courts do not engage into a broader search for legislative intent, even as confirmation of their textual analysis. To the extent that textualists are interested in legislative intent, it is only insofar as the text manifests that intent. Related, textualists generally reject the use of legislative history as an "authoritative" source for discerning statutory meaning. As detailed below, Justice Scalia, the most ardent textualist on the Supreme Court, refuses to join the part of any opinion that references legislative history, even if he agrees with the conclusion. Some espouse a weaker version of textualism, which regards text as the best indication of statutory meaning. On this view, a clear textual reading controls and cannot be subverted by contrary indications of legislative intent.

Although textualism has long existed, it has gained new life in recent years courtesy of several prominent judges and academics. Modern accounts often refer to "new textualism," by which they mean the version that has emerged in the last three decades or so. Justice Scalia, who we just mentioned, is the figure most responsible for shifting the debate about statutory interpretation toward textualism. His writings demonstrate the justifications for textualism as well as the corresponding criticisms of other theories, most notably intentionalism and purposivism.

The first point concerns the proper aim of statutory interpretation. For Justice Scalia, courts are obligated to determine the meaning of *the statute* based on the text. Part of the reason is constitutional. Only the text is enacted through the legislative process, and therefore, only the text constitutes law. Part of the reason is normative. Courts must give effect to the text as written or else their views dominate those of Congress. Note that this is precisely the same "legislative supremacy" or "representative democracy" justification that intentionalists and purposivists offer in support of their theories. The disagreement is whether a focus on the text alone or other sources better advances the goals of faithful agent theory. Textualists believe that the intent of the legislature as purportedly revealed in legislative history is far too subjective a basis on which to base an interpretation.

Consider the following comment from Justice Scalia:

> [D]espite frequent statements to the contrary, we do not really look for subjective legislative intent. We look for a sort of "objective" intent — the intent that a reasonable person would gather from the text of the law, placed alongside the remainder of the *corpus juris*. As Bishop's old treatise nicely put it, elaborating upon the usual formulation: "[T]he primary object of all rules for interpreting statutes is to ascertain the legislative intent;

or, exactly the meaning which the subject is authorized to understand the legislature intended." And the reason we adopt this objectified version is, I think, that it is simply incompatible with democratic government, or indeed, even with fair government, to have the meaning of a law determined by what the lawgiver meant, rather than by what the lawgiver promulgated. That seems to me one step worse than the trick the emperor Nero was said to engage in: posting edicts high up on the pillars, so that they could not easily be read. Government by unexpressed intent is similarly tyrannical. . . .

In reality, however, if one accepts the principle that the object of judicial interpretation is to determine the intent of the legislature, being bound by genuine by unexpressed legislative intent rather than the law is only the *theoretical* threat. The practical threat is that, under the guise or even the self-delusion of pursuing unexpressed legislative intents, common-law judges will in fact pursue their own objective desires, extending their lawmaking proclivities from the common law to the statutory field. When you are told to decide, not on the basis of what the legislature said, but on the basis of what it meant, and are assured that there is no necessary connection between the two, your best shot at figuring out what the legislature meant is to ask yourself what a wise and intelligent person should have meant; and that will surely bring you to the conclusion that the law means what you think it ought to mean—which is precisely how judges decide things under the common law. . . .

Textualism should not be confused with so-called strict constructionism, a degraded form of textualism that brings the whole philosophy into disrepute. . . . A text should not be construed strictly, and it should not be construed leniently; it should be construed reasonably, to contain all that it fairly means. . . . But while a good textualist is not a literalist, neither is he a nihilist. Words have a limited range of meaning, and no interpretation that goes beyond that range is permissible.

ANTONIN SCALIA, A MATTER OF INTERPRETATION 18-19, 23-24 (1997).

Professor John Manning offers another justification for textualism, grounded in public choice theory and the realities of the legislative process:

> [T]extualists argue that the (often unseen) complexities of the legislative process make it meaningless to speak of "legislative intent" as distinct from the meaning conveyed by a clearly expressed statutory command. It may be true that a majority of legislators, perhaps a large majority, would sometimes prefer statutory results different from those required by the statutory text. But legislative preferences do not pass unfiltered into legislation; they are distilled through a carefully designed process that requires legislation to clear several distinct institutions, numerous veto gates, the threat of a Senate filibuster, and countless other procedural devices that temper unchecked majoritarianism. Hence, the precise lines drawn by any statute may reflect unrecorded compromises among interest groups, unknowable strategic behavior, or even an implicit legislative decision to forgo costly bargaining over greater textual precision. So understood, the legislative process is simply too complex and too opaque to permit judges to get inside Congress's "mind." Textualists therefore believe that the only safe course for a faithful agent is to enforce the clear terms of the statutes that have emerged from that process.

John F. Manning, *The Absurdity Doctrine*, 116 HARV. L. REV. 2387, 2390 (2003).

Scholars and judges have debated virtually all of the central tenets of textualism. Consider the following.

a. Is Textualism Constitutionally Compelled?

Some textualists claim that statutory text is the only permissible source of statutory meaning because the text, and only the text, is enacted through the constitutionally required process of bicameralism and presentment to the President. This contention, if correct, is devastating to the other theories. These theories are not merely inferior but foreclosed. But intentionalists and purposivists do not dispute the claim that only the text is law. Rather, they maintain that it is permissible to rely on extrinsic sources of legislative intent, such as legislative history, to ascertain the meaning of the text. *See* Stephen G. Breyer, *On the Uses of Legislative History in Interpreting Statutes*, 65 S. CAL. L. REV. 845, 862-64 (1992); William N. Eskridge, Jr., *Legislative History Values*, 66 CHI.-KENT L. REV. 365, 374-75 (1990). Do textualists have a rejoinder? They also rely on extrinsic sources, such as dictionaries and industry customs. What is the difference between these tools and other tools?

b. Is Textualism More Constraining?

Because textualism commits courts to discern statutory meaning based solely on textual analysis, some contend that it is more constraining on judges than the other theories. *See* Peter J. Smith, *New Legal Fictions*, 95 GEO. L.J. 1435, 1475 (2007) (asserting that textualists are more interested in promoting a theory of judicial restraint than anything else). Is textualism more constraining? *See* Peter J. Smith, *Textualism and Jurisdiction*, 108 COLUM. L. REV. 1883 (2008) (arguing, based on empirical study of cases involving jurisdictional statutes, that it is more constraining than other theories). If so, does the constraint come from the fact that all arguments must be based on the text, not sources like legislative history? Or does the constraint come from the character of inferences from the text the textualist finds "fair" and "reasonable"? *See* Antonin Scalia, *Judicial Deference to Administrative Interpretations of Law*, 1989 DUKE L.J. 511, 521 (noting that he finds that the text has a plain meaning relatively more often than those inclined to consult legislative history). Is textualism constraining, or are textualists more accepting of textual arguments?

Some textualists argue that their theory, if uniformly applied, would better discipline the legislative process. *See, e.g.*, Frank H. Easterbrook, *Statutes' Domain*, 50 U. CHI. L. REV. 533, 548-49 (1983). Members of Congress would know that courts would only consider the text of statutes they enact, not committee reports and other forms of legislative history. They would put all important choices in the statute itself. Would textualism work to improve the legislative process, given the difficulties of obtaining consensus on legislation? *See* Jane Schacter, *Metademocracy: The Changing Structure of Legitimacy in Statutory Interpretation*, 108 HARV. L. REV. 593, 645 (1995) (questioning whether Congress can be induced to write better statutes). Are more specific statutes always better statutes? *See* Daniel J. Meltzer, *The Supreme Court's Judicial Passivity*, 2002 SUP. CT. REV. 343, 396 ("[N]ot only is it unrealistic to expect Congress to be able to resolve all issues up front in statutory text, but there are many instances in which a congressional effort to do so is likely to be less successful than leaving matters to be worked out by judicial decision."). Is improving the legislative process the proper aim of statutory interpretation? *See* Andre Marmor, *The Immorality of Textualism*, 38 LOY. L.A. L. REV. 2063, 2072

(2005) (arguing that "it should not be the business of the courts to enlighten the legislature on how to make laws or how to make them more precise").

c. Is Textualism Distinctive?

Textualism directs courts to discern the ordinary meaning of text "in context." This directive avoids the criticism that textualism is overly literalistic and insensitive to the broader statutory landscape. *See* William N. Eskridge, Jr. & Philip P. Frickey, *Statutory Interpretation as Practical Reasoning*, 42 STAN. L. REV. 321 (1990) (offering this critique). But does it go so far as to rob textualism of its distinctiveness? That depends on what exactly "in context" entitles courts to examine. For example, are courts permitted to consider the historical or social context in which the statute was enacted? If yes, then textualism is very close to purposivism. *See* Jonathan Molot, *The Rise and Fall of Textualism*, 106 COLUM. L. REV. 1, 37-40 (2006); *see also* Caleb Nelson, *What Is Textualism?*, 91 VA. L. REV. 347, 348 (2005) (arguing that objective meaning is close to subjective meaning because "textualists construct their sense of objective meaning from what the evidence that they are willing to consider tells them about the subjective intent of the enacting legislature"). Textualists still eschew reliance on legislative history and, more generally, seek "semantic context" rather than "policy context." John F. Manning, *What Divides Textualists from Purposivists?*, 106 COLUM. L. REV. 70, 92-93 (2006); John F. Manning, *Textualism and Legislative Intent*, 91 VA. L. REV. 419, 423-24 (2005) (arguing that objectified intent is different from subjective intent). Is this difference a semantic or substantial one? *See* Molot, *supra* (noting that legislative history is not often relevant to determining context); Nelson, *supra*, at 348-49 (noting that even in cases in with no relevant legislative history, textualists often come to the same conclusion as intentionalists); *cf.* Jonathan R. Siegel, *The Inexorable Radicalism of Textualism*, 158 U. PA. L. REV. 117 (2009) (arguing that textualism is growing more radical and more distinctive from the other theories). If textualism is not distinctive from the other theories, why take it so seriously?

d. Is Textualism Internally Consistent?

Textualists rely on some tools that do not fit well with their overarching theory. As previously mentioned, textualists do not confine themselves to the text itself; they consider extrinsic tools like dictionaries and industry customs. At least those are sources of meaning how words are used in the relevant context or community. What about tools that determine how words *should be* understood, as a normative matter, such as substantive canons? Why allow some normative values but not others to influence statutory interpretation? Are the ones on which courts generally rely sufficiently well rooted in our democratic tradition? Finally, what about the doctrines of avoiding absurd results and correcting scrivener's errors? These are also long held. Still, how can textualism allow courts to disregard the text in favor of what is right or what Congress really meant? Some advocates of textualism have argued that these doctrines should be abandoned. *See* John C. Nagle, *Textualism's Exceptions, Issues in Legal Scholarship,* available at http://www .bepress.com/ils/iss3/art15 (arguing that absurd results and scrivener's error doctrines "conflict with the theoretical argument for textualism"); John F. Manning, *The Absurdity Doctrine,* 116 HARV. L. REV. 2387, 2390 (2003) (arguing that the absurd results doctrine no longer reflects the realities of legislative behavior and therefore does not fit within textualism); *see also* ADRIAN VERMEULE, JUDGING UNDER UNCERTAINTY: AN INSTITUTIONAL THEORY OF LEGAL INTERPRETATION 192-205 (2006) (arguing, as part of a broader theory focusing on the costs and benefits of judicial statutory interpretation, that these doctrines carry costs without countervailing benefits; despite the work involved in applying them, they might lead courts astray more often than not). How much do you like textualism without these "safety valves"?

e. Is Legislative History an Impermissible Interpretive Tool?

Many of the critiques of legislative history have been fortified by the ascendance of new textualism. As we have noted previously, two questions about judicial reliance on legislative history are (1) what is the proper weight to accord different pieces of legislative history?, and (2) which pieces of legislative history are reliable indicators of legislative intent or statutory purpose? *See* Matthew C. Stephenson, *The Price of Public Action: Constitutional Doctrine and the Judicial Manipulation of Legislative Enactment Costs,* 118 YALE L.J. 2, 43-44 (2008); William N. Eskridge, Jr., *Legislative History Value,* 66 CHI.-KENT L. REV. 365, 365 (1990). Textualism raises a prior question: whether it is permissible at all for courts to consult legislative history as an aid to statutory interpretation. Textualism offers a resounding "no." The other questions never arise.

Justice Scalia has expressed his objection to judicial reliance on legislative history in numerous judicial opinions. *See, e.g.,* Green v. Bock Laundry Machine Co., 490 U.S. 504, 528 (1989) (Scalia, J., concurring in the judgment). He also has refused to join portions of opinions that discuss legislative history; numerous opinions indicate that Justice Scalia joins them except for the special portions, whether sections or footnotes, citing legislative history. *See, e.g.,* S.D. Warren Co. v. Maine Bd. of Environmental Protection, 547 U.S. 370 (2006) (Scalia, J., joining the opinion of the Court except as to Part III-C, discussing legislative history); Williams v. Taylor, 529 U.S. 362, 399 (2000) (Scalia, J., joining Justice O'Connor's opinion of the Court as to Part II except as to footnote discussing legislative history). Other justices know that if their opinions rely upon legislative history, even in a footnote, they will lose Justice Scalia's support at least for certain portions.

In his book, *A Matter of Interpretation,* Justice Scalia touches upon almost all the central issues in the legislative history debate. As you will see, his critiques of the use of legislative history are bound up with the justifications for textualism. He offers objections based on (1) the Constitution or the rule of law, (2) the reliability of legislative history as an indicator of legislative intent, (3) the way in which legislative history facilitates willful judging, (4) the cost of its use to lawyers and judges, and (5) the incentives it creates for the legislature.

Antonin Scalia, A Matter of Interpretation: Federal Courts and the Law

29-37 (1997)

Let me turn now . . . to an interpretive device whose widespread use is relatively new: legislative history, by which I mean the statements made in the floor debates, committee reports, and even committee testimony, leading up to the enactment of the legislation. My view that the objective indication of the words, rather than the intent of the legislature, is what constitutes the law leads me, of course, to the conclusion that legislative history should not be used as an authoritative indication of a statute's meaning. This was the traditional English, and the traditional American, practice. Chief Justice Taney wrote:

> In expounding this law, the judgment of the court cannot, in any degree, be influenced by the construction placed upon it by individual members of Congress in the debate which took place on its passage, nor by the motives or reasons assigned by them for supporting or opposing amendments that were offered. The law as it passed is the will of the majority of both houses, *and the only mode in which that will is spoken is in the act itself;* and we must gather their intention from the language there used, comparing it, when any ambiguity exists, with the laws upon the same subject, and looking, if necessary, to the public history of the times in which it was passed.[1]

That uncompromising view generally prevailed in this country until the present century. The movement to change it gained momentum in the late 1920s and 1930s, driven, believe it or not, by frustration with common-law judges' use of "legislative intent" and phonied-up canons to impose their own views — in those days views opposed to progressive social legislation. I quoted earlier an article by Dean Landis inveighing against such judicial usurpation. The solution he proposed was not the banishment of legislative intent as an interpretive criterion, but rather the use of legislative history to place that intent beyond manipulation.

Extensive use of legislative history in this country dates only from about the 1940s. It was still being criticized by such respected justices as Frankfurter and Jackson as recently as the 1950s. Jackson, for example, wrote in one concurrence:

> I should concur in this result more readily if the Court could reach it by analysis of the statute instead of by psychoanalysis of Congress. When we decide from legislative history, including statements of witnesses at hearings, what Congress probably had in mind, we must put ourselves in the place of a majority of Congressmen and act according to the impression we think this history should have made on them. Never having been a Congressman, I am handicapped in that weird endeavor. That process seems to me not interpretation of a statute but creation of a statute.[2]

In the past few decades, however, we have developed a legal culture in which lawyers routinely — and I do mean routinely — make no distinction

---

1. *Aldridge v. Williams*, 44 U.S. (3 How.) 9, 24 (1845) (emphasis added).
2. *United States v. Public Utils. Comm'n of Cal.*, 345 U.S. 295, 319 (1953) (Jackson, J., concurring).

between words in the text of a statute and words in its legislative history. My Court is frequently told, in briefs and in oral argument, that "Congress said thus-and-so"—when in fact what is being quoted is not the law promulgated by Congress, nor even any text endorsed by a single house of Congress, but rather the statement of a single committee of a single house, set forth in a committee report. Resort to legislative history has become so common that lawyerly wags have popularized a humorous quip inverting the oft-recited (and oft-ignored) rule as to when its use is appropriate: "One should consult the text of the statute," the joke goes, "only when the legislative history is ambiguous." Alas, that is no longer funny. Reality has overtaken parody. A few terms ago, I read a brief that *began* the legal argument with a discussion of legislative history and then continued (I am quoting it verbatim): "Unfortunately, the legislative debates are not helpful. Thus, we turn to the other guidepost in this difficult area, statutory language."[3]

As I have said, I object to the use of legislative history on principle, since I reject intent of the legislature as the proper criterion of the law. What is most exasperating about the use of legislative history, however, is that it does not even make sense for those who *accept* legislative intent as the criterion. It is much more likely to produce a false or contrived legislative intent than a genuine one. The first and most obvious reason for this is that, with respect to 99.99 percent of the issues of construction reaching the courts, there *is* no legislative intent, so that any clues provided by the legislative history are bound to be false. Those issues almost invariably involve points of relative detail, compared with the major sweep of the statute in question. That a majority of both houses of Congress (never mind the President, if he signed rather than vetoed the bill) entertained *any* view with regard to such issues is utterly beyond belief. For a virtual certainty, the majority was blissfully unaware of the *existence* of the issue, much less had any preference as to how it should be resolved.

But assuming, contrary to all reality, that the search for "legislative intent" is a search for something that exists, that something is not likely to be found in the archives of legislative history. In earlier days, when Congress had a smaller staff and enacted less legislation, it might have been possible to believe that a significant number of senators or representatives were present for the floor debate, or read the committee reports, and actually voted on the basis of what they heard or read. Those days, if they ever existed, are long gone. The floor is rarely crowded for a debate, the members generally being occupied with committee business and reporting to the floor only when a quorum call is demanded or a vote is to be taken. And as for committee reports, it is not even certain that the members of the issuing committees have found time to read them, as demonstrated by the following Senate

---

3. *Jett v. Dallas Indep. Sch. Dist.*, 491 U.S. 701 (1989), *quoted in Green v. Bock Laundry Machine Co.*, 490 U.S. 504, 530 (1989) (Scalia, J., concurring).

floor debate on a tax bill, which I had occasion to quote in an opinion written when I was on the Court of Appeals:

MR. ARMSTRONG: . . . My question, which may take [the chairman of the Committee on Finance] by surprise, is this: Is it the intention of the chairman that the Internal Revenue Service and the Tax Court and other courts take guidance as to the intention of Congress from the committee report which accompanies this bill?

MR. DOLE: I would certainly hope so. . . .

MR. ARMSTRONG: Mr. President, will the Senator tell me whether or not he wrote the committee report?

MR. DOLE: Did I write the committee report?

MR. ARMSTRONG: Yes.

MR. DOLE: No; the Senator from Kansas did not write the committee report.

MR. ARMSTRONG: Did any Senator write the committee report?

MR. DOLE: I have to check.

MR. ARMSTRONG: Does the Senator know of any Senator who wrote the committee report?

MR. DOLE: I might be able to identify one, but I would have to search. I was here all during the time it was written, I might say, and worked carefully with the staff as they worked. . . .

MR. ARMSTRONG: Mr. President, has the Senator from Kansas, the chairman of the Finance Committee, read the committee report in its entirety?

MR. DOLE: I am working on it. It is not a bestseller, but I am working on it.

MR. ARMSTRONG: Mr. President, did members of the Finance Committee vote on the committee report?

MR. DOLE: No.

MR. ARMSTRONG: Mr. President, the reason I raise the issue is not perhaps apparent on the surface, and let me just state it: . . . The report itself is not considered by the Committee on Finance. It was not subject to amendment by the Committee on Finance. It is not subject to amendment now by the Senate. . . .

. . . If there were matter within this report which was disagreed to by the Senator from Colorado or even by a majority of all Senators, there would be no way for us to change the report. I could not offer an amendment tonight to amend the committee report.

. . . [F]or any jurist, administrator, bureaucrat, tax practitioner, or others who might chance upon the written record of this proceeding, let me just make the point that this is not the law, it was not voted on, it is not subject to amendment, and we should discipline ourselves to the task of expressing congressional intent in the statute.[4]

Ironically, but quite understandably, the more courts have relied upon legislative history, the less worthy of reliance it has become. In earlier days, it was at least genuine and not contrived—a real part of the legislation's *history*, in the sense that it was part of the *development* of the bill, part of

---

4. 128 Cong. Rec. 16918-19, 97th Cong., 2d Sess. (July 19, 1982), *quoted in Hirschey v. Federal Energy Regulatory Comm'n*, 777 F.2d 1, 7 n.1 (D.C. Cir. 1985) (Scalia, J., concurring).

the attempt to inform and persuade those who voted. Nowadays, however, when it is universally known and expected that judges will resort to floor debates and (especially) committee reports as authoritative expressions of "legislative intent," affecting the courts rather than informing the Congress has become the primary purpose of the exercise. It is less that the courts refer to legislative history because it exists than that legislative history exists because the courts refer to it. One of the routine tasks of the Washington lawyer-lobbyist is to draft language that sympathetic legislators can recite in a prewritten "floor debate" — or, even better, insert into a committee report.

There are several common responses to these criticisms. One is "So what, if most members of Congress do not themselves know what is in the committee report. Most of them do not know the details of the legislation itself, either — but that is valid nonetheless. In fact, they are probably more likely to read and understand the committee report than to read and understand the text." That ignores the central point that genuine knowledge is a precondition for the supposed authoritativeness of a committee report, and not a precondition for the authoritativeness of a statute. The committee report has no claim to our attention except on the assumption that it was the *basis* for the house's vote and thus represents the house's "intent," which we (presumably) are searching for. A statute, however, has a claim to our attention simply because Article I, section 7 of the Constitution provides that since it has been passed by the prescribed majority (*with or without adequate understanding*), it is a law.

Another response simply challenges head-on the proposition that legislative history must reflect congressional thinking: "Committee reports are *not* authoritative because the full house presumably knows and agrees with them, but rather because the full house *wants* them to be authoritative — that is, leaves to its committees the details of its legislation." It may or may not be true that the houses entertain such a desire; the sentiments of Senator Armstrong quoted earlier suggest that it is not. But if it is true, it is unconstitutional. "All legislative Powers herein granted," the Constitution says, "shall be vested in a Congress of the United States, which shall consist of a Senate and House of Representatives."[5] The legislative power is the power to make laws, not the power to make legislators. It is nondelegable. Congress can no more authorize one committee to "fill in the details" of a particular law in a binding fashion than it can authorize a committee to enact minor laws. Whatever Congress has not *itself* prescribed is left to be resolved by the executive or (ultimately) the judicial branch. That is the very essence of the separation of powers. The only conceivable basis for considering committee reports authoritative, therefore, is that they are a genuine indication of the will of the entire house — which, as I have been at pains to explain, they assuredly are not.

---

5. U.S. Const. art. I, §1.

I think that Dean Landis, and those who joined him in the prescription of legislative history as a cure for what he called "willful judges," would be aghast at the results a half-century later. On balance, it has facilitated rather than deterred decisions that are based upon the courts' policy preferences, rather than neutral principles of law. Since there are no rules as to how much weight an element of legislative history is entitled to, it can usually be either relied upon or dismissed with equal plausibility. If the willful judge does not like the committee report, he will not follow it; he will call the statute not ambiguous enough, the committee report too ambiguous, or the legislative history (this is a favorite phrase) "as a whole, inconclusive." It is ordinarily very hard to demonstrate that this is false so convincingly as to produce embarrassment. To be sure, there are ambiguities involved, and hence opportunities for judicial willfulness, in other techniques of interpretation as well — the canons of construction, for example, which Dean Landis so thoroughly detested. But the manipulability of legislative history has not *replaced* the manipulabilities of these other techniques; it is has *augmented* them. There are still the canons of construction to play with, *and in addition* legislative history. Legislative history provides, moreover, a uniquely broad playing field. In any major piece of legislation, the legislative history is extensive, and there is something for everybody. As Judge Harold Leventhal used to say, the trick is to look over the heads of the crowd and pick out your friends. The variety and specificity of result that legislative history can achieve is unparalleled.

I think it is time to call an end to a brief and failed experiment, if not for reasons of principle then for reasons of practicality. I have not used legislative history to decide a case for, I believe, the past nine terms. Frankly, that has made very little difference (since legislative history is ordinarily so inconclusive). In the only case I recall in which, had I followed legislative history, I *would* have come out the other way, the rest of my colleagues (who *did* use legislative history) did not come out the other way either.[6] The most immediate and tangible change the abandonment of legislative history would effect is this: Judges, lawyers, and clients will be saved an enormous amount of time and expense. When I was head of the Office of Legal Counsel in the Justice Department, I estimated that 60 percent of the time of the lawyers on my staff was expended finding, and poring over, the incunabula of legislative history. What a waste. We did not use to do it, and we should do it no more. . . .

Notes and Questions

1. Justice Scalia argues that "legislative history should not be used as an authoritative indication of a statute's meaning" because the objective meaning of the words, not the subjective intent of the legislature,

---

6. *See Wisconsin Public Intervenor v. Mortier*, 501 U.S. 597 (1991); *id.*, at 616 (Scalia, J., concurring).

constitutes law. Other have suggested that reliance on legislative history violates the Constitution's procedures for enacting statutes because it treats
the intentions of Congress, as opposed to the text of the statute itself, as
having the force of law. *See, e.g.*, In re Sinclair, 870 F.2d 1340, 1344 (7th Cir.
1989) (Easterbrook, J.) ("The Constitution establishes a complex of procedures, including presidential approval (or support by two-thirds of each
house). It would demean the constitutionally prescribed method of legislating to suppose that its elaborate apparatus for deliberation on, amending,
and approving a text is just a way to create some *evidence* about the law, while
the *real* source of legal rules is the mental processes of legislators."). Still
others have argued that reliance on legislative history amounts to empowering a subset of the Congress, a committee or even an individual member, to
make law, contrary to the constitutionally prescribed procedures. *See* John
F. Manning, *Textualism as a Nondelegation Doctrine*, 97 Colum. L. Rev. 673
(1997). In a sense, we have already discussed the responses, but here are
some, encapsulated by Justice Breyer:

> The "statute-is-the-only-law" argument misses the point. No one claims that legislative
> history is a statute, or even that, in any strong sense, it is "law." Rather, legislative history
> is helpful in trying to understand the meaning of the words that do make up the statute
> or the "law." A judge cannot interpret the words of an ambiguous statute without look-
> ing beyond its words for the words have simply ceased to provide univocal guidance
> to decide the case at hand. Can the judge, for example, ignore a dictionary or the
> historical interpretive practice of the agency that customarily applies some words? Is
> a dictionary or an historic agency interpretive practice "law"? It is "law" only in a weak
> sense that does not claim the status of a statute, and in a sense that violates neither the
> letter nor the spirit of the Constitution.
>
> The delegation argument ("the Senator did not write, or even read, the report")
> is susceptible to the same type of criticism. After all, no one elected lexicographers or
> agency civil servants to Congress. The Constitution nowhere grants them legislative power.
> Yet, judges universally seek their help in resolving interpretive problems. More impor-
> tantly, this argument misunderstands how Congress works as an institution. The relevant
> point here is that nothing in the Constitution seems to prohibit Congress from using staff
> and relying upon groups and institutions in the way I have described. And, for purposes of
> establishing the legislator's personal responsibility, that description does not distinguish
> between different kinds of documents—between committee reports, floor statements, or
> statutory text. Rather, it holds the legislator personally responsible for the work of staff,
> and it correlates the legislator's direct personal involvement, not according to the kind
> of document, but according to the significance of the decision at issue. That is to say, the
> personal involvement of the individual legislator in the statute's text itself may or may not
> be greater than the legislator's involvement with report language or a floor statement.
> Involvement is a function of the importance of the substantive, procedural, or political
> *issue* facing the legislator, not of the "category" of the text that happens to embody that
> particular issue.

Stephen G. Breyer, *On the Uses of Legislative History in Interpreting Statutes*,
65 S. Cal. L. Rev. 845, 863-64 (1992). Another jurist and academic, Judge
Robert Katzmann, observes that committee reports "are often the principal
means by which staffs brief their principals before voting on a bill." Robert
A. Katzmann, *Statutes*, 87 N.Y.U. L. Rev. 637, 653 (2012). The system of
reliance on committee reports by legislative staff and legislators, he notes,

"works because the committee members and their staffs will lose influence with their colleagues as to future bills if they do not accurately represent the bills under consideration." *Id.* at 654. Judge Katzmann argues that the internal reliance by Congress on these sources also plays a role in their value to judicial construction:

> As to constraining judicial preferences, it seems to me that excluding legislative history when interpreting ambiguous statutes will just as likely expand a judge's discretion as reduce it. When a statute is unambiguous, resorting to legislative history is generally not necessary; in that circumstance, the inquiry ordinarily ends. But when a statute is ambiguous, barring legislative history leaves a judge only with words that could be interpreted in a variety of ways without contextual guidance as to what legislators may have thought. Lacking such guidance increases the probability that a judge will construe a law in a manner that the legislators did not intend. It is seemingly inconsistent that textualists, who look to such extratextual materials as the records of the Constitutional Convention and The Federalist in interpreting the Constitution, would look askance at the use of legislative history sources when interpreting legislation.
>
> The contention that the use of legislative history violates the constitutional proscription against self-delegation is premised on a mistaken view of the legislative process. Legislative history accompanying proposed legislation precedes legislative enactment. When Congress passes a law, it can be said to incorporate the materials that it or at least the law's principal sponsors (and others who worked to secure enactment) deem useful in interpreting the law. After all, Article I of the Constitution gives each chamber the authority to set its own procedures for the introduction, consideration, and approval of bills. And each chamber has established its own rules and practices, governing lawmaking — some favoring certain proceedings over others — establishing "a resultant hierarchy of internal communications." Those rules and procedures give particular legislators — such as committee chairs, floor managers, and party leaders — substantial control over the process by which legislation is enacted. Communications from such members as to the meaning of proposed statutes can provide reliable signals to the whole chamber. And, as I noted earlier, members and their staffs have every incentive to accurately represent the meaning of proposed statutes to colleagues, as written and discussed in legislative history.

2. Legislative history is often drafted by staffers, who are directly responsible to elected members of Congress, while statutory text is often drafted by professionals in the Senate or House Office of Legislative Counsel, who are not. Staffers strongly endorsed the use of legislative history in drafting and interpreting statutes. A large majority said that legislative history is a useful tool in the drafting process — for educating members of Congress, guiding agencies and courts, and housing details of the legislation that would otherwise bloat the text. A large majority stated that legislative history is a useful tool for courts to use if seeking to determine legislative intent, and nearly all stated that courts should not rely only on the text when interpreting statutes. At the same time, staffers differentiated among types of legislative history, based on a number of factors including the type of statute, the identity of the speaker, and the timing of the statement, and ranking committee and conference reports at the top. Does it matter what Congress thinks?

3. Professors James Brudney and Corey Ditslear have shown that in decisions involving workplace law, the Supreme Court's citation of legislative history has declined from nearly 50 percent during the Burger Court to less than 30 percent since 1985. *See* James J. Brudney & Corey Ditslear, *The Decline and Fall of Legislative History? Patterns of Supreme Court Reliance in the Burger and Rehnquist Eras*, 89 JUDICATURE 220 (2006). To what would you attribute the decline in reliance on legislative history? How does it affect the Court's decisions?

5. Dynamic Interpretation

Despite their differences, all of the prior theories have a central commonality: they all take the meaning of statutes as fixed at the time of their enactment. They commit courts to inquire into only what Congress wrote or intended. Thus, courts are asked to be faithful agents of Congress. The faithful-agent theory is normatively appealing in a representative democracy; elected officials — not unelected judges — should make the major policy decisions. But this ideal does not map reality. Statutes may stand still, but life does not. How does it serve democracy for courts to interpret statutes in a social, political, or technological vacuum?

T. Alexander Aleinikoff, Updating Statutory Interpretation

87 Mich. L. Rev. 20, 21-61 (1988)

[Consider] two different ways of thinking about statutory interpretation. The first is "archeological": the meaning of a statute is set in stone on the date of its enactment, and it is the interpreter's task to uncover and reconstruct that original meaning. . . . The second way to think about statutory interpretation is "nautical." At the risk of overextending a metaphor, it may be described as follows. Congress builds a ship and charts its initial course, but the ship's ports-of-call, safe harbors and ultimate destination may be a product of the ship's captain, the weather, and other factors not identified at the time the ship sets sail. This model understands a statute as an on-going process (a voyage) in which both the shipbuilder and subsequent navigators play a role. The dimensions and structure of the craft determine where it is capable of going, but the current course is set primarily by the crew on board. (Of course, Congress may send subsequent messages to the ship or change the waters in which the ship is sailing.) . . . The nautical metaphor is suggested by Justice Stevens' willingness to test [the result in a statutory decision] the *mores* of today. . . .

Most opinions display a decidedly archeological mind-set. Nevertheless nonoriginalism seems to exert a significant tug on statutory interpretation. Despite deeply ingrained notions of legislative supremacy, we seem to feel that statutes ought to be responsive to today's world. They ought to be made to fit, as best they can, into the current legal landscape. . . .

A. A NAUTICAL EXAMPLE: EXCLUSION OF HOMOSEXUAL ALIENS UNDER THE IMMIGRATION AND NATIONALITY ACT

In 1950, the Senate Judiciary Committee issued a massive report analyzing the existing immigration system and proposing a comprehensive rewriting of the statute. One of its recommendations was that the grounds excluding persons on the basis of mental disease be amended to specify the exclusion of "homosexuals and other sex perverts." When the bill came up in the Senate the next year, the proposed exclusion ground read: "aliens afflicted with psychopathic personality, epilepsy, or a mental defect." The Senate Report explained that "the Public Health Service has advised that the provision for the exclusion of aliens afflicted with psychopathic personality or a mental defect . . . is sufficiently broad to provide for the exclusion of homosexuals and sex perverts."

The Senate language was adopted, and the exclusion ground took its place among the other medical grounds for exclusion in section 212(a) of the McCarran-Walter Act. As enacted, the first six (of 33) grounds of exclusion were:

(1) Aliens who are feeble-minded;
(2) Aliens who are insane;
(3) Aliens who have had one or more attacks of insanity;
(4) Aliens afflicted with psychopathic personality, epilepsy, or a mental defect;
(5) Aliens who are narcotic drug addicts or chronic alcoholics;
(6) Aliens who are afflicted with tuberculosis in any form, or with leprosy, or any dangerous contagious disease.

In 1967, in *Boutilier v. INS*, the Supreme Court ruled that the phrase "psychopathic personality" in the 1952 provision included homosexuals and that the phrase was not unconstitutionally vague. The Court stated that "the legislative history of the Act indicates beyond a shadow of a doubt that the Congress intended the phrase 'psychopathic personality' to include homosexuals," and it specifically rejected the alien's claim that the term was "medically ambiguous": "The test here is what Congress intended, not what differing psychiatrists may think. It was not laying down a clinical test, but an exclusionary standard which it declared to be inclusive of those having homosexual and perverted characteristics."

Two years before *Boutilier*, Congress had amended section 212(a)(4) to include "sexual deviation" as a ground for exclusion. (*Boutilier* was based on the original provision and did not consider this phrase.) . . .

The immigration act provides for medical examinations of aliens to determine whether they are excludable on medical grounds. Exams made in the United States are usually done by the Public Health Service under the supervision of the Surgeon General. Until 1979, the Immigration and Naturalization Service referred aliens suspected of being homosexuals to the P.H.S. for examination. In that year, the Surgeon General announced that the P.H.S. would no longer carry out such examinations because (1) "according to 'current and generally accepted canons of medical practice', homosexuality *per se* is no longer considered to be a mental disorder"; and (2) "the determination of homosexuality is not made through a medical diagnostic procedure."

Assume that a homosexual alien appears at the border today and applies for admission, arguing that section 212(a)(4) should not be read to exclude him. Does he have a good case? The archeological interpreter would no doubt be startled by the claim. From an originalist perspective, the case for exclusion appears overwhelming. Congress twice and the Supreme Court once has said that the statute excludes homosexuals.

But suppose we start the analysis a different way. Suppose we treat the statute *as if it had been enacted yesterday* and try to make sense of it in today's world. We might pursue this present-minded analysis by asking the following kinds of questions. Would a reader of the statute today be likely to think it requires the exclusion of homosexuals? Why would a legislature enact this law? What could it have been trying to accomplish? If a legislature today sought to exclude aliens based on their sexual orientation, would it be likely to choose the words of the statute to do so? If the statute is read to exclude homosexuals, how would we then be inclined to state the objective of the statute? Would this reformulated purpose cover other cases that the words would lead us to believe ought to be covered? Would this reformulated purpose make us understand the words in a new way? If read to cover homosexual aliens, how would the statute fit with other laws on the books? Does such an interpretation appear consistent with broader prevailing common law and constitutional norms?

These questions, for the most part, should appear familiar. They are the stuff of statutory interpretation as practiced in our legal system. What is missing is talk of original intent, and what is added is a distinct present-mindedness. By treating the statute as if it had been enacted recently, we are attempting to weave it into today's legal system, to make it responsive to today's conditions. We are seeking, for lack of a better term, synchronic coherence.

A nautical interpreter ought to begin by noticing that the statute nowhere mentions homosexuality, and the phrase "psychopathic personality" does not spring to mind as a ready category into which to place it. "Sexual deviation" might well include homosexuality. But how should we decide if it does or does not? The location of the exclusion ground appears particularly significant; it is placed among the other medical exclusion grounds in section 212(a). Thus the structure of the current Act suggests that the paragraph might be limited to medically diagnosable diseases. This view is supported by the detailed provision relating to medical examinations by the P.H.S. which specifically refers to section 212(a)(4). Stated another way, the statutory language and structure suggest a *current* purpose to exclude persons with either physical or mental medical problems.

If the position of the highest medical officer of the United States government (which is charged with enforcement of the immigration laws) is that homosexuality per se is not a disease, and if that opinion is now the accepted view of the medical and psychiatric professions, then it would not be unreasonable to conclude that homosexuality ought not to be considered a medical ground of exclusion. That is, treating the statute as if recently enacted, one might well decide that section 212(a)(4) is limited to medical exclusions, and exclusion on the basis of homosexuality would not readily come within it. This interpretation does not read the phrase "sexual deviation" out of the statute; it limits the term to "deviations" that are currently considered pathological (perhaps pedophilia or exhibitionism). . . .

I should make clear that a nonoriginalist approach does not reject the idea of precedent. Stability, predictability, and reliance are terribly important norms of our legal system. Thus, under a nautical approach, a court may well reach a result following precedent that it would not reach if it were considering the question for the first time. But it should be clear that such an approach would not accord statutory precedents the current "super-strong presumption." The value that a nautical approach places on current coherence in the law would inform its stance towards precedent. . . .

C. IN DEFENSE OF THE NAUTICAL MODEL

Despite the established nonoriginalist elements in common law and constitutional adjudication, something rubs us the wrong way about nautical models of statutory interpretation. The legislature did something back then, our intuitions tell us, and until they act again it is not up to the courts (or any interpreter) to update the law. To update is to usurp the legislature's job, to violate important notions of legislative supremacy and separation of powers, to undermine the rule of law. Warren Lehman has, with irony, identified the allure of intentionalism: "we know no better way to express the ideas of sovereignty and legitimacy."

Perhaps somewhat curiously, it is possible to defend a nautical approach in intentionalist terms. The court that resolutely applies the original intent of the legislation (assuming we abide by the fiction) is often disserving that legislature. By leaving issues for subsequent interpreters, the legislature has necessarily recognized that it needs help in making the statute work in unprovided-for cases. An interpretation that makes no sense in today's world, even if it accurately reflects original meaning, can hardly be said to "work" today. . . .

Nautical models are built on an understanding of the nature of statutes and the role of interpreters that is fundamentally different from the view that underlies an archeological approach. Archeologists see statutes as once-shouted commands that continue simply to echo through time. Current readers of the statute are not interpreters; they are receivers of messages, capturing and recording the communication precisely as it was uttered long ago. This is a singularly inapt description of statutes and interpreters. Enactment of a statute represents the beginning of a journey, not the end. The statute "means" nothing until it takes its place in the legal system, until it begins to interact with judges, lawyers, administrators, and lay people. Each of these interactions changes, or fills out, the meaning of the statute. In deciding that an exclusion provision does (or does not) apply to homosexuals, we have made the statute something other than what it was before we picked it up. We have not *applied* the statute, as if it were a pre-existing, self-contained, unchangeable thing; we have operated within the statute, done something to it we have *interpreted* it. Interpreters are not reporters or historians, searching out the facts of the past. They are creators of meaning.

This view of statutes is not necessarily inconsistent with an originalist approach. A thoughtful archeologist recognizes that the profession is not about just digging up old pots; it is concerned with recreating and understanding the culture of which the pots are evidence. That is, the archeological process can attempt to give meaning to artifacts, rather than simply put them in a museum.

Thus a nautical approach must offer something more than simply a richer description of statutory interpretation. It must defend present-mindedness. To do so, it can begin with some very simple ideas that are universally recognized. Law is a tool for arranging today's social relations and expressing today's social values; and we fully expect our laws, no matter when enacted, to speak to us today. Statutes compiled in the United States Code are not color-coded based on date of enactment. Each is viewed as a present statement of the law and treated as such. . . . Charles Curtis has described how the past and present come together as follows:

> As soon as a statute is enacted, it joins the rest of the law, and together with all the rest it speaks to the judge at the moment he decides the case. When it is enacted, to be sure, it was a command, uttered at a certain time in certain circumstances, but it became more than that. It became a part of the law which is now telling the judge, with the case before him and a decision confronting him, what he should now do. And isn't this just what the legislature wanted? The legislature had fashioned the statute, not for any immediate occasion, but for an indefinite number of occasions to arise in an indefinite future, until it was repealed or amended.

There is another dimension implicit in a nautical approach beyond simply understanding law as an enterprise that exists in the present. It is the project described by Hart and Sacks of fitting the statute into the current legal system as a whole what I have called above synchronic coherence.

The case for coherence is based, in part, on traditional legal values of fairness and equality (treating like cases alike) and perhaps surprisingly notice (that is, lay persons consulting the statute may be more likely to read it in light of current understandings than by searching out the legislative history and the state of the law at the time of enactment). Most significantly, consistency in the present is important because we recognize that fundamental understandings, such as right and wrong, entitlement, responsibility, fairness, and duty, lie behind every aspect of our legal system. These notions provide a backdrop for legislative and judicial behavior, providing norms to be taken into account in making decisions and standards for judging the appropriateness of decisions. To fit statutes into the overall fabric of the law is to make them reflect, to make them responsive to, these evolving background norms. To the extent that archeological approaches aim at describing another time they risk undermining the moral force necessary to legitimate current positive law.

Finally, there is an important way in which law does more than simply fulfill present-mindness purposes. As Robert Cover has noted, law creates, and is part of, a normative universe. It is "a bridge linking a concept of a reality to an imagined alternative." When we decide whether our immigration law excludes homosexuals from the United States, we are implicitly making a statement about the kind of world we live in and want to live in. These judgments are complex and controversial. But we cannot even begin to approach them sensibly through an archeological analysis, which can only present us with images of the past rather than visions of a normative present and future.

It must be stressed that an interpretive approach based on a nautical understanding of statutes does not ask an interpreter to keep a statute "up to date" in the sense of predicting how a current legislature would answer the statutory question. The nautical approach suggests a process of interpretation that uses familiar tools of statutory construction — the language, structure, and purpose of a statute, related statutory provisions, and prevailing common law and constitutional norms. What the nautical approach demands is that the process of interpretation be carried out in a present-minded fashion, as if the statute had been recently enacted. . . .

It is crucial to see that while nautical models of statutory interpretation may be openly *nonarcheological*, they are not *nontextual*. The approach suggested here, similar to other nautical approaches, attributes meaning to printed words written by the enacting legislature. Ultimately the question is, what is the most plausible meaning today *that these words will bear*. Of course, this calls for judgment, and interpreters have a wide range of sources they may consult. Nonetheless, the fact that the statute is written at least as measured against the range of possible actions that may be taken to solve a social problem provides a significant restraint on judges. . . .

So far, I have tried to build a case for a nautical model of statutory interpretation. The approach I have sketched would treat statutes as if they were enacted yesterday and would refuse to make the search for original intent the central interpretive task. This is not, however, a complete theory of statutory interpretation. I have not considered the role that reliance, legislative acquiesence, stare decisis, the age of a statute, or agency action ought to play. Nor have I discussed how one can make coherent a statute whose parts have been interpreted at different times under different conditions. These topics must await another day. My limited purpose is to demonstrate that one can, and should, start the interpretive analysis in the present, not the past.

Notes and Questions

1. The nautical or dynamic approach asks courts to interpret statutes as part of the contemporary legal landscape. How would you describe the conception of the judicial role underlying this approach? Is it for courts to serve as faithful agents of the enacting Congress? A co-equal partner with Congress on an ongoing basis? A mediator on behalf of those whom statutes affect? To what extent does this theory emphasize legal values over democratic ones? Why might that be a good thing? For a classic defense of reliance on common law reasoning and precedent in constitutional law, see David A. Strauss, *Common Law Constitutional Interpretation*, 63 U. Chi. L. Rev. 877 (1996).

2. When we discussed the tools of statutory interpretation earlier in the chapter, we included tools for considering changed circumstances. These tools are useful for making dynamic interpretation operational. Note here that dynamic interpretation is subject to the criticisms of those tools.

3. A related criticism of dynamic interpretation is that it gives courts too much room to impose their own preferences. *See* Antonin Scalia, A Matter of Interpretation 22 (1997); Adrian Vermeule, Judging under Uncertainty: An Institutional Theory of Legal Interpretation 46-50 (2006) (arguing that courts, particularly lower courts, are not institutionally suited for projecting statutes forward; they are best suited to reading the text). One provocative response comes from Professor Einer Elhauge, who argues that courts should interpret statutes in light of the "enactable" preferences of Congress at the time of interpretation. Einer Elhauge, *Preference-Estimating Statutory Default Rules*, 102 Colum. L. Rev. 2027, 2082-83 (2002). Put simply, a court should figure out whether Congress would have enough votes today to enact the statute if interpreted one way or another. If applied in this fashion, Elhauge argues that dynamic interpretation is democratic or faithful to the will of Congress — perhaps more so than other theories. *Id.* Why might this be the case? Assuming you agree, can you imagine how a court would implement this approach? How would a court ascertain the current enactable preferences of Congress on a statutory issue?

4. Might dynamic interpretation have the "paradoxical" effect of preventing Congress from enacting new watershed legislation of the sort that we saw during the 1970s? Professors Daniel Rodriguez and Barry Weingast argue that dynamic interpretation may have this effect because it undoes the delicate compromises that Congress must make to obtain the support of moderate legislators on such progressive legislation. Daniel B. Rodriguez & Barry R. Weingast, *The Paradox of Expansionist Statutory Interpretations*, 101 Nw. U. L. Rev. 1207, 1215-19 (2007). Rodriguez and Weingast predict that moderate legislators, if aware of this judicial practice, will prefer the status quo to new watershed legislation. *Id.* at 1241-50. Does this paradoxical effect suggest that dynamic interpretation is a poor choice for interpreting those statutes that Congress succeeds in enacting?

5. Suppose that the question litigated in the *Boutilier* decision were presented to the Supreme Court again today. How should the Court resolve it? Consider in this regard Lawrence v. Texas, 539 U.S. 558 (2003), which invalidated a state law that criminalized sodomy. The Court held the liberty interest protected by the Due Process Clause gives the individuals who were prosecuted under the law and who were gay, "the full right to engage in their conduct without interventions from the government." *Id.* at 577. The Court wrote: "The State cannot demean their existence or control their destiny by making their private sexual conduct a crime. . . . The Texas statute furthers no legitimate state interest which can justify its intrusion into the personal and private life of the individual." *Id.* How should the Court resolve the *Boutilier* question today? What role does the Court's decision in *Lawrence* play in your analysis?

Now that you possess the major tools and theories of judicial statutory interpretation, we continue our discussion in the following chapters by factoring in agencies and how they implement statutes. As we do, you will see a fuller picture of the regulatory state. You will also acquire more tools and theories for operating as a lawyer (judge, political official, private party, or citizen) in our complex modern government.

4

Policy Making by Rule: A Case Study

Once a statute authorizing an agency to take action has been passed and the agency has decided, through some sort of interpretive process, what the statute means, it is time for the agency to take action. Some statutes only require research by the agency. The National Climate Program Act, Pub. L. 95-367, 92 Stat. 601 (1978), established a program office within the Department of Commerce to, inter alia, carry out "basic and applied research to improve the understanding of climate processes, natural and man induced, and the social, economic and political implications of climate change," but did not authorize any action. Some statutes authorize the government to acquire or distribute resources. The California Desert Protection Act of 1994, Pub. L. 103-433, created Death Valley National Park and Joshua Tree National Park, as well as various wilderness areas, and appropriated $300 million for land acquisition. But the most distinctive statutes in the modern state regulate some aspect of the economy or the society, and this is typically carried out by rulemaking, adjudication, or a combination of the two. The National Labor Relations Board notoriously relies on adjudication, even though it has been granted rulemaking authority. Most agencies, however, use rulemaking as the primary means of implementing a regulatory statute.

Chapter 5 describes and analyzes tools agencies rely on to implement their statutes, with a particular focus on the rulemaking process. It presents the procedures that govern that process, and then considers the use of statutory, scientific, economic, and political analysis to formulate rules. In addition, it addresses two other ways in which agencies make policy—adjudication and guidance.

This chapter provides an overview of the rulemaking process in operation by following the development of a single rule. Promulgating a rule with significant consequences is a complex process involving empirical research by the agency; consultation with experts; design and drafting of the rule itself; negotiations with the regulated parties, their competitors, and relevant public interest groups; and political challenges to the rule in Congress. While the judiciary intervenes in the process with some regularity, as you will see, the process itself involves a lot more than a series of judicial decisions. Do not conclude, on this basis, that there is something non-legal about it. This is law, the way law is instantiated in the modern administrative state. It is what lawyers do these days. Lawyers working for an agency are engaged in every aspect of the rulemaking process. Lawyers for a regulated party respond to every aspect of the process by helping their clients comply with the agency rules, negotiating with the agency, cajoling it, out-guessing it, and out-maneuvering it. This process is not reflected in the average casebook, but that is an indication of the limits of traditional legal education, not the realities of modern legal practice.

To depict those realities—the realities of law in the modern administrative state—we return to the subject of auto safety as an example. Look back at the Motor Vehicle Safety Act, and specifically at Section 103. This requires the implementing agency (NHTSA) to establish "Motor Vehicle Safety Standards." Now look at Section 119 of the Act, which grants the agency the general authority to issue rules. The difference between Section 103 and Section 119 is that Section 103 is mandatory, providing that the agency "shall" issue safety standards and prescribing a fixed timetable (Subsection (h)) by which those standards must be issued. But both provisions grant the agency rulemaking authority, and Congress clearly envisioned that it would use that authority.

Note that neither Section 103 nor Section 119 specifies any particular procedures. The reason is that it is not necessary for it to do so. The Administrative Procedure Act (APA) provides the procedures for any federal rulemaking or adjudication unless Congress provides otherwise. This is what is known as a default statute. We will discuss the APA in greater detail in Chapter 5. For now, what you need to know is the relatively simple procedures that the APA requires for the promulgation of a regulatory rule. They appear in APA §553(b) and (c):

> **(b)** General notice of proposed rule making shall be published in the Federal Register, unless persons subject thereto are named and either personally served or otherwise have actual notice thereof in accordance with law. The notice shall include—
>> **(1)** a statement of the time, place, and nature of public rule making proceedings;
>> **(2)** reference to the legal authority under which the rule is proposed; and
>> **(3)** either the terms or substance of the proposed rule or a description of the subjects and issues involved.
> **(c)** After notice required by this section, the agency shall give interested persons an opportunity to participate in the rule making through submission of written data, views, or arguments with or without opportunity for oral presentation. After consideration of the relevant matter presented, the agency shall incorporate in the rules adopted a concise general statement of their basis and purpose.

Here is the story of the process by which NHTSA promulgated one of its Motor Vehicle Safety Standards: Standard 208, involving passive restraints, arguably the most important and the most controversial of all the standards NHTSA adopted. You are familiar with the results of this rule; it is responsible for the presence of seatbelts and airbags in every automobile on the road in the United Sates. This chapter recounts the complex and often tumultuous process by which that happened.

A. NHTSA GETS ORGANIZED

The first director of the agency was William Haddon, a medical doctor who had worked on automobile safety for the New York State Department of Health and had written a book about the subject. Here is an account of the way he went about his assignment to issue Safety Standards under Section 103, and the vicissitudes that he encountered.

Michael R. Lemov, Car Safety Wars: One Hundred Years of Technology, Politics, and Death

115-18 (2015)

The infant agency raced against the clock to issue new safety standards within about one year of its creation by early 1968. It was not an easy task. Its buildings were scattered all over Washington and it was severely understaffed. Only 150 of its authorized 440 employees had been hired . . . . Haddon himself worked nights and weekends while building the structure of NHTSA and simultaneously writing the final safety standards. The standards were not finished until the day they were due to be issued: January 31, 1968. The administrator stayed awake until 5 o'clock in the morning to finish them on time . . . .

NHTSA's twenty-three "final" safety standards were drawn mostly from existing General Service Administration standards,[1] from the Society of Automotive Engineers' (SAE) voluntary "guides," and one—banning hubcaps that could become dangerous projectiles—based on a Swedish government standard. They were organized into three categories, paralleling Haddon's original accident matrix: 100-level standards designed to prevent crashes from occurring; 200-level standards designed to reduce the likelihood of injury when crashes occurred; and 300-level standards designed to reduce the risk of injury after a crash occurred. They were issued on time.

Once a federal standard was adopted it had real teeth. It became the law of the land and could not be ignored or offered only as an option by car makers selling motor vehicles in the United States. The scope of federal motor vehicle safety standards (FMVSS) started with the initial twenty-three, but it has expanded and now includes more than fifty major standards, covering passenger cars, pickup trucks, vans, SUVs, motorcycles, large trucks, buses, and school buses.

The initial 1968 standards ranged from relatively modest changes, such as uniform and visible labeling of dashboard controls, to groundbreaking rules, such as those requiring front seat shoulder harnesses and seat belts

---

1. That is, the standards that the federal government imposed on the vehicles it purchased for its own use—[Eds.]

built to the GSA standard. There were standards that represented major improvements, such as common transmission shifting sequences (Park-Reverse-Neutral-Drive-Low), warning lights for braking system failures, improved exterior lighting, front seat head restraints, collapsible, energy-absorbing steering columns, and safer door latches.

The first NHTSA standards were met with sharp criticism from automobile manufacturers. They derided them as "useless," "inadvisable," "illegal," and "impossible to meet." After the agency had first issued the standards in proposed form, Haddon solicited the manufacturers' further views and recommendations. By early January 1967, each of the four United States manufacturers had formally claimed that it would be unable to meet many of the proposed regulations in time for the production of their 1968 models. These rebuffs came in the form of bulky dossiers of engineering documents, veiled threats of legal challenges, and somber pronouncements that the standards could force the shuttering of auto factories and job layoffs.

. . .

Henry Ford II, chairman of Ford Motor Company, was one of the harshest critics of the proposed regulations. "Many of the standards are arbitrary and I think technically are not feasible." he said. "If we cannot meet the final version of the standards, we will have to shut down our production lines . . . depending on what the standards might be."

. . .

By January 1967, four months after the creation of NHTSA, after the sharp industry pushback, Haddon and the agency had softened many of the proposed standards before they became effective. The Act also required them to be reconsidered again before they became final standards in January 1968.

Of the first twenty-three proposed standards, NHTSA "temporarily withdrew" three in January 1967; fourteen others were amended and relaxed to assuage industry concerns (and then adopted); and six were amended and provisionally adopted, subject to further consultation with the industry. The altered standards included 109 (pneumatic tire quality standards), 110 (tire rim standards), and 202 (headrests). These now-weakened standards were changed to incorporate further concerns of the automobile industry. In addition to weakening some of the safety standards, NHTSA also granted the manufacturers an additional four months to comply with all of them, moving the deadline from September 1, 1967 to January 1, 1968.

The *Chicago Tribune* reported that the automakers felt they had gained "considerable ground" in getting the standards modified, but that there was certainly "no gloating." The industry was right not to gloat. The withdrawn standards on tires, rims, and headrests were all reissued in January 1969.

Despite their complaints, the manufacturers incorporated most of the requirements of nineteen of the remaining twenty initial NHTSA standards into their 1968 models as required by the new law. Foreshadowing future fights over passive restraint proposals, they argued that standard 201, a key effort to minimize the "second collision" with the interior of the vehicle during a crash, was simply impossible to meet. This was the standard that required vehicles to have padded vehicle parts, such as seat backs, knobs, and dashboards in order to cushion occupants when their bodies collided with the interior surfaces of a car during a crash. Detroit's hostility toward interior protection anticipated by a few years the commencement of its decades-long fight over another occupant protection standard for ' "passive restraints," the requirement for installing air bags in vehicles.

At first, the new administrator stood firm on standard 201, interior protection of occupants, refusing to change it barring compelling information from the automobile manufacturers as to why they could not comply. Then on March 30, 1967[,] the day after his announcement that he would not unilaterally weaken the standard again, the big four major manufacturers took their standard 201 challenge to court.

They filed petitions to set aside standard 201 as authorized under the Act in the U.S. Court of Appeals in Cincinnati. They claimed it was so strict that it violated a provision in the 1966 safety law stating that the "interim" standards must be "based upon existing safety standards." Ford threatened that if the standard was not revised it would "be unable to produce any automobiles for sale in the United States after December 31, 1967." This was a not-so-veiled threat to lay off a lot of American workers.

In May 1967 the government caved. The Sixth Circuit challenge was withdrawn. In a meeting with automobile manufacturers (which Haddon refused to attend), federal highway administrator Lowell K. Bridwell announced that the government would further weaken the interior protection, or "second collision" standard, based on industry input. Three months later, modified standard 201 was finalized. Automobiles would have some increased padding for interiors, including instrument panels, seat backs, arm rests, and sun visors. However, requirements for leg and knee impact protection were dropped. Some new cars now offer such protection as optional equipment, using small air bags at the knee and leg positions.

Notes and Questions

1. Do you think Congress should legislate hard deadlines by which agencies must issue regulations? Does that create perverse incentives for the agency? Does it lead to uninformed or premature judgments? *See* Jacob E. Gerson & Anne Joseph O'Connell, *Deadlines in Administrative Law*, 156 U. PA. L. REV. 923 (2007).

2. Why were all the automobile manufacturers so opposed to safety standards? The standards applied to all of them equally, so it would not seem that imposing these standards would alter the competitive balance. Alternatively, if there was some reason that one manufacturer could comply more readily, why wouldn't that manufacturer have been in favor of the standards? Did the manufacturers, as a group, think that the safety standards, and the increased costs that they imposed on consumers, would decrease overall car sales? Does that make sense?

3. Is this a story about a conscientious agency attempting to act in the public interest that had to compromise with self-interested, irresponsible private businesses? Or is it a story about the way that an overly eager or politically motivated agency, that does not know enough about the product it is regulating, negotiates with the manufacturers of that product to reach reasonable compromises?

4. Why didn't disputes about the practicality and effectiveness of the standards get resolved during the notice-and-comment process? Isn't that the purpose of this process?

B. STANDARD 208 TAKES SHAPE: 1967 TO 1971

Standard 208 had a modest beginning. It was one of the batch of regulations promulgated by NHTSA in its scramble to comply with the Congressional deadline. Here is the original Standard 208, in context.

National Highway Traffic Safety Administration, Title 23—Highways and Vehicles

Chapter II—Vehicle and Highway Safety

[Docket No. 3]

Part 255—Initial Federal Motor Vehicle Safety Standards

This order establishes Initial Federal Motor Vehicle Safety Standards for new motor vehicles and equipment. A notice of rule making proposing the Initial Standards was issued on November 30, 1966 (31 F.R. 15212, corrected 31 F.R. 15600). All pertinent matter in the written and oral comments received has been fully considered. Considerations of time prevent discussion of comments on individual standards.

The motor vehicle safety standards are rules as that term is defined in 5 U.S.C. sec. 551(4). The established practice is that the public record of

a rulemaking proceeding under 5 U.S.C. section 553 (former sec. 4 Administrative Procedure Act), Involving a substantive rule and instituted upon an agency's own initiative, begins with the notice of rule making. An agency is under no legal duty to reveal the internal processes that shaped the project, and interested persons are not entitled to comment thereon, 5 U.S.C. section 553(b)(3). Where, as here, the addressees of a proposed rule are themselves actively engaged as experts on the subject matter, their understanding of the meaning and effect of a rule is certainly not impaired by the absence of such a disclosure. As a practical proposition, this Agency intends to adopt a policy of the greatest possible disclosure of underlying considerations in future substantive rule making when it will not operate under an unusually tight time schedule. In this instance, such disclosure was not possible, and administrative due process required no more than publication of the

notice. The requirement that the standards be based on a record does not operate to require insertion in the record of matter not required as part of a rulemaking notice.

The following findings are made with respect to all standards—

(1) Each standard is a minimum standard for motor vehicle or equipment performance which is practicable and meets the need for motor vehicle safety, land provides objective criteria;

(2) Each standard is reasonable, practicable, and appropriate for the particular class of motor vehicle or item of equipment for which it is prescribed;

(3) Each standard will contribute substantially to the purpose of reducing traffic accidents, and deaths and injuries to persons resulting there from, in the United States; and

(4) The matter incorporated by reference is reasonably available to the

persons affected by this regulation.

. . . [T]he initial Standards as herein established introduce the new class of "multipurpose passenger vehicles." Only standards proposed in the Notice for vehicles now in this class are made applicable to this class. Each standard applies only to the class of vehicles to which it is made applicable by its terms.

The initial standards may be amended from time to time. Each standard remains in effect until rescinded or superseded by a Revised Standard actually becoming effective.

The requirements of Standard No. 209 were originally published on August 31, 1966 (31 F.R. 11528), as a revision to the existing seat belt standard that had been promulgated by the Secretary of Commerce under the authority of Public Law 88-201. At that time, it was provided that the revised standards would become mandatory after February 28, 1967, and would be an optional alternative to the existing standard until that date. As a result seat belt manufacturers had already taken steps to meet the March 1, 1967 date before the Notice for the initial Federal Motor Vehicle Safety Standards was issued on December 3, 1966. To preserve the continuity of this change to the new seat belt standard, the March 1, 1967 effective date was included in the proposed Initial Federal Motor Vehicle Safety Standards. This places no certification requirement on the vehicle manufacturer, however, until the effective date of the first Standard applicable to a motor vehicle rather than motor vehicle equipment.

In consideration of the foregoing, Chapter II of Title 23 of the Code of Federal Regulations is amended by adding a new Subchapter C—Motor Vehicle Safety Regulations, effective January 1, 1968 except Motor Vehicle Safety Standard No. 209, "Seat Belt Assemblies—Passenger Cars, Multipurpose Passenger Vehicles, Trucks, and Buses," which becomes effective March 1, 1967, to read as set forth below.

This regulation was proposed as Part 245 but will, for reasons of organization of subject matter, be issued as Part 255.

This rulemaking action is taken under the authority of sections 103 and 119 of the National Traffic and Motor Vehicle Safety Act of 1966 (15 TT.S.C. sec. 1392, 1407) and the delegations of authority of October 20, 1966 (31 FH. 13952) and January 24, 1967 (32 F.R. 1005).

Issued in Washington, D.C., on January 31, 1967.

. . .

SUBPART B— STANDARDS §255.21 FEDERAL MOTOR VEHICLE SAFETY STANDARDS.

The Federal Motor Vehicle Safety Standards are set forth in this subpart.

Motor vehicle safety standard numbers and titles

101 Control Location and Identification—Passenger Cars
102 Transmission Shift lever Sequence, Starter Interlock, and Transmission Braking Effect—Passenger Cars, Multipurpose Passenger Vehicles, Trucks, and Buses
103 Windshield Defrosting and Defogging—Passenger Cars and Multipurpose Passenger Vehicles
104 Windshield Wiping and Washing Systems—Passenger Cars
105 Hydraulic Service Brake, Emergency Brake, and Parking Brake Systems—Passenger Cars
106 Hydraulic Brake Hoses—Passenger Cars and Multipurpose Passenger Vehicles
107 Reflecting Surfaces—Passenger Cars, Multipurpose Passenger Vehicles, Trucks, and Buses
108 Lamps, Reflective Devices, and Associated Equipment—Multipurpose Passenger Vehicles, Trucks, Trailers, and Buses, 80 or More Inches Wide Overall
111 Rearview Mirrors—Passenger Cars and Multipurpose Passenger Vehicles
203 Impact Protection for the Driver Prom the Steering Control System—Passenger Cars
204 Steering Control Rearward Displacement—Passenger Cars
205 Glazing Materials—Passenger Cars, Multipurpose Passenger Vehicles, Motorcycles, Trucks, and Buses
206 Door Latches and Door Hinge Systems—Passenger Cars
207 Anchorage of Seats—Passenger Cars
208 Seat Belt Installations—Passenger Cars
209 Seat Belt Assemblies—Passenger Cars, Multipurpose Passenger Vehicles, Trucks, and Buses
210 Seat Belt Assembly Anchorages—Passenger Cars

211 Wheel Nuts, Wheel Discs, and Hub Caps— Passenger Cars and Multipurpose Passenger Vehicles

301 Fuel Tanks, Fuel Tank Filler Pipes, and Fuel Tank Connections— Passenger Cars

Motor Vehicle Safety Standard No. 208 Seat Belt Installations—Passenger Cars

S1. *Purpose and, scope.* This standard establishes requirements for seat belt installations.

S2. *Application.* This standard applies to passenger cars.

S3. *Requirements.*

S3.1 Except as provided in S3.1.1 and S3.1.2, a Type 1 or Type 2 seat belt assembly that conforms to Motor Vehicle Safety Standard No. 209 shall be installed in each passenger car seat position.

S3.1.1 Except in convertibles a Type 2 seat belt assembly that conforms to Motor Vehicle Safety Standard No. 209 shall be installed in each outboard passenger car seat position that includes the windshield header within the head impact area.

S3.1.2 The requirements of S3.1 do not apply to folding auxiliary jump seats, side-facing seats, and rearfacing seats.

Motor Vehicle Safety Standard No. 209 Seat Belt Assemblies—Passenger Cars, Multipurpose Passenger Vehicles, Trucks, and Buses

S1. *Purpose and scope.* This standard specifies requirements for seat belt assemblies.

S2. *Application.* This standard applies to seat belt assemblies for use in passenger cars, multipurpose passenger vehicles, trucks, and buses.

S3. *Requirements,* Seat belt assemblies shall meet the requirements of Department of Commerce, National Bureau of Standards, *Standards for Seat Belts for Use in Motor Vehicles* (15 CFR 9) (31 F.R. 11528).

This Standard supersedes Department of Commerce, National Bureau of Standards, *Standards for Seat Belts for Use in Motor Vehicles* (15 CFR 9) (30 F.R. 8432).

Notes and Questions

1. This is the way the rules NHTSA promulgated actually appear in the Federal Register. Because NHTSA was required to produce a multitude of rules on short notice, they do not quite conform to the standard form of agency rules. You will see more typical rules later on in this section. The final paragraph of the introductory statement is standard; you will see its equivalent in every NPRM and final regulation that appears in the Federal Register. It is required by §553(b)(2), which in turn reflects the basic requirement of statutory authorization for agency action that we have already discussed. The longer explanation of the way that the standards were drafted that precedes the final paragraph is atypical, however. Its defensive and somewhat apologetic tone probably reflects the level of stress that NHTSA experienced in drafting so many standards in so short a time, and the intensity of the criticism leveled at the agency from both the automobile industry and the rapidly growing auto safety lobby, particularly Ralph Nader (who disliked and distrusted Haddon). As discussed above, the NPRM, which usually comes quite late in the agency's decision-making process, is the first public disclosure about that process that the agency is required to make. The implicit statement that the agency is not required to adopt any procedures that are not specified in the APA was recognized doctrine at the time, and forcefully confirmed in the subsequent *Vermont Yankee* decision, see Chapter 6. But the "concise general statement of the [rule's] basis and purpose" required by §553(c) has mushroomed into an extensive explanation and justification, as you will see below. Its absence from the first promulgation of the NHTSA Standards is another result of the haste with which the agency was required to act.

2. As its name (or rather number) suggests, Standard 208 was part of the 200 series of NHTSA regulations. The numbering process described in the excerpt from Lemov's book—100s to prevent crashes from occurring, 200s to reduce injuries from crashes that did occur, and 300s to reduce injuries after the crash—was based on a matrix developed by Haddon that indicated which safety measures would be most effective at different points in the process. Here is a simplified version of the matrix:

	Human	Vehicle	Environment
Pre-Crash	X		
Crash		X	
Environment			X

3. Note the range of issues that NHTSA was addressing, and recall again our question about whether agencies should be compelled to act with so much celerity. On the one hand, such a requirement certainly communicates a sense of urgency, valid when the number of fatalities from auto accidents was running at about 50,000 per year at the time (and thus, as auto safety advocates pointed out, equal to all American combat deaths in all its wars every 12 years). On the other hand, each little line in the index represents a complex set of engineering and economic judgments, necessarily made with little opportunity to study the problem or negotiate with the manufacturers. Was this partially responsible for the level of industry resistance, and the vulnerability of the rules to subsequent attenuation, that Lemov describes?

4. The simplicity of Standard 208 itself, and its companion Standard 209, is achieved in part by incorporating standards from another set of rules, in this case the National Bureau of Standards, the first scientific laboratory established by the federal government (now renamed the National Institute of Standards and Technology). The practice of incorporating standards from other parts of government or from the regulated industry is common in federal regulations.

5. Note the exception for fold-out seats. These include additional seats in the rear part of the passenger compartment, and also the famous rumble seat on the back of the vehicle, outside the compartment. Rumble seats were discontinued by auto manufacturers by 1940. Why make the exception? You will find exceptions in almost all statutory enactments; the exceptions to §553 are a major feature of administrative law, as you have already seen,. For a general discussion, see Alfred C. Aman, Jr., *Administrative Equity: An Analysis of Exceptions to Administrative Rules*, 1982 DUKE L.J. 277 (1982); Peter H. Shuck, *When the Exception Becomes the Rule: Regulatory Equity and the Formulation of Energy Policy Through an Exceptions Process*, 1984 DUKE L.J. 163.

As you can see, the first version of Standard 208 required only that auto manufacturers install manual seatbelts. Manual seatbelts, if used properly, have always been (and continue to be) an effective means to reduce the occurrence of secondary collisions or the incidence of injury or death from such collisions when they do occur. But manual seatbelt use was so low during this initial period that traffic injuries and fatalities barely deceased. People simply refused to buckle up on their own. So the agency began to study the option of "passive" occupant restraint systems, which would not depend upon an affirmative action by the occupant to produce the safety benefits that result from seat belt use.

By this time, Richard Nixon was President, and Haddon had resigned from NHTSA and accepted an invitation from insurance industry companies to create a public interest organization, the Insurance Institute for Highway Safety (IIHS). His successor, appointed by Nixon, was Douglas Toms, an equally qualified auto safety expert deemed acceptable by Nader. In order to deal with the apparent ineffectiveness of manual seatbelts, NHTSA began to consider passive restraints. It focused on two different types: the automatic seatbelt and the airbag. The airbag was not new technology. A patent for a device of this type had been filed in 1952, and by the 1960s aircraft manufacturers were experimenting with it. An engineering firm, Eaton, Yale & Towne, carried out extensive research on the device at its facility in Southfield, Michigan, a few miles from Detroit, in the late 1960s, and was ready with a commercially viable model by the end of the decade. It had hoped to persuade the auto manufacturers to incorporate it into their products, but despite some initial interest from Ford, they rejected the idea.

On March 3, 1971, NHTSA promulgated a new version of Standard 208.

National Highway Traffic Safety Administration, Occupant Crash Protection in Passenger Cars, Multipurpose Passenger Vehicles, Trucks, and Buses

Part 571 — Federal Motor Vehicle Safety Standards

The purpose of this amendment to Standard No. 208, 49 CFR 571.21, is to specify occupant crash protection requirements for passenger cars, multipurpose passenger vehicles, trucks, and buses manufactured on or after January 1, 1972, with additional requirements coming into effect for certain of those vehicles on August 15, 1973, August 15, 1975, and August 15, 1977. The requirements effective for the period beginning on January 1,1972, were the subject of a notice of proposed rulemaking published September 25, 1970 (35 F.B. 14941), and appear today for the first time in the form of a rule. The requirements for subsequent periods were issued in rule form on November 3, 1970 (35 F.R. 16927), and are reissued today in amended form as the result of petitions for reconsideration.

The substantive rulemaking actions that preceded this amendment are as follows:

(a) May 7, 1970 (35 KB. 7187)—Proposed requirements and a schedule for the adoption of passive restraint systems and interim active systems.

(b) September 25, 1970 (35 F.R. 14941)—Proposal for a modified interim set of requirements effective January 1, 1972.

(c) November 3, 1970 (35 F.R. 16927)—Rule amending Standard No. 208 to specify requirements for passive restraints, effective July 1, 1973.

(d) November 3, 1970 (35 F.R. 16937)—Proposed additional requirements and conditions to be contained in Standard No. 208.

Following issuance of the November 3 amendment,

petitions for reconsideration were filed pursuant to §553.35 of the procedural rules (49 CFR 553.35, 35 F.R. 5119) . . .

Concurrently with the evaluation of the petitions, the Administration has reviewed the comments received in response to the September 25 and November 3 proposals, and the interim occupant protection requirements are combined herein with the requirements for later periods.

The standard establishes quantitative criteria for occupant injury, as determined by use of anthropomorphic test devices. . . .

For systems that provide complete passive protection there are three vehicle impact modes in which a vehicle is required to meet the injury criteria. In the frontal mode, the vehicle impacts a fixed collision barrier perpendicularly or at any angle up to and including 30° in either direction from the perpendicular while traveling longitudinally forward at any speed up to 30 m.p.h. In the lateral mode, the vehicle is impacted on its side by a barrier moving at 20 m.p.h. In the rollover mode, the vehicle is rolled over from a speed of 30 m.p.h.

On January 1, 1972, a passenger car will be required to provide one of three options for occupant protection: (1) Passive protection system that meets the above Injury criteria in all impact modes at all seating positions; (2) lap belts of all positions, with a requirement that the front outboard positions meet the Injury criteria with lap-belted dummies in a 30-m.p.h. perpendicular barrier crash; or (3) lap-and-shoulder-belt systems at the front outboard positions that restrain test dummies in a 30-m.p.h. barrier crash without belt or anchorage failure, and lap belts in other positions.

Both the second and third options require warning systems that activate a visible and audible signal if an occupant of either front outboard position has not extended his lap belt to a specified length. Lap belts furnished under the second or third options must have emergency-locking or automatic-locking retractors at all outboard positions, front and rear. Shoulder belts furnished under the third option must have either manual adjustment or emergency-locking retractors.

On August 15, 1973, a passenger car will be required to provide one of two options for occupant protection: (1) Passive protection that meets the injury criteria in all impact modes at all seating positions; or (2) a system that provides passive protection for the front positions in a perpendicular frontal fixed barrier crash, that includes lap belts at all seating positions such that the injury criteria are met at the front positions both, with and without lap belts fastened in a perpendicular frontal fixed barrier crash, and that has a seat belt warning system at the front outboard positions.

. . .

On and after August 15, 1975, a passenger car will be required to meet the injury criteria in all impact modes at all seating positions by passive means.

The remainder of this preamble is separated into sections dealing with (I) the comments received in response to the September 25 proposal for the interim system, (II) the petitions for reconsideration of the November 3 rule on the requirements for later periods, and (III) the comments received and action taken pursuant to the November 3

proposal for additional requirements.

I. The September 25 proposal specified a series of options for occupant protection in passenger cars manufactured on or after January 1, 1972. Each option represented a significant advance over the level of protection afforded occupants by present seat belt systems. Upon consideration of comments requesting postponement of the requirements, it has been determined that compliance with one or another of the options by January 1, 1972, is reasonable and practicable. In response to the comments and other available information, however, certain changes have been made.

. . .

The third option proposed in the September 25 notice has been adopted with some changes. It consists of an improved combination of lap and shoulder belts in the front outboard seating positions, with lap belts in other positions. The belts and anchorages at the front outboard positions must be capable of restraining a dummy in a 30-m.p.h. frontal perpendicular impact without separation of the belts or their anchorages.

The seat belt warning system required under the second and third options has been modified somewhat in the light of the comments, to clarify the requirements and to restrict its operation to situations where the vehicle is likely to be in motion. The notice proposed that the system operate when the driver or right front passenger, or both, occupied the seat but did not fasten the belt about them. It was stated in several comments such systems operating through the buckle are relatively complex and that leadtime would be a significant problem. Upon evaluation of the comments, it has been decided to provide for warning system operation when the driver's belt is not extended to a length that will accommodate a 5th-percentfie adult female, or when the right front passenger's seat is occupied and that belt is not extended far enough to fit a 50th-percentile 6-year-old. Keying the system to belt withdrawal is technologically simpler, and still provides protection against tampering. The notice had proposed that the system operate whenever the vehicle's ignition was in the "on" position. It was pointed out in the comments that situations arise in which the vehicle is at rest with the ignition on and the engine running, as when picking up or discharging passengers. To avoid the annoyance to vehicle occupants of the warning system in such situations, the standard provides that the system shall operate only if the ignition is in the "on" position and the transmission is in a drive position.

. . .

II. With few exceptions, the petitions for reconsideration of the November 3 amendment requested that the requirement for mandatory passive protection be postponed. . . .

However, considerable data was presented in the petitions to the effect that the development of passive systems for the various impact modes has not proceeded at an equal rate. It appears that a number of manufacturers may be unable to comply with the lateral crash protection requirements in 1973. Accordingly, it has been decided to establish two restraint options for the front seating positions of passenger cars manufactured on or after August 15, 1973, and before August 15, 1975. A manufacturer may choose, first, to provide a passive system

that meets the occupant crash protection requirements at all seating positions, in all impact modes. If he is unable to provide such full passive protection, he may choose to adopt a system that provides passive protection for the front occupants in a head-on collision, and also, includes a lap belt at each seating position with a seatbelt warning system for the front outboard positions. Under this option, the injury criteria must be met at each front position in a perpendicular barrier crash up to 30 m.p.h., both with and without the lap belts fastened. This option thus resembles the second option permitted during the interim period, except that the injury criteria must also be met with the test dummies unrestrained, and at the front center position as well as the front outboard positions.

. . .

The use of the anthropomorphic test device described in SAE J963 was objected to by several petitioners, on the grounds that further specifications are needed to ensure repeatability of test results. The Administration finds no sufficient reason to alter its conclusion that the SAB specification is the best available. The NHTSA is sponsoring further research and examining all available data, however, with a view to issuance of further specifications for these devices.

. . .

A number of other minor issues were raised by the petitions, and each has been carefully evaluated by the Administration. With respect to those objections and suggestions not specifically mentioned elsewhere in this notice, the petitions are hereby denied.

In light of the foregoing, Motor Vehicle Safety Standard No. 208 in §571.21

of Title 49, Code of Federal Regulations, is amended to read as follows, with effective dates as specified in the text of the standard. This amendment is issued under the authority of sections 103, 108, 112, 114, and 119 of the National Traffic and Motor Vehicle Safely Act, 15 U.S.C. 1392, 1347, 1401, 1403, 1407, and the delegation of authority at 49 CFR 1.51.

Issued on March 3, 1971.

Douglas W. Tolis,
Acting Administrator.

§571.21 Federal Motor Vehicle Safety Standards.

* * * *

Motor Vehicle Safety Standard No. 208 Occupant Crash Protection

S1. *Scope.* This standard specifies performance requirements for the protection of vehicle occupants in crashes.

S2. *Purpose.* The purpose of this standard is to reduce the number of deaths of vehicle occupants, and the severity of injuries, by specifying vehicle crashworthiness requirements in terms of forces and accelerations measured on anthropomorphic dummies in test crashes, and by specifying equipment requirements for active and passive restraint systems.

. . .

S4.1.2 *Passenger cars manufactured from August 15, 1973 to August 14, 1975.* Passenger cars manufactured from August 15, 1973, to August 14, 1975, inclusive, shall meet the requirements of S4.1.2.1 or S4.1.2.2. A protection, system that meets the requirements of S4.1.2.1 may be installed at one or more designated seating positions of a vehicle that otherwise meets the requirements of S4.1.2.2.

S4.1.2.1 *First option—complete passive protection system.* The vehicle shall meet the crash protection requirements of S5 by means that require no action by vehicle occupants.

S4.1.2.2 *Second option—head-on passive protection system.* The vehicle shall—

(a) At each designated seating position, have a Type 1 seatbelt assembly that conforms to Standard No. 209 and to S7.1 and S7.2 of this standard;

(b) At each front designated seating position, meet the frontal crash protection requirements of S5.1, in a perpendicular impact, by means that require no action by vehicle occupants;

(c) At each front designated seating position, meet the frontal crash protection requirements of S5.1, in a perpendicular impact, with a test device restrained by a Type 1 seatbelt assembly; and

(d) At each front outboard designated seating position, have a seatbelt warning system that conforms to S7.3.

S4.1.3 *Passenger cars manufactured on or after August 15, 1975.* Each passenger car manufactured on or after August 15, 1975, shall meet the occupant crash protection requirements of S5 by means that require no action by vehicle occupants.

Notes and Questions

1. In this edited version, you can see most of the typical features of an agency rule. There is no declaration of legal authority, since this is an amendment to an existing rule, but there is the statement of "basis and purpose" and the codified language of the rule itself. Note also that the amendments, being new regulatory requirements, followed the standard procedure in being preceded by an NPRM.

2. Note that in addition to commenting on the NPRM within the specified time, the manufacturers also petitioned for reconsideration of the rule in accordance with §553(e). This provision does not require the agency to do anything other than receive the petition, but a different section, §555(e), may require the agency to provide "a brief statement of the grounds for denial." The uncertainty arises because this second section is embedded in the provisions for formal adjudication under the heading of "Ancillary Matters" that include such adjudication-related issues as the right to counsel and the scope of agency subpoenas, which have no relevance to informal rulemaking. In any event, the Supreme Court has held that the agency's denial of a petition for rulemaking is subject to review, which effectively means that the agency must provide reasons for the denial. Massachusetts v. EPA, 549 U.S. 497 (2007). It is clear, of course (and at this point should be clear to you), that if a statute explicitly requires that agency to respond to petitions, that provision, not the APA provisions, is the controlling one. An example is Clean Air Act §307(d)(7)(B), 42 U.S.C. §7607(d)(7)(B); *see* Clean Air Council v. Pruitt, 862 F.3d 1 (D.C. Cir. 2017). The fact that *Massachusetts* involved the Bush Administration's response to climate change and that *Clean Air Council* involved the Trump Administration's policy regarding enforcement of anti-pollution laws is hardly surprising. It is often matters of intense public controversy that lead to extensive litigation and judicial intervention.

3. There is also no requirement in §553 that the agency respond to the comments submitted in the notice-and-comment process, but that fact that the agency's statement of basis and purpose is subject to review effectively requires such responses. The standard by which courts review these statements, as we will explore at greater length in this chapter, and in Chapter 6, is established by §706 of the APA, which instructs courts to set aside rules that are "arbitrary, capricious, and abuse of discretion or otherwise not in accordance with law." In the context of the notice-and-comment process, this is usually taken to mean that, at a minimum, the agency must respond to significant comments. Significance is usually determined by the identity of the commentator rather than the content of the comment, which would require technical expertise to assess. A comment from a firm that will be subject to the regulation, or its trade association, will almost always be considered significant, as will a comment from a leading public interest group. In contrast, the agency can safely ignore a comment from an unknown individual who claims that the automobile is an immoral machine or that economic regulation is unconstitutional. Note the quick dismissal of "minor issues" in the penultimate paragraphs of the agency's statement. Note also the way the agency responded to comments from the industry, and the way it changed its rule in response. Does this show that the notice-and-comment process is working well?

4. Look back at the Senate Report for the Motor Vehicle Safety Act, and specifically to the Committee's repeated assurances that it "was not empowering the Secretary to take over the design and manufacturing functions of private industry." To what extent does this version of Standard 208 reflect this orientation?

5. To what extent does the new standard reflect the general orientation of the Motor Vehicle Safety Act? As discussed in Chapter 2, the notorious adage that preceded passage of the Act was that the most dangerous part of a car was the "nut behind the wheel." Given that seat belts were proven to be effective in reducing deaths and injuries, and that NHTSA had now required their installation, it could be argued that any injuries resulting from failure to attach them was readily attributable to the nuts behind the wheel and in the passenger seats. Would this have represented a misunderstanding of the authorizing statute?

6. In its early days, NHTSA issued safety regulations regarding specific features of motor vehicles, such as headlamps, bumpers, and dashboards. According to Jerry L. Mashaw & David L. Harfst, The Struggle for Auto Safety 79 (1990):

> That technique placed the agency at an overwhelming strategic disadvantage in fulfilling its mandate. . . . By comparison with broadly articulated systems of performance criteria, component-specific rules greatly magnified the agency's information-gathering burdens; made coordination of regulatory activities complex and cumbersome; and exaggerated the agency's maintenance and housekeeping chores simply to keep the rules up to date. This approach virtually ensured that obstructionist tactics by recalcitrant manufacturers would succeed. Incremental rulemaking at the level of individual equipment items allowed manufacturers to focus attention repeatedly on production

feasibility. The manufacturers continuously portrayed equipment-specific rules as inherently disruptive of automobile production.

Note that the authors consider NHTSA's equipment-specific rules defective on both expertise and strategic grounds, that is, the agency lacked the knowledge to design these rules an induced a high level of industry resistance by promulgated them. As Mashaw and Harfst describe, the 1971 version of Standard 208 represented a major change in strategy. What is that change? What sort of requirements does the regulation adopt? In what way do they avoid the expertise and strategic problems of NHTSA's former strategy?

7. An "anthropomorphic test device" is of course the famous "crash test dummy" which became an icon of the auto safety era:

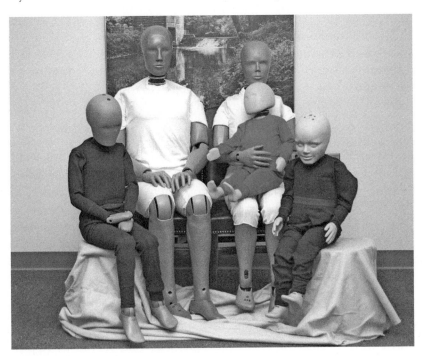

C. STANDARD 208 HITS A WALL: 1971 TO 1976

This new version catapulted Standard 208 to the forefront of industry concern about safety regulations, a position it would hold for the next two decades. An indication of the concern that auto company executives felt about the Standard's potential impact comes from the Nixon Tapes. This is a unique document. President Nixon kept a tape recorder running constantly in his office, allegedly for use in writing his memoirs after he retired with glory. He expected that he would be the only person who had access to the recordings, and he possibly forgot about their existence. Visitors to his office were, of course, entirely unaware that they were being recorded.

When Nixon's various defalcations were investigated, and he resigned in disgrace rather than glory, the tapes became publicly available. There is virtually no other case where we have transcripts of completely candid private conversations among public officials and private parties who met with them.

The transcript that follows includes comments from the following persons:

Richard Nixon: Nixon was faced with a heavily Democratic Congress that was, in fact, strongly progressive and intent on enacting sweeping legislation in civil rights, environmental protection, and consumer protection. He signed a good deal of this legislation. He did veto several of the major bills, such as the Clean Water Act, but was overridden.

Henry Ford II: The grandson of the company founder, "Hank the Deuce" was as close to the status of royalty as can exist in the United States, and he behaved—or misbehaved—accordingly. His fancy clothes, multiple mansions, and frequent philandering were matched by an imperious style of management. He was President of Ford from 1945 to 1960. At the time of this conversation, he had become Chairman of the Board and Chief Executive Officer.

Lee Iacocca: Born to an immigrant family in an industrial section of Pennsylvania, Iacocca worked his way up the ranks at Ford and became President of the Company in 1970. A genuinely charismatic figure, he was probably the most famous corporate executive in the United States at this time. He developed the Ford Mustang, a resounding success, but also the Ford Pinto, whose agonies we have recounted in Chapter 2. . Hank the Deuce fired him in 1978, famously declaring that he just didn't like him, perhaps because Iacocca was acting like Ford's social equal. Iacocca went on to become President of Chrysler.

John Volpe: Appointed by Nixon as Secretary of Transportation, a position he held from 1969 to 1973. Previously, he had served as Republican Governor of Massachusetts from 1961 to 1963 and 1965 to 1969. He had no particular expertise regarding transportation issues. Amtrak was created during his time as Secretary.

John Ehrlichman: Trained as a lawyer, he served as Nixon's White House Counsel and then Chief Domestic Advisor. He organized the Watergate break-in. Convicted of conspiracy, obstruction of justice, and perjury, he was sentenced to 18 months in prison. After his release, having been disbarred for his felony convictions, he appeared in television commercials for Dreyer's Ice Cream until consumers objected.

Transcript of Public Record; Conversation 488-15, Nixon Presidential Library and Museum, National Archives

April 27, 1971, 10:19-11:43 A.M., Oval Office

Part of a conversation among President Nixon, Lido Anthony Iacocca, Henry Ford II, and John S. Ehrlichman in the Oval Office on April 27, 1971 between 11:08 and 11:43 A.M. (Transcript provided by the Nixon Presidential Materials staff at the National Archives.)

PRESIDENT: Well, anyway, uh, I want to say first that, uh, on this subject that I'm glad to have you come in and, uh, talk about it. And let me introduce it by, by tr-trying to tell you what I know—about it and what I don't know. And then I want to hear directly from you and you can talk to me in complete confidence, I can assure you. And John is a lawyer who says nothing. . . .

PRESIDENT: Uh, but, uh, my views in this field, I'm just telling you my personal views. Uh, and, Henry, you will not be surprised at this, but, uh, we, uh, [unintelligible] tells me about, uh, the, uh, the, uh, uh, these back- grounds and so forth, but he, he may be surprised, but . . . [Unintelligible] views are, are, are frankly, uh, whether it's the environment or pollution or Naderism or consumerism, are extremely pro-business. Uh, we are fighting, frankly, a delaying action in many instances. Uh, we're fighting a delaying action due to the fact, now let me, let me separate two things out: there is pollution. We all know that. You can fly over various places and you can see the stuff in the air. Maybe, there are safety problems, I assume. [Unintelligible] I think they're greatly exaggerated, but there are some. But where there is pollution and where there is safety, the general principle that I believe in is that, well, then we'll do the best we can to, to, to, to, to, to, uh, eliminate the toxins. But we can't have a completely safe society or safe highways or safe cars and pollution-free and so forth. Or we could have, go back and live like a bunch of damned animals. Uh, that won't be too good either. But I also know that using this issue, and, boy, this is true. It's true in, in the environmentalists and it's true of the consumerism people. They're a group of people that aren't one really damn bit interested in safety or clean air. What they're interested in is destroying the system. They're enemies of the system. So, what I'm trying to say is this: that you can speak to me in terms that I am for the system.

UNKNOWN: Right.

PRESIDENT: Uh, uh, I, uh, I, I try to fight the demagogues, uh, to the extent that we can. Uh, I would say this: that I think we have to know that, uh, the tides run very strongly. I mean, you know, the, it's the kick now. You know, the environment kick is in your ads, of course. You're reflecting it. Kids are for it and all the rest, they say. Uh, the safety thing is the kick, 'cause Nader's running around, squealing around about this and that and the other thing. And so out of all this sort of thing what we have to do is to get beyond that: one, to do what is right to do, and then, second, what we, having determined what is right to do, we have to determine [unintelligible] we can do, and having in mind the political problem that we have, I mean, down in the Congress, in the things they will pass and the things that they will ask us to do. So, uh, it's, uh, with that in mind that's, that's, that's the background. Now, tell me the problems you've got with, uh, the industry, with the Department of Transportation, and all these things and let me listen. As [unintelligible].

FORD: Well, I'd like to say first, Mr. President, that, first, we appreciate your taking the time to see us [unintelligible].

PRESIDENT: [Unintelligible].

FORD: We fully understand your time is very limited. Uh, we, I have, have seen all those people: Ruckelshaus and Goalby [sp?] and particularly Thomas in the DOT. . . .

UNKNOWN: Toms.

FORD: . . . so we don't want to have anybody feel that, you know, we're trying to go over anybody's head. . .

FORD: Uh, so, we have, uh, the best we can, tried to keep as close as possible. We even set up a special office down here with engineers so that they can be right next door rather than having to come to Detroit and all that kind of thing. Secondly, I don't think, uh, we want to talk to you today about emissions. . . . I think the thing that concerns us more than anything else is this total safety problem. And, uh, what we're worried about really, basically, is—this isn't an industry problem—is really the economy of the United States, if you want to get into the broad picture because, uh, we represent the total automotive [unintelligible] supply, industry supplies, dealers, dealer [unintelligible] the whole bit, about one-sixth of G.N.P. Now, if the price of cars goes up because emission requirements is gonna be in there, even though we, though we've talked about this morning, safety requirements are in there, bumpers are in there. And these things are, and that's leaving out inflation and material costs increases, which are also there. We think that the price of cars are going to go up from next year through '75 anywhere from a hundred dollars to, up to maybe seven or eight hundred dollars in the next four years because of the requirements that are being, that's leaving out the inflation, which we don't need to discuss. . . .

PRESIDENT: Right.

FORD: . . . with you this morning.

PRESIDENT: That's a problem, too.

FORD: That's a big problem, but we can't do anything about it.

PRESIDENT: This, this is another, and all this will be reflected in the Consumer Price Index and so forth, even though you're uh, you're buying a hell of a lot more car, presumably. But, uh, I see, it—it is. In other words, it'll, it'll kick up the price of cars and all of them, the, the inexpensive ones and the others, too.

FORD: [Unintelligible] we see the price of a Pinto, which now sells for nineteen hundred and nineteen dollars going something like fifty percent in the next three years with inflation part of it, but that's not the big part of it. It's the safety requirements. Now, uh, what we're really talking about? We're talking about trying to put some sense into the Trans, to DOT and how they go about doing their business. Now, they've been in business for, since '66, supposedly. And, uh, they've had problems, we understand that. But, uh, the cost-effectiveness of what they ask us to do has got to be important. And, uh, they, uh, they are asking us to do things that, uh, in our opinion, are driving our people up the wall because they don't know what to do, and, secondly, they ask us one thing this week and then they cancel that and send us out another direction next week. They've got bumper standards for '73; they've got different bumper standards for '74; they've got, uh, air bag standards. All of these things, uh, the only thing that we want to try to, to, to talk to you about this morning is the fact that these things are all going to cost money. If these prices get so high that people stop buying cars. . . .

PRESIDENT: Uh-hum.

FORD: . . . they're gonna buy more foreign cars; you're going to have balance-of-payments problems. . . .

PRESIDENT: Right. I'm convinced. . . .

FORD: Granted, the foreign [unintelligible] have got to do the same thing, but they're doing it at a wage rate that's half [unintelligible].

PRESIDENT: I know, I know. Sure. Uh, what is, uh, let's talk a moment about the procedures. How do they come in? Do they have hearings on these sort of things at the DOT? And then they issue and order and it's [unintelligible] in the executive register. That's about all I know about it. Now, you understand, I haven't approved any policy on it. . . .

UNKNOWN: Oh, sure.

PRESIDENT: . . . yet, but I'm gonna take a look.

IACOCCA: Well, [unintelligible] you directly, Mr. President. They do, they, they have a, a rulemaking procedure. And they promulgate these, and the law, ha, gives us sixty days to respond to a rule they put out. After that sixty days they hear from everybody, foreign manufacturers, the Big Four here, and then they put out a standard. Then you have sixty days to decide what you want to do about that. And once it becomes standard, uh, we're approaching one right now. In fact, on Monday morning, we will in all probability—I'll tell you honestly 'cause our meeting isn't 'til Thursday this week—but our lawyers and engineers too—we have [unintelligible]—we will go to these, uh, court of appeals. We will have our first major confrontation for real this time. Uh, we've had threats before, bah, uh, this brings up this whole issue of, uh, how important is safety. Uh, it's, uh it's a case we're going through, it's not a fad. We. . . .

PRESIDENT: Right.

IACOCCA: . . . didn't have to kill fifty people on the highway. But I, I feel that, you know, we worry about inflation, and we should, 'cause it's eating us up alive right now, and in the next few years, we feel, it's still gonna be bad, as far as our labor contracts are concerned, our materials. . . .

PRESIDENT: Particularly your labor. . . .

IACOCCA: Right.

Transcript of Public Record, Nixon Presidential Library and Museum, National Archives

April 30, 1971

V—Volpe (Secretary of Transportation)
E—Ehrlichman (Assistant to the President for Domestic Affairs)
(Transcript provided by the Nixon Presidential Materials staff at the National Archives.)

V: There will be an avalanche, and I mean an avalanche, of protest in every news-paper in this country. I have absolutely no doubt we've postponed, as the letter we've sent to you pointed out, for a two year period listened to their complaints and their woes and done everything we possibly could to accommodate their requirements and we have allowed them to meet their goals in performance standards in several ways rather than the air bag. Now I suggest to you, John, very sincerely that I think the President and John Volpe and this Department particularly will receive some of the worst editorial comments that we have seen in this area because . . . well, we've had plenty of them recently because we eased up on the farm (foreign?) drivers situation because of a great many requests and we're reviewing it again. We eased up in two or three other areas where industry convinces (?) like I mentioned to you on the bumper situation because industry convices (?) they couldn't meet the five miles an hour—two and a half is the best they could do. We eased up on that and so forth and instead of get-ting patted on the back because we would establish a standard we got knocked because we supposedly got in bed with the manufacturers.

E: Well, I appreciate that the Nader element is very with their public relations and with their access to the press. At the same time the controlling consideration here . . . the two controlling considerations as far as the President's concerned are, first of all, the showing that was made to him that the idea is not a good idea—number one and basic. Number two that we're dealing here with an industry which are basically our friends.

V: Now, Mr. Ford isn't your friend.

E: He sure is.

V: Well, you know what he did in 1960 and what he did in 1964.

E: Yes sir, but I know where he is today. I know exactly where he is today. The point here is that pleasing Ralph Nader doesn't get us anything.

V: It isn't Ralph Nader I'm worried about. Christ, I've kicked him in the teeth several times. Ralph Nader doesn't bother me a damn bit. What I'm concerned about is the editorials of the newspapers of this nation.

E: Well, apparently, the President's willing to take that heat.

V: . . . the President will take the heat, it's John Volpe, as you know, unless, of course, the story gets out . . . won't get out from here, but these damn things have a way of leaking that we're ordered to do it.

E: Well, I have no doubt that that will be apparent before we're all done. The situation here though is not one of having any latitude as far as I'm concerned. I have very definite instructions from the President on this and the only thing that I can do is reconfirm to you the thing that I said to Charley Baker the other day which was very clear that the President wanted the order suspended.

V: Well, John, I don't know what to say to you, I'm trying to do a job over here, as you know. I frankly don't think the President has both sides of the story. Maybe our letter wasn't as good as it should have been. I will admit that I was working on a hell of a lot of other things when I signed this letter.

E: Well, I don't think it's a question of that and I'm sure he doesn't want to get into a trial court situation where he has to sit and listen to both sides and then render a judgment for somebody and against somebody else.

V: It's a natural course, John.

E: It's a situation where people have come to him with a complaint where there's a very, very short time schedule. We're, what, three days away from the deadline.

V: Yeah . . . but we had two years in which to do it. E: Well, that may be, but he feels that the selling was sufficiently strong that they should not be compelled to litigate that rather than that there should a suspensionary (?) order to obviate the necessity of litigating and that there should be a further examination of the problem because he doesn't feel that the solutions to which the bureau has come are reasonable solutions in the premises. Now, the bureau has a number of arguments, one of which interestingly enough in the memorandum, is that the manufacturers don't object to this. Well, we know from the personal representations of these top people that the manufacturers very vigorously do object to it.

V: Well, you and I know damn well, John, I was in industry I know how I fought occupational health hazard regulations on the part of the government.

E: Sure.

V: And you're going to fight. In industry you fight for anything you can get.

E: Well, but there was an affirmative representation in the memorandum that just isn't borne out. Now that's a minor point.

V: After we modified it, John, I'll be very truthful with you, after we modified this and gave them . . . I spoke to Ed Cole about this at Fairfax (?), he said if you can do it this way so that we're given the options and you can put this off until 1973 we can meet it.

E: Yeah, well.

V: Cole told me out there. . . .

E: I understand, but more recently both Ford and GM strongly . . . the point here is simply that the President has temporarily made his mind up at least through next Monday he does not want this order to remain in effect to compel these people to litigate. Now what happens after that I would say is an open question, but he definitely does want the order suspended as of today.

V: Well, is it possible, legally I can't determine, John, because I'm not a lawyer. But if we postpone the effective date for 30 days does that give the auto industry the additional 30 days and then give us a chance to further examine and present this case so that a decision can be made then to well, fine, we haven't made the case and the President decided this is the way he wants to go or that yes he's seen our side of the story.

E: I don't know.

V: Seen everything and so forth.

E: I don't know the answer to that. That's something your General Counsel would have to tell you. The only thing I can put it in terms of is the end result which is —

V: That you don't want the manufacturers to be able or have to go into court on Monday.

E: That's correct.

V: And if a postponement of 30 days prevents them from having to go into court on Monday that would give us a chance to see what can be worked out if anything can be worked out that will accommodate the situation without the kind of avalanche of protest that I'm sure will come down around our necks.

E: Well, the whole point here as far as the scope of my instructions is concerned is that I'm instructed to advise you that the President desires that the order be suspended. Now the reason for it is that he does not want them to be forced to litigate on Monday. The additional reason is that on the selling that has been made thus far he is persuaded that it is not a reasonable regulation. Now whether the suspension should be 30 days or indefinitely or permanently or what it should be I'm not prepared to say.

V: Well, let me check with my General Counsel, John, and I think that what the President decides can be accomplished by the postponement . . . in other words, they have to protect themselves within a certain time frame, right?

E: The Manufacturers?

V: That's correct. And as long as it's postponed and they have that additional 30 days beyond Monday which is the final day in which to enter a decree or judgment or—

E: Well, as you say, that's a technical question and I just don't know the answer to it.

V: Well, I know what the President has asked you to do and you're carrying out his instructions. I personally think it's a mistake but I will comply with it and check with my General Counsel to see whether or not the 30 day suspension is valid and can be done.

E: Alright, then would ask him to just give us a call and let us know which way he plans to proceed.

V: Fine.

E: Thank you.

Notes and Questions

1. Do you suppose that it is unusual for leading industrialists and leading contributors to appear in the Oval Office to plead their case? What about a union, or a public interest group (e.g, the Sierra Club, or the Insurance Institute for Highway Safety)?

2. Is Nixon's conversation with Ford and Iacocca inappropriate, apart from its tone? Is this a case of pandering to special interests, of listening to knowledgeable business leaders, or of answering to members of the electorate? Does it matter? Consider the long speech with which Nixon begins the conversation. What is he inviting Ford and Iacocca to say? What kinds of signals is he giving them about the kinds of issues that would be appropriate or inappropriate to raise?

3. How do Ford, and then Iacocca, respond? What arguments do they make? In terms of content (not tone, of course), do they say anything they would not be prepared to say in public? Are they responding to the implicit invitation in Nixon's opening statement or not?

4. What about Ehrlichman's phone call to Secretary Volpe? On the one hand, the Department of Transportation is an executive-branch agency subject to the President's direct control. No one questions a President's power to fire the Secretary of Transportation if he or she is displeased with the policies that the Secretary is adopting. On the other hand, the Department, specifically NHTSA, is implementing a statute that was passed by Congress for the express purpose of regulating auto safety. At one point in the conversation,

Volpe says: "Well, John, I don't know what to say to you. I'm trying to do a job over here." How is he defining that job?

5. Does the reason that Ehrlichman states for wanting to suspend the rule, namely to avoid litigation by auto manufacturers, eliminate any concern for impropriety? It does suggest that the President is responding to a threat, rather than doing a favor. Couldn't the President or the Secretary say publicly that he was suspending the regulation because he wanted to avoid a lawsuit? But that is not exactly the tone of the phone conversation, is it?

6. What role do public attitudes play in determining the behavior of the various actors? Note Volpe's comment: "There will be an avalanche, and I mean an avalanche, of protest in every newspaper in this country." Compare this with his other effort to resist (however ineffectively) Ehrlichman's demands—his statement that "I'm trying to do a job over here." Note again the interplay between politics and expertise. Volpe does not merely rely on expertise-based arguments against political control, but uses his own political argument as well.

7. Nixon and Ehrlichman seem obsessed with Ralph Nader. Why do they regard him as such a threat? After all, he was a non-partisan consumer advocate who was attacking private companies and urging an increase in government authority. He was harshly critical of Haddon, Johnson's appointment as the first head of NHTSA, and notably less critical of Nixon's appointment, Douglas Toms. After conceding that there are serious pollution and safety problems, Nixon says: "We can't have a completely safe society or safe highways or safe cars and pollution-free and so forth. Or we could have, go back and live like a bunch of damned animals." Is there any plausible interpretation of Nader's actions to suggest that he wanted to abolish automobiles or reverse the industrial revolution? What is Nixon talking about?

As it turned out, there was indeed litigation regarding Standard 208, Notice 9.

Chrysler Corp. v. Department of Transportation

472 F.2d 659 (6th Cir. 1972)

John W. PECK, Circuit Judge.

The petitioners, major domestic and foreign manufacturers of automobiles, have petitioned this Court for a review of an order of the National Highway Traffic Safety Administration of the Department of Transportation, adopted pursuant to the National Traffic and Motor Vehicle Safety Act of 1966, 15 U.S.C. §§1381-1461, entitled "Motor Vehicle Safety Standard #208, Occupant Crash Protection in Passenger Cars, Multipurpose Passenger Vehicles, Trucks and Buses." . . .

I

The standard under review requires the petitioners to build into their vehicles by a specified date a specified quantum of "passive protection" through the use of "passive restraint devices." An "airbag" is a passive inflatable occupant restraint system. Although the safety standard under review does not by its terms specify that airbags be used to meet the specified injury criteria, the petitioners unanimously contend that because the injury criteria of Standard 208 were established with the airbag in mind that the airbag is the only device which can be reasonably expected to satisfy these criteria, and that therefore, the standard is in reality an airbag requirement standard. Although nothing in the record justifies disagreement with the petitioners on this point, for the purposes of this opinion we do not find it necessary to distinguish between the airbag and any other form of passive restraint.

Standard 208 was first published as part of the initial federal standards issued pursuant to 15 U.S.C. §1392(h) on February 3, 1967 (32 F.R. 2415 (1967)) "Seat Belt Installation-Passenger Cars") and established the requirements for seat belt installations.

A proposed change in the initial Standard 208 was first announced in Notice 1, published on July 2, 1969, entitled "Inflatable Occupant Restraint Systems" (34 F.R. 11148).

After a lengthy evaluation of the comments of the manufacturers and other interested parties and newly developed technical information, the Agency issued a notice of a proposed safety standard entitled "Occupant Crash Protection; Passenger Cars, Multipurpose Passenger Vehicles, Trucks and Buses" (Notice 4, 35 F.R. 7187). The Agency held numerous formal and informal meetings and conferences; comments were submitted by more than 120 interested persons. After consideration of these comments and other relevant materials, the Agency issued the passive protection requirements of the standard as a final rule in Notice 7 on November 3, 1970 (35 F.R. 16927).

In response to a variety of objections raised in comments and in petitions for reconsideration, the Agency republished Standard 208 on March 10, 1971, as Notice 9 (36 F.R. 4600), a complete and final rule. This notice forms the basis of the Agency's action which is before this Court for review. Notice 12 (36 F.R. 19254) was issued on October 1, 1971, as a response to the petitions for reconsideration of Notice 9, and is the second of the two notices which this Court has been requested to review. This amendment clarifies the monitoring system requirements for a passive system, specifies the positioning and locations of the anthropomorphic test devices and changes the cargo weight to be used for testing multipurpose passenger vehicles and trucks. In the comments to Notice 9, the Agency acknowledged that the test dummy specifications were inadequate and that variances in dummies could jeopardize the test results of a vehicle attempting to comply with the standard. The Agency stated that it would issue, at a later date, proposed amendments to the standard detailing performance and descriptive specifications for the test dummies. In the interim, the Agency stated in the comments to Notice 12 that if a vehicle is found to comply with the existing standard under a properly conducted test by a manufacturer the negative results of an Agency test will not be used as the basis for a finding of non-compliance so long as the difference in the test results can be attributed to the test dummies.

Notice 13 (36 F.R. 19266), issued simultaneously with Notice 12, proposed an amendment to Standard 208 which would allow for an additional interim option of a seat belt interlock system which will not allow the engine starting system in a vehicle to operate unless the driver and any front seat passengers have fastened their seat belts. . . .

Chrysler, Jeep, American Motors, Ford and the Automobile Importers of America have petitioned this Court for a review of Notice 9; Ford, American Motors and Jeep have petitioned this Court for a review of Notice 12. These petitions for review were consolidated in this Court, and were argued together. Notice 9, as amended by Notices 10, 12, 15 and 16 is designed to be implemented in three stages, the first two of which offer a manufacturer the choice of several options for compliance:

STAGE ONE: A manufacturer must provide on all vehicles manufactured between January 1, 1972, and August 14, 1973, one of the following three options:

(1) "Complete Passive Protection," defined as a system which meets specified injury criteria for all seating positions in all impact modes, frontal (head-on into a fixed barrier at 30 mph), angular (30 degrees from either side of frontal into a fixed barrier), and side (90 degrees from frontal, impact at 20 mph with a lateral moving barrier) and which will prohibit any part of two test dummies from extending outside any part of the car in a rollover test (rollover in either lateral direction at 30 mph); or

(2) Sufficient interior padding plus lap belts such that the prescribed injury criteria are met at the front outboard positions with test dummies in a 30 mph frontal crash into a fixed barrier; or

(3) Lap and shoulder belt systems with warning signals at the front outboard positions that restrain test dummies in a 30 mph frontal test crash without complete separation of the belts themselves or their anchorages, plus lap belts at other seating positions.

STAGE TWO: A manufacturer must provide on all vehicles manufactured after August 15, 1973, one of the following three options:

(1) "Complete Passive Protection"; or

(2) Passive protection for front seat positions which will meet specified injury criteria in a 30 mph headon crash into a fixed barrier, plus lap belts at all other positions; or

(3) Seat belts with ignition interlocks[1] for front seat passengers, plus non-interlocked belts at other positions which must meet the specified injury criteria for front outboard occupants in a 30 mph impact into a fixed barrier.

STAGE THREE: By August 15, 1975, a manufacturer must provide "Complete Passive Protection." . . .

III

The petitioners' first argument is that the Automobile Safety Act of 1966 does not authorize the Agency to establish a safety standard which requires the improvement of existing technology, and that the Agency may only establish performance requirements which can be met with devices which, at the time of the rulemaking, are developed to the point that they may be readily installed. The explicit purpose of the Act, as amplified in its legislative history, is to enable the Federal government to impel automobile manufacturers to develop and apply new technology to the task of improving the safety design of automobiles as readily as possible. . . .

> "[T]his legislation reflects the faith that the restrained and responsible exercise of Federal authority can channel the creative energies and vast technology of the automobile industry into a vigorous and competitive effort to improve the safety of vehicles." S. REP. 1301, 89th Cong., 2d Sess., 2 U.S. Code, Cong. and Admin. News, 2709 (1966).

The same report continues:

> "While the bill reported by the committee authorizes the Secretary to make grants or award contracts for research in certain cases, a principal aim is to encourage the auto industry itself to engage in greater auto safety and safety-related research." *Id.* at 2718.

There is no suggestion in the Act that developed technology be in use by an automobile manufacturer or that any given procedure be an established industry practice prior to its incorporation into a federal motor vehicle safety standard. If the Agency were so limited, it would have little discretion to accomplish its primary mission of reducing the deaths and injuries resulting from highway accidents.

In fact, specific efforts by the Automobile Manufacturers Association to tie the rate of innovation imposed by safety standards to the pace of innovation of the manufacturers were rejected by the House Committee on Interstate and Foreign Commerce, and the reported bill proposed that safety standards be "practicable, meet the need for motor vehicle safety, and be stated in objective terms." . . .

In summary, the Agency is empowered to issue safety standards which require improvements in existing technology or which require the development of new technology, and it is not limited to issuing standards based solely

---

1. The interlock system must prevent the starting of the engine if any front seat occupant does not have his belt fastened. The occupant must be seated before the belt system is fastened, and unfastening a belt after the engine is started may not stop the engine, but must activate a light-sound warning system.

on devices already fully developed. This is in accord with the Congressional mandate that "safety shall be the overriding consideration in the issuance of standards." S. Rep. 1301 (1966).

The petitioners next contend that Standard 208 is not practicable because airbag technology is not, at present, developed to the point where airbags can be installed in all presently manufactured cars. In light of our preceding conclusion, we need not discuss this contention at length. But we will observe that, as the record indicates, many of the development problems with which the petitioners have concerned themselves in their briefs (such as noise, sensor reliability, danger to out of position occupants and effectiveness in certain nonfrontal impact modes), have been eliminated or are presently the subject of continuing development efforts. We need not detail here the immense amount of factual data contained in the record relevant to this issue; suffice it to here observe that present systems demonstrate considerable sophistication over earlier prototypes. In addition, several automobile manufacturers and several airbag developers have expressed a great deal of confidence in their present systems and an equal confidence that present developmental research programs will eliminate any obstacles which may presently remain. . . .

Since we have rejected the petitioners' contention that nonexisting technology may not be the subject of motor vehicle safety standards, and in view of the present state of the art of passive inflatable occupant restraint systems, we conclude that Standard 208 is practicable as that term is used in this legislation.[2]

The petitioners contend that Standard 208 does not meet the need for motor vehicle safety because belts offer better protection to occupants than do airbags. The Agency defends the standard by contending that airbags offer better protection to occupants than do belts. The record supports the conclusion that each type of occupant restraint offers protection in a slightly different form for differing impact situations. Neither is clearly superior to the other in every respect. Consequently, we conclude that the Agency's decision to abandon active restraints in favor of passive restraints was a proper exercise of its administrative discretion.

Paramount among the Agency's considerations in deciding to require all occupant restraint systems to be fully passive was the factor of low belt usage. It is uncontested that active restraints are not extensively used. The record indicates that usage rates for lap belts are about 20 to 30%, and for the lap and shoulder harness combination about 1 to 5%; it is projected that devices (or laws) to encourage or to force belt usage will not increase usage rates above 60%. The petitioners' position is that, if the Agency starts with the proposition that occupants are not now using belts, its consequent course of action should be an effort to increase belt usage through whatever means are available (e.g.: ignition interlocks, compulsory usage laws) rather

---

2. The House Report indicates that "practicable" requires consideration of all relevant factors, including the technological ability to achieve the goal of a particular standard. . . .

than to disregard active restraints entirely and require passive protection in all vehicles.

It is conceded that belts, when used, are extremely effective. The conclusive evidence on this point is a study of more than 28,000 accident cases in Sweden which showed that no occupant wearing a combined lap belt and shoulder harness was fatally injured in any accident occurring at speeds below 60 miles per hour. On the other hand, while belts are superior to airbags in some respects, most notably in rollovers and multiple impact situations, airbags have advantages over belts in other equally important respects. For example, airbags spread crash deceleration forces over most of the whole body, while belts concentrate them on the narrow area of the rigid belt. Airbags restrain the body evenly over a greater distance and a longer period of time by permitting occupants who are thrown forward in the crash to ride down the deceleration forces more gradually, over a distance of two or three feet. An airbag system, being passive, removes the elements of the occupants' will, memory and skill from the consideration of reliability. Furthermore, many people cannot properly use belt systems (e.g.: children under four years of age, persons under 55 inches in height, obese or very smallwaisted persons and pregnant women) and among those who can, there is an inevitable percentage who will not wear them properly. We cite these facts not to advocate belts over airbags or vice versa, but to indicate the myriad factors which must be carefully considered by the Agency in reaching a conclusion on this issue.

We conclude that the issue of the relative effectiveness of active as opposed to passive restraints is one which has been duly delegated to the Agency, with its expertise, to make; we find that the Agency's decision to require passive restraints is supported by substantial evidence, and we cannot say on the basis of the record before us that this decision does not meet the need for motor vehicle safety.

IV

We now turn to the final major substantive argument presented by the petitioners: that Standard 208 fails to meet the statutorily required criteria of objectivity. The necessity for objective certainty in the performance requirements of safety standards was clearly recognized by Congress in the Safety Act. The Act provides, as noted above, that "standard[s] shall be practicable, shall meet the need for motor vehicle safety, and shall be stated in objective terms." 15 U.S.C. §1392(a). These requirements are repeated in the statutory definition of motor vehicle safety standards: "'Motor vehicle safety standards' means a minimum standard for motor vehicle performance, or motor vehicle equipment performance, which is practicable, which meets the need for motor vehicle safety and which provides objective criteria." 15 U.S.C. §1391(2). The requirement of objectivity was emphasized in the following statement from the House Report: In order to insure that the question of whether there is compliance with the standard can be answered by objective measurements and without recourse to any subjective determination, every standard must be stated in objective terms." H.R. 1776, 89th Cong., 2d Sess. 1966, p. 16.

The importance of objectivity in safety standards cannot be overemphasized. The Act puts the burden upon the manufacturer to assure that his vehicles comply under pain of substantial penalties. In the absence of objectively defined performance requirements and test procedures, a manufacturer has no assurance that his own test results will be duplicated in tests conducted by the Agency. Accordingly, such objective criteria are absolutely necessary so that "the question of whether there is compliance with the standard can be answered by objective measurement and without recourse to any subjective determination."

Objective, in the context of this case, means that tests to determine compliance must be capable of producing identical results when test conditions are exactly duplicated, that they be decisively demonstrable by performing a rational test procedure, and that compliance is based upon the readings obtained from measuring instruments as opposed to the subjective opinions of human beings. Standard 208 requires that compliance be determined by specified tests using an anthropomorphic dummy built to the specifications of SAE Recommended Practice J963, "Anthropomorphic Test Device for Dynamic Testing." These specifications generally provide for the structural characteristics of the dummy, which is to simulate the basic human body components in size, shape, mass and kinematics. The petitioners contend that this test device will not produce consistent, reliable, or repeatable test results. The record supports the conclusions that the test procedures and the test device specified by Standard 208 are not objective in at least the following respects: (1) The absence of an adequate flexibility criteria for the dummy's neck; the existing specifications permit the neck to be very stiff, or very flexible, or somewhere in between, significantly affecting the resultant forces measured on the dummy's head. (2) Permissible variations in the test procedure for determining thorax dynamic spring rate (force deflection characteristics of the dummy's chest) permit considerable latitude in chest construction which could produce wide variations in maximum chest deceleration between two different dummies, each of which meets the literal requirements of SAE J963. (3) The absence of specific, objective specifications for construction of the dummy's head permits significant variation in forces imparted to the accelerometer by which performance is to be measured.

The shortcomings of the test device become understandable, if still not excusable, when one considers the minutes of a May 23, 1971, meeting of the SAE Crash Test Dummy Subcommittee, which are a part of the record in this case. That report points out that since SAE J963 only relates some limited performance specifications for an anthropomorphic test device, it should be used as a guide for specifications of such a device, with considerations given to certain enumerated shortcomings. Further, the report mentions that "[i]t should be noted that the original document [SAE J963] was intended to specify a research tool and, therefore, the document was written in general terms," and that until more definitive specifications are published, "[t]he subcommittee is of the opinion that SAE Recommended Practice J963 can only be used as a guide rather than as a rigid set of specifications." The Safety Systems Laboratory (formerly of the office of Vehicle Systems Research, National Bureau of Standards, now of the NHTSA) reported in September of 1971 that SAE J963 is not "sufficiently definitive to provide an adequate description of the dummies" and concluded that "further study is necessary to develop standard specifications for an anthropometric crash dummy."

Further recitation of statements from the record that the test procedure and devices of Standard 208 lack objectivity is unnecessary because, interestingly enough, the Agency has never asserted that its test criteria are fully objective. Although the Agency noted, at the time it first proposed the adoption of SAE J963, that these dummy specifications "may not provide totally reproducible results," it justified their adoption because they are "evidently the most complete set available at this time." 35 F.R. 7188. Specific comments were requested from interested parties; comments were submitted by each of the parties to this action. The Agency replied to these comments in Notice 7 by modifying the specifications slightly, but retained the requirement of the SAE J963 dummy, noting only that "dummies conforming to the SAE specifications are the most complete and satisfactory ones presently available." 35 F.R. 16928. In Notice 9, the Agency again remarked not that the SAE J963 dummy was adequate, but that it was the "best available," and that it was sponsoring research in this area and would therefore issue new specifications at some time in the future. Virtually all automobile manufacturers, including each of the present petitioners, submitted petitions for reconsideration to these requirements of Notice 9. General Motors went so far as to supply suggested modifications and additions to the SAE J963 test device specifications which it felt were necessary before a device would provide consistent test results.

The Agency makes two responses to the attacks upon the standard's lack of objectivity. First, it contends that the incompleteness of the dummy device is not fatal to the standard because it has assured the manufacturers that specifications for a suitable test device will be issued in the future. We do not think it necessary to dwell upon the obvious inadequacy of this response because it seems to us axiomatic that a manufacturer cannot be required to develop an effective restraint device in the absence of an effective testing device which will assure uniform, repeatable and consistent test results.

The Agency's second response is that it has assured the manufacturers that their position with regard to compliance will not be jeopardized by the variances in the test device. The Agency's solution to the problem was set out in Notice 12:

> "If the NHTSA concludes after investigation that a manufacturer's tests are properly conducted, with dummies meeting the specifications, and show compliance with the standard, and that differences in results from tests conducted by the agency are due to differences in the test dummies used by each, the Agency tests will not be considered to be the basis for a finding of noncompliance." 36 F.R. 19255.

This statement is illusory. This test allows as many as three subjective judgments to be made by the Agency, including the ultimate determination of whether the differences in results from tests conducted by the Agency are due to differences in the test dummies used by each. As noted above, objectivity requires that each essential element of compliance be made by specified measuring instruments; there is no room for an "agency investigation" in this procedure. The inherent uncertainty of this procedure is no substitute for the specification of an adequate test device, especially in light of the Agency's power to specify such a device. As the Agency noted in Notice 12:

> "[S]ince the dummy is merely a test instrument and not an item of regulated equipment, it is not necessary to describe it in performance terms; its design could legally be 'frozen' by detailed, blueprint-type drawings and complete equipment specifications." 36 F.R. 19255.

While we have concluded that automobile manufacturers can (and should) be compelled by automobile safety standards to develop new safety devices, we hold that the performance goals which they must meet must be clearly delineated by the Agency. That is to say, while they can be required to develop a new device not presently existing, we do not think that they can (or should) simultaneously be required to develop a testing device by which the safety device is to be measured.

The Amicus Center for Auto Safety cautions that if we were to hold that the standard is invalid because the test procedures are not objective we would be allowing "the tail to wag the dog." We think that the Center has misapprehended the anatomy of the animal. The Act requires the Agency to issue performance standards, which a manufacturer must then meet by any system of hardware it chooses. It is clear from a reading of the Act and its legislative history that the performance standards (injury criteria and test procedures) are in fact the "dog" to which a manufacturer is free to attach the tail of its choosing. To rule otherwise would be to permit the Agency to establish a "product standard" requiring airbags, without requiring it to establish adequate, objective and repeatable test procedures by which a manufacturer's airbags can be measured, by it or by the Agency, for compliance.

We conclude that [the paragraph] of Standard 208 which requires the use of the anthropomorphic test device as defined in SAE Recommended Practice J963 to be invalid; the remaining portions of the standard which do not depend for their effectiveness upon [that paragraph] are valid and remain in effect. . . . The proceeding is remanded to the Agency with instructions that any further specifications for test devices be made in objective terms which will assure comparable results among testing agencies, and that the effective date for the implementation of passive restraints be delayed until a reasonable time after such test specifications are issued.

William E. MILLER, Circuit Judge (concurring in part and dissenting in part).

The effect of Judge Peck's opinion, as I construe it, is to postpone indefinitely the development of an automobile safety device which, according to the record, holds definite promise of contributing materially to the reduction in the number of deaths and serious injuries from automobile accidents.

For the reasons discussed in this opinion, I do not believe that this result is required either by the National Traffic and Motor Vehicle Safety Act of 1966 nor by the motor vehicle safety standard as formulated by the administrative agency.

First, I disagree with the implication in the majority opinion that in all cases the National Traffic and Motor Vehicle Safety Act of 1966 makes no distinction between "motor vehicle safety standards" and "methods for inspecting and testing to determine compliance with motor vehicle safety standards." Second, I am not able to agree that in this case the form in which Standard 208 was promulgated precludes separating the motor vehicle safety standard from the compliance testing device and procedures. Third, I cannot agree with what I believe is an overly broad definition of the statutory word "objective." Fourth, I am in disagreement with the position that under this legislation the government has the sole burden of developing and perfecting methods of compliance testing and that the National Highway Traffic Safety Administration cannot require the automobile industry to develop or refine compliance testing devices or procedures as part of its development of new technological advances in automotive safety. Fifth, I am unable to agree that Standard 208 is invalid. . . . Confronted with the appalling statistics of death and debilitating injuries on American highways and the inexorable fact that the promotion of automotive safety through voluntary industry standards had proved inadequate, Congress responded with strong, sweeping federal legislation. The paramount intent of the National Traffic and Motor Vehicle Safety Act of 1966, evidenced by the Congressional declaration of purpose in 15 U.S.C. §1381, "is to reduce traffic accidents and deaths and injuries to persons resulting from traffic accidents." The definition of "motor vehicle safety" contained in the Act succinctly states this Congressional resolution as well.

> "'Motor vehicle safety' means the performance of motor vehicles or motor vehicle equipment in such a manner that the public is protected against unreasonable risk of accidents occurring as a result of the design, construction or performance of motor vehicles and is also protected against unreasonable risk of death or injury to persons in the event accidents do occur. . . ."

15 U.S.C. §1391(1). To accomplish this laudable objective of motor vehicle safety, Congress determined "that it is necessary to establish motor vehicle safety standards for motor vehicles and equipment. . . ." 15 U.S.C. §1381. It consequently placed an affirmative duty upon the Secretary of Transportation to promulgate such standards in the first sentence of 15 U.S.C. §1392(a): "The Secretary shall establish by order appropriate Federal motor vehicle safety standards." In addition to directing the formulation of such safety standards, Congress also specified the yardstick by which such motor vehicle safety standards are to be judged in this same section: "Each such Federal motor vehicle safety standard shall be practicable, shall meet the need for motor vehicle safety, and shall be stated in objective terms." 15 U.S.C. §1392(a). This section identifies three substantive restrictions upon each motor vehicle safety standard promulgated pursuant to the Act which

are repeated in the definition section characterizing a motor vehicle safety standard:

> " 'Motor vehicle safety standards' means a minimum standard for motor vehicle performance, or motor vehicle equipment performance, which is practicable, which meets the need for motor vehicle safety and which provides objective criteria."

15 U.S.C. §1391(2). Since only the third of the statutory requirements by which a motor vehicle safety standard is to be judged is in issue at this point, it deserves repeating that these sections speak only of a motor vehicle safety standard and do not mention compliance testing: "Each such Federal motor vehicle safety standard . . . shall be stated in objective *terms*." 15 U.S.C. §1392(a). [Emphasis added.] " 'Motor vehicle safety standards' means a minimum standard for motor vehicle performance, or motor vehicle equipment performance . . . which provides objective *criteria*." 15 U.S.C. §1391(2) [emphasis added]. Both these sections utilize the same terminology except that §1391(2) uses the word "criteria" while §1392(a) uses the word "terms." Consequently, it must be determined whether Congress in using the word "criteria" in §1391(2) expanded the requirement of objectivity to apply to more than just a motor vehicle safety standard and therefore intended that the objectivity test should be applicable to compliance testing devices and procedures as well. . . .

From a reading of the statutory text alone, it would appear that the requirement of objectivity applies only to a motor vehicle safety standard. Further support for this position is provided by the language of 15 U.S.C. §1396 which specifically separates and distinguishes these two concepts.

> The Secretary is authorized to advise, assist, and cooperate with, other Federal departments and agencies, and State and other interested public and private agencies, in the planning and development of—
>
> (1) *motor vehicle safety standards*;
> (2) *methods for inspecting and testing to determine compliance with motor vehicle safety standards*. [Emphasis added.]

In light of the fact that Congress was demonstrably cognizant of a difference between "motor vehicle safety standards" and "methods for inspecting and testing to determine compliance with motor vehicle safety standards," and in §§1391(2) and 1392(a) chose only the words "motor vehicle safety standards" when enumerating the substantive requirements by which such standards were to be judged, the proper interpretation of the Act would clearly appear to be that the objectivity requirement applies only to "motor vehicle safety standards" and does not mandate this requirement for testing devices or procedures. My understanding of Judge Peck's position is that these two clearly delineated statutory concepts are inseparable in all cases involving motor vehicle safety standards. I am in basic disagreement with this view. . . .

Since the Act makes clear that motor vehicle safety standards are distinct from methods for inspecting and testing to determine compliance with motor vehicle safety standards, that the statutory requirement of objectivity applies only to motor vehicle safety standards, and since the Agency has impliedly recognized these facts in Standard 208, in my opinion, it is a mistake to apply the objectivity test to the compliance test instrument (dummy).

The Act does not define "objective" but the House and Senate Committee Reports indicate what was meant by this word. The House Report states:

> In order to insure that the question of whether there is compliance with the standard can be answered by objective *measurement* and without recourse to any subjective determination, every standard must be stated in objective terms.

H.R. Rep. No. 1776, 89th Cong., 2d Sess. 16 (1966) [emphasis added]. The Senate Report, by incorporating an example states: "The Secretary would thus be concerned with the *measurable* performance of a braking system, but not its design details." S. Rep. No. 1301, 89th Cong., 2d Sess., 2 U.S. Code, Cong. and Admin. News, 2714 (1966) [emphasis added]. Since both these Reports use a derivative of the word "measure" in referring to a motor vehicle safety standard, the word "objective" in 15 U.S.C. §§1391(2) and 1392(a) means that a motor vehicle safety standard is to be prescribed in quantitative or measurable terms—as opposed to qualitative terms.

The majority opinion in defining "objective" states:

> Objective, in the context of this case, means that tests to determine compliance must be capable of producing identical results when test conditions are exactly duplicated, that they be decisively demonstrable by performing a rational test procedure, and that compliance is based upon the readings obtained from measuring instruments as opposed to the subjective opinions of human beings.

This expansive definition, in my opinion, is much broader than is necessary to decide this case and consequently should be avoided for several reasons. First, the opinion's statement supposedly limiting its definition of the word "objective" to "the context of this case" is unrealistic. Since this word is statutory language it cannot have a meaning all its own for this particular case, but rather must have a definition which is applicable to all cases arising under 15 U.S.C. §§1391(2) and 1392(a). Second, from this definition the opinion implies that the Agency has an affirmative duty to prescribe, contemporaneously with the issuance of a motor vehicle safety standard, a fully pre-developed compliance testing device. In my opinion, a proper construction of the Act only places a duty on the Agency to delineate a motor vehicle safety standard which is capable of measurement and not necessarily a compliance test instrument and procedure at the time the standard is promulgated. To avoid this unwarranted implication which makes the opinion's definition broader than is necessary to decide this case, the word "objective" should be defined to mean "measurable."

Although the opinion does not specifically deal with the petitioners' objection to the rollover requirement of Standard 208, this objection illustrates the danger of such a broad definition of the word. The first injury criterion of Standard 208 requires that all portions of any test device must be contained within the vehicle passenger compartment throughout the vehicle rollover procedure. This requirement anticipates measurement by visual inspection. In my view it is stated in objective terms since it may be measured by the eye, but under the opinion's definition of objective even this injury criterion is invalid because conformance would not be "based upon the readings obtained from measuring instruments. . . ." . . .

It follows from the foregoing that the proceeding should not be remanded to the Agency. On the contrary, the petitions should be dismissed and the determinations and orders of the Agency should be upheld.

Notes and Questions

1. The first part of the decision provides a good summary of the previous history of Standard 208. Think of the strategy sessions, the staff work, and the varied debates that occurred within NHTSA as these variations were proposed and superseded. This is not intended to make you feel sorry for the agency, which after all does not have feelings, but rather to provide some sense of the complexity of the administrative process.

2. Take a look at the Motor Vehicle Safety Act again, and specifically at Section 102(2), the definition of a Motor Vehicle Safety Standard, and Section 103(a). Did the terms used in those provisions strike you as significant at the time, or did they just seem to be general descriptions of an overall idea? Did the Court overinterpret them? Did the drafting error we pointed out in the notes to the Act contribute to the Court's approach (that is, that substituting the definition for the term used is Section 103 leads to the reading that "Each such [minimum standard . . . which is practicable, which meets the need for motor vehicle safety and which provides objective criteria] shall be practicable, shall meet the need for motor vehicle safety, and shall be stated in objective terms.")? The Court mentions both as if there is significance to the repetition, rather than just slovenly drafting. It does not point out the discrepancy between the two. Is there a difference between providing objective criteria (the definition) and stated in objective terms (the substantive provision)? Does the overlap produce a more demanding standard?

3. In which ways did the agency win, and in which ways did it lose? The court agrees wholeheartedly with NHTSA on the issue of technology-forcing, a matter that was in doubt when the regulation was drafted. This was a big win for the agency because it eliminated the automakers' best argument against passive restraints—that is, that passive restraints failed to conform to the statute's practicability requirement. But if the agency won big on technology forcing, it lost big on the objectivity of its crash tests. To evaluate the magnitude of this defeat, think about the consequences in the context of the agency's political environment. In trying to develop tests that will meet the objectivity standard, who will it need to contend with? What will that interaction look like?

4. The Court seems to express a lot of sympathy for the auto manufacturers and their inability to know what they were being required to do. Is this justified? After all, the domestic auto industry consisted of three extremely large companies and a fourth moderately large company (American Motors), all of which were in continuous contact with NHTSA. Why couldn't the requirements be developed by a more fluid process of negotiation between the agency and these four companies? Would that have been a violation of the law? Would it have changed the balance of power between the agency and the companies in a way that Congress did not want?

NHTSA responded to the *Chrysler* decision by providing new dummy specifications for passive restraints, using an existing dummy that had been developed by General Motors. It did not specify further action. What was left of Standard 208? It permitted automakers to install ignition interlocks, an inexpensive device that prevented the car from starting or buzzed continuously unless the seatbelt was fastened. After *Chrysler*, the ignition interlock was the only option left on the table, pending further developments consistent with the decision. Thus, automakers installed ignition interlocks in the 1974 models.

As it turned out, car owners did not like the ignition interlock. In fact, Congress received more negative mail about this device than it had about any other issue in the history of the United States. It responded as follows.

National Highway Traffic Safety Administration, Motor Vehicle and School Bus Safety Amendments of 1974

Pub. L. No. 93-492, 88 Stat. 1470, 1482

SEC. 109. OCCUPANT RESTRAINT SYSTEMS.

The National Traffic and Motor Vehicle Safety Act of 1986 is amended by inserting after section 124 the following new section:

"SEC. 125. (a) Not later than 60 days after the date of enactment of this section, the Secretary shall amend the Federal motor vehicle safety standard numbered 208 (49 CFR 571.208), so as to bring such standard into conformity with the requirements of paragraphs (1), (2), and (3) of subsection (b) of this section. Such amendment shall take effect not later than 120 days after the date of enactment of this section.

"(b) After the effective date of the amendment prescribed under subsection (a):

"(1) No Federal motor vehicle safety standard may—

"(A) have the effect of requiring, or

"(B) provide that a manufacturer is permitted to comply with such standard by means of, any continuous buzzer designed to indicate that safety belts are not in use, or any safety belt interlock system.

"(2) Except as otherwise provided in paragraph (3), no Federal motor vehicle safety standard respecting occupant restraint systems may—

"(A) have the effect of requiring, or

"(B) provide that a manufacturer is permitted to comply with such standard by means of, an occupant restraint system other than a belt system.

"(3) (A) Paragraph (2) shall not apply to a Federal motor vehicle safety standard which provides that a manufacturer is permitted to comply with such standard by equipping motor vehicles manufactured by him with either—

"(i) a belt system, or

"(ii) any other occupant restraint system specified in such standard,

"(B) Paragraph (2) shall not apply to any Federal motor vehicle safety standard which the Secretary elects to promulgate in accordance with the procedure specified in subsection (c), unless it is disapproved by both Houses of Congress by concurrent resolution m accordance with subsection (d).

"(C) Paragraph (2) shall not apply to a Federal motor vehicle safety standard if at the time of promulgation of such standard (i) the 60-day period determined under subsection (d) has expired with respect to any previously promulgated standard which the Secretary has elected to promulgate in accordance with subsection (c), and (ii) both Houses of Congress have not by concurrent resolution within such period disapproved such previously promulgated standard.

"(c) The procedure referred to in subsection (b)(3)(B) and (C) in accordance with which the Secretary may elect to promulgate a standard is as follows:

"(1) The standard shall be promulgated in accordance with section 103 of this Act, subject to the other provisions of this subsection.

"(2) Section 553 of title 5, "United States Code, shall apply to such standard; except that the Secretary shall afford interested persons an opportunity for oral as well as written presentation of data, views, or arguments. A transcript shall be kept of any oral presentation.

"(3) The chairmen and ranking minority members of the House Interstate and Foreign Commerce Committee and the Senate Commerce Committee shall be notified in writing of any proposed standard to which this section applies. Any Member of Congress may make an oral presentation of data, views, or arguments under paragraph (2).

"(4) Any standard promulgated pursuant to this subsection shall be transmitted to both Houses of Congress, on the same day and to each House while it is in session. In addition, such standard shall be transmitted, to the chairmen and ranking minority members of the committees referred to in paragraph (3).

"(d) (1) A standard which the Secretary has elected to promulgate in accordance with subsection (c) shall not be effective if, during the first period of 60 calendar days of continuous session, of Congress after the date of transmittal to Congress, both Houses of Congress pass a concurrent resolution the matter after the resolving clause of which reads as follows: 'The Congress disapproves the Federal motor vehicle safety standard transmitted to Congress on————, 19—.'; (the blank space being filled with date of transmittal of the standard to Congress). If both Houses do not pass such a resolution during such period, such standard shall not be effective until the expiration of such period (unless the standard specifies a later date).

"(f) For purposes of this section:

"(1) The term 'safety belt interlock' means any system designed to prevent starting or operation of a motor vehicle if one or more occupants of such vehicle are not using safety belts.

"(2) The term 'belt system' means an occupant restraint system consisting of integrated lap and shoulder belts for front outboard occupants and lap belts for other occupants. With respect to (A) motor vehicles other than passenger vehicles, (B) convertibles, and (C) open-body type vehicles, such term also includes an occupant restraint system consisting of hip belts or lap belts combined with detachable shoulder belts.

"(3) The term 'occupant restraint system' means a system the principal purpose of which is to assure that occupants of a motor vehicle, remain in their seats in the event of a collision or rollover. Such term does not include a warning device designed to indicate that seat belts are not in use.

"(4) The term 'continuous buzzer' means a buzzer other than a buzzer which operates only during the 8 second period after the ignition is turned to the 'start' or 'on' position."

Gerald R. Ford, Statement on Signing the Motor Vehicle and School Bus Safety Amendments of 1974

October 28, 1974

I have signed S. 355, the Motor Vehicle and School Bus Safety Amendments of 1974.

This act renews our national commitment to the promotion of highway safety, a goal shared not only by the Congress and my Administration but by every American. Last year, more than 56,000 people lost their lives on America's highways. Although the accident and death rates on our highways are declining, we can never be satisfied with the level of tragic loss and injury on our roads.

By signing S. 355, I believe we will accelerate our commitment to reduce deaths and injuries on the highway. It authorizes $55 million for the current fiscal year and $60 million for fiscal year 1976 to carry out the important mandate contained in the National Traffic and Motor Vehicle Safety Act of 1966. . . .

Finally, this act also does away with the so-called seat belt interlock systems. This system had the laudable goal of encouraging motorists to wear their safety belts. In practice, however, it has proved to be intensely unpopular with the American motorist. I can fully understand why drivers might object to being forced by the Federal Government, in effect, to buckle up. This constitutes an unacceptable governmental intrusion into the life of the individual.

However, in signing this removal of the interlock system, I am in no way encouraging drivers to desist from using their seat belts. To the contrary, safety restraints save lives and prevent injuries. I give my strongest recommendation that all Americans follow the sound advice which tells us to "buckle up for safety."

To emphasize my concern for highway safety, I want also to remind every American to observe sensible driving speeds and especially not to exceed 55 miles per hour. As we all know, the lowering of the highway speed limit has saved lives and conserved energy. Saving lives, saving fuel, and saving the motorist money in the operation of his vehicle are goals we can all find worthy in the months ahead.

Notes and Questions

1. The ignition interlock issue illustrates the ability of the people, in a democratic society such as ours, to transform a regulatory issue into a hot-button political one. Up until this point, the public was a mass of separate individuals who refused to comply with NHTSA's regulations. All of a sudden, they turned into a mobilized political force that could directly influence a decision maker superior to the agency. What do you suppose was the source of the widespread and vociferous reaction to the ignition interlock? Could NHTSA have anticipated this reaction?

2. Would there be this same reaction today? When you were little, did your parents insist that you wear a seatbelt? (Answer this question only if you were born after 1990.) If so, did you perceive it as an assault on your freedom? Do you use a seat belt today? Would you do so even if the car didn't buzz (intermittently, of course)?

3. Were the 1974 Amendments democracy at work? Or does the prohibition of the ignition interlock indicate a failure in the democratic system of government? Suppose the two major parties had agreed that the interlock would save lives, and that they would not amend the statute or use the issue against each other in political campaigns. Would that have been a betrayal of our system? This issue is generally referred to as paternalism. As discussed in Chapter 2, the term refers to action by government officials that goes against the preferences of the majority (most democratic legislation goes against the preferences of some minority) on the grounds that the officials know what is best for the people. A milder version, which may still count as paternalism depending on your views, occurs when government officials take action that they think is best for the people without making any effort to find out what a majority of the people want. This occurs all the time in administrative governance. Unless there is either a widespread reaction from the public, as there was in the ignition interlock case, the views of the public are generally ignored. They do not serve as a basis for judicial review of agency action (*see* APA §706).

4. Note the special procedure that the Amendments establish for the promulgation of new regulations regarding passive restraints. Clearly, it is a response to the extraordinarily strong reaction from the public. It consists of three elements. The lesser elements, provided in Subsections (c)(2) and (3), are that NHTSA must hold some sort of oral hearing when using the informal rulemaking procedures of §553, and that notice must be provided to the chair and ranking minority members of the House and Senate Commerce Committees. As you know, §553 does not require oral hearings, although agencies sometimes hold them voluntarily. What do you think Congress way trying to achieve by requiring them here, and by requiring the special notification of the two Congressional committees?

5. The more demanding element Congress' special procedure is the Subsection (c)(4) provision that it may block passive restraint regulations by means of a concurrent resolution. A concurrent resolution, as the Amendments provide, is a measure enacted by a majority of both Houses of Congress. It should be distinguished from a joint resolution, which follows the same procedure as a statute; that is, passage by both Houses and presentment to the President for signature or veto. Congress typically proceeds by joint resolution rather than statute for enactments that will not appear in the U.S. Code, such as single appropriations, foreign relations initiatives, and temporary modifications of existing laws. In contrast, a provision that enables Congress to block a proposed agency regulation by concurrent resolution, as in the 1974 Amendment, differs from a statute in that it is not presented to the President for signature. This is called a legislative veto. Provisions of this sort, which also included disapproval by simple resolution (action by one chamber only), were being regularly used by 1974. They were declared unconstitutional in Chadha v. INS, 462 U.S. 919 (1983), as violating the Presentment Clause, which the Court saw as requiring that any action affecting people's legal status must follow the constitutionally prescribed procedures for legislation, even if previously authorized by statute. (Joint resolutions create no constitutional problem, of course.) Concurrent resolutions are still used for internal congressional procedures. Why did Congress want to establish a legislative veto procedure in this case?

6. Most important statutes that are signed by the President (which is to say most important legislation, veto overrides being a rarity) are accompanied by signing statements that express the President's view of the legislation. The statement may address the general public, as here, or it may address the implementing administrative agency, expressing the President's view about the way the statute should be interpreted or applied. Is President Ford's attitude toward the abolition of the interlock an accurate reflection of the statute? How should the agency take signing statements into account? The legal force of such statements has been a matter of controversy. *See* Daniel B. Rodriguez, Edward H. Stiglitz & Barry R. Weingast, *Executive Opportunism, Presidential Signing Statements*, 8 J. LEGAL ANALYSIS 95 (2016).

Shortly after passage of the Motor Vehicle and School Bus Safety Amendment, NHTSA responded as follows.

---

40 C.F.R. 571

Seat Belt Interlock Option

[Docket No. 74-39; Notice 1]; October 31, 1974

[39 Fed. Reg. 38380]

This notice amends Standard No. 208, *Occupant crash protection,* 49 CFR 571.208, by eliminating the ignition interlock. Parallel changes are made to the passive seat belt provisions (S4.5.3) and the seat belt assembly requirements (S7.) of the standard.

This amendment is responsive to recently-enacted legislation which prohibits, after February 25, 1975, any Federal motor vehicle safety standard that requires or provides for use of a safety belt interlock system or a "continuous buzzer" warning. Pub. L 93-492; section 109 (Oct. 28, 1974). The legislation further specifies that lap and shoulder belt assemblies shall be installed until the NHTSA undertakes further rulemaking on alternative systems. The NHTSA concludes that immediate action to delete the interlock option conforms to the intent of the legislation. Accordingly, S4.1.2.3, S4.5.3. and S7.4 have been modified as necessary to specify seat belt assemblies without an interlock that inhibits operation of the vehicle engine.

The legislation does not list the exact specifications of the warning system which will replace the "continuous buzzer" after 120 days, but it restricts the buzzer portion of any future warning to an 8-second period following operation of the ignition. Because the legislation leaves considerable regulatory discretion concerning warning systems, and a new system may require components no presently in manufacturers' inventories, the NHTSA finds it necessary and desirable to propose the new requirements in a separate notice, permitting opportunity for consideration and submission of comments by interested persons. Final action will be taken by December 27, 1974, to specify a new warning system as required by the statute.

In consideration of the foregoing, Standard No. 208 (49 C.F.R. 571.208) is amended as follows. . . .

Effective date: October 29, 1974. Because this amendment relieves a restriction and responds to a Congressional mandate expressed in the Motor Vehicle and Schoolbus Safety Amendments of 1974, the National Highway Traffic and Safety Administration finds for good cause shown, that notice and public procedure hereon are impracticable and unnecessary, and that an immediate effective date is in the public interest. . . .

James B. Gregory
Administrator.

Notes and Questions

1. Note that this regulation was adopted without notice-and-comment under the good cause exception of §553, which applies "when the agency for good cause finds (and incorporates the finding and a brief statement of reasons therefor in the rules issued) that notice and public procedure thereon are impracticable, unnecessary, or contrary to the public interest. Why did NHTSA choose to invoke the exception in this case? Was that a valid interpretation of the statute? Was it desirable as a matter of policy?

2. The regulation is written in the usual formal and dispassionate language of agency pronouncements (or less charitably, in bureaucratize). Do you sense an underlying mood, however? How would you feel at this point if you were working for NHTSA, and specifically if you had been working on Standard 208 for the past ten years?

During the remainder of the Ford Administration, the Secretary of Transportation that Ford had appointed, William Coleman, held a public hearing and issued an NPRM on Standard 208, 41 Fed. Reg. 24070 (1976). He then delayed indefinitely the implementation of passive restraints and initiated a demonstration program, under which a limited number of new vehicles would have passive restraints, "to exhibit the effectiveness of passive restraint system." 42 Fed. Reg. 5071 (1977). By the time theAdministration ended with Ford's electoral defeat in 1976, the implementation of the passive restraints requirements had been derailed for nearly eight years.

D. STANDARD 208'S DEATH AND RESURRECTION: 1976 TO 1989

Jimmy Carter appointed Brock Adams as the Secretary of Transportation and explicitly instructed him to move forward aggressively with auto safety standards. Carter ensured that these instructions were taken seriously by appointing Joan Claybrook as the Administrator of NHTSA. Claybrook had worked with Nader in lobbying for passage of the Safety Act, and then for the Public Interest Research Group (PIRG), a Nader-inspired public interest organization focused on consumer protection. In 1977, a revivified NHTSA issued a new version of Standard 208.

National Highway Traffic Safety Administration, Part 571—Federal Motor Vehicle Safety Standards: Occupant Restraint Systems

C.F.R. Vol. 42, No. 128, Docket No. 75-14: Notice 10

AGENCY: Department of Transportation (DOT).

ACTION: Final Rule.

SUMMARY: The existing motor vehicle safety standard for occupant crash, protection in new passenger cars is amended to require the provision of "passive" restraint protection in passenger cars with wheelbases greater than 114 inches manufactured on and after September 1, 1981, in passenger cars with wheelbases greater than 100 inches on and after September 1, 1982, and in an passenger cars manufactured on or after September 1, 1983. The low usage rate of active seat belt systems negates much of their potential safety benefit. However, lap belts will continue to be required at most front and all rear seating positions in new cars, and the Department will continue to recommend their use to motorists. It is found that upgraded occupant crash protection is a reasonable and necessary exercise of the mandate of the National Traffic and Motor Vehicle Safety Act to provide protection through improved automotive design, construction, and performance.

DATES: Effective date September 1, 1981.

ADDRESSES: Petitions for reconsideration should refer to the docket number and be submitted to: Docket Section, Boom 5108 — Nassif Building, 400 Seventh Street, SW., Washington, D.C. 20590.

. . .

CONSIDERATIONS UNDERLYING THE STANDARD

Under the National Traffic and Motor Vehicle Safety Act, as amended, (the Act) (15 U.S.C. 1381 et seq.) the Department of Transportation is responsible for issuing motor vehicle safety standards that, among other things, protect the public against unreasonable risk of death or injury to persons in the event accidents occur. The Act directs the Department to consider whether a standard would contribute to carrying out the purposes of the Act and would be reasonable, practicable, and appropriate for a particular type of motor vehicle (15 U.S.C. 1392(f)(3)). The standard must, as formulated, be practicable, meet the need for motor vehicle safety, and be stated in objective terms (15 U.S.C. 1392(a)). The Senate Committee drafting the statute stated that safety would be the overriding consideration in the issuance of standards. S. Rep. No. 1301, 89th Cong., 2d Sess. (1960) at 6.

The total number of fatalities annually in motor vehicle accidents is approximately 46,000 (estimate for 1976), of which approximately 25,000 are estimated to be automobile front seat occupants. Two major hazards to which front seat occupants are exposed are ejection from the vehicle, which increases the probability of fatality greatly, and impact with the vehicle interior during the crash. Restraint of occupants to protect against these hazards has long been recognized as a means to substantially

reduce the fatalities and serious injuries experienced at the front seating positions.

One of the Department's first actions in implementing the Act was promulgation in 1967 of Standard No. 208, Occupant Crash Protection (49 CFR 571.208), to make it possible for vehicle occupants to help protect themselves against the hazards of a crash by engaging seat belts. The standard requires the installation of lap and shoulder seat belt assemblies (Type 2) at front outboard designated seating positions (except in convertibles) and lap belt assemblies (Type 1) at all other designated seating positions. The standard became effective January 1, 1968.

While it is generally agreed that when they are worn, seat belt assemblies are highly effective in preventing occupant impact with the vehicle interior or ejection from the vehicle, only a minority of motorists in the United States use seat belts. For all types of belt systems, National Highway Traffic Safety Administration (NHTSA) studies show that about 20 percent of belt systems are used (DOT HS 6 01340 (in process)). The agency's calculations show that only about 2,600 deaths (and corresponding numbers of injuries) of front seat occupants were averted during 1976 by the restraints required by Standard No. 208 as it is presently written.

Two basic approaches have been developed to increase the savings of life and mitigation of injury afforded by occupant restraint systems. More than 20 nations and two provinces of Canada have enacted mandatory seat belt use laws to increase usage and thereby the effective lifesaving potential of existing seat belt systems. The other approach is to install

automatic passive restraints in passenger cars in place of, or in conjunction with, active belt systems. These systems are passive in the sense that no action by the occupant is required to benefit from the restraint. Passive restraint systems automatically provide a high level of occupant crash protection to virtually 100 percent of front seat occupants.

The two forms of passive restraint that have been commercially produced are inflatable occupant restraints (commonly known as air bags) and passive belts. Air bags are fabric cushions that are rapidly filled with gas to cushion the occupant against colliding with the vehicle interior when a crash occurs that is strong enough to register on a sensor device in the vehicle. The deployment is accomplished by the rapid generation or release of a gas to inflate the bag. Passive belt systems are comparable to active belt systems in many respects, but are distinguished by automatic deployment around the occupant as the occupant enters the vehicle and closes the door.

. . . Standard No. 208 (49 CFR 571.208) is amended as follows:

1. S4.1.2 is amended to read:

S4.1.2 *Passenger cars manufactured from September 1, 1973, to August 31, 1983*. Each passenger car manufactured from September 1, 1973 to August 31, 1981, inclusive, shall meet the requirements of S4.1.2.1, S4.1.2.2, or S4.1.2.3. Each passenger car manufactured from September 1, 1981, to August 31, 1982, inclusive, shall meet the requirements of S4.1.2.1, S4.1.2.2. or S4.1.2.3, except that a passenger car with a wheelbase of more than 114 inches shall meet the requirements specified in S4.1.3. Each passenger car manufactured from September 1, 1982, to August 31, 1983, inclusive, shall meet the requirements of S4.1.2.1, S4.1.2.2, or S4.1.2.3, except that a passenger car with a wheelbase of more than 100 inches shall meet the requirements specified in S4.1.3. A protection system that meets the requirements of S4.1.2.1 or S4.1.2.2 may be installed at one or more designated seating positions of a vehicle that otherwise meets the requirements of S4.1.2.3.

2. A new S4.1.3 is added to read:

S4.1.3 *Passenger cars manufactured on or after*

September 1, 1983. Each passenger car manufactured on or after September 1, 1983, shall—

(a) At each front designated seating position meet the frontal crash protection requirements of S5.1 by means that require no action by vehicle occupants;

(b) At each rear designated seating position have a Type 1 or Type 2 seat belt assembly that conforms to Standard No. 209 and S7.1 and S7.2; and

(c) Either—

(1) Meet the lateral crash protection requirements of S5.2 and the roll-over

crash protection requirements of S5.3 by means that require no action by vehicle occupants; or

(2) At each front designated seating position have a Type 1 or Type 2 seat belt assembly that conforms to Standard No. 209 and S.7 through S7.3 and meet the requirements of S5.1 with front test dummies as required by S5.1, restrained by the Type 1 or Type 2 seat belt assembly (or the pelvic portion of any Type 2 seat belt assembly which has a detachable upper torso belt) in addition to the means that require no action by the vehicle occupant.

Notes and Questions

1. Note the recitation of the statutory standard at the beginning of this regulation, which is, after all, an amendment rather than a new regulation. The remainder of the agency's statement, omitted here, is a detailed history of Standard 208, captioned as such. Why do you suppose the agency included this material, instead of simply explaining the justification for the new (or more correctly renewed) requirements?

2. How do you feel about the other option mentioned by the agency, which is to require seat belt use by law? That does not require any modification to the car beyond installation of the belts, which was already required. Does that make it less expensive, and for whom? Why wasn't that an option in the United States?

3. Note the explicit reference to, and description of, the air bag as an alternative form of passive restraint.

––––––––––––

In 1981, Standard 208 faced yet another reversal in the hands of another new presidential administration. Ronald Reagan campaigned for President on a platform of deregulation. Upon taking office, he supported easing regulatory burdens on the ailing domestic auto industry. On April 6, 1981, NHTSA delayed compliance with the passive restraint requirement for large cars, moving it from September 1, 1981, to September 1, 1982. It also proposed a more dramatic overhaul of the passive restraint regulations. Here is a summary of its proposal as it appeared the Notice of Proposed Rulemaking, 46 Fed. Reg. 21205 (1981):

SUMMARY: The purpose of this notice is to seek comment on a series of alternative amendments to the automatic restraint requirements of Safety Standard No. 208, Occupant Crash Protection. As amended by a final rule published in today's Federal Register, those requirements are currently scheduled to become effective for large cars and mid-size cars on September 1, 1982, and for small cars on September 1, 1983.

Under the first alternative being considered, the sequence of compliance would be changed so that small cars would be required to comply on September 1, 1982, mid-size cars on September 1, 1983, and large cars on September 1, 1984.

The second alternative would require all cars sizes to begin compliance on March 1, 1983. In addition, the first and second alternatives would amend the automatic restraint requirements so that those restraints would not be required in the front center seating position.

The third alternative would rescind the automatic restraint requirements.

After duly receiving comments, NHTSA issued its final rule, 46 Fed. Reg. 53,419 (1981):

SUMMARY: The purpose of this notice is to amend Federal Motor Vehicle Safety Standard No. 208, Occupant Crash Protection, to rescind the requirements for installation of automatic restraints in the front seating positions of passenger cars. Those requirements were scheduled to become effective for large and mid-size cars on September 1, 1982, and for small cars on September 1, 1983.

The automatic restraint requirements are being rescinded because of uncertainty about the public acceptability and probable usage rate of the type of automatic restraint which the car manufacturers planned to make available to most new car buyers. This uncertainty and the relatively substantial cost of automatic restraints preclude the agency from determining that the standard is at this time reasonable and practicable. The reasonableness of the automatic restraint requirements is further called into question by the fact that all new car buyers would be required to pay for automatic belt systems that may induce only a few additional people to take advantage of the benefits of occupant restraints.

The agency is also seriously concerned about the possibility that adverse public reaction to the cost and presence of automatic restraints could have a significant adverse effect on present and future public acceptance of highway safety efforts.

The NPRM and final rule are reprinted in full in the following chapter as an example of the way that agencies formulate and justify rules; that is, the way they provide the rule and the statement of basis and purpose as required by APA §553(c). Even from this brief summary, you may notice that something is missing. The insurance industry certainly did, and brought suit to declare the rule invalid under the judicial review provisions of the APA.

Motor Vehicle Manufacturers Ass'n of the United States, Inc. v. State Farm Mutual Automobile Insurance Co.

463 U.S. 29 (1983)

Justice WHITE delivered the opinion of the Court.

The development of the automobile gave Americans unprecedented freedom to travel, but exacted a high price for enhanced mobility. Since 1929, motor vehicles have been the leading cause of accidental deaths and injuries in the United States. In 1982, 46,300 Americans died in motor vehicle accidents and hundreds of thousands more were maimed and injured. While a consensus exists that the current loss of life on our highways is unacceptably high, improving safety does not admit to easy solution. In 1966, Congress decided that at least part of the answer lies in improving the design and safety features of the vehicle itself. But much of the technology for building safer cars was undeveloped or untested. Before changes in automobile design could be mandated, the effectiveness of these changes had to be studied, their costs examined, and public acceptance considered. This task called for considerable expertise and Congress responded by enacting the National Traffic and Motor Vehicle Safety Act of 1966, (Act), 15 U.S.C. §§1381 et seq. (1976 and Supp. IV 1980). The Act, created for the purpose of "reduc[ing] traffic accidents and deaths and injuries to persons resulting from traffic accidents," 15 U.S.C. §1381, directs the Secretary of Transportation or his delegate to issue motor vehicle safety standards that "shall be practicable, shall meet the need for motor vehicle safety, and shall be stated in objective terms." 15 U.S.C. §1392(a). In issuing these standards, the Secretary is directed to consider "relevant available motor vehicle safety data," whether the proposed standard "is reasonable, practicable and appropriate" for the particular type of motor vehicle, and the "extent to which such standards will contribute to carrying out the purposes" of the Act. 15 U.S.C. §1392(f)(1), (3), (4).

The Act also authorizes judicial review under the provisions of the Administrative Procedure Act (APA), 5 U.S.C. §706 (1976), of all "orders establishing, amending, or revoking a Federal motor vehicle safety standard," 15 U.S.C. §1392(b). Under this authority, we review today whether NHTSA [the National Highway Transportation Safety Administration, to which the Secretary has delegated authority under the Act] acted arbitrarily and capriciously in revoking the requirement in Motor Vehicle Safety Standard 208 that new motor vehicles produced after September 1982 be equipped with passive restraints to protect the safety of the occupants of the vehicle in the event of a collision. Briefly summarized, we hold that the agency failed to present an adequate basis and explanation for rescinding the passive restraint requirement and that the agency must either consider the matter further or adhere to or amend Standard 208 along lines which its analysis supports.

I

The regulation whose rescission is at issue bears a complex and convoluted history. Over the course of approximately 60 rulemaking notices, the requirement has been imposed, amended, rescinded, reimposed, and now rescinded again. . . .

II

In a statement explaining the rescission, NHTSA maintained that it was no longer able to find, as it had in 1977, that the automatic restraint requirement would produce significant safety benefits. Notice 25, 46 Fed. Reg. 53,419 (Oct. 29, 1981). This judgment reflected not a change of opinion on the effectiveness of the technology, but a change in plans by the automobile industry. In 1977, the agency had assumed that airbags would be installed in 60% of all new cars and automatic seatbelts in 40%. By 1981 it became apparent that automobile manufacturers planned to install the automatic seatbelts in approximately 99% of the new cars. For this reason, the life-saving potential of airbags would not be realized. Moreover, it now appeared that the overwhelming majority of passive belts planned to be installed by manufacturers could be detached easily and left that way permanently. Passive belts, once detached, then required "the same type of affirmative action that is the stumbling block to obtaining high usage levels of manual belts." 46 Fed. Reg., at 53421. For this reason, the agency concluded that there was no longer a basis for reliably predicting that the standard would lead to any significant increased usage of restraints at all.

In view of the possibly minimal safety benefits, the automatic restraint requirement no longer was reasonable or practicable in the agency's view. The requirement would require approximately $1 billion to implement and the agency did not believe it would be reasonable to impose such substantial costs on manufacturers and consumers without more adequate assurance that sufficient safety benefits would accrue. In addition, NHTSA concluded that automatic restraints might have an adverse effect on the public's attitude toward safety. Given the high expense and limited benefits of detachable belts, NHTSA feared that many consumers would regard the standard as an instance of ineffective regulation, adversely affecting the public's view of safety regulation and, in particular, "poisoning popular sentiment toward efforts to improve occupant restraint systems in the future." 46 Fed. Reg., at 53424.

III

Unlike the Court of Appeals, we do not find the appropriate scope of judicial review to be the "most troublesome question" in these cases. Both the Act and the 1974 Amendments concerning occupant crash protection standards indicate that motor vehicle safety standards are to be promulgated under the informal rulemaking procedures of the Administrative Procedure Act. 5 U.S.C. §553. The agency's action in promulgating such standards therefore may be set aside if found to be "arbitrary, capricious, an abuse of discretion, or otherwise not in accordance with law." 5 U.S.C. §706(2)(A); *Citizens to Preserve Overton Park v. Volpe,* 401 U.S. 402, 401 U.S. 414 (1971). We believe that the rescission or modification of an occupant protection standard is subject to the same test. Section 103(b) of the Act, 15 U.S.C. §1392(b), states that the procedural and judicial review provisions of the Administrative Procedure Act "shall apply to all orders establishing, amending, or revoking a Federal motor vehicle safety standard," and suggests no difference in the scope of judicial review depending upon the nature of the agency's action.

Petitioner Motor Vehicle Manufacturers Association (MVMA) disagrees, contending that the rescission of an agency rule should be judged by the same standard a court would use to judge an agency's refusal to promulgate a rule in the first place — a standard petitioner believes considerably narrower than the traditional arbitrary and capricious test. We reject this view. The Act expressly equates orders "revoking" and "establishing" safety standards; neither that Act nor the APA suggests that revocations are to be treated as refusals to promulgate standards. Petitioner's view would render meaningless Congress' authorization for judicial review of orders revoking safety rules. Moreover, the revocation of an extant regulation is substantially different than a failure to act. Revocation constitutes a reversal of the agency's former views as to the proper course. A "settled course of behavior embodies the agency's informed judgment that, by pursuing that course, it will carry out the policies committed to it by Congress. There is, then, at least a presumption that those policies will be carried out best if the settled rule is adhered to." *Atchison, T. & S.F.R. Co. v. Wichita Bd. of Trade,* 412 U.S. 800, 412 U.S. 807-808 (1973). Accordingly, an agency changing its course by rescinding a rule is obligated to supply a reasoned analysis for the change beyond that which may be required when an agency does not act in the first instance.

In so holding, we fully recognize that "[r]egulatory agencies do not establish rules of conduct to last forever," *American Trucking Assns., Inc. v. Atchison, T. & S.F.R. Co.,* 387 U.S. 397, 387 U.S. 416 (1967), and that an agency must be given ample latitude to "adapt their rules and policies to the demands of changing circumstances." *Permian Basin Area Rate Cases,* 390 U.S. 747, 390 U.S. 784 (1968). But the forces of change do not always or necessarily point in the direction of deregulation. In the abstract, there is no more reason to presume that changing circumstances require the rescission of prior action, instead of a revision in or even the extension of current regulation. If Congress established a presumption from which judicial review should start, that presumption—contrary to petitioners' views—is not against safety regulation, but *against* changes in current policy that are not justified by the rulemaking record. While the removal of a regulation may not entail the monetary expenditures and other costs of enacting a new standard, and, accordingly, it may be easier for an agency to justify a deregulatory action, the direction in which an agency chooses to move does not alter the standard of judicial review established by law.

The Department of Transportation accepts the applicability of the "arbitrary and capricious" standard. It argues that under this standard, a reviewing court may not set aside an agency rule that is rational, based on consideration of the relevant factors and within the scope of the authority delegated to the agency by the statute. We do not disagree with this formulation. The scope of review under the "arbitrary and capricious" standard is narrow and a court is not to substitute its judgment for that of the agency.

Nevertheless, the agency must examine the relevant data and articulate a satisfactory explanation for its action including a "rational connection between the facts found and the choice made." *Burlington Truck Lines v. United States*, 371 U.S. 156, 168 (1962). In reviewing that explanation, we must "consider whether the decision was based on a consideration of the relevant factors and whether there has been a clear error of judgment." *Bowman Transp. Inc. v. Arkansas-Best Freight System*, 419 U.S., at 285; *Citizens to Preserve Overton Park v. Volpe*, 401 U.S., at 416. Normally, an agency rule would be arbitrary and capricious if the agency has relied on factors which Congress has not intended it to consider, entirely failed to consider an important aspect of the problem, offered an explanation for its decision that runs counter to the evidence before the agency, or is so implausible that it could not be ascribed to a difference in view or the product of agency expertise. The reviewing court should not attempt itself to make up for such deficiencies: "We may not supply a reasoned basis for the agency's action that the agency itself has not given." *SEC v. Chenery Corp.*, 332 U.S. 194, 196 (1947). We will, however, "uphold a decision of less than ideal clarity if the agency's path may reasonably be discerned." *Bowman Transp. Inc. v. Arkansas-Best Freight System*, 419 U.S., at 286. For purposes of this case, it is also relevant that Congress required a record of the rulemaking proceedings to be compiled and submitted to a reviewing court, 15 U.S.C. §1394, and intended that agency findings under the Motor Vehicle Safety Act would be supported by "substantial evidence on the record considered as a whole." S. Rep. No. 1301, 89th Cong., 2d Sess. p. 8 (1966).

IV

The Court of Appeals correctly found that the arbitrary and capricious test applied to rescissions of prior agency regulations, but then erred in intensifying the scope of its review based upon its reading of legislative events. It held that congressional reaction to various versions of Standard 208 "raise[d] doubts" that NHTSA's rescission "necessarily demonstrates an effort to fulfill its statutory mandate," and therefore the agency was obligated to provide "increasingly clear and convincing reasons" for its action. Specifically, the Court of Appeals found significance in three legislative occurrences:

> "In 1974, Congress banned the ignition interlock, but did not foreclose NHTSA's pursuit of a passive restraint standard. In 1977, Congress allowed the standard to take effect when neither of the concurrent resolutions needed for disapproval was passed. In 1980, a majority of each house indicated support for the concept of mandatory passive restraints, and a majority of each house supported the unprecedented attempt to require some installation of airbags."

From these legislative acts and nonacts, the Court of Appeals derived a "congressional commitment to the concept of automatic crash protection devices for vehicle occupants." This path of analysis was misguided, and the inferences it produced are questionable. It is noteworthy that, in this Court, respondent State Farm expressly agrees that the postenactment legislative history of the Act does not heighten the standard of review of NHTSA's actions. State Farm's concession is well taken, for this Court has never suggested that the standard of review is enlarged or diminished by subsequent congressional action. While an agency's interpretation of a statute may be confirmed or ratified by subsequent congressional failure to change that interpretation, *Bob Jones University v. United States,* 461 U.S. 574, 599-602 (1983), in the cases before us, even an unequivocal ratification—short of statutory incorporation—of the passive restraint standard would not connote approval or disapproval of an agency's later decision to rescind the regulation. That decision remains subject to the arbitrary and capricious standard.

That we should not be so quick to infer a congressional mandate for passive restraints is confirmed by examining the postenactment legislative events cited by the Court of Appeals. Even were we inclined to rely on inchoate legislative action, the inferences to be drawn fail to suggest that NHTSA acted improperly in rescinding Standard 208. First, in 1974, a mandatory passive restraint standard was technically not in effect; Congress had no reason to foreclose that course. Moreover, one can hardly infer support for a mandatory standard from Congress' decision to provide that such a regulation would be subject to disapproval by resolutions of disapproval in both Houses. Similarly, no mandate can be divined from the tabling of resolutions of disapproval which were introduced in 1977. The failure of Congress to exercise its veto might reflect legislative deference to the agency's expertise, and does not indicate that Congress would disapprove of the agency's action in 1981. And even if Congress favored the Standard in 1977, it—like NHTSA—may well reach a different judgment, given changed circumstances four years later. Finally, the Court of Appeals read too much into floor action on the 1980 authorization bill, a bill which was not enacted into law. Other contemporaneous events could be read as showing equal congressional hostility to passive restraints.

V

The ultimate question before us is whether NHTSA's rescission of the passive restraint requirement of Standard 208 was arbitrary and capricious. We conclude, as did the Court of Appeals, that it was. We also conclude, but for somewhat different reasons, that further consideration of the issue by the agency is therefore required. We deal separately with the rescission as it applies to airbags and as it applies to seatbelts.

A

The first and most obvious reason for finding the rescission arbitrary and capricious is that NHTSA apparently gave no consideration whatever to modifying the Standard to require that airbag technology be utilized. Standard 208 sought to achieve automatic crash protection by requiring automobile manufacturers to install either of two passive restraint devices: airbags or automatic seatbelts. There was no suggestion in the long rulemaking process that led to Standard 208 that if only one of these options were feasible, no passive restraint standard should be promulgated. Indeed, the agency's original proposed standard contemplated the installation of inflatable restraints in all cars.[1] Automatic belts were added as a means of complying with the standard because they were believed to be as effective as airbags in achieving the goal of occupant crash protection. 36 Fed. Reg. 12,858, 12,859 (July 8, 1971). At that time, the passive belt approved by the agency could not be detached.[2] Only later, at a manufacturer's behest, did the agency approve of the detachability feature—and only after assurances that the feature would not compromise the safety benefits of the restraint.[3] Although it was then foreseen that 60% of the new cars would contain air-bags and 40% would have automatic seatbelts, the ratio between the two was not significant as long as the passive belt would also assure greater passenger safety.

The agency has now determined that the detachable automatic belts will not attain anticipated safety benefits because so many individuals will detach the mechanism. Even if this conclusion were acceptable in its entirety, *see infra*, at 2871-2872, standing alone it would not justify any more than an amendment of Standard 208 to disallow compliance by means of the one technology which will not provide effective passenger protection. It does not cast doubt on the need for a passive restraint standard or upon the efficacy of airbag technology. In its most recent rulemaking, the agency again acknowledged the life-saving potential of the airbag:

> "The agency has no basis at this time for changing its earlier conclusions in 1976 and 1977 that basic airbag technology is sound and has been sufficiently demonstrated to be effective in those vehicles in current use. . . ." NHTSA Final Regulatory Impact Analysis (RIA) at XI-4.

Given the effectiveness ascribed to airbag technology by the agency, the mandate of the Safety Act to achieve traffic safety would suggest that the logical response to the faults of detachable seatbelts would be to require the installation of airbags. At the very least this alternative way of achieving the objectives of the Act should have been addressed and adequate reasons given for its abandonment. But the agency not only did not require compliance through airbags, it did not even consider the possibility in its 1981 rulemaking. Not one sentence of its rulemaking statement

---

1. While NHTSA's 1970 passive restraint requirement permitted compliance by means other than the airbag, 35 Fed. Reg. 16,927 (1970), "[t]his rule was [a] de facto air bag mandate since no other technologies were available to comply with the standard." J. Graham & P. Gorham, *NHTSA. Restraints: A Case of Arbitrary and Capricious Deregulation*, 35 Admin. L. Rev. 193, 197 (1983). . . .

2. Although the agency suggested that passive restraint systems contain an emerg. release mechanism to allow easy extrication of passengers in the event of an accident, the agency cautioned that "[i]n the case of passive safety belts, it would be required that the release not cause belt separation, and that the system be self-restoring after operation of the release." 36 Fed. Reg. 12,866 (July 8, 1971).

3. In April 1974, NHTSA adopted the suggestion of an automobile manufacturer that emergency release of passive belts be accomplished by a conventional latch-provided the restraint system was guarded by an ignition interlock and warning buzzer to encourage reattachment of the passive belt. 39 Fed. Reg. 14,593 (April 25, 1974). When the 1974 Amendments prohibited these devices, the agency simply eliminated the interlock and buzzer requirements, but continued to allow compliance by a detachable passive belt.

discusses the airbags-only option. Because, as the Court of Appeals stated, "NHTSA's . . . analysis of airbags was nonexistent," 680 F.2d, at 236, what we said in *Burlington Truck Lines v. United States*, 371 U.S., at 167, is apropos here:

> "There are no findings and no analysis here to justify the choice made, no indication of the basis on which the [agency] exercised its expert discretion. We are not prepared to and the Administrative Procedure Act will not permit us to accept such . . . practice. . . . Expert discretion is the lifeblood of the administrative process, but 'unless we make the requirements for administrative action strict and demanding, expertise, the strength of modern government, can become a monster which rules with no practical limits on its discretion.' *New York v. United States*, 342 U.S. 882, 884 (dissenting opinion)." (footnote omitted).

We have frequently reiterated that an agency must cogently explain why it has exercised its discretion in a given manner, *Atchison, T. & S.F.R. Co. v. Wichita Bd. of Trade*, 412 U.S. 800, 806 (1973) . . . ; and we reaffirm this principle again today.

The automobile industry has opted for the passive belt over the airbag, but surely it is not enough that the regulated industry has eschewed a given safety device. For nearly a decade, the automobile industry waged the regulatory equivalent of war against the airbag and lost—the inflatable restraint was proven sufficiently effective. Now the automobile industry has decided to employ a seatbelt system which will not meet the safety objectives of Standard 208. This hardly constitutes cause to revoke the standard itself. Indeed, the Motor Vehicle Safety Act was necessary because the industry was not sufficiently responsive to safety concerns. The Act intended that safety standards not depend on current technology and could be "technology-forcing" in the sense of inducing the development of superior safety design. *See Chrysler Corp. v. Dept. of Transp.*, 472 F.2d, at 672-673. If, under the statute, the agency should not defer to the industry's failure to develop safer cars, which it surely should not do, a fortiori it may not revoke a safety standard which can be satisfied by current technology simply because the industry has opted for an ineffective seatbelt design. . . .

B

Although the issue is closer, we also find that the agency was too quick to dismiss the safety benefits of automatic seatbelts. NHTSA's critical finding was that, in light of the industry's plans to install readily detachable passive belts, it could not reliably predict "even a 5 percentage point increase as the minimum level of expected usage increase." 46 Fed. Reg., at 53,423. The Court of Appeals rejected this finding because there is "not one iota" of evidence that Modified Standard 208 will fail to increase nationwide seatbelt use by at least 13 percentage points, the level of increased usage necessary for the standard to justify its cost. Given the lack of probative evidence, the court held that "only a well-justified refusal to seek more evidence could render rescission non-arbitrary."

Petitioners object to this conclusion. In their view, "substantial uncertainty" that a regulation will accomplish its intended purpose is sufficient reason, without more, to rescind a regulation. We agree with petitioners that just as an agency reasonably may decline to issue a safety standard if it is uncertain about its efficacy, an agency may also revoke a standard on the basis of serious uncertainties if supported by the record and reasonably explained. Rescission of the passive restraint requirement would not be arbitrary and capricious simply because there was no evidence in direct support of the agency's conclusion. It is not infrequent that the available data does not settle a regulatory issue and the agency must then exercise its judgment in moving from the facts and probabilities on the record to a policy conclusion. Recognizing that policymaking in a complex society must account for uncertainty, however, does not imply that it is sufficient for an agency to merely recite the terms "substantial uncertainty" as a justification for its actions. The agency must explain the evidence which is available, and must offer a "rational connection between the facts found and the choice made." *Burlington Truck Lines, Inc. v. United States*, 371 U.S., at 168. Generally, one aspect of that explanation would be a justification for rescinding the regulation before engaging in a search for further evidence.

In this case, the agency's explanation for rescission of the passive restraint requirement is not sufficient to enable us to conclude that the rescission was the product of reasoned decisionmaking. To reach this conclusion, we do not upset the agency's view of the facts, but we do appreciate the limitations of this record in supporting the agency's decision. We start with the accepted ground that if used, seatbelts unquestionably would save many thousands of lives and would prevent tens of thousands of crippling injuries. Unlike recent regulatory decisions we have reviewed . . . , the safety benefits of wearing seatbelts are not in doubt and it is not challenged that were those benefits to accrue, the monetary costs of implementing the standard would be easily justified. We move next to the fact that there is no direct evidence in support of the agency's finding that detachable automatic belts cannot be predicted to yield a substantial increase in usage. The empirical evidence on the record, consisting of surveys of drivers of automobiles equipped with passive belts, reveals more than a doubling of the usage rate experienced with manual belts.[4] Much of the agency's rulemaking statement—and much of the controversy in this case—centers on the conclusions that should be drawn from these studies. The agency maintained that the doubling of seatbelt usage in these studies could not be extrapolated to an across-the-board

---

4. Between 1975 and 1980, Volkswagen sold approximately 350,000 Rabbits equipped with detachable passive seatbelts that were guarded by an ignition interlock. General Motors sold 8,000 1978 and 1979 Chevettes with a similar system, but eliminated the ignition interlock on the 13,000 Chevettes sold in 1980. NHTSA found that belt usage in the Rabbits averaged 34% for manual belts and 84% for passive belts. Regulatory Impact Analysis (RIA) at IV-52. For the 1978-1979 Chevettes, NHTSA calculated 34% usage for manual belts and 71% for passive belts. On 1980 Chevettes, the agency found these figures to be 31% for manual belts and 70% for passive belts. Ibid.

mandatory standard because the passive seatbelts were guarded by ignition interlocks and purchasers of the tested cars are somewhat atypical.[5] Respondents insist these studies demonstrate that Modified Standard 208 will substantially increase seatbelt usage. We believe that it is within the agency's discretion to pass upon the generalizability of these field studies. This is precisely the type of issue which rests within the expertise of NHTSA, and upon which a reviewing court must be most hesitant to intrude.

But accepting the agency's view of the field tests on passive restraints indicates only that there is no reliable real-world experience that usage rates will substantially increase. To be sure, NHTSA opines that "it cannot reliably predict even a 5 percentage point increase as the minimum level of increased usage." Notice 25, 46 Fed. Reg., at 53,423. But this and other statements that passive belts will not yield substantial increases in seatbelt usage apparently take no account of the critical difference between detachable automatic belts and current manual belts. A detached passive belt does require an affirmative act to reconnect it, but—unlike a manual seat belt—the passive belt, once reattached, will continue to function automatically unless again disconnected. Thus, inertia—a factor which the agency's own studies have found significant in explaining the current low usage rates for seatbelts[6]—works in favor of, not against, use of the protective device. Since 20 to 50% of motorists currently wear seatbelts on some occasions,[7] there would seem to be grounds to believe that seatbelt use by occasional users will be substantially increased by the detachable passive belts. Whether this is in fact the case is a matter for the agency to decide, but it must bring its expertise to bear on the question.

The agency is correct to look at the costs as well as the benefits of Standard 208. The agency's conclusion that the incremental costs of the requirements were no longer reasonable was predicated on its prediction that the safety benefits of the regulation might be minimal. Specifically, the agency's fears that the public may resent paying more for the automatic belt systems is expressly dependent on the assumption that detachable automatic belts will not produce more than "negligible safety benefits." 46 Fed. Reg., at 53,424. When the agency reexamines its findings as to the likely increase in seatbelt usage, it must also reconsider its judgment of the reasonableness of

5. "NHTSA believes that the usage of automatic belts in Rabbits and Chevettes would have been substantially lower if the automatic belts in those cars were not equipped with a use-inducing device inhibiting detachment." Notice 25, 46 Fed. Reg., at 53,422.

6. NHTSA commissioned a number of surveys of public attitudes in an effort to better understand why people were not using manual belts and to determine how they would react to passive restraints. The surveys reveal that while 20% to 40% of the public is opposed to wearing manual belts, the larger proportion of the population does not wear belts because they forgot or found manual belts inconvenient or bothersome. RIA at IV-25. In another survey, 38% of the surveyed group responded that they would welcome automatic belts, and 25% would "tolerate" them. See RIA at IV-37. NHTSA did not comment upon these attitude surveys in its explanation accompanying the rescission of the passive restraint requirement.

7. Four surveys of manual belt usage were conducted for NHTSA between 1978 and 1980, leading the agency to report that 40% to 50% of the people use their belts at least some of the time. RIA, at IV-25.

the monetary and other costs associated with the Standard. In reaching its judgment, NHTSA should bear in mind that Congress intended safety to be the preeminent factor under the Motor Vehicle Safety Act:

"The Committee intends that safety shall be the overriding consideration in the issuance of standards under this bill. The Committee recognizes . . . that the Secretary will necessarily consider reasonableness of cost, feasibility and adequate leadtime." S. Rep. No. 1301, at 6, U.S. Code Cong. & Admin. News 1966, p. 2714.

"In establishing standards the Secretary must conform to the requirement that the standard be practicable. This would require consideration of all relevant factors, including technological ability to achieve the goal of a particular standard as well as consideration of economic factors. Motor vehicle safety is the paramount purpose of this bill and each standard must be related thereto." H. REP. No. 1776, at 16.

The agency also failed to articulate a basis for not requiring nondetachable belts under Standard 208. It is argued that the concern of the agency with the easy detachability of the currently favored design would be readily solved by a continuous passive belt, which allows the occupant to "spool out" the belt and create the necessary slack for easy extrication from the vehicle. The agency did not separately consider the continuous belt option, but treated it together with the ignition interlock device in a category it titled "option of use-compelling features." 46 Fed. Reg., at 53,424. The agency was concerned that use-compelling devices would "complicate extrication of [a]n occupant from his or her car." *Ibid.* "To require that passive belts contain use-compelling features," the agency observed, "could be counterproductive [given] . . . widespread, latent and irrational fear in many members of the public that they could be trapped by the seat belt after a crash." *Ibid.* In addition, based on the experience with the ignition interlock, the agency feared that use-compelling features might trigger adverse public reaction.

By failing to analyze the continuous seatbelts in its own right, the agency has failed to offer the rational connection between facts and judgment required to pass muster under the arbitrary and capricious standard. We agree with the Court of Appeals that NHTSA did not suggest that the emergency release mechanisms used in nondetachable belts are any less effective for emergency egress than the buckle release system used in detachable belts. In 1978, when General Motors obtained the agency's approval to install a continuous passive belt, it assured the agency that nondetachable belts with spool releases were as safe as detachable belts with buckle releases. 43 Fed. Reg. 21,912, 21,913-14 (1978). NHTSA was satisfied that this belt design assured easy extricability: "the agency does not believe that the use of [such] release mechanisms will cause serious occupant egress problems. . . ." 43 Fed. Reg. 52,493, 52,494 (1978). While the agency is entitled to change its view on the acceptability of continuous passive belts, it is obligated to explain its reasons for doing so.

The agency also failed to offer any explanation why a continuous passive belt would engender the same adverse public reaction as the ignition interlock, and, as the Court of Appeals concluded, "every indication in the record points the other way." 680 F.2d, at 234. We see no basis for equating the two devices: the continuous belt, unlike the ignition interlock, does not interfere with the operation of the vehicle. More importantly, it is the agency's responsibility, not this Court's, to explain its decision.

VI

"An agency's view of what is in the public interest may change, either with or without a change in circumstances. But an agency changing its course must supply a reasoned analysis. . . ." *Greater Boston Television Corp. v. FCC,* 444 F.2d 841, 852 (CADC 1971). We do not accept all of the reasoning of the Court of Appeals but we do conclude that the agency has failed to supply the requisite "reasoned analysis" in this case. Accordingly, we vacate the judgment of the Court of Appeals and remand the case to that court with directions to remand the matter to the NHTSA for further consideration consistent with this opinion.

So ordered.

Justice REHNQUIST, with whom THE CHIEF JUSTICE, Justice POWELL, and Justice O'CONNOR join, concurring in part and dissenting in part.

I join parts I, II, III, IV, and V-A of the Court's opinion. In particular, I agree that, since the airbag and continuous spool automatic seatbelt were explicitly approved in the standard the agency was rescinding, the agency should explain why it declined to leave those requirements intact. In this case, the agency gave no explanation at all. Of course, if the agency can provide a rational explanation, it may adhere to its decision to rescind the entire standard.

I do not believe, however, that NHTSA's view of detachable automatic seatbelts was arbitrary and capricious. The agency adequately explained its decision to rescind the standard insofar as it was satisfied by detachable belts.

The statute that requires the Secretary of Transportation to issue motor vehicle safety standards also requires that "[e]ach such . . . standard shall be practicable [and] shall meet the need for motor vehicle safety." 15 U.S.C. §1392(a). The Court rejects the agency's explanation for its conclusion that there is substantial uncertainty whether requiring installation of detachable automatic belts would substantially increase seatbelt usage. The agency chose not to rely on a study showing a substantial increase in seatbelt usage in cars equipped with automatic seatbelts and an ignition interlock to prevent the car from being operated when the belts were not in place and which were voluntarily purchased with this equipment by consumers. It is reasonable for the agency to decide that this study does not support any conclusion concerning the effect of automatic seatbelts that are installed in all cars whether the consumer wants them or not and are not linked to an ignition interlock system.

The Court rejects this explanation because "there would seem to be grounds to believe that seatbelt use by occasional users will be substantially increased by the detachable passive belts," and the agency did not adequately explain its rejection of these grounds. It seems to me that the agency's explanation, while by no means a model, is adequate. The agency acknowledged that there would probably be some increase in belt usage, but concluded that the increase would be small and not worth the cost of mandatory detachable automatic belts. 46 F.R. 53421-54323 (1981). The agency's obligation is to articulate a "rational connection between the facts found and the choice made." I believe it has met this standard.

The agency explicitly stated that it will increase its educational efforts in an attempt to promote public understanding, acceptance, and use of passenger restraint systems. 46 F.R. 53425 (1981). It also stated that it will "initiate efforts with automobile manufacturers to ensure that the public will have [automatic crash protection] technology available. If this does not succeed, the agency will consider regulatory action to assure that the last decade's enormous advances in crash protection technology will not be lost." *Id.*, at 53426.

The agency's changed view of the standard seems to be related to the election of a new President of a different political party. It is readily apparent that the responsible members of one administration may consider public resistance and uncertainties to be more important than do their counterparts in a previous administration. A change in administration brought about by the people casting their votes is a perfectly reasonable basis for an executive agency's reappraisal of the costs and benefits of its programs and regulations. As long as the agency remains within the bounds established by Congress, it is entitled to assess administrative records and evaluate priorities in light of the philosophy of the administration.

Notes and Questions

1. Why was the case initiated by the auto insurance industry rather than a public interest group? There seem to be three reasons: (1) the insurance industry had more resources; (2) insurers had long thought that they were losing money because of the extensive payouts that resulted from auto accidents; and (3) William Haddon. After leaving NHTSA, Haddon had convinced the industry to establish the Insurance Institute for Highway Safety, a research group funded by the industry. Like Nader, he served as what political scientists call a policy entrepreneur. His influence on the industry and the issue in general cannot be over-estimated.

2. The *State Farm* decision is not only an important event in the history of Standard 208, but also one of the two most important decisions in modern administrative law. The other one is Chevron U.S.A. Inc. v. Natural Resources Defense Council, Inc., 467 U.S. 837 (1984). Both decisions are central in defining the current role of the judiciary in reviewing agency actions, and thus in supervising the administrative apparatus. For that reason, we will return to them in later chapters and consider them in detail there. For the present, you should simply note the language in the last paragraph of Part III of the majority opinion, and specifically the sentence beginning with the word "Normally." This is the *State Farm* test. It is widely accepted as the operative formulation of the "arbitrary and capricious" standard of review provided for in APA §706.

3. In addition to establishing a test for determining whether an agency action is arbitrary and capricious, *State Farm* settled an open question about the standard of review for rescissions of agency rules. As in the case of its arbitrary and capricious test, *State Farm*'s resolution of this issue has become settled law, and currently elicits little controversy or disagreement. Note two aspects of the Court's holding and its supporting rationale. First, it emphasizes the similarity between a regulation and a statute. A statute remains in force perpetually (unless it contains a "sunset" provision) and can only be amended or terminated by another statute that is enacted by the same procedure as the original. Second, the Court declares that no deregulatory bias is built into our system of administrative procedure, that is, our law does not assume that non-regulation is the preferred condition. It is also important to note that the two main holdings in the case, first on the standard of review to be applied to rescissions, and second on the test for determining whether agency action is arbitrary and capricious, are both unanimous. Moreover, no Supreme Court justice has seriously challenged either holding since the decision was handed down.

4. As discussed at some length in Chapter 1, the economic theory of regulation assumes that an unregulated market (that is, exchange regulated only by contract law that enforces the parties' agreements) is the preferred condition because it is efficient. Regulation, according to this theory, should only be instituted when there is a demonstrable market failure and only in the form that responds to that specific failure. When Donald Trump took office, he promulgated Executive Order 13,771. Its central provision is as follows:

> Sec. 2. Regulatory Cap for Fiscal Year 2017. (a) Unless prohibited by law, whenever an executive department or agency (agency) publicly proposes for notice-and-comment or otherwise promulgates a new regulation, it shall identify at least two existing regulations to be repealed.
>
> (b) For fiscal year 2017, which is in progress, the heads of all agencies are directed that the total incremental cost of all new regulations, including repealed regulations, to be finalized this year shall be no greater than zero, unless otherwise required by law or consistent with advice provided in writing by the Director of the Office of Management and Budget (Director).

Does this reflect the economic theory of regulation or a deeper skepticism about regulation? Do you think it is a good idea? Do you think it will be effective? Suppose it had been imposed on NHTSA while Joan Claybrook was the administrator; how do you think the agency would have responded?

5. While the Supreme Court found that the Court of Appeals had employed the correct standard of review to the rescission—that is, the §706 arbitrary and capricious standard—it held that the lower court's intensification of that standard was error. In part, the difference between the two courts turns on their different treatment of the regulation's post-enactment history. The Court of Appeals found significance in the fact that Congress had not exercised its legislative veto authority to overturn the passive restraint standard, but the Supreme Court rejected this view. Why do you suppose it came to that conclusion, and how did it distinguish the case from *Bob Jones*, discussed in Chapter 3, which the Court cites? As stated above, the Supreme Court declared the legislative veto unconstitutional, in fact in the very same term as the *State Farm* decision. *See* INS v. Chadha, 462 U.S. 919 (1983). Over the past several years, there have been several pro-posals to require Congressional approval for all important regulations; what does the Court's treatment of the legislative veto issue in this case suggest about such proposals?

    6. Did you realize what was missing from NHTSA's explanation of its rescission regulation — that is, that the agency simply did not mention air-bags? After concluding that automatic seatbelts would be ineffective, it proceeded to the conclusion that the entirety of Standard 208 should be rescinded without considering the other major passive restraint that had been required in the regulation it was rescinding. Why do you think that happened? Was it a simple oversight? Or did the career employees respon-sible for drafting the regulation and its statement of basis and purpose (and who had devoted however long they had spent working for NHTSA to developing passenger safety mechanisms) purposely write a vulnerable statement to undermine the new administrator that President Reagan had appointed? We know that the Reagan administration's new NHTSA admin-istrator, Raymond Peck (a Republican lawyer opposed to regulatory expan-sion), instructed the agency to rescind the regulation, and we know that Michael Finkelstein, the highly experienced staff member who headed NHTSA's rulemaking department, greeted this decision with profanity-laden condemnation. *See* MARTIN ALBAUM, SAFETY SELLS: MARKET FORCE AND REGULATION IN THE DEVELOPMENT OF AIRBAGS 116 (2005). The extent to which a new presidential administration, and its political appointees, should control an agency, as opposed to the ongoing agency staff (who are protected from dismissal by the civil service laws) is a major issue in modern administration.

    What are the ethics involved? Are civil servants obligated to follow the instructions of their politically appointed agency head? Or are they entitled to push back and resist? If so, on what basis? Because they believe that the agency head is not following the law? Because they believe that he or she is not acting in the public interest? If they are permitted to resist, then the question is to what extent and in what way. Should they limit themselves to raising objections within the agency? (That's the easy part of the question. Of course they should be permitted to do so; any institution benefits from open discussion about policy options.) Should they go to the press? Are they entitled to engage in passive resistance? If so, in what circumstances? To test your own views on these questions, envision two cases: one where you agree, on substantive grounds, with the policy change the agency head is attempting to impose, and one where you disagree.

7. Although *State Farm* seems to push NHTSA back toward its rulemaking approach to passive restraints, the fairly intensive level of scrutiny that it deployed may have unintentionally moved the agency in the reverse direction. Professors Mashaw and Harfst have argued that in response to the decision, NHTSA adopted a wait-and-see posture of issuing recalls upon discovery that motor vehicles are unsafe rather than issuing rules to make them safe. *See* JERRY MASHAW & DAVID L. HARFST, THE STRUGGLE FOR AUTO SAFETY, 224-54 (1990). Recalls are adjudications, rather than rules. Look back at the Motor Vehicle Safety Act to see the procedure that the agency is required to follow to impose a recall; it is Section 113. What sort of adjudications are these? Hint: Does the statute say that the Secretary's decision must be made "on the record"? Does it require an ALJ?

8. While the majority recognized that deregulation is an issue in the case, it did not discuss the political context in which this issue arose. But Justice Rehnquist raised this issue in his separate opinion, joined by three other justices. He was willing to give the agency's rescission of the seat belt requirement some credence because he thought that it reflected the politics of the administration. Why was the Court less sympathetic?

On the relationship between politics and policy, consider the following.

Kathryn A. Watts, Proposing a Place for Politics in Arbitrary and Capricious Review

119 Yale L.J. 2, 6-9 (2009)

Ever since the Court handed down *State Farm*, agencies, courts, and scholars alike generally seem to have accepted the view that influences coming from one political branch or another cannot be allowed to explain administrative decisionmaking, even if such factors are influencing agency decisionmaking. Take agencies to begin with. Agencies today generally try to meet their reason-giving duties under *State Farm* by couching their decisions in technocratic, statutory, or scientific language, either failing to disclose or affirmatively hiding political factors that enter into the mix. A good example of this can be found by looking at the Food and Drug Administration's (FDA) attempt in the 1990s to regulate teen smoking. Even though President Clinton played a very active role in directing the rulemaking (going so far as to personally announce the final rule in a Rose Garden ceremony), the FDA's statement of basis and purpose accompanying the final rule relied upon statutory, scientific, and expert justifications—barely even hinting at President Clinton's role in the rulemaking.

Judicial review of agency action is similarly technocratic in focus. Courts applying arbitrary and capricious review today routinely search agency decisions to ensure they represent expert-driven decisionmaking. Decisions from the D.C. Circuit, for example, borrow from *State Farm*'s language and repeatedly frame arbitrary and capricious review in expert-driven terms, asking whether the agency "offered an explanation for its decision that runs counter to the evidence before the agency, or is so implausible that it could not be ascribed to a difference in view or the product of agency expertise."

This Article seeks to identify those rulemaking proceedings in which agencies acting as "mini legislatures" might most appropriately rely upon political influences coming from the President, other members of the executive branch, or Congress to justify agency decisions for purposes of arbitrary and capricious review. The heart of the argument is that what count as "valid" reasons under arbitrary and capricious review should be expanded to include certain political influences from the President, other executive officials, and members of Congress, so long as the political influences are openly and transparently disclosed in the agency's rulemaking record.

Acceptance of the argument set forth here would not mean that any and all political influences would be allowed to legitimize agency action. Although drawing a precise line between permissible and impermissible influences is difficult, legitimate political influences can roughly be thought of as those influences that seek to further policy considerations or public values, whereas illegitimate political influences can be thought of as those that seek to implement raw politics or partisan politics unconnected in any way to the statutory scheme being implemented.

Shortly after the State Farm decision, Reagan's Secretary of Transportation, Drew Lewis, resigned and was replaced by Elizabeth Dole, who had been a Federal Trade Commissioner and was married to Robert Dole, at that time Senate majority leader. With her in charge, an admonished NHTSA issued the following NPRM.

National Highway Traffic Safety Administration, Federal Motor Vehicle Safely Standards; Occupant Crash Protection

49 C.F.R Part 571

[Docket No. 74–14; Notice 32]

AGENCY: Department of Transportation (DOT).

ACTION: Notice of Proposed Rulemaking (NPRM).

SUMMARY: This notice proposes several alternative actions to provide protection for an automobile's front seat occupants in case of frontal, side-impact, and rollover accidents; This rulemaking is part of the further agency review contemplated by the recent Supreme Court decision that found the Department of Transportation's National Highway Traffic Safety Administration's (NHTSA's) October 1981 rescission, of the automatic-occupant restraint requirements of Federal Motor Vehicle Safety Standard 208, Occupant Crash Protection, to be arbitrary and capricious.

DATES: *Public Comments*—Comments on this notice must be received on or before December 19, 1983.

. . .

SUPPLEMENTARY INFORMATION:

I. Background

The 1981 Rescission

On October, 23, 1981, NHTSA issued an order pursuant to section 103 of the National Traffic and Motor Vehicle Safety Act, 15 U.S.C. 1392, amending Federal Motor Vehicle Safety Standard No. 208, *Occupant Crash Protection* (49 CFR 571.208; "FMVSS 208"), by rescinding the provisions that would have required the front seating positions in all new cars to be equipped with automatic restraints (46 FR 53419; October 29, 1981).

In rescinding the automatic restraint requirement, the agency noted that the facts had changed radically since the 1977 promulgation of the requirement. In 1977, the agency had assumed that airbags would be installed in 60 percent of new cars and automatic belts in the remaining 40 percent. However, based on comments by the car manufacturers in 1981, the NHTSA Administrator found that airbags would actually be used in less than one percent of new cars. He found, further, that the type of automatic belt that the manufacturers planned to install in most of the remaining 99 percent of new cars was readily detachable and was not equipped with any device to compel reattachment.

He considered data regarding the usage rates of various types of automatic belts, ones that were either not detachable or that were equipped with an ignition interlock, and concluded that there was no relevant evidence regarding the likely usage rates of detachable automatic belts without interlocks. He concluded also that the similarity of the detachable automatic belt to the conventional manual lap and shoulder belt might lead many motorists to treat and use that type of belt in the same fashion and to the same extent as they currently do the manual belts. The Administrator, therefore, stated that he has no reliable basis on which to predict that the detachable automatic belt without an interlock would increase belt usage. Accordingly, he stated that he was unable to find that the automatic restraint requirement would meet the need for safety.

Due to the possibly minimal safety benefits and substantial compliance costs of the requirement, the Administrator said that he was also unable to find that the requirement was practicable or reasonable as required by the Act. Finally, the Administrator noted that implementation of the requirements might cause long lasting damage to the ability of the agency to gain die public's cooperation in its safety efforts.

The Court of Appeals' Opinion

In late November 1981, petitions for judicial review of the agency's rescission were filed with the U.S. Court of Appeals for the D.C. Circuit by State Farm Mutual Automobile Insurance Company and by the National Association of Independent Insurers. On June 1, 1982, the Court entered an opinion overturning the rescission as arbitrary and capricious. *State Farm v. DOT,* 680, F.2d 206.

The Supreme Court's Opinion

In September 1982, the agency filed a petition for certiorari with the U.S. Supreme Court seeking review of the Court of Appeals' decision. Additional petitions for certiorari were filed by the Motor Vehicle Manufacturers Association, Consumer Alert and the Pacific Legal Foundation. The Supreme Court granted these petitions on November 8, 1982. In response, the Court of Appeals entered an order recalling its mandate.

On June 24, 1983, the Supreme court held that NHTSA's rescission of the automatic restraint requirement was arbitrary and capricious. *Motor Vehicle Manufacturer's Association v. State Farm Mutual Automobile Insurance Co.,* 103 S. Ct. 2856. (Subsequent references to this decision will be to "*State Farm*" and a page number from the decision.) It said that the agency had failed to present an adequate basis and explanation for rescinding the requirement. The Court stated, also, that the agency must either consider the matter further or adhere to or amend the standard along the lines that its analysis supports. Specifically, the Court unanimously held that the agency has not given adequate consideration to modifying the requirement to require installation of airbags; such consideration was necessary because airbags were both a policy and technological alternative within the existing automatic restraint requirement.

The Court found that, even if the agency were correct that detachable automatic belts without interlocks would yield few benefits, that fact alone would not justify rescission. Instead, it would justify only the modification of the requirement to prohibit the compliance by means of that type of automatic belt. The Court also unanimously held that NHTSA had not given adequate considation to requiring that automatic belts be continuous (i.e., nondetachable) instead of detachable.

By a five to four vote, the Court held that the agency had been too quick in dismissing the benefits of detachable automatic belts without interlocks. The Court stated that the agency's explanation of its rescission was not sufficient to enable the Court to conclude that the agency's action was the product of reasoned decision making. The Court found that the agency had hot taken account of the critical difference between detachable automatic belts without interlocks and current manual belts: "A detached passive belt does require an affirmative act to reconnect it, but—unlike a manual sealbelt—the passive belt, once reattached, will continue to function automatically unless again disconnected." *State Farm* at 2872.

Based on its rejection of the Court of Appeals' view regarding the standard of review and some of that Court's reasoning regarding the arbitrariness and capriciousness of the agency's rescission, the Supreme Court vacated the judgment of that court. It further remanded the case to the Court of Appeals with directions to remand the matter to the Department for further consideration consistent with the Supreme Court's opinion. In so doing, the Court noted that the agency had sufficient justification to suspend the automatic restraint requirement pending the further consideration required by its opinion.

The Court of Appeals remanded the matter to the Department effective September 23, 1983.

The 1983 Suspension

On September 1, 1983, the Department suspended the automatic restraint requirement for one year to ensure sufficient time was available for considering the issues raised by the Supreme Court's decision (48 FR 39908). The Department concluded that suspension was justified because compliance by that date would have been impracticable and it would have been inappropriate to require it during the review period.

The Department said that, at the completion of the rulemaking, it would establish an appropriate effective date either for the rule that was rescinded, if we decide to retain it, or for any other action that we take, including re-rescission of the rule.

. . .

III. Proposals

General

This notice is being issued to aid the Department in its strong commitment to carry out its vital mission of improving motor vehicle safety. No part of that mission is more important and can provide more benefits than protecting automobile passengers against injury when they are involved in a crash. Through this rulemaking, the Department is exploring various ways for providing reasonable and effective protection for these people.

The lengthy history of this rulemaking presents conflicting problems for the Department. On the one hand, we recognize that, in light of the amount of time that has elapsed since the Department initially proposed automatic restraints to reduce the number of passenger car occupant fatalities, we cannot permit our response to the Supreme Court decision to be unduly delayed. At the same time, we recognize that one of the reasons that such an extensive amount of time has been spent on this rulemaking is the controversy that it has generated. While we understand that concensus would be impossible, we do recognize that public acceptability is a very important ingredient of any rule. Experience has also clearly taught us that for any rule to be successful, the compliance method must be effective. In this regard, we are concerned about any changes in the state of the art as well as any new data being gathered on the effectiveness and efficiency of alternative devices.

In the section that follows, we have set forth proposals for Departmental action in accordance with the Supreme Court's decision. In discussing these proposals, we ask a number of questions or make a number of requests for data to help us obtain the kind of information we believe will facilitate our analysis. For easy reference, we have numbered the questions or requests consecutively throughout the document. We would like to stress, however, that we do not wish to limit public comment to these proposals or the questions and requests that we ask. We would also like to receive any other information that will aid our decision making and would like to solicit any other suggestions or alternatives for complying with the Department's statutory responsibilities and the Supreme Court decision.

In providing a comment on a particular matter or in responding to a particular question, please provide any relevant factual information to support your conclusions or opinions, including but not limited to statistical and cost data, and the source of such information. (In this regard, it is noteworthy that the Supreme Court stated that "[t]he agency is correct to look at the costs as well as the benefits of Standard 208." *State Farm* at 2873.)

Range of Proposals and Fundamental Issues.

There are three regulatory actions that the Department can take in response to the Supreme Court decision. They are as follows:

1. *Amend the automatic occupant restraint requirements of FMVSS 208:* We could amend FMVSS 208; that is, we could decide, for example, to permit compliance only with either airbags or nondetachable seatbelts.
2. *Retain the automatic occupant restraint requirements of FMVSS 208:* We could adhere to FMVSS 208; that is, we could retain the substantive requirement for an automatic occupant restraint and establish a compliance date.
3. *Rescind the automatic occupant restraint requirements of FMVSS 208:* We could rescind the existing automatic occupant restraint requirements of FMVSS 208, after we, as the Supreme Court said, "consider the matter further" and provide additional justification.

Other steps are possible in conjunction with, or as a supplement to, one or more of the basic alternative proposals. We propose three in the NPRM. They are:

1. *Conduct a demonstration program:* As a preliminary step to action on one of the regulatory alternatives, we could conduct a demonstration program to help us gather more detailed and definitive data on public acceptability.
2. *Seek mandatory state safety belt usage laws:* We could seek legislation that would establish requirements to provide incentives for the States to adopt and enforce safety belt usage laws.
3. *Seek legislation mandating consumer option:* We could seek legislation requiring manufacturers to provide consumers with an option of selecting airbags or automatic belts, if they prefer these over manual belts.

During the course of the rulemaking on automatic occupant restraints, three fundamental issues have been raised that are interwined with the alternative proposals set forth above. These three issues are:

1. *Compliance alternatives:* This issue essentially involves the question of whether we can make the rule more flexible and reasonable.
2. *Public acceptance:* This issue involves the willingness of the public to accept a standard; acceptability is a necessity for any standard to be fully effective.
3. *Cost and technology information:* This issue involves cost and technical matters related to the various proposals.

Notes and Questions

1. Note the description of the *State Farm* decision that precedes the regulation itself. Agency officials are concerned about the public image of their agency. This is a natural human instinct, but also a response to the possibility of oversight hearings by Congress and investigations by the Office of Inspector General (see below). How did the agency handle the harsh repudiation of its decision that the Supreme Court inflicted on it? Is its account of the decision accurate? Does it capture the Court's tone? Does it try to justify the agency's action, and if so, how?

2. The agency followed this summary with a lengthy (nine pages in the densely printed Federal Register) account of "The Safety Problem" and the "Current Occupant Restraint Technology," which we have omitted. It then proceeded to its proposals. As in the case of the previous NPRM, this is atypical; usually, the NPRM is a draft of the final rule. Why do you suppose the agency adopted this approach? Note also the three additional possibilities that the agency says it is considering, and their lesser impact on the auto industry. The agency also includes a list of three "fundamental issues" that arose during the course of its considerations. Is anything missing (Hint: How about maximum safety protection for the occupants of the car?)

3. Section 553 does not require hearings, and courts do not impose them. As already noted, the Supreme Court had already handed down a decision in Vermont Yankee Nuclear Power Cor. v. NRDC, 435 U.S. 519 (1978) declaring that federal courts should not require agency rulemaking to follow any procedures beyond those specified in §553. (We present this case in Chapter 6). But NHTSA decided to hold hearings (which it is of course free to do if it wishes). Why do you suppose it made this decision? Five hearings were held, one in Los Angeles, one in Kansas City, and three in Washington, D.C.; Claybrook, Haddon, and Nader all testified, as did an insurance industry representative. GM continued to oppose passive restraints, arguing that its improvements to their vehicles' interiors would be sufficient, but Ford was more amenable to an airbag requirement.

At some point during the months that followed, Dole personally become convinced that airbags should be installed in automobiles. The reason why is not clear. When subsequently elected Senator from North Carolina, her voting record was markedly conservative and she lost her bid for reelection when she accused her Democratic opponent, Kay Hagen, of atheism. Perhaps—despite the cynicism that prevails among political observers and seems confirmed by much of the preceding narrative—she concluded, as had John Volpe, that she should implement the law. The Reagan Administration, despite clear discomfort, apparently came to the same conclusion. Martin Albaum reports:

> While the DOT task force had been working on the problem, Mrs. Dole, [Deputy Secretary James] Burnley, and Diane Steed maintained open channels on the issue with Christopher DeMuth, head of OMB's Office of Information and Regulatory Affairs [OIRA] and executive director of the Presidential Task Force on Regulatory Relief. Although Burnley thought that they might have convinced DeMuth of their position, DeMuth recalled that he was not persuaded that the Supreme Court ruling presented an insuperable barrier to a reformulated rescission. In any event, DeMuth felt that it was his role to argue for deregulation in any close case, and he did just that in a couple of closed meetings with the President's counsel, Ed Meese. There were meetings in the West Wing of the White House, Burnley recalled, that also included James Baker, the President's chief of staff, and Boyden Grey, the Vice President's counsel. These meetings took place at the very end of the process. Burnley characterized them as more philosophical than political. When the White House senior staff had endorsed Mrs. Dole's decision, she met with President Reagan to get his final blessing. She had a neurosurgeon with ties to the President, Dr. Paul Meyer, waiting outside in a limousine to

brief the President on the medical aspects of passive restraints. But he was not needed. The President's assent was "pretty much a done deal," Burnley remembers.

MARTIN ALBAUM, SAFETY SELLS: MARKET FORCES AND REGULATION IN THE DEVELOPMENT OF AIRBAGS 122 (2005).

Here is NHTSA's final rule.

National Highway Traffic Safety Administration, Federal Motor Vehicle Safety Standard; Occupant Crash Protection

49 C.F.R Part 571

[Docket No. 74-14; Notice No. 36]

AGENCY: Department of Transportation (DOT).

ACTION: Final rule.

SUMMARY: This Rule requires the installation of automatic restraints in all new cars beginning with model year 1990 (September 1, 1989) unless, prior to that time, state mandatory belt usage laws are enacted that cover at least two-thirds of the U.S. population. The requirement would be phased in by an increasing percentage of production over a three-year period beginning with model year 1987 (September 1, 1986). To further encourage the installation of advanced technology, the rule would treat cars, equipped with such technology other than automatic belts as equivalent to 1.5 vehicles during the phase-in.

DATES: The amendments made by this rule to the text of the Code of Federal Regulations are effective August 16, 1984.

The principal compliance dates for the rule, unless two-thirds of the population are covered by mandatory use laws, are:

September 1, 1986—for phase-in requirement

September 1, 1989—for full implementation requirement.

In addition: February 1, 1985—for center seating position exemption from automatic restraint provisions.

ADDRESS: Petitions for reconsideration should refer to the docket and notice numbers set forth above and be submitted not later than August 16, 1984 to: Administrator, National Highway Traffic Safety Administration, 400 Seventh Street, SW., Washington, D.C. 20590.

FOR FURTHER INFORMATION CONTACT: Neil R. Eisner, Assistant General Counsel for Regulation and Enforcement, Department of Transportation, 400 Seventh Street, SW., Washington, D.C. 20590 (202-425-4723).

SUPPLEMENTARY INFORMATION:

I. Summary of the Final Rule

After a thorough review of the issue of automobile occupant protection, including the long regulatory history of the matter; the comments on the Notice of Proposed Rulemaking (NPRM) and the Supplemental Notice of Proposed Rulemaking (SNPRM); and extensive studies, analyses, and data on the subject; and the court decisions that have resulted from law suits over the different rulemaking actions, the Department of Transportation has reached a final decision that it believes will offer the best method of fulfilling the

objectives and purpose of the governing statute, the National Traffic and Motor Vehicle Safety Act. As part of this decision, the Department has reached three basic conclusions:

- Effectively enforced state mandatory seatbelt use laws (MULs) will provide the greatest safety benefits most quickly of any of the alternatives, with almost no additional cost.
- Automatic occupant restraints provide demonstrable safety benefits, and, unless a sufficient number of MULs are enacted, they must be required for the most frequently used seats in passenger automobiles.
- Automatic occupant protection systems that do not totally rely upon belts, such as airbags or passive interiors, offer significant additional potential for preventing fatalities and injuries, at least in part because the American public is likely to find them less intrusive; their development and availability should be encouraged through appropriate incentives.

As a result of these conclusions, the Department has decided to require automatic occupant protection in all passenger automobiles based on a phased-in schedule beginning on September 1, 1986, with full implementation being required by September 1, 1989, unless, before April 1, 1989, two-thirds of the population of the United States are covered by MULs meeting specified conditions. More specifically, the rule would require the following:

Passenger cars manufactured for sale in the United States after September 1, 1986, will have to have automatic occupant restraints based on the following phase-in schedule:

- Ten percent of all automobiles manufactured after September 1, 1986.
- Twenty-five percent of all automobiles manufactured after September 1, 1987.
- Forty percent of all automobiles manufactured after September 1, 1988.
- One-hundred percent of all automobiles manufactured after September 1, 1989.
- The requirement for automatic occupant restraints will be rescinded if MULs meeting specified conditions are passed by a sufficient number of states before April 1, 1989 to cover two-thirds of the population of the United States.
- During the phase-in period, each passenger automobile that is manufactured with a system that provides automatic protection to the driver without automatic belts will be given an extra credit equal to one-half of an automobile toward meeting

the percentage requirement.
- The front center seat of passenger cars will be exempt from the requirement for automatic occupant protection.

. . .

VIII. The Rule

PART 571 — FEDERAL MOTOR VEHICLE SAFETY STANDARDS

In consideration of the foregoing, Federal Motor Vehicle Safety Standard No. 208. *Occupant Crash Protection,* (49 CFR 571.208), is amended as set forth below.

§571.208 [Amended]

S4.1.2 through S4.1.2.2 of Standard No. 208 are revised to read as follows:

* * * * *

S4.1.2 *Passenger cars manufactured on or after September 1, 1973, and before September 1, 1986.* Each passenger car manufactured on or after September 1, 1973, and after September 1, 1986, shall meet the requirements of S4.1.2.1, S4.1.2.2 or S4.1.2.3. A protection system that meets the requirements of S4.1.2.1 or S4.1.2.2 may be installed at one or more designated seating positions of a vehicle that otherwise meets the requirements of S4.1.2.3.

S4.1.2.1 *First option—frontal/ angular automatic protection system. The vehicle shall:*

(a) At each front outboard designated seating position meet the frontal crash protection requirements of S5.1 by means that require no action by vehicle occupants;
(b) At the front center designated seating position and at each rear designated seating position have a Type 1 or Type 2 seat

belt assembly that conforms to Standard No. 209 and to S7.1 and S7.2; and
(c) *Either.* (1) Meet the lateral crash protection requirements of S5.2 and the rollover crash protection requirements of S5.3 by means that require no action by vehicle occupants; or
(2) At each front outboard designated seating position have a Type 1 or Type 2 seat belt assembly-that conforms to Standard No. 203 and S7.1 through S7.3, and that meets the requirements of S5.1 with front test dummies as required by S5.1, restrained by the Type 1 or Type 2 seat belt assembly (or the pelvic portion of any Type 2 seat belt assembly which has a detachable upper torso belt) in addition to the means that require no action by the vehicle occupant.

S4.1.2.2 *Second option—head-on automatic protection system.* The vehicle shall—

(a) At each designated seating position have a Type 1 seat belt assembly or Type 2 seat belt assembly with a detachable upper torso portion that conforms to S7.1 and S7.2 of this standard.
(b) At each front outbord designated seating position, meet the frontal crash protection requirements of S5.1, in a perpendicular impact, by means that require no action by vehicle occupants;

(c) At each front out-board designated seating position, meet the frontal crash protection requirements of S5.1 in a perpendicular impact, with a test device restrained by a Type 1 seat belt assembly; and

(d) At each front outboard designated seating position, have a seat belt warning system that conforms to S7.3

2. S4.1.3 of Standard No. 203 is revised to read as follows:

S4.1.3 *Passenger cars manufactured on or after September 1, 13S8, and before September 1, 1989.*

S4.1.3.1 *Passenger cars manufactured on or after September 1, 193S, and before September 1, 1987.*

S4.1.3.1.1 Subject to S4.1.3.1.2 and S4.1.3.4, each passenger car manufactured on or after September 1, 1988, and before September 1, 1987, shall comply with the requirements of S4.1.2.1. S4.1.2.2 or S4.1.2.3.

S4.1.3.1.2 Subject to S4.1.5, an amount of the cars specified in S4.1.3.1.1 equal to not less than 10 percent of the average annual production of passenger cars manufactured on or after September 1, 1983, and before September 1, 1986, by, each manufacturer, shall comply with the requirements of S4.1.2.1.

S4.1.3.2 *Passenger cars manufactured on or after September 1, 1987, and before September 1, 1988.*

S4.1.3.2.1 Subject to S4.1.3.2.2 and S4.1.3.4, each passenger car manufactured on or after September 1, 1987, and before September 1, 1988, shall comply with the requirements of S4.1.2.1, S4.1.2.2 or S4.1.2.3.

S4.1.3.2.2 Subject to S4.1.5, art amount of the cars specified in S4.1.3.2.1 equal to not less than 25 percent of the average annual production of passenger cars manufactured on or after September 1, 1984, and before September 1, 1987, by each manufacturer, shall comply with.the requirements of S4.1.2.1.

S4.1.3.3 *Passenger cars manufactured on or after September 1, 1988, and before September 1, 1989.*

S4.1.3.3.1 Subject to S4.1.3.3.2 and S4.1.3.4, each passenger car manufactured on or after September 1, 1988, and before September 1, 1989, shall comply with the requirements of S4.1.2.1, S4.1.2.2 or S4.1.2.3.

S4.1.3.3.2 Subject to S4.1.5, an amount of the cars specified in S4.1.3.3.1 equal to not less than 40 percent of the average annual production of passenger cars manufactured on or after September 1, 1985, and before September 1, 1988, by each manufacturer, shall comply with the requirements of S4.1.2.1.

S4.1.3.4 For the purposes of calculating the numbers of cars manufactured under S4.1.3.1.2, S4.1.3.2.2 or S4.1.3.3.2 to comply with S4.1.2.1, each car whose driver's seating position will comply with these requirements by means other than any type of seat belt is counted as 1.5 vehicles.

3. Standard No. 208 is amended by adding the following new sections:

S4.1.4 *Passenger cars manufactured on or after September 1, 1989.* Except as provided in S4.1.5, each passenger car manufactured on or after September 1, 1989, shall comply with the requirements of S4.1.2.1.

S4.1.5 *Mandatory seat-belt use laws.*

S4.1.5.1 If the Secretary of Transportation determines, by not later than April 1, 1989, that state mandatory safety belt usage laws have been enacted that meet the criteria specified in S4.1.5.2 and that are applicable to not less than two-thirds of the total population of the 50 states and the District of Columbia (based on the most recent Estimates of the Resident Population of States, by Age, Current Population Reports, Series P-25, Bureau of the Census), each passenger car manufactured under S4.1.3 or S4.1.4 on or after the date of that determination shall comply with the requirements of S4.1.2.1, S4.1.2.2 or S4.1.2.3.

S4.1.5.2 The minimum criteria for state mandatory safety belt usage laws are:

(a) Require that each front seat occupant of a passenger car equipped with safety belts under Standard No. 208 has a safety belt properly fastened about his or her body at all times when the vehicle is in forward motion.

(b) If waivers from the safety bolt usage requirement are to be provided, permit them for medical reasons only.

(c) Provide for the following enforcement measures:

(1) A penalty of not less than $25.00 (which may include court costs) for each occupant of a car who violates the bolt usage requirement.

(2) A provision specifying that the violation of

the belt usage requirement may be used to mitigate damages with respect to any person who is involved in a passenger car accident while violating the belt usage requirement and who seeks in any subsequent litigation to recover damages for injuries resulting from the accident. This requirement is satisfied if there is a rule of law in the State permitting such mitigation.

(3) A program to encourage compliance with the belt usage requirement.

(d) An effective date of not later than September 1, 1989.

(Sec. 103, 119, Pub. L. 89-563, 80 Stat. 710 (15 U.S.C. 1392, 1407)

Issued: July 11, 1984.

Elizabeth H, Dole,
Secretary of Transportation.

Notes and Questions

1. The statement of basis and purpose of this rule has a 112 item table of contents, and runs some 40 pages in the Federal Register, about the length of Hemingway's *The Old Man and the Sea.* Clearly, the agency did not want to suffer the same fate as it did when it promulgated its previous rule. Recall that the legal requirement is a "concise general statement." Does the tumescence of Standard 208's justification indicate a breakdown or an improvement of the administrative process? It is easy to satirize or excoriate the size of the Federal Register, but comparing a week's publications to the height of a giraffe may not be a meaningful way to analyze the issue. After all, the issue of passive restraints involves tens or hundreds of thousands of lives and hundreds of thousands of injuries, while the economic impact on the industry and on consumers, runs well into the billions. The cost of having a few staff members produce a comprehensive explanation for the decision is trivial by comparison. On the other hand, if all this material is grist for the judicial review mill, and leads to intensified scrutiny of the agency's decision, then the agency's ability to function, and the power of elected officials' to control it, may be challenged in ways that we find undesirable.

2. What do you think about the provision regarding Mandatory Use Laws (MULs)? Was it effectively a substitute for the passive restraint requirement, was it a surrender to the auto manufacturers, or was it a meaningless fig leaf in the raiment of American federalism that the agency was using to conceal its exercise of authority? It became known as the "trapdoor" provision, for obvious reasons. Auto safety advocates challenged it immediately as arbitrary and capricious, but the D.C. Circuit refused to reach the merits, arguing that the challenge lacked finality, a requirement for judicial review under APA §704 ("final agency action" is "subject to judicial review."). *See* State Farm Mut. Automobile Ins. Co. v. Dole, 802 F.2d 474 (1986).

After the regulation was promulgated, the auto manufacturers formed an organization called Traffic Safety Now to campaign for state MULs that would lead to rescission of the federal requirement. The problem for them was that this rather transparent strategy was easy enough to combat in those states that were favorable to auto safety measures—generally the large urban states that would need to act in order to cover the two-thirds of the population that would trigger the trapdoor. New York enacted an MUL that provided for a $50 maximum fine rather than the $25 minimum fine specified in the regulation. California went still further; borrowing a concept from corporate anti-acquisition practice, it added a "poison pill" to its MUL providing that the law would be automatically revoked if it triggered the trapdoor. It is not known whether Elizabeth Dole anticipated this result. In any event, the trapdoor never opened and Standard 208's passive restraint requirement went into effect on schedule. Thus, automakers had no choice and began to comply with the passive restraint rule, opting mostly to install airbags. In 1991, facing no further opposition from the industry, Congress enacted a statute that ordered NHTSA to enact a regulation requiring airbags in all new vehicles. *See* Pub. L. No. 102-240, §2508, 105 Stat. 1914, 2085 (1991).

Is this a happy ending? Many commentators do not think so. NHTSA's performance has been subject to continued criticism. *See, e.g.,* LEONARD EVANS, TRAFFIC SAFETY SERVING SOCIETY (2004); Lauren Pacelli, *Asleep at the Wheel of Auto Safety? Recent Air Bag Regulations by the National Highway Traffic Safety Administration,* 15 J. CONTEMP. HEALTH L. & POLICY 739 (1999). In his book, Evans includes the following chart:

Country	1979 Fatalities	2002 Fatalities	Percent Change
United States	51,093	42,815	−16.2%
Great Britain	6,352	3,431	−46.0%
Canada	5,863	2,936	−49.9%
Australia	3,508	1,715	−51.1%

It might seem unfair to compare the United States to a relatively small European nation such as Great Britain (or Germany, France, or Italy?) because the larger vehicles such as pickup trucks and SUVs that people tend to use in open spaces are inherently more dangerous. But Canada and Australia are much more sparsely populated than the United States, and Canada has the same mix of vehicles as we do. We just seem to be dying more.

Concluding Question

All three U.S. auto manufacturers were opposed to safety regulation, but GM was particularly hostile, as you have probably noticed from the preceding materials. GM was equally antagonistic toward fuel economy regulations (the CAFE, or Corporate Average Fuel Economy, standards) and anti-pollution regulations. Its opposition to these policies began when they were instituted in the late 1960s or early 1970s and continued unabated through the 1970s, '80s, '90s and into the new century. There seems to have been a sense of self-righteous fury against regulation among five decades of GM management, a belief that any government interference with their decision making was improper and un-American. After the *State Farm* decision, Roger Smith, Chairman of GM wrote a letter to Elizabeth Dole, arguing that none of the airbags currently on the market were effective. An executive of Allstate Insurance Co. responded:

> Mr. Smith is not a credible adviser upon this subject. He is an avowed opponent of automatic crash protection. He canceled the GM airbag program. He caused GM to submit the strategy upon which rescission of the safety standard was based. He included rescission of passive restraint standards on his first "wish list" when the Administration took office. His suggestions should be ignored.

MARTIN ALBAUM, SAFETY SELLS: MARKET FORCES AND REGULATION IN THE DEVELOPMENT OF AIRBAGS 122 (2005).

During this same period, GM underwent a sustained and prepreciptious decline in both its domestic and worldwide market share, with a good deal of the decline being attributed to Chairman Smith. In 1962, GM controlled a full half of the U.S. market (50.7%). Its Chevrolet division alone accounting for a quarter, nearly as much as all of Ford, which was in second place. At present, its share is 17 percent, a decline of two thirds. Because it was carrying the management, pension, and fixed-plant costs from its grander days, GM began piling up huge annual losses as its market share declined, and it declared bankruptcy under Chapter 11 in 2009. It only survived as a corporate entity through a $51 billion government bailout. Ford's market share has also declined, but by a lower proportion (about half, from 29% to 15%). Chrysler's market share has remained relatively steady and in fact grown somewhat (from 10% to 13%), but the company (which also went bankrupt in 2009) is now a subsidiary of Fiat, the Italian automaker.

GM's decline and fall is certainly one of the most dramatic and tragic tales in American business history. *See* ALEX TAYLOR III, SIXTY TO ZERO: AN INSIDE LOOK AT THE COLLAPSE OF GENERAL MOTORS—AND THE DETROIT AUTO INDUSTRY (2010). The company was seen as the very pinacle of American commercial prowess in the 1950s, an industrial behemoth and the ultimate "blue chip" investment. What happened? Competition from manufacturers in other nations is an obvious explanation, but why were these manufacturers able to invade and conquer the U.S. market so effectively, increasing their market share from under 10 percent in the early 1960s to nearly 60 percent today (even counting Chrysler as American)? And why wasn't a gigantic and well-financed company like GM able to score equivalent successes in foreign markets (its share of the non-U.S. market, not surprisingly, is even lower, about 8%).

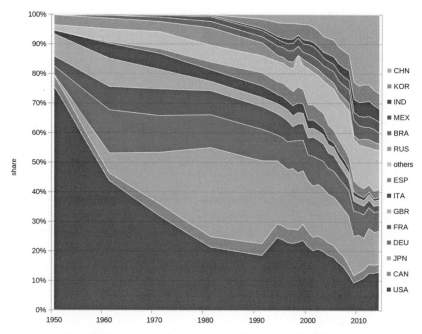

World Motor Vehicle Production, Selected Countries (thousands of vehicles) Bureau of Transportation Statistics

An explanation common in business literature is that GM was stodgy and insular, a victim of its own size and success. Maria von Neumann Whitman describes "a deeply embedded and profoundly dysfunctional culture" that operated as "a bulwark against reality" (THE MARTIAN'S DAUGHTER (2011)). But that seems more a description of the result than an explanation of its causes. In fact, GM engaged in a wide variety of efforts to halt its decline, some of which convey an air of frantic desperation. Beginning in 1960, it quickly came out with the Chevrolet Corvair to compete with imported Eurpean compacts, but the car was rushed into production and—though small and inexpensive—it—turned out to be "unsafe at any speed" (see Chapter 2). During the 1990s, GM tried new management. Its marketing was put in the hands of Vince Barraba, who had previously worked for Kodak and the U.S. Census Bureau and commuted to Detroit from his beach home in California. The European division was run by Lou "Mad Dog" Hughes, who took his subordinates on five-day Outward Bound excursions. GM was also one of the first companies to use robots in its manufacturing process; installed to spray paint on the vehicles coming off the assembly line, the robots ended up spraying each other. Far from being over-cautious, the company kept coming up with new designs, but—most of them just weren't very good, in one way or another. Saturn, an entirely new division, was established to make small cars that would compete, once again, with imported compacts, this time from Japan. The Saturns, whose most striking innovation was their plastic body panels, did not perform well, a problem that management tried to solve, over time, by making them larger. The much-touted Pontiac Aztek, described by one executive as looking like an angry kitchen appliance, is generally considered the ugliest car ever made in America.

Perhaps the explanation for GM's dramatic collapse is that the regulators knew more about its consumer base than its executives did. To design a product, particularly one like an anutomobile that takes at least five or six years to bring to market, one needs to have a clear idea of its potential buyers. Although GM, with its enormous range of product lines (too many perhaps) certainly aimed at a variety of demographic groups, many of its new models seemed to have been directed to a buyer who might be called "car guy"—a twenty- to forty-something small-town male who wanted a car that would say great things about himself. GM never seemed to realize that modern Americans might want safe cars, fuel efficient cars, and even—although it would bring them no direct benefit—non-polluting cars. Would it have done better if its leaders had cooperated with the regulators, rather than going to war against them? Would "soccer mom" and "eco-family" have been more promising potential markets?

Should GM's instransigence be blamed on its leadership, or do regulators such as NHTSA deserve a share of the blame? Could NHTSA have worked with American automakers to develop safety and fuel economy standards? Could it have convinced them that such standards would help them meet the challenge coming from the European and Japanese imports? Could the agency have presented its regulatory initiatives as a way to stop the hemmorhaging of the American manufacturers' market share? Based on the materials presented in this chapter, how do you think the agency might have implemented this approach, and do you think it would have been effective?

For one possibility, admittedly focused more on individual citizens than on regulated firms, consider the following.

Jody Freeman, Collaborative Governance in the Administrative State

45 UCLA Law Rev. 1, 22, 96-7 (1997)

Collaborative governance seeks to respond to the litany of criticisms about the quality, implementability, and legitimacy of rule making by reorienting the regulatory enterprise around joint problem solving and away from controlling discretion. Collaborative governance is characterized by the following features:

1. A problem-solving orientation. The focus is on solving regulatory problems. This requires information sharing and deliberation among parties with the knowledge most relevant to devising and implementing creative solutions.

2. Participation by interested and affected parties in all stages of the decision-making process. Broad participation has an independent democratic value and may facilitate effective problem solving. It may take different forms in different contexts.

3. Provisional solutions. Rules are viewed as temporary and subject to revision. This requires a willingness to move forward under conditions of uncertainty. It also demands a willingness to devise solutions to regulatory problems without foreclosing a rethinking of both solutions and goals. To this end, continuous monitoring and evaluation are crucial.

4. Accountability that transcends traditional public and private roles in governance. Parties are interdependent and accountable to each other. New arrangements, networks, institutions, or allocations of authority may replace or supplement traditional oversight mechanisms. These might include self-monitoring and disclosure, community oversight, and third-party certification. In these arrangements, traditional roles and functions are open to question.

5. A flexible, engaged agency. The agency is a convenor and facilitator of multi-stakeholder negotiations. It provides incentives for broader participation, information sharing, and deliberation. It acts as a capacity builder of parties and institutions by providing technical resources, funding, and organizational support when needed. While the agency may set floors and ceilings and act as the ultimate decisionmaker, it views regulatory success as contingent on the contributions of other participants. . . .

It may turn out that many kinds of knowledge are relevant to the design and implementation of rules, including knowledge that has not traditionally been regarded as expert. For example, local homeowners may have valuable information about how police might improve law enforcement; school administrators and teachers may offer expertise about how to accommodate children with special needs; tribal communities may possess important insight about ecosystem management; employees may know a great deal about preventing exposure to workplace hazards. The challenge is to resist the notion that agency cultivation of broader, more direct participation in governance, in specific regulatory contexts, necessarily erodes governmental power, or that it always undermines the legitimacy of the administrative regime. To argue that the government should cultivate the capacity of nongovernmental groups does not detract from the legitimacy of regulatory decisions; it increases legitimacy.

5

Statutory Implementation by Agencies

Agencies are the institutions primarily responsible for implementing regulatory statutes. This chapter examines how they perform that function. We discuss the different tools or types of analyses that agencies use in the implementation process—statutory, scientific, economic, and political. In doing so, we focus on one particular process that agencies use for implementing regulatory statutes: notice-and-comment rulemaking. This process generates rules, also called regulations, which are legally binding on government officials and private parties, similar to statutes. At the end of this chapter, we will discuss some other means of statutory implementation, including formal adjudication and guidance.

Before we begin, it is worth summarizing some of the features that make agencies distinctive as institutions for implementing statutes. First, and perhaps most fundamentally, agencies are designed to deploy technical expertise. A central reason why Congress creates agencies is to deploy their specialized skills. Agencies employ scientists, economists, and other professionals who are trained and knowledgeable about the important aspects of complex regulatory problems. Agencies also have the capacity to obtain and process technical information as well as to develop long-term experience with implementing policy in particular regulatory areas. Courts, by contrast, are generalists. They have relatively limited access to technical staff, limited ability to obtain and process technical information, and limited familiarity with regulatory schemes.

Second, most agency action is authorized by a relatively few identifiable statutes. Agencies work with these statutes day after day and develop familiarity with the key aspects of their operation. Any given court, by contrast, confronts any particular statute infrequently and often over an issue at the margins, rather than the core, of its operation.

Third, agencies have considerable control over their agenda. Although some statutes impose specific deadlines for when an agency must complete a specific task, most grant agencies discretion within a general area about which problems to tackle, when to tackle them, and through what means. Many agencies have the ability to refrain from taking any action at all; a statute grants them authority but imposes no obligation to use it. NHTSA is not such an agency; the 1966 Motor Vehicle Safety Act requires it to issue auto safety standards within a certain period. But even NHTSA has discretion concerning the content and timing of such standards. In this respect, agencies are like prosecutors or Congress; prosecutors can pick their cases and Congress has control over its agenda. In contrast, courts depend upon lawsuits to present issues for their resolution. While the Supreme Court has some ability to control the issues it decides, courts are generally reactive institutions.

Fourth, agencies are structured to be responsive, or accountable, to political officials. Agencies have an ongoing relationship with both of the political branches, and this relationship is most evident when agencies are making major policy decisions. Congress not only creates the statutes that grant agencies authority but continues to monitor how that authority is exercised. The President is also involved on an ongoing basis, particularly in the work of executive-branch agencies. If an agency does something unpopular, members of Congress and the President will hear about it. Federal courts, by contrast, are relatively insulated from politics, not only because federal judges have life tenure, but also because due process principles insulate adjudication from direct outside influences.

As you will see, these distinctive features affect how agencies implement their statutes. Indeed, it can be argued that agency statutory implementation replaces the basic conception of law that existed in the pre-administrative state. *See* EDWARD RUBIN, BEYOND CAMELOT: RETHINKING POLITICS AND LAW FOR THE MODERN STATE, 191-226 (2005). Take note of the ways in which these capabilities and constraints manifest themselves throughout the chapter.

A. THE NOTICE-AND-COMMENT RULEMAKING PROCESS

Just as Congress generally follows a relatively predictable process for enacting statutes, agencies generally follow a relatively predictable process for issuing regulations. In the case of agencies, however, that process is partially controlled by legislation, specifically the Administrative Procedure Act (APA). The Act's requirements are known as the "notice-and-comment" rulemaking process. A helpful overview of this process can be found at *www.regulations.gov* (under "Learn," you can find a detailed map of the regulatory process, *http://www.reginfo.gov/public/reginfo/Regmap/index.jsp*). In addition, *www.regulations.gov* provides information and facilitates public involvement in government regulations proceeding through that process.

The APA provision that establishes the notice and comment process is 5 U.S.C. §553, and reads as follows:

(a) This section applies, according to the provisions thereof, except to the extent that there is involved —

(1) a military or foreign affairs function of the United States; or

(2) a matter relating to agency management or personnel or to public property, loans, grants, benefits, or contracts.

(b) General notice of proposed rule making shall be published in the Federal Register, unless persons subject thereto are named and either personally served or otherwise have actual notice thereof in accordance with law. The notice shall include —

(1) a statement of the time, place, and nature of public rule making proceedings;

(2) reference to the legal authority under which the rule is proposed; and

(3) either the terms or substance of the proposed rule or a description of the subjects and issues involved.

Except when notice or hearing is required by statute, this subsection does not apply —

(A) to interpretative rules, general statements of policy, or rules of agency organization, procedure, or practice; or

(B) when the agency for good cause finds (and incorporates the finding and a brief statement of reasons therefor in the rules issued) that notice and public procedure thereon are impracticable, unnecessary, or contrary to the public interest.

(c) After notice required by this section, the agency shall give interested persons an opportunity to participate in the rule making through submission of written data, views, or arguments with or without opportunity for oral presentation. After consideration of the relevant matter presented, the agency shall incorporate in the rules adopted a concise general statement of their basis and purpose. When rules are required by statute to be made on the record after opportunity for an agency hearing, sections 556 and 557 of this title apply instead of this subsection.

(d) The required publication or service of a substantive rule shall be made not less than 30 days before its effective date, except

(1) a substantive rule which grants or recognizes an exemption or relieves a restriction;

(2) interpretative rules and statements of policy; or

(3) as otherwise provided by the agency for good cause found and published with the rule.

(e) Each agency shall give an interested person the right to petition for the issuance, amendment, or repeal of a rule.

Here is a description of the way these provisions function in context. For a more detailed account, see Jeffrey S. Lubbers, A Guide to Federal Agency Rulemaking (2006); *A Blackletter Statement of Federal Administrative Law*, 54 Admin. L. Rev. 1 (2002).

Initiating the Process.   The impetus to initiate the rulemaking process can come from many different sources. The agency can consider a rulemaking at its own initiative in response to its own statutory mandates, regulatory action plans, new scientific data, or triggering events, such as an increase in accidents or lawsuits based on those accidents. Likewise, the President can sometimes order that an agency initiate rulemaking or urge such action, often through OIRA (Office of Information and Regulatory Affairs) in the form of a prompt letter. An agency may also respond to recommendations by other agencies or government bodies or a Petition for Rulemaking from private parties or groups.

Formulating the Rule. The agency will typically the conduct an analysis to determine whether to formulate a proposed rule. Once an agency decides to proceed with a proposed rule, the first step usually is to issue a *Notice of Proposed Rulemaking* (NPRM), which contains one or more proposed rules and is published in the *Federal Register*. We reproduce a NPRM in the next section. Sometimes an agency will issue a document in advance of the NPRM, called (not surprisingly) an *Advanced Notice of Proposed Rulemaking* (ANPRM). This step is useful to winnow proposals prior to issuing an NPRM. When an executive-branch agency is in the initiation phase, it must submit any proposed rule with anticipated costs of $100 million or more for review to the Office of Information and Regulatory Affairs (OIRA) in the White House. *See* Exec. Order No. 12866, 58 Fed. Reg. 51735 §6 (Sept. 30, 1993), as amended by Exec. Order No. 13497, 74 Fed Reg. 6113 (Jan. 30, 2009). Note that this review requirement comes from executive order, not the APA. We reproduce this Executive Order and discuss its operation in Chapter 6.

Under APA §553, an NPRM must contain a "reference to the legal authority under which the rule is promulgated," "either the terms or substance of the proposed rule or description of the subjects involved," and a statement of time and place of any public proceedings. APA, 5 U.S.C. §553(b). These are minimum requirements in the sense that agencies are free to structure rulemakings with more elaborate procedures. As we will see in Chapter 6, the Supreme Court has prohibited reviewing courts from ordering agencies to adopt more elaborate procedures than those set forth in the APA. But courts have had some say, interpreting the existing procedures in the APA as requiring agencies to make available the data and studies that are the basis for its rule.

Conducting the Process. After the agency publishes the NPRM in the *Federal Register*, it must provide a reasonable time for interested parties to submit written comments on the proposed rule. These comments are the means for interested parties to be "heard" on the proposed rule. One purpose of the notice-and-comment rulemaking process is to replace an oral, trial-type hearing with a written one. Although agencies still occasionally hold hearings, they are not obliged to do so. To make the paper process meaningful, the agency is generally regarded as having an obligation to consider the comments that parties submit as part of the rulemaking docket; these written comments are now generally available for easy viewing on the Internet. *See, e.g., www.regulations.gov.* Many comments, particularly those from industry groups such as automakers or insurance companies, include detailed analysis of the proposals and are frequently drafted by lawyers. But any person may submit a comment on any proposal, and the agency has the same obligation to consider it.

After receiving comments, an agency sometimes realizes that a new proposal is worth consideration alongside, or in lieu of, existing ones. If that proposal is not a "logical outgrowth" of the existing proposals, the agency must conduct a new round of notice and comment. *See* Clean Air Act Council v. Pruitt, 862 F.3d 1 (D.C. Cir. 2017); CSX Transportation, Inc. v. Surface Transportation Bd., 584 F.3d 1076, 1079-80 (D.C. Cir. 2009) (NPRM is logical outgrowth if parties should have anticipated that change was possible and thus reasonably should have filed their comments during notice and comment). It typically does so by issuing a *Supplemental Notice of Proposed Rulemaking* (SNPRM). It is possible for an agency to conduct multiple rounds, although that is not the norm. Can you see why? An agency can gather a sense for the range of options before issuing an NPRM by seeking information through informal contacts with affected parties or by issuing an ANPRM.

Completing the Process. The agency completes the notice-and-comment rulemaking process by issuing a final rule. The APA requires the agency to include with its final rule a statement of the basis for the rule: "After consideration of the relevant matter presented, the agency shall incorporate in the rules adopted a concise general statement of their basis and purpose." APA, §553(c). The statement of "basis and purpose" must, at a minimum, forth the rationale and legal authority for the rule. Although the "basis and purpose" language in the APA is rather sparse, the Supreme Court has required agencies to provide an extensive explanation for their final rules, partially to facilitate judicial review of such rules under a different section of the APA, 5 U.S.C. §702. *See* Motor Vehicle Manufacturers Association of the United States, Inc. v. State Farm Mutual Automobile Insurance Co., 463 U.S. 29, 43-44 (1983); Citizens to Preserve Overton Park v. Volpe, 401 U.S. 402, 416 (1971). Sometimes an agency determines after completing the notice-and-comment rulemaking process that no final rule is warranted. The agency must provide an explanation for that decision as well. Note that a host of other statutes require agencies to evaluate the impact of their regulations on certain interests — for example, on small businesses and the environment. Agencies often include a section called "impact analyses" in their final rules, which demonstrates their compliance with these statutes. This section also may contain any cost-benefit analysis that an agency performed to comply with the executive order on this issue.

If an agency wants to amend or rescind a final rule, it also must do so through the notice-and-comment rulemaking process. Put differently, the agency must issue a new rule. This principle should be familiar by analogy to the legislative process: Congress can amend or repeal a statute only by enacting a new statute. For both Congress and agencies, this principle generally holds regardless of the magnitude of the change. Thus, even if an agency wants to change a relatively minor detail of a final rule, such as extending a phase-in schedule, it must issue a new rule.

Notes and Questions

1. We have said that the notice-and-comment rulemaking process is analogous to the legislative process in that it produces rules with effects similar to statutes. What are the most obvious differences from the legislative process? Why does the notice-and-comment rulemaking process look the way that it does? Why would Congress have designed it this way? What values does it serve? To what extent is it based on judicial process (notice, a hearing, a decision on the record), rather than legislative process? See Edward Rubin, *It's Time to Make Administrative Law Administrative*, 89 CORNELL L. REV. 95 (2003).

2. Based on the description above, do you have any sense about who writes NPRMs or final rules? Agency rulemaking staff? Agency lawyers? Agency political officials? All of the above? The agency head must sign every rule. Do you suppose that she has familiarity with the content of the rules, even if she did not pen all the words? Or is she, like Congress, relative to the committees responsible for bills? We will revisit questions like these as we go along in this chapter.

3. Does the notice-and-comment rulemaking process seem "burdensome" to you? Is it less burdensome than a trial-type hearing? What sort of alternative might the agency prefer?

4. Although notice-and-comment rulemaking is the primary means through which agencies issue legally binding rules, the APA contemplates that agencies will issue binding rules through other processes as well. It allows agencies to issue rules through a trial-like proceeding called formal rulemaking, *see* 5 U.S.C. §§556 and 557, but this is so rarely used that there is no need to discuss it further. The APA also provides for agencies to promulgate "direct final rules," which become effective after publication if no "adverse" comments are received. Likewise, it provides for agencies to issue "interim final rules," which are generally effective immediately upon publication, and to then solicit comments after the fact. *See* Ronald M. Levin, *Direct Final Rulemaking*, 64 GEO. WASH. L. REV. 1, 16-18 (1995) (describing the use of direct final rules); Anne Joseph O'Connell, *Political Cycles of Rulemaking: An Empirical Portrait of the Modern Administrative State*, 94 VA. L. REV. 889, 901, 902 & n.33, 903, 931 (2008) (describing formal rulemaking, direct final rules, and interim final rules, and documenting use of the latter two).

B. AN EXAMPLE OF NOTICE AND COMMENT RULEMAKING: NHTSA STANDARD 208

The cars that we drive today are equipped with airbags. We can trace that result in large part to the 1966 National Traffic and Motor Vehicle Safety Act (the Motor Vehicle Safety Act or the 1966 Act). Yet the 1966 Act did not mandate airbags, or any other safety feature, per se. Rather, it created an agency, the National Highway Traffic Safety Administration (NHTSA), located originally in the Department of Commerce but soon transferred to the newly-created Department of Transportation, to establish safety standards. NHTSA issued a final rule, so-called Standard 208, which is principally responsible for airbags. But, the story was far more complicated than that. Beginning in 1967 and unfolding over more than two decades, NHTSA issued the rule, amended the rule, suspended the rule, rescinded the rule, and reintroduced the rule. Thus, NHTSA went through an extended period of intense regulatory activity, mainly through successive notice-and-comment rulemaking proceedings, where it addressed what are called "passive restraints" — that is, vehicle safety devices that protect occupants without requiring them to buckle up (hence the name "passive"). The most familiar are automatic seatbelts (belts that typically attach to the door of car and swing forward to meet the occupant when the door closes) and airbags (inflatable cushions that deploy on impact). NHTSA finally settled on airbags.

In this section, we provide the two documents from the middle of the story: the 1981 Notice of Proposed Rulemaking and Final Rule. A more extensive set of documents, constituting a case study of the first decade of the process for Standard 208, is provided in Chapter 4 of this book. Here we focus on just two documents, an NPRM and a final rule.

Before turning to these two agency documents, it is first helpful to recall the provisions of the 1966 Act that required NHTSA to issue motor vehicle safety standards:

> Sec. 103. (a) The Secretary shall establish by order appropriate Federal motor vehicle safety standards. Each such Federal motor vehicle safety standard shall be practicable, shall meet the need for motor vehicle safety, and shall be stated in objective terms.
>
> (b) The Administrative Procedure Act shall apply to all orders establishing, amending, or revoking a Federal motor vehicle safety standard under this title.
>
> (c) Each order establishing a Federal motor vehicle safety standard shall specify the date such standard is to take effect which shall not be sooner than one hundred and eighty days or later than one year from the date such order is issued, unless the Secretary finds, for good cause shown, that an earlier or later effective date is in the public interest, and publishes his reasons for such finding.
>
> (d) Whenever a Federal motor vehicle safety standard established under this title is in effect, no State or political subdivision of a State shall have any authority either to establish, or to continue in effect, with respect to any motor vehicle or item of motor vehicle equipment any safety standard applicable to the same aspect of performance of such vehicle or item of equipment, which is not identical to the Federal standard. Nothing in this section shall be construed to prevent the Federal Government or the government of any State or political subdivision thereof from establishing a safety requirement applicable to motor vehicles or motor vehicle equipment procured for its own use if such

requirement imposes a higher standard of performance than that required to comply with the otherwise applicable Federal standard.

(e) The Secretary may by order amend or revoke any Federal motor vehicle safety standard established under this section. Such order shall specify the date on which such amendment or revocation is to take effect, which shall not be sooner than one hundred and eighty days or later than one year from the date the order is issued, unless the Secretary finds, for good cause shown, that an earlier or later effective date is in the public interest, and publishes his reasons for such finding.

(f) In prescribing standards under this section, the Secretary shall —

(1) consider relevant available motor vehicle safety data, including the results of research, development, testing and evaluation activities conducted pursuant to this Act;

(2) consult with the Vehicle Equipment Safety Commission, and such other State or interstate agencies (including legislative committees) as he deems appropriate;

(3) consider whether any such proposed standard is reasonable practicable and appropriate for the particular type of motor vehicle or item of motor vehicle equipment for which it is prescribed; and

(4) consider the extent to which such standards will contribute to carrying out the purposes of this Act.

Pub. L. No. 89-563, 80 Stat. 718, 719-20 (1966).

It is also helpful to have a sense of the broader political and social context of Standard 208. The history of that regulation is the subject of Chapter 4. Because it is complex, we summarize it here. For a more detailed account, see JERRY L. MASHAW & DAVID L. HARFST, THE STRUGGLE FOR AUTO SAFETY (1990).

In the Beginning: Manual Seatbelts. When the Department of Transportation initially promulgated Standard 208 in 1967, the agency did not require auto manufacturers to install passive restraints in new motor vehicles. Rather, it required only that auto manufacturers install manual seatbelts. Manual seatbelts, if used properly, have always been (and continue to be) an effective means to reduce the occurrence of secondary collisions or the incidence of injury or death from such collisions when they do occur. But manual seatbelt use was so low during this initial period that traffic injuries and fatalities remained high. People simply refused to buckle up on their own. So the agency began to study the option of "passive" occupant restraint systems, which would not depend upon an affirmative action by the occupant to produce safety benefits. The Department began investigating two different types of passive restraints: the automatic seatbelt and the airbag.

Enter Passive Restraints. In 1969, the Department issued a proposal (again, called a Notice of Proposed Rulemaking or NPRM) to require auto manufacturers to install passive restraints in new vehicles. In 1970 and 1972, it issued a final rule revising Standard 208 to require auto manufacturers to install passive restraints, ultimately for all front seat occupants in vehicles manufactured after 1975. In the interim before 1975, the agency required auto manufacturers either to install passive restraints or couple a manual seatbelt with an "ignition interlock," a device that emitted an audible warning buzzer and prevented the vehicle from starting if the seatbelts were not fastened. In 1972, the Court of Appeals for the Sixth Circuit upheld the Department's decision to require passive restraints, but concluded that the testing procedure involving anthropomorphic dummies did not define the dummies' characteristics with sufficient specificity to provide auto manufacturers with objective criteria to assess compliance, and thus did not satisfy the 1966 Act's requirement that the standards be "objective." *See* Chrysler Corp. v. Department of Transportation, 472 F.2d 659, 675-68 (6th Cir. 1972). This conclusion also invalidated the agency's airbag requirement because the efficacy of airbags depended upon crash-dummy testing. *Id.* at 681. The agency's standard regarding ignition interlock systems was unaffected by the Sixth Circuit's decision. Auto manufacturers began to comply with the still valid portions of the agency's passive restraint requirement by choosing to install ignition interlocks.

Drivers and Congress React; NHTSA responds. The American public had an extremely strong adverse reaction to ignition interlocks. Just as car owners resented the intrusion of manual seat belts, they opposed the annoying reminder to fasten them. Congress took note. In 1974, Congress amended the 1966 Motor Vehicle Safety Act to prohibit NHTSA from allowing an ignition interlock or an audible buzzer. *See* 49 U.S.C. §30124. In addition, Congress required the agency to submit any passive restraint regulation to Congress, which it could then veto for a 60-day period by a concurrent resolution of the House and Senate before the standard would be effective. *See* Motor Vehicle and Schoolbus Safety Amendments of 1974, Pub. L. No. 93-492, §109, 88 Stat. 1470, 1482. In 1975, William T. Coleman, the Secretary of Transportation under President Ford, postponed further development of passive restraint standards, and then suspended altogether the installation of passive restraints. Secretary Coleman instead established a demonstration project to facilitate public acceptance, allowing manufacturers to install passive restraints in up to 500,000 new cars.

A New Administration Weighs In. When President Carter took office in 1977, he replaced Secretary Coleman with Secretary Brock Adams. NHTSA also got a new leader: Joan Claybrook, a former congressional staffer who had worked on the Motor Vehicle Safety Act. Secretary Adams and Administrator Claybrook saw things differently from the prior administration. They believed that the demonstration project was unnecessary to facilitate public acceptance. Accordingly, NHTSA modified Standard 208 to require a phase-in of passive restraints by 1982 for large model cars, and by 1984 for small model cars, see 42 Fed. Reg. 34289 (1977), and Congress did not exercise the legislative veto it had reserved in the 1974 amendments.

The Court of Appeals for the D.C. Circuit upheld this version of Standard 208. *See* Pacific Legal Foundation v. Department of Transportation, 593 F.2d 1338, 1339 (D.C. Cir. 1979).

Another New Administration Changes Course. In 1981, Standard 208 faced yet another reversal in the hands of yet another new presidential administration. President Reagan campaigned for office on a platform of deregulation. As part of that plan, he supported easing regulatory burdens on the ailing domestic auto industry. On April 6, 1981, NHTSA delayed compliance with the passive restraint requirement for large cars, moving it from September 1, 1981, to September 1, 1982. It also proposed a more dramatic overhaul of the passive restraint regulations. On October 29, 1981, the agency issued a final rule rescinding the passive restraints requirement.

What follows are the two basic documents for NHTSA's 1981 notice-and-comment rulemaking: the Notice of Proposed Rulemaking and the Final Rule, as first published in the *Federal Register*. Read them as you would any written text, attending both to their formal features and their reasoning.

---

49 C.F.R. 571, Federal Motor Vehicle Safety Standards; Occupant Crash Protection

[Docket No. 74-14; Notice 22], April 6, 1981

[46 Fed. Reg. 21205 (1981)]

AGENCY: Department of Transportation

ACTION: Notice of proposed rulemaking

SUMMARY: The purpose of this notice is to seek comment on a series of alternative amendments to the automatic restraint requirements of Safety Standard No. 208, Occupant Crash Protection. As amended by a final rule published in today's Federal Register, those requirements are currently scheduled to become effective for large cars and mid-size cars on September 1, 1982, and for small cars on September 1, 1983.

Under the first alternative being considered, the sequence of compliance would be changed so that small cars would be required to comply on September 1, 1982, mid-size cars on September 1, 1983, and large cars on September 1, 1984.

The second alternative would require all cars sizes to begin compliance on March 1, 1983. In addition, the first and second alternatives would amend the automatic restraint requirements so that those restraints would not be required in the front center seating position.

The third alternative would rescind the automatic restraint requirements.

This action is being taken to ensure that Standard No. 208 reflects the changes in circumstances that have occurred since the automatic restraint requirements were issued in 1977, and to ensure that the standard meets the requirements of the National Traffic and Motor Vehicle Safety Act of 1966 and Executive Order 12291, "Federal Regulation," (February 17, 1981).

DATE: Comments on this proposal must be received by: May 26, 1981.

ADDRESS: Comments should refer to the docket number and to the number of this notice and be submitted to: Docket Section, Room 5109, Nassif Building, 400 Seventh Street, S.W., Washington, D.C. 20590. (Docket hours are 8:00 A.M. to 4:00 P.M.)

FOR FURTHER INFORMATION CONTACT: Mr. Michael Finkelstein, Office of Rulemaking, National Highway Traffic Safety Administration, Washington, D.C. 20590 (202-426-1810).

SUPPLEMENTARY INFORMATION: On February 12, 1981, the Department of Transportation published a proposal for a one year delay in the application of the automatic restraint requirements of Safety Standard No. 208 to large cars (46 FR 12033). That action was proposed in light of circumstances which made it necessary and appropriate to extend the effective date, and to provide an opportunity to review the requirements and determine the need for further revisions in the standard. In today's issue of Federal Register, the Department has published a final rule adopting the one year delay.

The purpose of this notice is to gather public comment to aid the review process. The notice proposes a wide range of possible changes to the automatic restraint requirements in order to encourage broad and creative public participation. The Department, desires to ensure that it is taking the most effective and reasonable approach to addressing the serious safety problem posed by the low rate of safety belt use in all cars and by the steadily decreasing average size of new cars sold in this country. As discussed below, the Department is also undertaking an intensive campaign to inform and encourage the public on the need for increased manual belt usage.

Background

The automatic restraint requirements of Standard No. 208 were adopted by the Department in 1977 (42 FR 34289; July 5, 1977). That decision was based on a variety of factors. The Department was confronted with a substantial safety problem. Approximately 25,000 occupants in the front seats of passenger cars were being killed annually in crashes. Although the cars were equipped with manual safety belts under Safety Standard No. 208, relatively few people were being protected since most people did not use manual belts. Studies showed that usage was about 20 percent for all types of belt systems.

The Department anticipated that this safety problem would progressively worsen as people began to switch to smaller, more fuel efficient cars. Generally, the chance of death or serious injury in a crash increases as car size decreases.

The Department concluded that there was no available way of increasing manual belt use. Although mandatory belt use laws had been used in combination in other countries to achieve dramatic increases in the rate of belt use, similar opportunities do not exist in this country. Based on Congressional action indicating disfavor with these laws and lack of State interest, enactment of mandatory use laws was not deemed to be a viable alternative.

To provide a solution to the problems of a high death and injury toll and of a low manual belt use rate, the Department turned to requiring the use of automatic restraints. Then, as now, the two systems that qualified as automatic restraints were air cushion restraints (air bags) and automatic seat belts (belts that automatically move into place when an occupant enters a vehicle and closes the door). Automatic restraints were found to be superior to manual belts because they were as effective as manual belts in preventing death and injury and would provide protection in a much higher percentage of crashes. (Persons wishing to learn additional details about that and earlier rulemaking relating to automatic restraints are urged to consult dockets 69-7, 73-8 and 74-14 and the rulemaking notices associated with those dockets.)

The Department anticipated substantial safety benefits from the automatic restraint requirements. According to NHTSA's analysis, 9,000 fatalities and 65,000 serious injuries would be prevented annually once all cars on the road had automated restraints, i.e., ten years after initial implementation.

As the Department indicated in its February 12, 1981 proposal, the 1977 decision was based on a variety of key assumptions which, in the light of subsequent events, are no longer valid. The Department assumed that consumers would freely be able to choose between air bags and automatic belts, with 60 percent of cars having the former and 40 percent having the latter. The air bag percentage was based on the expectation that all large cars and intermediates, and half of the compacts would be equipped with those systems. The Department also believed that some of the even smaller cars would be equipped with air bags. These factors, together with the greater design problems and absence of experience in installing air bags in smaller cars, led the Department to phase-in the automatic requirements beginning with large cars. Current manufacturer plans contemplate almost no installation of air bags, only about 1 percent of the total fleet of new cars. As a result, the phasing-in of the requirements with large cars first and small cars last requires reexamination.

The phase-in sequence is further called into question by the accelerated switch from large cars to less safe, smaller ones. The Department recognized that a switch would occur as a result of the 1973-74 oil shock and the impending implementation of fuel economy standards. It did not, however, anticipate that the switch would occur as rapidly as it had, due in large measure to the subsequent oil cut-off of 1979. In 1977, NHTSA estimated that size mix in the early 1980's would be 24 percent small cars, 53 percent mid-size cars, and 23 percent large cars. Now the expectation is that the new car fleet will consist of 1 percent large cars, 58 percent mid-size cars and 41 percent small cars. When the numbers of large and small cars in the early-mid 1980's was expected to be approximately the same, the sequence of implementation had no significance in terms of the cars equipped with automatic restraints. Given the currently expected fleet mix of large and small cars, the sequence has substantial significance, especially since smaller cars are less safe.

In 1977, NHTSA believed that automatic belts would cost only 34 dollars more than manual belts and that air bags would cost approximately 154 dollars more than manual belts. Today, NHTSA's comparable figures are 105 dollars for the incremental cost of automatic belts, and at least 400 dollars for air bags at high production volumes and as much as 1,100 dollars at low volumes.

The Department has now undertaken to review the automatic restraint requirements and their implementation schedule in view of changed circumstances which undermine the reasonableness of the existing implementation schedule, the substantial impact of automatic restraints on manufacturer and consumer costs and the accentuation of those manufacturer impacts by the economic difficulties of the automobile industry.

In the analysis which preceded the February 12 proposal, the Department determined that a number of additional factors were relevant. Among these factors is the unnecessary character of the costs which would be incurred by application of automatic restraint requirements to large cars scheduled to be phased out in the near future. These costs would arise largely from the loss of sales due to increased costs, and to the loss of the middle front seating position in large cars.

Another factor is the possibility that initial public acceptance of automatic restraints might have been adversely affected by the decision of large car manufacturers not to make air bags available in model year 1982. Still another factor was the effect of current automatic belt designs on public acceptance and usage.

Based on all of these factors, the Department decided to adopt the one year delay for installing those restraints in large cars.

In conjunction with this decision, the Department is preparing to undertake an intensive public education campaign to induce the public to use their safety belts: This campaign would affect not only the 1982 model year cars which now will be equipped almost exclusively with manual belts but also all other belt-equipped vehicles on the road today. The number of seat belt-equipped vehicles is over 150 million. Accordingly, it is expected that a properly conceived and sustained program, aided by manufacturers and other levels of government, would make an important contribution to vehicle safety.

The same factors underlying the one year delay also led the Department to issue this notice and propose three principal alternatives.

Principal Proposals

1. Reversal of phase-in sequence. Under this proposal, the automatic restraint requirements would become effective for small cars (wheelbase of 100 inches or less) on September 1, 1982, for mid-size cars (wheelbase greater than 100 inches and less than 114 inches) on September 1, 1983, and for large cars (wheelbase of 114 inches or greater) on September 1, 1984. This proposal would have the advantage of ensuring that automatic restraints are first placed in the car size class which presents the greatest safety risk.

If adopted as proposed, it could produce greater net benefits than implementation of the automatic restraint requirements in accordance with the original phase-in schedule established in 1977. This gain would result from the greater safety risk posed by small cars than by large cars and the increasingly greater number of small cars over large ones.

The Department notes also that requiring small cars instead of large cars to comply first would require

a much larger proportion of manufacturers to begin compliance simultaneously rather than under the original schedule. Thus, the new schedule would be more equitable and reasonable. Still another advantage of this proposal is that it would avoid, to a large extent, the necessity and extra cost of redesigning and equipping large cars with automatic restraints for the few years that these cars will continue to be produced. In view of the substantial experience of several manufacturers with designing and producing small cars with automatic belts, it is believed that there is sufficient leadtime to implement this proposal.

2. Simultaneous compliance. Under this proposal, all size classes would be required to begin compliance at the same time, i.e., March 1, 1983. This proposal allows compliance to begin a half year later than under the first proposal, to offset switching from a phase-in compliance schedule to a simultaneous one. Like the first proposal, this proposal could yield benefits greater than the original phase-in schedule by accelerating the date on which all cars must be equipped with automatic restraints. This proposal could be construed as even more equitable than the first in that all manufacturers would have to bring all of their cars into compliance at the same time.

3. Rescission. The third principal proposal is to rescind the automatic restraint requirements. The principal considerations underlying this proposal are the unlikelihood of public acceptability of automatic restraints in the absence of any significant degree of choice between automatic belts and air bags, the public acceptability of the specific automatic belt designs currently planned by the automobile manufacturers, uncertainties about the general public's rate of future usage of both automatic and manual belt systems, and the substantial cost of air bags even if produced in large volumes.

Additional Proposals

In conjunction with the first and second principal proposals, the Department is also proposing to except the front center seating position of cars from automatic restraint requirements. With that exception, manufacturers could equip that seating position with either a manual belt or with an automatic restraint. This exception is intended to solve a dilemma presented manufacturers in bringing six seat passenger cars into compliance with the current automatic restraint requirements. Since the only known type of automatic restraint for the center seating position is the air bag, manufacturers are faced with a choice of either equipping all three front seating positions with the relatively expensive air bags, or removing the center position and equipping the remaining two with automatic belts.

The latter choice permits use of the less expensive type of automatic restraint, but has the offsetting disadvantage of reducing the utility of the car. The advantage of such an exception is that it would enable manufacturers to retain the center position and equip the two outer front positions with automatic belts. If the automatic belts were the detachable type, they would permit ready access to the center position. The Department recognizes that the usage rate of detachable automatic belts may be less than that for nondetachable types.

The Department also seeks comment on the desirability of and authority for adopting a suggestion made by Volvo in commenting on the February 12 proposal. Out of concern about the perceived marketing need for flexibility in the beginning of new model years and about the relative inflexibility of the normal agency practice of treating September 1 as the beginning of the model year, Volvo suggested that effective dates be specified as "September 1 or the date of production start of the new model year if this date falls between September 1 and December 31."

Impacts of Proposals

The Department has considered the impacts of these proposals and determined that each of the three principal proposals in the notice is a major rulemaking within the meaning of E.O. 12291. A preliminary regulatory impact analysis is being placed in the docket simultaneously with the publication of this notice. A copy of the analysis may be obtained by contacting the docket at the address given at the beginning of this notice.

As noted above, it is expected that both the reversal proposal and the simultaneous compliance proposal could produce benefits equal or greater than the benefits of the revised schedule. This would result primarily from the earlier compliance by small cars which pose greater safety risks than large or mid-size cars. Rescission of the automatic restraint requirements could, after ten years, cause a loss of 750-7,500 lives annually based on the benefits to be expected from all cars on the road having been equipped with automatic restraints by that time.

The precise safety impacts of these and the other proposals depend largely on the usage rate of automatic belts and the effectiveness of the planned public information campaign. As set forth in more detail in the regulatory impact analysis accompanying the Final Rule published elsewhere in this issue of the Federal Register,

NHTSA now anticipates a usage rate in the range of 15-60 percent. The rate will ultimately depend on how the public reacts to the automatic belt designs, especially the detachable ones which now appear likely to become the predominant type.

The cost effects of the reversal and simultaneous compliance proposals would be mixed. For example, the reversal proposal would cause the manufacturing and consumer costs of model year 1983 small cars to increase and of model year 1983 mid-size and large cars to decrease. Some slight loss of sales or deferral of purchases of model year 1983 small cars and model year 1984 mid-size cars could occur, although such effects should be minimized by the market forces pushing consumers toward smaller, more fuel efficient cars.

The cost impacts of the simultaneous compliance proposal would depend on how near the manufacturers come to beginning compliance on March 1, 1983. If they begin precisely on that date, then the manufacturer and consumer costs would decrease for the mid-size and large cars produced during the first half of model year 1983 and would increase for the small cars produced during the latter half of that model year. The effect on individual company sales should be minimized by this proposal, since competitive effects among manufacturers and different car size classes would be eliminated.

The rescission proposal would produce substantial savings in manufacturer capital investments and variable costs and in consumer costs. The savings in capital investments alone would be at least several hundred million dollars. The annual savings in manufacturing and consumer costs would be much greater, based on the costs that would otherwise be incurred in installing automatic restraints in all new cars.

The effects of this notice on small entities have been considered under the Regulatory Flexibility Act. Interested persons should consult both the preliminary regulatory impact analysis prepared for this notice and also the final regulatory impact analysis for the one year delay notice published today.

Although almost none if the direct or indirect suppliers of air bags and automatic belts are considered to be "small businesses," the Department did examine the impact on those suppliers. It is believed that the impact of the reversal and simultaneous compliance proposals should be minimal, because those proposals accelerate the compliance of some cars while delaying the compliance of others and since, in the case of automatic belt manufacturers, these businesses produce both automatic and manual belts.

Rescission of the automatic restraint requirements would adversely affect both automatic belt manufacturers and air bag manufacturers. To the extent that the profit to these manufacturers from automatic belt sales exceeds that from manual belt sales, the revenue of these manufacturers will decrease. Given the decision of the car manufacturers to use automatic belts almost exclusively in complying with the automatic restraint requirements, the impact of a rescission on air bag manufacturers may actually be quite limited. Nevertheless, the Department notes that air bag suppliers responding to its February 12 proposal stated that any further delay or uncertainty regarding the automatic restraint effective dates would adversely affect their prospect.

The only proposal that would more than minimally affect small governments and other small fleet purchasers would appear to be rescission.

Its adoption would give them a cost savings similar to the one created for purchasers of large 1982 model year cars by the one year delay.

In accordance with the National Environmental Policy Act of 1969, the Department has considered the environmental impacts of the proposals in this notice. A Draft Environmental Impact Statement will be placed in the docket for this rulemaking.

Interested persons are also urged to consult the Final Environmental Impact Statement for the 1977 rule establishing the automatic restraint requirements.

Interested persons are invited to submit comments on the proposal. It is requested but not required that 10 copies be submitted.

All comments must be limited not to exceed 15 pages in length. Necessary attachments may be appended to these submissions without regard to the 15 page limit. This limitation is intended to encourage commenters to detail their primary arguments in a concise fashion.

If a commenter wishes to submit certain information under a claim of confidentiality, three copies of the complete submission, including purportedly confidential information, should be submitted to the Chief Counsel, NHTSA, at the street address given above, and seven copies from which the purportedly confidential information has been deleted should be submitted to the Docket Section. Any claim of confidentiality must be supported by a statement demonstrating that the information falls within 5 U.S.C. section 552(b)(4), and that disclosure of the information is likely to result in substantial competitive damage; specifying the period during which the information must be withheld to avoid that damage; and showing that earlier disclosure would result in that damage. In addition,

the commenter or, in the case of a corporation, a responsible corporate official authorized to speak for the corporation must certify in writing that each item for which confidential treatment is requested is in fact confidential within the meaning of section 552(b)(4) and that a diligent search has been conducted by the commenter or its employees to assure that none of the specified items has previously been disclosed or otherwise become available to the public.

All comments received before the close of business on the comment closing date indicated above will be considered, and will be available for examination in the docket at the above address both before and after that date. To the extent possible, comments filed after the closing date will also be considered. However, the rulemaking action may proceed at any time after that date, and comments received after the closing date and too late for consideration in regard to the action will be treated as suggestions for future rulemaking. NHTSA will continue to file relevant material as it becomes available in the docket after the closing date, and it is recommended that interested persons continue to examine the docket for new material.

Those persons desiring to be notified upon receipt of their comments in the rules docket should enclose, in the envelope with their comments, a self addressed stamped postcard. Upon receiving the comments, the docket supervisor will return the postcard by mail.

(Secs. 103, 119, Pub. L. 89-563, 80 Stat. 718 (15 U.S.C. 1392, 1407))

Issued on April 6, 1981.

Andrew L. Lewis, Jr.,
Secretary of Transportation
[FR Doc. 81-10709 Filed 4-6-81; 2:25 pm]
BILLING CODE 4910-59-M

Notes and Questions

1. Create an outline of the NPRM and describe the function or content of each section. Does the title of each indicate its purpose or seem to have a more specialized meaning? Why might the agency prepare the document in this form? Do you suppose that the form is typical for NHTSA? All agencies?

2. What reasons does the agency give for seeking a change to Standard 208? Was it incorrect about the safety benefits of the passive restraints requirement?

3. The NPRM contains three alternative proposals. Is each proposal equally supported by the information in the background section? If NHTSA favored one proposal, is there any indication of that? Can you think of any other proposal that NHTSA should have considered?

4. After NHTSA sets forth its proposals, it considers the "impacts" of those proposals. Which impacts does it assess? Why does it assess these particular impacts? Exec. Order 12,291 is an executive order issued by President Reagan that requires agencies to prepare a regulatory impact analysis, evaluating the costs and benefits of their proposals. We will discuss this below and again in Chapter 6. The Regulatory Flexibility Act, 5 U.S.C. §§601 *et seq.,* is a federal statute that requires agencies to consider the effect of their proposals on small entities, including businesses and governments. The National Environmental Policy Act of 1969, 42 U.S.C. §§4321 *et seq.,* is a federal statute that requires agencies to prepare an environmental impact statement, evaluating the effect of their proposals on the environment. We will also discuss these below.

5. As you might imagine, given the stakes for the domestic and foreign auto industries and the auto insurance industry, not to mention the public, NHTSA received a mountain of comments. If you were a lawyer for one of these organizations or for a consumer protection organization, what comments would you file with the agency?

Now read the final rule that NHTSA issued in 1981 rescinding the passive restraints requirement. As with the NPRM, you should pay careful attention to its formal features as well as the agency's reasoning. You should also seek to identify the ways in which it is similar to and different from the NPRM.

---

49 C.F.R. Part 571
National Highway Traffic Safety Administration

[Docket No. 74-14; Notice 25],
Thursday, October 29, 1981

[46 Fed. Reg. 53419 (1981)]

Federal Motor Vehicle Safety Standards; Occupant Crash Protection

AGENCY: National Highway Traffic Safety Administration, Department of Transportation.

ACTION: Final rule.

SUMMARY: The purpose of this notice is to amend Federal Motor Vehicle Safety Standard No. 208, Occupant Crash Protection, to rescind the requirements for installation of automatic restraints in the front seating positions of passenger cars. Those requirements were scheduled to become effective for large and mid-size cars on September 1, 1982, and for small cars on September 1, 1983.

The automatic restraint requirements are being rescinded because of uncertainty about the public acceptability and probable usage rate of the type of automatic restraint which the car manufacturers planned to make available to most new car buyers. This uncertainty and the relatively substantial cost of automatic restraints preclude the agency from determining that the standard is at this time reasonable and practicable. The reasonableness of the automatic restraint requirements is further called into question since the fact that all new car buyers would be required to pay for automatic belt systems that may induce only a few additional people to take advantage of the benefits of occupant restraints.

The agency is also seriously concerned about the possibility that adverse public reaction to the cost and presence of automatic restraints could have a significant adverse effect on present and future public acceptance of highway safety efforts.

Under the amended standard, car manufacturers will continue to have the current option of providing either automatic or manual occupant restraints.

DATES: The rescission of the automatic restraint requirements of Standard No. 208 is effective December 8, 1981. Any petitions for reconsideration must be received by the agency not later than December 3, 1981.

ADDRESS: Any petitions for reconsideration should refer to the docket number and notice number of this notice and be submitted to: Administrator, National Highway Traffic Safety Administration, 400 Seventh Street, S.W., Washington, D.C. 20590.

FOR FURTHER INFORMATION CONTACT: Mr. Michael Finkelstein, Associate Administrator for Rulemaking, National Highway Traffic Safety Administration, Washington, D.C. 20590 (202-426-1810).

SUPPLEMENTARY INFORMATION: On April 9, 1981, the Department of Transportation published a notice of proposed rulemaking (NPRM) setting forth alternative amendments to the automatic restraint requirements of Standard No. 208 (46 FR 21205). The purpose of proposing the alternatives was to ensure that Standard No. 208 reflects the changes in circumstances since the automatic restraint requirements were issued (42 FR 34289; July 5, 1977) and to ensure that the standard meets the requirements of the National Traffic and Motor Vehicle Safety Act of 1966 and Executive Order 12291, "Federal Regulations" (February 17, 1981).

Background and NPRM

The automatic restraint requirements were adopted in 1977 in response to the high number of passenger car occupants killed annually in crashes and to the persistent low usage rate of manual belts. The manual belt is the type of belt which is found in most cars today and which the occupant must place around himself or herself and buckle in order to gain its protection. Then, as now, there were two types of automatic restraints, i.e., restraints that require no action by vehicle occupants, such as buckling a belt, in order to be effective. One type is the air cushion restraint (air bag) and the other is the automatic belt (a belt which automatically envelops an occupant when the occupant enters a vehicle and closes the door).

In view of the greater experience with air bags in large cars and to spread out capital investments, the Department established a large-to-small car compliance schedule. Under that schedule, large cars were required to begin compliance on September 1, 1981, mid-size cars on September 1, 1982, and small cars on September 1, 1983.

On April 6, 1981, after providing notice and opportunity for comment, the Department delayed the compliance date for large cars from September 1, 1981, to September 1, 1982. As explained in the April 6, final rule, that delay was adopted . . . because of the effects of implementation in model year 1982 on large car manufacturers, because of the added significance which those effects assume due to the change in economic circumstances since the schedule was adopted in 1977, and because of the undermining by subsequent events of the rationale underlying the original phase-in schedule.

Simultaneous with publishing the one-year delay in the effective date for large cars, the Department also issued a proposal for making further changes in the automatic restraint requirements. This action was taken in response to a variety of factors that raised questions whether the automatic restraint requirements represented the most reasonable and effective approach to the problem of the low usage of safety belts. Among these factors were the uncertainty about public acceptability of automatic restraints in view of the absence of any significant choice between automatic belts and air bags and the nature of the automatic belt designs planned by the car manufacturers, the consequent uncertainties about the rate of usage of automatic restraints, and the substantial costs of air bags even if produced in large volumes.

The three principal proposals were reversal of phase-in sequence, simultaneous compliance, and rescission. The reversal proposal would have changed the large-to-small car order of compliance to a requirement that small cars commence compliance on September 1, 1982, mid-size cars on September 1, 1983, and large cars on September 1, 1984. The proposal for simultaneous compliance would have required all size classes to begin compliance on the same date, March 1, 1983. The rescission proposal would have retained the manufacturers' current option of equipping their cars with either manual or automatic restraints.

In addition, the Department proposed that, under both the first and second alternatives, the automatic restraint requirements be amended so that such restraints would not be required in the front center seating position.

Following the close of the period for written comments on the April NPRM, NHTSA decided, in its discretion, to hold a public meeting on the alternatives. The purpose of the meeting was to permit interested parties to present their views and arguments orally before the Administrator and ensure that all available data were submitted to the agency. The notice announcing the meeting indicated that participants at the hearing would be permitted to supplement their previous comments. The notice also urged participants to consider the issues raised in former Secretary Coleman's June 14, 1976 proposal regarding occupant restraints and in former Secretary Adams' March 24, 1977 proposal regarding automatic restraints.

Rationale for Agency Decision

The decision to rescind the automatic restraint requirements was difficult for the agency to make. NHTSA has long pursued the goal of achieving substantial increases in the usage of safety belts and other types of occupant restraints. Former Secretary Adams clearly believed that he had ensured the achievement of that goal in July 1977 when he promulgated the automatic restraint requirements. Now

that goal appears as elusive as ever. Instead of being equipped with automatic restraints that will protect substantially greater numbers of persons than current manual belts, most new cars would have had a type of automatic belt that might not have been any more acceptable to the public than manual belts. The usage of those automatic belts might, therefore, have been only slightly higher than that of manual belts. While most of the anticipated benefits have virtually disappeared, the costs have not. Vehicle price increases would have amounted to approximately $1 billion per year.

This turn of events may in part reflect the failure of the Department in the years following 1977 to conduct a long term effort to educate the public about the various types of restraints and the need to use them. The need for such an undertaking was seen by former Secretary Coleman in announcing his decision in 1976 to conduct an automatic restraint demonstration project prior to deciding whether to mandate automatic restraints. His instruction that NHTSA undertake significant new steps to promote safety belt usage was never effectively carried out. The result of such an effort could have been that a substantial portion of the public would have been receptive to a variety of automatic restraint designs. As a result of concern over public acceptance, manufacturers have designed their automatic restraints to avoid creating a significant adverse reaction. Unfortunately, the elements of design intended to minimize adverse reaction would also minimize the previously anticipated increases in belt usage and safety benefits of requiring new cars to have automatic restraints instead of manual belts.

The uncertainty regarding the usage of the predominant type of planned automatic restraint

has profound implications for the determinations which NHTSA must make regarding a standard under the National Traffic and Motor Vehicle Safety Act. NHTSA has a duty under the Vehicle Safety Act and E.O. 12291 to review the automatic restraint requirements in light of changing events and to ensure that the requirements continue to meet the criteria which each Federal Motor Vehicle Safety Standard must satisfy. If the criteria cannot be satisfied, the agency must make whatever changes in the standard are warranted. The agency must also have the flexibility to modify its standards and programs in its efforts to find effective methods for accomplishing its safety mission.

The agency believes that the post-1977 events have rendered it incapable of finding now, as it was able to do in 1977, that the automatic restraint requirements would meet all of the applicable criteria in the Vehicle Safety Act. Section 103(a) of the Vehicle Safety Act requires that each Federal Motor Vehicle Safety Standard meet the need for safety and be practicable and objective. Each standard must also be reasonable, practicable and appropriate for each type of vehicle or equipment to which it applies (Section 103(f)(3)). To meet the need for safety, a standard must be reasonably likely to reduce deaths and injuries. To be found practicable, the agency must conclude that the public will in fact avail themselves of the safety devices installed pursuant to the standard. (*Pacific Legal Foundation v. Department of Transportation*, 593 F.2d 1338, at 1345-6 (D.C. Cir. 1979).) To be reasonable and practicable, a standard must be economically and technologically feasible, and the costs of implementation must be reasonable. (S. Rep. No. 1301, 89th Cong., 2d Sess. 6 (1966).)

In reaching the decision announced by this notice, NHTSA has reviewed the enormous record compiled by this agency over the past decade on automatic restraints. Particular attention was paid to the information and issues relating to the notices which the Agency or Department has issued regarding automatic restraints since 1976. All comments submitted in response to the April 1981 proposal by proponents and opponents of the automatic restraint requirements have been thoroughly considered. A summary of the major comments is included as an appendix to this notice. The agency's analysis of those comments may be found in this notice and the final regulatory impact analysis. A copy of the analysis has been placed in the public docket.

Usage of automatic restraints and safety benefits. As in the case of the comments submitted concerning the one-year delay in automatic restraint requirements for large cars, the commenters on the April 1981 proposal expressed sharply divergent views and arguments and reached widely differing conclusions concerning the likely usage rates and benefits of the automatic restraints planned for installation in response to the automatic restraint requirements. The wide distance between the positions of the proponents and opponents of these requirements stems primarily from the lack of any directly relevant data on the most important issue, i.e., the public reaction to and usage rate of detachable automatic belts. These disagreements once again demonstrate the difficulty in reaching reliable conclusions due to the uncertainty created by the lack of adequate data.

In issuing the automatic restraint requirements in 1977, NHTSA assumed that the implementation of those requirements would produce substantial benefits. According to the analysis which NHTSA performed in that year, automatic restraints were expected to prevent 9,000 deaths and 65,000 serious injuries once all cars on the road were equipped with those devices. That prediction was premised on several critical assumptions. Most important among the assumptions were those concerning the safety benefits of automatic restraints — reductions in death and injury — which in turn are a function of the types of automatic restraints to be placed in each year's production of new cars.

The agency assumed that the combination of air bags and lap belts would be approximately 66 percent effective in preventing fatalities and that automatic belts would have a 50% level of effectiveness. The agency assumed also that air bags would be placed in more than 60 percent of new cars and that automatic belts would be placed in the remaining approximately 40 percent. The agency's analysis predicted that air bags would provide protection in virtually all crashes of sufficient severity to cause deployment of the air bags. It was further assumed that the automatic belts would be used by 60 to 70 percent of the occupants of those cars.

As to public reaction, the agency anticipated that the public would, as a whole, accept automatic restraints because it could choose between the two types of those restraints. Those not wanting automatic belts would select an air bag. Partly as a function of the expected large volume of air bag installation, the agency projected that the cost of air bags would be only slightly more than $100 (in 1977 dollars) more than manual belts.

As part of its efforts to monitor and facilitate implementation of the automatic restraint requirements, the agency continued its gathering of data about the use and effectiveness of air bags and of automatic belts with use-inducing features, the only type of automatic belt available to the public. With respect to automatic belts, this effort was carried out through a contract with Opinion Research Corporation. Under that contract, observations were made of seat belt usage during the two year period beginning November 1977. These observations provided data on usage of manual and automatic belts in model year 1975-79 VW Rabbits and of manual belts in model year 1978-79 GM Chevettes, As a result of voluntary decisions by VW and GM, a number of the Rabbits and Chevettes were equipped with automatic belts. The observation data showed usage rates of about 36 percent for manual belts and about 81 percent for automatic belts in the Rabbits. The observed rate of manual belt usage in Chevettes was 11 percent. There were insufficient numbers of model year 1978-79 Chevettes equipped with automatic belts to develop reliable usage figures.

Several telephone surveys were also made under contract with Opinion Research. The first survey involved owners of model year 1979 VW Rabbits and GM Chevettes equipped with automatic belts and was conducted during 1979. This survey showed that 89 percent of Rabbit owners and 72 percent of Chevette owners said that they used their automatic belts. A second survey was conducted in late 1979 and early 1980. It covered owners of model year 1980 Rabbits and Chevettes. The usage rates found by the second survey were almost identical to those in the first survey.

Now, however, the validity of the benefit predictions in 1977 and the relevancy of the extensive data gathered by NHTSA on air bags and on automatic belts with use-inducing features have been substantially if not wholly undermined by drastic changes in the types of automatic restraints that would have been installed under the automatic restraint requirements. Instead of installing air bags in approximately 60 percent of new cars, the manufacturers apparently planned to install them in less than 1 percent of new cars. Thus, automatic belts would have been the predominant means of compliance, and installed in approximately 99% of new cars. Thus, the assumed life-saving potential of air bags would not have been realized.

Manufacturers have stated that they chose belt systems for compliance because of the competitive disadvantage of offering the relatively expensive, inadequately understood air bag when other manufacturers would have been providing automatic belts. These explanations seem credible.

The other drastic change concerns the type of automatic belt to be installed. Although some aspects of the car manufacturers' automatic belt plans are still tentative, it now appears reasonably certain that if the automatic restraint requirements were implemented, the overwhelming majority of new cars would be equipped with automatic belts that are detachable, unlike the automatic belts in Rabbits and Chevettes. Most planned automatic belts would be like today's manual lap and shoulder belts in that they can be easily detached and left that way permanently.

Again, this design choice would appear to have arisen out of concern that without such features emergency exit could be inhibited, and, in part as a result of a perception of this fact, public refusal to accept new designs would be widespread. The agency shares this concern, and has since 1977 required that all such belts provide for emergency exit. Agency concerns on this point have been validated by recent

related attitudinal research, discussed below.

In its final rule delaying the initial effective date of the automatic restraint requirements, the April 1981 proposal and the associated documents analyzing the impacts of those actions, NHTSA expressly confronted the lack of usage data directly relevant to the type of automatic belts now planned to be installed in most new cars. The agency stated that there were several reasons why the available data was of limited utility in attempting to make any reliable predictions about the usage of easily detachable automatic belts. The most important reason, which has already been noted, is that the predominant type of planned automatic belt would not have had features to ensure that these belts are not detached.

Second, all of the available data relate to only two subcompacts, the Rabbit and the Chevette. Due to a combination of owner demographics and a correlation between driver perception of risk and the size of the car being driven, belt usage rates are typically higher in small cars than in larger ones. Therefore, the usage rates for the two subcompacts cannot simply be adopted as the usage rates for automatic belts in all car size classes.

Third, most of the Rabbit and Chevette owners knew that their new car would come with an automatic belt and had it demonstrated for them, even if many state that they did not consciously choose that type of belt. Having voluntarily invested in automatic restraints, they are more likely to use those restraints than someone who is compelled to buy them.

The significance of the fundamental difference between the nondetachable and detachable automatic belt bears further discussion. The Rabbit automatic belts are, as a practical matter, not permanently detachable since they are equipped with

an ignition interlock. If the belt is disconnected, the interlock prevents the starting of the car. Each successive use would therefore require re-connection before engine start. The Chevette automatic belts were initially equipped with an ignition interlock. Beginning in model year 1980, the Chevette belts were made both practically and literally nondetachable. They consist of a continuous, nondetachable shoulder belt. Additional webbing can be played out to produce slack in the belt; however, the belt remains attached at both ends.

By contrast, the automatic belts now planned for most cars do not have any effect on the starting of the cars and are easily detachable. Some belt designs may be detached and permanently stowed as readily as the current manual lap and shoulder belts. Once a detachable automatic belt is detached, it becomes identical to a manual belt. Contrary to assertions of some supporters of the standard, its use thereafter requires the same type of affirmative action that is the stumbling block to obtaining high usage levels of manual belts. If the car owners perceive the belts as simply a different configuration of the current manual belts, this stumbling block is likely to remain. They may treat the belt as a manual one and thus never develop the habit of simply leaving the belt attached so that it can act as an automatic belt.

The agency recognizes the possibility that the exposure of some new car purchasers to attached automatic belts may convert some previously occasional users of manual belts to full time belt users. Present attitudinal survey data clearly establish the existence of a population of such occupants who could be influenced by some external factor to convert to relatively constant users. However, the agency believes that many purchasers of new cars having detachable automatic belts would not experience the potential use-inducing character of attached automatic belts unless they had taken the initiative themselves to attach the belts.

Thus, the change in car manufacturers' plans has left the agency without any factual basis for reliably predicting the likely usage increases due to detachable automatic belts, or for even predicting the likelihood of any increase at all. The only tentative conclusion that can be drawn from available data is that the installation of nondetachable automatic belts in other subcompacts could result in usage rates near those found in Rabbits and Chevettes. Even that use of the Rabbit and Chevette data may be questionable, however, given the element of voluntarism in the purchase of automatic belts by many of the Rabbit and Chevette owners. Thus, the data on automatic belt use in Rabbits and Chevettes may do little more than confirm the lesson of the model year 1974-75 cars equipped with manual belts and ignition interlocks, i.e., that the addition to a belt system of a feature that makes the belt nondetachable or necessitates its attachment before a car can be started can substantially increase the rate of belt usage.

In estimating automatic belt usage rates for the purposes of the April final rule and proposal, the agency recognized the substantial uncertainty regarding the effects of easily detachable automatic belts on belt usage. NHTSA attempted to compensate for the lack of directly relevant data by using two different techniques to predict a potential range of usage.

One technique was to assume a consistent multiplier effect, whereby belt usage in cars of all size classes would be assumed to be more than slightly double as it had in Rabbits. A doubling of the current 10-11 percent manual belt usage rate projected over the general car fleet

would mean a 22 percent rate could be achieved with the installation of automatic belts. The other technique was to assume that there would be a consistent additive effect, whereby the same absolute percentage point increase in belt usage would occur as there had been in the case with Rabbits. Use of this method would result in a predicted 50 percentage point increase in belt usage, over the entire fleet, from the current 10-11 percent to approximately 60 percent.

The agency used the results of these two techniques in an attempt to construct a range of possible increases in belt usage. Thus, a range of 15 to 60 percent was used in both the final regulatory impact analysis for the April rulemaking to defer the effective date for one year and the preliminary analysis for the current action. The figure of 15 percent was derived by doubling the observed 7 percent usage levels in the large type cars affected by the deferral. A figure of 22 percent would have been more appropriate as the low end of the range for the current action, since it would represent a doubling of the current usage rate of the car fleet as a whole. This latter figure has been used in addressing this question in the current final regulatory analysis.

Although the agency had no definitive way of resolving the uncertainty about the usage of detachable automatic belts, the agency estimated that belt usage with automatic belts would most likely fall near the lower end of either range. This estimate was based on a variety of factors. Most relate to the previously discussed limitations in the relevancy of the observations and surveys of Rabbit and Chevette owners. In addition, those data were on their face inconsistent with data regarding automatic belt usage in crashes involving Rabbits. Those crash data indicated

a usage rate of 55-57 percent instead of the better than 80 percent rate indicated by the observation study and telephone surveys.

Thus, the agency made the preliminary judgment in its impact analyses that the switch from manual belts to detachable automatic belts could approximately double belt usage. However, the April 1981 final rule noted that the actual belt usage might be lower, even substantially so. With respect to cars with current low usage rates, that notice stated that the usage rate of detachable automatic belts might only approach levels similar to those currently achieved with manual belts.

The commenters on the April 1981 NPRM did not present any new factual data that could have reduced the substantial uncertainty confronting the agency. Instead, the commenters relied on the same data examined by the agency in its impact analyses.

The commenters were sharply divided on the question of usage rates. Proponents of the automatic restraint requirements did not in their analyses address the significance of the use-inducing nature of the nondetachable automatic belts in the Rabbits and Chevettes or the demographic factors relating to those car purchasers. Instead, they asserted that the usage rates achieved in Rabbits and Chevettes would, with slight adjustments, also be achieved in other car size classes. In reaching this conclusion, they asserted that the usage rate increases of automatic belts shown by Rabbit and Chevette owners were the same regardless of whether the automatic belts were purchased knowingly or unknowingly. There was an exception to this pattern of comment among the proponents. One public spokesperson for an interest group acknowledged that automatic belts could be designed in a way that they so closely resembled manual belts that their usage rates would be the same.

Opponents of the automatic restraint requirements, relying on the similarity of detachable automatic belts to manual belts, predicted that the automatic belts would not have any substantial effect on belt usage. The opponents of the requirements also dismissed the experience of the Rabbit and Chevette owners on the grounds that the automatic belts in those cars had been voluntarily purchased and were nondetachable.

While the public comments did not provide the agency with any different or more certain basis for estimating belt usage than it already had, they did induce the agency to reexamine its assumption about the possible automatic belt usage rates. Although it is nearly impossible to sort out with precision the individual contributions made by nondetachability, interlocks, car size, demographics and other factors, NHTSA believes that the usage of automatic belts in Rabbits and Chevettes would have been substantially lower if the automatic belts in those cars were not equipped with a use-inducing device inhibiting detachment.

In the agency's judgment, there is a reasonable basis for believing that most of the increase in automatic belt Rabbits and Chevettes is due to the nondetachability feature, whether an interlock or other design feature, of their belt systems. Necessitating the attachment of belts by the addition of interlocks to 1974-75 cars resulted in an increase in manual belt usage by as much as 40 percent in cars subject to that requirement. A similar effect in the case of the Rabbit would account for four-fifths of the increase observed in the automatic belt vehicles. A significant portion of the remaining increase could in

fact be attributable to the fact many owners of automatic belt Rabbits and Chevettes knowingly and voluntarily bought the automatic belts. By the principle of self-selection, these people would be more inclined to use their belts than the purchasers of 1974-75 Rabbits who did not have any choice regarding the purchase of a manual belt equipped with an interlock. This factor would not, of course, be present in the fleet subject to the standard.

The most appropriate way of accounting for the detachability problem and other limitations on the validity of that Rabbit and Chevette data would be to recognize that the levels of usage resulting from both the point estimates are based on uncertain conclusion and adjust each appropriately. The agency's estimate in the final regulatory impact analysis for the April 1981 final rule that usage would likely fall near the lower end of the range had the effect of substantially adjusting downward the usage rate (60 percent) produced by the technique relying on the absolute percentage point increase (50 percentage points) in belt usage in automatic belt Rabbits and Chevettes. A similar adjustment could also be made in the usage rate (15 percent) indicated by the multiplier technique.

Throughout these sequential analyses, the agency has examined the extremely sparse factual data, applied those factors which are known to externally affect usage rates, and defined for analytical purposes the magnitude of potential safety effects. Aside from the initial data points, all such analyses in all cases necessarily involve exercises of discretion and informed judgment. Resultant conclusions are indications of probable usage which always have been and always must be relied upon by the agency in the absence of additional objective data.

The agency believes that the results produced by both techniques must be adjusted to account for the effects of detachability and the other factors affecting usage rates. Therefore, as the April 1981 final rule recognized, the incremental usage attributable to the automatic aspect of the subject belts may be substantially less than 11 percent.

The agency's analysis of the public comments and other available information leads it to conclude that it cannot reliably predict even a 5 percentage point increase as the minimum level of expected usage increase. The adoption of a few percentage points increase as the minimum would, in the agency's judgment, be more consistent with the substantial uncertainty about the usage rate of detachable automatic belts. Based on the data available to it, NHTSA is unable to assess the probability that the actual incremental usage would fall nearer a 0 percentage point increase or nearer some higher value like a 5 or 10 percentage point increase.

Thus, the agency concludes that the data on automatic belt usage in Rabbits and Chevettes does not provide a sufficient basis for reliably extrapolating the likely range of usage of detachable automatic belts by the general motoring public in all car size classes. Those data are not even sufficient for demonstrating the likelihood that those belts would be used in perceptibly greater numbers than the current manual belts. If the percentage increase is zero or extremely small due to the substantial similarity of the design and methods of using detachable automatic belts and manual belts, then the data regarding manual belt usage would be as reliable a guide to the effects of detachable automatic belts on belt usage as data regarding usage of nondetachable automatic belts. Indeed, the manual belt data may even be a more reliable guide since the data are based on usage by the general motoring public in cars from all size and demographic classes.

In view of the uncertainty about the incremental safety benefits of detachable automatic belts, it is difficult for the agency to determine that the automatic restraint requirements in their present form meet the need for safety.

In concluding that for this reason detachable automatic belts may contribute little to achieving higher belt usage rates, the question then arises whether the agency should amend the standard to require that automatic belts have a use-inducing feature like that of the Rabbit and Chevette automatic belts. NHTSA believes that such features would increase belt usage. The agency does not, however, believe that such devices should be mandated, for the reasons discussed in detail below.

Costs of automatic restraints

In view of the possibly minimal safety benefits and substantial costs of implementing the automatic restraint requirements, the agency is unable to conclude that the incremental costs of the requirements are reasonable. The requirements are, in that respect, impracticable. While the car manufacturers have already made some of the capital expenditures necessary to comply with the automatic restraint requirements, they still face substantial, recurring variable costs. The average price increase per car is estimated to be $89. The costs of air bags and some designs of automatic belts would be substantially higher. With a total annual production of more than 10 million cars for sale in this country, there would be a price effect of approximately $1 billion.

While the car manufacturers might be able to pass along some or all of their costs to consumers, the necessary price increases would reduce sales. There might not be any net revenue loss since the extra revenue from the higher prices could offset the revenue loss from the lower volume of sales. However, those sale losses would cause net employment losses. Additional sales losses might occur due to consumer uncertainty about or antipathy toward the detachable automatic belts which do not stow so unobtrusively as current manual lap and shoulder belts.

Consumers would probably not be able to recoup their loss of disposable income due to the higher car prices. There does not appear to be any certainty that owners of cars with detachable automatic belts would receive offsetting discounts in insurance costs. Testimony and written comments submitted to the agency indicate premium reductions generally are available only to owners of cars equipped with air bags, not automatic belts. Some large insurance companies do not now offer discounts to any automatic restraint-equipped cars, even those with air bags. If insurance cost discounts were to be given owners of cars having detachable automatic belts, such discounts would be given only after the automatic belts had produced significant increases in belt usage, and in turn significant decreases in deaths and serious injuries. The apparent improbability of any economic effect approaching the magnitude of the consumer cost means that the discounts would not likely materialize on a general basis.

Insurance company statements at the August 1981 public meeting reaffirmed this belief as they state that they could not now assure reductions in insurance premiums but would have to first collect a considerable amount of claim data.

Finally, the weight added to cars by the installation of automatic belts would cause either increased fuel costs for consumers or further new car price increases to cover the incorporation of offsetting fuel economy improvements.

The agency does not believe that it would be reasonable to require car manufacturers or consumers to bear such substantial costs without more adequate assurance that they will produce benefits. Given the plans of the car manufacturers to rely primarily on detachable automatic belts and the absence of relevant data to resolve the usage question, implementation of the automatic restraint requirements amounts to an expensive federal regulatory risk. The result if the detachable automatic belts fail to achieve significant increases in belt usage could be a substantial waste of resources.

The agency believes that the costs are particularly unreasonable in view of the likelihood that other alternatives available to the agency, the states and the private sector could accomplish the goal of the automatic restraint requirements at greatly reduced cost. Like those requirements, the agency's planned educational campaign is addressed primarily to the substantial portion of the motoring public who are currently occasional users of manual belts.

Effect on public attitude toward safety

Although the issue of public acceptance of automatic restraints has already been discussed as it relates to the usage rate of detachable automatic restraints, there remains the question of the effect of automatic restraints on the public attitude toward safety regulation in general. Whether or not there would be more than minimal safety benefits, implementation of the automatic restraint requirements might cause significant long run harm to the safety program.

No regulatory policy is of lasting value if it ultimately proves unacceptable to the public. Public acceptability is at issue in any vehicle safety rulemaking proceeding in which the required safety equipment would be obtrusive, relatively expensive and beneficial only to the extent that significant portions of the motoring public will cooperate and use it. Automatic belt requirements exhibit all of those characteristics. The agency has given the need for public acceptability of automatic restraints substantial weight since it will clearly determine not only the level of safety benefits but also the general public attitude toward related safety initiatives by the government or the private sector.

As noted above, detachable automatic belts may not be any more acceptable to the public than manual belts at any given point in time. If the detachable automatic belts do not produce more than negligible safety benefits, then regardless of the benefits attributable to the small number of other types of automatic restraints planned to be installed, the public may resent being required to pay substantially more for the automatic systems. Many if not most consumers could well conclude that the automatic belts would in fact provide them with no different freedom of choice about usage or levels of protection than manual belts currently offer. As a result, it is not unreasonable to conclude that the public may regard the automatic restraint requirements as an expensive example of ineffective regulation.

Thus, whether or not the detachable automatic belts might have been successful in achieving higher belt usage rates, mandates requiring such belts could well adversely affect public attitude toward the automatic restraint requirements in particular and safety measures in general. As noted in more detail in the 1976 Decision of Secretary Coleman.

Rejection by the public would lead to administrative or Congressional reversal of a passive restraint requirement that could result in hundreds of millions of dollars of wasted resources, severe damage to the nation's economy, and, equally important, a poisoning of popular sentiment toward efforts to improve occupant restraint systems in the future.

It can only be concluded that the public attitude described by the Secretary at that time is at least as prevalent today. The public might ultimately have sought the legislative rescission of the requirements. Action-forcing safety measures have twice before been overturned by Congress. In the mid-1970's, Congress rescinded the ignition interlock provision and provided that agency could not require the States to adopt and enforce motorcycle helmet use laws. Some people might also have cut the automatic belts out of their cars, thus depriving subsequent owners of the cars of the protection of any occupant restraint system. These are serious concerns for an agency charged by statute with taking steps appropriate for addressing safety problems that arise not only in the short term but also the long term. The agency must be able to react effectively to the expected increases in vehicle deaths and injuries during the 1980's.

Equity

Another relevant factor affecting the reasonableness of the automatic restraint requirements and of their costs is the equity of the distribution of such costs among the affected consumers. Responsible regulatory policy should generally strive to ensure that the beneficiaries of regulation bear the principal costs of that regulation. The higher the costs of a given regulation, the more serious the potential equity problem. The automatic restraint requirements of the standard would have required the current regular user of manual belts not only to pay himself for a system that affords him no additional safety protection, but in part to subsidize the current nonuser of belts who may or may not be induced by the automatic restraints to commence regular restraint usage.

Option of Adopting Use-Compelling Features

As noted above, some commenters have suggested that the only safety belts which are truly "passive" are those with use-compelling features. Such commenters have recommended that the agency amend the standard so as to require such features. For example, an ignition interlock which prohibits the car from starting unless the belt is secured is a use-compelling feature. Another example is a passive belt design which is simply not detachable, because no buckle and latch release mechanism is provided. While NHTSA agrees that such use-compelling features could significantly increase usage of passive belts, NHTSA cannot agree that use-compelling features could be required consistent with the interests of safety. In the case of the ignition interlock, NHTSA clearly has no authority to require such a use-compelling feature. The history of the Congressional action which removed this authority from NHTSA suggests that Congress would look with some disfavor upon any similar attempt to impose a use-compelling feature on a belt system.

But, even if NHTSA were to require that passive belts contain use-compelling features, the agency believes that the requirement could be counterproductive. Recent attitudinal research conducted by NHTSA confirms a widespread, latent and irrational fear in many members of the public that they could be trapped by the seat belt after a crash. Such apprehensions may well be contributing factors in decisions by many people not to wear a seat belt at all. This apprehension is clearly a question which can be addressed through education, but pending its substantial reduction, it would be highly inappropriate to impose a technology which by its very nature could heighten or trigger that concern.

In addition, the agency believes there are compelling safety reasons why it should not mandate use-compelling features on passive belts. In the event of accident, occupants wearing belts suffer significantly reduced risk of loss of consciousness, and are commonly able to extricate themselves with relative ease. However, the agency would be unable to find the cause of safety served by imposing any requirement which would further complicate the extrication of any occupant from his or her car, as some use-compelling features would. NHTSA's regulations properly recognize the need for all safety belts to have some kind of release mechanism, either a buckle and latch mechanism or a spool-out release which feeds a length of belt long enough to extricate a car occupant.

Alternative methods of increasing restraint usage

Finally, the agency believes that it is possible to induce increased belt usage, and enhance public understanding and awareness of belt mechanisms in general, by means that are at least as effective but much less

costly than the installation of millions of detachable automatic belts.

In the decision noted above, Secretary Coleman noted the obligation of the Department of Transportation to undertake efforts to encourage the public to use occupant restraints, active or passive. Toward this point, Secretary Coleman directed the Administrator of NHTSA to undertake significant new steps to promote seat belt usage during the demonstration program. This instruction of the Secretary was not effectively carried out and, unfortunately, we do not enjoy today the benefits of a prolonged Departmental campaign to encourage seat belt usage. Had such a program been successfully carried out, increased seat belt usage could have saved many lives each year, beginning in 1977.

Rather than allowing the Coleman demonstration program and its accompanying education effort to come to fruition, the Department reconsidered Secretary Coleman's 1976 decision during 1977. At the conclusion of the reconsideration period, the Department reversed that decision, and amended the standard to require the provision of automatic restraints in new passenger cars, in accordance with a phased-in schedule.

The benefits of any such belt use enhancement efforts could have already substantially exceeded those projected for the automatic restraint requirements of this standard. Over the next ten years, the requirements of the standard would have addressed primarily those occasional belt users amenable to change who buy new cars during the mid and late 1980's.

Prior to the initiation of rulemaking in February of this year, the Department had resolved to undertake a major educational effort to enhance

voluntary belt usage levels. Such efforts will be closely coordinated with new and preexisting major initiatives at the State level and in the private sector, many of which were discussed at the public meeting on the present rulemaking. These efforts will address not only those users/purchasers amenable to change, but also those currently driving and riding in cars, multipurpose passenger vehicles and trucks on the road today. The potential for immediate impact is thus many times greater. Further, with the much greater number of persons directly impacted, educational efforts would need to raise safety belt usage in the vehicles on the road during the 1980's by only a few percentage points to achieve far greater safety benefits than the automatic restraint requirements could have achieved during the same time period.

This is in no sense to argue or suggest that nonregulatory alternatives are or should be considered in all cases appropriate to limit Federal regulation. However, the existence of such efforts, and their relevance to calculations of benefits in the present case, must be and has been considered to the extent discussed herein.

Summary of Agency Conclusion

As originally conceived, the automatic restraint requirement was a far reaching technology forcing regulation that could have resulted in a substantial reduction in injuries and loss of life on our highways.

As it would be implemented in the mid-1980's, however, the requirement has turned into a billion dollar Federal effort whose main technological advance would be to require seat belts that are anchored to the vehicle door rather than the vehicle body, permitting these belts to be used either as conventional active belts or as automatic belts.

To gain this advantage, under the standard as drafted, consumers would see the end of the six passenger car and an average vehicle price increase on the order of $89 per car. The almost certain benefits that had been anticipated as a result of the use of air bag technology have been replaced by the gravely uncertain benefit estimates associated with belt systems that differ little from existing manual belts.

In fact, with the change in manufacturers' plans that in essence replaced air bags with automatic belts, the central issue in this proceeding has become whether automatic belts would induce higher belt usage rates than are occurring with manual belts.

Many of the comments in the course of this rulemaking were directed specifically at the question of belt use. Most addressed themselves to the information in the docket on the usage witnessed in the VW Rabbit and Chevette equipped with automatic belts.

The Agency's own analysis of the available information concludes that it is virtually impossible to develop an accurate and supportable estimate of future belt use increases based upon the Rabbit and Chevette automatic belt observations. The Agency further believes that it is impossible to disaggregate the roles that demographics, use inducing devices, and automatic aspects of the belt played in the observed increases.

Faced with this level of uncertainty, and the wide margins of possible error, the agency is simply unable to comply with its statutory mandate to consider and conclude that the automatic restraint requirements are at this time practicable or reasonable within the meaning of the Vehicle Safety Act. On the other hand, the agency is not able to agree

with assertions that there will be absolutely no increase in belt use as a result of automatic belts. Certainly, while a large portion of the population appears to find safety belts uncomfortable or refuses to wear them for other reasons, there is a sizeable segment of the population that finds belts acceptable but still does not use them. It is plausible to assume that some people in this group who would not otherwise use manual belts would not disconnect automatic belts.

It is this same population that will generate all of the benefits that result directly and solely from this regulation. This is a population that can also be reached in other ways. The Agency, state governments and the private sector are in the process of expanding and initiating major national belt use educational programs of unprecedented scale. While undertaken entirely apart from the pending proceeding, the fact remains that this effort will predominantly affect the same population that the automatic belts would be aimed at.

On the one hand, it could be argued that, the success of any belt use program would only be enhanced by the installation of automatic belts. Individuals who can be convinced of the utility of safety belts would presumably have an easier time accepting an automatic belt. On the other hand, there is little evidence that the standard itself will materially increase usage levels above those otherwise achievable.

However, the agency is not merely faced with uncertainty as to the actual benefits that would result from detachable automatic safety belts. When the uncertain nature of the benefits is considered together with the risk of adverse safety consequences that might result from the maintenance of this regulation, the agency must conclude that such retention would not be

reasonable, and would not meet the need for motor vehicle safety.

It is useful to summarize precisely what the agency believes these risks might be. The principal risk is that adverse public reaction could undermine the effectiveness of both the standard itself and future or related efforts.

The agency also concludes, however, that retention would present serious risk of jeopardizing other separate efforts to increase manual belt usage by the Federal government, States and the private sector. A public that believes it is the victim of too much government regulation by virtue of the standard might well resist such parallel efforts to enhance voluntary belt usage. Further, to the extent that States begin to consider belt use laws as an option, a Federal regulation addressing the same issue could undermine those attempts as well.

While one cannot be certain of the adverse effects on net belt usage increases, it would be irresponsible to fail to consider them. A decision to retain the regulation under any of the schedules now being considered would not get automatic belts on the road until 1983 and would not apply to the entire fleet of new cars until 1984. By the end of the 1984 model year, under most options, there would have been fewer than 20 million vehicles equipped with automatic belts on the road.

By the same time, however, there will be upward of 150 million vehicles equipped with only manual belts, drivers and occupants of which will have been exposed to interim belt usage encouragement efforts.

Agency analysis indicates that external efforts of whatever kind that increase usage by only 5 percent, will save more than 1300 lives per year beginning in 1983. Installation of automatic belts could save an equal number of lives in 1983 only with 95 percent belt usage.

Further, even if one is convinced that automatic belts can double belt usage and alternative efforts would only increase usage by 5 percent, it would not be until 1989 that total life savings attributable to automatic belts installed under the automatic restraint requirements would reach the total life savings achieved through such other efforts.

NHTSA fully recognizes that neither outcome is a certainty. Much closer to the truth is that both outcomes are uncertain. However, neither is significantly more likely than the other. That being the case, to impose the $1 billion cost on the public does not appear to be reasonable.

It is particularly unreasonable in light of the fact that the rescission does not foreclose the option to again reopen rulemaking if enhanced usage levels of both manual and automatic belts do not materialize. Long before there would have been any substantial number of vehicles on the road mandatorily equipped with automatic belts as a result of this standard, NHTSA will conclusively know whether other efforts to increase belt use have succeeded either in achieving acceptable usage levels or in increased public understanding and acceptance of the need for further use-inducing or automatic protection alternatives. If so obviously no further action would be needed. If such is not the case, rulemaking would again be a possibility. Any such rulemaking, following even partially successful efforts to increase belt use, would be much less likely to face public rejection.

It has been said that the Vehicle Safety Act is a "technology-forcing" statute. The agency concurs completely.

However, the issue of automatic restraints now before the agency is not a "technology-forcing" issue. The manual seat belt available in every car sold today offers the same, or more, protection than either the automatic seat belt or the air bag. Instead, the agency today faces a decision to force people to accept protection that they do not choose for themselves. It is difficult to conclude that the Vehicle Safety Act is, or in light of past experience could become, a "people-forcing" statute.

NHTSA cannot find that the automatic restraint requirements meet the need for motor vehicle safety by offering any greater protection than is already available.

After 12 years of rulemaking, NHTSA has not yet succeeded in its original intent, the widespread offering of automatic crash protection that will produce substantial benefits. The agency is still committed to this goal and intends immediately to initiate efforts with automobile manufacturers to ensure that the public will have such types of technology available. If this does not succeed, the agency will consider regulatory action to assure that the last decade's enormous advances in crash protection technology will not be lost.

Impact Analyses

NHTSA has considered the impacts of this final rule and determined that it is a major rulemaking within the meaning of E.O. 12291 and a significant rule within the meaning of the Department of Transportation regulatory policies and procedures. A final regulatory impact analysis is being placed in the public docket simultaneously with the publication of this notice. A copy of the analysis may be obtained by writing to: National Highway Traffic Safety Administration, Docket Section, Room 5109, 400 Seventh Street, S.W., Washington, D.C. 20590.

The agency's determination that the rule is major and significant is based primarily upon the substantial savings in variable manufacturing costs and in consumer costs that result from the rescission of the automatic restraint requirements. These costs would have amounted to approximately $1 billion once all new cars became subject to the requirements. The costs would have recurred annually as long as the requirements remained in effect. There is also a recurring savings in fuel costs of approximately $150 million annually. Implementation of the automatic restraint requirements would have increased the weight of cars and reduced their fuel economy. In addition, the car manufacturers will be able to reallocate $400 million in capital investment that they would have had to allocate for the purpose of completing their efforts to comply with the automatic restraint requirements.

The agency finds it difficult to provide a reliable estimate of any adverse safety effects of rescinding the automatic restraint requirements. There might have been significant safety loss if the installation of detachable automatic belts resulted in a doubling of belt usage and if the question were simply one of the implementation or rescission of the automatic restraint requirements. The April 1981 NPRM provided estimates of the additional deaths that might occur as a result of rescission. However, those estimates included carefully drafted caveats. The notice expressly stated that the impacts of rescission would depend upon the usage rate of automatic belts and of the effectiveness of the agency's educational campaign. The agency has now determined that there is no certainty that the detachable automatic belts would produce more than a several percentage point increase in usage. The small number of cars that would have been equipped with automatic belts having use-inducing features or with air bags would not have added more than several more percentage points to that amount. Further, any potential safety losses associated with the rescission must be balanced against the expected results of the agency's planned educational program about safety belts. That campaign will be addressed to the type of person who might be induced by the detachable automatic belts to begin regular safety belt usage, i.e., the occasional user of manual belts. Since that campaign will affect occasional users in all vehicles on the road today instead of only those in new cars, the campaign can yield substantially greater benefits than the detachable automatic belts even with a much lower effectiveness level.

The agency has also considered the impact of this action on automatic restraint suppliers, new car dealers and small organizations and governmental units. Since the agency certifies that the rescission would not have a significant effect on a substantial number of small entities, a final regulatory flexibility analysis has not been prepared. However, the impacts of the rescission on the suppliers, dealers and other entities are discussed in the final Regulatory Impact Analysis.

The impact on air bag manufacturers is likely to be minimal. Earlier this year, General Motors, Ford and most other manufacturers cancelled their air bag programs for economic reasons. These manufacturers planned instead to rely almost wholly on detachable automatic belts. Therefore, it is not accurate to say, as some commenters did, that rescission of the automatic restraint requirements will "kill" the air bag. Rescission will not affect the air bag manufacturers to any

significant degree. Further, the agency plans to undertake new steps to promote the continued development and production of air bags.

The suppliers of automatic belts are generally the same firms that supply manual belts. Thus, the volume of sales of these firms is not expected to be affected by the rescission. However, there will be some loss of economic activity that would have been associated with developing and producing the more sophisticated automatic belts.

The effects of the rescission on new car dealers would be positive. Due to reduced new car purchase prices and more favorable reaction to manual belts than to automatic belts, sales increases of 395,000 cars were estimated by GM and 235,000 cars by Ford. While these figures appear to be overstated, the agency agrees that rescission will increase new car sales.

Small organizations and governmental units would be benefited by the reduced cost of purchasing and operating new cars. Given the indeterminacy of the usage rate that detachable automatic belts would have achieved, it is not possible to estimate the effects, if any, of the rescission on the safety of persons employed by these groups.

In accordance with the National Environmental Policy Act of 1969, NHTSA has considered the environmental impacts of the rescission and the alternatives proposed in the April 1981 NPRM. The option selected is disclosed by the analysis to result in the largest reductions in the consumption of plastics, steel, glass and fuel/energy. A Final Environmental Impact Statement is being placed in the public docket simultaneously with the publication of this notice.

This amendment is being made effective in less than 180 days because the date on which the car manufacturers

would have to make expenditure commitments to meet the automatic restraint requirements for model year 1983 falls within that 180-day period.

Part 571 Federal Motor Vehicle Safety Standards 49 C.F.R. §571.208

In consideration of the foregoing, Federal Motor Vehicle Safety Standard No. 208, Occupant Crash Protection (49 CFR 571.208), is amended as set forth below.

49 C.F.R. §571.208 §571.208 [Amended]

1. §4.1.2 is amended by revising it to read:
§4.1.2 Passenger cars manufactured on or after September 1, 1973. Each passenger car manufactured on or after September 1, 1973, shall meet the requirements of §4.1.2.1, §4.1.2.2 or §4.1.2.3. A protection system that meets the requirements of §4.1.2.1 or §4.1.2.2 may be installed at one or more designated seating positions of a vehicle that otherwise meets the requirements of §4.1.2.3.
2. The heading of §4.1.2.1 is amended by revising it to read:
§4.1.2.1 First option — Frontal/Angular Automatic protection system.

. . .

§4.1.3 [Removed]
3. §4.1.3. is removed.
(Secs. 103, 119, Pub. L. 89-563, 80 Stat. 718 (15 Stat. 1392, 1407); delegation of authority at 49 CFR 1.50)

Issued on October 23, 1981. Raymond A. Peck, Jr., Administrator.

Appendix
Editorial

Note. — This appendix will not appear in the Code of Federal Regulations.

Following is a summary of the major comments submitted in response to the April 9, 1981 notice of proposed rulemaking. A more detailed summary of comments has been placed in NHTSA Docket No. 74-14; Notice 22. This summary is organized in broad terms according to the interest groups from which the comments were received.

Insurance Companies

All commenting insurance companies strongly favored retention of the automatic restraint requirements. Many favored maintaining the present implementation schedule (i.e., September 1, 1982, for large and medium-sized cars and September 1, 1983, for small cars), although several companies stated they would support a change to require that small cars are phased in first or a simultaneous implementation date. Several insurance companies stated that air bags offer the best technology for saving lives and reducing injuries. These companies pointed out that repeated surveys have indicated that consumers appear to favor air bags, even if higher costs are likely. Several insurers argued that a retreat from the standard represents a breach of the Secretary's statutory obligation to reduce traffic accidents and deaths and injuries which result from them. One company argued that a delay in the standard (i.e., the delay and reversal alternative) would produce no measurable economic benefit to car makers and might possibly result in an economic loss to them. Nearly all the companies argued that the standard is cost-beneficial and represents the optimum approach to resolving this country's most pressing public health problem. Many companies stated that reduced insurance premiums resulting from the lives saved and injuries prevented by automatic restraints would help offset the cost of those systems to consumers.

A majority of the insurance companies argued that seat belt use campaigns will not be effective in raising the current use rate of manual belts significantly. The companies pointed to the failures of all past campaigns to have any substantial impact on use rates. On the other hand, these companies believe that the use rate of automatic belts will be significant. The companies point to the current use data for automatic belts on VW Rabbits and Chevettes as evidence that automatic belt use will be significant. The companies believe that seat belt use campaigns should only be complementary to automatic restraints, not a substitute.

Several insurance companies pointed to the huge economic losses resulting from traffic accidents. One company stated that these losses mount to over 1 billion dollars per year and result in recurring costs because of continuing medical problems such as epilepsy and quadriplegia. One company cited Professor William Nordhaus's analysis of the consequences of rescinding the standard as being equivalent to society's loss if the tuberculosis vaccine had not been developed, or if Congress repealed the Clean Air Act. In his submission on behalf of the insurance companies, Professor Nordhaus stated that fatalities will increase by 6,400 each year and injuries by 120,000 if the standard is rescinded. One company argued that the standard is cost-beneficial if automatic belt use rates increase usage only 5 percent. However, this company stated that use rates as high as 70 percent could be expected, and that the costs of rescinding the standard could reach as much as 2 billion dollars per year. This company also argued that the economic condition of the vehicle industry is no excuse for any delay in the standard and is not a statutorily justified reason for rescinding the standard.

Consumer Groups and Health Organizations

There were many consumer groups and health-related organizations which strongly urged that the automatic restraint requirements be maintained and that there be no further delays in the implementation schedule. Most of these groups argued that the cost of both air bags and automatic belts are greatly exaggerated by vehicle manufacturers. One group stated that the three alternative proposals are "naive and exhibit a callous disregard for human lives that flouts the agency's mandated safety mission." This group argued that a worst alternative is to rescind the standard and rely on education programs to increase the use of manual belts, since seat belt campaigns have failed repeatedly in this country. The group stated that the simultaneous implementation alternative in March 1983 ignores the industry's background of introducing safety changes only at the beginning of a new model year. Regarding a reversed phase-in schedule, the group stated that the requirement that small cars have automatic restraints by September 1, 1982, would not likely provide sufficient lead time for small car manufacturers. Additionally, with approximately 2 to 1 difference in seat belt use in small cars versus larger cars, it is not at all clear that the proposed reversal would make up for the delay in implementation in the larger cars in terms of lives saved. The group argued that the best alternative is to maintain the existing implementation schedule.

Several consumer groups argued that the center seating position should not be eliminated from the requirements for several reasons. First, they argued, this position is likely to be occupied by children. Second, the center seat requirement is one factor that will lead to the installation of air bags in some vehicles since current automatic belt designs cannot be applied to the center seat. Nearly all consumer groups argued that benefits of the automatic restraint standard far outweigh the costs.

One association stated that the air bag supplier industry could be forced out of business if substantial modifications and further delays are made to the standard. This would mean, the association argued, that the life-saving air bag technology could be lost forever. The association would support some modifications to the standard if there were some clear commitment by the Department that some car models would be required to offer the consumer the choice of air bags. The group noted that air bag suppliers have indicated that a sufficient production volume would result in air bag systems priced in the 200 to 300 dollar range.

Various health groups and medical experts argued that the pain and suffering resulting from epilepsy and paraplegia, as well as mental suffering and physical disfigurement, could be greatly reduced by the automatic restraint standard. These persons argued that the standard should be implemented as soon as possible.

One consumer oriented group did not support the automatic restraint standard. That foundation argued that the standard is not justified, particularly if it is complied with by means of air bags. The group stated that air bag effectiveness is overestimated since the agency does not include non-frontal crashes in its statistics. The organization argued that in many situations air bags are actually unsafe. This group also argued that the public acceptability of automatic seat belts is uncertain, and

that a well-founded finding of additional safety benefits by the Department is required in order to justify retention of the standard.

Vehicle Manufacturers

The vehicle manufacturers, both foreign and domestic, were unanimously opposed to retention of the automatic restraint standard. Most manufacturers stated the predominant means of complying with the standard would be with automatic belts, and that such belts are not likely to increase usage substantially. This is because most automatic belts will be designed to be easily detachable because of emergency egress considerations and to avoid a potential backlash by consumers that would be counterproductive to the cause of motor vehicle safety. The domestic manufacturers argued that the public would not accept coercive automatic belts (i.e., automatic belts with interlocks or some other use-inducing feature). Eliminating any coercive element produces, in effect, a manual belt, which will be used no more than existing manual systems.

The domestic manufacturers also argued that air bags would not be economically practicable and would, therefore, be unacceptable to the public. One manufacturer noted that current belt users will object strenuously to paying additional money for automatic belts that will not offer any more protection than their existing belts.

One manufacturer argued that the injury criteria specified in the standard is not representative of real injuries and should be replaced with only static test requirements for belt systems. The company argued that there are many problems with test repeatability under the 208 requirements.

All manufacturers of small cars stated that it would

be impossible for them to comply with the standard by September 1, 1982, i.e., under the reversal proposal. These manufacturers stated that there is insufficient lead time to install automatic restraints in small cars by that date, and several foreign manufacturers stated they would not be able to sell their vehicles in that model year if the schedule is reversed. Most of the manufacturers, both domestic and foreign, stated that it is also too late to install automatic restraints in their small cars even six months earlier than the existing schedule, i.e., under the March 1983 simultaneous implementation proposal. Many manufacturers supported a simultaneous implementation if the standard is not rescinded, but requested that the effective date be September 1, 1983, or later. The manufacturers argued that an effective date for small cars prior to September 1, 1983, would not allow enough time to develop acceptable, reliable and high quality automatic belts.

Nearly all vehicle manufacturers believe that an intensive seat belt education campaign can be just as effective as automatic restraints and without the attendant high costs of automatic restraints. Additionally, most foreign manufacturers recommended that mandatory seat belt use laws be enacted in lieu of automatic restraints.

One foreign manufacturer requested that any effective date for automatic restraints be "September 1 or the date of production start of the new model year if this date falls between September 1 and December 31." The company stated that this would allow manufacturers to continue production for several months of models that would then be phased out of production. However, a domestic vehicle manufacturer argued that this would give foreign manufacturers an unfair competitive advantage, and that current practice of September 1 effective dates should be retained.

Most manufacturers supported the proposal to exclude the center seating position from the automatic restraint requirements, in order to give manufacturers more design flexibility. However, the two domestic manufacturers which would be most affected by such an exception stated that it is too late for them to make use of such an exception for 1983 models. The two companies stated that such an exception would have benefits in the long run, however, and would allow them to continue production of six-seat passenger cars in the mid-1980's.

Suppliers and Trade Groups

Suppliers of air bag system components supported continuation of the automatic restraint requirements. One commenter stated that having to buckle-up is an act which requires a series of psychological and physical reactions which are responsible for the low rate of manual seat belts. Also, this company stated that educational campaigns to increase belt use will not work.

One motor vehicle trade group stated that a study by the Canadian government has established the superiority of manual seat belt systems. This group argued that the automatic restraint requirements cannot be justified because any expected benefits are speculative.

One trade group voiced its concern about sodium azide (an air bag propellant) as it pertains to possible hazards posed to the scrap processing industry.

A group representing seat belt manufacturers stated that the most effective way of guaranteeing belt use is through mandatory belt use

laws. That group believes that belt usage can be increased through public education, and that simple, easy to use automatic belts such as are currently on the VW Rabbit will also increase belt usage. This group did not support a simultaneous implementation date for automatic restraints, stating that this could put a severe strain on the supplier industry. The group did support elimination of the automatic restraint requirements for center seating positions.

An automobile association recommended equipping small cars with automatic restraints first. The association stated that a reversed phase-in schedule would protect a significantly large segment of the public at an earlier date, would reduce a foreign competitive advantage (under the existing schedule), and would give needed economic relief to large car manufacturers. This organization also recommended that, as an alternative, automatic restraints be required only at the driver's position. This would achieve three-quarters of the reductions in deaths and serious injuries now projected for full-front seat systems, yet cost only half as much.

Congressional comments

Mr. Timothy E. Wirth, Chairman of the House Subcommittee on Telecommunications, Consumer Protection and Finance, made the following comments:

- The automatic restraint requirements would produce benefits to society far in excess of costs.
- The Committee findings strongly point to the necessity of requiring the installation of automatic crash protection systems, at a minimum, on a

substantial portion of the new car fleet at the earliest possible date. Mr. Wirth suggested that the effective date for small cars be September 1, 1982, and for intermediate and large cars September 1, 1983.

- The economic conditions of the automobile industry should not be relevant to the NHTSA's decision on matters of safety. NHTSA's decision must be guided solely by safety-related concerns.
- The agency should not discount its own findings indicating high use of automatic belts (referring to the existing VW and Chevette automatic belt use data).

In a joint letter to the Secretary, eighteen Congressmen urged that the automatic restraint requirements be maintained. This letter noted that over 50,000 people are killed each year on the highways and stated: "While the tragedy of their deaths cannot be measured in economic terms, the tragedy of their serious injuries cost all of us billions of dollars each year in higher insurance costs, increased welfare payments, unemployment and social security payments and rehabilitation costs paid to support the injured and the families of those who have been killed." The letter stressed the Congressmen's belief that the automatic crash protection standard would produce benefits to society far in excess of its cost.

In a letter addressed to Administrator Peck, fifty-nine Congressmen urged that the automatic restraint standard be rescinded. That letter stated: "The 208 standard persists as one of the more controversial federal regulations to be forced on the automobile industry. . . . The industry continues to spend hundreds of thousands of dollars every day in order to meet this standard, despite considerable evidence that any safety benefits realized by enforcing the standard would be minimal."

Private Citizens

In addition to comments from the above groups and organizations, the agency also received general comments from numerous private citizens. These comments

were almost equally divided in their support or opposition to the automatic restraint standard.

[FR Doc. 81-31189 Filed 10-23-81; 3:46 pm]

BILLING CODE 4910-59-M

Notes and Questions

1. What are the differences between the final rule and the NPRM? In terms of format, the final rule is similar to the NPRM. It contains similar headings (e.g., summary, supplementary information, etc.). In terms of effect, the final rule is not the same as the NPRM. It sets forth the agency's final action. Simply put, those subject to the rule — the so-called regulated entities, which are automakers in this instance — face legal sanctions for noncompliance with the requirements or prohibitions in the final rule. Furthermore, the agency itself is obligated to follow the rule unless and until it changes the rule through another round of notice-and-comment rulemaking. Thus, NHTSA cannot reintroduce a passive restraint requirement in any other way. What substantive differences can you identify between the NPRM and the final rule? Read them side by side to see what the agency learned from the rulemaking process.

2. In the NPRM, the agency set forth three principal proposals, and in the final rule, it adopted just one. How did it make that decision? In the remaining questions, let's try to break down the agency's rationale.

> **a.** What words of the statute were relevant? How does NHTSA decide what those words mean in relation to passive restraints?

> **b.** NHTSA includes a discussion of the Rabbit/Chevette study. What did that study show? Why did the agency discount it? Was doing so reasonable?

> **c.** What is the role of economic analysis in the decision? What was the cost of the rule? Who felt the effects — automakers, consumers, others? Why was $89 per car such an indefensible amount to pay for safety, given the overall cost of new cars?

> **d.** What is the role of public attitudes? How does the agency factor them in? What are the options for addressing public attitudes? Did NHTSA select a rational course?

> **e.** As we recounted above, President Reagan was committed to easing burdens on the ailing domestic auto industry. Passive restraints contributed significantly to such burdens. Where is that factor mentioned in the rationale for the final rule? Should it be mentioned?

C. THE STANDARD FORM OF REGULATIONS

You have just read an NPRM and a final rule. To what extent do other NPRMs and final rules resemble these? Quite a bit, as it happens. Although every rulemaking document is suited to its own issues, such documents have distinctive and predictable features. To really appreciate those features, it is useful to compare them to the structural features of statutes.

Recall the features of statutes:

- Title ("*An Act to . . .*")
- Enacting clause
- Short title
- Statement of purpose
- Definitions
- Principal operative provisions
- Subordinate operative provisions
- Implementation provisions
- Temporary provisions
- Specific repeals
- Preemption provision
- Savings clause
- Expiration date
- Effective date

Do the agency documents mirror these sections? The answer is not exactly. But the organization of NHTSA's final rule does reflect the general structure for agency final rules. The elements of a final rule can be described as follows:

- **Caption:** The caption of a final rule serves a similar purpose as the title of a statute. It identifies the regulation, not by short name but by citation, subject, and agency. Agencies issue too many regulations, even on a single subject, to distinguish them by casual reference. That said, some of the more significant rules or repeat players are identified for purposes of discussion by number, such as Standard 208.
- **Summary:** In some sense, the summary of a rule is like the title or purpose of a statute ("*An Act to . . .* "). The summary indicates upfront, in brief, the purpose of the rule. It generally contains more elaboration than the purpose clause of a statute, but then again, the rule generally contains more elaboration than a statute.
- **Supplementary Information:** This section contains the explanation for the rule. First, it supplies the *background* for the rule, which is analogous, if you will, to the factual and procedural posture section of a judicial opinion. It also provides a *rationale* for the rule. As part of the rationale for the rule, the agency addresses the comments that parties submitted. Statutes rarely contain explicit rationales (or responses to

citizen suggestions); as we have seen, rationales are often produced in the legislative history, if at all. The Supplementary Information also contains *impact analyses*. When issuing regulations, agencies are obligated to consider the effect of their decisions on certain interests. By executive order, many must perform a regulatory impact analysis, including a cost-benefit analysis, for all major regulations (basically, those with costs of $100 million or more). *See, e.g.,* Exec. Order No. 12,866, 58 Fed. Reg. 51735 (Sept. 30, 1993), *as amended by* Exec. Order No. 13,497, 74 Fed. Reg. 6113 (Jan. 30, 2009) and Exec. Order No. 13,563 (Jan. 18, 2011). Under the Regulatory Flexibility Act, 5 U.S.C. §§601, 604, agencies must prepare a "regulatory flexibility analysis" (RFA) if the rulemaking could "have a significant impact on a substantial number of small entities," including businesses and governments. Under the National Environmental Policy Act, 42, U.S.C. §§4321 *et seq.,* and related statutes and executive orders, agencies must prepare an environmental impact statement for "major Federal actions significantly affecting the quality of the human environment." 42 U.S.C. §4332. Agencies face other legal obligations as well. For example, under the Unfunded Mandates Act, 2 U.S.C. §1532, an agency must prepare a written statement about benefits and costs of their rules that may result in aggregate expenditure by State, local, and tribal governments, or by the private sector, of $100 million or more in any one year (adjusted annually for inflation). Under the Paperwork Reduction Act, 44 U.S.C. §§3501 *et seq.,* agencies must consider whether their rules (or other actions) will create any additional information collection, paperwork, or recordkeeping burdens. Agencies include a summary of their impact analyses in their final rules (as well as in their NPRMs). Statutes include no equivalent section because Congress faces no similar obligation to analyze the impacts of legislation.

- **Appendix:** The agency's final rule may contain an appendix that includes a summary of party comments or technical data — basically material that is necessary to support the explanation for the rule. The NPRM may also have an appendix section, particularly if technical data is necessary for parties to meaningfully comment on the proposals. The appendix of the final rule is a part of the record on which the agency's decision will be reviewed. Statutes rarely contain such backup material, although they do occasionally contain "findings" sections. But the legislative history frequently contains testimony transcripts and written submissions.

- **Codification:** After the agency publishes its final rule in the *Federal Register*, the operative provisions of the rule will be codified in the *Code of Federal Regulations* (C.F.R.). These operative provisions are what alter the legal requirements imposed on private parties. Thus, these provisions are most closely analogous to actual text of a statute codified in the *United States Code*.

Note on the Formalization of the Agency Explanation

The most striking difference between an agency's statement of basis and purpose and a statute is the narrative style. In this respect, the agency rule seems more like the Senate Report that you have read, see Chapter 2 or perhaps a judicial opinion. But there is a very important difference. The narrative explanation is necessary to the validity of the rule. Recall that when an agency engages in notice-and-comment rulemaking, the APA requires the agency, "[a]fter consideration of the relevant matter presented [in the comment period,]" to "incorporate in the rules adopted a concise statement of their basis and purpose." APA, §553(c). An agency that issued a rule without a concise statement of its basis and purpose would violate this requirement of the APA and face judicial reversal on that ground. Furthermore, the Supreme Court has required a more detailed explanation to facilitate judicial review of agency rules, as we discuss here only briefly in the note below and more extensively elsewhere in the book. No constitutional procedure or legislative rule requires Congress to provide an explanation, though it may provide more or less detail in the purpose section of a statute.

But agencies generally feel obligated to provide a much more extensive explanation for their rules than the relatively minimal requirements in §553 of the APA demand. The most likely reason is that the Supreme Court has required such explanations to facilitate judicial review. The APA directs courts to reverse agency action that is "arbitrary, capricious, [or] an abuse of discretion," APA, §706. In its famous decision, Motor Vehicle Manufacturers Ass'n v. State Farm Mutual Insurance Co.,463 U.S. 29 (1983), the Court required that agencies provide an explanation containing the reasons for their rules in order for those rules to survive review under the "arbitrary and capricious" standard. This decision actually involves judicial review of the very rule that you just read. For now, just observe that the result of *State Farm* and other decisions is to require that agencies provide fairly extensive explanations for their decisions. Drawing on those decisions, it is fair to say that, at a minimum, an agency must demonstrate that it has:

- Based its decision on relevant factors and no irrelevant factors;
- Considered all important aspects of the problem;
- Considered alternatives within the ambit of existing regulation;
- Made a rational connection between the evidence and its conclusions;
- Offered a plausible policy, even if not the one that a court would adopt;
- Justified changes in course from prior policy;
- Disclosed scientific or other data upon which it relied; and
- Considered comments submitted in response to the NPRM.

In addition, the Court has insisted that agencies furnish these extensive explanations at the time when they act; a reviewing court will not uphold an agency decision "unless the grounds upon which the agency acted in exercising its power were those upon which its action can be sustained." SEC v. Chenery Corp., 318 U.S. 80, 95 (1943). Thus, the agency cannot supply a "post hoc" rationale for a rule, say, in the course of defending such a rule in court. Nor will a court supply a rationale, as it might when reviewing a statute or a lower court decision. *See* Kevin M. Stack, *The Constitutional Foundation of* Chenery, 116 YALE L.J. 952, 955, 966-71 (2007).

The result of these judicial doctrines has been to "formalize" informal, notice-and-comment rulemaking. If agencies are interested in protecting their regulations from judicial reversal and remand — an order returning the regulation to the agency for further proceedings consistent with the opinion of the court — they must produce explanations that contain the basis for their decisions. Of course, agencies may have other reasons for providing explanations for their decisions. For example, they might think that this exercise not only protects their decisions from judicial reversal and remand but from political reprisal. In other words, offering an explanation reduces the chance of the President or Congress reacting adversely. Agencies may also think that providing an explanation increases compliance by regulated entities and approval by citizens. If parties understand a regulation, they are more likely to follow and accept it. And agencies may think that providing an explanation reflects best practices from an internal management standpoint. If forced to explain their regulations in rational terms, agency officials will be encouraged to develop regulations in rational terms. Similarly, agency officials will be encouraged to follow a regularized process across diverse issues. The bottom line is that for some or all of these reasons, agencies have come to provide extensive explanations in the predictable form that you have seen.

D. THE TOOLS OF STATUTORY IMPLEMENTATION

In a certain sense, the explanation that an agency provides reveals the factors that it considered or analyses that it performed when making a decision. Consider what NHTSA stated in its explanation when amending Standard 208 in response to a 1998 airbags statute:

> Before we made decisions on which provisions should be included in this rule to improve air bag performance as required by TEA 21 [The Transportation Equity Act for the 21st Century, 49 U.S.C. §30127], we carefully considered the available information and the public comments, the underlying safety problems, the performance of air bag systems in current motor vehicles, the ability (including lead time needs) of vehicle manufacturers to achieve better performance in future motor vehicles, the air bag technology (including advanced air bag technology) currently available or being developed, the cost of compliance, and other factors. Because the comments on the SNPRM [Supplemental Notice of Proposed Rulemaking] focused on the alternatives for improving the protection provided by air bags, we were particularly careful in considering the comments concerning the costs, benefits and risks associated with each of those alternatives.
>
> The requirements in today's rule for improving protection and minimizing risk are challenging and will push the vehicle manufacturers to make needed safety improvements in air bag performance. Our decisions regarding the selection of those requirements [were] based on available test data and analysis, and our informed judgment about the best way of implementing the requirements of TEA 21.

See Department of Transportation, Federal Motor Vehicle Safety Standards; Occupant Crash Protection, Final Rule, 65 Fed. Reg. 30680 (May 12, 2001). In this section, we explore the factors that agencies consider and the modes of analysis that they employ when issuing notice-and-comment rules. It is important for lawyers to understand these "tools" of agency statutory implementation. They often furnish the grounds for influencing, challenging, defending, or applying agency decisions. Here is a brief overview of the ones that we will highlight, with references back to the story of Standard 208:

- **Statutory:** The agency considers the authority that the statute grants (e.g., "establish . . . appropriate Federal motor vehicle safety standards") and the instructions that it provides (e.g., establish standards that are "practicable" and "meet the need for auto safety") to determine what actions are required and permitted; it often interprets the language of its statute before applying that language, just as courts do.
- **Scientific:** The agency examines the scientific data that the problem requires (e.g., on the potential of passive restraints to prevent crashes or save lives and minimize injuries in the event of crashes, relying on existing studies or producing new ones). Moreover, it considers the existing and potential technology for responding to risks (e.g., advanced airbags).
- **Economic:** The agency assesses the costs (e.g., to automakers and consumers of passive restraints requirements) in relation to the benefits (e.g., to passengers and others of such requirements) of different alternatives.
- **Political:** The agency considers other important aspects of the problem, like public attitudes (e.g., public resistance to future auto safety regulation) and political preferences (e.g., presidential desire to minimize federal regulation, especially burdens on the domestic auto industry, though such consideration is not evident in the final rule rescinding passive restraints).

Note that agencies do not perform all of these analyses for every regulation. For example, an agency may issue a regulation without scientific or technical analysis if that regulation simply interprets a statutory term, such as "take" for purposes of the Endangered Species Act, as you may recall from the *Sweet Home* decision in Chapter 3. Or it may forgo statutory analysis if the regulation is clearly authorized and purely technical. In addition, a particular statute may preclude or limit a particular mode of analysis. The Clean Air Act, for example, precludes EPA from allowing the costs of regulating pollutants to control. A statute may restrict particular policy considerations, like the financial health of the regulated industry (did the Motor Vehicle Safety Act restrict this consideration?). A statute may require an agency to rely on the conclusions of a particular expert body. Given these possibilities, an agency may have to determine as part of its *statutory* analysis whether its statute precludes or limits other analyses, such as economic or scientific analyses. Lawyers working with regulatory statutes are never relieved of the responsibility to read actual statutes to see what they specify.

Note also that agencies must find a way to integrate these tools when making a decision. Regulations reflect all-things-considered judgments, not a series of isolated considerations. Similarly, agencies must find a way to integrate the people who apply these tools, from political appointees to career staff, policymakers to lawyers to scientists to economists. These individuals within an agency possess expertise in different areas. Some internal structure is necessary to ensure that they work in a cooperative fashion rather than a counter-productive one.

In each of the four sections of this exploration, we will begin with an exemplary regulation that highlights the mode of analysis in question.

1. Statutory Analysis

An agency must ensure that its regulations are (a) within the scope of its statute and (b) consistent with the terms of its statute. Both are issues of statutory interpretation. The first issue is one of "jurisdiction": does this statute authorize this agency to reach a particular subject. A statute that authorizes an agency to regulate "vehicles" does not allow it to regulate air conditioners no matter what "vehicles" means (interestingly, it might authorize an agency to regulate air pollutants, at least indirectly, as part of regulating vehicle fuel economy).

Even if an agency has jurisdiction over a particular subject, it may only regulate that subject in the manner that the statute permits. Thus, the second issue: an agency may not rely on prohibited or irrelevant statutory factors and it must consider mandatory or relevant statutory factors. For example, a statute might prohibit reliance on a particular policy factor, such as the health of the auto industry, notwithstanding the President's contrary wishes. Or a statute might make that factor irrelevant in light of the interests that it does prioritize, such as the safety of auto occupants. Furthermore, a statute might require an agency to consider certain factors, such as whether an auto safety standard is "practicable" or meets "the need for auto safety." The agency is not entitled to disregard statutorily mandated factors. Nor is it entitled to ignore a factor that the statute makes relevant among others, but not necessarily determinative in the overall judgment. We hope that this distinction is helpful. Bear in mind, however, that the Supreme Court has held that there is no difference between jurisdictional and substantive factors from a doctrinal perspective. City of Arlington v. FCC, 569 U.S. 290 (2013).

Logically, issues of statutory interpretation come before all other analyses, such as scientific, economic, and political. The agency has to resolve questions about its authority before it proceeds to exercise that authority. Indeed, such questions may determine how an agency conducts the other analyses. For example, the word "feasible" in a statute might require (or prohibit) a particular type of economic analysis. As a practical matter, agencies often engage in statutory analysis concurrently or even after other analyses. In some cases, it is only once a viable policy alternative has surfaced based on other tools that the agency will seriously engage in statutory analysis; and of course, at that point, or if the agency has a strong policy preference, it may conduct statutory analysis in light of the policy it has already chosen. You can consider this issue from the personnel perspective as well: often, agency lawyers are brought onto a matter at the same time as or even after agency policymakers, scientists, and economists have begun to work.

You have already seen some agency statutory analysis or interpretation in Chapter 3. For example, consider *Sweet Home*, in which the Court addressed the meaning of "take" for purposes of the Endangered Species Act. It found that "take," which was further defined to include "harm," could be understood to apply to significant habitat modification or degradation. The Department of Interior had issued that interpretation through notice-and-comment rulemaking before the Court ever got there. We did not focus on the role of the agency when discussing that case. Now we address it directly. In so doing, we emphasize the way agency lawyers address questions of statutory interpretation and whether they do so differently from courts. Statutory analysis is the bread and butter for agency lawyers, and a central occupation for lawyers who seek to influence agency action.

a. Two Examples of Statutory Analysis

In this case, two automakers petitioned to retroactively reduce the fuel economy standards the agency had set for cars in a certain model year. The automakers filed the petition after they had failed to meet the fuel economy standards and were subject to significant penalties as a result. In denying the petition, NHTSA provided a detailed statutory analysis. This document is not a notice of proposed rulemaking or a final rule but the denial of petition for rulemaking.

---

49 C.F.R. 531
Passenger Automobile Average Fuel Economy Standards; Denial of Petitions for Rulemaking

[Docket No. FE-87-02; Notice 1], April 28, 1988

[53 Fed. Reg. 39115 (1988)]

AGENCY: National Highway Traffic Safety Administration (NHTSA), DOT.
ACTION: Denial of petitions for rulemaking.

SUMMARY: This notice denies petitions for rulemaking submitted by Mercedes-Benz of North America and the General Motors Corporation. Mercedes asked the agency to retroactively reduce the model year 1984 and 1985 corporate average fuel economy (CAFE) standards for passenger automobiles to 26.0 miles per gallon or below. General Motors asked the agency to retroactively reduce the model year 1985 standard to 26.0 miles per gallon or below. The model year 1984 standard was set by the agency; the model year 1985 standard, by Congress in the CAFE statute. The agency is denying both petitions for the reasons set forth in this notice. . . .

SUPPLEMENTARY INFORMATION:
. . . Title V of the Motor Vehicle Information and Cost Savings Act (Cost Savings Act), which is codified at 15 U.S.C. 2001-2012, provides for an automotive fuel economy regulatory program under which standards are established for the corporate average fuel economy (CAFE) of the annual production fleets of passenger automobiles and of light trucks. Title V was added in 1975 to the Cost Savings Act by the Energy Policy and Conservation Act (EPCA). Responsibility for the automotive fuel economy program was delegated by the

Secretary of Transportation to the Administrator of NHTSA....

Section 502 [of Title V] specified CAFE standards for passenger automobiles of 18, 19 and 20 mpg for model years 1978, 1979, and 1980, respectively, and 27.5 mpg for model year 1985 and thereafter. The Secretary of Transportation was required to establish standards for model years 1981-84 by July 1, 1977. Section 502(a)(3) requires that the standards for each of those model years be set at a level which (1) is the maximum feasible average fuel economy level and (2) would result in steady progress toward meeting the standard for model year 1985. On June 30, 1977, NHTSA adopted CAFE standards for passenger automobiles for model years 1981-84 (42 FR 33534). These standards were 22 mpg for 1981, 24 mpg for 1982, 26 mpg for 1983, and 27 mpg for 1984.

Section 502(f)(1) provides that the model year 1981-84 standards may be amended, from time to time, as long as the amended standards are set at the maximum feasible level and at a level representing steady progress toward the model year 1985 standard. In 1979, General Motors and Ford did informally request that rulemaking be initiated to reduce the model year 1981-84 standards. NHTSA denied the request on the ground that there was no showing that the standards were infeasible, but invited petitions in the future if there were any inaccuracies in the agency's analysis of the requests or any new facts significant enough to warrant commencing rulemaking. (See "Report on Requests by General Motors and Ford to Reduce Fuel Economy Standards for MY 1981-84 Passenger Automobiles" June 1979, and the accompanying notice of availability, June 25, 1979; 44 FR 37104.) General Motors and Ford did suggest in August 1986 in their comments on a supplemental NPRM on the reduction of the model year 1987-88 standards for passenger automobiles that the agency retroactively reduce the model year 1984-85 standards if it did not reduce the model year 1987-88 standards to 26.0 mpg.... [T]he standards for model year 1987-88 were reduced to 26.0 mpg. No petition for rulemaking to reduce the model year 1984-85 standards was submitted until August 1987.

Section 502(a)(4) authorizes (but does not require) the agency to amend the standard of 27.5 mpg for model year 1985 or any subsequent model year if it finds that the maximum feasible fuel economy level is higher or lower than 27.5 mpg in that year and sets the standard at that level. The agency has not previously amended the statutory standard of 27.5 for model year 1985, and did affirm the feasibility of that standard on several occasions. (For example, see the preamble to the June 1977 final rule adopting the model year 1981-1984 standards, and the June 1979 report on requests by General Motors and Ford to reduce the model year 1981-84 standards.) In response to timely petitions, the agency did reduce the passenger automobile standards for model years 1986-88 from 27.5 mpg to 26.0 mpg (50 FR 40528, October 4, 1985, for model year 1986 and 51 FR 35594, October 6, 1986, for model years 1987-88). Also, in response to a timely petition, the agency did reduce the 1985 light truck CAFE standard. (October 22, 1984; 49 FR 41250.) ...

Title V provides for civil penalties for violating a CAFE standard and credits for exceeding one, in the amount of $5 for each 0.1 mpg that a manufacturer's fleet is below (above, in the case of credits) the standard, multiplied by the number of automobiles in that fleet. The credits may be used to offset a shortfall that occurs when a manufacturer does not achieve in a model year the CAFE required by the standard for that year. Manufacturers may carry credits as far back as three model years before the year in which they are earned or as far forward as three model years after the year in which they are earned. (See sections 502(l), 507 and 508 of the Cost Savings Act.)

If information available to the agency indicates that a manufacturer's CAFE for a model year fell below the standard for that year, and the manufacturer does not have sufficient carry-forward credits to offset the shortfall, the agency is required by section 502(l)(1)(C)(iv) to notify the manufacturer of that fact and provide a reasonable period for the manufacturer to submit a plan for earning sufficient credits in the three following model years to offset that shortfall completely. If a carry-back plan is not submitted and approved, the agency is required by section 508 to commence a proceeding under that section to determine whether the manufacturer has violated section 507(a)(1), which makes it unlawful to fail to comply with a CAFE standard for passenger automobiles. If the agency makes that determination, on the record following opportunity for agency hearing, the agency assesses civil penalties according to the formula described above.

Finally, under section 508, penalties may be compromised, modified or remitted in only three circumstances: If necessary to prevent insolvency or bankruptcy of a manufacturer; if a manufacturer shows that the violation was the result of an act of God, strike, or fire; or if the Federal Trade Commission certifies (in response to a request by a manufacturer for relief) that a modification of the penalty is necessary to prevent a substantial lessening of competition. . . .

Petitions for rulemaking to reduce the model year 1984-85 standards were submitted after the agency notified several manufacturers of apparent noncompliance with one or both of those standards. . . .

The agency has concluded that such retroactive amendment [i.e., amending a CAFE standard for a past year, namely 1984-1985] is inconsistent with several aspects of the statutory scheme. First, the agency believes that the statutory scheme of establishing annual standards, but permitting the attainment of compliance through the earning and applying of credits to handle shortfalls, is not consistent with retroactive amendment of a standard after the end of the applicable model year. Congress included a one year carry-back/carry-forward provision in Title V in 1975 to provide the manufacturers some flexibility in dealing with the problems created by falling short of a standard. When Congress amended Title V in 1980 to extend the availability of credits from one year to three, and provided for the submission of carry-back plans for the use of credits in advance of their actually being earned, the legislative history made it clear that Congress believed it was increasing the manufacturers flexibility regarding the problems associated with shortfalls. The Senate Report stated that the extension "to provide greater flexibility in the application of existing rules covering carry-forward/carry-back of civil penalties (sic; should have read "credits") will relieve some of the burden of present regulation on automobile manufacturers." Sen. Rpt. No 96-642, March 25, 1980, page 4. With respect to the requirement for submittal of a plan, the Report stated that:

[S]ubmittal of such a plan offers useful deterrent to a scenario (improbable though

it may be) in which a manufacturer might fail over a successive period of as many as 3 years to meet each year's CAFE standard and then appeal for economic relief from a massive civil penalty accrued over that period. *Ibid*, page 7.

The flexibility of carry-forward and carry-back credits would not have been needed if the agency could (or must, as the petitions imply) retroactively amend standards to account for industrywide shortfalls. The fact that Congress did extend the availability of credits suggests that retroactive amendment was not thought to be an available option. It further suggests that Congress recognized that there would be some years in which shortfalls might occur for a variety of reasons. Instead of directing the agency to remedy such shortfalls through retroactive rulemaking, Congress chose to expand the availability of credits to offset these potential shortfalls.

Other aspects of the statutory scheme that would be disturbed by retroactive amendments are the precise and narrow provisions for commencing a proceeding to determine the existence of a noncompliance and to assess civil penalties and for mitigation of civil penalties in the event that a shortfall cannot be offset by credits. Congress chose to restrict this authority of the Secretary of Transportation quite specifically. With respect to mitigation of penalties, Congress provided for mitigation in three specific instances only, specifying express limitations on the exercise of discretion in two of the instances and requiring consultation with the Federal Trade Commission in the other instance. If retroactive rulemaking amounted to an indirect attempt by the agency to remit penalties, it would

be contrary to the statutory scheme.

Finally, the statutory scheme for making refunds to manufacturers for civil penalties already paid would also be disturbed by retroactive amendment. Sections 507 and 508 together provide that a manufacturer which has violated a standard (i.e., has fallen short of a standard and has not obtained agency approval of a plan projecting its earning of sufficient credits in the three following years to completely offset its shortfall) must pay the civil penalty for the shortfall, and later apply for a partial refund in the amount of any credits actually earned during those subsequent three years. The provision in section 508 regarding the refund of civil penalties is the only provision in Title V dealing with that subject. Yet, the retroactive amendment sought by these two petitioners would cause refunds to be made in excess of $3 million to two manufacturers that paid civil penalties for one or both of model years 1984-85. These refunds would be made, not because those manufacturers earned credits in subsequent years, as the statute contemplates, but because the standards would have been retroactively amended.

Further, reducing a standard for a model year after the year is over would raise questions about equity of such an amendment for manufacturers which absorbed the costs of compliance with the standard for a particular model year. While not directly disturbing the statutory scheme in the same manner as the examples above, these perceived inequities must be considered by the agency in the context of whether the manufacturers that did comply (with or without credits) might decline to make efforts in the future, counting instead on retroactive amendment. If this were to occur, the statutory scheme would indeed be disturbed. . . .

In its 1984 interpretation, the agency noted that while the statute does not contain explicit language concerning an amendment which lowers a CAFE standard, it does contain language that suggests that reductions are to be made prospectively, i.e., before the beginning of the model year in question. The agency cited arguments by Chrysler that amendments reducing the stringency of standards must be made at least 18 months before the beginning of the model year and that, therefore, Ford's petition regarding model year 1984-5 light truck standards was too late with respect to both models years. Chrysler argued that section 502(b) calls for 18 months leadtime for any light truck standards being prescribed and that changes in standards come within that requirement. Chrysler argued also that the 18 month requirement of section 502(f)(2) was applicable since granting Ford's request would in effect make the standards more stringent for Chrysler. Section 502(f)(2) applies to amendments to passenger automobile standards as well as those to light truck standards.

On the other hand, there are other statutory provisions that some past commenters have interpreted to the opposite effect. Section 502(f)(1) provides that amendments to the 1981-84 car standards may be made "from time to time." Some manufacturers have interpreted that language to indicate that there is no temporal limitation on amendments reducing standards. They have also noted the absence of any express limitation in the statute on the time period in which an amendment reducing a standard may be adopted.

To aid in resolving this issue, the agency carefully examined the legislative history of section 502. The relevant legislative history of section 502 is found in the Conference Report on EPCA which contains the following discussion:

Average fuel economy standards prescribed by the ST (Secretary of Transportation) for passenger automobiles in model years after 1980, for non-passenger automobiles, and for passenger automobiles manufactured by manufacturers of fewer than 10,000 passenger automobiles may be amended from time to time as long as each such amendment satisfies the 18 month rule — i.e., any amendment which has the effect of making an average fuel economy standard more stringent must be promulgated at least 18 months prior to the beginning of the model year to which such amendment will apply. An amendment which has the effect of making an average fuel economy standard less stringent can be promulgated at any time prior to the beginning of the model year in question. *See* Sen. Rep. 94-516, 94th Cong., 1st Sess. (1975) at 157.

The agency reaffirms its belief that the language in the legislative history is clear. Amendments increasing standards may be made at any time up to 18 months before the model year, while amendments reducing a standard may be made at any time up to the beginning of the model year. If no limit on the timing of amendments reducing the standards had been intended, the second-quoted sentence would have ended with the words "promulgated at any time."

As to the petitioners arguments about the absence of any express deadline in Title V for amendments reducing a standard, the agency notes that deadlines are generally specified in Title V, as in the agency's other vehicle regulatory statutes, to ensure that the agency completes its rulemaking establishing new requirements far enough in advance of the effective date to provide adequate leadtime for regulated parties to achieve compliance. Although Title V does not contain an express requirement that an amendment reducing a standard be issued before the beginning of the model year to which it applies, the agency does not interpret the fact of that absence to indicate that Congress permits retroactive amendment of the standards. In light of the legislative history, it is likely that Congress viewed a provision expressly specifying such a deadline as unnecessary.

General Motors made a related argument that the conference committee's choice of the House's 18-month deadline for amendments increasing standards over the Senate's 18 month deadline for all amendments to standards indicates that Congress desired that there be no deadline for amendments reducing standards. The legislative history of Title V provides no indication that Congress wanted to authorize retroactive rulemaking. The agency believes that the choice of the House version indicates only that Congress recognized that no leadtime was necessary to enable manufacturers to conform their conduct to a relaxing amendment and sought to allow the issuance of such amendments right up to the beginning of the model year. Cutting these amendments off 18 months before the beginning of the model year would have been inconsistent with the provision in the APA allowing a rule relieving a restriction to become effective immediately upon issuance.

Notes and Questions

1. Which provisions of the statute were relevant to NHTSA's decision?

2. Think back to Chapter 3. What tools of statutory interpretation does NHTSA use? Specifically, see if you can identify the canons of construction on which it relies. Do you have a sense that NHTSA uses the tools differently than a court would? *See* General Motors Corp. v. National Highway Traffic & Safety Administration, 898 F.2d 165 (D.C. Cir. 1990).

3. How does the agency use legislative history? On which sources does it rely? What inferences does it draw from them? Does NHTSA use legislative history any differently than a court would?

4. Later in 1988, GM again asked NHTSA to grant a retroactive amendment, and NHTSA again denied the petition. *See* 53 Fed. Reg. 39115 (Oct. 5, 1988). Two months after the agency denied GM's second petition, the Supreme Court issued a new decision on the issue of retroactive rulemaking. Bowen v. Georgetown University Hospital, 488 U.S. 204 (1988). In that decision, the Court held that a statute will not be understood "to encompass the power to promulgate retroactive rules unless that power is conveyed in express terms." *Id.* at 208. This rule is the agency analogue to the presumption against retroactivity that we discussed in Chapter 3. If NHTSA applied this rule, how would it change its analysis?

Here is a second example of agency statutory interpretation, this time serving as the basis for a rule, rather than a basis for denying a petition. It relates to NHTSA's enforcement of the civil penalties provided for by the Motor Vehicle Safety Act, which were previously discussed in Chapter 2. Initiating civil actions, like any other power that an agency possesses, depends on statutory authorization. NHTSA changed in its enforcement practices based on its interpretation of statutory language.

DEPARTMENT OF TRANSPORTATION

National Highway Traffic Safety Administration

49 CFR Part 578

. . .

Civil Penalty Procedures and Factors

AGENCY: National Highway Traffic Safety Administration (NHTSA), Department of Transportation.

ACTION: Notice of proposed rulemaking (NPRM).

. . .

I. Executive Summary

The Moving Ahead for Progress in the 21st Century Act (MAP-21 or the Act) was signed into law on July 6, 2012 (Pub. L. 112-141). Section 31203(a) of MAP-21 amends the civil penalty provision of the Safety Act, as amended and recodified, 49 U.S.C. chapter 301, by requiring the Secretary of Transportation to consider various factors in determining the amount of a civil penalty or compromise. This statutory language confirms that the Secretary has the power to assess civil penalties. The factors that the Secretary shall consider in determining the amount of civil penalty or compromise are codified in amendments to 49 U.S.C. 30165(c). Section 31203(b) of MAP-21 requires the Secretary to issue a final rule, in accordance with 5 U.S.C. 553, providing an interpretation of the penalty factors set forth in MAP-21. . . . This NPRM proposes an interpretation of the civil penalty factors in 49 U.S.C. 30165(c) for NHTSA to consider in determining the amount of civil penalty or compromise and proposes procedures for NHTSA to assess civil penalties under a delegation from the Secretary, 49 CFR 1.95 and 1.81. The proposed procedure for assessing civil penalties and the proposed interpretation of the civil penalty factors is intended to apply only to matters falling under section 30165.

This rulemaking also sets forth NHTSA's amendment of its penalty regulation, 49 CFR 578.6, to conform it to the statutory language and maximums enacted in MAP–21.

II. Civil Penalties Under the Safety Act Prior to MAP-21

Prior to the enactment of MAP-21, 49 U.S.C. 30165(c) stated, "In determining the amount of a civil penalty or compromise, the appropriateness of the penalty or compromise to the size of the business of the person charged and the gravity of the violation shall be considered." 49 U.S.C. 30165(c) (2011). The statute did not specify who would assess the civil penalties. However, the statute specifically stated that "The Secretary of Transportation may compromise the amount of a civil penalty imposed under this section." 49 U.S.C. 30165(b)(1). Construing these provisions, NHTSA, through the authority delegated from the Secretary of Transportation pursuant to 49 CFR 1.50 (2011), compromised civil penalties, but did not assess them.

NHTSA has in fact compromised, or settled, many civil penalty actions. However, if the action was not compromised, NHTSA had relied on the U.S. Department of Justice to initiate an action in U.S. District Court for the assessment of civil penalties.

Congress has revised the language in 49 U.S.C. 30165(c), which now states in part that "In determining the amount of a civil penalty or compromise under this section, the Secretary of Transportation shall consider the nature, circumstances, extent, and gravity of the violation." The plain language of the statute indicates Congress' intent that the Secretary of Transportation is authorized to determine the amount of a civil penalty and to impose such penalty.

NHTSA's reading of the statute, as amended, is supported by the legislative history. For example, on July 29, 2011, Senator Pryor introduced S. 1449, the Motor Vehicle and Highway Safety Improvement Act of 2011 (Mariah's Act). This bill contained language listing the factors that the Secretary of Transportation shall consider in determining the amount of civil penalty or compromise. According to a Senate report, the provisions of S. 1449 were enacted into law, with modifications, as title I of division C of the Moving Ahead for Progress in the 21st Century Act (MAP-21, 126 Stat. 732), which was signed into law on July 6, 2012. The Report of the Senate Committee on Commerce, Science, and Transportation made clear that NHTSA was authorized to impose "fines." For example, it stated, "Before issuing a fine, the Secretary would be required to consider several relevant factors in setting the level of the fine, including the nature of the violation; the severity of the risk of injury; the actions taken by the person charged to identify, investigate,

or mitigate the violation; the nature of the defect or noncompliance; and the size of the company." The use of the words "issuing a fine" indicates that the monetary amount is due and owing to the public treasury. *See, e.g., Black's Law Dictionary* (10th ed. 2014) (defining "fine" as "[a] pecuniary criminal punishment or civil penalty payable to the public treasury.").

NHTSA historically has considered the gravity of the violation when compromising civil penalties. Consideration of the gravity of the violation has involved a variety of factors, depending on the case. The factors that have been important or germane have included the nature of the violation, the nature of a safety-related defect or noncompliance with Federal Motor Vehicle Safety Standards ("FMVSS"), the safety risk, the number of motor vehicles or items of motor vehicle equipment involved, the delay in submitting a defect and noncompliance information report, the information in the possession of the violator regarding the violation, other actions by the violator, and the relationship of the violation to the integrity and administration of the agency's programs.

In the past, NHTSA also has considered the size of the violator when compromising civil penalties. With respect to civil penalties involving small businesses, among the factors that have been considered are the violator's ability to pay, including its ability to pay over time, and any effect on the violator's ability to continue to do business.

Notes and Questions

1. NHTSA insists here that it is interpreting the statute. NHTSA also specifies the procedures it will use to carry out the penalty-imposing authority it asserts. Although NHTSA solicited comments on this proposed rule, it treated it as exempt from the notice-and-comment requirement, and therefore as able to go into effect without a final version or a statement of basis and purpose. Both the interpretation and the procedures were considered exempt under §553(b) ("this subsection does not apply (A) to interpretative [sic] rules, general statements of policy, or rules of agency organization, procedure, or practice").

2. Once again, consider the tools of statutory interpretation that the agency uses, including its reliance on legislative history. Could its statement have appeared in a judicial opinion, or is there a difference in the way a court would analyze the issue?

3. Agencies that are not granted the power to bring cases to court on their own or the greater power to impose their own civil penalties must rely on the Department of Justice to bring their enforcement actions to court. But Justice does not simply follow the agency's orders to file a case in federal court. Instead, it exercises supervisory authority, determining on its own whether the agency's position is likely to prevail. In doing so, it is establishing its own credibility with the judiciary, and thus increases the likelihood that it will prevail in cases that it chooses to initiate. It is also providing one more means (in addition to the review of rules by OMB, as will be discussed in Chapter 6) by which the President can control administrative agencies, since the Department of Justice is headed by the Attorney General, a member of the cabinet and traditionally a close ally of the President. *See* CORNELL W. CLAYTON, THE POLITICS OF JUSTICE: THE ATTORNEY GENERAL AND THE MAKING OF LEGAL POLICY (1992); REBECCA M. SALOKAR, THE SOLICITOR GENERAL: THE POLITICS OF LAW (1992); Neal Devins, *Unitariness and Independence: Solicitor General Control over Independent Agency Litigation*, 82 CALIF. L. REV. 255 (1994). This means that the ability of NHTSA to impose penalties on its own represents a major expansion of the agency's authority and autonomy. Do you think that the statutory language or legislative history supports such a significant change?

b. The "Discovery" of Agency Interpretation: *Chevron*

From the very beginning of the administrative state, everyone understood that an agency must take its instructions from an authorizing statute, and that this required the agency to read and understand that statute. As the previous example demonstrates, agencies can apply the tools of statutory interpretation in a manner similar to courts. Why might they fall roughly in line with judicial practice? The reason is not necessarily because that is the only way or even the best way to interpret statutes. In fact, agencies might place greater emphasis on particular tools or draw different inferences from them because of their deep familiarity with the statutory scheme and their overall responsibility for implementing the scheme. Nevertheless, agencies have incentives to interpret their statutes in ways that are likely to survive judicial review. *See* William N. Eskridge, Jr. & John Ferejohn, *The Article I, Section 7 Game*, 80 GEO. L.J. 523, (1992). The leading decision on judicial review of agency statutory interpretations is Chevron U.S.A. Inc. v. Natural Resources Defense Council, Inc., 467 U.S. 837 (1984). There is much to be said about *Chevron*. We reproduce the entire decision in Chapter 6. For now, read this short excerpt for the "test" it contains and consider how that test relates to how agencies render those interpretations. What would agency lawyers find significant for their work in the decision?

Chevron Oil Refinery, Richmond, California

Chevron U.S.A. Inc. v. Natural Resources Defense Council, Inc.

467 U.S. 837 (1984)

Justice MARSHALL and Justice REHNQUIST took no part in the consideration or decision of these cases.

Justice O'CONNOR took no part in the decision of these cases.

Justice STEVENS delivered the opinion of the Court.

. . . In the Clean Air Act Amendments of 1977, Pub. L. 95-95, 91 Stat. 685, Congress enacted certain requirements applicable to States that had not achieved the national air quality standards established by the Environmental Protection Agency (EPA) pursuant to earlier legislation. The amended Clean Air Act required these "nonattainment" States to establish a permit program regulating "new or modified major stationary sources" of air pollution. Generally, a permit may not be issued for a new or modified major stationary source unless several stringent conditions are met. The EPA regulation promulgated to implement this permit requirement allows a State to adopt a plantwide definition of the term "stationary source." Under this definition, an existing plant that contains several pollution-emitting devices may install or modify one piece of equipment without meeting the permit conditions if the alteration will not increase the total emissions from the plant. The question presented by these cases is whether EPA's decision to allow States to treat all of the pollution-emitting devices within the same industrial grouping as though they were encased within a single "bubble" is based on a reasonable construction of the statutory term "stationary source." . . .

I [OMITTED]

II

. . . When a court reviews an agency's construction of the statute which it administers, it is confronted with two questions. First, always, is the question whether Congress has directly spoken to the precise question at issue. If the intent of Congress is clear, that is the end of the matter; for the court, as well as the agency, must give effect to the unambiguously expressed intent of Congress.[1] If, however, the court determines Congress has not directly addressed the precise question at issue, the court does not simply impose its own construction on the statute, as would be necessary in the absence of an administrative interpretation. Rather, if the statute is silent or ambiguous with respect to the specific issue, the question for the court is whether the agency's answer is based on a permissible construction of the statute.

The power of an administrative agency to administer a congressionally created . . . program necessarily requires the formulation of policy and the making of rules to fill any gap left, implicitly or explicitly, by Congress. *Morton v. Ruiz*, 415 U.S. 199, 231 (1974). If Congress has explicitly left a gap for the agency to fill, there is an express delegation of authority to the agency to elucidate a specific provision of the statute by regulation. Such legislative regulations are given controlling weight unless they are arbitrary, capricious, or manifestly contrary to the statute. Sometimes the legislative delegation to an agency on a particular question is implicit, rather than explicit. In such a case, a court may not substitute its own construction of a statutory provision for a reasonable interpretation made by the administrator of an agency . . . .

Policy

. . . The arguments over policy that are advanced in the parties' briefs create the impression that respondents are now waging in a judicial forum a specific policy battle which they ultimately lost in the agency and in the 32 jurisdictions opting for the "bubble concept," but one which was never waged in the Congress. Such policy arguments are more properly addressed to legislators or administrators, not to judges.

---

1. The judiciary is the final authority on issues of statutory construction and must reject administrative constructions that are contrary to clear congressional intent. If a court, employing the traditional tools of statutory construction, ascertains that Congress has an intention on the precise question at issue, that intention is the law and must be given effect.

In these cases, the Administrator's interpretation represents a reasonable accommodation of manifestly competing interests, and is entitled to deference: the regulatory scheme is technical and complex, the agency considered the matter in a detailed and reasoned fashion, and the decision involves reconciling conflicting policies. Congress intended to accommodate both interests, but did not do so itself on the level of specificity presented by these cases. Perhaps that body consciously desired the Administrator to strike the balance at this level, thinking that those with great expertise and charged with responsibility for administering the provision would be in a better position to do so; perhaps it simply did not consider the question at this level; and perhaps Congress was unable to forge a coalition on either side of the question, and those on each side decided to take their chances with the scheme devised by the agency. For judicial purposes, it matters not which of these things occurred.

Judges are not experts in the field, and are not part of either political branch of the Government. Courts must, in some cases, reconcile competing political interests, but not on the basis of the judges' personal policy preferences. In contrast, an agency to which Congress has delegated policymaking responsibilities may, within the limits of that delegation, properly rely upon the incumbent administration's views of wise policy to inform its judgments. While agencies are not directly accountable to the people, the Chief Executive is, and it is entirely appropriate for this political branch of the Government to make such policy choices—resolving the competing interests which Congress itself either inadvertently did not resolve, or intentionally left to be resolved by the agency charged with the administration of the statute in light of everyday realities.

When a challenge to an agency construction of a statutory provision, fairly conceptualized, really centers on the wisdom of the agency's policy, rather than whether it is a reasonable choice within a gap left open by Congress, the challenge must fail. In such a case, federal judges—who have no constituency—have a duty to respect legitimate policy choices made by those who do. The responsibilities for assessing the wisdom of such policy choices and resolving the struggle between competing views of the public interest are not judicial ones: "Our Constitution vests such responsibilities in the political branches." *TVA v. Hill*, 437 U.S. 153, 195 (1978).

We hold that the EPA's definition of the term "source" is a permissible construction of the statute which seeks to accommodate progress in reducing air pollution with economic growth. . . .

Notes and Questions

1. It is important to distinguish between the interpretive process that the *Chevron* case establishes and the rationale that underlies this process. The interpretive process is the famous two-step test. Be sure you can articulate it. We return to it in Chapter 6. In the excerpt reprinted above, you can also identify the rationale for prescribing this test.

2. Focus first on the two-step test. As you know, the standard rule for appellate review of a trial court decision is that the appellate court defers to findings of fact, but reviews determinations of law de novo. The ratio-nale is that the trial judge is in a better position to determine facts because she has seen the witnesses testify, examined the physical evidence, and watched the case develop, but the appellate court is in as good a position to interpret the law, and should do so in its supervisory and coordinating role. *Chevron* changes this rule for review of appellate review of agency decisions, and defers to the body being reviewed (an agency not a court) on questions of law as well as questions of fact under certain circumstances.

3. The rationale for the test contains three separate justifications. The first is: when Congress assigns implementation of a statute to an agency, the agency should be the primary interpreter of its language. The second is that federal judges, unlike agencies, are not experts on the subject matter of the statute. The third is that federal judges, unlike agencies, are not accountable to elected officials. Which of these is most persuasive or most important from the agency's perspective?

4. In answering the previous question, consider that *Chevron* test applies only when an agency is interpreting "its own" statute; that is, the statute that it is assigned to implement. When an agency is interpreting any other law, including—significantly—the APA, *Chevron* does not apply. We will study the rules that determine whether *Chevron*'s two-step test will apply to a par-ticular agency interpretation as well as the pre-*Chevron* standard of judicial review in Chapter 6. Which of *Chevron*'s rationales explain this limitation on *Chevron*'s application? In answering, consider for example which agency is more "expert" on environmental hazards created by cars, NHTSA or EPA? Perhaps you will find the question a close one, and the agencies might well disagree with each other. Which agency do you think will be given *Chevron* deference on interpretations of the law that authorizes the creation of those standards?

5. As you know from Chapter 3, many commentators feel that legislative intent is a fictional concept. *See* Kenneth A. Shepsle, *Congress Is a "They," Not an "It": Legislative Intent as Oxymoron*, 12 INT'L REV. L. & ECON. 239, 239 (1993) ("Legislative intent is an internally inconsistent, self-contradictory expression. Therefore, it has no meaning."). Commentators have applied this observation to the congressional delegation rationale of *Chevron*. David J. Barron & Elena Kagan, *Chevron's Nondelegation Doctrine*, 2001 SUP. CT. REV. 201, 212 ("Because Congress so rarely makes its intentions about deference clear, *Chevron* doctrine at most can rely on a fictionalized statement of leg-islative desire, which in the end must rest on the Court's view of how best to allocate interpretive authority."); Thomas W. Merrill, *Judicial Deference to Executive Precedent*, 101 YALE L.J. 969, 998 (1992) (*Chevron* relies on the "dubi-ous fiction of delegated authority"); Mark Seidenfeld, Chevron's *Foundation*, 86 NOTRE DAME L. REV. 273, 278 (2001) ("By most accounts, Congress does not directly address the question of which institution—agency or court—is authorized to fill gaps or resolve ambiguities in the vast majority of regu-latory statutes. In that sense, congressional intent about interpretive pri-macy is a fiction."). But this argument has been challenged on the basis of empirical investigation. *See* Lisa Schultz Bressman, *Reclaiming the Legal Fiction of Congressional Delegation*, 97 VA. L. REV. 2009 (2009) (members of Congress are aware of the delegation and interpretation argument).

6. Does *Chevron* track how agencies interpret their statutes? If you were an agency head, you might select a policy and confirm with your lawyers that it is permissible under the statute. Isn't that approach the exact opposite of *Chevron* — statute first, policy second? What is the advantage of starting with policy? *See* Elizabeth V. Foote, *Statutory Interpretation or Policy Administration: How* Chevron *Misconceives the Function of Agencies and Why It Matters*, 59 ADMIN. L. REV. 673 (2007). Might *Chevron* interfere?

7. Now return to the NHTSA retroactive amendment example. What did *Chevron* mean for that regulation? On judicial review, it meant that the Court of Appeals for the D.C. Circuit determined whether the statute was ambiguous (it was), and whether the NHTSA's interpretation was reasonable (it was). *See* General Motors Corp. v. National Highway Traffic & Safety Administration, 898 F.2d 165 (D.C. Cir. 1990). What about when NHTSA was making its decision? How did *Chevron* factor in at that stage? NHTSA did not cite *Chevron* in the final rule. Why not? Was it not aware of the decision? Perhaps agencies do not think primarily in terms of surviving judicial review. Perhaps agencies do not think in terms of rigid categories, as squaring the interpretation with the text and the legislative history *or* as squaring it with the overall implementation of the statutory scheme. It's a mix of both. Consider this issue again after reading the next section.

Chevron is the most widely cited case in modern administrative law, and it is difficult to overestimate its importance. There had been a few cases decided prior to the APA that focused on statutory interpretation, e.g., Skidmore v. Swift & Co., 323 U.S. 134 (1944); NLRB v. Hearst Pub., Inc., 322 U.S. 111 (1944); and Gray v. Powell, 314 U.S. 402 (1941). But it was not until *Chevron* that the Court focused on statutory interpretation as a distinct element of the agency implementation process and a distinct mode of analysis in the agency's policy-making process. Even then, the Court did not immediately become aware of the wide-ranging implications of its own decision. *See* Jack M. Beermann, *End the Failed Chevron Experiment Now: How* Chevron *Has Failed and Why It Can and Should Be Overruled*, 42 CONN. L. Rev. 779, 829-32 (2010); William N. Eskridge, Jr. & Lauren E. Bauer, *The Continuum of Deference: Supreme Court Treatment of Agency Interpretation from,* Chevron *to* Hamdan 96 GEO. L.J. 1083, 1142 (2008); Thomas W. Merrill, *Judicial Deference to Executive Precedent*, 101 YALE L.J. 969, 980-83 (1992).

Here are three major implications of *Chevron*:

1. *Statutory interpretation is an intrinsic part of an administrative agency's implementation process.* The agency is the first, and often the sole interpreter of the statute. Procedurally, this is because most challenges to regulatory actions are based on the way the agency is applying the statute, which means that it has already interpreted the statute.

2. *Open-ended statutory language is a tool of agency implementation not a drafting oversight.* Although the *Chevron* decision continues to employ the term "ambiguity," for language whose meaning a reviewing court cannot readily discern, it treats such language as an implicit grant of authority to the implementing agency. According to the three different explanations that Justice Stevens provided when discussing legislative behavior, open-ended language (perhaps a better term than "ambiguous") can represent a conscious intent to grant the implementing agency authority to choose the precise meaning, an avoidable result of the legislators' inability to anticipate all the vagaries of future events, or a by-product of the legitimate process of legislative compromise. Regardless of the reason, the gap-filling authority flows to the agency.

3. *The appellate court's relationship to an agency is different from its relationship to a trial court.* When an appellate court is reviewing a decision by a trial court, it is dealing with a statute or a system (common law) whose implementation is assigned to the judiciary. In other words, it is exercising a direct supervisory function, reviewing decisions made by its hierarchical subordinates in its own institution. In contrast, when an appellate court is reviewing a decision by an agency, it is dealing with a statute that assigns implementation authority to a different institution. In this case, it is carrying out what can be called a control or checking function rather than a supervisory one. Why should the traditional rules regarding de novo review of legal decisions, which evolved for review of trial courts, apply to review of agency decisions? The relationship between reviewing courts and agencies should be analyzed separately, on its own terms, which is what *Chevron* does. This last implication relates more closely to judicial control of agency action, and we will return to it in Chapter 6.

c. The Practice of Agency Interpretation

Now that we recognize the crucial role that agencies play in interpreting the statutes they administer, the question is how they carry out this function. Although we have extensive knowledge of how courts interpret statutes, we have sorely little for agencies. Do they apply the same tools of statutory interpretation as courts do, with the same emphasis, and for the same reasons? What about the theories that we have used to describe particular approaches to statutory interpretation? Are agencies intentionalists or purposivists or textualists? Are there theoretical divisions among different agencies or officials as there are among courts or judges? How do agencies *really* interpret statutes?

Agency lawyers must be attentive to how courts interpret statutes, and in particular to how courts are likely to interpret what a statute requires or clearly prohibits. Overlooking those features of judicial practice invites judicial reversal of agency action. But how courts interpret statutes is only one part of what agencies consider when *they* interpret statutes. In this respect, it is important not to assume that agencies interpret statutes in the same manner as courts do. They are different institutions, with different capacities and constraints.

Agencies can gather information about statutes that courts cannot. They are often involved in the development of legislation and have more familiarity with the regulatory scheme. They are situated with respect to their statutes in a way that both expands and narrows their interpretive horizon. They see interpretation as one part of a larger task (i.e., statutory implementation).

Professor Jerry Mashaw has drawn together these observations and more, offering a preliminary account of agency statutory interpretation.

Jerry L. Mashaw, Agency Statutory Interpretation

www.bepress.com/ils/iss3/art9 (2002)

How do administrators go about the business of statutory interpretation? The question has two related parts: (1) What are the occasions, forms and processes for agency statutory interpretation? (2) How do administrators interpret; what is their interpretive methodology?

The first issue requires scrutiny in part because both courts and commentators have argued that the occasion, form and process for agency statutory interpretation bear directly on the respect that courts should give to agency determinations of statutory meaning. These arguments presume to greater or lesser degree that occasion, form and process are probative both about whether an agency is exercising authoritative lawmaking power when interpreting a statute and about the degree to which the agency's views are "well-considered" and, therefore, highly persuasive if not authoritative. Are these presumptions correct?

These issues also bear examination in their own right. We know the answer to occasion, form and process questions when considering judicial interpretation of statutes. The occasion is a lawsuit. The form of interpretation is a judicial opinion rationalizing the court's resolution of the lawsuit. The process is the conventional judicial process of adversary argument followed by independent judicial consideration.

Agency interpretations, by contrast, take myriad forms: legislative rules, interpretative rules, statements of policy, manual issuances, advisory opinions, letters, press releases, after dinner speeches, formal adjudications, informal adjudications, interpretive memoranda, guidelines, "rulings" and so on, and on. The occasions for interpretation are not just disputes, but queries, political provocations, and autonomous policy decisions. And the process through which interpretations are formulated vary with the occasion for interpretation and the form in which it will or must be rendered. It would be surprising for agency interpretive methodology to be invariant across these differing contexts (although it may be). Hence, if we are to understand "how," we must extend our interest to "when," "what," and "through what process." . . .

For purposes of this essay, I made two brief forays into [agency] interpretive practice, both limited to published legislative rules in the post-*Chevron* era. Querying the Federal Register rules database yielded well over 600 hits where statutory interpretation was at least mentioned. From that set I selected two agencies, EPA, and HHS for a closer look. Both had substantial numbers of issuances and they are engaged in disparate administrative tasks and politico-legal contexts. For the same agencies I selected a few rulemaking activities that resulted in judicial review. . . .

A search in the Lexis Federal Register data base for EPA and HHS rules that at least mentioned statutory interpretation produced 60 hits for HHS and 179 for EPA. This was an obviously underinclusive approach, but broader searches yielded thousands of results which Lexis would not display. The intuitive underpinning of the search was simply to find some instances in which the agencies are attending self-consciously to statutory interpretation. Of the returned hits, I selected approximately a dozen rules from each agency where interpretive practice was most prominently on display.

The surprise here, if there is one, is how unsurprising agency practice appears from this type of sampling. At both agencies much of the discussion of statutory interpretation comes in the agencies' replies to comments. Although the agencies sometimes anticipated interpretive problems and noted them in setting forth the rules, I focused my analysis primarily on the agencies' responses to comments which attacked their proposed interpretations in an attempt to influence the agencies to change proposed rules. In other words, I focused on instances in which statutory interpretation was conflictual.

In both sets of rules "textualism" is often in evidence, including some highly formalistic "plain meaning" arguments. Legislative history is not as prominent as one might have expected. On the other hand, the agencies do not apologize (as many contemporary courts do) when invoking legislative history nor do they question its reliability. Floor statements from the Congressional Record are used occasionally, but most reliance is on committee reports. Neither agency makes much of anything of its relationship to other "political" actors. There is some reliance on congressional acquiescence in past practice and the necessity of complying with general executive orders. These agencies may be relying on the dynamics of their political environment to inform their interpretations, but their enunciation of interpretive reasons leaves these factors decidedly in the background.

As one might expect, there is no attempt to address methodological issues in interpretation. Those sorts of methodological controversies bubble up in multi-member judicial panels where the judges or justices disagree about outcome and pursue their disagreements through the medium of methodological controversy. These agency final rules "lay down the law" with one voice, and their drafters seem to use whatever methods come to hand in dealing with the questions before them.

This small sample suggests some differences between HHS and EPA practice that are probably not unexpected to those who know something of both agencies and their regulatory context. HHS interpretations seem much more straightforward and focused. They simply answer the question raised by a commentator and go on to the next question. Case authority is very sparse in HHS issuances, and there seems a decided lack of strategic posturing in anticipation of judicial review.

EPA explanations are noticeably different. The interpretive analysis is more elaborate. This is probably a result both of more extensive commentary by well-organized interests, high levels of litigation, and a continuous need at EPA to harmonize technical sections of multiple statutes which have been passed at different times and are potentially working at cross purposes. Not surprisingly one finds EPA citing and using the *Chevron* two-step criterion to structure its interpretive arguments. After all, *Chevron* is an EPA case.

The EPA rules also are heavier on judicial jurisprudence and the use of interpretive presumptions gleaned from Supreme Court opinions, such as the requirement that there be a "clear statement" for a statute to preempt state action or the dictum that statutes should be construed for the benefit of Indian tribes.

In at least one of the rules reviewed EPA proceduralized *Chevron*. In its Notice of Proposed Rulemaking it articulated the reasons for finding the relevant statutory provisions ambiguous and invited comments on alternative interpretations of the Act. Indeed, the EPA rulemaking responses often move the discussion rapidly away from "meaning" (*Chevron* step 1) to the question of "reasonableness" (*Chevron* step 2). The agency then relies on a host of sources to demonstrate the reasonableness of its approach, including everything from the overall purposes of the act, to canons of statutory construction to practical problems of enforcement and administration. There is considerable emphasis on its own past practice and on its prior interpretations, whether or not they have ever been blessed by a reviewing court.

In a few instances agency practices seem to mirror some of the normative expectations previously discussed. In one of HHS's rulemaking proceedings, commentators attacked the constitutionality of the rules. HHS dismissed the constitutional claims without extended discussion, and certainly without any suggestion that its policies should be trimmed to avoid constitutional challenge. Not much should be made of this finding, of course. The sample here was small and these constitutional claims bordered on the frivolous.

In addition, in one of its rulemaking proceedings EPA had to deal with explicitly contrary circuit court authority. It clearly announced its refusal to acquiesce in the circuit court determination, save in the case in which it was rendered, and explained at length why it believed that the circuit court opinion had been wrong. . . .

My short field trip into agency statutory interpretation included a top down sampling of a few rules (four each) promulgated by HHS and EPA and subjected to subsequent circuit court review. Some of these rules were relatively high profile controversies, such as the HHS rules concerning parental notification requirements applicable to family planning services and the EPA regulation establishing its nitrogen oxide emission reduction program. Others are more run of the mine, technical rules which may have important impacts on particular parties, but are hardly the stuff of high political controversy.

The story here is much the same as that pieced together in the preceding section. EPA interpretive analyses were in general much more extensive than those provided by HHS, and EPA constantly invoked *Chevron* and emphasized the "reasonableness" of its interpretations. At both agencies examination of judicial precedent was scant and there was considerable reliance on past agency practice, technical industry or scientific understandings of terms and legislative history.

Looking at agency interpretive discussions side by side with reviewing court opinions allows some further tentative comparisons. Agency effort at explaining or justifying interpretations in their final rules does not seem to correlate with judicial acceptance of the agencies' positions. This may, of course, simply reflect that agency effort is correlated positively with agency uncertainty about the acceptability of its interpretations.

Perhaps most striking are the cases in which an agency's highly nuanced interpretation—based on text, legislative history, statutory history, past agency practice, the balance of competing congressional purposes, and industry or scientific understandings—were rejected in favor of judicial approaches based on pure textual analysis, plain meaning or the invocation of grammatical rules. These cases highlight the strikingly different context of agency and court interpretive activity. They also obviously raise again the question of how "deferential" judicial review can be when agency and court interpretations are informed by different political, administrative, and procedural contexts that lead to differing methodological commitments.

Notes and Questions

1. According to Mashaw, what are the most prominent "tools" of agency statutory interpretation? Are those tools for ascertaining statutory meaning based principally on text? Do they involve other indicia of legislative intent or statutory purpose? Are any suited to considering changed circumstances? Are they relevant to discerning the statute's clear meaning, or something else?

2. Does Mashaw view agencies as adhering to any particular theory of statutory interpretation? Are they textualists? Intentionalists? Purposivists? Dynamic or nautical interpreters? If you had to pick a theory of interpretation that best describes the agency approach, which would you choose?

3. Mashaw intended his summary to prompt debate. What justifies the contrasts that Mashaw draws between courts and agencies? In particular, does Mashaw over- or understate the differences in the way agencies approach interpretive tasks with regard to statutes that they administer? For further analysis of the questions provoked by Mashaw's inquiry, see *Symposium: Administrative Statutory Interpretation*, 2009 MICH. ST. L. REV. 1 (2009).

As a normative matter, should agencies interpret statutes using the same tools and theories that courts use? Might we think instead that the different institutional capacities of courts and agencies support different interpretive approaches? In this regard, note that some of the tools that courts use depend in some measure on the fact that a court, not an executive officer or an agency, is doing the interpreting. One example is the constitutional avoidance canon, discussed in Chapter 3. The traditional justification for the avoidance canon is grounded in the assumption that Congress legislates in light of constitutional limitations and on the judiciary's desire to avoid, when possible, passing on the constitutionality of legislation enacted by democratically elected representatives. As Professor Trevor Morrison has argued, interpretations by the executive branch do not have the same institutional effects as those by courts, and therefore, the norm of avoidance, if it is to apply to the executive branch, must be justified independently. *See* Trevor W. Morrison, *Constitutional Avoidance in the Executive Branch*, 106 COLUM. L. REV. 1189, 1206-07 (2006).

Although much work remains to be done in this area, the thought is that many other tools of statutory interpretation may fare differently depending on which institution is using them. Consider Professor Mashaw again, this time with a chart comparing agency and judicial practice:

CANONS FOR INSTITUTIONALLY RESPONSIBLE STATUTORY
INTERPRETATION

	Agency	Court
1. Follow presidential directions unless clearly outside your authority.	+*	-*
2. Interpret to avoid raising constitutional questions.	-	+
3. Use legislative history as a primary interpretive guide.	+	-
4. Interpret to give energy and breadth to all legislative programs within your jurisdiction.	+	-
5. Engage in activist lawmaking.	+	-
6. Respect all judicial precedent.	-	+
7. Interpret to lend coherence to the overall legal order.	-	+
8. Pay particular attention to the strategic parameters of interpretive efficiency.	+	-
9. Interpret to insure hierarchical control over subordinates.	+	-
10. Pay constant attention to your contemporary political milieu.	+	-
* "+" means appropriate; "-" inappropriate. Given my discussion, many of these notations might realistically be more nuanced, "++" or "+/-," or even "+/?," for example.		

Jerry L. Mashaw, *Norms, Practices, and the Paradox of Deference: A Preliminary Inquiry into Agency Statutory Interpretation*, 57 ADMIN. L. REV. 501, 523 (2005).

4. Following up on Professor Bressman and Gluck's study on congressional staffers' knowledge of canons of statutory interpretation, Professor

Christopher Walker conducted a survey of agency rule makers, asking about their knowledge of the same canons of statutory interpretation. *See* Christopher J. Walker, *Inside Agency Statutory Interpretation*, 67 STAN. L. REV. 999 (2015). Professor Walker asked agency staff members how frequently agency drafters used the interpretive tools of these canons. His results are reported below in his Figure 2, indicating use of the interpretive principle by name, except where indicated with an asterisk, in which case the use is reported by concept. Do these results support or undermine Professor Mashaw's suppositions about agency statutory interpretation?

FIGURE 2
Agency Rule Drafters' Use of Interpretive Tools

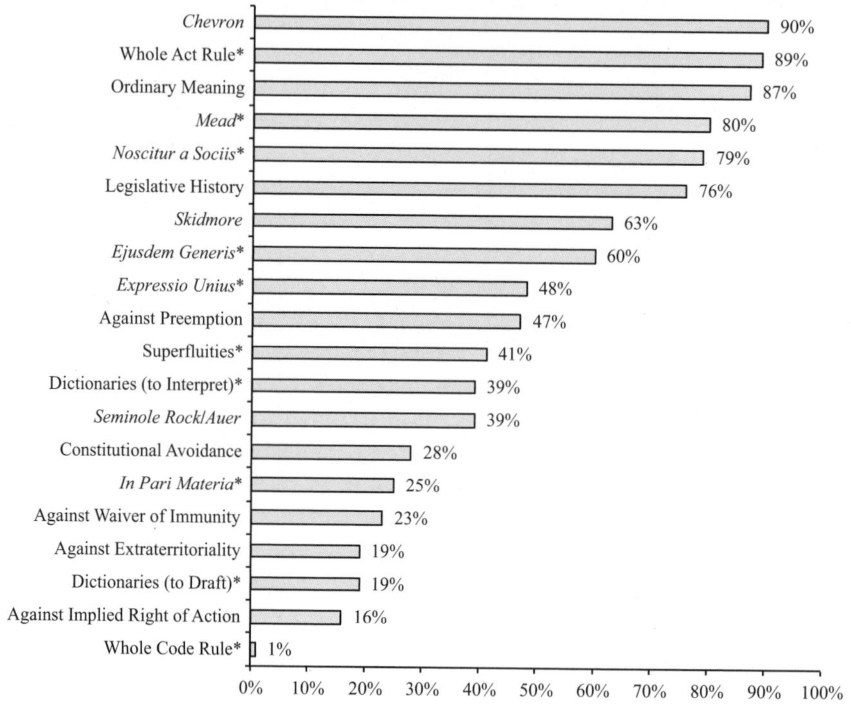

Now consider Professor Mashaw on the topic of agency reliance on legislative history.

Jerry L. Mashaw, Agency Statutory Interpretation

www.bepress.com/ils/iss3/art9 (2002)

In recent years, much controversy about statutory interpretation has centered on the evidentiary materials that should be relevant to the judicial task. Textualists are at war with purposivists; plain language advocates joust with those prepared to seek meaning in legislative history. But, whatever one thinks of judicial use of non-statutory, legislative material, Peter Strauss has argued persuasively that these materials are critical to the interpretive task of agencies. Although Professor Strauss does not put the argument precisely in "faithful agent" terms, his basic case is that agencies have a direct relationship with Congress that gives them insights into legislative purposes and meaning that are likely to be much more sure-footed than those available to courts in episodic litigation. For a faithful agent to forget this content, to in some sense ignore its institutional memory, would be to divest itself of critical resources in carrying out congressional designs.

Perhaps even more importantly, in Strauss' view, the loss of these resources would be devastating to agency defense of statutory integrity against the pressures of subsequent political coalitions. Statutes persist while presidents and congresses change. In this context the agency becomes the guardian or custodian of the legislative scheme as enacted. If we believe that agencies are meant to implement the statute, not the preferences of sitting presidents or senators or representatives, then to denude them of the use of legislative history as a defense against contemporary political importuning is to leave the statutory custodians naked before their enemies.

Hence, even if you think, as I do, that the use of legislative history has no constitutional consequences for courts, that is, that there is no constitutional basis for textualism — one might take a different view with respect to agencies. Not only might they as a prudential matter have a better chance of understanding the real political context only partially revealed by legislative history as argued to courts in litigation, they might need to wrap themselves tightly in the blanket of pre-legislative congressional utterances in order to maintain the integrity of the statutory scheme in the face of powerful political controllers intent on wrenching statutory schemes loose from their historical, contextual foundations. In some instances only the skillful deployment of legislative history will permit agencies to fulfill their constitutional role as faithful agents in the statute's implementation.

Yet, one wonders how far to push this position. As I have argued elsewhere, legislative history is almost always more specific than statutory language. The concrete and particularized problems memorialized in congressional hearings and reports usually give rise to generalized legislative responses. Legislative history is anecdotal, statutory language may approach the Delphic. The suggestion that maintaining historic meaning through the use of legislative history is the defense of integrity begs the question of what integrity means when implementing statutory terms whose breadth allows development and reorientation.

Indeed to the extent that we believe that agencies should be subject to presidential direction in shaping statutory meaning, we commit ourselves to a form of dynamic interpretation that downplays the relevance of the original context of statutory enactments. Nor are presidents the only ones who engage in post-enactment political activity relevant to statutory implementation. Agencies are subjected to legislative oversight of their implementing activity. They consult with congress continuously about proposals relevant to their jurisdictions. They appear before congressional appropriations committees who often have strong views about the directions that agency implementation should take. If it is the immersion of agencies in this continuous interaction with both executive branch offices and sub-parts of congress that provide us with constitutional security concerning the political accountability of our administrative institutions, should not all of this political context be constitutionally relevant to administrators when pondering the appropriate interpretation of their statutory mandates?

To put the matter slightly differently, one can understand the judiciary's constitutional qualms about using non-enacted legislative materials as a basis for interpretation, particularly post-enactment congressional activities not leading to subsequent legislation. If courts are to maintain their independent status as both defenders and declarers of "the law," they risk at least the appearance of illegitimacy the more they immerse themselves in the politics of legislative enactment and particularly the politics of post-enactment implementation. Therein lies, I take it, one strategic constitutional underpinning for the *Chevron* doctrine. If courts are to act as faithful agents and yet avoid immersing themselves in contemporary political processes, one way to go about it is to give discretion to those who cannot avoid it.

But these considerations suggest that whatever constitutional scruples there may be about judicial use of evidence bearing on political struggles and political context, agency use of this "political" material is a part of maintaining their democratic legitimacy. It is precisely their job as agents of past congresses and sitting politicians to synthesize the past with the present. To be a faithful agent of the political branches is to engage in forms of interpretation that satisfy Bill Eskridge's description of a "dynamic" interpretive process, as Ed Rubin argues in his contribution to this symposium.

Other structural aspects of agencies' constitutional position point in the same direction. Agencies are not passive interpreters dependent upon discrete occasions of adversary contest to present them with interpretive choices. They are, instead, active implementers who are expected to pick and choose their occasions for interpretation and the forms those interpretive utterances will take. Agency control of what might be called its "interpretative agenda" argues for an interpretative approach that engages a more wide ranging set of policy considerations and a more straightforward attention to political context than would be constitutionally appropriate for the judiciary.

Moreover, in many situations agencies have clear lawmaking authority. They are the implementers of non-self-executing legislation, laws that are not capable of application as rules of conduct until the agency gives them meaning by adopting binding interpretations. Here again the *Chevron* doctrine recognizes a convergence of interpretation and policymaking that both counsels judicial caution and establishes administrative responsibility. As a part of the Court's *Chevron* opinion put it, the combination of law making and interpretive responsibility in administrative institutions is constitutionally appropriate because it can be directed, checked and controlled by the political branches.

Notes and Questions

1. Professor Mashaw, citing Professor Peter Strauss, suggests that reliance on legislative history is more appropriate for agencies than courts. He suggests that agencies have greater knowledge of the legislative history, and a greater need to rely on it. Why?

2. Mashaw states that he does find persuasive the constitutional objection to reliance on legislative history. But he goes on to address the proper role of legislative history in agency statutory interpretation. What is his view?

3. What would Justice Scalia say in response to Professor Mashaw's suggestions about the role of legislative history in agency statutory interpretation?

4. The rule drafters who Professor Walker studied were also asked about their perceptions regarding the purposes of legislative history. Agency and congressional drafters had the greatest agreement on the following two purposes: "Explain the Purposes of the Statute" (Agency drafters: 93% v. congressional drafters: 96%) and "Indicate a Decision to Leave a Deliberate Ambiguity in the Statute" (agency drafters: 54% v. congressional drafters: 55%). The two sets of drafters had the greatest disagreements on the following three purposes: "Shape the Way Individuals or Courts Will Interpret Contested Terms" (agency drafters: 67% v. congressional drafters: 91%); "Shape the Way Agencies Will Interpret Deliberate Ambiguities (agency drafters: 65% v. congressional drafters: 94%); "Shape the Way Individuals or Courts Will Interpret Deliberate Ambiguities" (agency drafters: 62% v. congressional drafters: 93%). *See* Christopher J. Walker, *Inside Agency Statutory Interpretation*, 67 STAN. L. REV. 999, 1041 (2015) (Figure 7). What explains these points of agreement and disagreement between agency and congressional drafters on these points?

5. More generally, can you think of how interpretive theories might have different meaning when agencies rather than courts use them? Professor Michael Herz argues that "the standard critiques of purposivism in statutory interpretation have been articulated with judges, not administrators, in mind." *See* Michael Herz, *Purposivism and Institutional Competence in Statutory Interpretation*, 2009 MICH. ST. L. REV. 89, 121. If an objection to purposivism is that it leaves courts relatively free to determine statutory purpose in a particular case and therefore do not provide fair notice of legally required or prohibited conduct, can you see how the use of purposivist interpretation by an implementing agency through notice-and-comment rulemaking would not raise the same concerns? *See id.* at 102-03. If agencies interpret their organic statutes differently than courts do, whose approach should be regarded as normatively preferable? Recall that *Chevron* gives courts primacy in determining whether statutory language is ambiguous. What if courts are more likely than agencies to find clarity because of the tools that they use or the theories upon which they rely? If so, is this result wrong? And if courts are to defer to agency interpretations, are they to defer on the basis of the agency's own interpretive methods or the courts'? We will confront these questions when we return to *Chevron* in Chapter 6.

Kevin M. Stack, Purposivism in the Executive Branch: How Agencies Interpret Statutes

109 Nw. U. L. Rev. 871, (2015)

Over the last thirty years, a sophisticated understanding of judicial statutory interpretation has emerged. The debate over how courts do and should interpret statutes has narrowed to two primary interpretive approaches: textualism and purposivism. These approaches represent different theories of interpretation in the sense that they offer different accounts of the goals of interpretation, the sources of interpretation, and the relationship among those sources. Textualists take understanding the meaning of enacted text as the sole object of interpretation. In contrast, purposivists treat the text as the best evidence of statutory purposes and a source of constraint, but understand interpretation as a process of implementing statutory purposes, not merely adhering to statutory text.

At the same time that the lines of distinction between textualism and purposivism have been refined, there has been a robust debate over how courts should review an agency's interpretation of a statute that grants the agency lawmaking power. *Chevron* famously requires a reviewing court to accept an agency's construction of a statute the agency administers so long as it is permissible under the statute and reasonable, as opposed to imposing the court's own construction on the statute as it would do for statutes not administered by the agency. But to judge the permissibility of an agency's interpretation under *Chevron* requires an approach to statutory interpretation. The methodology of judicial statutory interpretation has thus become a critical question for administrative law—and how a court is to judge the permissibility of the agency's interpretation under *Chevron* has become a critical flashpoint for debates over statutory interpretation.

For all the prominence and color of these debates, they overlook much of the interpretive activity in the federal administrative state. This neglect can be classified along two primary dimensions. First, as to the sources of law, the traditional focus on judicial statutory interpretation overlooks notice-and-comment regulations, which are widely viewed as creating more legal obligations than federal statutes. Recent scholarship has begun to address the interpretive issues posed by regulations. Second, as to the identity of the interpreter, scholars have long recognized that administrative agencies make many more statutory interpretations than federal courts, and that agencies' decisions are frequently not reviewed by courts, and thus are often final. But how do agencies interpret the statutes they administer? In other words, how do agencies reach the very interpretations that courts review, whether under the *Chevron* standard or otherwise?

At a basic level, the agency's duty is not simply to implement (go make rules!), but to implement in furtherance of the principles or purposes of the statute (go make rules to "protect[] the public against unreasonable risk of accidents" or to protect consumers from "unfair, deceptive, or abusive act[s] or practice[s]." The agency's obligation to implement is thus an obligation to conform its conduct in accordance with the purposes Congress has established, and at a minimum, the intelligible principle that validates the statute constitutionally.

This duty of implementation structures the agency's reasoning in concrete ways. First and most obviously, the agency must develop an understanding of the principle or purposes the statute sets forth. That understanding will depend upon the level of specificity or generality of the statute, and the way in which the general aims of the statute interact with its more specific provisions. But having identified the statute's purposes or principles, the agency has an obligation to do something with them. Second, and in particular, it must evaluate alternatives in light of those purposes, and, third, ultimately select an alternative that, other things equal, best carries them forward. Of course, other things are rarely equal. Statutes may narrowly prescribe the means available or put some purposes in conflict with others. Directions from political supervisors can also reduce the range of options available to the agency. But the core prima facie duty a regulatory statute imposes is to carry forward its principles or purposes within the means the statute permits—a duty I refer to as "the purposive duty to implement."

But it should also be clear that this duty has important implications for the role of law for the agency. By obliging the agency to conform its action to a principle or purpose, the law does not inform the agency's decision-making only in a binary way—sorting actions into those that are permitted and those that are prohibited, but otherwise leaving the agency free to exercise its discretion. Rather, regulatory statutes impose teleological obligations. They oblige agencies to pursue ends and principles, and as a result, law continues to make demands on agencies' reasoning even within the set of actions the law does not otherwise prohibit. In short, for the agency's implementation of regulatory statutes, the law does not merely authorize and prohibit—it also guides.

Perhaps the most straightforward position on this question is that the duty to implement commits the agency to a particular structure of practical reasoning. . . . [T]he agency must develop an understanding of the purposes of the statute, evaluate alternatives in light of those purposes, and select a course of action that, other things equal, best furthers those purposes within the scope of textually permitted actions. This structure of practical reasoning is the basic structure of reasoning that purposive interpretive theories commend. In a sense, the point is that once this purposive duty to implement is understood in these terms, it clearly commits the agency to a purposive method of interpretation.

How the interpreter "attributes" purposes to a statute and its subordinate provisions constitutes "[t]he principal problem in the development of a workable technique of interpretation," and a principal focus of criticism of Hart and Sacks's theory. . . . [But] Agencies are far better positioned than courts to discern statutory purposes. To the extent statutory purpose is gleaned in part from nontextual sources, agencies have an even clearer advantage. Unlike courts, as noted in Part I, agencies have frequently "lived" the process of statutory drafting, have access to congressional overseers, and must make credible representations as to the compromises the legislation embodies.

With regard to agencies' own capacities to assess whether their actions fall within the range of permissible understandings of the powers granted by statute, several contrasting considerations are at play. On the one hand, agencies have specialized commitments, and "an agent with a specific substantive commitment may go further than its more neutral principal would approve" in implementing its specific end. By taking statutory purpose as the lodestar of interpretation, especially when situated within an institution committed to those ends, the agency may "lose sight of Congress's choice of means." Agencies may also face greater political incentives than courts to push the boundaries of Congress's choice of words to implement statutory ends. On the other hand, agencies' greater familiarity with the statutes they administer makes them more expert at determining their scope. Further, to the extent agency action is challenged in court, agencies face reversal if they do not heed how a court is likely to define what the statute permits. The process of regulatory review also frequently involves vetting agencies' construction of their statutes through an institution with distinct and more general incentives, such as with the Office of Information and Regulatory Affairs (OIRA). Exactly how one balances these countervailing considerations depends on one's perspective and the context. Surely agencies sometimes do push beyond the boundaries of their authority as judged by courts. But just as clearly, agencies also have the institutional capacities to assess the boundaries of their statutory authority and strong incentives to accurately do so.

Notes and Questions

1. The reference to Hart and Sacks is HENRY M. HART, JR. & ALBERT M. SACKS, THE LEGAL PROCESS: BASIC PROBLEMS IN THE MAKING AND APPLICATION OF LAW (William N. Eskridge, Jr. & Philip P. Frickey eds., 1994). Legal Process is an academic legal movement that was dominant during the 1950s and '60s, and that continues to be influential. One of its basic features is comparative institutional analysis; that is, an inquiry into which institution (president, agency, legislature, courts) can best carry out particular tasks. For a later elaboration, see NEIL K. KOMESAR, IMPERFECT ALTERNATIVES: CHOOSING INSTITUTIONS IN LAW, ECONOMICS AND PUBLIC POLICY (1994). An example is that courts can effectively adjudicate disputes between parties who appear before them, but are ill-equipped to allocate resources among a large number of potential recipients or targets. *See* Lon L. Fuller, *The Forms and Limits of Adjudication*, 92 HARV. L. REV. 353 (1978). (Both Hart & Sacks and Fuller were written during the 1950s, but remained in draft form until their later publication dates.) One of the principal themes of the Legal Process School was the purposive interpretation of statutes, which Hart and Sacks defined as based on the assumption that the legislature consists of "reasonable persons pursuing reasonable purposes reasonably," *supra* at 1378. Does this assumption still seem plausible today? Does the increasing partisanship in Congress (much increased, by most measures, since the 1950s and '60s) call it into question? If so, what premise about Congress would you substitute, and what interpretive principle would you derive from that premise?

2. John F. Manning, *The New Purposivism*, 2011 SUP. CT. REV. 113, argues that modern-day purposivists have moved in a textualist direction based on the relative specificity of the statute that they are interpreting. He says: "even if one believes that law is inescapably purposive and that interpreters should interpret a statute to fulfill its purpose, an interpreter must take seriously the signals that Congress sends through the level of generality reflected in its choice of words. A precise and specific command signals an implemental purpose to leave relatively little discretion to the law's implementer. An open-ended and general one signals the opposite." *Id.* at 116. Professor Manning is writing about judicial interpretation. Does the same apply to agency interpretation? Should it? Look back at the Motor Vehicle Safety Act. Can you identify the parts of that statute that have more specific or definitive language? Is the level of specificity a relative or an absolute determination? If parts of the Motor Vehicle Safety Act are more specific than others, does this mean that the others should be given a more purposive interpretation?

3. Can you make an argument for textualist interpretation by an administrative agency? Think about changes in the composition of Congress and of the role of oversight hearings.

4. How relevant is agency rule makers' own understanding of the tools of statutory interpretation upon which they rely?

2. Scientific Analysis

In our daily lives, science and technology are all around us—in cars, phones, medication, food safety—and science and technology pervade many of the issues that agencies confront when implementing their statutes. In a general sense, we can trace the role of science and technology in society and regulatory policy to the Scientific Revolution of the seventeenth century, which transformed our understanding of the natural world by first discovering some of the underlying principles that govern its behavior. That understanding has led to a historically unique proliferation of knowledge in a wide range of fields. Modern technology is based on this vast body of knowledge and is only comprehensible in those terms. This creates a serious dilemma for governance; the welfare of the citizenry now depends on information that no generalist can possibly understand. As late as the Renaissance and Reformation Eras, an intelligent government official could fully comprehend the operation of every human product in the society—its windmills and watermills, its plows and harrows, its carriages and sailing ships, its cannons and crossbows, its printed books and messenger systems. Stonemasons and stained-glass makers possessed astounding levels of skill, and these skills were subjects of study. *See* HENRY ADAMS, MONT-SAINT-MICHEL AND CHARTRES (1913); RICHARD CORDOBA, ED., CRAFT TREATISES AND HANDBOOKS: THE DISSEMINATION OF TECHNICAL KNOWLEDGE IN THE MIDDLE AGES (2013). But the basics of those techniques could be readily understood. What contemporary political official can understand, even approximately, the operation of an oil refinery or a nuclear power plant, a farm combine or a food processor, an automobile or a container ship, a computer or a cell phone?

In some sense, the administrative state can be viewed as a result of this proliferation of specialized knowledge. Instead of a general chief executive, legislature, and judiciary, it features an array of subject-specific agencies with full-time credentialed employees chosen on the basis of their expertise. But this creates three readily-identifiable sets of problems. First, how do these experts deploy accepted bodies of scientific knowledge to solve practical problems? Second, how do they communicate their conclusions to generalist political officials who do not understand the bases for their conclusions? And, third, what does everyone do when all our science, despite its sophistication, fails to provide definitive answers?

a. Two Examples of Scientific Analysis

The following NHTSA final rule shows the agency wrestling with many of these aspects of scientific analysis.

---

49 C.F.R. 552, 571, 585, 595

Federal Motor Vehicle Safety Standards; Occupant Crash Protection

[Docket No. NHTSA 00-7013; Notice 1], Friday, May 12, 2000

[65 Fed. Reg. 30680 (2000)]

AGENCY: National Highway Traffic Safety Administration (NHTSA), DOT.

ACTION: Final rule; interim final rule.

SUMMARY: This rule amends our occupant crash protection standard to require that future air bags be designed to create less risk of serious air bag-induced injuries than current air bags, particularly for small women and young children; and provide improved frontal crash protection for all occupants, by means that include advanced air bag technology. To achieve these goals, it adds a wide variety of new requirements, test procedures, and injury criteria, using an assortment of new dummies. It replaces the sled test with a rigid barrier crash test for assessing the protection of unbelted occupants.

The issuance of this rule completes the implementation of our 1996 comprehensive plan for reducing air bag risks. It is also required by the Transportation Equity Act for the 21st Century (TEA 21), which was enacted in 1998. . . .

The number of lives saved annually by air bags is continuing to increase as the percentage of air bag-equipped vehicles on the road increases. We estimate that air bags will save more than 3,200 lives annually in passenger cars and light trucks when all light vehicles on the road are equipped with driver and passenger air bags. This estimate is based on an anticipated fleet of vehicles meeting all of the requirements in this rule and on 1997 seat belt use rates (66.9 percent, according to State-reported surveys). However, if observed seat belt use rates were to reach 85 percent, the annual savings of lives due to air bags would be reduced to approximately 2,400. . . .

While air bags are saving an increasing number of

people in moderate and high speed crashes, they have occasionally caused fatalities, especially to unrestrained, out-of-position children, in relatively low speed crashes. As of April 1, 2000, NHTSA's Special Crash Investigation (SCI) program had confirmed a total of 158 fatalities induced by the deployment of an air bag. Of that total, 92 were children, 60 were drivers, and 6 were adult passengers. An additional 38 fatalities were under investigation by SCI on that date, but they had not been confirmed as having been induced by air bags.

Changes have already occurred that are reducing the number of persons killed by air bags. Some changes are behavioral. As a result of public education programs, improved labeling and media coverage, the public is much more aware of the dangers air bags pose to children in the front seat and to drivers sitting too close to the air bag and is taking steps to reduce those dangers. For example, more children are being put in the back seat. More short-statured drivers are moving back from the steering wheel.

Other changes are technological. First, as NHTSA noted in its report, "Air Bag Technology in Light Passenger Vehicles" (December 1999), the air bag outputs (i.e., pressure rise rate and the peak pressure) were reduced significantly in many MY 1998 and later motor vehicles in comparison to the earlier vehicles. Hence, the sled test option successfully expedited the depowering of existing air bags. While there are many means by which air bag aggressiveness can be reduced, reducing air bag outputs is a quick means of accomplishing this goal. The agency's analyses also show that, between MY 1997 and MY 1998, 50 to 60 percent of the vehicles

in the fleet covered by the 1997 IR lowered the output of the driver-side air bag, while about 40 to 50 percent of the vehicles in that fleet lowered the output for the passenger side. Comparison of the data for MY 1997 and MY 1998 vehicles shows that, on average, the pressure rise rate in MY 1998 vehicles decreased about 22 percent for the driver air bag and 14 percent for the passenger air bags. . . .

To address the problems that arose with the air bags installed in many motor vehicles, the agency announced a comprehensive plan in November 1996. The plan set forth an array of immediate, interim and long-term measures. The immediate and interim measures focused on behavioral changes and relatively modest technological changes. The long-term measures focused on more significant technological changes, i.e., advanced air bag technologies. The immediate steps included expanding efforts to persuade parents to place their children in the rear seat; requiring new labels with eye-catching graphics and colors and strong, clear warning messages; extending the period of time for permitting the installation of original equipment on-off switches in new vehicles which either lacked a rear seat or had a rear seat too small to permit the installation of a child restraint system; and permitting the installation of retrofit on-off switches in vehicles-in-use to protect people in at-risk groups. Because of the lead time needed to develop and install advanced air bag technologies, NHTSA announced plans to propose an interim measure to accelerate manufacturer efforts to redesign their air bags. In the long term, the agency said that it would

conduct rulemaking to require the installation of advanced air bags. . . .

To implement the interim phase of the comprehensive plan and speed the redesigning and recertifying of air bags to reduce the risks to out-of-position occupants, we amended Standard No. 208, Occupant Crash Protection, 49 CFR 571.208, to establish a temporary option under which vehicle manufacturers could certify their vehicles based on a 48 km/h (30 mph) unbelted sled test using a 50th percentile adult male dummy, instead of the 48 km/h (30 mph) unbelted rigid barrier crash test using that dummy. 62 F.R. 12960; March 19, 1997.

Available data indicate that the redesigned air bags, together with behavioral changes, such as placing more children in the back seat, have reduced the risks from air bags for the at-risk populations. Although these real-world data reflect only about two years of field experience with redesigned air bags, they preliminarily indicate that the redesigned air bags in model year (MY) 1998 and 1999 vehicles provide the same level of frontal crash protection as that provided by earlier air bags.

While the redesigned air bags in current motor vehicles have contributed to the reduction in the risk of air bag-induced injuries, they can still cause death or serious injury to unrestrained occupants. We selected the provisions adopted in this rule to ensure that future air bags provide more frontal crash protection, and reduce risk further, than either the current redesigned air bags or air bags that would have been minimally compliant with the sled test. . . .

The rule will improve protection and minimize risk by requiring new tests and injury criteria and specifying the use of an entire family of test dummies: the existing dummy representing 50th percentile adult males, and new dummies representing 5th percentile adult females, six-year old children, three-year old children, and one-year old infants. With the addition of those dummies, our occupant crash protection standard will more fully reflect the range in sizes of vehicle occupants. As noted above, most aspects of this rule are supported by most commenters on this rulemaking, including vehicle manufacturers, air bag manufacturers, insurance companies, public interest groups, academia, and the NTSB [National Transportation Safety Board]. . . .

The provisions of this rule, particularly the maximum test speed for the unbelted rigid barrier test, reflect the uncertainty associated with simultaneously achieving the twin goals of TEA 21.* This uncertainty leads us to take an approach that best assures improved air bag protection for occupants of all sizes, without compromising efforts to reduce the risks of injury to vulnerable occupants, including children and short women seated very close to air bags and out-of-position occupants. Such an approach is one that involves the least uncertainty for the occupants who have been most at risk. As long as the manufacturers improve the already substantial overall level of real world protection provided by current redesigned air bags,

the uncertainty associated with the challenge of simultaneously achieving the twin goals of TEA 21 is best resolved at this point in favor of minimizing risk. This is especially true in the early stages of the introduction of advanced air bag technologies.

In light of that uncertainty, we are selecting the lower of two proposed speeds as the maximum test speed for the unbelted rigid barrier crash test and issuing that part of this rule as an interim final rule. To resolve that uncertainty, we are planning a multi-year effort to obtain additional data. We will issue a final decision regarding the maximum test speed after giving notice and seeking public comment. If we were to increase the speed, we would provide leadtime commensurate with the extent of that increase. . . .

The agency drafted the risk minimization requirements to give vehicle manufacturers a broad choice among those advanced air bag technologies that can be used either to turn air bags off in appropriate circumstances or cause air bags to deploy in a low risk manner. Thus, the vehicle manufacturers will have the freedom to choose from a variety of available technological solutions or to innovate by developing new ones if they so desire.

We estimate that if advanced air bag technologies (suppression and low risk deployment) are 100 percent reliable, they could have eliminated 95 percent of the known air bag fatalities that have occurred to date in low speed crashes. For example, weight sensors can be installed in the passenger seat so that

the passenger air bag is turned off when children, from infants up to the typical 6-year-old, are present. The use of weight sensors for that purpose should essentially eliminate the risk of air bag-induced fatal injuries for children in that size and age range. Based on available data, it does not appear that turning air bags off for those young children would result in the loss of any benefits. There is an element of uncertainty about the level of reliability and effectiveness of the suppression for children from 0 to 6 years old and low risk deployment designs that will be actually installed in vehicles. We also note that we do not currently have a dummy suitable for assessing the effectiveness of suppression and low risk deployment for children ages 7-12. (See the section below entitled, "Future Rulemaking Plans.") Our decision concerning the maximum test speed for the unbelted rigid barrier test reflects, in part, these uncertainties and limitations.

The availability of advanced air bag technologies for minimizing risks is not just a theoretical possibility. Vehicle manufacturers are very actively working on completing their development and testing of weight sensor systems so that they will be ready for installation for the passenger air bags in their motor vehicles. Installation could begin as early as the next model year. Means of reducing risk for drivers, including dual-stage air bags coupled with sensors for driver seat belt use and driver seat position, are already being installed in some vehicles. . . .

---

* [The Transportation Equity Act for the 21st Century (TEA 21), 49 U.S.C. §30127, enacted by Congress in June 1998, requires NHTSA to issue a rule amending Federal Motor Vehicle Safety Standard No. 208, Occupant Crash Protection: "to improve occupant protection for occupants of different sizes, belted and unbelted, under Federal Motor Vehicle Safety Standard No. 208, while minimizing the risk to infants, children, and other occupants from injuries and deaths caused by air bags, by means that include advanced air bags." — EDS.]

Notes and Questions

1. Airbags have significant health and safety benefits, but they are not an unmitigated good. In particular, they can cause significant injuries and fatalities to children and small-stature adults. How does NHTSA estimate the risks from airbags to children and small-stature adults?

2. How does NHTSA address these risks? Note the role of behavioral changes and technological changes. How do they affect the standards that NHTSA adopts?

3. NHTSA states that scientific "uncertainty" plays a role. What is the uncertainty? How does it affect the standards that NHTSA adopts?

Here is another example, NHTSA's current rule regarding bumper standards.

National Highway Traffic Safety Administration, Part 581 — Bumper Standard

49 C.F.R. Ch. V (10-1-11 Edition)

AUTHORITY: 49 U.S.C. 32502; 322, 30111, 30115, 30117 and 30166; delegation of authority at 49 CFR 1.50.
SOURCE: 42 FR 24059, May 12, 1977, unless otherwise noted.

---

§581.1 Scope.

This standard establishes requirements for the impact resistance of vehicles in low speed front and rear collisions.

§581.2 Purpose.

The purpose of this standard is to reduce physical damage to the front and rear ends of a passenger motor vehicle from low speed collisions.

§581.3 Application.

This standard applies to passenger motor vehicles other than multipurpose passenger vehicles and low-speed vehicles as defined in 49 CFR part 571.3(b).
. . .

§581.5 Requirements.

(a) Each vehicle shall meet the damage criteria of §§581.5(c)(1) through 581.5(c)(9) when impacted by a pendulum-type test device in accordance with the procedures of §581.7(b), under the conditions of §581.6, at an impact speed of 1.5 m.p.h., and when impacted by a pendulum-type test device in accordance with the procedures of §581.7(a) at 2.5 m.p.h., followed by an impact into a fixed collision barrier that is perpendicular to the line of travel of the vehicle, while traveling longitudinally forward, then longitudinally rearward, under the conditions of §581.6, at 2.5 m.p.h.
. . .

(c) *Protective criteria.*
(1) Each lamp or reflective device except license plate lamps shall be free of cracks and shall comply with applicable visibility requirements of S5.3.1.1 of Standard No. 108 (§571.108 of this chapter). The aim of each headlamp installed on the vehicle shall be adjustable to within the beam aim inspection limits specified in Table 1 of SAE Recommended Practice J599 AUG-97, measured with the aiming method appropriate for that headlamp.
(2) The vehicle's hood, trunk, and doors shall operate in the normal manner.
(3) The vehicle's fuel and cooling systems shall have no leaks or constricted fluid passages and all sealing devices and caps shall operate in the normal manner.
(4) The vehicle's exhaust system shall have no leaks or constrictions.
(5) The vehicle's propulsion, suspension, steering, and braking systems shall remain in adjustment and shall operate in the normal manner.
(6) A pressure vessel used to absorb impact energy in an exterior protection system by the accumulation of

gas pressure or hydraulic pressure shall not suffer loss of gas or fluid accompanied by separation of fragments from the vessel.

(7) The vehicle shall not touch the test device, except on the impact ridge shown in Figures 1 and 2, with a force that exceeds 2000 pounds on the combined surfaces of Planes A and B of the test device.

(8) The exterior surfaces shall have no separations of surface materials, paint, polymeric coatings, or other covering materials from the surface to which they are bonded, and no permanent deviations from their original contours 30 minutes after completion of each pendulum and barrier impact, except where such damage occurs to the bumper face bar and the components and associated fasteners that directly attach the bumper face bar to the chassis frame.

(9) Except as provided in §581.5(c)(8), there shall be no breakage or release of fasteners or joints.

. . .

§581.6 Conditions.

The vehicle shall meet the requirements of §581.5 under the following conditions.

(a) *General.* (1) The vehicle is at unloaded vehicle weight.

(2) The front wheels are in the straight ahead position.

(3) Tires are inflated to the vehicle

manufacturer's recommended pressure for the specified loading condition.

(4) Brakes are disengaged and the transmission is in neutral.

(5) Trailer hitches, license plate brackets, and headlamp washers are removed from the vehicle. Running lights, fog lamps, and equipment mounted on the bumper face bar are removed from the vehicle if they are optional equipment.

(b) *Pendulum test conditions.* The following conditions apply to the pendulum test procedures of §581.7 (a) and (b).

(1) The test device consists of a block with one side contoured as specified in Figure 1 and Figure 2 with the impact ridge made of A1S1 4130 steel hardened to 34 Rockwell "C." The impact ridge and the surfaces in Planes A and B of the test device are finished with a surface roughness of 32 as specified by SAE Recommended Practice J449A, June 1963. Prom the point of release of the device until the onset of rebound, the pendulum suspension system holds Plane A vertical, with the arc described by any point on the impact line lying in a vertical plane (for §581.7(a), longitudinal; for §581.7(b), at an angle of 30° to a vertical longitudinal

plane) and having a constant radius of not less than 11 feet.

(2) With Plane A vertical, the impact line shown in Figures 1 and 2 is horizontal at the same height as the test device's center of percussion.

(3) The effective impacting mass of the test device is equal to the mass of the tested vehicle.

(4) When impacted by the test device, the vehicle is at rest on a level rigid concrete surface.

(c) *Barrier test condition.* At the onset of a barrier impact, the vehicle's engine is operating at idling speed in accordance with the manufacturer's specifications. Vehicle systems that are not necessary to the movement of the vehicle are not operating during impact.

. . .

§581.7 Test procedures.

(a) *Longitudinal impact test procedures.* (1) Impact the vehicle's front surface and its rear surface two times each with the impact line at any height from 16 to 20 inches, inclusive, in accordance with the following procedure.

(2) For impacts at a height of 20 inches, place the test device shown in Figure 1 so that Plane A is vertical and the impact line is horizontal at the specified height.

(3) For impacts at a height between 20 inches and 16 inches, place the test device shown in Figure 2 so that

Plane A is vertical and the impact line is horizontal at a height within the range.

(4) For each impact, position the test device so that the impact line is at least 2 inches apart in vertical direction from its position in any prior impact, unless the midpoint of the impact line with respect to the vehicle is to be more than 12 inches apart laterally from its position in any prior impact.

(5) For each impact, align the vehicle so that it touches, but does not move, the test device, with the vehicle's longitudinal centerline perpendicular to the plane that includes Plane A of the test device and with the test device inboard of the vehicle corner test positions specified in § 581.7(b).

(6) Move the test device away from the vehicle, then release it to impact the vehicle.

(7) Perform the impacts at intervals of not less than 30 minutes.

(b) *Corner impact test procedure.*
(1) Impact a front corner and a rear corner of the vehicle once each with the impact line at a height of 20 inches and impact the other front corner and the other rear corner once each with the impact line at any height from 16 to 20 inches, inclusive, in accordance with the following procedure.

(2) For an impact at a height of 20 inches, place the test device shown in Figure 1 so that Plane A is vertical and the impact line is horizontal at the specified height.

(3) For an impact at a height between 16 inches and 20 inches, place the test device shown in Figure 2 so that Plane A is vertical and the impact line is horizontal at a height within the range.

(4) Align the vehicle so that a vehicle corner touches, but does not move, the lateral center of the test device with Plane A of the test device forming an angle of 60 degrees with a vertical longitudinal plane.

(5) Move the test device away from the vehicle, then release it to impact the vehicle.

(6) Perform the impact at intervals of not less than 30 minutes.

Notes and Questions

1. Did you read every word of the Bumper Standard, or did your eye skip down the page? If the latter, it is because you are not an automobile engineer. It is hard to read something unless it is meaningful to you, and technical standards of this nature are only meaningful to those with training in the field. That is why NHTSA hires people with the relevant engineering credentials. They—and the engineers at the regulated companies—read this sort of material with careful attention. Should the NHTSA administrator have such training? The first two, William Haddon and Douglas Toms, did, but that has not been the pattern since then.

2. Should the Secretary of Transportation have expertise in automotive safety? In addition to this subject, NHTSA also administers fuel economy standards, and the Department of Transportation also regulates trucks, railroads, airplanes, ships, pipelines, highways, and various other matters. Do you think that the regulations regarding those items are less technical than the ones you just read? Is there anyone who has the requisite level of expertise in all these fields? How then should the Secretary evaluate recommendations from expert staff on these matters?

3. Should the Secretary of Transportation have executive skills rather than expertise in any related field, given the broad scope of the Department's coverage? Here is an excerpt of the Secretary's biography, taken from the NHTSA website when this edition of the coursebook was written:

> Secretary Elaine L. Chao is currently the U.S. Secretary of Transportation. This is her second cabinet position. She served as U.S. Secretary of Labor from 2001-January 2009. Secretary Chao comes to the U.S. Department of Transportation with extensive experience in the transportation sector. Early in her career, she specialized in transportation financing in the private sector. Prior to the Department of Labor, Secretary Chao was President and Chief Executive Officer of United Way of America, where she restored public trust and confidence in one of America's premier institutions of private charitable giving, after it had been tarnished by financial mismanagement and abuse. Secretary Chao also served as Director of the Peace Corps, where she established the first programs in the Baltic nations and the newly independent states of the former Soviet Union.

The biography also gives the names of Secretary Chao's parents, but it does not mention that she is married to Mitch McConnell, U.S. Senator from Kentucky and Majority Leader of the Senate at the time of her appointment.

4. In Chrysler Corp. v. DOT, 472 F.2d 659 (6th Cir. 1972), reprinted in Chapter 4, the reviewing court struck down one version of NHTSA's passive restraint regulation (Standard 208) because it relied on the use of crash test dummies that were not precisely engineered, and thus failed the test for objectivity established by the statute, see the Motor Vehicle Safety Act § 102 (standards must provide "objective criteria"). The Court seemed to be using a definition of "objective" derived from natural science, which is that "tests . . . must be capable of producing identical results when test conditions are exactly duplicated." Is that the correct legal conclusion; must a regulatory standard meet the test for scientific validity to be considered "objective"? Does the Bumper Standard appear to meet it?

b. The Use of Science

Science in regulatory policy often does not involve just one scientific discipline but many. To develop a rule that depends on scientific or technical knowledge, agency scientists must coordinate with each other as well as agency economists, lawyers, and policymakers. Consider the following, which discusses EPA and the use of science.

Thomas O. McGarity, The Internal Structure of EPA Rulemaking

54 L. & Contemp. Prob. 57, 60-65 (1991)

EPA's regulations must protect many classes of beneficiaries from a multitude of harms resulting from an enormous variety of sources ranging from industrial effluent to household garbage. The extraordinarily ambitious statutes that Congress has written for EPA require the application of a wide variety of expertise. For example, to regulate photochemical oxidants under the Clean Air Act, EPA must draw upon expertise in toxicology, epidemiology, and the etiology of lung diseases to establish the national primary ambient air quality standards; expertise in atmospheric chemistry to understand the complex relationships between precursor pollutants (reactive hydrocarbons and oxides of nitrogen) and the photochemical oxidants that cause smog; expertise in air pollution dispersion modeling to understand the extent to which individual sources contribute to the overall problem; expertise in stationary source technology to understand what individual sources can do to limit direct and fugitive emissions into the atmosphere; expertise in mobile source technology to understand what manufacturers can do to limit emissions from automobiles, trucks, trains and airplanes; expertise in transportation and urban planning to understand how modifying driving patterns and urban mass transportation can reduce mobile source emissions. . . .

No individual within EPA has genuine expertise in all of the required areas. . . .

The expertise upon which the rulemaking edifice rests is thus an "institutional expertise" that transcends the knowledge and experience of any individual person or office within the agency. The success of a rulemaking initiative depends to a substantial degree upon the capacity of the institution to integrate the contributions of widely varying professional perspectives into a single coherent product. . . .

Health scientists are trained to relate environmental exposures to disease endpoints in sensitive populations. Materials scientists are interested in how pollutants interact with metals and other materials to cause damage. Ecologists are trained to identify complex and subtle changes in interactingecological systems that result from externally induced stimuli like pollutants. The primary professional concern of all three groups is protecting health and the environment. These groups are less concerned with how exposures can be reduced (and how much that will cost) than with what will happen if they are not reduced or if they increase.

Environmental engineers, on the other hand, are trained to design and implement pollution control technologies. They focus almost exclusively on how pollutants can be eliminated from waste streams and then managed. For them a pound of pollutant removed is a benefit, irrespective of the damage that it would have caused had it remained in the waste stream. Although the engineers are cost-conscious, they are not especially concerned that the cost of a pollution reduction technology is exceeded by its monetized benefits. Instead, they prefer to search for the "knee of the cost curve"—the point at which the cost per pound of pollutant removed begins to rise at a very rapid rate—in deciding whether costs are excessive. . . .

Sidney Shapiro, Elizabeth Fisher & Wendy Wagner, The Enlightenment of Administrative Law: Looking Inside the Agency for Legitimacy

47 Wake Forest L. Rev. 463, 492-500 (2015)

A. THE NAAQS PROCESS

Section 109 of the Clean Air Act requires the EPA to review, at five-year intervals, the standards for six criteria or general pollutants that the EPA identifies under Section 108 of the Act. These NAAQS must be set at a level "requisite to protect the public health" with "an adequate margin of safety." While the Supreme Court interprets the statute as allowing the EPA to consider only scientific, not economic, factors in setting the primary health standards for these criteria pollutants, there is still a great deal of room for technical maneuvering within scientifically plausible options. Indeed, the remaining agency discretion is so great that a majority in one D.C. Circuit judgment concluded that this section of the Act violated the nondelegation doctrine of the Constitution.

Given their national role in specifying the lowest acceptable air quality for any region in the United States, the selection of the NAAQS has significant regulatory consequences. Elaborate regulatory permits and state implementation plans ensure that these specific NAAQS are met. Billions of dollars, both in health protection and compliance costs, hinge on adjustments as small as even one-thousandth of a part per million for the standard for any given criteria pollutant. Presidential elections also can turn on, or at least be affected by, an administration's decision to make NAAQS more stringent or not.

1. The Old Way

Until a recent change of direction, the EPA's approach to setting the NAAQS largely followed the rational-instrumental paradigm. From the 1980s to mid-2005, the EPA produced assessments that grew increasingly voluminous and were considered relatively impenetrable to anyone other than air quality experts, and even these experts were challenged by the document. Producing these reports was so unwieldy that the EPA itself could not complete them in a five-year time frame as required by statute and was perpetually at risk of being in contempt of court. The agency also found itself under constant attack for the judgments reached in its decisions.

2. The New Way

This all changed in 2006 when the EPA redesigned the NAAQS process. The current approach involves five separate analytical steps and products.

a. The Planning Report

The first step sets the stage for the integration of scientists, stakeholders, public health advocates, and professional agency staff by convening a "kick-off" workshop that is followed by a staff-authored report that articulates the overarching policy questions that will guide the process. The report is reviewed by the "Clean Air Science Advisory Committee" ("CASAC"), a statutorily required standing committee of top scientists chartered under the Federal Advisory Committee Act ("FACA"), and by the public before it is final.

The resulting final planning report is thus a professional, staff-authored document that has been reviewed iteratively by the public and external scientists. This planning report, moreover, is integral to enhancing transparency of the NAAQS review process. By framing the relevant science-policy questions, the planning report focuses the EPA's subsequent NAAQS review, which stretches over a four-year process.

b. Integrated Scientific Assessment Report

At the next step of the NAAQS review process, the EPA compiles an integrated scientific assessment ("ISA") that reviews all of the scientific evidence. In stark contrast to the EPA's earlier version of this assessment in previous NAAQS processes, the new and improved ISA is more concise and focuses the assessment on the specific questions framed in the planning report. More detailed information is reserved for annexes, which can sometimes be longer than the body of the report itself.

The document is prepared in a way that is roughly equivalent to a large team-authored scientific review paper. Academics generally are contracted to draft the individual chapters of the ISA, with multiple points of review (at least three) from intra-agency reviewers, CASAC, and the public before the ISA is considered final. Like other NAAQS documents, the ISA includes a detailed list of the EPA executive staff, authors, contributors, and peer reviewers. Authors and peer reviewers outside the agency are also listed by name and affiliation in the front matter. Staff members who disagree with the scientific analysis may remove their names. At the same time, those who agree are held accountable for the contents.

c. Risk/Exposure Assessment Report

Based on the analysis of the scientific evidence in the ISA, the EPA staff then prepares a separate risk assessment report that applies this evidence to predict the effects of alternate standards on public health. The goal at this stage is to employ multiple models to produce quantitative risk estimates, accompanied by expressions of the underlying uncertainties and variability for various endpoints, such as the impacts of a pollutant on susceptible populations and ecosystems. The risk assessment process itself begins with a planning/scoping stage, which again involves CASAC review and public comment, followed by two more periods of intra-agency, CASAC, and public comment on the draft risk assessment reports.

d. Policy Assessment Report

The last document in the process is a policy assessment that "bridges" these more science-intensive (ISA and risk assessment) reports with the policy questions at hand. In summarizing the evidence in a way that relates to the overarching policy question, the report offers alternative health protection scenarios and standards, accompanied by discussions of unknowns and uncertainties. The policy analysis also identifies questions for further research. The policy assessment is, in and of itself, an extensive document (in the EPA's review of the particulate matter standard, the policy assessment was over 450 pages in length, including appendices), but the discussion is written for laypersons who do not have an extensive background in the relevant science.

The policy assessment is reviewed by internal EPA staff and by CASAC, sometimes several times, to ensure that important scientific information is not lost in translation. It is worth noting that even at this late stage, CASAC review and comment is rigorous and extensive. For example, the second CASAC review of the EPA's Policy Assessment for the Review of the Particulate Matter ("PM") NAAQS consisted of over seventy pages of single-spaced comments.

e. The Proposed and Final Rulemaking Process

Based on this wealth of deliberative science-policy work, the EPA management identifies a standard and prepares a proposed rule that is cleared through the Office of Management and Budget ("OMB") and then published in the Federal Register. At this point, the outside-in model kicks in. Stakeholders appreciate that if they wish to preserve their challenges for judicial review, they must submit comments that raise every issue of concern. After notice and comment and further inter-governmental deliberations, the EPA promulgates a final rule.

---

c. Assessing Risk

As you have seen, many regulatory statutes grant agencies authority to address risks to human health and safety, to the environment, to animal populations, and more. But what exactly constitutes a risk? Professor Kip Viscusi defines risk as follows:

> It is helpful to distinguish among risk, uncertainty, and ignorance. In the situation of risk, we know that states of the world that may prevail (a flipped coin will show one or two faces) and the precise probability of each state (heads and tails are equally likely). In the case of uncertainty, we may not even be able to define what states of the world are possible.
>
> The real world is rife with uncertainty. Even if we can make direct environmental measurements (e.g., for atmospheric pollution), interpretation of our observations may be problematic. Does an unusually high temperature this year indicate an upward trend, or does it represent random variation around an unchanging mean?
>
> As our technological capabilities grow and economic activity imposes further strains on the environment, we will increasingly find ourselves in situations of ignorance. As we enter apparently benign but uncharted territory, we cannot be confident that if there were threats, we would detect them. Many individual decisions, as well as

scientific risk analyses, are afflicted by ignorance. California studies of transportation safety in the event of an earthquake, for example, failed to capture the full range of effects that may have led to the highway damage experienced in October 1989. Under ignorance, the potential for bad society decisions is particularly great. Conceivably, for example, environmental releases of genetically engineered organisms might alter the current ecological balance in ways we cannot anticipate.

KIP VISCUSI, FATAL TRADEOFFS 153-54 (1992).

One important aspect of how agencies use science is how they respond to uncertainty. NHTSA helps to demonstrate the point in concrete, not overly technical, terms. In its rule rescinding passive restraints, NHTSA stated that "the changes in car manufacturers' plans has left the agency without any factual basis for reliably predicting the likely usage increases due to detachable automatic seat belts, or for even predicting the likelihood of any increase at all." 46 Fed. Reg. 53422. This is a claim of factual uncertainty, analogous to scientific uncertainty.

In general, how should an agency respond in the face of scientific uncertainty? This question is the subject of intense academic debate. Many agencies actually believe it supports precautionary action. Consider the following from Professor Viscusi:

> Government efforts aimed at developing risk information are not guided by the formal statistical properties of the risk but rather by administrative procedures incorporating various types of "conservatism." Although risk assessment biases may operate in both directions, most approved procedures tend to overstate the actual risk. In regulated toxic substances, for example, results from the most sensitive animal species are often used, and government agencies such as the EPA routinely focus on the upper end of the 95 confidence interval as the risk level rather than use the mean of the distribution. A series of such conservative assumptions (e.g., on exposure by focusing on the most sensitive humans) can overstate the mean probability of an unfavorable outcome by several orders of magnitude.

KIP VISCUSI, FATAL TRADEOFFS, 156-57.

When lives are at stake, the impulse in the face of scientific uncertainty often is to follow a conservative approach (which tends to justify more regulation, not less). But where do we stop? Would you ban cell phones because of the risk that they cause brain tumors as a result of radiation emitted to the brain? There is scientific uncertainty on the causal link. If not, would you mandate potentially life-saving devices (e.g., an earpiece that puts distance between the phone and the brain) in excess of caution? In other contexts, would you withhold potentially life-saving precautions (e.g., drugs or vaccines) until the science can demonstrate their safety?

Agencies are inconsistent in their responses to scientific uncertainty. As a practical matter, agencies often respond to scientific uncertainty by offering ranges of risk reduction. This is how NHTSA dealt with factual uncertainty in its final rule rescinding passive restraints requirements. After determining that the Rabbit/Chevette study was not reliable because of the demographics of the subjects and type of automatic restraints in their cars, the agency considered two different methods for using that study to construct a range of possible increases in belt usage as a result of the installation of automatic seatbelts (15-60%). In the end, it concluded that usage would likely be at the low end of the range.

The task of many regulatory agencies can be described as transforming uncertainty into risk and then managing that risk. Consider NHTSA and EPA, the two agencies whose use of expertise is described above. When NHTSA was first organized, the true causes of traffic injuries were not known; that is, they were uncertain. NHTSA was charged with determining those causes—was it driver error, the internal design of the car, the strength of the bumpers, etc.? The agency was commanded to carry out research to determine these causes, thus transforming the uncertainty into risk, and to then adopt measures to reduce the risk. EPA was charged with carrying out the same process with respect to air pollution—to find out where was it coming from, and then what might be done to abate it.

In other words, agencies charged with protecting citizens generally follow a two-step process. They first acquire and process information that will transform uncertainty into risk. This step is known as "risk assessment." They then determine how to respond to such risk. This step is known as "risk management." Professors Celia Campbell-Mohn and John Applegate provide a succinct account of the difference between risk assessment and risk management in the toxic substances context:

> Risk assessment is a process for calculating the probability and magnitude of identified adverse effects, most commonly excess deaths from cancer caused by exposure to a chemical or radiological agent. The process is used to identify activities that require regulatory attention, to select the nature and stringency of an appropriate regulatory response, and to choose among the many potential objects of regulators' efforts. Risk assessment aims to "organize and express what can be stated about risks that are not subject to direct observation and measurement" based on an analysis of data concerning toxicity and exposure.
>
> A 1983 NAS [National Academy of Sciences] report, *Risk Assessment in the Federal Government: Managing the Process* (the "Red Book") set out the general methodology for human-health-related risk assessment. . . .
>
> The Red Book distinguished this process from *risk management*, the substantive decision to take or withhold regulatory action. The latter, unlike risk assessment, explicitly involves political, social, and economic policy questions, such as the acceptable level of risk and the appropriate regulatory response. As a rigid dichotomy, of course, this split is an unrealistic view of government action and of science. Political and judgmental factors pervade the entire assessment function. Operating in a world of uncertainty, incomplete data, and genuine differences between scientists in interpretation of and inferences from the available data, risk assessors must make many assumptions and estimates. The choice, for example, among conservative, risk-preferring, or middle-ground assumptions is clearly a policy question. Rather than paper over the role of policy in risk assessment, the relationship between risk assessment and risk management should be acknowledged.

Celia Campbell-Mohn & John S. Applegate, *Learning from NEPA: Guidelines for Responsible Risk Legislation*, 23 HARV. ENVTL. L. REV. 93, 95-98 (1999).

Note that the distinction between scientific questions and policy questions separates risk assessment from risk management. There are some questions that science can answer and some questions that science cannot.

A decision how or whether to regulate cannot turn solely on the scientific "facts." It involves "political, social, and economic policy questions, such as the acceptable level of risk and the appropriate regulatory response." But, as Professors Campbell-Mohn and Applegate acknowledge, judgment calls pervade the principal methodologies for performing risk assessment — that is, for obtaining the scientific "facts." The next excerpt outlines those methodologies and shows some of the junctures where the distinction between science and policy blurs.

David Ropeik & George Gray, Risk!

8-13 (2002)

As we try to judge what's risky and what's not, we look to science for answers. But even with all the facts that science can provide, much uncertainty remains, for a number of reasons. First, the sciences by which risk is investigated-toxicology, epidemiology, and statistical analysis are inherently imprecise. Second, there are a lot of risk questions science simply hasn't asked yet. New risks like using a cell phone while driving or eating genetically modified food haven't been studied nearly enough for us to have all the answers. And third, even for risks that have been studied, the facts as we know them are constantly changing as scientific answers to one set of questions reveal more questions. . . .

TOXICOLOGY

Most simply described, toxicology is the study of poisons: But because of that very definition, you can understand why toxicologists usually can't test the agent they're investigating on human subjects. So animals are used as surrogates. But toxicologists admit that they can't say for sure what a compound will do in humans based on evidence of what it does in animals. As one toxicologist says, "With stuff that might kill people, animal testing, as imprecise as it is, is the best we can do. But despite what you might think of your boss or some people you don't like, humans aren't rats." Toxicologists don't know which lab animal species serve as the best indicators of what would happen in people, nor do they know which species are better indicators for which kinds of hazards. So extrapolating from lab animals to humans is imprecise. As one example, cyclamate, an artificial sweetener, causes one type of liver tumor in only one species of rat, and then only in males, and doesn't cause it in any other test animals. Yet test data from the experiments on those rats caused the food additive to be banned for human consumption.

Another imprecision from toxicology arises because testing of lab animals often involves subjecting the animals to massive doses of an agent. In testing for carcinogenicity, animals routinely get doses, each day, far greater than you would be exposed to in your entire lifetime. Toxicologists call this dose the MTD, for "maximum tolerated dose." They use this technique when testing for cancer in order to maximize the chance that they'll find any effect that might occur and that might not show up from a milder dose.

Using these [maximum tolerated doses], toxicologists presume that if the substance they're testing causes an effect at a high dose, it might cause the same effect at a lower dose. This approach seems like a rational way to deal with potentially dangerous chemicals and other agents; if high doses cause harm, assume that low doses might too. But sometimes the size of the dose is what's really causing the harm. Think of aspirin, for example. One or two aspirin are fine. Too many will kill you. The standard toxicological approach of subjecting lab animals to high doses of a test compound can reveal subtle effects, but it can also produce misleading results.

A further imprecision arises in toxicology because in vivo tests in living lab animals, or in vitro tests of cells in a lab dish or beaker, isolate and test just one compound at a time. That's a smart way to find out with precision whether that particular agent is hazardous. But in the real world we're exposed to a stew of agents, and the mix can lead to different outcomes than exposure to any individual component. (Radon and smoking, for instance, apparently work synergistically and increase the risk of lung cancer more than the sum of one risk plus the other risk.) In addition, while the environment in the lab is stable and uniform, the real world is full of variables such as our environment, our health, our food, our emotional states, and our genetic makeup from one generation to the next and from one person to the next. These factors and many others affect how we react to a compound or circumstance.

In short, while toxicology can tell us a lot about the biological hazard of a particular chemical or element or compound, it can't tell us with absolute accuracy just what the substance being tested—at high doses to another species in a controlled lab—will do at lower doses to humans in the complicated real world.

EPIDEMIOLOGY

When we can't test a substance or hazard on people but we want to know whether it might be a threat to public health, we look around for circumstances in which people might already have been exposed. Studying what has happened, or is currently happening, to real populations in the real world, and trying to make sense of which hazards and exposures might be associated with which consequences, is the essence of epidemiology.

Like toxicologists, epidemiologists readily acknowledge that their science is imprecise. Epidemiology can usually provide only associations, not absolute proof, that some particular exposure may be what's causing some particular consequence. For example, in one kind of study epidemiologists investigate a specific small group of people who get sick. The book and movie *A Civil Action*, for instance, made famous the polluted drinking water in Woburn, Massachusetts.

A higher-than-expected number of cases of childhood leukemia showed up in just a few years in a small neighborhood. Epidemiologists investigated to find out what sources of exposure to potential hazards the neighbors shared.

They discovered that one thing the neighbors had in common was that those who drank from a certain water supply had a higher rate of illness. Therefore, something about the water was the likely cause of the leukemia. They tested the water for chemicals suspected to cause that illness and estimated how much of the water people drank, for how long, and how polluted it was when people drank it. In the end, a peer-reviewed epidemiological study showed an association between how much of the well water pregnant mothers drank and the frequency of childhood leukemia in their offspring. The more they drank, the more likely it was that their children developed leukemia.

But that's not proof. Perhaps a couple of the neighbors were exposed to something else the researchers didn't ask about. Maybe the researchers never detected something else in the well water. These other factors are known as "confounders," hidden clues that can muddy the epidemiological waters and lead to an inaccurate assumption that A caused B. Hidden confounders can never be completely ruled out.

This isn't to suggest that the findings of epidemiology are weak or of little use in judging risks. In good epidemiological studies, researchers give the research subjects in-depth questionnaires about their health, their lifestyle, their diet, their social and economic characteristics, even their residential history (where they have lived and when), trying to rule out all confounders. They compare a group of people suffering some kind of health problem, like those families in Woburn, with other "control" groups, populations of similar size and socioeconomic status somewhere else, who presumably were not exposed to the same things. For the bigger long-term population studies, epidemiologists carry out multiple research programs in different places at different times to see if their results agree. With such techniques, epidemiologists can rule out every other possibility they can think of. They can become more and more certain of the associations they find.

But, like toxicologists, they can rarely be completely sure.

STATISTICAL ANALYSIS

In addition to the findings of toxicology and epidemiology, risk analysts also look for their clues among large sets of statistics. Those data collections are compilations of real-world information, on either morbidity (nonfatal health problems) or mortality (deaths). These databases can offer rich details, like how many people were injured or killed in motor vehicle accidents, categorized by speed, vehicle size, whether the victim was male, female, old, young, wearing a seat belt or not, and so on. There are data sets on hundreds of risks that offer information on the age, gender, and race of the affected population and the circumstances that led to the death or illness, such as the number of food poisoning cases connected with restaurants, or the number of workers murdered on the job. Other data collections provide risk analysts with information about hazardous materials emissions, local water or air pollution levels, or the presence of harmful chemicals in our blood or the food we eat. These details all offer insights about the hazard, exposure, consequence, and probability of various risks.

But the numbers in these data collections usually suffer from some imprecision. Not everybody who suffers food poisoning after dining at a restaurant, for example, actually goes to a doctor to report his illness. Not every police officer fills out every last detail on every accident report. Not every factory keeps accurate, or honest, records of its emissions. And not every government information collection system gathers the information and enters it into its database accurately.

Numbers are also subject to interpretation. Here's an example. According to national motor vehicle crash statistics, drivers 75 years old or over are involved in four times as many fatal crashes as the average of all other age groups. But does that mean that elderly drivers are killing other people, or just that because of frail health they're more likely to die themselves whenever they're in a crash? You can't tell by that statistic. The numbers don't tell you everything you need to know. As Mark Twain said, "There are three kinds of lies—lies, damned lies, and statistics."

Finally, no matter how precise and narrow statistical categories are, they lump everybody in that category together. For example, federal motor vehicle crash statistics group data by age, gender, the day and time of crashes, and the kind of vehicle involved. So you can determine how many 15- to 24-year-old males were involved in crashes on Sundays at 5 P.M. in pickup trucks. As narrow as that seems, that's still a large group of people and not everyone in it is the same. Individuals within that group have all sorts of differences in health, lifestyle, education, genetics, body size and shape, and on and on.

Risk statistics are generalities, and by definition cannot specifically answer the question we all want answered: "What is the risk to *me*?" . . . As we've stated, because you are unique none of those numbers will accurately and precisely answer your question. Risk numbers can be only a general guide. They give you a sense of which risks are bigger and which ones are smaller, and sometimes they can tell you which risks are higher or lower for the demographic groups to which you belong. But even risk numbers that define the categories as narrowly as possible still can't calculate the risk for each unique individual.

In sum, the sciences that supply the facts about risk, while growing more and more powerful, are still imprecise. They can provide us with valuable insights. But their results are uncertain and open to interpretation. There are very few unequivocal answers when it comes to defining and quantifying the risks we face. That's why in this guide our approach is to offer information in ranges: the *range* of exposures, the *range* of consequences, and so forth. . . .

Notes and Questions

1. No methodology for evaluating risk answers every question. For example, any test that does not rely on human subjects to estimate risk about human populations is inherently imprecise. What are the sources of imprecision in the various methodologies?

Consider that question in the context of estimating low-dose exposure to radiation, a question that authorities regulating nuclear energy must consider. The effects of large radiation doses are well established from the victims of severe incidents, such as the Life Span Studies of the 120,321 survivors of the Hiroshima and Nagasaki atomic bombs. These high-dosage survival studies show that roughly half the individuals who are exposed to instantaneous doses of radiation at a high level (300 rem, "rem" being the unit of measurement for the biological effects of radiation in humans) will die within a few weeks with minimal medical treatment, and roughly half of the population exposed to extremely high levels of radiation (450 rem) will die within a few weeks even with medical treatment. Though there is no threshold below which health risks are entirely absent, there are few epidemiological studies of relatively small radiation doses (a single dose of 10 rem, or sustained dosage of 1 to 5 rem a year). A National Cancer Institute study compares cancer rates in counties in the United States that housed nuclear facilities and those that do not, from 1950 to 1984, finding no greater incidence of cancer in the counties that housed the nuclear facilities. Is the National Cancer Institute study relevant to estimating the risk of low-dose exposure? Are the Life Span Studies? For a classic articulation of how these and other studies are evaluated, see V. Mubayi et al., *Cost-Benefit Considerations in Regulatory Analysis*, NUREG/CR-6349, 2-1 to 2-9 (1995).

2. Agencies rely on scientific analyses despite their imprecision. How does an agency determine whether a particular mouse study (or a Rabbit study) is reliable? The answer is: the agency makes a judgment call based on its estimation of the relevant similarities and differences of mice and men or owners of Rabbits and other cars with respect to the particular risk at issue. Mice may have biological systems that are sufficiently similar for one purpose, say the effect of a drug on the nervous system, but not for others, say the effect on the endocrine system. *See* Junhee Seok, H. Shaw Warren, et al., *Genomic Responses in Mouse Models Poorly Mimic Human Inflammatory Diseases*, Proceedings of the National Academy of Sciences (Early Edition) (Feb. 11, 2013).

3. Where do crash-test-dummy studies, like the ones that NHTSA uses, fit among the methodologies that Ropeik and Gray describe? What are the limits of such simulations? You might imagine that computers often perform simulations without the need to crash an actual car or airplane or other craft.

4. Assuming agencies can acquire information about risk, they must process such information when using it to make a decision. Let's say a mouse study predicted a small risk of non-fatal side effects in humans from a particular drug. Is this a significant risk or a trivial risk? Would more information help? Suppose that the drug is intended for children. Further suppose that the drug may disrupt normal growth and have lasting reproductive effects. How are you responding now to the "small risk of non-fatal side effects"?

5. If policy judgment inheres in every aspect of risk assessment, perhaps the most important question is who within the agency should decide. Are scientists best able to evaluate whether the particular biological system of mice is similar enough to the comparable system of people? What about whether Rabbit owners are representative of the average car passenger? Aren't judgment calls supposed to be made by political officials within agencies because only those officials have the requisite accountability? We will return to the question of "who should decide" below, but it pervades this entire discussion of agency statutory implementation. The allocation of authority within an agency affects the ultimate decision as much as the allocation between agencies and other institutions.

6. OMB has offered guidelines to agency heads for performing risk assessment. These guidelines have a fairly complicated history. In 1995, OMB and the Office of Science and Technology Policy in the Executive Office of the President first provided a set of principles. *See* U.S. Office of Mgmt. and Budget (OMB), Memo for Regulatory Working Group, Principles for Risk Analysis (1995). In 2006, OMB issued a Proposed Risk Assessment Bulletin for comment, and requested that the National Academy of Sciences conduct an expert peer review on the 2006 Bulletin. The National Academy found that the 2006 Bulletin was "fundamentally flawed," and it recommended that OMB withdraw it. *See* Scientific Review of the Proposed Risk Assessment Bulletin from the Office of Management and Budget 6 (National Research Council, 2007). In response, OMB declined to issue the 2006 Bulletin in final form, and instead issued a memorandum to heads of executive departments and agencies specifying its guidelines for risk assessment. *See* Memorandum to Heads of Exec. Departments and Agencies from Susan Dudley & Sharon Hays, Updated Principles of Risk Analysis (Sept. 17, 2007). These guidelines require the assumptions, both quantitative and qualitative, underlying risk assessments to be explicitly stated. They also direct agencies to make significant risk management decisions in a manner that creates the greatest net improvement in social welfare.

d. The Misuse and Abuse of Science

Even if science can produce good information about the level of risk, it does not reveal the proper response to that risk. This insight is often startling to those who regard risk assessment as a "science" rather than an art. But it is central to the distinction between risk assessment and risk management. To really appreciate the point, consider the following.

Wendy E. Wagner, The Science Charade in Toxic Risk Regulation

95 Colum. L. Rev. 1613, 1619-28 (1995)

I. THE SCIENCE-POLICY NATURE OF TOXIC RISK PROBLEMS

A. The Mixture of Science and Policy

Science-based regulations are typically based on a vague statutory mandate that requires the agency to set standards or take action at the point at which a chemical substance "presents or will present an unreasonable risk of injury to health or the environment." The initial step of translating "unreasonable risk" into a quantitative goal is often resolved with a single, express policy choice, such as a risk averse goal that no more than one in one million persons be adversely affected. The second and final step — determining the concentration at which any particular toxic substance actually poses a predetermined quantitative heath risk — requires a more extended inquiry and presents several significant challenges. These difficulties and their implications for policymaking are considered below.

1. Limits of Science. — First, and despite appearances to the contrary, contemporary science is incapable of completely resolving the level at which a chemical will pose some specified, quantitative risk to humans. In assessing the health risks of formaldehyde, for example, scientific experimentation can establish the effects of high doses of formaldehyde on the total number of nasal tumors in laboratory mice, but quantification of the effects of low doses on humans currently lies beyond the reach of science.

Nuclear physicist Alvin Weinberg first identified these gaps in knowledge as "trans-science" — "questions which can be asked of science and yet which cannot be answered by science." In contrast to the uncertainty that is characteristic of all of science, in which "the answer" is accompanied by some level of unpreventable statistical noise or uncertainty, trans-scientific questions are uncertain because scientists cannot even perform the experiments to test the hypotheses. This can be due to a variety of technological, informational, and ethical constraints on experimentation. For example, ethical mores prohibit direct testing on humans, leaving investigators to extrapolate the effects of a toxic substance on humans from studies conducted on animals. Even when some segment of the human population has been exposed to a toxic substance, isolating that substance's impact may be statistically impossible because of the many other factors that adversely affect human health.

Since trans-scientific issues arise from a variety of practical and theoretical limitations on scientific experimentation, the ability of science to quantify adverse health effects of low levels of toxins can be quite limited. To reach a final quantitative standard, policy considerations must fill in the gaps that science cannot inform. This combination of science and policy necessary to the resolution of issues concerning toxics regulation has led to the classification of these issues as "science-policy" problems.

2. The Fragmented Contributions of Science. — A second problem arising in the attempt to quantify health risks is that those insights which science is able to provide are fragmented and occur sporadically throughout the larger investigation. The search for a "safe" concentration of a chemical, which poses only minimal risks to human health, immediately breaks down into a sequence of smaller sub-questions that often alternate between questions that can be resolved with science and others that cannot. . . .

Even for those questions that cannot be resolved by science, however, science plays a small but important role in defining the scientifically plausible "default options" available at each trans-scientific juncture. For example, although the ultimate selection of an extrapolatory model that predicts the effects of a substance at low doses based on high dose data must be based on policy factors, the types of curves which are possible originate in scientific theory. . . . As a result, the contributions of science and policy, although generally separable, are mixed in complicated ways. . . .

This mix of science and policy can be illustrated by depicting a few hypothetical stages in an agency's effort to determine the maximum concentration of a carcinogen, such as formaldehyde, acceptable in public drinking water. Typically, the best information available on carcinogenicity consists of laboratory studies in which animals have been exposed to high concentrations of the specified chemical. One of the first trans-scientific questions that arises (Q1) is whether to count all tumors found in test animals after exposure or only those tumors that prove to be malignant. Although the decision will dramatically affect quantification of the hazard posed by the chemical, guidance provided by science in selecting among the options is limited. Once this trans-scientific question has been resolved with a nonscientific determination, the statistical results will provide valuable quantitative information on the effects of high levels of the substance on animals (Q2). Extrapolating these results to potential effects of low levels of the substance on humans then presents the next two trans-scientific junctures, which are often collapsed into one. First (Q3), an extrapolatory model must be selected that will predict low-dose effects on animals based solely on high-dose data. Although there are several scientifically plausible extrapolatory models, . . . the choice of one model over another cannot be resolved by science and thus must be determined by policy factors. This policy choice will have significant implications for the level ultimately chosen as adequate to protect public health. Second (Q4), since the similarities between animals and humans with regard to their sensitivity to carcinogens are largely unknown and incapable of being studied directly, a policy choice must again be made. For example, in many standard-setting efforts decision makers adopt the risk adverse assumption that humans are one hundred times more sensitive to the adverse effects of a carcinogen than test animals. After these trans-scientific junctures have been bridged with policy choices, further resolution of the inquiry then turns back to science for estimates of the average daily adult intake of water (Q5) and scientifically plausible models for absorption of the carcinogen in an adult (Q6). The absorption model ultimately selected will again be based on policy considerations.

Since dozens of such issues arise in determining the concentration at which a chemical causes adverse health effects, the number of scientific and trans-scientific subquestions that must be addressed in the course of a single standard-setting project is substantial, and the cumulative effect of these subquestions can have profound policy implications. Fortunately, the National Research Council of the National Academy of Sciences identified most, if not all, of these subquestions in its 1983 study and specifically listed the dozens of trans-scientific questions that must be resolved with policy considerations.

These dual characteristics of science-policy problems substantially complicate policymaking by limiting those capable of separating science and policy to persons proficient in science. Although trans-scientific questions cannot be answered by science, they generally appear to outside observers to be resolvable by contemporary science and thus are often mistaken for straightforward scientific questions. In fact, virtually all trans-scientific questions are capable of being framed as working scientific hypotheses, and in many cases the experiments needed to answer these hypotheses can be designed in theory. As a consequence, distinguishing between questions resolvable by science and those that must remain trans-scientific requires familiarity with the current capabilities and limitations of scientific experimentation.

The difficulties in identifying which questions are trans-scientific and which can be addressed by scientific experimentation are exacerbated by the fact that the gaps in scientific knowledge are not clustered at the beginning or end of the inquiry, but are located at numerous, intermittent points, often alternating with questions that science can resolve. Moreover, while resolution of a trans-scientific question must ultimately be determined by policy considerations, the plausible options available for resolving a trans-scientific question often originate in scientific theory. Thus, even with some appreciation of the limits of scientific experimentation, a nonscientist would have a difficult time identifying all of the questions that cannot be resolved by science and the scientifically plausible options available for each trans-scientific question.

II. THE PREVALENCE OF THE SCIENCE CHARADE

In a perfect world, scientists and policy specialists would strive to separate trans-scientific issues from issues that can be resolved with scientific experimentation. Policy choices would be made at each trans-scientific juncture, the basis for each choice would be explained, and the public would find the agency's policy decisions clear and accessible.

Not surprisingly, in the real world a completely different picture emerges. Agency scientists and bureaucrats engage in a "science charade" by failing first to identify the major interstices left by science in the standard-setting process and second to reveal the policy choices they made to fill each trans-scientific gap. Toxics standards promulgated under science-based mandates are covered—from the preamble to the regulatory impact analysis—with scientific explanations, judgments, and citations. Major policy decisions that undergird a quantitative toxic risk standard are at best acknowledged as "agency judgments" or "health policies," terms that receive no elaboration in the often hundreds of pages of agency explanations given for a proposed or final toxic standard and appear in a context that gives readers the impression they are based on science. Although this science charade appears to pervade virtually every toxics rule promulgated since the late 1970s, whether the agency engaged in the charade deliberately or inadvertently appears to vary from standard to standard.

A. The Unintentional Charade

In many instances agency officials charged with formulating toxic standards seem to engage in a science charade rather unwittingly. A statutory mandate that appears to require protective standards to be based at least in part on science, coupled with a deficient understanding of the science-policy nature of risk assessment, may lead these officials to reach for science in setting protective standards. In such cases, and without any apparent bureaucratic reflection, the agency officials mechanically assign the standard-setting task to agency scientists and associated technocrats.

Once given responsibility for setting a single, quantitative standard, agency scientists generally take one of two approaches: 1) they continue indefinitely to look to science to resolve the trans-scientific questions; or 2) they substitute their own values for the policy choices needed at the trans-scientific junctures and characterize the final science-policy decisions as the result of scientific experimentation and scientific judgment. In either case, the results are disturbing.

A cautious scientist typically takes the first, more "scientific" approach and declines to impose her values on a national toxic risk standard that has wide-ranging economic and related public policy consequences. In so doing, however, the scientist nevertheless continues the charade by embarking on an endless search for nonexistent scientific answers, thereby halting many standards in the research phase and leaving significant gaps in the regulation of toxics. The small number of toxic risk standards promulgated under science-based mandates, coupled with the fact that the standard-setting task often begins and ends with agency scientists, supports the likelihood that at least some standards have been stalled in this way.

If the second path is followed, significant public policy judgments are made by technocrats who have not been appointed as policymakers and who are unlikely to be held accountable for their decisions. In some cases a scientist may become convinced that the highly controversial issues will never be resolved unless she steps in and resolves the trans-scientific questions herself. In other cases a scientist may enjoy being the source of public policy, particularly when her hidden value choices are likely to be free from oversight by high level governmental officials and the public at large. Finally, a scientist may deceive herself into believing that her scientific expertise gives her the professional legitimacy to resolve a vast range of trans-scientific questions without assistance from appointed officials or other designated policymakers.

B. The Intentional Charade

In contrast to the unintentional charade, where bureaucrats inadvertently characterize the standard-setting task as a problem for science, in the intentional charade agency bureaucrats consciously disguise policy choices as science. The intentional charade typically occurs only after agency scientists have begun developing a standard. Once the wide-ranging political and/or economic implications of a standard proposed by agency scientists are understood, high-level agency officials become aware of the scientific uncertainties and begin to consider whether a weaker or a more stringent standard could be set by substituting different policy assumptions at the trans-scientific junctures. Although this means the decision on a final standard is often made arbitrarily (for example by selecting some undefined low- or mid-point between science-policy options), the result presented to the public is again masked in science, leaving no trace of the policy compromise that formed the basis for the standard.

A vivid illustration of the intentional science charade can be seen when one compares EPA's actual decision making process for revising the ozone standard under the Clean Air Act with the agency's public account of that decision published in the Federal Register. Scientific knowledge about ozone was so limited at the time of the EPA revision in the late 1970s that agency scientists were unable to reach consensus on a single quantitative standard, leaving scientifically justified possibilities ranging from 0.25 parts per million (ppm) to 0.08 ppm. In selecting a final standard, the EPA Administrator essentially struck a compromise between White House concerns for the economy on the one hand and public health concerns on the other. Administrator Costle later admitted that in selecting 0.12 ppm over the leading alternatives of 0.08, 0.10, or 0.15, "[i]t was [going to be] a political loser no matter what you did. . . . The minute you picked a number . . . everybody can argue that it can't be that number, or it could just as easily be another number. . . . [It] was a value judgment."

Despite the Administrator's subsequent candor, EPA's public account of its rationale in selecting the 0.12 standard revealed none of the underlying policy considerations, but rather gave readers the opposite impression that the standard was selected based on scientific evidence. EPA concluded its fifteen page presentation of mind-numbing scientific justification in the final rulemaking with a single acknowledgment that to the extent "[t]here is no collection of facts or medical evidence that permits selecting an undisputed value for the standard level," "[t]he Administrator must exercise the informed scientific judgment that Congress has authorized him to bring to bear on these difficult problems." The economic impact of the selected standard or alternate standards, which were clearly considered by the Administrator, were publicly disregarded by EPA as statutorily irrelevant and summarized in four sentences near the end of the lengthy preamble. In reviewing a challenge brought by both industrial and environmental groups, the District of Columbia Circuit Court of Appeals refused to overrule the Administrator's decision, finding that in selecting the 0.12 standard EPA had taken "into account all the relevant studies . . . [and] did so in a rational manner" using "informed judgment."

C. The Premeditated Charade

A final agency approach to standard-setting is to make a specific policy choice, whether it is pro-industry or favors overprotection of public health and the environment, and to introduce science only after the fact in order to scientifically justify the predetermined standard. In contrast to the intentional charade, which has been identified as those instances where gaps in scientific knowledge become apparent only near the end of a standard-setting endeavor, the premeditated charade occurs when policy decisions are made in advance and guide selection of the science ultimately cited as support for a quantitative standard. The standard may not only exploit the policy flexibility permitted by the trans-scientific junctures, but also may disregard the available scientific evidence. Nevertheless, the standard, or the decision not to promulgate a standard, is presented to the public clothed in the mantle of science and supported by studies carefully selected to favor the agency's position.

Accounts of the premeditated charade in the early years of the Reagan Administration are the most abundant. During that period high-level officials attempted to eliminate or substantially weaken protective standards, and in each case these decisions were framed as decisions based on principles of "good science" which, according to the Administration, necessitated "hard proof of damage to health" before toxic materials could be regulated. One of the best examples of Reagan's premeditated charade is EPA's decision in 1982 not to regulate formaldehyde under the Toxic Substances Control Act (TSCA) because of the lack of conclusive data on the risk formaldehyde presented to human health. EPA presented its decision as based almost exclusively on science and insisted that risk assessment was a " 'scientific and not a legal matter.'" EPA's supporting scientific explanations, however, deviated significantly from both the prevailing scientific evidence regarding health effects of formaldehyde and accepted EPA risk assessment assumptions — deviations which EPA uniformly failed to identify or explain. Close observers of the decision alleged that EPA was simply manipulating science after-the-fact in order to justify a predetermined political decision that would benefit an important industry. In fact, circumstantial evidence supports the charge that EPA's decision not to regulate formaldehyde was actually made prior to its scientific reassessment of the data. Not surprisingly, after a series of congressional hearings and considerable controversy within the scientific community, EPA rescinded its decision and determined in 1984 that formaldehyde did present a major health risk and should be regulated, a decision that was based on the same scientific information available in 1982. This 180-degree reversal is attributable largely, if not exclusively, to the appointment of a new EPA Administrator who was selected specifically in order to restore the agency's tarnished image.

Notes and Questions

1. Trans-scientific questions "arise from a variety of practical and theoretical limitations on scientific experimentation." As a result, agency decisions that are based on scientific data or conclusions (e.g., the decision to limit exposure of a toxin at a particular concentration, the decision to require the installation of passive restraints) reflect substantial numbers of policy judgments. The mixture is inevitable; both science and trans-science are necessary to a final agency regulation, but typically, neither is sufficient. Who should decide trans-scientific questions? Even if your answer is political officials, why must agency scientists nonetheless maintain some sort of a role?

2. Professors Campbell-Mohn and Applegate, who earlier gave us the distinction between risk assessment and risk management, caution against too rigid a separation at EPA:

> The call to keep these two functions distinct was originally articulated in response to a widespread perception that EPA was making judgments on the risk posed by a particular substance not on the basis of science, but rather on the basis of its willingness to regulate the substance. The purpose of separation, however, was not to prevent any exercise of policy judgment at all when evaluating science or to prevent risk managers from influencing the type of information that assessors would collect, analyze, or present. Indeed, the Red Book made it clear that judgment (also referred to as risk-assessment policy or science policy) would be required even during the phase of risk assessment. The present committee concludes further that the science-policy judgments that EPA makes in the course of risk assessment would be improved if they were more clearly informed by the agency's priorities and goals in risk management. Protecting the integrity of the risk assessment, while building more productive linkages to make risk assessment more accurate and relevant to risk management, will be essential as the agency proceeds to regulate the residual risks of hazardous air pollutants.

Celia Campbell-Mohn & John S. Applegate, *Learning from NEPA: Guidelines for Responsible Risk Legislation*, 23 HARV. ENVTL. L. REV. 93, 97-98 (1999) (citing National Research Council, Committee on Risk Assessment of Hazardous Air Pollutants, Science and Judgment in RISK ASSESSMENT 259-60 (1994)). If separation is not the answer, then what is?

3. Think back to NHTSA's reason for discounting the Rabbit/Chevette study: the owners of those smaller cars were not representative of the average passenger, and the automatic belt systems in those cars were not representative of the one that the agency was considering. These determinations concerning the relevance of the study were not scientific conclusions but trans-scientific judgments. What were the scientific facts or conclusions that the Rabbit/Chevette study revealed? How forthcoming was NHTSA about its reasons for discounting the Rabbit/Chevette study? Look back at the final rule. Do you detect signs that the agency was making the decision to rescind the passive restraints requirement seem more scientific than it was?

4. One scholar has found political polarization in the U.S. has led to more skepticism about scientific studies and a consequent decline in the stringency of U.S. health and environmental regulations compared to Europe. *See* DAVID VOGEL, THE POLITICS OF PRECAUTION: REGULATING HEALTH, SAFETY, AND ENVIRONMENTAL RISKS IN EUROPE AND THE UNITED STATES (2012).

5. One way to think about the "science charade" is in terms of who perpetrates it. Two forms (i.e., unintentional and intentional) involve agency scientists. Science blurs into policy, yet the scientists fail to draw the line (either inadvertently or deliberately). The third form involves agency political appointees (or officials within the White House). Policy comes first, and political officials enlist science to justify the choice. Does the direction matter? In either case, interested observers (i.e., regulated entities, regulatory beneficiaries, courts, politicians) cannot determine which parts of the decision are subjective and therefore most susceptible to challenge. From this perspective, the effect is equally bad. Ask yourself whether it makes the agency's rationale for its decision something of a sham or a scam. Perhaps the problem runs even deeper. Is it worse for an agency to engage in results-oriented decision making than to hide the ball?

6. Another way to think about the science charade is in terms of motivation. The unintentional charade reflects the difficulty of separating scientific and trans-scientific questions. The intentional and premeditated charade reflects the decision makers' calculated effort to impose their own policy preferences. Yet the effect is largely the same: interested observers cannot determine which parts of the decision are fact and which are judgment. Still, it seems worse from a normative perspective to deliberately mislead outsiders for the pursuit of self-interested policy ends.

7. On March 9, 2009, President Obama issued a memorandum to the heads of executive departments on scientific integrity. In his memorandum, he endorsed the following principles to guide the scientific integrity in the executive branch:

(a) The selection and retention of candidates for science and technology positions in the executive branch should be based on the candidate's knowledge, credentials, experience, and integrity;

(b) Each agency should have appropriate rules and procedures to ensure the integrity of the scientific process within the agency;

(c) When scientific or technological information is considered in policy decisions, the information should be subject to well-established scientific processes, including peer review where appropriate, and each agency should appropriately and accurately reflect that information in complying with and applying relevant statutory standards;

(d) Except for information that is properly restricted from disclosure under procedures established in accordance with statute, regulation, Executive Order, or Presidential Memorandum, each agency should make available to the public the scientific or technological findings or conclusions considered or relied on in policy decisions;

(e) Each agency should have in place procedures to identify and address instances in which the scientific process or the integrity of scientific and technological information may be compromised; and

(f) Each agency should adopt such additional procedures, including any appropriate whistleblower protections, as are necessary to ensure the integrity of scientific and technological information and processes on which the agency relies in its decisionmaking or otherwise uses or prepares.

Which, if any, of these principles is most important in addressing the unintentional or intentional science charades?

3. Economic Analysis

When moving from risk assessment to risk management, an agency must decide whether to regulate, and if so, how stringently. One of the major tools for making such policy judgments is economic analysis. Agencies use economic analysis, for example, to assign a dollar amount to the benefits of a regulation and then to examine those benefits in relation to their costs. Economic considerations play a pivotal role in the work of agencies and therefore in the work of lawyers, both inside and outside of those agencies.

Where does economic analysis come from? When agencies make decisions, common sense suggests that they ought to consider costs in some respect, even if they ultimately choose to prioritize another factor. We live in a world of finite resources; agencies should determine whether we are getting the most for our money. Furthermore, we run our lives generally in consideration of the costs and benefits of our actions. When deciding whether to cross a street against the light, you (at least implicitly) weigh the benefits of crossing against the costs of such action. If you wait to walk, it is because you are better off that way.

Common sense is not the only factor that prompts agencies to consider costs and benefits. Many statutes invite consideration of costs and benefits, and some require it. Only a very few prohibit it. In addition, as noted above, executive orders since President Reagan have required cost-benefit analysis (CBA) for all proposed major regulations (basically, those with costs of $100 million or more). Thus, there is a standing presidential requirement of CBA, backed by an executive order. We discuss this requirement in Chapter 6. Here, we examine the technique itself as a means by which agencies use economic analysis to implement their statutory mission. Note that CBA is not the only form of economic analysis that statutes demand or agencies perform, and we present other forms toward the end of this section. But CBA is the dominant form, so we focus on it here.

NHTSA is a good example. When NHTSA originally mandated the installation of passive restraints in 1977, it estimated that its rule would yield significant benefits:

> According to the analysis which NHTSA performed [when it first instituted Standard 208], automatic restraints were expected to prevent 9,000 deaths and 65,000 serious injuries once all cars on the road were equipped with those devices. That prediction was premised on several critical assumptions. Most important among the assumptions were those concerning the safety benefits of automatic restraints—reductions in death and injury—which in turn are a function of the types of automatic restraints to be placed in each year's production of new cars.

The agency assumed that the combination of airbags and lap belts would be approximately 66 percent effective in preventing fatalities and that automatic belts would have a 50 percent level of effectiveness. The agency assumed also that airbags would be placed in more than 60 percent of new cars and that automatic belts would be placed in the remaining approximately 40 percent. The agency's analysis predicted that airbags would provide protection in virtually all crashes of sufficient severity to cause deployment of the airbags. It was further assumed that the automatic belts would be used by 60 to 70 percent of the occupants of those cars.

NHTSA, Federal Vehicle Safety Standards, Final Rule, 46, Fed. Reg. 53419, 53420 (Oct. 29, 1981).

NHTSA's assumptions about the benefits of its passive restraints requirements did not materialize because automakers overwhelmingly chose to install automatic seatbelts rather than airbags. Furthermore, the agency found that the benefits of automatic seatbelts were uncertain: no data existed showing that people would use such seatbelts any more often than they were using manual seatbelts. As a result, it concluded that Standard 208 would cost $89 per vehicle (the cost to install automatic seatbelts) and eliminate the middle seat or sixth seat passenger position without any countervailing benefits. The quality of the CBA depends on the accuracy of the assumptions the agency makes when conducting it. How do agencies perform CBA? What are the criticisms of that approach? What are the other variations of economic analysis that statutes prescribe or agencies perform? We consider these issues in some detail because, for good or bad, the regulatory state is at present a "cost-benefit state." *See* CASS R. SUNSTEIN, THE COST-BENEFIT STATE (2002). Economic considerations play a pivotal role in the work of agencies and therefore in the work of lawyers, both inside and outside of those agencies.

a. An Example of Cost-Benefit Analysis

Consider the following example, which we introduce with a so-called return letter from OIRA, followed by NHTSA's response. We discuss return letters in Chapter 6 as a means of presidential control. For now, think about how OIRA's letter affects NHTSA's cost-benefit analysis.

Section 13 of the Transportation Recall Enhancement, Accountability, and Documentation Act (TREAD Act), 49 U.S.C. §30123, requires NHTSA to issue regulations for monitoring tire pressure to ensure proper inflation. NHTSA drafted a rule prescribing two different systems: direct and indirect. The direct system requires a sensor in each wheel to measure tire pressure. The indirect system infers tire pressure from information provided by a vehicle's anti-lock brake system (ABS). During the phase-in period of the new regulation, manufacturers could choose to install either system. But thereafter, manufacturers would have to install the direct system. As required, NHTSA sent this rule to OIRA for approval. OIRA disapproved it by the usual method of a return letter, which prevents the agency from publishing the proposed regulation in the Federal Register. By virtue of APA §552 (the publication requirement), this means that the regulation cannot go into effect. NHTSA then responded with a new regulation. The return letter and the new regulation are reprinted below.

Office of Information and Regulatory Affairs, Return Letter

February 12, 2002

Mr. Kirk K. Van Tine
General Counsel
U.S. Department of Transportation
400 Seventh Street, S.W., Room 10428
Washington, DC 20590

Dear Mr. Van Tine:

The Office of Management and Budget (OMB) has been conducting an expedited review under Executive Order No. 12866 of the draft final rule prepared by the National Highway Traffic Safety Administration (NHTSA) entitled "Tire Pressure Monitoring Systems." In accordance with recent legislation passed by Congress, the draft final rule addresses an important public safety issue: the traffic crashes, injuries and fatalities that result from operating a vehicle with underinflated tires.

OMB supports NHTSA's establishment of a safety standard in this area. However, the analysis NHTSA has performed to date does not adequately demonstrate that NHTSA has selected the best available method of achieving the regulatory objective: enhanced highway safety. Therefore, we are returning this rule to NHTSA for reconsideration of two analytic concerns related to safety. First, we have identified a regulatory alternative—one that NHTSA has not explicitly analyzed—that may provide more safety to the consumer than the draft version of the final rule. In order to analyze this alternative with care, NHTSA needs to consider the impact of regulatory alternatives on the availability of anti-lock brake systems (ABS). Second, the technical foundation for NHTSA's estimates of safety benefits needs to be better explained and subjected to sensitivity analysis. My staff is available and eager to work with NHTSA to complete this analysis and the rulemaking as expeditiously as possible.

Many vehicles on the road do not have any tire pressure monitoring system. For these vehicles, the owner or driver must take the initiative to periodically check the pressure of the vehicle's tires to ensure that each of the tires is inflated to the proper pressure level. The available evidence suggests that many people do not regularly check their tires, or at least do not take the steps to achieve optimal tire inflation. As envisioned by Congress, the draft final rule would establish a Federal Motor Vehicle Safety Standard under which tire pressure monitoring systems would have to be installed in all new passenger cars, light trucks, multi-purpose vehicles and buses weighing up to 10,000 pounds.

There are two types of tire pressure monitoring systems, both now used in some vehicles, that NHTSA believes are possible compliance choices for vehicle manufacturers. "Direct" systems monitor pressure by means of instruments installed in each wheel. Indirect systems infer tire pressure from information already available in vehicles that are equipped with anti-lock brake systems. In particular, the indirect system detects pressure differences between wheels by sensing differences in their rotational speeds. Underinflated tires have smaller diameters and thus rotate faster.

The draft final rule would establish, over a four-year phase-in period, a standard under which all new vehicles would be required to have some tire pressure monitoring system. During the phase-in period, compliance could be achieved with either indirect or direct systems. However, after the phase-in, the performance standard would be altered in a way that effectively prohibits compliance with a purely indirect system. The vehicle manufacturer would instead be compelled to comply with a direct system. NHTSA believes a so-called "hybrid" system, which would combine elements of direct and indirect tire pressure monitoring, could also meet the rule's performance standard. However, no such hybrid systems have yet been installed in vehicles and the public record provides little information about their likely performance or cost.

OMB believes that a rule permitting indirect systems may provide more overall safety than a rule that permits only direct or hybrid systems. This additional safety may be available at a lower total cost to the public. Although direct systems are capable of detecting low pressure under a greater variety of circumstances than indirect systems, the indirect system captures a substantial portion of the benefit provided by direct systems. Moreover, allowing indirect systems will reduce the incremental cost of equipping vehicles with anti-lock brakes, thereby accelerating the rate of adoption of ABS technology. About one-third of new vehicle sales currently lack anti-lock brakes necessary for an indirect system. Both experimental evidence and recent real-world data have indicated a modest net safety benefit from anti-lock brakes. Before NHTSA finalizes a rule that disallows indirect systems, OMB believes that the potential safety benefits from more vehicles with anti-lock brakes need to be considered. In a preliminary analysis attached to this memorandum, OIRA staff show that a rule permitting indirect systems may provide more overall public safety at less cost to the consumer than NHTSA's preferred alternative.

OMB is also concerned that NHTSA's estimates of the number of crashes, injuries and fatalities prevented by direct systems are based on limited data and/or assumptions that have not been fully explained or analyzed. For example, NHTSA assumes that 95% of consumers would respond promptly and effectively to a warning light indicating that the vehicle has a tire inflation problem. No data, such as estimates of driver response rates to existing safety-related warning lights, are provided to support this figure. While the safety benefit estimates stemming from reduced skidding and better control are based on a well-done study, that study unfortunately was published in 1977, before the widespread existence of front-wheel drive, radial tires and SUVs and minivans. It also appears that NHTSA's use of experimental data on shorter stopping distances from proper tire inflation was based on insufficient consideration of all of the available data. In light of the limited data and insufficiently supported assumptions, OMB suggests that NHTSA's regulatory analysis should include more sensitivity analysis of the type that is found in many previous regulatory analyses prepared by NHTSA. NHTSA should also provide additional explanation of the data choices and uncertainties underlying its analysis.

In conclusion, OMB believes that, before issuing a final rule, NHTSA needs to provide a stronger analysis of the safety issues and benefits, including a formal analysis of a regulatory alternative that would permit indirect systems after the phase-in period. Moreover, NHTSA could analyze an option that would defer a decision about the ultimate fate of indirect systems for several more years, until the potential impact on installation of anti-lock brake systems is better understood. In addition to representing sound public policy, the consideration of the suggested regulatory alternative is required under Sections 202 and 205 of the Unfunded Mandates Act (2 U.S.C. 1532 and 1535) and under Section 1(b)(5), (8), and (11) of E.O. 12866.

Accordingly, I am returning the draft final rule for reconsideration. My staff and I are available to work with the agency in the reconsideration of this matter and in the prompt promulgation of an important safety rule.

Sincerely,

John D. Graham, Ph.D.
Administrator
Office of Information and Regulatory Affairs

Enclosure
cc: Dr. Jeffrey W. Runge

This enclosure describes in detail our concerns with the draft Final Economic Assessment (FEA). It presents—for illustrative purposes— an analysis of an option that has the potential to achieve substantially greater safety at lower cost than the draft final rule. The enclosure also includes a discussion of some of the major uncertainties and potential biases associated with key assumptions in the FEA and suggests possible ways to address them.

BACKGROUND

After a four-year phase-in, the draft final rule would require that tire pressure monitoring systems (TPMS) be able to detect when up to four tires are 25 percent or more underinflated. The FEA includes analysis of direct and "hybrid" TPMS. Direct systems monitor tire pressure directly by means of sensors installed in each wheel. Hybrid systems would monitor tire pressure by combining elements from a direct system with elements from an in- direct system. Indirect systems infer tire pressure from information already available in vehicles equipped with anti-lock brake systems (ABS). They detect pressure differences between tires by sensing differences in wheel rotational speeds. Underinflated tires have smaller diameters and thus rotate faster. No indirect systems currently available can meet a four-tire standard. The rulemaking record is also unclear on whether hybrid systems could do so.[1] Nevertheless, we assume for the sake of argument that NHTSA is correct in its belief that hybrid systems could meet a four-tire requirement.

The FEA presents quantified estimates of two components of cost: "vehicle" (e.g., hardware) and maintenance costs for each system. The benefit estimates include the value of fuel savings and reduced tire tread wear that would result from each system. The FEA presents the difference between costs and the fuel and tire wear savings as "net costs." The FEA also includes three categories of quantified safety benefits: reduced skidding and better control, shorter stopping distances, and fewer flat tires and blowouts. For direct systems, the FEA estimates a net cost (i.e., total cost minus the value of fuel economy and tire tread wear benefits) of $1,240 million per year and safety benefits of 10,271 injuries and 141 fatalities averted per year when applied to the entire on-road fleet. For hybrid systems, the FEA estimates a net cost of $862 million per year with safety benefits of 8,722 injuries and 124 fatalities averted per year.

1. Evaluation of Alternatives

The FEA does not meaningfully compare viable alternatives. Specifically, NHTSA did not analyze the benefits and costs associated with an alternative requirement that would allow indirect systems to continue to be used indefinitely (i.e., a 30 percent underinflation, 1-tire standard). There are in excess

---

1. We were unable to locate anything in the rulemaking record indicating that hybrid systems would be able to detect four simultaneously low tires. The rulemaking record on the performance and cost of hybrid systems appears to be limited to two paragraphs in one comment. That comment stated, "The current releases of indirect TPMS will require the equivalent of the addition of two direct tire pressure sensors and a radio-frequency receiver to meet the requirement to detect *two* simultaneously low tires under *alternative 2* [emphasis added]." Under the proposed rule, "alternative 2" would have required the detection of up to three, not four, simultaneously low tires. That comment also asserted, ". . . the maximum cost to implement these changes to be about 60% of the cost of a full direct TPMS for vehicles already equipped with an ABS." The commenter provided no further information on the performance or cost of such a system. To date, no such system has ever been produced or installed on a vehicle.

of 2 million TPMS-equipped vehicles on the road today, the vast majority of which are indirect systems.

Based on information in the Preliminary Economic Assessment (PEA) and the FEA, a requirement that allowed indirect systems indefinitely could achieve comparable and, quite possibly, substantially greater safety benefits at lower cost than those associated with the final rule. An option that allows indirect systems will provide an inducement to install anti-lock brakes (ABS) on more vehicles. We present the following analysis for illustrative purposes only. We believe that the example shows that indirect systems warrant a com- plete and careful analysis. At the same time, we do not consider our example to be definitive. Further refinements by NHTSA may be necessary.

A. Costs and Benefits of an Indirect System

Based on information contained in the PEA, and consistent with assumptions in the FEA, we estimate that an indirect system would cost an average of about $30 per vehicle in "vehicle" (e.g., hardware) costs and an additional $13 in maintenance costs, or a total of about $720 million per year. Indirect systems would result in about $200 million in fuel and tread wear savings combined for a net cost of about $520 million per year. We estimate this option could achieve safety benefits of about 5,000 injuries and 70 fatalities averted per year when applied to the entire on-road fleet.

B. The Anti-lock Brake Effect — Induced ABS

Indirect versus direct systems—Allowing indirect systems likely would induce vehicle manufacturers to equip a greater percentage of the new vehicle fleet with ABS.[2] This is because vehicles not equipped with ABS will need a more-expensive, direct system to comply with the rule. For direct systems, the FEA estimates vehicle cost of $66.50 per vehicle. For vehicles already equipped with ABS, the vehicle cost of an indirect system would be $13.29 per vehicle.[3]

Thus, a manufacturer who decided to install ABS in a vehicle that would not have ABS otherwise can reduce the (vehicle) cost of compliance by about $53 per vehicle. In other words, a rule that would allow indirect systems would reduce the incremental cost of adding ABS by $53, since the manufacturer could avoid the cost of a direct system.[4]

---

2. For model year 2000 about 68 percent of new cars and light trucks were equipped with ABS. Although the percentage of new vehicles equipped with ABS generally has increased in recent years, it appears to be leveling off. In 1999, 68.3 percent of the fleet was equipped with ABS.

3. The average cost of $30 mentioned above is higher because it is a weighted average of both direct and indirect systems, since vehicles without ABS would require direct systems.

4. The remainder of this analysis assumes that the consumer does not correctly perceive the difference in maintenance cost. If he or she did, the effective "discount" on ABS would be substantially greater—an additional $40 or so when comparing direct with indirect systems.

According to NHTSA, the average cost of ABS is about $240. Therefore, a manufacturer could save about 22 percent ($53/$240) of the cost of equipping a vehicle with ABS by avoiding the cost of a direct TPMS. Assuming a price elasticity of demand for ABS of 1[5] (i.e., each 1 percent decline in the price of ABS induces a 1 percent increase in quantity demanded), a 22 percent reduction in the cost of ABS would result in a 22 percent increase in the number of new vehicles equipped with ABS. Thus, we could reasonably expect about 7.4 percent of the new vehicle fleet (22 percent of the 33 percent of the new vehicle fleet without ABS), or about 1.1 million vehicles, to be equipped with ABS as a direct result of this option.

A recent study in a peer-reviewed journal[6] estimated that light-duty vehicles equipped with ABS are between 4 and 9 percent less likely to be involved in fatal crashes of all types. (These estimates are not statistically significant. However, they appear to represent the best estimates available at this time.) Overall, there are about 40,000 fatalities per year involving these vehicles. Thus 7.4 percent of the fleet accounts for about 2,960 fatalities per year. Reducing these by 4 to 9 percent would mean 118 to 266 fatalities[7] averted per year as a result of additional ABS induced by the rule. Adding these to the 70 fatalities averted from indirect systems without the additional ABS yields a total of 188-336 fatalities averted or between 47 and 195 more than with direct systems.

We calculated the nationwide aggregate cost of the additional ABS systems as follows: About 1.1 million (7.4% × 15 million new vehicles/yr.) more vehicles would be equipped with ABS. Since the FEA already accounted for these vehicles having to install direct systems, the increment to the FEA aggregate cost estimate is about $206 million per year (1.1 million vehicles × $187 ($240 – $53)). This brings the net cost of the indirect system approach (including the cost of additional ABS systems) to about $726 ($520 + $206) million per year, or about $514 million per year less than the net cost of direct systems.

Indirect versus hybrid systems—The FEA estimated the vehicle cost of a hybrid system to be $39.90 per vehicle. This is about $26.50 less than the

---

5. We do not have an empirically-based estimate of the price elasticity of demand for anti-lock brakes. However, NHTSA reported in the draft preamble to the final rule that one vehicle manufacturer said it would add ABS to an additional 400,000 vehicles if indirect systems are permitted. This alone accounts for more than 1/3 of the additional ABS our illustrative example assumes. In public comments, all vehicle manufacturers supported a 30%, 1-tire standard. Thus it does not appear that this manufacturer made this statement in the context of a standard that today's indirect systems cannot meet.

6. Farmer, Charles M., "*New evidence concerning fatal crashes of passenger vehicles before and after adding antilock braking systems,*" ACCIDENT ANALYSIS AND PREVENTION, 33 (2001), 361-69.

7. The study we relied upon did not estimate ABS effectiveness rates for injuries. We estimated injury reduction benefits attributable to ABS by assuming that injury reduction benefits would occur in the same proportion to fatalities (i.e., between 70 and 75 injuries per fatality) as NHTSA estimated in the FEA.

vehicle cost of a direct system, or about half of the savings per vehicle associated with indirect systems. Following the approach we used for indirect systems, manufacturers who choose a hybrid option over a direct system can also effectively capture the savings as a cost reduction for providing ABS. Under the same assumptions we used above, this would result in an additional 3.7% of the new vehicle fleet (about 550,000 vehicles) being equipped with ABS. This, in turn translates into an additional 59-133 more fatalities averted and about $117 million additional net cost compared with hybrid systems with no ABS effect. The total benefits for hybrid systems would then be 183-257 (124 + 59 and 124 + 133) fatalities averted per year and the net cost would be about $979 million per year. Including the ABS effect, allowing indirect systems would avert between 5 (188-183) and 79 (336-257) more fatalities and about $250 million in cost per year than would hybrid systems.

The table below summarizes these estimates.

System	Cost per vehicle	National Estimates (without ABS Effect)[8]			National Estimates (with ABS Effect)		
		Annual Net Cost ($ millions)	Annual Injuries Averted	Annual Fatalities Averted	Annual Net Cost ($ millions)	Annual Injuries Averted	Annual Fatalities Averted
Direct	$66.50	$1,240	10,271	141	$1,240	10,271	141
Hybrid	$39.30	$862	8,733	124	$979	12,888-18,099	183-257
Indirect	$13.29	$520	5,000	70	$726	13,429-24,000	188-336

Because of this possibility, NHTSA should carefully evaluate the benefits and costs of an option that would allow indefinite use of today's indirect systems. We hope that the illustrative example we provide here will serve as a useful starting point for such an analysis. As a longer-term project, NHTSA should also evaluate the on-road performance of current direct and indirect systems.

The quantified safety benefits in the FEA are divided among 3 categories: reduced skidding and better control, shorter stopping distances, and fewer flat tires and blowouts. The magnitude of each is directly related to vehicle owners' responses to low pressure warning lights. This section describes some assumptions about several uncertain or unknown key parameters that affect the magnitude of the safety benefit estimates. Each assumption warrants some empirical grounding and/or sensitivity analysis.

---

8. The estimates for the direct and hybrid systems are take from the draft FEA. The estimates for an indirect system are OMB estimates based on information in the PEA and, to the maximum extent possible, consistent with assumptions NHTSA made in its draft FEA.

A. Vehicle Owner Response to Warning Light

The safety benefits from a TPMS system depend critically on how vehicle owners respond when the low pressure warning light comes on. There can be no benefit if owners ignore the warning light. The FEA assumes that 95 percent of all vehicle owners will respond to the warning light promptly and appropriately. In the Preliminary Economic Assessment, NHTSA assumed 60 percent of vehicle owners would respond to a light that did not specify which tire(s) was low by inflating their tires to the correct pressure and 80 percent in cases where the dashboard light indicated which tire was low. Neither the PEA nor the FEA provides an empirical basis for any of these response rates. At the same time, it is also likely that some vehicle owners will come to rely exclusively on the warning light to inform them of tire pressure and will reduce the frequency with which they normally check their tires. To the extent that this occurs, the benefits of the rule may decline, and may do so at different rates depending on the technology.

To provide a stronger foundation for its analysis, NHTSA should provide some empirical basis for this critical component of the analysis. NHTSA could, for example, perform an analysis of responses to other dashboard warnings. In any event, NHTSA should perform sensitivity analyses using alternative response rates. We believe that a carefully conducted survey and analysis of driver behavior and corresponding tire pressures in TPMS-equipped vehicles currently on the road would go a long way toward refining the estimates based on this parameter.

B. Reduced Skidding and Better Control

In the PEA, NHTSA stated it was not able to quantify this category of benefits. No commenters disagreed or suggested ways that NHTSA might do so. In the FEA, NHTSA estimated the benefits from reduced skidding and better control using a 1977 study, "Tri-Level Study of the Causes of Traffic Accidents, Final Report (Report)." This Report provides great detail on the circumstances associated with 420 crashes. It was well-done and for a long time served as a useful data source for understanding the causes of crashes. Unfortunately, because of changes in the nature of vehicles on the road, the report's value has diminished with the passage of time. The skidding and control component of the benefit estimates for this rule appears to stem from analysis of about six of the 420 crashes analyzed in the report. The small sample size alone is enough to warrant a sensitivity analysis. Perhaps more importantly, though, the relevance of the vehicles and tires involved to the fleet of vehicles that this rule will affect is not clear. For example, none of the six vehicles in the Report had front-wheel drive, none were sport utility vehicles (SUVs) or minivans, and, in all likelihood, none were equipped with radial tires. The newest of the vehicles involved in these crashes was a 1972 Pontiac. One of the six involved a 1960 Ford Falcon—a vehicle produced more than

45 years before the final rule will be fully effective. NHTSA should also provide more support for the assumption that these crashes are directly relevant to this rule.

C. *Shorter Stopping Distances*

Stopping distances vary greatly among vehicles and road and tire conditions. They also vary from test to test under the same vehicle, road, and tire conditions. All of the improved stopping distance benefits were based on tests of two vehicles: a Dodge Caravan minivan and a Ford Ranger pickup truck. The FEA appears to rely exclusively on the Caravan test results to estimate benefits for the passenger car fleet (but not for the minivan or SUV fleet). The FEA also appears to rely exclusively on the Ford Ranger test results to estimate benefits for the light truck fleet (including minivans and SUVs).

NHTSA chose not to continue to use results from a passenger car tested on a NHTSA test track. These results had formed part of the basis for benefit estimates in the PEA. They showed little, if any, effect of reduced pressure on stopping distances. This result is not surprising, for the same reason that the rule is expected to yield fuel economy and tread wear benefits — reduced pressure increases rolling resistance, and could be expected to improve stopping distances under at least some conditions. Although NHTSA received no comments suggesting these results were unrepresentative, it did not use them because of a belief that the test road surface was not sufficiently worn to be representative.

NHTSA does not explain why it believes the minivan test results better represent passenger car performance than NHTSA's own passenger car results. NHTSA also does not explain why it believes the pickup truck test results better represent minivan and SUV performance than the minivan test results.

Given the small sample size and variability of stopping distances, it is unclear whether any of the test results available to NHTSA are representative of much more than those particular vehicles. NHTSA should estimate benefits using its passenger car test results to represent passenger cars, the minivan test results to represent minivans and SUVs, and the pickup truck test results to represent pickup trucks. NHTSA should also perform some sensitivity calculations around the corresponding benefit estimates.

D. *Flat Tires and Blowouts*

In the PEA, NHTSA stated it did not have sufficient data to reliably estimate the magnitude of this category of benefits. Commenters agreed that there will be some benefits in this area.

However, no commenters disagreed with NHTSA's initial assessment that they could not be quantified. As was the case with skidding and control, none suggested ways NHTSA might estimate them. In the FEA, NHTSA produced an estimate of these benefits by assuming that 20 percent of blow-outs are caused by low tire pressure. This new assumption warrants further justification and a sensitivity analysis, at the least.

Notes and Questions

1. In this return letter, OIRA recommended that NHTSA allow automakers to install indirect systems in new cars rather than direct systems, at their discretion. Why? OIRA claimed that allowing automakers to install indirect systems would increase the installation of ABS and therefore improve "overall safety." How does OIRA know whether manufacturers would install more ABS? If it cannot be sure, why would OIRA prefer this option?

2. OIRA also claimed that the draft rule was based on unreliable data about the safety benefits of direct systems. Who is in a better position to evaluate such data, OIRA or NHTSA? What kind of training do the professionals in each agency possess? Who is in closer contact with the regulated industry? Who has more experience with the subject matter?

3. Could it be argued that OIRA's cost-benefit analysis is equivalent to judicial review—the supervision of agency decision making by an outside body of generalists who are trained to bring a different but relevant methodology to bear on the decisions of those with subject area expertise. What are the similarities and differences between the two types of review?

4. Two auto safety public interest groups, Public Citizen (founded by Ralph Nader, with Joan Claybrook as its first Executive Director) and Consumers Union, filed strong objections to the return letter. The Public Citizen letter stated that OMB had relied upon "unproven assumptions about the cost and market effects of combining indirect systems with a requirement for anti-lock brakes (ABS) (a long-controversial area outside the focus of the agency's current rulemaking mandate), which, in turn, has only statistically insignificant and highly disputed safety effects."

Here is part of the final rule that NHTSA promulgated after receiving the return letter. (Part One was a more lenient interim standard that would apply until November 2006.) The rule uses an asterisk as its multiplication sign.

NHTSA, Final Rule (Part Two)

Federal Motor Vehicle Safety Standard No. 138, 49 C.F.R. §571.138 (2002)

Based on the record compiled to this date, the results of the study, and any other new information (including, for example, information on the overall safety benefits of ABS) submitted to the agency, NHTSA will issue the second part of this final rule. The second part will be issued by March 1, 2005, to ensure vehicle manufacturers have sufficient lead time before November 1, 2006, when all new light vehicles must be equipped with a TPMS.

Based on the record now before the agency, NHTSA tentatively believes that a four-tire, 25 percent requirement would best meet the TPMS mandate in the TREAD Act. Nevertheless, it is possible that the new information may be sufficient to justify a continuation of the requirements in the first part of this final rule, or even some other alternative.

BENEFITS

Following is a summary of the benefits associated with this final rule. For purposes of this analysis, the agency assumes that 95 percent of drivers will respond to a low tire pressure warning by re-inflating their tires to the placard pressure. OMB questioned this assumption in its return letter. NHTSA has little hard evidence supporting this assumption. As discussed in the FEA, a recent study indicated that 97 percent of respondents stated they would respond to a dashboard warning light informing them that their tire pressure was low.

Under-inflation affects many different types of crashes. These include crashes which result from: (1) skidding and/or losing control of the vehicle in a curve, such as a highway off-ramp, or in a lane-change maneuver; (2) hydroplaning on a wet surface, which can cause increases in stopping distance and skidding or loss of control; (3) increases in stopping distance; and (4) flat tires and blowouts; (5) overloading the vehicle.

The agency was able to identify target populations for skidding and loss of control crashes, stopping distance (which involves any vehicle that brakes during a crash sequence), flat tires, and blowouts. The agency was not able to identify, from crash files and other reports, a target population for crashes caused by hydroplaning and overloading the vehicle.

A. Tire Safety Benefits

1. Skidding/Loss of Control

Under-inflation reduces tire stiffness, which causes the tire to generate lower cornering force. When a tire is under-inflated, the vehicle requires a greater steering angle to generate the same cornering force in a curve or in a lane-change maneuver. This can result in skidding or loss of control of the vehicle in a tight curve or a quick lane change maneuver. The agency estimates that if all light vehicles meet the four-tire, 25 percent compliance option, 46 fatalities will be prevented and 4,345 injuries will be prevented or reduced in severity per year due to reductions in these types of crashes. If all light vehicles meet the one-tire, 30 percent compliance option, 30 fatalities will be prevented and 2,817 injuries will be prevented or reduced in severity per year due to reductions in these types of crashes.

2. Stopping Distance

As explained in greater detail above, tires are designed to maximize their performance capabilities at a specific inflation pressure. When a tire is under-inflated, the shape of its footprint and the pressure it exerts on the road surface are both altered. This degrades the tire's ability to transmit braking force to the road surface, and increases a vehicle ís stopping distance, especially on wet surfaces. Decreasing stopping distance is beneficial in several ways. Some crashes can be completely avoided. Other crashes will still occur, but at a lower impact speed because the vehicle is able to decelerate more quickly. The agency estimates that if all light vehicles meet the four-tire, 25 percent compliance option, 39 fatalities will be prevented and 3,410 injuries will be prevented or reduced in severity per year due to reductions in vehicles' stopping distances. If all light vehicles meet the one-tire, 30 percent compliance option, 17 fatalities will be prevented and 1,562 injuries will be prevented or reduced in severity per year due to reductions in vehicles' stopping distances.

3. Flat Tires and Blowouts

Under-inflation, along with high speed and overloading, can cause tire blowouts. A blowout in one of the front tires can cause the vehicle to veer off the road or into oncoming traffic. A blowout in one of the rear tires can cause spinning and loss of control of the vehicle. The agency estimates that if all light vehicles meet the four-tire, 25 percent compliance option, 39 fatalities will be prevented and 967 injuries will be prevented or reduced in severity per year due to reductions in crashes involving blowouts and flat tires. Thus, the agency estimates that more fatalities and injuries will be reduced as a result of reductions in crashes that occur on dry surfaces than crashes that occur on wet surfaces. If all light vehicles meet the one-tire, 30 percent compliance option, 32 fatalities will be prevented and 797 injuries will be prevented or reduced in severity per year due to reductions in crashes involving blowouts and flat tires.

4. Unquantified Benefits

The agency cannot quantify the benefits from a reduction in crashes associated with hydroplaning and overloading vehicles. The primary reason that the agency has been unable to quantify these benefits is the lack of crash data indicating tire pressure and how often these conditions are the cause or contributing factors in a crash. The agency does not collect tire pressure in its crash investigations. NHTSA also has not been able to quantify the benefits associated with reductions in property damage and travel delays that will result from fewer crashes or reductions in the severity of crashes.

B. Non-Tire Safety Benefits

In its return letter, OMB stated that issuing a final rule that allowed current indirect TPMSs to comply would encourage vehicle manufacturers to install ABS on additional vehicles. OMB recommended that NHTSA consider the potential safety benefits of additional vehicles being equipped with ABS. However, as noted above, there is no reliable basis for concluding that permitting current indirect TPMSs to comply would lead to a significant increase in installation of ABS in light vehicles. Moreover, there is no statistically reliable basis for concluding that ABS reduces fatalities in light vehicles.

Thus, the agency does not believe that, even if vehicle manufacturers install ABS on additional vehicles, additional safety benefits would be experienced.

C. Total Quantified Safety Benefits

The agency estimates that the total quantified safety benefits from reductions in crashes due to skidding/loss of control, stopping distance, and flat tires and blowouts, therefore, will be 124 fatalities prevented and 8,722 injuries prevented or reduced in severity each year, if all light vehicles meet the four-tire, 25 percent compliance option; and 79 fatalities prevented and 5,176 injuries prevented or reduced in severity each year, if all light vehicles meet the one-tire, 30 percent compliance option.

D. Economic Benefits

1. Fuel Economy

Correct tire pressure improves a vehicle's fuel economy. Recent data provided by Goodyear indicate that a vehicle's fuel efficiency is reduced by one percent for every 2.96 psi that its tires are below the placard pressure. The agency estimates that if all light vehicles meet the four-tire, 25 percent compliance option, vehicles' higher fuel economy will translate into an average discounted value of $16.43 per vehicle over the lifetime of the vehicle. If all light vehicles meet the one-tire, 30 percent compliance option, vehicles' higher fuel economy will translate into an average discounted value of $2.06 per vehicle over the lifetime of the vehicle.

2. Tread Life

Correct tire pressure also increases a tire's tread life. Data from Goodyear indicate that for every 1 psi drop in tire pressure, tread life decreases by 1.78 percent. NHTSA estimates that if all light vehicles meet the four-tire, 25 percent compliance option, average tread life will increase by 1,143 miles. If all light vehicles meet the one-tire, 30 percent compliance option, average tread life will increase by 15 miles. This will delay new tire purchases. The agency estimates that the average discounted value of these delays in tire purchases will be $5.09, if all light vehicles meet the four-tire, 25 percent compliance option; and $0.65 if all light vehicles meet the one-tire, 30 percent compliance option.

COSTS

A. Indirect TPMSs

NHTSA estimates that the cost of an indirect TPMS that will meet the one-tire, 30 percent compliance option will be $13.29 per vehicle, if the vehicle already has a four-wheel, four-channel (four wheel-speed sensors) ABS. In the 2000 model year, about 67 percent of all new light vehicles were equipped with a four-wheel ABS. However, about 31 percent of these vehicles only had a three-channel system. A three-channel system has one wheel speed sensor for each front wheel and one for the rear axle. Thus, in order to meet the requirement that the TPMS be able to detect when any tire is significantly under-inflated, a vehicle with a three-channel ABS must be redesigned from having one wheel speed sensor for the rear axle to a wheel speed sensor for each rear wheel. The agency estimates that this will cost $25 per vehicle. Accordingly, the agency estimates that the average cost of providing an indirect TPMS to a vehicle already equipped with ABS will be $21.13 ($13.29 + $25 * .3135) per vehicle.

For vehicles not currently equipped with ABS, manufacturers would have to install either four wheel speed sensors at a cost of $130 per vehicle, or ABS at a cost of $240 per vehicle, in addition to an indirect TPMS. Thus, the average cost of providing an indirect TPMS to a vehicle not already equipped with ABS will be $143.29 ($130 + $13.29) if the manufacturer installs four-wheel speed sensors, or $253.29 ($240 + $13.29) per vehicle if the manufacturer installs ABS.

B. Direct TPMSs

NHTSA estimates that the cost of a direct TPMS that will meet the four-tire, 25 percent compliance option will be $70.35 per vehicle, if the manufacturer chooses to install an individual tire pressure display. This includes $7.50 for each tire pressure sensor ($30 per vehicle), $19 for the control module, $3.85 for an individual tire pressure display, $6 for four valves, and $11.50 for the combination of an instrument panel telltale, assembly, and miscellaneous wiring. The agency assumes that about one percent of vehicles currently comply. Thus, the agency estimates that the incremental cost will be $69.65 per vehicle ($70.35 * 99 percent) if manufacturers install an individual tire pressure display. If manufacturers install only a warning telltale, the agency estimates that the incremental cost will be $65.84 ($70.35 − $3.85 (the cost of an individual tire pressure display) * 99 percent).

C. Hybrid TPMSs

A hybrid TPMS consists of an indirect TPMS for vehicles equipped with an ABS and two direct pressure sensors and a radio frequency receiver. As noted above, insofar as NHTSA is aware, no manufacturer is currently planning to produce a hybrid TPMS. If a manufacturer were to produce a hybrid TPMS, the agency believes that such a system would be able to detect when one to four tires are 25 percent or more below placard. TRW estimated that the cost of such a system would be about 60 percent of the cost of a direct TPMS. Since the hybrid TPMS would not be able to tell drivers the inflation pressure in all four tires, the agency assumes that this type of TPMS would not be accompanied by a display system that would allow the driver to see the pressure for each tire. Consequently, the agency estimates that the cost of a hybrid TPMS that would meet the four-tire, 25 percent compliance option would be $39.90 ($70.35 − $3.85 (the cost of an individual tire pressure display) * .60).

D. Vehicle Cost

If all light vehicles meet the four-tire, 25 percent compliance option, the agency assumes that manufacturers will install hybrid TPMSs on the

67 percent of vehicles that are currently equipped with an ABS and direct TPMSs on the 33 percent of vehicles that are not so equipped. Thus, the agency estimates that the average incremental cost if all vehicles meet the four-tire, 25 percent compliance option will be $48.19 per vehicle [$39.90 × .67 + $66.50 × .33] × .99 (to account for one percent current compliance). Since approximately 16 million vehicles are produced for sale in the U.S. each year, the total annual vehicle cost will be about $771 million per year.

If all light vehicles meet the one-tire, 30 percent compliance option, the agency assumes that manufacturers will install an indirect TPMS on vehicles currently equipped with ABS (about 67 percent of new light vehicles), and a direct TPMS on vehicles not equipped with ABS (about 33 percent of new light vehicles). The agency also assumes that about five percent of vehicles currently meet the one-tire, 30 percent compliance option. Thus, the average incremental cost if all vehicles meet the one-tire, 30 percent compliance option will be $33.34 [($21.13 * .67) + ($66.5079 * .33) * .95]. ($66.50 is the cost of a direct TPMS with only a warning telltale.). Since approximately 16 million vehicles are produced for sale in the U.S. each year, the total annual vehicle cost will be about $533 million per year.

E. Maintenance Costs

Each pressure sensor in direct TPMSs needs a battery. Currently, these batteries last five to ten years. Thus, they will have to be replaced to keep the system functioning over the full life of a vehicle. At this time, all tire pressure sensors are enclosed packages that do not open so that the battery can be replaced. Thus, when the battery is depleted, the entire sensor must be replaced.

To estimate the present discounted value of this cost, the agency is making the following assumptions. First, the agency assumes that the pressure sensors will be replaced the second time the vehicle's tires are changed, in the 90,000 to 100,000 mile range. The agency multiplied the cost of the sensor ($7.50 each, or $30 for the vehicle) by three to account for typical aftermarket markups. After applying discount factors, the agency estimates that the maintenance costs for direct TPMSs will be $40.91 per vehicle. For hybrid TPMSs, with direct pressure sensors in two wheels, the agency estimates the average maintenance costs will be half the maintenance costs of direct TPMSs, or $20.45. Thus, the agency estimates that if all light vehicles meet the four-tire, 25 percent compliance option, the present discounted value of the maintenance costs will be $27.20 ($20.45 × .67 + $40.91 × .33) per vehicle. Since approximately 16 million vehicles are produced for sale in the Unites States each year, the total annual maintenance costs will be about $435 million.

NHTSA notes that the maintenance costs associated with direct and hybrid TPMSs may decrease significantly in the future if manufacturers are able to mass produce a pressure sensor that does not require a battery. One

TPMS manufacturer, IQmobil Electronics of Germany, commented that it has developed a "batteryless transponder chip" that "costs half as much as the battery transmitter it replaces." Indirect TPMSs do not need a battery, and are assumed to have no maintenance costs for purposes of this analysis. If all light vehicles meet the one-tire, 30 percent compliance option, the agency assumes that manufacturers will install an indirect TPMS on vehicles currently equipped with ABS (about 67 percent of new light vehicles), and a direct TPMS on vehicles not equipped with ABS (about 33 percent of new light vehicles). Thus, the agency estimates that if all light vehicles meet the one-tire, 30 percent compliance option, the present discounted value of the maintenance costs will be $13.50 ($40.91 * .33) per vehicle.

F. Testing Costs

The agency estimates that the man-hours required to complete the necessary compliance testing will be 6 hours for a manager, 30 hours for a test engineer, and 30 hours for a technician/driver. The agency estimates that the labor costs will be $75 per hour for a manager, $53 per hour for a test engineer, and $31 per hour for a technician/driver. Thus, the agency estimates that the total costs will be $2,970 per vehicle model under both compliance options.

G. Unquantified Costs

The agency anticipates that there may be other maintenance costs for both direct and indirect TPMS. For example, with indirect TPMSs, there may be problems with wheel speed sensors and component failures. With direct TPMSs, the pressure sensors may be broken off when tires are changed. The agency requested comments on this issue in the NPRM, but received none. Without estimates of these maintenance problems and costs, the agency is unable to quantify their impact. The agency also notes that in order to benefit from the TPMS, drivers must respond to a warning by re-inflating their tires. To accomplish this, most drivers will either make a separate trip to a service station or take additional time to inflate their tires when they are at a service station for fuel. The process of checking and re-inflating tires is relatively simple, and probably would take from three to five minutes. The time it would take to make a separate trip to a service station would vary depending on the driver's proximity to a station at the time he or she was notified.

It is likely that drivers who take the time to re-inflate their tires would consider this extra time to be fairly trivial. Since the action is voluntary, by definition, they would consider it to be worth the potential benefits they will derive from properly inflated tires. However, when tallied across the entire driving population, the total effort involved in terms of man-hours may be significant. NHTSA has no data to indicate what portion of drivers would make a separate trip or wait to re-inflate their tires when they next visited a service station. Thus, the agency has not been able to quantify this cost.

H. ABS Costs

As noted above, the agency estimates that the average cost of equipping a vehicle with ABS is $240.

I. Net Costs and Costs Per Equivalent Life Saved

The agency estimates that if all light vehicles meet the four-tire, 25 percent compliance option, the net cost [vehicle cost + maintenance costs (fuel savings + tread life savings)] will be $53.87 [$48.19 + $27.20 − ($16.43 + $5.09)]. As noted above, the agency estimates the total annual cost will be about $771 million. The agency estimates the total annual net cost will be about $862 million [$771 million + $435 million − ($263 million + $81 million)]. NHTSA estimates that the net cost per equivalent life saved will be about $4.3 million. The agency estimates that if all light vehicles meet the one-tire, 30 percent compliance option, the net cost will be $44.13 [$33.34 + $13.50 − ($2.06 + $0.65)]. The agency estimates that the total annual cost will be about $533 million per year, and the total annual net cost will be about $706 million [$533 million + $216 million − ($33 million + $10 million)]. NHTSA estimates that the net cost per equivalent life saved will be about $5.8 million.

Notes and Questions

1. As you can see, NHTSA rejected OIRA's suggestions. On what basis did it do so?

2. In justifying its final rule, NHTSA calculated the cost per life saved. Are you convinced by these calculations? Look at each of the benefit and cost items. How were the calculations made? What was the factual basis for them?

3. If you are not satisfied with NHTSA's calculations, how do you think the decision should be made? How much cost should be imposed on car manufacturers (and ultimately car buyers) to avoid accidents related to tire pressure?

4. Although NHTSA did not allow automakers generally to choose indirect systems in place of direct systems, it did allow them to install indirect systems during a phase-in period before November 2006, that being Part One of the rule. The Court of Appeals for the Second Circuit reversed and remanded the rule to the agency because the rule allowed automakers to install indirect systems even for a limited time. *See* Public Citizen, Inc. v. Minetta, 340 F.3d 39 (2d Cir. 2003). Specifically, the court found that the rule in this respect was (a) contrary to the statute and (b) arbitrary and capricious under the APA. Can you make the textual argument that the rule is contrary to the statute? Section 13 of the TREAD Act provides: "The Secretary of Transportation shall complete a rulemaking for a regulation to require a warning system in new motor vehicles to indicate to the operator when *a* tire is significantly under-inflated" (emphasis added). Do both indirect and direct systems satisfy this language? Or does the language preclude one?

b. The Mechanics of Cost-Benefit Analysis

At a basic level, conducting cost-benefit analysis involves monetizing—or assigning a dollar value to—the benefits and costs of a regulation. That can be a difficult task. It involves complex determinations such a putting a value on human life and taking account of the changes in the value of money over time.

The "bottom line" of NHTSA's computation was that, at a 25 percent compliance rate, the net cost per equivalent life saved will be about $4.3 million. To reach a legal conclusion about whether or not to impose the requirement, it now becomes necessary to decide whether a human life is worth $4.3 million. Whenever agencies monetize the benefits for regulations that protect human health and safety, they confront the question of what a human life is worth in dollars. To set a dollar value, agencies use a statistical "value of human life" number. That number can vary wildly among agencies—from $50,000 per life to more than $8 million per life. What is the basis for these numbers? Consider the following.

W. Kip Viscusi, Fatal Tradeoffs

17-19 (1992)

2.1 VALUATION METHODOLOGY

Traditionally, issues pertaining to the valuation of human life had been treated as strictly moral concepts, not matters to be degraded through economic analysis of choices and tradeoffs. However, as Schelling (1968) observed, substantial insight can be obtained by assessing the benefits of risk reduction in the same manner as we value other economic effects. In general, the appropriate benefit measure for risk reductions is the willingness to pay to produce the particular outcome. Similarly, the selling price for changes in risk establishes the value for risk increases. In the usual risk policy decision—for example, determining what safety characteristics to provide in automobiles—the policy result to be assessed is an incremental risk reduction rather than a shift involving the certainty of life or death. This need to think in terms of statistical lives as opposed to certain lives defines the main character of our choice problems. In particular, the matter of interest is individuals' valuation of lotteries involving life and death.

Addressing value-of-life issues by focusing on our attitudes toward lotteries involving small risks of death provides a methodology for formulating these issues in a sound economic manner. This approach also avoids the more difficult task of confronting the valuation of lives at risk of certain death, which understandably raises a different class of ethical issues. Nevertheless, even when only small risks are involved, the concerns involved remain inherently sensitive, and we should not be cavalier in making these judgments. Because of the central role of individual preferences, individual values of life may differ considerably, just as do other tastes. A central concern is who is valuing the life and for what reason. A particular life may have one value to the individual, another to his or her family, and still another to society at large.

As the willingness-to-pay methodology has become better understood, the controversy surrounding the entire line of research on the value of life has diminished. Much of the early opposition to the economic valuation of life stemmed from the reliance on value-of-life concepts that had been developed to inform decisions on compensating survivors rather than on reducing risks to life. Initial efforts consequently sought to value life using the human capital approach. In particular, [some early analyses] estimated values of life based on various measures of earnings. This technique, which continues to be used throughout the United States court system to assess damages for personal injury, addresses only the financial losses involved. The death of a family member, for example, would impose a financial loss on survivors, which would be measured as the present value of the income the deceased would have earned net of taxes and his or her consumption. Similarly, the present value of taxes the deceased would have paid represents the financial loss to the rest of society. . . .

2.2 THE VALUE OF STATISTICAL LIVES

The ultimate purpose of the value-of-life literature is to provide some basis for sensitive social decisions. Before investigating how society should make decisions involving the saving of lives, we will first assess whether we can establish an empirical reference point for making tradeoffs involving life and health. In the absence of such empirical information, there will be few operational contexts in which economic analysis of value-of-life decisions is instructive. Some sense of the order of magnitude of the value-of-life estimates will also assuage many of the concerns expressed about the morality of this line of work. If the appropriate economic value of life is over $1 million, resistance to this methodology will probably be much less than if the estimate is, say, $200,000.

The basic approach to establishing a value of risk reduction parallels the technique for benefit assessment for other contexts. If, for example, one were attempting to assign benefits to the building of a new public parking garage, the appropriate benefit measure would be the sum of the willingness to pay of all the residents for this new facility. In a similar manner, when assessing the benefits of risk reduction, the pertinent value is the willingness to pay for the risk reduction. What we are purchasing with our tax dollars is not the certainty of survival. Rather, it is the incremental reduction in the probability of an adverse outcome that might otherwise have affected some random member of our community. What is at stake is consequently statistical lives, not certain identified lives.

In the case of risks that we must bear, the concern shifts from our willingness to pay for added safety to the amount that we require to bear the risk, which is usually termed our willingness-to-accept amount. For sufficiently small changes in risk, the willingness-to-pay and willingness-to-accept amounts should be approximately equal, but in practice they are not. [T]here is often an alarmist reaction to increases in risk above the accustomed level so that willingness-to-accept amounts may dwarf the willingness-to-pay amounts if we respond irrationally to the risks.

In each case, the underlying concern is with a lottery involving a small probability of an adverse outcome. Our attitude toward this lottery defines the terms of trade that we believe are appropriate, where these terms of trade represent our risk dollar tradeoff.

Notes and Questions

1. The statistical value of a human life is different from tort measures of economic damages, such as lost earnings. Why is it more appropriate when monetizing the benefits of regulation to ask individuals what they would be willing to pay for a small reduction in the risk of harm?

2. What does "statistical" mean? When economists survey individuals concerning their willingness to pay for risk reduction, those individuals are not valuing their own lives or the lives of those they know. Rather, they are placing a price tag on "the incremental reduction in the probability of an adverse outcome that might otherwise have affected some random member of our community." Why is this the proper question to ask when estimating the benefits of regulation?

Further Note on Monetization

Professor Viscusi provides the basic framework for valuing statistical lives, but other issues arise in the process. Consider the following:

Heterogeneity of Life.   Are all lives worth the same? What if a regulation mainly benefits future generations? Suppose people tend to value their own lives more. What about a regulation that mainly benefits the elderly? Or the poor? Suppose people tend to value the lives of the elderly or the poor less. What are the pros and cons of allowing the heterogeneity of statistical life to enter into the calculation? For a critical analysis of these issues, see RICHARD L. REVESZ & MICHAEL LIVERMORE, RETAKING RATIONALITY: HOW COST-BENEFIT ANALYSIS CAN BETTER PROTECT THE ENVIRONMENT AND OUR HEALTH 77-84 (elderly), 107-18 (future generations) (2008).

Stated Preferences vs. Revealed Preferences.   How do economists measure "willingness to pay"? Is what we say different from how we behave — put simply, do we put our money where our mouths are? The answer is: not always. To account for the divergence, economists measure both stated and revealed preferences. They measure stated preferences by surveying individuals about how much they are willing to pay to avoid increased risks. They measure revealed preferences by, for example, observing in job market data how much workers demand in hazard pay to accept risky jobs. These studies seek to understand the "wage premium" that workers receive for higher-risk employment. Professor Viscusi terms this measure "willingness to accept" and says it is useful for risks that we must bear. He also notes that what individuals are willing to accept to incur exposure to a risk and willing to pay to avoid exposure are different; the former is higher. Think about your own behavior. Can you explain why?

Critics have challenged reliance on wage premium studies as a basis for monetizing the value of life. Consider a coal miner who receives a higher wage than a bookkeeper working at the same company with similar levels of skills. Under what conditions does it make sense to treat the pay difference between the coal miner and the bookkeeper as a wage premium to compensate for the increased risk? In particular, does that assume that employees are informed about the scope of job risks? "If workers don't appreciate the risks of death that they face, one can draw no valuation inferences from their decisions." Frank Cross & Charles Silver, *In Texas, Life Is Cheap*, 59 VAND. L. REV. 1875, 1879 (2006). "An alternative explanation is the absence of a truly competitive wage market, with non-unionized workers unable to bargain for wage increases to compensate for risk." *Id.*

Variations Among Agencies and Issues. When economists perform studies and evaluate market data, they can particularize the analysis for differences among risks across agencies or even within a single agency. That is why different agencies maintain divergent valuations and why some agencies use different numbers for different problems. For an extended discussion, see KIP VISCUSI, FATAL TRADEOFFS 34-39; RICHARD REVESZ & MICHAEL LIVERMORE, RETAKING RATIONALITY: HOW COST-BENEFIT ANALYSIS CAN BETTER PROTECT THE ENVIRONMENT AND OUR HEALTH 47-48.

Updating Valuations over Time. The value of a statistical life can be expected to change over time as people's preferences about risk change. Economists update the numbers periodically. And so do agencies. But not all updates are on the up and up. For example, in 2008, EPA set the value of a statistical life at $6.9 million, a drop of $1 million from 2005. *See* Seth Borenstein, *An American Life Worth Less Today*, ASSOCIATED PRESS (July 10, 2008). The agency itself did not call attention to the change; rather, the Associated Press discovered it after reviewing the cost-benefit analyses in EPA regulations. *See id.* Professor Viscusi was quoted in the Associated Press article as saying that EPA's change "doesn't make sense" because "[a]s people become more affluent, the value of statistical lives go up as well." *Id.* By contrast, the Department of Transportation increased its statistical life valuation twice over this same time. *See id.* Consider another example. In 2002, the EPA decided to reduce the value of statistical life by 38 percent for the elderly but then reversed itself when the change became public. *Id.* Do these experiences suggest that valuation is not only driven by economics? Under the circumstances, perhaps the question we ought to be asking is *who* should select the appropriate valuation? Agency career economists? Agency political appointees? OIRA officials who combine economics with politics when performing regulatory review on behalf of the White House? Elected officials themselves? As in the scientific context, "who decides" questions are crucial to the policy that results.

Cognitive Biases.   People suffer from predictable irrationalities or cognitive biases that cause them to misperceive risk. These biases then affect the statistical life valuation. What people are willing to pay for a small reduction in risk depends on how they view that risk. Here is Professor Viscusi:

MISTAKES IN ESTIMATION
        Whereas people generally overestimate the likelihood of low-probability events (death by tornado), they underestimate higher risk levels (heart disease or stroke). We are particularly likely to overestimate previously unrecognized risks in the aftermath of an unfavorable outcome. Such perceptional biases account for the emotional public response to such events as Three Mile Island, or occasional incidents of deliberate poisoning of foodstuffs or medicines.
        Risk perceptions may also be affected by the visibility of a risk, by fear associated with it, and by the extent to which individuals believe they can exercise control over it. Consider the greenhouse effect. Although global warming is a prime concern of the Environmental Protection Agency, it ranks only twenty-third among the U.S. public's environmental concerns. The high risk of automobile fatality-car accidents kill one in 5,000 Americans each year might perhaps be reduced significantly if drivers informed with a more realistic sense of what they can and cannot do to control the risk drank less alcohol and wore seat belts more often.
        Because experience tells us little about low-probability risks, we appropriately examine correlated indicators that pose less serious problems. For example, the record high temperatures of 1988 may or may not have been signals of an impending greenhouse effect. Unfortunately, such signals are seldom as informative as canaries in the coal mine. Adverse events may occur without warning; witness the San Francisco earthquake in October 1989. Moreover, happenstance warnings may bear little relation to the magnitude, likelihood, or nature of a problem. Forest management efforts should not have to await the chance burning of national parks and forests.

DISTORTIONS IN MONETARY VALUATION
        Economic valuations of risk also tend to be distorted by underlying misweighting of risks. For example, from an expected utility perspective, individuals generally place too high a value on preventing increases in a risk from its current level (the so-called status quo bias or reference risk effect). These tendencies are reflected in government policy. Products causing new forms of cancer tend to arouse greater public concern and new technologies are often regulated much more strictly than are old technologies and familiar risks. Man-made carcinogens are carefully scrutinized, while much higher levels of natural carcinogens may be tolerated. Because of this imbalance, we pay more dollars for our products and end up with greater risks to our lives.
        Studies of consumers show that many individuals would be willing to pay a premium for the assured elimination of a risk. The Russian roulette problem illustrates. Consider

two alternative scenarios for a forced round of play. In the first, you have the option to purchase and remove one bullet from a gun that has three bullets in its six chambers. How much would you pay for this reduction in risk? (Assume you are unmarried, with no children.) In the second situation, the gun has only a single bullet. How much would you pay to buy back this bullet? From an economic standpoint, you should always be willing to pay at least as much and typically more in the first situation since there is some chance you will be killed by one of the remaining bullets, in which case money is worthless (or worth less). However, experiments find respondents are typically willing to pay more when a single bullet is in the gun, because its removal will ensure survival. . . .

The valuation of a risk is likely to depend on how the risk is generated. We tolerate voluntarily assumed risks more than those, such as environmental hazards over which we have no control. We regard acts of commission as much more serious than acts of omission. In pharmaceutical screening, for example, the Food and Drug Administration (FDA) worries more about introducing harmful new drugs than about missing opportunities for risk reduction offered by new pharmaceutical products.

KIP VISCUSI, FATAL TRADEOFFS 152-54.

In monetizing the benefits of a regulation, agencies often make other assumptions. For example, in a 2008 rule, NHTSA made the following assumption about the price of a gallon of gasoline to calculate the costs and benefits of improved fuel economy standards:

> The total costs for manufacturers just complying with the [fuel economy] standards for [model year or "MY"] 2011-2015 passenger cars would be approximately $16 billion, compared to the costs they would incur if the standards remained at the adjusted baseline. The resulting vehicle price increases to buyers of MY 2015 passenger cars would be recovered or paid back in additional fuel savings in an average of 56 months, assuming fuel prices ranging from $2.26 per gallon in 2016 to $2.51 per gallon in 2030. The total costs for manufacturers just complying with the standards for MY2011-2015 light trucks would be approximately $31 billion, compared to the costs they would incur if the standards remained at the adjusted baseline. The resulting vehicle price increases to buyers of MY 2015 light trucks would be paid back in additional fuel savings in an average of 50 months, assuming fuel prices ranging from $2.26 to $2.51 per gallon.

73 Fed. Reg. 24352, 24356 (May 2, 2008).

When NHTSA made this assumption about gas prices in May 2008, those prices were hovering around the $4.00/gallon mark. (What are gas prices as you read this material?) But models projecting future gas prices were optimistic about a decline in the price. What is the effect of the agency's low-ball assumption on the economic analysis that it is performing? What is the effect on the fuel economy standards that it is proposing?

It is useful to know how people today value a life and what they are willing to pay to avoid a risk. But many of the costs and benefits of regulation affect the future. What is a small reduction in the risk of cancer in 25 years worth to you in today's dollars? Similarly, what does a gallon of gas priced at $2.51 in the year 2030 cost in today's dollars? To deal with this aspect of regulation, agencies select a discount rate to convert future costs and benefits to present dollars. But the choice is often quite difficult to make.

Cass R. Sunstein, Cost-Benefit Default Principles

99 Mich. L. Rev. 1651, 1704-17 (2001)

Perhaps the most difficult issue here, from the theoretical point of view, involves the selection of the appropriate discount rate. How should the agency value future gains and losses? In terms of ultimate outcomes, the choice matters a great deal. If an agency chooses a discount rate of 2%, the outcome will be very different from what it would be if an agency were to choose a discount rate of 10%; the benefits calculation will shift dramatically as a result. If a human life is valued at $8 million, and if an agency chooses a 10% discount rate, a life saved 100 years from now is worth only $581. "At a discount rate of 5%, one death next year counts for more than a billion deaths in 500 years." OMB suggests a 7% discount rate . . . but this is highly controversial. A key question is therefore: What legal constraints should be imposed on the agency's choice? . . .

Usually statutes are silent on the question of appropriate discount rate. In fact, I have been unable to find any statute that specifies a discount rate for agencies to follow. On judicial review, the question will therefore involve a claim that the agency's choice is arbitrary. Here the national government shows strikingly (and inexplicably) variable practices. As noted, the Office of Management and Budget suggests a 7% discount rate, departing from a 10% rate in the 1980s. But agencies are not bound by OMB guidelines, and they have ranged from as low as 0% (EPA, latency period for cancer from arsenic) and 3% (Food and Drug Administration, Department of Housing and Urban Development) to as high as 10% (EPA). In fact the same agency sometimes endorses different discount rates for no apparent reason — with EPA, for example, selecting a 3% rate for regulation of lead-based paint as compared to 7% for regulation of drinking water, and 10% rates, respectively, for regulation of emissions from locomotives. Here government practice seems extremely erratic.

From the purely economic standpoint, there are serious conundrums here. The impetus for discounting future effects stems from the judgment that, in the context of money, discounting future benefits and losses is entirely rational, even simple: a dollar today is worth more than a dollar tomorrow. There are two reasons: investment value (or opportunity cost) and pure time preference. A dollar today can be invested, and for this reason it is worth more than a dollar a year from now. An emphasis on the investment value of money yields a discount rate of roughly 5% - 7%. Quite apart from this point, people generally seem to have a preference for receiving money sooner rather than later. People value current consumption more than they value future consumption. An inquiry into pure time preference produces lower discount rates of 1% - 3%. Though they lead to different numbers, both points justify discounting future income gains and losses.

So far, so good. The problem is that, notwithstanding conventional wisdom among economists, these points are not easily taken to justify a discount rate for the nonmonetary benefits of regulation. . . . If a regulation will save ten lives this year and ten lives annually for the next ten years, it cannot plausibly be urged that the future savings are worth less than the current savings on the ground that a current life saved can be immediately "invested." The point about investment value, or the opportunity cost of using capital, seems utterly irrelevant here. With time preference, things are less clear. Perhaps people would rather save ten lives today than ten lives in a decade. But it is unclear that this is so. And even if it is, what moral status would such a time preference have? Almost certainly it makes sense to say that it would be worse for you to lose your limb now than to lose it in ten years; in the latter case, you will have ten years' use of the limb. And probably it makes sense to say that agencies should attend to life-years saved, not only lives saved. But holding all this constant, the death of a thirty-five-year-old in 2004 does not seem worth more than the death of a thirty-five-year-old in 2044. And since different people are involved, the moral problem is serious: the preference of the chooser in 2002 is certainly relevant to determining that chooser's own fate, and the timing of risks that might come to fruition for that chooser. But the chooser's preference cannot easily be used to determine the fate of someone not yet born.

These points suggest that, as Richard Revesz argues, it is important to distinguish two issues that go under the name of "discounting" and that have yet to be separated in administrative practice: (a) latent harms, in the form of exposures whose consequences will occur late in someone's lifetime; and (b) harms to future generations. It is reasonable to say that latent harms should count for less than immediate ones, since they remove fewer years from people's lives and because people do seem to prefer, other things being equal, a harm in the future to a present harm. For latent harms, some kind of discount rate is sensible. Consider, for example, the case of arsenic. In its regulation, the EPA treated an arsenic death in the future as equivalent to an arsenic death in the present, even though an arsenic death is likely to come, if it does come, many years after exposure. On this count, the EPA's judgment seems wrong, even arbitrary; some kind of discount rate is clearly appropriate here. It would be easy to imagine a challenge to the failure to discount the latent harms here. On the other hand, OMB's 7% figure, based on the investment value of money is probably too high. There is no reason to believe that the discount rate for future health harms is equal to the discount rate for future income effects, and considerable reason to believe otherwise. Indeed, the use of a 7% discount rate, if it decisively affects the ultimate decision, would seem to be legally doubtful — arbitrary in its own way.

But the case of harms to future generations, or people not yet born, is altogether different, and in that case the usual grounds for discounting monetary benefits are quite inapplicable. For this reason some people think that no discounting is appropriate for the nonmonetary benefits of regulation. On this view, a life-year saved is a life-year saved, and it does not matter, for purposes of valuation, when the saving occurs.

But there seems to be a major objection to this way of proceeding: it would appear to require truly extraordinary sacrifices from the present for the sake of the (infinite) future. Perhaps the "failure to discount would leave all generations at a subsistence level of existence, because benefits would be postponed perpetually for the future." On the other hand, it is not clear that the assumption behind this objection is convincing. Technological and other advances made by the current generation benefit future generations as well, and hence impoverishment of the current generation would inevitably harm those who will come later. In any case there is a hard ethical question here — how much the current generation should suffer for the benefit of the future — and a judgment against discounting would not answer that question unless we were sure that as a matter of policy, we should be engaging in maximizing some aggregate welfare function. It is not at all clear that this form of maximization is the appropriate choice to make.

At this point it should be clear that these issues are exceedingly complex and that agencies asked to engage in cost-benefit analysis have no clear path to an appropriate choice of discount rate for future generations.

Notes and Questions

1. Professor Sunstein makes several points about selecting an appropriate discount rate. First, regulatory statutes do not specify a discount rate and therefore leave agencies discretion to choose the appropriate one. Second, selecting a discount rate for monetary benefits and costs — such as future fuel savings — can be complicated because there tends to be more than one possibility. As a result, different agencies choose different discount rates, and sometimes the same agency chooses different discount rates for different issues. Third, the issue becomes even more difficult regarding non-monetary benefits because it acquires a moral dimension. Is a life saved in ten years worth less than a life saved today? As Sunstein suggests, avoiding latent injuries or deaths may be worth less because we value avoiding present harms more highly. This makes sense: we are given ten more years to live unaffected. But it is not inevitable. Fourth, what about harms to people who do not yet exist? Sunstein writes that agencies have "no clear path to an appropriate discount rate for future generations." How much should the present generation be made to suffer for benefits to future generations?

2. Given these considerations, who should select the appropriate discount rate? Agency career economists? Agency political appointees? OIRA officials? Elected officials themselves? Perhaps Congress *should* specify discount rates in regulatory statutes. Does Professor Sunstein's analysis help you answer these questions?

The choice of discount rate is an issue that arises frequently. Agencies often propose different discount rates and seek comment on the proper choice. Even when agencies do not solicit input on the discount rate or propose more than one, commentators often challenge their selection. As you can gather, understanding and questioning the discount rate (as well as the other components of cost-benefit analysis) is the work of lawyers and not just economists. To see the importance of discount rates from a lawyer's perspective, consider this example from another regulation setting fuel economy standards:

49 C.F.R. Parts 523, 533, and 537

Average Fuel Economy Standards for Light Trucks Model Years 2008-2011

[Docket No. NHTSA 2006-24306], Thursday, April 6, 2006

[71 Fed. Reg. 17566 (2006)]

AGENCY: National Highway Traffic Safety Administration (NHTSA), Department of Transportation.
ACTION: Final rule.

. . .

Discounting future fuel savings and other benefits is intended to measure the reduction in the value to society of these benefits when they are deferred until some future date rather than received immediately. The discount rate expresses the percent decline in the value of these benefits — as viewed from today's perspective — for each year they are deferred into the future. The agency used a discount rate of 7 percent per year to discount the value of future fuel savings and other benefits when it analyzed the CAFE standards proposed in the NPRM.

The Alliance, General Motors, the Mercatus Center, and Criterion Economics all argued that in assessing benefits and costs associated with the CAFE standards, the agency should rely on a discount rate greater than 7 percent. The Alliance stated that the Congressional Budget Office discounts consumers' fuel savings at a rate of 12 percent per year and that other recent studies of CAFE standards have also used that rate. According to the Alliance, that rate is slightly higher than the average interest rate that consumers reported paying to finance used car purchases in the most recent Consumer Expenditure Survey. The Alliance argued further that consumers can be expected to discount the value of future fuel savings at a rate at least as high as their cost for financing the purchase of a vehicle whose higher price was justified by its higher fuel economy.

The Alliance based its assertion for use of 12 percent because, as it stated, this value was used in the NAS [National Academy of Science] report and approximates the used car loan rate published in the Consumer Expenditure Survey. However, we note that the NAS report did not use a single discount rate. Instead, the NAS used both 12 percent and 0 percent discount rates due to the assumption that the proper discount rate was "subjective." Therefore, NAS did not advocate a discount rate. As explained below, the

vehicle loan rate faced by consumers is an appropriate measure of the discount rate.

General Motors suggested a discount rate of 9 percent, based on its assertions that new vehicles are financed at 8 percent and used vehicles at 10 percent. Essentially, General Motors is recommending that the agency rely on the interest for a car loan as the discount rate. General Motors also argued that fuel economy is not the only thing which consumers value and that the agency should take efforts to separate private benefits from public externalities. While we are uncertain as to what General Motors is recommending, we assume that its comment suggests that a higher discount rate, based on car loan rates, is appropriate for discounting private benefits (those to buyers), while a lower rate is appropriate for social benefits (such as reductions in externalities). Criterion Economics also recommended use of a 9 percent discount rate in its comments, which it suggested is a conservative rate between the average real rates for new and used cars that adequately accounts for volatility in future energy prices.

As discussed further below, we agree in that loan rates for new and used cars should be considered when determining the appropriate discount rate. However, loan estimates made by both General Motors and Criterion Economics are considerably higher than data provided by the Federal Reserve Board, which estimates new loan rates (as of October 2005) of 6 percent for new cars and 9 percent for used cars.

The Mercatus Center stated that the 7 percent discount rate selected by the agency is too low, and as a result, it results in the setting of standards that are inequitable, particularly to low-income households. According to published academic research referenced by the Mercatus Center, most households have discount rates higher than 7 percent, with low-income households having particularly high discount rate. Therefore, the Mercatus Center urged NHTSA to rely on discount rates of 12 percent for all households and as high as 20 percent for low-income households in evaluating proposed standards. However, the studies cited by Mercatus Center to justify these discount rates examine the implied discount rate for future energy savings that result when households purchase more energy-efficient appliances such as furnaces and air conditioners. These studies were generally conducted in the late 1970's and early 1980's and may not be representative of the discount rates for motor vehicles of the economic conditions 20-25 years later.

Environmental Defense, NRDC [Natural Resources Defense Council], and the Union of Concerned Scientists provided comments endorsing use of a lower discount rate. These organizations expressed their belief that a 7 percent discount rate is too high, proposing instead a rate of 3 percent. Environmental Defense and NRDC stated that OMB Circular A-4, Regulatory analysis (2003), recommends a discount rate of 3 percent when the regulation directly affects private consumption. These commenters asserted that the proposed CAFE

regulation primarily and directly affects private consumption (i.e., by affecting the sales price of new vehicles and reducing the per-mile cost of driving). NRDC also argued that OMB Circular A-4 further indicates that lower rates may be appropriate for rules that produce benefits over multiple generations. Thus, these commenters recommended that a discount rate reflecting the social rate of time preference (i.e., a 3 percent real rate) should be used.

In response to Environmental Defense, the Union of Concerned Scientists, and NRDC, the guidelines in OMB circular A-4, New Guidelines for the Conduct of Regulatory Analysis, state that the agency should analyze the costs and benefits of a regulation at 3 percent and 7 percent discount rates, as suggested by guidance issued by the federal OMB. The 3 percent and 7 percent rates reflect two potential evaluations of impacts: Foregone private consumption and foregone capital investment, respectively. In accordance with these guidelines, the agency analyzes the impacts of costs and benefits using both discount rates. However, this guidance does not state what discount rate should be used to determine the standards.

There are several reasons for the agency's choice of 7 percent as the appropriate discount rate to determine the standards. First, OMB Circular A-4 indicates that this rate reflects the economy-wide opportunity cost of capital. The agency believes that a substantial portion of the cost of this regulation may come at the expense of other investments the auto manufacturers might otherwise make. Several large manufacturers are resource-constrained with respect to their engineering and product-development capabilities. As a result, other

uses of these resources will be foregone while they are required to be applied to technologies that improve fuel economy.

Second, 7 percent is also an appropriate rate to the extent that the costs of the regulation come at the expense of consumption as opposed to investment. As explained below, the agency believes a car loan rate is an appropriate discount rate because it reflects the opportunity cost faced by consumers when buying vehicles with greater fuel economy and a higher purchase price. The agency assumed that a majority of both new and used vehicles is financed and since the vast majority of the benefits of higher fuel economy standards accrue to vehicle purchasers in the form of fuel savings, the appropriate discount rate is the car loan interest rate paid by consumers.

According to the Federal Reserve, the interest rate on new car loans made through commercial banks has closely tracked the rate on 10-year treasury notes, but exceeded it by about 3 percent. The official Administration forecast is that real interest rates on 10-year treasury notes will average about 3 percent through 2016, implying that 6 percent is a reasonable forecast for the real interest rate on new car loans. During the last five years, the interest rate on used car loans made through automobile financing companies has closely tracked the rate on new car loans made through commercial banks, but exceeded it by about 3 percent. Consideration is given to the loan rate of used cars because some of the fuel savings resulting from improved fuel economy accrue to used car buyers. Given the 6 percent estimate for new car loans, a reasonable forecast for used car loans is 9 percent. Since the benefits of fuel economy accrue to both new and used car owners, a discount rate between 6 percent and 9 percent is appropriate. Assuming that new car buyers discount fuel savings at 6 percent for 5 years (the average duration of a new car loan) and that used car buyers discount fuel savings at 9 percent for 5 years (the average duration of a used car loan), the single constant discount rate that yields equivalent present value fuel savings is very close to 7 percent.

Further, reliance on the consumer borrowing rate is consistent with that of the Department of Energy (DOE) program for energy efficient appliances. For more than a decade, the Department of Energy has used consumer borrowing interest rates or "finance cost" to discount the value of future energy savings in establishing minimum energy efficiency standards for household appliances. This includes (1) the financial cost of any debt incurred to purchase appliances, principally interest charges on debt, or (2) the opportunity cost of any equity used to purchase appliances, principally interest earnings on household equity. For example, for appliances purchased in conjunction with a new home, DOE uses real mortgage interest rates to discount future energy savings. This approach is analogous to NHTSA's use of real auto loan rates to discount future gasoline savings in establishing CAFE standards.

Notes and Questions

1. You can see that lawyering in the regulatory state involves economics, but some of the economics are not surprising. For example, it probably did not surprise you that the automakers were arguing for a higher discount rate while the public interest groups were arguing for a lower one. Which parts of the arguments reflect common sense rather than hard-core economics?

2. As you will see immediately below, OMB asks those agencies to submit a list of monetized costs and benefits in undiscounted terms. Can you understand the reason why?

Once an agency has monetized the benefits and costs of a regulation, including settling on a discount rate, what does it do with that information? How does it produce a cost-benefit analysis document? OMB has provided a guidance document for executive-branch agencies on what sort of cost-benefit analysis they should produce and submit to OIRA pursuant to the Executive Order in place since the Reagan era. It provides close to 50 pages of guidelines; here are the first few paragraphs of the section on developing cost-benefit estimates.

OMB, Circular A-4, To the Heads of Executive Agencies and Establishments, Subject: Regulatory Analysis [effective date January 1, 2004]

http://www.whitehouse.gov/omb/assets/regulatory_matters_pdf/a-4.pdf

SOME GENERAL CONSIDERATIONS

The analysis document should discuss the expected benefits and costs of the selected regulatory option and any reasonable alternatives. How is the proposed action expected to provide the anticipated benefits and costs? What are the monetized values of the potential real incremental benefits and costs to society? To present your results, you should:

- Include separate schedules of the monetized benefits and costs that show the type and timing of benefits and costs, and express the estimates in this table in constant, undiscounted dollars (for more on discounting see "*Discount Rates*" below);
- list the benefits and costs you can quantify, but cannot monetize, including their timing;
- describe benefits and costs you cannot quantify; and
- identify or cross-reference the data or studies on which you base the benefit and cost estimates.

When benefit and cost estimates are uncertain . . . , you should report benefit and cost estimates (including benefits of risk reductions) that reflect the full probability distribution of potential consequences. Where possible, present probability distributions of benefits and costs and include the upper and lower bound estimates as complements to central tendency and other estimates.

If fundamental scientific disagreement or lack of knowledge prevents construction of a scientifically defensible probability distribution, you should describe benefits or costs under plausible scenarios and characterize the evidence and assumptions underlying each alternative scenario. . . .

To the extent possible, you should monetize any such forgone benefits and add them to the other costs of that alternative. You should also try to monetize any cost savings as a result of an alternative and either add it to the benefits or subtract it from the costs of that alternative. . . .

Estimating benefits and costs when market prices are hard to measure or markets do not exist is more difficult. In these cases, you need to develop appropriate proxies that simulate market exchange. . . . For instance, a house is a product characterized by a variety of attributes including the number of rooms, total floor area, and type of heating and cooling. If there are enough data on transactions in the housing market, it is possible to develop an estimate of the implicit price for specific attributes, such as the implicit price of an additional bathroom or for central air conditioning. This technique can be extended, as well, to develop an estimate for the implicit price of public goods that are not directly traded in markets. An analyst can develop implicit price estimates for public goods like air quality and access to public parks by assessing the effects of these goods on the housing market. Going through the analytical process of deriving benefit estimates by simulating markets may also suggest alternative regulatory strategies that create such markets.

Notes and Questions

1. Agency officials and lawyers are likely to give the Circular A-4 guidelines careful attention; as OMB later clarified, "OMB may return a rule to an agency if its regulatory analysis does not conform to Circular A-4." *See* Memorandum for President's Management Council, From John G. Graham,

OMB's Circular A-4, New Guidelines for the Conduct of Regulatory Analysis (Mar. 2, 2004). But Circular A-4 is not only important for surviving OIRA review. How might Circular A-4 affect the way that an agency performs cost-benefit analysis at the early stages?

2. Circular A-4 addresses costs and benefits that agencies cannot monetize or quantify. What might these look like? Often the problem is that the risk itself is difficult to quantify, for example risks to the ecosystem. *See* Frank Ackerman & Lisa Heinzerling, *Pricing the Priceless: Cost-Benefit Analysis of Environmental Protection*, 150 U. PA. L. REV. 1553, 1554 (2002). Other times the risk is new, and economists lack enough information to generate quantitative estimates. How does Circular A-4 handle costs and benefits that are difficult to monetize or quantify?

3. What is the relationship between cost-benefit analysis and scientific analysis? Was that relationship evident in NHTSA's decision to rescind its passive restraints requirement? The agency lacked scientific evidence on the benefits of automatic seatbelts, and thus could not assign those benefits a number, even though common sense suggested to the agency that surely some passengers would not go to the trouble of detaching them. When science is uncertain, agencies frequently talk in terms of benefit or cost "ranges," as the OMB circular suggests that they do.

c. The Controversy over Cost-Benefit Analysis

Although the centrality of CBA is unarguable, the wisdom of relying on it as a critical tool for determining regulatory policy is controversial. Compare the following.

Cass R. Sunstein, Cost-Benefit Default Principles

99 Mich. L. Rev. 1651, 1656-63 (2001)

The rise of interest in cost-benefit balancing signals a dramatic shift from the initial stages of national risk regulation. Those stages were undergirded by what might be called "1970s environmentalism," which placed a high premium on immediate responses to long-neglected problems, which emphasized the existence of problems rather than their magnitude, and which was often rooted in moral indignation directed at the behavior of those who created pollution and other risks to safety and health. Defining aspects of 1970s environmentalism can be found in the apparently cost-blind national ambient air quality provisions of the Clean Air Act and in statutory provisions requiring that standards be set on the basis of "standards of performance" for which costs are a secondary consideration.

No one should deny that 1970s environmentalism has done an enormous amount of good, helping to produce dramatic improvements in many domains, above all in the context of air pollution, where ambient air quality has improved for all major pollutants. Indeed, 1970s environmentalism appears, by most accounts, to survive cost-benefit balancing, producing aggregate benefits in the trillions of dollars, well in excess of the aggregate costs. The EPA's own estimates suggest that, as a result of the Clean Air Act, there were 184,000 fewer premature deaths among people thirty years of age or older in 1990—and also that there were 39,000 fewer cases of congestive heart failure, 89,000 fewer cases of hospital admissions for respiratory problems, 674,000 fewer cases of chronic bronchitis, and 850,000 fewer asthma attacks. The EPA finds annual costs of air pollution control at $37 billion, hardly a trivial number, but less than 4% of the annual health and welfare benefits of $1.1 trillion. Even if the EPA's own numbers show an implausibly high ratio, more conservative valuations of likely beneficial effects still reveal benefits far higher than costs.

More generally, the Office of Management and Budget ("OMB") has, for the last several years, engaged in a full accounting of the costs and benefits of all regulation. The report shows that regulatory benefits, in the aggregate, exceed regulatory costs. While the government's own numbers should be discounted—agency accounts may well be self-serving—at least they provide a good place to start. In its 2000 report, OMB finds total regulatory benefits ranging from $254 billion to $1.8 trillion, with total costs ranging from $146 billion to $229 billion, for net benefits ranging from $25 billion to $1.65 trillion. A more disaggregated picture is also encouraging. In the transportation sector, the benefits range from $84 billion to $110 billion, with the costs from $15 billion to $18 billion, for net benefits of $66 billion to $95 billion. In the net, benefits range from $9 billion to $12 billion. Much of the uncertainty stems from uncertainty about environmental benefits and costs, producing a possible range from $73 billion in net costs to over $1.5 trillion in net benefits.

For most government action, however, the benefits do seem to exceed the costs. As especially good examples, consider the following regulations, all from recent years:

Table 1: Regulations Yielding Net Benefits

Regulation	2000 (net benefits in millions of dollars)	2005	2010	2015
Head impact protection	310-370	1,210-1,510	1,210-1,510	1,210-1,510
Conservation reserve program	1100	1100	1100	1100
Restriction on sale and distribution of tobacco	9,020-9820	9,020-9820	9,020-10,220	9,020-9820
Acid rain controls	260-1900	260-1900	260-1900	260-1900
Energy conservation standards for refrigerators	330	330-360	510-580	440-500
New surface water treatment	50-1,200	50-1,200	50-1,200	50-1,200
Emission standards for new highway heavy-duty engines	0	110-1200	110-1200	110-1200
Disposal of PCBs	136-736	136-736	136-736	136-736
Particulates standard	0	0	12,000-113,000	-20,000-86,000

But even though the overall picture shows no cause for alarm, a closer look at federal regulatory policy shows a wide range of problems. Perhaps foremost is exceptionally poor priority setting, with substantial resources sometimes going to small problems, and with little attention to some serious problems. There are also unnecessarily high costs, with no less than $400 billion being attributable to compliance costs each year, including $130 billion on environmental protection alone. OMB's own report shows some disturbing numbers. For the next fifteen years, OSHA's methylene chloride regulation will have annual costs of $100 million and annual benefits of $40 million; a regulation calling for roadway worker protection has benefits of $30 million, but equivalent costs; the cost-benefit ratio for airbag technology innovations seems bad, though there is uncertainty in the data; EPA's regulation for financial assurance for municipal solid waste landfills has monetized benefits of $0, but costs of $100 million, and this is expected for the next fifteen years. By way of general illustration, consider the following table, all drawn from recent regulations:

Table 2: Regulations Failing to Yield Net Benefits

Regulation	2000 (net benefits in millions of dollars)	2005	2010	2015
Exposure to methylene chloride	-60	-60	-60	-60
Roadway worker protection	0	0	0	0
Financial assurance for municipal solid waste landfills	-100	-100	-100	-100
Pulp and paper effluent guidelines	-150 to 0	-150 to 0	-150 to 0	-240 to 0
Ozone standards	0	-235 to 240	-840 to 1190	-9,200 to -1000
Child restraint system	-40 to 40	-40 to 40	-40 to 40	-40 to 40
Vessel response plans	-220	-220	-220	-220
Nitrogen oxide emission from new fossil fuel fired steam generating units	-57 to 29	-57 to 29	-57 to 29	-57 to 29

These figures, based on the anticipated costs and benefits of each regulation adopted in a single year, show a less than coherent overall pattern, especially when Table 1 is put together with Table 2. According to one study, better allocations of health expenditures could save, each year, 60,000 more lives at no additional cost—and such allocations could maintain the current level of lives saved with $31 billion in annual savings. The point has been dramatized by repeated demonstrations that some regulations create significant substitute risks — and that with cheaper, more effective tools, regulation could achieve its basic goals while saving billions of dollars.

In these circumstances, the most attractive parts of the movement for cost-benefit analysis have been rooted not in especially controversial judgments about what government ought to be doing, but instead in a more mundane search for pragmatic instruments designed to reduce three central problems: poor priority setting, excessively costly tools, and inattention to the unfortunate side-effects of regulation. By drawing attention to costs and benefits, it should be possible to spur the most obviously desirable regulations, to deter the most obviously undesirable ones, to encourage a broader view of consequences, and to promote a search for least-cost methods of achieving regulatory goals. Notice that, so defended, cost-benefit analysis functions not only as an obstacle to unjustified regulation but also as a spur to government as well, showing that it should attend to neglected problems. If cost-benefit balancing is supported on these highly pragmatic grounds, it might well attract support from many different people with diverse theoretical commitments.

In fact, the record of cost-benefit analysis, at least within the EPA, is generally encouraging. Assessments of costs and benefits have, for example, helped produce more stringent and rapid regulation of lead in gasoline, promoted more stringent regulation of lead in drinking water, led to stronger controls on air pollution at the Grand Canyon and the Navaho Generating Station, and produced a reformulated gasoline rule that promotes stronger controls on air pollutants. In these areas, cost-benefit analysis, far from being only a check on regulation, has indeed spurred governmental attention to serious problems.

Cost-benefit analysis has also led to regulations that accomplish statutory goals at lower cost, or that do not devote limited private and public resources to areas where they are unlikely to do much good. With respect to asbestos, for example, an analysis of benefits and costs led the EPA to tie the phase-down schedules to the costs of substitutes, and also to exempt certain products from a flat ban. With respect to lead in gasoline and control of CFCs (destructive of the ozone layer), cost-benefit analysis helped promote the use of economic incentives rather than command-and-control regulation; economic incentives are much cheaper and can make more stringent regulation possible in the first place. For regulation of sludge, protection of farm workers, water pollution regulation for the Great Lakes, and controls on organic chemicals, cost-benefit analysis helped regulators produce modifications that significantly reduced costs. For modern government, one of the most serious problems appears to be not agency use of cost-benefit analysis, but frequent noncompliance with executive branch requirements that agencies engage in such analysis.

Of course cost-benefit analysis is hardly uncontroversial. Insofar as both costs and benefits are being measured by the economic criterion of "private willingness to pay," there are many problems. Poor people often have little

ability, and hence little willingness, to pay, and some people will be inadequately informed and therefore show unwillingness to pay for benefits that
would improve their lives. In some circumstances, regulatory agencies should
seek not private willingness to pay, but reflective public judgments as expressed
in public arenas. Society is not best taken as some maximizing machine, in
which aggregate output is all that matters. Sometimes a regulation producing
$5 million in benefits but $6 million in costs will be worthwhile, if those who
bear the costs (perhaps representing dollar losses alone?) can do so easily,
and if those who receive the benefits (perhaps representing lives and illnesses
averted?) are especially needy. Sometimes public deliberation, with its own
norms and constraints, will reveal that government should proceed even if
the costs exceed the benefits, measured in terms of private willingness to pay.

In view of these problems, the strongest arguments for cost-benefit balancing are based not only on neoclassical economics, but also on an understanding of human cognition, on democratic considerations, and on an
assessment of the real-world record of such balancing. Begin with cognition.
People have a hard time understanding the systemic consequences of one-
shot interventions. Unless they are asked to seek a full accounting, they are
likely to focus on small parts of problems, producing inadequate or even
counterproductive solutions. Cost-benefit analysis is a way of producing that
full accounting. Ordinary people also have difficulty in calculating probabilities, and they tend to rely on rules of thumb, or heuristics, that can lead
them to make systematic errors. Cost-benefit analysis is a natural corrective
here. Because of intense emotional reactions to particular incidents, people
often make mistakes in thinking about the seriousness of certain risks. Cost-
benefit balancing should help government resist demands for regulation
that are rooted in misperceptions of facts. The idea here is not that the
numbers are all that matter, but that the numbers can inform public debate
simply by providing relevant information.

With respect to democracy, the case for cost-benefit analysis is strengthened by the fact that interest groups are often able to use these cognitive
problems strategically, thus fending off regulation that is desirable or pressing
for regulation when the argument on its behalf is fragile. Here cost-benefit
analysis, taken as an input into decisions, can protect democratic processes
by exposing an account of consequences to public view. Of course, public
deliberation might reveal that private willingness to pay greatly understates
the actual benefits of the project at issue. Values will inevitably play a role
in the characterization and assessment of costs and especially benefits, but
a review of the record suggests that cost-benefit balancing leads to improvements, not on any controversial view of how to value the goods at stake, but
simply because such balancing leads to more stringent regulation of serious
problems, less costly ways of achieving regulatory goals, and a reduction in
expenditures for problems that are, by any account, relatively minor.

None of these points suggests that cost-benefit analysis is a panacea
for the problems that I have identified. Everything depends on questions

of implementation, and there are also hard questions about appropriate valuation, questions to which I shall return. It is possible that cost-benefit balancing could provide a form of "paralysis by analysis," and thus prevent desirable regulations from going forward. I have emphasized that the numbers should not be decisive. Sometimes respect for rights, or concerns about irreversibility, justify a rejection of cost-benefit balancing. Interest groups will undoubtedly portray both costs and benefits in a self-serving manner. The central point is that cost-benefit analysis can be seen, not as opposition to some abstraction called "regulation," and not as an endorsement of the economic approach to valuation, but as a real-world instrument designed to ensure that the consequences of regulation are placed before relevant officials and the public as a whole, and intended to spur attention to neglected problems while at the same time ensuring that limited resources will be devoted to areas where they will do the most good. Thus understood, cost-benefit analysis promises to attract support from a wide range of people with diverse perspectives on contested issues — a promise realized in the apparently growing bipartisan consensus on some form of cost-benefit balancing in many domains of regulatory policy.

Frank Ackerman & Lisa Heinzerling, Pricing the Priceless: Cost-Benefit Analysis of Environmental Protection

150 U. Pa. L. Rev. 1553, 1554-81 (2002)

1. THE LIMITS OF QUANTIFICATION

Cost-benefit studies of regulations focus on quantified benefits of the proposed action and generally ignore other, nonquantified, health and environmental benefits. This raises a serious problem because many benefits of environmental programs — including the prevention of many nonfatal diseases and harms to the ecosystem — either have not been quantified or are not capable of being quantified at this time. Indeed, for many environmental regulations, the only benefit that can be quantified is the prevention of cancer deaths. On the other hand, one can virtually always come up with some number for the costs of environmental regulations. Thus, in practice, cost-benefit analysis tends to skew decision making against protecting public health and the environment.

For example, regulation of workers' exposure to formaldehyde is often presented as the extreme of inefficiency, supposedly costing $72 billion per life saved. This figure is based on the finding that the regulation prevents cancers that occur only in small numbers, but which have been thoroughly evaluated in numerical terms. But the formaldehyde regulation also prevents many painful but nonfatal illnesses excluded from the $72 billion figure. If described solely as a means of reducing cancer, the regulation indeed would be very expensive. But if described as a means of reducing cancer and other diseases, the regulation would make a good deal of sense. Workplace regulation of formaldehyde is not a bad answer, but it does happen to be an answer to a different question.

The formaldehyde case is by no means unique. Often, the only regulatory benefit that can be quantified is the prevention of cancer, yet cancer has a latency period of between five and forty years. When discounted at five percent, a cancer death forty years from now has a "present value" of only one-seventh of a death today. Thus, one of the benefits that most often can be quantified — allowing it to be folded into cost-benefit analysis — is also one that is heavily discounted, making the benefits of preventive regulation seem trivial.

A. Ignoring What Cannot Be Counted

A related practical problem is that even when the existence of unquantified or unquantifiable benefits is recognized, their importance is frequently ignored. Many advocates of cost-benefit analysis concede that the decision-making process must make some room for non-quantitative considerations. Some environmental benefits never have been subjected to rigorous economic evaluation. Other important considerations in environmental protection (such as the fairness of the distribution of environmental risks) cannot be quantified and priced.

In practice, however, this kind of judgment is often forgotten, or even denigrated, once all the numbers have been crunched. No matter how many times the EPA, for example, says that one of its rules will produce many benefits — like the prevention of illness or the protection of ecosystems — that cannot be quantified, the non-quantitative aspects of its analyses are almost invariably ignored in public discussions of its policies.

When the Clinton administration's EPA proposed, for example, strengthening the standard for arsenic in drinking water, it cited many human illnesses that would be prevented by the new standard but that could not be expressed in numerical terms. Subsequent public discussion of the EPA's cost-benefit analysis of this standard, however, inevitably referred only to the EPA's numerical analysis and forgot about the cases of avoided illness that could not be quantified.

B. Overstated Costs

There is also a tendency, as a matter of practice, to overestimate the costs of regulations in advance of their implementation. This happens in part because regulations often encourage new technologies and more efficient ways of doing business; these innovations reduce the cost of compliance. It is also important to keep in mind, when reviewing cost estimates, that they are usually provided by the regulated industry itself, which has an obvious incentive to offer high estimates of costs as a way of warding off new regulatory requirements.

One study found that costs estimated in advance of regulation were more than twice the actual costs in eleven out of twelve cases. Another study found that advance total cost estimates were more than 25% higher than actual costs for fourteen out of twenty-eight regulations; advance estimates were more than 25% too low in only three of the twenty-eight cases. Before the 1990 Clean Air Act Amendments took effect, industry anticipated that the cost of sulfur reduction under the amendments would be $1500 per ton: In 2000, the actual cost was under $150 per ton. Of course, not all cost-benefit analyses overstate the actual costs of regulation, but given the technology-forcing character of environmental regulations, it is not surprising to find a marked propensity to overestimate the costs of such rules.

In a related vein, many companies have begun to discover that environmental protection actually can be good for business in some respects. Increased energy efficiency, profitable products made from waste, and decreased use of raw materials are just a few of the cost-saving or even profit-making results of turning more corporate attention to environmentally protective business practices. Cost-benefit analyses typically do not take such money-saving possibilities into account in evaluating the costs of regulation.

Notes and Questions

1. What are the advantages of CBA? What are the disadvantages? Is it possible to be more specific in our assessment? For example, are there certain types of regulatory problems which are more amenable to CBA or allow less controversial applications of CBA? Are their certain problems which are less amendable? Consider the views of John Graham, OIRA Administrator during the George W. Bush administration:

> Public health, safety, and environmental regulation, launched with optimism during the Progressive Era, the New Deal, and the Great Society, survived the deregulatory impulses of the early Reagan years and the Gingrich era. Sometimes called "lifesaving" regulation for short, these rules differ from curative medicine because they do not seek to improve the health of identifiable individuals. Unlike an effort to save a trapped coal miner or a patient dying from kidney disease, administrative law saves lives by reducing small probabilities of premature death, injury, or illness among large numbers of anonymous workers, consumers, travelers, and residents. The names of those whose lives will be saved are unknown when the rule is adopted and may never be known. They are sometimes called "statistical lives."
>
> Thanks to advances in probability research and statistics, we now know that federal lifesaving regulations do save lives, and there is no basis for believing that these lives are any less real than the lives saved by physicians and nurses in emergency rooms. Although the evaluation literature is not as comprehensive and robust as one would prefer, there is a variety of studies showing that specific federal rules (or combinations

of rules) have saved lives, and, in fact, such rules now account for a majority of the major rules issued each year by the U.S. federal government. . . .

Who are the lifesaving regulators? Measured by recent rulemaking activity, they include the Department of Agriculture (USDA), the Food and Drug Administration (FDA), the Environmental Protection Agency (EPA), the Occupational Safety and Health Administration (OSHA), and the Department of Transportation (DOT). Independent agencies such as the Nuclear Regulatory Commission (NRC) and the Consumer Product Safety Commission (CPSC) play an important role outside the purview of White House oversight.

John D. Graham, *Saving Lives Through Administrative Law and Economics*, 157 U. PA. L. REV. 395, 397-99 (2008). Which issues or agencies are not on the list?

2. Given the stakes of CBA for regulations and how much variance there is on monetizing benefits and costs, what sorts of internal checks should an agency have to help improve the quality of its analysis?

3. How does the involvement of OIRA and OMB affect the analysis? Does Circular A-4 help address any of the issues that Professors Ackerman and Heinzerling raise? Might OIRA review harm in other respects? What if OIRA career economists or political officials injected their own biases, perhaps focusing more heavily on costs than benefits, thereby tilting in a deregulatory direction? *See* Nicholas Bagley & Richard Revesz, *Centralized Oversight of the Regulatory State*, 106 COLUM. L. REV. 1260, 1267-70 (2006), Lisa Schultz Bressman & Michael P. Vandenbergh, *Inside the Administrative State: A Critical Look at the Practice of Presidential Control*, 105 MICH. L. REV. 47, 72-74 (2006); RICHARD REVESZ & MICHAEL LIVERMORE, RETAKING RATIONALITY: HOW COST-BENEFIT ANALYSIS CAN BETTER PROTECT THE ENVIRONMENT AND OUR HEALTH 24-45 (2011). What if the lobbyists for private firms, and litigation by those firms, distort the process? *See* Jason Scott Johnston, *A Game Theoretic Analysis of Institutions for Cost-Benefit Analysis*, 150 U. PA. L. REV. 1343 (2002). We will discuss these issues further in Chapter 6.

4. Consider the following response to general criticisms of cost-benefit analysis:

> First, a common criticism of CBA—that it sometimes produces morally unjustified outcomes—overlooks the fact that CBA is a decision procedure, not a moral standard. A decision procedure is a method for achieving desirable results, and some decision procedures are more accurate or less costly than others. CBA is justified, even if it sometimes produces undesirable outcomes, as long as the total costs associated with CBA (the costs of undesirable outcomes, plus procedural costs) are lower than the total costs associated with alternative decision procedures. We argue that alternatives that are proposed in the literature—risk-risk analysis, feasibility-based assessment, direct interpersonal comparisons, and so on—will typically be costlier than CBA, as long as CBA is used in the right way.
>
> Second, CBA will produce reasonably accurate results only as long as it is used in the right way, and this means that under certain conditions agencies may need to modify the traditional understanding of CBA, or even depart from CBA entirely. When a proposed project would affect people who have highly unequal levels of wealth, or who are poorly informed about the consequences of the project, or whose preferences

fail for other reasons to register projects that would enhance their well-being, agencies should modify or depart from CBA. One possible modification to CBA is the weighting of costs and benefits by a factor that reflects the marginal utility of money for the persons affected. Another is a revision of the standard methodology for computing costs and benefits, the "willingness to pay" and "willingness to accept" methodology, so as to take account of the disjunction between the mere satisfaction of a person's preferences and the enhancement of his well-being. The proper adjustments to standard CBA cannot be described at a high level of abstraction, but depend on such things as the competence of agencies, the degree to which they can be monitored by politically responsive actors, and the extent to which people's stated preferences and market choices track their own welfare.

Third, CBA suitably revised to reflect these concerns is consistent with a broad array of popular theories of the proper role of government. It is commonly and mistakenly believed that CBA presupposes a particular form of utlitarianism that assumes that the governement should maximize the satisfaction of people's preferences, even when these preferences are uninformed or distorted. By contrast, we argue that CBA, properly understood, is consistent with every political theory that holds that the government should care about the overall well-being of its citizens — including non-utilitarian theories that supplement "overall well-being" with additional moral considerations, and non-preference-based theories that incorporate a different view about the nature of well-being. The use of CBA by agencies in suitable circumstances is consistent with commitments to distributive justice, deontological rights, and other moral values, and it is consistent with the view that objective values, hedonic pleasures, and other factors beyond preference-satisfaction figure in human welfare.

Matthew D. Adler & Eric A. Posner, *Rethinking Cost-Benefit Analysis*, 109 YALE L.J. 165, 167-68 (1999).

5. Perhaps the most insistent response by proponents of CBA is that the critics have offered very little by way of an alternative. One intriguing proposal was offered by Professors Sidney Shapiro and Christopher Schroeder, which they refer to as a pragmatic regulatory impact analysis or pragmatic RIA. *See* Sidney A. Shapiro & Christopher H. Schroeder, *Beyond Cost-Benefit Analysis: A Pragmatic Reoreintation*, 32 HARV. ENVTL. L. REV. 433, 476-81 (2008). Their approach focuses on two steps: determining the "risk trigger" and then the level of regulation set by the statutory standard. The risk trigger requires the agency to make a prediction of a particular risk. If the risk were above a particular threshold, the agency would then regulate to the level of a statutory standard, which is rarely an explicitly CBA standard. This approach aims to focus the level of regulation on the statutory standard, not the monetizing of benefits and costs, which can distort decisionmaking. Another alternative is the Social Welfare Function proposed by MATTHEW D. ADLER, WELL-BEING AND FAIR DISTRIBUTION BEYOND COST-BENEFIT ANALYSIS (2011), which draws on recent scholarship regarding well-being and hedonic experience.

d. Statutory Variations in Economic Analysis

Organic statutes frequently have something to say about economic analysis. Some statutes require CBA and some prohibit it. Some statutes mandate a different or more limited form of analysis. Some are silent on the issue, leaving the choice to the agency itself. Ultimately, these are questions of statutory interpretation. An agency may have to decide as part of its legal analysis whether its organic statute specifies a form of economic analysis. We addressed the topic of agency statutory analysis earlier in this chapter. Now, we direct your attention to some rules of thumb for assessing how organic statutes generally treat economic analysis.

Cass R. Sunstein, Cost-Benefit Default Principles

99 Mich. L. Rev. 1651, 1664-67 (2001)

I order the statutes roughly in accordance with their treatment of cost-benefit balancing, beginning with those that most flatly reject it, and ending with those that unambiguously embrace it.

1. Flat bans on consideration of costs. Some statutes, exemplifying 1970s environmentalism, appear to forbid any consideration of cost. Perhaps the most famous example is the Delaney Clause, which for a long period prohibited food additives that "induce cancer in man or animal." In the face of that language, the government sought to permit additives that, while carcinogenic, created only the most minuscule risks of cancer — lower risks, in fact than those that would come from eating one peanut with the FDA-permitted level of aflatoxins every 250 days, and much lower risks than come from spending about seventeen hours every year in Denver (with its high elevation and radiation levels) rather than the District of Columbia. Nonetheless, the Delaney Clause was taken to forbid any form of balancing. But a far more important example comes from the most fundamental provisions of the Clean Air Act, governing national ambient air quality standards. For a long time, the national ambient air quality standards set under that Act have been understood to be based on "public health" alone. The EPA's judgment is to be grounded only in benefits; the cost of compliance is irrelevant.

2. Significant risk requirements. An alternative formulation is to require the agency to address only "significant" or "unacceptable" risks. On this view, risks that do not reach a certain level need not and perhaps may not be addressed. This is the prevailing interpretation of the Occupational Safety and Health Act, under both the toxic substance provisions and the more general provisions of the Act. A requirement of a "significant risk" falls short of cost-benefit analysis in the sense that it is entirely benefits-based; costs are irrelevant as such. Once benefits fall below a certain threshold, regulation is not required and in fact is banned. Once benefits rise above that threshold, regulation is permissible, even if the benefits seem low in comparison to the costs.

3. Substitute risks and health-health tradeoffs. Some statutes require agencies to consider whether a regulation controlling one risk would, in so doing, create a substitute risk. If so, agencies are permitted to decline to regulate, or to regulate to a different point. These are clear statutory recognition of health-health tradeoffs, which arise when there are health concerns on both sides of the equation, from both more and less regulation. Many statutory "consideration" requirements have an unambiguous feature of this sort, for example by requiring agencies entrusted with reducing air pollution problems to take account as well of "non-air quality health and environmental impact and energy requirements." Here is an explicit recognition that the EPA is allowed to consider the danger that a regulation that decreases air pollution will also create water pollution or some other environmental problem. The reformulated gasoline program takes this basic form, as does the provision governing emissions standards for new vehicles, which authorizes the EPA to examine "safety factors" as well as cost and energy issues. Thus the EPA is instructed to ask whether a program designed to reduce air pollution might thereby make cars more dangerous; if so, the EPA should reconsider the program. Under the fuel regulation program of the Clean Air Act, the EPA is not allowed to prohibit a fuel or fuel additive unless "he finds, and published such finding, that in his judgment such prohibition will not cause the use of any other fuel or fuel additive which will produce emissions which will endanger the public health or welfare to the same or greater degree than the prohibited item." The Toxic Substances Control Act similarly requires the EPA to take account of substitute risks.

4. *Feasibility requirements.* Some statutes require agencies to regulate "to the extent feasible" or "achievable." These expressions are far from transparent. But as generally understood, such statutes put the focus not on benefits but solely on costs, and on costs in a particular way. They forbid an agency from regulating to a point that is neither (a) technically feasible, because the relevant control technology does not exist, nor (b) economically feasible, because the industry cannot bear the cost without significant or massive business failures. The line between (a) and (b), usually treated as crisp and simple, is hardly that. Whether a requirement is technically feasible will usually depend on the level of resources that are devoted to it. In practice, (a) and (b) therefore overlap, with (b) serving as a separate category only on those occasions when even massive expenditure of existing resources cannot bring the technology into existence. Noteworthy here is the fact that, while a significant risk requirement is entirely benefits-based, a feasibility requirement looks exclusively at the cost side of the equation. Such a requirement is a "block" of excessively expensive regulation.

5. *"Consideration" requirements.* A large number of statutes ask agencies to "take into consideration" various factors, including cost, in addition to the principal factor to which the statute draws the agency's attention (such as clean air or water). The most common formulation, now standard, asks

the agency to produce the "maximum degree of reduction" that is "achievable," after "taking into consideration [1] the cost of achieving such emission reduction, and [2] any [a] non-air quality health and environmental impacts and [b] energy requirements." The basic idea here is that the agency is supposed to qualify the pursuit of the "maximum" achievable reduction by asking (a) whether the cost is excessive, (b) whether energy requirements would be adversely affected, and (c) whether the "maximum" requirement might create health and environmental harms by, for example, increasing water pollution though reducing air pollution.

6. Cost-benefit requirements. Several statutes ask agencies to balance costs against benefits, mostly through a prohibition of "unreasonable risks," alongside a definition of "unreasonable" that refers to both costs and benefits. The most prominent examples are the Toxic Substances Control Act and the Federal Insecticide, Fungicide, and Rodenticide Act. Under these statutes, the agency is required to calculate both costs and benefits and to compare them against each other. If the costs exceed the benefits, regulation is unacceptable. More recently, cost-benefit analysis has been mandated by the Safe Drinking Water Act Amendments. Under the Act, the EPA is asked to conduct a careful risk-cost analysis and to back away from the maximum feasible level if the benefits of the stricter standard "would not justify the costs of complying with the level." While Congress has thus far resisted efforts to impose a cost-benefit "supermandate" calling for a general decision rule based on cost-benefit balancing, Congress has enacted legislation requiring assessment, and public disclosure, of costs and benefits of major regulations. OMB itself has been required to produce annual accounting of costs and benefits.

In the abstract, the distinctions among these kinds of provisions should be clear enough. A statute that calls for consideration of substitute risks does not require cost-benefit balancing, because it is more narrowly concerned to ensure that risks (generally to health) do not increase on balance; under a statute calling for health-health tradeoffs, it is irrelevant that costs as such exceed benefits. A statute that requires that regulations be "feasible" is ordinarily taken to entail no comparison between costs and benefits, but a cost-focused inquiry into what industry is able to do. A statute that regulates "significant risks," by contrast, is ordinarily taken to entail no comparison between costs and benefits, but a benefit-centered inquiry into the magnitude of the risk to be addressed.

Notes and Questions

1. Professor Sunstein sets out a variety of useful rules of thumb for an initial assessment of whether a statute allows, prohibits, or requires the agency to engage in economic analysis of its regulations. But remember these are just rules of thumb; they are not reasons to forgo careful consideration of the statutes that you encounter.

2. Provisions to permit, prohibit, or require the agency to engage in economic analysis of its regulations are, like all other statutory design choices, a product of politics. With regard to an auto safety statute such as the Motor Vehicle Safety Act, which interest groups are likely to be the most vocal proponents of any provisions prohibiting, allowing, or requiring economic analysis? What about other consumer protection statutes or environmental statutes?

3. When a statute prohibits an agency from considering costs and benefits as a basis for its decision, may the White House nonetheless require that agency to perform CBA by executive order? We will take up this question in Chapter 6 when discussing presidential control of agency action. The short answer is probably.

4. Political Analysis

Agencies consider other factors that do not fall neatly into one of the previous categories, including public attitudes, distributional effects, and political preferences. We group these considerations into the broad category of political analysis, although nothing in particular turns on this label. These factors, which are the most difficult to describe in abstract terms, are often the ones that have the most significant effect on regulatory policy.

When regulating, agencies often consider public attitudes as part of their broader contextual analysis. Consider NHTSA. NHTSA was reluctant to impose automatic seatbelts because it believed citizens resisted them and would develop a dislike of future auto safety regulations. In addition, it was reluctant to experiment with nondetachable automatic seatbelts because citizens viewed them as traps in emergency situations.

Agencies not only consider how the public is likely to react to a regulation but whom a regulation is likely to affect. Thus, agencies take into account distributional and fairness concerns. For example, NHTSA was reluctant to impose costs on new car buyers because those buyers would be effectively subsidizing members of the public who refused to wear their manual belts. This issue can be captured in terms of the costs and benefits of a rule. NHTSA expressed the concern as one for "equity." Distributional concerns more typically arise when a problem burdens a discrete portion of the public — for example, when air quality is particularly bad in low-income neighborhoods because industrial plants have market incentives to locate there (e.g., available and inexpensive property). *See* Christopher W. Tessum, et al., Inequality in Consumption of Goods and Services Adds to Racial-Ethnic Disparities in Air Pollution Exposure, Proceedings of the Nat'l Acad. of Sciences, USA, March 11, 2019 https://doi.org/10.1073/pnas.1818859116. Then agencies may frame regulation as alleviating fairness concerns raised by market forces.

In addition to considering public impacts, agencies consider political preferences. Here we are not speaking about the preferences that motivated Congress to enact a statute. Rather, we mean the preferences of current political officials, including the President and members of Congress, concerning the implementation of the statute. Recall that President Reagan campaigned on a platform of deregulation that included reducing government burdens on the ailing domestic auto industry. NHTSA may have considered that political agenda in issuing the rule that rescinded passive restraints, as then-Justice Rehnquist observed in his dissenting opinion in the case reviewing that rule:

> The agency's changed view of the standard seems to be related to the election of a new President of a different political party. It is readily apparent that the responsible members of one administration may consider public resistance and uncertainties to be more important than do their counterparts in a previous administration. A change in administration brought about by the people casting their votes is a perfectly reasonable basis for an executive agency's reappraisal of the costs and benefits of its programs and regulations. As long as the agency remains within the bounds established by Congress. . . .

Motor Vehicle Manufacturers Ass'n v. State Farm Insurance Co., 463 U.S. 29, 59 (1983) (Rehnquist, J., dissenting).

Of course, if NHTSA had relied on this basis in issuing its rule, it was not evident on the face of the NPRM or the final rule. Agencies are not always forthright about their political considerations. Think for a moment why NHTSA excluded political considerations from its explanation for the rescission of Standard 208; would President Reagan's platform have been a permissible basis for the rescission?

A. An Example of Political Analysis

Still, sometimes political considerations appear as an explicit part of the agency's rationale, alongside statutory, scientific, and economic considerations. Here is an example of explicit reliance on political preferences in an EPA document denying a petition for rulemaking.

Environmental Protection Agency

[FRL-7554-7]

[68 Fed. Reg. 52922 (2003)]

Control of Emissions From New Highway Vehicles and Engines

Monday, September 8, 2003
AGENCY: Environmental Protection Agency (EPA).
ACTION: Notice of denial of petition for rulemaking.

SUMMARY: A group of organizations petitioned EPA to regulate emissions of carbon dioxide and other greenhouse gases from motor vehicles under the Clean Air Act. For the reasons set forth in this notice, EPA is denying the petition. . . .

SUPPLEMENTARY INFORMATION:

I. Background

On October 20, 1999, the International Center for Technology Assessment (ICTA) and a number of other organizations petitioned EPA to regulate certain greenhouse gas (GHG) emissions from new motor vehicles and engines under section 202(a)(1) of the Clean Air Act (CAA). Specifically, petitioners seek EPA regulation of carbon dioxide (CO_2), methane (CH_4), nitrous oxide (N_2O), and hydrofluorocarbon (HFCs) emissions from new motor vehicles and engines. Petitioners claim these emissions are significantly contributing to global climate change.

EPA is authorized to regulate air pollutants from motor vehicles under title II of the CAA. In particular, section 202(a)(1) provides that "the Administrator [of EPA] shall by regulation prescribe . . . in accordance with the provisions of [section 202], standards applicable to the emission of any air pollutant from any class or classes of new motor vehicle . . . , which in his judgment cause, or contribute to, air pollution which may reasonably be anticipated to endanger public health or welfare." . . .

V. EPA Response

After careful consideration of petitioners' arguments and the public comments, EPA concludes that it cannot and should not regulate GHG emissions from U.S. motor vehicles under the CAA. Based on a thorough review of the CAA, its legislative history, other congressional action and Supreme Court precedent, EPA believes that the CAA does not authorize regulation to address global climate change. Moreover, even if CO_2 were an air pollutant generally subject to regulation under the CAA, Congress has not authorized the Agency to regulate CO_2 emissions from motor vehicles to the extent such standards would effectively regulate car and light truck fuel economy, which is governed by a comprehensive statute administered by DOT.

In any event, EPA believes that setting GHG emission standards for motor vehicles is not appropriate at this time. President Bush has established a comprehensive global climate change policy designed to (1) answer questions about the causes, extent, timing and effects of global climate change that are critical to the formulation of an effective, efficient long-term policy, (2) encourage the development of advanced technologies that will enable dramatic reductions in GHG emissions, if needed, in the future, and (3) take sensible steps in the interim to reduce the risk of global climate change. The international nature of global climate change also has implications for foreign policy, which the President directs. In view of EPA's lack of CAA regulatory authority to address global climate change, DOT's

authority to regulate fuel economy, the President's policy, and the potential foreign policy implications, EPA declines the petitioners' request to regulate GHG emissions from motor vehicles. . . .

D. Different Policy Approach

Beyond issues of authority and interference with fuel economy standards, EPA disagrees with the regulatory approach urged by petitioners. We agree with the President that "we must address the issue of global climate change" (February 14, 2002). We do not believe, however, that it would be either effective or appropriate for EPA to establish GHG standards for motor vehicles at this time. As described in detail below, the President has laid out a comprehensive approach to climate change that calls for near-term voluntary actions and incentives along with programs aimed at reducing scientific uncertainties and encouraging technological development so that the government may effectively and efficiently address the climate change issue over the long term. . . .

Knowledge of the climate system and of projections about the future climate is derived from fundamental physics, chemistry and observations. Data are then incorporated in global circulation models. However, model projections are limited by the paucity of data available to evaluate the ability of coupled models to simulate important aspects of climate. The U.S. and other countries are attempting to overcome these limitations by developing a more comprehensive long-term observation system, by making more extensive regional measurements of greenhouse gases, and by increasing the computing power required to handle these expanded data sets.

A central component of the President's policy is to reduce key uncertainties that exist in our understanding of global climate change. Important efforts are underway to address these uncertainties. In particular, the Federal Government has expanded scientific research efforts through its Climate Change Research Initiative (CCRI). President Bush announced this new initiative in June 2001 and called for it "to study areas of uncertainty and identify priority areas where investments can make a difference." The CCRI recently issued its final "Strategic Plan for the Climate Change Research Program" to ensure that scientific efforts are focused where they are most critical and that the key scientific uncertainties identified are addressed in a timely and effective manner for decision makers.

The President has also stated, however, that "while scientific uncertainties remain, we can begin now to address the factors that contribute to climate change" (June 11, 2001). Thus, along with stepped-up efforts to reduce scientific uncertainties, the President's policy calls for public-private partnerships to develop break-through technologies that could dramatically reduce the economy's reliance on fossil fuels without slowing its growth. Large-scale shifts away from traditional energy sources, however, will require not only the development of abundant, cost-effective alternative fuels, but potentially wholesale changes in the way industrial processes and consumer products use fuel. Such momentous shifts do not take place quickly. As the President has explained, "[a]ddressing global climate change will require a sustained effort, over many generations' (*www.whitehouse.gov/ news/releases/2002/02/ climatechange.html*).

By contrast, establishing GHG emission standards for U.S. motor vehicles at this time would require EPA to make scientific and technical judgments without the benefit of the studies being developed to reduce uncertainties and advance technologies. It would also result in an inefficient, piecemeal approach to addressing the climate change issue. The U.S. motor vehicle fleet is one of many sources of GHG emissions both here and abroad, and different GHG emission sources face different technological and financial challenges in reducing emissions. A sensible regulatory scheme would require that all significant sources and sinks of GHG emissions be considered in deciding how best to achieve any needed emission reductions.

Unilateral EPA regulation of motor vehicle GHG emissions could also weaken U.S. efforts to persuade key developing countries to reduce the GHG intensity of their economies. Considering the large populations and growing economies of some developing countries, increases in their GHG emissions could quickly overwhelm the effects of GHG reduction measures in developed countries. Any potential benefit of EPA regulation could be lost to the extent other nations decided to let their emissions significantly increase in view of U.S. emission reductions. Unavoidably, climate change raises important foreign policy issues, and it is the President's prerogative to address them.

In light of the considerations discussed above, EPA would decline the petitioners' request to regulate motor vehicle GHG emissions even if it had authority to promulgate such regulations. Until more is understood about the causes, extent and significance of climate change and the potential options for addressing it, EPA believes it is inappropriate to regulate GHG emissions from motor vehicles.

In any event, the President's policy includes efforts to reduce motor vehicle petroleum consumption through increases in motor vehicle fuel economy. As noted previously, petitioners specifically suggested that EPA set a "corporate average fuel economy-based standard," but only DOT is authorized to set motor vehicle fuel economy standards. DOT considered increasing fuel economy standards and recently promulgated a final rule increasing the CAFE standards for light trucks, including sports utility vehicles, by 1.5 miles per gallon over a three-year period beginning with model year 2005. The new standards are projected to result in savings of approximately 3.6 billion gallons of gasoline over the lifetime of the affected vehicles, with the corresponding avoidance of 31 million metric tons of carbon dioxide emissions. For the longer term, the President has established a new public-private partnership with the nation's automobile manufacturers to promote the development of hydrogen as a primary fuel for cars and trucks, with the goal of building a commercially viable zero-emissions hydrogen-powered vehicle. In the near-term, the President has sought $3 billion in tax credits over 11 years for consumers to purchase fuel cell and hybrid vehicles.

Notes and Questions

1. Describe the President's stated goals or initiatives for addressing climate change. Did the agency "agree" with those goals and initiatives or simply follow them? Is it possible to tell the difference? Should it matter?

2. What if an agency relied not on the views of the President but on the views of OIRA concerning the benefits and costs of a regulation? As you will recall, OIRA is the agency within the White House responsible for reviewing significant proposed agency rules from an economic perspective. Is relying on the views of OIRA problematic?

3. To what extent can an agency follow political preferences when those preferences conflict with other factors, whether statutory, scientific, or economic? Consider the relationship between political and scientific analysis in EPA's document: "A central component of the President's policy is to reduce key uncertainties that exist in our understanding of global climate change." What if the President's view of uncertainty was different from the National Academy of Sciences or other experts? Is uncertainty more of a political question than a scientific one? See Edward L. Rubin, Beneficial Precaution: A Proposed Approach to Uncertain Technological Dangers, 21 JETLaw (forthcoming 2019). Now do you have a sense for why NHTSA declined to rely explicitly on President Reagan's preference for rescinding passive restraints?

4. More generally, to the extent that agencies take into account current political preferences, will an agency's interpretation or implementation of a statute end up more dynamic than a court's interpretation of the same statutory provisions?

EPA also considered contemporary congressional preferences concerning climate change as it understood those preferences from statutes in the area.

Environmental Protection Agency

[FRL-7554-7]

[68 Fed. Reg. 52922 (2003)]

Control of Emissions From New Highway Vehicles and Engines

Monday, September 8, 2003

AGENCY: Environmental Protection Agency (EPA).

ACTION: Notice of denial of petition for rulemaking.

. . . Congress was well aware of the global climate change issue when it last comprehensively amended the CAA in 1990. During the 1980s, scientific discussions about the possibility of global climate change led to public concern both in the U.S. and abroad. In response, the U.S. and other nations developed the United Nations Framework Convention on Climate Change (UNFCCC). President George H. W. Bush signed, and the U.S. Senate approved, the UNFCCC in 1992, and the UNFCCC took effect in 1994.

The UNFCCC established the "ultimate objective" of "stabiliz[ing] greenhouse gas concentrations in the atmosphere at a level that would prevent dangerous anthropogenic interference with the climate system" (Article 2 of the UNFCCC). All parties to the UNFCCC agreed on the need for further research to determine the level at which GHG concentrations should be stabilized, acknowledging that "there are many uncertainties in predictions of climate change, particularly with regard to the timing, magnitude and regional patterns thereof" (findings section of UNFCCC).

Shortly before the UNFCCC was adopted in May 1992, Congress developed the 1990 CAA amendments. A central issue for the UNFCCC — whether binding emission limitations should be set — was also considered in the context of the CAA amendments. As several commenters noted, a Senate committee included in its bill to amend the CAA a provision requiring EPA to set CO_2 emission standards for motor vehicles. However, that provision was removed from the bill on which the full Senate voted, and the bill eventually enacted was silent with regard to motor vehicle CO_2 emission standards. During this same time period, other legislative proposals were made to control GHG emissions, some in the context of national energy policy, but none were passed (see, e.g., S. 324, 101st Cong. (1989); S. 1224, 101st Cong. (1989); H.R. 5966, 101st Cong. (1990)).

In the CAA Amendments of 1990 as enacted, Congress called on EPA to develop information concerning global climate change and "nonregulatory" strategies for reducing CO_2 emissions. Specifically, uncodified section 821 of the CAA Amendments requires measurement of CO_2 emissions from utilities subject to permitting under title V of the CAA. New section 602 of the CAA directs EPA to determine the "global warming potential" of substances that deplete stratospheric ozone. And new section 103(g) calls on EPA to develop "nonregulatory" measures for the prevention of multiple air pollutants and lists several air pollutants and CO_2 for that purpose.

Notably, none of these provisions authorizes the imposition of mandatory requirements, and two of them expressly preclude their use for regulatory purposes (sections 103(g) and 602). Only the research and development provision of the CAA — section 103 — specifically mentions CO_2, and the legislative history of that section indicates that Congress was focused on seeking a sound scientific basis on which to make future decisions on global climate change, not regulation under the CAA as it was being amended. Representatives Roe and Smith, two of the principal authors of section 103 as amended, explained that EPA's "science mandate" needed updating to deal with new, more complex issues, including "global warming" (A Legislative History of the Clean Air Act Amendments of 1990, 103 Cong., 1st Sess., S. Prt. 103-38, Vol. 2, pp. 2776 and 2778). They

expressed concern that EPA's research budget had been too heavily focused on supporting existing regulatory actions when the Agency also needed to conduct long-term research to "enhance EPA's ability to predict the need for future action" (id. at 2777).

In providing EPA with expanded research and development authority, however, Congress did not provide commensurate regulatory authority. In section 103(g), Congress directed EPA to establish a "basic engineering research and technology program to develop, evaluate and demonstrate" strategies and technologies for air pollution prevention and specifically called for improvements in such measures for preventing CO_2 as well as several specified air pollutants. But it expressly provided that nothing in the subsection "shall be construed to authorize the imposition on any person of air pollution control requirements." As if to drive home the point, section 103(g) was revised in conference to include the term "nonregulatory" to describe the "strategies and technologies" the subsection was intended to promote. In its treatment of the global climate change issue in the CAA amendments, Congress made clear that it awaited further information before making decisions on the need for regulation.

Beyond Congress' specific CAA references to CO_2 and global warming, another aspect of the Act cautions against construing its provisions to authorize regulation of emissions that may contribute to global climate change. The CAA provisions addressing stratospheric ozone depletion

demonstrate that Congress has understood the need for specially tailored solutions to global atmospheric issues, and has expressly granted regulatory authority when it has concluded that controls may be needed as part of those solutions. Like global climate change, the causes and effects of stratospheric ozone depletion are global in nature. Anthropogenic substances that deplete stratospheric ozone are emitted around the world and are very long-lived; their depleting effects and the consequences of those effects occur on a global scale. In the CAA prior to its amendment in 1990, Congress specifically addressed the problem in a separate portion of the statute (part B of title I) that recognized the global nature of the problem and called for negotiation of international agreements to ensure world-wide participation in research and any control of stratospheric ozone-depleting substances. In the 1990 CAA amendments, Congress again addressed the issue in a discrete portion of the statute (title VI) that similarly provides for coordination with the international community. Moreover, both incarnations of the CAA's stratospheric ozone provisions contain express authorization for EPA to regulate as scientific information warrants. In light of this CAA treatment of stratospheric ozone depletion, it would be anomalous to conclude that Congress intended EPA to address global climate change under the CAA's general regulatory provisions, with no provision recognizing the international dimension of the issue and any solution, and no express authorization to regulate.

Notes and Questions

1. EPA considered these legislative actions as part of its statutory analysis. The agency found, in light of these actions, that Congress did not authorize it to regulate greenhouse gases under the "general regulatory provisions" of the CAA. What is the relationship between statutory analysis and political analysis? Did these actions *really* determine the clear meaning of a prior-enacted statutory provision? Were these statutes reliable indications of congressional preferences for any purpose? For example, were they as strong as President Bush's statements on the issue? If not, why was the agency leaning on them so heavily?

2. It is more complicated for Congress to make known its views than the President because of the multi-member problem. How can an agency be certain what a majority of Congress (or even the median legislator) prefers concerning the implementation of a statute? An agency might have a sense for the views of certain members — for example, recall that members of Congress submitted comments on the passive restraints rule rescission. Is it less justifiable for an agency to rely heavily on the views of some members than on the views of the President?

E. OTHER POLICYMAKING FORMATS

In this chapter, we have illustrated how agencies implement their statutes through notice-and-comment rules. But agencies also use other policymaking forms, including *adjudication* and *guidance.* To provide a more complete picture of agency statutory implementation, we briefly consider these forms.

1. Adjudication

Some agencies rely heavily on adjudication as a means of setting policy. In addition, there is an inherent element of policy making in most adjudicatory systems. Administrative adjudication comes in a wide variety of forms. One way to categorize them is according to the legal rules that govern them. From least to most restrictive (very roughly), these are:

   a. *No rules.* The governing statute does not specify any rules, and no one's rights are involved. The Department of Transportation Act of 1966 and the Federal-Aid Highway Act of 1968 prohibit the Secretary of Transportation from authorizing the use of federal funds to finance the construction of highways through public parks if a "feasible and prudent" alternative route exists. But neither act specifies the procedures that the Secretary must use, and no private citizen's rights are at stake (parks don't have rights). Thus, the Secretary is free to devise whatever procedures seem appropriate. A challenge to one of these determinations came before the Supreme Court in *Citizens to Preserve Overton Park v. Volpe.*

b. *Due process.* If the rights of individuals are involved, but there is no procedure specified by statute, then the Due Process Clause of the Fifth or Fourteenth Amendments applies. In the administrative law context, due process, as defined by Goldberg v. Kelly, 397 U.S. 254 (1970) and Mathews v. Eldridge 424 U.S. 319 (1976), requires notice, a hearing, an impartial decision maker, and a decision on the record. The rights that trigger these requirements are "life, liberty, or property" as stated in the Amendments and interpreted in Board of Regents of State Colleges v. Roth, 408 U.S. 564 (1974). Unlike the previous category, the imposition of due process rules necessarily results in a procedure that we generally recognize as a trial.

c. *Statutory rules.* A statute cannot reduce due process protection because that is a constitutional requirement, but it can add other procedural requirements. Of course, if the Due Process Clause is not triggered, then the statutory rules can be less restrictive than due process requirements, which is why this is only a rough categorization. You have seen an example of such statutory rules in detail, namely, the rules governing recalls of automobiles that violate motor vehicle safety standards, which appear in the Motor Vehicle Safety Act. Given the existence of formal adjudication, it is tempting to call these adjudications "informal," and to apply that term to the preceding category as well. Recall however, that the term "informal adjudication" is used as a residual category for all agency action that is not formal adjudication or rulemaking. Thus, hearings that are governed by statutory rules or due process certainly count as adjudications in administrative law lingo, but so do hearings governed by no rules at all, as do educational brochures, no-action letters, inspections, negotiations, etc.

d. *Formal adjudication.* The rules for formal adjudication by agencies are specified in §§554-557 of the APA. They are only required when a statute provides that determinations by the agency must be made "on the record" after an agency hearing. *See* United States v. Florida East Coast Railway, 410 U.S. 224 (1973). Think of formal adjudication as analogous to a judicial bench trial. In other words, the procedural requirements go considerably beyond the requirements of due process. The official who presides over the initial agency hearing is typically an Administrative Law Judge, or ALJ. In formal adjudication, the parties have a right to present their position "by oral or documentary evidence." APA, 5 U.S.C. §556(d). Furthermore, the parties also have a right to "conduct cross-examination as may be required for a full and true disclosure of the facts." *Id.* The Federal Rules of Evidence do not apply in formal adjudication, which means that some evidence, like hearsay, is permissible, but the hearing official must "provide for the exclusion of irrelevant, immaterial, or unduly repetitive evidence." *Id.* Whereas trial court judges do not have a specific legal obligation to justify their decisions with reasons and findings, ALJs do. The APA specifically requires that all decisions include a statement of "findings and conclusions, and the reasons or basis thereof." *Id.*

e. *Civil trial.* Formal adjudication is generally the most procedurally restrictive type of adjudication carried out by agencies themselves because most agencies are not authorized to impose monetary penalties on firms that violate their orders. Instead, a suit against the party must be filed in federal court, and the somewhat greater formality of a civil trial then results. Moreover, although some agencies have the authority to initiate suit in federal court on their own, many others must rely on the Department of Justice to act on their behalf. This was true for NHTSA prior to 2012. Given that the Attorney General is part of the Cabinet and traditionally a close ally of the President, this requirement provides the President with another means of exercising control over agencies. Unlike the cost-benefit analysis requirement enforced by OIRA, it often applies to independent agencies as well as executive-branch agencies. For example, the Federal Trade Commission, like NHTSA, had to enforce its cease and desist orders through suit filed by the Department of Justice. However, again like NHTSA, recent legislation has granted it authority to bring suit in federal court on its own. If an agency must bring enforcement actions in civil court, and particularly if it must rely on the Department of Justice to do so, it will have difficulty developing policy through the adjudicatory process.

a. Formal Adjudication

Formal adjudication is generally regarded as the most direct alternative to rulemaking as a means of policy making by federal agencies. Any system of adjudication in which decisions are recorded and precedent is respected can serve as a source of policy, but it is the appellate structure of administrative adjudication that provide the most extensive policy-making possibilities. Agencies typically have at least one level and sometimes two levels of internal review, with the first level being as of right, and the second level being discretionary. This parallels the federal court and most state court systems. The final adjudicatory authority of the agency is vested in the agency head or commission, unless delegated to another decision maker. *See Blackletter Statement of Federal Administrative Law,* 54 ADMIN. L. REV. 1, 28 (2002). Unlike federal or state court systems, however, this final source of review is not another adjudicatory body, insulated from other governmental roles, but rather the person or collegium in charge of the entire agency, including all its rulemaking and enforcement functions. This produces a tendency for the final discretionary review to be conceived in terms of policy in addition to (some would say in place of) disposition of the specific case at issue.

The poster child for this approach is the National Labor Relations Board. The NLRB was clearly granted rulemaking authority in its organic statute, the National Labor Relations Act (Wagner Act), 49 Stat. 449, 29 U.S.C. §§151-169 (1935), but has virtually never used this authority. Instead, it makes policy by adjudication. The general view is that it does so because of the highly controversial nature of its mission. In fact, the union activities that the Wagner Act was designed to encourage were significantly limited just

12 years later by the Taft-Hartley Act, 61 Stat. 136 (1947), and the NLRB has been the target of extensive criticism. *See* Mark H. Grunewald, The *NLRB's First Rulemaking: An Exercise in Pragmatism,* 41 DUKE L.J. 274 (1991)

Boston Medical Center Corporation and House Officers' Association/Committee of Interns and Residents, Petitioner

330 NLRB 152 (1999)

November 26, 1999
DECISION ON REVIEW AND DIRECTION OF ELECTION
BY CHAIRMAN TRUESDALE AND MEMBERS FOX,
LIEBMAN, HURTGEN, AND BRAME

On October 17, 1997, the Regional Director for Region 1 issued a Decision and Order dismissing a petition seeking certification of a unit of interns, residents, and fellows (house officers or house staff) because the house officers are not employees within the meaning of Section 2(3) of the Act. The Regional Director relied on *Cedars-Sinai Medical Center* [223 NLRB 251 (1976)] and *St. Clare's Hospital & Health Center* [229 NLRB 1000 (1977)], which held that medical interns, residents, and fellows are primarily students and, therefore, not "employees" within the meaning of Section 2(3) of the Act. The Regional Director also found that the Petitioner, inasmuch as it does not admit individuals into membership other than house officers, is not a labor organization within the meaning of Section 2(5) of the Act. . . .

[Petitioner and Employer both filed timely petitions to review the Regional Director's decision; the Board granted those requests for review.]

The Petitioner, mindful of the *Cedars-Sinai* and *St. Clare's Hospital* precedent, requests that the Board overrule that precedent. Boston Medical Center (BMC or the Employer) asserts, *inter alia,* that the Board should adhere to that precedent, that, under *Cedars-Sinai* and *St. Clare's Hospital,* the Petitioner is not a labor organization because it is not an organization in which "employees" participate, and that the unit is inappropriate because the individuals sought are primarily students rather than "employees."

Having carefully reviewed the entire record in this proceeding, including the briefs of the Employer and the Petitioner and the briefs of the various *amici curiae,*[1] with respect to the issues under review, the Board has decided

---

1. Amicus status was granted to the following interested organizations, all of which filed briefs: the American Federation of Labor-Congress of Industrial Organizations (AFL-CIO) and the American Nurses Association; the Association of American Medical Colleges, the American Hospital Association, the American Council on Education, the American Board of Medical Specialties, and the Council of Medical Specialty Societies; the American Medical Students Association; the University of Michigan House Officers Association; the Medical Society of the State of New York; the Ad Hoc Committee for House Staff Rights at University Hospital, Inc. and the Ad Hoc Committee for House Staff Rights at Prince George's Hospital Center; the California Medical Association; the American Medical Association and the Massachusetts Medical Society; and the American Public Health Association. Additionally, the American Medical Women's Association filed a position statement.

to overrule *Cedars-Sinai, St. Clare's Hospital,* and other decisions following those cases, and to find that the interns, residents, and fellows employed by BMC, while they may be students learning their chosen medical craft, are also "employees" within the meaning of Section 2(3) of the Act.

I. THE FACTS

The Regional Director fully set forth the salient facts in her Decision and Order We will not attempt to repeat all of those facts but will highlight those necessary for a cogent understanding of our decision.

BMC operates a 432-bed, nonprofit, acute-care teaching hospital in Boston, Massachusetts. It provides both inpatient and outpatient services, maintains a 24-hour emergency care facility, and serves as the primary teaching facility for the Boston University School of Medicine. As such, BMC sponsors some 37 different residency programs varying in length from 3 to 5 years, with some lasting longer. Fellowships last from 1 to 4 additional years. There are about 430 house officers in the unit sought by the Petitioner. . . .

House officers enter a residency or fellowship program in order to become certified specialists in their chosen medical specialty. To become an intern, an individual must have graduated from medical school and passed Parts 1 and 2 of the U.S. medical licensing exam. The appropriate state board of registration in medicine then issues interns a temporary license, which permits them to practice only under the aegis of their particular residency program. The state boards require that in order for medical school graduates to practice as fully licensed physicians, they must successfully complete the 1-year internship and then pass part 3 of the U.S. medical licensing exam. This then allows them to practice outside their residency program, as well.

Residents who successfully complete their program receive a diploma from the Boston University School of Medicine. . . .

III. ANALYSIS

Over 20 years ago, this Agency — despite the dissent of one member — concluded that hospital house staff were "primarily" students, and thus were not employees within the meaning of Section 2(3) of the Act. *Cedars-Sinai,* 223 NLRB at 253. The Board "clarified" its position shortly thereafter to explain that it did not mean to find that private sector house staff were not covered by the statute, but that as a particular type of student they were not entitled to collective-bargaining rights. *St. Clare's Hospital,* 229 NLRB at 1003.

We are convinced by normal statutory and legal analysis, including resort to legislative history, experience, and the overwhelming weight of judicial and scholarly opinion, that the Board reached an erroneous result in *Cedars-Sinai.* Accordingly, we overrule that decision and its offspring, conclude that house staff are employees as defined by the Act, and find that such individuals are therefore entitled to all the statutory rights and obligations that flow from our conclusion.

A. Background

In *Cedars-Sinai Medical Center*, 223 NLRB 251 (1976), decided shortly after the enactment of the Health Care Amendments to the Act, a Board majority concluded that interns, residents and fellows were not statutory employees. Although recognizing that house staff received many benefits characteristic of employee status, the Board majority concluded that house staff were primarily engaged in graduate educational training, and therefore were students rather than employees entitled to bargaining rights under the Act. The majority reasoned that house staff entered into a relationship with a hospital not primarily to earn a living, but to fulfill educational requirements of state or specialty boards. The majority placed little reliance on the fact that house staff spent most of their time in direct patient care, finding that "this is simply the means by which the learning process is carried out." Concerning the stipends house staff received, the Board majority concluded that such pay was more in the nature of a living allowance than compensation for services. The Board majority noted that stipends were fixed depending on the year of training, and did not vary depending on hours worked or with the nature of the services rendered. The majority further found significant that house staff tenure was related to the particular education program, that such a relationship was of relatively short duration, and that there was little chance that a regular employment relationship would be established following completion of the program. . . .

B. Section 2(3) of the Act

We find the Board's determination in *Cedars-Sinai* and *St. Clare's Hospital* of the status of house staff to be flawed in many respects. We begin our analysis with reference to Section 2(3) of the Act. That key statutory language is as follows:

> The term "employee" shall include any employee . . . unless the Act [this subchapter] explicitly states otherwise . . . but shall not include any individual employed as an agricultural laborer, or in the domestic service of any family or person at his home, or any individual employed by his parent or spouse, or any individual employed as an independent contractor. . . .

The "breadth of §2(3)'s definition is striking. The Act specifically applies to 'any employee.'" *Sure-Tan, Inc. v. NLRB*, 467 U.S. 883, 891-892 (1984) (undocumented aliens "plainly come within the broad statutory definition of 'employee'"). The exclusions listed in the statute are limited and narrow, and do not, on their face, encompass the category "students." Thus, unless there are other statutory or policy reasons for excluding house staff, they literally and plainly come within the meaning of "employee" as defined in the Act. We find no such reasons.

In his dissent in *Cedars-Sinai*, then-Member Fanning traced the Act's definition of "employee" as an outgrowth of the common law concept of the "servant." 223 NLRB at 254. In turn, the master-servant relationship itself finds its antecedents in common law agency doctrine. *Id.* at 254-255. *See also*

NLRB v. Town & Country, 516 U.S. 85, 93-95 (1995). At common law, a servant was one who performed services for another and was subject to the other's control or right of control. Consideration, i.e., payment, is strongly indicative of employee status. *Id. Cf.* WBAI Pacifica Foundation, 328 NLRB 1273 (1999). We agree with this analysis.

The Supreme Court in *Town & Country* echoed the same logic in its analysis of Section 2(3). Specifically, the Court noted that the Board's definition of the term "employee" as used in the Act reflected the common law agency doctrine of the conventional master-servant relationship. 516 U.S. at 93-95. In this recent case, the Court reiterated that the language of this section of the statute is "broad":

> The ordinary dictionary definition of "employee" includes any "person who works for another in return for financial or other compensation." American Heritage Dictionary 604 (3d ed. 1992). *See also* Black's Law Dictionary 525 (6th ed. 1990) (an employee is a "person in the service of another under any contract of hire, express or implied, oral or written, where the employer has the power or right to control and direct the employees in the material details of how the work is to be performed"). The phrasing of the Act seems to reiterate the breadth of the ordinary dictionary definition, for it says "[t]he term 'employee' shall include *any* employee." 29 U.S.C. §152(3) (1988 ed.) [Emphasis added.]
>
> For another thing, the Board's broad, literal interpretation of the word "employee" is consistent with several of the Act's purposes, such as protecting "the right of employees to organize for mutual aid without employer interference" . . . and "encouraging and protecting the collective-bargaining process." . . . And, insofar as one can infer purpose from congressional reports and floor statements, those sources too are consistent with the Board's broad interpretation of the word. It is fairly easy to find statements to the effect that an "employee" simply "means someone who works for another for hire." H.R. Rep. No. 245, 80th Cong., 1st Sess., 18 (1947), and includes "every man on a payroll." 79 Cong. Rec. 9686 (1935) (colloquy between Reps. Taylor and Connery). . . . At the same time, contrary statements, suggesting a narrow or qualified view of the word, are scarce, or nonexistent — except, of course, those made in respect to the specific (here inapplicable) exclusions written into the statute.

Town & Country Electric, 516 U.S. at 90-91 (some citations omitted). As the Court noted, the Board's historic, broad, literal reading of the statute finds support in Supreme Court precedent. *Id.* at 91-92; *Sure-Tan, supra*; *NLRB v. Hendricks County Rural Electric Membership Corp.*, 454 U.S. 170, 189-190 (1981); *Phelps Dodge Corp. v. NLRB*, 313 U.S. 177, 185-186 (1941).

We believe, therefore, that whatever other description may be fairly applied to house staff, it does not preclude a finding that individuals in such positions are, among other things, employees as defined by the Act.

Ample evidence exists here to support our finding that interns, residents and fellows fall within the broad definition of "employee" under Section 2(3), notwithstanding that a purpose of their being at a hospital may also be, in part, educational. That house staff may also be students does not thereby change the evidence of their "employee" status. As stressed above, nothing in the statute suggests that persons who are students but also employees should be exempted from the coverage and protection of the Act. The essential elements of the house staff's relationship with the Hospital obviously define an employer-employee relationship.

First, house staff work for an employer within the meaning of the Act. Second, house staff are compensated for their services. The house staff, as noted, receive compensation in the form of a stipend. There is no exclusion under the Internal Revenue Code for such stipends. The Hospital withholds Federal and state income taxes, as well as social security, on their salaries.

Further, the interns, residents, and fellows receive fringe benefits and other emoluments reflective of employee status. Workers' compensation is provided. They receive paid vacations and sick leave, as well as parental and bereavement leave. The Hospital provides health, dental, and life insurance, as well as malpractice insurance, for house staff and other Hospital employees.

Third, house staff provide patient care for the Hospital. Most noteworthy is the undisputed fact that house staff spend up to 80 percent of their time at the Hospital engaged in direct patient care. The advanced training in the specialty the individual receives at the Hospital is not inconsistent with "employee" status. It complements, indeed enhances, the considerable services the Hospital receives from the house staff, and for which house staff are compensated. That they also obtain educational benefits from their employment does not detract from this fact. Their status as students is not mutually exclusive of a finding that they are employees.

As "junior professional associates,"[4] interns, residents, and fellows bear a close analogy to apprentices in the traditional sense. It has never been doubted that apprentices are statutory employees eligible to vote in elections with their more experienced colleagues. *See, e.g., The Vanta Co.*, 66 NLRB 912 (1946).[5] Nor does the fact that interns, residents and fellows are continually acquiring new skills negate their status as employees. . . . Plainly, many employees engage in long-term programs designed to impart and improve skills and knowledge. Such individuals are still employees, regardless of other intended benefits and consequences of these programs.

Additionally, while house staff possess certain attributes of student status, they are unlike many others in the traditional academic setting. Interns, residents, and fellows do not pay tuition or student fees.[6] They do not take typical examinations in a classroom setting, nor do they receive grades as such. They do not register in a traditional fashion. Their education and student status is geared to gaining sufficient experience and knowledge to become Board-certified in a specialty.

---

4. 1 Leg. Hist. 540 (LMRA 1947).

5. Indeed, in the construction industry, it has long been the case that apprentices are included in units with journeymen. The practice is so well established that it has rarely been litigated. *See, e.g.,* Heating, Piping & Air Conditioning Contractors, 110 NLRB 261, 263 (1954) (plumber and pipefitter apprentices included in respective craft units).

6. The only exception appears to be that several dental residents pay some tuition.

C. Other Statutory Considerations

Our interpretation of Section 2(3) of the Act to include house staff as statutory employees is further supported by reference to Section 2(12) of the Act. That provision defines a professional employee as:

> (a) any employee engaged in work . . . (iv) requiring knowledge of an advanced type in a field of science or learning customarily acquired by a prolonged course of specialized intellectual instruction and study in an institution of higher learning or a hospital . . . or
>
> (b) any employee who (i) has completed the courses of specialized intellectual instruction and study described in clause (iv) of paragraph (a) and (ii) is performing related work under the supervision of a professional person to qualify himself to become a professional employee as defined in paragraph (a).

Literally read, Section 2(12)(b) embraces house staff. Interns, residents, and fellows clearly are individuals who have completed a course of specialized intellectual instruction and study "in an institution of higher learning or a hospital." Just as plainly, they are "performing related work under the supervision of a professional to qualify" to be a professional as defined in the Act. The legislative history of the Taft-Hartley amendments (the Labor Management Relations Act) supports the conclusion that this section of the Act was crafted to include "such persons as legal, engineering, scientific and *medical personnel along with their junior professional associates.*" I Leg. Hist. 540 (LMRA 1947) (emphasis added). As Member Fanning stated in his *Cedars-Sinai* dissent, this "definition fits, precisely, housestaff officers." 223 NLRB at 258. *See also Physicians Nat. House Staff Assn. v. Fanning,* 642 F.2d 492, 500 (D.C. Cir. 1980) (Chief Judge Wright, dissenting).[7] We find, therefore, based on the foregoing and the record as a whole, that house staff clearly fit within the statutory definition of "employee."

D. Legislative History of the 1974 Healthcare Amendments

Were there any lingering doubt about our interpretation of Section 2(3) as applied to interns, residents, and fellows, it is put to rest by consideration of the legislative history of the 1974 Healthcare Amendments.[8] Member Fanning, in his dissent in *Cedars-Sinai*, as well as Chief Judge Wright in his dissent in *Physicians Nat. House Staff,* extensively analyzed this history. In agreement with them, we believe, based on our own review, that the legislative history amply demonstrates that Congress, to the extent it considered the question, thought house staff to be statutory employees.[9]

---

7. The *Cedars-Sinai* majority responded to this argument with sleight of hand simply by stating that since house staff are not employees within the meaning of the Act, there is no reason to refer to other sections of the Act (223 NLRB at 253 fn. 4).

8. Legislative History of the Coverage of Nonprofi t Hospitals Under the National Labor Relations Act, 1974 (P.L. 93-360) (S. 3203).

9. It is telling that the Board majority failed to address this legislative history in *Cedars-Sinai. See* Note, *Student-Workers or Working Students? A Fatal Question for Collective Bargaining of Hospital House Staff,* 38 U. Pitt. L. Rev. 762, 767 (1977) (hereafter Student-Workers); Physicians Nat. House Staff, 642 F.2d at 505-506.

In 1974, Congress extended the Board's jurisdiction to nonprofit health-care facilities. In repealing the exemption of private, nonprofit hospitals from the definition of "employer," Congress was responding to the spate of recognition strikes in the healthcare industry, *Physicians Nat. House Staff*, 642 F.2d at 505, and stressed the need for continuous health services.[10] In Senate hearings on the amendments, representatives for the house staff, while urging that Congress adopt the amendments, advanced a new provision that would have excluded house staff from the ambit of Section 2(11) of the Act, which sets forth the definition of "supervisor," thus ensuring that house staff were not excluded from coverage of the Act on that basis. The committee report on why this legislative provision was not adopted bears reciting:

> Various organizations representing health care professionals have urged an amendment to Section 2(11) of the Act so as to exclude such professionals from the definition of "supervisor." The Committee has studied this definition with particular reference to health care professionals, such as . . . interns, residents, fellows . . . and concludes that the proposed amendment is unnecessary because of existing Board decisions. The Committee notes that the Board has carefully avoided applying the definition of a "supervisor" to a health care professional who gives directions to other employees, which direction is incidental to the professional's treatment of patients and thus is not the exercise of supervisory authority in the interest of the employer.[11]

This statement clearly assumes that house staff are employees. For if they were thought to be students, their status as supervisors would not be pertinent. *Physicians Nat. House Staff*, 642 F.2d at 505; *Student-Workers* at 768.

This view is underscored by the remarks of Senator Cranston, cosponsor and floor manager of the Senate bill. Senator Cranston, in introducing the bill, explained that one of the conditions the bill was designed to remedy was the "notoriously underpaid . . . average annual salary for all hospital employees — including doctors. . . . According to [the] president of the Physicians National House staff Association, the average house staff officer — intern, resident, or fellow — works 70 to 100 hours per week, and earns about $10,000 per year. His hourly wage then ranges from $1.92 to $2.74."[12] Senator Cranston's remarks about interns, residents, and fellows obviously reflect his assumption that they were to be covered by the legislation he was offering. *Physicians Nat. House Staff*, 642 F.2d at 505-506.

This legislative history is very persuasive. Yet, the Employer does not address it. Rather, the Employer argues that the failure of Congress to pass legislation, formally considered in 1979, that would have set aside the

---

10. *Student-Workers* at 767.

11. Legislative History of the Coverage of Nonprofit Hospitals at 13; S. Rept. 93-766, 93d Cong., 2d Sess. 6 (1974). *See also* Legislative History of the Coverage of Nonprofit Hospitals at 275, H.R. Rep. No. 1051 at 7 (1974).

12. Legislative History of the Coverage of Nonprofit Hospitals at 93, 120 Cong. Rec. 12937 (1974). As the dissent noted in *Physicians Nat. House Staff*, even the opponents of the 1974 Amendments assumed that house staff were employees. Senator Dominick "referred repeatedly to the coverage of house staff under the bill, grouping house staff together with other hospital employees." 642 F.2d at 506. See 120 Cong. Rec. 12971, 12580 (remarks of Senator Dominick).

Board's *Cedars-Sinai* and *St. Clare's Hospital* decisions, means that Congress approved the Board's decisions in those cases, and thus we are not free to overrule them. The argument lacks merit.

It is a canon of statutory construction that opinions of legislatures expressed years after an Act was passed should not be given weight as to the meaning of the earlier Act. *Teamsters v. U.S.*, 431 U.S. 324, 354 fn. 39 (1977) ("views of members of a later Congress . . . are entitled to little if any weight"); *U.S. v. Mine Workers*, 330 U.S. 258 (1947); Physicians Nat. House Staff, 642 F.2d at 509-510. Indeed, when the language of a statute is plain — as it is here — one is to give the words their plain meaning. *American Tobacco Co. v. Patterson*, 456 U.S. 63, 68, 75 (1982).

It is a dubious proposition indeed that the inaction of one house of Congress could be relevant evidence of what a previous entire Congress meant to do when it acted in its "full constitutional cycle." *Physicians Nat. House Staff*, 642 F.2d at 510. The germaneness of subsequent congressional action is further diminished where, as here, the alleged "action" is, in fact, inaction. Our reconsideration of *Cedars-Sinai* and related cases cannot appropriately be foreclosed merely because of the failure of one house of Congress to reverse that and related cases.[13]

E. Other Considerations

. . . Further, we reach our decision here to overrule *Cedars-Sinai* and its progeny on the basis of our experience and understanding of developments in labor relations in the intervening years since the Board rendered those decisions. Almost without exception, every other court, agency, and legal analyst to have grappled with this issue has concluded that interns, residents, and fellows are, in large measure, employees. *Regents of the University of Michigan v. ERC*, 204 N.W.2d at 225 (evidence on doctors' pay, benefits, amount of time devoted to patient care, and duties and responsibilities to diagnose and prescribe patient care program and put it into effect "far more indicative of an employee (i.e. — in this case a doctor) than a student"); *House Officers Assn. for the University of Nebraska Medical Center v. University of Nebraska Medical Center*, 255 N.W.2d 258 (Neb. 1977) ("the obvious conclusion from the recitation of facts is that House Officers are both students and employees"); *University Hospital v. SERB*, 587 N.E.2d 835 (Ohio 1992), rehearing denied 590 N.E.2d 753 (May 6, 1992); *The Regents of the University of California v. PERB*, 715 P.2d 590 (Cal. 1986); *Walls v. North Mississippi Medical Center*, 568 So. 2d 712 (Miss. 1990); *Long Beach Veterans Administration Medical Center, Long Beach, CA*, 7 FLRA 134 (1981); *Veterans Administration Medical Center, Brooklyn, NY*, 8 FLRA 289 (1982); *Veterans Administration Medical Center,*

---

13. To the extent that post–*Cedars-Sinai* congressional responses might be deemed relevant to consideration of the issue of employee status of house staff, we note that Representative Frank Thompson, a co-sponsor of the 1974 Health Care Amendments, stated that "[w]hen we passed the . . . Amendments in 1974 . . . we all thought, proponent and opponent alike, that medical house staff were included." 125 Cong. Rec. 33943 (1979).

East Orange, NJ, 20 FLRA 900 (1985); *City of Cambridge,* 2 MLC 1450 (Mass. Lab. Rel. Comm. 1976). . . .

These judicial bodies, and other commentators, have concluded that house staff are employees, in addition to being students, on similar facts as exist here. In each case, the courts and others have rejected the analysis the Board adopted in *Cedars-Sinai.* In its stead, these courts and commentators have assessed the realities of the relationship between house staff and the hospitals that they serve, and have concluded that the relationship exhibits sufficient factors to warrant a finding of employee status. . . .

Member HURTGEN, dissenting.

For more than 20 years, the Board has held that interns, residents, and fellows (house staff) are not employees entitled to bargain collectively under the Act.[1] As discussed infra, the courts have endorsed this position, as has the Congress of the United States. I see no reason now to proceed 180 degrees in the opposite direction. Instead, I agree with the result and rationale reached in those cases. I incorporate by reference the rationale of those cases, and thus need not repeat it here. I need only to add a few further thoughts.

First, the majority relies on two Supreme Court decisions that have issued since *Cedars-Sinai* and *St. Clare's.*[2] Those cases do not support the position of the majority. Those cases hold only that it is permissible for the Board to treat illegal aliens and paid union organizers as employees. They do not require that these employees be included in bargaining units. Similarly, it may be permissible for the Board to treat house staff as employees. But surely the Board is not compelled to take the position that they are entitled to be in bargaining units. Rather, in all these cases, the Board makes a policy choice to include or exclude the group at issue. This is precisely what the Board did in *Cedars-Sinai* and *St. Clare's.* The Board there exercised its discretion by holding that "collective bargaining should not be applied to what is fundamentally an educational relationship."[3]

The majority goes to some length to establish that house staff fall within the statutory definition of employee. They thereby miss my essential point. I am not necessarily suggesting that house staff cannot fall within the statutory definition. Rather, I conclude that, as a policy matter, the Board should continue to exercise its discretion to exclude them for purposes of collective bargaining.

No case has held that the Act compels a conclusion that house staff are employees for purposes of collective bargaining. Nor does the language

---

1. *Cedars-Sinai Medical Center,* 223 NLRB 251 (1976); *St. Clare's Hospital & Health Center,* 229 NLRB 1000 (1977).

2. *NLRB v. Town & Country Electric,* 516 U.S. 85 (1995); *Sure-Tan v. NLRB,* 467 U.S. 883 (1984).

3. *St. Clare's Hospital,* 229 NLRB at 1004. In *St. Clare's,* the Board made it clear that it was "not renouncing entirely our jurisdiction over [house staff]." *Id.* at 1003. Rather, the Board was simply declining, for policy reasons, to place house staff in units for purposes of collective bargaining.

In view of my position stated herein, I do not pass on the issue of whether house staff are employees under Sec. 2(3) of the Act. I assume arguendo that they are.

of Section 2(3) compel that result. That section provides that "the term 'employee' shall include any employee." Thus, the Act defines the word "employee" by reference to the word itself. This is hardly a statutory command that house staff must be regarded as employees for bargaining purposes.[4]

Second, I note that all courts considering the matter have upheld the Board's discretion to exclude house staff from the status of employees who are entitled to the collective-bargaining provisions of the Act.[5]

Further, I note that, in 1979, Congress was presented with a bill that would have specifically overruled *Cedars-Sinai/St. Clare's*, and would have required the Board to treat house staff as unit employees. The proposed legislation was rejected.

With respect to the legislative history of the 1974 healthcare amendments, the majority notes that Congress rejected a bill that would have excluded house staff from the ambit of supervisory status under Section 2(11) of the Act. They argue that this legislative action demonstrates that house staff are statutory employees. The argument has no merit. The legislative proposal was based on a concern that house staff would be supervisors, and the proponents of the proposal wished to avoid that result. The rejection of the proposal was based on a desire to leave things as they were. . . . The proposal and its rejection dealt only with the issue of whether these persons are Section 2(11) supervisors. The debate did not focus at all on the issue of whether house staff are employees within the meaning of Section 2(3). Thus, that legislative history does not support the proposition that house staff must be treated as employees. Indeed, I think it ironic that the majority is quick to draw an inference from this rejection of a legislative bill, but seeks to reject the much clearer inference to be drawn from the rejection of the 1979 bill that would have specifically endorsed the proposition that house staff are Section 2(3) employees.[6]

The majority observes that no problems have developed in the public sector where house staff are involved in collective bargaining. I would remind them that these governmental employees do not have the right to strike. The majority would now thrust house staff into the NLRA sector where there is a right to strike. In these circumstances, it surely does not follow that the

---

4. The section contains explicit exceptions (*e.g.*, agricultural laborers). These persons must be excluded. As explained above, others may be excluded.

Sec. 2(12) of the Act (defining professional employees) does not compel a finding of employee status. House staff have not "completed" their education within the meaning of that section. Rather, their work at the hospital includes continuing education. Further, even if house staff fit the statutory definition of professional employees, the Board, as a matter of policy, can choose to exclude them from bargaining units.

5. *Physicians National House Staff Assn. v. Fanning*, 642 F.2d 492 (D.C. Cir. 1980), cert. denied, 450 U.S. 917 (1981); *NLRB v. Committee of Interns & Residents*, 566 F.2d 810 (1977), cert. denied, 435 U.S. 904 (1978).

6. I note that, in both cases, Congress was dealing with a proposed amendment of earlier legislation. In 1974, the proposal was to amend Sec. 2(11); in 1979, the proposal was to amend Sec. 2(3).

absence of strikes in the public sector will translate to an absence of strikes under the NLRA. . . .

Although the Board has the power to change longstanding precedent, that change should be grounded in experience. An agency can change its rules and policies if there are "change[d] circumstances."[7] But, there is no record evidence herein of "change[d] circumstances." More particularly, there is no record evidence that the essentially educational nature of the house staff experience has changed to any appreciable degree in the past 20 years. Indeed, the Regional Director found, in the instant case, that the graduate medical programs of Respondent are substantially the same as those in *Cedars-Sinai* and *St. Clare's.*

In essence, there is no change in circumstances, but only a change in Board member composition. I would not alter longstanding and workable precedent simply because of a change in Board membership. In my view, the interests of stability and predictability in the law require that established precedent be reversed only upon a showing of manifest need. There is no such showing here. . . .

Notes and Questions

1. In the *Boston Medical* decision, the NLRB changed its longstanding precedent concerning whether medical interns and residents are employees under §2(3) of the National Labor Relations Act, 29 U.S.C. §152(3), the *Boston Medical* decision is similar to the notice-and-comment rule underlying the *Chevron* decision discussed above — both involve a switch in statutory interpretation. It is also similar to the rule rescinding passive restraints, which reversed a prior policy. Given the similar postures, consider the following:

a. How different were the opportunities for participation? What do you infer from the list of amicus briefs filed in the *Boston Medical* case, as noted in footnote 1 of the opinion? If you were a lawyer representing the American Hospital Association, which did not want medical residents to be considered "employees" under the Act, which would you have preferred in terms of opportunities for participation on behalf of your client — this adjudication or notice-and-comment rulemaking?

b. How different is the effect? The NLRB's decision in *Boston Medical Corp.,* like a court decision, binds the parties to the proceeding and has precedential effect. If you represented the American Hospital Association, is there any practical difference in the advice you would give your clients following the *Boston Medical* decision or a rulemaking reaching the same conclusion (that medical residents and interns are "employees" under §3(2) of the Act)?

---

7. *See Permian Basin Area Rate Cases,* 390 U.S. 747, 784 (1968).

c. How significant is the fact that formal adjudication is routinely retroactive, applying the new rule to the parties in the case? Does this seem to you be unfair, particularly in contrast with the advance notice that rulemaking provides? What about the fact that the outcome of the case may depend upon the capabilities of the advocates for the opposing sides, or the closely related matter of the relative amount of money that the opposing sides can devote to the case. If these issues trouble you, are you equally troubled by common law, which suffers from some of the same limitations as a means for articulating generally applicable policy?

2. In reaching its new interpretation, what tools of statutory interpretation does the Board invoke? Does the agency give those tools different weight than a court would? What theory of statutory interpretation best describes the agency's analysis? Related, does the agency have an obligation to interpret its statute in the same way that a court would? For example, is the agency obligated to decide whether the statute is clear or ambiguous? Member Hurtgen raises this issue in dissent.

3. The Supreme Court has established that agencies have discretion to choose between formal adjudication and notice-and-comment rulemaking. This conclusion predates the APA, *see* SEC v. Chenery Corp., 332 U.S. 194, 203 (1947). Subsequently, the Court suggested that reliance on policymaking by adjudication might be regarded as arbitrary and capricious under the APA, NLRB v. Wyman-Gordon, 394 U.S. 759 (1969), and some commentators articulated reasons to support this conclusion, see Lisa Schultz Bressman, *Beyond Accountability: Arbitrariness and Legitimacy in the Administrative State,* 78 N.Y.U. L. Rev. 461, 535-36 (2003); Richard J. Pierce, *Two Problems in Administrative Law: Political Polarity on the District of Columbia Circuit and Judicial Deterrence of Agency Rulemaking,* 1988 Duke L.J. 300, 308-09. But the Court rejected this possibility in NLRB v. Bell Aerospace, 416 U.S. 267 (1974), and has not reopened the issue since then.

4. The NLRB is not the only agency to have changed its mind on the medical resident issue. In 2004, the Treasury Department issued a ruling that medical residents should be treated as employees, not students, in determining whether they must pay Federal Insurance Contributions Act (FICA) taxes. A hospital (the famous Mayo Clinic) challenged the ruling on the ground that the applicable statute defined "student" in a way that necessarily included medical residents, thus exempting them from FICA. In Mayo Foundation v. U.S., 562 U.S. 44 (2010), the Supreme Court ruled in favor of the government, granting *Chevron* deference to the Treasury's interpretation of the statute.

b. "Informal" Adjudication

In addition to formal adjudication, agencies carry out a great many activities that are characterized as informal adjudication. This is the residual category that emerges from the APA's structure (i.e., defining rulemaking and adjudication, then defining formal and informal action) but not actually addressed by the statute itself. Some of the actions that fall into this category are recognizable as adjudications; they are informal in the sense that they are not subject to the formal adjudication provisions of the APA. This is determined by statute; formal adjudication is only required if the statute imposes that requirement, usually by stating that the determination is to be made "on the record." In the absence of that requirement, or some other procedural rule stated in the statute, the agency is free to fashion its own procedures. Many important types of agency adjudications, including deportation hearings, patent determinations, and nuclear regulatory licensing proceedings are informal adjudications in this sense. These are often similar to formal adjudications, in part because they are subject to the Due Process Clause of the Constitution, in part because of deeply embedded cultural understandings about the nature of an adjudication. They are more varied in character, however, and some differ from formal adjudication in significant ways. *See* Kent H. Barnett & Russell Weaver, *Non-ALJ Adjudications in Federal Agencies: Status, Selection, Oversight and Removal*, 53 Ga. L. Rev. 1 (2019).

In our discussion of statutory analysis as a policy-making tool, we have reprinted NHTSA's interpretation of the MAP-21 Act as authorizing the agency to impose civil penalties on its own, rather than bringing suit in federal court (either directly or through the Department of Justice). This interpretation was part of an interim final rule that NHTSA proposed and that subsequently went into effect. NHTSA's rule went on to specify the procedures that it will follow in imposing civil penalties. It is, in effect, a mini-treatise on administrative adjudication and merits close attention.

NHTSA's Proposed Procedures for Its Assessment of Civil Penalties Under the Safety Act

MAP-21 vests authority, responsibility, and discretion in the Secretary to impose civil penalties for violations of the Safety Act and regulations thereunder. Pursuant to 49 C.F.R. 1.95, this authority has been delegated to NHTSA. The amendments to MAP-21 providing the Secretary with the authority to assess civil penalties do not establish procedures for the assessment of those penalties. In order to ensure that NHTSA's assessment of civil penalties, as delegated to NHTSA by the Secretary, comports with the constitutional requirements of due process, NHTSA is proposing to adopt informal procedures to assess civil penalties pursuant to 49 U.S.C. §30165. These procedures include three options for the respondent to elect after NHTSA makes an initial demand for civil penalties: (1) Pay the demanded penalty; (2) provide an informal response, or (3) request a hearing. Here is more:

. . . The procedures for a hearing to assess civil penalties need not take all the formal trappings of a trial in a court of law. The Supreme Court has recognized that due process is flexible and that the procedural protections needed to ensure due process differ as the situation demands. *See Mathews v. Eldridge*, 424 U.S. 319, 334 (1976). An Agency has discretion to formulate its procedures, Vermont *Yankee Nuclear Power Corp. v. Natural Resources Defense Council, Inc.,* 435 U.S. 519, 524 (1978).

NHTSA does not believe that a formal adjudication is required in order to impose civil penalties for a violation of the Motor Vehicle Safety Act or regulations thereunder. If Congress wanted a proceeding with a formal adjudication on the record, it would have made that intent clear. Indeed, in another statute administered by NHTSA, such a procedure is required to determine certain violations. *See e.g.,* 49 U.S.C. §32911(a) (stating that "The Secretary of Transportation shall conduct a proceeding, with an opportunity for a hearing on the record, to decide whether a person has committed a violation."). As NHTSA does not believe that a formal adjudication falling within the purview of sections 5, 7, and 8 of the Administrative Procedure Act (5 U.S.C. §§554, 556, 557) is required, NHTSA is adopting informal procedures that provide respondents with administrative due process, that will allow for the efficient enforcement of statutes administered by NHTSA, and that will lead to the creation of a record in each individual proceeding that can form the basis for judicial review without a new trial of all the facts and issues in the district court. NHTSA anticipates that judicial review of orders assessing civil penalties issued pursuant to these procedures will consist of the "arbitrary, capricious, an abuse of discretion, or otherwise not in accordance with law" standard prescribed by 5 U.S.C. §706(2)(A).

A. Initiation of the Proceeding by NHTSA

Under the proposed procedures, NHTSA, through the Assistant Chief Counsel for Litigation and Enforcement, will begin a civil penalty proceeding by serving a notice of initial demand for civil penalties on a person (*i.e.* respondent] charging him or her with having violated one or more laws administered by NHTSA. This notice of initial demand for civil penalties will include a statement of the provision(s) which the respondent is believed to have violated as of the date of the initial demand for civil penalties; a statement of the factual allegations upon which the proposed civil penalty is being sought; notice of the maximum amount of civil penalty for which the respondent may be liable as of that date for the violations alleged; notice of the amount of the civil penalty proposed to be assessed; a description of the manner in which the respondent should make payment of any money to the United States; a statement of the respondent's right to present written explanations, information or any materials in answer to the charges or in mitigation of the penalty; and a statement of the respondent's right to request a hearing and the procedures for requesting a hearing. The notice will include a statement that failure: (i) To pay the amount of the civil penalty; (ii) to elect to provide an informal response; or (iii) to request a hearing within 30 days of the date of the initial demand authorizes the NHTSA Chief Counsel, without further notice to the respondent, to find the facts to be as alleged in the initial demand for civil penalties and to assess an appropriate civil penalty.

The notice will also include documentation that the Assistant Chief Counsel for Litigation and Enforcement relied on to determine the alleged violations of a statute or regulation administered by NHTSA giving rise to liability for civil penalties or the amount of civil penalties in the initial demand. This notice may be amended at any time prior to the entry of an order assessing a civil penalty, including amendment to the amount of civil penalties demanded. The notice of initial demand for civil penalties may contain proposed civil penalties for multiple unrelated violations. The maximum civil penalty stated in the notice of initial demand for civil penalties will reflect whether the violations in the notice are related or unrelated.

B. Election of Process by the Respondent

1. Payment of the Civil Penalty Proposed

The respondent may elect to pay the civil penalty that was proposed in the initial demand. If the respondent elects to make the payment, NHTSA will direct the respondent as to how to make the payment, including any installment plan permitted.

2. Election of Informal Response

If the respondent to the initial demand for civil penalties elects to make an informal response, that person must submit to the Chief Counsel and to the Assistant Chief Counsel for Litigation and Enforcement in writing any arguments, views or supporting documentation that dispute or mitigate that person's liability for, or the amount of, civil penalties to be imposed. The respondent must submit these materials within 30 days of the date on which the initial demand for civil penalties is issued. A person who has elected to make an informal response to an initial demand for civil penalties may also request a conference with the Chief Counsel. Because traveling to the Department of Transportation's headquarters in Washington, DC may be burdensome for some smaller companies responding to an initial demand for civil penalties, we are proposing to allow a person responding to an initial demand for civil penalties to request that the conference with the Chief Counsel be conducted by telephone. If the respondent elects to request a conference with the Chief Counsel and fails to attend the conference without good cause shown, the Chief Counsel may, without further notice to the respondent, find the facts to be as alleged in the initial demand for civil penalties and assess an appropriate civil penalty. This decision will constitute final agency action and no appeal to the Administrator will be permitted.

The Assistant Chief Counsel for Litigation and Enforcement would be permitted to provide rebuttal information to the Chief Counsel, replying to the information submitted by the respondent. After consideration of the submissions of the Assistant Chief Counsel and the Respondent, including any relevant information presented at a conference, the Chief Counsel may dismiss the initial demand for civil penalties in whole or in part. If the Chief Counsel does not dismiss the demand in its entirety, he or she may issue an order assessing a civil penalty. For civil penalty orders exceeding $1,000,000, the decision of the Chief Counsel becomes a final decision 20 days (including weekends and holidays) after it is issued unless the respondent files a timely appeal with the Administrator. If the respondent elects not to appeal to the Administrator within the 20-day period, then the Chief Counsel's decision is a final decision subject to judicial review. Civil penalty orders of $1,000,000 or less are final upon issuance by the Chief Counsel and subject to judicial review at that time.

Any assessment of civil penalties will be made only after considering the nature, circumstances, extent and gravity of the violation. As appropriate, the determination will include consideration of the nature of the defect or noncompliance; knowledge by the respondent of its obligations under 49 U.S.C. chapter 301; the severity of the risk of injury posed by the defect or non-compliance; the occurrence or absence or injury; the number of motor vehicles or items of motor vehicle equipment distributed with the defect or noncompliance; actions taken by the respondent to identify, investigate, or mitigate the condition; the appropriateness of such penalty in relation to the size of the business of the respondent, including the potential for undue adverse economic impacts; and other relevant and appropriate factors.

NHTSA intends for this informal response process to be less rigid than the procedures for conducting a hearing discussed below. For example, a respondent that elects an informal response would be permitted to bring in employees or other representatives (within reason) to explain facts and circumstances relating to the events described in the initial demand for civil penalties or any other factors that the respondent believes are relevant. A respondent may find it beneficial to be able to present the views of employees or representatives to the Chief Counsel in person, considering that if the respondent elects a hearing the presentation of witness testimony will be committed to the discretion of the Hearing Officer. Further, NHTSA envisions that any written materials that the respondent provides as part of an informal response would not have the formality of legal briefs submitted pursuant to the hearing procedures in this proposal and would allow for flexibility in the respondent's response. It is also NHTSA's intent that the conference between the Chief Counsel and the respondent consist of informal discussion and would not take on the structure of an adversarial proceeding.

3. Election of a Hearing

If, in response to an initial demand for civil penalties, a person requests a hearing, the Chief Counsel will designate a Hearing Officer to preside over the hearing. The Hearing Officer appointed by the Chief Counsel may have no other responsibility, either direct or supervisory, for the investigation or enforcement of the violation for which the initial demand for civil penalties relates and will not have any prior connection to the case.

The Hearing Officer will have the authority to conduct the proceeding and arrange for NHTSA and the person served with the initial demand for civil penalties to submit additional documents for the administrative record, regulate the course of the hearing, and take notice of matters that are not subject to a bona fide dispute and are commonly known in the community or are ascertainable from readily available sources of known accuracy.

With respect to the type of hearing proposed, NHTSA believes that most civil penalty determinations can be made based solely on written submissions because in the vast majority of instances, the evidence to establish, or refute, a respondent's liability for civil penalties and facts for the application of the penalty factors will consist of documents. Therefore, we are proposing that the Hearing Officer will have the discretion to conduct an in-person hearing and allow witness testimony only if an in-person hearing is needed, in the opinion of the Hearing Officer, to resolve any factual and/or legal issues that cannot be easily resolved by written submissions.

If the respondent elects to request a hearing, the respondent must submit to the Assistant Chief Counsel for Litigation and Enforcement two complete copies via hand delivery, use of an overnight or express courier service, facsimile, or electronic mail containing: (1) A detailed statement of factual and legal issues in dispute; and (2) all statements and documents supporting the respondent's case within 30 days of the date on which the initial demand for civil penalties is issued. If the respondent wishes for the hearing to be conducted in-person, the respondent must also submit the basis for its request for the in-person hearing (*i.e.* why an in-person hearing and witness testimony are necessary to resolve any factual or legal issues present in the case), a list of witnesses that the respondent wishes to call at the hearing, a description of each witness's expected testimony, a description of the factual basis for each witness's expected testimony, and whether the respondent will arrange to have a verbatim transcript prepared at its own expense.[10] These materials must be provided within 30 days of the date on which the initial demand for civil penalties is issued. If an in-person hearing is requested, the Hearing Officer will notify the respondent and NHTSA in writing of his or her decision to grant or deny a request for an in-person hearing.

If an in-person hearing is granted and the respondent fails to attend the in-person hearing without good cause shown, the Hearing Officer is authorized, without further notice to the respondent, to find the facts as alleged in the initial demand for civil penalties and to assess an appropriate civil penalty. This decision will constitute final agency action and no appeal to the Administrator will be permitted.

NHTSA may supplement the record with additional information, including disclosure of proposed witnesses and their expected testimony, prior to the hearing. A copy of such information will be provided to the respondent no later than 3 days before the hearing. These procedures allow the Hearing Officer to focus the inquiry at the hearing and eliminate the need

---

10. NHTSA has determined that in order to minimize the expense of conducting a hearing, a verbatim transcript of any in-person hearing will not normally be prepared. Any person requesting an in-person hearing in response to an initial demand for civil penalties may arrange for a transcript to be created at its own expense if an in-person hearing is granted.

for discovery because both the agency and respondent will be in possession of the documents on which the other party intends to rely and appraised of all expected witness testimony. Therefore, we propose that discovery not be permitted in any hearing conducted pursuant to these procedures.

The administrative record of an in-person hearing shall contain the notice of initial demand for civil penalties and any supporting documentation that accompanied the initial demand; any documentation submitted by the respondent, any further documentation submitted by the Agency as a reply to the request for a hearing or presented at an in-person hearing; any additional materials presented at an in-person hearing; the transcript of the hearing (if any); and any other materials that the Hearing Officer determines are relevant In considering the admission of evidence into the administrative record the Hearing Officer will not be bound by the Federal Rules of Evidence.

In the event that the Hearing Officer determines that witness testimony is not necessary, the Assistant Chief Counsel for Litigation and Enforcement will submit a written reply with the agency' responses to the arguments and documents included in the respondent's request for a hearing. With respect to the administrative record where there is no in-person hearing, NHTSA proposes that all documents contained in and with its initial demand, any response thereto, or any reply automatically would be part of the administrative record. In considering the admission of evidence into the administrative record the Hearing Officer will not be bound by the Federal Rules of Evidence.

At the hearing, NHTSA will have the evidentiary burden of establishing the violation giving rise to civil penalties under 49 U.S.C. 30165. In the event that the hearing is conducted by written submission, the Hearing Officer will make his or her decision based on NHTSA's initial demand for civil penalties and any included documents, the respondent's request for a hearing and any included documents, NHTSA's reply (including any documents) to the arguments and documents provided in the respondent's request for a hearing, and any other evidence in the record.

In the event that the Hearing Officer grants an in-person hearing, NHTSA will first present any evidence the agency believes is relevant for the administrative record. If permitted by the Hearing Officer, NHTSA may call witnesses. No later than three days prior to the hearing NHTSA will provide a list of witnesses that it expects to call at the hearing, a description of the witnesses' expected testimony and the factual basis for the expected testimony to the respondent. At the close of NHTSA's presentation of evidence, the respondent will have the right to respond to and rebut evidence and arguments presented by NHTSA. The respondent or his or her counsel may offer relevant information including testimony (if permitted) regarding the respondent's liability for civil penalties and the application of the penalty factors. At the close of the respondent's presentation of evidence, the Hearing Officer may allow the presentation of rebuttal evidence by NHTSA. The Hearing Officer, in his or her discretion, may allow the respondent to reply to any such rebuttal evidence submitted.

In the event that the Hearing Officer grants an in-person hearing, the Assistant Chief Counsel for Litigation and Enforcement and the respondent may present arguments on the issues involved in the case after all the evidence has been presented.

A respondent challenging the amount of a civil penalty proposed to be assessed will have the burden of proving the mitigating circumstances. For example, a respondent challenging the amount of a civil penalty on the grounds that the penalty would have an undue adverse economic impact would have the burden of proving that undue impact. It is appropriate that the burden is placed on the respondent as the respondent is more likely to have relevant financial evidence than NHTSA.

After the hearing is completed, the Hearing Officer will issue a written decision based solely on the administrative record, including any testimony offered at an in-person hearing. Any assessment of civil penalties will be made only after considering the nature, circumstances, extent and gravity of the violation. As appropriate, the determination will include consideration of the nature of the defect or noncompliance, knowledge by the respondent of its obligations under 49 U.S.C. chapter 301, the severity of the risk of injury, the occurrence or absence or injury, the number of motor vehicles or items of motor vehicle equipment distributed with the defect or noncompliance, actions taken by the respondent to identify, investigate, or mitigate the condition, the appropriateness of such penalty in relation to the size of the business of the respondent, including the potential for undue adverse economic impacts, and other relevant and appropriate factors, including those discussed below.

For civil penalties exceeding $1,000,000, the decision of the Hearing Officer will become a final decision 20 calendar days (including weekends and holidays) after it is issued, unless the respondent files a timely appeal with the Administrator before the expiration of 20 days. If the respondent elects not to appeal to the Administrator within the 20-day period, then the Hearing Officer's decision is a final decision subject to judicial review. Civil penalty orders of $1,000,000 or less are final upon issuance by the Hearing Officer and subject to judicial review at that time.

C. Administrative Appeal

In matters where the civil penalties assessed by either the Chief Counsel or the Hearing Officer exceed $1,000,000, the proposed regulations provide an opportunity for the respondent aggrieved by the order assessing a civil penalty to file an appeal with the Administrator.

The Administrator will affirm the order unless the Administrator finds that the order was unsupported by the record as a whole; based on a mistake of law; or that new evidence, not available at the hearing, is available. Appeals that fail to allege and provide supporting basis for one of these grounds of appeal will be summarily dismissed. If the Administrator finds that the order was unsupported, based on a mistake of law, or that new evidence is available, then the Administrator may assess or modify a civil penalty; rescind the initial demand for civil penalty; or remand the case for new or additional proceedings. In the absence of a remand, the decision of the Administrator in an appeal is a final agency action.

If the Administrator affirms the order assessing civil penalties and the respondent does not pay the civil penalty in the manner specified by the order within thirty (30) days after the Administrator's decision on appeal is issued, the matter may be referred to the Attorney General with a request that an action to collect the penalty be brought in the appropriate United States District Court pursuant to 49 U.S.C. 30163(c). *See also* 28 U.S.C. 1331. A party aggrieved by a final order from the Administrator or a final order from the Hearing Officer or Chief Counsel, may file a civil action in United States District Court seeking review of the final order pursuant to the Administrative Procedure Act. *See* 5 U.S.C. 706.

D. The Proposed Procedures Comport with Due Process

The proposed procedures for adjudicating civil penalties are consistent with the requirements for due process established by the U.S. Supreme Court in *Mathews* v. *Eldridge*. In that case the Court stated that three factors should be considered when determining what procedures must be provided before the government deprives a person of a property interest. The factors that the Court considers are:

> the private interest that will be affected by the official action; . . . the risk of an erroneous deprivation of such interest through the procedures used, and the probable value, if any, of additional or substitute procedural safeguards; and . . . the Government's interest, including the function involved and the fiscal and administrative burdens that the additional or substitute procedural requirement would entail. *See Eldridge,* 424 U.S. at 335.

In examining whether the private interest at stake requires additional procedural safeguards, the Supreme Court looks to the "degree of potential deprivation," and the gravity of the hardship borne by an entity wrongfully deprived of a property interest. *See id.* at 341, 343. In determining whether additional procedures would add to the fairness and reliability of the proceeding, the courts consider the nature of the issue at controversy. *See id.* Factors that the court considers include the nature of the evidence to be presented, such as whether the evidence consists mainly of documents or whether the resolution of the controversy hinges on the credibility of witness testimony. *See id.* at 343-44. When considering the government interest at stake, the courts examine the administrative burdens created by additional procedures and other societal costs that additional procedures would impose. *See id.* at 347.

NHTSA believes that the private interest at stake in a proceeding to assess civil penalties, while substantial for some of the entities NHTSA regulates, does not rise to the level of hardship for which the Supreme Court has required heightened procedural protections.[11] In many cases in which NHTSA has settled civil penalty liability with motor vehicle manufacturers,

---

11. *See Goldberg v. Kelly,* 397 U.S. 254 (1970) (holding that because the wrongful deprivation of a person's interest in welfare would deny the person of their means for subsistence, due process required a pre-termination evidentiary hearing).

the total civil penalty amount was a small percentage of the company's annual revenue. NHTSA will also apply its Civil Penalty Policy Under the Small Business Regulatory Enforcement Fairness Act when assessing a civil penalty against a small entity. As NHTSA considers a business' size in determining the penalty amount under this policy, the relative magnitude of the potential deprivation of the interest of smaller entities subject to civil penalties is minimized.

NHTSA does not believe that additional procedural safeguards beyond what are proposed in today's NPRM would add to the fairness and reliability of civil penalty determinations under the proposed procedures. NHTSA believes that most of the evidence regarding a person's liability for civil penalties will consist of documents such as test reports, documents submitted in compliance with 49 CFR part 579 subpart C, vehicle owner questionnaires submitted by consumers; and documents and responses submitted in response to Information Requests, General Orders, and Special Orders. This is the type of evidence for which witness demeanor and credibility is not at issue and a hearing conducted by written submission is appropriate. In the rare instance in which liability for civil penalties hinges on issues that involve witness credibility, the Hearing Officer will have the discretion to permit witness testimony and cross examination.

NHTSA also does not believe that additional procedures for conducting administrative discovery before the hearing would increase the reliability or fairness of a hearing to determine liability for civil penalties. *See Eldridge,* 424 U.S. at 343. Under the proposed hearing procedures, the Assistant Chief Counsel for Litigation and Enforcement must attach to the notice of initial demand for civil penalties any documentation that he or she relied on in determining an alleged violation of a statute or regulation that NHTSA contends gives rise to liability for civil penalties or the amount of civil penalties in the initial demand. If NHTSA later wishes to present materials not provided with the initial demand, NHTSA must provide these materials to the respondent. These procedures will ensure that the respondent receives all of the materials that the agency will rely on to establish a violation giving rise to civil penalties and to support its demanded amount.[15]

Finally, the procedures for determining civil penalties proposed in today's NPRM will advance the government's interest in increasing the administrative efficiency of the resolution of civil penalty cases. The proposed procedures will also serve society's interests by allowing NHTSA to more efficiently and effectively enforce the Safety Act and regulations prescribed thereunder by allowing the Agency to assess civil penalties without protracted proceedings. Fair, timely, and efficient imposition of civil penalties on persons who violate the statutes administered by NHTSA and

---

15. NHTSA may rely on documents not provided to the respondent with the initial demand for civil penalties to rebut statements made on behalf of the respondent.

regulations prescribed thereunder should lead to greater compliance with those statutes and regulations.

Moreover, a final order on civil penalties would be a final agency action subject to judicial review under the Administrative Procedure Act, 5 U.S.C. 701 *et seq.* A challenge to a NHTSA civil penalty final order could be brought in the appropriate United State district court and subject to all of the procedural rights and protections afforded by federal courts in reviewing final agency orders. *See e.g.*, 49 U.S.C. 30163(c), 28 U.S.C. 1331. We anticipate that the standard of review in the U.S. district court would be the "arbitrary, capricious, an abuse of discretion, or otherwise not in accordance with law" standard prescribed by 5 U.S.C. 706(2)(A).

For these reasons NHTSA believes that the procedures in today's NPRM would provide due process to persons alleged to have violated the statutes or regulations administered by NHTSA and regulations prescribed thereunder.

Notes and Questions

1. Note the three alternative procedures that the rule establishes. The first and third are not surprising. Someone who has in fact violated the law will often simply pay the fine; most NHTSA fines, while not trivial, are relatively lenient. The third alternative outlines a fairly typical administrative hearing. The second alternative may not seem as familiar—there is nothing like it in the Federal Rules of Civil Procedure, for example—but it is also quite standard. Most civil cases are resolved by agreement (i.e., a settlement), and this is typically the outcome of a negotiation. Judges often play an active role in these negotiations, motivated powerfully by considerations of judicial economy. *See* Marc Galanter & Mia Cahill, *Most Cases Settle: Judicial Promotion and Regulation of Settlements*, 46 STAN. L. REV. 1339 (1994); Judith Resnick, *Managerial Judges*, 96 HARV. L. REV. 374 (1982). Here the agency, which is the moving party but has a quasi-judicial role, engages in similar negotiations, motivated by the same economic considerations. A full-scale hearing consumes a substantial amount of the agency's limited resources (NHTSA had a mere 591 employees in 2015); given the size of the automobile industry and the number of firms involved (not only the 14 major producers but hundreds of component manufacturers), it is essential for NHTSA to resolve disputes or violations in an expeditious manner.

2. The third alternative, of course, is the "informal" adjudication. What is NHTSA's justification for relying on this rather than on formal adjudication? Does it amount to much more than a statement that "we've got the power?" But if the agency has the power, isn't it justified, if not obligated, to use that power when carrying out its congressionally assigned responsibilities, particularly when human life and limb is at stake? What motivated NHTSA to avoid formal adjudication in this setting?

3. The Due Process Clause of the Fifth Amendment applies to any federal action, and the equivalent clause in the Fourteenth Amendment applies to actions by state governments. Mathews v. Eldridge, 424 U.S. 319 (1976), cited in the decision, involved a challenge to Social Security Administration (SSA) disability hearings, and is in fact the leading case that determines the content of due process protection in administrative adjudications. The test that it established seems inspired by cost-benefit analysis, right? As we discussed, cost-benefit analysis is a central element in economic analysis. Is it appropriate for determining the contours of a constitutional right? *See* Jerry Mashaw, *The Supreme Court's Due Process Calculus for Administrative Adjudication in Mathews v. Eldridge: Three Factors in Search of a Theory of Value*, 44 U. CHI. L. REV. 28 (1976).

4. The requirements of the Due Process Clause, as *Mathews* makes clear, vary with the specific circumstances of the adjudication. Administrative adjudications often involve the legal status of individuals, many of whom may be vulnerable. NHTSA's hearings do not; only business firms produce cars or car components. Does this make a difference?

5. How exactly does the informal hearing that the rule provides for differ from a formal adjudication? Here are some wrong answers:

It can be based entirely on written submissions. That is true of formal adjudications as well. In fact, the specific holding of *Mathews* is that SSA disability determinations may be based entirely on written submissions. SSA determinations are certainly an important category of formal adjudications, since there are close to one million of them each year, nearly ten times as many as the number of federal district court cases.

The record can be supplemented prior to the hearing. That is true for many formal adjudications, including SSA disability determinations.

The Federal Rules of Evidence do not apply. They do not apply in formal adjudications either. One major consequence is that hearsay testimony is generally admitted in administrative adjudications, although its probative value is of course subject to scrutiny.

Discovery can be limited by the presiding officer. Again, true for both.

6. Note that there is only one level of appeal here, not the two levels that we described above as typical. Note also that only the private party can appeal. What do you suppose is responsible for the difference? Perhaps it is that NHTSA safety hearings are not mass justice; each case is likely to be significant. In any event, the last stage of any appeal, as with agency adjudication in general, is to the hierarchical head of the agency, whether a board or, as with NHTSA, a single administrator. This is central to the use of adjudication as a means of policy formation by the agency.

The residual category of informal adjudication also includes many agency actions that are not recognizable as adjudications at all. These include guidance (described below), other informational communications, inspections, negotiations, agreements, and a wide range of other ways in which agencies interact with private parties. All of them can potentially be used as policy-making instruments.

Here again as an example, we briefly consider one such mode of informal adjudication: complaint handling. When an agency is charged with policing a large number of individual items or locations, such as workplace safety (Occupational Safety and Health Administration), workplace labor practices (National Labor Relations Board), banks (various banking agencies), restaurants (state and local health departments), toys (Consumer Products Safety Commission), or automobiles (you know who), it must rely partially or primarily on complaints for the necessary information. In 2014, the (Acting) Administrator of NHTSA was called before a Senate oversight committee to explain the way the agency had dealt with the General Motors ignition switch crisis.

The problem was that certain GM cars were equipped with ignition switches that shut off during driving; this not only caused the vehicle to be involved in crashes, but also prevented the airbag from deploying. The defect was ultimately responsible for over 100 fatalities. GM did not begin recalling cars until 2014, when complaints from consumers brought the problem to national attention. Ultimately, nearly 30 million cars were recalled, and the company paid a $900 million fine. A question arose about whether NHTSA knew, or should have known about the defect, and why it failed to take action in response to the complaints. The Acting Administrator was called before a Senate subcommittee to explain.

Statement of David Friedman, Acting Administrator, NHTSA, Before the Subcommittee on Consumer Protection, Product Safety, and Insurance of the Senate Committee on Commerce, Science and Transportation

April 2, 2014

STATEMENT OF THE HONORABLE DAVID FRIEDMAN
ACTING ADMINISTRATOR, NATIONAL HIGHWAY TRAFFIC
SAFETY ADMINISTRATION

BEFORE THE

SENATE COMMITTEE ON COMMERCE, SCIENCE,
AND TRANSPORTATION SUBCOMMITTEE
ON CONSUMER PROTECTION,
PRODUCT SAFETY, AND INSURANCE

"Examining the GM Recall and NHTSA's Defect Investigation Process."

April 2, 2014

Chairman McCaskill, Ranking Member Heller, and Members of the Subcommittee:

Thank you for the opportunity to appear before you today to discuss the recall process of the National Highway Traffic Safety Administration (NHTSA) and the General Motors (GM) ignition switch recall.

Let me begin my testimony by saying, on behalf of everyone at NHTSA, that we are deeply saddened by the loss of life in vehicle crashes involving the GM ignition switch defect. Our deepest sympathies are with the families and friends.

. . .

NHTSA is not a large agency. We currently have 591 employees. The President's budget for fiscal year 2015 requests $5.2 million for additional staff to help strengthen our ability to address the enormous safety mission that this agency faces.

NHTSA is a data-driven organization that approaches highway safety by considering both the behavioral and the vehicle aspects of crashes. Human behavior remains the leading cause of highway crashes and deaths, so NHTSA places an emphasis on reducing impaired driving, encouraging seat belt use at all times, and underscoring the dangers of distracted driving. These programs have shown enormous success over the years in driving down the number of deaths involving alcohol and driving up the percentages of vehicle occupants who wear seat belts. More work, however, is required, as nearly one-third of fatalities involve alcohol and more than half involve an unbelted occupant.

As those efforts seek to change human behavior, NHTSA's vehicle safety program focuses on ways to save lives through safety improvements to vehicles, ensuring that vehicles meet all safety standards, and eliminating vehicle defects that pose an unreasonable risk to safety.

. . .

For vehicles and vehicle equipment in the U.S., manufacturers must certify that their products meet applicable Federal Motor Vehicle Safety Standards (FMVSS). The Office of Vehicle Safety Compliance (OVSC) tests a sample of new vehicles and equipment each year to determine whether they meet those standards. If the vehicles or equipment do not comply, manufacturers must recall them and provide a remedy to the consumer.

The Office of Defects Investigation (ODI) has a different mission. ODI searches through consumer complaints, manufacturer data, data from NHTSA's National Center for Statistics and Analysis (NCSA), special crash investigations, and other sources for information that might indicate the presence of a defect or defect trend. Where it can find a possible defect or defect trend posing an unreasonable risk to safety, it investigates. If NHTSA can demonstrate that a defect exists and that it poses an unreasonable safety risk, the agency can order a recall.

NHTSA's ability to influence or order recalls is its greatest strength in safeguarding against problems in the vehicles traveling our roads today. Since 2000, NHTSA has influenced, on average, the recall of nearly 9 million vehicles every year, as well as millions of items of equipment, for safety related defects.

An Overview of the Defects Investigation and Recall Process

Defects Investigations

Each potential defect investigation is unique and dependent on the data gathered in each case. NHTSA uses a number of tools and techniques to gather and analyze data and look for trends that warrant a vehicle safety investigation, and possibly a recall. These tools include customer complaints to NHTSA, early warning data, as well as other sources that might provide related information, such as crash investigations and industry-related websites. Additionally, the law requires manufacturers to inform NHTSA within five business days of any noncompliance or defects that create an unreasonable risk to safety. They are then required to initiate a recall to remedy the defect and notify affected consumers.

NHTSA's defects investigation office, ODI, has a staff of 51 people. Their goal is to find possible defects or defect trends that may indicate significant safety risks in particular makes, models, and model years; determine whether there is an unreasonable safety risk apparently being caused by a defect; and, if so, persuade—or require—the manufacturer to conduct a recall. . . .

The defects investigation process begins with the screening of incoming information for evidence of a potential safety defect. Complaints from consumers are the primary source of information. NHTSA receives over 45,000 complaints a year through *SaferCar.gov* and the Vehicle Safety Hotline, and reviews each one promptly. Human eyes review every single complaint. Follow-up is sometimes required to get additional information, and in cases of interest, NHTSA staff will contact the complainants directly to obtain clarifying information. Screeners also look at technical service bulletins issued by manufacturers, reports of foreign recalls, crash investigations done by NHTSA's Special Crash Investigations office, and supplemental information such as occasional reports from insurance companies and information available on the Internet. When appropriate, the screeners consult NHTSA's crash databases, including the Fatality Analysis Reporting System (FARS) and National Automotive Sampling System (NASS). Also, members of the public may file petitions asking NHTSA to investigate and order a recall on a particular matter. The agency carefully reviews each petition before making a decision on whether to grant or deny it. If granted, a formal investigation is opened. Since 2004, the agency has opened 980 investigations. These safety defect investigations have resulted in 1,299 recalls involving more than 95 million vehicles, equipment, tires, and child restraints, which have helped reduce vehicle fatalities to historic lows. For example, a NHTSA investigation recently led to the recall of over 4 million child safety seats and is still underway regarding the possible recall of infant seats.

Another important source of information is Early Warning Reporting (EWR) data submitted quarterly by manufacturers of vehicles, tires, and child seats. For light vehicle manufacturers, the data include counts of property damage claims, warranty reports, consumer complaints, and field reports, which are efforts by the automaker to look into specific incidents. These aggregate data are broken down by make, model, and model year and by component category (e.g., steering, braking, engine, speed control). Manufacturers must also submit brief reports on each claim against the company for death or injury allegedly related to a possible vehicle defect. The volume of the data received is enormous. NHTSA uses sophisticated data mining techniques to identify trends in the data that may be evidence of a safety defect. When potential trends are found, the EWR division can make a referral to the team involved in the screening process.

Those who screen NHTSA's various sources of information are in constant communication and support each other in their efforts to identify potential defect issues. When patterns emerge from any source, the screeners look very carefully at what may be behind the patterns. Where there is possible evidence of a defect trend, the screening staff recommends that the appropriate investigating division consider opening an investigation. ODI staff meets regularly to determine which recommendations warrant opening an investigation and which may warrant continued monitoring. With preliminary evidence and 16 investigators, ODI must analyze all of the fact patterns and discern whether potential defects likely involve more serious risks or are likely to reveal a defect trend.

If it is determined that an investigation is warranted, a preliminary evaluation begins. This often entails detailed interviews with complainants, requesting relevant information from the manufacturer, and analysis to determine whether there is sufficient evidence either to seek a recall or continue to a more in-depth investigation. If it is determined that sufficient evidence exists, the next stage is the engineering analysis, which involves gathering additional information from consumers and the manufacturer, perhaps testing of vehicles or equipment by NHTSA's Ohio based test facility, surveys of peer vehicle experience, and further in-depth analysis of the underlying problem.

If, at any stage, ODI staff believes there is enough information to determine that a specific defect exists and that it creates an unreasonable risk to safety, they urge the manufacturer to conduct a recall. Where the manufacturer is not persuaded by NHTSA to undertake a recall, NHTSA's Associate Administrator for Enforcement may issue an initial decision requiring that the manufacturer conduct the recall. Following the initial decision, NHTSA convenes a public meeting in which interested parties—including the manufacturer, consumers, suppliers, public interest groups—may provide testimony. The manufacturer is given another opportunity to submit comments on the testimony heard at the public meeting. If, after review of all the information generated by the administrative process, the Administrator concludes that a recall should occur, the Administrator issues a recall order. A recall order is not self-enforcing. If the manufacturer does not follow the order, NHTSA would seek enforcement. To prevail in court, NHTSA must be able to prove that a defect exists and that the defect creates an unreasonable safety risk.

Sounds pretty good, right? Now consider this analysis by an independent government investigatory agency.

Office of Inspector General, Audit Report: Inadequate Data and Analysis Undermine NHTSA's Efforts to Identify and Investigate Vehicle Safety Concerns

June 18, 2015

BACKGROUND

NHTSA, established by the Highway Safety Act of 1970, administers highway safety and consumer programs intended to reduce deaths, injuries, and economic losses resulting from motor vehicle crashes. NHTSA's ODI is responsible for reviewing vehicle safety data, identifying and investigating potential vehicle safety issues, and requiring and overseeing manufacturers' vehicle and equipment recalls (see table 1). NHTSA reports that it has influenced, on average, the recall of nearly 9 million vehicles every year since 2000. ODI's pre-investigative phase includes four key elements:

Table 1. ODI's Vehicle Safety Oversight Process

Phase	Number of Staff	Description
Pre-Investigation	13	ODI collects and analyzes vehicle safety data to identify and select potential safety issues for further investigation.
Investigation	20	ODI investigates the potential safety issue to determine whether a recall is warranted.
Recall management	8	ODI ensures that manufacturer recalls comply with statutory requirements.

Source: OIG analysis

- **Collection and analysis of early warning reporting data.** The Transportation Recall Enhancement, Accountability, and Documentation (TREAD) Act of 2000 authorized NHTSA to require manufacturers to report on a variety of early warning data. These data include property damage claims, consumer complaints, warranty claims, and field reports from incidents involving certain vehicle components and conditions defined in NHTSA regulations. In addition, manufacturers are required to report all death and injury claims and notices. ODI's Early Warning Division staff are responsible for verifying that manufacturers submit these data, prioritizing the data using statistical tests, and identifying and referring potential safety trends to the Defects Assessment Division for further analysis.

- **Collection and analysis of consumer complaints.** ODI receives consumer complaints through a variety of sources including letters, vehicle safety hotline calls, and submissions through NHTSA's safercar.gov Web site. ODI's Defects Assessment Division screens all complaints and forwards ones with potential safety significance for additional review.[10]
- **Identification of potential safety issues.** If a potential safety issue is identified, the Defects Assessment Division researches and analyzes available safety data and prepares an investigation proposal for ODI's investigative division chiefs to review.[11]
- **Selection of potential safety issues to investigate.** ODI's investigative division chiefs review investigation proposals and recommend to the Director of ODI whether to open an investigation, decline an investigation, or refer the proposal to the Defects Assessment Panel for further review.

. . .

ODI LACKS EFFECTIVE PROCESSES FOR COLLECTING COMPLETE AND ACCURATE VEHICLE SAFETY DATA

ODI's processes for collecting vehicle safety data are insufficient to ensure complete and accurate data. Deficiencies in ODI's vehicle safety data are due in part to the Agency's lack of detailed guidance on what information manufacturers and consumers should report. Further, ODI does not verify the completeness and accuracy of manufacturers' early warning reporting data, or take timely action to correct identified inaccuracies and omissions. In the GM case, ODI received data on the ignition switch defect as early as 2003. Some of these data specifically described the ignition switch problems; however, other information lacked sufficient detail or was inconsistently categorized.

. . .

ODI's assessment of early warning reporting data is greatly influenced by the codes manufacturers assign to incidents. While regulations specify 24 broad vehicle codes (see exhibit D for a complete list of codes), ODI notes that an average vehicle may have over 15,000 components, and categorizing them can be open to interpretation. For example, ODI staff told us that a manufacturer could categorize a malfunction of an air bag component located in a seat using three different vehicle codes: air bags, seats, or electrical system. Additionally, the regulations allow manufacturers to decide if an incident not included in the 24 defined codes should be reported. However, this does not apply to death and injury claims, all of which must be reported.

---

10. The Defect Assessment Division currently has nine staff including eight screeners and a Division Chief.

11. ODI has three investigative divisions: the Vehicle Control Division, Vehicle Integrity Division, and the Medium and Heavy Duty Vehicle Division.

Despite this complexity, ODI does not provide detailed guidance to help ensure manufacturers interpret and apply the appropriate codes. According to ODI staff, additional rulemaking would be required in order to provide more guidance to manufacturers. ODI analysts told us that when a manufacturer asks for specific guidance on assigning codes, their practice is not to provide guidance and instead allow each manufacturer to make its own decisions. However, ODI investigative chiefs and vehicle safety advocates told us that ODI's early warning aggregate data are ultimately of little use due to the inconsistencies in manufacturers' categorizations of safety incidents.

. . .

ODI Does Not Provide Sufficient Guidance to Consumers on the Type of Information to Include When Submitting Complaints

ODI relies primarily on consumer complaints to identify potential safety concerns. However, consumer complaints often do not provide enough detail to determine the existence of safety concerns or do not correctly identify the vehicle systems involved.

The majority of consumer complaints are submitted through NHTSA's safercar.gov Web site, which prompts consumers to provide details about the vehicles and incidents in question. The online complaint submission form requires consumers to select up to 3 affected parts from a drop-down list of 18 options, such as air bags and electronic stability control (see figure 1). Additionally, the Web site provides a text field for consumers to describe the incidents underlying their complaints.

. . .

According to ODI's initial screener, roughly 50 to 75 percent of complaints incorrectly identify the affected parts, and roughly 25 percent do not provide adequate information to determine the existence of safety concerns. These data quality issues occur in part because ODI does not provide consumers with detailed guidance on submitting complaints. For example, safercar.gov does not define the 18 affected parts categories—some of which may be unfamiliar to consumers, such as "adaptive equipment." Furthermore, safercar.gov does not allow consumers to submit, or encourage them to retain, supporting documentation (such as photographs or police reports), which ODI's screeners and management have indicated are valuable in identifying potential safety concerns. In contrast, the U.S. Consumer Product Safety Commission's complaint Web site (saferproducts .gov) allows consumers to upload as many as 25 documents or photos related to their complaints.

ODI Received Early Warning and Consumer Complaint Data Related to the GM Ignition Switch Defect

ODI received early warning reporting data and consumer complaints related to the GM ignition switch defect for more than a decade before GM notified ODI of the recall on February 7, 2014. However, some of this information lacked sufficient detail or was inconsistently categorized. From 2003 through 2013, GM submitted about 15,600 non-dealer field reports and about 2,000 death and injury reports on vehicles subject to the ignition switch recall—especially related to the 2005 to 2010 Chevrolet Cobalt (see table 3). In a 2011 ODI early warning reporting analysis of 22 vehicles with potential air bag issues, the 2005 to 2010 Chevrolet Cobalt ranked fourth for fatal incidents and second for injury incidents involving air bags.

Table 3. Early Warning Reporting Data Related to Vehicles Subject to GM Ignition Switch Defect

Non-dealer field reports	GM submitted about 15,600 non-dealer field reports.	The Cobalt represented 36 percent of these non-dealer field reports.
Death and injury claims and notices	GM submitted about 2,000 death and injury reports. About 90 indicated at least 1 fatality.	The Cobalt represented 63 percent of the death and injury reports—and 74 percent of these reports indicated at least one fatality.

Source: OIG analysis

GM inconsistently categorized some of the early warning reporting data it submitted to ODI. For example, GM assigned different codes for similar non-dealer field reports related to the ignition switch defect.

- In March 2005, GM submitted a non-dealer field report in which a GM employee described the ignition switch defect in a 2005 Chevrolet Cobalt. The employee wrote that the vehicle stalled on a highway when the employee's knee "hit the GM brown leather key holder." The employee concluded that minor impact to the ignition key could easily cause the engine to shut off. GM categorized this report using the "Engine and Engine Cooling" code.
- In May 2007, GM submitted another non-dealer field report in which a GM employee describes the ignition switch defect in a 2006 Pontiac Solstice. The employee wrote that the vehicle ignition system turned off several times while driving when his knee hit the accessories attached to the key ring. GM categorized this report using the "Electrical" code.

In addition, GM's categorization of a death and injury report pertaining to a fatal accident involving a 2005 Chevrolet Cobalt was inconsistent with supporting documentation. NHTSA regulations state that manufacturers must identify each vehicle system or component that allegedly contributed to the incident when reporting death and injury claims and notices. GM categorized the accident as not involving any of the systems, components, or conditions defined in regulations. However, underlying documentation for the report included a Wisconsin State trooper's report indicating that the ignition switch and air bags were both involved in the accident:

> The ignition switch on the . . . vehicle appears to have been in the accessory position when it impacted the trees preventing the air bags from deploying. A search of the [NHTSA] web site indicates five complaints of 2005 Chevrolet Cobalt ignition switches turning off while the vehicle was being driven. Three of the complaints talk about the knee or leg touching the ignition or key chain causing the engine to turn off. . . . It appears likely that the vehicles' key turned to accessory as a result of the low key cylinder torque/effort.

In February 2007, a GM technical service bulletin uploaded to Artemis—ODI's primary database for storing data used to identify and address potential safety defects—described inadvertent turning of the key cylinder and loss of electrical systems. The bulletin applied to vehicle models and model years that would eventually be subject to the February 2014 recall. Although the bulletin does not describe the potential for the vehicle to stall as a result of inadvertent turning of the ignition switch, it does state that the problem was more likely to occur when the vehicle was turning. GM categorized this bulletin using the "Steering" code.

From January 1, 2003, through February 7, 2014, ODI received 9,266 complaints involving the vehicles subject to the GM ignition switch recall—including 72 complaints indicating at least 1 injury and 3 complaints indicating at least 1 fatality. The majority of these complaints involved the 2005 to 2010 Chevrolet Cobalt and the 2003 to 2007 Saturn Ion.

Some consumer complaints were miscategorized or lacked sufficient detail to link them to the ignition switch defect. For example, a June 2005 complaint stated only that an accident had destroyed a 2005 Chevrolet Cobalt and injured one person and that the air bags did not deploy. The complaint did not specify whether this accident occurred on or off the road, or whether the impact was to the front, side, or back of the vehicle—details that were essential to ODI's analysis of air bag non-deployment in these vehicles.

However, some consumer complaints described the ignition switch defect in detail. For example, in June 2005, a consumer sent NHTSA a copy of a letter that she sent to the GM customer service department describing how her 2005 Chevrolet Cobalt had turned off on three occasions while driving. The letter stated that the service manager tested the vehicle and was able to turn the ignition switch when his knee hit the bottom of the "opener gadget" on the keychain. The letter goes on:

> This is a safety/recall issue if there ever was one. Forget the bulletin. I have found the cause of the problem. Not suggested causes as listed in bulletin. The problem is the ignition turn switch is poorly installed. Even with the slightest touch, the car will shut off while in motion. I don't have to list to you the safety problems that may happen, besides an accident or death. . . .

Furthermore, ODI contractors miscategorized some consumer complaints related to ignition switch defects. For example, in September 2003, a driver of a 2003 Saturn Ion reported experiencing engine shutoff on three occasions when the driver's knee accidently hit the car keys. According to the complaint, two of these events occurred when the car was traveling at 65 miles per hour on a freeway. When entering this complaint into Artemis, ODI contractors miscategorized this complaint using the codes "Unknown or Other" and "Exterior Lighting: Headlights: Switch" rather than the correct code "Electrical Systems: Ignition: Switch."

WEAK DATA ANALYSES AND REVIEWS UNDERMINE ODI'S EFFORTS TO IDENTIFY VEHICLE DEFECTS

ODI does not follow standard statistical practices when analyzing early warning reporting data, conduct thorough reviews of consumer complaints, or provide adequate supervision or training for staff responsible for reviewing these data and complaints. As a result, it cannot reliably identify the most statistically significant safety issues to pursue. ODI's complaints process is not thorough and in the case of GM, ODI missed multiple opportunities to link the GM ignition switch defect to air bag non-deployments because ODI staff lacked technical expertise and did not consider all available information.

ODI Does Not Follow Standard Statistical Practice When Analyzing Early Warning Reporting Data

ODI uses four statistical tests to analyze aggregate early warning reporting data (such as consumer complaints, warranty claims, and property damage claims) — as well as a fifth test to analyze non-dealer field reports (see table 4).

Table 4. ODI's Statistical Tests for Analyzing Early Warning Reporting Data

Statistical test	Description
Crow-AMSAA	Trend analysis used to analyze aggregate data
Mahalanobis distance	Test used to analyze aggregate data
Probability measure	Test used to analyze aggregate data
Logistic regression	Regression test used to analyze death and injury aggregate data
CRM-114	Filter used to analyze non-dealer field reports

Source: OIG analysis

While the statistical experts we consulted note that conducting multiple tests provides a sound basis for analysis, ODI does not follow standard statistical practices when implementing the tests of the aggregate data. Specifically, ODI does not consistently identify a model (a set of assumptions) for the aggregate data to establish a base case—that is, what the test results would be in the absence of safety defects. According to the statistical experts, identifying assumptions and models—and checking to see whether they fit the data—are essential for establishing a base case. Without a base case, ODI cannot differentiate trends and outliers that represent random variation from those that are statistically significant—that is, scores that indicate a safety issue should be pursued.

. . .

ODI Does Not Thoroughly Screen Consumer Complaints

In October 2010, ODI established a two-tiered process for screening consumer complaints, its primary source for identifying potential vehicle safety concerns. Currently, one employee reviews all submitted consumer complaints, determines which complaints have potential safety implications, and forwards those complaints to eight advanced screeners who perform more in-depth reviews (see figure 2). In 2011, we recommended that ODI conduct a workforce assessment to determine the number of staff required for ODI to meet its objectives and determine the most effective mix of skill sets. ODI has recently completed its workforce assessment. We are conducting a separate audit to assess NHTSA's actions to implement our 2011 recommendations—including the workforce assessment—and plan to report our findings on this topic later this year.

Figure 2. ODI's Consumer Complaint Review Process

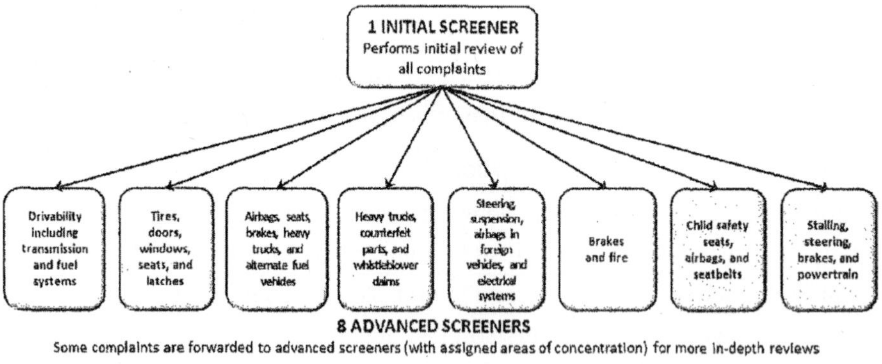

Source: OIG analysis

Since 2010, ODI has received at least 40,000 complaints a year. In 2014, it received nearly 78,000 complaints (see figure 3). In other words, the initial screener's workload is roughly 330 complaints each day. Determinations of whether complaints warrant further review are made within a matter of seconds—in part because the initial screener spends roughly half of the day carrying out other work responsibilities.

Figure 3. ODI's Annual and Average Daily Complaint Volume

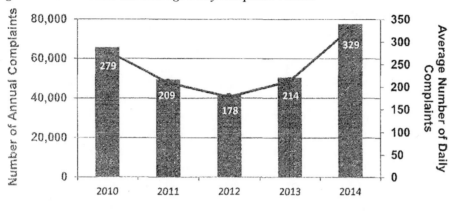

▓▓ Annual Complaint Volume   ─●─Average Daily Complaint Volume

Note: Calculation of average daily complaint volume assumes 236 working days per year.
Source: OIG analysis of complaint data in Artemis

According to the initial screener and our independent verification, about 10 percent of complaints are forwarded to advanced screeners for in-depth reviews,[26] leaving no assurance that the remaining 90 percent of complaints receive additional review.

In making determinations, the initial screener relies on his professional experience and judgment, as well as informal guidance and precedent. While he noted that ODI informally established certain complaint categories that automatically warrant further analysis—including most air bag non-deployments and seatbelt issues — ODI lacks formal guidance for initial screening. The initial screener further noted that he prioritizes incidents that occur suddenly, with little warning for the consumer, but assigns lower priority to engine, transmission, and vehicle body issues and generally does not forward certain incidents that most likely do not lead to investigations, such as sharp door edges. The initial screener also does not forward complaints he believes are covered by existing recalls.

ODI's process for initially screening consumer complaints leaves the office vulnerable to a single point of failure and the risk that complaints with potential safety significance may not be selected for further review.

Like the initial screener, ODI's eight advanced screeners have access to a variety of data sources—such as technical service bulletins and special crash investigation reports—and have the authority to reach out to consumers

26. We independently verified that, in 1 week of review, the initial screener forwarded about 10 percent of complaints to advanced screeners.

and perform field inspections to augment their research. However, three advanced screeners told us that they rely mainly on consumer complaints to identify safety concerns, and four advanced screeners said they only occasionally use other sources of data. While screeners are encouraged to query all complaints for issues in their areas of concentration, four screeners told us they do not consistently do this—in some cases because it takes too much time. Advanced screeners also have access to early warning reporting data; however, four advanced screeners told us that they are less likely to rely on these data because they are untimely. Two screeners were also concerned about the early warning reporting data's lack of usefulness because they felt the data provided no significant additional detail.

In 2013, ODI began requiring advanced screeners to annotate the complaints they review by documenting the condition that led to the incident and their reasons for deciding not to pursue potential issues. According to the Defects Assessment Division Chief, the annotations are intended to identify and correct inconsistencies and inaccuracies in complaints—and thereby enable ODI to properly link them to relevant safety concerns—and provide a record of review. However, an ODI internal audit found that roughly half the complaints were incorrectly annotated or lacked critical information. Additionally, we analyzed annotations for complaints received in the fourth quarter of 2013 and found that about 57 percent of the complaints that screeners determined did not warrant further review lacked justifications. Advanced screeners told us that annotating complaints is time consuming.

ODI's Pre-Investigation Staff Lack the Training and Supervision To Effectively Analyze Vehicle Safety Data

While NHTSA has a training plan, it has not been implemented effectively. As a result, ODI staff who review early warning reporting data and consumer complaints lack adequate training to carry out their responsibilities. For example:

- ODI staff charged with interpreting statistical test results for early warning reporting data told us they have no training or background in statistics. Three screeners assigned to analyze air bag incidents lacked training in air bags. One screener who was originally hired to review child seat restraint issues was assigned in 2008 to review air bag issues—without any air bag training and without an engineering or automotive background.
- Screeners told us that training to maintain professional certifications—such as the Automotive Service Excellence certification for automotive mechanics—must be completed on their own time and generally at their own expense.
- Screeners also noted that ODI lacked the funding to allow them to attend training to stay abreast of the latest developments in vehicle technology.

Further, ODI has not established an adequate supervisory review process to evaluate the quality of screeners' work in identifying potential safety issues. Except for reviews of final investigation proposals, we found no documentation of supervisory review. In addition, ODI staff told us that their data analysis and screening efforts were generally not reviewed and that they received little feedback on the quality of their work.

For example, the Defects Assessment Division Chief characterized his oversight of the initial complaint screener's work as "minimal" and acknowledged that he does not provide much guidance to the initial screener. Instead, ODI relies on the screener's years of experience and professional judgment to identify complaints warranting further analysis. Advanced screeners also told us that supervisory review is often informal and that the Defects Assessment Division Chief does not regularly review their complaint annotations.

Inadequate training and supervisory review have led to deficient analyses of early warning reporting and complaint data. For example, the developer of one statistical test that ODI uses to analyze early warning reporting data stated that the test should produce the same results every time for the same data input in the same order. However, ODI staff told us that different test runs produce different results, and management has not considered this to be a problem,

ODI Staff Overlooked Documentation Pointing to the GM Ignition Switch Defect

NHTSA staff and contractors reviewed non-dealer field reports that described the GM ignition switch defect, and reviewed death and injury and special crash investigation reports that explicitly linked the ignition switch defect and air bag non-deployments. However, ODI staff missed opportunities to connect the ignition switch defect to air bag non-deployments because they did not consider all available information.

For example, in 2007, two ODI employees reviewed the underlying documentation for a death and injury report on a fatal accident involving a 2005 Chevrolet Cobalt, which contained evidence that linked the ignition switch defect to the vehicle's air bag non-deployment. However, neither employee—an early warning reporting analyst and an ODI air bag investigator—made this connection during their analyses of the documentation. The death and injury report documentation specifically included:

- A Wisconsin State Trooper's report that identified the ignition switch defect as a possible cause of air bag non-deployment during the accident. However, the two ODI staff who reviewed the report did not note this finding when documenting their reviews of the report.
- Event data recorder data[27] showed the vehicle's power mode status had been in the "accessory" position during the accident—a key indicator of the ignition switch defect. However, the ODI analyst reviewing

---

27. An event data recorder is a device installed in a vehicle to record technical vehicle and occupant information for a brief period of time (seconds, not minutes) before, during, and after a crash.

this report did not include this information in his annotation. The air bag investigator noted this information in his review but ultimately concluded that the air bag non-deployment was caused by the long delay between the first and final impacts.

A NHTSA special crash investigation report on the same fatal accident also suggested a link between the ignition switch defect and air bag non-deployments. Specifically, the report concluded that the vehicle's air bags failed to deploy possibly due to "power loss due to movement of the ignition switch just prior to the impact," among other potential reasons. NHTSA's special crash investigation staff told us that they submitted their report to ODI for review in April 2007. However, ODI told us its staff did not review the report.[28]

Between the second quarter of 2012 and the fourth quarter of 2013, ODI received 13 non-dealer field reports on the 2005 to 2010 Chevrolet Cobalts that GM categorized as air bag-related and that we determined may be related to the ignition switch defect.[29] However, ODI staff reviewed only one of these non-dealer field reports before the February 2014 recall. According to ODI staff, they did not review the majority of these reports because in the second quarter of 2012, GM began using a new file format for most of their document submissions (.docx), which could not be read by the statistical test ODI uses to analyze these reports.[30] ODI staff acknowledged that they did not notice the reports were not analyzed until after the recall.

In addition to the non-dealer reports, ODI received 9,266 consumer complaints between January 1, 2003, and February 7, 2014, that involved GM vehicles subject to the ignition switch recall. Because ODI's screeners were not required to annotate their reviews of complaints until 2013, ODI cannot establish a full picture of why it did not investigate complaints related to the GM ignition switch and air bag non-deployment issues prior to 2013. From the time that the annotations were required to the date of the recall, ODI received 926 consumer complaints involving the recalled vehicles. ODI's initial screener advanced 27—or 3 percent—of these complaints for further review, compared to the average of 10 percent that are typically forwarded. ODI's advanced screeners noted in their annotations that 11 of the 27 complaints included allegations of front air bag non-deployment, but they did not advance these complaints for further consideration because they concluded there was either "no actionable trend indicated" or "minimal

28. Artemis records for the GM air bag non-deployment issue contain a preliminary version of the special crash investigation report (IN-06-033) completed in December 2006. According to the preliminary report, evidence showed that the ignition switch was in the "accessory" position at the time of the crash and that the contractor was "continuing its investigation into this aspect of the crash."

29. To determine which non-dealer field reports were related to the ignition switch recall, we limited this analysis to vehicle models, model years, facts, and circumstances that would make an accident eligible for compensation through the GM ignition switch compensation fund.

30. ODI's written instructions to vehicle manufacturers for submitting early warning reporting documents specify seven acceptable electronic file formats (including .doc and .html), but .docx is not one of those specified. Docx is the Microsoft Office extensible markup language file format.

hazard." ODI staff did not thoroughly understand when air bags were supposed to deploy in these vehicles, which prevented them from linking the ignition switch defect to the air bag non-deployment. This may be explained by ODI staffs acknowledged lack of training on air bags.

ODI prepared three investigation proposals for the Chevrolet Cobalt and Saturn Ion about loss of electric power steering and air bag non-deployment. Each proposal was supported by early warning reporting referrals identifying these potential safety concerns. However, ODI staff did not establish the ignition switch defect as a potential root cause for these issues. For example, in September 2007, an ODI screener submitted an investigation proposal on front air bag non-deployment in the 2005 and 2006 Chevrolet Cobalt and the 2003 through 2005 Saturn Ion. The proposal attributed 4 fatalities, 11 injuries, and 29 crashes to the potential safety defect, and it explained that "driver and passenger side frontal air bags fail to deploy during crash events where [data] suggest the air bags should have deployed." However, the proposal did not link the air bag non-deployment to the ignition switch defect, even though proposal documentation included an interview with a vehicle owner who mentioned the special crash investigation report that identified the position of the ignition switch as a possible cause of the air bag non-deployments. ODI officials told us that they did not understand the safety consequences of the ignition switch defect before the GM recall.

Notes and Questions

1. For many purposes, including legal actions and congressional oversight, NHTSA is treated as a single entity. Note, however, that even within an agency that is relatively small, as Acting Administrator Friedman points out, there is a complex internal structure. Testing is done by the Office of Vehicle Safety Compliance (OVSC), while the Office of Defects Investigation (ODI) gathers information about possible defects. Within ODI, the Defects Assessment Division does the initial screening on complaints and forwards those it considers significant. Look at the chart (Figure 2) in the Inspector General's Report showing the way advanced screeners are assigned. When an agency's performance is questioned, as here, there is a tendency to look at its substantive policies and practices (see below). But the organizational structure of the agency may be a source of problems as well. Should the complaint handling department have been separate from the rest of the agency? Should top-level administrators rotate from one department to another, as in Japan? Should the advanced screeners be assigned tasks on the basis of the different parts of a car? To what extent does ODI's leadership supervise subdivisions such as the Defects Assessment Division, and to what extent does NHTSA leadership supervise ODI? To what extent are the activities of these various divisions coordinated. Obviously, the Administrator must answer to Congress for all of them.

2. Note that ODI has (at least) two sources of information. One is reports about safety problems filed by the manufacturing firms, which are required by statute. The other is consumer complaints. That is the one we focus on here, as a type of adjudication, but the required reports are obviously important; in fact, they are a major element of the administrative process.

3. Acting Administrator Friedman states, in his testimony: "Human behavior remains the leading cause of highway crashes and deaths." Is this a return to the "nut behind the wheel" explanation that was, in essence, rejected by the Motor Vehicle Safety Act?

4. Does consumer complaint handling require expertise, meaning specialized training and experience? We can assume that most consumers are honest, but their knowledge of cars, their verbal skills, and their ability to fill out an online form will vary considerably. (As a test, pick an auto defect, then go to *www.safecar.gov* and see whether it is readily captured by the form.) What sort of policy decisions go into the design of the form, and what sorts of decisions go into the way that the information is interpreted?

5. The Inspector General states that "ODI staff charged with interpreting statistical test results from early warning reporting told us they have no training or background in statistics." Given the issues raised by the preceding note (4), was this good policy? What sort of training did these staff members have? What training or credentials should they have had?

6. Look at the description of the GM ignition issue in the Inspector General's report. At what points did NHTSA's approach break down? See if you can determine what should have been done instead at those points, what the general approach to complaint handling should have been, and what general policy it should have been intended to instantiate.

7. Consider the following statement by the Inspector General: "Deficiencies in ODI's vehicle safety data are due in part to the Agency's lack of detailed guidance on what information manufacturers and consumers should report." In other words, the Inspector General sees a positive and important, if not essential role, for guidance issued by an administrative agency. Keep that conclusion in mind as you read the material in the following section.

2. Guidance

Agencies also implement their statutes through procedures that are less formal than notice-and-comment rulemaking (which generates what can be referred to "legislative rules"), formal adjudication, or even "informal" adjudication (that is, adjudication not governed by APA §§554, 556-557). They routinely issue interpretive rules, statements of policy, informative brochures, and no-action letters, as well as enforcement handbooks or manuals, and rules of "agency organization, procedure, or practice." There is no general term for these actions in the APA, and they have thus been consigned to the residual category of informal adjudication (although, as you can see, they bear little resemblance to the ordinary language use of this term). More commonly, they are described as forms of *guidance*. We use the term "guidance" to refer to agency action that is expressly exempted from the requirements of notice-and-comment rulemaking, either as "interpretative [sic] rules, general statements of policy, or rules of agency organization, procedure or practice." 5 U.S.C. §553(b)(A). But without a legal definition, a great deal of uncertainty afflicts the term.

Professor Nina Mendelson describes the prevalence of guidance in contemporary agency practice: "In setting policy, federal regulatory agencies regularly bypass the requirements of the Administrative Procedure Act (APA) public notice-and-comment process for issuing legislative rules. They instead use the statutory exception for general statements of policy and interpretative rules. Compared with notice-and-comment rules, the volume of these materials, which I will collectively call "guidance documents," is massive. Examples range from the Forest Service's nonbinding Directive System regarding national forest management, to the Federal Aviation Administration (FAA) Advisory Circulars on air safety, to the Treasury Department's Examination Handbook on the operation of thrift institutions. In response to congressional requests, the Environmental Protection Agency (EPA) catalogued over two thousand guidance documents it had issued between 1996 and 1999, and the Occupational Safety and Health Administration of the Department of Labor (OSHA) catalogued over three thousand. During the same period, the EPA issued one hundred "significant" rules subject to Office of Management and Budget (OMB) review, and the entire Department of Labor, including OSHA, issued twenty such rules. A recent study of the Food and Drug Administration (FDA) suggests that on average it issues at least twice as many guidances as it does rules. According to another source, the FDA's use of guidance documents continues to increase. This use of guidances dwarfs agencies' production of notice-and-comment rules. Nina Mendelson, *Regulatory Beneficiaries and Informal Agency Policymaking*, 92 CORNELL L. REV. 397, 398-401 (2007).

Here is NHTSA's description of the range of situations where it uses this device:

National Highway Traffic Safety Administration, Laws & Regulations: Guidance Documents

https://www.nhtsa.gov/laws-regulations/guidance-documents

TYPES OF GUIDANCE

To enable the public to better understand the various types of documents that NHTSA issues that could provide information on our interpretation of, or policy concerning, our rules, statutes, or technical issues and the extent to which the public may rely on them, we have prepared the following descriptions. The following examples of NHTSA guidance are approved by appropriate agency officials in accordance with procedures approved by the head of the agency, and they may be relied on by the party or parties to whom they are provided:

- Preambles. Preambles to final rules promulgated by the agency. They are issued at the time of, and as part of, the final rule signed by the head of the agency or another senior official with delegated authority from the agency head.

- Generally Applicable Interpretations or Policy Statements Issued or Approved by the Agency Head (or designee). These are normally published in the Federal Register or posted on the agency's website.
- Letters to Specific Individuals or Entities. These letters respond to requests from individuals or entities and provide an interpretation of particular regulatory or statutory provisions. These letters represent the definitive view of the agency on the questions addressed and may be relied upon by the regulated industry and members of the public. However, the agency strongly cautions that these letters are based on specific facts that are critical to the agency's interpretation. NHTSA posts these letters on the agency's website.
- Oral Guidance Statements by Senior Agency Officials. If there is a record of such statements, such as prepared statements from senior officials testifying at a Congressional committee hearing, the statements are posted on the agency's website.
- Grant Guidelines. These documents provide information about the agency's grant program criteria. They are published in the Federal Register for notice and comment and/or posted on the agency's website. Compliance Guides. Generally, compliance guides restate or summarize statutory and regulatory requirements to provide assistance to the public or regulated entities.

In theory, guidance documents are not legally binding, but the agency has the obligation to make them widely available, which now means posting that material on its website. *See* 5 U.S.C. §552(a)(1) and (2). Regulated entities often feel obligated to follow these statements because they assume the agency will do so. One agency that makes extensive use of guidance is the Food and Drug Administration (FDA). For example, it has chosen to address one of the most controversial issues within its jurisdiction, the safety of genetically modified organisms (GMOs) for food use, exclusively through a guidance document, rather than by using its authority to promulgate a rule under §553. *See* Edward L. Rubin & Joanna K. Sax, *Administrative Guidance and Genetically Modified Food*, 60 Ariz. L. Rev. 539 (2018). The FDA has explained the legal effect of its guidance documents in, of all things, a guidance document. Here is an excerpt from the FDA guidance on guidance.

Food and Drug Administration, §10.115 Good Guidance Practices

21 CFR Ch. I (4-1-12 Edition)

(a) *What are good guidance practices?* Good guidance practices (GGP's) are FDA's policies and procedures for developing, issuing, and using guidance documents.

(b) *What is a guidance document?* (1) Guidance documents are documents prepared for FDA staff, applicants/sponsors, and the public that describe the agency's interpretation of or policy on a regulatory issue.

(2) Guidance documents include, but are not limited to, documents that relate to: The design, production, labeling, promotion, manufacturing, and testing of regulated products; the processing, content, and evaluation or approval of submissions; and inspection and enforcement policies.

(3) Guidance documents do not include: Documents relating to internal FDA procedures, agency reports, general information documents provided to consumers or health professionals, speeches, journal articles and editorials, media interviews, press materials, warning letters, memoranda of understanding, or other communications directed to individual persons or firms.

(c) *What other terms have a special meaning?* (1) "Level 1 guidance documents" include guidance documents that:

(i) Set forth initial interpretations of statutory or regulatory requirements;

(ii) Set forth changes in interpretation or policy that are of more than a minor nature;

(iii) Include complex scientific issues; or

(iv) Cover highly controversial issues.

(2) "Level 2 guidance documents" are guidance documents that set forth existing practices or minor changes in interpretation or policy. Level 2 guidance documents include all guidance documents that are not classified as Level 1.

(3) "You" refers to all affected parties outside of FDA.

(d) *Are you or FDA required to follow a guidance document?* (1) No. Guidance documents do not establish legally enforceable rights or responsibilities. They do not legally bind the public or FDA.

(2) You may choose to use an approach other than the one set forth in a guidance document. However, your alternative approach must comply with the relevant statutes and regulations. FDA is willing to discuss an alternative approach with you to ensure that it complies with the relevant statutes and regulations.

(3) Although guidance documents do not legally bind FDA, they represent the agency's current thinking. Therefore, FDA employees may depart from guidance documents only with appropriate justification and supervisory concurrence.

(e) *Can FDA use means other than a guidance document to communicate new agency policy or a new regulatory approach to a broad public audience?* The agency may not use documents or other means of communication that are excluded from the definition of guidance document to informally communicate new or different regulatory expectations to a broad public audience for the first time. These GGP's must be followed whenever regulatory expectations that are not readily apparent from the statute or regulations are first communicated to a broad public audience.

(f) *How can you participate in the development and issuance of guidance documents?* (1) You can provide input on guidance documents that FDA is developing under the procedures described in paragraph (g) of this section.

(2) You can suggest areas for guidance document development. Your suggestions should address why a guidance document is necessary.

(3) You can submit drafts of proposed guidance documents for FDA to consider

(4) You can, at any time, suggest that FDA revise or withdraw an already existing guidance document. Your suggestion should address why the guidance document should be revised or withdrawn and, if applicable, how it should be revised.

(g) *What are FDA's procedures for developing and issuing guidance documents?* (1) FDA's procedures for the development and issuance of Level 1 guidance documents are as follows:

(i) Before FDA prepares a draft of a Level 1 guidance document, FDA can seek or accept early Input from individuals or groups outside the agency. For example, FDA can do this by participating in or holding public meetings and workshops.

(ii) After FDA prepares a draft of a Level 1 guidance document, FDA will:

(A) Publish a notice in the FEDERAL REGISTER announcing that the draft guidance document is available;

(B) Post the draft guidance document on the Internet and make it available in hard copy; and

(C) Invite your comment on the draft guidance document. Paragraph (h) of this section tells you how to submit your comments.

(iii) After FDA prepares a draft of a Level 1 guidance document, FDA also can:

(A) Hold public meetings or workshops; or

(B) Present the draft guidance document to an advisory committee for review.

(iv) After providing an opportunity for public comment on a Level 1 guidance document, FDA will:

(A) Review any comments received and prepare the final version of the guidance document that incorporates suggested changes, when appropriate;

(B) Publish a notice in the FEDERAL REGISTER announcing that the guidance document is available;

(C) Post the guidance document on the Internet and make it available in hard copy; and

(D) Implement the guidance document.

(v) After providing an opportunity for comment, FDA may decide that it should issue another draft of the guidance document. In this case, FDA will follow the steps in paragraphs (g)(1)(ii), (g)(1)(iii), and (g)(1)(iv) of this section.

(2) FDA will not seek your comment before it implements a Level 1 guidance document if the agency determines that prior public participation is not feasible or appropriate.

(3) FDA will use the following procedures for developing and issuing Level 1 guidance documents under the circumstances described in paragraph (g)(2) of this section:

(i) After FDA prepares a guidance document, FDA will:

(A) Publish a notice in the FEDERAL REGISTER announcing that the guidance document is available;

(B) Post the guidance document on the Internet and make it available in hard copy;

(C) Immediately implement the guidance document; and

(D) Invite your comment when it issues or publishes the guidance document. Paragraph (h) of this section tells you how to submit your comments.

(ii) If FDA receives comments on the guidance document, FDA will review those comments and revise the guidance document when appropriate.

(4) FDA will use the following procedures for developing and issuing Level 2 guidance documents:

(2) Guidance documents must not include mandatory language such as "shall," "must," "required," or "requirement," unless FDA is using these words to describe a statutory or regulatory requirement.

(j) *Who, within FDA, can approve issuance of guidance documents?* Bach center and office must have written procedures for the approval of guidance documents. Those procedures must ensure that issuance of all documents is approved by appropriate senior PDA officials.

(k) *How will FDA review and revise existing guidance documents?* (1) The agency will periodically review existing guidance documents to determine whether they need to be changed or withdrawn.

(2) When significant changes are made to the statute or regulations, the agency will review and, if appropriate, revise guidance documents relating to that changed statute or regulation.

(3) As discussed in paragraph (f)(3) of this section, you may at any time suggest that PDA revise a guidance document.

(1) *How will FDA ensure that FDA staff are following GGP's?* (1) All current and new PDA employees involved in the development, issuance, or application of guidance documents will be trained regarding the agency's GGP's.

(2) PDA centers and offices will monitor the development and issuance of guidance documents to ensure that GGP's are being followed.

(o) *What can you do if you believe that someone at FDA is not following these GGP's?* If you believe that someone at FDA did not follow the procedures in this section or that someone at FDA treated a guidance document as a binding requirement, you should contact that person's supervisor in the center or office that issued the guidance document. If the issue cannot be resolved, you should contact the next highest supervisor. You can also contact the center or office ombudsman for assistance in resolving the issue. If you are unable to resolve the issue at the center or office level or if you feel that you are not making progress by going through the chain of command, you may ask the Office of the Chief Mediator and Ombudsman to become involved.

[65 Fed. Reg. 56477 (Sept. 19, 2000)]

Notes and Questions

1. The Office of Management and Budget (OMB) relied on this document in producing its own bulletin on guidance practices, Final Bulletin for Agency Good Guidance Practices, 72 Fed. Reg. 3432 (Jan. 25, 2017).

2. The procedure by which the FDA develops and issues guidance documents seems fairly elaborate. What is the difference between this procedure and the requirements for issuing an informal rule under §553? Which of those differences do you suppose motivates the agency to make such extensive use of guidance?

3. Level 2 guidance documents, as defined by the FDA Guidance, seem unobjectionable. But what about the Level 1 documents? Should this mechanism be used for "initial interpretations," or "changes in interpretations or policy that are of more than a minor nature," or "highly controversial issues"? For an argument that these kind of issues, particularly the last, are precisely the ones that should be subject to the notice-and-comment rulemaking process, see Rubin & Sax, *supra.*

4. According to this document, are FDA guidances legally binding on regulated parties? Can you identify the different places in the document where the agency asserts that they are not? Now consider the statement in (d)(3) that "FDA employees may depart from guidance documents only with appropriate justification and supervisory concurrence." Is that a reassuring promise of agency regularity or a contravention of its asserted flexibility? If you were giving legal advice to a regulated party, what would you recommend that it should do with respect to a relevant guidance document?

5. A number of commentators have advanced proposals for dealing with the legal issues that agency guidances present. One possibility is to allow regulated parties to challenge the legality of a guidance in court as soon as it is issued, instead of relying on the usual rule that only allows a challenge after the agency has taken some final or definitive action based on the guidance. Richard Epstein, *The Role of Guidances in Modern Administrative Procedure: The Case for De Novo Review*, 8 J. LEGAL ANALYSIS 47 (2016); Mark Seidenfeld, *Substituting Substantive for Procedural Review of Guidance Documents*, 90 TEX. L. REV. 331 (2011). A different proposal is that a document that has not gone through the § 553 notice-and-comment rulemaking process (i.e., is not a "legislative rule") cannot be used by the agency as a basis for action; the agency would need to justify any enforcement proceeding against a private party on some other basis (statute, regulations). Jacob Gerson, *Legislative*

Rules Revisited, 74 U. CHI. L. REV. 1705 (2007); John F. Manning, *Nonlegislative Rules,* 72 GEO. WASH. L. REV. 893 (2004). Do you see any problems with these suggestions? *See* David Franklin, *Legislative Rules, Non-Legislative Rules, and the Perils of the Shortcut,* 120 YALE L.J. 276 (2010).

Why or when would an agency prefer to use guidance documents than the notice-and-comment rulemaking process?

Nina Mendelson, Regulatory Beneficiaries and Informal Agency Policymaking

92 Cornell L. Rev. 397, 408-12 (2007).

[A]gencies have several reasons to prefer using guidance documents to following the APA notice-and-comment procedure. First, issuing a guidance is relatively cheap compared with the costs of notice-and-comment rulemaking. The agency also retains flexibility to change the guidance inexpensively and quickly. These increased costs undoubtedly sharpen the incentive to use guidance documents. The agency may also hope to forestall expensive litigation over the policy's validity and avoid the possibility of an adverse judicial ruling. Since guidance documents are generally not published in the Federal Register, they are also less likely to be subject to congressional oversight or attention in the media. As described in more detail below, guidances have not been subject to executive oversight either. In short, by issuing a guidance document, an agency can obtain a rule-like effect while minimizing political oversight and avoiding the procedural discipline, public participation, and judicial accountability required by the APA. The prospect of "compliance for less" is almost certainly among the reasons that agencies use guidance documents rather than go through the effort of notice-and-comment rulemaking. Meanwhile, the lack of procedural discipline can raise the risk of agency action that serves rent-seeking interests or does not properly engage public preferences. This has led legislators and scholars to complain about agencies' illegitimate use of guidance documents.

By issuing a policy in a guidance document, an agency will forgo some benefits it might have received from notice-and-comment rulemaking. The agency will not, for example, receive useful information from previously unknown sources, and its decision will not be subjected to the discipline of having to respond to comments received.

An agency can have very good reasons to use a guidance document unrelated to its resemblance to a legislative rule. For instance, an agency may simply wish to supervise its employees. Agencies rely on handbooks, directives, and other similar guidance documents to ensure that lower-level employees complete forms correctly and make consistent (and thus more predictable) decisions. Legislative rules could serve the same purpose, but guidance documents allow the agency to supply information to lower-level employees more cheaply and without risking an outside suit based on later noncompliance with the legislative rule. An agency may also use guidance documents to experiment with new approaches to implementing a program before committing the policies to the binding, less flexible form of the legislative rule. Finally, because an agency cannot realistically define and set forth every nuance of its approach in a rule document, guidance documents may supplement legislative rules. It would be highly cumbersome to require rulemaking every time a detail is explained or amplified.

From the perspective of a regulated entity, however, an agency's use of a policy or guidance document raises significant reliance concerns. Unlike a notice-and-comment rule, the agency is generally not bound to comply with the statement in the guidance document. Guidance documents sometimes contain explicit disclaimers to this effect. Indeed, courts will rarely hold an agency to the terms of such a document.

Moreover, although they may participate informally to some degree, regulated entities generally lack the entitlement they would possess in rulemaking to participate in the guidance development process. Besides the extent of public access, the agency also has discretion regarding how much data to disclose. The agency is not obligated to respond to comments or to supply the "concise general statement of their basis and purpose" that the APA would require for rulemaking.

Guidance documents receive very limited review from Congress and the White House. For example, guidance documents to date have been exempt from the Office of Management and Budget (OMB) review normally applied to legislative rules. On January 18, 2007, however, President Bush issued Executive Order 13,422, which gives OMB the option to demand consultation with an agency prior to its issuing a "significant" guidance document. Given OMB's resource constraints, it is unclear how frequently it will exercise this option. Meanwhile, guidance documents also are not subject to Congressional Review Act requirements. While Congress can, of course, exercise oversight of any agency action, such oversight is generally ad hoc. Congressional review of policy and guidance documents is highly limited at best.

Finally, judicial review of these decisions is often difficult to obtain. If a guidance document is not signed by the head of the agency, is a staff-level document, or states it is not binding, then a policy contained in the document may not be considered a "final agency action." Even if a court considers the document to be a final action, it may not be "ripe" for review outside the context of a particular situation. Courts have only occasionally recognized the immediate practical effect a guidance document may have as a basis for finding the document ripe for review. More often, courts have declined to review the guidance document, especially if the agency has specifically disclaimed any binding effect.

———————————

Now you know that guidance documents exist and even a bit about how agencies use them. What do they actually look like? They take a wide variety of forms, depending on the agency and the issue. Consider this example:

Before the
Federal Communications Commission

Washington, D.C. 20554

In the Matter of	)	
	)	
Industry Guidance on the Commission's	)	File No. EB-00-IH-0089
Case Law Interpreting 18 U.S.C. §1464	)	
and Enforcement Policies Regarding	)	
Broadcast Indecency	)	
	)	

POLICY STATEMENT

Adopted: March 14, 2001   **Released:** April 6, 2001

By the Commission: Commissioners Ness and Furchtgott-Roth issuing separate statements; Commissioner Tristani dissenting and issuing a statement.

II. STATUTORY BASIS/JUDICIAL HISTORY

2. It is a violation of federal law to broadcast obscene or indecent programming. Specifically, Title 18 of the United States Code, Section 1464 (18 U.S.C. §1464), prohibits the utterance of "any obscene, indecent, or profane language by means of radio communication." Congress has given the Federal Communications Commission the responsibility for administratively enforcing 18 U.S.C. §1464. In doing so, the Commission may revoke a station license, impose a monetary forfeiture, or issue a warning for the broadcast of indecent material. *See* 47 U.S.C. Sections 312(a)(6) and 503(b)(1)(D).

3. The FCC's enforcement policy under Section 1464 has been shaped by a number of judicial and legislative decisions. In particular, because the Supreme Court has determined that obscene speech is not entitled to First Amendment protection, obscene speech cannot be broadcast at any time. In contrast, indecent speech is protected by the First Amendment, and thus, the government must both identify a compelling interest for any regulation it may impose on indecent speech and choose the least restrictive means to further that interest. Even under this restrictive standard, the courts have consistently upheld the Commission's authority to regulate indecent speech, albeit with certain limitations.

4. *FCC v. Pacifica Foundation,* 438 U.S. 726 (1978), provides the judicial foundation for FCC indecency enforcement. In that case, the Supreme Court held that the government could constitutionally regulate indecent broadcasts. In addition, the Court quoted the Commission's definition of indecency with apparent approval. The definition, "language or material that, in context, depicts or describes, in terms patently offensive as measured by contemporary community standards for the broadcast medium, sexual or excretory activities or organs," has remained substantially unchanged since the time of the *Pacifica* decision.

5. Although the D.C. Circuit approved the FCC's definition of indecency in the *ACT* cases, it also established several restrictive parameters on FCC enforcement. The court's decisions made clear that the FCC had to identify the compelling government interests that warranted regulation and also explain how the regulations were narrowly tailored to further those interests. [It remanded a subsequent case] to the Commission "with instructions to limit its ban on the broadcasting of indecent programs to the period from 6:00 a.m. to 10:00 p.m."

6. Thus, outside the 10:00. P.M. to 6:00 A.M. safe harbor, the courts have approved regulation of broadcast indecency to further the compelling government interests in supporting parental supervision of children and more generally its concern for children's well being. The principles of enforcement articulated below are intended to further these interests.

III. INDECENCY DETERMINATIONS

A. Analytical Approach

7. Indecency findings involve at least two fundamental determinations. First, the material alleged to be indecent must fall within the subject matter scope of our indecency definition — that is, the material must describe or depict sexual or excretory organs or activities. *WPBN/WTOM License Subsidiary, Inc. (WPBN-TV and WTOM-TV),* 15 FCC Rcd 1838, 1840-41 (2000).

8. Second, the broadcast must be *patently offensive* as measured by contemporary community standards for the broadcast medium. In applying the "community standards for the broadcast medium" criterion, the Commission has stated: The determination as to whether certain programming is patently offensive is not a local one and does not encompass any particular geographic area. Rather, the standard is that of an average broadcast viewer or listener and not the sensibilities of any individual complainant. *WPBN/WTOM License Subsidiary, Inc.,* 15 FCC Rcd at 1841.

9. In determining whether material is patently offensive, the *full context* in which the material appeared is critically important. It is not sufficient, for example, to know that explicit sexual terms or descriptions were used, just as it is not sufficient to know only that no such terms or descriptions were used. Explicit language in the context of a *bona fide* newscast might not be patently offensive, while sexual innuendo that persists and

is sufficiently clear to make the sexual meaning inescapable might be. Moreover, contextual determinations are necessarily highly fact-specific, making it difficult to catalog comprehensively all of the possible contextual factors that might exacerbate or mitigate the patent offensiveness of particular material. An analysis of Commission case law reveals that various factors have been consistently considered relevant in indecency determinations. By comparing cases with analogous analytical structures, but different outcomes, we hope to highlight how these factors are applied in varying circumstances and the impact of these variables on a finding of patent offensiveness.

B. Case Comparisons

10. The principal factors that have proved significant in our decisions to date are: (1) the *explicitness or graphic nature* of the description or depiction of sexual or excretory organs or activities; (2) whether the material *dwells on or repeats at length* descriptions of sexual or excretory organs or activities; (3) *whether the material appears to pander or is used to titillate,* or *whether the material appears to have been presented for its shock value.* In assessing all of the factors, and particularly the third factor, the overall context of the broadcast in which the disputed material appeared is critical. Each indecency case presents its own particular mix of these, and possibly other, factors, which must be balanced to ultimately determine whether the material is patently offensive and therefore indecent. No single factor generally provides the basis for an indecency finding. To illustrate the noted factors, however, and to provide a sense of the weight these considerations have carried in specific factual contexts, a comparison of cases has been organized to provide examples of decisions in which each of these factors has played a particularly significant role, whether exacerbating or mitigating, in the indecency determination made.

11. It should be noted that the brief descriptions and excerpts from broadcasts that are reproduced in this document are intended only as a research tool and should not be taken as a meaningful selection of words and phrases to be evaluated for indecency purposes without the fuller context that the tapes or transcripts provide. The excerpts from broadcasts used in this section have often been shortened or compressed. In order to make the excerpts more readable, however, we have frequently omitted any indication of these ellipses from the text. Moreover, in cases where material was included in a complaint but not specifically cited in the decision based on the complaint, we caution against relying on the omission as if it were of decisional significance. For example, if portions of a voluminous transcript are the object of an enforcement action, those portions not included are not necessarily deemed not indecent. The omissions may be the result of an editing process that attempted to highlight the most significant material within its context. No inference should be drawn regarding the material deleted.

1. Explicitness/Graphic Description versus Indirectness/Implication

12. The more explicit or graphic the description or depiction, the greater the likelihood that the material will be considered patently offensive. Merely because the material consists of double entendre or innuendo, however, does not preclude an indecency finding if the sexual or excretory import is unmistakable.

13. Following are examples of decisions where the explicit/graphic nature of the description of sexual or excretory organs or activities played a central role in the determination that the broadcast was indecent.

WYSP(FM), Philadelphia, PA   **"Howard Stern Show"**

God, my testicles are like down to the floor . . . you could really have a party with these. . . . Use them like Bocci balls.

(As part of a discussion of lesbians) I mean to go around porking other girls with vibrating rubber products. . . .

Have you ever had sex with an animal? Well, don't knock it. I was sodomized by Lambchop.

Indecent—Warning Issued. *Infinity Broadcasting Corporation of Pennsylvania (WYSP(FM))*, 2 FCC Rcd 2705 (1987), *aff'd* 3 FCC Rcd 930 (1987), *aff'd in part, vacated in part on other grounds, remanded sub nom. ACT I*, 852 F.2d 1332 (D.C. Cir. 1988) (subsequent history omitted). Excerpted material (only some of which is cited above) consisted of "vulgar and lewd references to the male genitals and to masturbation and sodomy broadcast in the context of . . . 'explicit references to masturbation, ejaculation, breast size, penis size, sexual intercourse, nudity, urination, oral-genital contact, erections, sodomy, bestiality, menstruation and testicles.'" 3 FCC Rcd at 932.

KSJO(FM), San Jose, CA   **Song to Tune of "Beverly Hillbillies"**

Come a listen to a story about a man named Boas, a poor politician that barely kept his winky fed, then one day he's poking a chick and up from his pants came a bubbling crude. Winky oil. Honey pot. Jail Bait. . . . So, he loaded up his winky and he did it with Beverly.

Indecent—NAL Issued. *Narragansett Broadcasting Company of California, Inc. (KSJO(FM))*, 5 FCC Rcd 3821 (1990) (forfeiture paid). "Even in the cases of double entendre, not only was the language understandable and clearly capable of a specific sexual or excretory meaning but, because of the context, the sexual and excretory import was inescapable." 5 FCC Rcd at 3821.

2. Dwelling/Repetition versus Fleeting Reference

17. Repetition of and persistent focus on sexual or excretory material have been cited consistently as factors that exacerbate the potential offensiveness of broadcasts. In contrast, where sexual or excretory references have been made once or have been passing or fleeting in nature, this characteristic has tended to weigh against a finding of indecency. . . .

3. Presented in a Pandering or Titillating Manner or for Shock Value

20. The apparent purpose for which material is presented can substantially affect whether it is deemed to be patently offensive as aired. In adverse indecency findings, the Commission has often cited the pandering or titillating character of the material broadcast as an exacerbating factor. Presentation for the shock value of the language used has also been cited. As Justice Powell stated in his opinion in the Supreme Court's decision affirming the Commission's determination that the broadcast of a comedy routine was indecent, "[T]he language employed is, to most people, vulgar and offensive. It was chosen specifically for this quality, and it was repeated over and over as a sort of verbal shock treatment." *FCC v. Pacifica Foundation,* 438 U.S. 726, 757 (1978) (Powell, J., concurring in part and concurring in the judgment). On the other hand, the manner and purpose of a presentation may well preclude an indecency determination even though other factors, such as explicitness, might weigh in favor of an indecency finding. In the following cases, the decisions looked to the manner of presentation as a factor supporting a finding of indecency.

WXTB(FM), Clearwater, FL   **"Bubba, The Love Sponge"**

Take the phone and I want you to rub it on it hard. I want to hear the telephone, okay? Okay honey. (Rubbing noises) You hear that? A little bit longer though please. I'm on the edge right now. A little bit faster. (Rubbing noises) You get that? That's nice. Could you do it again and then scream my name out, please? Like you're having an orgasm? Yeah. Go ahead. Okay. (Rubbing noises) Mm mm. That's it? It's got to be longer than that Ginny, come on work with me. Be a naughty girl. Be a little slutty bitch that you are. One more time. Okay. (Rubbing noises).

Indecent—NAL Issued. *Citicasters Co. (WXTB(FM)),* 13 FCC Rcd 15381 (MMB 1998) (forfeiture paid).

21. In determining whether broadcasts are presented in a pandering or titillating manner, the context of the broadcast is particularly critical. Thus, even where language is explicit, the matter is graphic, or where there is intense repetition of vulgar terms, the presentation may not be pandering or titillating, and the broadcast may not be found actionably indecent.

KING-TV, Seattle, WA   **"Teen Sex: What About the Kids?"**

Broadcast of portions of a sex education class in a local high school that included the use of very realistic sex organ models and simulated demonstrations of various methods of birth control as well as frank discussions of sexual topics.

Not Indecent. *King Broadcasting Co. (KING-TV),* 5 FCC Rcd 2971 (1990). The Commission held that although the program dealt explicitly with sexual issues and included the use of very graphic sex organ models, "the material presented was clinical or instructional in nature and not presented in a pandering, titillating or vulgar manner." 5 FCC Rcd at 2971.

WSMC-FM, Collegedale, TN   **"All Things Considered"**
[National Public Radio]

Mike Schuster has a report and a warning. The following story contains some very rough language. [Excerpt from wiretap of telephone conversation in which organized crime figure John Gotti uses "fuck" or "fucking" 10 times in 7 sentences (110 words).]

Not Indecent. *Peter Branton,* 6 FCC Rcd 610 (1991) (subsequent history omitted). Explicit language was integral part of a bona fide news story concerning organized crime; the material aired was part of a wiretap recording used as evidence in Gotti's widely reported trial. The Commission explained that it did "not find the use of such [coarse] words in a legitimate news report to have been gratuitous, pandering, titillating or otherwise "patently offensive" as that term is used in our indecency definition." 6 FCC Rcd at 610.

WPBN-TV, Traverse City, MI   **"Schindler's List" Film**
WTOM-TV, Cheboygan, MI

"Schindler's List" is a film that depicted a historical view of World War II and wartime atrocities. The movie contained depictions of adult frontal nudity.

Not Indecent. *WPBN/WTOM License Subsidiary, Inc. (WPBN-TV and WTOM-TV),* 15 FCC Rcd 1838 (2000). The Commission ruled that full frontal nudity is not *per se* indecent. Rather, the "full context" of the nudity is controlling. Looking at "the subject matter of the film, the manner of its presentation, and the warnings that accompanied the broadcast," the Commission held that the nudity in "Schindler's List" was not actionably indecent. . . .

IV. ENFORCEMENT PROCESS

24. The Commission does not independently monitor broadcasts for indecent material. Its enforcement actions are based on documented complaints of indecent broadcasting received from the public. Given the sensitive

nature of these cases and the critical role of context in an indecency determination, it is important that the Commission be afforded as full a record as possible to evaluate allegations of indecent programming. In order for a complaint to be considered, our practice is that it must generally include: (1) a full or partial tape or transcript or significant excerpts of the program; (2) the date and time of the broadcast; and (3) the call sign of the station involved.

25. If a complaint does not contain the supporting material described above, or if it indicates that a broadcast occurred during "safe harbor" hours or the material cited does not fall within the subject matter scope of our indecency definition, it is usually dismissed by a letter to the complainant advising of the deficiency. In many of these cases, the station may not be aware that a complaint has been filed.

26. If, however, the staff determines that a documented complaint meets the subject matter requirements of the indecency definition and the material complained of was aired outside "safe harbor" hours, then the broadcast at issue is evaluated for patent offensiveness. Where the staff determines that the broadcast is not patently offensive, the complaint will be denied. If, however, the staff determines that further enforcement action might be warranted, the Enforcement Bureau, in conjunction with other Commission offices, examines the material and decides upon an appropriate disposition, which might include any of the following: (1) denial of the complaint by staff letter based upon a finding that the material, in context, is not patently offensive and therefore not indecent; (2) issuance of a Letter of Inquiry (LOI) to the licensee seeking further information concerning or an explanation of the circumstances surrounding the broadcast; (3) issuance of a Notice of Apparent Liability (NAL) for monetary forfeiture; and (4) formal referral of the case to the full Commission for its consideration and action. Generally, the last of these alternatives is taken in cases where issues beyond straightforward indecency violations may be involved or where the potential sanction for the indecent programming exceeds the Bureau's delegated forfeiture authority of $25,000 (47 C.F.R. §0.311).

27. Where an LOI is issued, the licensee's comments are generally sought concerning the allegedly indecent broadcast to assist in determining whether the material is actionable and whether a sanction is warranted. If it is determined that no further action is warranted, the licensee and the complainant will be so advised. Where a *preliminary* determination is made that the material was aired and was indecent, an NAL is issued. If the Commission previously determined that the broadcast of the same material was indecent, the subsequent broadcast constitutes egregious misconduct and a higher forfeiture amount is warranted. *KGB, Inc. (KGB-FM),* 13 FCC Rcd 16396 (1998) ("higher degree of culpability for the subsequent broadcast of material previously determined by the Commission to be indecent").

28. The licensee is afforded an opportunity to respond to the NAL, a step which is required by statute. 47 U.S.C. §503(b). Once the Commission or its staff has considered any response by the licensee, it may order payment of a monetary penalty by issuing a Forfeiture Order. Alternatively, if

the preliminary finding of violation in the NAL is successfully rebutted by the licensee, the NAL may be rescinded. If a Forfeiture Order is issued, the monetary penalty assessed may either be the same as specified in the NAL or it may be a lesser amount if the licensee has demonstrated that mitigating factors warrant a reduction in forfeiture.

29. A Forfeiture Order may be appealed by the licensee through the administrative process under several different provisions of the Commission's rules. The licensee also has the legal right to refuse to pay the fine. In such a case, the Commission may refer the matter to the U.S. Department of Justice, which can initiate a trial *de novo* in a U.S. District Court. The trial court may start anew to evaluate the allegations of indecency.

V. CONCLUSION

30. The Commission issues this Policy Statement to provide guidance to broadcast licensees regarding compliance with the Commission's inde- cency regulations.[1] By summarizing the regulations and explaining the Commission's analytical approach to reviewing allegedly indecent material, the Commission provides a framework by which broadcast licensees can assess the legality of airing potentially indecent material. Numerous exam- ples are provided in this document in an effort to assist broadcast licens- ees. However, this document is not intended to be an all-inclusive summary of every indecency finding issued by the Commission and it should not be relied upon as such. There are many additional cases that could have been cited. Further, as discussed above, the excerpts from broadcasts quoted in this document are intended only as a research tool. A complete understand- ing of the material, and the Commission's analysis thereof, requires review of the tapes or transcripts and the Commission's rulings thereon.

Separate Statement of Commissioner Susan Ness

Our enforcement of the broadcast indecency statute compels the FCC to reconcile two competing fundamental obligations: (1) to ensure that the air- waves are free of indecent programming material during prescribed hours when children are most likely to be in the audience; and (2) to respect the First Amendment rights of broadcasters regarding program content.

Understandably, the public is outraged by the increasingly coarse con- tent aired on radio and television at all hours of the day, including times when children are likely to be listening or watching. The flood of letters and e-mails we receive reflect a high degree of anger. As a parent, I share the

---

1. This Policy Statement addresses the February 22, 1994, Agreement for Settlement and Dismissal with Prejudice between the United States of America, by and through the Department of Justice and Federal Communications Commission, and Evergreen Media Corporation of Chicago, AM, Licensee of Radio Station WLUP(AM). Specifically, in paragraph 2(b) of the settlement agreement, the Commission agreed to "publish industry guidance relating to its caselaw interpreting 18 U.S.C. §1464 and the FCC's enforcement policics with respect to broadcast indecency. . . ."

public's frustration. Many parents feel that they cannot enjoy watching daytime or primetime television with their children for fear that their youngsters will be exposed to indecent material — content that just a few years ago would have been unimaginable on broadcast television.

Despite an onslaught of on-air smut, the Commission necessarily walks a delicate line when addressing content issues, and must be careful not to tread on the First Amendment — the constitutional bulwark of our free society. Even words that might be construed as indecent are subject to some constitutional protection against government regulation.

That said, the Supreme Court has seen fit, despite declining broadcast audience shares, to reaffirm the FCC's broadcast indecency enforcement role, given the "pervasive" and "invasive" characteristics of the free over the air broadcast medium. Our Policy Statement on indecency reconciles our statutory mandate and constitutional obligation by providing helpful guidance to broadcasters and the public alike. The guidance we offer — a restatement of existing statutory, regulatory, and judicial law — establishes a measure of clarity in an inherently subjective area. . . .

Recommended Procedural Improvements

We should strive to make our complaint procedures as user-friendly as possible. I believe that our complaint process could be improved if, prior to acting on an indecency complaint, the Commission routinely forwarded the complaint to the licensee in question. The Policy Statement concedes that in "many [indecency] cases, the station may not be aware that a complaint has been filed." Moreover, many consumers feel that the Commission mechanically dismisses their complaints. I do not believe that broadcasters' First Amendment rights would be threatened if we were to send broadcasters a courtesy copy of complaints filed with the FCC. Indeed, most broadcasters *want* to be made aware of audience complaints. And consumers would be reassured that their views were being treated seriously.

Broadcasters Are Part of a National Community

Release of this Policy Statement alone will not solve the festering problem of indecency on the airwaves. However, it is entirely within the power of broadcasters to address it — and to do so *without government intrusion*. It is not a violation of the First Amendment for broadcasters on their own to take responsibility for the programming they air, and to exercise that power in a manner that celebrates rather than debases humankind.

It is time for broadcasters to consider reinstating a voluntary code of conduct. I encourage broadcasters, the Bush Administration, and Congress swiftly to resolve any antitrust impediments to such action and move ahead.

We all are part of a National Community. As stewards of the airwaves, broadcasters play a vital leadership role in setting the cultural tone of our society. They can choose to raise the standard or to lower it. I hope that broadcasters will rise to the occasion by reaffirming the unique role of broadcasting as a family friendly medium. The public deserves no less. . . .

Dissenting Statement of Commissioner Gloria Tristani

I dissent from the issuance of this "Policy Statement" (hereinafter "Statement") for three reasons. First, the Statement creates a false impression that it satisfies an obligation assumed by the Commission in 1994. Second, the Statement perpetuates the myth that broadcast indecency standards are too vague and compliance so difficult that a Policy Statement is necessary to provide further guidance. Most importantly, this Statement diverts this Agency's attention and resources away from the ongoing problem of lax enforcement, which is a pressing concern of America's citizens.

. . .

I turn next to the underpinnings of the need for this statement. The Statement provides:

The Commission issues this Policy Statement to provide guidance to the broadcast industry regarding our case law interpreting 18 U.S.C. §1464 and our enforcement policies with respect to broadcast indecency.

First, settlement of a case involving a single licensee [Evergreen] should not compel the FCC to adopt our most significant industry-wide Policy Statement on this subject, particularly when doing so does not serve the public interest. Second, there is nothing in the record demonstrating that Evergreen Media failed to understand the FCC's, or the U.S. Supreme Court's, cases on broadcast indecency. In fact Evergreen agreed to issue to its employees a "policy statement" that was to be based upon "the FCC's definition of broadcast indecency." It is difficult to understand how Evergreen could both issue a policy statement containing the FCC's definition of indecency to its employees *and* simultaneously be unable to understand the FCC's definition. But leaving that quirk aside, there is simply no proof that broadcast licensees are in need of this Policy Statement. No factual basis exists for concluding that confusion about the standards or overreaching enforcement by the FCC requires this Statement.

Moreover, I am aware of no rush of inquiries by broadcast licensees seeking to learn whether their programs comply with our indecency case law. In the absence of such requests, this Policy Statement will likely become instead a "how-to" manual for those licensees who wish to tread the line drawn by our cases. It likely may lead to responses to future enforcement actions that cite the Statement as establishing false safe harbors. In the absence of proof that the Statement addresses concerns supported by the FCC's history of enforcement, or the record of the Evergreen case, the Statement is nothing more than a remedy in search of a problem. It would better serve the public if the FCC got serious about enforcing the broadcast indecency standards. For these reasons, I dissent.

Notes and Questions

1. Guidance often involves the interpretation of a rule or of the authorizing statute. This is guidance regarding a series of adjudications. In other words, it is advising regulated parties about a quasi-common law process that the agency is using. Should courts be more or less permissive about the use of guidance in this context, or should both uses of guidance be treated the same?

2. Even a document that is regarded as nonbinding from a legal perspective can have real world effects. Suppose the FCC document is a valid, nonbinding guidance. If you were a lawyer representing a radio station before the FCC, how would you use the FCC document in advising your client on whether to settle a claim involving the following statement made by announcers on your client's station against an announcer on a competitor's network?

Announcers referred to complainant, Chuck Harder, as "Suck Harder," "Suck," and "Suckie" throughout the broadcast and called the complainant a "useless piece of crap." They also referred to complainant's network, the Sun Radio Network as "Suck Harder Radio Network."

3. The *Pacifica* case, referred to in the FCC's Policy Statement, involved a routine by George Carlin (1937-2008, pictured below), a stand-up comedian who had five Grammy-award winning albums and was the first host of *Saturday Night Live.* The routine centered on "seven words you can never say on television." Carlin described the words as "the heavy seven. Those are the ones that'll infect your soul, curve your spine, and keep the country from winning the war."

4. The FCC's Policy Statement has attracted many hilarious (and accurate) parodies. Perhaps the best is from *South Park*, which airs on a cable channel not subject to the strict licensing requirements of public broadcasters. In the episode, entitled "It Hits the Fan," the word "shit" was said 162 times, but that was far from all. Here is Eric Cartman saying the word for the first time during the show (South Park, Season 5, Episode 502). We also particularly like the song about the FCC from another television show, *Family Guy* (Family Guy, Season 4, Episode 14). On a more serious note, we will return to the judicial aftermath of the FCC's policy statement in Chapter 6.

Guidance includes more individualized communications with regulated parties that can range from blistering threats to genial advice. Many agencies will respond to letter requests from interested parties with advice about the way that the agency will treat a proposed product or practice. The Securities and Exchange Commission (SEC) developed this approach extensively; a response indicating that the agency regarded the proposal as legally permitted is called a no-action letter. NHTSA also uses this approach. Here is the agency's description of it, followed by a fairly typical example that involves a cutting-edge innovation in automotive design.

NHTSA's Interpretation Files Search

https://isearch.nhtsa.gov/search.htm

NHTSA's Chief Counsel interprets the statutes that the agency administers and the regulations that it promulgates. When members of the public ask the agency a question about motor vehicles or motor vehicle equipment that involves these statutes and regulations, the Chief Counsel responds with a letter of interpretation that looks at the particular facts presented in the question and explains how the law applies given those facts. These letters of interpretation, signed by the Chief Counsel, represent the opinion of the agency on the questions addressed at the time of signature and may be helpful in determining how the agency might answer a question that you have if that question is similar to a previously-considered question. Please remember, however, that interpretation letters represent the opinion of the Chief Counsel based on the facts of individual cases at the time the letter was written. Do not assume that a prior interpretation will necessarily apply to your situation! There are a number of reasons why the interpretation letters in this database might not be applicable to your situation, such as:

- Your facts may be sufficiently different from those presented in prior interpretations, such that the agency's answer to you might be different from the answer in the existing interpretation letter;
- Your situation may be completely new to the agency and not addressed in an existing interpretation letter;
- The database may be incomplete (the agency is currently working to ensure that all prior interpretation letters are contained in the database);
- The agency's standards and regulations may have changed since the time when the existing interpretation letter was written and the agency's interpretation no longer applies; or
- Some combination of all of the above, or other factors.

Paul Hemmersbaugh, NHTSA Chief Counsel, to Brian Latour, Exec. Director of Global Safety and Field Investigations, General Motors Corp.

Letter of Nov. 18, 2016

Dear Mr. Latouf,

This responds to your letter dated March 18, 2016 requesting an interpretation with respect to the meaning of "vehicle hazard warning signal operating unit" in Federal Motor Vehicle Safety Standard ("FMVSS") No. 108; Lamps, reflective devices, and associated equipment, as applied to a new cruise control system General Motors ("GM") is developing.

You state that GM is developing a new adaptive cruise control system with lane following (which GM has referred to as "Super Cruise") that controls steering, braking, and acceleration in certain freeway environments. When Super Cruise is in use, the driver must always remain attentive to the road, supervise Super Cruise's performance, and be ready to steer and brake at all times. In some situations, Super Cruise will alert the driver to resume steering, for example, when the system detects a limit or fault. If the driver is unable or unwilling to take control of the wheel (if, for example, the driver is incapacitated or unresponsive), Super Cruise may determine that the safest thing to do is to bring the vehicle slowly to a stop in or near the roadway, and the vehicle's brakes will hold the vehicle until overridden by the driver.

You indicate that GM plans to develop Super Cruise so that, in this situation, once Super Cruise has brought the vehicle to a stop, the vehicle's automated system will activate the vehicle's hazard lights. You state that you believe that this automatic activation of the hazard lights complies with the requirements of FMVSS No. 108 for several reasons. You state that the system's activation of the hazard lights in this situation alerts other drivers that the vehicle is stopped and ensures overall traffic safety. Your letter cites and discusses several past agency interpretations, and asserts that automatic activation of the hazard lights in the situation GM describes is similar to at least one situation in which NHTSA has previously interpreted the standard to permit automatic activation of the hazard lights immediately following a crash event. You state that you believe that there would be no ambiguity about the meaning of the hazard lights in this situation, and it would be the safe thing to do. You ask NHTSA to confirm that activation of the hazard lights by the vehicle's automated system in the unresponsive/incapacitated driver situation described above complies with FMVSS No. 108. As we explain below, we interpret FMVSS No. 108 to allow the type of automatic hazard activation described in GM's letter.

FMVSS No. 108 requires that all vehicles to which the standard applies, except trailers and motorcycles, be equipped with, among other things, a vehicular hazard warning operating unit and a vehicular hazard warning signal flasher. A vehicular hazard warning signal operating unit is a driver controlled device which causes all required turn signal lamps to flash simultaneously to indicate to approaching drivers the presence of a vehicular hazard. A vehicular hazard warning signal flasher is a device which, as long as it is turned on, causes all the required turn signal lamps to flash. These requirements for hazard lights have been in the standard, largely unchanged, since it was first enacted in 1967.[4] The purpose of the hazard warning is to indicate to approaching drivers that the vehicle is stopped or is proceeding at a slower rate than surrounding traffic.

As an initial matter, although not explicitly stated in GM's letter, we assume for purposes of this interpretation that the vehicle GM describes has a manually-activated hazard warning control that satisfies the requirements

---

4. Before 2012, the hazard warning requirements were largely incorporated by reference to standards promulgated by SAE (formerly the Society of Automotive Engineers). In a 2007 final rule NHTSA reorganized FMVSS No. 108 by streamlining the regulatory text and clarifying the standard's requirements. The final rule, among other things, reduced reliance on third-party documents incorporated by reference by incorporating those requirements directly into the regulatory text. This final rule, which incorporated the hazard warning requirements directly into the regulatory text, became effective on December 1, 2012. 76 FR 48009 (Aug. 8, 2011).

in S6.6.2 and S4 for a driver controlled hazard warning operating unit, and also satisfies the requirements in FMVSS No. 101 for a hazard warning signal control and telltale. Nothing in GM's letter indicates otherwise. Moreover, this is consistent with the vehicle having, as GM describes, a Level 2 automated system.

Past agency interpretations of automatic activation of hazard lights have reached different conclusions about their permissibility. FMVSS No. 108 defines the hazard warning operating unit as a "driver controlled device which causes all required turn signal lamps to flash simultaneously to indicate to approaching drivers the presence of a vehicular hazard." Some past agency interpretations have construed this language to preclude automatic operation of the hazard warning lights, on the basis that automatic activation would not be "driver controlled."[7]

However, since those interpretations were issued, NHTSA has clarified that automatic activation is permissible in certain circumstances. In a 2002 interpretation letter issued to Bartlett Industries, Inc., NHTSA explained that the hazard lights may be automatically actuated following a vehicle crash:

> [A] series of . . . letters reflect our opinion that hazard warning system lamps must be activated and deactivated by the driver. This conclusion was based upon the definition of hazard warning systems by the Society of Automotive Engineers (SAE) as "driver actuated."
>
> The one exception to driver actuation that our recent letters reflect is automatic activation of the hazard warning system in the aftermath of a vehicle crash. As we informed Mr. Steele, we would not view automatic activation of the hazard signals in the event of a crash as a noncompliance with Standard No. 108 since there can be no ambiguity about the signal's meaning at that point.[8]

GM states that in the event that a human driver fails to respond to Super Cruise's request that the human retake control of the vehicle, and Super Cruise consequently determines that the safest thing to do is to bring the vehicle slowly to a stop in or near the roadway, Super Cruise-equipped vehicles will activate the vehicle's hazard lights automatically once the vehicle is stopped. We agree with GM that the situation it describes is similar to the situation in which the Steele (and Bartlett) letters that interpreted FMVSS No.

---

7. Letter from Frank Seales, Jr., Chief Counsel, to Mark Steele, Steele Enterprises (Dec. 6, 1999) ("This means that the hazard warning signal unit must be activated by the driver and not automatically."), *available at* http://isearch.nhtsa.gov/files/20856.ztv.html. Letter from Frank Seales, Jr., Chief Counsel, to Eric Reed (Feb. 29, 2000) ("An automatic activation of the hazard warning unit would not be "driver controlled" and is therefore not permitted."), *available at* http://isearch.nhtsa.gov/files/reed.ztv.html. Letter from Jacqueline Glassman, Chief Counsel, to Ted Gaston, Muncie Indiana Transit System (Apr. 25, 2005) ("We have previously interpreted "driver controlled" to mean that the hazard warning signal system must be activated and deactivated by the driver and not by automatic means. . . ."), *available at* http://isearch.nhtsa.gov/files/GF002470.html.

8. Letter from John Womack, Acting Chief Counsel, to Timothy Bartlett, Bartlett Industries, Inc. (Jan. 28, 2002) ("Bartlett letter") (citations omitted), *available at* http://isearch.nhtsa.gov/files/23695.ztv.html (quoting Letter from Frank Seales, Jr., Chief Counsel, to Steele Enterprises (Feb. 25, 2000) ("Steele letter"), *available at* http://isearch.nhtsa.gov/files/21171.ztv.html. As noted above, *see supra* n.4, the referenced SAE document is now incorporated into the text of FMVSS No. 108.

108 to permit automatic actuation of the hazard lights. Although GM's system does not activate the hazard warning signal after a crash has occurred, it does activate the hazard lights when the vehicle has already stopped. This is the prototypical situation in which the hazard lights are intended to be used, and it is one of the situations that other motorists have come to expect when they see the hazard signal. There would appear to be no ambiguity about the signal's meaning in this situation, and we believe that it is unlikely that the use of the hazard lights would confuse other motorists. Therefore, the automatic activation of the hazard lights in the circumstances described by GM would be permissible.[10] Any other automatic activation of hazard warning lights would need to be evaluated on a case-by-case basis. NHTSA may also consider amending the relevant provisions of FMVSS No. 108 at some point in the future in order to clarify situations when hazard lights may activate automatically.

We note that GM indicates that when the driver is unable or unwilling to take control of the vehicle the system will bring the vehicle to a stop in or near the roadway. A vehicle system that stops a vehicle directly in a roadway might—depending on the circumstances—be considered to contain a safety-related defect, i.e., it may present an unreasonable risk of an accident occurring or of death and injury in an accident. Federal law requires the recall of a vehicle that contains a safety-related defect. We urge GM to fully consider the likely operation of the system it is contemplating and ensure that it will not present such a risk.

Sincerely,

Paul Hemmersbaugh

Chief Counsel

---

10. Since the mid-1990s, several interpretations have addressed situations in which automatic activation of hazard lights would *not* be permissible because the message that the hazard lights would convey in those instances would not be consistent with the purpose of hazards, i.e., to indicate to approaching drivers that the vehicle is stopped or is proceeding at a slower rate than surrounding traffic. *See, e.g.*, Letter from Frank Seales, Jr., Chief Counsel, to David Coburn, Steptoe & Johnson LLP (Aug. 6, 1999) ("We believe that a hazard warning system should not be used for the auxiliary purpose of indicating sudden accelerator release, a signal that bears no relationship to a hazard warning signal and one which could create confusion were the hazard warning signal used for an unrelated purpose."), *available at* http://isearch.nhtsa.gov/files/19886.ztv.html; Letter from Frank Seales, Jr., Chief Counsel, to Mark Steele, Steele Enterprises (Oct. 7, 1999) (FMVSS No. 108 does not permit the hazard lights to signal the activation of the anti-lock brake system because that could result in confusing signals), *available at* http://isearch.nhtsa.gov/files/20662.ztv.htm. NHTSA would continue to consider automatic activation of hazard lights in such situations to be inconsistent with FMVSS No. 108.

Notes and Questions

1. Does this mechanism seem useful to you? In its absence, what should GM do? Proceed to market its innovation and take the chance that the agency will take action against it as a violation of the safety standards or avoid marketing it until the agency has clarified the rules on its own? What effect do you suppose that would have on the company's incentive to innovate?

2. Why does NHTSA provide that letters of this sort be addressed to the Chief Counsel, and (if your answer is that the Chief Counsel can direct the letter to another staff member) why does the Chief Counsel respond? What is the basis for the response? To what extent is the answer based on the statute, and to what extent is it based on prior answers? Consider not only the text of the letter but also footnotes 7, 8, and 10. Does this extensive citation of prior letters remind you of anything? How about common law? Why do you suppose NHTSA relies so extensively on a common law-type process in answering these letters?

3. Suppose an agency official makes a mistake and gives someone incorrect information in response to a request. In private law, the doctrine of equitable estoppel provides a remedy in the analogous situation. If an insurance agent mistakenly tells a customer that he is covered for a particular loss, when according to the contract he would have had to pay an additional fee to obtain the coverage, the insurance company is "estopped" from denying coverage on the basis of the non-payment. In Federal Crop Ins. Corp. v. Merrill, 332 U.S. 380 (1947), a farmer bought insurance from a federal agency because he was incorrectly informed by an agency official that his crop was insurable. When his crop was destroyed, the agency refused to pay him. The Court held that estoppel is a private law doctrine that cannot be applied to government because it would interfere with government efficiency and allow a careless agent to, in effect, appropriate money from the public treasury. Does that make sense, or should the *Merrill* doctrine be repudiated?

As we close this chapter, return your focus to the notice-and-comment rulemaking process, the dominant mode of agency policy making and the one that we have considered in most detail. Proposed and final rules have a predictable form and are based on standard analyses — statutory, scientific, economic, and political. Although many believe that these analyses do not well explain the complexities of agency behavior, they are the building blocks of the regulatory state. Because agencies use them to frame their regulations, lawyers use them to frame their arguments. Now that you have seen one, you can handle them all.

We are now ready to situate agency regulation in their broader political and judicial context. Agency regulations do not exist in isolation — or even only in terms of the political influence that you have seen explicitly in the rulemaking documents themselves. In some sense, such influence is only the tip of iceberg. Both political officials and courts make a difference as to how agencies implement their statutes. In the next and final chapter, we will turn to a more extended discussion of political and judicial control of agency action.

6

Control of Agency Action

When agencies implement their statutes, they understand that each branch of government will have an interest in how they do so. Roughly speaking, political officials, most notably the President or members of Congress, will seek to ensure that agency action tracks their preferences. Courts will seek to ensure that agency action comports with legal standards. They do so because agencies are the primary means of implementing the law in our modern state. In this chapter, we examine various tools that each branch uses in asserting control of agency action. We discuss the efficacy of these tools as well as the normative implications of their use, such as promoting (or undermining) accountability and expertise.

Lawyers have ample reason to study control of agency action. Not only is that subject important for a complete understanding of how agencies implement their statutes, but lawyers are involved in how political officials and courts assert control over agencies. When agency decision making is underway, gaining the attention of OMB in the White House or a congressional committee, for example, can help prompt intervention in the agency action. Once agency action is final, lawyers are the ones who seek to invoke judicial control through litigation challenging such action.

Although we introduce control on a branch-by-branch and tool-by-tool basis, all of the branches may assert control over the same agency action and use more than one tool. Might we then end up with a battle among political officials or between political officials and courts over the fate of agency action? Keep this question in mind as you read.

A. PRESIDENTIAL CONTROL OF AGENCY ACTION

In looking at the regulatory state, one fact is certain: the President seeks to assert control of agency action. The President does so in a number of ways that differ in terms of their formality, transparency, and effectiveness. At one end of the spectrum, the President can request that an agency voluntarily take a particular action and can make such a request in a meeting or other informal, non-public manner. At the other end, the President can take the formal, visible, and effective step of replacing recalcitrant agency officials with individuals more amenable to administration views or withhold funding until agency officials change course. Perhaps in the middle, the President can set up an entire process for requiring agencies to submit their proposed regulations to the White House for review under specified principles. In this section, we introduce you to these tools and more. We will not focus on the informal means per se but rather on the more formal and transparent means by which presidential administrations assert control over agencies. We also examine the different officials who exert influence.

At the outset, you might ask why the President seeks to assert control of agency action. Many believe that the President asserts control to ensure that agency action roughly tracks administration preferences. In this way, the President can better implement his agenda and enhance the prospects of reelection. Or the President can build a lasting legacy. "Because voters and history judge presidents for the performance of the entire federal government during their tenure," Presidents have incentives "to ensure that policy outcomes, both legislative and administrative, are under their control." DAVID E. LEWIS, THE POLITICS OF PRESIDENTIAL APPOINTMENTS 55 (2008).

The President also has a responsibility to supervise agency action. The Constitution provides that the President "shall take Care that the laws be faithfully executed." U.S. CONST. art. II, §3, cl. 3. Some believe that the Take Care Clause, combined with other structural features of the Constitution means that the President has an obligation to oversee agency action. *See, e.g.,* Gillian M. Metzger, The *Constitutional Duty* to *Supervise*, 124 Yale L.J. 1836 (2015); Elena Kagan, *Presidential Administration*, 114 HARV. L. REV. 2245, 2331-32 (2001); Jerry L. Mashaw, *Prodelegation: Why Administrators Should Make Political Decisions*, 1 J.L. ECON. & ORG. 81, 95 (1985). On this account, the President asserts control of agency action as the President deems necessary to ensure that such action is consistent with administration priorities.

What are the normative implications of presidential control? First and foremost, presidential control may enhance the accountability of agency action. The President is the one official elected by a national constituency and can confer his unique brand of representation on unelected agency officials by asserting control of their actions. In addition, voters can hold the President responsible for agency actions that they dislike. Second, presidential control may improve the efficacy of agency action. The President can coordinate the actions of agencies across the government, avoiding redundant or conflicting regulations. The President can spur a sluggish agency into action or require agencies to consider factors that they may have neglected or misapplied, including the costs and benefits of their proposed regulations. In this last respect, presidential control may improve the efficiency of agency action. Note, however, that presidential control is not without potential downsides. What if the President seeks to influence agency action in a way that contravenes scientific findings or statutory considerations? In such instances, presidential control can be said to decrease the expertise and even the legality of agency action.

Before turning to the specific tools of presidential control over agency action, we first consider the constitutional framework that concerns the operation of such control. The doctrine in this area has been most explicitly drawn in connection with the President's efforts to control agency action by removing (or firing) agency officials. We highlight those cases below.

1. The Constitutionality of Independent Agencies and Presidential Control Thereof

The creation of independent agencies has placed a considerable amount of conceptual stress on the three-branch structure that the Constitution employs to describe the government that it creates. If independent agencies are not under the President's direct supervision—for example, if he cannot give them orders or freely fire the leaders he has appointed—then can they really be placed in the branch headed by the Chief Executive? Even though many of these agencies perform functions that can be more accurately described as legislative or judicial rather than executive, as they make rules and adjudicate the rights of private parties, so do executive-branch agencies. Independent agencies cannot be plausibly located in either of the two other branches because they are more like an executive-branch agency than a legislature or a court. Franklin Roosevelt's President's Committee on Administrative Management (called the Brownlow Committee after its chair) described them as a "headless fourth branch." This quandary has led a number of scholars to argue that independent agencies are unconstitutional and that Congress must place any agency it creates under the President's direct supervision. This idea is sometimes called the "unitary executive" theory. *See* Steven Calabresi & Kevin Rhodes, *The Structural Constitution: Unitary Executive, Plural Judiciary*, 105 HARV. L. REV. 1155 (1992); Geoffrey Miller, *Independent Agencies*, 1986 SUP. CT. REV. 41.

The constitutionality of independent agencies and consequent limitations on presidential control came before the Supreme Court in three famous cases that are excerpted below, Myers v. United States, Humphrey's Executor v. United States, and Morrison v. Olson. The *Myers* case involved a postmaster who, according to an 1876 statute, was appointed to a four-year term and could be removed by the President before the conclusion of that term "by and with the advice and consent of the Senate." *Humphrey's Executor*, decided nine years later, involved a member of the Federal Trade Commission who, according to the FTC's organic statute, was appointed by the President and could be removed by the President, but only for cause. *Morrison* was a challenge to the constitutionality of the Independent Counsel, a specially appointed official who, according to the Ethics in Government Act, could only be removed by "the personal action of the Attorney General and only for good cause, physical disability, mental incapacity, or any other condition that substantially impairs the performance of such independent counsel's duties."

The opinions themselves are complex. You might find at times that the Court's arguments are convoluted, vague, and ultimately indeterminate. Harness them as best you can.

Myers v. United States

272 U.S. 52 (1926)

Chief Justice TAFT delivered the opinion of the Court.

This case presents the question whether, under the Constitution, the President has the exclusive power of removing executive officers of the United States whom he has appointed by and with the advice and consent of the Senate. . . .

By the 6th section of the Act of Congress of July 12, 1876, 19 Stat. 80, 81, c. 179, under which Myers was appointed with the advice and consent of the Senate as a first-class postmaster, it is provided that

> "Postmasters of the first, second and third classes shall be appointed and may be removed by the President by and with the advice and consent of the Senate and shall hold their offices for four years unless sooner removed or suspended according to law." . . .

The Government maintains that the [statutory requirement of Senate consent] is invalid for the reason that, under Article II of the Constitution the President's power of removal of executive officers appointed by him with the advice and consent of the Senate is full and complete without consent of the Senate. . . .

The vesting of the executive power in the President [by the Constitution] was essentially a grant of the power to execute the laws. But the President, alone and unaided, could not execute the laws. He must execute them by the assistance of subordinates. . . . As he is charged specifically to take care that they be faithfully executed, the reasonable implication, even in the absence of express words, was that, as part of his executive power, he should select those who were to act for him under his direction in the execution of the laws. The further implication must be, in the absence of any express limitation respecting removals, that, as his selection of administrative officers is essential to the execution of the laws by him, so must be his power of removing those for whom he cannot continue to be responsible. It was urged that the natural meaning of the term "executive power" granted the President included the appointment and removal of executive subordinates. . . .

The power to prevent the removal of an officer who has served under the President is different from the authority to consent to or reject his appointment. When a nomination is made, it may be presumed that the Senate is, or may become, as well advised as to the fitness of the nominee as the President, but in the nature of things the defects in ability or intelligence or loyalty in the administration of the laws of one who has served as an officer under the President are facts as to which the President, or his trusted subordinates, must be better informed than the Senate, and the power to remove him may, therefore, be regarded as confined, for very sound and practical reasons, to the governmental authority which has administrative control. The power of removal is incident to the power of appointment, not to the power of advising and consenting to appointment, and when the grant of the executive power is enforced by the express mandate to take care that the laws be faithfully executed, it emphasizes the necessity for including within the executive power as conferred the exclusive power of removal.

. . . The degree of guidance in the discharge of their duties that the President may exercise over executive officers varies with the character of their service as prescribed in the law under which they act. The highest and most important duties which his subordinates perform are those in which they act for him. In such cases they are exercising not their own but his discretion. This field is a very large one. It is sometimes described as political. . . . Each head of a department is and must be the President's alter ego in the matters of that department where the President is required by law to exercise authority. . . .

In all such cases, the discretion to be exercised is that of the President in determining the national public interest and in directing the action to be taken by his executive subordinates to protect it. In this field, his cabinet officers must do his will. He must place in each member of his official family, and his chief executive subordinates, implicit faith. The moment that he loses confidence in the intelligence, ability, judgment or loyalty of anyone of them, he must have the power to remove him without delay. To require him to file charges and submit them to the consideration of the Senate might make impossible that unity and coordination in executive administration essential to effective action.

The duties of the heads of departments and bureaus in which the discretion of the President is exercised and which we have described are the most important in the whole field of executive action of the Government. There is nothing in the Constitution which permits a distinction between the removal of the head of a department or a bureau, when he discharges a political duty of the President or exercises his discretion, and the removal of executive officers engaged in the discharge of their other normal duties. The imperative reasons requiring an unrestricted power to remove the most important of his subordinates in their most important duties must, therefore, control the interpretation of the Constitution as to all appointed by him.

But this is not to say that there are not strong reasons why the President should have a like power to remove his appointees charged with other duties than those above described. The ordinary duties of officers prescribed by statute come under the general administrative control of the President by virtue of the general grant to him of the executive power, and he may properly supervise and guide their construction of the statutes under which they act in order to secure that unitary and uniform execution of the laws which Article II of the Constitution evidently contemplated in vesting general executive power in the President alone. Laws are often passed with specific provision for the adoption of regulations by a department or bureau head to make the law workable and effective. The ability and judgment manifested by the official thus empowered, as well as his energy and stimulation of his subordinates, are subjects which the President must consider and supervise in his administrative control. Finding such officers to be negligent and inefficient, the President should have the power to remove them. Of course, there may be duties so peculiarly and specifically committed to the discretion of a particular officer as to raise a question whether the President may overrule or revise the officer's interpretation of his statutory duty in a particular instance. Then there may be duties of a quasi-judicial character imposed on executive officers and members of executive tribunals whose decisions after hearing affect interests of individuals, the discharge of which the President cannot in a particular case properly influence or control. But even in such a case, he may consider the decision after its rendition as a reason for removing the officer, on the ground that the discretion regularly entrusted to that officer by statute has not been, on the whole, intelligently or wisely exercised. Otherwise, he does not discharge his own constitutional duty of seeing that the laws be faithfully executed. . . .

[The Court then considered the argument that the removal provision could be sustained because postmasters were "inferior officers" within the meaning of the Appointments Clause:]

The power to remove inferior executive officers, like that to remove superior executive officers, is an incident of the power to appoint them, and is in its nature an executive power. The authority of Congress given by the excepting clause to vest the appointment of such inferior officers in the heads of departments carries with it authority incidentally to invest the heads of departments with power to remove. It has been the practice of Congress to do so and this Court has recognized that power. The Court also has recognized in the *Perkins* case [which challenged the constitutionality of the Civil Service Reform] that Congress, in committing the appointment of such inferior officers to the heads of departments, may prescribe incidental regulations controlling and restricting the latter in the exercise of the power of removal. But the Court never has held, nor reasonably could hold, although it is argued to the contrary on behalf of the appellant, that the excepting clause enables Congress to draw to itself, or to either branch of it, the power to remove or the right to participate in the exercise of that power. To do this would be to go beyond the words and implications of that clause and to infringe the constitutional principle of the separation of governmental powers.

Assuming then the power of Congress to regulate removals as incidental to the exercise of its constitutional power to vest appointments of inferior officers in the heads of departments, certainly so long as Congress does not exercise that power, the power of removal must remain where the Constitution places it, with the President, as part of the executive power. . . .

Our conclusion on the merits, sustained by the arguments before stated, is that Article II grants to the President the executive power of the

Government, i.e., the general administrative control of those executing the laws, including the power of appointment and removal of executive officers—a conclusion confirmed by his obligation to take care that the laws be faithfully executed; that Article II excludes the exercise of legislative power by Congress to provide for appointments and removals, except only as granted therein to Congress in the matter of inferior offices; that Congress is only given power to provide for appointments and removals of inferior officers after it has vested, and on condition that it does vest, their appointment in other authority than the President with the Senate's consent; that the provisions of the second section of Article II, which blend action by the legislative branch, or by part of it, in the work of the executive are limitations to be strictly construed, and not to be extended by implication; that the President's power of removal is further established as an incident to his specifically enumerated function of appointment by and with the advice of the Senate, but that such incident does not, by implication, extend to removals the Senate's power of checking appointments, and finally that to hold otherwise would make it impossible for the President, in case of political or other differences with the Senate or Congress, to take care that the laws be faithfully executed. Judgment affirmed.

Justice HOLMES, dissenting.

. . . The arguments drawn from the executive power of the President, and from his duty to appoint officers of the United States (when Congress does not vest the appointment elsewhere), to take care that the laws be faithfully executed, and to commission all officers of the United States, seem to me spider's webs inadequate to control the dominant facts.

We have to deal with an office that owes its existence to Congress, and that Congress may abolish tomorrow. Its duration and the pay attached to it while it lasts depend on Congress alone. Congress alone confers on the President the power to appoint to it and at any time may transfer the power to other hands. With such power over its own creation, I have no more trouble in believing that Congress has power to prescribe a term of life for it free from any interference than I have in accepting the undoubted power of Congress to decree its end. I have equally little trouble in accepting its power to prolong the tenure of an incumbent until Congress or the Senate shall have assented to his removal. The duty of the President to see that the laws be executed is a duty that does not go beyond the laws or require him to achieve more than Congress sees fit to leave within his power.

Justice BRANDEIS, dissenting.

. . . The ability to remove a subordinate executive officer, being an essential of effective government, will, in the absence of express constitutional provision to the contrary, be deemed to have been vested in some person or body. But it is not a power inherent in a chief executive. The President's power of removal from statutory civil inferior offices, like the power of appointment to them, comes immediately from Congress. It is true that the exercise of the power of removal is said to be an executive act; and that when the Senate grants or withholds consent to a removal by the President, it participates in an executive act. But the Constitution has confessedly granted to Congress the legislative power to create offices, and to prescribe the tenure thereof; and it has not in terms denied to Congress the power to control removals. . . .

The separation of the powers of government did not make each branch completely autonomous. It left each in some measure, dependent upon the others, as it left to each power to exercise, in some respects, functions in their nature executive, legislative and judicial. Obviously the President cannot secure full execution of the laws, if Congress denies to him adequate means of doing so. Full execution may be defeated because Congress declines to create offices indispensable for that purpose. Or, because Congress, having created the office, declines to make the indispensable appropriation. Or because Congress, having both created the office and made the appropriation, prevents, by restrictions which it imposes, the appointment of officials who in quality and character are indispensable to the efficient execution of the law. If, in any such way, adequate means are denied to the President, the fault will lie with Congress. The President performs his full constitutional duty, if, with the means and instruments provided by Congress and within the limitations prescribed by it, he uses his best endeavors to secure the faithful execution of the laws enacted.

Checks and balances were established in order that this should be "a government of laws and not of men." . . . The doctrine of the separation of powers was adopted by the convention of 1787 not to promote efficiency but to preclude the exercise of arbitrary power. The purpose was not to avoid friction, but, by means of the inevitable friction incident to the distribution of the governmental powers among three departments, to save the people from autocracy. In order to prevent arbitrary executive action, the Constitution provided in terms that presidential appointments be made with the consent of the Senate, unless Congress should otherwise provide; and this clause was construed by Alexander Hamilton in The Federalist, No. 77, as requiring like consent to removals. . . . In America, as in England, the conviction prevailed then that the people must look to representative assemblies for the protection of their liberties. And protection of the individual, even if he be an official, from the arbitrary or capricious exercise of power was then believed to be an essential of free government.

Humphrey's Executor v. United States

295 U.S. 602 (1935)

Justice SUTHERLAND delivered the opinion of the Court.

Plaintiff brought suit in the Court of Claims against the United States to recover a sum of money alleged to be due the deceased for salary as a Federal Trade Commissioner from October 8, 1933, when the President undertook to remove him from office, to the time of his death on February 14, 1934. . . .

William E. Humphrey, the decedent, on December 10, 1931, was nominated by President Hoover to succeed himself as a member of the Federal Trade Commission, and was confirmed by the United States Senate. He was duly commissioned for a term of seven years, expiring September 25, 1938; and, after taking the required oath of office, entered upon his duties. On July 25, 1933, President Roosevelt addressed a letter to the commissioner asking for his resignation, on the ground "that the aims and purposes of the Administration with respect to the work of the Commission can be carried out most effectively with personnel of my own selection," but disclaiming any reflection upon the commissioner personally or upon his services. The commissioner replied, asking time to consult his friends. After some further correspondence upon the subject, the President on August 31, 1933, wrote the commissioner expressing the hope that the resignation would be forthcoming, and saying: "You will, I know, realize that I do not feel that your mind and my mind go along together on either the policies or the administering of the Federal Trade Commission, and, frankly, I think it is best for the people of this country that I should have a full confidence."

The commissioner declined to resign; and on October 7, 1933, the President wrote him: "Effective as of this date you are hereby removed from the office of Commissioner of the Federal Trade Commission." Humphrey never acquiesced in this action, but continued thereafter to insist that he was still a member of the commission, entitled to perform its duties and receive the compensation provided by law at the rate of $10,000 per annum. Upon these and other facts set forth in the certificate, which we deem it unnecessary to recite, the following questions are certified:

> "1. Do the provisions of section 1 of the Federal Trade Commission Act, stating that 'any commissioner may be removed by the President for inefficiency, neglect of duty, or malfeasance in office,' restrict or limit the power of the President to remove a commissioner except upon one or more of the causes named?
>
> "If the foregoing question is answered in the affirmative, then—
>
> "2. If the power of the President to remove a commissioner is restricted or limited as shown by the foregoing interrogatory and the answer made thereto, is such a restriction or limitation valid under the Constitution of the United States?"

The Federal Trade Commission Act creates a commission of five members to be appointed by the President by and with the advice and consent of the Senate, . . . for terms of seven years, except that any person chosen to fill a vacancy shall be appointed only for the unexpired term of the commissioner whom he shall succeed. The commission shall choose a chairman from its own membership. No commissioner shall engage in any other business, vocation, or employment. Any commissioner may be removed by the President for inefficiency, neglect of duty, or malfeasance in office. . . .

First. The question first to be considered is whether, by the provisions of section 1 of the Federal Trade Commission Act already quoted, the President's power is limited to removal for the specific causes enumerated therein. . . . The statute fixes a term of office, in accordance with many precedents. The first commissioners appointed are to continue in office for terms of three, four, five, six, and seven years, respectively; and their successors are to be appointed for terms of seven years—any commissioner being subject to removal by the President for inefficiency, neglect of duty, or malfeasance in office. The words of the act are definite and unambiguous. . . .

. . . But if the intention of Congress that no removal should be made during the specified term except for one or more of the enumerated causes were not clear upon the face of the statute, as we think it is, it would be made clear by a consideration of the character of the commission and the legislative history which accompanied and preceded the passage of the act.

The commission is to be nonpartisan; and it must, from the very nature of its duties, act with entire impartiality. It is charged with the enforcement of no policy except the policy of the law. Its duties are neither political nor executive, but predominantly quasi-judicial and quasi-legislative. Like the Interstate Commerce Commission, its members are called upon to exercise the trained judgment of a body of experts "appointed by law and informed by experience."

The legislative reports in both houses of Congress clearly reflect the view that a fixed term was necessary to the effective and fair administration of the law. . . . The debates in both houses demonstrate that the prevailing view was that the Commission was not to be "subject to anybody in the government but . . . only to the people of the United States"; free from "political domination or control" or the "probability or possibility of such a thing"; to be "separate and apart from any existing department of the government—not subject to the orders of the President." . . .

Thus, the language of the act, the legislative reports, and the general purposes of the legislation as reflected by the debates, all combine to demonstrate the congressional intent to create a body of experts who shall gain experience by length of service—a body which shall be independent of executive authority, except in its selection, and free to exercise its judgment without the leave or hindrance of any other official or any department of the government. To the accomplishment of these purposes, it is clear that Congress was of opinion that length and certainty of tenure would vitally contribute. And to hold that, nevertheless, the members of the commission continue in office at the mere will of the President, might be to thwart, in large measure, the very ends which Congress sought to realize by definitely fixing the term of office.

We conclude that the intent of the act is to limit the executive power of removal to the causes enumerated, the existence of none of which is claimed here; and we pass to the second question.

Second. To support its contention that the removal provision of §1, as we have just construed it, is an unconstitutional interference with the executive power of the President, the government's chief reliance is *Myers v. United States.* That case has been so recently decided, and the prevailing and dissenting opinions so fully review the general subject of the power of executive removal, that further discussion would add little of value to the wealth of material there collected. Nevertheless, the narrow point actually decided was only that the President had power to remove a postmaster of the first class, without the advice and consent of the Senate as required by act of Congress. . . . In so far as they are out of harmony with the views here set forth, these expressions are disapproved. . . .

The office of a postmaster is so essentially unlike the office now involved that the decision in the *Myers* Case cannot be accepted as controlling our decision here. A postmaster is an executive officer restricted to the performance of executive functions. He is charged with no duty at all related to either the legislative or judicial power. The actual decision in the *Myers* Case finds support in the theory that such an officer is merely one of the units in the executive department and, hence, inherently subject to the exclusive and illimitable power of removal by the Chief Executive, whose subordinate and aid he is. Putting aside *dicta*, which may be followed if sufficiently persuasive but which are not controlling, the necessary reach of the decision goes far enough to include all purely executive officers. It goes no farther—much less does it include an officer who occupies no place in the executive department and who exercises no part of the executive power vested by the Constitution in the President.

The Federal Trade Commission is an administrative body created by Congress to carry into effect legislative policies embodied in the statute in accordance with the legislative standard therein prescribed, and to perform other specified duties as a legislative or as a judicial aid. Such a body cannot in any proper sense be characterized as an arm or an eye of the executive. Its duties are performed without executive leave and, in the contemplation of the statute, must be free from executive control. In administering the provisions of the statute in respect of "unfair methods of competition"—that is to say, in filling in and administering the details embodied by that general standard—the commission acts in part quasi-legislatively and in part quasi-judicially. In making investigations and reports thereon for the information of Congress under § 6, in aid of the legislative power, it acts as a legislative agency. Under §7, which authorizes the commission to act as a master in chancery under rules prescribed by the court, it acts as an agency of the judiciary. To the extent that it exercises any executive function, as distinguished from executive power in the constitutional sense, it does so in the discharge and effectuation of its quasi-legislative or quasi-judicial powers, or as an agency of the legislative or judicial departments of the government.[1]

If Congress is without authority to prescribe causes for removal of members of the trade commission and limit executive power of removal accordingly, that power at once becomes practically all-inclusive in respect of civil

---

1. The provision of section 6(d) of the act 15 U.S.C. § 46(d) which authorizes the President to direct an investigation and report by the Commission in relation to alleged violations of the anti-trust acts, is so obviously collateral to the main design of the act as not to detract from the force of this general statement as to the character of that body.

officers with the exception of the judiciary provided for by the Constitution. The Solicitor General, at the bar, apparently recognizing this to be true, with commendable candor, agreed that his view in respect of the removability of members of the Federal Trade Commission necessitated a like view in respect of the Interstate Commerce Commission and the Court of Claims. We are thus confronted with the serious question whether not only the members of these quasi-legislative and quasi-judicial bodies, but the judges of the legislative Court of Claims, exercising judicial power, continue in office only at the pleasure of the President.

We think it plain under the Constitution that illimitable power of removal is not possessed by the President in respect of officers of the character of those just named. The authority of Congress, in creating quasi-legislative or quasi-judicial agencies, to require them to act in discharge of their duties independently of executive control cannot well be doubted; and that authority includes, as an appropriate incident, power to fix the period during which they shall continue "in office," and to forbid their removal except for cause in the meantime. For it is quite evident that one who holds his office only during the pleasure of another, cannot be depended upon to maintain an attitude of independence against the latter's will.

The fundamental necessity of maintaining each of the three general departments of government entirely free from the control or coercive influence, direct or indirect, of either of the others, has often been stressed and is hardly open to serious question. So much is implied in the very fact of the separation of the powers of these departments by the Constitution; and in the rule which recognizes their essential co-equality. The sound application of a principle that makes one master in his own house precludes him from imposing his control in the house of another who is master there. . . .

The result of what we now have said is this: Whether the power of the President to remove an officer shall prevail over the authority of Congress to condition the power by fixing a definite term and precluding a removal except for cause will depend upon the character of the office; the *Myers* decision, affirming the power of the President alone to make the removal, is confined to purely executive officers; and as to officers of the kind here under consideration, we hold that no removal can be made during the prescribed term for which the officer is appointed, except for one or more of the causes named in the applicable statute.

To the extent that, between the decision in the *Myers* case, which sustains the unrestrictable power of the President to remove purely executive officers, and our present decision that such power does not extend to an office such as that here involved, there shall remain a field of doubt, we leave such cases as may fall within it for future consideration and determination as they may arise.

In accordance with the foregoing, the questions submitted are answered.

Question No. 1, Yes.

Question No. 2, Yes.

Morrison v. Olson

487 U.S. 654 (1988)

Chief Justice REHNQUIST delivered the opinion of the Court.

This case presents us with a challenge to the independent counsel provisions of the Ethics in Government Act of 1978, 28 U.S.C. §§49, 591 *et seq.* (1982 ed., Supp. V). We hold today that these provisions of the Act do not violate the Appointments Clause of the Constitution, Art. II, §2, cl. 2, or the limitations of Article III, nor do they impermissibly interfere with the President's authority under Article II in violation of the constitutional principle of separation of powers.

I

Briefly stated, Title VI of the Ethics in Government Act (Title VI or the Act), allows for the appointment of an "independent counsel" to investigate and, if appropriate, prosecute certain high-ranking Government officials for violations of federal criminal laws. The Act requires the Attorney General, upon receipt of information that he determines is "sufficient to constitute grounds to investigate whether any person [covered by the Act] may have violated any Federal criminal law," to conduct a preliminary investigation of the matter. When the Attorney General has completed this investigation, or 90 days has elapsed, he is required to report to a special court (the Special Division) created by the Act "for the purpose of appointing independent counsels." If the Attorney General has determined that there are "reasonable grounds to believe that further investigation or prosecution is warranted," then he "shall apply to the division of the court for the appointment of an independent counsel." The Attorney General's application to the court "shall contain sufficient information to assist the [court] in selecting an independent counsel and in defining that independent counsel's prosecutorial jurisdiction." Upon receiving this application, the Special Division "shall appoint an appropriate independent counsel and shall define that independent counsel's prosecutorial jurisdiction." . . .

Two statutory provisions govern the length of an independent counsel's tenure in office. The first defines the procedure for removing an independent counsel. Section 596(a)(1) provides:

> "An independent counsel appointed under this chapter may be removed from office, other than by impeachment and conviction, only by the personal action of the Attorney General and only for good cause, physical disability, mental incapacity, or any other condition that substantially impairs the performance of such independent counsel's duties." . . .

The other provision governing the tenure of the independent counsel defines the procedures for "terminating" the counsel's office. Under §596(b)(1), the office of an independent counsel terminates when he or she notifies the Attorney General that he or she has completed or substantially completed any investigations or prosecutions undertaken pursuant to the Act. . . .

The Appointments Clause of Article II reads as follows:

"[The President] shall nominate, and by and with the Advice and Consent of the Senate, shall appoint Ambassadors, other public Ministers and Consuls, Judges of the Supreme Court, and all other Officers of the United States, whose Appointments are not herein otherwise provided for, and which shall be established by Law: but the Congress may by Law vest the Appointment of such inferior Officers, as they think proper, in the President alone, in the Courts of Law, or in the Heads of Departments." U.S. Const., Art. II, §2, cl. 2.

The parties do not dispute that "[t]he Constitution for purposes of appointment . . . divides all its officers into two classes." "[P]rincipal officers are selected by the President with the advice and consent of the Senate. Inferior officers Congress may allow to be appointed by the President alone, by the heads of departments, or by the Judiciary." The initial question is, accordingly, whether appellant is an "inferior" or a "principal" officer. If she is the latter, as the Court of Appeals concluded, then the Act is in violation of the Appointments Clause.

The line between "inferior" and "principal" officers is one that is far from clear, and the Framers provided little guidance into where it should be drawn. We need not attempt here to decide exactly where the line falls between the two types of officers, because in our view appellant clearly falls on the "inferior officer" side of that line. Several factors lead to this conclusion.

First, appellant is subject to removal by a higher Executive Branch official. Although appellant may not be "subordinate" to the Attorney General (and the President) insofar as she possesses a degree of independent discretion to exercise the powers delegated to her under the Act, the fact that she can be removed by the Attorney General indicates that she is to some degree "inferior" in rank and authority. Second, appellant is empowered by the Act to perform only certain, limited duties. An independent counsel's role is restricted primarily to investigation and, if appropriate, prosecution for certain federal crimes. Admittedly, the Act delegates to appellant "full power and independent authority to exercise all investigative and prosecutorial functions and powers of the Department of Justice," but this grant of authority does not include any authority to formulate policy for the Government or the Executive Branch, nor does it give appellant any administrative duties outside of those necessary to operate her office. The Act specifically provides that in policy matters appellant is to comply to the extent possible with the policies of the Department.

Third, appellant's office is limited in jurisdiction. Not only is the Act itself restricted in applicability to certain federal officials suspected of certain serious federal crimes, but an independent counsel can only act within the scope of the jurisdiction that has been granted by the Special Division pursuant to a request by the Attorney General. Finally, appellant's office is limited in tenure. There is concededly no time limit on the appointment of a particular counsel. Nonetheless, the office of independent counsel is "temporary" in the sense that an independent counsel is appointed essentially to accomplish a single task, and when that task is over the office is terminated, either by the counsel herself or by action of the Special Division. . . .

This does not, however, end our inquiry under the Appointments Clause. Appellees argue that even if appellant is an "inferior" officer, the Clause does not empower Congress to place the power to appoint such an officer outside the Executive Branch. They contend that the Clause does not contemplate congressional authorization of "interbranch appointments," in which an officer of one branch is appointed by officers of another branch. The relevant language of the Appointments Clause is worth repeating. It reads: ". . . but the Congress may by Law vest the Appointment of such inferior Officers, as they think proper, in the President alone, in the courts of Law, or in the Heads of Departments." On its face, the language of this "excepting clause" admits of no limitation on interbranch appointments. Indeed, the inclusion of "as they think proper" seems clearly to give Congress significant discretion to determine whether it is "proper" to vest the appointment of, for example, executive officials in the "courts of Law." . . .

We do not mean to say that Congress' power to provide for interbranch appointments of "inferior officers" is unlimited. In addition to separation-of-powers concerns, which would arise if such provisions for appointment had the potential to impair the constitutional functions assigned to one of the branches, [*Ex parte Siebold*] suggested that Congress' decision to vest the appointment power in the courts would be improper if there was some "incongruity" between the functions normally performed by the courts and the performance of their duty to appoint. . . .

In this case, however, we do not think it impermissible for Congress to vest the power to appoint independent counsel in a specially created federal court. We thus disagree with the Court of Appeals' conclusion that there is an inherent incongruity about a court having the power to appoint prosecutorial officers. . . .

V

We now turn to consider whether the Act is invalid under the constitutional principle of separation of powers. Two related issues must be addressed: The first is whether the provision of the Act restricting the Attorney General's power to remove the independent counsel to only those instances in which he can show "good cause," taken by itself, impermissibly interferes with the President's exercise of his constitutionally appointed functions. The second is whether, taken as a whole, the Act violates the separation of powers by reducing the President's ability to control the prosecutorial powers wielded by the independent counsel.

A

Two Terms ago we had occasion to consider whether it was consistent with the separation of powers for Congress to pass a statute that authorized a

Government official who is removable only by Congress to participate in what we found to be "executive powers." *Bowsher v. Synar*, 478 U.S. 714, 730 (1986). We held in *Bowsher* that "Congress cannot reserve for itself the power of removal of an officer charged with the execution of the laws except by impeachment." A primary antecedent for this ruling was our 1926 decision in *Myers v. United States*, 272 U.S. 52 (1926). *Myers* had considered the propriety of a federal statute by which certain postmasters of the United States could be removed by the President only "by and with the advice and consent of the Senate." There too, Congress' attempt to involve itself in the removal of an executive official was found to be sufficient grounds to render the statute invalid. As we observed in *Bowsher*, the essence of the decision in *Myers* was the judgment that the Constitution prevents Congress from "draw[ing] to itself . . . the power to remove or the right to participate in the exercise of that power. To do this would be to go beyond the words and implications of the [Appointments Clause] and to infringe the constitutional principle of the separation of governmental powers."

Unlike both *Bowsher* and *Myers*, this case does not involve an attempt by Congress itself to gain a role in the removal of executive officials other than its established powers of impeachment and conviction. The Act instead puts the removal power squarely in the hands of the Executive Branch; an independent counsel may be removed from office, "only by the personal action of the Attorney General, and only for good cause." There is no requirement of congressional approval of the Attorney General's removal decision, though the decision is subject to judicial review. In our view, the removal provisions of the Act make this case more analogous to *Humphrey's Executor v. United States*, and *Wiener v. United States*, than to *Myers* or *Bowsher*.

In *Humphrey's Executor*, the issue was whether a statute restricting the President's power to remove the Commissioners of the Federal Trade Commission (FTC) only for "inefficiency, neglect of duty, or malfeasance in office" was consistent with the Constitution. We stated that whether Congress can "condition the [President's power of removal] by fixing a definite term and precluding a removal except for cause, will depend upon the character of the office." Contrary to the implication of some dicta in *Myers*, the President's power to remove Government officials simply was not "all-inclusive in respect of civil officers with the exception of the judiciary provided for by the Constitution." At least in regard to "quasi-legislative" and "quasi-judicial" agencies such as the FTC, "[t]he authority of Congress, in creating [such] agencies, to require them to act in discharge of their duties independently of executive control . . . includes, as an appropriate incident, power to fix the period during which they shall continue in office, and to forbid their removal except for cause in the meantime." In *Humphrey's Executor*, we found it "plain" that the Constitution did not give the President "illimitable power of removal" over the officers of independent agencies. Were the President to have the power to remove FTC Commissioners at will, the "coercive influence" of the removal power would "threate[n] the independence of [the] commission." . . .

Appellees contend that *Humphrey's Executor* and *Wiener* are distinguishable from this case because they did not involve officials who performed a "core executive function." They argue that our decision in *Humphrey's Executor* rests on a distinction between "purely executive" officials and officials who exercise "quasi-legislative" and "quasi-judicial" powers. In their view, when a "purely executive" official is involved, the governing precedent is *Myers*, not *Humphrey's Executor*. And, under *Myers*, the President must have absolute discretion to discharge "purely" executive officials at will.

We undoubtedly did rely on the terms "quasi-legislative" and "quasi-judicial" to distinguish the officials involved in *Humphrey's Executor* and *Wiener* from those in *Myers*, but our present considered view is that the determination of whether the Constitution allows Congress to impose a "good cause"-type restriction on the President's power to remove an official cannot be made to turn on whether or not that official is classified as "purely executive." The analysis contained in our removal cases is designed not to define rigid categories of those officials who may or may not be removed at will by the President, but to ensure that Congress does not interfere with the President's exercise of the "executive power" and his constitutionally appointed duty to "take care that the laws be faithfully executed" under Article II. *Myers* was undoubtedly correct in its holding, and in its broader suggestion that there are some "purely executive" officials who must be removable by the President at will if he is to be able to accomplish his constitutional role. But as the Court noted in *Wiener*:

> "The assumption was short-lived that the *Myers* case recognized the President's inherent constitutional power to remove officials no matter what the relation of the executive to the discharge of their duties and no matter what restrictions Congress may have imposed regarding the nature of their tenure."

At the other end of the spectrum from *Myers*, the characterization of the agencies in *Humphrey's Executor* and *Wiener* as "quasi-legislative" or "quasi-judicial" in large part reflected our judgment that it was not essential to the President's proper execution of his Article II powers that these agencies be headed up by individuals who were removable at will. We do not mean to suggest that an analysis of the functions served by the officials at issue is irrelevant. But the real question is whether the removal restrictions are of such a nature that they impede the President's ability to perform his constitutional duty, and the functions of the officials in question must be analyzed in that light.

Considering for the moment the "good cause" removal provision in isolation from the other parts of the Act at issue in this case, we cannot say that the imposition of a "good cause" standard for removal by itself unduly trammels on executive authority. There is no real dispute that the functions performed by the independent counsel are "executive" in the sense that they are law enforcement functions that typically have been undertaken by officials within the Executive Branch. As we noted above, however, the independent counsel is an inferior officer under the Appointments Clause, with limited jurisdiction and tenure and lacking policymaking or significant administrative authority. Although the counsel exercises no small amount of discretion and judgment in deciding how to carry out his or her duties under the Act, we simply do not see how the President's need to control the exercise of that discretion is so central to the functioning of the Executive Branch as to require as a matter of constitutional law that the counsel be terminable at will by the President.

Nor do we think that the "good cause" removal provision at issue here impermissibly burdens the President's power to control or supervise the independent counsel, as an executive official, in the execution of his or her duties under the Act. This is not a case in which the power to remove an executive official has been completely stripped from the President, thus providing no means for the President to ensure the "faithful execution" of the laws. Rather, because the independent counsel may be terminated for "good cause," the Executive, through the Attorney General, retains ample authority to assure that the counsel is competently performing his or her statutory responsibilities in a manner that comports with the provisions of the Act. Although we need not decide in this case exactly what is encompassed within the term "good cause" under the Act, the legislative history of the removal provision also makes clear that the Attorney General may remove an independent counsel for "misconduct." Here, as with the provision of the Act conferring the appointment authority of the independent counsel on the special court, the congressional determination to limit the removal power of the Attorney General was essential, in the view of Congress, to establish the necessary independence of the office. We do not think that this limitation as it presently stands sufficiently deprives the President of control over the independent counsel to interfere impermissibly with his constitutional obligation to ensure the faithful execution of the laws.

B

The final question to be addressed is whether the Act, taken as a whole, violates the principle of separation of powers by unduly interfering with the role of the Executive Branch. Time and again we have reaffirmed the importance in our constitutional scheme of the separation of governmental powers into the three coordinate branches. . . . [T]he system of separated powers and checks and balances established in the Constitution was regarded by the Framers as "a self-executing safeguard against the encroachment or aggrandizement of one branch at the expense of the other." We have not hesitated to invalidate provisions of law which violate this principle. On the other hand, we have never held that the Constitution requires that the three branches of Government "operate with absolute independence." . . .

We observe first that this case does not involve an attempt by Congress to increase its own powers at the expense of the Executive Branch. . . . Indeed, with the exception of the power of impeachment—which applies to all officers of the United States—Congress retained for itself no powers of control or supervision over an independent counsel.

Similarly, we do not think that the Act works any judicial usurpation of properly executive functions. As should be apparent from our discussion of the Appointments Clause above, the power to appoint inferior officers such as independent counsel is not in itself an "executive" function in the constitutional sense, at least when Congress has exercised its power to vest the appointment of an inferior office in the "courts of Law." . . .

Finally, we do not think that the Act "impermissibly undermine[s]" the powers of the Executive Branch, or "disrupts the proper balance between the coordinate branches [by] prevent[ing] the Executive Branch from accomplishing its constitutionally assigned functions. It is undeniable that the Act reduces the amount of control or supervision that the Attorney General and, through him, the President exercises over the investigation and prosecution of a certain class of alleged criminal activity. The Attorney General is not allowed to appoint the individual of his choice; he does not determine the counsel's jurisdiction; and his power to remove a counsel is limited. Nonetheless, the Act does give the Attorney General several means of supervising or controlling the prosecutorial powers that may be wielded by an independent counsel. Most importantly, the Attorney General retains the power to remove the counsel for "good cause," a power that we have already concluded provides the Executive with substantial ability to ensure that the laws are "faithfully executed" by an independent counsel. No independent counsel may be appointed without a specific request by the Attorney General, and the Attorney General's decision not to request appointment if he finds "no reasonable grounds to believe that further investigation is warranted" is committed to his unreviewable discretion. The Act thus gives the Executive a degree of control over the power to initiate an investigation by the independent counsel. In addition, the jurisdiction of the independent counsel is defined with reference to the facts submitted by the Attorney General, and once a counsel is appointed, the Act requires that the counsel abide by Justice Department policy unless it is not "possible" to do so. Notwithstanding the fact that the counsel is to some degree "independent" and free from executive supervision to a greater extent than other federal prosecutors, in our view these features of the Act give the Executive Branch sufficient control over the independent counsel to ensure that the President is able to perform his constitutionally assigned duties. . . .

Reversed.

Justice SCALIA, dissenting.

. . . Article II, §1, cl. 1, of the Constitution provides:

"The executive Power shall be vested in a President of the United States."

. . . [T]his does not mean *some* of the executive power, but *all of* the executive power. It seems to me, therefore, that the decision of the Court of Appeals invalidating the present statute must be upheld on fundamental separation-of-powers principles if the following two questions are answered affirmatively: (1) Is the conduct of a criminal prosecution (and of an

investigation to decide whether to prosecute) the exercise of purely executive power? (2) Does the statute deprive the President of the United States
of exclusive control over the exercise of that power? Surprising to say, the
Court appears to concede an affirmative answer to both questions, but seeks
to avoid the inevitable conclusion that since the statute vests some purely
executive power in a person who is not the President of the United States it
is void.

The Court concedes that "[t]here is no real dispute that the functions
performed by the independent counsel are 'executive,'" though it qualifies
that concession by adding "in the sense that they are law enforcement functions that typically have been undertaken by officials within the Executive
Branch." The qualifier adds nothing but atmosphere. In what *other* sense
can one identify "the executive Power" that is supposed to be vested in the
President (unless it includes everything the Executive Branch is given to
do) *except* by reference to what has always and everywhere—if conducted
by government at all—been conducted never by the legislature, never by
the courts, and always by the executive. There is no possible doubt that the
independent counsel's functions fit this description. . . .

As for the second question, whether the statute before us deprives the
President of exclusive control over that quintessentially executive activity: The Court does not, and could not possibly, assert that it does not. That is
indeed the whole object of the statute. Instead, the Court points out that the
President, through his Attorney General, has at least *some* control. That concession is alone enough to invalidate the statute, but I cannot refrain from
pointing out that the Court greatly exaggerates the extent of that "some"
Presidential control. "Most importan[t]" among these controls, the Court
asserts, is the Attorney General's "power to remove the counsel for 'good
cause.'" This is somewhat like referring to shackles as an effective means of
locomotion. As we recognized in *Humphrey's Executor v. United States*—indeed,
what *Humphrey's Executor* was all about—limiting removal power to "good
cause" is an impediment to, not an effective grant of, Presidential control.
We said that limitation was necessary with respect to members of the Federal
Trade Commission, which we found to be "an agency of the legislative and
judicial departments," and "wholly disconnected from the executive department," because "it is quite evident that one who holds his office only during
the pleasure of another, cannot be depended upon to maintain an attitude
of independence against the latter's will." What we in *Humphrey's Executor*
found to be a means of eliminating Presidential control, the Court today
considers the "most importan[t]" means of assuring Presidential control.
Congress, of course, operated under no such illusion when it enacted this
statute, describing the "good cause" limitation as "protecting the independent counsel's ability to act independently of the President's direct control"
since it permits removal only for "misconduct." . . .

As I have said, however, it is ultimately irrelevant how *much* the statute
reduces Presidential control. The case is over when the Court acknowledges,
as it must, that "[i]t is undeniable that the Act reduces the amount of control

or supervision that the Attorney General and, through him, the President exercises over the investigation and prosecution of a certain class of alleged criminal activity." . . .

Notes and Questions

1. There are several other Supreme Court decisions on the subject of presidential removal, but they have dealt with subsidiary issues, such as whether independent agency status can be implied without explicit statutory language, see Wiener v. United States, 357 U.S. 349 (1958), and whether independent agency status can be further attenuated by, for example, making an agency official removable for cause by other agency officials who themselves are removable only for cause. We discuss this latter case below. *See* Free Enterprise Fund v. Public Company Accounting Oversight Board, 130 S. Ct. 3138 (2010). The basic doctrine is stated in the three cases excerpted above. Did you have trouble stating the rule of these cases? If so, one source of your trouble may be the second to last paragraph of *Humphrey's Executor.* Isn't the Court admitting its own uncertainty or confusion? In fact, the issue raised in the case remains unresolved to this day. We know, courtesy of the Court's decision, that Congress can constitutionally limit the President's removal authority over some agency officials to removal for cause, which places these officials beyond the President's direct policy control. But which ones? Are there limits on Congress's power to make certain officials or agencies independent of the Chief Executive?

2. *Humphrey's Executor* seems to suggest that the test concerns which type of functions an agency performs. Does the agency perform (quasi) legislative or (quasi) judicial functions in addition to any executive ones? If so, Congress can create the agency "independent" of plenary presidential removal authority and therefore control. But if the agency performs functions that are purely executive, removal restrictions are a no-go. Most agencies, and certainly most of the ones with broad jurisdiction, perform all three kinds of functions, as you have seen throughout the course. Is this test viable?

3. *Morrison* seems to suggest another possible test—has Congress interfered with the President's exercise of the "executive power" and duty to "take care that the laws be faithfully executed" under Article I? The difficulty here is that Article II does not define the executive power or the take-care duty. How can we know if Congress has interfered if we don't know what is protected from interference? The most that can be discerned is that external relations—war and diplomacy—are the President's particular preserve. This isn't much, by contemporary standards, as it does not reach the Department of Justice or the Department of the Treasury. It does preserve a larger sphere of action for the President than the *Humphrey's Executor* test, however. (The military is a core function if ever there was one, but it performs a lot of judicial actions—think of courts martial—and it certainly promulgates a lot of rules.)

At the end of the day, how would you describe the boundary between permissible and impermissible independent agencies? What factors might matter more than (or in addition to) the categories of functions that the agency can be said to perform? The scope of an agency's power, the duration of that power, the existence of rules to confine the exercise of that power? All of these, some of them?

4. Note the most basic difference between Chief Justice Taft and Justice Scalia on the one hand, and Justices Brandeis, Holmes, Sutherland, and Chief Justice Rehnquist on the other. Taft and Scalia subscribe to the unitary executive theory and argue that the constitutional provision stating "The executive Power shall be vested in a President of the United States of America" (Art. II, cl. 1) means *all* the executive power. Are you convinced by this textual reading? The prevailing interpretation is the one adopted by the other justices, which is to the contrary.

5. One pragmatic basis for the unitary executive theory, apart from textual or historical arguments, is the principle of hierarchy: that the executive power must be organized as an ordered ranking of officials, each one supervised by a higher-ranking official. This is often regarded as an essential feature of modern bureaucracy. It is modeled on the development of modern military forces. How essential is this feature? Does it conflict with the principle of checks and balances?

6. How should we conceptualize the President's relationship to his or her subordinates in the vast and varied executive apparatus? The *Myers* opinion states that "[e]ach head of a department is and must be the President's alter ego in the matters of that department where the President is required by law to exercise authority." *Humphrey's Executor* states that a body such as the FTC "cannot in any proper sense be characterized as an arm or an eye of the executive." Is the entire concept of three branches that we have relied on for so long (or four branches, one of which is headless) obsolete, given that most governmental functions in the modern state are now carried out by administrative agencies? *See* Edward Rubin, Beyond Camelot: Rethinking Politics and Law for the Modern State 39-73 (2005).

7. Taft, who wrote the majority opinion in *Myers*, was President of the United States from 1908 to 1912. He was appointed Chief Justice in 1921 and served in that capacity until 1930. *Myers* is probably his best-known opinion. To what extent would you ascribe its conclusion to Taft's experience as President, and to what extent would you ascribe it to bias in favor of the office?

8. Although insistent on the need for presidential control of the executive branch, Chief Justice Taft is also solicitous of the Civil Service System. The constitutionality of that system was challenged almost immediately, but the Supreme Court rejected this challenge in United States v. Perkins, 116 U.S. 483 (1886). Taft works hard to distinguish the *Perkins* case in *Myers*. "Distinguishing" is another form of legal argument by analogy; it means that the opinion writer tries to demonstrate that two cases, despite apparently related factual patterns, are not analogous to each other and should not be decided the same way. How does Taft distinguish between *Myers* and *Perkins*; that is, on what basis does he argue that political appointees, who he claims the President must have the power to remove, are different from civil service appointees, who, by the nature of that system, can only be removed for cause?

9. Note the distinction between principal and inferior offices, as established by Article II, §2 of the Constitution. It refers to appointments, not removal. Aren't appointments a more important way for the President to control agencies than removal? Appointing a like-minded person, who will follow the President's policies voluntarily, is easier than monitoring the person's actions and deciding which ones should be reversed. You might think that Congress would focus more on appointment than removal. But Congress has less room to limit presidential appointment of principal officers because the Court has held that this authority cannot be taken away from the President. Congress does have some say: the President must exercise this authority with the "Advice and Consent" of the Senate. Can you see a relationship between the appointments power and the removal power? Why might Congress have a strong reason for limiting removal and the President have a strong reason against limiting removal?

What about "inferior officers"? It would be impossible to operate a modern administrative state if the appointment of "inferior" officers could not be vested in "Heads of Departments." That is one of the basic features of a hierarchically organized staff. If agencies have relative freedom to appoint their own officers, would you expect Congress to seek more or less control over removal of these officers? Should the President have a greater or lesser interest in removal?

10. Is Justice Scalia correct in arguing that a "for cause" removal provision cannot be regarded as preserving sufficient presidential control? Presidential control means the ability to control the policy judgments that the officer makes, and that is thought to involve the ability to remove the officer "at will," that is, for no reason at all. "For cause" is the civil service standard, and means that there must be a reason for the dismissal, typically at the level of malfeasance, incompetence, or dishonesty, which the person dismissed can challenge in some adjudicatory setting. Note, however, that the "good cause" provision of the Ethics in Government Act includes "any other condition that substantially impairs the performance of such independent counsel's duties." Does this give the President more authority than a simple "good cause" provision? Is that enough authority for the clause to do the work that the majority wants it to do, or is Justice Scalia right in saying that the majority's argument is like treating shackles as a means of locomotion?

Why might Congress seek to create an independent agency? The obvious answer is that Congress wants considerations other than politics to control agency decisions, but this begs the basic question: why don't we want politics — or more specially, political officials, who are, after all, the people we have chosen to run our government — to make particular decisions?

There are two classic cases that present the concern about politics driving agency decisions. One is when the agency is adjudicating the rights of individuals. It would be odious to find someone guilty of a crime, or judge her liable for a civil injury, because of her political views. This is one reason why the Constitution provides for the independence of the federal courts. Of course, it isn't necessary to make the entire agency independent in order to achieve this goal. The adjudicators within the agency can be made independent of political officials, can't they? The other classic case is when an agency is involved in central banking — that is, exercising control of the money supply. The possibility of inflating the currency to secure short-term political gains is regarded as simply too great a temptation for elected officials. The Federal Reserve Board of Governors, and the Chairman of the Fed, can attribute their independence to these sorts of arguments. No two government tasks could be as different from each other as adjudicating the rights of individuals and controlling the money supply. Is there a general principle that would encompass these disparate functions?

The independent counsel statute at issue in *Morrison* reflects another rationale for creating an independent agency. The independent counsel statute at issue in *Morrison* was enacted in response to the Watergate scandal, during which President Nixon decided to dismiss the Watergate Special Prosecutor, Archibald Cox, in the midst of his investigation. Since the prosecutor had been appointed by the Attorney General, Nixon proceeded by ordering the Attorney General to fire Cox. Instead he resigned, and so did his second in command. The third person in line at the Department of Justice was Robert Bork, the Solicitor General, and he dutifully fired Cox. This occurred late on Saturday, October 20, 1973, and became known as the Saturday Night Massacre. In response, Congress enacted the Special Prosecutor statute, which established the office and provided the limitation on presidential removal at issue in the case. It was used on several occasions, but was finally pushed too far when Kenneth Starr expanded his investigation of President Clinton's Whitewater transactions to include his affair with Monica Lewinsky. In 1999, the statute, which had to be reauthorized in order to remain in effect, was allowed to lapse. (Incidentally, most statutes don't have to be reauthorized, but continue in perpetuity, unless of course they are repealed. A provision in a statute that requires that it be reauthorized is called a sunset provision.) Does the Starr investigation demonstrate that Justice Scalia was right in his *Morrison* dissent? Was the problem with the independent counsel statute that the prosecutor was independent?

Just recently, another congressional innovation triggered another Supreme Court pronouncement on the constitutional status of independent agencies. Now that you have the established doctrine clearly in mind (it must be clear; how could there be constitutional uncertainty about a basic operational unit of our governmental system?), see how you would apply that doctrine to the conflicting opinions in the following case.

Free Enterprise Fund v. Public Company Accounting Oversight Board

130 S. Ct. 3138 (2010)

Chief Justice ROBERTS delivered the opinion of the Court.

Since 1789, the Constitution has been understood to empower the President to keep these officers accountable—by removing them from office, if necessary. *See generally Myers v. United States*. This Court has determined, however, that this authority is not without limit. In *Humphrey's Executor v. United States*, we held that Congress can, under certain circumstances, create independent agencies run by principal officers appointed by the President, whom the President may not remove at will but only for good cause. Likewise, in *United States v. Perkins*, the Court sustained similar restrictions on the power of principal executive officers—themselves responsible to the President—to remove their own inferiors. The parties do not ask us to reexamine any of these precedents, and we do not do so.

We are asked, however, to consider a new situation not yet encountered by the Court. The question is whether these separate layers of protection may be combined. May the President be restricted in his ability to remove a principal officer, who is in turn restricted in his ability to remove an inferior officer, even though that inferior officer determines the policy and enforces the laws of the United States?

We hold that such multilevel protection from removal is contrary to Article II's vesting of the executive power in the President. The President cannot "take Care that the Laws be faithfully executed" if he cannot oversee the faithfulness of the officers who execute them. Here the President cannot remove an officer who enjoys more than one level of good-cause protection, even if the President determines that the officer is neglecting his duties or discharging them improperly. That judgment is instead committed to another officer, who may or may not agree with the President's determination, and whom the President cannot remove simply because that officer disagrees with him. This contravenes the President's "constitutional obligation to ensure the faithful execution of the laws." *Morrison v. Olson*.

I

A

After a series of celebrated accounting debacles, Congress enacted the Sarbanes-Oxley Act of 2002 (or Act). Among other measures, the Act introduced tighter regulation of the accounting industry under a new Public

Company Accounting Oversight Board. The Board is composed of five members, appointed to staggered 5-year terms by the Securities and Exchange Commission. It was modeled on private self-regulatory organizations in the securities industry—such as the New York Stock Exchange—that investigate and discipline their own members subject to Commission oversight. Congress created the Board as a private "nonprofit corporation," and Board members and employees are not considered Government "officer[s] or employee[s]" for statutory purposes. The Board can thus recruit its members and employees from the private sector by paying salaries far above the standard Government pay scale.

Unlike the self-regulatory organizations, however, the Board is a Government-created, Government-appointed entity, with expansive powers to govern an entire industry. Every accounting firm—both foreign and domestic—that participates in auditing public companies under the securities laws must register with the Board, pay it an annual fee, and comply with its rules and oversight. The Board is charged with enforcing the Sarbanes-Oxley Act, the securities laws, the Commission's rules, its own rules, and professional accounting standards. To this end, the Board may regulate every detail of an accounting firm's practice, including hiring and professional development, promotion, supervision of audit work, the acceptance of new business and the continuation of old, internal inspection procedures, professional ethics rules, and "such other requirements as the Board may prescribe." . . .

The Act places the Board under the SEC's oversight, particularly with respect to the issuance of rules or the imposition of sanctions (both of which are subject to Commission approval and alteration). But the individual members of the Board—like the officers and directors of the self-regulatory organizations—are substantially insulated from the Commission's control. The Commission cannot remove Board members at will, but only "for good cause shown," "in accordance with" certain procedures.

Those procedures require a Commission finding, "on the record" and "after notice and opportunity for a hearing," that the Board member

> "(A) has willfully violated any provision of th[e] Act, the rules of the Board, or the securities laws;
>
> "(B) has willfully abused the authority of that member; or
>
> "(C) without reasonable justification or excuse, has failed to enforce compliance with any such provision or rule, or any professional standard by any registered public accounting firm or any associated person thereof." . . .

The parties agree that the [SEC] Commissioners cannot themselves be removed by the President except under the *Humphrey's Executor* standard of "inefficiency, neglect of duty, or malfeasance in office," and we decide the case with that understanding.

III

A

We hold that the dual for-cause limitations on the removal of Board members contravene the Constitution's separation of powers.

The Constitution provides that "[t]he executive Power shall be vested in a President of the United States of America." Art. II, §1, cl. 1. . . . The landmark case of *Myers v. United States* reaffirmed the principle that Article II confers on the President "the general administrative control of those executing the laws." It is *his* responsibility to take care that the laws be faithfully executed. The buck stops with the President, in Harry Truman's famous phrase. As we explained in *Myers*, the President therefore must have some "power of removing those for whom he can not continue to be responsible."

Nearly a decade later in *Humphrey's Executor*, this Court held that *Myers* did not prevent Congress from conferring good-cause tenure on the principal officers of certain independent agencies. That case concerned the members of the Federal Trade Commission, who held 7-year terms and could not be removed by the President except for "'inefficiency, neglect of duty, or malfeasance in office.'" The Court distinguished *Myers* on the ground that *Myers* concerned "an officer [who] is merely one of the units in the executive department and, hence, inherently subject to the exclusive and illimitable power of removal by the Chief Executive, whose subordinate and aid he is." By contrast, the Court characterized the FTC as "quasi-legislative and quasi-judicial" rather than "purely executive," and held that Congress could require it "to act . . . independently of executive control." Because "one who holds his office only during the pleasure of another, cannot be depended upon to maintain an attitude of independence against the latter's will," the Court held that Congress had power to "fix the period during which [the Commissioners] shall continue in office, and to forbid their removal except for cause in the meantime."

Humphrey's Executor did not address the removal of inferior officers, whose appointment Congress may vest in heads of departments. If Congress does so, it is ordinarily the department head, rather than the President, who enjoys the power of removal.

We again considered the status of inferior officers in *Morrison*. That case concerned the Ethics in Government Act, which provided for an independent counsel to investigate allegations of crime by high executive officers. The counsel was appointed by a special court, wielded the full powers of a prosecutor, and was removable by the Attorney General only "'for good cause.'" We recognized that the independent counsel was undoubtedly an executive officer, rather than "'quasi-legislative'" or "'quasi-judicial,'" but we stated as "our present considered view" that Congress had power to impose good-cause restrictions on her removal. The Court noted that the statute "g[a]ve the Attorney General," an officer directly responsible to the President and "through [whom]" the President could act, "several means of supervising or controlling" the independent counsel—"[m]ost importantly . . . the power to remove the counsel for good cause." Under those circumstances, the Court sustained the statute. *Morrison* did not, however, address the consequences of more than one level of good-cause tenure—leaving the issue, as both the court and dissent below recognized, "a question of first impression" in this Court.

B

As explained, we have previously upheld limited restrictions on the President's removal power. In those cases, however, only one level of protected tenure separated the President from an officer exercising executive power. It was the President—or a subordinate he could remove at will—who decided whether the officer's conduct merited removal under the good-cause standard.

The Act before us does something quite different. It not only protects Board members from removal except for good cause, but withdraws from the President any decision on whether that good cause exists. That decision is vested instead in other tenured officers—the Commissioners—none of whom is subject to the President's direct control. The result is a Board that is not accountable to the President, and a President who is not responsible for the Board.

The added layer of tenure protection makes a difference. Without a layer of insulation between the Commission and the Board, the Commission could remove a Board member at any time, and therefore would be fully responsible for what the Board does. The President could then hold the Commission to account for its supervision of the Board, to the same extent that he may hold the Commission to account for everything else it does.

A second level of tenure protection changes the nature of the President's review. Now the Commission cannot remove a Board member at will. The President therefore cannot hold the Commission fully accountable for the Board's conduct, to the same extent that he may hold the Commission accountable for everything else that it does. The Commissioners are not responsible for the Board's actions. They are only responsible for their own determination of whether the Act's rigorous good-cause standard is met. And even if the President disagrees with their determination, he is powerless to intervene—unless that determination is so unreasonable as to constitute "inefficiency, neglect of duty, or malfeasance in office." *Humphrey's Executor.*

This novel structure does not merely add to the Board's independence, but transforms it. Neither the President, nor anyone directly responsible to him, nor even an officer whose conduct he may review only for good cause, has full control over the Board. The President is stripped of the power our precedents have preserved, and his ability to execute the laws—by holding his subordinates accountable for their conduct—is impaired.

That arrangement is contrary to Article II's vesting of the executive power in the President. Without the ability to oversee the Board, or to attribute the Board's failings to those whom he can oversee, the President is no longer the judge of the Board's conduct. He is not the one who decides whether Board members are abusing their offices or neglecting their duties. He can neither ensure that the laws are faithfully executed, nor be held responsible for a Board member's breach of faith. This violates the basic principle that the President "cannot delegate ultimate responsibility or the active obligation to supervise that goes with it," because Article II "makes a single President responsible for the actions of the Executive Branch."

Indeed, if allowed to stand, this dispersion of responsibility could be multiplied. If Congress can shelter the bureaucracy behind two layers of good-cause tenure, why not a third? At oral argument, the Government was unwilling to concede that even five layers between the President and the Board would be too many. The officers of such an agency—safely encased within a Matryoshka doll of tenure protections—would be immune from Presidential oversight, even as they exercised power in the people's name. . . .

By granting the Board executive power without the Executive's oversight, this Act subverts the President's ability to ensure that the laws are faithfully executed—as well as the public's ability to pass judgment on his efforts. The Act's restrictions are incompatible with the Constitution's separation of powers.

C

Respondents and the dissent resist this conclusion, portraying the Board as "the kind of practical accommodation between the Legislature and the Executive that should be permitted in a 'workable government.'" According to the dissent, Congress may impose multiple levels of for-cause tenure between the President and his subordinates when it "rests agency independence upon the need for technical expertise." The Board's mission is said to demand both "technical competence" and "apolitical expertise," and its powers may only be exercised by "technical professional experts." In this respect the statute creating the Board is, we are told, simply one example of the "vast numbers of statutes governing vast numbers of subjects, concerned with vast numbers of different problems, [that] provide for, or foresee, their execution or administration through the work of administrators organized within many different kinds of administrative structures, exercising different kinds of administrative authority, to achieve their legislatively mandated objectives."

The Framers created a structure in which "[a] dependence on the people" would be the "primary control on the government." THE FEDERALIST NO. 51, at 349 (J. Madison). That dependence is maintained, not just by "parchment barriers," *id.*, No. 48, at 333 (same), but by letting "[a]mbition . . . counteract ambition," giving each branch "the necessary constitutional means, and personal motives, to resist encroachments of the others," *id.*, No. 51, at 349. A key "constitutional means" vested in the President—perhaps *the* key means—was "the power of appointing, overseeing, and controlling those who execute the laws." 1 Annals of Cong., at 463. And while a government of "opposite and rival interests" may sometimes inhibit the smooth functioning of administration, THE FEDERALIST NO. 51, at 349, "[t]he Framers recognized that, in the long term, structural protections against abuse of power were critical to preserving liberty." *Bowsher.*

Calls to abandon those protections in light of "the era's perceived necessity," are not unusual. Nor is the argument from bureaucratic expertise limited only to the field of accounting. The failures of accounting regulation may be a "pressing national problem," but "a judiciary that licensed extraconstitutional government with each issue of comparable gravity would, in the long run, be far worse." Neither respondents nor the dissent explains why the Board's task, unlike so many others, requires *more* than one layer of insulation from the President—or, for that matter, why only two. The point is not to take issue with for-cause limitations in general; we do not do that. The question here is far more modest. We deal with the unusual situation, never before addressed by the Court, of two layers of for-cause tenure. And though it may be criticized as "elementary arithmetical logic," two layers are not the same as one.

The President has been given the power to oversee executive officers; he is not limited, as in Harry Truman's lament, to "persuad[ing]" his unelected subordinates "to do what they ought to do without persuasion." In its pursuit of a "workable government," Congress cannot reduce the Chief Magistrate to a cajoler-in-chief.

D

The parties have identified only a handful of isolated positions in which inferior officers might be protected by two levels of good-cause tenure. . . . The dissent here suggests that other such positions might exist, and complains that we do not resolve their status in this opinion. The dissent itself, however, stresses the very size and variety of the Federal Government, and those features discourage general pronouncements on matters neither briefed nor argued here. In any event, the dissent fails to support its premonitions of doom; none of the positions it identifies are similarly situated to the Board.

For example, many civil servants within independent agencies would not qualify as "Officers of the United States," who "exercis[e] significant authority pursuant to the laws of the United States," *Buckley*. The parties here concede that Board members are executive "Officers," as that term is used in the Constitution. We do not decide the status of other Government employees, nor do we decide whether "lesser functionaries subordinate to officers of the United States" must be subject to the same sort of control as those who exercise "significant authority pursuant to the laws." *Buckley*.

Nor do the employees referenced by the dissent enjoy the same significant and unusual protections from Presidential oversight as members of the Board. Senior or policymaking positions in government may be excepted from the competitive service to ensure Presidential control, see 5 U.S.C. §§2302(a)(2)(B), 3302, 7511(b)(2), and members of the Senior Executive Service may be reassigned or reviewed by agency heads (and entire agencies may be excluded from that Service by the President), *see, e.g.*, §§3132(c), 3395(a), 4312(d), 4314(b)(3), (c)(3); *cf.* §2302(a)(2)(B)(ii). While the full extent of that authority is not before us, any such authority is of course wholly absent with respect to the Board. Nothing in our opinion, therefore, should be read to cast doubt on the use of what is colloquially known as the civil service system within independent agencies.[1]

Justice BREYER, with whom Justice STEVENS, Justice GINSBURG, and Justice SOTOMAYOR join, dissenting.

. . . The Necessary and Proper Clause does not grant Congress power to free *all* Executive Branch officials from dismissal at the will of the President. Nor does the separation-of-powers principle grant the President an absolute authority to remove *any and all* Executive Branch officials at will. Rather, depending on, say, the nature of the office, its function, or its subject matter, Congress sometimes may, consistent with the Constitution, limit the President's authority to remove an officer from his post. See *Humphrey's Executor v. United States*, overruling in part *Myers; Morrison v. Olson*. And we must here decide whether the circumstances surrounding the statute at issue justify such a limitation.

. . . In *Myers*, the Court invalidated—for the first and only time—a congressional statute on the ground that it unduly limited the President's authority to remove an Executive Branch official. But soon thereafter the Court expressly disapproved most of *Myers'* broad reasoning. *See Humphrey's Executor*, overruling in part *Myers; Wiener v. United States*, (stating that *Humphrey's Executor* "explicitly 'disapproved'" of much of the reasoning in *Myers*). Moreover, the Court has since said that "the essence of the decision in *Myers* was the judgment that the Constitution prevents Congress from '*draw[ing] to itself*. . . the power to remove or the right to participate in the exercise of that power.'" *Morrison*. And that feature of the statute—a feature that would *aggrandize* the power of Congress—is not present here. Congress has not granted itself any role in removing the members of the Accounting Board. Compare *Myers* (striking down statute where Congress granted itself removal authority over Executive Branch official), with *Humphrey's Executor* (upholding statute where such aggrandizing was absent); *Wiener* (same); *Morrison* (same).

In short, the question presented lies at the intersection of two sets of conflicting, broadly framed constitutional principles. And no text, no history, perhaps no precedent provides any clear answer. . . .

The upshot is that today vast numbers of statutes governing vast numbers of subjects, concerned with vast numbers of different problems, provide for, or foresee, their execution or administration through the work

---

1. For similar reasons, our holding also does not address that subset of independent agency employees who serve as administrative law judges. *See, e.g.,* 5 U.S.C. §§556(c), 3105. Whether administrative law judges are necessarily "Officers of the United States" is disputed. *See, e.g., Landry v. FDIC.* And unlike members of the Board, many administrative law judges of course perform adjudicative rather than enforcement or policymaking functions, see §§554(d), 3105, or possess purely recommendatory powers. The Government below refused to identify either "civil service tenure-protected employees in independent agencies" or administrative law judges as "precedent for the PCAOB." 537 F.3d 667, 699, n.8 (C.A.D.C. 2008) (Kavanaugh, J., dissenting). [Footnote 10 in the Opinion. — Eds.]

of administrators organized within many different kinds of administrative structures, exercising different kinds of administrative authority, to achieve their legislatively mandated objectives. And, given the nature of the Government's work, it is not surprising that administrative units come in many different shapes and sizes.

The functional approach required by our precedents recognizes this administrative complexity and, more importantly, recognizes the various ways presidential power operates within this context—and the various ways in which a removal provision might affect that power. As human beings have known ever since Ulysses tied himself to the mast so as safely to hear the Sirens' song, sometimes it is necessary to disable oneself in order to achieve a broader objective. Thus, legally enforceable commitments—such as contracts, statutes that cannot instantly be changed, and, as in the case before us, the establishment of independent administrative institutions—hold the potential to empower precisely because of their ability to constrain. If the President seeks to regulate through impartial adjudication, then insulation of the adjudicator from removal at will can help him achieve that goal. And to free a technical decisionmaker from the fear of removal without cause can similarly help create legitimacy with respect to that official's regulatory actions by helping to insulate his technical decisions from nontechnical political pressure. . . .

But even if we put all these other matters to the side, we should still conclude that the "for cause" restriction before us will not restrict presidential power significantly. For one thing, the restriction directly limits, not the President's power, but the power of an already independent agency. The Court seems to have forgotten that fact when it identifies its central constitutional problem: According to the Court, the President "is powerless to intervene" if he has determined that the Board members' "conduct merit[s] removal" because "[t]hat decision is vested instead in other tenured officers—the Commissioners—none of whom is subject to the President's direct control." But so long as the President is legitimately foreclosed from removing the Commissioners except for cause (as the majority assumes), nullifying the Commission's power to remove Board members only for cause will not resolve the problem the Court has identified: The President will still be "powerless to intervene" by removing the Board members if the Commission reasonably decides not to do so.

In other words, the Court fails to show why two layers of "for cause" protection—Layer One insulating the Commissioners from the President, and Layer Two insulating the Board from the Commissioners—impose any more serious limitation upon the *President's* powers than *one* layer. . . .

At the same time, Congress and the President had good reason for enacting the challenged "for cause" provision. First and foremost, the Board adjudicates cases. *See* 15 U.S.C. §7215. This Court has long recognized the appropriateness of using "for cause" provisions to protect the personal independence of those who even only sometimes engage in adjudicatory functions. *Humphrey's Executor*, see also *Wiener*. . . . Indeed, as early as 1789

James Madison stated that "there may be strong reasons why an" executive "officer" such as the Comptroller of the United States "should not hold his office at the pleasure of the Executive branch" if one of his "principal dut[ies]" "partakes strongly of the judicial character." 1 Annals of Congress 611-612. . . . The Court, however, all but ignores the Board's adjudicatory functions when conducting its analysis. And when it finally does address that central function (in a footnote), it simply asserts that the Board *does not* "*perform* adjudicative . . . functions," n.10 (emphasis added), an assertion that is inconsistent with the terms of the statute. *See* §7215(c)(1) (governing "proceeding[s] by the Board to determine whether a registered public accounting firm, or an associated person thereof, should be disciplined").

Moreover, in addition to their adjudicative functions, the Accounting Board members supervise, and are themselves, technical professional experts. *See* §7211(e)(1) This Court has recognized that the "difficulties involved in the preparation of" sound auditing reports require the application of "scientific accounting principles." And this Court has recognized the constitutional legitimacy of a justification that rests agency independence upon the need for technical expertise. *See Humphrey's Executor.* . . .

One last question: How can the Court simply *assume* without deciding that the SEC Commissioners themselves are removable only "for cause"? . . . I am not aware of any other instance in which the Court has similarly (on its own or through stipulation) *created* a constitutional defect in a statute and then relied on that defect to strike a statute down as unconstitutional. . . . [T]the statute that established the Commission says nothing about removal. It *is silent* on the question. . . .

The Court then, by assumption, . . . reads *into* the statute books a "for cause removal" phrase that does not appear in the relevant statute. . . . And it does so in order to strike down, not to uphold, another statute. This is not a statutory construction that seeks to avoid a constitutional question, but its opposite. . . .

Notes and Questions

1. The PCAOB, universally known as "Peekaboo," is certainly an unusual government agency. Regardless of whether you side with the majority or the dissent, it is difficult to disagree with the dissent's statement that the Board reflects a government system that consists of "many different kinds of administrative structures, exercising different kinds of administrative authority, to achieve their legislatively mandated objectives." Why do you think Congress chose to create an agency of this sort? Note that the case was a 5-4 decision, following the Court's standard ideological fault lines, and Justice Kennedy casting the deciding vote. Why does a technical question of administrative structure divide the Court in this manner?

2. Justice Breyer characterizes his own approach as functional and the majority's approach as formalist. This is a fairly standard way to label the

two sides in structural cases; that is, cases involving separation of powers, federalism, and related issues. *See, e.g.,* Rebecca Brown, *Separated Powers and Ordered Liberty,* 139 U. Pa. L. Rev. 1513 (1991); Harold Krent, *Separating the Strands in Separation of Powers Controversies,* 74 Va. L. Rev. 1253 (1988); Gary Lawson, *The Rise and Rise of the Administrative State,* 107 Harv. L. Rev. 1231 (1994); M. Elizabeth Magill, *The Real Separation in Separation of Powers Law,* 86 Va. L. Rev. 1127 (2007); Peter Strauss, *Formal and Functionalist Approaches to Separation-of-Powers—A Foolish Inconsistency?,* 72 Cornell L. Rev. 482 (1987); Cass Sunstein, *Constitutionalism After the New Deal,* 101 Harv. L. Rev. 421 (1987). Formalist arguments tend to focus on the language of the Constitution, the original intent of the Framers, and the importance of retaining the boundaries of the different branches of government. Functionalist arguments focus on the purpose of the Constitution, its evolving meaning over time, and the overlap and interaction among the branches. We have seen formalism versus functionalism in all of the Court's independent agency decisions (which opinions are which?) and we will see it again in the congressional control section of this Chapter.

3. Both the majority and the dissent in *Free Enterprise Fund* cite the whole succession of independent agency cases—*Myers, Humphrey's Executor, Wiener,* and *Morrison.* Neither side attempts to cast any doubt on the validity of these decisions, but they reach opposite results on the basis of them. In what ways are they reading these cases differently, and who has the preferable interpretation?

4. What do you think of Justice Breyer's point that the Court cannot avail itself of the argument that Sarbanes-Oxley limits presidential power too severely because even one layer of "for cause" removal requirements, which is unquestionably constitutional, would insulate an agency from presidential control? How does the Court respond to this? What underlying assumptions do these conflicting views reveal about the actual operation of the regulatory state, the nature of political supervision, and the incentives of agency officials?

5. To what extent does the *Free Enterprise Fund* decision influence the constitutional foundation for single-level removal provisions? In this light, consider the following argument made by Professor Strauss:

> PCAOB authority could be preserved, the majority found, because this statutory flaw could be cured by severing the offensive "for cause" removal provisions from the statute. Once this had been done, the PCAOB's affirmative responsibilities and authority could persist unimpaired. It is simply that its members would now perform their functions under the same possibility of discipline as direct SEC employees face, leaving "the President separated from Board members by only a single level of good-cause tenure. The Commission is then fully responsible for the Board's actions, which are no less subject than the Commission's own actions to Presidential oversight." As that level of control over SEC staff was constitutionally sufficient to recognize the President's necessary authority to oversee the actions of the executive branch, it must be sufficient for the Board as well. While the majority said only that it had not been invited to reexamine *Humphrey's Executor* and was not doing so, the necessary implication of its finding of PCAOB constitutionality on this rationale is to reaffirm the result in *Humphrey's Executor.*

In at least some settings, Congress can create elements of the executive branch whose heads are removable only "for cause." The constitutionality of the PCAOB's authority could not conscionably have been sustained without accepting the single level of "for cause" protection the majority attributed to the SEC.

Peter L. Strauss, *On the Difficulties of Generalization—* PCAOB *in the Footsteps of* Myers, Humphrey's, Morrison, *and* Freytag, 32 CARDOZO L. REV. 2255, 2274 (2011).

6. The decision has also been read as implicating separation of functions.

[T]he dual layer of removal protection was not what decided the case. If it were, the PCAOB decision would have swept aside the constitutional foundation for good-cause protections for the many adjudicators operating in independent agencies who also have two layers of good-cause protection, a conclusion the *PCAOB* Court resists. The question, then, is what distinguished the Board's removal protections from the removal protections of officers who only have adjudicative functions (i.e., dedicated adjudicators) in independent agencies. The answer . . . is the Board's combination of functions. The Board possesses rulemaking, enforcement, and adjudicative functions. This combination of functions sets the Board's removal protections apart from those of dedicated adjudicators within independent agencies whose removal protections the Court sought to preserve, and furnishes the key ground of the decision. *PCAOB*'s principle, then, is that the consistency of good-cause removal protections with separation of powers depends in part on the combination of functions of the officials whose tenure those provisions protect. At base, this principle reflects a significant reversal of the constitutional baseline for assessing removal protections: Whereas formerly adjudicative functions provided a sufficient ground for upholding good-cause removal protections for an agency with a combination of functions, under *PCAOB*'s principle, enforcement and policymaking functions take primacy over adjudicative functions, and provide a sufficient ground for requiring at-will removal power. . . .

Kevin M. Stack, *Agency Independence After* PCAOB, 32 CARDOZO L. REV. 2391 (2011). On that view, does the decision undermine *Humphrey's?*

7. On the practical significance of independence, as we discussed in Chapter 1, both independent and executive agencies are subject to the APA and the same standards of judicial review. In addition, the President typically selects the Chair of independent agencies.

2. Control of Agency Personnel

Chief among the President's powers for asserting control of agency action is the power to appoint and to fire the heads of agencies.[2] Through appointment of Senate-confirmed officers, the President is able to select individuals who will follow administration priorities either because they share those priorities or are loyal on party or personal grounds. If the President makes the

---

2. The President also influences agency policy by appointing other officials, including members of the Senior Executive Service and individuals with so-called Schedule C appointments whose responsibilities are of a confidential or policymaking nature. *See* LEWIS, THE POLITICS OF PRESIDENTIAL APPOINTMENTS at 23-25.

right appointments, he will rarely need means for later exerting control over an agency; the political appointee will know what needs to be done.

In the event of disagreement over general priorities or specific policies, the President has the authority to fire the heads of executive-branch agencies. The President can replace those officials with individuals more amenable to administration views.

The actual removal of high-level officials can be politically costly for the President. Such removal attracts considerable publicity and creates the need for a replacement acceptable to the Senate. How can the President avoid some of the spectacle and still control an official? The threat of removal often creates strong incentives for agency leaders to comply with the President's wishes or to resign "voluntarily" from their positions. (On the flip side, the threat of resigning can put pressure on a President who wishes to avoid the appearance of cabinet officials making a noisy exit.) On May 1, 2019, Deputy Attorney General Rod J. Rosenstein, the number two official in the Department of Justice, sent his resignation letter to President Trump. Rosenstein was involved in overseeing the investigation into Russian election interference and collusion with the Trump campaign—a highly political matter, and not one of regulatory policy. Nevertheless, it illustrates the basic relationship between resignation and removal. Many were angered that Rosenstein did not dismiss the investigation and, as the Associated Press summed it up, "his relationship with the president waffled over time and his job often appeared in the balance." *See https://apnews.com/0a5d5a8f141446b98b26d2ed8412c71d.* In his resignation letter, Rosenstein began by praising the work of the Department of Justice and then stated: "As I submit my resignation effective on May 11, I am grateful to you for the opportunity to serve; for the courtesy and humor you often display in our personal conversations; and for the goals you set in your inaugural address: patriotism, unity, safety, education, and prosperity, because 'a nation exists to serve its citizens.' " Rosenstein, after praising the impartiality and fairness of the Justice Department, closed his letter with a phrase from President Trump's campaign: "We keep the faith, we follow the rules, and we always put America first."

As we have just seen, control of agency officials plays out differently for independent agencies. The President cannot fire the commissioners or board members of independent agencies for policy disagreements, even if inclined to take the heat and find a replacement. Those officials, for the most part, are protected by statute from presidential removal except for specified cause, as we just saw when discussing the constitutionality of these statutory removal restrictions. But the President still has the ability to assert some control over those agencies and their political officials. A good cause restriction is not complete insulation from presidential removal or presidential control. Furthermore, the President possesses other means to assert control of independent agencies. As with executive-branch agencies,

as a "de facto" matter, fully "in the stream of every policy decision made by the federal government." As a former political appointee in charge of one of the RMOs has explained, "You sit at the pure epicenter of policy. You're in a position to make a difference. And eventually, everything will come across your desk." The RMOs' influence over independent agencies is especially striking, as independent agencies are not subject to OIRA's regulatory review but do generally fall under OMB's budget purview.

Does the RMOs' work reflect *presidential* control, as opposed to OMB control or RMO control? It depends. Because the RMOs provide a direct link into every agency, they are a valuable conduit for policy and political direction from the President, as well as from other senior advisors who might be said to speak for the President.

At the same time, because the RMOs possess deep knowledge about agency work and policy context, decisions made by the President and senior advisors may simply be those that the RMOs recommend. And given the vast number of decisions made throughout the budgeting process, only a small fraction will ever make it to the President's desk, or even the OMB director's, leaving RMO staff members in practice as the final decision-makers on a wide range of issues. This is not to suggest that RMO staff members routinely impose their own preferences on the agencies they oversee, but rather that at least some of the RMOs' control of agency policy choices reflects choices made by civil servants and the non-Senate-confirmed political appointees who oversee each of the RMOs.

What ought we to make of the extent to which the RMOs influence the choices agencies make? At some level, the RMOs' work deserves praise for the valuable coordinating function it serves, furthering both the efficiency and effectiveness of agency action. Overall, RMO staff members are of an extremely high caliber, and they may well improve the substance of agency decisions.

Yet at the same time, the RMOs' work raises a series of concerns about accountability, many of which echo concerns scholars and others have raised about OIRA's own work over the years. For one thing, the RMOs' work suffers from a lack of transparency, both as to process and substance. Which interest groups meet with which RMO staff? How frequently do they meet and what issues do they discuss? How has RMO oversight changed different agencies' priorities over different administrations? It is hard to hold government officials accountable when it is almost impossible to find out what they are doing or what is happening in their offices.

Additionally, the structure of the RMOs gives a lot of discretion to civil servants and lower-level political appointees to direct the choices of Senate-confirmed agency officials. Although some of the RMOs' direction is no doubt an interpretation of presidential goals, the structure also allows the White House to distance itself from the RMOs' decisions when convenient.

Admittedly, the RMOs' work sounds technocratic, sometimes portrayed merely as "bean counting" by staff who wear green eyeshades. Yet despite the image of day-to-day budget decisions as routine and unimportant for the public to track, even the smallest budgetary decisions involve tradeoffs and value choices, which the complexity and opacity of the RMOs' work only obscures.

Opportunities to address these accountability concerns exist both inside and outside the executive branch. For example, the President could issue an executive order governing the RMOs' work, just as each President for the last thirty years has issued an executive order governing OIRA's. An RMO executive order would both tie the RMOs' work more closely to the President's authority and also make that work more transparent.

From outside the executive branch, Congress could increase the RMOs' accountability by paying closer attention to their work. It might, for example, ask agencies about policy alternatives that OMB rejected, as Congress currently does now with the military services' budget requests. It might also ask the political appointees at the helm of each RMO to testify about their priorities.

More generally, though, scholars and others who watch the administrative state ought to include the RMOs in their thinking about presidential control. More than a thousand law review articles discussing OIRA have been published in the last twenty years. Only a handful mention the RMOs. But the RMOs' ability to influence policy through the budget process is significant. . . .

Notes and Questions

1. The "budget side" of presidential control over agency action is extremely significant. Professor Pasachoff recommends that the President issue an executive order to both increase transparency of the way in which RMOs do their work and also increase the connection between the President and the actions RMOs take. How far should transparency go? For instance, should there be required disclosure of contacts between RMOs and the agency? Or would that create additional incentives for agencies to behave strategically in their negotiations with their RMOs? *See* Eloise Pasachoff, *The President's Budget as a Source of Agency Policy Control*, 125 YALE L.J. 2182 (2016). Even if there is greater disclosure, the budget issues are often obscure, requiring some experience or diligence to figure out the effects of decision. As a result, transparency in the process must be coupled with interest group and other forms of civil society oversight.

2. What are the virtues of the President exerting some control over how agencies spend their funds? On the one hand, it seems like a direct way of implementing presidential priorities in agency action. As long as it is transparent, one might say that it merely increases accountability. On the other hand, our constitutional structure puts Congress in charge of the purse strings. If there is some inevitable discretion in the process of spending appropriated funds, shouldn't the President's preferences matter?

3. The President's control over agency spending also has to be examined in light of the President's formal review and supervision of agency policy, which happens under what is known as regulatory planning and review, to which we now turn.

4. Regulatory Planning and Review

In Chapter 5, we noted that every President since Ronald Reagan has issued an executive order requiring executive-branch agencies to perform cost-benefit analysis. We now situate cost-benefit analysis in its broader political context. It is a critical part of a larger process for centralizing regulatory planning and review in the White House. In relatively short order, that process has become one of the most important tools for the President to assert control of agency action.

The concept of centralizing regulatory planning and review in the White House first emerged during the 1970s as a means of controlling inflation. It was transformed in 1982, when President Reagan issued an executive order establishing a process for centralizing regulatory planning and review in the White House specifically as a means of downsizing government. The executive order authorized the Office of Management and Budget (OMB) and, more particularly, its subunit, the Office of Information and Regulatory Affairs (OIRA), to coordinate and evaluate major rulemaking proposals. Exec. Order No. 12,291, 3 C.F.R. §127 (1982), *reprinted in* 5 U.S.C. §601 (2000). President George H.W. Bush retained the OIRA process, creating the Council on Competitiveness in Vice President Dan Quayle's office to oversee it. President Clinton also retained the OIRA process, though he abolished the Council on Competitiveness. *See* Exec. Order No. 12,866, 3 C.F.R. §638 (1993), *reprinted in* 5 U.S.C. §601 (2001). But he justified the process differently, as part of an effort to reinvent government rather than reduce it. By the time President George W. Bush arrived, preserving the OIRA process was a foregone conclusion. But President Bush made several changes that sparked considerable controversy, including extending regulatory review not only to proposed rules but to proposed guidance documents and installing a presidentially selected Regulatory Review Compliance Officer in each executive-branch agency. *See* Exec. Order No. 13,422, 72 Fed. Reg. 2763 (2007). On January 30, 2009, President Obama revoked the Bush version, returning the executive order to the form that had prevailed between 1993 and 2007. On January 18, 2011, President Obama issued Executive Order No. 13, 563, which maintained the same basic structure but, significantly, also required agencies to perform retrospective analysis of existing rules. President Trump has largely maintained that structure of regulatory review, with one very significant change. President Trump has imposed a requirement that agencies repeal two existing regulations for each new regulation they issue, and perhaps even more significantly, not adopt any regulations that impose addition net costs for compliance. *See* Reducing Regulation and Controlling Regulatory Costs, Exec. Order No. 13771 (Jan. 30, 2017).

Under Executive Order No. 12,866, note that planning and review are distinctive mechanisms within the OIRA process. Only the planning mechanism applies to independent agencies. During the Reagan administration, the Office of Legal Counsel issued a memorandum stating that the President could, as a legal matter, subject independent agencies to regulatory review. *See* Memorandum for the Hon. David Stockman, Dir., Office of Mgmt. & Budget, from Larry L. Simms, Acting Ass't Atty. Gen., Office of Legal Counsel (Feb. 12, 1981), *reprinted in part in* PETER M. SHANE & HAROLD H. BRUFF, SEPARATION OF POWERS LAW: CASES AND MATERIALS 495-497 (3D ED. 2011). Can you make the legal arguments for applying the regulatory review mechanism to independent agencies? Even if legal, how might Congress respond?

Before turning to Executive Order No. 12,866, it is useful to note some general information about executive orders. Executive orders are binding on the executive-branch institutions or officials to whom they are directed (including, in some circumstances, independent agencies), create no cause of action against the government, and apply only to the extent permitted by law (statutory and constitutional). Executive orders are published in the *Federal Register* when issued and also compiled in the *Code of Federal Regulations* on an annual basis. The President can revoke or amend an executive order at any time. New Presidents can follow existing executive orders, replace them with new executive orders, or revoke them entirely.

Executive Order No. 12,866, Regulatory Planning and Review

3 C.F.R. §638 (1993), *reprinted in* 5 U.S.C. §601 (2001)

The American people deserve a regulatory system that works for them, not against them: a regulatory system that protects and improves their health, safety, environment, and well-being and improves the performance of the economy without imposing unacceptable or unreasonable costs on society; regulatory policies that recognize that the private sector and private markets are the best engine for economic growth; regulatory approaches that respect the role of State, local, and tribal governments; and regulations that are effective, consistent, sensible, and understandable. We do not have such a regulatory system today.

With this Executive order, the Federal Government begins a program to reform and make more efficient the regulatory process. The objectives of this Executive order are to enhance planning and coordination with respect to both new and existing regulations; to reaffirm the primacy of Federal agencies in the regulatory decision-making process; to restore the integrity and legitimacy of regulatory review and oversight; and to make the process more accessible and open to the public. In pursuing these objectives, the regulatory process shall be conducted so as to meet applicable statutory requirements and with due regard to the discretion that has been entrusted to the Federal agencies.

Accordingly, by the authority vested in me as President by the Constitution and the laws of the United States of America, it is hereby ordered as follows:

Section 1. *Statement of Regulatory Philosophy and Principles.*

(a) *The Regulatory Philosophy.* Federal agencies should promulgate only such regulations as are required by law, are necessary to interpret the law, or are made necessary by compelling public need, such as material failures of private markets to protect or improve the health and safety of the public, the environment, or the well-being of the American people. In deciding whether and how to regulate, agencies should assess all costs and benefits of available regulatory alternatives, including the alternative of not regulating. Costs and benefits shall be understood to include both quantifiable measures (to the fullest extent that these can be usefully estimated) and qualitative measures of costs and benefits that are difficult to quantify, but nevertheless essential to consider. Further, in choosing among alternative regulatory approaches, agencies should select those approaches that maximize net benefits (including potential economic, environmental, public health and safety, and other advantages; distributive impacts; and equity), unless a statute requires another regulatory approach.

(b) *The Principles of Regulation.* To ensure that the agencies' regulatory programs are consistent with the philosophy set forth above, agencies should adhere to the following principles, to the extent permitted by law and where applicable:

(1) Each agency shall identify the problem that it intends to address (including, where applicable, the failures of private markets or public institutions that warrant new agency action) as well as assess the significance of that problem.

(2) Each agency shall examine whether existing regulations (or other law) have created, or contributed to, the problem that a new regulation is intended to correct and whether those regulations (or other law) should be modified to achieve the intended goal of regulation more effectively.

(3) Each agency shall identify and assess available alternatives to direct regulation, including providing economic incentives to encourage the desired behavior, such as user fees or marketable permits, or providing information upon which choices can be made by the public.

(4) In setting regulatory priorities, each agency shall consider, to the extent reasonable, the degree and nature of the risks posed by various substances or activities within its jurisdiction.

(5) When an agency determines that a regulation is the best available method of achieving the regulatory objective, it shall design its regulations in the most cost-effective manner to achieve the regulatory objective. In doing so, each agency shall consider incentives for innovation, consistency, predictability, the costs of enforcement and compliance (to the government, regulated entities, and the public), flexibility, distributive impacts, and equity.

(6) Each agency shall assess both the costs and the benefits of the intended regulation and, recognizing that some costs and benefits are difficult to quantify, propose or adopt a regulation only upon a reasoned determination that the benefits of the intended regulation justify its costs.

(7) Each agency shall base its decisions on the best reasonably obtainable scientific, technical, economic, and other information concerning the need for, and consequences of, the intended regulation.

(8) Each agency shall identify and assess alternative forms of regulation and shall, to the extent feasible, specify performance objectives, rather than specifying the behavior or manner of compliance that regulated entities must adopt.

(9) Wherever feasible, agencies shall seek views of appropriate State, local, and tribal officials before imposing regulatory requirements that might significantly or uniquely affect those governmental entities. Each agency shall assess the effects of Federal regulations on State, local, and tribal governments, including specifically the availability of resources to carry out those mandates, and seek to minimize those burdens that uniquely or significantly affect such governmental entities, consistent with achieving regulatory objectives. In addition, as appropriate, agencies shall seek to harmonize Federal regulatory actions with related State, local, and tribal regulatory and other governmental functions.

(10) Each agency shall avoid regulations that are inconsistent, incompatible, or duplicative with its other regulations or those of other Federal agencies.

(11) Each agency shall tailor its regulations to impose the least burden on society, including individuals, businesses of differing sizes, and other entities (including small communities and governmental entities), consistent with obtaining the regulatory objectives, taking into account, among other things, and to the extent practicable, the costs of cumulative regulations.

(12) Each agency shall draft its regulations to be simple and easy to understand, with the goal of minimizing the potential for uncertainty and litigation arising from such uncertainty.

Section 2. *Organization.* An efficient regulatory planning and review process is vital to ensure that the Federal Government's regulatory system best serves the American people.

(a) *The Agencies.* Because Federal agencies are the repositories of significant substantive expertise and experience, they are responsible for developing regulations and assuring that the regulations are consistent with applicable law, the President's priorities, and the principles set forth in this Executive order.

(b) *The Office of Management and Budget.* Coordinated review of agency rulemaking is necessary to ensure that regulations are consistent with applicable law, the President's priorities, and the principles set forth in this Executive order, and that decisions made by one agency do not conflict with the policies or actions taken or planned by another agency. The Office of Management and Budget (OMB) shall carry out that review function. Within OMB, the Office of Information and Regulatory Affairs (OIRA) is the repository of expertise concerning regulatory issues, including methodologies and procedures that affect more than one agency, this Executive order, and the President's regulatory policies. To the extent permitted by law, OMB shall provide guidance to agencies and assist the President, the Vice President, and other regulatory policy advisors to the President in regulatory planning and shall be the entity that reviews individual regulations, as provided by this Executive order.

(c) *The Vice President.* The Vice President is the principal advisor to the President on, and shall coordinate the development and presentation of recommendations concerning, regulatory policy, planning, and review, as set forth in this Executive order. In fulfilling their responsibilities under this Executive order, the President and the Vice President shall be assisted by the regulatory policy advisors within the Executive Office of the President and by such agency officials and personnel as the President and the Vice President may, from time to time, consult.

Section 3. *Definitions.* For purposes of this Executive order:

(a) "Advisors" refers to such regulatory policy advisors to the President as the President and Vice President may from time to time consult, including, among others:

(1) the Director of OMB;

(2) the Chair (or another member) of the Council of Economic Advisers;

(3) the Assistant to the President for Economic Policy;

(4) the Assistant to the President for Domestic Policy;

(5) the Assistant to the President for National Security Affairs;

(6) the Assistant to the President for Science and Technology;

(7) the Assistant to the President for Intergovernmental Affairs;

(8) the Assistant to the President and Staff Secretary;

(9) the Assistant to the President and Chief of Staff to the Vice President;

(10) the Assistant to the President and Counsel to the President;

(11) the Deputy Assistant to the President and Director of the White House Office on Environmental Policy; and

(12) the Administrator of OIRA, who also shall coordinate communications relating to this Executive order among the agencies, OMB, the other Advisors, and the Office of the Vice President.

(b) "Agency," unless otherwise indicated, means any authority of the United States that is an "agency" under 44 U.S.C. 3502(1), other than those considered to be independent regulatory agencies, as defined in 44 U.S.C. 3502(10).

(c) "Director" means the Director of OMB.

(d) "Regulation" or "rule" means an agency statement of general applicability and future effect, which the agency intends to have the force and effect of law, that is designed to implement, interpret, or prescribe law or policy or to describe the procedure or practice requirements of an agency. It does not, however, include:

(1) Regulations or rules issued in accordance with the formal rulemaking provisions of 5 U.S.C. 556, 557;

(2) Regulations or rules that pertain to a military or foreign affairs function of the United States, other than procurement regulations and regulations involving the import or export of non-defense articles and services;

(3) Regulations or rules that are limited to agency organization, management, or personnel matters; or

(4) Any other category of regulations exempted by the Administrator of OIRA.

(e) "Regulatory action" means any substantive action by an agency (normally published in the *Federal Register*) that promulgates or is expected to lead to the promulgation of a final rule or regulation, including notices of inquiry, advance notices of proposed rulemaking, and notices of proposed rulemaking.

(f) "Significant regulatory action" means any regulatory action that is likely to result in a rule that may:

(1) Have an annual effect on the economy of $100 million or more or adversely affect in a material way the economy, a sector of the economy, productivity, competition, jobs, the environment,

public health or safety, or State, local, or tribal governments or communities;

(2) Create a serious inconsistency or otherwise interfere with an action taken or planned by another agency;

(3) Materially alter the budgetary impact of entitlements, grants, user fees, or loan programs or the rights and obligations of recipients thereof; or

(4) Raise novel legal or policy issues arising out of legal mandates, the President's priorities, or the principles set forth in this Executive order.

Section 4. *Planning Mechanism.* In order to have an effective regulatory program, to provide for coordination of regulations, to maximize consultation and the resolution of potential conflicts at an early stage, to involve the public and its State, local, and tribal officials in regulatory planning, and to ensure that new or revised regulations promote the President's priorities and the principles set forth in this Executive order, these procedures shall be followed, to the extent permitted by law:

(a) *Agencies' Policy Meeting.* Early in each year's planning cycle, the Vice President shall convene a meeting of the Advisors and the heads of agencies to seek a common understanding of priorities and to coordinate regulatory efforts to be accomplished in the upcoming year.

(b) *Unified Regulatory Agenda.* For purposes of this subsection, the term "agency" or "agencies" shall also include those considered to be independent regulatory agencies, as defined in 44 U.S.C. 3502(10). Each agency shall prepare an agenda of all regulations under development or review, at a time and in a manner specified by the Administrator of OIRA. The description of each regulatory action shall contain, at a minimum, a regulation identifier number, a brief summary of the action, the legal authority for the action, any legal deadline for the action, and the name and telephone number of a knowledgeable agency official. Agencies may incorporate the information required under 5 U.S.C. 602 and 41 U.S.C. 402 into these agendas.

(c) *The Regulatory Plan.* For purposes of this subsection, the term "agency" or "agencies" shall also include those considered to be independent regulatory agencies, as defined in 44 U.S.C. 3502(10).

(1) As part of the Unified Regulatory Agenda, beginning in 1994, each agency shall prepare a Regulatory Plan (Plan) of the most important significant regulatory actions that the agency reasonably expects to issue in proposed or final form in that fiscal year or thereafter. The Plan shall be approved personally by the agency head and shall contain at a minimum:

(A) A statement of the agency's regulatory objectives and priorities and how they relate to the President's priorities;

(B) A summary of each planned significant regulatory action including, to the extent possible, alternatives to be considered and preliminary estimates of the anticipated costs and benefits;

(C) A summary of the legal basis for each such action, including whether any aspect of the action is required by statute or court order;

(D) A statement of the need for each such action and, if applicable, how the action will reduce risks to public health, safety, or the environment, as well as how the magnitude of the risk addressed by the action relates to other risks within the jurisdiction of the agency;

(E) The agency's schedule for action, including a statement of any applicable statutory or judicial deadlines; and

(F) The name, address, and telephone number of a person the public may contact for additional information about the planned regulatory action.

(2) Each agency shall forward its Plan to OIRA by June 1st of each year.

(3) Within 10 calendar days after OIRA has received an agency's Plan, OIRA shall circulate it to other affected agencies, the Advisors, and the Vice President.

(4) An agency head who believes that a planned regulatory action of another agency may conflict with its own policy or action taken or planned shall promptly notify, in writing, the Administrator of OIRA, who shall forward that communication to the issuing agency, the Advisors, and the Vice President.

(5) If the Administrator of OIRA believes that a planned regulatory action of an agency may be inconsistent with the President's priorities or the principles set forth in this Executive order or may be in conflict with any policy or action taken or planned by another agency, the Administrator of OIRA shall promptly notify, in writing, the affected agencies, the Advisors, and the Vice President.

(6) The Vice President, with the Advisors' assistance, may consult with the heads of agencies with respect to their Plans and, in appropriate instances, request further consideration or interagency coordination.

(7) The Plans developed by the issuing agency shall be published annually in the October publication of the Unified Regulatory Agenda. This publication shall be made available to the Congress; State, local, and tribal governments; and the public. Any views on any aspect of any agency Plan, including whether any

planned regulatory action might conflict with any other planned or existing regulation, impose any unintended consequences on the public, or confer any unclaimed benefits on the public, should be directed to the issuing agency, with a copy to OIRA.

(d) *Regulatory Working Group.* Within 30 days of the date of this Executive order, the Administrator of OIRA shall convene a Regulatory Working Group ("Working Group"), which shall consist of representatives of the heads of each agency that the Administrator determines to have significant domestic regulatory responsibility, the Advisors, and the Vice President. The Administrator of OIRA shall chair the Working Group and shall periodically advise the Vice President on the activities of the Working Group. The Working Group shall serve as a forum to assist agencies in identifying and analyzing important regulatory issues (including, among others (1) the development of innovative regulatory techniques, (2) the methods, efficacy, and utility of comparative risk assessment in regulatory decision-making, and (3) the development of short forms and other streamlined regulatory approaches for small businesses and other entities). The Working Group shall meet at least quarterly and may meet as a whole or in subgroups of agencies with an interest in particular issues or subject areas. To inform its discussions, the Working Group may commission analytical studies and reports by OIRA, the Administrative Conference of the United States, or any other agency.

(e) *Conferences.* The Administrator of OIRA shall meet quarterly with representatives of State, local, and tribal governments to identify both existing and proposed regulations that may uniquely or significantly affect those governmental entities. The Administrator of OIRA shall also convene, from time to time, conferences with representatives of businesses, nongovernmental organizations, and the public to discuss regulatory issues of common concern.

Section 5. *Existing Regulations.* In order to reduce the regulatory burden on the American people, their families, their communities, their State, local, and tribal governments, and their industries; to determine whether regulations promulgated by the executive branch of the Federal Government have become unjustified or unnecessary as a result of changed circumstances; to confirm that regulations are both compatible with each other and not duplicative or inappropriately burdensome in the aggregate; to ensure that all regulations are consistent with the President's priorities and the principles set forth in this Executive order, within applicable law; and to otherwise improve the effectiveness of existing regulations:

(a) Within 90 days of the date of this Executive order, each agency shall submit to OIRA a program, consistent with its resources and regulatory priorities, under which the agency will periodically review its existing significant regulations to determine whether any such regulations should be modified or eliminated so as to make the agency's regulatory program more effective in achieving the regulatory objectives, less burdensome, or in greater alignment with the President's priorities and the principles set forth in this Executive order. Any significant regulations selected for review shall be included in the agency's annual Plan. The agency shall also identify any legislative mandates that require the agency to promulgate or continue to impose regulations that the agency believes are unnecessary or outdated by reason of changed circumstances.

(b) The Administrator of OIRA shall work with the Regulatory Working Group and other interested entities to pursue the objectives of this section. State, local, and tribal governments are specifically encouraged to assist in the identification of regulations that impose significant or unique burdens on those governmental entities and that appear to have outlived their justification or be otherwise inconsistent with the public interest.

(c) The Vice President, in consultation with the Advisors, may identify for review by the appropriate agency or agencies other existing regulations of an agency or groups of regulations of more than one agency that affect a particular group, industry, or sector of the economy, or may identify legislative mandates that may be appropriate for reconsideration by the Congress.

Section 6. *Centralized Review of Regulations.* The guidelines set forth below shall apply to all regulatory actions, for both new and existing regulations, by agencies other than those agencies specifically exempted by the Administrator of OIRA:

(a) *Agency Responsibilities.*

(1) Each agency shall (consistent with its own rules, regulations, or procedures) provide the public with meaningful participation in the regulatory process. In particular, before issuing a notice of proposed rulemaking, each agency should, where appropriate, seek the involvement of those who are intended to benefit from and those expected to be burdened by any regulation (including, specifically, State, local, and tribal officials). In addition, each agency should afford the public a meaningful opportunity to comment on any proposed regulation, which in most cases should include a comment period of not less than 60 days. Each agency also is directed to explore and, where appropriate, use consensual mechanisms for developing regulations, including negotiated rulemaking.

(2) Within 60 days of the date of this Executive order, each agency head shall designate a Regulatory Policy Officer who shall report to the agency head. The Regulatory Policy Officer shall be involved at each stage of the regulatory process to foster the

development of effective, innovative, and least burdensome regulations and to further the principles set forth in this Executive order.

(3) In addition to adhering to its own rules and procedures and to the requirements of the Administrative Procedure Act, the Regulatory Flexibility Act, the Paperwork Reduction Act, and other applicable law, each agency shall develop its regulatory actions in a timely fashion and adhere to the following procedures with respect to a regulatory action:

(A) Each agency shall provide OIRA, at such times and in the manner specified by the Administrator of OIRA, with a list of its planned regulatory actions, indicating those which the agency believes are significant regulatory actions within the meaning of this Executive order. Absent a material change in the development of the planned regulatory action, those not designated as significant will not be subject to review under this section unless, within 10 working days of receipt of the list, the Administrator of OIRA notifies the agency that OIRA has determined that a planned regulation is a significant regulatory action within the meaning of this Executive order. The Administrator of OIRA may waive review of any planned regulatory action designated by the agency as significant, in which case the agency need not further comply with subsection (a)(3)(B) or subsection (a)(3)(C) of this section.

(B) For each matter identified as, or determined by the Administrator of OIRA to be, a significant regulatory action, the issuing agency shall provide to OIRA:

(i) The text of the draft regulatory action, together with a reasonably detailed description of the need for the regulatory action and an explanation of how the regulatory action will meet that need; and

(ii) An assessment of the potential costs and benefits of the regulatory action, including an explanation of the manner in which the regulatory action is consistent with a statutory mandate and, to the extent permitted by law, promotes the President's priorities and avoids undue interference with State, local, and tribal governments in the exercise of their governmental functions.

(C) For those matters identified as, or determined by the Administrator of OIRA to be, a significant regulatory action within the scope of section 3(f)(1), the agency shall also provide to OIRA the following additional information developed as part of the agency's decision-making process (unless prohibited by law):

> (i) An assessment, including the underlying analysis, of benefits anticipated from the regulatory action (such as, but not limited to, the promotion of the efficient functioning of the economy and private markets, the enhancement of health and safety, the protection of the natural environment, and the elimination or reduction of discrimination or bias) together with, to the extent feasible, a quantification of those benefits;

> (ii) An assessment, including the underlying analysis, of costs anticipated from the regulatory action (such as, but not limited to, the direct cost both to the government in administering the regulation and to businesses and others in complying with the regulation, and any adverse effects on the efficient functioning of the economy, private markets (including productivity, employment, and competitiveness), health, safety, and the natural environment), together with, to the extent feasible, a quantification of those costs; and

> (iii) An assessment, including the underlying analysis, of costs and benefits of potentially effective and reasonably feasible alternatives to the planned regulation, identified by the agencies or the public (including improving the current regulation and reasonably viable nonregulatory actions), and an explanation why the planned regulatory action is preferable to the identified potential alternatives.

(D) In emergency situations or when an agency is obligated by law to act more quickly than normal review procedures allow, the agency shall notify OIRA as soon as possible and, to the extent practicable, comply with subsections (a)(3)(B) and (C) of this section. For those regulatory actions that are governed by a statutory or court-imposed deadline, the agency shall, to the extent practicable, schedule rulemaking proceedings so as to permit sufficient time for OIRA to conduct its review, as set forth below in subsection (b)(2) through (4) of this section.

(E) After the regulatory action has been published in the *Federal Register* or otherwise issued to the public, the agency shall:

> (i) Make available to the public the information set forth in subsections (a)(3)(B) and (C);

(ii) Identify for the public, in a complete, clear, and simple manner, the substantive changes between the draft submitted to OIRA for review and the action subsequently announced; and

(iii) Identify for the public those changes in the regulatory action that were made at the suggestion or recommendation of OIRA.

(F) All information provided to the public by the agency shall be in plain, understandable language.

(b) *OIRA Responsibilities.* The Administrator of OIRA shall provide meaningful guidance and oversight so that each agency's regulatory actions are consistent with applicable law, the President's priorities, and the principles set forth in this Executive order and do not conflict with the policies or actions of another agency. OIRA shall, to the extent permitted by law, adhere to the following guidelines:

(1) OIRA may review only actions identified by the agency or by OIRA as significant regulatory actions under subsection (a)(3)(A) of this section.

(2) OIRA shall waive review or notify the agency in writing of the results of its review within the following time periods:

(A) For any notices of inquiry, advance notices of proposed rulemaking, or other preliminary regulatory actions prior to a Notice of Proposed Rulemaking, within 10 working days after the date of submission of the draft action to OIRA;

(B) For all other regulatory actions, within 90 calendar days after the date of submission of the information set forth in subsections (a)(3)(B) and (C) of this section, unless OIRA has previously reviewed this information and, since that review, there has been no material change in the facts and circumstances upon which the regulatory action is based, in which case, OIRA shall complete its review within 45 days; and

(C) The review process may be extended (1) once by no more than 30 calendar days upon the written approval of the Director and (2) at the request of the agency head.

(3) For each regulatory action that the Administrator of OIRA returns to an agency for further consideration of some or all of its provisions, the Administrator of OIRA shall provide the issuing agency a written explanation for such return, setting forth the pertinent provision of this Executive order on which OIRA is relying.

If the agency head disagrees with some or all of the bases for the return, the agency head shall so inform the Administrator of OIRA in writing.

(4) Except as otherwise provided by law or required by a Court, in order to ensure greater openness, accessibility, and accountability in the regulatory review process, OIRA shall be governed by the following disclosure requirements:

(A) Only the Administrator of OIRA (or a particular designee) shall receive oral communications initiated by persons not employed by the executive branch of the Federal Government regarding the substance of a regulatory action under OIRA review;

(B) All substantive communications between OIRA personnel and persons not employed by the executive branch of the Federal Government regarding a regulatory action under review shall be governed by the following guidelines:

(i) A representative from the issuing agency shall be invited to any meeting between OIRA personnel and such person(s);

(ii) OIRA shall forward to the issuing agency, within 10 working days of receipt of the communication(s), all written communications, regardless of format, between OIRA personnel and any person who is not employed by the executive branch of the Federal Government, and the dates and names of individuals involved in all substantive oral communications (including meetings to which an agency representative was invited, but did not attend, and telephone conversations between OIRA personnel and any such persons); and

(iii) OIRA shall publicly disclose relevant information about such communication(s), as set forth below in subsection (b)(4)(C) of this section.

(C) OIRA shall maintain a publicly available log that shall contain, at a minimum, the following information pertinent to regulatory actions under review:

(i) The status of all regulatory actions, including if (and if so, when and by whom) Vice Presidential and Presidential consideration was requested;

(ii) A notation of all written communications forwarded to an issuing agency under subsection (b)(4)(B)(ii) of this section; and

(iii) The dates and names of individuals involved in all substantive oral communications, including meetings and telephone conversations, between OIRA personnel and any person not employed by the executive branch of the Federal Government, and the subject matter discussed during such communications.

(D) After the regulatory action has been published in the *Federal Register* or otherwise issued to the public, or after the agency has announced its decision not to publish or issue the regulatory action, OIRA shall make available to the public all documents exchanged between OIRA and the agency during the review by OIRA under this section.

(5) All information provided to the public by OIRA shall be in plain, understandable language.

Section 7. *Resolution of Conflicts.* To the extent permitted by law, disagreements or conflicts between or among agency heads or between OMB and any agency that cannot be resolved by the Administrator of OIRA shall be resolved by the President, or by the Vice President acting at the request of the President, with the relevant agency head (and, as appropriate, other interested government officials). Vice Presidential and Presidential consideration of such disagreements may be initiated only by the Director, by the head of the issuing agency, or by the head of an agency that has a significant interest in the regulatory action at issue. Such review will not be undertaken at the request of other persons, entities, or their agents.

Resolution of such conflicts shall be informed by recommendations developed by the Vice President, after consultation with the Advisors (and other executive branch officials or personnel whose responsibilities to the President include the subject matter at issue). The development of these recommendations shall be concluded within 60 days after review has been requested.

During the Vice Presidential and Presidential review period, communications with any person not employed by the Federal Government relating to the substance of the regulatory action under review and directed to the Advisors or their staffs or to the staff of the Vice President shall be in writing and shall be forwarded by the recipient to the affected agency(ies) for inclusion in the public docket(s). When the communication is not in writing, such Advisors or staff members shall inform the outside party that the matter is under review and that any comments should be submitted in writing.

At the end of this review process, the President, or the Vice President acting at the request of the President, shall notify the affected agency and the Administrator of OIRA of the President's decision with respect to the matter.

Section 8. *Publication.* Except to the extent required by law, an agency shall not publish in the *Federal Register* or otherwise issue to the public any regulatory action that is subject to review under section 6 of this Executive order until (1) the Administrator of OIRA notifies the agency that OIRA has waived its review of the action or has completed its review without any requests for further consideration, or (2) the applicable time period in section 6(b)(2) expires without OIRA having notified the agency that it is returning the regulatory action for further consideration under section 6(b)(3), whichever occurs first. If the terms of the preceding sentence have not been satisfied and an agency wants to publish or otherwise issue a regulatory action, the head of that agency may request Presidential consideration through the Vice President, as provided under section 7 of this order. Upon receipt of this request, the Vice President shall notify OIRA and the Advisors. The guidelines and time period set forth in section 7 shall apply to the publication of regulatory actions for which Presidential consideration has been sought.

Section 9. *Agency Authority.* Nothing in this order shall be construed as displacing the agencies' authority or responsibilities, as authorized by law.

Section 10. *Judicial Review.* Nothing in this Executive order shall affect any otherwise available judicial review of agency action. This Executive order is intended only to improve the internal management of the Federal Government and does not create any right or benefit, substantive or procedural, enforceable at law or equity by a party against the United States, its agencies or instrumentalities, its officers or employees, or any other person.

Section 11. *Revocations.* Executive Orders Nos. 12291 and 12498; all amendments to those Executive orders; all guidelines issued under those orders; and any exemptions from those orders heretofore granted for any category of rule are revoked.

WILLIAM CLINTON

Notes and Questions

1. You can now see that Executive Order No. 12,866 has two basic mechanisms: a planning mechanism and a review mechanism. What does the planning mechanism specifically require agencies to do? What does it specifically require OIRA to do? How does it achieve control of agency action when viewed from the White House's perspective?

2. The same questions for the review mechanism. What does that mechanism specifically require agencies to do? What does it specifically require OIRA to do? How does it achieve control of agency action when viewed from the White House's perspective?

3. Under Executive Order No. 12,866, is an agency required to perform and submit a cost-benefit analysis even if its organic statute prohibits or restricts cost considerations? What would OIRA argue? What is the opposite view?

4. In Chapter 5, we discussed cost-benefit analysis as a tool of statutory implementation that agencies employ. Is OIRA likely to apply cost-benefit analysis in the same manner as agencies do? Does it depend on who works for OIRA and how they were trained? Although OIRA houses high-level policy officials, career economists review many routine regulations. Some of those career economists have been there for decades, applying the economic methodologies that they learned in graduate school. *See* Lisa Schultz Bressman & Michael P. Vandenbergh, *Inside the Administrative State: A Critical Look at the Practice of Presidential Control*, 105 MICH. L. REV. 47, 74 (2006). These individuals are viewed by some as unduly focused on minimizing costs, fueling criticism that OIRA review has an anti-regulatory effect. *See* Nicholas Bagley & Richard L. Revesz, *Centralized Oversight of the Regulatory State*, 106 COLUM. L. REV. 1260, 1267-70 (2006). We will return to these issues below.

5. What happens in cases of conflict between OIRA and an agency? Under Executive Order No. 12,866, how are such conflicts resolved? As a practical matter, how often do you suppose it reaches that level? What other recourse might an agency have in cases of conflict?

6. Executive Order No. 12,866 requires OIRA to adhere to certain requirements concerning communications, meetings, and documents. For example, only the OIRA Administrator may receive oral communications with persons outside the agency whose proposed regulation is being reviewed. A person from the agency must be present at all meetings between OIRA and outsiders regarding the agency's regulation. Written communications from outsiders must be forwarded to the agency within ten days of receipt. OIRA must maintain a public log containing the status of all actions and the receipt of written communications. After the regulation has been issued, OIRA must make available all documents exchanged between OIRA and the agency. What is the purpose of these requirements, taken together?

7. Finally, note that Executive Order No. 12,866 functions not only as a tool for asserting control of agency action but also as a tool for obtaining information about agency action. The White House otherwise would face a seemingly insurmountable task of acquiring such information, which is a prerequisite to exercising control. How else would the White House know which among the thousands of proposed regulations require attention? This need for information about agency action is a persistent problem that also affects Congress, as we will discuss below. Certain tools allow political officials to improve the efficiency of monitoring agency action. Executive Order No. 12,866 is one because it identifies all significant proposed regulations and provides information to OIRA about them. Look for others as we go along.

a. Return and Prompt Letters

To communicate its preferences in response to information learned about planned or proposed regulations, OIRA can issue "return letters" and "prompt letters." Both are formal, publicly accessible documents addressed to particular agency officials, but with different roles. Return letters remit proposed regulations to the agency that produced them for reconsideration, providing an explanation of the deficiencies and suggestions for further development. Prompt letters address an agency's plans or priorities for a given year. Such letters might suggest that an agency "explore a promising regulatory issue for agency action, accelerate its efforts on an ongoing

regulatory matter, or consider rescinding or modifying an existing rule."
John D. Graham, OIRA Administrator, Memorandum for the President's
Management Council, Sept. 20, 2001. OIRA will request an agency response
to the prompt letter, usually within 30 days.

Read the letters below to get a sense for how OIRA actually asserts control of agency action. The first is a return letter, and the latter two are prompt letters with agency responses. Ask yourself how easy it is for an agency to disregard letters of this sort. If the answer is "not very," pinpoint what about the letters makes that so.

EXECUTIVE OFFICE OF THE PRESIDENT
OFFICE OF MANAGEMENT AND BUDGET
WASHINGTON. D.C. 20503
ADMINISTRATOR
OFFICE OF INFORMATION
AND REGULATORY AFFAIRS

Aug. 22, 2003
Ms. Rosalind A. Knapp
Deputy General Counsel
Department of Transportation
400 Seventh Street, S.W.
Washington, D.C. 20590

Dear Ms. Knapp:

On June 6, 2003, the Department of Transportation (DOT) submitted a Research and Special Programs Administration (RSPA) draft final rule titled "Hazardous Materials: Transportation of Lithium Batteries" to the Office of Management and Budget (OMB) for review under Executive Order No. 12866. This final rule would make changes to the test methods for lithium batteries, eliminate existing exceptions from the hazard communication, and packaging requirements of the Hazardous Materials Regulations (HMR) for larger batteries and revise the exceptions for smaller batteries.

After discussions with staff at the Small Business Administration, we are returning the final rule for your reconsideration. We believe a full Initial Regulatory Flexibility Analysis (IRFA) should be prepared in order to receive additional public comment and to provide further support for RSPA's certification that the rule would not have a significant impact on a substantial number of small entities. The IRFA should include additional information that will allow RSPA to more fully address comments disputing the need for regulating lithium ion batteries, and we believe it would also be beneficial for RSPA to provide as much detail as possible on their cost estimates as there is some amount of disagreement concerning the cost of this rulemaking. It may also be prudent to gather additional information on the number of small businesses impacted and their annual revenues as some commentators have indicated this rule will cause them to incur significant costs.

Please note that the preparation of an IRFA does not necessarily mean a Supplemental Notice of Proposed Rulemaking (SNPRM) must be prepared. An IRFA can be prepared independently and published in the *Federal Register* seeking public comment. The results of the IRFA process will determine if the next step for the rulemaking should be a Final Rule or a SNPRM.

Our staff and the staff at SBA are available for further discussion with you on the concerns that have been raised. We look forward to working with you to improve this important rulemaking effort.

Sincerely,

/s/

John D. Graham, Ph.D.
Administrator

Here are the prompt letters, with agency responses. The first requests accelerated action of an issue that the agency was undertaking. The second requests consideration of an issue that the agency had not made a priority.

April 16, 2004

Benjamin Grumbles
Acting Assistant Administrator
Office of Water
U.S. Environmental Protection Agency
1200 Pennsylvania Avenue, NW
Washington, DC 20460

Dear Mr. Grumbles:

Thank you for recently briefing us on EPA's efforts to protect our oceans and beaches. We appreciate your attention to this top Administration priority as we look forward to the upcoming draft report of the U.S. Commission on Ocean Policy. In the meantime, please provide us with more information on EPA's action plan to protect our nation's beaches and ensure compliance with the BEACH Act of 2000.

As you know, the Beaches, Environmental Assessment and Coastal Health (BEACH) Act of 2000 requires coastal States, including those bordering the Great Lakes, to adopt up-to-date pathogen criteria by April 10, 2004, to protect beachgoers from harmful bacteria. The Act further provides that, if a

State fails to meet this deadline, EPA must promptly propose and promulgate Federal standards to protect that State's beaches. It is our understanding that to date, only 11 of the 35 affected States and Territories apparently have adopted criteria for pathogens as required by the BEACH Act.[3] An additional 4 States[4] have adopted criteria for some, but apparently not all, of their eligible coastal recreational waters, 14 States and Territories[5] are in the processing of adopting the required criteria, and 6 States[6] apparently have not begun the process of adopting these criteria.

Under the Clean Water Act, EPA issues criteria which serve as guidance to States in adopting standards. EPA issued criteria for *e-coli* and *enterococci* in 1986, but many States still rely on outdated standards for total or fecal coliforms. We understand that EPA's research indicates that there is little correlation between coliform levels and swimming-related illness (gastroenteritis) in either marine or fresh waters. In contrast, correlations for *e-coli* (in fresh waters) and *enterococci* (in marine waters) are high, demonstrating that these bacteria are reliable indicators for the presence of harmful pathogens.

We share your concern that American families deserve safe beaches. While we believe that it is generally preferable for States to adopt and implement their own water quality standards, as envisioned by the Clean Water Act, EPA also needs to fulfill its oversight responsibility to promote scientifically defensible, protective beach standards.

As the 2004 beach season is fast approaching, we would appreciate a prompt response to this letter. Our staffs would be happy to assist you to move forward quickly with this important initiative. Please do not hesitate to contact Jim Laity or Kameran Onley of our staffs if you would like to discuss this matter further.

Sincerely,

/s/	/s/
John D. Graham	James L. Connaughton
Administrator	Chairman
Office of Information and Regulatory Affairs	Council on Environmental Quality

---

3. [American Samoa, Connecticut, Delaware, Guam, Indiana, Maine, Michigan, New Hampshire, Ohio, Texas, Virginia.]

4. [California, Hawaii, New Jersey, Puerto Rico.]

5. [Alabama, Florida, Georgia, Illinois, Maryland, Massachusetts, Minnesota, Mississippi, North Carolina, Northern Marianas, Pennsylvania, South Carolina, Virgin Islands, Wisconsin.]

6. [Alaska, Louisiana, New York, Oregon, Rhode Island, Washington.]

April 19, 2004

Mr. James L. Connaughton
Chairman, Council on Environmental Quality
730 Jackson Place NW
Washington, DC 20503

Dr. John D. Graham
Administrator, Office of Information and Regulatory Affairs
Eisenhower Executive Office Building
725 Seventeenth Street NW
Washington, DC 20503

Dear Mr. Connaughton and Dr. Graham:

Thank you for your April 19, 2004, letter reiterating this Administration's priority of ensuring clean beaches and oceans, including the successful implementation by States and EPA of the Beaches Environmental Assessment and Coastal Health (BEACH) Act of 2000.

Over the last several years, EPA has worked with States and Territories to adopt up-to-date water quality standards to help protect recreational users of coastal beaches. We have provided more than $20 million in grants to States and Territories for developing and implementing improved standards, coastal water quality monitoring, and public notification programs. In 2002, we issued detailed guidance to States and Territories for monitoring and assessing coastal recreation waters and for notifying America's beach-going public when those waters exceed water quality standards.

As your letter affirms, EPA firmly believes that American families deserve safe beaches. We and the States and Territories must all work together to accelerate progress towards adoption of protective standards.

I am pleased to enclose our action plan to accelerate progress and to meet the requirements of the BEACH Act. Today, I signed letters to key State and Territory leaders reiterating the BEACH Act requirements and describing the steps EPA will take to make sure protective standards are in place. Shortly, EPA will announce an additional $10 million in grants to States and Territories for FY 2004 to further their monitoring and public notification programs for coastal beaches. The Administrator of EPA will also promptly sign a notice of proposed rulemaking establishing more protective standards as required by the BEACH Act for those States and Territories that have not yet met the statutory requirement to do so. The enclosed action plan also describes numerous other actions we are taking to help States and Territories protect families at coastal beaches.

We share a common desire to ensure clean and safe water at America's beaches, to collaborate with States and Territories, and, where necessary, to issue protective Federal water quality standards to advance the goals of the BEACH Act and the Clean Water Act.

Sincerely,

/s/

Benjamin H. Grumbles
Acting Assistant Administrator

Enclosure

September 18, 2001

Honorable John Henshaw
Assistant Secretary of Labor
Occupational Safety and Health Administration
Washington, DC 20210

Dear John:

The purpose of this letter is to draw your attention to a promising lifesaving technology, automatic external defibrillators (AEDs), and request that you consider whether promotion of AEDs should be elevated to a priority at the Occupational Safety and Health Administration.

When used promptly and properly, AEDs can be used to increase the rate of survival after cardiac arrest. A recent survey article in the JOURNAL OF THE AMERICAN MEDICAL ASSOCIATION concluded that: The [sic] AED represents an efficient method of delivering defibrillation to persons experiencing out-of-hospital cardiac arrest and its use by both traditional and nontraditional first responders appears to be safe and effective. [sic]

Recent articles in the NEW ENGLAND JOURNAL OF MEDICINE examined the effectiveness of AED programs in different settings. One study documented a 38% effectiveness rate in lifesaving among 148 people who suffered cardiac arrest in casinos. The other study documented a 17% AED effectiveness rate in lifesaving when available on 627,956 American Airline flights with trained flight attendants.

AEDs cost about $3,000 plus maintenance costs, primarily for batteries, of about $150 per year. A recent study in CIRCULATION found that untrained sixth graders following automated voice prompts performed almost as well in use of AEDs as well trained emergency medical technicians or paramedics. Nevertheless, for organizations that commit to AED use, there is also an incremental cost of training personnel for proper use of this technology.

In a recent editorial in the NEW ENGLAND JOURNAL OF MEDICINE, Dr. Marie Robertson noted that only 2 to 5% of the 225,000 persons who have sudden and unexpected cardiac arrest each year outside a hospital are successfully resuscitated compared to the 17 to 38% success rates found with AEDs. I do not know how many of these cases of sudden cardiac arrest occur in the workplace but it seems that this is a worthwhile question to investigate. One of my senior staff members, John Morrall, has performed some preliminary cost effectiveness calculations and determined that AEDs in the workplace might prove to be a very cost-effective intervention.

If you should determine that this matter is a priority for OSHA, a number of questions will need be investigated. The National Institute for Occupational Safety and Health, through its surveillance resources, may be able to determine the incidence of sudden cardiac arrest in the workplace. A survey of small and large private employers might need to be conducted to determine the extent of AED use in US workplaces and barriers to increased AED use.

I am aware that steps have been taken by other federal agencies to promote use of AEDs. On April 12, 2001, after OMB review, the US Department of Transportation issued a final rule (proposed in the previous Administration) that requires AEDs on all those air carriers for which at least one flight attendant is required. The accompanying regulatory impact analysis indicated that about nine lives per year would be saved, producing $25.2 million in annual benefits compared to $2.4 million in annual costs. It has also been brought to my attention that the Department of Health and Human Services and the General Services Administration have jointly developed guidelines for public access to AEDs in public buildings. The guidelines, which were published in the FEDERAL REGISTER on May 23, 2001, were developed pursuant to a May 19th 2000 Presidential memorandum. Although these steps are promising, I am not aware of any steps by the Federal government to promote the use of AEDs in private workplaces.

If you should decide that the AED issue is worthy of investigation, a series of complex questions will need to be addressed. For example, the cost-effectiveness of AED availability will depend on how many AEDs are provided in a workplace setting and what the incremental effectiveness rate for multiple AEDs proves to be. Moreover, an important question is whether AED use should be promoted by information, economic incentives, voluntary agreement, or compulsory regulation.

In requesting that OSHA consider making AEDs a priority for promotion, I understand that OSHA faces limited resources, legislative constraints, and numerous areas where steps can be taken to enhance the health and safety of workers. At this stage, I am simply asking OSHA to consider whether this matter should be a priority in the foreseeable future. I would appreciate an initial response to this inquiry within 60 days. Please do not hesitate to contact me or John Morrall if you would like to discuss this matter further.

Sincerely,

/s/

John D. Graham
Administrator
Office of Information and Regulatory Affairs

U.S. Department of Labor
Assistant Secretary for
Occupational Safety and Health
Washington, D.C. 20210

December 3, 2001

John D. Graham
Administrator
Office of Information and Regulatory Affairs
Executive Office of the President
Office of Management and Budget
Washington, D.C. 20503

Dear Dr. Graham:

This is in response to your letter of September 18, 2001, regarding automatic external defibrillators (AEDs). The Occupational Safety and Health Administration agrees that employers in America's workplaces should be made more aware of this important lifesaving technology and should be encouraged to implement AED programs where appropriate. Thirteen percent of workplace fatalities reported to OSHA during the past two years were due to cardiac arrests.

Much work has already been done to promote the use of AEDs in the workplace. For instance, the Department of Health and Human Services and the General Services Administration have developed guidelines on the use of AEDs in the Federal workplace. Similarly, the American College of Occupational and Environmental Medicine (ACOEM), the professional organization representing occupational physicians, has also developed guidelines for workplace programs. I enclose a copy of these ACOEM guidelines for your reference.

As you know, emergency medical service personnel have historically provided the initial response and treatment of sudden cardiac arrest. When such personnel utilize AEDs, early defibrillation has been shown to be a safe and effective medical intervention.

Some groups, such as the American Heart Association, have proposed more far-reaching programs under which lay personnel—as opposed to trained emergency medical service personnel—would be given greater access to AEDs. In particular, as your letter and subsequent correspondence note, the American Heart Association has proposed a public access defibrillation program which would encourage or require placement of defibrillators at readily accessible sites (*i.e.,* sites that permit a response time of five minutes or less) for use by trained lay personnel.

OSHA is aware of the American Heart Association proposal. However, there remain questions whether providing lay personnel with greater access to AEDs would actually save lives. The National Heart, Lung and Blood Institute of the National Institutes of Health, in collaboration with the American Heart Association, is currently studying the question whether or not trained volunteers can be as effective as EMS personnel. This study will be completed in 2003. We expect this study to provide important information regarding the effectiveness of the American Heart Association's proposed program.

While it awaits the results of this study, OSHA will continue to consider issues related to AED use. For example, OSHA will continue to evaluate the cost of having AEDs in workplaces in effective numbers. As noted above, the American Heart Association suggests that AEDs are most effective when placed so that the response time is five minutes or less. If the American Heart Association is correct that AEDs are optimally effective when placed so that an AED can be found and utilized within five minutes, workplaces would require numerous AEDs, which would dramatically increase the cost of an effective AED program. Similarly, the ACOEM guidelines indicate that an AED program should be part of a more general worksite emergency response plan, and should include clearly defined medical direction and control. A program following the ACOEM guidelines would likely be much more costly than some advocates' estimates.

In summary, we agree with you that more widespread awareness of this promising lifesaving technique will encourage employers to give serious consideration to installing and using AEDs in their workplaces. OSHA is in the process of preparing a Technical Information Bulletin (TIB) and an information card outlining to employers the potential benefits of AEDs in the workplace. OSHA is also compiling a Technical Link page on AEDs to add to OSHA's web site. This page will reference the guidelines mentioned above, and other sources employers may wish to consult when determining the appropriateness of an AED program for their workplaces. The web page reference will also be included on the TIB and the information card to direct employers to this more extensive information source. In addition to placing the information on the OSHA website which received over 340 million hits last year, OSHA will distribute the TIB and information card to all state plan partners and consultation programs and more then [sic] 125 trade, professional and union organizations for further dissemination.

We appreciate your interest in this important occupational safety and health issue. If you or your staff have any further questions or comments, please feel free to contact us.

Sincerely,

/s/

John L. Henshaw
Assistant Secretary

Enclosure

b. The Debate About Regulatory Planning and Review

Few doubt that the OIRA process is an effective tool for asserting control of agency action. But many question whether this is a good thing. Because the process is so central to presidential control, we take some time to explore the debate.

Supporters of the OIRA process believe that it improves the legitimacy of agency action because it increases the accountability of decisions that would otherwise be made by unelected bureaucrats. Some argue, moreover, that presidential involvement is the best way to achieve accountability; elected by a national constituency, the President arguably embodies the popular will more fully than any other elected official, including the members of

Congress. For arguments along these lines, see JERRY L. MASHAW, GREED, CHAOS, AND GOVERNANCE (1997); Elena Kagan, *Presidential Administration*, 114 HARV. L. REV. 2245 (2001). Some also argue that, because of its coordination function and cost-benefit focus, the OIRA process improves the efficacy and efficiency of agency rulemaking. OIRA is uniquely situated to provide coordination across federal agencies. By considering all planned regulations, it can ensure that there is no conflict or redundancy among them. In addition, its "outsider's" view of cost-benefit analysis encourages the production of more rational or efficient regulation. Agencies, if left to their own devices, may suffer from a certain mission orientation or "tunnel vision" that causes them to overestimate benefits or underestimate costs. For arguments along these lines, see Christopher C. Demuth & Douglas H. Ginsburg, *White House Review of Agency Rulemaking*, 99 HARV. L. REV. 1075 (1986). Finally, OIRA can spur dilatory agencies into action, providing energy or inspiration that is otherwise missing.

Critics of the OIRA process see it differently, especially the CBA component. In Chapter 5, we highlighted some general objections to cost-benefit analysis—for example, some risks are difficult to monetize, such as those to the environment or future generations. Scholars have also criticized how OIRA performs cost-benefit analysis. They argue that OIRA focuses more on costs than benefits and thus systematically undervalues regulations. *See* Nicholas Bagley & Richard L. Revesz, *Centralized Oversight of the Regulatory State*, 106 COLUM. L. REV. 1260 (2006). On this account, OIRA generally weakens rules that impose high costs as opposed to strengthening rules that promise large benefits. Part of the cause is that OIRA employs career staffers who have been around since the Reagan era and are committed to deregulation. In short, critics contend that OIRA interposes a cost-based veto that merely inhibits or delays necessary and beneficial agency regulations.

Critics also point to broader flaws in the OIRA process. Some argue that OIRA has neither the staff nor the time to perform review in an adequate manner. *See, e.g.*, Robert V. Percival, *Presidential Management of the Administrative State: The Not-So-Unitary Executive*, 51 DUKE L.J. 963, 1006-08 (2001); Mark Seidenfeld, *A Big Picture Approach to Presidential Influence on Agency Policy-Making*, 80 IOWA L. REV. 1, 14 (1994); *but see* Steven Croley, *White House Review of Agency Rulemaking: An Empirical Investigation*, 70 U. CHI. L. REV. 821 (2003). Others contend that OIRA intervenes too late in the rulemaking process to offer meaningful input. *See, e.g.*, Alan B. Morrison, *OMB Interference with Agency Rulemaking: The Wrong Way to Write a Regulation*, 99 HARV. L. REV. 1059, 1064 (1986). Some note that the OIRA process is not an open process but a secret conduit by which regulated entities can exercise undue influence over the regulatory process. *See, e.g.*, Oliver A. Houck, *President X and the New (Approved) Decisionmaking*, 36 AM. U. L. REV. 535, 551 n.94 (1987); Morrison, *OMB Interference with Agency Rulemaking*, 99 HARV. L. REV. at 1067; Erik D. Olson, *The Quiet Shift of Power: Office of Management &*

Budget Supervision of Environmental Protection Agency Rulemaking under Executive Order 12,291, 4 VA. J. NAT. RESOURCES L. 1, 28-40 (1984).

Now consider the following prompt letter to NHTSA. Ask yourself whether the letter reveals a different limitation of OIRA—not based on the quality of its analysis but on the selectivity of its intervention. Why did OIRA choose this problem from among all those that NHTSA confronts? Does the letter offer an explanation? What if OIRA fails to issue a prompt letter in response to equally or more pressing problems—for example, NHTSA's lax investigation and regulation of faulty acceleration systems that led to a massive recall of Toyotas in 2009 and 2010, only after significant public harm? *See* Auto Safety Regulator Under Scrutiny After the Toyota Fiasco, available at *http://www.ombwatch.org/node/10851*.

December 7, 2001

The Honorable Michael P. Jackson
Deputy Secretary
Department of Transportation
400 Seventh Street, SW
Washington, DC 20590

Dear Mr. Jackson:

The purpose of this letter is to request that the Department of Transportation and the National Highway Traffic Safety Administration (NHTSA) consider giving greater priority to modifying its frontal occupant protection standard by establishing a high-speed, frontal offset crash test. Such a test would seek to improve protection for the lower extremities of automobile and light truck occupants. A frontal offset crash test—which is currently conducted in the European New Car Assessment Program and by the Insurance Institute for Highway Safety—involves crashing a portion of the test vehicle's front end (instead of the entire front end) to evaluate the structural integrity of the vehicle, including the "toe pan," which helps protect the feet and legs of occupants.

Historically, one of NHTSA's principal safety goals has been to enhance the protection of vehicle occupants involved in crashes that result in life-threatening injuries to the head, neck, and chest. Safety standards requiring the installation of seat belts and air bags have reduced the frequency and severity of such injuries. As a result, more people are surviving previously fatal crashes. However, I believe there is room for improvement in the area of lower extremity injuries. I believe that paying more attention to the protection of lower extremities could build upon NHTSA's impressive record of success in addressing upper-body injury risks. I was therefore encouraged to see an offset test rulemaking in NHTSA's recent

Regulatory Agenda and urge the agency to provide this initiative significant priority.

Substantial safety improvements may be possible. Despite the existing occupant protection systems in cars and light trucks, about 3,300 people are killed and 400,000 are injured annually in frontal offset crashes. Although lower-body injuries are rarely fatal, they are often serious enough to require lengthy hospitalization and rehabilitation, and they sometimes result in years of chronic pain and impairment.

Although I realize that more thorough benefit assessment needs to be done, I suspect that the benefits of such action could substantially exceed its costs. As NHTSA noted in November 2000, a report prepared for the Australian government estimates that a new offset test may result in a 15 percent reduction in the "cost of trauma" (the product of the frequency of injuries and the cost to the public). Most of these benefits would result from a reduction in lower body and leg injuries. NHTSA's preliminary estimates then were that, for vehicles that would not currently pass this test, structural modifications would cost $14 per vehicle. Assuming that 25 percent of the fleet would need to be modified, the total annual cost to consumers would be $60 million.

If you determine that this matter should be given greater priority, a number of questions would still need to be investigated. Most importantly, NHTSA would have to refine its estimates of the specific safety benefits that a new offset test would generate. Such estimates would need to take into account potential losses in existing safety benefits due to possible changes in vehicle structure and design. For example, NHTSA would need to examine whether implementing a new offset test might create disbenefits in other crash modes such as side impacts. NHTSA would also need to estimate the number of existing vehicles that would have to be modified to pass the revised safety standard. In exploring these issues, NHTSA should assess the incremental benefits and costs of setting the new crash test at different speeds. NHTSA should also evaluate the relative merits of using different types of barriers as a potential test device. I would also encourage NHTSA to consider the possible benefits of subjecting the supporting technical and economic analyses to external peer review. I believe that taking these steps would help NHTSA ascertain the cost effectiveness of instituting the contemplated test and develop an appropriate phase-in schedule.

In requesting that NHTSA give greater priority to considering the expansion of its frontal occupant protection standard, I recognize that NHTSA faces resource constraints and other legislative mandates, such as the TREAD Act. Accordingly, I simply request that NHTSA consider whether this matter should be given greater priority in the foreseeable future. I would appreciate an initial response to this inquiry within 60 days. Please do not hesitate to contact me or Jeff Hill if you would like to discuss this matter further.

Sincerely,

/s/

John D. Graham
Administrator
Office of Information and Regulatory Affairs

cc: The Honorable Jeffrey W. Runge

Notes and Questions

1. Take the prompt letter on its own merits for a moment. It has a very different tone than the previous return letter. It identifies an aspect of the agency's planned agenda and suggests that that aspect should be given greater priority. If you were Deputy Secretary Jackson, how might you consider responding to the letter? If you were the general counsel of an automaker, how might the letter inform the advice you give to your client? What actions might you recommend that your client take?

2. Now answer the broader question that precedes this prompt letter. Should OIRA better explain which action it chooses to prompt? What exactly would OIRA say to show that its intervention, while selective, is not arbitrary? Would such an explanation help the agency respond to the recommendation? Would it enhance the legitimacy of OIRA involvement and, ultimately, agency action?

3. Why isn't it enough for OIRA to say, "We want this policy, and we are the ones who sit in the White House"? On this score, consider whether there are any reasons to doubt whether OIRA reflects presidential preferences. We discuss this issue further below.

5. Presidential Directives

The President can assert control of agency action by issuing pre-regulatory directives in the form of official memoranda to executive-branch agency heads. Such directives, particularly notable during the Clinton administration, instruct an agency to take a particular action under its existing regulatory authority—such as telling the FDA to regulate cigarettes and other tobacco products under the Food, Drug and Cosmetics Act. They are different from prompt letters because they are signed by the President not another White House official, like the OIRA Administrator. There can be no doubt that a presidential directive reflects presidential preferences.

Now Justice Elena Kagan, who brought the use of presidential directives to academic attention, argued that the practice had positive normative implications for agency action. *See* Elena Kagan, *Presidential Administration*, 114 HARV. L. REV. 2245 (2001). Because these directives come from the President, they enhance the accountability of the resulting agency action more than other measures, whether from other White House officials or members of Congress. Because they are open to public view, they also enhance the accountability of agency action. Voters cannot evaluate what they cannot see; nor can they, even in theory, hold any official responsible for such action. Thus, presidential directives do not suffer from the black-box quality of much White House involvement in agency rulemaking (though return and prompt letters are also publicly available). In addition, these directives may spur a dilatory agency into action, perhaps more powerfully than an OIRA prompt letter, and thereby increase regulatory efficacy.

Despite these arguments, presidential directives raise difficult legal questions. Where does the President derive authority to order an agency to take a particular action? It is one thing to review such actions to ensure that the agency is "faithfully executing" the laws or even to recommend certain actions as part of this duty. But most regulatory statutes delegate final say to agencies, not the President. Do those statutes grant implied authority to the President? *See* Kevin M. Stack, *The President's Statutory Powers to Administer the Laws*, 106 COLUM. L. REV. 263 (2006). What is the difference between making policy, by issuing a presidential directive, and influencing policy, by issuing a prompt letter or return letter or threatening to remove the agency head?

Even if legally authorized, what are the dangers of presidential directives? Perhaps they allow the President to alter agency decisions too powerfully and easily, without incurring the costs of legislation. Thus, if widely used, they would be an effective end-run around the rigors of the legislative process. Or perhaps they make it impossible for agencies to honestly evaluate other considerations, such as statutory arguments against cigarette regulation. Thus, they have a kind of a skewing effect on the administrative process in favor of presidential preferences. Do you agree? We revisit this question following Food & Drug Administration v. Brown & Williamson Tobacco Corp., 529 U.S. 120 (2000), excerpted below.

Although presidential directives have attracted a lot of attention, their use appears to be quite limited. *See* David J. Barron, *From Takeover to Merger: Reforming Administrative Law in the Age of Agency Politicization*, 76 GEO. WASH. L. REV. 1095, 1117-21 (2008) (suggesting that President Clinton issued at most half a dozen directives a year). The President only has so much time and personally intervenes in an official capacity (or any capacity, for that matter) on a highly selective basis. OIRA involvement, which we discussed above, is much more prevalent, as is other White House and agency involvement, which we discuss below.

6. Other White House and Agency Involvement

Beyond the President and OIRA, many other officials or offices also attempt to influence various agencies to change their regulations. In the White House, they include or have included: Chief of Staff, Legislative Affairs, Public Liaison, Intergovernmental Liaison, Press Secretary, White House Counsel, Domestic Policy Counsel, National Economic Council, Political Affairs, Office of the Vice President (including the Council on Competitiveness in the Bush I administration), Office of Policy Development, Office of Management and Budget (other than OIRA), Council of Economic Advisors, Council on Environmental Quality, Office of the United States Trade Representative, Office of Science and Technology Policy, and the National Security Council (chaired by the President).

White House offices often contact an agency in informal and invisible ways, through phone calls or meetings. Sometimes they contact OIRA to advocate on their behalf in the regulatory review process. Moreover, they can hold views that conflict with one another, raising difficult questions of which office represents the President's views. If these offices impart their own views rather than the President's views, do they render agency regulations more "accountable"? Note that, of the offices mentioned above, less than half are run by officials who are elected or subject to Senate confirmation. Those include the last five, as well as the Office of the Vice President. OIRA, within OMB, is also run by a Senate-confirmed official.

Other federal agencies are involved in the rulemaking activities of their siblings. The Department of Energy might contact the Department of Transportation or EPA concerning their respective regulations. The Secretary of the Treasury might contact the Chair of the Federal Reserve Board or the SEC. In United States v. Nova Scotia Food Products, Inc., excerpted below, you will see the Bureau of Commercial Fisheries contacting the Food and Drug Administration (to no effect as it turned out), about the impact of an FDA regulation on the affected industry. Such contacts, even if informal and largely invisible to outside participants, might promote inter-agency coordination. When agencies work together, they are less likely to produce overlapping or conflicting regulations. Other agencies also might transmit presidential preferences or executive-branch interests, particularly if the "target" agency is independent. Thus, other federal agencies may be an indirect source of political accountability. *See* Keith Bradley, *The Design of Agency Interactions*, 111 Colum. L. Rev. 745 (2011); Jody Freeman & James Rossi, *Agency Coordination in Shared Regulatory Space*, 125 Harv. L. Rev. 1131 (2012); Jason Marisam, *The Interagency Marketplace*, 96 Miss. L. Rev. 886 (2012). At the same time, these agencies might make things worse not better. They might contribute to a sense of turf warfare rather than collaboration, or they might convey narrow interests rather than broader governmental ones. *See* Jacob E. Gerson, *Overlapping and Underlapping Jurisdiction in Administration Law*, 2006 Sup. Ct. Rev. 201; Louis J. Sirico, Jr., *Agencies in Conflict: Overlapping Agencies and the Legitimacy of the Administrative Process*, 33 Vand. L. Rev. 101 (1980).

B. CONGRESSIONAL CONTROL OF AGENCY ACTION

Like the President, Congress seeks to assert control of agency action. Perhaps this surprises you: after all, Congress agreed to give the power away to the agency in the first place. But the impulse to delegate does not negate the impulse to control; indeed, the two go hand in hand. Once Congress decides to delegate, it has an immediate and ongoing interest in ensuring that subsequent agency action roughly tracks legislative preferences. What does this interest reflect? Similar to the President, Congress may assert control for strategic reasons—to ensure that agency action reflects the preferences of the constituents who can help its members get reelected. Or Congress may assert control for more public-regarding reasons—to ensure that agency action comports with statutory mandates and popular preferences. What are the normative implications of congressional control? It may enhance (or decrease) political accountability, agency expertise, and other important values.

This section examines the main tools of congressional control. As with the tools of presidential control, we do not focus here on informal contacts per se, such as telephone calls or office meetings between members of Congress and agency officials. Rather, we concentrate on more formal and public means used to ensure compliance with the preferences of members of Congress, such as enacting restrictive legislation or conducting oversight hearings. We also discuss tools that Congress has sought to use but the Supreme Court has declared unconstitutional. In some sense, these tools occupy a middle ground between the informal contacts and the formal statutes that Congress can use to assert control of agency action. We will ask why the Court has rejected them.

As you explore these tools, consider how each works for Congress. As with the tools of presidential control, consider the varying degrees of formality, transparency, and effectiveness. Also consider their normative implications. Can Congress confer on agency action the same level of accountability, efficacy, or efficiency as the President? Why or why not? What dangers does congressional control of agency action impose?

Before we continue, note an additional complication: Congress must obtain information about agency action to know whether legislative intervention is necessary. We have already noted that the President also confronts this problem. How can members of Congress know when agency action departs from their preferences if they lack information about such action? Some actions are the sort that members of Congress have a personal interest in watching or are too high profile to ignore. For example, members of Congress may have a personal interest in auto safety, health care, or financial reform, and they may constantly monitor the agencies in charge. Issues like the terrorist attacks of 9-11 or Hurricane Katrina are known to all, and members of Congress join the rest of the country in watching the agencies that handle them. But most issues do not fall into either category, and members of Congress face considerable costs in monitoring them. Consider that every minute spent monitoring agency action is a minute less spent on other important (or electorally significant) activities. We have noted that Executive Order No. 12,866 is quite helpful to the White House for reducing the costs of monitoring agency action because it produces relevant information about planned and proposed regulations. On the basis of this information, the White House can decide whether intervention is necessary. Thus, the OIRA process is an informational tool as well as a control tool.

Congress also possesses informational tools that require agencies to report their activities, but those tools have not been nearly as effective for legislative monitoring. For example, Congress sometimes writes specific reporting requirements into organic statutes. NHTSA was subject to a reporting requirement in the 1966 Motor Vehicle Safety Act:

> SEC. 120. (a) The Secretary shall prepare and submit to the President for transmittal to the Congress on March 1 of each year a comprehensive report on the administration of this Act for the preceding calendar year. Such report shall include but not be restricted to (1) a thorough statistical compilation of the accidents and injuries occurring in such year; (2) a list of Federal motor vehicle safety standards prescribed or in effect in such year; (3) the degree of observance of applicable Federal motor vehicle standards; (4) a summary of all current research grants and contracts together with a description of the problems to be considered by such grants and contracts; (5) an analysis and evaluation, including relevant policy recommendations, of research activities completed and technological progress achieved during such year; and (6) the extent to which technical information was disseminated to the scientific community and consumer-oriented information was made available to the motoring public.

This reporting requirement has limitations as a monitoring mechanism; it pertains to implementation activities in the *preceding* calendar year. It does not furnish information about agency action at the earlier point in the process when political intervention is likely to be more effective precisely because the activities are under active consideration.

In 1996, Congress enacted a generally applicable provision that goes further. It is called the Congressional Review Act (CRA), 5 U.S.C. §§801-803, and we discuss it in its own right below. The CRA requires both independent and executive-branch agencies to submit "major" rules, as well as other information including any cost-benefit analysis of the rule, to Congress and the General Accounting Office before the rule may take effect. *See* 5 U.S.C. §801(a)(1)(B). Major rules do not become effective for at least 60 days, allowing time for congressional review. *See* 5 U.S.C. §801(a)(2)(B)(3). The Act provides expedited procedures by which a member of Congress may propose a joint resolution of disapproval of the rule. *See* 5 U.S.C. §802. A joint resolution has the same requirements as ordinary legislation: it can overturn a rule by a vote of both Houses of Congress and the President's approval or with a super-majority vote over the President's veto. *See* 5 U.S.C. §801(a). (The only difference is that joint resolutions are typically used for enactments that will not be incorporated into the U.S. Code.) Despite the potential of the CRA, Congress has rarely used it. Perhaps Congress is confronted with too much information, which can be just as problematic as too little information. Facing a mountain of agency documents, congressional staff members (who have lots of other work to do) have no idea even where to begin. Perhaps Congress simply lacks the capacity to act with the requisite dispatch. How quickly can Congress muster the support to enact a joint resolution, even with expedited procedures? Or perhaps the information comes too late in the rulemaking process to make less-draconian adjustments than complete disapproval of a generally desirable rule.

How else may Congress obtain information about agency action? That is a question that pervades our discussion of congressional control. As you read below, watch for tools that serve an informational function in addition to or in support of a control function.

1. New Legislation

To assert control of agency action, Congress can enact new legislation. Legislation might abolish an agency or restrict its authority. Less drastically, it might preclude a particular agency regulation or compel a different regulation. The amendment to the 1966 Motor Vehicle Safety Act prohibiting ignition interlock devices, which appears later in this chapter, is a good example. Congress enacted this amendment because of widespread public resistance to the ignition interlock option that NHTSA had permitted automakers to adopt. Some might say that such legislation is absolute vindication of popular will by a politically accountable Congress. Some might regard Congress as having more self-interested motives: the electoral benefits from the legislation outweighed the costs.

Often, Congress can assert control of agency action by simply threatening to restrict an agency's authority or reverse an agency's rule. From a political standpoint, you can see that such threats have an advantage and disadvantage, which are actually flip sides of the same coin. The advantage is that threats are far easier to make than new legislation is to enact. Threats can come from any member of Congress or any congressional committee, in private settings, such as a phone call or meeting, or in public contexts, such as a press statement or oversight hearing. New legislation comes only one way—subject to the requirements of bicameralism and presentment. These requirements were designed to be onerous in order to slow the production of hasty and improvident law and have been made even more so by the complexities of the modern legislative process. The disadvantage of threats is that agencies can ignore them. Agencies are free to evaluate whether Congress has the requisite political support to follow through. This is a fairly high-stakes game of chicken. Nevertheless, only new legislation is certain to produce change. When Congress amends a statute, the agency has no choice but to implement it. Pause to consider whether threats have the same normative implications as actually enacting new legislation. What if the threat only comes from one member or one committee or even one house of Congress? If the threat works to control agency action, does it enhance accountability to the same degree as a statutory amendment would?

2. Appropriations Legislation

Congress can also use appropriations legislation to restrict funding for a particular agency or regulatory program. When Congress creates an agency or regulatory program, it ordinarily funds them on an annual basis through separate appropriations legislation. Here is a concise description of the types of appropriations legislation:

Congress annually considers several appropriations measures, which provide funding for numerous activities, such as national defense, education, and homeland security, as well as general government operations. Appropriations acts are characteristically annual, and generally provide funding authority that expires at the end of the federal fiscal year, September 30.

These measures are considered by Congress under certain rules and practices, referred to as the *congressional appropriations process*. . . .

When considering appropriations measures, Congress is exercising the power granted to it under the Constitution, which states, "No money shall be drawn from the Treasury, but in Consequence of Appropriations made by Law." The power to appropriate is a legislative power. Congress has enforced its prerogatives through certain laws. The so-called Antideficiency Act, for example, strengthened the application of this section by, in part, explicitly prohibiting federal government employees and officers from making contracts or other obligations in advance of or in excess of an appropriation, unless authorized by law; and providing administrative and criminal sanctions for those who violate the act. Under law, public funds, furthermore, may only be used for the purpose(s) for which Congress appropriated the funds. . . .

The House and Senate Committees on Appropriations have jurisdiction over the annual appropriations measures. Each committee has 12 subcommittees and each subcommittee has jurisdiction over one regular annual appropriations bill that provides funding for departments and agencies under the subcommittee's jurisdiction.

The jurisdictions of the House and Senate appropriations subcommittees are generally parallel. That is, each House appropriations subcommittee is paired with a Senate appropriations subcommittee and the two subcommittees' jurisdictions are generally identical. As currently organized, there are 12 subcommittees:

- Agriculture, Rural Development, Food and Drug Administration, and Related Agencies;
- Commerce, Justice, Science, and Related Agencies;
- Defense;
- Energy and Water Development, and Related Agencies;
- Financial Services and General Government;
- Homeland Security;
- Interior, Environment, and Related Agencies;
- Labor, Health and Human Services, Education, and Related Agencies;
- Legislative Branch;
- Military Construction, Veterans Affairs, and Related Agencies;
- State, Foreign Operations, and Related Programs; and
- Transportation, and Housing and Urban Development, and Related Agencies. . . .

The appropriations process assumes the consideration of 12 regular appropriations measures annually. Each House and Senate appropriations subcommittee has jurisdiction over one regular bill.

Regular appropriations bills contain a series of unnumbered paragraphs with headings, generally reflecting a unique budget account. The basic unit of regular and supplemental appropriations bills is the account. Under these measures, funding for each department and large independent agency is distributed among several accounts. Each account, generally, includes similar programs, projects, or items, such as a research and development account or salaries and expenses account. For small agencies, a single account may fund all of the agency's activities. These acts typically provide a lump-sum amount for each account as well as any conditions, provisos, or specific requirements that apply to that account. A few accounts include a single program, project, or item, which the appropriations act funds individually.

In report language, the House and Senate Committees on Appropriations may provide more detailed directions to the departments and agencies on the distribution of funding among various activities funded within an account.

Appropriations measures may also provide transfer authority. *Transfers* shift budget authority from one account or fund to another or allow agencies to make such shifts. For example, an agency moving new budget authority from a salaries and expenses account to a research and development account would be a transfer. Agencies are prohibited from making such transfers without statutory authority. Agencies may, however, generally shift budget authority from one activity to another within an account without additional statutory authority. This is referred to as *reprogramming*. The appropriations subcommittees have established notification and other oversight procedures for various agencies to follow regarding reprogramming actions. Generally, these procedures differ with each subcommittee. . . .

Congress has traditionally considered and approved each regular appropriations bill separately, but Congress has also combined several bills together. These packages are referred to as omnibus appropriation measures. In these cases, Congress typically begins consideration of each regular bill separately, but generally has combined some of the bills together at the conference stage. During conference on one of the regular appropriations bills, the conferees have typically added to the conference report the final agreements on other outstanding regular appropriations bills, thereby creating an omnibus appropriations measure.

Omnibus acts may provide the full text of each regular appropriations bill included in the act or may incorporate the full text by reference. Omnibus acts may also be in the form of full-year continuing resolutions. Those that provide funding either by including the text of the regular bills or by incorporating them by reference may be considered omnibus bills, but those resolutions providing spending rates, such as is typically included in continuing resolutions, would not.

Packaging regular appropriations bills can be an efficient means for resolving outstanding differences within Congress or between Congress and the President. The negotiators may be able to make more convenient trade-offs between issues among several bills and complete consideration of appropriations using fewer measures. Omnibus measures may also be used to achieve a timely end to the annual appropriations process. . . .

Regular appropriations expire at the end of the fiscal year, September 30. If action on one or more regular appropriations measures has not been completed by the start of the next fiscal year, on October 1, the agencies funded by these bills must cease non-excepted activities due to lack of budget authority. Traditionally, *continuing appropriations* have been used to maintain temporary funding for agencies and programs until the regular bills are enacted. Such appropriations continuing funding are usually provided in a joint resolution, hence the term *continuing resolution* (or *CR*).

In only four instances since FY1977 (FY1977, FY1989, FY1995, and FY1997) were all regular appropriations enacted by the start of the fiscal year. In all other instances, at least one continuing resolution was necessary to fund governmental activities until action on the remaining regular appropriations bills was completed. On or before the start of the fiscal year, Congress and the President generally complete action on an initial continuing resolution that temporarily funds the outstanding regular appropriations bills.

In contrast to funding practices in regular bills (i.e., providing separate appropriations levels for each account), temporary continuing resolutions generally provide funding at a rate or formula, with certain exceptions. Recently, the continuing resolutions have generally provided a rate at the levels provided in the previous fiscal year for all accounts in each regular bill covered, with some account-specific adjustments. The initial CR typically provides temporary funding until a specific date or until the enactment of the applicable regular appropriations acts, if earlier.

Once the initial CR becomes law, additional interim continuing resolutions are frequently used to sequentially extend the expiration date. These subsequent continuing resolutions sometimes change the funding methods.

Less frequently, Congress may adopt a full-year continuing resolution that continues funding, at a specific rate or formula for accounts in outstanding regular bills, with numerous account-specific exceptions, through the end of the fiscal year. For example, the FY2007 full-year CR (P.L. 110-5) funded 9 regular bills and the FY2011 full-year CR (P.L. 112-10) covered 11 regular bills. . . .

Congress frequently considers one or more supplemental appropriations measures (or supplementals) for a fiscal year that generally increase funding for selected activities previously funded in the regular bills. Recent supplementals have also been used to provide funds for the wars in Iraq and Afghanistan. Supplementals may provide funding for unforeseen needs (such as funds to recover from a hurricane, earthquake, or flood); or increase or provide funding for other activities. These measures, like regular appropriations bills, provide specific amounts of funding for individual accounts in the bill. Sometimes Congress includes supplemental appropriations in regular bills and continuing resolutions rather than in a separate supplemental bill. During a calendar year, Congress typically considers at least

- 12 regular appropriations bills for the fiscal year that begins on October 1 (often referred to as the budget year),
- several continuing resolutions for the same fiscal year, and
- one or more supplementals for the current fiscal year. . . .

CONG. RESEARCH SERV., THE CONGRESSIONAL APPROPRIATIONS PROCESS: AN INTRODUCTION 1, 11-12 (Feb. 23, 2012).

The appropriations process enables Congress to assert continuous control of agency action. A funding reduction can put a halt to an agency program. But agencies are likely to adjust their policies to legislative preferences in response to a threat of a budget cut. Agencies need funding to run their programs, so money is a powerful motivator. If a threat is enough, then this tool is less costly than mustering the political support to actually cut funding. Will a threat always be enough? As with any threat, agencies are free to determine whether those making them have the political support to back them up. In other words, agencies are free to determine whether the threat is credible. There is a coordination problem that complicates the analysis. The committee responsible for appropriations is different from the committee responsible for the substantive mandate, like auto safety. If the substantive committee is the one displeased with agency action, it must communicate that dissatisfaction to the appropriations committee, and the appropriations committee must agree to follow through. Still, funding threats are seen as quite powerful. Perhaps the reason is the unique nature of appropriations legislation. Funding for any particular agency program is just one item in a larger bill that reflects many diverse legislative interests and that Congress intends to pass. Funding is therefore relatively easier to alter than provisions in other bills (including bills to reduce an agency's authority or reverse an agency's rule).

3. Oversight Hearings

Congress can use oversight hearings in a variety of ways to control agency action. It can use hearings to uncover facts in aid of further legislative activity, such as statutory amendments or funding reductions. In this respect, oversight hearings can function as an informational tool. Congress can use hearings to pressure agencies to conform their policy to legislative preferences without further legislative action. This use enables Congress to hold the agency accountable in a sense that we have emphasized — as a superior that issues instructions to a subordinate. *See* Edward Rubin, *The Myth of Accountability and the Anti-Administrations Impulse*, 103 MICH. L. REV. 2073 (2005). Congress can also use hearings to hold officials "accountable" for their actions in the traditional sense of the word — a public airing or blaming. Even if such hearings cannot change past conduct, they may enable voters to better judge those responsible for it, or they may serve as a warning for the future. The advantage of oversight hearings as a tool for controlling agency action is their relative informality. Congress need not enact legislation to move agency action in a direction consistent with its preferences. At the same time, the visibility of oversight hearings may improve their effectiveness as compared to less formal control tools, such as closed-door meetings or other contacts. Agency officials may find it more difficult to resist when doing so occurs in public view. Despite the advantages of oversight hearing has long been conceived as not a particularly strong form of control, in part because they are indirect. Recent empirical research suggests the picture may be more complicated. Consider the following by Professor Brian Feinstein.

Brian D. Feinstein, Congress in the Administrative State
95 Wash. U. L. Rev. 1187, 1187-93 (2018)

[I]n the summer of 2000, tire safety held the public's attention. That summer, the nation learned that failed Firestone tires were responsible for over one hundred deaths during the previous several years. Concerned about the perceived inability of the National Highway Traffic Safety Administration (NHTSA) to identify and adequately address the defect, Congress enacted legislation requiring the agency to establish a data-reporting and analysis system by mid-2002 under which manufacturers must submit to NHTSA information on accident-related claims.

Yet NHTSA, with more industry-friendly officials at the helm following the 2000 election, dragged its feet. In 2002, a House subcommittee convened a hearing where several legislators sharply criticized NHTSA's administrator for the agency's inaction concerning the defect information system. Following the hearing, NHTSA made swift progress, completing the first phase of the system just nine months later. Two years after that, the agency issued the first recall based on analysis using the new system—which, incredibly, had become the government's largest non-military computer database.

This sequence of events—Congress passes a law, the agency delays implementation, Congress critiques the agency's inaction, and the agency improves–suggests that congressional pressure caused an otherwise recalcitrant agency to act. Yet the episode stands outside of the accepted view of congressional power. When scholars typically discuss Congress's role, they tend to focus on the branch's well-known, direct powers: primarily its lawmaking function, along with appropriations and appointments. Recent work on Congress's other powers—most notably Josh Chafetz's study of Congress's "soft powers" concerning the freedom of speech or debate and each chamber's powers to establish cameral rules and discipline its members—has begun to challenge this conventional focus on the institution's legislative powers. Yet mechanisms, like oversight, that lie beyond those delineated in the Constitution remain underappreciated—despite the significant resources that Congress expends performing these functions. Given this incomplete picture, it is not surprising that the received wisdom holds that Congress's role in policymaking, relative to that of the President, is diminished.

This Article provides a corrective. It contends that, as NHTSA's response to congressional oversight hearings exemplifies, hearings provide Congress with a powerful tool to influence administration. This Article tests this theory with an original dataset of 14,431 agency "infractions," which . . . comprise the set of issues from which Congress tends to select its subjects for oversight hearings. These infractions include critiques regarding a wide variety of regulatory implementation, enforcement, and personnel issues across all executive departments and major independent agencies, as raised in inspector-general reports, Government Accountability Office "top challenges" lists, and newspaper editorials. For each infraction, I identify, first, whether Congress held a hearing on the subject within one year after its mention and, second, whether the infraction reappeared in the dataset in the next year.

The use of this large-scale dataset allows for the comparison of agency actions that are subject to oversight hearings with otherwise similar agency actions for which Congress does not hold hearings. After all, one cannot know the independent effect of the Transportation Recall Enhancement, Accountability and Documentation (TREAD) Act implementation hearing on NHTSA's later actions without comparing that episode to a (hypothetical) other NHTSA implementation issue on which Congress did not hold hearings. This effort, the first large-scale, quantitative study of congressional oversight, answers two questions: under what conditions will oversight occur, and is this activity consequential? Taken together, answers to these questions will shed light on the broader question of whether oversight enables

Congress to exert a degree of *ex post* control over the administrative state following legislative enactments.

Empirical analysis concerning the first question shows that the particular preference alignment of Congress, the relevant committee, and the relevant agency affect whether oversight occurs concerning a given infraction. This finding is attributable to Congress's bifurcated structure: committees are empowered to convene hearings, but only the full legislature may sanction agencies for continued non-compliance following hearings. This structure encourages committees to ignore some infractions that Congress might prefer to probe, based on the committees' fears that convening hearings could motivate Congress to enact legislative changes that the committees oppose. Essentially, committees—mindful that their parent chamber's preferences may differ from their own—make strategic decisions concerning which agencies they take to task and which they ignore.

A second analysis finds that, when it occurs, oversight often is consequential, changing agency behavior for a statistically significant 18.5% of infractions, relative to otherwise similar infractions for which oversight does not occur. To put that figure in perspective: agencies commit an average of 656 infractions per year, of which 239 infractions continue (or reoccur) the next year; by holding oversight hearings, Congress prevents an additional forty-seven infractions per year from reappearing in the dataset in the next year on average. Oversight alters agency behavior—moving it towards congressional preferences on issues ranging from the level of regulatory enforcement to the creation of programs that stretch agencies' statutory authority, as well as concerning more run-of-the-mill issues such as waste, fraud, and abuse—an average of 89 times per year.

. . . The finding that oversight can substantially alter agency behavior indicates that Congress's position vis-à-vis the White House is not as diminished as some suggest. In recent years, scholars have begun to push back against the conventional perception of an enfeebled Congress. This Article contributes to this nascent reassessment by adding oversight as among Congress's soft powers that provide the branch with a source of control over administrative agencies.

[In addition], these findings suggest that concerns that administrative law doctrines leave the executive branch without supervision deserve reconsideration. In recent years, a growing chorus of jurists and scholars has voiced concerns that deference doctrines strip agencies of any checks, judicial or legislative, on their actions. That oversight provides Congress with a powerful mechanism to influence agency behavior—and that Congress has the ability to restructure its internal institutions to promote even greater oversight, should it so desire—belies this notion. Thus, these findings provide a rejoinder to critics of judicial deference to agencies on these grounds.

To the extent that oversight hearings ensure that agency action tracks the preferences of elected officials rather than unelected bureaucrats, they can enhance the accountability of such action.

Depending on your standpoint, the frequency of oversight hearings is a downside. When agency officials' time, energy, and attention are consumed by oversight hearings, they cannot attend to the jobs for which they were appointed and confirmed. Even well-intentioned oversight hearings divert agency resources from their intended purposes. The claim of interference is weaker for former agency officials.

Of course, not all oversight hearings are well intentioned. They may serve political purposes but no obviously public-regarding ones. For example, oversight hearings can be used to harass or scapegoat agency officials or administrations. They can be used to improve the profile of members of Congress or their association with politically salient issues. In this regard, consider that oversight hearings are more likely in response to high-profile events and in times of divided government. (Recall the arguments from Chapter 2 concerning delegation. Congress has less reason to monitor agency action during times of unified government because it has less reason to worry that such action will depart from its preferences.)

How do oversight hearings work and what are the obstacles to their success? When a congressional committee convenes an oversight hearing, it sends a letter requesting that an agency official appear and sometimes produce documents. What happens if an agency official refuses to voluntarily appear or produce documents? In many cases, the committee will work out a compromise with the official, perhaps to provide more limited testimony or produce documents without appearing. But Congress can also use its subpoena power to compel compliance, holding officials who defy those subpoenas in contempt of Congress. A contempt citation can originate in either the House or the Senate. It is debated like any other resolution, subject to the same filibuster and procedural rules, and requires a majority vote for approval. Once approved, the House speaker or the Senate president pro tem refers it to the U.S. Attorney for the District of Columbia for prosecution. *See* 2 U.S.C. §§1992-1994. Contempt of Congress is a federal misdemeanor, punishable by a maximum $100,000 fine and a maximum one-year sentence in federal prison. *See* Josh Chafetz, *Executive Branch Contempt of Congress*, 76 U. Chi. L. Rev. 1083 (2009).

In some instances, the President may assert a claim of executive privilege on behalf of agency officials. Executive privilege enables the President to protect the confidentiality of executive communications from legislative or judicial investigations. The Supreme Court has held that executive privilege, though not mentioned in the Constitution, is implicit in the notion of separation of powers. *See* United States v. Nixon, 418 U.S. 683 (1974). But the Court has left the privilege ill defined: To what extent may the interests of the other branches overcome it? What sorts of information does it protect? Disputes between the executive and legislative branches can lead to lawsuits, although courts are reluctant to intervene and may ask the parties to work it out. The "resolution" can be quite messy for both sides.

4. Fire Alarms

In the previous section, we mentioned that oversight hearings can function not only as a tool for asserting control of agency action but also as a tool for obtaining information about agency action. In this section, we explore other tools for obtaining information about agency action. This issue is critical because without information, Congress does not know when to intervene in agency action. We have already noted that Congress has enacted statutes requiring agencies to submit information directly to it. These mechanisms, like oversight hearings, are costly from a legislative perspective. To obtain information, Congress must devote time to calling witnesses or reading documents.

Political scientists have argued that Congress has means that enable it to monitor agency action more efficiently by shifting the responsibility and cost to others. In this regard, political scientists have distinguished between *police patrols*, which are tools that require Congress itself to monitor agency action, and *fire alarms*, which are tools that position constituents to monitor agency action and alert Congress (i.e., sound a "fire alarm") when legislative intervention is necessary. Mathew McCubbins & Thomas Schwartz, *Congressional Oversight Overlooked: Police Patrols Versus Fire Alarms*, 28 Am. J. Pol. Sci. 165 (1984). If oversight hearings and reporting requirements are examples of police patrols, what are examples of fire alarms?

Administrative procedures can serve as fire alarms. The prime example is notice-and-comment rulemaking, which allows any interested party to participate in the development of agency policy, acquiring information about such policy along the way and triggering legislative intervention when it departs from their preferences. *See* Mathew D. McCubbins, Roger G. Noll & Barry R. Weingast, *Administrative Procedures as Instruments of Political Control*, 3 J.L. Econ. & Org. 243 (1987). Congress has enacted other statutes that require agencies to furnish certain sorts of information while formulating policy that may be relevant to particular groups in seeking legislative intervention. *See* 42 U.S.C. §§4321-4347 (2000) (National Environmental Policy Act); 5 U.S.C. §§601-612 (Regulatory Flexibility Act); Pub. L. No. 1040121, 110 Stat. 857 (1996) (codified in scattered sections of 5, 15, and 28 U.S.C.) (Small Business Regulatory Enforcement Fairness Act). Note that some political scientists question whether administrative procedures can function as information-control mechanisms. Some contend that the connection between administrative procedures and legislative monitoring is too general and cannot be tested as an empirical matter. *See* John D. Huber & Charles R. Shipan, Deliberate Discretion? The Institutional Foundations of Bureaucratic Autonomy 26, 36 (2002). Others argue that providing information is insufficient to make administrative procedures useful to Congress; Congress still needs the will and the means to assert control of agency action.

See Jerry L. Mashaw, *Explaining Administrative Process: Normative, Positive, and Critical Stories of Legal Development*, 6 J.L. ECON. & ORG. (Special Issue) 267 (1990). Note also that legal scholars tend to view administrative procedures as legal, not political, tools. They see administrative procedures, such as notice-and-comment rulemaking, as promoting notice, fairness, deliberation, and the like. But most have not really considered the simultaneous political function that administrative procedures may serve. *See* Lisa Schultz Bressman, *Procedures as Politics in Administrative Law*, 107 COLUM. L. REV. 1749 (2007).

In addition to obtaining information by placing citizens in the administrative process, Congress can obtain information by placing citizens in the judicial process. Thus, Congress has enacted so-called citizen-suit provisions, which authorize "any person" to seek judicial review of agency action. *See, e.g.,* 16 U.S.C. §1540(g) (citizen-suit provision in Endangered Species Act). The right to seek judicial review gives citizens a greater incentive to watch agency action and report to Congress when such action departs from their preferences, in addition to or in lieu of later filing a lawsuit. It may also give agencies a greater incentive to share information with citizens; "[a]gencies are more inclined to involve and accommodate those who have the power to challenge their decisions later." Bressman, *Procedures as Politics in Administrative Law*, 107 COLUM. L. REV. at 1796. In these ways, citizen-suit provisions shift monitoring costs to citizens. They also shift monitoring costs to courts. A judicial decision can serve as a signal to Congress that legislative intervention may be necessary. As we discuss in the judicial control section, the Constitution limits the extent to which Congress can rely on citizen-suit provisions as monitoring mechanisms. As a result, citizen-suit provisions do not allow Congress to shift the costs of monitoring as broadly as it might prefer.

Finally, Congress has enacted other statutes that furnish citizens information outside the context of an administrative or judicial proceeding. For example, the Freedom of Information Act directs agencies to provide records to "any person" upon a request that "reasonably describes such records." *See* 5 U.S.C. §552 (2000); *see also* 5 U.S.C. §552b (Government in the Sunshine Act, which requires independent agencies to give reasonable notice of their meetings and make every portion of their meetings open to public observation). Although these statutes provide a number of exemptions that shield certain agency information from public view, they are important mechanisms for citizens to obtain information, on the basis of which they may invoke legislative intervention.

5. Legislative Vetoes

Now we turn to tools that Congress has created to assert control of agency action, but that the Supreme Court has subsequently invalidated on constitutional grounds. Thus, these are tools that Congress may not use today. Because Congress is not likely to stop searching for innovative mechanisms, it is important to understand the political advantage of these tools, as well as the constitutional objections and normative implications. We start with the legislative veto.

A legislative veto is a statutory provision that enables Congress to reverse an agency decision without enacting a new statute. There are several forms of the legislative veto: one-house, two-house, or committee. You can understand almost immediately the political appeal of such a tool. Above all else, a legislative veto enables Congress to reverse an agency decision without obtaining a presidential signature or two-thirds majority to override a presidential veto. In addition, a one-house veto dispenses with the need for bicameral consensus. Most extreme, and most tempting, is the committee veto, which places control in the small group of senators or representatives who deal with the agency on a regular basis and conduct the oversight of that agency. Yet a legislative veto, regardless of its form, has the same legal effect. It is binding on the agency, reversing its decision as if through new legislation. Therefore, even the mere threat of a veto is powerful. If you think an agency official is generally in a tough spot when called to testify at an oversight hearing, think how much more pressure the official faces if the committee can, on its own, reverse the agency's regulations.

Not surprisingly, the legislative veto has been a popular tool. As a leading legislation casebook reports, "[a] library of Congress study for period 1932 to 1975 found 295 congressional review provisions in 196 federal statutes; for the year 1975 alone, there were 58 provisions in 21 statutes." WILLIAM N. ESKRIDGE, JR. ET AL., LEGISLATION: STATUTES AND THE CREATION OF PUBLIC POLICY 1149 (4th ed. 2007). The authors found that the trend accelerated in the late 1970s, and offer the following table:

Form of Legislative Veto	1932-78	1979-82
One-House	71	24
Two-House	65	23
Committee	0	26
Other	0	5
Totals	205	78

This list includes congressional review provisions other than "negative" legislative vetoes, which have the effect of reversing an agency decision. For example, Congress can require an agency to obtain legislative approval before a decision becomes effective, which is known as a "positive" legislative veto. Congress can also require an agency to report a decision to a specified committee and wait for a period to allow legislative review, which is known as "laying over."

In 1983, the Court held that the negative form of the legislative veto is unconstitutional. With that decision, the Court invalidated more federal legislation in one day than it had invalidated in the 194 years of the republic that preceded it.

Here is the decision.

Immigration & Naturalization Service v. Chadha

462 U.S. 919 (1983)

CHIEF JUSTICE BURGER delivered the opinion of the Court.

[This case] presents a challenge to the constitutionality of the provision in §244(c)(2) of the Immigration and Nationality Act, 8 U.S.C. §1254(c)(2), authorizing one House of Congress, by resolution, to invalidate the decision of the Executive Branch, pursuant to authority delegated by Congress to the Attorney General of the United States, to allow a particular deportable alien to remain in the United States.

Chadha is an East Indian who was born in Kenya and holds a British passport. He was lawfully admitted to the United States in 1966 on a non-immigrant student visa. His visa expired on June 30, 1972. On October 11, 1973, the District Director of the Immigration and Naturalization Service ordered Chadha to show cause why he should not be deported for having "remained in the United States for a longer time than permitted." Pursuant to §242(b) of the Immigration and Nationality Act (Act), 8 U.S.C. §1252(b), a deportation hearing was held before an immigration judge on January 11, 1974. On the basis of evidence adduced at the hearing, affidavits submitted with the application, and the results of a character investigation conducted by the INS, the immigration judge, on June 25, 1974, ordered that Chadha's deportation be suspended. The immigration judge found that Chadha met the requirements of §244(a)(1): he had resided continuously in the United States for over seven years, was of good moral character, and would suffer "extreme hardship" if deported.

Pursuant to §244(c)(1) of the Act, 8 U.S.C. §1254(c)(1), the immigration judge suspended Chadha's deportation and a report of the suspension was transmitted to Congress. Section 244(c)(1) provides:

> "Upon application by any alien who is found by the Attorney General to meet the requirements of subsection (a) of this section the Attorney General may in his discretion suspend deportation of such alien. If the deportation of any alien is suspended under the provisions of this subsection, a complete and detailed statement of the facts and pertinent provisions of law in the case shall be reported to the Congress with the reasons for such suspension. Such reports shall be submitted on the first day of each calendar month in which Congress is in session."

Once the Attorney General's recommendation for suspension of Chadha's deportation was conveyed to Congress, Congress had the power under §244(c)(2) of the Act, 8 U.S.C. §1254(c)(2), to veto the Attorney General's determination that Chadha should not be deported. Section 244(c)(2) provides:

> "(2) In the case of an alien specified in paragraph (1) of subsection (a) of this subsection—
>
> if during the session of the Congress at which a case is reported, or prior to the close of the session of the Congress next following the session at which a case is reported, either the Senate or the House of Representatives passes a resolution

stating in substance that it does not favor the suspension of such deportation, the Attorney General shall thereupon deport such alien or authorize the alien's voluntary departure at his own expense under the order of deportation in the manner provided by law. If, within the time above specified, neither the Senate nor the House of Representatives shall pass such a resolution, the Attorney General shall cancel deportation proceedings."

On December 12, 1975, [one week before the time to exercise the legislative veto was set to expire] Representative Eilberg, Chairman of the Judiciary Subcommittee on Immigration, Citizenship, and International Law, introduced a resolution opposing "the granting of permanent residence in the United States to [six] aliens", including Chadha. The resolution was referred to the House Committee on the Judiciary. On December 16, 1975, the resolution was discharged from further consideration by the House Committee on the Judiciary and submitted to the House of Representatives for a vote. The resolution had not been printed and was not made available to other Members of the House prior to or at the time it was voted on. So far as the record before us shows, the House consideration of the resolution was based on Representative Eilberg's statement from the floor that

> "[i]t was the feeling of the committee, after reviewing 340 cases, that the aliens contained in the resolution [Chadha and five others] did not meet these statutory requirements, particularly as it relates to hardship; and it is the opinion of the committee that their deportation should not be suspended."

The resolution was passed without debate or recorded vote. Since the House action was pursuant to §244(c)(2), the resolution was not treated as an Article I legislative act; it was not submitted to the Senate or presented to the President for his action.

[The Court first addressed questions concerning the availability of judicial review, including its jurisdiction and standing. It concluded that it had authority to review Chadha's claims.]

III

We turn now to the question whether action of one House of Congress under §244(c)(2) violates strictures of the Constitution. We begin, of course, with the presumption that the challenged statute is valid. Its wisdom is not the concern of the courts; if a challenged action does not violate the Constitution, it must be sustained. By the same token, the fact that a given law or procedure is efficient, convenient, and useful in facilitating functions of government, standing alone, will not save it if it is contrary to the Constitution. Convenience and efficiency are not the primary objectives—or the hallmarks—of democratic government and our inquiry is sharpened rather than blunted by the fact that Congressional veto provisions are appearing with increasing frequency in statutes which delegate authority to executive and independent agencies.

Explicit and unambiguous provisions of the Constitution prescribe and define the respective functions of the Congress and of the Executive in the legislative process. Since the precise terms of those familiar provisions are critical to the resolution of this case, we set them out verbatim. Art. I provides:

> "All legislative Powers herein granted shall be vested in a Congress of the United States, which shall consist of a Senate *and* a House of Representatives." Art. I, §1. (Emphasis added).
>
> "Every Bill which shall have passed the House of Representatives *and* the Senate, *shall*, before it becomes a Law, be presented to the President of the United States; . . ." Art. I, §7, cl. 2. (Emphasis added).
>
> "*Every* Order, Resolution, or Vote to which the Concurrence of the Senate and House of Representatives may be necessary (except on a question of Adjournment) *shall be* presented to the President of the United States; and before the Same shall take Effect, *shall be* approved by him, or being disapproved by him, *shall be* repassed by two thirds of the Senate and House of Representatives, according to the Rules and Limitations prescribed in the Case of a Bill." Art. I, §7, cl. 3. (Emphasis added).

These provisions of Art. I are integral parts of the constitutional design for the separation of powers. We have recently noted that "[t]he principle of separation of powers was not simply an abstract generalization in the minds of the Framers: it was woven into the documents that they drafted in Philadelphia in the summer of 1787." *Buckley v. Valeo*, 424 U.S., at 124. Just as we relied on the textual provision of Art. II, §2, cl. 2, to vindicate the principle of separation of powers in *Buckley*, we find that the purposes underlying the Presentment Clauses, Art. I, §7, cls. 2, 3, and the bicameral requirement of Art. I, §1 and §7, cl. 2, guide our resolution of the important question presented in this case. The very structure of the articles delegating and separating powers under Arts. I, II, and III exemplify the concept of separation of powers and we now turn to Art. I.

B

The Presentment Clauses

The records of the Constitutional Convention reveal that the requirement that all legislation be presented to the President before becoming law was uniformly accepted by the Framers. Presentment to the President and the Presidential veto were considered so imperative that the draftsmen took special pains to assure that these requirements could not be circumvented. During the final debate on Art. I, §7, cl. 2, James Madison expressed concern that it might easily be evaded by the simple expedient of calling a proposed law a "resolution" or "vote" rather than a "bill." 2 M. Farrand, The Records of the Federal Convention of 1787 301-302. As a consequence, Art. I, §7, cl. 3, was added. *Id.*, at 304-305.

The decision to provide the President with a limited and qualified power to nullify proposed legislation by veto was based on the profound conviction of the Framers that the powers conferred on Congress were the powers to be most carefully circumscribed. It is beyond doubt that lawmaking was a power to be shared by both Houses and the President. In *The Federalist* No. 73 (H. Lodge ed. 1888), Hamilton focused on the President's role in making laws:

> "If even no propensity had ever discovered itself in the legislative body to invade the rights of the Executive, the rules of just reasoning and theoretic propriety would of themselves teach us that the one ought not to be left to the mercy of the other, but ought to possess a constitutional and effectual power of self-defense." *Id.*, at 457-458.

The President's role in the lawmaking process also reflects the Framers' careful efforts to check whatever propensity a particular Congress might have to enact oppressive, improvident, or ill-considered measures. The President's veto role in the legislative process was described later during public debate on ratification:

> "It establishes a salutary check upon the legislative body, calculated to guard the community against the effects of faction, precipitancy, or of any impulse unfriendly to the public good which may happen to influence a majority of that body. . . . The primary inducement to conferring the power in question upon the Executive is to enable him to defend himself; the secondary one is to increase the chances in favor of the community against the passing of bad laws through haste, inadvertence, or design." THE FEDERALIST No. 73, at 458 (A. Hamilton).

The Court also has observed that the Presentment Clauses serve the important purpose of assuring that a "national" perspective is grafted on the legislative process:

> "The President is a representative of the people just as the members of the Senate and of the House are, and it may be, at some times, on some subjects, that the President elected by all the people is rather more representative of them all than are the members of either body of the Legislature whose constituencies are local and not country-wide. . . ." *Myers v. United States*, 272 U.S., at 123.

C

Bicameralism

The bicameral requirement of Art. I, §§1, 7 was of scarcely less concern to the Framers than was the Presidential veto and indeed the two concepts are interdependent. By providing that no law could take effect without the concurrence of the prescribed majority of the Members of both Houses, the Framers reemphasized their belief, already remarked upon in connection with the Presentment Clauses, that legislation should not be enacted unless it has been carefully and fully considered by the Nation's elected officials. In the Constitutional Convention debates on the need for a bicameral legislature, James Wilson, later to become a Justice of this Court, commented:

> "Despotism comes on mankind in different shapes. Sometimes in an Executive, sometimes in a military, one. Is there danger of a Legislative despotism? Theory & practice both proclaim it. If the Legislative authority be not restrained, there can be neither liberty nor stability; and it can only be restrained by dividing it within itself, into distinct and independent branches. In a single house there is no check, but the inadequate one, of the virtue & good sense of those who compose it." 1 M. Farrand, at 254.

Hamilton argued that a Congress comprised of a single House was antithetical to the very purposes of the Constitution. Were the Nation to adopt a Constitution providing for only one legislative organ, he warned:

> "we shall finally accumulate, in a single body, all the most important prerogatives of sovereignty, and thus entail upon our posterity one of the most execrable forms of government that human infatuation ever contrived. Thus we should create in reality that very tyranny which the adversaries of the new Constitution either are, or affect to be, solicitous to avert." THE FEDERALIST No. 22, at 135.

These observations are consistent with what many of the Framers expressed, none more cogently than Hamilton in pointing up the need to divide and disperse power in order to protect liberty:

> "In republican government, the legislative authority necessarily predominates. The remedy for this inconveniency is to divide the legislature into different branches; and to render them, by different modes of election and different principles of action, as little connected with each other as the nature of their common functions and their common dependence on the society will admit." THE FEDERALIST No. 51 at 324.

See also THE FEDERALIST No. 62.

However familiar, it is useful to recall that apart from their fear that special interests could be favored at the expense of public needs, the Framers were also concerned, although not of one mind, over the apprehensions of the smaller states. Those states feared a commonality of interest among the larger states would work to their disadvantage; representatives of the larger states, on the other hand, were skeptical of a legislature that could pass laws favoring a minority of the people. *See* 1 M. Farrand, 176-177, 484-491. It need hardly be repeated here that the Great Compromise, under which one House was viewed as representing the people and the other the states, allayed the fears of both the large and small states.

We see therefore that the Framers were acutely conscious that the bicameral requirement and the Presentment Clauses would serve essential constitutional functions. The President's participation in the legislative process was to protect the Executive Branch from Congress and to protect the whole people from improvident laws. The division of the Congress into two distinctive bodies assures that the legislative power would be exercised only after opportunity for full study and debate in separate settings. The President's unilateral veto power, in turn, was limited by the power of two-thirds of both Houses of Congress to overrule a veto thereby precluding final arbitrary action of one person. *See* 1 M. Farrand, at 99-104. It emerges clearly that the prescription for legislative action in Art. I, §§1, 7 represents the Framers' decision that the legislative power of the Federal government be exercised in accord with a single, finely wrought and exhaustively considered, procedure.

IV

The Constitution sought to divide the delegated powers of the new federal government into three defined categories, legislative, executive and judicial, to assure, as nearly as possible, that each Branch of government would confine itself to its assigned responsibility. The hydraulic pressure inherent within each of the separate Branches to exceed the outer limits of its power, even to accomplish desirable objectives, must be resisted.

Although not "hermetically" sealed from one another, *Buckley v. Valeo*, 424 U.S., at 121, the powers delegated to the three Branches are functionally identifiable. When any Branch acts, it is presumptively exercising the power the Constitution has delegated to it. *See Hampton & Co. v. United States*, 276 U.S. 394, 406. When the Executive acts, it presumptively acts in an executive or administrative capacity as defined in Art. II. And when, as here, one House of Congress purports to act, it is presumptively acting within its assigned sphere.

Beginning with this presumption, we must nevertheless establish that the challenged action under §244(c)(2) is of the kind to which the procedural requirements of Art. I, §7 apply. Not every action taken by either House is subject to the bicameralism and presentment requirements of Art. I. . . . Whether actions taken by either House are, in law and fact, an exercise of legislative power depends not on their form but upon "whether they contain matter which is properly to be regarded as legislative in its character and effect."

Examination of the action taken here by one House pursuant to §244(c)(2) reveals that it was essentially legislative in purpose and effect. In purporting to exercise power defined in Art. I, §8, cl. 4 to "establish an uniform Rule of Naturalization," the House took action that had the purpose and effect of altering the legal rights, duties and relations of persons, including the Attorney General, Executive Branch officials and Chadha, all outside the legislative branch. Section 244(c)(2) purports to authorize one House of Congress to require the Attorney General to deport an individual alien whose deportation otherwise would be cancelled under §244. The one-House veto operated in this case to overrule the Attorney General and mandate Chadha's deportation; absent the House action, Chadha would remain in the United States. Congress has acted and its action has altered Chadha's status.

The legislative character of the one-House veto in this case is confirmed by the character of the Congressional action it supplants. Neither the House of Representatives nor the Senate contends that, absent the veto provision in §244(c)(2), either of them, or both of them acting together, could effectively require the Attorney General to deport an alien once the Attorney General, in the exercise of legislatively delegated authority,[1] had determined the alien should remain in the United States. Without the challenged provision

---

1. Congress protests that affirming the Court of Appeals in this case will sanction "lawmaking by the Attorney General. . . . Why is the Attorney General exempt from submitting his proposed changes in the law to the full bicameral process?" Brief of the United States House of Representatives 40. To be sure, some administrative agency action-rule making, for example-may resemble "lawmaking." See 5 U.S.C. §551(4), which defines an agency's "rule" as "the whole or part of an agency statement of general or particular applicability and future effect designed to implement, interpret, or prescribe *law* or policy. . . ." This Court has referred to agency activity as being "quasi-legislative" in character. *Humphrey's Executor v. United States*, 295 U.S. 602, 628 (1935). Clearly, however, "[i]n the framework of our Constitution, the President's power to see that the laws are faithfully executed refutes the idea that he is to be a

in §244(c)(2), this could have been achieved, if at all, only by legislation requiring deportation. Similarly, a veto by one House of Congress under §244(c)(2) cannot be justified as an attempt at amending the standards set out in §244(a)(1), or as a repeal of §244 as applied to Chadha. Amendment and repeal of statutes, no less than enactment, must conform with Art. I.

The nature of the decision implemented by the one-House veto in this case further manifests its legislative character. After long experience with the clumsy, time consuming private bill procedure, Congress made a deliberate choice to delegate to the Executive Branch, and specifically to the Attorney General, the authority to allow deportable aliens to remain in this country in certain specified circumstances. It is not disputed that this choice to delegate authority is precisely the kind of decision that can be implemented only in accordance with the procedures set out in Art. I. Disagreement with the Attorney General's decision on Chadha's deportation—that is, Congress' decision to deport Chadha—no less than Congress' original choice to delegate to the Attorney General the authority to make that decision, involves determinations of policy that Congress can implement in only one way; bicameral passage followed by presentment to the President. Congress must abide by its delegation of authority until that delegation is legislatively altered or revoked.

This does not mean that Congress is required to capitulate to "the accretion of policy control by forces outside its chambers." Javits and Klein, Congressional Oversight and the Legislative Veto: A Constitutional Analysis, 52 N.Y.U. L. Rev. 455, 462 (1977). The Constitution provides Congress with abundant means to oversee and control its administrative creatures. Beyond the obvious fact that Congress ultimately controls administrative agencies in the legislation that creates them, other means of control, such as durational limits on authorizations and formal reporting requirements, lie well within Congress' constitutional power.

---

lawmaker." *Youngstown Sheet & Tube Co. v. Sawyer,* 343 U.S. 579, 587 (1952). See *Buckley v. Valeo,* 424 U.S. 1, 123 (1976). When the Attorney General performs his duties pursuant to §244, he does not exercise "legislative" power. See *Ernst & Ernst v. Hochfelder,* 425 U.S. 185, 213-214 (1976). The bicameral process is not necessary as a check on the Executive's administration of the laws because his administrative activity cannot reach beyond the limits of the statute that created it-a statute duly enacted pursuant to Art. I, §§1, 7. The constitutionality of the Attorney General's execution of the authority delegated to him by §244 involves only a question of delegation doctrine. The courts, when a case or controversy arises, can always "ascertain whether the will of Congress has been obeyed," *Yakus v. United States,* 321 U.S. 414, 425 (1944), and can enforce adherence to statutory standards. See *Youngstown Sheet & Tube Co. v. Sawyer,* 343 U.S. 579, 585 (1952); *Ethyl Corp. v. EPA,* 541 F.2d 1, 68 (CADC) (en banc) (separate statement of Leventhal, J.), *cert. denied,* 426 U.S. 941 (1976); L. Jaffe, Judicial Control of Administrative Action 320 (1965). It is clear, therefore, that the Attorney General acts in his presumptively Art. II capacity when he administers the Immigration and Nationality Act. Executive action under legislatively delegated authority that might resemble "legislative" action in some respects is not subject to the approval of both Houses of Congress and the President for the reason that the Constitution does not so require. That kind of Executive action is always subject to check by the terms of the legislation that authorized it; and if that authority is exceeded it is open to judicial review as well as the power of Congress to modify or revoke the authority entirely. A one-House veto is clearly legislative in both character and effect and is not so checked; the need for the check provided by Art. I, §§1, 7 is therefore clear. Congress' authority to delegate portions of its power to administrative agencies provides no support for the argument that Congress can constitutionally control administration of the laws by way of a Congressional veto.

Finally, we see that when the Framers intended to authorize either House of Congress to act alone and outside of its prescribed bicameral legislative role, they narrowly and precisely defined the procedure for such action. There are but four provisions in the Constitution, explicit and unambiguous, by which one House may act alone with the unreviewable force of law, not subject to the President's veto:

(a) The House of Representatives alone was given the power to initiate impeachments. Art. I, §2, cl. 6;

(b) The Senate alone was given the power to conduct trials following impeachment on charges initiated by the House and to convict following trial. Art. I, §3, cl. 5;

(c) The Senate alone was given final unreviewable power to approve or to disapprove presidential appointments. Art. II, §2, cl. 2;

(d) The Senate alone was given unreviewable power to ratify treaties negotiated by the President. Art. II, §2, cl. 2.

Clearly, when the Draftsmen sought to confer special powers on one House, independent of the other House, or of the President, they did so in explicit, unambiguous terms. These carefully defined exceptions from presentment and bicameralism underscore the difference between the legislative functions of Congress and other unilateral but important and binding one-House acts provided for in the Constitution. . . .

Since it is clear that the action by the House under §244(c)(2) was not within any of the express constitutional exceptions authorizing one House to act alone, and equally clear that it was an exercise of legislative power, that action was subject to the standards prescribed in Article I. The bicameral requirement, the Presentment Clauses, the President's veto, and Congress' power to override a veto were intended to erect enduring checks on each Branch and to protect the people from the improvident exercise of power by mandating certain prescribed steps. To preserve those checks, and maintain the separation of powers, the carefully defined limits on the power of each Branch must not be eroded. To accomplish what has been attempted by one House of Congress in this case requires action in conformity with the express procedures of the Constitution's prescription for legislative action: passage by a majority of both Houses and presentment to the President.

The veto authorized by §244(c)(2) doubtless has been in many respects a convenient shortcut; the "sharing" with the Executive by Congress of its authority over aliens in this manner is, on its face, an appealing compromise. In purely practical terms, it is obviously easier for action to be taken by one House without submission to the President; but it is crystal clear from the records of the Convention, contemporaneous writings and debates, that the Framers ranked other values higher than efficiency. The records of the Convention and debates in the States preceding ratification underscore the common desire to define and limit the exercise of the newly created federal powers affecting the states and the people. There is unmistakable expression of a determination that legislation by the national Congress be a step-by-step, deliberate and deliberative process.

The choices we discern as having been made in the Constitutional Convention impose burdens on governmental processes that often seem clumsy, inefficient, even unworkable, but those hard choices were consciously made by men who had lived under a form of government that permitted arbitrary governmental acts to go unchecked. There is no support in the Constitution or decisions of this Court for the proposition that the cumbersomeness and delays often encountered in complying with explicit Constitutional standards may be avoided, either by the Congress or by the President. *See Youngstown Sheet & Tube Co. v. Sawyer*, 343 U.S. 579 (1952). With all the obvious flaws of delay, untidiness, and potential for abuse, we have not yet found a better way to preserve freedom than by making the exercise of power subject to the carefully crafted restraints spelled out in the Constitution. . . .

We hold that the congressional veto provision in §244(c)(2) . . . is unconstitutional. Accordingly, the judgment of the Court of Appeals is
Affirmed.

Justice POWELL, concurring in the judgment.

The Court's decision, based on the Presentment Clauses, Art. I, §7, cls. 2 and 3, apparently will invalidate every use of the legislative veto. The breadth of this holding gives one pause. Congress has included the veto in literally hundreds of statutes, dating back to the 1930s. Congress clearly views this procedure as essential to controlling the delegation of power to administrative agencies. One reasonably may disagree with Congress' assessment of the veto's utility, but the respect due its judgment as a coordinate branch of Government cautions that our holding should be no more extensive than necessary to decide this case. In my view, the case may be decided on a narrower ground. When Congress finds that a particular person does not satisfy the statutory criteria for permanent residence in this country it has assumed a judicial function in violation of the principle of separation of powers. Accordingly, I concur only in the judgment.

. . . The Court thus has been mindful that the boundaries between each branch should be fixed "according to common sense and the inherent necessities of the governmental co-ordination." *J.W. Hampton, Jr. & Co. v. United States*, 276 U.S. 394, 406 (1928). But where one branch has impaired or sought to assume a power central to another branch, the Court has not hesitated to enforce the doctrine. *See Buckley v. Valeo*, 424 U.S., at 123.

Functionally, the doctrine may be violated in two ways. One branch may interfere impermissibly with the other's performance of its constitutionally assigned function. *See Nixon v. Administrator of General Services*, 433 U.S. 425, 433 (1977); *United States v. Nixon*, 418 U.S. 683 (1974). Alternatively, the doctrine may be violated when one branch assumes a function that more properly is entrusted to another. *See Youngstown Sheet & Tube Co. v. Sawyer*, 343 U.S., at 587 (1952). . . . This case presents the latter situation.

On its face, the House's action appears clearly adjudicatory. The House did not enact a general rule; rather it made its own determination that six specific persons did not comply with certain statutory criteria. It thus undertook the type of decision that traditionally has been left to other branches. Even if the House did not make a de novo determination, but simply reviewed the Immigration and Naturalization Service's findings, it still assumed a function ordinarily entrusted to the federal courts. *See* 5 U.S.C. §704 (providing generally for judicial review of final agency action). . . . Where, as here, Congress has exercised a power "that cannot possibly be regarded as merely in aid of the legislative function of Congress," *Buckley v. Valeo*, 424 U.S., at 138, the decisions of this Court have held that Congress impermissibly assumed a function that the Constitution entrusted to another branch, *see id.* at 138-41.

The impropriety of the House's assumption of this function is confirmed by the fact that its action raises the very danger the Framers sought to avoid—the exercise of unchecked power. In deciding whether Chadha deserves to be deported, Congress is not subject to any internal constraints that prevent it from arbitrarily depriving him of the right to remain in this country. Unlike the judiciary or an administrative agency, Congress is not bound by established substantive rules. Nor is it subject to the procedural safeguards, such as the right to counsel and a hearing before an impartial tribunal, that are present when a court or an agency adjudicates individual rights. The only effective constraint on Congress' power is political, but Congress is most accountable politically when it prescribes rules of general applicability. When it decides rights of specific persons, those rights are subject to "the tyranny of a shifting majority."

Chief Justice Marshall observed: "It is the peculiar province of the legislature to prescribe general rules for the government of society; the application of those rules would seem to be the duty of other departments." *Fletcher v. Peck*, 6 Cranch 87, 136 (1810). In my view, when Congress undertook to apply its rules to Chadha, it exceeded the scope of its constitutionally prescribed authority. I would not reach the broader question whether legislative vetoes are invalid under the Presentment Clauses.

Justice WHITE, dissenting.

Today the Court not only invalidates §244(c)(2) of the Immigration and Nationality Act, but also sounds the death knell for nearly 200 other statutory provisions in which Congress has reserved a "legislative veto." For this reason, the Court's decision is of surpassing importance. And it is for this reason that the Court would have been well-advised to decide the case, if possible, on the narrower grounds of separation of powers, leaving for full consideration the constitutionality of other congressional review statutes operating on such varied matters as war powers and agency rulemaking, some of which concern the independent regulatory agencies.

[T]he legislative veto is more than "efficient, convenient, and useful." . . . It is an important if not indispensable political invention that allows the President and Congress to resolve major constitutional and policy differences, assures the accountability of independent regulatory agencies, and preserves Congress' control over lawmaking. Perhaps there are other means of accommodation and accountability, but the increasing reliance of Congress upon the legislative veto suggests that the alternatives to which Congress must now turn are not entirely satisfactory.

The history of the legislative veto also makes clear that it has not been a sword with which Congress has struck out to aggrandize itself at the expense of the other branches — the concerns of Madison and Hamilton. Rather, the veto has been a means of defense, a reservation of ultimate authority necessary if Congress is to fulfill its designated role under Article I as the nation's lawmaker. While the President has often objected to particular legislative vetoes, generally those left in the hands of congressional committees, the Executive has more often agreed to legislative review as the price for a broad delegation of authority. To be sure, the President may have preferred unrestricted power, but that could be precisely why Congress thought it essential to retain a check on the exercise of delegated authority.

For all these reasons, the apparent sweep of the Court's decision today is regrettable. The Court's Article I analysis appears to invalidate all legislative vetoes irrespective of form or subject. Because the legislative veto is commonly found as a check upon rulemaking by administrative agencies and upon broad-based policy decisions of the Executive Branch, it is particularly unfortunate that the Court reaches its decision in a case involving the exercise of a veto over deportation decisions regarding particular individuals. Courts should always be wary of striking statutes as unconstitutional; to strike an entire class of statutes based on consideration of a somewhat atypical and more-readily indictable exemplar of the class is irresponsible.

The reality of the situation is that the constitutional question posed today is one of immense difficulty over which the executive and legislative branches — as well as scholars and judges — have understandably disagreed. In my view, neither Article I of the Constitution nor the doctrine of separation of powers is violated by this mechanism by which our elected representatives preserve their voice in the governance of the nation. The power to exercise a legislative veto is not the power to write new law without bicameral approval or presidential consideration. The veto must be authorized by statute and may only negative what an Executive department or independent agency has proposed. On its face, the legislative veto no more allows one House of Congress to make law than does the presidential veto confer such power upon the President. Accordingly, the Court properly recognizes that it "must establish that the challenged action under §244(c)(2) is of the kind to which the procedural requirements of Art. I, §7 apply" and admits that "not every action taken by either House is subject to the bicameralism and presentation requirements of Art. I."

The Court's holding today that all legislative-type action must be enacted through the lawmaking process ignores that legislative authority is routinely delegated to the Executive branch, to the independent regulatory agencies, and to private individuals and groups.

"The rise of administrative bodies probably has been the most significant legal trend of the last century. . . . They have become a veritable fourth branch of the Government, which has deranged our three-branch legal theories. . . ." *Federal Trade Commission v. Ruberoid Co.*, 343 U.S. 470, 487 (1952) (Jackson, J. dissenting).

If Congress may delegate lawmaking power to independent and executive agencies, it is most difficult to understand Article I as forbidding Congress from also reserving a check on legislative power for itself. Absent the veto, the agencies receiving delegations of legislative or quasi-legislative power may issue regulations having the force of law without bicameral approval and without the President's signature. It is thus not apparent why the reservation of a veto over the exercise of that legislative power must be subject to a more exacting test. In both cases, it is enough that the initial statutory authorizations comply with the Article I requirements.

The Court also takes no account of perhaps the most relevant consideration: However resolutions of disapproval under §244(c)(2) are formally characterized, in reality, a departure from the status quo occurs only upon the concurrence of opinion among the House, Senate, and President. Reservations of legislative authority to be exercised by Congress should be upheld if the exercise of such reserved authority is consistent with the distribution of and limits upon legislative power that Article I provides.

The central concern of the presentation and bicameralism requirements of Article I is that when a departure from the legal status quo is undertaken, it is done with the approval of the President and both Houses of Congress — or, in the event of a presidential veto, a two-thirds majority in both Houses. This interest is fully satisfied by the operation of §244(c)(2). The President's approval is found in the Attorney General's action in recommending to Congress that the deportation order for a given alien be suspended. The House and the Senate indicate their approval of the Executive's action by not passing a resolution of disapproval within the statutory period. Thus, a change in the legal status quo — the deportability of the alien — is consummated only with the approval of each of the three relevant actors. The disagreement of any one of the three maintains the alien's pre-existing status: the Executive may choose not to recommend suspension; the House and Senate may each veto the recommendation. The effect on the rights and obligations of the affected individuals and upon the legislative system is precisely the same as if a private bill were introduced but failed to receive the necessary approval. "The President and the two Houses enjoy exactly the same say in what the law is to be as would have been true for each without the presence of the one-House veto, and nothing in the law is changed absent the concurrence of the President and a majority in each House." *Atkins v. United States*, 556 F.2d 1028, 1064 (Ct. Claims, 1977).

[T]he history of the separation of powers doctrine is also a history of accommodation and practicality. Apprehensions of an overly powerful branch have not led to undue prophylactic measures that handicap the effective working of the national government as a whole. The Constitution does not contemplate total separation of the three branches of Government. *Buckley v. Valeo*, 424 U.S. 1, 121 (1976). "[A] hermetic sealing off of the three branches of Government from one another would preclude the establishment of a Nation capable of governing itself effectively." *Ibid.*

"[I]n determining whether the Act disrupts the proper balance between the coordinate branches, the proper inquiry focuses on the extent to which it prevents the Executive Branch from accomplishing its constitutionally assigned functions. *United States v. Nixon*, 418 U.S. [683] at 711-712. Only where the potential for disruption is present must we then determine whether that impact is justified by an overriding need to promote objectives within the constitutional authority of Congress." 433 U.S., at 443.

Section 244(c)(2) survives this test. The legislative veto provision does not "prevent the Executive Branch from accomplishing its constitutionally assigned functions." First, it is clear that the Executive Branch has no "constitutionally assigned" function of suspending the deportation of aliens. "'Over no conceivable subject is the legislative power of Congress more complete than it is over' the admission of aliens." *Kleindienst v. Mandel*, 408 U.S. 753, 766 (1972), quoting *Oceanic Steam Navigation Co. v. Stranahan*, 214 U.S. 320, 339 (1909). Nor can it be said that the inherent function of the Executive Branch in executing the law is involved. Here, §244 grants the executive only a qualified suspension authority and it is only that authority which the President is constitutionally authorized to execute.

Moreover, the Court believes that the legislative veto we consider today is best characterized as an exercise of legislative or quasi-legislative authority. Under this characterization, the practice does not, even on the surface, constitute an infringement of executive or judicial prerogative. The Attorney General's suspension of deportation is equivalent to a proposal for legislation. The nature of the Attorney General's role as recommendatory is not altered because §244 provides for congressional action through disapproval rather than by ratification. In comparison to private bills, which must be initiated in the Congress and which allow a Presidential veto to be overridden by a two-thirds majority in both Houses of Congress, §244 augments rather than reduces the executive branch's authority. So understood, congressional review does not undermine, as the Court of Appeals thought, the "weight and dignity" that attends the decisions of the Executive Branch.

Nor does §244 infringe on the judicial power, as Justice Powell would hold. Section 244 makes clear that Congress has reserved its own judgment as part of the statutory process. Congressional action does not substitute for judicial review of the Attorney General's decisions. The Act provides for judicial review of the refusal of the Attorney General to suspend a deportation and to transmit a recommendation to Congress. *INS v. Wang*, 450 U.S. 139 (1981) (per curiam). But the courts have not been given the authority to review whether an alien should be given permanent status; review is limited to whether the Attorney General has properly applied the statutory standards for essentially denying the alien a recommendation that his deportable status be changed by the Congress. Moreover, there is no constitutional obligation to provide any judicial review whatever for a failure to suspend deportation. "The power of Congress, therefore, to expel, like the power to exclude aliens, or any specified class of aliens, from the country, may be exercised entirely through executive officers; or Congress may call in the aid of the judiciary to ascertain any contested facts on which an alien's right to be in the country has been made by Congress to depend." *Fong Yue Ting v. United States*, 149 U.S. 698, 713-714 (1893).

I do not suggest that all legislative vetoes are necessarily consistent with separation of powers principles. A legislative check on an inherently executive function, for example that of initiating prosecutions, poses an entirely different question. But the legislative veto device here—and in many other settings—is far from an instance of legislative tyranny over the Executive. It is a necessary check on the unavoidably expanding power of the agencies, both executive and independent, as they engage in exercising authority delegated by Congress.

Notes and Questions

1. The majority invalidated all negative legislative vetoes as a violation of the constitutional lawmaking requirements of bicameralism and presentment. Justice Powell would have invalidated the legislative veto at issue in the case because it involved the exercise of judicial power. Why did the majority and Justice Powell have different understandings?

2. How do we think about the majority's focus on the legislative process? On the one hand, that focus seems overly formalistic, given the reality of the regulatory state. On the other hand, the INS and the Attorney General accorded Chadha the full rigors of the administrative process only to have that process overturned by Congress, without the full rigors of the legislative process. Perhaps the great danger of the legislative veto in Chadha's case *was* the process (or lack thereof). In the individual rights context, a version of Justice Powell's argument is that legislators should not assume the role of adjudicators because they lack an individualized, trial-type process. Does that argument prove too much? Could Congress pass a statute deporting Chadha? In any event, the larger question posed by both the majority and the concurrence is this one: what is a better option—the administrative process or the legislative veto?

3. Note that most legislative vetoes reverse an agency regulation of general application rather than an adjudicatory order involving a specific person's legal status. Consider a legislative veto provision in an energy statute, which authorizes either House to disapprove by resolution certain NHTSA "energy actions" involving fuel economy and pricing. *See* Energy Policy and

Conservation Act, 42 U.S.C. §6421(c) (authorizing either House to disapprove certain presidentially proposed "energy actions" involving fuel economy and pricing). Opponents of a certain energy action would only need to persuade one House of Congress to veto the action. The legislative veto makes it cheaper for private groups to skew legislation in their preferred direction. Isn't this the sort of arbitrary action that the formal legislative process is designed to inhibit (i.e., hasty and improvident law)?

4. While the decision in *Chadha* is viewed as highly consequential, prior to the decision, Congress rarely exercised the veto to overrule a regulatory decision. As reflected in a study by the Congressional Research Service, Congress exercised the legislative veto 255 times between 1932 and 1983. *See* C.L. Norton, *Usage of the Congressional Veto: Approval and Disapproval Resolutions Introduced, Adopted, Rejected or Not Acted Upon*, 1932-1983, Washington, DC: Library of Congress, Congressional Research Service, Report No. 84-114 Gov 11 (1984). Only a small percentage of this set of actions involved regulatory policy; Congress used a legislative veto to reject agency rules and regulations less than 20 times. *Id.* at 2. That amounts to an extremely small percentage of rulemaking activity during that period. To say the least, Congress's exercise of the veto did not match its zeal for including legislative veto provisions in legislation. At the same time, in a period of divided government, it is hard to imagine that the House or Senate would not use the legislative veto more vigorously today. Is that merely a reflection of the increasingly polarized character of our politics?

5. Now consider whether the legislative veto might encourage Congress to enact especially vague statutes. Can you see why it might have this effect? Is this a *constitutional* reason to reject the legislative veto? What kind of bicameralism are we getting if Congress has a tool that allows it to retain a measure of control even when it enacts vague statutes?

6. The legislative veto also might elevate the preferences of the current Congress above those of the enacting Congress in the implementation of a statute. Suppose the enacting Congress intended the "extreme hardship" provision to be liberally applied, but a subsequent committee or coalition took a different view, which it implemented through the veto. Is this what happened in the case? If so, whose view should count?

7. Justice White argued in dissent that nothing in the Constitution prohibits the legislative veto and that the legislative veto operates as a safety valve against ever-expanding agency authority. In effect, the legislative veto restores to Congress the level of control it lost when the complexity of modern industrial society compelled it to grant broad authority to agencies. Once we acknowledge that broad delegation is necessary, shouldn't we be prepared to accept a congressional check? Does that suggest that Justice White's view is correct?

8. Think about the issue from a slightly different angle. The President possesses means short of legislation to assert control of agency action (although the President cannot possess a "line item" veto). Doesn't Congress deserve a comparable tool? Why is it restricted to the seemingly all-or-nothing choice between statutory amendments and oversight hearings?

9. Following the *Chadha* decision, Congress continued to enact statutes that contained legislative veto provisions. *See* Louis Fisher, *The Legislative Veto: Invalidated, It Survives,* 56 LAW & CONTEMP. PROBS. 273, 275-84 (1993). Although the legislative veto provisions are not constitutional if acted upon, Congress appears to believe that agencies will take them as a warning. In 1996, Congress came up with an alternative mechanism to provide review of agency regulations as part of the Contract with America Advancement Act of 1996. It is the granddaddy of all "laying over" provisions, the Congressional Review Act (CRA), 5 U.S.C. §§801-803. It requires agencies to submit their regulations to Congress and then wait for a certain period of time before those regulations become effective, during which time Congress can override them by joint resolution. Why is the CRA constitutional after *Chadha?* We also noted that Congress has only repealed a single rule under the CRA, as of 2008. What does this suggest about the CRA? Is it too formal to work?

6. Congressional Review Act

The Congressional Review Act (CRA) was enacted in 1996. *See* Subtitle E ("Congressional Review") of the Small Business Regulatory Enforcement Fairness Act of 1996, Title II of the Contract with America Advancement Act of 1996, P.L. 104-121, 101 Stat. 847 at 868-74, codified at Title 5 U.S.C. Sections 801-808. It requires agencies, when publishing "rules" in the Federal Register, to submit those rules to Congress, which then has 60 legislative days to pass a joint resolution overturning them. Until recently, Congress had used the CRA only once, in 2001, to overturn an agency rule. In 2017, during the first 100 days of the Trump administration, Congress used the CRA to overturn 14 rules that the Obama administration had approved in its final weeks. The overturned rules concerned education, environment, gun control, health, labor, and telecommunications. The CRA prohibits the agencies from issuing a new rule that is "substantially the same form" as the overturned rule, absent new legislative authorization. *See* 5 U.S.C. §801(b)(2).

The CRA defines "rules" based on the APA, but notably includes guidance as well as notice-and-comment rules. As a result, Congress has an opportunity to disapprove guidance through the CRA's procedures, even though such guidance is often difficult to challenge in court. Of course, a rule must be submitted to Congress to trigger review, which is not always the case, especially for guidance, which agencies may not view as final agency action. An agency rule that was not submitted to Congress for this reason or any other may be submitted at any time. This feature is what makes the CRA a potentially powerful tool for new administrations—with the cooperation of Congress—to undo the policies of the previous administration. The new administration does not have to issue a new notice-and-comment rule rescinding the old one, which would take more than 60 days, or withdraw the old guidance. Withdrawing the guidance does not sound particularly onerous, but the CRA has lasting effect—the agency is prohibited from issuing the guidance in substantially the same form unless Congress enacts new legislation.

The Government Accounting Office administers the submission process. From the GOA's website, *www.gao.gov*:

> The Congressional Review Act requires GAO to report on major rules that federal agencies make, including summaries of the procedural steps taken by the agencies.
>
> Federal agencies promulgating rules must submit a copy to both houses of Congress and GAO before the rules can take effect. (Congressional Review Act, 5 U.S.C. §801(a)(1)(A)). We track all rules (major and non-major) submitted to us.
>
> Federal agencies can submit rules to GAO using the Submission of Federal Rules under the Congressional Review Act. We also provide Congress with related Legal Opinions, upon request.
>
> **GAO Contact**
> Please send comments and suggestions to FedRules@gao.gov.

Here is an example of a submission by the FDA:

April 1, 2019

The Honorable Lamar Alexander, Chairman
The Honorable Patty Murray, Ranking Member
Committee on Health, Education, Labor, and Pensions
United States Senate

The Honorable Frank Pallone, Jr., Chairman
The Honorable Greg Walden, Ranking Member
Committee on Energy and Commerce
House of Representatives

Subject: *Department of Health and Human Services, Food and Drug Administration: Standards for the Growing, Harvesting, Packing, and Holding of Produce for Human Consumption; Extension of Compliance Dates for Subpart E*

Pursuant to section 801(a)(2)(A) of title 5, United States Code, this is our report on a major rule promulgated by Department of Health and Human Services, Food and Drug Administration (FDA) entitled "Standards for the Growing, Harvesting, Packing, and Holding of Produce for Human Consumption; Extension of Compliance Dates for Subpart E" (RIN: 0910-AH93). We received the rule on March 13, 2019. It was published in the *Federal Register* as a final rule on March 18, 2019. 84 Fed. Reg. 9706.

The final rule extends for covered produce other than sprouts, the dates for compliance with the agricultural water provisions in the "Standards for the Growing, Harvesting, Packing, and Holding of Produce for Human Consumption" rule published in November 2015 (November 2015 Rule). FDA is extending the compliance dates to address questions about the practical implementation of compliance with certain provisions and to consider how it might further reduce the regulatory burden or increase flexibility while continuing to protect public health.

The Congressional Review Act (CRA) requires a 60-day delay in the effective date of a major rule from the date of publication in the *Federal Register* or receipt of the rule by Congress, whichever is later. 5 U.S.C. §801(a)(3)(A). The November 2015 rule had a stated effective date of January 26, 2016. 80 Fed. Reg. 74,354, 74,527 (Nov. 27, 2015). In our major rule report for the November 2015 rule, we reported that it did not have the required 60-day delay in effective date because it was not received until December 1, 2015. GAO, *Department of Health and Human Services, Food and Drug Administration: Standards for the Growing, Harvesting, Packing and Holding of Produce for Human Consumption*, GAO-16-299R (Washington, D.C.: Dec. 16, 2015). The November 2015 Rule had staggered compliance dates ranging from 1 to 6 years from the effective date, depending on the size of the farm and the specific requirement; The notice of proposed rulemaking for this rule was published in the *Federal Register* on September 13, 2017, and this final rule was published on March 18, 2019. 82 Fed. Reg. 42,963; 84 Fed. Reg. 9706. The rule was received by the House of Representatives on March 19, 2019, and the Senate received the rule March 18, 2019. 165 Cong. Rec. H2793 (Mar. 25, 2019); 165 Cong. Rec. S2039 (Mar. 27, 2019). The rule states that as of March 18, 2019, the compliance dates for certain provisions of the November 2015 Rule are delayed to January 26, 2024. Therefore the final rule does not have the required 60-day delay in its effective date.

Enclosed is our assessment of FDA's compliance with the procedural steps required by section 801(a)(1)(B)(i) through (iv) of title 5 with respect to the rule. If you have any questions about this report or wish to contact GAO officials responsible for the evaluation work relating to the subject matter of the rule, please contact Janet Temko-Blinder at (202) 512-7104.

Shirley A. Jones
Managing Associate General Counsel

Enclosure

cc: Kenneth Cohen
    Director, Regulations Policy and Management Staff
    Food and Drug Administration
    Department of Health and Human Services

ENCLOSURE

REPORT UNDER 5 U.S.C. §801(a)(2)(A) ON A MAJOR RULE
ISSUED BY THE
DEPARTMENT OF HEALTH AND HUMAN SERVICES,
FOOD AND DRUG ADMINISTRATION
ENTITLED
"STANDARDS FOR THE GROWING, HARVESTING, PACKING, AND
HOLDING OF PRODUCE FOR HUMAN CONSUMPTION;
EXTENSION OF COMPLIANCE DATES FOR SUBPART E"
(RIN: 0910-AH93)

(i) Cost-benefit analysis

Food and Drug Administration (FDA) included in this final rule an economic analysis of its impacts. FDA found that all initial startup costs and recurring costs remain the same as estimated in the final regulatory impact analysis for the "Standards for the Growing, Harvesting, Packing, and Holding of Produce for Human Consumption" rule (November 2015 Rule). However, FDA found the annualized total costs decrease from $291 million to $280 million, resulting in a savings of $12 million, when calculated with a 3 percent discount rate over 10 years or decrease from $265 million to $254 million resulting in a savings of $10 million, when calculated with a 7 percent discount rate over 10 years. FDA found that the present value of total costs, discounted at 3 percent over 10 years, decreases from about $2.5 billion to about $2.4 billion, resulting in a savings of about $99 million or, discounted at 7 percent over 10 years, decreases from about $1.9 billion to about $1.8 billion, resulting in a savings of about $74 million.

FDA also found that there is a reduction in benefits associated with extending the compliance dates. Consumers eating non-sprout covered produce will not enjoy the potential health benefits (*i.e.,* reduced risk of illness) provided by the provisions of the November 2015 Rule until 2 to 4 years later than originally established in the produce safety regulation. Thus, FDA estimated the annualized total benefits to consumers, discounted at 3 percent over 10 years, decrease by $104 million from $800 million to $696 million or discounted at 7 percent over 10 years, decrease by $96 million from $740 million to $644 million. According to FDA, the present value of total benefits, discounted at 3 percent over 10 years, decreases from about $6.8 billion to about $5.9 billion or, discounted at 7 percent over 10 years, decreases from about $5.2 billion to about $4.5 billion.

(ii) Agency actions relevant to the Regulatory Flexibility Act (RFA), 5 U.S.C. §§603-605, 607, and 609

FDA certified that this final rule will not have a significant economic impact on a substantial number of small entities.

(iii) Agency actions relevant to sections 202-205 of the Unfunded Mandates Reform Act of 1995, 2 U.S.C. §§1532-1535

FDA determined that this final rule will not result in expenditure by state, local, and tribal governments, in the aggregate, in any year that meets or exceeds $150 million ($100 million adjusted for inflation).

(iv) Other relevant information or requirements under acts and executive orders

Administrative Procedure Act, 5 U.S.C. §§551 et seq.

On September 13, 2017, FDA published a proposed rule. 82 Fed. Reg. 42,963. FDA received comments from covered farms, consumer protection groups, groups representing these stakeholders, and state governments. FDA responded to comments within the scope of the proposed rule in the final rule.

Paperwork Reduction Act (PRA), 44 U.S.C. §§3501-3520

FDA determined that this final rule contains no collection of information.

Statutory authorization for the rule

FDA promulgated the November 2015 Rule under the authorities of the Federal Food, Drug, and Cosmetic Act (FD&C Act) as amended by the Food Safety Modernization Act (FSMA), and the Public Health Service Act (PHS Act). FDA specifically cited the authorities in section 105 of FSMA, sections 419, 701(a), and 709 of the FD&C Act and sections 311, 361, and 368 of the PHS Act. 21 U.S.C. §§350h, 371(a), 379a; 42 U.S.C. §§243, 264, 271. FDA did not identify statutory authority to delay the November 2015 Rule in this final rule.

Executive Order No. 12866 (Regulatory Planning and Review)

FDA determined that this final rule is an economically significant regulatory action as defined by the Order.

Executive Order No. 13132 (Federalism)

FDA determined that this final rule does not contain policies that have federalism implications as defined by the Order.

Notes and Questions

1. The CRA, enacted 10 years after the Court invalidated the legislative veto in *Chada*, was not an effective tool of congressional control until a motivated presidential administration set it in motion. Does that make the CRA better or worse? Both political branches are involved in repealing agency rules, just as the constitutional requirements for lawmaking intend. That's good, right?

2. Or does the CRA result in a "diffusion of accountability," to use Chief Justice Roberts's phrase from *Free Enterprise* (the *PCAOB* case), excerpted above? The Congressional Review Act seems to be as much a tool a presidential control, under the right circumstances. But it is Congress that undertakes the review and commences the joint resolution process. Which branch is responsible for reversing the agency rules?

3. The Trump administration did not escape accountability for the repeal of the 14 regulations from the Obama administration; to the contrary, it sought responsibility. Where is the worry when a newly elected administration acts to reverse rules that the outgoing administration sought to entrench in its last weeks? The outgoing administration was attempting a "dead hand of the law" maneuver, wasn't it?

4. Is there a worry in the speed with which the law shifts? The APA contemplates a participatory and deliberative process for issuing, amending, and rescinding notice-and-comment rules. Does the CRA replace administrative procedure with politics?

5. Consider the FDA's letter to the House and Senate committee leaders. Is this document sufficient for adequate review? Does it have to provide much information when agency has already published the final rule with full explanation? Is it merely a screening device for Congress? If it is a screening device, what sort of information does it provide?

7. Congressional Control of Agency Officials

Another tool that Congress has created and the Court has rejected concerns control of agency officials. As you know, Congress has many (valid) means to assert control of agency officials. Congress has a constitutional role in the appointment of agency officials. The Constitution provides that presidential appointment of "Officers of the United States" must be made with the "Advice and Consent" of the Senate. U.S. CONST. art. II, §2. Moreover, Congress has the ability to bring pressure to bear on particular officials once appointed, for example, by calling them to appear for an oversight hearing. The question, however, is whether Congress can seek more formal or direct means to assert control of agency officials. What if Congress created a scheme that granted itself a role in removing an agency head? Congress could then use that removal power to compel compliance with its preferences, much as the President is able to do. The Court held that such a strategy is unconstitutional.

Bowsher v. Synar

478 U.S. 714 (1986)

CHIEF JUSTICE BURGER delivered the opinion of the Court.

The question presented by these appeals is whether the assignment by Congress to the Comptroller General of the United States of certain functions under the Balanced Budget and Emergency Deficit Control Act of 1985 [Gramm-Rudman-Hollings] violates the doctrine of separation of powers.

I

. . . The purpose of the [Gramm-Rudman-Hollings] Act is to eliminate the federal budget deficit. To that end, the Act sets a "maximum deficit amount" for federal spending for each of fiscal years 1986 through 1991. The size of that maximum deficit amount progressively reduces to zero in fiscal year 1991. If in any fiscal year the federal budget deficit exceeds the maximum deficit amount by more than a specified sum, the Act requires across-the-board cuts in federal spending to reach the targeted deficit level, with half of the cuts made to defense programs and the other half made to nondefense programs.

These "automatic" reductions are accomplished through a rather complicated procedure, spelled out in §251, the so-called "reporting provisions" of the Act. Each year, the Directors of the Office of Management and Budget (OMB) and the Congressional Budget Office (CBO) independently estimate the amount of the federal budget deficit for the upcoming fiscal year. If that deficit exceeds the maximum targeted deficit amount for that fiscal year by more than a specified amount, the Directors of OMB and CBO independently calculate, on a program-by-program basis, the budget reductions necessary to ensure that the deficit does not exceed the maximum deficit amount. The Act then requires the Directors to report jointly their deficit estimates and budget reduction calculations to the Comptroller General.

The Comptroller General, after reviewing the Directors' reports, then reports his conclusions to the President. §251(b). The President in turn must issue a "sequestration" order mandating the spending reductions specified by the Comptroller General. §252. There follows a period during which Congress may by legislation reduce spending to obviate, in whole or in part, the need for the sequestration order. If such reductions are not enacted, the sequestration order becomes effective and the spending reductions included in that order are made. . . .

Within hours of the President's signing of the Act, Congressman Synar, who had voted against the Act, filed a complaint seeking declaratory relief that the Act was unconstitutional. Eleven other Members later joined Congressman Synar's suit. A virtually identical lawsuit was also filed by the National Treasury Employees Union. The Union alleged that its members had been injured as a result of the Act's automatic spending reduction provisions, which have suspended certain cost-of-living benefit increases to the Union's members.

II

[The Court first addressed the issuing of standing and found that one of the appellants, a member of the Union, had an injury in fact.]

III

We noted recently that "[t]he Constitution sought to divide the delegated powers of the new Federal Government into three defined categories, Legislative, Executive, and Judicial." *INS v. Chadha*, 462 U.S. 919, 951 (1983). The declared purpose of separating and dividing the powers of government, of course, was to "diffus[e] power the better to secure liberty." *Youngstown Sheet & Tube Co. v. Sawyer*, 343 U.S. 579, 635 (1952) (Jackson, J., concurring). . . .

Other, more subtle, examples of separated powers are evident as well. Unlike parliamentary systems such as that of Great Britain, no person who is an officer of the United States may serve as a Member of the Congress. Art. I, §6. Moreover, unlike parliamentary systems, the President, under Article II, is responsible not to the Congress but to the people, subject only to impeachment proceedings which are exercised by the two Houses as representatives of the people. Art. II, §4. And even in the impeachment of a President the presiding officer of the ultimate tribunal is not a member of the Legislative Branch, but the Chief Justice of the United States. Art. I, §3.

That this system of division and separation of powers produces conflicts, confusion, and discordance at times is inherent, but it was deliberately so structured to assure full, vigorous, and open debate on the great issues affecting the people and to provide avenues for the operation of checks on the exercise of governmental power.

The Constitution does not contemplate an active role for Congress in the supervision of officers charged with the execution of the laws it enacts. The President appoints "Officers of the United States" with the "Advice and Consent of the Senate. . . ." Art. II, §2. Once the appointment has been made and confirmed, however, the Constitution explicitly provides for removal of Officers of the United States by Congress only upon impeachment by the House of Representatives and conviction by the Senate. An impeachment by the House and trial by the Senate can rest only on "Treason, Bribery or other high Crimes and Misdemeanors." Article II, §4. A direct congressional role in the removal of officers charged with the execution of the laws beyond this limited one is inconsistent with separation of powers.

This Court first directly addressed this issue in *Myers v. United States*, 272 U.S. 52 (1925). At issue in *Myers* was a statute providing that certain postmasters could be removed only "by and with the advice and consent of the Senate." The President removed one such Postmaster without Senate approval, and a lawsuit ensued. Chief Justice Taft, writing for the Court, declared the statute unconstitutional on the ground that for Congress to "draw to itself, or to either branch of it, the power to remove or the right to participate in the exercise of that power . . . would be . . . to infringe the constitutional principle of the separation of governmental powers." *Id.*, at 161.

A decade later, in *Humphrey's Executor v. United States*, 295 U.S. 602 (1935), relied upon heavily by appellants, a Federal Trade Commissioner who had been removed by the President sought backpay. *Humphrey's Executor* involved an issue not presented either in the *Myers* case or in this case — i.e., the power of Congress to limit the President's powers of removal of a Federal Trade Commissioner. 295 U.S., at 630.[1] The relevant statute permitted removal "by the President," but only "for inefficiency, neglect of duty, or malfeasance in office." Justice Sutherland, speaking for the Court, upheld the statute, holding that "illimitable power of removal is not possessed by the President [with respect to Federal Trade Commissioners]." *Id.*, at 628-629. The Court distinguished *Myers*, reaffirming its holding that congressional participation in the removal of executive officers is unconstitutional. Justice Sutherland's opinion for the Court also underscored the crucial role of separated powers in our system:

> "The fundamental necessity of maintaining each of the three general departments of government entirely free from the control or coercive influence, direct or indirect, of either of the others, has often been stressed and is hardly open to serious question. So much is implied in the very fact of the separation of the powers of these departments by the Constitution; and in the rule which recognizes their essential co-equality." 295 U.S., at 629-630.

The Court reached a similar result in *Wiener v. United States,* 357 U.S. 349 (1958), concluding that, under *Humphrey's Executor,* the President did not have unrestrained removal authority over a member of the War Claims Commission.

In light of these precedents, we conclude that Congress cannot reserve for itself the power of removal of an officer charged with the execution of the laws except by impeachment. To permit the execution of the laws to be vested in an officer answerable only to Congress would, in practical terms, reserve in Congress control over the execution of the laws. As the District Court observed: "Once an officer is appointed, it is only the authority that can remove him, and not the authority that appointed him, that he must fear and, in the performance of his functions, obey." 626 F. Supp., at 1401. The structure of the Constitution does not permit Congress to execute the laws; it follows that Congress cannot grant to an officer under its control what it does not possess.

Our decision in *INS v. Chadha,* 462 U.S. 919 (1983), supports this conclusion. To permit an officer controlled by Congress to execute the laws would be, in essence, to permit a congressional veto. Congress could simply remove, or threaten to remove, an officer for executing the laws in any

---

1. Appellants therefore are wide of the mark in arguing that an affirmance in this case requires casting doubt on the status of "independent" agencies because no issues involving such agencies are presented here. The statutes establishing independent agencies typically specify either that the agency members are removable by the President for specified causes, *see, e.g.,* 15 U.S.C. §41 (members of the Federal Trade Commission may be removed by the President "for inefficiency, neglect of duty, or malfeasance in office"), or else do not specify a removal procedure, *see, e.g.,* 2 U.S.C. §437c (Federal Election Commission). This case involves nothing like these statutes, but rather a statute that provides for direct congressional involvement over the decision to remove the Comptroller General. Appellants have referred us to no independent agency whose members are removable by the Congress for certain causes short of impeachable offenses, as is the Comptroller General. . . .

fashion found to be unsatisfactory to Congress. This kind of congressional control over the execution of the laws, *Chadha* makes clear, is constitutionally impermissible.

. . . With these principles in mind, we turn to consideration of whether the Comptroller General is controlled by Congress.

IV

Appellants urge that the Comptroller General performs his duties independently and is not subservient to Congress. We agree with the District Court that this contention does not bear close scrutiny.

The critical factor lies in the provisions of the statute defining the Comptroller General's office relating to removability. Although the Comptroller General is nominated by the President from a list of three individuals recommended by the Speaker of the House of Representatives and the President pro tempore of the Senate, *see* 31 U.S.C. §703(a)(2), and confirmed by the Senate, he is removable only at the initiative of Congress. He may be removed not only by impeachment but also by joint resolution of Congress "at any time" resting on any one of the following bases:

"(i) permanent disability;
"(ii) inefficiency;
"(iii) neglect of duty;
"(iv) malfeasance; or
"(v) a felony or conduct involving moral turpitude."

31 U.S.C. §703(e)(1)B.[2]

This provision was included, as one Congressman explained in urging passage of the Act, because Congress "felt that [the Comptroller General] should be brought under the sole control of Congress, so that Congress at any moment when it found he was inefficient and was not carrying on the duties of his office as he should and as the Congress expected, could remove him without the long, tedious process of a trial by impeachment." 61 Cong. Rec. 1081 (1921).

The removal provision was an important part of the legislative scheme, as a number of Congressmen recognized. Representative Hawley commented: "[H]e is our officer, in a measure, getting information for us. . . . If he does not do his work properly, we, as practically his employers, ought to be able to discharge him from his office." 58 Cong. Rec. 7136 (1919). Representative Sisson observed that the removal provisions would give "[t]he Congress of the United States . . . absolute control of the man's destiny in office." 61 Cong. Rec. 987 (1921). The ultimate design was to "give the legislative branch of the Government control of the audit, not through the

---

2. Although the President could veto such a joint resolution, the veto could be overridden by a two-thirds vote of both Houses of Congress. Thus, the Comptroller General could be removed in the face of Presidential opposition. Like the District Court, 626 F. Supp., at 1393, n.21, we therefore read the removal provision as authorizing removal by Congress alone.

power of appointment, but through the power of removal." 58 Cong. Rec. 7211 (1919) (Rep. Temple).

The statute permits removal for "inefficiency," "neglect of duty," or "malfeasance." These terms are very broad and, as interpreted by Congress, could sustain removal of a Comptroller General for any number of actual or perceived transgressions of the legislative will. The Constitutional Convention chose to permit impeachment of executive officers only for "Treason, Bribery, or other high Crimes and Misdemeanors." It rejected language that would have permitted impeachment for "maladministration," with Madison arguing that "[s]o vague a term will be equivalent to a tenure during pleasure of the Senate." 2 M. Farrand, Records of the Federal Convention of 1787, p. 550 (1911).

We need not decide whether "inefficiency" or "malfeasance" are terms as broad as "maladministration" in order to reject the dissent's position that removing the Comptroller General requires "a feat of bipartisanship more difficult than that required to impeach and convict." Surely no one would seriously suggest that judicial independence would be strengthened by allowing removal of federal judges only by a joint resolution finding "inefficiency," "neglect of duty," or "malfeasance." . . .

It is clear that Congress has consistently viewed the Comptroller General as an officer of the Legislative Branch. The Reorganization Acts of 1945 and 1949, for example, both stated that the Comptroller General and the GAO are "a part of the legislative branch of the Government." 59 Stat. 616. Similarly, in the Accounting and Auditing Act of 1950, Congress required the Comptroller General to conduct audits "as an agent of the Congress." 64 Stat. 835. . . .

Against this background, we see no escape from the conclusion that, because Congress has retained removal authority over the Comptroller General, he may not be entrusted with executive powers. The remaining question is whether the Comptroller General has been assigned such powers in the Balanced Budget and Emergency Deficit Control Act of 1985. . . .

Appellants suggest that the duties assigned to the Comptroller General in the Act are essentially ministerial and mechanical so that their performance does not constitute "execution of the law" in a meaningful sense. On the contrary, we view these functions as plainly entailing execution of the law in constitutional terms. Interpreting a law enacted by Congress to implement the legislative mandate is the very essence of "execution" of the law. Under §251, the Comptroller General must exercise judgment concerning facts that affect the application of the Act. He must also interpret the provisions of the Act to determine precisely what budgetary calculations are required. Decisions of that kind are typically made by officers charged with executing a statute.

The executive nature of the Comptroller General's functions under the Act is revealed in §252(a)(3) which gives the Comptroller General the ultimate authority to determine the budget cuts to be made. Indeed, the Comptroller

General commands the President himself to carry out, without the slightest variation (with exceptions not relevant to the constitutional issues presented), the directive of the Comptroller General as to the budget reductions:

> "The [Presidential] order *must provide* for reductions in the manner specified in section 251(a)(3), *must incorporate* the provisions of the [Comptroller General's] report submitted under section 251(b), and *must be consistent with such report in all respects.* The President *may not modify or recalculate any of the estimates, determinations, specifications, bases, amounts, or percentages* set forth in the report submitted under section 251(b) in determining the reductions to be specified in the order with respect to programs, projects, and activities, or with respect to budget activities, within an account. . . ." §252(a)(3) (emphasis added).

See also §251(d)(3)(A).

Congress of course initially determined the content of the Balanced Budget and Emergency Deficit Control Act; and undoubtedly the content of the Act determines the nature of the executive duty. However, as *Chadha* makes clear, once Congress makes its choice in enacting legislation, its participation ends. Congress can thereafter control the execution of its enactment only indirectly—by passing new legislation. *Chadha*, 462 U.S., at 958. By placing the responsibility for execution of the Balanced Budget and Emergency Deficit Control Act in the hands of an officer who is subject to removal only by itself, Congress in effect has retained control over the execution of the Act and has intruded into the executive function. The Constitution does not permit such intrusion.

Justice STEVENS, with whom Justice MARSHALL joins, concurring in the judgment.

When this Court is asked to invalidate a statutory provision that has been approved by both Houses of the Congress and signed by the President, particularly an Act of Congress that confronts a deeply vexing national problem, it should only do so for the most compelling constitutional reasons. I agree with the Court that the "Gramm-Rudman-Hollings" Act contains a constitutional infirmity so severe that the flawed provision may not stand. I disagree with the Court, however, on the reasons why the Constitution prohibits the Comptroller General from exercising the powers assigned to him by §251(b) and §251(c)(2) of the Act. It is not the dormant, carefully circumscribed congressional removal power that represents the primary constitutional evil. Nor do I agree with the conclusion of both the majority and the dissent that the analysis depends on a labeling of the functions assigned to the Comptroller General as "executive powers." . . . Rather, I am convinced that the Comptroller General must be characterized as an agent of Congress because of his longstanding statutory responsibilities; that the powers assigned to him under the Gramm-Rudman-Hollings Act require him to make policy that will bind the Nation; and that, when Congress, or a component or an agent of Congress, seeks to make policy that will bind the Nation, it must follow the procedures mandated by Article I of the Constitution—through passage by both Houses and presentment to the President. In short, Congress may not exercise its fundamental power to formulate national policy by delegating that power to one of its two Houses, to a legislative committee, or to an individual agent of the Congress such as the Speaker of the House of Representatives, the Sergeant at Arms of the Senate, or the Director of the Congressional Budget Office. *INS v. Chadha*, 462 U.S. 919 (1983). That principle, I believe, is applicable to the Comptroller General.

Justice WHITE, dissenting.

The Court, acting in the name of separation of powers, takes upon itself to strike down the Gramm-Rudman-Hollings Act, one of the most novel and far-reaching legislative responses to a national crisis since the New Deal. The basis of the Court's action is a solitary provision of another statute that was passed over 60 years ago and has lain dormant since that time. I cannot concur in the Court's action. Like the Court, I will not purport to speak to the wisdom of the policies incorporated in the legislation the Court invalidates; that is a matter for the Congress and the Executive, both of which expressed their assent to the statute barely half a year ago. I will, however, address the wisdom of the Court's willingness to interpose its distressingly formalistic view of separation of powers as a bar to the attainment of governmental objectives through the means chosen by the Congress and the President in the legislative process established by the Constitution. Twice in the past four years I have expressed my view that the Court's recent efforts to police the separation of powers have rested on untenable constitutional propositions leading to regrettable results. *See Northern Pipeline Construction Co. v. Marathon Pipe Line Co.*, 458 U.S. 50, 92-118 (1982) (White, J., dissenting); *INS v. Chadha*, 462 U.S. 919, 967-1003 (1983) (White, J., dissenting). Today's result is even more misguided. As I will explain, the Court's decision rests on a feature of the legislative scheme that is of minimal practical significance and that presents no substantial threat to the basic scheme of separation of powers. In attaching dispositive significance to what should be regarded as a triviality, the Court neglects what has in the past been recognized as a fundamental principle governing consideration of disputes over separation of powers:

> "The actual art of governing under our Constitution does not and cannot conform to judicial definitions of the power of any of its branches based on isolated clauses or even single Articles torn from context. While the Constitution diffuses power the better to secure liberty, it also contemplates that practice will integrate the dispersed powers into a workable government." *Youngstown Sheet & Tube Co. v. Sawyer*, 343 U.S. 579, 635 (1952) (Jackson, J., concurring).

I have no quarrel with the proposition that the powers exercised by the Comptroller under the Act may be characterized as "executive" in that they involve the interpretation and carrying out of the Act's mandate. I can also accept the general proposition that although Congress has considerable authority in designating the officers who are to execute legislation, . . . the constitutional scheme of separated powers does prevent Congress from reserving an executive role for itself or for its "agents." . . . I cannot accept, however, that the exercise of authority by an officer removable for cause by a joint resolution of Congress is analogous to the impermissible execution of the law by Congress itself, nor would I hold that the congressional role in the removal process renders the Comptroller an "agent" of the Congress, incapable of receiving "executive" power.

As the majority points out, the Court's decision in *INS v. Chadha*, 462 U.S. 919 (1983), recognizes limits on the ability of Congress to participate in or influence the execution of the laws. As interpreted in *Chadha*, the Constitution prevents Congress from interfering with the actions of officers of the United States through means short of legislation satisfying the demands of bicameral passage and presentment to the President for approval or disapproval. *Id.*, at 954-955. Today's majority concludes that the same concerns that underlay *Chadha* indicate the invalidity of a statutory provision allowing the removal by joint resolution for specified cause of any officer performing executive functions. Such removal power, the Court contends, constitutes a "congressional veto" analogous to that struck down in *Chadha*, for it permits Congress to "remove, or threaten to remove, an officer for executing the laws in any fashion found to be unsatisfactory." The Court concludes that it is "[t]his kind of congressional control over the execution of the laws" that *Chadha* condemns.

The deficiencies in the Court's reasoning are apparent. First, the Court baldly mischaracterizes the removal provision when it suggests that it allows Congress to remove the Comptroller for "executing the laws in any fashion found to be unsatisfactory"; in fact, Congress may remove the Comptroller only for one or more of five specified reasons, which "although not so narrow as to deny Congress any leeway, circumscribe Congress' power to some extent by providing a basis for judicial review of congressional removal." Second, and more to the point, the Court overlooks or deliberately ignores the decisive difference between the congressional removal provision and the legislative veto struck down in *Chadha*: under the Budget and Accounting Act, Congress may remove the Comptroller only through a joint resolution, which by definition must be passed by both Houses and signed by the President. *See United States v. California*, 332 U.S. 19, 28 (1947). In other words, a removal of the Comptroller under the statute satisfies the requirements of bicameralism and presentment laid down in *Chadha*. The majority's citation of *Chadha* for the proposition that Congress may only control the acts of officers of the United States "by passing new legislation," in no sense casts doubt on the legitimacy of the removal provision, for that provision allows Congress to effect removal only through action that constitutes legislation as defined in *Chadha*.

To the extent that it has any bearing on the problem now before us, *Chadha* would seem to suggest the legitimacy of the statutory provision making the Comptroller removable through joint resolution, for the Court's opinion in *Chadha* reflects the view that the bicameralism and presentment requirements of Art. I represent the principal assurances that Congress will remain within its legislative role in the constitutionally prescribed scheme of separated powers. Action taken in accordance with the "single, finely wrought, and exhaustively considered, procedure" established by Art. I, *Chadha*, at 951, should be presumptively viewed as a legitimate exercise of legislative power. That such action may represent a more or less successful attempt by Congress to "control" the actions of an officer of the United States surely does not in itself indicate that it is unconstitutional, for no one would dispute that Congress has the power to "control" administration through legislation imposing duties or substantive restraints on executive officers, through legislation increasing or decreasing the funds made available to such officers, or through legislation actually abolishing a particular office. . . .

That a joint resolution removing the Comptroller General would satisfy the requirements for legitimate legislative action laid down in *Chadha* does not fully answer the separation of powers argument, for it is apparent that even the results of the constitutional legislative process may be unconstitutional if those results are in fact destructive of the scheme of separation-of-powers. *Nixon v. Administrator of General Services*, 433 U.S. 425 (1977). The question to be answered is whether the threat of removal of the Comptroller General for cause through joint resolution as authorized by the Budget and Accounting Act renders the Comptroller sufficiently subservient to Congress that investing him with "executive" power can be realistically equated with the unlawful retention of such power by Congress itself; more generally, the question is whether there is a genuine threat of "encroachment or aggrandizement of one branch at the expense of the other," *Buckley v. Valeo*, 424 U.S., at 122. Common sense indicates that the existence of the removal provision poses no such threat to the principle of separation of powers.

The statute does not permit anyone to remove the Comptroller at will; removal is permitted only for specified cause, with the existence of cause to be determined by Congress following a hearing. Any removal under the statute would presumably be subject to post-termination judicial review to ensure that a hearing had in fact been held and that the finding of cause for removal was not arbitrary. These procedural and substantive limitations on the removal power militate strongly against the characterization of the Comptroller as a mere agent of Congress by virtue of the removal authority. Indeed, similarly qualified grants of removal power are generally deemed to protect the officers to whom they apply and to establish their independence from the domination of the possessor of the removal power. *See Humphrey's Executor v. United States*, 295 U.S., at 625-626, 629-630, 55 S. Ct., at 874-875. Removal authority limited in such a manner is more properly viewed as motivating adherence to a substantive standard established by law than as inducing subservience to the particular institution that enforces that standard. . . .

More importantly, the substantial role played by the President in the process of removal through joint resolution reduces to utter insignificance the possibility that the threat of removal will induce subservience to the Congress. As I have pointed out above, a joint resolution must be presented to the President and is ineffective if it is vetoed by him, unless the veto is overridden by the constitutionally prescribed two-thirds majority of both Houses of Congress. The requirement of Presidential approval obviates the possibility that the Comptroller will perceive himself as so completely at the mercy of Congress that he will function as its tool. If the Comptroller's conduct in office is not so unsatisfactory to the President as to convince the latter that removal is required under the statutory standard, Congress will have no independent power to coerce the Comptroller unless it can muster a two-thirds majority in both Houses—a feat of bipartisanship more difficult than that required to impeach and convict. The incremental in terrorem effect of the possibility of congressional removal in the face of a Presidential veto is therefore exceedingly unlikely to have any discernible impact on the extent of congressional influence over the Comptroller.

The practical result of the removal provision is not to render the Comptroller unduly dependent upon or subservient to Congress, but to render him one of the most independent officers in the entire federal establishment. Those who have studied the office agree that the procedural and substantive limits on the power of Congress and the President to remove the Comptroller make dislodging him against his will practically impossible.

Realistic consideration of the nature of the Comptroller General's relation to Congress thus reveals that the threat to separation of powers conjured up by the majority is wholly chimerical. The power over removal retained by the Congress is not a power that is exercised outside the legislative process as established by the Constitution, nor does it appear likely that it is a power that adds significantly to the influence Congress may exert over executive officers through other, undoubtedly constitutional exercises of legislative power and through the constitutionally guaranteed impeachment power. Indeed, the removal power is so constrained by its own substantive limits and by the requirement of Presidential approval "that, as a practical matter, Congress has not exercised, and probably will never exercise, such control over the Comptroller General that his non-legislative powers will threaten the goal of dispersion of power, and hence the goal of individual liberty, that separation of powers serves." *Ameron, Inc. v. United States Army Corps of Engineers*, 787 F.2d, at 895 (Becker, J., concurring in part).

The wisdom of vesting "executive" powers in an officer removable by joint resolution may indeed be debatable—as may be the wisdom of the entire scheme of permitting an unelected official to revise the budget enacted by Congress—but such matters are for the most part to be worked out between the Congress and the President through the legislative process, which affords each branch ample opportunity to defend its interests. The Act vesting budget-cutting authority in the Comptroller General represents Congress' judgment that the delegation of such authority to counteract ever-mounting deficits is "necessary and proper" to the exercise of the powers granted the Federal Government by the Constitution; and the President's approval of the statute signifies his unwillingness to reject the choice made by Congress. *Cf. Nixon v. Administrator of General Services*, 433 U.S., at 441. Under such circumstances, the role of this Court should be limited to determining whether the Act so alters the balance of authority among the branches of government as to pose a genuine threat to the basic division between the lawmaking power and the power to execute the law. Because I see no such threat, I cannot join the Court in striking down the Act.

Notes and Questions

1. The Court held that Congress cannot possess the authority to remove the Comptroller General, relying on formal categories: the power to balance the budget is "executive" and therefore cannot be vested in an agency subject to congressional control. Are you confident that you can distinguish "executive" power from "legislative" power in this case? Is there a way to reach the same conclusion even if the power is legislative? Does Justice Stevens help?

2. Does the holding in this case imperil the validity of independent agencies, those subject to a presidential "for cause" removal limitation?

3. Consider that Congress can terminate the Comptroller General only upon joint resolution, which requires the agreement of both Houses and a presidential signature. Congress could use the equivalent process (i.e., the legislative process) to cut the agency's authority or budget. Why not allow it to fire the agency's head? Will this tool be more effective as a means of controlling agency action? Is that why Congress wants it?

4. As in *Chadha*, Justice White dissents. He views the removal provision as part of a useful scheme for controlling runaway budgets. If Congress cannot be trusted to cut the budget because of the realities of the legislative process, why not allow it to use an agency for this purpose? In addition, he notes that Congress does not possess complete control over the Comptroller General any more than the President possesses complete control over independent agency officials. Congress can remove the Comptroller General only for "good cause." Isn't this a better way to view the case? Congress does not gain much control of agency action through this scheme but overcomes its own limitations by placing authority to cut the budget in agency hands.

5. Independent agencies are insulated from presidential control to a certain extent, but they are not any further insulated from Congress. From the perspective of congressional control, the distinction between an executive agency and an independent agency is largely invisible; Congress can exercise the same types of control over independent agencies as it exercises over executive-agencies, including overturning regulations under the Congressional Review Act (*see* 5 U.S.C §804(1)), new legislation, appropriations legislation, and the oversight that is described above. If Congress really wants an agency to be independent, can it also insulate that agency from itself? It probably cannot prevent a future Congress from changing an enacted statute, but it can provide an agency with an independent source of funds that frees it from the direct control of the appropriations process. The most notable case of a self-funded agency is the Federal Reserve Board, which in fact enjoys a high degree of independence as a result. *See* Edward Rubin, *Hyperdepoliticization*, 47 Wake Forest L. Rev. 631 (2012).

C. JUDICIAL CONTROL OF AGENCY ACTION

We now turn to judicial control of agency action. Judicial control comes later than many forms of political control. As we have seen, presidential control routinely occurs in the midst of agency decision making, and congressional control often does as well. Courts exercise control of agency action only by reviewing challenges to such action; generally, that process occurs only after agency action is complete or "final." For the same reason, courts exercise more limited control of agency action than political officials. Judges cannot pick up the telephone and call an agency to express their views. They cannot haul an agency in for hearings on their own initiative. They must wait until someone files a lawsuit challenging agency action. It is fair to say, however, that agencies anticipate judicial review of their actions and incorporate that prospect into their decision making. They certainly know that significant regulations are likely to end up in front of a judge.

Although judicial review is last, it is certainly not least—in terms of the treatment in this book or courses in law school. Judicial review is a main topic of administrative law. We do not seek to replicate the entire administrative law course but introduce the central cases and key concepts, as well as some of the more influential scholarship.

1. Judicial Control of Agency Statutory Interpretation

We begin with the doctrine that the Court has developed for reviewing agency statutory interpretations. In connection with the discussion of agency statutory interpretation in Chapter 5, we have already mentioned the leading case: Chevron U.S.A. Inc. v. Natural Resources Defense Council, Inc., 467 U.S. 837 (1984). It is difficult to over-emphasize the importance of this decision. First, it defines important features of the relationship between agencies and statutes—agencies must implement legislative enactments and their range of discretion in doing so is determined primarily by the language of those statutes. Note that the decision addresses this second issue in terms of the first one. It says that the stringency of judicial review (i.e., how intensely or deferentially courts examine agency interpretations) should be governed by the extent to which Congress delegated basic policy decisions to the agency. If Congress wanted to constrain agency discretion by drafting precise language, then the courts should make sure that the agency abides by that language. But if Congress wanted to increase agency discretion by drafting a vaguely worded or ambiguous statute, then the courts should respect that choice and defer to the agency as long as the agency chose a reasonable interpretation.

There are cases both before and after *Chevron.* In some sense, each of the cases gives courts different tools for controlling agency statutory interpretations rather than simply deferring to them. We present the major ones below. Note that there are other decisions that we could present. Scholars have identified nearly a dozen different deference regimes that courts apply to agency interpretations. We focus on the basic decisions because they are complex enough, as scholars too numerous to mention have demonstrated. (For a sampling, see Jack M. Beermann, *End the Failed* Chevron *Experiment Now: How* Chevron *Failed and Why It Can and Should Be Overruled,* 42 CONN. L. REV. 779 (2010) (arguing that *Chevron* has outlived its usefulness); Lisa Schultz Bressman, Chevron*'s Mistake,* 58 DUKE L.J. 549 (2009) (arguing that *Chevron* allows courts to find statutory meaning where none exists and should be reworked); Elizabeth V. Foote, *Statutory Interpretation or Public Administration: How* Chevron *Misconceives the Function of Agencies and Why It Matters,* 59 ADMIN. L. REV. 673 (2007) (arguing that *Chevron* ignores the reality of agency statutory implementation); Matthew C. Stephenson & Adrian Vermeule, Chevron *Has Only One Step,* 95 VA. L. REV. 597 (2009) (arguing that *Chevron* does not really have two distinct steps and should be reinterpreted); Peter L. Strauss, *"Deference" Is Too Confusing—Let's Call Them* "Chevron *Space"* and *"Skidmore Weight,"* 112 COLUM. L. REV. 1143 (2012) (arguing that *Chevron's* first step of assessing whether the agency acts within its delegated area of discretion, or its "*Chevron* space," is determined by a judge according the agency's construction "*Skidmore*" weight).

a. Before *Chevron: Skidmore*

Skidmore v. Swift & Co.

323 U.S. 134 (1944)

Mr. Justice JACKSON delivered the opinion of the Court.

Seven employees of the Swift and Company packing plant at Fort Worth, Texas, brought an action under the Fair Labor Standards Act, 29 U.S.C.A. §201 et seq., to recover overtime, liquidated damages, and attorneys' fees, totalling approximately $77,000. The District Court rendered judgment denying this claim wholly, and the Circuit Court of Appeals for the Fifth Circuit affirmed. 136 F.2d 112.

It is not denied that the daytime employment of these persons was working time within the Act. Two were engaged in general fire hall duties and maintenance of fire-fighting equipment of the Swift plant. The others operated elevators or acted as relief men in fire duties. They worked from 7:00 A.M. to 3:30 P.M., with a half-hour lunch period, five days a week. They were paid weekly salaries.

Under their oral agreement of employment, however, petitioners undertook to stay in the fire hall on the Company premises, or within hailing distance, three and a half to four nights a week. This involved no task except to answer alarms, either because of fire or because the sprinkler was set off for some other reason. No fires occurred during the period in issue, the alarms were rare, and the time required for their answer rarely exceeded an hour. For each alarm answered the employees were paid in addition to their fixed compensation an agreed amount, fifty cents at first, and later sixty-four cents. The Company provided a brick fire hall equipped with steam heat and air-conditioned rooms. It provided sleeping quarters, a pool table, a domino table, and a radio. The men used their time in sleep or amusement as they saw fit, except that they were required to stay in or close by the fire hall and be ready to respond to alarms. It is stipulated that "they agreed to remain in the fire hall and stay in it or within hailing distance, subject to call, in event of fire or other casualty, but were not required to perform any specific tasks during these periods of time, except in answering alarms." The trial court found the evidentiary facts as stipulated; it made no findings of fact as such as to whether under the arrangement of the parties and the circumstances of this case, which in some respects differ from those of the *Armour* case (*Armour & Co. v. Wantock et al.*, 323 U.S. 126), the fire hall duty or any part thereof constituted working time. It said, however, as a "conclusion of law" that "the time plaintiffs spent in the fire hall subject to call to answer fire alarms does not constitute hours worked, for which overtime compensation is due them under the Fair Labor Standards Act, as interpreted by the Administrator and the Courts," and in its opinion (53 F. Supp. 1020, 1021) observed, "of course we know pursuing such pleasurable occupations or performing such personal chores does not constitute work." The Circuit Court of Appeals affirmed. . . .

Congress did not utilize the services of an administrative agency to find facts and to determine in the first instance whether particular cases fall within or without the Act. Instead, it put this responsibility on the courts. *Kirschbaum v. Walling*, 316 U.S. 517, 523. But it did create the office of Administrator, impose upon him a variety of duties, endow him with powers to inform himself of conditions in industries and employments subject to the Act, and put on him the duties of bringing injunction actions to restrain violations. Pursuit of his duties has accumulated a considerable experience in the problems of ascertaining working time in employments involving periods of inactivity and a knowledge of the customs prevailing in reference to their solution. From these he is obliged to reach conclusions as to conduct without the law, so that he should seek injunctions to stop it, and that within the law, so that he has no call to interfere. He has set forth his views of

IV

The Clean Air Act Amendments of 1977 are a lengthy, detailed, technical, complex, and comprehensive response to a major social issue. A small portion of the statute—91 Stat. 745-751 (Part D of Title I of the amended Act, 42 U.S.C. §§7501-7508)—expressly deals with nonattainment areas. The focal point of this controversy is one phrase in that portion of the Amendments.

Basically, the statute required each State in a nonattainment area to prepare and obtain approval of a new SIP by July 1, 1979. In the interim, those States were required to comply with the EPA's interpretative Ruling of December 21, 1976. 91 Stat. 745. The deadline for attainment of the primary NAAQS's was extended until December 31, 1982, and in some cases until December 31, 1987, but the SIP's were required to contain a number of provisions designed to achieve the goals as expeditiously as possible.

Most significantly for our purposes, the statute provided that each plan shall

> (6) require permits for the construction and operation of new or modified major stationary sources in accordance with section 173. . . .

Id. at 747. Before issuing a permit, §173 requires (1) the state agency to determine that there will be sufficient emissions reductions in the region to offset the emissions from the new source and also to allow for reasonable further progress toward attainment, or that the increased emissions will not exceed an allowance for growth established pursuant to §172(b)(5), (2) the applicant to certify that his other sources in the State are in compliance with the SIP, (3) the agency to determine that the applicable SIP is otherwise being implemented, and (4) the proposed source to comply with the lowest achievable emission rate (LAER).

The 1977 Amendments contain no specific reference to the "bubble concept." Nor do they contain a specific definition of the term "stationary source," though they did not disturb the definition of "stationary source" contained in §111(a)(3), applicable by the terms of the Act to the NSPS program. Section 302(j), however, defines the term "major stationary source" as follows:

> (j) Except as otherwise expressly provided, the terms "major stationary source" and "major emitting facility" mean any stationary facility or source of air pollutants which directly emits, or has the potential to emit, one hundred tons per year or more of any air pollutant (including any major emitting facility or source of fugitive emissions of any such pollutant, as determined by rule by the Administrator).

91 Stat. 770.

V

The legislative history of the portion of the 1977 Amendments dealing with nonattainment areas does not contain any specific comment on the "bubble concept" or the question whether a plantwide definition of a stationary source is permissible under the permit program. It does, however, plainly disclose that in the permit program Congress sought to accommodate the conflict between the economic interest in permitting capital improvements to continue and the environmental interest in improving air quality. Indeed, the House Committee Report identified the economic interest as one of the "two main purposes" of this section of the bill. It stated:

> Section 117 of the bill, adopted during full committee markup establishes a new section 127 of the Clean Air Act. The section has two main purposes: (1) to allow reasonable economic growth to continue in an area while making reasonable further progress to assure attainment of the standards by a fixed date; and (2) to allow States greater flexibility for the former purpose than EPA's present interpretative regulations afford.
>
> The new provision allows States with nonattainment areas to pursue one of two options. First, the State may proceed under EPA's present "tradeoff" or "offset" ruling. The Administrator is authorized, moreover, to modify or amend that ruling in accordance with the intent and purposes of this section.
>
> The State's second option would be to revise its implementation plan in accordance with this new provision.

H.R. Rep. No. 95-294, p. 211 (1977). . . .

VI

. . .

In 1981, a new administration took office and initiated a "Government-wide reexamination of regulatory burdens and complexities." 46 Fed. Reg. 16281. In the context of that review, the EPA reevaluated the various arguments that had been advanced in connection with the proper definition of the term "source" and concluded that the term should be given the same definition in both nonattainment areas and PSD areas.

In explaining its conclusion, the EPA first noted that the definitional issue was not squarely addressed in either the statute or its legislative history, and therefore that the issue involved an agency "judgment as how to best carry out the Act." *Ibid.* It then set forth several reasons for concluding that the plantwide definition was more appropriate. It pointed out that the dual definition "can act as a disincentive to new investment and modernization by discouraging modifications to existing facilities" and can actually retard progress in air pollution control by discouraging replacement of older, dirtier processes or pieces of equipment with new, cleaner ones. Moreover, the new definition would simplify EPA's rules by using the same definition of "source" for PSD, nonattainment new source review, and the construction moratorium. This reduces confusion and inconsistency. Finally, the agency explained that additional requirements that remained in place would accomplish the fundamental purposes of achieving attainment with NAAQS's as expeditiously as possible. These conclusions were expressed in a proposed rulemaking in August, 1981, that was formally promulgated in October. *See id.* at 50766.

VII

In this Court, respondents expressly reject the basic rationale of the Court of Appeals' decision. That court viewed the statutory definition of the term "source" as sufficiently flexible to cover either a plantwide definition, a narrower definition covering each unit within a plant, or a dual definition that could apply to both the entire "bubble" and its components. It interpreted the policies of the statute, however, to mandate the plantwide definition in programs designed to maintain clean air and to forbid it in programs designed to improve air quality. Respondents place a fundamentally different construction on the statute. They contend that the text of the Act requires the EPA to use a dual definition—if either a component of a plant, or the plant as a whole, emits over 100 tons of pollutant, it is a major stationary source. They thus contend that the EPA rules adopted in 1980, insofar as they apply to the maintenance of the quality of clean air, as well as the 1981 rules which apply to nonattainment areas, violate the statute.

Statutory Language

The definition of the term "stationary source" in §111(a)(3) refers to "any building, structure, facility, or installation" which emits air pollution. This definition is applicable only to the NSPS program by the express terms of the statute; the text of the statute does not make this definition applicable to the permit program. Petitioners therefore maintain that there is no statutory language even relevant to ascertaining the meaning of stationary source in the permit program aside from §302(j), which defines the term "major stationary source." We disagree with petitioners on this point.

The definition in §302(j) tells us what the word "major" means—a source must emit at least 100 tons of pollution to qualify—but it sheds virtually no light on the meaning of the term "stationary source." It does equate a source with a facility—a "major emitting facility" and a "major stationary source" are synonymous under §302(j). The ordinary meaning of the term "facility" is some collection of integrated elements which has been designed and constructed to achieve some purpose. Moreover, it is certainly no affront to common English usage to take a reference to a major facility or a major source to connote an entire plant, as opposed to its constituent parts. Basically, however, the language of §302(j) simply does not compel any given interpretation of the term "source."

Respondents recognize that, and hence point to §111(a)(3). Although the definition in that section is not literally applicable to the permit program, it sheds as much light on the meaning of the word "source" as anything in the statute. As respondents point out, use of the words "building, structure, facility, or installation," as the definition of source, could be read to impose the permit conditions on an individual building that is a part of a plant. A "word may have a character of its own not to be submerged by its association." *Russell Motor Car Co. v. United States*, 261 U.S. 514, 519 (1923). On the other hand, the meaning of a word must be ascertained in the context of achieving particular objectives, and the words associated with it may indicate that the true meaning of the series is to convey a common idea. The language may reasonably be interpreted to impose the requirement on any discrete, but integrated, operation which pollutes. This gives meaning to all of the terms—a single building, not part of a larger operation, would be covered if it emits more than 100 tons of pollution, as would any facility, structure, or installation. Indeed, the language itself implies a "bubble concept" of sorts: each enumerated item would seem to be treated as if it were encased in a bubble. While respondents insist that each of these terms must be given a discrete meaning, they also argue that §111(a)(3) defines "source" as that term is used in §302(j). The latter section, however, equates a source with a facility, whereas the former defines "source" as a facility, among other items.

We are not persuaded that parsing of general terms in the text of the statute will reveal an actual intent of Congress. We know full well that this language is not dispositive; the terms are overlapping, and the language is not precisely directed to the question of the applicability of a given term in the context of a larger operation. To the extent any congressional "intent" can be discerned from this language, it would appear that the listing of overlapping, illustrative terms was intended to enlarge, rather than to confine, the scope of the agency's power to regulate particular sources in order to effectuate the policies of the Act.

Legislative History

In addition, respondents argue that the legislative history and policies of the Act foreclose the plantwide definition, and that the EPA's interpretation is not entitled to deference, because it represents a sharp break with prior interpretations of the Act.

Based on our examination of the legislative history, we agree with the Court of Appeals that it is unilluminating. The general remarks pointed to by respondents "were obviously not made with this narrow issue in mind, and they cannot be said to demonstrate a Congressional desire. . . ." *Jewell Ridge Coal Corp. v. Mine Workers*, 325 U.S. 161, 168-169 (1945). Respondents' argument based on the legislative history relies heavily on Senator Muskie's observation that a new source is subject to the LAER requirement. But the full statement is ambiguous, and, like the text of §173 itself, this comment does not tell us what a new source is, much less that it is to have an inflexible definition. We find that the legislative history as a whole is silent on the precise issue before us. It is, however, consistent with the view that the EPA should have broad discretion in implementing the policies of the 1977 Amendments.

More importantly, that history plainly identifies the policy concerns that motivated the enactment; the plantwide definition is fully consistent with one of those concerns—the allowance of reasonable economic growth—and, whether or not we believe it most effectively implements the other, we must recognize that the EPA has advanced a reasonable explanation for its conclusion that the regulations serve the environmental objectives as well. Indeed, its reasoning is supported by the public record developed in the rulemaking process, as well as by certain private studies.

Our review of the EPA's varying interpretations of the word "source"—
both before and after the 1977 Amendments—convinces us that the agency
primarily responsible for administering this important legislation has consistently interpreted it flexibly—not in a sterile textual vacuum, but in the
context of implementing policy decisions in a technical and complex arena.
The fact that the agency has from time to time changed its interpretation
of the term "source" does not, as respondents argue, lead us to conclude
that no deference should be accorded the agency's interpretation of the
statute. An initial agency interpretation is not instantly carved in stone. On
the contrary, the agency, to engage in informed rulemaking, must consider
varying interpretations and the wisdom of its policy on a continuing basis.
Moreover, the fact that the agency has adopted different definitions in different contexts adds force to the argument that the definition itself is flexible, particularly since Congress has never indicated any disapproval of a
flexible reading of the statute.

Significantly, it was not the agency in 1980, but rather the Court of
Appeals that read the statute inflexibly to command a plantwide definition
for programs designed to maintain clean air and to forbid such a definition
for programs designed to improve air quality. The distinction the court drew
may well be a sensible one, but our labored review of the problem has surely
disclosed that it is not a distinction that Congress ever articulated itself, or
one that the EPA found in the statute before the courts began to review
the legislative work product. We conclude that it was the Court of Appeals,
rather than Congress or any of the decisionmakers who are authorized by
Congress to administer this legislation, that was primarily responsible for
the 1980 position taken by the agency.

Policy

The arguments over policy that are advanced in the parties' briefs create the
impression that respondents are now waging in a judicial forum a specific
policy battle which they ultimately lost in the agency and in the 32 jurisdictions opting for the "bubble concept," but one which was never waged in the
Congress. Such policy arguments are more properly addressed to legislators
or administrators, not to judges.

In these cases, the Administrator's interpretation represents a reasonable accommodation of manifestly competing interests, and is entitled to
deference: the regulatory scheme is technical and complex, the agency considered the matter in a detailed and reasoned fashion, and the decision
involves reconciling conflicting policies. Congress intended to accommodate
both interests, but did not do so itself on the level of specificity presented
by these cases. Perhaps that body consciously desired the Administrator to
strike the balance at this level, thinking that those with great expertise and
charged with responsibility for administering the provision would be in a
better position to do so; perhaps it simply did not consider the question at
this level; and perhaps Congress was unable to forge a coalition on either
side of the question, and those on each side decided to take their chances

with the scheme devised by the agency. For judicial purposes, it matters not which of these things occurred.

Judges are not experts in the field, and are not part of either political branch of the Government. Courts must, in some cases, reconcile competing political interests, but not on the basis of the judges' personal policy preferences. In contrast, an agency to which Congress has delegated policymaking responsibilities may, within the limits of that delegation, properly rely upon the incumbent administration's views of wise policy to inform its judgments. While agencies are not directly accountable to the people, the Chief Executive is, and it is entirely appropriate for this political branch of the Government to make such policy choices—resolving the competing interests which Congress itself either inadvertently did not resolve, or intentionally left to be resolved by the agency charged with the administration of the statute in light of everyday realities.

When a challenge to an agency construction of a statutory provision, fairly conceptualized, really centers on the wisdom of the agency's policy, rather than whether it is a reasonable choice within a gap left open by Congress, the challenge must fail. In such a case, federal judges—who have no constituency—have a duty to respect legitimate policy choices made by those who do. The responsibilities for assessing the wisdom of such policy choices and resolving the struggle between competing views of the public interest are not judicial ones: "Our Constitution vests such responsibilities in the political branches." *TVA v. Hill,* 437 U.S. 153, 195 (1978).

We hold that the EPA's definition of the term "source" is a permissible construction of the statute which seeks to accommodate progress in reducing air pollution with economic growth.

The Regulations which the Administrator has adopted provide what the agency could allowably view as . . . [an] effective reconciliation of these two-fold ends. . . . *United States v. Shimer,* 367 U.S. at 383.

The judgment of the Court of Appeals is reversed.

It is so ordered.

Notes and Questions

1. Step One of *Chevron* directs reviewing courts to ask whether "Congress has directly spoken to the precise issue in question," or, put differently, whether "the intent of Congress is clear." Under Step One, how clear is "clear"? The Court indicates that Congress need not resolve all doubt about the meaning of a provision in the text of the statute. Rather, courts are called upon to interpret statutory provisions applying the "traditional tools of statutory construction." That phrase should be familiar: we identified the tools of statutory interpretation in Chapter 3. Are all the tools of statutory interpretation fair game under Step One? You can see the Court applying text-based tools, including textual canons, and intent or purpose-based tools, including legislative history. What about substantive canons? Is there any reason to believe that these are off limits? How about evidence of changed circumstances? May a court consult subsequent legislative, executive, or judicial activity? Does the Court offer any clues as to the status of these tools? We will have more to say on this subject below.

2. Step Two applies when Congress has not specified a statutory meaning. It directs courts to defer to the agency interpretation as long as that interpretation is "reasonable." Can you determine from the opinion what "reasonable" means? We will have more to say about this, too.

3. One important aspect of *Chevron* is that it permits agencies to change their interpretations of ambiguous provisions in response to changing technological, social, or political circumstances. In this case, the Reagan administration preferred the "bubble" interpretation to the prior individual smokestack interpretation. The Court deferred to the change. Why is such "flip-flopping" permissible, and under what circumstances? Could a future administration change back to the "smokestack" concept?

4. What exactly does "judicial deference" mean? When a court defers to an agency interpretation, it gives that interpretation the force of law. The interpretation binds the parties in the case, as well as future parties and government officials, including the agency and the courts. The only way to depart from an agency interpretation is for the agency to change it by issuing another rule or for Congress to repeal it by enacting another statute. So you can see why *Chevron* deference is a big deal for agencies and those affected by their choices. The Court agrees and has complicated *Chevron* on this force-of-law point, as we discuss below.

5. *Chevron* is sometimes described as a canon of construction, one that instructs reviewing courts to defer to agency interpretations of ambiguous statutory provisions so long as those interpretations are reasonable. The Court has offered normative reasons in support of such deference: congressional delegation, agency expertise, and political accountability. Are these justifications equally persuasive? Many scholars and justices have labeled the congressional delegation rationale a "fiction"—they do not believe that Congress intends for agencies to resolve ambiguities. *See, e.g.,* David J. Barron & Elena Kagan, Chevron*'s Nondelegation Doctrine*, 2001 Sup. Ct. Rev. 201, 203 (2001); Stephen Breyer, *Judicial Review of Questions of Law and Policy*, 38 Admin. L. Rev. 363, 370 (1986); Evan J. Criddle, Chevron*'s Consensus*, 88 B.U. L. Rev. 1271, 1285 (2008); Ronald J. Krotoszynski, Jr., *Why Deference?: Implied Delegationism, Agency Expertise, and the Misplaced Legacy of* Skidmore, 54 Admin. L. Rev. 735, 753 (2002); Antonin Scalia, *Judicial Deference to Administrative Interpretations of Law*, 1989 Duke L.J. 511, 517; Mark Seidenfeld, Chevron*'s Foundation*, 86 Notre Dame L. Rev. 273, 311 (2011). Why would the Court rely on this fiction in *Chevron*? What if the fiction is now a reality because congressional staffers are aware of and rely on *Chevron* when they draft legislation? *See* Abbe R. Gluck & Lisa Schultz Bressman, *Statutory Interpretation from the Inside—An Empirical Study of Congressional Drafting, Delegation, and the Canons: Part I*, 65 Stan. L. Rev. 901 (2013).

i. Step One: Clear Statutory Meaning

To be sure, *Chevron* had the effect of changing the mood of courts when interpreting statutes. Think back to Babbitt v. Sweet Home Chapter of Communities for a Great Oregon, 515 U.S. 687 (1995), a decision excerpted in Chapter 3 as an example of the "battle of the textual canons." Justice Stevens—the author of *Chevron*—wrote for the majority in that case. After examining the text, structure, and legislative history of the Endangered Species Act, Justice Stevens concluded that the Secretary of Interior's interpretation of "harm" to include significant habitat modification or degradation was a reasonable interpretation. Here is a portion of his opinion that we did not include in Chapter 3:

> When it enacted the ESA, Congress delegated broad administrative and interpretive power to the Secretary. *See* 16 U.S.C. §§1533, 1540(f). The task of defining and listing endangered and threatened species requires an expertise and attention to detail that exceeds the normal province of Congress. Fashioning appropriate standards for issuing permits under §10 for takings that would otherwise violate §9 necessarily requires the exercise of broad discretion. The proper interpretation of a term such as "harm" involves a complex policy choice. When Congress has entrusted the Secretary with broad discretion, we are especially reluctant to substitute our views of wise policy for his. *See Chevron*, 467 U.S., at 865-866. In this case, that reluctance accords with our conclusion, based on the text, structure, and legislative history of the ESA, that the Secretary reasonably construed the intent of Congress when he defined "harm" to include "significant habitat modification or degradation that actually kills or injures wildlife."

Sweet Home, 515 U.S. at 708.

Justice Stevens ultimately deferred to the Secretary's interpretation, despite his heavy use of the tools of statutory construction that he ordinarily employs ("the text, structure, and legislative history of the ESA"). But Justice Scalia, in dissent, saw the matter differently. Using the tools of statutory construction that *he* ordinary applies, Justice Scalia read the ESA as clearly foreclosing the Secretary of Interior's interpretation:

> I think it unmistakably clear that the legislation at issue here (1) forbade the hunting and killing of endangered animals, and (2) provided federal lands and federal funds *for the acquisition of private lands,* to preserve the habitat of endangered animals. The Court's holding that the hunting and killing prohibition incidentally preserves habitat on private lands imposes unfairness to the point of financial ruin not just upon the rich, but upon the simplest farmer who finds his land conscripted to national zoological use.

Sweet Home, 515 U.S. at 714 (Scalia, J., dissenting).

How often do courts find clear statutory meaning using the traditional tools of statutory construction? Although this is a difficult empirical question, the possibility of finding a clear meaning exists in every case. Courts can assert control of agency interpretations, even though *Chevron* sets a mood of deference. (And don't courts assert control whether they reject or uphold the agency interpretation? Justice Scalia plainly would have asserted control by rejecting the Secretary's interpretation of "harm," but what if Justice Stevens has said that the statute clearly mandates the Secretary's interpretation? To see the point, consider whether the Department of Interior could change its interpretation in the future, as the EPA did in *Chevron*.)

The following decisions are leading examples of this phenomenon. As you read these decisions, note the interpretive tools and theories that the Court uses. Ask yourself whether certain tools or theories give courts relatively more ability to control agency interpretations. Also consider whether certain interpretive tools or theories ought to be off limits to courts to maintain fidelity to the underlying justifications of *Chevron*. Finally, consider which normative values are served (and which, if any, are sacrificed) when courts find clear meaning. Is that what Congress intended? Does it promote the rule of law? Or does it reflect judicial overreaching at the expense of congressional delegation, agency expertise, and political accountability?

MCI Telecommunications Corp. v. American Telephone & Telegraph Co.

512 U.S. 218 (1994)

Justice SCALIA delivered the opinion of the Court.

Section 203(a) of Title 47 of the United States Code requires communications common carriers to file tariffs with the Federal Communications Commission, and §203(b) authorizes the Commission to "modify" any requirement of §203. These cases present the question whether the Commission's decision to make tariff filing optional for all nondominant long-distance carriers is a valid exercise of its modification authority.

I

[Section 203 requires that telephone carriers, or common carriers, file their rates with the Commission and charge only the filed rate. In the 1970s and 1980s, the Commission issued a series of rules that relaxed the procedures requiring filing of rates for nondominant carriers in long-distance markets. It first relaxed the requirements of filing rates for nondominant carriers by making the filing of tariffs permissive, then in 1985, it prohibited nondominant carriers from filing tariffs. The Court of Appeals for the D.C. Circuit struck down the Commission's rule that prohibited nondominant carriers from filing tariffs, reasoning that §203(a)'s provision that "[e]very common carrier . . . shall . . . file" tariffs was mandatory, and although §203(b) authorizes the Commission to "modify any requirement" in the section, the Court of Appeals concluded that that phrase "suggest[ed] circumscribed alterations—not, as the FCC now would have it, wholesale abandonment or elimination of a requirement."

Following the D.C. Circuit's decision, MCI continued its practice of not filing tariffs pursuant to the Commission's rules making filing of tariffs permissive. AT&T sued arguing that the Commission lacked authority to make the filing of tariffs permissive. The D.C. Circuit granted AT&T's request for summary reversal of the Commission's permissive detariffing policy. Both

MCI and the United States (together with the Commission) petitioned for certiorari, which the Court granted.]

II

Section 203 of the Communications Act contains both the filed rate provisions of the Act and the Commission's disputed modification authority. It provides in relevant part:

"(a) Filing; public display.

"Every common carrier, except connecting carriers, shall, within such reasonable time as the Commission shall designate, file with the Commission and print and keep open for public inspection schedules showing all charges . . . , whether such charges are joint or separate, and showing the classifications, practices, and regulations affecting such charges. . . .

"(b) Changes in schedule; discretion of Commission to modify requirements.

"(1) No change shall be made in the charges, classifications, regulations, or practices which have been so filed and published except after one hundred and twenty days notice to the Commission and to the public, which shall be published in such form and contain such information as the Commission may by regulations prescribe.

"(2) The Commission may, in its discretion and for good cause shown, modify any requirement made by or under the authority of this section either in particular instances or by general order applicable to special circumstances or conditions except that the Commission may not require the notice period specified in paragraph (1) to be more than one hundred and twenty days.

"(c) Overcharges and rebates.

"No carrier, unless otherwise provided by or under authority of this chapter, shall engage or participate in such communication unless schedules have been filed and published in accordance with the provisions of this chapter and with the regulations made thereunder; and no carrier shall (1) charge, demand, collect, or receive a greater or less or different compensation for such communication . . . than the charges specified in the schedule then in effect, or (2) refund or remit by any means or device any portion of the charges so specified, or (3) extend to any person any privileges or facilities in such communication, or employ or enforce any classifications, regulations, or practices affecting such charges, except as specified in such schedule." 47 U.S.C. §203 (1988 ed. and Supp. IV).

The dispute between the parties turns on the meaning of the phrase "modify any requirement" in §203(b)(2). Petitioners argue that it gives the Commission authority to make even basic and fundamental changes in the scheme created by that section. We disagree. The word "modify"—like a number of other English words employing the root "mod-" (deriving from the Latin word for "measure"), such as "moderate," "modulate," "modest," and "modicum"—has a connotation of increment or limitation. Virtually every dictionary we are aware of says that "to modify" means to change moderately or in minor fashion. *See, e.g.,* Random House Dictionary of the English Language 1236 (2d ed. 1987) ("to change somewhat the form or qualities of; alter partially; amend"); Webster's Third New International Dictionary 1452 (1981) ("to make minor changes in the form or structure of: alter without transforming"); 9 Oxford English Dictionary 952 (2d ed. 1989) ("[t]o make partial changes in; to change (an object) in respect of some of its qualities; to alter or vary without radical transformation"); Black's Law Dictionary 1004 (6th ed. 1990) ("[t] o alter; to change in incidental or subordinate features; enlarge; extend; amend; limit; reduce").

In support of their position, petitioners cite dictionary definitions contained in, or derived from, a single source, *Webster's Third New International Dictionary* 1452 (1981) (*Webster's Third*), which includes among the meanings of "modify," "to make a basic or important change in."[1] Petitioners contend that this establishes sufficient ambiguity to entitle the Commission to deference in its acceptance of the broader meaning, which in turn requires approval of its permissive detariffing policy. *See Chevron U.S.A. Inc. v. Natural Resources Defense Council, Inc.*, 467 U.S. 837, 843 (1984). In short, they contend that the courts must defer to the agency's choice among available dictionary definitions. Most cases of verbal ambiguity in statutes involve a selection between accepted alternative meanings shown as such by many dictionaries. One can envision (though a court case does not immediately come to mind) having to choose between accepted alternative meanings, one of which is so newly accepted that it has only been recorded by a single lexicographer. (Some dictionary must have been the very first to record the widespread use of "projection," for example, to mean "forecast.") But what petitioners demand that we accept as creating an ambiguity here is a rarity even rarer than that: a meaning set forth in a single dictionary (and, as we say, its progeny) which not only supplements the meaning contained in all other dictionaries, but contradicts one of the meanings contained in virtually all other dictionaries. Indeed, contradicts one of the alternative meanings contained in the out-of-step dictionary itself—for as we have observed, *Webster's Third* itself defines "modify" to connote both (specifically) major change and (specifically) minor change. It is hard to see how that can be. When the word "modify" has come to mean both "to change in some respects" and "to change fundamentally" it will in fact mean neither of those things. It will simply mean "to change," and some adverb will have to be called into service to indicate the great or small degree of the change.

---

1. Petitioners also cite *Webster's Ninth New Collegiate Dictionary* 763 (1991), which includes among its definitions of "modify," "to make basic or fundamental changes in often to give a new orientation to or to serve a new end." They might also have cited the eighth version of *Webster's New Collegiate Dictionary* 739 (1973), which contains that same definition; and *Webster's Seventh New Collegiate Dictionary* 544 (1963), which contains the same definition as *Webster's Third New International Dictionary* quoted in text. The *Webster's New Collegiate Dictionaries*, published by G. & C. Merriam Company of Springfield, Massachusetts, are essentially abridgments of that company's *Webster's New International Dictionaries*, and recite that they are based upon those lengthier works. The last *New Collegiate* to be based upon *Webster's Second New International*, rather than *Webster's Third*, does not include "basic or fundamental change" among the accepted meanings of "modify." See Webster's New Collegiate Dictionary 541 (6th ed. 1949).

If that is what the peculiar *Webster's Third* definition means to suggest has happened—and what petitioners suggest by appealing to *Webster's Third*—we simply disagree. "Modify," in our view, connotes moderate change. It might be good English to say that the French Revolution "modified" the status of the French nobility—but only because there is a figure of speech called understatement and a literary device known as sarcasm. And it might be unsurprising to discover a 1972 White House press release saying that "the Administration is modifying its position with regard to prosecution of the war in Vietnam"—but only because press agents tend to impart what is nowadays called "spin." Such intentional distortions, or simply careless or ignorant misuse, must have formed the basis for the usage that *Webster's Third*, and *Webster's Third* alone, reported. It is perhaps gilding the lily to add this: In 1934, when the Communications Act became law—the most relevant time for determining a statutory term's meaning, *see Perrin v. United States*, 444 U.S. 37, 42-45 (1979) — *Webster's Third* was not yet even contemplated. To our knowledge all English dictionaries provided the narrow definition of "modify," including those published by G. & C. Merriam Company. *See* Webster's New International Dictionary 1577 (2d ed. 1934); Webster's Collegiate Dictionary 628 (4th ed. 1934). We have not the slightest doubt that is the meaning the statute intended.

Beyond the word itself, a further indication that the §203(b)(2) authority to "modify" does not contemplate fundamental changes is the sole exception to that authority which the section provides. One of the requirements of §203 is that changes to filed tariffs can be made only after 120 days' notice to the Commission and the public. §203(b)(1). The only exception to the Commission's §203(b)(2) modification authority is as follows: "except that the Commission may not require the notice period specified in paragraph (1) to be more than one hundred and twenty days." Is it conceivable that the statute is indifferent to the Commission's power to eliminate the tariff-filing requirement entirely for all except one firm in the long-distance sector, and yet strains out the gnat of extending the waiting period for tariff revision beyond 120 days? We think not. The exception is not as ridiculous as a Lilliputian in London only because it is to be found in Lilliput: in the small-scale world of "modifications," it is a big deal.

Bearing in mind, then, the enormous importance to the statutory scheme of the tariff-filing provision, we turn to whether what has occurred here can be considered a mere "modification." The Commission stresses that its detariffing policy applies only to nondominant carriers, so that the rates charged to over half of all consumers in the long-distance market are on file with the Commission. It is not clear to us that the proportion of customers affected, rather than the proportion of carriers affected, is the proper measure of the extent of the exemption (of course all carriers in the long-distance market are exempted, except AT & T). But even assuming it is, we think an elimination of the crucial provision of the statute for 40% of a major sector of the industry is much too extensive to be considered a "modification." What we have here, in reality, is a fundamental revision of the statute, changing it from a scheme of rate regulation in long-distance common-carrier communications to a scheme of rate regulation only where effective competition does not exist. That may be a good idea, but it was not the idea Congress enacted into law in 1934.

Finally, petitioners earnestly urge that their interpretation of §203(b) furthers the Communications Act's broad purpose of promoting efficient telephone service. They claim that although the filing requirement prevented price discrimination and unfair practices while AT & T maintained a monopoly over long-distance service, it frustrates those same goals now that there is greater competition in that market. Specifically, they contend that filing costs raise artificial barriers to entry and that the publication of rates facilitates parallel pricing and stifles price competition. We have considerable sympathy with these arguments (though we doubt it makes sense, if one is concerned about the use of filed tariffs to communicate pricing information, to require filing by the dominant carrier, the firm most likely to be a price leader). . . .

But our estimations, and the Commission's estimations, of desirable policy cannot alter the meaning of the federal Communications Act of 1934. For better or worse, the Act establishes a rate-regulation, filed-tariff system for common-carrier communications, and the Commission's desire "to 'increase competition' cannot provide [it] authority to alter the well-established statutory filed rate requirements," "such considerations address themselves to Congress, not to the courts," *Armour Packing*, 209 U.S., at 82.

We do not mean to suggest that the tariff-filing requirement is so inviolate that the Commission's existing modification authority does not reach it at all. Certainly the Commission can modify the form, contents, and location of required filings, and can defer filing or perhaps even waive it altogether in limited circumstances. But what we have here goes well beyond that. It is effectively the introduction of a whole new regime of regulation (or of free-market competition), which may well be a better regime but is not the one that Congress established.

The judgment of the Court of Appeals is

Affirmed.

Justice STEVENS, with whom Justice BLACKMUN and Justice SOUTER join, dissenting.

The communications industry has an unusually dynamic character. In 1934, Congress authorized the Federal Communications Commission (FCC or Commission) to regulate "a field of enterprise the dominant characteristic of which was the rapid pace of its unfolding." *National Broadcasting Co. v. United States*, 319 U.S. 190, 219 (1943). The Communications Act of 1934 (Act) gives the FCC unusually broad discretion to meet new and unanticipated problems in order to fulfill its sweeping mandate "to make available, so far as possible, to all the people of the United States, a rapid, efficient, Nation-wide and world-wide wire and radio communication service with adequate facilities at reasonable charges." 47 U.S.C. §151. This Court's consistent interpretation of the Act has afforded the Commission ample leeway to interpret and apply its statutory powers and responsibilities. *See, e.g., United States v. Southwestern Cable Co.*, 392 U.S. 157, 172-173 (1968); *FCC v. Pottsville Broadcasting Co.*, 309 U.S. 134, 138 (1940). The Court today abandons that approach in favor of a rigid literalism that deprives the FCC of the flexibility Congress meant it to have in order to implement the core policies of the Act in rapidly changing conditions.

I

At the time the Act was passed, the telephone industry was dominated by the American Telephone & Telegraph Company (AT & T) and its affiliates. Title II of the Act, which establishes the framework for FCC regulation of common carriers by wire, was clearly a response to that dominance. As the Senate Report explained, "[u]nder existing provisions of the Interstate Commerce Act the regulation of the telephone monopoly has been practically nil. This vast monopoly which so immediately serves the needs of the people in their daily and social life must be effectively regulated." S. Rep. No. 781, 73d Cong., 2d Sess., 2 (1934)....

Section 203, modeled upon the filed rate provisions of the Interstate Commerce Act, requires that common carriers other than connecting carriers "file with the Commission and print and keep open for public inspection schedules showing all charges for itself and its connecting carriers." 47 U.S.C. §203(a). A telephone carrier must allow a 120-day period of lead time before a tariff goes into effect, and, "unless otherwise provided by or under authority of this Chapter," may not provide communication services except according to a filed schedule, §§203(c), (d). The tariff-filing section of the Act, however, contains a provision that states:

> "(b) Changes in schedule; discretion of Commission to modify requirements....
>
> "(2) The Commission may, in its discretion and for good cause shown, modify any requirement made by or under the authority of this section either in particular instances or by general order applicable to special circumstances or conditions except that the Commission may not require the notice period specified in paragraph (1) to be more than one hundred and twenty days." 47 U.S.C. §203(b)(2) (1988 ed., Supp. IV).

Congress doubtless viewed the filed rate provisions as an important mechanism to guard against abusive practices by wire communications monopolies. But it is quite wrong to suggest [as the Court does,] that the mere process of filing rate schedules—rather than the substantive duty of reasonably priced and nondiscriminatory service—is "the heart of the common-carrier section of the Communications Act."

III

... In my view, each of the Commission's detariffing orders was squarely within its power to "modify any requirement" of §203. Section 203(b)(2) plainly confers at least some discretion to modify the general rule that carriers file tariffs, for it speaks of "any requirement." Section 203(c) of the Act, ignored by the Court, squarely supports the FCC's position; it prohibits carriers from providing service without a tariff "unless otherwise provided by or under authority of this Act." Section 203(b)(2) is plainly one provision that "otherwise provides," and thereby authorizes, service without a filed schedule. The FCC's authority to modify §203's requirements in "particular instances" or by "general order applicable to special circumstances or conditions" emphasizes the expansive character of the Commission's authority: modifications may be narrow or broad, depending upon the Commission's appraisal of current conditions. From the vantage of a Congress seeking to regulate an almost completely monopolized industry, the advent of competition is surely a "special circumstance or condition" that might legitimately call for different regulatory treatment.

The only statutory exception to the Commission's modification authority provides that it may not extend the 120-day notice period set out in §203(b)(1). *See* §203(b)(2). The Act thus imposes a specific limit on the Commission's authority to stiffen that regulatory imposition on carriers, but does not confine the Commission's authority to relax it. It was no stretch for the FCC to draw from this single, unidirectional statutory limitation on its modification authority the inference that its authority is otherwise unlimited. *See* 7 FCC Rcd, at 8075.

According to the Court, the term "modify," as explicated in all but the most unreliable dictionaries, rules out the Commission's claimed authority to relieve nondominant carriers of the basic obligation to file tariffs. Dictionaries can be useful aids in statutory interpretation, but they are no substitute for close analysis of what words mean as used in a particular statutory context. *Cf. Cabell v. Markham*, 148 F.2d 737, 739 (CA2 1945) (Hand, J.). Even if the sole possible meaning of "modify" were to make "minor" changes, further elaboration is needed to show why the detariffing policy should fail. The Commission came to its present policy through a series of rulings that gradually relaxed the filing requirements for nondominant carriers. Whether the current policy should count as a cataclysmic or merely an incremental departure from the §203(a) baseline depends on whether one focuses on particular carriers' obligations to file (in which case the Commission's policy arguably works a major shift) or on the statutory policies behind the tariff-filing requirement (which remain satisfied because market constraints on nondominant carriers obviate the need for rate filing). When §203 is viewed as part of a statute whose aim is to constrain monopoly power, the Commission's decision to exempt nondominant carriers is a rational and "measured" adjustment to novel circumstances—one that remains faithful to the core purpose of the tariff-filing section. *See* Black's Law Dictionary 1198 (3d ed. 1933) (defining "modification" as "A change; an alteration which introduces new elements into the details, or cancels some of them, but leaves the general purpose and effect of the subject-matter intact").

The Court seizes upon a particular sense of the word "modify" at the expense of another, long-established meaning that fully supports the Commission's position. That word is first defined in *Webster's Collegiate Dictionary* 628 (4th ed. 1934) as meaning "to limit or reduce in extent or degree."[1] The Commission's permissive detariffing policy fits comfortably within this common understanding of the term. The FCC has in effect adopted a general rule stating that "if you are dominant you must file, but if you are nondominant you need not." The Commission's partial detariffing policy—which excuses nondominant carriers from filing on condition that they remain nondominant—is simply a relaxation of a costly regulatory requirement that recent developments had rendered pointless and counterproductive in a certain class of cases. . . .

The filed tariff provisions of the Communications Act are not ends in themselves, but are merely one of several procedural means for the Commission to ensure that carriers do not charge unreasonable or discriminatory rates. *See* 84 F.C.C.2d, at 483. The Commission has reasonably concluded that this particular means of enforcing the statute's substantive mandates will prove counterproductive in the case of nondominant long-distance carriers. Even if the 1934 Congress did not define the scope of the Commission's modification authority with perfect scholarly precision, this is surely a paradigm case for judicial deference to the agency's interpretation, particularly in a statutory regime so obviously meant to maximize administrative flexibility. Whatever the best reading of §203(b)(2), the Commission's reading cannot in my view be termed unreasonable. It is informed (as ours is not) by a practical understanding of the role (or lack thereof) that filed tariffs play in the modern regulatory climate and in the telecommunications industry. Since 1979, the FCC has sought to adapt measures originally designed to control monopoly power to new market conditions. It has carefully and consistently explained that mandatory tariff-filing rules frustrate the core statutory interest in rate reasonableness. The Commission's use of the "discretion" expressly conferred by §203(b)(2) reflects "a reasonable accommodation of manifestly competing interests and is entitled to deference: the regulatory scheme is technical and complex, the agency considered the matter in a detailed and reasoned fashion, and the decision involves reconciling conflicting policies." *Chevron U.S.A. Inc. v. Natural Resources Defense Council, Inc.*, 467 U.S. 837, 865 (1984) (footnotes omitted). The FCC has permissibly interpreted its §203(b)(2) authority in service of the goals Congress set forth in the Act. We should sustain its eminently sound, experience-tested, and uncommonly well-explained judgment.

---

1. See also 9 Oxford English Dictionary 952 (2d ed. 1989) ("2. To alter in the direction of moderation or lenity; to make less severe, rigorous, or decided; to qualify, tone down. . . .1610 Donne Pseudomartyr 184 'For so Mariana modefies his Doctrine, that the Prince should not execute any Clergy man, though he deser[v]e it' "); Random House Dictionary of the English Language 1236 (2d ed. 1987) ("5. to reduce or lessen in degree or extent; moderate; soften; to modify one's demands"); Webster's Third New International Dictionary 1452 (1981) ("1: to make more temperate and less extreme: lessen the severity of; . . . 'traffic rules were modified to let him pass' "); Webster's New Collegiate Dictionary 739 (1973) ("1. to make less extreme; MODERATE"); Webster's Seventh New Collegiate Dictionary 544 (1963) (same); Webster's Seventh New International Dictionary 1577 (2d ed. 1934) ("2. To reduce in extent or degree; to moderate; qualify; lower; as, to modify heat, pain, punishment"); N. Webster, American Dictionary of the English Language (1828) ("To moderate; to qualify; to reduce in extent or degree. Of his grace He modifies his first severe decree. Dryden").

Notes and Questions

1. List the tools of statutory interpretation that the Court used in arriving at its interpretation. Now list the tools that the dissent used. What explains the difference? On the FCC's interpretation, the provision at issue gave the agency the power to alter its statute by waiving a central requirement for all but the dominant long-distance carrier. How much did this influence the Court? *See* Whitman v. American Trucking Ass'ns, 531 U.S. 457, 468 (2001) (citing *MCI Telecomms. Corp. v. American Tel. & Tel. Co.* for the proposition that Congress does not "hide elephants in mouseholes").

2. So, how clear is clear anyway? Did the Court determine that the word "modify" was clear in all respects? Or did it simply find that the word cannot mean what the FCC said?

3. Is this a faithful application of Step One? Or do the traditional tools of statutory construction, and in particular the textual tools, make it far too easy for courts to deny "agency-liberating ambiguity" and assert judicial control, as Justice Scalia happily acknowledged. Antonin Scalia, *Judicial Deference to Administrative Interpretations of Law*, 1989 Duke L.J. 511, 521 (1989). There is some empirical support for this view. *See* Thomas J. Miles & Cass R. Sunstein, *Do Judges Make Regulatory Policy? An Empirical Investigation of* Chevron, 73 U. Chi. L. Rev. 823, 831-32 (2006) (finding that Justice Scalia defers the least of all the justices). As you move along, consider whether another approach might better balance the values at stake. For example, should the Court look for more reliable signals of congressional delegation than statutory ambiguity? Do such signals exist? Or does it just come down to whether judicial control or agency control of statutory interpretation is preferable?

4. Assume the Court was correct about the meaning of "modify." Who should determine the magnitude of the change in terms of the overall statutory scheme, the Court or the agency? What is the danger of each? The majority and dissent also disagreed on this issue.

5. Did the dissent find the provision clear or ambiguous? Again, think about why it might matter whether a court declares a provision clear or not. Relative clarity or ambiguity determines not only the validity of an agency's interpretation but the scope of the agency's authority.

Here is another important example of judicial control under Step One.

Food & Drug Administration v. Brown & Williamson Tobacco Corp.

529 U.S. 120 (2000)

Justice O'Connor delivered the opinion of the Court.

This case involves one of the most troubling public health problems facing our Nation today: the thousands of premature deaths that occur each year because of tobacco use. In 1996, the Food and Drug Administration

(FDA), after having expressly disavowed any such authority since its inception, asserted jurisdiction to regulate tobacco products. The FDA concluded that nicotine is a "drug" within the meaning of the Food, Drug, and Cosmetic Act (FDCA or Act), 52 Stat. 1040, as amended, 21 U.S.C. §301 et seq., and that cigarettes and smokeless tobacco are "combination products" that deliver nicotine to the body. Pursuant to this authority, it promulgated regulations intended to reduce tobacco consumption among children and adolescents. The agency believed that, because most tobacco consumers begin their use before reaching the age of 18, curbing tobacco use by minors could substantially reduce the prevalence of addiction in future generations and thus the incidence of tobacco-related death and disease.

Regardless of how serious the problem an administrative agency seeks to address, however, it may not exercise its authority "in a manner that is inconsistent with the administrative structure that Congress enacted into law." *ETSI Pipeline Project v. Missouri*, 484 U.S. 495, 517 (1988). And although agencies are generally entitled to deference in the interpretation of statutes that they administer, a reviewing "court, as well as the agency, must give effect to the unambiguously expressed intent of Congress." *Chevron U.S.A. Inc. v. Natural Resources Defense Council, Inc.*, 467 U.S. 837, 842-843 (1984). In this case, we believe that Congress has clearly precluded the FDA from asserting jurisdiction to regulate tobacco products. Such authority is inconsistent with the intent that Congress has expressed in the FDCA's overall regulatory scheme and in the tobacco-specific legislation that it has enacted subsequent to the FDCA. In light of this clear intent, the FDA's assertion of jurisdiction is impermissible.

I

The FDCA grants the FDA, as the designee of the Secretary of Health and Human Services (HHS), the authority to regulate, among other items, "drugs" and "devices." *See* 21 U.S.C. §§321(g)-(h), 393 (1994 ed. and Supp. III). The Act defines "drug" to include "articles (other than food) intended to affect the structure or any function of the body." 21 U.S.C. §321(g)(1)(C). It defines "device," in part, as "an instrument, apparatus, implement, machine, contrivance, . . . or other similar or related article, including any component, part, or accessory, which is . . . intended to affect the structure or any function of the body." §321(h). The Act also grants the FDA the authority to regulate so-called "combination products," which "constitute a combination of a drug, device, or biological product." §353(g)(1). The FDA has construed this provision as giving it the discretion to regulate combination products as drugs, as devices, or as both.

On August 11, 1995, the FDA published a proposed rule concerning the sale of cigarettes and smokeless tobacco to children and adolescents. The rule, which included several restrictions on the sale, distribution, and advertisement of tobacco products, was designed to reduce the availability and attractiveness of tobacco products to young people. A public comment period followed, during which the FDA received over 700,000 submissions, more than "at any other time in its history on any other subject."

On August 28, 1996, the FDA issued a final rule entitled "Regulations Restricting the Sale and Distribution of Cigarettes and Smokeless Tobacco to Protect Children and Adolescents." The FDA determined that nicotine is a "drug" and that cigarettes and smokeless tobacco are "drug delivery devices," and therefore it had jurisdiction under the FDCA to regulate tobacco products as customarily marketed—that is, without manufacturer claims of therapeutic benefit. First, the FDA found that tobacco products "'affect the structure or any function of the body'" because nicotine "has significant pharmacological effects." Specifically, nicotine "exerts psychoactive, or mood-altering, effects on the brain" that cause and sustain addiction, have both tranquilizing and stimulating effects, and control weight. Second, the FDA determined that these effects were "intended" under the FDCA because they "are so widely known and foreseeable that [they] may be deemed to have been intended by the manufacturers"; consumers use tobacco products "predominantly or nearly exclusively" to obtain these effects; and the statements, research, and actions of manufacturers revealed that they "have 'designed' cigarettes to provide pharmacologically active doses of nicotine to consumers." Finally, the agency concluded that cigarettes and smokeless tobacco are "combination products" because, in addition to containing nicotine, they include device components that deliver a controlled amount of nicotine to the body.

Having resolved the jurisdictional question, the FDA next explained the policy justifications for its regulations, detailing the deleterious health effects associated with tobacco use. It found that tobacco consumption was "the single leading cause of preventable death in the United States." According to the FDA, "[m]ore than 400,000 people die each year from tobacco-related illnesses, such as cancer, respiratory illnesses, and heart disease." . . .

Based on these findings, the FDA promulgated regulations concerning tobacco products' promotion, labeling, and accessibility to children and adolescents. *See id.*, at 44615-44618. The access regulations prohibit the sale of cigarettes or smokeless tobacco to persons younger than 18. . . . The promotion regulations require that any print advertising appear in a black-and-white, text-only format unless the publication in which it appears is read almost exclusively by adults; prohibit outdoor advertising within 1,000 feet of any public playground or school. The labeling regulation requires that the statement, "A Nicotine-Delivery Device for Persons 18 or Older," appear on all tobacco product packages. *Id.*, at 44617. . . .

Respondents, a group of tobacco manufacturers, retailers, and advertisers, filed suit in United States District Court for the Middle District of North Carolina challenging the regulations. *See Coyne Beahm, Inc. v. FDA,* 966 F. Supp. 1374 (1997). [The district court denied their motion for summary judgment on the grounds that the FDA lacked jurisdiction to regulate tobacco products. The Court of Appeals for the Fourth Circuit reversed, holding that Congress had not granted the FDA jurisdiction to regulate tobacco products. The Court granted the federal parties' petition for certiorari to determine whether the FDA had authority under the FDCA to regulate tobacco products as customarily marketed.]

II

The FDA's assertion of jurisdiction to regulate tobacco products is founded on its conclusions that nicotine is a "drug" and that cigarettes and smokeless tobacco are "drug delivery devices." Again, the FDA found that tobacco products are "intended" to deliver the pharmacological effects of satisfying addiction, stimulation and tranquilization, and weight control because those effects are foreseeable to any reasonable manufacturer, consumers use tobacco products to obtain those effects, and tobacco manufacturers have designed their products to produce those effects. As an initial matter, respondents take issue with the FDA's reading of "intended," arguing that it is a term of art that refers exclusively to claims made by the manufacturer or vendor about the product. That is, a product is not a drug or device under the FDCA unless the manufacturer or vendor makes some express claim concerning the product's therapeutic benefits. We need not resolve this question, however, because assuming, arguendo, that a product can be "intended to affect the structure or any function of the body" absent claims of therapeutic or medical benefit, the FDA's claim to jurisdiction contravenes the clear intent of Congress.

A threshold issue is the appropriate framework for analyzing the FDA's assertion of authority to regulate tobacco products. Because this case involves an administrative agency's construction of a statute that it administers, our analysis is governed by *Chevron U.S.A. Inc. v. Natural Resources Defense Council, Inc.*, 467 U.S. 837 (1984). Under *Chevron*, a reviewing court must first ask "whether Congress has directly spoken to the precise question at issue." *Id.*, at 842. If Congress has done so, the inquiry is at an end; the court "must give effect to the unambiguously expressed intent of Congress." *Id.*, at 843. . . . But if Congress has not specifically addressed the question, a reviewing court must respect the agency's construction of the statute so long as it is permissible. *See INS v. Aguirre-Aguirre*, 526 U.S. 415, 424 . . . (1999). Such deference is justified because "[t]he responsibilities for assessing the wisdom of such policy choices and resolving the struggle between competing views of the public interest are not judicial ones," *Chevron*, at 866, and because of the agency's greater familiarity with the ever-changing facts and circumstances surrounding the subjects regulated, *see Rust v. Sullivan*, 500 U.S. 173, 187 (1991).

In determining whether Congress has specifically addressed the question at issue, a reviewing court should not confine itself to examining a particular statutory provision in isolation. The meaning—or ambiguity—of certain words or phrases may only become evident when placed in context. *See Brown v. Gardner*, 513 U.S. 115, 118 (1994) ("Ambiguity is a creature not of definitional possibilities but of statutory context"). It is a "fundamental canon of statutory construction that the words of a statute must be read in their context and with a view to their place in the overall statutory scheme." *Davis v. Michigan Dept. of Treasury*, 489 U.S. 803, 809 (1989). A court must therefore interpret the statute "as a symmetrical and coherent regulatory scheme," *Gustafson v. Alloyd Co.*, 513 U.S. 561, 569 (1995), and "fit, if possible, all parts into an harmonious whole," *FTC v. Mandel Brothers, Inc.*, 359 U.S. 385, 389 (1959). Similarly, the meaning of one statute may be affected by other Acts, particularly where Congress has spoken subsequently and more specifically to the topic at hand. *See United States v. Estate of Romani*, 523 U.S. 517, 530-531 (1998); *United States v. Fausto*, 484 U.S. 439, 453 (1988). In addition, we must be guided to a degree by common sense as to the manner in which Congress is likely to delegate a policy decision of such economic and political magnitude to an administrative agency. *Cf. MCI Telecommunications Corp. v. American Telephone & Telegraph Co.*, 512 U.S. 218, 231 (1994).

With these principles in mind, we find that Congress has directly spoken to the issue here and precluded the FDA's jurisdiction to regulate tobacco products.

A

Viewing the FDCA as a whole, it is evident that one of the Act's core objectives is to ensure that any product regulated by the FDA is "safe" and "effective" for its intended use. *See* 21 U.S.C. §393(b)(2) (1994 ed., Supp. III) (defining the FDA's mission). . . . This essential purpose pervades the FDCA. For instance, 21 U.S.C. §393(b)(2) (1994 ed., Supp. III) defines the FDA's "[m]ission" to include "protect[ing] the public health by ensuring that . . . drugs are safe and effective" and that "there is reasonable assurance of the safety and effectiveness of devices intended for human use." . . . [T]he Act generally requires the FDA to prevent the marketing of any drug or device where the "potential for inflicting death or physical injury is not offset by the possibility of therapeutic benefit." *United States v. Rutherford*, 442 U.S. 544, 556 (1979).

In its rulemaking proceeding, the FDA quite exhaustively documented that "tobacco products are unsafe," "dangerous," and "cause great pain and suffering from illness." It found that the consumption of tobacco products presents "extraordinary health risks," and that "tobacco use is the single leading cause of preventable death in the United States." . . .

These findings logically imply that, if tobacco products were "devices" under the FDCA, the FDA would be required to remove them from the market. Consider, first, the FDCA's provisions concerning the misbranding of drugs or devices. The Act prohibits "[t]he introduction or delivery for introduction into interstate commerce of any food, drug, device, or cosmetic that is adulterated or misbranded." 21 U.S.C. §331(a). In light of the FDA's findings, two distinct FDCA provisions would render cigarettes and smokeless tobacco misbranded devices. First, §352(j) deems a drug or device misbranded "[i]f it is dangerous to health when used in the dosage or manner, or with the frequency or duration prescribed, recommended, or suggested in the labeling thereof." The FDA's findings make clear that tobacco products are "dangerous to health" when used in the manner prescribed. Second, a drug or device is misbranded under the Act "[u]nless its labeling bears . . . adequate directions for use . . . in such manner and form, as are necessary for the protection of users," except where such directions are "not necessary for the protection of the public health." §352(f)(1). Given the FDA's conclusions concerning the health consequences of tobacco use, there are no directions that could adequately protect consumers. That is, there are no directions that could make tobacco products safe for obtaining their intended effects. Thus, were tobacco products within the FDA's jurisdiction, the Act would deem them misbranded devices that could not be introduced into interstate commerce. Contrary to the dissent's contention, the Act admits no remedial discretion once it is evident that the device is misbranded. . . .

The FDCA's misbranding . . . provisions therefore make evident that were the FDA to regulate cigarettes and smokeless tobacco, the Act would require the agency to ban them. . . .

Congress, however, has foreclosed the removal of tobacco products from the market. A provision of the United States Code currently in force states that "[t]he marketing of tobacco constitutes one of the greatest basic industries of the United States with ramifying activities which directly affect interstate and foreign commerce at every point, and stable conditions therein are necessary to the general welfare." 7 U.S.C. §1311(a). More importantly, Congress has directly addressed the problem of tobacco and health through legislation on six occasions since 1965. [Citing statutes.] When Congress enacted these statutes, the adverse health consequences of tobacco use were well known, as were nicotine's pharmacological effects . . . [citing extensive studies]. Nonetheless, Congress stopped well short of ordering a ban. Instead, it has generally regulated the labeling and advertisement of tobacco products, expressly providing that it is the policy of Congress that "commerce and the national economy may be . . . protected to the maximum extent consistent with" consumers "be[ing] adequately informed about any adverse health effects." 15 U.S.C. §1331. Congress' decisions to regulate labeling and advertising and to adopt the express policy of protecting "commerce and the national economy . . . to the maximum extent" reveal its intent that tobacco products remain on the market. Indeed, the collective premise of these statutes is that cigarettes and smokeless tobacco will continue to be sold in the United States. A ban of tobacco products by the FDA would therefore plainly contradict congressional policy. . . .

Considering the FDCA as a whole, it is clear that Congress intended to exclude tobacco products from the FDA's jurisdiction. A fundamental precept of the FDCA is that any product regulated by the FDA—but not banned—must be safe for its intended use. . . . If they cannot be used safely for any therapeutic purpose, and yet they cannot be banned, they simply do not fit.

B

In determining whether Congress has spoken directly to the FDA's authority to regulate tobacco, we must also consider in greater detail the tobacco-specific legislation that Congress has enacted over the past 35 years. At the time a statute is enacted, it may have a range of plausible meanings. Over time, however, subsequent acts can shape or focus those meanings. The "classic judicial task of reconciling many laws enacted over time, and getting them to 'make sense' in combination, necessarily assumes that the implications of a statute may be altered by the implications of a later statute." *United States v. Fausto*, 484 U.S., at 453. This is particularly so where the scope of the earlier statute is broad but the subsequent statutes more specifically address the topic at hand. As we recognized recently in *United States v. Estate of Romani*, "a specific policy embodied in a later federal statute should control our construction of the [earlier] statute, even though it ha[s] not been expressly amended." 523 U.S., at 530-531.

Congress has enacted six separate pieces of legislation since 1965 addressing the problem of tobacco use and human health. Those statutes, among other things, require that health warnings appear on all packaging and in all print and outdoor advertisements, *see* 15 U.S.C. §§1331, 1333, 4402; prohibit the advertisement of tobacco products through "any medium of electronic communication" subject to regulation by the Federal Communications Commission (FCC), *see* §§1335, 4402(f); require the Secretary of HHS to report every three years to Congress on research findings concerning "the addictive property of tobacco," 42 U.S.C. §290aa-2(b)(2); and make States' receipt of certain federal block grants contingent on their making it unlawful "for any manufacturer, retailer, or distributor of tobacco products to sell or distribute any such product to any individual under the age of 18," §300x-26(a)(1).

In adopting each statute, Congress has acted against the backdrop of the FDA's consistent and repeated statements that it lacked authority under the FDCA to regulate tobacco absent claims of therapeutic benefit by the manufacturer. In fact, on several occasions over this period, and after the health consequences of tobacco use and nicotine's pharmacological effects had become well known, Congress considered and rejected bills that would have granted the FDA such jurisdiction. Under these circumstances, it is evident that Congress' tobacco-specific statutes have effectively ratified the FDA's long-held position that it lacks jurisdiction under the FDCA to regulate tobacco products. Congress has created a distinct regulatory scheme to address the problem of tobacco and health, and that scheme, as presently constructed, precludes any role for the FDA. . . .

Subsequent tobacco-specific legislation followed a similar pattern. By the FCLAA's own terms, the prohibition on any additional cigarette labeling or advertising regulations relating to smoking and health was to expire July 1, 1969. *See* §10, 79 Stat. 284. In anticipation of the provision's expiration, both the FCC and the FTC proposed rules governing the advertisement of cigarettes. . . . After debating the proper role for administrative agencies in the regulation of tobacco, *see generally* Cigarette Labeling and Advertising—1969: Hearings before the House Committee on Interstate and Foreign Commerce, 91st Cong., 1st Sess., pt. 2 (1969), Congress amended the FCLAA by banning cigarette advertisements "on any medium of electronic communication subject to the jurisdiction of the Federal Communications Commission" and strengthening the warning required to appear on cigarette packages. Public Health Cigarette Smoking Act of 1969, Pub. L. 91-222, §§4, 6, 84 Stat. 88-89. Importantly, Congress extended indefinitely the prohibition on any other regulation of cigarette labeling with respect to smoking and health (again despite the importance of labeling regulation under the FDCA). §5(a), 84 Stat. 88 (codified at 15 U.S.C. §1334(a)). Moreover, it expressly forbade the FTC from taking any action on its pending rule until July 1, 1971, and it required the FTC, if it decided to proceed with its rule thereafter, to notify Congress at least six months in advance of the rule's becoming effective. §7(a), 84 Stat. 89. As the chairman of the House committee in which the bill originated stated, "the Congress—the body elected by the people—must make the policy determinations involved in this legislation—and not some agency made up of appointed officials." 116 Cong. Rec. 7920 (1970) (remarks of Rep. Staggers). . . .

Meanwhile, the FDA continued to maintain that it lacked jurisdiction under the FDCA to regulate tobacco products as customarily marketed. In 1972, FDA Commissioner Edwards testified before Congress that "cigarettes recommended for smoking pleasure are beyond the Federal Food, Drug, and Cosmetic Act." 1972 Hearings 239, 242. He further stated that the FDA believed that the Public Health Cigarette Smoking Act "demonstrates that the regulation of cigarettes is to be the domain of Congress," and that "labeling or banning cigarettes is a step that can be take[n] only by the Congress. Any such move by FDA would be inconsistent with the clear congressional intent." *Ibid.* [The Court documented statements by FDA Commissioners to similar effect in 1977 and in 1980.] . . .

In 1983, Congress again considered legislation on the subject of smoking and health. . . . Nonetheless, Assistant [of HHS] Secretary Brandt maintained [in testimony] that "the issue of regulation of tobacco . . . is something that Congress has reserved to itself, and we do not within the Department have the authority to regulate nor are we seeking such authority." *Id.*, at 74. He also testified before the Senate, stating that, despite the evidence of tobacco's health effects and addictiveness, the Department's view was that "Congress has assumed the responsibility of regulating . . . cigarettes." Smoking Prevention and Education Act: Hearings on S. 772 before the Senate Committee on Labor and Human Resources, 98th Cong., 1st Sess., 56 (1983) (hereinafter 1983 Senate Hearings).

Against this backdrop, Congress enacted three additional tobacco-specific statutes over the next four years that incrementally expanded its regulatory scheme for tobacco products. In 1983, Congress adopted the Alcohol and Drug Abuse Amendments, Pub. L. 98-24, 97 Stat. 175 (codified at 42 U.S.C. §290aa *et seq.*), which require the Secretary of HHS to report to Congress every three years on the "addictive property of tobacco" and to include recommendations for action that the Secretary may deem appropriate. A year later, Congress enacted the Comprehensive Smoking Education Act, Pub. L. 98-474, 98 Stat. 2200, which amended the FCLAA by again modifying the prescribed warning. Notably, during debate on the Senate floor, Senator Hawkins argued that the FCLAA was necessary in part because "[u]nder the Food, Drug and Cosmetic Act, the Congress exempted tobacco products." 130 Cong. Rec. 26953 (1984). And in 1986, Congress enacted the Comprehensive Smokeless Tobacco Health Education Act of 1986 (CSTHEA), Pub. L. 99-252, 100 Stat. 30 (codified at 15 U.S.C. §4401 et seq.), which essentially extended the regulatory provisions of the FCLAA to smokeless tobacco products. Like the FCLAA, the CSTHEA provided that "[n]o statement relating to the use of smokeless tobacco products and health, other than the statements required by [the Act], shall be required by any Federal agency to appear on any package . . . of a smokeless tobacco product." §7(a), 100 Stat. 34 (codified at 15 U.S.C. §4406(a)). Thus, as with cigarettes, Congress reserved for itself an aspect of smokeless tobacco regulation that is particularly important to the FDCA's regulatory scheme. . . .

Taken together, these actions by Congress over the past 35 years preclude an interpretation of the FDCA that grants the FDA jurisdiction to regulate tobacco products. We do not rely on Congress' failure to act—its consideration and rejection of bills that would have given the FDA this authority—in reaching this conclusion. Indeed, this is not a case of simple inaction by Congress that purportedly represents its acquiescence in an agency's position. To the contrary, Congress has enacted several statutes addressing the particular subject of tobacco and health, creating a distinct regulatory scheme for cigarettes and smokeless tobacco. In doing so, Congress has been aware of tobacco's health hazards and its pharmacological effects. It has also enacted this legislation against the background of the FDA repeatedly and consistently asserting that it lacks jurisdiction under the FDCA to regulate tobacco products as customarily marketed. Further, Congress has persistently acted to preclude a meaningful role for any administrative agency in making policy on the subject of tobacco and health. Moreover, the substance of Congress' regulatory scheme is, in an important respect, incompatible with FDA jurisdiction. Although the supervision of product labeling to protect consumer health is a substantial component of the FDA's regulation of drugs and devices, *see* 21 U.S.C. §352 (1994 ed. and Supp. III), the FCLAA and the CSTHEA explicitly prohibit any federal agency from imposing any health-related labeling requirements on cigarettes or smokeless tobacco products, *see* 15 U.S.C. §§1334(a), 4406(a).

Under these circumstances, it is clear that Congress' tobacco-specific legislation has effectively ratified the FDA's previous position that it lacks jurisdiction to regulate tobacco. As in *Bob Jones Univ. v. United States*, 461 U.S. 574 (1983), "[i]t is hardly conceivable that Congress—and in this setting, any Member of Congress—was not abundantly aware of what was going on." *Id.*, at 600-601. Congress has affirmatively acted to address the issue of tobacco and health, relying on the representations of the FDA that it had no authority to regulate tobacco. It has created a distinct scheme to regulate the sale of tobacco products, focused on labeling and advertising, and premised on the belief that the FDA lacks such jurisdiction under the FDCA. As a result, Congress' tobacco-specific statutes preclude the FDA from regulating tobacco products as customarily marketed. . . .

C

Finally, our inquiry into whether Congress has directly spoken to the precise question at issue is shaped, at least in some measure, by the nature of the question presented. Deference under *Chevron* to an agency's construction of a statute that it administers is premised on the theory that a statute's ambiguity constitutes an implicit delegation from Congress to the agency to fill in the statutory gaps. *See Chevron*, at 844. In extraordinary cases, however, there may be reason to hesitate before concluding that Congress has intended such an implicit delegation. Cf. Breyer, *Judicial Review of Questions of Law and Policy*, 38 Admin. L. Rev. 363, 370 (1986) ("A court may also ask whether the legal question is an important one. Congress is more likely to have focused upon, and answered, major questions, while leaving interstitial matters to answer themselves in the course of the statute's daily administration.").

This is hardly an ordinary case. Contrary to its representations to Congress since 1914, the FDA has now asserted jurisdiction to regulate an industry constituting a significant portion of the American economy. . . . Congress, for better or for worse, has created a distinct regulatory scheme for tobacco products, squarely rejected proposals to give the FDA jurisdiction over tobacco, and repeatedly acted to preclude any agency from exercising significant policymaking authority in the area. Given this history and the breadth of the authority that the FDA has asserted, we are obliged to defer not to the agency's expansive construction of the statute, but to Congress' consistent judgment to deny the FDA this power.

Our decision in *MCI Telecommunications Corp. v. American Telephone & Telegraph Co.*, 512 U.S. 218 (1994), is instructive. That case involved the proper construction of the term "modify" in §203(b) of the Communications Act of 1934. The FCC contended that, because the Act gave it the discretion to "modify any requirement" imposed under the statute, it therefore possessed the authority to render voluntary the otherwise mandatory requirement that long distance carriers file their rates. *Id.*, at 225. We rejected the FCC's construction, finding "not the slightest doubt" that Congress had directly spoken to the question. *Id.*, at 228. In reasoning even more apt here, we concluded that "[i]t is highly unlikely that Congress would leave the determination of whether an industry will be entirely, or even substantially, rate-regulated to agency discretion—and even more unlikely that it would achieve that through such a subtle device as permission to 'modify' rate-filing requirements." *Id.*, at 231.

As in *MCI*, we are confident that Congress could not have intended to delegate a decision of such economic and political significance to an agency in so cryptic a fashion. To find that the FDA has the authority to regulate tobacco products, one must not only adopt an extremely strained understanding of "safety" as it is used throughout the Act—a concept central to the FDCA's regulatory scheme—but also ignore the plain implication of Congress' subsequent tobacco-specific legislation. It is therefore clear, based on the FDCA's overall regulatory scheme and the subsequent tobacco legislation, that Congress has directly spoken to the question at issue and precluded the FDA from regulating tobacco products. . . .

Reading the FDCA as a whole, as well as in conjunction with Congress' subsequent tobacco-specific legislation, it is plain that Congress has not given the FDA the authority that it seeks to exercise here. For these reasons, the judgment of the Court of Appeals for the Fourth Circuit is affirmed.

It is so ordered.

Justice BREYER, with whom Justice STEVENS, Justice SOUTER, and Justice GINSBURG join, dissenting.

The Food and Drug Administration (FDA) has the authority to regulate "articles (other than food) intended to affect the structure or any function of the body. . . ." Federal Food, Drug, and Cosmetic Act (FDCA), 21 U.S.C. §321(g)(1)(C). Unlike the majority, I believe that tobacco products fit within this statutory language.

In its own interpretation, the majority nowhere denies the following two salient points. First, tobacco products (including cigarettes) fall within the scope of this statutory definition, read literally. Cigarettes achieve their mood-stabilizing effects through the interaction of the chemical nicotine and the cells of the central nervous system. Both cigarette manufacturers and smokers alike know of, and desire, that chemically induced result. Hence, cigarettes are "intended to affect" the body's "structure" and "function," in the literal sense of these words.

Second, the statute's basic purpose—the protection of public health—supports the inclusion of cigarettes within its scope. *See United States v. Article of Drug Bacto-Unidisk*, 394 U.S. 784, 798 (1969) (FDCA "is to be given *a liberal construction consistent with [its] overriding purpose to protect the public health*" (emphasis added)). Unregulated tobacco use causes "[m]ore than 400,000 people [to] die each year from tobacco-related illnesses, such as cancer, respiratory illnesses, and heart disease." Indeed, tobacco products kill more people in this country every year "than . . . AIDS . . . , car accidents, alcohol, homicides, illegal drugs, suicides, and fires, *combined*." *Ibid.* (emphasis added).

I [OMITTED]

II

A

The tobacco companies contend that the FDCA's words cannot possibly be read to mean what they literally say. The statute defines "device," for example, as "an instrument, apparatus, implement, machine, contrivance, implant, in vitro reagent, or other similar or related article . . . intended to affect the structure or any function of the body. . . ." 21 U.S.C. §321(h). . . . One can readily infer from this language that at least an article that does achieve its primary purpose through chemical action within the body and that is dependent upon being metabolized is a "drug," provided that it otherwise falls within the scope of the "drug" definition. And one need not hypothesize about air conditioners or thermal pajamas to recognize that the chemical nicotine, an important tobacco ingredient, meets this test.

Although I now oversimplify, the FDA has determined that once nicotine enters the body, the blood carries it almost immediately to the brain. Nicotine then binds to receptors on the surface of brain cells, setting off a series of chemical reactions that alter one's mood and produce feelings of sedation and stimulation. Nicotine also increases the number of nicotinic receptors on the brain's surface, and alters its normal electrical activity. And nicotine stimulates the transmission of a natural chemical that "rewards" the body with pleasurable sensations (dopamine), causing nicotine addiction. The upshot is that nicotine stabilizes mood, suppresses appetite, tranquilizes, and satisfies a physical craving that nicotine itself has helped to create—all through chemical action within the body after being metabolized. . . .

B

The tobacco companies' principal definitional argument focuses upon the statutory word "intended." *See* 21 U.S.C. §321(g)(1)(C). The companies say that "intended" in this context is a term of art. They assert that the statutory word "intended" means that the product's maker has made an express claim about the effect that its product will have on the body. . . .

The FDCA, however, does not use the word "claimed"; it uses the word "intended." And the FDA long ago issued regulations that say the relevant "intent" can be shown not only by a manufacturer's "expressions," but also "by the circumstances surrounding the distribution of the article." . . .

Courts ordinarily reverse an agency interpretation of this kind only if Congress has clearly answered the interpretive question or if the agency's interpretation is unreasonable. *Chevron U.S.A. Inc. v. Natural Resources Defense Council, Inc.*, 467 U.S. 837, 842-843 (1984). . . .

C

The majority nonetheless reaches the "inescapable conclusion" that the language and structure of the FDCA as a whole "simply do not fit" the kind of public health problem that tobacco creates. That is because, in the majority's view, the FDCA requires the FDA to ban outright "dangerous" drugs or devices (such as cigarettes); yet, the FDA concedes that an immediate and total cigarette-sale ban is inappropriate.

This argument is curious because it leads with similarly "inescapable" force to precisely the opposite conclusion, namely, that the FDA does have jurisdiction but that it must ban cigarettes. More importantly, the argument fails to take into account the fact that a statute interpreted as requiring the FDA to pick a more dangerous over a less dangerous remedy would be a perverse statute, causing, rather than preventing, unnecessary harm whenever a total ban is likely the more dangerous response. And one can at least imagine such circumstances. . . .

In my view, where linguistically permissible, we should interpret the FDCA in light of Congress' overall desire to protect health. That purpose requires a flexible interpretation that both permits the FDA to take into account the realities of human behavior and allows it, in appropriate cases, to choose from its arsenal of statutory remedies. A statute so interpreted easily "fit[s]" this, and other, drug- and device-related health problems.

III

In the majority's view, laws enacted since 1965 require us to deny jurisdiction, whatever the FDCA might mean in their absence. But why? Do those laws contain language barring FDA jurisdiction? The majority must concede that they do not. Do they contain provisions that are inconsistent with the FDA's exercise of jurisdiction? With one exception, the majority points to no such provision. Do they somehow repeal the principles of law (discussed in Part II, supra) that otherwise would lead to the conclusion that the FDA has jurisdiction in this area? The companies themselves deny making any such claim. . . .

Regardless, the later statutes do not support the majority's conclusion. That is because, whatever individual Members of Congress after 1964 may have assumed about the FDA's jurisdiction, the laws they enacted did not embody any such "no jurisdiction" assumption. . . .

IV

I now turn to the final historical fact that the majority views as a factor in its interpretation of the subsequent legislative history: the FDA's former denials of its tobacco-related authority. . . . When it denied jurisdiction to regulate cigarettes, the FDA consistently stated why that was so. . . .

What changed? For one thing, the FDA obtained evidence sufficient to prove the necessary "intent" despite the absence of specific "claims." This evidence, which first became available in the early 1990's, permitted the agency to demonstrate that the tobacco companies knew nicotine achieved appetite-suppressing, mood-stabilizing, and habituating effects through chemical (not psychological) means, even at a time when the companies were publicly denying such knowledge.

Moreover, scientific evidence of adverse health effects mounted, until, in the late 1980's, a consensus on the seriousness of the matter became firm. . . .

Finally, administration policy changed. Earlier administrations may have hesitated to assert jurisdiction for the reasons prior Commissioners expressed. Commissioners of the current administration simply took a different regulatory attitude.

Nothing in the law prevents the FDA from changing its policy for such reasons. By the mid-1990's, the evidence needed to prove objective intent—even without an express claim—had been found. The emerging scientific consensus about tobacco's adverse, chemically induced, health effects may have convinced the agency that it should spend its resources on this important regulatory effort.

V

One might nonetheless claim that, even if my interpretation of the FDCA and later statutes gets the words right, it lacks a sense of their "music." *See Helvering v. Gregory*, 69 F.2d 809, 810-811 (C.A.2 1934) (L. Hand, J.) ("[T]he meaning of a [statute] may be more than that of the separate words, as a melody is more than the notes . . ."). Such a claim might rest on either of two grounds.

First, one might claim that, despite the FDA's legal right to change its mind, its original statements played a critical part in the enactment of the later statutes and now should play a critical part in their interpretation. . . .

The majority also believes that subsequently enacted statutes deprive the FDA of jurisdiction. But the later laws say next to nothing about the FDA's tobacco-related authority. Previous FDA disclaimers of jurisdiction may have helped to form the legislative atmosphere out of which Congress' own tobacco-specific statutes emerged. But a legislative atmosphere is not a law, unless it is embodied in a statutory word or phrase. And the relevant words and phrases here reveal nothing more than an intent not to change the jurisdictional status quo.

The upshot is that the Court today holds that a regulatory statute aimed at unsafe drugs and devices does not authorize regulation of a drug (nicotine) and a device (a cigarette) that the Court itself finds unsafe. Far more than most, this particular drug and device risks the life-threatening harms that administrative regulation seeks to rectify. The majority's conclusion is counterintuitive. And, for the reasons set forth, I believe that the law does not require it.

Consequently, I dissent.

Notes and Questions

1. Similar to *MCI, Brown & Williamson* involves a battle between the majority and the dissent as to whether the statute was sufficiently clear to preclude the agency's interpretation. What tools did the justices use in this case to determine whether the statute was clear? Are all of them equally appropriate for this purpose? Focus specifically on the use of subsequent legislative history. Why was this fair game? Are any tools of statutory interpretation not among the "traditional tools of statutory construction" that the Court uses at Step One?

2. Relying on *MCI*, the Court stated that Congress does not delegate matters of great economic and social significance to an agency through mere ambiguity. This principle is often called the major questions doctrine—as in, Congress does not implicitly delegate authority to an agency to resolve major questions through ambiguous language. How significant must the issue be before the Court will refuse to read ambiguity as a delegation to the agency? If you cannot answer that question, can you see how much control this principle gives reviewing courts?

3. The major questions doctrine is sometimes referred to as the elephants-in-mouseholes doctrine. This label comes courtesy of Justice Scalia, writing for the Court in another case, Whitman v. American Trucking Association, Inc., 531 U.S. 457 (2001). The question in *Whitman* was whether the Clean Air Act (CAA) violated the constitutional nondelegation doctrine because it directed the EPA to set National Ambient Air Quality Standards (NAAQS) at a level "the attainment and maintenance of which are requisite to protect the public health with 'an adequate margin of safety.'" Respondents argued that unless this language was read to permit EPA to consider costs in setting NAAQS, the agency would have virtually unlimited authority to determine the quality of our air, and the CAA thus would violate the nondelegation doctrine. The Court disagreed. In a prior case involving a different provision of the CAA, the Court had refused to interpret ambiguous language as granting the EPA implicit authority to consider costs when many other provisions in the statute granted such authority expressly. Accordingly, Justice Scalia stated that respondents would have to show "a texual commitment" for EPA to consider costs in setting NAAQS. Furthermore, that textual commitment would have to be "a clear one" because the NAAQS provision was the "engine" of the CAA. Citing *MCI* and *Brown & Williamson*, Justice Scalia continued, "Congress, we have held, does not alter the fundamental details of a regulatory scheme in vague terms or ancillary provisions—it does not, one might say, hide elephants in mouseholes." Although Justice Scalia found no clear texual commitment, the Court nevertheless found that NAAQS provision, as written, contained a sufficient intelligible principle to survive a nondelegation challenge.

4. What is the justification for this principle? Is it true that Congress does not intend to delegate matters of great economic and social significance to an agency through mere ambiguity? A number of congressional staffers who draft legislation seem to strongly agree. *See* Abbe R. Gluck & Lisa Schultz Bressman, *Statutory Interpretation from the Inside—An Empirical Study of Congressional Drafting, Delegation, and the Canons: Part I*, 65 STAN. L. REV. 901 (2013). According to a majority of those interviewed, drafters intend to delegate the details of implementation, not the major policy questions. *Id.*

5. Suppose, as was the case, that the FDA was under significant pressure from the Clinton administration to issue its regulations regarding cigarettes. Can you make any inference about the role (or sufficiency) of presidential involvement for validating agency action? Why wasn't political accountability enough to carry the day? Did the importance of tobacco regulation to the Clinton administration actually trigger heightened judicial review?

King v. Burwell

135 S. Ct. 2480 (2015)

Chief Justice ROBERTS delivered the opinion of the Court.

[The opinion and dissent appear in Chapter 3. The question in the case was whether the phrase "established by "an Exchange established by the State" could include health care exchanges established by the federal government. The IRS had issued a notice-and-comment rule interpreting this phrase as including federal exchanges, and as a result, making tax credits available to qualified individuals who purchased health insurance on federal exchanges. The first question the Court confronted is whether it should afford *Chevron* deference to the IRS's position. Only after it resolved that question did the Court go on to independently interpret the statute. Below is the entirety of the Court's analysis of whether the IRS's rule warranted consideration under *Chevron*.]

The Affordable Care Act addresses tax credits in what is now Section 36B of the Internal Revenue Code. That section provides: "In the case of an applicable taxpayer, there shall be allowed as a credit against the tax imposed by this subtitle . . . an amount equal to the premium assistance credit amount." 26 U.S.C. §36B(a). Section 36B then defines the term "premium assistance credit amount" as "the sum of the *premium assistance amounts* determined under paragraph (2) with respect to all *coverage months* of the taxpayer occurring during the taxable year." §36B(b)(1) (emphasis added). Section 36B goes on to define the two italicized terms — "premium assistance amount" and "coverage month" — in part by referring to an insurance plan that is enrolled in through "an Exchange established by the State under [42 U.S.C. §18031]." 26 U.S.C. §§36B(b)(2)(A), (c)(2)(A)(i).

The IRS issued a rule interpreting Section 36B to authorize tax credits for individuals who enroll in an insurance plan through a Federal Exchange as well as a State Exchange. Petitioners argue that a Federal Exchange is not "an Exchange established by the State under [42 U.S.C. §18031]," and that the IRS Rule therefore contradicts Section 36B. Brief for Petitioners 18-20. The Government responds that the IRS Rule is lawful because the phrase "an Exchange established by the State under [42 U.S.C. §18031]" should be read to include Federal Exchanges. Brief for Respondents 20-25.

When analyzing an agency's interpretation of a statute, we often apply the two-step framework announced in *Chevron*, 467 U.S. 837. Under that framework, we ask whether the statute is ambiguous and, if so, whether the agency's interpretation is reasonable. *Id.*, at 842-843. This approach "is premised on the theory that a statute's ambiguity constitutes an implicit delegation from Congress to the agency to fill in the statutory gaps." *FDA* v. *Brown & Williamson Tobacco Corp.*, 529 U.S. 120, 159 (2000). "In extraordinary cases, however, there may be reason to hesitate before concluding that Congress has intended such an implicit delegation." *Ibid.*

This is one of those cases. The tax credits are among the Act's key reforms, involving billions of dollars in spending each year and affecting the price of health insurance for millions of people. Whether those credits are available on Federal Exchanges is thus a question of deep "economic and political significance" that is central to this statutory scheme; had Congress wished to assign that question to an agency, it surely would have done so expressly. *Utility Air Regulatory Group* v. *EPA*, 573 U.S. ___, (2014) (slip op., at 19) (quoting *Brown & Williamson*, 529 U.S., at 160). It is especially unlikely that Congress would have delegated this decision to the IRS, which has no expertise in crafting health insurance policy of this sort. See *Gonzales* v. *Oregon*, 546 U.S. 243-267 (2006). This is not a case for the IRS.

Notes and Questions

1. What does *King v. Burwell* add to the "major questions" doctrine relied upon in *Brown & Williamson*? How would you state the "major questions" factors that oust a case from consideration under *Chevron*? Does the issue have to be a significant one to economy, or merely a significant one for the statutory scheme? How important is the relative expertise of the agency in making that evaluation?

2. Practically, what was the difference between upholding the position the agency took under *Chevron* or upholding the agency's position on the grounds that the issue is one that is too important to presume Congress would have delegated it to the agency? At the time *King v. Burwell* was decided in 2015, there was a divided government, with a Democrat, President Obama, in the White House, and a Republican majority in both the Senate and the House, and the 2016 election was on the horizon. If the Court had decided to uphold the agency's interpretation under *Chevron*—after all, the Court did find the statute ambiguous on the question—how could the subsequent Trump administration have reversed course? Considered in this light, the Court's decision not to treat the issue under *Chevron* was extremely significant for the future of the health care law.

ii. Step Two: Unreasonable Agency Interpretations

Although courts often assert control by finding that a statutory term is clear under Step One, they do so less often by finding that an agency interpretation is unreasonable under Step Two. In fact, the Supreme Court did so for the first time only in 1999 and has seldom done so since. *See* AT&T Corp. v. Iowa Utilities Board, 525 U.S. 366 (1999). Thus, for the Supreme Court, Step Two has not served as a major tool of judicial control. Many lower courts, for their part, often provide only a cursory analysis at Step Two. As long as an interpretation is within the outer boundaries of the statute under Step One, it is "permissible" under the statute under Step Two. Some might say that this approach is most consistent with *Chevron* and its normative defense of judicial deference: congressional delegation, agency expertise, and political accountability.

Yet other lower courts do perform a more rigorous analysis under Step Two, and thereby assert control of agency action. These courts tend to view reasonableness review as overlapping with arbitrary and capricious review—a topic that we will discuss below. *See* Ronald M. Levin, *The Anatomy of* Chevron: *Step Two Reconsidered*, 72 CHI.-KENT L. REV. 1253, 1264-67 (1997) (examining decisions in which courts regard Step Two this way). Briefly described, many courts seek to ensure that the agency interpretation is thoroughly considered and well explained, and in this sense, not "arbitrary or capricious," in line with the Court's decisions (e.g., *State Farm*, reprinted below) elaborating that language from the APA's judicial review provision, §706. This approach can be understood as "provid[ing] a structural check for the very presumptions of agency accountability, rationality, and expertise upon which *Chevron* deference is based." Kevin M. Stack, *The Constitutional Foundations of* Chenery, 116 YALE L.J. 952, 959 (2007).

Finally, certain judges may treat reasonableness review as a means to assert control for a different sort of reason and with a different sort of effect. These judges are textualists. They may regard reasonableness review as an opportunity to revisit the statutory language and use tools of statutory interpretation that they reject under Step One. Justice Scalia demonstrated this approach in Christensen v. Harris County, 529 U.S. 576, 590-91 (2000) (Scalia, J., concurring in part and concurring in the judgment). He found an agency interpretation unreasonable because it was not the best reading of a provision when that provision was viewed in the context of the overall statute. *Id.* at 591. In essence, he read the provision perhaps more broadly or even more purposively than he would under Step One. Is this fair game under Step Two?

c. After *Chevron*: *Mead* and *Barnhart*

In 2001, the Supreme Court unsettled the two-step structure of *Chevron* in United States v. Mead Corp., 533 U.S. 218 (2001). *Mead* announced what appeared to be a new doctrinal step, sometimes referred to as *Chevron* Step Zero, see Cass R. Sunstein, Chevron *Step Zero*, 92 VA. L. REV. 187 (2006). Under that step, a court asks, as threshold matter, whether an agency interpretation meets certain requirements that entitle it to the application of *Chevron*. If so, the court reviews the interpretation using the two-step test of *Chevron*. If not, the court reviews the interpretation using the old standard from Skidmore

v. Swift & Co., 323 U.S. 134 (1944). Recall that, under *Skidmore,* courts provide their own interpretations of the statutory provision at issue but accord "some deference" to agency interpretations that they find "persuasive." To make matters more complicated, just one term after *Mead,* the Court issued Barnhart v. Walton, 535 U.S. 212 (2002), which courts sometimes consult in applying *Mead,* but which has requirements that are dissimilar from *Mead.* We reproduce both *Mead* and *Barnhart* below.

As you can imagine, *Mead* has created considerable controversy and confusion. By imposing new requirements for the application of *Chevron,* the decision appears to reverse at least part of the presumption in *Chevron* that ambiguity in a statute is read to delegate interpretive authority to the agency charged with implementing that statute. *See* Adrian Vermeule, *Introduction:* Mead *in the Trenches,* 71 GEO. WASH. L. REV. 347, 348 (2003). Before attempting to understand the difficulties and curiosities that *Mead* introduces, try to articulate the conditions that *Mead* establishes as prerequisites to the application of *Chevron.*

United States v. Mead Corp.

533 U.S. 218 (2001)

Justice SOUTER delivered the opinion of the Court.

The question is whether a tariff classification ruling by the United States Customs Service deserves judicial deference. The Federal Circuit rejected Customs's invocation of *Chevron U.S.A. Inc. v. Natural Resources Defense Council, Inc.,* 467 U.S. 837 (1984), in support of such a ruling, to which it gave no deference. We agree that a tariff classification has no claim to judicial deference under *Chevron,* there being no indication that Congress intended such a ruling to carry the force of law, but we hold that under *Skidmore v. Swift & Co.,* 323 U.S. 134 (1944), the ruling is eligible to claim respect according to its persuasiveness.

I

A

Imports are taxed under the Harmonized Tariff Schedule of the United States (HTSUS), 19 U.S.C. §1202. Title 19 U.S.C. §1500(b) provides that Customs "shall, under rules and regulations prescribed by the Secretary [of the Treasury,] . . . fix the final classification and rate of duty applicable to . . . merchandise" under the HTSUS. Section 1502(a) provides that

> "[t]he Secretary of the Treasury shall establish and promulgate such rules and regulations not inconsistent with the law (including regulations establishing procedures for the issuance of binding rulings prior to the entry of the merchandise concerned), and may disseminate such information as may be necessary to secure a just, impartial, and uniform appraisement of imported merchandise and the classification and assessment of duties thereon at the various ports of entry."

See also §1624 (general delegation to Secretary to issue rules and regulations for the admission of goods).

The Secretary provides for tariff rulings before the entry of goods by regulations authorizing "ruling letters" setting tariff classifications for particular imports. 19 CFR §177.8 (2000). A ruling letter

> "represents the official position of the Customs Service with respect to the particular transaction or issue described therein and is binding on all Customs Service personnel in accordance with the provisions of this section until modified or revoked. In the absence of a change of practice or other modification or revocation which affects the principle of the ruling set forth in the ruling letter, that principle may be cited as authority in the disposition of transactions involving the same circumstances." §177.9(a).

After the transaction that gives it birth, a ruling letter is to "be applied only with respect to transactions involving articles identical to the sample submitted with the ruling request or to articles whose description is identical to the description set forth in the ruling letter." §177.9(b)(2). As a general matter, such a letter is "subject to modification or revocation without notice to any person, except the person to whom the letter was addressed," §177.9(c), and the regulations consequently provide that "no other person should rely on the ruling letter or assume that the principles of that ruling will be applied in connection with any transaction other than the one described in the letter," *ibid.* Since ruling letters respond to transactions of the moment, they are not subject to notice and comment before being issued, may be published but need only be made "available for public inspection," 19 U.S.C. §1625(a), and, at the time this action arose, could be modified without notice and comment under most circumstances, 19 CFR §177.10(c) (2000). A broader notice-and-comment requirement for modification of prior rulings was added by statute in 1993, Pub. L. 103-182, §623, 107 Stat. 2186, codified at 19 U.S.C. §1625(c), and took effect after this case arose.

Any of the 46 port-of-entry Customs offices may issue ruling letters, and so may the Customs Headquarters Office, in providing "[a]dvice or guidance as to the interpretation or proper application of the Customs and related laws with respect to a specific Customs transaction [which] may be requested by Customs Service field offices . . . at any time, whether the transaction is prospective, current, or completed," 19 CFR §177.11(a) (2000). Most ruling letters contain little or no reasoning, but simply describe goods and state the appropriate category and tariff. A few letters, like the Headquarters ruling at issue here, set out a rationale in some detail.

B

Respondent, the Mead Corporation, imports "day planners," three-ring binders with pages having room for notes of daily schedules and phone numbers and addresses, together with a calendar and suchlike. The tariff schedule on point falls under the HTSUS heading for "[r]egisters, account books, notebooks, order books, receipt books, letter pads, memorandum pads, diaries and similar articles," HTSUS subheading 4820.10, which comprises two subcategories. Items in the first, "[d]iaries, notebooks and address books, bound; memorandum pads, letter pads and similar articles," were subject to a tariff of 4.0% at the time in controversy. 185 F.3d 1304, 1305 (C.A. Fed. 1999) (citing subheading 4820.10.20). Objects in the second, covering "[o]ther" items, were free of duty. . . .

Between 1989 and 1993, Customs repeatedly treated day planners under the "other" HTSUS subheading. In January 1993, however, Customs changed its position, and issued a Headquarters ruling letter classifying Mead's day planners as "Diaries . . . , bound" subject to tariff under subheading 4820.10.20. That letter was short on explanation, but after Mead's protest, Customs Headquarters issued a new letter, carefully reasoned but never published, reaching the same conclusion. . . . [Mead filed suit in the Court of International Trade. The Court of International Trade granted the Government's motion for summary judgment. Mead appealed to the United States Circuit Court for the Federal Circuit, which reversed.]

We granted certiorari, in order to consider the limits of *Chevron* deference owed to administrative practice in applying a statute. We hold that administrative implementation of a particular statutory provision qualifies for *Chevron* deference when it appears that Congress delegated authority to the agency generally to make rules carrying the force of law, and that the agency interpretation claiming deference was promulgated in the exercise of that authority. Delegation of such authority may be shown in a variety of ways, as by an agency's power to engage in adjudication or notice-and-comment rulemaking, or by some other indication of a comparable congressional intent. The Customs ruling at issue here fails to qualify, although the possibility that it deserves some deference under *Skidmore* leads us to vacate and remand.

II

A

When Congress has "explicitly left a gap for an agency to fill, there is an express delegation of authority to the agency to elucidate a specific provision of the statute by regulation," *Chevron*, 467 U.S., at 843-844, and any ensuing regulation is binding in the courts unless procedurally defective, arbitrary or capricious in substance, or manifestly contrary to the statute. *See id.*, at 844; *United States v. Morton*, 467 U.S. 822, 834, (1984); APA, 5 U.S.C. §§706(2)(A), (D). But whether or not they enjoy any express delegation of authority on a particular question, agencies charged with applying a statute necessarily make all sorts of interpretive choices, and while not all of those choices bind judges to follow them, they certainly may influence courts facing questions the agencies have already answered. "[T]he well-reasoned views of the agencies implementing a statute 'constitute a body of experience and informed judgment to which courts and litigants may properly resort for guidance,'"

Bragdon v. Abbott, 524 U.S. 624, 642 (1998) (quoting *Skidmore,* 323 U.S., at 139-140), and "[w]e have long recognized that considerable weight should be accorded to an executive department's construction of a statutory scheme it is entrusted to administer...." *Chevron,* at 844 (footnote omitted).... The fair measure of deference to an agency administering its own statute has been understood to vary with circumstances, and courts have looked to the degree of the agency's care,[1] its consistency,[2] formality,[3] and relative expertness,[4] and to the persuasiveness of the agency's position, *see Skidmore,* at 139-140. The approach has produced a spectrum of judicial responses, from great respect at one end, *see, e.g., Aluminum Co. of America v. Central Lincoln Peoples' Util. Dist.,* 467 U.S. 380, 389-390 (1984) ("'substantial deference'" to administrative construction), to near indifference at the other, see, *e.g., Bowen v. Georgetown Univ. Hospital,* 488 U.S. 204, 212-213 (1988) (interpretation advanced for the first time in a litigation brief). Justice Jackson summed things up in *Skidmore v. Swift & Co.*:

> "The weight [accorded to an administrative] judgment in a particular case will depend upon the thoroughness evident in its consideration, the validity of its reasoning, its consistency with earlier and later pronouncements, and all those factors which give it power to persuade, if lacking power to control." 323 U.S., at 140.

Since 1984, we have identified a category of interpretive choices distinguished by an additional reason for judicial deference. This Court in *Chevron* recognized that Congress not only engages in express delegation of specific interpretive authority, but that "[s]ometimes the legislative delegation to an agency on a particular question is implicit." 467 U.S., at 844. Congress, that is, may not have expressly delegated authority or responsibility to implement a particular provision or fill a particular gap. Yet it can still be apparent from the agency's generally conferred authority and other statutory circumstances that Congress would expect the agency to be able to speak with the force of law when it addresses ambiguity in the statute or fills a space in the enacted law, even one about which "Congress did not actually have an intent" as to a particular result. *Id.,* at 845. When circumstances implying such an expectation exist, a reviewing court has no business rejecting an agency's exercise of its generally conferred authority to resolve a particular statutory ambiguity simply because the agency's chosen resolution seems unwise, *see id.,* at 845-846, but is obliged to accept the agency's position if Congress has not previously spoken to the point at issue and the agency's interpretation is reasonable, *see id.,* at 842-845; *cf.* 5 U.S.C. §706(2) (a reviewing court shall set

1. *See, e.g., General Elec. Co. v. Gilbert,* 429 U.S. 125, 142 (1976) (courts consider the "'thoroughness evident in [the agency's] consideration'" (quoting *Skidmore v. Swift & Co.,* 323 U.S. 134, 140 (1944))).

2. *See, e.g., Good Samaritan Hospital v. Shalala,* 508 U.S. 402, 417 (1993) ("[T]he consistency of an agency's position is a factor in assessing the weight that position is due").

3. *See, e.g., Reno v. Koray,* 515 U.S. 50, 61 (1995) (internal agency guideline that is not "subject to the rigors of the [APA], including public notice and comment," is entitled only to "some deference" (internal quotation marks omitted)).

4. *See, e.g., Aluminum Co. of America v. Central Lincoln Peoples' Util. Dist.,* 467 U.S. 380, 390 (1984).

aside agency action, findings, and conclusions found to be "arbitrary, capricious, an abuse of discretion, or otherwise not in accordance with law").

We have recognized a very good indicator of delegation meriting *Chevron* treatment is express congressional authorizations to engage in the process of rulemaking or adjudication that produces regulations or rulings for which deference is claimed. *See, e.g., EEOC v. Arabian American Oil Co.,* 499 U.S. 244, 257 (1991) (no *Chevron* deference to agency guideline where congressional delegation did not include the power to "'promulgate rules or regulations'" (quoting *General Elec. Co. v. Gilbert,* 429 U.S. 125, 141 (1976))); *see also Christensen v. Harris County,* 529 U.S. 576, 596-597 (2000) (Breyer, J., dissenting) (where it is in doubt that Congress actually intended to delegate particular interpretive authority to an agency, *Chevron* is "inapplicable"). It is fair to assume generally that Congress contemplates administrative action with the effect of law when it provides for a relatively formal administrative procedure tending to foster the fairness and deliberation that should underlie a pronouncement of such force. *Cf. Smiley v. Citibank (South Dakota), N.A.,* 517 U.S. 735, 741 (1996) (APA notice and comment "designed to assure due deliberation"). Thus, the overwhelming number of our cases applying *Chevron* deference have reviewed the fruits of notice-and-comment rulemaking or formal adjudication. That said, and as significant as notice-and-comment is in pointing to *Chevron* authority, the want of that procedure here does not decide the case, for we have sometimes found reasons for *Chevron* deference even when no such administrative formality was required and none was afforded, see, *e.g., NationsBank of N.C., N.A. v. Variable Annuity Life Ins. Co.,* 513 U.S. 251, 256-257, 263 (1995).[5] The fact that the tariff classification here was not a product of such formal process does not alone, therefore, bar the application of *Chevron.*

There are, nonetheless, ample reasons to deny *Chevron* deference here. The authorization for classification rulings, and Customs's practice in making them, present a case far removed not only from notice-and-comment process, but from any other circumstances reasonably suggesting that Congress ever thought of classification rulings as deserving the deference claimed for them here.

B

No matter which angle we choose for viewing the Customs ruling letter in this case, it fails to qualify under *Chevron.* On the face of the statute, to begin with, the terms of the congressional delegation give no indication that Congress meant to delegate authority to Customs to issue classification

---

5. In *NationsBank of N.C., N.A. v. Variable Annuity Life Ins. Co.,* 513 U.S., at 256-257 (internal quotation marks omitted), we quoted longstanding precedent concluding that "[t]he Comptroller of the Currency is charged with the enforcement of banking laws to an extent that warrants the invocation of [the rule of deference] with respect to his deliberative conclusions as to the meaning of these laws." *See also* 1 M. Malloy, Banking Law and Regulation §1.3.1, p. 1.41 (1996) (stating that the Comptroller is given "personal authority" under the National Bank Act).

rulings with the force of law. We are not, of course, here making any global statement about Customs's authority, for it is true that the general rulemaking power conferred on Customs, *see* 19 U.S.C. §1624, authorizes some regulation with the force of law, or "legal norms," as we put it in *Haggar*, 526 U.S., at 391. It is true as well that Congress had classification rulings in mind when it explicitly authorized, in a parenthetical, the issuance of "regulations establishing procedures for the issuance of binding rulings prior to the entry of the merchandise concerned," 19 U.S.C. §1502(a). The reference to binding classifications does not, however, bespeak the legislative type of activity that would naturally bind more than the parties to the ruling, once the goods classified are admitted into this country. And though the statute's direction to disseminate "information" necessary to "secure" uniformity, *ibid.*, seems to assume that a ruling may be precedent in later transactions, precedential value alone does not add up to *Chevron* entitlement; interpretive rules may sometimes function as precedents, *see* Strauss, The Rulemaking Continuum, 41 Duke L.J. 1463, 1472-1473 (1992), and they enjoy no *Chevron* status as a class. In any event, any precedential claim of a classification ruling is counterbalanced by the provision for independent review of Customs classifications by the CIT, *see* 28 U.S.C. §§2638-2640; the scheme for CIT review includes a provision that treats classification rulings on par with the Secretary's rulings on "valuation, rate of duty, marking, restricted merchandise, entry requirements, drawbacks, vessel repairs, or similar matters," §1581(h); *see* §2639(b). It is hard to imagine a congressional understanding more at odds with the *Chevron* regime.

It is difficult, in fact, to see in the agency practice itself any indication that Customs ever set out with a lawmaking pretense in mind when it undertook to make classifications like these. Customs does not generally engage in notice-and-comment practice when issuing them, and their treatment by the agency makes it clear that a letter's binding character as a ruling stops short of third parties; Customs has regarded a classification as conclusive only as between itself and the importer to whom it was issued, 19 CFR §177.9(c) (2000), and even then only until Customs has given advance notice of intended change, §§177.9(a), (c). Other importers are in fact warned against assuming any right of detrimental reliance. §177.9(c).

Indeed, to claim that classifications have legal force is to ignore the reality that 46 different Customs offices issue 10,000 to 15,000 of them each year. Any suggestion that rulings intended to have the force of law are being churned out at a rate of 10,000 a year at an agency's 46 scattered offices is simply self-refuting. Although the circumstances are less startling here, with a Headquarters letter in issue, none of the relevant statutes recognizes this category of rulings as separate or different from others; there is thus no indication that a more potent delegation might have been understood as going to Headquarters even when Headquarters provides developed reasoning, as it did in this instance. . . .

In sum, classification rulings are best treated like "interpretations contained in policy statements, agency manuals, and enforcement guidelines." *Christensen*, 529 U.S., at 587. They are beyond the *Chevron* pale.

C

To agree with the Court of Appeals that Customs ruling letters do not fall within *Chevron* is not, however, to place them outside the pale of any deference whatever. *Chevron* did nothing to eliminate *Skidmore*'s holding that an agency's interpretation may merit some deference whatever its form, given the "specialized experience and broader investigations and information" available to the agency, 323 U.S., at 139, and given the value of uniformity in its administrative and judicial understandings of what a national law requires, *id.*, at 140. *See generally Metropolitan Stevedore Co. v. Rambo,* 521 U.S. 121, 136 (1997) (reasonable agency interpretations carry "at least some added persuasive force" where *Chevron* is inapplicable); *Reno v. Koray,* 515 U.S. 50, 61 (1995) (according "some deference" to an interpretive rule that "do[es] not require notice and comment"); *Martin v. Occupational Safety and Health Review Comm'n,* 499 U.S. 144, 157 (1991) ("some weight" is due to informal interpretations though not "the same deference as norms that derive from the exercise of . . . delegated lawmaking powers").

There is room at least to raise a *Skidmore* claim here, where the regulatory scheme is highly detailed, and Customs can bring the benefit of specialized experience to bear on the subtle questions in this case: whether the daily planner with room for brief daily entries falls under "diaries," when diaries are grouped with "notebooks and address books, bound; memorandum pads, letter pads and similar articles," HTSUS subheading 4820.10.20; and whether a planner with a ring binding should qualify as "bound," when a binding may be typified by a book, but also may have "reinforcements or fittings of metal, plastics, etc.," Harmonized Commodity Description and Coding System Explanatory Notes to Heading 4820, p. 687 (cited in Customs Headquarters letter). A classification ruling in this situation may therefore at least seek a respect proportional to its "power to persuade," *Skidmore,* at 140; *see also Christensen,* 529 U.S., at 587; *id.,* at 595 (Stevens, J., dissenting); *id.,* at 596-597 (Breyer, J., dissenting). Such a ruling may surely claim the merit of its writer's thoroughness, logic, and expertness, its fit with prior interpretations, and any other sources of weight. . . .

Since the *Skidmore* assessment called for here ought to be made in the first instance by the Court of Appeals for the Federal Circuit or the [Court of International Trade], we go no further than to vacate the judgment and remand the case for further proceedings consistent with this opinion.

It is so ordered.

Justice SCALIA, dissenting.

Today's opinion makes an avulsive change in judicial review of federal administrative action. Whereas previously a reasonable agency application of an ambiguous statutory provision had to be sustained so long as it represented the agency's authoritative interpretation, henceforth such an application can be set aside unless "it appears that Congress delegated authority to the agency generally to make rules carrying the force of law," as by giving an agency "power to engage in adjudication or notice-and-comment rulemaking, or . . . some other [procedure] indicati[ng] comparable congressional intent," and "the agency interpretation claiming deference was promulgated in the exercise of that authority." What was previously a general presumption of authority in agencies to resolve ambiguity in the statutes they have been authorized to enforce has been changed to a presumption of no such authority, which must be overcome by affirmative legislative intent to the contrary. And whereas previously, when agency authority to resolve ambiguity did not exist the court was free to give the statute what it considered the best interpretation, henceforth the court must supposedly give the agency view some indeterminate amount of so-called *Skidmore* deference. *Skidmore v. Swift & Co.*, 323 U.S. 134 (1944). We will be sorting out the consequences of the *Mead* doctrine, which has today replaced the *Chevron* doctrine, *Chevron U.S.A. Inc. v. Natural Resources Defense Council, Inc.*, 467 U.S. 837 (1984), for years to come. I would adhere to our established jurisprudence, defer to the reasonable interpretation the Customs Service has given to the statute it is charged with enforcing, and reverse the judgment of the Court of Appeals. . . .

The basis in principle for today's new doctrine can be described as follows: The background rule is that ambiguity in legislative instructions to agencies is to be resolved not by the agencies but by the judges. Specific congressional intent to depart from this rule must be found—and while there is no single touchstone for such intent it can generally be found when Congress has authorized the agency to act through (what the Court says is) relatively formal procedures such as informal rulemaking and formal (and informal?) adjudication, and when the agency in fact employs such procedures. The Court's background rule is contradicted by the origins of judicial review of administrative action. But in addition, the Court's principal criterion of congressional intent to supplant its background rule seems to me quite implausible. There is no necessary connection between the formality of procedure and the power of the entity administering the procedure to resolve authoritatively questions of law. The most formal of the procedures the Court refers to—formal adjudication—is modeled after the process used in trial courts, which of course are not generally accorded deference on questions of law. The purpose of such a procedure is to produce a closed record for determination and review of the facts—which implies nothing about the power of the agency subjected to the procedure to resolve authoritatively questions of law.

As for informal rulemaking: While formal adjudication procedures are *prescribed* (either by statute or by the Constitution), *see* 5 U.S.C. §§554, 556; *Wong Yang Sung v. McGrath*, 339 U.S. 33, 50 (1950), informal rulemaking is more typically *authorized* but not required. Agencies with such authority are free to give guidance through rulemaking, but they may proceed to administer their statute case-by-case, "making law" as they implement their program (not necessarily through formal adjudication). *See NLRB v. Bell Aerospace Co.*, 416 U.S. 267, 290-295 (1974); *SEC v. Chenery Corp.*, 332 U.S. 194, 202-203 (1947). Is it likely—or indeed even plausible—that Congress meant, when such an agency chooses rulemaking, to accord the administrators of that agency, *and their successors,* the flexibility of interpreting the ambiguous statute now one way, and later another; but, when such an agency chooses case-by-case administration, to eliminate all future agency discretion by having that same ambiguity resolved authoritatively (and forever) by the courts? Surely that makes no sense. It is also the case that certain significant categories of rules—those involving grant and benefit programs, for example, are exempt from the requirements of informal rulemaking. *See* 5 U.S.C. §553(a)(2). Under the Court's novel theory, when an agency takes advantage of that exemption its rules will be deprived of *Chevron* deference, *i.e.,* authoritative effect. Was this either the plausible intent of the APA rulemaking exemption, or the plausible intent of the Congress that established the grant or benefit program?

Some decisions that are neither informal rulemaking nor formal adjudication are required to be made personally by a Cabinet Secretary, without any prescribed procedures. *See, e.g., United States v. Giordano,* 416 U.S. 505, 508 (1974) (involving application of 18 U.S.C. §2516 (1970 ed.), requiring wiretap applications to be authorized by "[t]he Attorney General, or any Assistant Attorney General specially designated by the Attorney General"); [citing other cases]. Is it conceivable that decisions specifically committed to these high-level officers are meant to be accorded no deference, while decisions by an administrative law judge left in place without further discretionary agency review, *see* 5 U.S.C. §557(b), are authoritative? This seems to me quite absurd, and not at all in accord with any plausible actual intent of Congress.

B

1

The principal effect will be protracted confusion. As noted above, the one test for *Chevron* deference that the Court enunciates is wonderfully imprecise: whether "Congress delegated authority to the agency generally to make rules carrying the force of law, . . . as by . . . adjudication[,] notice-and-comment rulemaking, or . . . some other [procedure] indicati[ng] comparable congressional intent." . . . It is hard to know what the lower courts are to make of today's guidance.

Another practical effect of today's opinion will be an artificially induced increase in informal rulemaking. Buy stock in the GPO. Since informal rulemaking and formal adjudication are the only more-or-less safe harbors from the storm that the Court has unleashed; and since formal adjudication is not an option but must be mandated by statute or constitutional command; informal rulemaking—which the Court was once careful to make voluntary unless required by statute, *see Bell Aerospace,* and *Chenery*—will now become a virtual necessity. As I have described, the Court's safe harbor requires not merely that the agency have been given rulemaking authority, but also that the agency have *employed* rulemaking as the means of resolving the statutory ambiguity. (It is hard to understand why that should be so. Surely the mere *conferral* of rulemaking authority demonstrates—if one accepts the Court's logic—a congressional intent to allow the agency to resolve ambiguities. And given that intent, what difference does it make that the agency chooses instead to use another perfectly permissible means for that purpose?) . . .

3

Worst of all, the majority's approach will lead to the ossification of large portions of our statutory law. Where *Chevron* applies, statutory ambiguities remain ambiguities subject to the agency's ongoing clarification. They create a space, so to speak, for the exercise of continuing agency discretion. As *Chevron* itself held, the Environmental Protection Agency can interpret "stationary source" to mean a single smokestack, can later replace that interpretation with the "bubble concept" embracing an entire plant, and if that proves undesirable can return again to the original interpretation. 467 U.S., at 853-859, 865-866. For the indeterminately large number of statutes taken out of *Chevron* by today's decision, however, ambiguity (and hence flexibility) will cease with the first judicial resolution. *Skidmore* deference gives the agency's current position some vague and uncertain amount of respect, but it does not, like *Chevron, leave* the matter within the control of the Executive Branch for the future. Once the court has spoken, it becomes *unlawful* for the agency to take a contradictory position; the statute now *says* what the court has prescribed. *See Neal v. United States,* 516 U.S. 284, 295 (1996). . . . It will be bad enough when this ossification occurs as a result of judicial determination (under today's new principles) that there is no affirmative indication of congressional intent to "delegate"; but it will be positively bizarre when it occurs simply because of an agency's failure to act by rulemaking (rather than informal adjudication) before the issue is presented to the courts. . . .

III

To decide the present case, I would adhere to the original formulation of *Chevron.* " 'The power of an administrative agency to administer a congressionally created . . . program necessarily requires the formulation of policy and the making of rules to fill any gap left, implicitly or explicitly, by Congress,' " 467 U.S., at 843 (quoting *Morton v. Ruiz,* 415 U.S. 199, 231 (1974)). We accordingly presume—and our precedents have made clear to Congress that we presume—that, absent some clear textual indication to the contrary, "Congress, when it left ambiguity in a statute meant for implementation by an agency, understood that the ambiguity would be resolved, first and foremost, by the agency, and desired the agency (rather than the courts) to possess whatever degree of discretion the ambiguity allows," *Smiley,* 517 U.S., at 740-741 (citing *Chevron,* at 843-844). *Chevron* sets forth an across-the-board presumption, which operates as a background rule of law against which Congress legislates: Ambiguity means Congress intended agency discretion. Any resolution of the ambiguity by the administering agency that is authoritative—that represents the official position of the agency—must be accepted by the courts if it is reasonable.

Nothing in the statute at issue here displays an intent to modify the background presumption on which *Chevron* deference is based. . . .

There is no doubt that the Customs Service's interpretation represents the authoritative view of the agency. Although the actual ruling letter was signed by only the Director of the Commercial Rulings Branch of Customs Headquarters' Office of Regulations and Rulings, the Solicitor General of the United States has filed a brief, cosigned by the General Counsel of the Department of the Treasury, that represents the position set forth in the ruling letter to be the official position of the Customs Service. *Cf. Christensen,* 529 U.S., at 591 (Scalia, J., concurring in part and concurring in judgment). No one contends that it is merely a "*post hoc* rationalizatio[n]" or an "agency litigating positio[n] wholly unsupported by regulations, rulings, or administrative practice," *Bowen v. Georgetown Univ. Hospital,* 488 U.S. 204, 212 (1988).

There is also no doubt that the Customs Service's interpretation is a reasonable one, whether or not judges would consider it the best. I will not belabor this point, since the Court evidently agrees: An interpretation that was unreasonable would not merit the remand that the Court decrees for consideration of *Skidmore* deference. . . .

* * *

For the reasons stated, I respectfully dissent from the Court's judgment. I would uphold the Customs Service's construction of Subheading 4820.10.20 of the Harmonized Tariff Schedule of the United States, 19 U.S.C. §1202, and would reverse the contrary decision of the Court of Appeals. I dissent even more vigorously from the reasoning that produces the Court's judgment, and that makes today's decision one of the most significant opinions ever rendered by the Court dealing with the judicial review of administrative action. Its consequences will be enormous, and almost uniformly bad.

Notes and Questions

1. It is first important (and difficult enough) to understand what *Mead* says. What are the conditions that *Mead* establishes for an agency interpretation to qualify for the application of *Chevron*? Is there one condition or two? Why didn't the Customs Service's revenue ruling letter warrant the application of *Chevron*?

2. *Mead* has produced confusion among the lower courts, as Justice Scalia warned. *See* Adrian Vermeule, *Introduction:* Mead *in the Trenches,* 71 GEO. WASH. U. L. REV. 347 (2003). *Mead* requires a very detailed inquiry to determine whether *Chevron* or *Skidmore* review is appropriate. One study found that lower courts were so uncertain about this inquiry that they actually sought to avoid it, when possible, by simply stating that the agency wins under any standard. *See* Lisa Schultz Bressman, *How* Mead *Has Muddled*

Judicial Review of Agency Action, 58 VAND. L. REV. 1443, 1465 (2005). Does it matter how an agency wins? The answer depends on whether the agency wants to change its interpretation in the future. If it originally won under Step Two, then *Chevron* says that it can change its interpretation (as long as it explains the change). If it originally won under *Skidmore,* then it will have to persuade that court that the new interpretation is a better interpretation of the statute. That is because the court technically retains interpretive authority under *Skidmore. See* Kristen E. Hickman & Mathew D. Kruger, *In Search of the Modern* Skidmore *Standard,* 107 COLUM. L. REV. 1235 (2007). Agencies may have a tough time persuading a court that a new interpretation is better. But there is a third possibility: if the agency originally won under *Skidmore* only because it failed to use a *Chevron*-worthy procedure, such as notice-and-comment rulemaking or formal adjudication, although it was authorized by its statute to do so, then it can change the interpretation through the *Chevron*-worthy procedure. *See* National Cable & Telecommunications Ass'n v. Brand X Internet Services, 545 U.S. 967, 982-83 (2002). Are you confused? Imagine how courts (and agencies) must feel. How should a court treat a subsequent agency interpretation when a prior court was not clear on the status of the prior interpretation?

3. One larger question raised by *Mead* is whether the Court picked sensible criteria for the application of *Chevron,* assuming the need for some prerequisites. The Court makes clear that when a statute authorizes an agency to engage in notice-and-comment rulemaking or in formal adjudication, and the agency uses these procedures to issue the interpretation in question, *Mead* is satisfied and *Chevron* is applicable. Justice Scalia argued in his dissent that *Chevron* should apply to "all authoritative agency interpretations of statutes they are charged with administering." Thus, as long as the agency is charged with administering the statute—which in most cases will involve a delegation to act in ways that "carry the force of law"—what matters is that the agency had taken an authoritative position, not that it has followed particular procedures. Similarly, scholars have argued that *Chevron* deference should depend on who within the agency acted, not on the format of their action. For instance, Elena Kagan and David Barron argue that *Chevron*'s political accountability rationale would be served if *Chevron* were limited to actions by statutory delegatees, those individuals expressly granted authority under the statute. *See* David J. Barron & Elena Kagan, Chevron's *Nondelegation Doctrine,* 2001 SUP. CT. REV. 201, 238. Others have countered that these views too quickly dismiss the valuable kernel of *Mead*: that deference should attach to agency interpretations only if they are sufficiently deliberative and transparent to warrant it. *See* Bressman, *How* Mead *Has Muddled Judicial Review of Agency Action,* 58 VAND. L. REV. at 1479-80. Some have argued that *Mead*'s insistence on a particular type of delegation is appropriate, but not that the agency, in addition, act through a particular format. *See* Ronald M. Levin, Mead *and the Prospective Exercise of Discretion,* 54 ADMIN. L. REV. 771, 791-804 (2001). Still others have maintained that *Mead* is too complex to be worthwhile. What is your view? Is there a justification for insisting on a congressional delegation of authority to bind with the force of law? Can you think of a reason why Congress might actually prefer that agencies issue interpretations in certain, relatively formal ways? Should that matter to the standard of review?

Barnhart v. Walton

535 U.S. 212 (2002)

BREYER, J., delivered the opinion of the Court, Parts I and III of which were unanimous, and Part II of which was joined by REHNQUIST, C.J., and STEVENS, O'CONNOR, KENNEDY, SOUTER, THOMAS, and GINSBURG, JJ. SCALIA, J., filed an opinion concurring in part and concurring in the judgment.

Justice BREYER delivered the opinion of the Court.

The Social Security Act authorizes payment of disability insurance benefits and Supplemental Security Income to individuals with disabilities. See 49 Stat. 622, as amended, 42 U.S.C. §401 *et seq.* (1994 ed. and Supp. V) (Title II disability insurance benefits); §1381 *et seq.* (Title XVI supplemental security income). For both types of benefits the Act defines the key term "disability" as an

> "*inability* to engage in any substantial gainful activity *by reason of* any medically determinable physical or mental *impairment* which can be expected to result in death or *which has lasted or can be expected to last for a continuous period of not less than 12 months.*" §423(d)(1)(A) (1994 ed.) (Title II) (emphasis added); accord, §1382c(a)(3)(A) (1994 ed., Supp. V) (Title XVI).

This case presents two questions about the Social Security Administration's interpretation of this definition.

First, the Social Security Administration (which we shall call the Agency) reads the term "inability" as including a "12 month" requirement. In its view, the "inability" (to engage in any substantial gainful activity) must last, or must be expected to last, for *at least 12 months*. Second, the Agency reads the term "expected to last" as applicable only when the "inability" has *not yet* lasted 12 months. In the case of a later Agency determination—where the "inability" *did not* last 12 months—the Agency will automatically assume that the claimant failed to meet the duration requirement. It will not look back to decide hypothetically whether, despite the claimant's actual return to work before 12 months expired, the "inability" nonetheless *might have been* expected to last that long.

The Court of Appeals for the Fourth Circuit held both these interpretations of the statute unlawful. We hold, to the contrary, that both fall within the Agency's lawful interpretive authority. See *Chevron U.S.A. Inc. v. Natural Resources Defense Council, Inc.,* 467 U.S. 837 (1984). Consequently, we reverse.

I

. . . The Agency concluded that Walton's mental illness had prevented him from engaging in any significant work, *i.e.,* from "engag[ing] in any substantial gainful activity," for 11 months—from October 31, 1994 (when he lost his teaching job) until the end of September 1995 (when he earned income sufficient to rise to the level of "substantial gainful activity"). *See* 20 CFR §§404.1574, 416.974 (2001). And because the statute demanded an "inability to engage in any substantial gainful activity" lasting 12, not 11, months, Walton was not entitled to benefits. . . .

II

The statutory definition of "disability" has two parts. First, it requires a certain kind of "inability," namely, an "inability to engage in any substantial gainful activity." Second, it requires an "impairment," namely, a "physical or mental impairment," which provides "reason" for the "inability." The statute adds that the "impairment" must be one that "has lasted or can be expected to last . . . not less than 12 months." But what about the "inability"? Must it also last (or be expected to last) for the same amount of time?

The Agency has answered this question in the affirmative. Acting pursuant to statutory rulemaking authority, 42 U.S.C. §§405(a) (Title II), 1383(d)(1) (Title XVI), it has promulgated formal regulations that state that a claimant is not disabled "regardless of [his] medical condition," if he is doing "substantial gainful activity." 20 CFR §404.1520(b) (2001). And the Agency has interpreted this regulation to mean that the claimant is not disabled if "within 12 months after the onset of an impairment . . . the impairment no longer prevents substantial gainful activity." 65 Fed. Reg. 42774 (2000). Courts grant an agency's interpretation of its own regulations considerable legal leeway. *Auer v. Robbins,* 519 U.S. 452, 461 (1997); *Udall v. Tallman,* 380 U.S. 1, 16-17 (1965). And no one here denies that the Agency has properly interpreted its own regulation.

Consequently, the legal question before us is whether the Agency's interpretation of the statute is lawful. This Court has previously said that, if the statute speaks clearly "to the precise question at issue," we "must give effect to the unambiguously expressed intent of Congress." *Chevron,* 467 U.S., at 842-843. If, however, the statute "is silent or ambiguous with respect to the specific issue," we must sustain the Agency's interpretation if it is "based on a permissible construction" of the Act. *Id.,* at 843. Hence we must decide (1) whether the statute unambiguously forbids the Agency's interpretation, and, if not, (2) whether the interpretation, for other reasons, exceeds the bounds of the permissible. *Ibid.; see also United States v. Mead Corp.,* 533 U.S. 218, 227 (2001). . . .

Walton also asks us to disregard the Agency's interpretation of its formal regulations on the ground that the Agency only recently enacted those regulations, perhaps in response to this litigation. We have previously rejected similar arguments. *Smiley v. Citibank (South Dakota), N.A.,* 517 U.S. 735, 741 (1996); *United States v. Morton,* 467 U.S. 822, 835-836, n.21 (1984).

Regardless, the Agency's interpretation is one of long standing. And the fact that the Agency previously reached its interpretation through means less formal than "notice and comment" rulemaking, *see* 5 U.S.C. §553, does not automatically deprive that interpretation of the judicial deference otherwise its due. *Cf. Chevron,* 467 U.S., at 843 (stating, without delineation of means, that the "'power of an administrative agency to administer a congressionally created . . . program necessarily requires the formulation of policy'" (quoting *Morton v. Ruiz,* 415 U.S. 199, 231 (1974)). If this Court's opinion in *Christensen v. Harris County,* 529 U.S. 576 (2000), suggested an absolute rule to the contrary, our later opinion in *United States v. Mead Corp.,* 533 U.S. 218 (2001), denied the suggestion. *Id.,* at 230-231 ("[T]he want of" notice and comment "does not decide the case"). Indeed, *Mead* pointed to instances in which the Court has applied *Chevron* deference to agency interpretations that did not emerge out of notice-and-comment rulemaking. 533 U.S., at 230-231 (citing *NationsBank of N.C., N.A. v. Variable Annuity Life Ins. Co.,* 513 U.S. 251, 256-257 (1995)). It indicated that whether a court should give such deference depends in significant part upon the interpretive method used and the nature of the question at issue. 533 U.S., at 229-231. And it discussed at length why *Chevron* did not require deference in the circumstances there present—a discussion that would have been superfluous had the presence or absence of notice-and-comment rulemaking been dispositive. 533 U.S., at 231-234.

In this case, the interstitial nature of the legal question, the related expertise of the Agency, the importance of the question to administration of the statute, the complexity of that administration, and the careful consideration the Agency has given the question over a long period of time all indicate that *Chevron* provides the appropriate legal lens through which to view the legality of the Agency interpretation here at issue. *See United States v. Mead Corp.; cf. also* 1 K. Davis & R. Pierce, Administrative Law Treatise §§1.7, 3.3 (3d ed. 1994).

For these reasons, we find the Agency's interpretation lawful. . . .

We conclude that the Agency's regulation is lawful.

* * *

The judgment of the Fourth Circuit is
Reversed.

Notes and Questions

1. A big question here: Is *Barnhart* consistent with *Mead?* On what grounds is an interpretation contained at various points in a Social Security Administration letter, manual, and ruling entitled to *Chevron* deference? The Court relied upon "the interstitial nature of the legal question, the related expertise of the Agency, the importance of the question to the administration of the statute, the complexity of that administration, and the careful consideration the Agency has given the question over a long period of time."

Does *Barnhart* suggest that *Mead* has given way to a totality-of-the-circumstances analysis for all non-traditional formats? Does *Barnhart* instead furnish an alternative test for courts to use as they wish? Does it provide a test for courts to apply if an agency interpretation flunks *Mead*? While we are on the topic of relationship to prior decisions, how is *Barnhart* different from *Skidmore* when the factors seem so similar?

2. This is not a case involving an agency flip-flop or change in position, as we have seen many times including in *Chevron* itself. To the contrary, Justice Breyer emphasizes that the SSA's interpretation has been constant since it was first announced, shortly after the statute was enacted. How important is this factor? Perhaps, given the complexity of this scheme, Congress anticipated that the SSA would have to determine all the details necessary to administer its statute, and the SSA followed through early and definitively. In other words, Congress and the SSA were partners from the start. Does this help to explain why the SSA interpretation was entitled to the application of *Chevron*?

3. Confused? So are lower courts. They have vacillated uncomfortably between the factors set forth in *Mead* and *Barnhart*, often applying different analyses and reaching different conclusions for identical interpretive formats. *See* Lisa Schultz Bressman, *How* Mead *Has Muddled Judicial Review of Agency Action*, 58 VAND. L. REV. 1443, 1458-63 (2005).

d. The Debate Over *Chevron*

The debate over *Chevron* has many facets. In articles too numerous to cite, scholars have debated whether the framework is too complicated for courts to apply, whether judicial deference does not turn on the framework but on a judge's interpretive method or political leaning, whether the rationale of congressional delegation is a legal fiction or legislative reality, and more. Many of these are largely empirical questions. As for the normative side, some have defended *Chevron* for enhancing presidential accountability for agency action, *see, e.g.*, Elena Kagan, *Presidential Administration*, 114 HARV. L. REV. 2245 (2001), while others have castigated *Chevron* as an abdication of legislative and judicial power. To this latter point, consider the views of two sitting Justices, first Justice Thomas followed by Justice Gorsuch:

> As I have explained elsewhere, "[T]he judicial power, as originally understood, requires a court to exercise its independent judgment in interpreting and expounding upon the laws." *Perez v. Mortgage Bankers Assn.*, (2015) (opinion concurring in judgment). Interpreting federal statutes—including ambiguous ones administered by an agency—"calls for that exercise of independent judgment." *Id. Chevron* deference precludes judges from exercising that judgment, forcing them to abandon what they believe is "the best reading of an ambiguous statute" in favor of an agency's construction. *Brand X, supra*, at 983. It thus wrests from Courts the ultimate interpretative authority to "say what the law is," *Marbury v. Madison*, 1 Cranch 137, 177 (1803), and hands it over to the Executive. See *Brand X, supra*, at 983 (noting that the judicial construction of an ambiguous statute is "not authoritative"). Such a transfer is in tension with Article III's Vesting Clause, which vests the judicial power exclusively in Article III courts, not administrative agencies. U. S. Const., Art. III, §1.

In reality . . . , agencies "interpreting" ambiguous statutes typically are not engaged in acts of interpretation at all. Instead, as *Chevron* itself acknowledged, they are engaged in the " 'formulation of policy.' " 467 U. S., at 843. Statutory ambiguity thus becomes an implicit delegation of rule-making authority, and that authority is used not to find the best meaning of the text, but to formulate legally binding rules to fill in gaps based on policy judgments made by the agency rather than Congress.

Although acknowledging this fact might allow us to escape the jaws of Article III's Vesting Clause, it runs headlong into the teeth of Article I's, which vests "[a]ll legislative Powers herein granted" in Congress. U. S. Const., Art I., §1. For if we give the "force of law" to agency pronouncements on matters of private conduct as to which " 'Congress did not actually have an intent,' " *Mead* at 229, we permit a body other than Congress to perform a function that requires an exercise of the legislative power. See *Department of Transportation v. Association of American Railroads,* (2015) (Thomas, J., concurring in judgment).

Michigan v. EPA, 135 S. Ct. 2699 (2015) (Thomas, J., concurring).

When the political branches disagree with a judicial interpretation of existing law, the Constitution prescribes the appropriate remedial process. It's called legislation. Admittedly, the legislative process can be an arduous one. But that's no bug in the constitutional design: it is the very point of the design. The framers sought to ensure that the people may rely on judicial precedent about the meaning of existing law until and unless that precedent is overruled or the purposefully painful process of bicameralism and presentment can be cleared. Indeed, the principle of *stare decisis* was one "entrenched and revered by the framers' precisely because they knew its importance 'as a weapon against . . . tyranny."

Transferring the job of saying what the law is from the judiciary to the executive unsurprisingly invites the very sort of due process (fair notice) and equal protection concerns the framers knew would arise if the political branches intruded on judicial functions. . . . [One] must always remain alert to the possibility that the agency will reverse its current view 180 degrees anytime based merely on the shift of political winds and still prevail. Neither, too, will agencies always deign to announce their views in advance; often enough they seek to impose their 'reasonable' new interpretations only retroactively in administrative adjudications. Perhaps allowing agencies rather than courts to declare the law's meaning bears some advantages, but it also bears its costs. And the founders were wary of those costs, knowing that, when unchecked by independent courts exercising the job of declaring the law's meaning, executives throughout history had sought to exploit ambiguous laws as license for their own prerogative.

For whatever the agency may be doing under *Chevron*, the problem remains that courts are not fulfilling their duty to interpret the law and declare invalid agency actions inconsistent with those interpretations in the cases and controversies that come before them. . . . That's a problem for the judiciary. And it is a problem for the people whose liberties may now be impaired not by an independent decisionmaker seeking to declare the law's meaning as fairly as possible—the decisionmaker promised to them by law—but by an avowedly politicized administrative agent seeking to pursue whatever policy whim may rule the day. . . .

Chevron invests the power to decide the meaning of the law, and to do so with legislative policy goals in mind, in the very entity charged with enforcing the law. . . . It's an arrangement, too, that seems pretty hard to square with the Constitution of the founders' design and, as Justice Frankfurter once observed, "[t]he accretion of dangerous power does not come in a day. It does come, however slowly, from the generative force of unchecked disregard of the restrictions' imposed by the Constitution. . . ."

All of which raises this question: what would happen in a world without *Chevron*? . . . Of course, courts could and would consult agency views and apply the agency's interpretation when it accords with the best reading of a statute. But de novo judicial review of the law's meaning would limit the ability of an agency to alter and amend existing law. It would avoid the due process and equal protection problems of the kind documented in our decisions. It would promote reliance interests by allowing citizens to organize their affairs with some assurance that the rug will not be pulled from under them tomorrow, the next day, or after the next election. And an agency's recourse for a judicial declaration of the law's meaning that it dislikes would be precisely the recourse the Constitution prescribes—an appeal to higher judicial authority or a new law enacted consistent with bicameralism and presentment.

Gutierrez-Brizuela v. Lynch, 834 F.3d 1142 (2016) (Gorsuch. J.).

Consider also Justice Breyer's view that *Chevron* is not an abdication of either judicial or legislative authority, but a rule of thumb for courts to apply out of respect for how Congress (permissibly) delegates to agencies:

> In referring to *Chevron*, I do not mean that courts are to treat that case like a rigid, black-letter rule of law, instructing them always to allow agencies leeway to fill every gap in every statutory provision. . . . Rather, I understand *Chevron* as a rule of thumb, guiding courts in an effort to respect that leeway which Congress intended the agencies to have. I recognize that Congress does not always consider such matters, but if not, courts can often implement a more general, virtually omnipresent congressional purpose—namely, the creation of a well-functioning statutory scheme—by using a canon-like, judicially created construct, the hypothetical reasonable legislator, and asking what such legislators would likely have intended had Congress considered the question of delegating gap-filling authority to the agency.

SAS Institute Inc. v. IANCU (2018) (Breyer, J., dissenting). Interestingly, Justice Kagan joined Justice Breyer's dissent, with the exception of this part. She has joined other opinions in which *Chevron* was applied in its more traditional sense. *See, e.g.*, City of Arlington v. FCC (2013).

Along these general lines, Professor Jonathan Siegel has offered a concise reply to the claim that *Chevron* violates the judicial role under Article III of the Constitution:

> Even the critics accept that, insofar as Article III is concerned, Congress could have expressly authorized the EPA to make the decision it made. Suppose that the Clean Air Act had set forth its permit requirements and had then provided:
> The EPA shall by rule determine whether the permit requirements of this Act shall apply:
> (a) to every new or modified piece of pollution-emitting equipment within a plant, or
> (b) only to a new plant or a plant that as a whole increases its emission of pollutants.
> In such a case, even the critics would accept that Article III would pose no barrier to the agency's exercising the authority conferred by the statute. Congress would simply have conferred on the agency discretion to make a policy choice. Congress does that all the time. The barrier to such delegation of discretion would, if anything, be the nondelegation doctrine, not Article III. *Chevron* deference, however, is nothing more than the generalized functional equivalent of the statute just hypothesized. It merely confers on agencies discretion to make the policy choice among the potential reasonable interpretations of ambiguous statutory language.

Jonathan R. Siegel, *The Constitutional Case for* Chevron *Deference*, 71 Vand. L. Rev. 937, 973 (2018).

Some have suggested that *Chevron* may be on shaky ground, not from a constitutional standpoint but a political one. In January 2017, when Congress was in session and before President Trump had been inaugurated, the House passed the Regulatory Accountability Act of 2017, in part to put an end to *Chevron* deference. The bill, in relevant part, provides:

TITLE II—SEPARATION OF POWERS RESTORATION ACT

Separation of Powers Restoration Act

Sec. 202. This title modifies the scope of judicial review of agency actions to authorize courts reviewing agency actions to decide de novo (without giving deference to the agency's interpretation) all relevant questions of law, including the interpretation of: (1) constitutional and statutory provisions, and (2) rules made by agencies. If the reviewing court determines that a statutory or regulatory provision relevant to its decision contains a gap or ambiguity, the court shall not interpret or rely on that gap or ambiguity as: (1) an implicit delegation to the agency of legislative rulemaking authority, or (2) a justification for interpreting agency authority expansively or for deferring to the agency's interpretation on the question of law.

No law may exempt such a civil action from the application of the amendments made by this bill except by specific reference to these provisions.

The Regulatory Accountability Act of 2017, if enacted, would have many other consequences for agency action, for example amending the APA's rulemaking requirements. The preamble in the bill provides:

AN ACT

To reform the process by which Federal agencies analyze and formulate new regulations and guidance documents, to clarify the nature of judicial review of agency interpretations, to ensure complete analysis of potential impacts on small entities of rules, and for other purposes.

What is the future of *Chevron* and its progeny? Only time will tell.

2. Judicial Control of Agency Regulatory Interpretation

Statutes are not the only legal sources that agencies interpret. Agencies frequently interpret their own regulations as well. They do so in adjudications when the meaning or application of the agency's regulations are at issue. They do so in guidance documents that spell out the agency's interpretation of its own regulations. They also do so in briefs, including amicus briefs, as well as in other informal documents.

The question arises whether an agency's interpretation of its own regulations should receive judicial deference when challenged in court and if so, what sort of deference? The story of judicial deference to agency interpretation of their own regulations begins with Bowles v. Seminole Rock & Sand Co., 325 U.S. 410 (1945). The regulations at issue in *Seminole Rock* were issued by the Office of Price Administration (OPA), which had broad powers to establish price controls. Congress established the OPA in 1942 to combat inflation produced by the wartime economy, and sought to contain it through price controls to be set by OPA. OPA faced significant pressure to issue price controls that would provide a binding interpretation that could be relied upon as private parties engaged in commerce. OPA pursued its job of establishing price controls through a set of so-called General Max regulations which established a general price freeze on thousands of commodities. *See* Sanne H. Knudsen & Amy J. Wildermuth, *Unearthing the Lost History of Seminole Rock*, 65 EMORY L.J. 47 (2015) (providing account of historical context of *Seminole Rock*).

One of these General Max regulations, Maximum Price Regulation No. 188, was at issue in *Seminole Rock*. It established the maximum price for rock at the March 1942 levels. The question in *Seminole Rock* was whether the price cap was for the price of crushed stone delivered in March 1942 or the price of crushed stone contracted for sale in March 1942. Seminole Rock had delivered crushed stone in March 1942 based on a 1941 contract at 60 cents a ton, but entered a contract in January 1942 for the sale of crushed stone at $1.50 a ton. *Seminole Rock*, 325 U.S. at 412-14. When Seminole Rock entered into a subsequent contract to sell crushed stone for 85 cents a ton, OPA sued to enjoin the sale on the ground that the price exceed that set in Maximum Price Regulation No. 188. *Id.* at 412. The regulation provides "the maximum price for any article which was delivered or offered for delivery in March, 1942, shall be the highest price charged by the manufacture during March, 1942." The OPA's Administrator has also issued a widely distributed bulletin, *What Every Retailer Should Know About the General Maximum Price Regulation*, which clarified that the "The highest price charged during March 1942 means the highest price which the retailer charged for an article actually delivered during that month, or if he did not make any such delivery of that article during March, his highest offering price for delivery of that article during March." *Id.* at 417. OPA claimed that the actual delivery of crushed stones in March 1942 is the highest maximum price under its Maximum Price Regulation No. 188. The Supreme Court resolved the issue by announcing the following standard:

> Since this involves an interpretation of an administrative regulation a court must necessarily look to the administrative construction of the regulation if the meaning of the words used is in doubt. The intention of Congress or the principles of the Constitution in some situations may be relevant in the first instance in choosing between various constructions. But the ultimate criterion is the administrative interpretation, which becomes of controlling weight unless it is plainly erroneous or inconsistent with the regulation.

Seminole Rock, 325 U.S. at 413-14. The Court provided no rationale for deference, in contrast to the detailed rational the *Chevron* court would provide for its framework some 40 years later. Perhaps the Court viewed the issue as simply unexceptional because of the practical need for uniform interpretations of price controls during wartime. In the years immediately following *Seminole Rock*, courts most frequently applied *Seminole Rock* deference—that an agency's interpretation of its own regulation is "controlling" unless "it is plainly erroneous or inconsistent with the regulation"—in the context of price control regulations. *See* Knudsen & Wildermuth, *Unearthing the Lost History of* Seminole Rock, 65 EMORY L.J. at 65. By the 1960s the doctrine had expanded, with courts relying on it far beyond the context of price control regulations. By the late 1960s, *Seminole Rock* deference had become an established doctrine of administrative law. Since 1997, this doctrine of judicial deference to agency interpretations of their own regulation has been known as *Auer* deference after the following decision.

Auer v. Robbins

519 U.S. 452 (1997)

SCALIA, J., delivered the opinion for a unanimous Court.

The Fair Labor Standards Act of 1938 (FLSA), 52 Stat. 1060, as amended, 29 U.S.C. §§201 *et seq.,* exempts "bona fide executive, administrative, or professional" employees from overtime pay requirements. This case presents the question whether the Secretary of Labor's "salary-basis" test for determining an employee's exempt status reflects a permissible reading of the statute as it applies to public-sector employees. We also consider whether the Secretary has reasonably interpreted the salary-basis test to deny an employee salaried status (and thus grant him overtime pay) when his compensation may "as a practical matter" be adjusted in ways inconsistent with the test.

I

Petitioners are sergeants and a lieutenant employed by the St. Louis Police Department. They brought suit in 1988 against respondents, members of the St. Louis Board of Police Commissioners, seeking payment of overtime pay that they claimed was owed under §7(a)(1) of the FLSA, 29 U.S.C. §207(a)(1). Respondents argued that petitioners were not entitled to such pay because they came within the exemption provided by §213(a)(1) for "bona fide executive, administrative, or professional" employees.

Under regulations promulgated by the Secretary, one requirement for exempt status under §213(a)(1) is that the employee earn a specified minimum amount on a "salary basis." 29 C.F.R. §§541.1(f), 541.2(e), 541.3(e) (1996). According to the regulations, "[a]n employee will be considered to be paid 'on a salary basis' . . . if under his employment agreement he regularly receives each pay period on a weekly, or less frequent basis, a predetermined amount constituting all or part of his compensation, which amount is not subject to reduction because of variations in the quality or quantity of the work performed." §541.118(a). Petitioners contended that the salary-basis test was not met in their case because, under the terms of the St. Louis Metropolitan Police Department Manual, their compensation could be reduced for a variety of disciplinary infractions related to the "quality or quantity" of work performed. Petitioners also claimed that they did not meet the other requirement for exempt status under §213(a)(1): that their duties be of an executive, administrative, or professional nature. See §§541.1(a)-(e), 541.2(a)-(d), 541.3(a)-(d).

. . .

III

. . .

The Secretary of Labor, in an *amicus* brief filed at the request of the Court, interprets the salary-basis test to deny exempt status when employees are covered by a policy that permits disciplinary or other deductions in pay "as a practical matter." That standard is met, the Secretary says, if there is either an actual practice of making such deductions or an employment policy that creates a "significant likelihood" of such deductions. The Secretary's approach rejects a wooden requirement of actual deductions, but in their absence it requires a clear and particularized policy—one which "effectively communicates" that deductions will be made in specified circumstances. This avoids the imposition of massive and unanticipated overtime liability (including the possibility of substantial liquidated damages, see, *e.g., Kinney v. District of Columbia, supra,* at 12) in situations in which a vague or broadly worded policy is nominally applicable to a whole range of personnel but is not "significantly likely" to be invoked against salaried employees.

Because the salary-basis test is a creature of the Secretary's own regulations, his interpretation of it is, under our jurisprudence, controlling unless "'plainly erroneous or inconsistent with the regulation.'" *Robertson v. Methow Valley Citizens Council,* 490 U.S. 332, 359, 109 S. Ct. 1835, 1850, 104 L. Ed. 2d 351 (1989) (quoting *Bowles v. Seminole Rock & Sand Co.,* 325 U.S. 410, 414, 65 S. Ct. 1215, 1217, 89 L. Ed. 1700 (1945)). That deferential standard is easily met here. The critical phrase "subject to" comfortably bears the meaning the Secretary assigns. *See* American Heritage Dictionary 1788 (3d ed.1992) (def. 2: defining "subject to" to mean "prone; disposed"; giving as an example "a child who is subject to colds"); Webster's New International Dictionary 2509 (2d ed.1950) (def. 3: defining "subject to" to mean "[e]xposed; liable; prone; disposed"; giving as an example "a country subject to extreme heat").

The Secretary's approach is usefully illustrated by reference to this case. The policy on which petitioners rely is contained in a section of the police manual that lists a total of 58 possible rule violations and specifies the range of penalties associated with each. All department employees are nominally covered by the manual, and some of the specified penalties involve disciplinary deductions in pay. Under the Secretary's view, that is not enough to render petitioners' pay "subject to" disciplinary deductions within the meaning of the salary-basis test. This is so because the manual does not "effectively communicate" that pay deductions are an anticipated form of punishment for employees *in petitioners' category,* since it is perfectly possible to give full effect to every aspect of the manual without drawing any inference of that sort. If the statement of available penalties applied solely to petitioners, matters would be different; but since it applies both to petitioners and to employees who are unquestionably not paid on a salary basis, the expressed availability of disciplinary deductions may have reference only to the latter. No clear inference can be drawn as to the likelihood of a sanction's being applied to employees such as petitioners. Nor, under the Secretary's approach, is such a likelihood established by the one-time deduction in a sergeant's pay, under unusual circumstances.

Petitioners complain that the Secretary's interpretation comes to us in the form of a legal brief; but that does not, in the circumstances of this case, make it unworthy of deference. The Secretary's position is in no sense a "*post hoc* rationalizatio[n]" advanced by an agency seeking to defend past agency action against attack, *Bowen v. Georgetown Univ. Hospital*, 488 U.S. 204, 212, 109 S. Ct. 468, 474, 102 L. Ed. 2d 493 (1988). There is simply no reason to suspect that the interpretation does not reflect the agency's fair and considered judgment on the matter in question. Petitioners also suggest that the Secretary's approach contravenes the rule that FLSA exemptions are to be "narrowly construed against . . . employers" and are to be withheld except as to persons "plainly and unmistakably within their terms and spirit." *Arnold v. Ben Kanowsky, Inc.*, 361 U.S. 388, 392, 80 S. Ct. 453, 456, 4 L. Ed. 2d 393 (1960). But that is a rule governing judicial interpretation of statutes and regulations, not a limitation on the Secretary's power to resolve ambiguities in his own regulations. A rule requiring the Secretary to construe his own regulations narrowly would make little sense, since he is free to write the regulations as broadly as he wishes, subject only to the limits imposed by the statute.

In the decades following the Court's decision in *Auer*, the doctrine came under challenge from academics, most prominently, John F. Manning, *Constitutional Structure and Judicial Deference to Agency Interpretations of Agency Rules*, 96 COLUM. L. REV. 612, 660-69 (1996). In a sequence of concurring opinions over a decade, Justice Scalia then expressed doubts and eventually argued that the doctrine should be overruled, a view that Justice Thomas also embraced. Chief Justice Roberts and Justice Alito have also expressed interest in reconsidering the doctrine. *See* Talk Am., Inc. v. Mich. Bell Tel. Co., 564 U.S. 50, 67 (2011) (Scalia, J., concurring) (doubting the validity of the doctrine); Perez v. Mortg. Bankers Ass'n, 135 S. Ct. 1199, 1212 (2015) (Scalia, J., concurring in the judgment) (calling for the Court to overrule *Auer*); *id.* at 1213, 1224 (Thomas, J., concurring in the judgment) (arguing *Auer* should be overruled); Decker v. Nw. Envtl. Def. Ctr., 133 S. Ct. 1326, 1338 (2013) (Roberts, C.J., concurring) (joining with Justice Alito in noting that "[i]t may be appropriate to reconsider"

Seminole Rock/Auer in another case); *id.* at 1339, 1342 (Scalia, J., concurring in part and dissenting in part) (urging the Court to overturn *Seminole Rock/Auer*).

The main challenges to Auer were framed in separation of powers terms. Justice Scalia's concurring opinion in *Decker* presses this point, in distinguishing *Auer* deference from *Chevron* deference:

> Another conceivable justification for *Auer* deference, though not one that is to be found in our cases, is this: If it is reasonable to defer to agencies regarding the meaning of statutes that *Congress* enacted, as we do per *Chevron,* it is *a fortiori* reasonable to defer to them regarding the meaning of regulations *that they themselves crafted.* To give an agency less control over the meaning of its own regulations than it has over the meaning of a congressionally enacted statute seems quite odd.
>
> But it is not odd at all. The theory of *Chevron* (take it or leave it) is that when Congress gives an agency authority to administer a statute, including authority to issue interpretive regulations, it implicitly accords the agency a degree of discretion, which the courts must respect, regarding the meaning of the statute. See *Smiley v. Citibank (South Dakota), N.A.,* 517 U.S. 735, 740-741 (1996). While the implication of an agency power to clarify the statute is reasonable enough, there is surely no congressional implication that the agency can resolve ambiguities in its own regulations. For that would violate a fundamental principle of separation of powers—that the power to write a law and the power to interpret it cannot rest in the same hands. "When the legislative and executive powers are united in the same person . . . there can be no liberty; because apprehensions may arise, lest the same monarch or senate should enact tyrannical laws, to execute them in a tyrannical manner." Montesquieu, Spirit of the Laws bk. XI, ch. 6, pp. 151-152 (O. Piest ed., T. Nugent transl. 1949). Congress cannot enlarge its *own* power through *Chevron*—whatever it leaves vague in the statute will be worked out *by someone else. Chevron* represents a presumption about who, as between the Executive and the Judiciary, that someone else will be. (The Executive, by the way—the competing political branch—is the less congenial repository of the power as far as Congress is concerned.) So Congress's incentive is to speak as clearly as possible on the matters it regards as important.
>
> But when an agency interprets its *own* rules—that is something else. Then the power to prescribe is augmented by the power to interpret; and the incentive is to speak vaguely and broadly, so as to retain a "flexibility" that will enable "clarification" with retroactive effect. "It is perfectly understandable" for an agency to "issue vague regulations" if doing so will "maximiz[e] agency power." *Thomas Jefferson Univ., supra,* at 525, 114 S. Ct. 2381 (Thomas, J., dissenting). Combining the power to prescribe with the power to interpret is not a new evil: Blackstone condemned the practice of resolving doubts about "the construction of the Roman laws" by "stat[ing] the case to the emperor in writing, and tak[ing] his opinion upon it." 1 W. Blackstone, Commentaries on the Laws of England 58 (1765). And our Constitution did not mirror the British practice of using the House of Lords as a court of last resort, due in part to the fear that he who has "agency in passing bad laws" might operate in the "same spirit" in their interpretation. The Federalist No. 81, pp. 543-544 (J. Cooke ed. 1961). *Auer* deference encourages agencies to be "vague in framing regulations, with the plan of issuing 'interpretations' to create the intended new law without observance of notice and comment procedures." Anthony, The Supreme Court and the APA: Sometimes They Just Don't Get It, 10 Admin. L.J. Am. U. 1, 11-12 (1996). *Auer* is not a logical corollary to *Chevron* but a dangerous permission slip for the arrogation of power. See *Talk America,* 131 S. Ct., at 2266 (Scalia, J., concurring); Manning, Constitutional Structure and Judicial Deference to Agency Interpretations of Agency Rules, 96 Colum. L. Rev. 612 (1996).

Decker v. Nw. Envtl. Def. Ctr., 568 U.S. 597, 619-21 (2013).

When the Court granted certiorari in a case that directly raised the validity of *Auer*, observers were certain, invoking the inevitable pun, that "its hour [had] come round at last." But the Court surprised most observers.

Kisor v. Wilkie, Secretary of Veterans Affairs

588 U.S. ____ (2019)

Justice KAGAN announced the judgment of the Court and delivered the opinion of the Court with respect to Parts I, II-B, III-B, and IV, and an opinion with respect to Parts II-A and III-A, in which Justice GINSBURG, Justice BREYER, and Justice SOTOMAYOR join.

This Court has often deferred to agencies' reasonable readings of genuinely ambiguous regulations. We call that practice *Auer* deference, or sometimes *Seminole Rock* deference, after two cases in which we employed it. See *Auer v. Robbins*, 519 U.S. 452 (1997); *Bowles v. Seminole Rock & Sand Co.*, 325 U.S. 410 (1945). The only question presented here is whether we should overrule those decisions, discarding the deference they give to agencies. We answer that question no. *Auer* deference retains an important role in construing agency regulations. But even as we uphold it, we reinforce its limits. *Auer* deference is sometimes appropriate and sometimes not. Whether to apply it depends on a range of considerations that we have noted now and again, but compile and further develop today. The deference doctrine we describe is potent in its place, but cabined in its scope.

We begin by summarizing how petitioner James Kisor's case made its way to this Court. Truth be told, nothing recounted in this Part has much bearing on the rest of our decision. The question whether to overrule *Auer* does not turn on any single application, whether right or wrong, of that decision's deference doctrine. [Following Justice Kagan's advice, the facts of the case are omitted.]

A

Begin with a familiar problem in administrative law: For various reasons, regulations may be genuinely ambiguous. They may not directly or clearly address every issue; when applied to some fact patterns, they may prove susceptible to more than one reasonable reading. Sometimes, this sort of ambiguity arises from careless drafting—the use of a dangling modifier, an awkward word, an opaque construction. But often, ambiguity reflects the well-known limits of expression or knowledge. The subject matter of a rule "may be so specialized and varying in nature as to be impossible"—or at any rate, impracticable—to capture in its every detail. *SEC v. Chenery Corp.*, 332 U.S. 194, 203 (1947). Or a "problem[] may arise" that the agency, when drafting the rule, "could not [have] reasonably foresee[n]." *Id.*, at 202.

Whichever the case, the result is to create real uncertainties about a regulation's meaning.

. . . [I]nterpreting the regulation involves a choice between (or among) more than one reasonable reading. To apply the rule to some unanticipated or unresolved situation, the court must make a judgment call. How should it do so?

In answering that question, we have often thought that a court should defer to the agency's construction of its own regulation. For the last 20 or so years, we have referred to that doctrine as *Auer* deference, and applied it often. But the name is something of a misnomer. Before the doctrine was called *Auer* deference, it was called *Seminole Rock* deference—for the 1945 decision in which we declared that when "the meaning of [a regulation] is in doubt," the agency's interpretation "becomes of controlling weight unless it is plainly erroneous or inconsistent with the regulation." 325 U.S., at 414. And *Seminole Rock* itself was not built on sand. Deference to administrative agencies traces back to the late nineteenth century, and perhaps beyond.

We have explained *Auer* deference (as we now call it) as rooted in a presumption about congressional intent—a presumption that Congress would generally want the agency to play the primary role in resolving regulatory ambiguities. . . . Congress, we have pointed out, routinely delegates to agencies the power to implement statutes by issuing rules. See *id.*, at 151. In doing so, Congress knows (how could it not?) that regulations will sometimes contain ambiguities. But Congress almost never explicitly assigns responsibility to deal with that problem, either to agencies or to courts. Hence the need to presume, one way or the other, what Congress would want. And as between those two choices, agencies have gotten the nod. We have adopted the presumption—though it is always rebuttable—that "the power authoritatively to interpret its own regulations is a component of the agency's delegated lawmaking powers." . . . Or otherwise said, we have thought that when granting rulemaking power to agencies, Congress usually intends to give them, too, considerable latitude to interpret the ambiguous rules they issue.

In part, that is because the agency that promulgated a rule is in the "better position [to] reconstruct" its original meaning. *Id.*, at 152. Consider that if you don't know what some text (say, a memo or an e-mail) means, you would probably want to ask the person who wrote it. And for the same reasons, we have thought, Congress would too (though the person is here a collective actor) (1986). Want to know what a rule means? Ask its author.

In still greater measure, the presumption that Congress intended *Auer* deference stems from the awareness that resolving genuine regulatory ambiguities often "entail[s] the exercise of judgment grounded in policy concerns." . . . Agencies (unlike courts) have "unique expertise," often of a scientific or technical nature, relevant to applying a regulation "to complex or changing circumstances." . . . Agencies (unlike courts) can conduct factual investigations, can consult with affected parties, can consider how their experts have handled similar issues over the long course of administering a regulatory program. . . . And agencies (again unlike courts) have political accountability, because they are subject to the supervision of the President, who in turn answers to the public. See *Free Enterprise Fund v. Public Company Accounting Oversight Bd.*, 561 U.S. 477, 499 (2010). It is because of those features that Congress, when first enacting a statute, assigns rulemaking power to an agency and thus authorizes it to fill out the statutory scheme. And so too, when new issues demanding new policy calls come up within that scheme, Congress presumably wants the same agency, rather than any court, to take the laboring oar. . . .

B

But all that said, *Auer* deference is not the answer to every question of interpreting an agency's rules. Far from it. As we explain in this section, the possibility of deference can arise only if a regulation is genuinely ambiguous. And when we use that term, we mean it—genuinely ambiguous, even after a court has resorted to all the standard tools of interpretation. . . . To make that effort, a court must "carefully consider[]" the text, structure, history, and purpose of a regulation, in all the ways it would if it had no agency to fall back on. Doing so will resolve many seeming ambiguities out of the box, without resort to *Auer* deference. . . .

If genuine ambiguity remains, moreover, the agency's reading must still be "reasonable." . . . In other words, it must come within the zone of ambiguity the court has identified after employing all its interpretive tools. . . . Still, we are not done—for not every reasonable agency reading of a genuinely ambiguous rule should receive *Auer* deference. . . . The inquiry on this dimension does not reduce to any exhaustive test. But we have laid out some especially important markers for identifying when *Auer* deference is and is not appropriate. To begin with, the regulatory interpretation must be one actually made by the agency. . . . In other words, it must be the agency's "authoritative" or "official position," rather than any more ad hoc statement not reflecting the agency's views. . . . Next, the agency's interpretation must in some way implicate its substantive expertise. Administrative knowledge and experience largely "account [for] the presumption that Congress delegates interpretive lawmaking power to the agency." . . . Finally, an agency's reading of a rule must reflect "fair and considered judgment" to receive *Auer* deference. *Christopher*, 567 U.S., at 155. That means, we have stated, that a court should decline to defer to a merely "convenient litigating position" or "post hoc rationalizatio[n] advanced" to "defend past agency action against attack." *Ibid.* And a court may not defer to a new interpretation, whether or not introduced in litigation, that creates "unfair surprise" to regulated parties. . . . That disruption of expectations may occur when an agency substitutes one view of a rule for another . . . [or when] an interpretation that would have imposed retroactive liability on parties for longstanding conduct that the agency had never before addressed.

III

That brings us to the lone question presented here—whether we should abandon the longstanding doctrine just described. In contending that we should, Kisor raises statutory, policy, and constitutional claims (in that order). But he faces an uphill climb. He must first convince us that *Auer* deference is wrong. And even then, he must overcome *stare decisis*—the special care we take to preserve our precedents. In the event, Kisor fails at the first step: None of his arguments provide good reason to doubt *Auer* deference. And even if that were not so, Kisor does not offer the kind of special justification needed to overrule *Auer*, and *Seminole Rock*, and all our many other decisions deferring to reasonable agency constructions of ambiguous rules.

A

Kisor first attacks *Auer* as inconsistent with the judicial review provision of the Administrative Procedure Act (APA). See 5 U.S.C. §706. As Kisor notes, Congress enacted the APA in 1946—the year after *Seminole Rock*—to serve as "the fundamental charter of the administrative state." Section 706 of the Act, governing judicial review of agency action, states (among other things) that reviewing courts shall "determine the meaning or applicability of the terms of an agency action" (including a regulation). According to Kisor, *Auer* violates that edict by thwarting "meaningful judicial review" of agency rules. Courts under *Auer*, he asserts (now in the language of Section 706), "abdicate their office of determining the meaning" of a regulation.

To begin with, that argument ignores the many ways, discussed above, that courts exercise independent review over the meaning of agency rules. As we have explained, a court must apply all traditional methods of interpretation to any rule, and must enforce the plain meaning those methods uncover. There can be no thought of deference unless, after performing that thoroughgoing review, the regulation remains genuinely susceptible to multiple reasonable meanings and the agency's interpretation lines up with one of them. . . . All of that figures as "meaningful judicial review."

And even when a court defers to a regulatory reading, it acts consistently with Section 706. That provision does not specify the standard of review a court should use in "determin[ing] the meaning" of an ambiguous rule. 5 U.S.C. §706. One possibility, as Kisor says, is to review the issue *de novo*. But another is to review the agency's reading for reasonableness. To see the point, assume that a regulatory (say, an employment) statute expressly instructed courts to apply *Auer* deference when reviewing an agency's interpretations of its ambiguous rules. Nothing in that statute would conflict with Section 706. Instead, the employment law would simply make clear *how* a court is to "determine the meaning" of such a rule—by deferring to an agency's reasonable reading.

Kisor next claims that *Auer* circumvents the APA's rulemaking requirements. Section 553, as Kisor notes, mandates that an agency use notice-and-comment procedures before issuing legislative rules. See 5 U.S.C.

§§553(b), (c). But the section allows agencies to issue "interpret[ive]" rules without notice and comment. See §553(b)(A). A key feature of those rules is that (unlike legislative rules) they are not supposed to "have the force and effect of law"—or, otherwise said, to bind private parties. *Perez v. Mortgage Bankers Assn.*, 575 U.S. 92, ___ (2015). Instead, interpretive rules are meant only to "advise the public" of how the agency understands, and is likely to apply, its binding statutes and legislative rules. *Ibid.* But consider, Kisor argues, what happens when a court gives *Auer* deference to an interpretive rule. The result, he asserts, is to make a rule that has never gone through notice and comment binding on the public. Or put another way, the interpretive rule ends up having the "force and effect of law" without ever paying the procedural cost. *Mortgage Bankers*, 575 U.S., at ___ (slip op., at 3).

But this Court rejected the identical argument just a few years ago, and for good reason. In *Mortgage Bankers*, we held that interpretive rules, even when given *Auer* deference, do *not* have the force of law. See 575 U.S., at ___, and n. 4. An interpretive rule itself never forms "the basis for an enforcement action"—because, as just noted, such a rule does not impose any "legally binding requirements" on private parties. . . . An enforcement action must instead rely on a legislative rule, which (to be valid) must go through notice and comment. And in all the ways discussed above, the meaning of a legislative rule remains in the hands of courts, even if they sometimes divine that meaning by looking to the agency's interpretation.

To supplement his two APA arguments, Kisor turns to policy, leaning on a familiar claim about the incentives *Auer* creates. According to Kisor, *Auer* encourages agencies to issue vague and open-ended regulations, confident that they can later impose whatever interpretation of those rules they prefer. That argument received its fullest elaboration in a widely respected law review article pre-dating *Auer*. See Manning, 96 Colum. L. Rev., at 654-669. More recently, the concern about such self-delegation has appeared in opinions from this Court, starting with several from Justice Scalia calling for *Auer*'s reconsideration.

But the claim has notable weaknesses, empirical and theoretical alike. First, it does not survive an encounter with experience. No real evidence—indeed, scarcely an anecdote—backs up the assertion. As two noted scholars (one of whom reviewed thousands of rules during four years of government service) have written: "[W]e are unaware of, and no one has pointed to, any regulation in American history that, because of *Auer*, was designed vaguely." Sunstein & Vermeule, 84 U. Chi. L. Rev., at 308. And even the argument's theoretical allure dissipates upon reflection. For strong (almost surely stronger) incentives and pressures cut in the opposite direction. "[R]egulators want their regulations to be effective, and clarity promotes compliance." Too, regulated parties often push for precision from an agency, so that they know what they can and cannot do. And ambiguities in rules pose risks to the long-run survival of agency policy. Vagueness increases the chance of adverse judicial rulings. And it enables future administrations, with different views, to reinterpret the rules to their own liking. Add all of that up and Kisor's ungrounded theory of incentives contributes nothing to the case against *Auer*.

Finally, Kisor goes big, asserting (though fleetingly) that *Auer* deference violates "separation-of-powers principles." In his view, those principles prohibit "vest[ing] in a single branch the law-making and law-interpreting functions." If that objection is to agencies' usurping the interpretive role of courts, this opinion has already met it head-on. Properly understood and applied, *Auer* does no such thing. In all the ways we have described, courts retain a firm grip on the interpretive function. If Kisor's objection is instead to the supposed commingling of functions (that is, the legislative and judicial) within an agency, this Court has answered it often before. See, *e.g.*, *Withrow v. Larkin*, 421 U.S. 35, 54 (1975) (permitting such a combination of functions); *FTC v. Cement Institute*, 333 U.S. 683, 702 (1948) (same). That sort of mixing is endemic in agencies, and has been "since the beginning of the Republic." *Arlington*, 569 U.S., at 304-305, n. 4. It does not violate the separation of powers, we have explained, because even when agency "activities take 'legislative' and 'judicial' forms," they continue to be "exercises of[] the 'executive Power'"—or otherwise said, ways of executing a statutory plan.

II

If all that were not enough, stare decisis cuts strongly against Kisor's position. "Overruling precedent is never a small matter." . . . Adherence to precedent is "a foundation stone of the rule of law." . . . And that is even more than usually so in the circumstances here. First, Kisor asks us to overrule not a single case, but a "long line of precedents" . . . . This Court alone has applied *Auer* or *Seminole Rock* in dozens of cases, and lower courts have done so thousands of times. Deference to reasonable agency interpretations of ambiguous rules pervades the whole corpus of administrative law. Second, because that is so, abandoning *Auer* deference would cast doubt on many settled constructions of rules. As Kisor acknowledged at oral argument, a decision in his favor would allow relitigation of any decision based on *Auer*, forcing courts to "wrestle [with] whether or not *Auer*" had actually made a difference. (Solicitor General agreeing that "every single regulation that's currently on the books whose interpretation has been established under *Seminole Rock* now [would have] to be relitigated anew"). It is the rare overruling that introduces so much instability into so many areas of law, all in one blow.

Chief Justice ROBERTS, concurring in part.

I join Parts I, II–B, III–B, and IV of the Court's opinion. [Chief Justice ROBERTS concurred on the basis of the plurality's stare decisis argument]. I write separately to suggest that the distance between the majority and Justice GORSUCH is not as great as it may initially appear.

Justice GORSUCH, with whom Justice THOMAS joins, with whom Justice KAVANAUGH joins as to Parts I, II, III, IV, and V, and with whom Justice ALITO joins as to Parts I, II, and III, concurring in the judgment.

It should have been easy for the Court to say goodbye to *Auer v. Robbins*. In disputes involving the relationship between the government and the people, *Auer* requires judges to accept an executive agency's interpretation of its own regulations even when that interpretation doesn't represent the best and fairest reading. This rule creates a "systematic judicial bias in favor of the federal government, the most powerful of parties, and against everyone else."

Still, today's decision is more a stay of execution than a pardon. The Court cannot muster even five votes to say that *Auer* is lawful or wise. Instead, a majority retains *Auer* only because of *stare decisis*. And yet, far from standing by that precedent, the majority proceeds to impose so many new and nebulous qualifications and limitations on *Auer* that the Chief Justice claims to see little practical difference between keeping it on life support in this way and overruling it entirely. So the doctrine emerges maimed and enfeebled—in truth, zombified.

II. THE ADMINISTRATIVE PROCEDURE ACT

[Justice GORSUCH raises the issues involving the APA which Justice KAGAN addresses in the plurality opinion.]

III. THE CONSTITUTION

Not only is *Auer* incompatible with the APA; it also sits uneasily with the Constitution. Article III, §1 provides that the "judicial Power of the United States" is vested exclusively in this Court and the lower federal courts. A core component of that judicial power is "'the duty of interpreting [the laws] and applying them in cases properly brought before the courts.'" As Chief Justice Marshall put it, "[i]t is emphatically the province and duty of the judicial department to say what the law is."

A

Our Nation's founders were painfully aware of the dangers of executive and legislative intrusion on judicial decision-making. One of the abuses of royal power that led to the American Revolution was King George's attempt to gain influence over colonial judges. Colonial legislatures, too, had interfered with the courts' independence "at the behest of private interests and factions." These experiences had taught the founders that "'there is no liberty if the power of judgment be not separated from the legislative and executive powers.'" They knew that when political actors are left free not only to adopt and enforce written laws, but also to control the interpretation of those laws, the legal rights of "litigants with unpopular or minority causes or . . . who belong to despised or suspect classes" count for little. Maybe the powerful, well-heeled, popular, and connected can wheedle favorable outcomes from a system like that—but what about everyone else? They are left always a little unsure what the law is, at the mercy of political actors and the shifting winds of popular opinion, and without the chance for a fair hearing before a neutral judge. The rule of law begins to bleed into the rule of men.

Experiencing all this in their own time, the founders designed a judiciary that would be able to interpret the laws "free from potential domination by other branches of government." . . . [T]hey gave federal judges life tenure, subject only to removal by impeachment; and they guaranteed that the other branches could not reduce judges' compensation so long as they remained in office. The founders afforded these extraordinary powers and protections not for the comfort of judges, but so that an independent judiciary could better guard the people from the arbitrary use of governmental power. And sitting atop the judicial branch, this Court has always carried a special duty to "jealously guar[d]" the Constitution's promise of judicial independence. So we have long resisted any effort by the other branches to "'usurp a court's power to interpret and apply the law to the circumstances before it.'"

Auer represents no trivial threat to these foundational principles. Under the APA, substantive rules issued by federal agencies through notice-and-comment procedures bear "the 'force and effect of law'" and are part of the body of federal law, binding on private individuals, that the Constitution charges federal judges with interpreting. Yet *Auer* tells the judge that he must interpret these binding laws to mean not what he thinks they mean, but what an executive agency says they mean. Unlike Article III judges, executive officials are not, nor are they supposed to be, "wholly impartial." They have their own interests, their own constituencies, and their own policy goals—and when interpreting a regulation, they may choose to "press the case for the side [they] represen[t]" instead of adopting the fairest and best reading. *Auer* thus means that, far from being "kept distinct," the powers of making, enforcing, and interpreting laws are united in the same hands—and in the process a cornerstone of the rule of law is compromised.

Notes and Questions

1. As Justice Kagan's opinion emphasizes, the *Auer* doctrine is much older than *Chevron*. In his 1951 treatise, *Administrative Law*, Professor Kenneth Culp Davis, commenting on *Seminole Rock*, noted that giving an agency's interpretation of its own regulation greater weight than its interpretation of a statute "seems plausible. One of the main ingredients of the interpretation is administrative intent, and an agency should know more about its own intent than about the intent of Congress." The advent of the *Chevron* doctrine, to which the Court continues to adhere, would seem to strengthen

Auer, and Justice Kagan emphasizes the connection between the two in her opinion (which, incidentally, provides a good review of the rationale for *Chevron*). Those opposed to *Auer*, therefore, like Justices Scalia or Gorsuch, need to articulate the distinction between them, and have generally adopted Professor Manning's argument, as the quoted language from the *Decker* case indicates. That argument depends on the view that the *Auer* doctrine, in combining the rulemaking and rule-interpreting functions, incentivizes the agency to write vague regulations that grant it latitude to reach subsequent decisions that advance its policy goals. Justice Kagan responds that there is no evidence for this, and that agencies are subject to opposite incentives to specify the behaviors that they want to encourage or prevent. By this point, you know something about the internal structure and operative strategy of one agency, NHTSA. Whose view of the agency and its incentives strikes you as more plausible?

2. A related question involves the more general view of regulation that one maintains. Assuming that *Auer* empowers the agency to some extent, does this create a threat to liberty (akin to George III's oppression of the American colonists, according to Justice Gorsuch) or does it enable the agency to protect citizens from threats, such as the danger of being sold an unsafe vehicle? Were the differing answers to this question the basis for the disagreement among the Justices. Note the political alignment on what would otherwise seem to be a highly technical question of administrative law doctrine.

3. Suppose the Court had overruled *Auer* and imposed *Skidmore* deference instead. How much of a difference would this make? Has Justice Kagan attenuated *Auer* with the qualifications she offers (and which she says are established doctrine) to the point where it is indistinguishable from *Skidmore*? Is Justice Roberts correct in saying that there is not much difference between the two Justices' views, despite the energy, and length, with which they argue for their positions. As the deciding vote, after all, it is his opinion that is law.

4. Justice Gorsuch, like Justice Scalia, is somewhat coy about the implications of the separation of powers argument. Suppose Congress enacted a statue, either generally or in a particular case, requiring courts to grant deference to an agency's interpretation of its regulations. Would Justice Gorsuch actually strike down that statute on constitutional grounds? Should he?

Note on the Interpretation of Regulations

Regardless of the standard of judicial deference, if any, that applies to an agency's interpretation of its own regulations, reviewing courts still need a method for interpreting those regulations. Under *Auer*, the court must interpret the regulation to decide whether the agency's interpretation is "inconsistent" with it. Just as the court's method of interpreting a statute can determinative of the outcome of review under *Chevron*, the court's method of regulatory interpretation can be determinative of the outcome under *Auer*. Absent *Auer*, the court faces an even more evident and pressing need to interpret the agency's regulation. How should courts approach the task of regulatory interpretation? Given the scope of legal obligations fixed by regulations, the question is an important one.

The method of regulatory interpretation by courts has not received much consideration. Professor Stack summarizes:

> [C]ourts have not developed a consistent approach to regulatory interpretation under these doctrines or elsewhere. Decisions sometimes rely exclusively on the regulation's text and canons of construction, but in other instances courts invoke aspects of the regulation's procedural history, the court's construction of the authorizing statute's purposes or congressional intent, or the agency's own justification for the regulation, among other tools. Courts not only lack a consistent approach but also generally invoke one interpretive tool or another without stating reasons for doing so — nor manifesting a compunction to consider how similar interpretive issues have been handled in the past. As a result, little law or considered practice on interpretive methodology applicable to regulations is developing. Indeed, it is hard to avoid the impression that the judiciary does not recognize regulatory interpretation as an aspect of judicial practice, like statutory interpretation, that merits independent and systematic consideration.

Kevin M. Stack, *Interpreting Regulations*, 111 MICH. L. REV. 355, 359-60 (2012). How would you characterize the Supreme Court's approach to regulatory interpretation in *Kisor*? What sources and maxims of interpretation does it rely upon?

In principle, does it make sense to interpret regulations in accordance with the same principles of statutory interpretation? On the one hand, that view has some appeal because both regulations and statutes are forms of positive (i.e., enacted) law. As such, both consist of text that establishes or changes the law, and both frequently state binding, prospective, and general norms. On the other hand, regulations and statutes have distinctive features from one another. The bodies that produce them and the processes through which they are produced differ significantly. Unlike statutes, regulations are accompanied by statements of basis and purpose (also called the preamble), and these explanatory statements are necessary to the validity of the rules. Regulations might also be thought of as serving a different function; they are designed to implement the statutes. Based on these differences, Professor Stack proposes a method of regulatory interpretation:

> Our initial inquiry into the legal character of regulations suggested, as starting points, that a goal of regulatory interpretation is to implement the purpose or aim of the regulation, and that the privileged interpretive sources are the regulatory text and accompanying statement of basis and purpose. Hart and Sacks's theory provides a model for integrating those elements into a comprehensive interpretive technique. The basic elements of the technique could track those of a purposive approach to statutes: the court's aim is to discern the purpose of the regulation and

its provisions, and to interpret the regulation to carry out those purposes to the extent permitted by its text while remaining consistent with policies and principles of clear statement.

As to the implementation of this approach, the critical difference between regulations and statutes is how the court discerns purposes. With regard to statutes, Hart and Sacks divided the inquiry into an initial consultation of the enacted statement of purpose, and only when such a statement is lacking or unhelpful, an inference into purpose from a broad range of sources. Statutes, however, are frequently enacted without statements of purpose. As a result, with regard to statutes, the paradigm for discerning purpose for a statute involves inferring purpose from a broad array of sources. This highlights that the critical appraisal of Hart and Sacks has a point: with the majority of statutes enacted without statements of purpose, purposive statutory interpretation will typically require the court to attribute, through broad inferences from the text and policy context, a reasonable aim of the legislation or its provisions.

In contrast, the administrative process generates much more consistent resources, analogous to enacted statements of purpose, for attributing purpose to regulations. With narrow exceptions, agencies must issue statements of basis and purpose for their rule to be procedurally valid, and the standards of judicial review make the agency's reasoning necessary to the validity of their rules. In response to these demands, agencies today issue statements of basis and purpose that are far from mere preambles; they are extremely detailed rationales for, and explanations of, their regulations. These explanations ordinarily include the agency's analysis of the data, how that data supports their regulations, the justification of the agency's choices in view of alternatives, how the regulations meet statutory purposes, and engagement with commentators. Moreover, the agency typically provides some explanation as to each regulatory provision or choice. When an agency does not offer a provision-specific justification, the statement typically includes a justification of the purpose at a higher level of generality—as it must for the regulation to be valid. . . .

It is not hard to imagine how these provision-specific justifications [in the statement of basis and purpose]. . . . could be used by lawyers and courts to understand the scope of the rule's prohibitions in relation to the rule's general purposes. And even where a specific justification did not pertain, the more general grounding of the regulation in protecting the integrity of the markets suggests a guidepost for interpretation. This is not to say that these statements eliminate the need for interpretative judgments about how to balance the overall aims of the regulations, the provision-specific justifications, and the text. But in contrast to statutes, it will be a relatively rare case in which the statement of basis and purpose provides no guidance on an interpretive question, either in a specific or more general justification for the regulation.

To the extent that courts and commentators have considered the interpretive role of the agency's statement of basis and purpose, they have generally seen it as analogous to a legislative committee report or statutory preamble. But the better analogy is to an enacted statement of purpose. In scope and detail, the analogy to legislative committee reports makes a lot of sense (as it does for those who embrace the bearing of committee reports for legislative interpretation). But treating statements of basis and purpose as analogous to legislative committee reports neglects critical differences between these agency statements and legislative reports. Most important is that the agency's statement of basis and purpose is itself necessary to the validity of a regulation, whereas legislative committee reports are not. Further, whereas legislative committee reports are statements of a subgroup of legislators and not made on behalf of the institution, statements of basis and purpose, like enacted statements of purposes, speak for the agency, not a subgroup or committee.

So what does this regulatory purposive technique look like? The central tenet of the approach is to read the text of the regulation in light of the regulation's statement of basis and purpose. The D.C. Circuit's decision in *Secretary of Labor, Mine Safety & Health Administration ex rel. Bushnell v. Cannelton Industries, Inc.*, 867 F.2d 1432 (D.C. Cir. 1989), delivered by then–Judge Ruth Bader Ginsburg, provides a nice illustration. The Secretary of Labor had issued regulations to protect miners with pneumoconiosis, a lung disease, providing that miners with evidence of pneumoconiosis could obtain a transfer to a position with lower dust concentrations. In addition, the regulations protected the miners' compensation, providing that "[w]henever" such a miner is transferred "the operator shall compensate the miner at not less than the regular rate of pay received by that miner immediately before the transfer." In the case at issue, the eligible miner had initially been transferred to work as a dispatcher at his mining wage, and then to an inside laborer position at a reduced wage as part of a general realignment due to economic conditions. The question was whether the regulations protected the miner from compensation decreases solely for transfers to meet the respiratory dust standards, as the employer maintained, or for all subsequent transfers, as the Secretary maintained.

The court agreed with the Secretary, finding the Secretary's position "consistent" with the regulations' text ("whenever") and also "fully consonant" with the "administrative history and purposes." The court relied on both the general and more specific purposes set forth in the Secretary's statement of basis and purpose for the regulations. At a general level, the court noted that the Secretary had observed that existing law discouraged eligible miners from claiming protections, and had sought in the regulations to "provide eligible miners with significant additional protections against fears of job security, adverse economic consequences," and other undesirable working and wage conditions. More specifically, as the court noted, the Secretary's statement of basis and purpose had stated that an eligible miner, "'should not suffer *any* loss in pay *whenever* an operator transfers the miner' because '[i]f any eligible miner perceived that their rate of pay could be decreased upon *any* transfer, the incentive to exercise the Part 90 option would be reduced.'" The court found that these grounds "strongly support[ed]" the Secretary's reading of the regulations to protect against wage decreases given that existing law already protected the miner's rate of pay upon initial transfer to less dusty work. The court thus located a reading of the regulations that was both permitted by the text and that carried out the regulations' purposes, which the court discerned from the regulations' statement of basis and purpose.

Notes and Questions

1. Suppose a court adopted this approach of interpreting a regulation in light of its statement of basis and purpose, paying particular attention to the aims the agency provides for the regulation. *See, e.g.*, Halo v. Yale Health Plan, 819 F.3d 42, 51-53 (2d Cir. 2016) (relying on regulatory preamble in regulatory interpretation). Would that give more notice of the meaning of the regulation in ways that might address some of the notice concerns raised by critics of the *Auer* doctrine? The answer might depend. If any interpretations that contradicted the statement of basis and purpose were viewed as contradicting the regulation, then there would be a smaller range of possible interpretations to which *Auer* deference would potentially apply. That would seem to promote notice of the regulation's possible meanings. But it would come with some cost to agency flexibility. The agency would be committed to abide by its statement of basis and purpose. Is that a worthy tradeoff—more notice but reduced agency flexibility?

2. Do you agree that a regulation's statement of basis and purpose is a stronger source for interpreting the meaning than legislative history is for statutes? If these explanatory statements are treated in this way, would it exacerbate an agency's incentives to including material upon which agency officials could not agree in the statement of basis and purpose rather than in the regulation? Are there other administrative law constraints that counteract those incentives, such as arbitrary and capricious review, or political constraints, such as OIRA review?

3. Empirical Evidence on Deference Frameworks

The frameworks for judicial deference to agency's interpretive judgments—under *Chevron*, *Skidmore*, and *Auer*—certainly have grown complex. It is worth pausing to consider whether the particular framework matters to the chances that a reviewing court will uphold or reverse an agency's position.

As to statutory interpretation, observers have long speculated that the chances of agency reversal under *Chevron* and *Skidmore* were not all that different. Consider the following logic. Any agency decision that a court would uphold under *Skidmore* should be upheld under *Chevron* (because *Skidmore* is less deferential than *Chevron*). So too, any decision reversed under *Chevron* should be reversed under *Skidmore* (for the same reason). So the difference between the frameworks would seem to boil down to the set of cases in which it would be upheld under *Chevron* but reversed under *Skidmore*. How many cases is that? Different people had different impressions, but it seemed like a rather small set. Indeed, in 2011, Professor Richard Pierce concluded based on the existing studies, mostly of Supreme Court decisions, "[t]here is no empirical support for the widespread belief that choice of doctrine plays a major role in judicial review of agency actions." Richard J. Pierce, Jr., *What Do the Studies of Judicial Review of Agency Actions Mean?*, 63 ADMIN. L. REV. 77, 93 (2011). In 2016, Professors Kent Barnett and Christopher Walker deepened the understanding of affirmance rates under *Chevron*. They conducted a study of eleven years (2003-2013) of published circuit court decisions citing *Chevron*. Here are some of their findings.

Kent Barnett & Christopher J. Walker, *Chevron* in the Circuits

116 Mich. L. Rev. 1 (2016)

As detailed in Figure 1, the agency prevailed at a higher rate than the overall agency-win rate (77.4% to 71.4%) when the court determined that *Chevron* applied. Conversely, the win rate dropped considerably when the court did not apply the *Chevron* standard: 66.4% when the court refused to decide which standard applies; 56.0% under the *Skidmore* standard; and 38.5% when the court applied de novo review.

Figure 1. Agency-Win Rates by Deference Standard (n=1558)

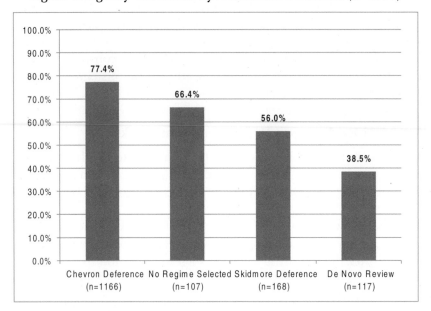

Again, comparison between deference regimes based on the decisions reviewed should be done carefully, since the dataset only includes decisions in which circuit courts expressly mentioned *Chevron* deference. It would not include decisions in which the court only mentioned *Skidmore* or reviewed interpretations de novo without mentioning *Chevron* — perhaps decisions in which one may expect higher agency-win rates whose inclusion would alter the results that we found. But at least in instances in which the court recognizes *Chevron* expressly in its opinion, the application of the *Chevron* framework seems to make a meaningful difference as to whether agencies prevail on the interpretive question. Indeed, there was nearly a twenty-four-percentage-point difference in win rates when the circuit courts applied *Chevron* deference (77.4%) than when they refused to apply it (53.6%). The agency was twice as likely (77.4% to 38.5%) to prevail if the court applied *Chevron* deference as opposed to reviewing the interpretation de novo and nearly three-fourths more likely (77.4% to 56.0%) to prevail under *Chevron* than *Skidmore*. In other words, agencies won more in the circuit courts when *Chevron* deference applied, at least when the court expressly considered whether to apply *Chevron* deference.

These findings challenge certain conclusions based on earlier studies. Evaluating affirmance rates in the Supreme Court and circuit courts from earlier studies, Richard Pierce found that, as relevant here, the affirmance ranges for de novo, *Skidmore*, and *Chevron* review overlap: 66% for de novo review, 55.1% to 70.9% for *Skidmore*, and 64% to 81.3% for *Chevron*. He concluded that "a court's choice of which doctrine to apply in reviewing an agency action is not an important determinant of outcomes in the Supreme Court or the circuit courts." Contrary to his conclusion concerning the circuit courts, our findings suggest that agency-win rates are meaningfully different under different deference regimes. . . .

Of the 1,558 total interpretations reviewed, the circuit courts applied the *Chevron* framework in 1,166 of them (74.8%). Of those 1,166 interpretations, the agency prevailed 902 times (77.4%). The more interesting questions, however, may concern how the circuit courts applied the two-step framework. In other words, how many decisions were decided at step one? How many were decided at step two? And, perhaps most importantly, what were the agency-win rates at each step? Figure 2 depicts the overall win/ loss numbers at both steps, with the percentages reflecting the portion of the set of interpretations in which the circuit courts applied the *Chevron* framework.

Figure 2. Agency Win/Loss Rates by *Chevron* Step for Interpretations Where *Chevron* Framework Applied (n=1166)

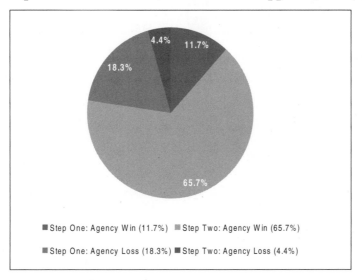

Consistent with prior studies, the vast majority of agency interpretations (817 interpretations, or 70.0%) made it to step two. And an even greater percentage of interpretations that made it to step two (766 interpretations, or 93.8%) were upheld. Indeed, we found that the agency won slightly more under step two (whether the court describes its analysis as one of "reason-ableness" in one step or two) than in an earlier study. In comparison to our agency-win rate of 93.8% under step two, [Orin] Kerr found that agencies in 1995 and 1996 won at step two or in a one-step "reasonableness" inquiry a combined total of 84.7% (156 out of 184 interpretations) of the time. To be sure, it is not true that *Chevron*, at least as an empirical matter, has collapsed into just one step of statutory ambiguity. In particular, fifty-one agency statu-tory interpretations in our dataset—6.2% of those cases that made it to step two—were deemed unreasonable even though the court found the statute to be ambiguous as to the question at issue.

What happens at step one is perhaps even more noteworthy. Courts decided 30.0% of interpretations at *Chevron*'s step one. . . . Our data indi-cated that the agencies still prevailed 39.0% of the time, meaning that the agency's interpretation was the only possible one under the statute.

. . .

Figure 3. Agency-Win Rates by Deference Standard, Including *Chevron* Steps One and Two (n=1558)

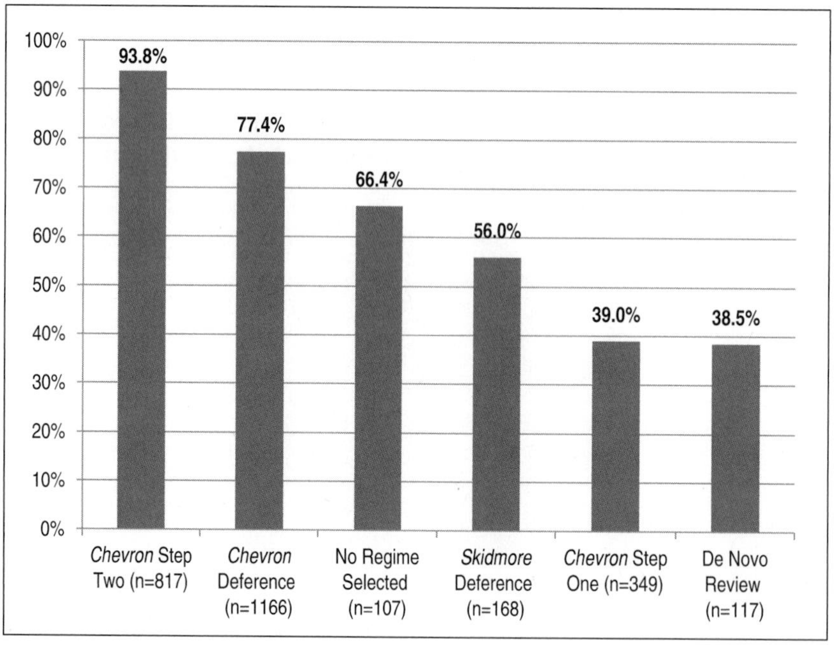

Notes and Questions

1. Lawyers still needs to know the doctrine to determine whether a case is likely to be resolved under *Chevron* or *Skidmore*, and whether there are strong arguments at *Chevron* Step One—how else would you write a brief on behalf of your client challenging or defending an agency interpretation? Courts still want to know which deference regime to apply. Yet knowing the likelihood of success that follows from those categorization is pretty powerful. It might be the most important information for advising your client, whether that client wishes to challenge or defend an agency interpretation. Do you see why?

2. Barnett and Walker's study also examines the different affirmance rates for different types of agency action. They find that notice-and-comment rules are upheld 74.7% when *Chevron* applies, but only 54.3% when *Chevron* does not apply. Formal adjudication is upheld 81.7% when *Chevron* applies, but only 51.9% when *Chevron* does not apply. *See* Kent Barnett & Christopher J. Walker, *Chevron in the Circuit Courts*, 116 MICH. L. REV. 1, 39 (2017). Why would rules be struck down at a greater rate than adjudications? Do these win rates provide incentives for agencies to develop new norms through adjudication?

3. Affirmance rates under the *Auer* framework are generally similar to *Chevron*. Professor Cynthia Barmore's study of *Auer* cases in the courts of appeals found the following: "Between 2011 and 2012, courts granted *Auer* deference in 82.3% of cases. Since the Court's 2013 decision in Decker v. Northwest Environmental Defense Center, that rate has fallen to 70.6%." Cynthia Barmore, Auer *in Action: Deference After Talk America*, 76 OHIO ST. L.J. 813, 815-16 (2015). Barmore attributes the decline in agency win rates under *Auer* to lower courts taking account of Justices Scalia and Thomas's dissatisfaction with *Auer*, and the Court's narrowing of the doctrine in *SmithKline*.

4. Judicial Control of Agency Statutory Implementation

We now turn to judicial review of agency statutory implementation. Whether the federal courts have the authority to review agency implementation (as well as agency interpretation) depends on the statute itself. A statute can either authorize courts to review the implementing agency's actions or preclude them from doing so. Most federal statutes do neither. Instead, they rely on the general review procedures specified in the Administrative Procedure Act (the APA) of 1946. As you may recall, the APA sets default procedures for regulatory statutes when those statutes are silent on the matter. For example, the APA specifies the procedures for notice-and-comment rulemaking and formal adjudication. The APA also contains provisions related to judicial review.

The APA's judicial review provisions authorize courts to determine whether the agencies have in fact followed the APA's procedures (as well as any other applicable law, such as the Constitution). In §702, entitled "Right of Review," it provides that "[a] person suffering legal wrong because of agency action, or adversely affected or aggrieved by agency action within the meaning of a relevant statute, is entitled to judicial review thereof." Section 704 states that "[a]gency action made reviewable by statute and final agency action for which there is no other adequate remedy in a court are subject to judicial review."

In addition to authorizing review, the APA, §706, specifies the standards that courts are to employ in carrying out this review. For notice-and-comment rulemaking, as well as other informal action, the APA directs the court to hold unlawful and set aside agency action that is "arbitrary, capricious, and abuse of discretion, or otherwise not in accordance with law." This standard is known as the "arbitrary and capricious" test. Decisions based on formal procedures are also subject to the requirement that they will be deemed unlawful if they are "unsupported by substantial evidence." There is controversy about whether this substantial evidence test is more demanding than the arbitrary and capricious test, or whether it is the same test applied in the context of formal adjudication. For the latter view (more or less), see Dickinson v. Zurko, 527 U.S. 150 (1999), citing ADPSO v. Board of Governors, 745 F.2d 677, 683-84 (D.C. Cir. 1984) (Scalia, J.).

These standards of review are default provisions, just like the rest of the APA. An organic statute can vary them; the Occupational Safety and Health Act (OSHA), for example, authorizes reviewing courts to set aside a notice-and-comment rule if it is "unsupported by substantial evidence." (Ask yourself why a statute would vary the standard of review in this manner? Which interests involved in the legislative process might push for more stringent judicial review? What might they seek to accomplish?)

a. Review of Agency Policy

We begin by examining decisions that elaborate the "arbitrary and capricious" standard of APA §706(2)(A). These decisions determine how much control courts possess in reviewing the way that an agency implements its statute, setting aside what the Court regards as a discrete issue of how the agency interprets its statute (i.e., the *Chevron* issue). They are among the most famous and often cited in administrative law.

Citizens to Preserve Overton Park, Inc. v. Volpe

401 U.S. 402 (1971)

Opinion of the Court by Mr. Justice MARSHALL, announced by Mr. Justice STEWART.

The growing public concern about the quality of our natural environment has prompted Congress in recent years to enact legislation designed to curb the accelerating destruction of our country's natural beauty. We are concerned in this case with §4(f) of the Department of Transportation Act of 1966, as amended, and §18(a) of the Federal-Aid Highway Act of 1968, 82 Stat. 823, 23 U.S.C. §138. These statutes prohibit the Secretary of Transportation from authorizing the use of federal funds to finance the construction of highways through public parks if a "feasible and prudent" alternative route exists. If no such route is available, the statutes allow him to approve construction through parks only if there has been "all possible planning to minimize harm" to the park.

Petitioners, private citizens as well as local and national conservation organizations, contend that the Secretary has violated these statutes by authorizing the expenditure of federal funds for the construction of a six-lane interstate highway through a public park in Memphis, Tennessee. Their claim was rejected by the District Court, which granted the Secretary's motion for summary judgment, and the Court of Appeals for the Sixth Circuit affirmed. After oral argument, this Court granted a stay that halted construction and, treating the application for the stay as a petition for certiorari, granted review. . . . We now reverse the judgment below and remand for further proceedings in the District Court.

Overton Park is a 342-acre city park located near the center of Memphis. The park contains a zoo, a nine-hole municipal golf course, an outdoor theater, nature trails, a bridle path, an art academy, picnic areas, and 170 acres of forest. The proposed highway, which is to be a six-lane, high-speed, expressway, will sever the zoo from the rest of the park. Although the roadway will be depressed below ground level except where it crosses a small creek, 26 acres of the park will be destroyed. The highway is to be a segment of Interstate Highway I-40, part of the National System of Interstate and Defense Highways. I-40 will provide Memphis with a major east-west expressway which will allow easier access to downtown Memphis from the residential areas on the eastern edge of the city.

. . . In April, 1968, the Secretary announced that he concurred in the judgment of local officials that I-40 should be built through the park. And in September, 1969, the State acquired the right-of-way inside Overton Park from the city. Final approval for the project—the route as well as the design—was not announced until November, 1969, after Congress had reiterated in §138 of the Federal-Aid Highway Act that highway construction through public parks was to be restricted. Neither announcement approving the route and design of I-40 was accompanied by a statement of the

Secretary's factual findings. He did not indicate why he believed there were no feasible and prudent alternative routes or why design changes could not be made to reduce the harm to the park.

Petitioners contend that the Secretary's action is invalid without such formal findings and that the Secretary did not make an independent determination but merely relied on the judgment of the Memphis City Council. They also contend that it would be "feasible and prudent" to route I-40 around Overton Park either to the north or to the south. And they argue that, if these alternative routes are not "feasible and prudent," the present plan does not include "all possible" methods for reducing harm to the park. Petitioners claim that I-40 could be built under the park by using either of two possible tunneling methods, and they claim that, at a minimum, by using advanced drainage techniques, the expressway could be depressed below ground level along the entire route through the park, including the section that crosses the small creek.

Respondents argue that it was unnecessary for the Secretary to make formal findings, and that he did, in fact, exercise his own independent judgment, which was supported by the facts. In the District Court, respondents introduced affidavits, prepared specifically for this litigation, which indicated that the Secretary had made the decision and that the decision was supportable. These affidavits were contradicted by affidavits introduced by petitioners, who also sought to take the deposition of a former Federal Highway Administrator who had participated in the decision to route I-40 through Overton Park.

The District Court and the Court of Appeals found that formal findings by the Secretary were not necessary, and refused to order the deposition of the former Federal Highway Administrator because those courts believed that probing of the mental processes of an administrative decisionmaker was prohibited. And, believing that the Secretary's authority was wide, and reviewing courts' authority narrow, in the approval of highway routes, the lower courts held that the affidavits contained no basis for a determination that the Secretary had exceeded his authority.

We agree that formal findings were not required. But we do not believe that, in this case, judicial review based solely on litigation affidavits was adequate. . . .

Section 4(f) of the Department of Transportation Act and §138 of the Federal-Aid Highway Act are clear and specific directives. Both the Department of Transportation Act and the Federal-Aid Highway Act provide that the Secretary "shall not approve any program or project" that requires the use of any public park land "unless (1) there is no feasible and prudent alternative to the use of such land, and (2) such program includes all possible planning to minimize harm to such park." . . .

Despite the clarity of the statutory language, respondents argue that the Secretary has wide discretion. They recognize that the requirement that there be no "feasible" alternative route admits of little administrative discretion. For this exemption to apply, the Secretary must find that, as a matter of sound engineering, it would not be feasible to build the highway along any other route. Respondents argue, however, that the requirement that there be no other "prudent" route requires the Secretary to engage in a wide-ranging balancing of competing interests. They contend that the Secretary should weigh the detriment resulting from the destruction of park land against the cost of other routes, safety considerations, and other factors, and determine on the basis of the importance that he attaches to these other factors whether, on balance, alternative feasible routes would be "prudent."

But no such wide-ranging endeavor was intended. It is obvious that, in most cases, considerations of cost, directness of route, and community disruption will indicate that park land should be used for highway construction whenever possible. Although it may be necessary to transfer funds from one jurisdiction to another, there will always be a smaller outlay required from the public purse when park land is used, since the public already owns the land, and there will be no need to pay for right-of-way. And since people do not live or work in parks, if a highway is built on park land, no one will have to leave his home or give up his business. Such factors are common to substantially all highway construction. Thus, if Congress intended these factors to be on an equal footing with preservation of park land, there would have been no need for the statutes.

Congress clearly did not intend that cost and disruption of the community were to be ignored by the Secretary. But the very existence of the statutes indicates that protection of park land was to be given paramount importance. The few green havens that are public parks were not to be lost unless there were truly unusual factors present in a particular case or the cost or community disruption resulting from alternative routes reached extraordinary magnitudes. If the statutes are to have any meaning, the Secretary cannot approve the destruction of park land unless he finds that alternative routes present unique problems.

Plainly, there is "law to apply," and thus the exemption for action "committed to agency discretion" is inapplicable. But the existence of judicial review is only the start: the standard for review must also be determined. For that, we must look to §706 of the Administrative Procedure Act, 5 U.S.C. §706, which provides that a "reviewing court shall . . . hold unlawful and set aside agency action, findings, and conclusions found" not to meet six separate standards. In all cases, agency action must be set aside if the action was "arbitrary, capricious, an abuse of discretion, or otherwise not in accordance with law" or if the action failed to meet statutory, procedural, or constitutional requirements. Even though there is no *de novo* review in this case and the Secretary's approval of the route of I-40 does not have ultimately to meet the substantial evidence test, the generally applicable standards of §706 require the reviewing court to engage in a substantial inquiry. . . .

. . . To make this finding, the court must consider whether the decision was based on a consideration of the relevant factors and whether there has been a clear error of judgment. Although this inquiry into the facts is to be searching and careful, the ultimate standard of review is a narrow one. The court is not empowered to substitute its judgment for that of the agency.

The final inquiry is whether the Secretary's action followed the necessary procedural requirements. Here, the only procedural error alleged is the failure of the Secretary to make formal findings and state his reason for allowing the highway to be built through the park.

Undoubtedly, review of the Secretary's action is hampered by his failure to make such findings, but the absence of formal findings does not necessarily require that the case be remanded to the Secretary. Neither the Department of Transportation Act nor the Federal-Aid Highway Act requires such formal findings. Moreover, the Administrative Procedure Act requirements that there be formal findings in certain rulemaking and adjudicatory proceedings do not apply to the Secretary's action here. Here, there is an administrative record that allows the full, prompt review of the Secretary's action that is sought without additional delay which would result from having a remand to the Secretary.

That administrative record is not, however, before us. The lower courts based their review on the litigation affidavits that were presented. These affidavits were merely "*post hoc*" rationalizations, which have traditionally been found to be an inadequate basis for review. And they clearly do not constitute the "whole record" compiled by the agency: the basis for review required by §706 of the Administrative Procedure Act.

Thus, it is necessary to remand this case to the District Court for plenary review of the Secretary's decision. That review is to be based on the full administrative record that was before the Secretary at the time he made his decision. But since the bare record may not disclose the factors that were considered or the Secretary's construction of the evidence, it may be necessary for the District Court to require some explanation in order to determine if the Secretary acted within the scope of his authority and if the Secretary's action was justifiable under the applicable standard.

The court may require the administrative officials who participated in the decision to give testimony explaining their action. Of course, such inquiry into the mental processes of administrative decisionmakers is usually to be avoided. And where there are administrative findings that were made at the same time as the decision . . . there must be a strong showing of bad faith or improper behavior before such inquiry may be made. But here there are no such formal findings, and it may be that the only way there can be effective judicial review is by examining the decisionmakers themselves.

The District Court is not, however, required to make such an inquiry. It may be that the Secretary can prepare formal findings including the information required by DOT Order 5610.1 that will provide an adequate explanation for his action. Such an explanation will, to some extent, be a "*post hoc* rationalization," and thus must be viewed critically. If the District Court decides that additional explanation is necessary, that court should consider which method will prove the most expeditious so that full review may be had as soon as possible.

Reversed and remanded.

Notes and Questions

1. *Overton Park* does not involve either rulemaking or formal adjudication under the APA. (The Transportation Act or the Highway Act could have imposed these procedures, but they did not.) Instead, the decision falls into that vast and vague residual category of agency actions that has been (less than usefully) described as "informal adjudication." The APA does not specify any procedures for informal adjudications. Nonetheless, informal adjudications are reviewable, as the decision establishes (*Overton Park* is one of the leading cases on this issue), and subject to the arbitrary and capricious standard of review under the APA, which applies to all "agency action." The decision characterizes this standard of review as an inquiry into "whether the decision was based on a consideration of the relevant factors and whether there has been a clear error of judgment." What are the "relevant factors" of agency policy—are they the same ones that agencies consider as part of statutory implementation, see Chapter 5? What is a "clear error of judgment"? What if the reviewing court simply disagrees with the policy?

2. Professor Peter Strauss is critical of *Overton Park* on grounds that relate to how and to what extent courts should control administrative agencies. *See* Peter Strauss, *Revisiting* Overton Park: *Political and Judicial Controls over Actions Affecting the Community*, 39 UCLA L. REV. 1251, 1266-68, 1319-22 (1992):

> Recall the intellectual process of the *Overton Park* passage quoted in text two paragraphs above: the Court decides to introduce an artificially structured legal constraint because—in its estimation, unsupported by reference to the actualities of administration during the intervening period—the policy judgment Congress "intended" cannot otherwise be implemented. But did Congress make that judgment, or was it the Court that was making it?
>
> Given the conceded indeterminacy of the congressional debates, talk about what Congress "intended" was not helpful. What faced the Court, rather, was the clash between two conventional views of statutory interpretation. Is a statute to be given meaning as a political act, with attention to the actual indeterminacies, compromises and imperfections a sensitive historian might find on full acquaintance with its political history? Or should it be treated as a text drawing force from its words as such, as a thoughtful (but not particularly historical or politically inclined) reader might find them?
>
> Suppose the possible workability of a political remedy were taken more seriously than the Court appears to have done, either because that may have been the historic congressional choice of remedy or because the Court, admitting its own responsibility for decision on this issue and understanding its own political susceptibilities, undertook to inquire rather than simply assert a conclusion on the question. An inquiry sympathetic to the possibility might proceed along either of two lines: first, there is the question of how the Secretary of Transportation might have placed this new statutory provision in the general context of statutes under his aegis, and of any trends

he might have noted in their evolution. Second would be the question how political controls appeared to have worked in this case—whether and to what extent CPOP had succeeded in drawing attention to its views and securing accommodation to them. Sections A and B address these questions in turn, suggesting that the case for the Secretary's choice is reasonably strong, and that the political effectiveness of CPOP in securing recognition if not full satisfaction of its claims was reasonably high.

In a number of recent opinions, the Supreme Court appears to have taken serious account of political controls over agency behavior as alternatives to judicial controls. These accounts not only acknowledge the existence of political controls over what agencies do, but also suggest that in some contexts they may be normatively superior, providing affirmative reasons for the judiciary to refrain from acting. In *Chevron*, for example, the possibility of presidential guidance respecting an agency's administration of a statute of uncertain meaning was given as a reason for judicial acceptance of the agency's reasonable interpretations.

The trust of political processes stated in these and other recent opinions, reflected back on *Overton Park*, suggests that the contemporary Court might find it easier to accept assignment of the 4(f) judgment to constrained politics in the first instance. The understanding of the statute that the Secretary exposed to the Senate Committee in hearings would be accepted as setting the framework within which his judgment was to be reached; and then that judgment, not one influenced by the much more restrictive statute-reading given by the *Overton Park* Court, would be subject to review for abuse of discretion. The location decision would almost certainly have survived such a challenge, leaving a statutory question the Court did not have to reach in the case as decided, whether the design Secretary Volpe approved had embodied "all possible planning to minimize harm" to the park.

3. One consequence of *Overton Park*, which you know if you have visited Memphis, is that Overton Park has been preserved. Another consequence, which you know if you have tried to drive through Memphis, is that no alternative route through the city for the I-40 freeway was ever agreed upon, and through traffic is routed into two wide loops around the city. Do these consequences suggest that the Court made the right decision or the wrong decision, or are they irrelevant?

The next decision is not only one of the most important in administrative law but the natural culmination of this book. It involves the NHTSA's passive restraints rescission—from airbags and seatbelts to neither of those options. That decision, Motor Vehicle Manufacturers Ass'n v. State Farm Insurance Co., 463 U.S. 29 (1983), is central to establishing the framework for arbitrary and capricious review.

Motor Vehicle Manufacturers Ass'n of the United States, Inc. v. State Farm Mutual Automobile Insurance Co.

463 U.S. 29 (1983)

[See pp. 406-417 in Chapter 4.]

Notes and Questions

1. *State Farm* tells reviewing courts that they can hold a regulation "arbitrary and capricious" and remand it to the agency for further explanation or consideration based on a host of factors short of outright policy disagreement. These factors mainly pertain to how the agency reached its decision, not what the agency decided. In this sense, *State Farm* authorizes courts to police the agency's decision-making process but not the substantive outcome. It imposes what many have called a "reasoned decision-making" requirement, encouraging agencies to issue rules that are logically sound, factually supported, and thoroughly considered. It is known as containing the "hard look" doctrine, which enables courts to take a hard look at whether agencies have taken a hard look at their rules.

2. The Court could have interpreted the arbitrary and capricious standard to authorize less intensive judicial review. The language in the APA actually comes from an old formulation of the Due Process Clause, which required courts to uphold statutes unless patently unreasonable. The Court could have directed reviewing courts to uphold an agency rule unless no reasonable agency could have adopted it. Why did it go further? Put differently, what is gained by the reasoned decision-making requirement?

3. Should the Court have interpreted the arbitrary and capricious test to authorize more searching review? What good is reviewing the agency's process if the agency's policy choice is unsound? Should courts also review the wisdom of the policy choice?

4. How successful was the Court in holding *itself* to the line that it established between the administrative process and the outcome? What did the Court hold on the facts of the case? It identified two problems with the rescission. Can you identify both? Where did it arguably overstep its bounds?

5. Missing from the Court's analysis was a discussion of politics. As we mentioned before, Justice Rehnquist raised this issue in his separate opinion, joined by three other justices. He was willing to give the agency's rescission of the seat belt requirement some credence because he thought that it reflected the politics of the administration. Why was the Court less sympathetic? On the relationship between politics and policy, consider the following from Kathryn A. Watts, *Proposing a Place for Politics in Arbitrary and Capricious Review*, 119 YALE L.J. 2, 6-9 (2009):

> Ever since the Court handed down *State Farm*, agencies, courts, and scholars alike generally seem to have accepted the view that influences coming from one political branch or another cannot be allowed to explain administrative decisionmaking, even if such factors are influencing agency decisionmaking. Take agencies to begin with. Agencies today generally try to meet their reason-giving duties under *State Farm* by couching their decisions in technocratic, statutory, or scientific language, either failing to disclose or affirmatively hiding political factors that enter into the mix. A good example of this can be found by looking at the Food and Drug Administration's (FDA) attempt in the 1990s to regulate teen smoking. Even though President Clinton played a very active role in directing the rulemaking (going so far as to personally announce the final rule in a Rose Garden ceremony), the FDA's statement of basis and purpose accompanying

the final rule relied upon statutory, scientific, and expert justifications—barely even hinting at President Clinton's role in the rulemaking.

Judicial review of agency action is similarly technocratic in focus. Courts applying arbitrary and capricious review today routinely search agency decisions to ensure they represent expert-driven decisionmaking. Decisions from the D.C. Circuit, for example, borrow from *State Farm*'s language and repeatedly frame arbitrary and capricious review in expert-driven terms, asking whether the agency "offered an explanation for its decision that runs counter to the evidence before the agency, or is so implausible that it could not be ascribed to a difference in view or the product of agency expertise."

This Article seeks to identify those rulemaking proceedings in which agencies acting as "mini legislatures" might most appropriately rely upon political influences coming from the President, other members of the executive branch, or Congress to justify agency decisions for purposes of arbitrary and capricious review. The heart of the argument is that what count as "valid" reasons under arbitrary and capricious review should be expanded to include certain political influences from the President, other executive officials, and members of Congress, so long as the political influences are openly and transparently disclosed in the agency's rulemaking record.

Acceptance of the argument set forth here would not mean that any and all political influences would be allowed to legitimize agency action. Although drawing a precise line between permissible and impermissible influences is difficult, legitimate political influences can roughly be thought of as those influences that seek to further policy considerations or public values, whereas illegitimate political influences can be thought of as those that seek to implement raw politics or partisan politics unconnected in any way to the statutory scheme being implemented.

6. In addition to its elaboration of the arbitrary and capricious standard and its (at least implicit) rejection of politics as a justification for administrative decision making, *State Farm* is famous for its holding that rescission of a regulation will be held to the same standard as the regulation when initially adopted. The Court of Appeals found this issue "troublesome," but the Supreme Court was dismissive of its concern, readily concluding that "an agency changing its course by rescinding a rule is obligated to supply a reasoned analysis for the change beyond that which may be required when an agency does not act in the first instance." Despite the ease with which the Court reached its conclusion, the issue is complex and goes to the general question of judicial control over agencies. The countervailing argument is that rescission of an existing regulation should be treated like the decision not to enact a statute in the first place. Such a decision is generally regarded by courts as within the agency's discretion and thus non-reviewable because, like other instances of "prosecutorial discretion," it involves an allocation of resources that courts are ill equipped to make. *See* Lon Fuller, *The Forms and Limits of Adjudication*, 92 HARV. L. REV. 353 (1978) (arguing that courts are not competent to make "polycentric decisions" involving resource allocation). Is the decision not to rescind a regulation like the decision not to regulate or prosecute, or can the situations be distinguished?

7. One year after the Supreme Court decided *State Farm,* NHTSA re-imposed mandatory passive restraints in the rule. The new rule required passive restraints unless by 1989 state laws required seat belts and met other conditions for two-thirds of the U.S. population. Although most states required seat belts by that date, they failed to comply with other conditions.

Thus, automakers had no choice and began to comply with the passive restraints rule, opting mostly to install airbags. In 1991, Congress enacted a statute that required auto manufacturers to install airbags. *See* Pub. L. No. 102-240, §2508, 105 Stat. 1914, 2085 (1991). Does this suggest that the Court got it right?

8. Even if the Court got passive restraints right, *State Farm* may have unintended consequences for agency action more generally. Professors Mashaw and Harfst have argued that in response to the decision, NHTSA adopted a wait-and-see posture of issuing recalls upon discovery that motor vehicles are unsafe rather than issuing rules to make them safe. *See* JERRY L. MASHAW & DAVID L. HARFST, THE STRUGGLE FOR AUTO SAFETY 224-54 (1990). Many argue that the hard look doctrine has the effect of "ossifying" agency action. *See* Thomas O. McGarity, *Some Thoughts on "Deossifying" the Rulemaking Process*, 41 DUKE L. J. 1385 (1992). The prospect of judicial review causes agencies to refrain from issuing rules until they have built an unassailable case, often delaying so long that the rule fails to keep pace with scientific advances or effectively address statutory goals. *See* STEPHEN BREYER, BREAKING THE VICIOUS CIRCLE 49 (1993). Agencies also may choose to forgo issuing rules altogether. Empirical studies suggest that the concern for ossification may be overstated. Despite hard look review, agencies continue to make plenty of rules at a reasonable speed. *See* Cary Coglianese, *Empirical Analysis and Administrative Law*, 2002 U. ILL. L. REV. 1111, 1125-31; William S. Jordan, III, *Ossification Revisited: Does Arbitrary and Capricious Review Significantly Interfere with Agency Ability to Achieve Regulatory Goals Through Informal Rulemaking?*, 94 NW. U. L. REV. 393, 403-07 (2000); Jason Webb Yackee & Susan Webb Yackee, *Testing the Ossification Thesis: An Empirical Examination of Federal Regulatory Volume and Speed, 1950-1990*, 80 GEO. WASH. L. REV. 1414 (2012). For a general critique of ossification, *see* Mark Seidenfeld, *Demystifying Deossification: Rethinking Recent Proposals to Modify Judicial Review of Notice and Comment Rulemaking*, 75 TEX. L. REV. 483 (1997).

Overton Park and *State Farm* are still the defining decisions on the arbitrary and capricious test, but a more recent one has something to say about judicial review of agency policy when that policy changes. In particular, how much explanation must an agency provide when it departs from a prior position? You will see that this decision generated a remarkable number of separate opinions from the justices. See if you can determine why so many felt the need to underscore their views.

FCC v. Fox Television Stations, Inc.

556 U.S. 502 (2009)

Justice SCALIA delivered the opinion of the Court, except as to Part III-E.

Federal law prohibits the broadcasting of "any . . . indecent . . . language," 18 U.S.C. §1464, which includes expletives referring to sexual or excretory activity or organs, see *FCC v. Pacifica Foundation*, 438 U.S. 726

(1978). This case concerns the adequacy of the Federal Communications Commission's explanation of its decision that this sometimes forbids the broadcasting of indecent expletives even when the offensive words are not repeated.

Statutory and Regulatory Background

The Communications Act of 1934, 48 Stat. 1064, 47 U.S.C. §151 et seq. (2000 ed. and Supp. V), established a system of limited-term broadcast licenses subject to various "conditions" designed "to maintain the control of the United States over all the channels of radio transmission," §301 (2000 ed.). Twenty-seven years ago we said that "[a] licensed broadcaster is granted the free and exclusive of a limited and valuable part of the public domain; when he accepts that franchise it is burdened by enforceable public obligations." *CBS, Inc. v. FCC,* 453 U.S. 367, 395 (1981) (internal quotation marks omitted).

One of the burdens that licensees shoulder is the indecency ban—the statutory proscription against "utter[ing] any obscene, indecent, or profane language by means of radio communication," 18 U.S.C. §1464—which Congress has instructed the Commission to enforce between the hours of 6 A.M. and 10 P.M. Public Telecommunications Act of 1992, §16(a), 106 Stat. 954, note following 47 U.S.C. §303. Congress has given the Commission various means of enforcing the indecency ban, including civil fines, see §503(b)(1), and license revocations or the denial of license renewals, see §§309(k), 312(a)(6).

The Commission first invoked the statutory ban on indecent broadcasts in 1975, declaring a daytime broadcast of George Carlin's "Filthy Words" monologue actionably indecent. At that time, the Commission announced the definition of indecent speech that it uses to this day, prohibiting "language that describes, in terms patently offensive as measured by contemporary community standards for the broadcast medium, sexual or excretory activities or organs, at times of the day when there is a reasonable risk that children may be in the audience."

In *FCC v. Pacifica Foundation,* we upheld the Commission's order against statutory and constitutional challenge. We rejected the broadcasters' argument that the statutory proscription applied only to speech appealing to the prurient interest, noting that "the normal definition of 'indecent' merely refers to nonconformance with accepted standards of morality." *Id.,* at 740. And we held that the First Amendment allowed Carlin's monologue to be banned in light of the "uniquely pervasive presence" of the medium and the fact that broadcast programming is "uniquely accessible to children." *Id.,* at 748-749.

In the ensuing years, the Commission took a cautious, but gradually expanding, approach to enforcing the statutory prohibition against indecent broadcasts. Shortly after *Pacifica,* 438 U.S. 726, the Commission expressed its "inten[tion] strictly to observe the narrowness of the *Pacifica* holding," which "relied in part on the repetitive occurrence of the 'indecent' words" contained in Carlin's monologue. When the full Commission next considered its indecency standard, however, it repudiated the view that its enforcement power was limited to "deliberate, repetitive use of the seven words actually contained in the George Carlin monologue." . . . The Court of Appeals for the District of Columbia Circuit upheld this expanded enforcement standard against constitutional and Administrative Procedure Act challenge.

Although the Commission had expanded its enforcement beyond the "repetitive use of specific words or phrases," it preserved a distinction between literal and nonliteral (or "expletive") uses of evocative language. The Commission explained that each literal "description or depiction of sexual or excretory functions must be examined in context to determine whether it is patently offensive," but that "deliberate and repetitive use . . . is a requisite to a finding of indecency" when a complaint focuses solely on the use of nonliteral expletives.

Over a decade later, the Commission emphasized that the "full context" in which particular materials appear is "critically important," but that a few "principal" factors guide the inquiry, such as the "explicitness or graphic nature" of the material, the extent to which the material "dwells on or repeats" the offensive material, and the extent to which the material was presented to "pander," to "titillate," or to "shock." "No single factor," the Commission said, "generally provides the basis for an indecency finding," but "where sexual or excretory references have been made once or have been passing or fleeting in nature, this characteristic has tended to weigh against a finding of indecency."

In 2004, the Commission took one step further by declaring for the first time that a nonliteral (expletive) use of the F- and S-Words could be actionably indecent, even when the word is used only once. The first order to this effect dealt with an NBC broadcast of the Golden Globe Awards, in which the performer Bono commented, " 'This is really, really, f***ing brilliant.' " . . .

The Commission first declared that Bono's use of the F-Word fell within its indecency definition, even though the word was used as an intensifier rather than a literal descriptor. "[G]iven the core meaning of the 'F-Word,' " it said, "any use of that word . . . inherently has a sexual connotation." The Commission determined, moreover, that the broadcast was "patently offensive" because the F-Word "is one of the most vulgar, graphic and explicit descriptions of sexual activity in the English language," because "[i]ts use invariably invokes a coarse sexual image," and because Bono's use of the word was entirely "shocking and gratuitous."

The Commission observed that categorically exempting such language from enforcement actions would "likely lead to more widespread use."

Commission action was necessary to "safeguard the well-being of the nation's children from the most objectionable, most offensive language." The order noted that technological advances have made it far easier to delete ("bleep out") a "single and gratuitous use of a vulgar expletive," without adulterating the content of a broadcast. . . .

The Present Case

This case concerns utterances in two live broadcasts aired by Fox Television Stations, Inc., and its affiliates prior to the Commission's *Golden Globes Order*. The first occurred during the 2002 Billboard Music Awards, when the singer Cher exclaimed, "I've also had critics for the last 40 years saying that I was on my way out every year. Right. So f*** 'em." The second involved a segment of the 2003 Billboard Music Awards, during the presentation of an award by Nicole Richie and Paris Hilton, principals in a Fox television series called "The Simple Life." Ms. Hilton began their interchange by reminding Ms. Richie to "watch the bad language," but Ms. Richie proceeded to ask the audience, "Why do they even call it 'The Simple Life?' Have you ever tried to get cow s*** out of a Prada purse? It's not so f***ing simple." Following each of these broadcasts, the Commission received numerous complaints from parents whose children were exposed to the language.

On March 15, 2006, the Commission released Notices of Apparent Liability for a number of broadcasts that the Commission deemed actionably indecent, including the two described above. Multiple parties petitioned the Court of Appeals for the Second Circuit for judicial review of the order, asserting a variety of constitutional and statutory challenges. Since the order had declined to impose sanctions, the Commission had not previously given the broadcasters an opportunity to respond to the indecency charges. It therefore requested and obtained from the Court of Appeals a voluntary remand so that the parties could air their objections. The Commission's order on remand upheld the indecency findings for the broadcasts described above.

The order first explained that both broadcasts fell comfortably within the subject-matter scope of the Commission's indecency test because the 2003 broadcast involved a literal description of excrement and both broadcasts invoked the "F-Word," which inherently has a sexual connotation. The order next determined that the broadcasts were patently offensive under community standards for the medium. Both broadcasts, it noted, involved entirely gratuitous uses of "one of the most vulgar, graphic, and explicit words for sexual activity in the English language." It found Ms. Richie's use of the "F-Word" and her "explicit description of the handling of excrement" to be "vulgar and shocking," as well as to constitute "pandering," after Ms. Hilton had playfully warned her to " 'watch the bad language.' " And it found Cher's statement patently offensive in part because she metaphorically suggested a sexual act as a means of expressing hostility to her critics. The order relied upon the "critically important" context of the utterances, noting that they were aired during prime-time awards shows "designed to draw a large nationwide audience that could be expected to include many children interested in seeing their favorite music stars." Indeed, approximately 2.5 million minors witnessed each of the broadcasts.

. . . The order stated . . . that the pre-*Golden Globes* regime of immunity for isolated indecent expletives rested only upon staff rulings and Commission dicta, and that the Commission itself had never held "that the isolated use of an expletive . . . was not indecent or could not be indecent." In any event, the order made clear, the *Golden Globes Order* eliminated any doubt that fleeting expletives could be actionably indecent, and the Commission disavowed the bureau-level decisions and its own dicta that had said otherwise. Under the new policy, a lack of repetition "weigh[s] against a finding of indecency," but is not a safe harbor.

The order explained that the Commission's prior "strict dichotomy between 'expletives' and 'descriptions or depictions of sexual or excretory functions' is artificial and does not make sense in light of the fact that an 'expletive's' power to offend derives from its sexual or excretory meaning." In the Commission's view, "granting an automatic exemption for 'isolated or fleeting' expletives unfairly forces viewers (including children)" to take " 'the first blow' " and would allow broadcasters "to air expletives at all hours of a day so long as they did so one at a time." . . .

The Court of Appeals reversed the agency's orders, finding the Commission's reasoning inadequate under the Administrative Procedure Act. . . .

Analysis

Governing Principles

. . . In overturning the Commission's judgment, the Court of Appeals here relied in part on Circuit precedent requiring a more substantial explanation for agency action that changes prior policy. The Second Circuit has interpreted the Administrative Procedure Act and our opinion in *State Farm* as requiring agencies to make clear " 'why the original reasons for adopting the [displaced] rule or policy are no longer dispositive' " as well as " 'why the new rule effectuates the statute as well as or better than the old rule.' " 489 F.3d, at 456-457 (quoting *New York Council, Assn. of Civilian Technicians v. FLRA*, 757 F.2d 502, 508 (C.A.2 1985); emphasis deleted). The Court of Appeals for the District of Columbia Circuit has similarly indicated that a court's standard of review is "heightened somewhat" when an agency reverses course. *NAACP v. FCC*, 682 F.2d 993, 998 (1982).

We find no basis in the Administrative Procedure Act or in our opinions for a requirement that all agency change be subjected to more searching review. The Act mentions no such heightened standard. And our opinion in *State Farm* neither held nor implied that every agency action representing a policy change must be justified by reasons more substantial than those required to adopt a policy in the first instance. That case, which involved the rescission of a prior regulation, said only that such action requires "a reasoned analysis for the change beyond that which may be required when an agency *does not act* in the first instance." 463 U.S., at 42 (emphasis added). Treating failures to act and rescissions of prior action differently for purposes of the standard of review makes good sense, and has basis in the text of the statute, which likewise treats the two separately. It instructs a reviewing court to "compel agency action unlawfully withheld or unreasonably delayed," 5 U.S.C. §706(1), and to "hold unlawful and set aside agency action, findings, and conclusions found to be [among other things] . . . arbitrary [or] capricious," §706(2)(A). The statute makes no distinction, however, between initial agency action and subsequent agency action undoing or revising that action.

To be sure, the requirement that an agency provide reasoned explanation for its action would ordinarily demand that it display awareness that it is changing position. An agency may not, for example, depart from a prior policy *sub silentio* or simply disregard rules that are still on the books. See *United States v. Nixon*, 418 U.S. 683, 696 (1974). And of course the agency must show that there are good reasons for the new policy. But it need not demonstrate to a court's satisfaction that the reasons for the new policy are *better* than the reasons for the old one; it suffices that the new policy is permissible under the statute, that there are good reasons for it, and that the agency *believes* it to be better, which the conscious change of course adequately indicates. This means that the agency need not always provide a more detailed justification than what would suffice for a new policy created on a blank slate. Sometimes it must—when, for example, its new policy rests upon factual findings that contradict those which underlay its prior policy; or when its prior policy has engendered serious reliance interests that must be taken into account. *Smiley v. Citibank (South Dakota), N.A.*, 517 U.S. 735, 742 (1996). It would be arbitrary or capricious to ignore such matters. In such cases it is not that further justification is demanded by the mere fact of policy change; but that a reasoned explanation is needed for disregarding facts and circumstances that underlay or were engendered by the prior policy.

[T]he broadcasters' arguments have repeatedly referred to the First Amendment. If they mean to invite us to apply a more stringent arbitrary-and-capricious review to agency actions that implicate constitutional liberties, we reject the invitation. The so-called canon of constitutional avoidance is an interpretive tool, counseling that ambiguous statutory language be construed to avoid serious constitutional doubts. See *Edward J. DeBartolo Corp. v. Florida Gulf Coast Building & Constr. Trades Council*, 485 U.S. 568, 575 (1988). We know of no precedent for applying it to limit the scope of authorized executive action. . . .

Application to This Case

Judged under the above described standards, the Commission's new enforcement policy and its order finding the broadcasts actionably indecent were neither arbitrary nor capricious. First, the Commission forthrightly acknowledged that its recent actions have broken new ground, taking account of inconsistent "prior Commission and staff action" and explicitly disavowing them as "no longer good law." To be sure, the (superfluous) explanation in its *Remand Order* of why the Cher broadcast would even have violated its earlier policy may not be entirely convincing. But that unnecessary detour is irrelevant. There is no doubt that the Commission knew it was making a change. That is why it declined to assess penalties; and it relied on the *Golden Globes Order* as removing any lingering doubt.

Moreover, the agency's reasons for expanding the scope of its enforcement activity were entirely rational. It was certainly reasonable to determine that it made no sense to distinguish between literal and nonliteral uses of offensive words, requiring repetitive use to render only the latter indecent. As the Commission said with regard to expletive use of the F-Word, "the word's power to insult and offend derives from its sexual meaning." And the Commission's decision to look at the patent offensiveness of even isolated uses of sexual and excretory words fits with the context-based approach we sanctioned in *Pacifica*, 438 U.S., at 750. Even isolated utterances can be made in "pander[ing,] . . . vulgar and shocking" manners, and can constitute harmful " 'first blow[s]' " to children. It is surely rational (if not inescapable) to believe that a safe harbor for single words would "likely lead to more widespread use of the offensive language."

When confronting other requests for *per se* rules governing its enforcement of the indecency prohibition, the Commission has declined to create safe harbors for particular types of broadcasts. The Commission could rationally decide it needed to step away from its old regime where nonrepetitive use of an expletive was *per se* nonactionable because that was "at odds with the Commission's overall enforcement policy."

The fact that technological advances have made it easier for broadcasters to bleep out offending words further supports the Commission's stepped-up enforcement policy. And the agency's decision not to impose any forfeiture or other sanction precludes any argument that it is arbitrarily punishing parties without notice of the potential consequences of their action. . . .

The Court of Appeals' Reasoning

The Court of Appeals found the Commission's action arbitrary and capricious on three grounds. First, the court criticized the Commission for failing to explain why it had not previously banned fleeting expletives as "harmful 'first blow[s].' " 489 F.3d, at 458. . . . As explained above, the fact that an agency had a prior stance does not alone prevent it from changing its view or create a higher hurdle for doing so. And it is not the Commission, but Congress that has proscribed "any . . . indecent . . . language." 18 U.S.C. §1464.

There are some propositions for which scant empirical evidence can be marshaled, and the harmful effect of broadcast profanity on children is one of them. One cannot demand a multiyear controlled study, in which some children are intentionally exposed to indecent broadcasts (and insulated from all other indecency), and others are shielded from all indecency. It is one thing to set aside agency action under the Administrative Procedure Act because of failure to adduce empirical data that can readily be obtained. See, e.g., *State Farm*, 463 U.S., at 46-56 (addressing the costs and benefits of mandatory passive restraints for automobiles). It is something else to insist upon obtaining the unobtainable. Here it suffices to know that children mimic the behavior they observe — or at least the behavior that is presented to them as normal and appropriate. Programming replete with one-word indecent expletives will tend to produce children who use (at least) one-word indecent expletives. Congress has made the determination that indecent material is harmful to children, and has left enforcement of the ban to the Commission. If enforcement had to be supported by empirical data, the ban would effectively be a nullity.

The Commission had adduced no quantifiable measure of the harm caused by the language in *Pacifica*, and we nonetheless held that the "government's interest in the 'well-being of its youth' . . . justified the regulation of otherwise protected expression." 438 U.S., at 749, 98 S. Ct. 3026 (quoting *Ginsberg v. New York*, 390 U.S. 629, 640 (1968)). If the Constitution itself demands of agencies no more scientifically certain criteria to comply with the First Amendment, neither does the Administrative Procedure Act to comply with the requirement of reasoned decisionmaking.

The court's second objection is that fidelity to the agency's "first blow" theory of harm would require a categorical ban on *all* broadcasts of expletives; the Commission's failure to go to this extreme thus undermined the coherence of its rationale. 489 F.3d, at 458-459. This objection, however, is not responsive to the Commission's actual policy under review — the decision to include patently offensive fleeting expletives within the definition of indecency. The Commission's prior enforcement practice, unchallenged here, already drew distinctions between the offensiveness of particular words based upon the context in which they appeared. Any complaint about the Commission's failure to ban only some fleeting expletives is better directed at the agency's context-based system generally rather than its inclusion of isolated expletives.

More fundamentally, however, the agency's decision to consider the patent offensiveness of isolated expletives on a case-by-case basis is not arbitrary or capricious. "Even a prime-time recitation of Geoffrey Chaucer's Miller's Tale," we have explained, "would not be likely to command the attention of many children who are both old enough to understand and young enough to be adversely affected." *Pacifica*, at 750, n.29. The same rationale could support the Commission's finding that a broadcast of the film Saving Private Ryan was not indecent — a finding to which the broadcasters point as supposed evidence of the Commission's inconsistency. The frightening suspense and the graphic violence in the movie could well dissuade the most vulnerable from watching and would put parents on notice of potentially objectionable material. The agency's decision to retain some discretion does not render arbitrary or capricious its regulation of the deliberate and shocking uses of offensive language at the award shows under review—shows that were expected to (and did) draw the attention of millions of children.

Finally, the Court of Appeals found unconvincing the agency's prediction (without any evidence) that a *per se* exemption for fleeting expletives would lead to increased use of expletives one at a time. But even in the absence of evidence, the agency's predictive judgment (which merits deference) makes entire sense. To predict that complete immunity for fleeting expletives, ardently desired by broadcasters, will lead to a substantial increase in fleeting expletives seems to us an exercise in logic rather than clairvoyance. . . .

Respondents' Arguments

Respondents press some arguments that the court did not adopt. They claim that the Commission failed to acknowledge its change in enforcement policy. That contention is not tenable in light of the *Golden Globes Order's* specific declaration that its prior rulings were no longer good law. . . .

The broadcasters also make much of the fact that the Commission has gone beyond the scope of authority approved in *Pacifica*, which it once regarded as the farthest extent of its power. But we have never held that *Pacifica* represented the outer limits of permissible regulation, so that fleeting expletives may not be forbidden. To the contrary, we explicitly left for another day whether "an occasional expletive" in "a telecast of an Elizabethan comedy" could be prohibited. 438 U.S., at 748. . . .

Finally, the broadcasters claim that the Commission's repeated appeal to "context" is simply a smokescreen for a standardless regime of unbridled discretion. But we have previously approved Commission regulation based "on a nuisance rationale under which context is all-important," *Pacifica*, at 750, and we find no basis in the Administrative Procedure Act for mandating anything different.

The Dissents' Arguments

Justice Breyer purports to "begin with applicable law," but in fact begins by stacking the deck. He claims that the FCC's status as an "independent" agency sheltered from political oversight requires courts to be "all the more" vigilant in ensuring "that major policy decisions be based upon articulable reasons." The independent agencies are sheltered not from politics but from the President, and it has often been observed that their freedom from presidential oversight (and protection) has simply been replaced by increased subservience to congressional direction. Indeed, the precise policy change at issue here was spurred by significant political pressure from Congress.[1] . . .

---

1. A Subcommittee of the FCC's House oversight Committee held hearings on the FCC's broadcast indecency enforcement on January 28, 2004. "Can You Say That on TV?": An Examination of the FCC's Enforcement with respect to Broadcast Indecency, Hearing before the Subcommittee on Telecommunications and the Internet of the House Committee on Energy and Commerce, 108th Cong., 2d Sess. Members of the Subcommittee specifically "called on the full Commission to reverse [the staff ruling in the *Golden Globes* case]" because they perceived a "feeling amongst many Americans that some

Regardless, it is assuredly not "applicable law" that rulemaking by independent regulatory agencies is subject to heightened scrutiny. The Administrative Procedure Act, which provides judicial review, makes no distinction between independent and other agencies, neither in its definition of agency, 5 U.S.C. §701(b)(1), nor in the standards for reviewing agency action, §706. Nor does any case of ours express or reflect the "heightened scrutiny" Justice Breyer and Justice Stevens would impose. Indeed, it is hard to imagine any closer scrutiny than that we have given to the Environmental Protection Agency, which is not an independent agency. There is no reason to magnify the separation-of-powers dilemma posed by the headless Fourth Branch, by letting Article III judges—like jackals stealing the lion's kill—expropriate some of the power that Congress has wrested from the unitary Executive.

Justice Breyer and Justice Stevens rely upon two supposed omissions in the FCC's analysis that they believe preclude a finding that the agency did not act arbitrarily. Neither of these omissions could undermine the coherence of the rationale the agency gave, but the dissenters' evaluation of each is flawed in its own right.

First, both claim that the Commission failed adequately to explain its consideration of the constitutional issues inherent in its regulation. We are unaware that we have ever before reversed an executive agency, not for violating our cases, but for failure to discuss them adequately. But leave that aside. According to Justice Breyer, the agency said "next to nothing about the relation between the change it made in its prior 'fleeting expletive' policy and the First-Amendment-related need to avoid 'censorship.'"

TV broadcasters are engaged in a race to the bottom, pushing the decency envelope to distinguish themselves in the increasingly crowded entertainment field." *Id.*, at 2 (statement of Rep. Upton); see also, *e.g.*, *id.*, at 17 (statement of Rep. Terry), 19 (statement of Rep. Pitts). They repeatedly expressed disapproval of the FCC's enforcement policies, see, *e.g.*, *id.*, at 3 (statement of Rep. Upton) ("At some point we have to ask the FCC: How much is enough? When will it revoke a license?"); *id.*, at 4 (statement of Rep. Markey) ("Today's hearing will allow us to explore the FCC's lackluster enforcement record with respect to these violations").

About two weeks later, on February 11, 2004, the same Subcommittee held hearings on a bill increasing the fines for indecency violations. Hearings on H. R 3717 before the Subcommittee on Telecommunications and the Internet of the House Committee on Energy and Commerce, 108th Cong., 2d Sess. All five Commissioners were present and were grilled about enforcement shortcomings. See, *e.g.*, *id.*, at 124 (statement of Rep. Terry) ("Chairman Powell, . . . it seems like common sense that if we had . . . more frequent enforcement instead of a few examples of fines . . . that would be a deterrent in itself"); *id.*, at 7 (statement of Rep. Dingell) ("I see that apparently . . . there is no enforcement of regulations at the FCC"). Certain statements, moreover, indicate that the political pressure applied by Congress had its desired effect. See *ibid.* ("I think our committee's work has gotten the attention of FCC Chairman Powell and the Bush Administration. And I'm happy to see the FCC now being brought to a state of apparent alert on these matters"); see also *id.*, at 124 (statement of Michael Copps, FCC Commissioner) (noting "positive" change in other Commissioners' willingness to step up enforcement in light of proposed congressional action). A version of the bill ultimately became law as the Broadcast Decency Enforcement Act of 2005, 120 Stat. 491.

The FCC adopted the change that is the subject of this litigation on March 3, 2004, about three weeks after this second hearing. See *Golden Globes Order*, 19 FCC Rcd. 4975. [Footnote 4 in the Opinion.—Eds.]

The *Remand Order* does, however, devote four full pages of small-type, single-spaced text (over 1,300 words not counting the footnotes) to explaining why the Commission believes that its indecency-enforcement regime (which includes its change in policy) is consistent with the First Amendment—and therefore not censorship as the term is understood. More specifically, Justice Breyer faults the FCC for "not explain[ing] why the agency changed its mind about the line that *Pacifica* draws or its policy's relation to that line." But in fact (and as the Commission explained) this Court's holding in *Pacifica*, 438 U.S. 726, 1073, drew no constitutional line; to the contrary, it expressly declined to express any view on the constitutionality of prohibiting isolated indecency. Justice Breyer and Justice Stevens evidently believe that when an agency has obtained this Court's determination that a less restrictive rule is constitutional, its successors acquire some special burden to explain why a more restrictive rule is not *un*constitutional. We know of no such principle.

Second, Justice Breyer looks over the vast field of particular factual scenarios unaddressed by the FCC's 35-page *Remand Order* and finds one that is fatal: the plight of the small local broadcaster who cannot afford the new technology that enables the screening of live broadcasts for indecent utterances. The Commission has failed to address the fate of this unfortunate, who will, he believes, be subject to sanction. . . .

The fundamental fallacy of Justice Breyer's small-broadcaster gloomy scenario is its demonstrably false assumption that the *Remand Order* makes no provision for the avoidance of unfairness—that the single-utterance prohibition will be invoked uniformly, in all situations. The *Remand Order* made very clear that this is not the case. It said that in determining "what, if any, remedy is appropriate" the Commission would consider the facts of each individual case, such as the "possibility of human error in using delay equipment." Thus, the fact that the agency believed that Fox (a large broadcaster that used suggestive scripting and a deficient delay system to air a prime-time awards show aimed at millions of children) "fail[ed] to exercise 'reasonable judgment, responsibility and sensitivity,'" says little about how the Commission would treat smaller broadcasters who cannot afford screening equipment. Indeed, that they would not be punished for failing to purchase equipment they cannot afford is positively suggested by the *Remand Order*'s statement that "[h]olding Fox responsible for airing indecent material in this case does not . . . impose undue burdens on broadcasters." . . .

Constitutionality

The Second Circuit did not definitively rule on the constitutionality of the Commission's orders, but respondents nonetheless ask us to decide their validity under the First Amendment. This Court, however, is one of final review, "not of first view. . . ." We decline to address the constitutional questions at this time. . . .

The judgment of the United States Court of Appeals for the Second Circuit is reversed, and the case is remanded for further proceedings consistent with this opinion.

Justice THOMAS, concurring. [omitted]

Justice KENNEDY, concurring in part and concurring in the judgment.

. . . This separate writing is to underscore certain background principles for the conclusion that an agency's decision to change course may be arbitrary and capricious if the agency sets a new course that reverses an earlier determination but does not provide a reasoned explanation for doing so. In those circumstances I agree with the dissenting opinion of Justice Breyer that the agency must explain why "it now reject[s] the considerations that led it to adopt that initial policy."

The question whether a change in policy requires an agency to provide a more reasoned explanation than when the original policy was first announced is not susceptible, in my view, to an answer that applies in all cases. There may be instances when it becomes apparent to an agency that the reasons for a longstanding policy have been altered by discoveries in science, advances in technology, or by any of the other forces at work in a dynamic society. If an agency seeks to respond to new circumstances by modifying its earlier policy, the agency may have a substantial body of data and experience that can shape and inform the new rule. In other cases the altered circumstances may be so new that the agency must make predictive judgments that are as difficult now as when the agency's earlier policy was first announced. Reliance interests in the prior policy may also have weight in the analysis.

The question in each case is whether the agency's reasons for the change, when viewed in light of the data available to it, and when informed by the experience and expertise of the agency, suffice to demonstrate that the new policy rests upon principles that are rational, neutral, and in accord with the agency's proper understanding of its authority. That showing may be required if the agency is to demonstrate that its action is not "arbitrary, capricious, an abuse of discretion, or otherwise not in accordance with law." 5 U.S.C. §706(2)(A). And, of course, the agency action must not be "in excess of statutory jurisdiction, authority, or limitations, or short of statutory right." §706(2)(C). . . .

Where there is a policy change the record may be much more developed because the agency based its prior policy on factual findings. In that instance, an agency's decision to change course may be arbitrary and capricious if the agency ignores or countermands its earlier factual findings without reasoned explanation for doing so. An agency cannot simply disregard contrary or inconvenient factual determinations that it made in the past, any more than it can ignore inconvenient facts when it writes on a blank slate.

. . . Rather than base its prior policy on its knowledge of the broadcast industry and its audience, the FCC instead based its policy on what it considered to be our holding in *FCC v. Pacifica Foundation*, 438 U.S. 726 (1978). The FCC did not base its prior policy on factual findings.

The FCC's *Remand Order* explains that the agency has changed its reading of *Pacifica*. The reasons the agency announces for this change are not so precise, detailed, or elaborate as to be a model for agency explanation. But, as the opinion for the Court well explains, the FCC's reasons for its action were the sort of reasons an agency may consider and act upon. The Court's careful and complete analysis—both with respect to the procedural history of the FCC's indecency policies, and the reasons the agency has given to support them—is quite sufficient to sustain the FCC's change of course against respondents' claim that the agency acted in an arbitrary or capricious fashion. . . .

Justice STEVENS, dissenting [omitted]

While I join Justice Breyer's cogent dissent, I think it important to emphasize two flaws in the Court's reasoning. Apparently assuming that the Federal Communications Commission's (FCC or Commission) rulemaking authority is a species of executive power, the Court espouses the novel proposition that the Commission need not explain its decision to discard a longstanding rule in favor of a dramatically different approach to regulation. Moreover, the Court incorrectly assumes that our decision in *FCC v. Pacifica Foundation*, 438 U.S. 726 (1978), decided that the word "indecent," as used in 18 U.S.C. §1464, permits the FCC to punish the broadcast of *any* expletive that has a sexual or excretory origin. *Pacifica* was not so sweeping, and the Commission's changed view of its statutory mandate certainly would have been rejected if presented to the Court at the time.

I

. . . The FCC, like all agencies, may revise its regulations from time to time, just as Congress amends its statutes as circumstances warrant. But the FCC is constrained by its congressional mandate. There should be a strong presumption that the FCC's initial views, reflecting the informed judgment of independent commissioners with expertise in the regulated area, also reflect the views of the Congress that delegated the Commission authority to flesh out details not fully defined in the enacting statute. The rules adopted after *Pacifica*, 438 U.S. 726, have been in effect for decades and have not proved unworkable in the intervening years. . . .

II

The Court commits a second critical error by assuming that *Pacifica* endorsed a construction of the term "indecent," as used in 18 U.S.C. §1464, that would include any expletive that has a sexual or excretory origin. Neither the opinion of the Court, nor Justice Powell's concurring opinion, adopted such a far-reaching interpretation. . . .

The narrow treatment of the term "indecent" in *Pacifica* defined the outer boundaries of the enforcement policies adopted by the FCC in the ensuing years. . . .

[T]he Commission has adopted an interpretation of "indecency" that bears no resemblance to what *Pacifica* contemplated. Most distressingly, the Commission appears to be entirely unaware of this fact, and today's majority seems untroubled by this significant oversight. Because the FCC has failed to demonstrate an awareness that it has ventured far beyond *Pacifica*'s reading of §1464, its policy choice must be declared arbitrary and set aside as unlawful. . . .

Justice GINSBURG dissenting. [omitted]

Justice BREYER, with whom Justice STEVENS, Justice SOUTER, and Justice GINSBURG join, dissenting.

In my view, the Federal Communications Commission failed adequately to explain *why* it *changed* its indecency policy from a policy permitting a single "fleeting use" of an expletive, to a policy that made no such exception. . . .

I

I begin with applicable law. That law grants those in charge of independent administrative agencies broad authority to determine relevant policy. But it does not permit them to make policy choices for purely political reasons nor to rest them primarily upon unexplained policy preferences. Federal Communications Commissioners have fixed terms of office; they are not directly responsible to the voters; and they enjoy an independence expressly designed to insulate them, to a degree, from "'the exercise of political oversight.'" *Freytag v. Commissioner*, 501 U.S. 868, 916 (1991) (Scalia, J., concurring in part and concurring in judgment). That insulation helps to secure important governmental objectives, such as the constitutionally related objective of maintaining broadcast regulation that does not bend too readily before the political winds. But that agency's comparative freedom from ballot-box control makes it all the more important that courts review its decisionmaking to assure compliance with applicable provisions of the law—including law requiring that major policy decisions be based upon articulable reasons. . . .

To explain a change requires more than setting forth reasons why the new policy is a good one. It also requires the agency to answer the question, "Why did you change?" And a rational answer to this question typically requires a more complete explanation than would prove satisfactory were change itself not at issue. An (imaginary) administrator explaining why he chose a policy that requires driving on the right-side, rather than the left-side, of the road might say, "Well, one side seemed as good as the other, so I flipped a coin." But even assuming the rationality of that explanation for an initial choice, that explanation is not at all rational if offered to explain why the administrator changed driving practice, from right-side to left-side, 25 years later.

... [T]he [*State Farm*] Court described the need for explanation in terms that apply, not simply to pure *rescissions* of earlier rules, but rather to changes of policy as it more broadly defined them. It said that the law required an explanation for such a *change* because the earlier policy, representing a " 'settled course of behavior[,] embodies the agency's informed judgment that, by pursuing that course, it will carry out the policies . . . best if the settled rule is adhered to.' " *State Farm*, at 41-42. Thus, the agency must explain *why* it has come to the conclusion that it should now change direction. Why does it now reject the considerations that led it to adopt that initial policy? What has changed in the world that offers justification for the change? What other good reasons are there for departing from the earlier policy?

... [This dissent] would not (and *State Farm* does not) require a "heightened standard" of review. Rather, the law requires application of the *same standard* of review to different circumstances, namely circumstances characterized by the fact that *change* is at issue. It requires the agency to focus upon the fact of change where change is relevant, just as it must focus upon any other relevant circumstance. It requires the agency here to focus upon the reasons that led the agency to adopt the initial policy, and to explain why it now comes to a new judgment.

I recognize that *sometimes* the ultimate explanation for a change may have to be, "We now weigh the relevant considerations differently." But at other times, an agency can and should say more. Where, for example, the agency rested its previous policy on particular factual findings; or where an agency rested its prior policy on its view of the governing law, or where an agency rested its previous policy on, say, a special need to coordinate with another agency, one would normally expect the agency to focus upon those earlier views of fact, of law, or of policy and explain why they are no longer controlling. . . . [C]*hange* is sometimes (not always) a relevant background feature that sometimes (not always) requires focus (upon prior justifications) and explanation lest the adoption of the new policy (in that circumstance) be "arbitrary, capricious, an abuse of discretion."

... Where does, and why would, the APA grant agencies the freedom to change major policies on the basis of nothing more than political considerations or even personal whim? . . .

II

. . . Consider the requirement that an agency at least minimally "consider . . . important aspect[s] of the problem." *State Farm*, at 43. The FCC failed to satisfy this requirement, for it failed to consider two critically important aspects of the problem that underlay its initial policy judgment (one of which directly, the other of which indirectly). First, the FCC said next to nothing about the relation between the change it made in its prior "fleeting expletive" policy and the First-Amendment-related need to avoid "censorship," a matter as closely related to broadcasting regulation as is health to that of the environment. The reason that discussion of the matter is particularly important here is that the FCC had *explicitly* rested its prior policy in large part upon the need to avoid treading too close to the constitutional line. . . .

. . . What then did it say, when it changed its policy, about *why* it abandoned this Constitution-based reasoning? The FCC devoted "four full pages of small-type, single-spaced text," responding to industry arguments that, e.g., changes in the nature of the broadcast industry made *all* indecency regulation, i.e., 18 U.S.C. §1464, unconstitutional. In doing so it repeatedly *reaffirmed* its view that *Pacifica* remains good law. All the more surprising then that, in respect to *why* it abandoned its prior view about the critical relation between its prior fleeting expletive policy and Justice Powell's *Pacifica* concurrence, it says no more than the following: "[O]ur decision is not inconsistent with the Supreme Court ruling in *Pacifica*. The Court explicitly left open the issue of whether an occasional expletive could be considered indecent." And, (repeating what it already had said), "[*Pacifica*] specifically reserved the question of 'an occasional expletive' and noted that it addressed only the 'particular broadcast' at issue in that case."

These two sentences are not a summary of the FCC's discussion about why it abandoned its prior understanding of *Pacifica*. They *are* the discussion. These 28 words (repeated in two opinions) do not acknowledge that an entirely different understanding of *Pacifica* underlay the FCC's earlier policy; they do not explain why the agency changed its mind about the line that *Pacifica* draws or its policy's relation to that line; and they tell us nothing at all about what happened to the FCC's earlier determination to search for "compelling interests" and "less restrictive alternatives." They do not explain the transformation of what the FCC had long thought an insurmountable obstacle into an open door. The result is not simply Hamlet without the prince, but Hamlet with a prince who, in mid-play and without explanation, just disappears. . . .

Second, the FCC failed to consider the potential impact of its new policy upon local broadcasting coverage. This "aspect of the problem" is particularly important because the FCC explicitly took account of potential broadcasting impact. Indeed, in setting forth "bleeping" technology changes (presumably lowering bleeping costs) as justifying the policy change, it implicitly reasoned that lower costs, making it easier for broadcasters to install bleeping equipment, made it less likely that the new policy would lead broadcasters to reduce coverage, say by canceling coverage of public events.

What then did the FCC say about the likelihood that smaller independent broadcasters, including many public service broadcasters, still would not be able to afford "bleeping" technology and, as a consequence, would reduce local coverage, indeed cancel coverage, of many public events? It said nothing at all. . . .

I cannot agree with the plurality . . . that the new policy obviously provides smaller independent broadcasters with adequate assurance that they will not be fined. The new policy removes the "fleeting expletive" exception, an exception that assured smaller independent stations that they would not be fined should someone swear at a public event. In its place, it puts a policy that places all broadcasters at risk when they broadcast fleeting expletives, including expletives uttered at public events. The best it can provide by way of assurance is to say that "it *may* be inequitable to hold a licensee responsible for airing offensive speech during live coverage of a public event *under some circumstances.*" It does list those circumstances as including the "possibility of human error in using delay equipment." But it says *nothing* about a station's *inability to afford* delay equipment (a matter that in individual cases could itself prove debatable). All the FCC had to do was to *consider* this matter and either grant an exemption or explain why it did not grant an exemption. But it did not. And the result is a rule that may well chill coverage — the kind of consequence that the law has considered important for decades, to which the broadcasters pointed in their arguments before the FCC, and which the FCC nowhere discusses. . . .

III [OMITTED]

IV

Were the question a closer one, the doctrine of constitutional avoidance would nonetheless lead me to remand the case. . . . The doctrine assumes that Congress would prefer a less-than-optimal interpretation of its statute to the grave risk of a constitutional holding that would set the statute entirely aside. . . .

In sum, the FCC's explanation of its change leaves out two critically important matters underlying its earlier policy, namely *Pacifica* and local broadcasting coverage. Its explanation rests upon three considerations previously known to the agency ("coarseness," the "first blow," and running single expletives all day, one at a time). With one exception, it provides no empirical or other information explaining why those considerations, which did not justify its new policy before, justify it now. Its discussion of the one exception (technological advances in bleeping/delay systems), failing to take account of local broadcast coverage, is seriously incomplete.

I need not decide whether one or two of these features, standing alone, would require us to remand the case. Here all come together. And taken together they suggest that the FCC's answer to the question, "Why change?" is, "We like the new policy better." This kind of answer, might be perfectly satisfactory were it given by an elected official. But when given by an agency, in respect to a major change of an important policy where much more might be said, it is not sufficient. . . .

Notes and Questions

1. What reasons did the FCC give for its policy change? Why did Justice Scalia find them acceptable? What test did he apply? What does it mean for an agency to justify a change if not to explain why the new policy is better than the old policy?

2. Justice Breyer finds the FCC's reasons unpersuasive and insufficient. What test does he apply? If an old policy is workable, is the agency precluded from changing it, even if a new policy would be permissible if writing on blank slate? Recall Justice Breyer's dissenting opinion in *Milner v. Dep't of Navy*, 131 S. Ct. 1259, 1273 (2011) (Breyer, J., dissenting), excerpted in Chapter 4. There, he lamented the Court's willingness to jettison old but "workable" judicial interpretations in favor of new ones. Is this the agency counterpart? Aren't agencies created in part because they can interpret statutes dynamically? How might Justice Breyer respond?

3. Is this a case of "Congress made me do it"? Is this the independent-agency equivalent of "the President made me do it"? Recall *State Farm*. To what extent is politics a permissible basis for policy change? Is this the feature that divides Justice Scalia and Justice Breyer?

4. Related, should a heightened standard apply to independent agencies? Justice Scalia rejects any distinction, and Justice Breyer does not purport to create one. But why not create one?

5. What about Justice Breyer's suggestion of avoiding a constitutional question? Why does Justice Scalia dismiss that strategy? Based on your understanding, who has the better view of the avoidance canon?

6. And, finally, why were the other justices so motivated to write separately in this case? Focus especially on Justice Kennedy because he joined all but Part III-E of the Court's opinion. The FCC clearly lost here, but what is the law?

b. Empirical Evidence on Judicial Control of Agency Policymaking

Scholars have examined how often agencies are affirmed under arbitrary and capricious review. The leading study was conducted by Professor Cass Sunstein and Thomas Miles.

Cass R. Sunstein & Thomas J. Miles, Depoliticizing Administrative Law

58 Duke L.J. 2193, 2199-2207 (2009)

For a number of years, we have been studying judicial judgments in the domain of administrative law, in an effort to see whether those judgments reflect policy choices on the part of federal judges. For present purposes, our method can be simply described.

Within the courts of appeals, our focus has been on judicial review of decisions by the Environmental Protection Agency (EPA) and the National Labor Relations Board (NLRB). This approach has the advantage of investigating one important executive agency (the EPA) and one important independent agency (the NLRB); it also presents certain advantages in terms of coding. . . . [W]e attempted to categorize agency decisions as "liberal" or "conservative" by asking whether the challenge was made by a company or instead by a public interest group or a labor union. If, for example, the Sierra Club objected to an EPA decision, the decision was coded as conservative; if General Motors made the objection, the decision was coded as liberal. This method greatly eases the coding exercise, avoids controversial judgments that might divide reviewers, and thus improves administrability. It can also be defended in principle, because what matters is not whether the agency's decision is liberal or conservative in the abstract, but the political valence of the particular challenge before the court. . . . Admittedly, however, our proxy is crude. For that reason, we read the cases ourselves, and when our method led to an incorrect or contestable result, we adjusted the coding accordingly. . . .

We also examined whether judicial votes were issued by Republican or Democratic appointees to the federal bench, with the hypothesis that the division should operate as a proxy for political predilections, and with the further thought that the effect of the political affiliation of the appointing president is of considerable independent interest. With this method, we can investigate "liberal voting rates" for Democratic and Republican appointees in different domains. We can also compare the validation rate of both sets of appointees for conservative agency decisions and for liberal agency decisions. In addition to studying the effects of party, we can study the effects of panels, by asking whether the votes of Democratic or Republican appointees are affected by the political affiliation of the president who appointed the two other judges on the panel. . . .

The baseline case, for purposes of studying neutrality and partisanship, would show no significant disparities between Republican and Democratic appointees. If no such disparities were shown, existing administrative law doctrines would be "working" in the sense that they would be serving to filter out any effect from the most obvious and salient difference among appointees to the federal bench. And indeed, there are important areas of federal law in which partisan differences are not observed.

For the Supreme Court, we took the same basic approach. Here, however, we examined all decisions that cited *Chevron*; we did not restrict ourselves to the EPA or the NLRB. And instead of distinguishing between Republican and Democratic appointees, we assessed voting patterns for each of the individual justices and (to obtain greater statistical power) for "blocks" of justices corresponding to conventional judgments about ideological divisions. With this approach, we are able to see if political predilections affect the justices' voting in administrative law cases. Because only a small number of "arbitrariness" cases reach the Supreme Court, making statistical tests impossible, we did not investigate those cases. . . .

C. COURTS OF APPEALS: ARBITRARINESS CASES

. . . Here the question is not whether the agency's decision conforms to the governing statute, but whether its judgments of policy or fact are arbitrary on the merits (or unsupported by substantial evidence). Return to our three key tests for politicized voting, and notice the closely analogous pattern in *Chevron* cases:

1. When the agency's decision is liberal, the Democratic validation rate is 71%; when the agency's decision is conservative, the rate falls to 56%. The pattern is the opposite for Republican appointees—very close to the mirror image. When the agency's decision is liberal, the validation rate is 58%; when the agency's decision is conservative, the validation rate jumps to 72%.

2. When the agency's decision is liberal, Democratic appointees are 13% more likely to vote to validate it than are Republican appointees. When the agency's decision is conservative, Democratic appointees are 17% less likely to validate it than are Republican appointees.

3. The overall liberal voting rate is 68 percent for Democratic appointees; for Republican appointees, it is 56 percent. . . .

[H]ere too, unified panels explain a significant part of these disparities. On politically unified panels of Democratic appointees, the average validation rate is 23 percentage points higher when the agency decision is liberal than when it is conservative. And on politically unified panels of Republican appointees, the average validation rate is 28 percentage points lower when the agency decision is liberal than when it is conservative. Here as well, a form of group polarization seems to be at work. On mixed panels, by contrast, the partisan differences are greatly muted, perhaps because of a moderating or whistleblower effect. In those panels, existing doctrine is again "working," in the sense that judges' arbitrariness judgments do not greatly differ depending on the political affiliation of the appointing president.

Just one question, similar to one we raised above in connection with the deference frameworks: How important are these findings for advising your clients?

c. Judicial Control of Agency Procedure

Although reviewing courts have many tools for asserting control of agency action, there was a time when courts used a tool that the Supreme

Court subsequently prohibited. Specifically, these courts reversed notice-and-comment rules and remanded them with instructions that agencies add certain procedures—for example, oral hearings. Why would courts ask agencies to add such procedures? For about 800 years, the Anglo-American judicial process has relied on oral hearings, including cross-examination of live witnesses. The legislative process relies heavily on oral hearings as well; the transcript for the committee hearings regarding an important statutory proposal can run thousands of pages. There is thus a deeply embedded tendency in our legal system to see oral hearings as a means of obtaining the information necessary for a decision. In the adjudicatory setting, oral hearings also provide face-to-face participation that has a dignity value, but this value is of greatest concern when individual rights are involved.

The APA acknowledges the tendency toward oral hearings for some forms of agency action, but it does not require oral hearings for informal rulemaking—a major victory for the New Deal, or pro-agency forces when the APA was being drafted. *See* George B. Shepherd, *Fierce Compromise: The Administrative Procedure Act Emerges from New Deal Politics*, 90 Nw. U. L. Rev. 1557 (1996). Are supervising courts ever justified in imposing such a requirement and, if so, under what circumstances? In a number of cases, federal courts imposed what came to be known as "hybrid rulemaking" because it combined elements of informal rulemaking and formal adjudication, largely through the imposition of oral hearings or additional discovery. This practice came to an end as a result of the case that appears below.

Before we turn to the case, some background is helpful. The case involves the disposal of radioactive nuclear waste, which industrialized countries struggle to safely store. The Atomic Energy Commission (AEC) is responsible for licensing private companies to operate nuclear power plants and ensuring proper disposal of waste that they generate. Although the agency handles licensing on an individualized, plant-by-plant basis through adjudication, it decided to address waste disposal at a generalized level through notice-and-comment rulemaking. You can appreciate the advantage of this way of proceeding from the agency's perspective: the waste disposal issue arises in every license application and can be addressed simultaneously for all. After issuing the rule, the AEC granted Vermont Yankee its operating license, relying on the rule to address the issue of waste disposal from the proposed Vermont Yankee plant. The Natural Resources Defense Council (NRDC) challenged the AEC decision to grant the license by arguing that the rule was invalid and therefore the agency could not rely on it to deal with the waste disposal issue.

The Vermont Yankee nuclear power plant, in a photo taken for its license renewal application in 2006

In August 2007, one of the cooling towers at the plant collapsed

Vermont Yankee Nuclear Power Corp. v. Natural Resources Defense Council, Inc.

435 U.S. 519 (1978)

Mr. Justice REHNQUIST delivered the opinion of the Court.

In 1946, Congress enacted the Administrative Procedure Act, which as we have noted elsewhere was not only "a new, basic and comprehensive regulation of procedures in many agencies," *Wong Yang Sung v. McGrath*, 339 U.S. 33 (1950), but was also a legislative enactment which settled "long-continued and hard-fought contentions, and enacts a formula upon which opposing social and political forces have come to rest." *Id.*, at 40. Section 4 of the Act, 5 U.S.C. §553 (1976 ed.), dealing with rulemaking, requires in subsection (b) that "notice of proposed rulemaking shall be published in the *Federal Register* . . . ," describes the contents of that notice, and goes on to require in subsection (c) that after the notice the agency "shall give interested persons an opportunity to participate in the rule making through submission of written data, views, or arguments with or without opportunity for oral presentation. After consideration of the relevant matter presented, the agency shall incorporate in the rules adopted a concise general statement of their basis and purpose." Interpreting this provision of the Act in *United States v. Allegheny-Ludlum Steel Corp.*, 406 U.S. 742 (1972), and *United States v. Florida East Coast R. Co.*, 410 U.S. 224 (1973), we held that generally speaking this section of the Act established the maximum procedural requirements which Congress was willing to have the courts impose upon agencies in conducting rulemaking procedures. Agencies are free to grant additional procedural rights in the exercise of their discretion, but reviewing courts are generally not free to impose them if the agencies have not chosen to grant them. This is not to say necessarily that there are no circumstances which would ever justify a court in overturning agency action because of a failure to employ procedures beyond those required by the statute. But such circumstances, if they exist, are extremely rare.

Even apart from the Administrative Procedure Act this Court has for more than four decades emphasized that the formulation of procedures was basically to be left within the discretion of the agencies to which Congress had confided the responsibility for substantive judgments. In *FCC v. Schreiber*, 381 U.S. 279, 290 (1965), the Court explicated this principle, describing it as "an outgrowth of the congressional determination that administrative agencies and administrators will be familiar with the industries which they regulate and will be in a better position than federal courts or Congress itself to design procedural rules adapted to the peculiarities of the industry and the tasks of the agency involved."

It is in the light of this background of statutory and decisional law that we granted certiorari to review two judgments of the Court of Appeals for the District of Columbia Circuit because of our concern that they had seriously misread or misapplied this statutory and decisional law cautioning reviewing courts against engrafting their own notions of proper procedures upon agencies entrusted with substantive functions by Congress. 429 U.S. 1090 (1977). We conclude that the Court of Appeals has done just that in these cases, and we therefore remand them to it for further proceedings. . . .

I

A

Under the Atomic Energy Act of 1954, 68 Stat. 919, as amended, 42 U.S.C. §2011 *et seq.*, the Atomic Energy Commission was given broad regulatory authority over the development of nuclear energy. Under the terms of the Act, a utility seeking to construct and operate a nuclear power plant must obtain a separate permit or license at both the construction and the operation stage of the project. *See* 42 U.S.C. §§2133, 2232, 2235, 2239. In order to obtain the construction permit, the utility must file a preliminary safety analysis report, an environmental report, and certain information regarding the antitrust implications of the proposed project. *See* 10 CFR §§2.101, 50.30(f), 50.33a, 50.34(a) (1977). This application then undergoes exhaustive review by the Commission's staff and by the Advisory Committee on Reactor Safeguards (ACRS), a group of distinguished experts in the field of atomic energy. Both groups submit to the Commission their own evaluations, which then become part of the record of the utility's application. *See* 42 U.S.C. §§2039, 2232(b). The Commission staff also undertakes the review required by the National Environmental Policy Act of 1969 (NEPA), 83 Stat. 852, 42 U.S.C. §4321 et seq., and prepares a draft environmental impact statement, which, after being circulated for comment, 10 CFR §§51.22-51.25 (1977), is revised and becomes a final environmental impact statement. §51.26. Thereupon a three-member Atomic Safety and Licensing Board conducts a public adjudicatory hearing, 42 U.S.C. §2241, and reaches a decision which can be appealed to the Atomic Safety and Licensing Appeal Board, and currently, in the Commission's discretion, to the Commission itself. 10 CFR §§2.714, 2.721, 2.786, 2.787 (1977). The final agency decision may be appealed to the courts of appeals. 42 U.S.C. §2239; 28 U.S.C. §2342. The same sort of process occurs when the utility applies for a license to operate the plant, 10 CFR §50.34(b) (1977), except that a hearing need only be held in contested cases and may be limited to the matters in controversy. *See* 42 U.S.C. §2239(a); 10 CFR §2.105 (1977); 10 CFR pt. 2, App. A, V(f) (1977).

These cases arise from two separate decisions of the Court of Appeals for the District of Columbia Circuit. In the first, the court remanded a decision of the Commission to grant a license to petitioner Vermont Yankee Nuclear Power Corp. to operate a nuclear power plant. *Natural Resources Defense Council v. NRC*, 547 F.2d 633 (1976).

B

In December 1967, after the mandatory adjudicatory hearing and necessary review, the Commission granted petitioner Vermont Yankee a permit to build a nuclear power plant in Vernon, Vt. Thereafter, Vermont Yankee applied for an operating license. Respondent Natural Resources Defense Council (NRDC) objected to the granting of a license, however, and therefore a hearing on the application commenced on August 10, 1971. Excluded from consideration at the hearings, over NRDC's objection, was the issue of the environmental effects of operations to reprocess fuel or dispose of wastes resulting from the reprocessing operations. This ruling was affirmed by the Appeal Board in June 1972.

In November 1972, however, the Commission, making specific reference to the Appeal Board's decision with respect to the Vermont Yankee license, instituted rulemaking proceedings "that would specifically deal with the question of consideration of environmental effects associated with the uranium fuel cycle in the individual cost-benefit analyses for light water cooled nuclear power reactors." The notice of proposed rulemaking offered two alternatives, both predicated on a report prepared by the Commission's staff entitled Environmental Survey of the Nuclear Fuel Cycle. The first would have required no quantitative evaluation of the environmental hazards of fuel reprocessing or disposal because the Environmental Survey had found them to be slight. The second would have specified numerical values for the environmental impact of this part of the fuel cycle, which values would then be incorporated into a table, along with the other relevant factors, to determine the overall cost-benefit balance for each operating license. Much of the controversy in this case revolves around the procedures used in the rulemaking hearing which commenced in February 1973. In a supplemental notice of hearing the Commission indicated that while discovery or cross-examination would not be utilized, the Environmental Survey would be available to the public before the hearing along with the extensive background documents cited therein. All participants would be given a reasonable opportunity to present their position and could be represented by counsel if they so desired. Written and, time permitting, oral statements would be received and incorporated into the record. All persons giving oral statements would be subject to questioning by the Commission. At the conclusion of the hearing, a transcript would be made available to the public and the record would remain open for 30 days to allow the filing of supplemental written statements. *See generally id.*, at 361-363. More than 40 individuals and organizations representing a wide variety of interests submitted written comments. On January 17, 1973, the Licensing Board held a planning session to schedule the appearance of witnesses and to discuss methods for compiling a record. The hearing was held on February 1 and 2, with participation by a number of groups, including the Commission's staff, the United States Environmental Protection Agency, a manufacturer of reactor equipment, a trade association from the nuclear industry, a group of electric utility companies, and a group called Consolidated National Intervenors which represented 79 groups and individuals including respondent NRDC.

After the hearing, the Commission's staff filed a supplemental document for the purpose of clarifying and revising the Environmental Survey. Then the Licensing Board forwarded its report to the Commission without rendering any decision. The Licensing Board identified as the principal procedural question the propriety of declining to use full formal adjudicatory procedures. The major substantive issue was the technical adequacy of the Environmental Survey.

In April 1974, the Commission issued a rule which adopted the second of the two proposed alternatives described above. The Commission also approved the procedures used at the hearing, and indicated that the record, including the Environmental Survey, provided an "adequate data base for the regulation adopted." *Id.*, at 392. Finally, the Commission ruled that to the extent the rule differed from the Appeal Board decisions in Vermont Yankee "those decisions have no further precedential significance," *id.*, at 386, but that since "the environmental effects of the uranium fuel cycle have been shown to be relatively insignificant, . . . it is unnecessary to apply the amendment to applicant's environmental reports submitted prior to its effective date or to Final Environmental Statements for which Draft Environmental Statements have been circulated for comment prior to the effective date," *id.*, at 395.

Respondents appealed from both the Commission's adoption of the rule and its decision to grant Vermont Yankee's license to the Court of Appeals for the District of Columbia Circuit. . . .

D

With respect to the challenge of Vermont Yankee's license, the court first ruled that in the absence of effective rulemaking proceedings, the Commission must deal with the environmental impact of fuel reprocessing and disposal in individual licensing proceedings. The court then examined the rulemaking proceedings and, despite the fact that it appeared that the agency employed all the procedures required by 5 U.S.C. §553 (1976 ed.) and more, the court determined the proceedings to be inadequate and overturned the rule. Accordingly, the Commission's determination with respect to Vermont Yankee's license was also remanded for further proceedings. . . .

II

A

. . . [Vermont Yankee questions whether] the Commission may consider the environmental impact of the fuel processes when licensing nuclear reactors. In addition to the weight which normally attaches to the agency's determination of such a question, other reasons support the Commission's conclusion.

Vermont Yankee will produce annually well over 100 pounds of radioactive wastes, some of which will be highly toxic. The Commission itself, in a pamphlet published by its information office, clearly recognizes that these wastes "pose the most severe potential health hazard. . . ." U.S. Atomic Energy Commission, Radioactive Wastes 12 (1965). Many of these substances must be isolated for anywhere from 600 to hundreds of thousands of years. It is hard to argue that these wastes do not constitute "adverse environmental effects which cannot be avoided should the proposal be implemented," or that by operating nuclear power plants we are not making "irreversible and irretrievable commitments of resources." 42 U.S.C. §§4332(2)(C)(ii), (v). As the Court of Appeals recognized, the environmental impact of the radioactive wastes produced by a nuclear power plant is analytically indistinguishable from the environmental effects of "the stack gases produced by a coal-burning power plant." 547 F.2d, at 638. For these reasons we hold that the Commission acted well within its statutory authority when it considered the back end of the fuel cycle in individual licensing proceedings.

B

We next turn to the invalidation of the fuel cycle rule. . . .

[T]he majority of the Court of Appeals struck down the rule because of the perceived inadequacies of the procedures employed in the rulemaking proceedings. The court first determined the intervenors' primary argument to be "that the decision to preclude 'discovery or cross-examination' denied them a meaningful opportunity to participate in the proceedings as guaranteed by due process." 547 F.2d, at 643. The court then went on to frame the issue for decision thus:

> "Thus, we are called upon to decide whether the procedures provided by the agency were sufficient to ventilate the issues." *Ibid.*, at 346, 547 F.2d, at 643.

. . . [T]he ineluctable mandate of the court's decision is that the procedures afforded during the hearings were inadequate. This conclusion is particularly buttressed by the fact that after the court examined the record, particularly the testimony of Dr. Pittman, and declared it insufficient, the court proceeded to discuss at some length the necessity for further procedural devices or a more "sensitive" application of those devices employed during the proceedings. *Ibid.* The exploration of the record and the statement regarding its insufficiency might initially lead one to conclude that the court was only examining the sufficiency of the evidence, but the remaining portions of the opinion dispel any doubt that this was certainly not the sole or even the principal basis of the decision. Accordingly, we feel compelled to address the opinion on its own terms, and we conclude that it was wrong.

In prior opinions we have intimated that even in a rulemaking proceeding when an agency is making a " 'quasi-judicial' " determination by which a very small number of persons are " 'exceptionally affected, in each case upon individual grounds,' " in some circumstances additional procedures may be required in order to afford the aggrieved individuals due process. *United States v. Florida East Coast R. Co.*, 410 U.S., at 242-245, quoting from

Bi-Metallic Investment Co. v. State Board of Equalization, 239 U.S. 441, 446 (1915). It might also be true, although we do not think the issue is presented in this case and accordingly do not decide it, that a totally unjustified departure from well-settled agency procedures of long standing might require judicial correction.

But this much is absolutely clear. Absent constitutional constraints or extremely compelling circumstances the "administrative agencies 'should be free to fashion their own rules of procedure and to pursue methods of inquiry capable of permitting them to discharge their multitudinous duties.'" *FCC v. Schreiber*, 381 U.S., at 290, quoting from *FCC v. Pottsville Broadcasting Co.*, 309 U.S., at 143. Indeed, our cases could hardly be more explicit in this regard. The Court has, as we noted in *FCC v. Schreiber*, at 290, and n.17, upheld this principle in a variety of applications, including that case where the District Court, instead of inquiring into the validity of the Federal Communications Commission's exercise of its rulemaking authority, devised procedures to be followed by the agency on the basis of its conception of how the public and private interest involved could best be served. Examining §4(j) of the Communications Act of 1934, the Court unanimously held that the Court of Appeals erred in upholding that action. And the basic reason for this decision was the Court of Appeals' serious departure from the very basic tenet of administrative law that agencies should be free to fashion their own rules of procedure. . . .

"At least in the absence of substantial justification for doing otherwise, a reviewing court may not, after determining that additional evidence is requisite for adequate review, proceed by dictating to the agency the methods, procedures, and time dimension of the needed inquiry and ordering the results to be reported to the court without opportunity for further consideration on the basis of the new evidence by the agency. Such a procedure clearly runs the risk of 'propel[ling] the court into the domain which Congress has set aside exclusively for the administrative agency.' *SEC v. Chenery Corp.*, 332 U.S. 194, 196 (1947)." *Ibid.*

Respondent NRDC argues that §4 of the Administrative Procedure Act, 5 U.S.C. §553 (1976 ed.), merely establishes lower procedural bounds and that a court may routinely require more than the minimum when an agency's proposed rule addresses complex or technical factual issues or "Issues of Great Public Import." We have, however, previously shown that our decisions reject this view. We also think the legislative history, even the part which it cites, does not bear out its contention. The Senate Report explains what eventually became §4 thus:

> "This subsection states . . . the minimum requirements of public rule making procedure short of statutory hearing. Under it agencies might in addition confer with industry advisory committees, consult organizations, hold informal 'hearings,' and the like. Considerations of practicality, necessity, and public interest . . . will naturally govern the agency's determination of the extent to which public proceedings should go. Matters of great import, or those where the public submission of facts will be either useful to the agency or a protection to the public, should naturally be

accorded more elaborate public procedures." S. Rep. No. 752, 79th Cong., 1st Sess., 14-15 (1945).

The House Report is in complete accord. . . . And the Attorney General's Manual on the Administrative Procedure Act 31, 35 (1947), a contemporaneous interpretation previously given some deference by this Court because of the role played by the Department of Justice in drafting the legislation, further confirms that view. In short, all of this leaves little doubt that Congress intended that the discretion of the agencies and not that of the courts be exercised in determining when extra procedural devices should be employed.

There are compelling reasons for construing §4 in this manner. In the first place, if courts continually review agency proceedings to determine whether the agency employed procedures which were, in the court's opinion, perfectly tailored to reach what the court perceives to be the "best" or "correct" result, judicial review would be totally unpredictable. And the agencies, operating under this vague injunction to employ the "best" procedures and facing the threat of reversal if they did not, would undoubtedly adopt full adjudicatory procedures in every instance. Not only would this totally disrupt the statutory scheme, through which Congress enacted "a formula upon which opposing social and political forces have come to rest," *Wong Yang Sung v. McGrath*, 339 U.S., at 40, but all the inherent advantages of informal rulemaking would be totally lost.

Secondly, it is obvious that the court in these cases reviewed the agency's choice of procedures on the basis of the record actually produced at the hearing, 547 F.2d, at 644, and not on the basis of the information available to the agency when it made the decision to structure the proceedings in a certain way. This sort of Monday morning quarterbacking not only encourages but almost compels the agency to conduct all rulemaking proceedings with the full panoply of procedural devices normally associated only with adjudicatory hearings.

Finally, and perhaps most importantly, this sort of review fundamentally misconceives the nature of the standard for judicial review of an agency rule. The court below uncritically assumed that additional procedures will automatically result in a more adequate record because it will give interested parties more of an opportunity to participate in and contribute to the proceedings. But informal rulemaking need not be based solely on the transcript of a hearing held before an agency. Indeed, the agency need not even hold a formal hearing. *See* 5 U.S.C. §553(c) (1976 ed.). Thus, the adequacy of the "record" in this type of proceeding is not correlated directly to the type of procedural devices employed, but rather turns on whether the agency has followed the statutory mandate of the Administrative Procedure Act or other relevant statutes. If the agency is compelled to support the rule which it ultimately adopts with the type of record produced only after a full adjudicatory hearing, it simply will have no choice but to conduct a full adjudicatory hearing prior to promulgating every rule. In sum, this sort of unwarranted judicial examination of perceived procedural shortcomings of a rulemaking proceeding can do nothing but seriously interfere with that process prescribed by Congress. . . .

There remains, of course, the question of whether the challenged rule finds sufficient justification in the administrative proceedings that it should be upheld by the reviewing court. Judge Tamm, concurring in the result reached by the majority of the Court of Appeals, thought that it did not. There are also intimations in the majority opinion which suggest that the judges who joined it likewise may have thought the administrative proceedings an insufficient basis upon which to predicate the rule in question. We accordingly remand so that the Court of Appeals may review the rule as the Administrative Procedure Act provides. We have made it abundantly clear before that when there is a contemporaneous explanation of the agency decision, the validity of that action must "stand or fall on the propriety of that finding, judged, of course, by the appropriate standard of review. If that finding is not sustainable on the administrative record made, then the Comptroller's decision must be vacated and the matter remanded to him for further consideration." *Camp v. Pitts*, 411 U.S. 138, 143 (1973). *See also SEC v. Chenery Corp.*, 318 U.S. 80 (1943). The court should engage in this kind of review and not stray beyond the judicial province to explore the procedural format or to impose upon the agency its own notion of which procedures are "best" or most likely to further some vague, undefined public good.

1. Of course, the court must determine whether the agency complied with the procedures mandated by the relevant statutes. *Citizens to Preserve Overton Park v. Volpe*, 401 U.S. 402, 417, 91 S. Ct. 814, 824, 28 L. Ed. 2d 136 (1971). But, as we indicated above, there is little doubt that the agency was in full compliance with all the applicable requirements of the Administrative Procedure Act.

III

. . . Reversed and remanded.

Mr. Justice BLACKMUN and Mr. Justice POWELL took no part in the consideration or decision of these cases.

Notes and Questions

1. Given the national significance of the issue in the case, why did the agency only provide a cursory explanation of its policy? Should it have said more, or was the problem that it should have done more? What might additional procedures have done to improve safety?

2. Why did the Court reject the claim for procedures beyond those required by the APA? Does the APA clearly prohibit what has been called "hybrid rulemaking"—a process with elements of both formal and informal (notice-and-comment) rulemaking? Why is hybrid rulemaking different, or worse, than the reasoned decision-making requirement of *State Farm*? *See* Jack M. Beerman & Gary Lawson, *Reprocessing* Vermont Yankee, 75 GEO. WASH. L. REV. 856, 880-82 (2007). Are there any arguments that it is better? Answer the question by pondering which an agency would prefer: a remand for further consideration/explanation or a remand for further oral testimony/cross-examination? Note that *Vermont Yankee* speaks only to whether *courts* can require agencies to use procedures in addition to those required by the APA. Congress may require additional procedures in an organic statute and has done so from time to time. Agencies also may adopt additional procedures if they determine that such procedures are beneficial to their decision making.

3. How do we reconcile *Mead* and *Vermont Yankee*? *Mead* encourages agencies to choose certain procedural forms, such as notice-and-comment rulemaking, by conditioning *Chevron* deference on that choice. Is *Mead* distinguishable from *Vermont Yankee* because it encourages certain procedures rather than requires them? Note that the decisions together suggest that the agency will be subject to less judicial control if it acts through notice-and-comment rulemaking. Can you explain why?

4. Return to the fact that the APA explicitly permits an agency to proceed without an oral hearing when undertaking informal rulemaking, and that this provision was the result of a sustained political debate, carried out at the highest levels of our government, about the role of administrative agencies in the wake of the New Deal reforms. Consider also that it has turned out to be literally impossible for agencies to promulgate rules using the formal rulemaking procedures of the APA (§§553, 556, and 557), which require oral hearings. On the other hand, isn't there some value to demanding that agencies justify their rules more fully and gather adequate information to support their decisions? Given that this case involves the construction of a nuclear power plant, perhaps we should demand that regulations making it easier to construct such facilities be supported by adequate evidence?

A court cannot impose additional procedures, but it can insist that the ones that APA §553 affords are meaningful. What if the agency's decision is based on facts not disclosed in the record and therefore not available for public comment or judicial review? In a sense, *State Farm* involved this problem; if NHTSA had relied on President Reagan's platform of deregulation when issuing the passive restraints rescission, as Justice Rehnquist assumed, where was the evidence in the record? Surely an agency is not obligated to provide notice of or solicit comment on every piece of information that it receives. But what are the limits? When will it be arbitrary and capricious to fail to disclose information?

Perez v. Mortgage Bankers Assn.

135 S. Ct. 1199 (2015)

Justice SOTOMAYOR delivered the opinion of the Court.

When a federal administrative agency first issues a rule interpreting one of its regulations, it is generally not required to follow the notice-and-comment rulemaking procedures of the Administrative Procedure Act (APA or Act). See 5 U.S.C. §553(b)(A). The United States Court of Appeals for the District of Columbia Circuit has nevertheless held, in a line of cases beginning with *Paralyzed Veterans of Am. v. D.C. Arena L.P.*, 117 F. 3d 579 (1997), that an agency must use the APA's notice-and-comment procedures when it wishes to issue a new interpretation of a regulation that deviates significantly from one the agency has previously adopted. The question in these cases is whether the rule announced in *Paralyzed Veterans* is consistent with the APA. We hold that it is not.

I

A

The APA establishes the procedures federal administrative agencies use for "rulemaking," defined as the process of "formulating, amending, or repealing a rule." §551(5). "Rule," in turn, is defined broadly to include "statement[s] of general or particular applicability and future effect" that are designed to "implement, interpret, or prescribe law or policy." §551(4).

Section 4 of the APA, 5 U.S.C. §553, prescribes a three-step procedure for so-called "notice-and-comment rulemaking." First, the agency must issue a "[g]eneral notice of proposed rulemaking," ordinarily by publication in the Federal Register. §553(b). Second, if "notice [is] required," the agency must "give interested persons an opportunity to participate in the rule making through submission of written data, views, or arguments." §553(c). An agency must consider and respond to significant comments received during the period for public comment. See *Citizens to Preserve Overton Park, Inc. v. Volpe*, 401 U.S. 402, 416 (1971). Third, when the agency promulgates the final rule, it must include in the rule's text "a concise general statement of [its] basis and purpose." §553(c). Rules issued through the notice-and-comment process are often referred to as "legislative rules" because they have the "force and effect of law." Chrysler Corp. v. *Brown*, 441 U.S. 281, 302-303 (1979) (internal quotation marks omitted).

Not all "rules" must be issued through the notice-and-comment process. Section 4(b)(A) of the APA provides that, unless another statute states otherwise, the notice-and-comment requirement "does not apply" to "interpretative rules, general statements of policy, or rules of agency organization, procedure, or practice." 5 U.S.C. §553(b)(A). The term "interpretative rule," or "interpretive rule," is not further defined by the APA, and its precise meaning is the source of much scholarly and judicial debate. For our purposes, it suffices to say that the critical feature of interpretive rules is that they are "issued by an agency to advise the public of the agency's construction of the statutes and rules which it administers." *Shalala v. Guernsey Memorial Hospital*, 514 U.S. 87, 99 (1995) (internal quotation marks omitted). The absence of a notice-and-comment obligation makes the process of issuing interpretive rules comparatively easier for agencies than issuing legislative rules. But that convenience comes at a price: Interpretive rules "do not have the force and effect of law and are not accorded that weight in the adjudicatory process." *Ibid.*

B

These cases began as a dispute over efforts by the Department of Labor to determine whether mortgage-loan officers are covered by the Fair Labor Standards Act of 1938 (FLSA). The FLSA "establishe[s] a minimum wage and overtime compensation for each hour worked in excess of 40 hours in each workweek" for many employees. *Integrity Staffing Solutions, Inc. v. Busk*, 574 U.S. ___, ___ (2014) (slip op., at 3). Certain classes of employees, however, are exempt from these provisions. Among these exempt individuals are those "employed in a bona fide executive, administrative, or professional capacity . . . or in the capacity of outside salesman. . . ." §213(a)(1). The exemption for such employees is known as the "administrative" exemption.

The FLSA grants the Secretary of Labor authority to "defin[e]" and "delimi[t]" the categories of exempt administrative employees. *Ibid.* The Secretary's current regulations regarding the administrative exemption were promulgated in 2004 through a notice-and-comment rulemaking. As relevant here, the 2004 regulations differed from the previous regulations in that they contained a new section providing several examples of exempt administrative employees. See 29 CFR §541.203. One of the examples is "[e]mployees in the financial services industry," who, depending on the nature of their day-to-day work, "generally meet the duties requirements for the administrative exception." §541.203(b). The financial services example ends with a caveat, noting that "an employee whose primary duty is selling financial products does not qualify for the administrative exemption." *Ibid.*

In 1999 and again in 2001, the Department's Wage and Hour Division issued letters opining that mortgage-loan officers do not qualify for the administrative exemption. In other words, the Department concluded that the FLSA's minimum wage and maximum hour requirements applied to mortgage-loan officers. When the Department promulgated its current FLSA regulations in 2004, respondent Mortgage Bankers Association (MBA), a national trade association representing real estate finance companies, requested a new opinion interpreting the revised regulations. In 2006, the Department issued an opinion letter finding that mortgage loan officers fell within the administrative exemption under the 2004 regulations.

Four years later, however, the Wage and Hour Division again altered its interpretation of the FLSA's administrative exemption as it applied to mortgage-loan officers. Reviewing the provisions of the 2004 regulations and judicial decisions addressing the administrative exemption, the Department's 2010 Administrator's Interpretation concluded that mortgage-loan officers "have a primary duty of making sales for their employers, and, therefore, do not qualify" for the administrative exemption. The Department accordingly withdrew its 2006 opinion letter, which it now viewed as relying on "misleading assumption[s] and selective and narrow analysis" of the exemption example in §541.203(b). Like the 1999, 2001, and 2006 opinion letters, the 2010 Administrator's Interpretation was issued without notice or an opportunity for comment.

C

MBA filed a complaint in Federal District Court challenging the Administrator's Interpretation. MBA contended that the document was inconsistent with the 2004 regulation it purported to interpret, and thus arbitrary and capricious in violation of . . . the APA, 5 U.S.C. §706. More pertinent to this case, MBA also argued that the Administrator's Interpretation was procedurally invalid in light of the D. C. Circuit's decision in *Paralyzed Veterans*, 117 F. 3d 579. Under the *Paralyzed Veterans* doctrine, if "an agency has given its regulation a definitive interpretation, and later significantly revises that interpretation, the agency has in effect amended its rule, something it may not accomplish" under the APA "without notice and comment." *Alaska Professional Hunters Assn., Inc. v. FAA*, 177 F.3d 1030, 1034 (CADC 1999).

The District Court granted summary judgment to the Department. Though it accepted the parties' characterization of the Administrator's Interpretation as an interpretive rule, the District Court determined that the *Paralyzed Veterans* doctrine was inapplicable because MBA had failed to establish its reliance on the contrary interpretation expressed in the Department's 2006 opinion letter. The Administrator's Interpretation, the District Court further determined, was fully supported by the text of the 2004 FLSA regulations. The court accordingly held that the 2010 interpretation was not arbitrary or capricious.

The D.C. Circuit reversed. In the court's view, "[t]he only question" properly before it was whether the District Court had erred in requiring MBA to prove that it relied on the Department's prior interpretation. Explaining that reliance was not a required element of the *Paralyzed Veterans* doctrine, and noting the Department's concession that a prior, conflicting interpretation of the 2004 regulations existed, the D.C. Circuit concluded that the 2010 Administrator's Interpretation had to be vacated.

II

The *Paralyzed Veterans* doctrine is contrary to the clear text of the APA's rulemaking provisions, and it improperly imposes on agencies an obligation beyond the "maximum procedural requirements" specified in the APA, *Vermont Yankee Nuclear Power Corp. v. Natural Resources Defense Council, Inc.*, 435 U.S. 519, 524 (1978).

A

Section 4 of the APA provides that "notice of proposed rulemaking shall be published in the Federal Register." 5 U.S.C. §553(b). When such notice is required by the APA, "the agency shall give interested persons an opportunity to participate in the rule making." §553(c). But §4 further states that unless "notice or hearing is required by statute," the Act's notice-and-comment requirement "does not apply . . . to interpretative rules." §553(b)(A). This exemption of interpretive rules from the notice-and-comment process is categorical, and it is fatal to the rule announced in *Paralyzed Veterans*.

Rather than examining the exemption for interpretive rules contained in §4(b)(A) of the APA, the D.C. Circuit in *Paralyzed Veterans* focused its attention on §1 of the Act. That section defines "rulemaking" to include not only the initial issuance of new rules, but also "repeal[s]" or "amend[ments]" of existing rules. See §551(5). Because notice-and-comment requirements may apply even to these later agency actions, the court reasoned, "allow[ing] an agency to make a fundamental change in its interpretation of a substantive regulation without notice and comment" would undermine the APA's procedural framework. 117 F.3d, at 586.

This reading of the APA conflates the differing purposes of §§1 and 4 of the Act. Section 1 defines what a rulemaking is. It does not, however, say what procedures an agency must use when it engages in rulemaking. That is the purpose of §4. And §4 specifically exempts interpretive rules from the notice-and-comment requirements that apply to legislative rules. So, the D.C. Circuit correctly read §1 of the APA to mandate that agencies use the same procedures when they amend or repeal a rule as they used to issue the rule in the first instance. See *FCC v. Fox Television Stations, Inc.*, 556 U.S. 502, 515 (2009) (the APA "make[s] no distinction . . . between initial agency action and subsequent agency action undoing or revising that action"). Where the court went wrong was in failing to apply that accurate understanding of §1 to the exemption for interpretive rules contained in §4: Because an agency is not required to use notice-and-comment procedures to issue an initial interpretive rule, it is also not required to use those procedures when it amends or repeals that interpretive rule.

B

The straightforward reading of the APA we now adopt harmonizes with longstanding principles of our administrative law jurisprudence. Time and again, we have reiterated that the APA "sets forth the full extent of judicial authority to review executive agency action for procedural correctness." *Fox Television Stations, Inc.*, 556 U.S., at 513. Beyond the APA's minimum requirements, courts lack authority "to impose upon [an] agency its own notion of which procedures are 'best' or most likely to further some vague, undefined public good." *Vermont Yankee*, 435 U.S., at 549. To do otherwise would violate "the very basic tenet of administrative law that agencies should be free to fashion their own rules of procedure." *Id.*, at 544.

These foundational principles apply with equal force to the APA's procedures for rulemaking. We explained in *Vermont Yankee* that §4 of the Act "established the maximum procedural requirements which Congress was willing to have the courts impose upon agencies in conducting rulemaking procedures." *Id.*, at 524. "Agencies are free to grant additional procedural rights in the exercise of their discretion, but reviewing courts are generally not free to impose them if the agencies have not chosen to grant them." *Ibid.*

The *Paralyzed Veterans* doctrine creates just such a judge-made procedural right: the right to notice and an opportunity to comment when an agency changes its interpretation of one of the regulations it enforces. That requirement may be wise policy. Or it may not. Regardless, imposing such an obligation is the responsibility of Congress or the administrative agencies, not the courts. We trust that Congress weighed the costs and benefits of placing more rigorous procedural restrictions on the issuance of interpretive rules. See *id.*, at 523 (when Congress enacted the APA, it "settled long continued and hard-fought contentions, and enact[ed] a formula upon which opposing social and political forces have come to rest" (internal quotation marks omitted)). In the end, Congress decided to adopt standards that permit agencies to promulgate freely such rules —whether or not they are consistent with earlier interpretations. That the D.C. Circuit would have struck the balance differently does not permit that court or this one to overturn Congress' contrary judgment.

A [omitted]

B

In the main, MBA attempts to justify the *Paralyzed Veterans* doctrine on practical and policy grounds. MBA contends that the doctrine reinforces the APA's goal of "procedural fairness" by preventing agencies from unilaterally and unexpectedly altering their interpretation of important regulations.

There may be times when an agency's decision to issue an interpretive rule, rather than a legislative rule, is driven primarily by a desire to skirt notice-and-comment provisions. But regulated entities are not without recourse in such situations. Quite the opposite. The APA contains a variety of constraints on agency decisionmaking—the arbitrary and capricious standard being among the most notable. As we held in *Fox Television Stations*, and underscore again today, the APA requires an agency to provide more substantial justification when "its new policy rests upon factual findings that contradict those which underlay its prior policy; or when its prior policy has engendered serious reliance interests that must be taken into account. It would be arbitrary and capricious to ignore such matters." 556 U.S., at 515 (citation omitted); see also *id.*, at 535 (Kennedy, J., concurring in part and concurring in judgment). In addition, Congress is aware that agencies sometimes alter their views in ways that upset settled reliance interests. For that reason, Congress sometimes includes in the statutes it drafts safe-harbor provisions that shelter regulated entities from liability when they act in conformance with previous agency interpretations. . . . These safe harbors will often protect parties from liability when an agency adopts an interpretation that conflicts with its previous position . . .

For the foregoing reasons, the judgment of the United States Court of Appeals for the District of Columbia Circuit is reversed.

It is so ordered.

Notes and Questions

1. In the *Perez* opinion, you see the APA sections with which you are familiar referred to by unfamiliar section numbers. Don't let the unfamiliar section numbers confuse you; the U.S. Code reference usually follows. For example, the Court states that "Section 4 of the APA provides that 'notice of proposed rulemaking shall be published in the Federal Register.' 5 U.S.C. §553(b)."

2. When an agency amends its prior interpretation of a regulation, does it call into question whether the first (and second) interpretive rule is mere interpretation, entitled to exemption from notice-and-comment rulemaking procedures? Perhaps the interpretive rules make a substantive change to the regulation, which would require notice-and-comment rulemaking. The Court refused to consider whether the interpretive rules were really "legislative rules" because no one had made this claim in the case.

3. When an agency amends a prior interpretive rule, is it simply saying that the interpretive rule wrong from the start? If an agency can misinterpret its own regulation, how do we continue to justify *Auer* and its progeny, which accord agencies deference in interpreting their own regulations, in part on the ground that agencies best know what they mean?

4. *Perez* was a 9-0 decision. The Justices agree that courts may not impose procedures beyond what the APA specifies. Yet the Court is not unanimous as to what *State Farm* and the arbitrary and capricious test require when agencies change prior policy, see *Fox.* The Court is certain as to what procedures the APA requires but not as to what sort of explanation the APA requires to survive judicial review. What justifies this result? Is one an issue of congressional intent and the other a matter of judicial discretion? Would Congress see it that way?

United States v. Nova Scotia Food Products, Inc.

568 F.2d 240 (2d Cir. 1977)

Before WATERMAN and GURFEIN, Circuit Judges, and BLUMENFELD, District Judge.

GURFEIN, Circuit Judge:

. . . Appellant Nova Scotia receives frozen or iced whitefish in interstate commerce which it processes by brining, smoking and cooking. The fish are then sold as smoked whitefish.

The regulations . . . require that hot-process smoked fish be heated by a controlled heat process that provides a monitoring system positioned in as many strategic locations in the oven as necessary to assure a continuous temperature through each fish of not less than 180° F. for a minimum of 30 minutes for fish which have been brined to contain 3.5% water phase salt or at 150° F. for a minimum of 30 minutes if the salinity was at 5% water phase. Since *each* fish must meet these requirements, it is necessary to heat an entire batch of fish to even higher temperatures so that the lowest temperature for *any* fish will meet the minimum requirements.

Government inspection of appellants' plant established without question that the minimum T-T-S requirements were not being met. Appellants, on their part, do not defend on the ground that they were in compliance, but rather that the requirements could not be met if a marketable whitefish was to be produced. They defend upon the grounds that the regulation is invalid (1) because it is beyond the authority delegated by the statute; (2) because the FDA improperly relied upon undisclosed evidence in promulgating the regulation and because it is not supported by the administrative record; and (3) because there was no adequate statement setting forth the basis of the regulation. We reject the contention that the regulation is beyond the authority delegated by the statute, but we find serious inadequacies in the procedure followed in the promulgation of the regulation and hold it to be invalid as applied to the appellants herein.

The hazard which the FDA sought to minimize was the outgrowth and toxin formation of Clostridium botulinum Type E spores of the bacteria which sometimes inhabit fish. The Commissioner of Food and Drugs ("Commissioner"), employing informal "notice-and-comment" procedures . . . issued a proposal for the control of C. botulinum bacteria Type E in fish. Responding to the Commissioner's invitation in the notice of proposed rulemaking, members of the industry, including appellants and the intervenor-appellant, submitted comments on the proposed regulation.

The Commissioner thereafter issued the final regulations in which he adopted certain suggestions made in the comments, including a suggestion by the National Fisheries Institute, Inc. ("the Institute"), the intervenor herein.

The Commissioner did not answer the suggestion by the Bureau of Fisheries that nitrite and salt as additives could safely lower the high temperature otherwise required, a solution which the FDA had accepted in the case of chub. Nor did the Commissioner respond to the claim of Nova Scotia through its trade association, the Association of Smoked Fish Processors, Inc., Technical Center that "[t]he proposed process requirements suggested by the FDA for hot processed smoked fish are neither commercially feasible nor based on sound scientific evidence obtained with the variety of smoked fish products to be included under this regulation."

Nova Scotia, in its own comment, wrote to the Commissioner that "the heating of certain types of fish to high temperatures will completely destroy the product." It suggested, as an alternative, that "specific processing procedures could be established for each species after adequate work and experimention [sic] has been done but not before." We have noted above that the response given by the Commissioner was in general terms. He did not specifically aver that the T-T-S requirements as applied to whitefish were, in fact, commercially feasible.

When, after several inspections and warnings, Nova Scotia failed to comply with the regulation, an action by the United States Attorney for injunctive relief was filed on April 7, 1976, six years later, and resulted in the judgment here on appeal. . . .

The history of botulism occurrence in whitefish, as established in the trial record, which we must assume was available to the FDA in 1970, is as follows. Between 1899 and 1964 there were only eight cases of botulism reported as attributable to hot-smoked whitefish. In all eight instances, vacuum-packed whitefish was involved. All of the eight cases occurred in 1960 and 1963. The industry has abandoned vacuum-packing, and there has not been a single case of botulism associated with commercially prepared whitefish since 1963, though 2,750,000 pounds of whitefish are processed annually. Thus, in the seven-year period from 1964 through 1970, 17.25 million pounds of whitefish have been commercially processed in the United States without a single reported case of botulism. The evidence also disclosed that defendant Nova Scotia has been in business some 56 years, and that there has never been a case of botulism illness from the whitefish processed by it.

Interested parties were not informed of the scientific data, or at least of a selection of such data deemed important by the agency, so that comments could be addressed to the data. Appellants argue that unless the scientific data relied upon by the agency are spread upon the public records, criticism of the methodology used or the meaning to be inferred from the data is rendered impossible.

We agree with appellants in this case, for although we recognize that an agency may resort to its own expertise outside the record in an informal rulemaking procedure, we do not believe that when the pertinent research material is readily available and the agency has no special expertise on the precise parameters involved, there is any reason to conceal the scientific data relied upon from the interested parties. This is not a case where the agency methodology was based on material supplied by the interested parties themselves. Here all the scientific research was collected by the agency, and none of it was disclosed to interested parties as the material upon which the proposed rule would be fashioned. Nor was an articulate effort made to connect the scientific requirements to available technology that would make commercial survival possible, though the burden of proof was on the agency. . . .

Though a reviewing court will not match submission against countersubmission to decide whether the agency was correct in its conclusion on scientific matters (unless that conclusion is arbitrary), it will consider whether the agency has taken account of all "relevant factors and whether there has been a clear error of judgment." *Citizens to Preserve Overton Park v. Volpe*, 401 U.S. 402, 415-16 (1971). In this circuit we have said that "it is 'arbitrary or capricious' for an agency not to take into account all relevant factors in making its determination."

If the failure to notify interested persons of the scientific research upon which the agency was relying actually prevented the presentation of relevant comment, the agency may be held not to have considered all "the relevant factors." We can think of no sound reasons for secrecy or reluctance to expose to public view (with an exception for trade secrets or national security) the ingredients of the deliberative process. Indeed, the FDA's own regulations now specifically require that every notice of proposed rulemaking contain "references to all data and information on which the Commissioner relies for the proposal (copies or a full list of which shall be a part of the administrative file on the matter . . .)." . . .

We think that the scientific data should have been disclosed to focus on the proper interpretation of "insanitary conditions." When the basis for a proposed rule is a scientific decision, the scientific material which is believed to support the rule should be exposed to the view of interested parties for their comment. One cannot ask for comment on a scientific paper without allowing the participants to read the paper. Scientific research is sometimes rejected for diverse inadequacies of methodology; and statistical results are sometimes rebutted because of a lack of adequate gathering technique or of supportable extrapolation. Such is the stuff of scientific debate. To suppress meaningful comment by failure to disclose the basic data relied upon is akin to rejecting comment altogether. For unless there is common ground, the comments are unlikely to be of a quality that might impress a careful agency. The inadequacy of comment in turn leads in the direction of arbitrary decision-making. We do not speak of findings of fact, for such are not technically required in the informal rulemaking procedures. We speak rather of what the agency should make known so as to elicit comments that probe the fundamentals. Informal rulemaking does not lend itself to a rigid pattern. Especially, in the circumstance of our broad reading of statutory authority in support of the agency, we conclude that the failure to disclose to interested persons the scientific data upon which the FDA relied was procedurally erroneous. Moreover, the burden was upon the agency to articulate rationally why the rule should apply to a large and diverse class, with the same T-T-S parameters made applicable to all species. . . .

Appellants additionally attack the "concise general statement" required by APA, 5 U.S.C. § 553, as inadequate. We think that, in the circumstances, it was less than adequate. It is not in keeping with the rational process to leave vital questions, raised by comments which are of cogent materiality, completely unanswered. The agencies certainly have a good deal of discretion in expressing the basis of a rule, but the agencies do not have quite the prerogative of obscurantism reserved to legislatures. "Congress did not purport to transfer its legislative power to the unbounded discretion of the regulatory body." F.C.C. v. RCA Communications, Inc., 346 U.S. 86, 90 (1953) (Frankfurter, J.). . . .

The test of adequacy of the "concise general statement" was expressed by Judge McGowan in the following terms:

> "We do not expect the agency to discuss every item of fact or opinion included in the submissions made to it in informal rulemaking. We do expect that, if the judicial review which Congress has thought it important to provide is to be meaningful, the 'concise general statement of . . . basis and purpose' mandated by Section 4 will enable us to see what major issues of policy were ventilated by the informal proceedings and why the agency reacted to them as it did." Automotive Parts & Accessories Ass'n v. Boyd, 132 U.S. App. D.C. 200, 208, 407 F.2d 330, 338 (1968). . . .

The Secretary was squarely faced with the question whether it was necessary to formulate a rule with specific parameters that applied to all species of fish, and particularly whether lower temperatures with the addition of nitrite and salt would not be sufficient. Though this alternative was suggested by an agency of the federal government, its suggestion, though acknowledged, was never answered.

Moreover, the comment that to apply the proposed T-T-S requirements to whitefish would destroy the commercial product was neither discussed nor answered. We think that to sanction silence in the face of such vital questions would be to make the statutory requirement of a "concise general statement" less than an adequate safeguard against arbitrary decision-making. . . .

One may recognize that even commercial infeasibility cannot stand in the way of an overwhelming public interest. Yet the administrative process should disclose, at least, whether the proposed regulation is considered to be commercially feasible, or whether other considerations prevail even if commercial infeasibility is acknowledged. This kind of forthright disclosure and basic statement was lacking in the formulation of the T-T-S standard made applicable to whitefish. It is easy enough for an administrator to ban everything. In the regulation of food processing, the worldwide need for food also must be taken into account in formulating measures taken for the protection of health. In the light of the history of smoked whitefish to which we have referred, we find no articulate balancing here sufficient to make the procedure followed less than arbitrary. . . .

We hold in this enforcement proceeding, therefore, that the regulation, as it affects non-vacuum-packed hot-smoked whitefish, was promulgated in an arbitrary manner and is invalid.

Notes and Questions

1. Isn't the purpose of the notice-and-comment requirement to allow people to comment on the proposed rule and induce the agency to change the proposed rule where it can be improved? If so, doesn't the court's demanding requirement in this case create the danger of an infinite regress? The court addressed this issue in a footnote, stating: "We recognize the problem that a proceeding might never end if such submission required a reply ad infinitum." Its response was that "the exposure of the scientific research relied on simply would have required a single round of comment addressed thereto." Is this response adequate? In Rybacheck v. EPA, 904 F.2d 1276 (9th Cir. 1990), "Rosalie A. Rybacheck, North Pole, Alaska, pro se," and others complained that the EPA had added "6,000 pages to the administrative record, after the public review-and-comment period had ended." In rejecting the claim that this violated the APA, the court said: "Nothing prohibits the Agency from adding supporting documentation for a final rule in response to public comments. In fact, adherence to the Rybachecks' view might result in the EPA's never being able to issue a final rule capable of standing up to review: every time the Agency responded to public comments, such as those in this rulemaking, it would trigger a new comment period. Thus, either the comment period would continue in a never-ending circle, or, if the EPA chose not to respond to the last set of public comments, any final rule could be struck down for lack of support in the record." Is that response adequate? Is there a basic contradiction between the purpose of notice (to alert or warn) and the purpose of the comments (to revise) in the way §553 is designed?

2. Was the court especially critical of the agency's failure to disclose the basis for its decision because the missing information was scientific data? Why might the failure to disclose scientific data be of particular concern for a court? Would it constitute a "science charade," in Professor Wagner's terms (see Chapter 5)?

3. Why was the FDA so unwilling to make distinctions among different kinds of fish? Did you notice that "species by species" determination was proposed not only by the fishing industry's trade organization but also by the Department of the Interior's Bureau of Commercial Fisheries? It is one thing to reject suggestions from an interested party, but quite another to reject suggestions from another federal agency that has greater expertise on an issue (the FDA deals with food generally, but the Bureau specializes in commercial fish).

4. Stepping back, was the court enforcing the procedural requirements of the APA in this case, or was it reversing a substantively unfair and sloppy decision by the agency? Was it serving notice to agencies that they need to cooperate with each other, that one agency should not ignore the more expert advice of another just because it has jurisdiction of the matter? Are these appropriate roles for the courts to play? The obverse of the issue of turf battles, noted above, is the issue of effective cooperation among agencies.

———————

Now consider "*ex parte* contacts," which are communications between the agency and an individual off the record. The APA prohibits an agency from receiving *ex parte* contacts or relying on them when making decisions "on the record after opportunity for agency hearing," §557—in other words, when making decisions through formal adjudication or formal rulemaking. But the APA does not speak to *ex parte* contacts in the context of informal actions, such as notice-and-comment rulemaking. Should courts take this silence as permitting *ex parte* contacts in notice-and-comment rulemaking? Should courts nevertheless treat such contacts like the President's plat-form—requiring disclosure of all information that the agency considered under the arbitrary and capricious standard? The Supreme Court has not addressed the issue of *ex parte* contacts in notice-and-comment rulemaking. Consider the following decision.

Home Box Office v. FCC

567 F.2d 9 (D.C. Cir. 1977)

Before WRIGHT and MACKINNON, Circuit Judges, and WEIGEL, District Judge.

PER CURIAM:

In these 15 cases, consolidated for purposes of argument and deci-sion, petitioners challenge various facets of four orders of the Federal Communications Commission which, taken together, regulate and limit the program fare "cablecasters" and "subscription broadcast television stations" may offer to the public for a fee set on a per-program or per-channel basis.

At the heart of these cases are the Commission's "pay cable" rules [which] restrict sharply the ability of cablecasters to present feature film and sports programs if a separate program or channel charge is made for this material.

[After considering various other challenges to these rules, the Court proceeded to the following:]

During the pendency of this proceeding Mr. Henry Geller, a participant before the Commission and an *amicus* here, filed with the Commission a "Petition for Revision of Procedures or for Issuance of Notice of Inquiry or Proposed Rule Making." In this petition *amicus* Geller sought to call the Commission's attention to what were alleged to be violations in these pro-ceedings of the *ex parte* communications doctrine set out by this court in *Sangamon Valley Television Corp. v. United States,* 106 U.S. App. D.C. 30, 269 F.2d 221 (1959). The Commission took no action in response to the peti-tion, and *amicus* now presses us to set aside the orders under review here because of procedural infirmity in their promulgation.

It is apparently uncontested that a number of participants before the Commission sought out individual commissioners or Commission employ-ees for the purpose of discussing *ex parte* and in confidence the merits of the rules under review here. In fact, the Commission itself solicited such communications in its notices of proposed rulemaking. In an attempt to clarify the facts this court *sua sponte* ordered the Commission to provide "a list of all of the *ex parte* presentations, together with the details of each, made to it, or to any of its members or representatives, during the rulemaking proceedings." In response to this order the Commission filed a document over 60 pages long which revealed, albeit imprecisely, widespread *ex parte* communications involving virtually every party before this court, including *amicus* Geller.

Although it is impossible to draw any firm conclusions about the effect of *ex parte* presentations upon the ultimate shape of the pay cable rules, the evidence is certainly consistent with often-voiced claims of undue industry influence over Commission proceedings, and we are particularly concerned that the final shaping of the rules we are reviewing here may have been by compromise among the contending industry forces, rather than by exercise of the independent discretion in the public interest the Communications Act vests in individual commissioners. Our concern is heightened by the submission of the Commission's Broadcast Bureau to this court which states that in December 1974 broadcast representatives "described the kind of pay cable regulation that, in their view, broadcasters 'could live with.'" If actual positions were not revealed in public comments, as this statement would suggest, and, further, if the Commission relied on these apparently more candid private discussions in framing the final pay cable rules, then the elaborate public discussion in these dockets has been reduced to a sham.

Even the possibility that there is here one administrative record for the public and this court and another for the Commission and those "in the know" is intolerable. Whatever the law may have been in the past, there can now be no doubt that implicit in the decision to treat the promulgation of rules as a "final" event in an ongoing process of administration is an assumption that an act of reasoned judgment has occurred, an assumption which further contemplates the existence of a body of material—documents, comments, transcripts, and statements in various forms declaring agency expertise or policy—with reference to which such judgment was exercised. Against this material, "the full administrative record that was before [an agency official] at the time he made his decision," *Citizens to Preserve Overton Park, Inc. v. Volpe,* 401 U.S. at 420, it is the obligation of this court to test the actions of the Commission for arbitrariness or inconsistency with delegated authority. Yet here agency secrecy stands between us and fulfillment of our obligation. As a practical matter, *Overton Park*'s mandate means that the public record must reflect what representations were made to an agency so that relevant information supporting or refuting those representations may be brought to the attention of the reviewing courts by persons participating in agency proceedings. This course is obviously foreclosed if communications are made to the agency in secret and the agency itself does not disclose the information presented. Moreover, where, as here, an agency justifies its actions by reference only to information in the public file while failing to disclose the substance of other relevant information that has been presented to it, a reviewing court cannot presume that the agency has acted properly, but must treat the agency's justifications as a fictional account of the actual decisionmaking process and must perforce find its actions arbitrary.

The failure of the public record in this proceeding to disclose all the information made available to the Commission is not the only inadequacy we find here. Even if the Commission had disclosed to this court the substance of what was said to it *ex parte*, it would still be difficult to judge the truth of what the Commission asserted it knew about the television industry because we would not have the benefit of an adversarial discussion among the parties. The importance of such discussion to the proper functioning of the agency decisionmaking and judicial review processes is evident in our cases. We have insisted, for example, that information in agency files or consultants' reports which the agency has identified as relevant to the proceeding be disclosed to the parties for adversarial comment. Similarly, we have required agencies to set out their thinking in notices of proposed rulemaking. This requirement not only allows adversarial critique of the agency but is perhaps one of the few ways that the public may be apprised of what the agency thinks it knows in its capacity as a repository of expert opinion. From a functional standpoint, we see no difference between assertions of fact and expert opinion tendered by the public, as here, and that generated internally in an agency: each may be biased, inaccurate, or incomplete — failings which adversary comment may illuminate. Indeed, the potential for bias in private presentations in rulemakings which resolve "conflicting private claims to a valuable privilege," seems to us greater than in cases where we have reversed agencies for failure to disclose internal studies. We do not understand the rulemaking procedures adopted by the Commission to be inconsistent with these views since those procedures provide for a dialogue among interested parties through provisions for comment, reply-comment, and subsequent oral argument. What we do find baffling is why the Commission, which apparently recognizes that ready availability of private contacts saps the efficacy of the public proceedings, nonetheless continues the practice of allowing public and private comments to exist side by side.

Equally important is the inconsistency of secrecy with fundamental notions of fairness implicit in due process and with the ideal of reasoned decisionmaking on the merits which undergirds all of our administrative law. This inconsistency was recognized in *Sangamon,* and we would have thought that the principles announced there so clearly governed the instant proceeding that there could be no question of the impropriety of *ex parte* contacts here. Certainly any ambiguity in how *Sangamon* should be interpreted has been removed by recent congressional and presidential actions. In the Government in the Sunshine Act, for example, Congress has declared it to be "the policy of the United States that the public is entitled to the fullest practicable information regarding the decisionmaking processes of the Federal Government," and has taken steps to guard against *ex parte* contacts in formal agency proceedings. Perhaps more closely on point is Executive Order 11920 (1976), which prohibits *ex parte* contacts with members of the White House staff by those seeking to influence allocation of international air routes during the time route certifications are before the President for his approval. The President's actions under Section 801 of the Federal

Aviation Act are clearly not adjudication, nor even quasi-judicial. Instead, the closest analogue is precisely that of *Sangamon*: informal official action allocating valuable privileges among competing private parties. Thus this is a time when all branches of government have taken steps "designed to better assure fairness and to avoid suspicions of impropriety," White House Fact Sheet on Executive Order 11920 (June 10, 1976), and consequently we have no hesitation in concluding with *Sangamon* that due process requires us to set aside the Commission's rules here.

From what has been said above, it should be clear that information gathered *ex parte* from the public which becomes relevant to a rulemaking will have to be disclosed at some time. On the other hand, we recognize that informal contacts between agencies and the public are the "bread and butter" of the process of administration and are completely appropriate so long as they do not frustrate judicial review or raise serious questions of fairness. Reconciliation of these considerations in a manner which will reduce procedural uncertainty leads us to conclude that communications which are received prior to issuance of a formal notice of rulemaking do not, in general, have to be put in a public file. Of course, if the information contained in such a communication forms the basis for agency action, then, under well-established principles, that information must be disclosed to the public in some form. Once a notice of proposed rulemaking has been issued, however, any agency official or employee who is or may reasonably be expected to be involved in the decisional process of the rulemaking proceeding, should "refus[e] to discuss matters relating to the disposition of a [rulemaking proceeding] with any interested private party, or an attorney or agent for any such party, prior to the [agency's] decision," Executive Order 11920, §4. If *ex parte* contacts nonetheless occur, we think that any written document or a summary of any oral communication must be placed in the public file established for each rulemaking docket immediately after the communication is received so that interested parties may comment thereon. *Compare* Executive Order 11920, §5.

Therefore, we today remand the record to the Commission for supplementation with instructions "to hold, with the aid of a specially appointed hearing examiner, an evidential hearing to determine the nature and source of all *ex parte* pleas and other approaches that were made to" the Commission or its employees after the issuance of the first notice of proposed rulemaking in these dockets. "All parties to the former proceeding and to the present review may on request participate fully in the evidential hearing," and may further participate in any proceedings before the Commission which it may hold for the purpose of evaluating the report of the hearing examiner.

Notes and Questions

1. *Home Box Office* involves a tension between the operation of modern administrative governance and the basic principle of democratic governance.

Agencies often must rely on outside contacts to gain information about decisions; an agency must do considerable work in order to commence a rulemaking, and it must continue to listen and learn throughout the process. Without the ability to talk to affected interests, the agency would be severely limited in its ability to identify problems and formulate proposed responses. For this reason, as the court in *Home Box Office* recognized, *ex parte* contacts are the "bread and butter" of notice-and-comment rulemaking. At the same time, *ex parte* contacts run counter to the requirement that the people, and the representatives who they elect, know what government agents are doing. Agencies should not receive or share information in private or secret, off the record.

As noted in the *Home Box Office* opinion, all of the three governmental actors that are discussed in this chapter have made concerted efforts to resolve this tension. The President promulgated an executive order to prohibit *ex parte* contacts in certain circumstances; Congress passed the Government in the Sunshine Act, which increases transparency of meetings and documents; and courts (though not the Supreme Court) have handed down opinions requiring agencies to disclose any *ex parte* contacts on which they rely. We have already looked at the nature of executive orders and legislation as means of control; the focus here is on judicial decisions. The court uses the actions of the other two branches as a justification for its own action, arguing that they reflect a general public policy of disclosure. Should courts reflect the same policy as the other branches or should they be more deferential for the same sort of reasons that they should be deferential under *Chevron* (i.e., the agency is best suited to balance the need for off-the-record information against the need for public disclosure)?

2. To what extent is *Home Box Office* a natural outgrowth of *Overton Park*? A reviewing court needs a record, and *ex parte* contacts may subvert that record precisely because they occur outside the record. This logic seems sound enough, but isn't there a worry? Once a court demands a record, isn't there a natural tendency to actually *expand* the scope of items included in that record? It is hard to argue against the idea that the court will be better able to determine the quality of the agency's decision if it has more information about the basis of that decision. If *Home Box Office* allows courts to demand that agencies keep more extensive records of their meetings, contacts, research, etc., what is the stopping point? Is there a way to formulate the rule in *Home Box Office* to keep courts in check?

3. Does the whole concept of *ex parte* contacts make sense in the informal rulemaking setting? *See* Edward Rubin, *It's Time to Make the Administrative Procedure Act Administrative*, 89 CORNELL L. REV. 95, 111-12, 119-20 (2003):

> [T]he pre-administrative model on which informal rulemaking is based, the enactment of a statute by a legislature, does not include procedural requirements. While there are techniques for legislation, and every legislature adopts internal rules of procedure, the only procedural requirements involve the rules for valid enactment. . . . [T]he APA, finding that the analogy between informal rulemaking and legislation provides no guidance for procedural requirements, resorts to the only other model of traditional

governmental action, namely, adjudication. The APA's requirements of notice, comments, and a statement of basis and purpose reiterate, in a diluted and adapted form, the due process requirements of notice, a hearing, and an impartial decision maker for adjudicatory decisions. As Peter Strauss, Todd Rakoff, and Cynthia Farina have suggested, [Gellhorn and Byse's ADMINISTRATIVE LAW: CASES AND COMMENTS 510-15, 549 (10th ed. 2003),] courts expand the adjudicatory implications of the statute because of their own familiarity with the adjudicatory process. The result is that rulemaking, although conceived as agency legislation, has been subjected to requirements that are largely judicial in nature.

The prohibition of ex parte contacts emanates from the basic character of adjudication as an adversary proceeding with a decision "on the record" by an impartial decision maker. Ex parte contacts deprive one party of an opportunity to become aware of and contest the assertions that the other party is advancing. To the extent that ex parte contacts serve as the basis for decision, they violate the principle that the decision may refer only to evidence presented as part of a formal record. In addition, because these contacts are not monitored by any outside party, they create a risk that the decision maker's neutrality may be compromised by threats, bribes, or flattery. These provisions do not apply to informal rulemaking under §553, of course, and their underlying rationale is equally inapplicable. Informal rulemaking is not an adversarial proceeding—it is explicitly not a decision on the record—and it does not require an impartial decision maker. On the contrary, policy makers are expected to collect empirical data on a wide variety of issues from a wide variety of sources, and much of this data gathering is necessarily ex parte. Moreover, the diffuse and open-ended nature of the comment process means that there will be no parties, in the traditional sense, but rather a number of interest groups with complex, cross-cutting relationships to each other.

The quasi-adjudicatory conception that lies behind the notice and comment provisions of §553, however, seems to demand some limit on ex parte contacts. If the agency can consult anyone it chooses at any time, what is the point of the comment process? There is something vaguely troubling, especially to a judge, about the image of all those legally required written comments flowing in, to be time-stamped and filed by the back-room myrmidons, while interest group representatives whisper into the ears of the agency's top officials over steak and champagne dinners. Having promulgated its preliminary regulation and established a delimited comment period of sixty or ninety days, it would seem that these officials should devote their attention to the comments and make their revisions on the basis of the ideas and information they receive. A ban on ex parte contacts during this period seems necessary if the ultimate decision is to be based on the reasoned arguments of the commenting parties.

4. The general view is that *Home Box Office* is not a valid interpretation of the APA. It has been disparaged by commentators, and another panel of the same court handed down a contrary decision shortly thereafter, Action for Children's Television v. FCC, 564 F.2d 458 (D.C. Cir. 1977):

Citizens to Preserve Overton Park, Inc. v. Volpe, a somewhat Delphic opinion concerning informal administrative action rather than informal rulemaking . . . should not be read as mandating that the public record upon which our review is based reflect every informational input that may have entered into the decisionmaker's deliberative process. If we go as far as *Home Box Office* does in its ex parte ruling in ensuring a "whole record" for our review, why not go further to require the decisionmaker to summarize and make available for public comment every status inquiry from a Congressman or any germane material[—]say a newspaper editorial[—]that he or she reads or their evening-hour ruminations? In the end, why not administer a lie-detector test to ascertain whether the required summary is an accurate and complete one? The problem is obviously a matter of degree, and the appropriate line must be drawn somewhere. In light of what must be presumed to be Congress' intent not to prohibit or require disclosure of all ex parte contacts during or after the public comment stage, we would draw that line at the point where the rulemaking proceedings involve "competing claims to a valuable privilege." It is at that point where the potential for unfair advantage outweighs the practical burdens, which we imagine would not be insubstantial, that such a judicially conceived rule would place upon administrators.

[R]ule making is a vital part of the administrative process, particularly adapted to and needful for sound evolution of policy . . . [and] is not to be shackled, in the absence of clear and specific Congressional requirement, by importation of formalities developed for the adjudicatory process and basically unsuited for policy rule making. [W]e believe that the nature of the proceedings was not of the kind that made this rulemaking action susceptible to poisonous ex parte influence. Private groups were not competing for a specific valuable privilege. Furthermore, this case does not raise serious questions of fairness. Not only were no rules adopted for the time being in our case, but the Commission's Children's Television Report demonstrates that the agency in good faith examined all the relevant factors raised during the comment stage, and comprehensively and rationally justified its decision to proceed cautiously by giving industry self-regulation a chance to prove that it could be effective.

5. Despite this judicial view, the principle of *Home Box Office* seems to have prevailed as a matter of administrative practice. Most agencies have codified its holding as a matter of their own internal procedures. This can be read as executive control, not judicial control, and to some extent, it is. But the executive has exercised this control by presenting its commands as a means of ensuring that the regulation in question is not invalidated by the courts, which means of course, that the executive is responding to, or reflecting, judicial control. On the other hand, because it is unclear that other courts will in fact follow *Home Box Office*, something more complex may be going on. Perhaps judicial decisions, even if they will not necessarily be followed in the future, can exercise powerful in terrorem effects, inducing major alterations in behavior as agency officials seek to avoid even a remote risk of judicial reversal.

d. Judicial Control of Agency Fact-Finding

When an agency is required to follow formal procedures, the "substantial evidence" standard of APA §706 applies to agency fact-finding.[7] That standard sounds more "substantial" than the arbitrary and capricious test. But what exactly does it entail?

Universal Camera v. National Labor Relations Board

340 U.S. 474 (1951)

Justice FRANKFURTER delivered the opinion of the Court.

The essential issue raised by this case . . . is the effect of the Administrative Procedure Act and the legislation colloquially known as the Taft-Hartley Act,

---

7. The Supreme Court has stated that an agency is not required to use formal rulemaking procedures, as opposed to informal rulemaking procedures, unless the relevant statute uses the exact formulation "on the record after opportunity for an agency hearing" from APA §553. *See* United States v. Florida East Coast Ry., 410 U.S. 224 (1973).

on the duty of Courts of Appeals when called upon to review orders of the National Labor Relations Board.

The Court of Appeals for the Second Circuit granted enforcement of an order directing, in the main, that petitioner reinstate with back pay an employee found to have been discharged because he gave testimony under the Wagner Act, and cease and desist from discriminating against any employee who files charges or gives testimony under that Act. The court below, Judge Swan dissenting, decreed full enforcement of the order. Because the views of that court regarding the effect of the new legislation on the relation between the Board and the courts of appeals in the enforcement of the Board's orders conflicted with those of the Court of Appeals for the Sixth Circuit we brought both cases here. . . .

I

Want of certainty in judicial review of Labor Board decisions partly reflects the intractability of any formula to furnish definiteness of content for all the impalpable factors involved in judicial review. But in part doubts as to the nature of the reviewing power and uncertainties in its application derive from history, and to that extent an elucidation of this history may clear them away.

The Wagner Act provided: "The findings of the Board as to the facts, if supported by evidence, shall be conclusive." Act of July 5, 1935, §10(e), 49 Stat. 449, 454, 29 U.S.C. §160(e), 29 U.S.C.A. §160(e). This Court read "evidence" to mean "substantial evidence," *Washington, V. & M. Coach Co. v. Labor Board*, 301 U.S. 142, and we said that "[s]ubstantial evidence is more than a mere scintilla. It means such relevant evidence as a reasonable mind might accept as adequate to support a conclusion." *Consolidated Edison Co. v. National Labor Relations Board*, 305 U.S. 197, 229. Accordingly, it "must do more than create a suspicion of the existence of the fact to be established . . . it must be enough to justify, if the trial were to a jury, a refusal to direct a verdict when the conclusion sought to be drawn from it is one of fact for the jury." *National Labor Relations Board v. Columbian Enameling & Stamping Co.*, 306 U.S. 292, 300.

The very smoothness of the "substantial evidence" formula as the standard for reviewing the evidentiary validity of the Board's findings established its currency. But the inevitably variant applications of the standard to conflicting evidence soon brought contrariety of views and in due course bred criticism. Even though the whole record may have been canvassed in order to determine whether the evidentiary foundation of a determination by the Board was "substantial," the phrasing of this Court's process of review readily lent itself to the notion that it was enough that the evidence supporting the Board's result was "substantial" when considered by itself. If is fair to say that by imperceptible steps regard for the fact-finding function of the Board led to the assumption that the requirements of the Wagner Act were met when the reviewing court could find in the record evidence which, when viewed in isolation, substantiated the Board's findings. . . .

Criticism of so contracted a reviewing power reinforced dissatisfaction felt in various quarters with the Board's administration of the Wagner Act in the years preceding the war. The scheme of the Act was attacked as an inherently unfair fusion of the functions of prosecutor and judge. Accusations of partisan bias were not wanting. The "irresponsible admission and weighing of hearsay, opinion, and emotional speculation in place of factual evidence" was said to be a "serious menace." No doubt some, perhaps even much, of the criticism was baseless and some surely was reckless. What is here relevant, however, is the climate of opinion thereby generated and its effect on Congress. Protests against "shocking injustices and intimations of judicial abdication" with which some courts granted enforcement of the Board's order stimulated pressures for legislative relief from alleged administrative excesses.

The strength of these pressures was reflected in the passage in 1940 of the Walter-Logan Bill. It was vetoed by President Roosevelt, partly because it imposed unduly rigid limitations on the administrative process, and partly because of the investigation into the actual operation of the administrative process then being conducted by an experienced committee appointed by the Attorney General. It is worth noting that despite its aim to tighten control over administrative determinations of fact, the Walter-Logan Bill contented itself with the conventional formula that an agency's decision could be set aside if "the findings of fact are not supported by substantial evidence."

The final report of the Attorney General's Committee was submitted in January, 1941. The majority concluded that "[d]issatisfaction with the existing standards as to the scope of judicial review derives largely from dissatisfaction with the fact-finding procedures now employed by the administrative bodies." Departure from the "substantial evidence" test, it thought, would either create unnecessary uncertainty or transfer to courts the responsibility for ascertaining and assaying matters the significance of which lies outside judicial competence. Accordingly, it recommended against legislation embodying a general scheme of judicial review.

Three members of the Committee registered a dissent. Their view was that the "present system or lack of system of judicial review" led to inconsistency and uncertainty. They reported that under a "prevalent" interpretation of the "substantial evidence" rule "if what is called 'substantial evidence' is found anywhere in the record to support conclusions of fact," the courts are said to be obliged to sustain the decision without reference to how heavily the countervailing evidence may preponderate—unless indeed the stage of arbitrary decision is reached. Under this interpretation, the courts need to read only one side of the case and, if they find any evidence there, the administrative action is to be sustained and the record to the contrary is to be ignored. Their view led them to recommend that Congress enact principles of review applicable to all agencies not excepted by unique characteristics. One of these principles was expressed by the formula that judicial review could extend to "findings, inferences, or conclusions of fact unsupported, upon the whole record, by substantial evidence." So far as the history of this movement for enlarged review reveals, the phrase "upon the whole record" makes its first appearance in this recommendation of the minority of the Attorney General's Committee. This evidence of the close relationship between the phrase and the criticism out of which it arose is important, for the substance of this formula for judicial review found its way into the statute books when Congress with unquestioning—we might even say uncritical—unanimity enacted the Administrative Procedure Act.

One is tempted to say "uncritical" because the legislative history of that Act hardly speaks with that clarity of purpose which Congress supposedly furnishes courts in order to enable them to enforce its true will. On the one hand, the sponsors of the legislation indicated that they were reaffirming the prevailing "substantial evidence" test. But with equal clarity they expressed disapproval of the manner in which the courts were applying their own standard. The committee reports of both houses refer to the practice of agencies to rely upon "suspicion, surmise, implications, or plainly incredible evidence," and indicate that courts are to exact higher standards "in the exercise of their independent judgment" and on consideration of "the whole record."

Similar dissatisfaction with too restricted application of the "substantial evidence" test is reflected in the legislative history of the Taft-Hartley Act. The bill as reported to the House provided that the "findings of the Board as to the facts shall be conclusive unless it is made to appear to the satisfaction of the court either (1) that the findings of fact are against the manifest weight of the evidence, or (2) that the findings of fact are not supported by substantial evidence." The bill left the House with this provision. Early committee prints in the Senate provided for review by "weight of the evidence" or "clearly erroneous" standards. But, as the Senate Committee Report relates, "it was finally decided to conform the statute to the corresponding section of the Administrative Procedure Act where the substantial evidence test prevails." In order to clarify any ambiguity in that statute, however, the committee inserted the words "questions of fact, if supported by substantial evidence on the record considered as a whole." . . .

This phraseology was adopted by the Senate. The House conferees agreed. They reported to the House: "It is believed that the provisions of the conference agreement relating to the courts' reviewing power will be adequate to preclude such decisions as those in *N.L.R.B. v. Nevada Consol. Copper Corp.*, 316 U.S. 105, and in the *Wilson, Columbia Products, Union Pacific Stages, Hearst, Republic Aviation*, and *Le Tourneau*, etc. cases, without unduly burdening the courts." The Senate version became the law.

It is fair to say that in all this Congress expressed a mood. And it expressed its mood not merely by oratory but by legislation. As legislation that mood must be respected, even though it can only serve as a standard for judgment and not as a body of rigid rules assuring sameness of application. Enforcement of such broad standards implies subtlety of mind and solidity of judgment. But it is not for us to question that Congress may assume such qualities in the federal judiciary.

From the legislative story we have summarized, two concrete conclusions do emerge. One is the identity of aim of the Administrative Procedure Act and the Taft-Hartley Act regarding the proof with which the Labor Board must support a decision. The other is that now Congress has left no room for doubt as to the kind of scrutiny which a Court of Appeals must give the record before the Board to satisfy itself that the Board's order rests on adequate proof. . . .

Whether or not it was ever permissible for courts to determine the substantiality of evidence supporting a Labor Board decision merely on the basis of evidence which in and of itself justified it, without taking into account contradictory evidence or evidence from which conflicting inferences could be drawn, the new legislation definitively precludes such a theory of review and bars its practice. The substantiality of evidence must take into account whatever in the record fairly detracts from its weight. This is clearly the significance of the requirement in both statutes that courts consider the whole record. . . .

II

. . . The decision of the Court of Appeals is assailed on two grounds. It is said (1) that the court erred in holding that it was barred from taking into account the report of the examiner on questions of fact insofar as that report was rejected by the Board, and (2) that the Board's order was not supported by substantial evidence on the record considered as a whole, even apart from the validity of the court's refusal to consider the rejected portions of the examiner's report.

The latter contention is easily met. It is true that two of the earlier decisions of the court below were among those disapproved by Congress. But this disapproval, we have seen, may well have been caused by unintended intimations of judicial phrasing. And in any event, it is clear from the court's opinion in this case that it in fact did consider the "record as a whole," and did not deem itself merely the judicial echo of the Board's conclusion. The testimony of the company's witnesses was inconsistent, and there was clear evidence that the complaining employee had been discharged by an officer who was at one time influenced against him because of his appearance at the Board hearing. On such a record we could not say that it would be error to grant enforcement.

The first contention, however, raises serious questions to which we now turn.

III

The Court of Appeals deemed itself bound by the Board's rejection of the examiner's findings because the court considered these findings not "as unassailable as a master's." They are not. Section 10(c) of the Labor Management Relations Act provides that "If upon the preponderance of the testimony taken the Board shall be of the opinion that any person named in the complaint has engaged in or is engaging in any such unfair labor practice, then the Board shall state its findings of fact. . . ." The responsibility for decision thus placed on the Board is wholly inconsistent with the notion that it has power to reverse an examiner's findings only when they are "clearly erroneous." Such a limitation would make so drastic a departure from prior administrative practice that explicitness would be required.

The Court of Appeals concluded from this premise "that, although the Board would be wrong in totally disregarding his findings, it is practically impossible for a court, upon review of those findings which the Board itself substitutes, to consider the Board's reversal as a factor in the court's own decision. This we say, because we cannot find any middle ground between doing that and treating such a reversal as error, whenever it would be such, if done by a judge to a master in equity." Much as we respect the logical acumen of the Chief Judge of the Court of Appeals, we do not find ourselves pinioned between the horns of his dilemma.

We are aware that to give the examiner's findings less finality than a master's and yet entitle them to consideration in striking the account, is to introduce another and an unruly factor into the judgmatical process of review. But we ought not to fashion an exclusionary rule merely to reduce the number of imponderables to be considered by reviewing courts.

The Taft-Hartley Act provides that "The findings of the Board with respect to questions of fact if supported by substantial evidence on the record considered as a whole shall be conclusive." Surely an examiner's report is as much a part of the record as the complaint or the testimony. According to the Administrative Procedure Act, "All decisions (including initial, recommended, or tentative decisions) shall become a part of the record." . . . We found that this Act's provision for judicial review has the same meaning as that in the Taft-Hartley Act. The similarity of the two statutes in language and purpose also requires that the definition of "record" found in the Administrative Procedure Act be construed to be applicable as well to the term "record" as used in the Taft-Hartley Act.

It is therefore difficult to escape the conclusion that the plain language of the statutes directs a reviewing court to determine the substantiality of evidence on the record including the examiner's report. The conclusion is confirmed by the indications in the legislative history that enhancement of the status and function of the trial examiner was one of the important purposes of the movement for administrative reform. . . .

We do not require that the examiner's findings be given more weight than in reason and in the light of judicial experience they deserve. The "substantial evidence" standard is not modified in any way when the Board and its examiner disagree. We intend only to recognize that evidence supporting a conclusion may be less substantial when an impartial, experienced examiner who has observed the witnesses and lived with the case has drawn conclusions different from the Board's than when he has reached the same conclusion. The findings of the examiner are to be considered along with the consistency and inherent probability of testimony. The significance of his report, of course, depends largely on the importance of credibility in the particular case. To give it this significance does not seem to us materially more difficult than to heed the other factors which in sum determine whether evidence is "substantial." . . .

We therefore remand the cause to the Court of Appeals. On reconsideration of the record it should accord the findings of the trial examiner the relevance that they reasonably command in answering the comprehensive question whether the evidence supporting the Board's order is substantial. But the court need not limit its reexamination of the case to the effect of that report on its decision. We leave it free to grant or deny enforcement as it thinks the principles expressed in this opinion dictate.

Notes and Questions

1. *Universal Camera* stands for two propositions: (1) the evidence on the whole record, not just the part that favors the agency, must be substantial; and (2) the hearing examiner's determination is part of the whole record. Who determines the extent of the record—the court or the agency?

2. When would the agency ever be justified in disregarding the hearing examiner's determination?

3. How intensively should courts review agency fact-finding? Isn't this where agency expertise is at its height? What is gained through interpreting the substantial evidence standard to impose more than nominal judicial scrutiny? What do the facts of a decision like *Universal Camera*, involving a credibility determination in a union context, suggest about the role of courts in policing agency fact-finding? Would the agency likely reflect a bias toward one side or another that might imperil its fact-finding function (what sort of bias might the National Labor Relations Board, charged with protecting employees and promoting unions against employers, reflect)?

If the facts of *Universal Camera* suggest a role for courts, consider the facts of *Allentown Mack*, where the fairness of the agency is specifically on the line.

Allentown Mack Sales and Service, Inc. v. NLRB

522 U.S. 359 (1998)

Justice SCALIA delivered the opinion of the Court.

Under longstanding precedent of the National Labor Relations Board, an employer who believes that an incumbent union no longer enjoys the support of a majority of its employees has three options: to request a formal, Board-supervised election, to withdraw recognition from the union and refuse to bargain, or to conduct an internal poll of employee support for the union. The Board has held that the latter two are unfair labor practices unless the employer can show that it had a "good-faith reasonable doubt" about the union's majority support. We must decide whether the Board's standard for employer polling is rational and consistent with the National Labor Relations Act, and whether the Board's factual determinations in this case are supported by substantial evidence in the record.

I

Mack Trucks, Inc., had a factory branch in Allentown, Pennsylvania, whose service and parts employees were represented by Local Lodge 724 of the International Association of Machinists and Aerospace Workers, AFL-CIO (Local 724). Mack notified its Allentown managers in May 1990 that it intended to sell the branch, and several of those managers formed Allentown Mack Sales & Service, Inc., the petitioner here, which purchased the assets of the business on December 20, 1990, and began to operate it as an independent dealership. From December 21, 1990, to January 1, 1991, Allentown hired 32 of the original 45 Mack employees.

During the period before and immediately after the sale, a number of Mack employees made statements to the prospective owners of Allentown Mack Sales suggesting that the incumbent union had lost support among employees in the bargaining unit. In job interviews, eight employees made statements indicating, or at least arguably indicating, that they personally no longer supported the union. In addition, Ron Mohr, a member of the union's bargaining committee and shop steward for the Mack Trucks service department, told an Allentown manager that it was his feeling that the employees did not want a union, and that "with a new company, if a vote was taken, the Union would lose." And Kermit Bloch, who worked for Mack Trucks as a mechanic on the night shift, told a manager that the entire night shift (then five or six employees) did not want the union.

On January 2, 1991, Local 724 asked Allentown Mack Sales to recognize it as the employees' collective-bargaining representative, and to begin negotiations for a contract. The new employer rejected that request by letter dated January 25, claiming a "good faith doubt as to support of the Union among the employees." The letter also announced that Allentown had "arranged for an independent poll by secret ballot of its hourly employees to be conducted under guidelines prescribed by the National Labor Relations Board." The poll, supervised by a Roman Catholic priest, was conducted on February 8, 1991; the union lost 19 to 13. Shortly thereafter, the union filed an unfair-labor-practice charge with the Board.

The Administrative Law Judge (ALJ) concluded that Allentown was a "successor" employer to Mack Trucks, Inc., and therefore inherited Mack's bargaining obligation and a presumption of continuing majority support for the union. The ALJ held that Allentown's poll was conducted in compliance with the procedural standards enunciated by the Board in *Struksnes Constr. Co.*, 165 N.L.R.B. 1062 (1967), but that it violated §§8(a)(1) and 8(a)(5) of the National Labor Relations Act (Act), 49 Stat. 452, as amended, 29 U.S.C. §§158(a)(1) and 158(a)(5), because Allentown did not have an "objective reasonable doubt" about the majority status of the union. The Board adopted the ALJ's findings and agreed with his conclusion that Allentown "had not demonstrated that it harbored a reasonable doubt, based on objective considerations, as to the incumbent Union's continued majority status after the transition." The Board ordered Allentown to recognize and bargain with Local 724.

On review in the Court of Appeals for the District of Columbia Circuit, Allentown challenged both the facial rationality of the Board's test for employer polling and the Board's application of that standard to the facts of this case. The court enforced the Board's bargaining order, over a vigorous dissent. We granted certiorari.

II

[The Court rejected Allentown Mack's argument that "because the Board's 'reasonable doubt' standard for employer polls is the same as its standard for unilateral withdrawal of recognition and for employer initiation of a Board-supervised election . . . , the Board irrationally permits employers to poll only when it would be unnecessary and legally pointless to do so."]

III

The Board held Allentown guilty of an unfair labor practice in its conduct of the polling because it "ha[d] not demonstrated that it held a reasonable doubt, based on objective considerations, that the Union continued to enjoy the support of a majority of the bargaining unit employees." We must decide whether that conclusion is supported by substantial evidence on the record as a whole. . . . *Universal Camera Corp. v. NLRB*, 340 U.S. 474 (1951). Put differently, we must decide whether on this record it would have been possible for a reasonable jury to reach the Board's conclusion. . . .

The question presented for review . . . is whether, on the evidence presented to the Board, a reasonable jury could have found that Allentown lacked a genuine, reasonable uncertainty about whether Local 724 enjoyed the continuing support of a majority of unit employees. In our view, the answer is no. The Board's finding to the contrary rests on a refusal to credit probative circumstantial evidence, and on evidentiary demands that go beyond the substantive standard the Board purports to apply.

The Board adopted the ALJ's finding that 6 of Allentown's 32 employees had made "statements which could be used as objective considerations supporting a good-faith reasonable doubt as to continued majority status by the Union." (These included, for example, the statement of Rusty Hoffman that "he did not want to work in a union shop," and "would try to find another job if he had to work with the Union.") The Board seemingly also accepted (though this is not essential to our analysis) the ALJ's willingness to assume that the statement of a seventh employee (to the effect that he "did not feel comfortable with the Union and thought it was a waste of $35 a month,") supported good-faith reasonable doubt of his support for the union—as in our view it unquestionably does. And it presumably accepted the ALJ's assessment that "7 of 32, or roughly 20 percent of the involved employees" was not alone sufficient to create "an objective reasonable doubt of union majority support. . . ." The Board did not specify how many express disavowals would have been enough to establish reasonable doubt, but the number must presumably be less than 16 (half of the bargaining unit), since that would establish reasonable certainty. Still, we would not say that 20% first-hand-confirmed opposition (even with no countering evidence of union support) is alone enough to *require* a conclusion of reasonable doubt. But there was much more.

For one thing, the ALJ and the Board totally disregarded the effect upon Allentown of the statement of an eighth employee, Dennis Marsh, who said that "he was not being represented for the $35 he was paying." The ALJ, whose findings were adopted by the Board, said that this statement "seems more an expression of a desire for better representation than one for no representation at all." It seems to us that it is, more accurately, simply an expression of dissatisfaction with the union's performance—which *could* reflect the speaker's desire that the union represent him more effectively, but *could also* reflect the speaker's desire to save his $35 and get rid of the union. The statement would assuredly engender an *uncertainty* whether the speaker supported the union, and so could not be entirely ignored.

But the most significant evidence excluded from consideration by the Board consisted of statements of two employees regarding not merely their own support of the union, but support among the work force in general. Kermit Bloch, who worked on the night shift, told an Allentown manager "the entire night shift did not want the Union." The ALJ refused to credit this, because "Bloch did not testify and thus could not explain how he formed his opinion about the views of his fellow employees." Unsubstantiated assertions that other employees do not support the union certainly do not establish the *fact of that disfavor* with the degree of reliability ordinarily demanded in legal proceedings. But under the Board's enunciated test for polling, it is not the fact of disfavor that is at issue (the poll itself is meant to establish that), but rather the existence of a reasonable uncertainty on the part of the employer regarding that fact. On that issue, absent some reason for the employer to know that Bloch had no basis for his information, or that Bloch was lying, reason demands that the statement be given considerable weight.

Another employee who gave information concerning overall support for the union was Ron Mohr, who told Allentown managers that "if a vote was taken, the Union would lose" and that "it was his feeling that the employees did not want a union." The ALJ again objected irrelevantly that "there is no evidence with respect to how he gained this knowledge." In addition, the Board held that Allentown "could not legitimately rely on [the statement] as a basis for doubting the Union's majority status," because Mohr was "referring to Mack's existing employee complement, not to the individuals who were later hired by [Allentown]." This basis for disregarding Mohr's statements is wholly irrational. Local 724 had never won an election, or even an informal poll, within the actual unit of 32 Allentown employees. Its claim to represent them rested entirely on the Board's presumption that the work force of a successor company has the same disposition regarding the union as did the work force of the predecessor company, if the majority of the new work force came from the old one. The Board cannot rationally adopt that presumption for purposes of imposing the duty to bargain, and adopt precisely the opposite presumption (i.e., contend that there is no relationship between the sentiments of the two work forces) for purposes of determining what evidence tends to establish a reasonable doubt regarding union support. Such irrationality is impermissible even if . . . it would further the Board's political objectives.

It must be borne in mind that the issue here is not whether Mohr's statement clearly establishes a majority in opposition to the union, but whether it contributes to a reasonable uncertainty whether a majority in favor of the union existed. We think it surely does. Allentown would reasonably have given great credence to Mohr's assertion of lack of union support, since he was not hostile to the union, and was in a good position to assess anti-union sentiment. Mohr was a union shop steward for the service department, and a member of the union's bargaining committee; according to the ALJ, he "did not indicate personal dissatisfaction with the Union." It seems to us that Mohr's statement has undeniable and substantial probative value on the issue of "reasonable doubt."

Accepting the Board's apparent (and in our view inescapable) concession that Allentown received reliable information that 7 of the bargaining-unit employees did not support the union, the remaining 25 would have had to support the union by a margin of 17 to 8—a ratio of more than 2 to 1—if the union commanded majority support. The statements of Bloch and Mohr would cause anyone to doubt that degree of support, and neither the Board nor the ALJ discussed any evidence that Allentown should have weighed on the other side. The most pro-union statement cited in the ALJ's opinion was Ron Mohr's comment that he personally "could work with or without the Union," and "was there to do his job." The Board cannot covertly transform its presumption of continuing majority support into a working assumption that *all* of a successor's employees support the union until proved otherwise. Giving fair weight to Allentown's circumstantial evidence, we think it quite impossible for a rational factfinder to avoid the conclusion that Allentown had reasonable, good-faith grounds to doubt—to be *uncertain about*—the union's retention of majority support.

IV

That conclusion would make this a fairly straightforward administrative-law case, except for the contention that the Board's factfinding here was not an aberration. Allentown asserts that, although "the Board continues to cite the words of the good faith doubt branch of its withdrawal of recognition standard," a systematic review of the Board's decisions will reveal that "it has in practice eliminated the good faith doubt branch in favor of a strict head count." The Board denies (not too persuasively) that it has insisted upon a strict head count, but does defend its factfinding in this case by saying that it has regularly rejected similarly persuasive demonstrations of reasonable good-faith doubt in prior decisions. . . .

It is certainly conceivable that an adjudicating agency might consistently require a particular substantive standard to be established by a quantity or character of evidence so far beyond what reason and logic would require as to make it apparent that the *announced* standard is not *really* the effective one. And it is conceivable that in certain categories of cases an adjudicating agency which purports to be applying a preponderance standard of proof might so consistently demand in fact more than a preponderance, that all should be on notice from its case law that the genuine burden of proof is more than a preponderance. The question arises, then, whether, if that should be the situation that obtains here, we ought to measure the evidentiary support for the Board's decision against the standards consistently applied rather than the standards recited. As a theoretical matter (and leaving aside the question of legal authority), the Board could certainly have raised the bar for employer polling or withdrawal of recognition by imposing a more stringent requirement than the reasonable-doubt test, or by adopting a formal requirement that employers establish their reasonable doubt by more than a preponderance of the evidence. Would it make any difference if the Board achieved precisely the same result by formally leaving in place the reasonable-doubt and preponderance standards, but consistently applying them as though they meant something other than what they say? We think it would.

The Administrative Procedure Act, which governs the proceedings of administrative agencies and related judicial review, establishes a scheme of "reasoned decisionmaking." *Motor Vehicle Mfrs. Assn. of United States, Inc. v. State Farm Mut. Automobile Ins. Co.,* 463 U.S. 29 (1983). Not only must an agency's decreed result be within the scope of its lawful authority, but the process by which it reaches that result must be logical and rational. Courts enforce this principle with regularity when they set aside agency regulations which, though well within the agencies' scope of authority, are not supported by the reasons that the agencies adduce. The National Labor Relations Board, uniquely among major federal administrative agencies, has chosen to promulgate virtually all the legal rules in its field through adjudication rather than rulemaking. . . . But adjudication is subject to the requirement of reasoned decisionmaking as well. It is hard to imagine a more violent breach of that requirement than applying a rule of primary conduct or a standard of proof which is in fact different from the rule or standard formally announced. And the consistent repetition of that breach can hardly mend it.

Reasoned decisionmaking, in which the rule announced is the rule applied, promotes sound results, and unreasoned decisionmaking the opposite. The evil of a decision that applies a standard other than the one it enunciates spreads in both directions, preventing both consistent application of the law by subordinate agency personnel (notably ALJ's), and effective review of the law by the courts. . . .

. . . If revision of the Board's standard of proof can be achieved thus subtly and obliquely, it becomes a much more complicated enterprise for a court of appeals to determine whether substantial evidence supports the conclusion that the required standard has or has not been met. It also becomes difficult for this Court to know, when certiorari is sought, whether the case involves the generally applicable issue of the Board's adoption of an unusually high standard of proof, or rather just the issue of an allegedly mistaken evidentiary judgment in the particular case. An agency should not be able to impede judicial review, and indeed even political oversight, by disguising its policymaking as factfinding.

Because reasoned decisionmaking demands it, and because the systemic consequences of any other approach are unacceptable, the Board must be required to apply in fact the clearly understood legal standards that it enunciates in principle, such as good-faith reasonable doubt and preponderance of the evidence. Reviewing courts are entitled to take those standards to mean what they say, and to conduct substantial-evidence review on that basis. Even the most consistent and hence predictable Board departure from proper application of those standards will not alter the legal rule by which the agency's factfinding is to be judged. . . .

The Board can, of course, forthrightly and explicitly adopt counterfactual evidentiary presumptions (which are in effect substantive rules of law) as a way of furthering particular legal or policy goals. . . . The Board might also be justified in forthrightly and explicitly adopting a rule of evidence that categorically excludes certain testimony on policy grounds, without reference to its inherent probative value. (Such clearly announced rules of law or of evidentiary exclusion would of course be subject to judicial review for their reasonableness and their compatibility with the Act.) That is not the sort of Board action at issue here, however, but rather the Board's allegedly systematic undervaluation of certain evidence, or allegedly systematic exaggeration of what the evidence must prove. When the Board purports to be engaged in simple factfinding, unconstrained by substantive presumptions or evidentiary rules of exclusion, it is not free to prescribe what inferences from the evidence it will accept and reject, but must draw all those inferences that the evidence fairly demands. "Substantial evidence" review exists precisely to ensure that the Board achieves minimal compliance with this obligation, which is the foundation of all honest and legitimate adjudication. . . .

We conclude that the Board's "reasonable doubt" test for employer polls is facially rational and consistent with the Act. But the Board's factual finding that Allentown Mack Sales lacked such a doubt is not supported by substantial evidence on the record as a whole. The judgment of the Court of Appeals for the District of Columbia Circuit is therefore reversed, and the case is remanded with instructions to deny enforcement.

It is so ordered.

[Concurrence in part and dissent in part of Chief Justice REHNQUIST, with whom Justice O'CONNOR, Justice KENNEDY, and Justice THOMAS join, omitted.]

Justice BREYER, with whom Justice STEVENS, Justice SOUTER, and Justice GINSBURG join, concurring in part and dissenting in part.

In Parts III and IV, the Court holds unlawful an agency conclusion on the ground that it is "not supported by substantial evidence." In deciding [that issue], the Court has departed from the half-century old legal standard governing this type of review. See *Universal Camera Corp. v. NLRB*, 340 U.S. 474, 490-491 (1951). It has rewritten a National Labor Relations Board (Board) rule without adequate justification. It has ignored certain evidentiary presumptions developed by the Board to provide guidance in the application of this rule. And it has failed to give the kind of leeway to the Board's factfinding authority that the Court's precedents mandate.

. . . To decide whether an agency's conclusion is supported by substantial evidence, a reviewing court must identify the conclusion and then examine and weigh the evidence. . . . As this Court said in 1951, "[w]hether on the record as a whole there is substantial evidence to support agency findings is a question which Congress has placed in the keeping of the Courts of Appeals." *Universal Camera*, 340 U.S., at 491. The Court held that it would "intervene only in what ought to be the rare instance when the standard appears to have been *misapprehended or grossly misapplied.*" *Ibid.* (emphasis added). . . . Consequently, if the majority is to overturn a court of appeals' "substantial evidence" decision, it must identify the agency's conclusion, examine the evidence, and then determine whether the evidence is so obviously inadequate to support the conclusion that the reviewing court must have seriously misunderstood the nature of its legal duty.

The majority opinion begins by properly stating the Board's conclusion, namely, that the employer, Allentown Mack Sales & Service, Inc., did not demonstrate that it "held a reasonable doubt, *based on objective considerations,* that the Union continued to enjoy the support of a majority of the bargaining unit employees." The opinion, however, then omits the words I have italicized and transforms this conclusion, rephrasing it as: "Allentown lacked a genuine, reasonable uncertainty about whether Local 724 enjoyed the continuing support of a majority of unit employees." Key words of a technical sort that the Board has used in hundreds of opinions written over several decades to express what the Administrative Law Judge (ALJ) here called "*objective* reasonable doubt" have suddenly disappeared, leaving in their place what looks like an ordinary jury standard that might reflect not an agency's specialized knowledge of the workplace, but a court's common understanding of human psychology. . . . In any event, the majority's interpretation departs from settled principles permitting agencies broad leeway to interpret their own rules, see, *e.g., Thomas Jefferson Univ. v. Shalala,*

512 U.S. 504, 512 (1994) (courts "must give substantial deference to an agency's interpretation of its own regulations").

. . . According to the ALJ, [Allentown Mack] sought to show that it had an "objective" good-faith doubt primarily by presenting the testimony of Allentown managers, who, in turn, reported statements made to them by 14 employees. The ALJ set aside the statements of 5 of those employees as insignificant for various reasons—for example because the employees were not among the rehired 32, because their statements were equivocal, or because they made the statements at a time too long before the transition. The majority does not take issue with the ALJ's reasoning with respect to these employees. The ALJ then found that statements made by six, and possibly seven, employees (22% of the 32) helped Allentown show an "objective" reasonable doubt. The majority does not quarrel with this conclusion. The majority does, however, take issue with the ALJ's decision not to count in Allentown's favor three further statements, made by employees Marsh, Bloch, and Mohr. The majority says that these statements *required* the ALJ and the Board to find for Allentown. I cannot agree.

Consider Marsh's statement. Marsh said, as the majority opinion notes, that " 'he was not being represented for the $35 he was paying.' " The majority says that the ALJ was wrong not to count this statement in the employer's favor. But the majority fails to mention that Marsh made this statement to an Allentown manager while the manager was interviewing Marsh to determine whether he would, or would not, be one of the 32 employees whom Allentown would reemploy. The ALJ, when evaluating all the employee statements, wrote that statements made to the Allentown managers during the job interviews were "somewhat tainted as it is likely that a job applicant will say whatever he believes the prospective employer wants to hear." In so stating, the ALJ was reiterating the Board's own normative general finding that employers should not "rely in asserting a good-faith doubt" upon "[s]tatements made by employees during the course of an interview with a prospective employer." *Middleboro Fire Apparatus, Inc.,* 234 N.L.R.B. 888, 894, 1978 WL 7283, enf'd, 590 F.2d 4 (C.A.5 1978). The Board also has found that " '[e]mployee statements of dissatisfaction with a union are not deemed the equivalent of withdrawal of support for the union.' " *Torch Operating Co.,* 322 N.L.R.B. 939, 943, 1997 WL 34911 (1997) (quoting *Briggs Plumbingware, Inc. v. NLRB,* 877 F.2d 1282, 1288 (C.A.6 1989)). . . . Either of these general Board findings (presumably known to employers advised by the labor bar), applied by the ALJ in this particular case, provides more than adequate support for the ALJ's conclusion that the employer could not properly rely upon Marsh's statement as help in creating an "objective" employer doubt.

I do not see how, on the record before us, one could plausibly argue that these relevant general findings of the Board fall outside the Board's lawfully delegated authority. The Board in effect has said that an employee statement *made during a job interview with an employer who has expressed an interest in a nonunionized work force* will often tell us precisely *nothing* about that employee's true feelings. That Board conclusion represents an exercise of the kind of discretionary authority that Congress placed squarely within the Board's administrative and factfinding powers and responsibilities. See *Radio Officers v. NLRB*, 347 U.S. 17, 49-50. Nor is it procedurally improper for an agency, rather like a common-law court, (and drawing upon its accumulated expertise and exercising its administrative responsibilities) to use adjudicatory proceedings to develop rules of thumb about the likely weight assigned to different kinds of evidence.

Consider next Bloch's statement, made during his job interview with Worth, that those on the night shift (five or six employees) "did not want the Union." The ALJ thought this statement failed to provide support, both for reasons that the majority mentions ("'Bloch did not testify and thus could not explain how he formed his opinion about the views of his fellow employees'"), and for reasons that the majority does not mention ("no showing that [the other employees] made independent representations about their union sympathies to [Allentown] and they did not testify in this proceeding").

The majority says that "reason demands" that Bloch's statement "be given considerable weight." But why? The Board, drawing upon both reason and experience, has said it will "view with suspicion and caution" one employee's statements "purporting to represent the views of other employees." *Wallkill Valley General Hospital*, 288 N.L.R.B. 103, 109, 1988 WL 213698 (1988), enf'd as modified, 866 F.2d 632 (C.A.3 1989). Indeed, the Board specifically has stated that this type of evidence does not qualify as "objective" within the meaning of the "objective reasonable doubt" standard. *Wallkill Valley General Hospital*, at 109-110 (finding that statement by one employee that other employees opposed the union "cannot be found to provide *objective* considerations" because statement was a "bare assertion," was "subjective," and "lacking in demonstrable foundation"; statement by another employee about the views of others was similarly "insufficiently reliable and definite to contribute to a finding of *objective* considerations" (emphases added)).

How is it unreasonable for the Board to provide this kind of guidance, about what kinds of evidence are more likely, and what kinds are less likely, to support an "objective reasonable doubt" (thereby helping an employer understand just when he may refuse to bargain with an established employee representative, in the absence of an employee-generated union decertification petition)? Why is it unreasonable for an ALJ to disregard a highly general conclusory statement such as Bloch's, a statement that names no names, is unsupported by any other concrete testimony, and was made during a job interview by an interviewer who foresees a nonunionized workforce? To put the matter more directly, how can the majority substitute its own judgment for that of the Board and the ALJ in respect to such detailed workplace-related matters, particularly on the basis of this record, where the question whether we should set aside this kind of Board rule has not even been argued?

Finally, consider the Allentown manager's statement that Mohr told him that "if a vote was taken, the Union would lose. . . ."

One can find reflected in the majority opinion some of the reasons the ALJ gave for discounting the significance of Mohr's statement. The majority says of the ALJ's first reason (namely, that "'there is no evidence with respect to how'" Mohr "'gained this knowledge'") that this reason is "irrelevan[t]." But why so? The lack of any specifics provides some support for the possibility that Mohr was overstating a conclusion, say, in a job-preserving effort to curry favor with Mack's new managers. More importantly, since the absence of detail or support brings Mohr's statement well within the Board's pre-existing cautionary evidentiary principle (about employee statements regarding the views of other employees), it diminishes the reasonableness of any employer reliance.

The majority discusses a further reason, namely, that Mohr was referring to a group of 32 employees of whom Allentown hired only 23, and "the composition of the complement of employees hired would bear on whether this group did or did not support the Union." The majority considers this reason "wholly irrational," because, in its view, the Board cannot "rationally" assume that "the work force of a successor company has the same disposition regarding the union as did the work force of the predecessor company, if the majority of the new work force came from the old one," while adopting an opposite assumption "for purposes of determining what evidence tends to establish a reasonable doubt regarding union support." The irrationality of these assumptions, however, is not obvious. The primary objective of the National Labor Relations Act is to secure labor peace. To preserve the status quo ante may help to preserve labor peace; the first presumption may help to do so by assuming (in the absence of contrary evidence) that workers wish to preserve that status quo; the second, by requiring detailed evidence before dislodging the status quo, may help to do the same. Regardless, no one has argued that these presumptions are contradictory or illogical.

The majority fails to mention the ALJ's third reason for discounting Mohr's statement, namely, that Mohr did not indicate "whether he was speaking about a large majority of the service employees being dissatisfied with the Union or a small majority." It fails to mention the ALJ's belief that the statement was "almost off-the-cuff." It fails to mention the ALJ's reference to the "Board's historical treatment of unverified assertions by an employee about other employees' sentiments" (which, by itself, would justify a considerable discount). And, most importantly, it leaves out the ALJ's conclusion. The ALJ did not conclude that Mohr's statement lacked evidentiary significance. Rather, the ALJ concluded that the statement did not provide "*sufficient* basis, even when considered with other employee statements relied upon, to meet the Board's objective reasonable doubt standard" (emphasis added).

Given this evidence, and the ALJ's reasoning, the Court of Appeals found the Board's conclusion adequately supported. That conclusion is well within the Board's authority to make findings and to reach conclusions on the basis of record evidence, which authority Congress has granted, and this Court's many precedents have confirmed.

In sum, the majority has failed to focus upon the ALJ's actual conclusions, it has failed to consider all the evidence before the ALJ, it has transformed the actual legal standard that the Board has long administered without regard to the Board's own interpretive precedents, and it has ignored the guidance that the Board's own administrative interpretations have sought to provide to the bar, to employers, to unions, and to its own administrative staff. The majority's opinion will, I fear, weaken the system for judicial review of administrative action that this Court's precedents have carefully constructed over several decades.

For these reasons, I dissent.

Notes and Questions

1. Did the Court overreach in applying the substantial evidence test, as Justice Breyer contends? In terms of applying the test, which side is right?

2. Was the Court particularly unsympathetic because the Board had attempted, without adequate process, to establish a presumption that effectively altered the application of that standard? Why wasn't Justice Breyer similarly unsympathetic?

3. Based on your reading of the last two decisions, is the substantial evidence test different from the arbitrary and capricious test? The tests use different linguistic formulations, but is it possible to distinguish them, especially in a case like this where fact-finding was contingent on policymaking?

3. Availability of Judicial Review

Courts are limited in their ability to assert control of agency action in broader and more significant ways. As you know, they must wait to assert control until someone files a lawsuit challenging agency action. Here we consider the additional fact that they can hear only certain cases—ones involving a proper plaintiff raising a proper claim at the proper time. Thus, judicial review is not always available, even if someone is willing to sue. In this section, we provide a brief overview of the most significant limits on the power of courts to review agency action.

a. Standing

Standing doctrine bars courts from hearing cases at the behest of certain plaintiffs. By limiting which plaintiffs can challenge agency action, standing doctrine limits the opportunities for judicial review (and hence judicial control) of agency action. Moreover, because the standing doctrine is based in part in constitutional law, it can provide a barrier to judicial review of agency action even when Congress has contemplated such review.

Standing doctrine is a complex body of law, typically covered in courses in constitutional law, administrative law, and federal courts. We provide a recent Supreme Court decision to illustrate how standing relates to judicial control of agency action. In Chapter 5, you saw excerpts of the agency document that the case concerns: EPA's denial of a petition for rulemaking to regulate greenhouse gases under the Clean Air Act. A court only needs one plaintiff to satisfy standing requirements to hear a case. Why does Massachusetts qualify?

Massachusetts v. EPA

549 U.S. 497 (2007)

Justice STEVENS delivered the opinion of the Court.

A well-documented rise in global temperatures has coincided with a significant increase in the concentration of carbon dioxide in the atmosphere. Respected scientists believe the two trends are related. For when carbon dioxide is released into the atmosphere, it acts like the ceiling of a greenhouse, trapping solar energy and retarding the escape of reflected heat. It is therefore a species—the most important species—of a "greenhouse gas."

Calling global warming "the most pressing environmental challenge of our time," a group of States, local governments, and private organizations, alleged in a petition for certiorari that the Environmental Protection Agency (EPA) has abdicated its responsibility under the Clean Air Act to regulate the emissions of four greenhouse gases, including carbon dioxide. Specifically, petitioners asked us to answer two questions concerning the meaning of §202(a)(1) of the Act: whether EPA has the statutory authority to regulate greenhouse gas emissions from new motor vehicles; and if so, whether its stated reasons for refusing to do so are consistent with the statute.

In response, EPA, supported by 10 intervening States and six trade associations, correctly argued that we may not address those two questions unless at least one petitioner has standing to invoke our jurisdiction under Article III of the Constitution. Notwithstanding the serious character of that jurisdictional argument and the absence of any conflicting decisions construing §202(a)(1), the unusual importance of the underlying issue persuaded us to grant the writ. 548 U.S., 126 S. Ct. 2960 (2006).

I

Section 202(a)(1) of the Clean Air Act, as added by Pub. L. 89-272, §101(8), 79 Stat. 992, and as amended by, inter alia, 84 Stat. 1690 and 91 Stat. 791, 42 U.S.C. §7521(a)(1), provides:

> "The [EPA] Administrator shall by regulation prescribe (and from time to time revise) in accordance with the provisions of this section, standards applicable to the emission of any air pollutant from any class or classes of new motor vehicles or new motor vehicle engines, which in his judgment cause, or contribute to, air pollution which may reasonably be anticipated to endanger public health or welfare. . . ."

The 1970 version of §202(a)(1) used the phrase "which endangers the public health or welfare" rather than the more-protective "which may reasonably be anticipated to endanger public health or welfare." *See* §6(a) of the Clean Air Amendments of 1970, 84 Stat. 1690. Congress amended §202(a)(1) in 1977 to give its approval to the decision in *Ethyl Corp. v. EPA*, 541 F.2d 1, 25 (C.A.D.C. 1976) (en banc), which held that the Clean Air Act "and common sense . . . demand regulatory action to prevent harm, even if the regulator is less than certain that harm is otherwise inevitable." *See* §401(d)(1) of the Clean Air Act Amendments of 1977, 91 Stat. 791; *see also* H.R. Rep. No. 95-294, p. 49 (1977), U.S. Code Cong. & Admin. News 1977, p. 1077.

The Act defines "air pollutant" to include "any air pollution agent or combination of such agents, including any physical, chemical, biological, radioactive . . . substance or matter which is emitted into or otherwise enters the ambient air." §7602(g). "Welfare" is also defined broadly: among other things, it includes "effects on . . . weather . . . and climate." §7602(h). . . .

IV

Article III of the Constitution limits federal-court jurisdiction to "Cases" and "Controversies." Those two words confine "the business of federal courts to questions presented in an adversary context and in a form historically viewed as capable of resolution through the judicial process." *Flast v. Cohen*, 392 U.S. 83, 95 (1968). It is therefore familiar learning that no justiciable "controversy" exists when parties seek adjudication of a political question, *Luther v. Borden*, 7 How. 1, 12 L. Ed. 581 (1849), when they ask for an advisory opinion, *Hayburn's Case*, 2 Dall. 409 (1792), *see also Clinton v. Jones*, 520 U.S. 681, 700, n.33 (1997), or when the question sought to be adjudicated has been mooted by subsequent developments, *California v. San Pablo & Tulare R. Co.*, 149 U.S. 308 (1893). This case suffers from none of these defects.

The parties' dispute turns on the proper construction of a congressional statute, a question eminently suitable to resolution in federal court. Congress has moreover authorized this type of challenge to EPA action. *See* 42 U.S.C. §7607(b)(1). That authorization is of critical importance to the standing inquiry: "Congress has the power to define injuries and articulate chains of causation that will give rise to a case or controversy where none existed before." [Lujan v. Defenders of Wildlife, 504 U.S. 505, 580 (1992)] (Kennedy, J., concurring in part and concurring in judgment). "In exercising this power, however, Congress must at the very least identify the injury it seeks to vindicate and relate the injury to the class of persons entitled to bring suit." *Ibid.* We will not, therefore, "entertain citizen suits to vindicate the public's nonconcrete interest in the proper administration of the laws." *Id.*, at 581.

EPA maintains that because greenhouse gas emissions inflict widespread harm, the doctrine of standing presents an insuperable jurisdictional obstacle. We do not agree. At bottom, "the gist of the question of standing" is whether petitioners have "such a personal stake in the outcome of the controversy as to assure that concrete adverseness which sharpens the presentation of issues upon which the court so largely depends for illumination." *Baker v. Carr*, 369 U.S. 186, 204 (1962). As Justice Kennedy explained in his *Lujan* concurrence:

> "While it does not matter how many persons have been injured by the challenged action, the party bringing suit must show that the action injures him in a concrete and personal way. This requirement is not just an empty formality. It preserves the vitality of the adversarial process by assuring both that the parties before the court have an actual, as opposed to professed, stake in the outcome, and that the legal questions presented . . . will be resolved, not in the rarified atmosphere of a debating society, but in a concrete factual context conducive to a realistic appreciation of the consequences of judicial action." 504 U.S., at 581 (internal quotation marks omitted).

To ensure the proper adversarial presentation, *Lujan* holds that a litigant must demonstrate that it has suffered a concrete and particularized injury that is either actual or imminent, that the injury is fairly traceable to the defendant, and that it is likely that a favorable decision will redress that injury. *See id.*, at 560-561. However, a litigant to whom Congress has "accorded a procedural right to protect his concrete interests," *id.*, at 572, n.7—here, the right to challenge agency action unlawfully withheld, §7607(b)(1)—"can assert that right without meeting all the normal standards for redressability and immediacy," *ibid*. When a litigant is vested with a procedural right, that litigant has standing if there is some possibility that the requested relief will prompt the injury-causing party to reconsider the decision that allegedly harmed the litigant. *Ibid.*; *see also Sugar Cane Growers Cooperative of Fla. v. Veneman*, 289 F.3d 89, 94-95 (C.A.D.C. 2002) ("A [litigant] who alleges a deprivation of a procedural protection to which he is entitled never has to prove that if he had received the procedure the substantive result would have been altered. All that is necessary is to show that the procedural step was connected to the substantive result").

Only one of the petitioners needs to have standing to permit us to consider the petition for review. *See Rumsfeld v. Forum for Academic and Institutional Rights, Inc.*, 547 U.S. 47, 52, n.2 (2006). We stress here, as did Judge Tatel below, the special position and interest of Massachusetts. It is of considerable relevance that the party seeking review here is a sovereign State and not, as it was in *Lujan*, a private individual.

Well before the creation of the modern administrative state, we recognized that States are not normal litigants for the purposes of invoking federal jurisdiction. . . .

When a State enters the Union, it surrenders certain sovereign prerogatives. Massachusetts cannot invade Rhode Island to force reductions in greenhouse gas emissions, it cannot negotiate an emissions treaty with China or India, and in some circumstances the exercise of its police powers to reduce in-state motor-vehicle emissions might well be pre-empted. *See Alfred L. Snapp & Son, Inc. v. Puerto Rico ex rel. Barez*, 458 U.S. 592, 607 (1982) ("One helpful indication in determining whether an alleged injury to the health and welfare of its citizens suffices to give the State standing to sue *parens patriae* is whether the injury is one that the State, if it could, would likely attempt to address through its sovereign lawmaking powers").

These sovereign prerogatives are now lodged in the Federal Government, and Congress has ordered EPA to protect Massachusetts (among others) by prescribing standards applicable to the "emission of any air pollutant from any class or classes of new motor vehicle engines, which in [the Administrator's] judgment cause, or contribute to, air pollution which may reasonably be anticipated to endanger public health or welfare." 42 U.S.C. §7521(a)(1). Congress has moreover recognized a concomitant procedural right to challenge the rejection of its rulemaking petition as arbitrary and capricious. §7607(b)(1). Given that procedural right and Massachusetts' stake in protecting its quasi-sovereign interests, the Commonwealth is entitled to special solicitude in our standing analysis.

With that in mind, it is clear that petitioners' submissions as they pertain to Massachusetts have satisfied the most demanding standards of the adversarial process. EPA's steadfast refusal to regulate greenhouse gas emissions presents a risk of harm to Massachusetts that is both "actual" and "imminent." *Lujan*, 504 U.S., at 560 (internal quotation marks omitted). There is, moreover, a "substantial likelihood that the judicial relief requested" will prompt EPA to take steps to reduce that risk. *Duke Power Co. v. Carolina Environmental Study Group, Inc.*, 438 U.S. 59, 79 (1978).

The Injury

The harms associated with climate change are serious and well recognized. Indeed, the NRC Report itself—which EPA regards as an "objective and independent assessment of the relevant science," 68 Fed. Reg. 52930—identifies a number of environmental changes that have already inflicted significant harms, including "the global retreat of mountain glaciers, reduction in snow-cover extent, the earlier spring melting of rivers and lakes, [and] the accelerated rate of rise of sea levels during the 20th century relative to the past few thousand years. . . ." NRC Report 16.

Petitioners allege that this only hints at the environmental damage yet to come. According to the climate scientist Michael MacCracken, "qualified scientific experts involved in climate change research" have reached a "strong consensus" that global warming threatens (among other things) a precipitate rise in sea levels by the end of the century, "severe and irreversible changes to natural ecosystems," a "significant reduction in water storage in winter snowpack in mountainous regions with direct and important economic consequences," and an increase in the spread of disease. He also observes that rising ocean temperatures may contribute to the ferocity of hurricanes.

That these climate-change risks are "widely shared" does not minimize Massachusetts' interest in the outcome of this litigation. *See Federal Election Comm'n v. Akins*, 524 U.S. 11, 24 (1998) ("[W]here a harm is concrete, though widely shared, the Court has found 'injury in fact'"). According to petitioners' unchallenged affidavits, global sea levels rose somewhere between 10 and 20 centimeters over the 20th century as a result of global warming. These rising seas have already begun to swallow Massachusetts' coastal land. Because the Commonwealth "owns a substantial portion of the state's coastal property," it has alleged a particularized injury in its capacity as a landowner. The severity of that injury will only increase over the course of the next century: If sea levels continue to rise as predicted, one Massachusetts official believes that a significant fraction of coastal property will be "either permanently lost through inundation or temporarily lost through periodic storm surge and flooding events." Remediation costs alone, petitioners allege, could run well into the hundreds of millions of dollars.[1]

Causation

EPA does not dispute the existence of a causal connection between man-made greenhouse gas emissions and global warming. At a minimum, therefore, EPA's refusal to regulate such emissions "contributes" to Massachusetts' injuries.

EPA nevertheless maintains that its decision not to regulate greenhouse gas emissions from new motor vehicles contributes so insignificantly to petitioners' injuries that the agency cannot be haled into federal court to answer for them. For the same reason, EPA does not believe that any realistic possibility exists that the relief petitioners seek would mitigate global climate change and remedy their injuries. That is especially so because predicted increases in greenhouse gas emissions from developing nations, particularly China and India, are likely to offset any marginal domestic decrease.

But EPA overstates its case. Its argument rests on the erroneous assumption that a small incremental step, because it is incremental, can never be attacked in a federal judicial forum. Yet accepting that premise would doom most challenges to regulatory action. Agencies, like legislatures, do not generally resolve massive problems in one fell regulatory swoop. *See Williamson v. Lee Optical of Okla., Inc.*, 348 U.S. 483, 489 (1955) ("[A] reform may take one step at a time, addressing itself to the phase of the problem which seems most acute to the legislative mind"). They instead whittle away at them over time, refining their preferred approach as circumstances change and as they develop a more-nuanced understanding of how best to proceed. *Cf. SEC v. Chenery Corp.*, 332 U.S. 194, 202 (1947) ("Some principles must await

---

1. "For example, the [Massachusetts Department of Conservation and Recreation] owns, operates and maintains approximately 53 coastal state parks, beaches, reservations, and wildlife sanctuaries. [It] also owns, operates and maintains sporting and recreational facilities in coastal areas, including numerous pools, skating rinks, playgrounds, playing fields, former coastal fortifications, public stages, museums, bike trails, tennis courts, boathouses and boat ramps and landings. Associated with these coastal properties and facilities is a significant amount of infrastructure, which the Commonwealth also owns, operates and maintains, including roads, parkways, stormwater pump stations, pier[s], sea wal[l] revetments and dams."

their own development, while others must be adjusted to meet particular, unforeseeable situations"). That a first step might be tentative does not by itself support the notion that federal courts lack jurisdiction to determine whether that step conforms to law.

And reducing domestic automobile emissions is hardly a tentative step. Even leaving aside the other greenhouse gases, the United States transportation sector emits an enormous quantity of carbon dioxide into the atmosphere-according to the MacCracken affidavit, more than 1.7 billion metric tons in 1999 alone. That accounts for more than 6% of worldwide carbon dioxide emissions. To put this in perspective: Considering just emissions from the transportation sector, which represent less than one-third of this country's total carbon dioxide emissions, the United States would still rank as the third-largest emitter of carbon dioxide in the world, outpaced only by the European Union and China. Judged by any standard, U.S. motor-vehicle emissions make a meaningful contribution to greenhouse gas concentrations and hence, according to petitioners, to global warming.

The Remedy

While it may be true that regulating motor-vehicle emissions will not by itself reverse global warming, it by no means follows that we lack jurisdiction to decide whether EPA has a duty to take steps to slow or reduce it. *See also Larson v. Valente*, 456 U.S. 228, 244, n.15 (1982) ("[A] plaintiff satisfies the redressability requirement when he shows that a favorable decision will relieve a discrete injury to himself. He need not show that a favorable decision will relieve his every injury"). Because of the enormity of the potential consequences associated with man-made climate change, the fact that the effectiveness of a remedy might be delayed during the (relatively short) time it takes for a new motor-vehicle fleet to replace an older one is essentially irrelevant. Nor is it dispositive that developing countries such as China and India are poised to increase greenhouse gas emissions substantially over the next century: A reduction in domestic emissions would slow the pace of global emissions increases, no matter what happens elsewhere.

We moreover attach considerable significance to EPA's "agree[ment] with the President that 'we must address the issue of global climate change,'" 68 Fed. Reg. 52929 (quoting remarks announcing Clear Skies and Global Climate Initiatives, 2002 *Public Papers of George W. Bush*, Vol. 1, Feb. 14, p. 227 (2004)), and to EPA's ardent support for various voluntary emission-reduction programs, 68 Fed. Reg. 52932. As Judge Tatel observed in dissent below, "EPA would presumably not bother with such efforts if it thought emissions reductions would have no discernable impact on future global warming." 415 F.3d, at 66.

In sum—at least according to petitioners' uncontested affidavits—the rise in sea levels associated with global warming has already harmed and will continue to harm Massachusetts. The risk of catastrophic harm, though remote, is nevertheless real. That risk would be reduced to some extent if petitioners received the relief they seek. We therefore hold that petitioners have standing to challenge EPA's denial of their rulemaking petition.

[On the merits, the Court found that the Clean Air Act authorizes EPA to regulate greenhouse gas emissions from new vehicles if certain conditions are met, and that EPA failed to provide a reasoned explanation for refusing to regulate greenhouse gas emissions.]

CHIEF JUSTICE ROBERTS, with whom Justice SCALIA, Justice THOMAS, and Justice ALITO join, dissenting.

Global warming may be a "crisis," even "the most pressing environmental problem of our time." Pet. for Cert. 26, 22. Indeed, it may ultimately affect nearly everyone on the planet in some potentially adverse way, and it may be that governments have done too little to address it. It is not a problem, however, that has escaped the attention of policymakers in the Executive and Legislative Branches of our Government, who continue to consider regulatory, legislative, and treaty-based means of addressing global climate change.

Apparently dissatisfied with the pace of progress on this issue in the elected branches, petitioners have come to the courts claiming broad-ranging injury, and attempting to tie that injury to the Government's alleged failure to comply with a rather narrow statutory provision. I would reject these challenges as nonjusticiable. Such a conclusion involves no judgment on whether global warming exists, what causes it, or the extent of the problem. Nor does it render petitioners without recourse. This Court's standing jurisprudence simply recognizes that redress of grievances of the sort at issue here "is the function of Congress and the Chief Executive," not the federal courts. *Lujan v. Defenders of Wildlife*, 504 U.S. 555, 576 (1992). I would vacate the judgment below and remand for dismissal of the petitions for review.

I

Article III, §2, of the Constitution limits the federal judicial power to the adjudication of "Cases" and "Controversies." "If a dispute is not a proper case or controversy, the courts have no business deciding it, or expounding the law in the course of doing so." *DaimlerChrysler Corp. v. Cuno*, 126 S. Ct. 1854 (2006). "Standing to sue is part of the common understanding of what it takes to make a justiciable case," *Steel Co. v. Citizens for Better Environment*, 523 U.S. 83, 102 (1998), and has been described as "an essential and unchanging part of the case-or-controversy requirement of Article III," *Defenders of Wildlife*, at 560.

Our modern framework for addressing standing is familiar: "A plaintiff must allege personal injury fairly traceable to the defendant's allegedly unlawful conduct and likely to be redressed by the requested relief." . . . Applying that standard here, petitioners bear the burden of alleging an injury that is fairly traceable to the Environmental Protection Agency's failure to promulgate new motor vehicle greenhouse gas emission standards, and that is likely to be redressed by the prospective issuance of such standards.

Before determining whether petitioners can meet this familiar test, however, the Court changes the rules. It asserts that "States are not normal litigants for the purposes of invoking federal jurisdiction," and that given "Massachusetts' stake in protecting its quasi-sovereign interests, the Commonwealth is entitled to *special solicitude* in our standing analysis." (emphasis added).

Relaxing Article III standing requirements because asserted injuries are pressed by a State, however, has no basis in our jurisprudence, and support for any such "special solicitude" is conspicuously absent from the Court's opinion. The general judicial review provision cited by the Court, 42 U.S.C. §7607(b)(1), affords States no special rights or status. The Court states that "Congress has ordered EPA to protect Massachusetts (among others)" through the statutory provision at issue, §7521(a)(1), and that "Congress has . . . recognized a concomitant procedural right to challenge the rejection of its rulemaking petition as arbitrary and capricious." The reader might think from this unfortunate phrasing that Congress said something about the rights of States in this particular provision of the statute. Congress knows how to do that when it wants to, *see, e.g.,* §7426(b) (affording States the right to petition EPA to directly regulate certain sources of pollution), but it has done nothing of the sort here. Under the law on which petitioners rely, Congress treated public and private litigants exactly the same. . . .

What is more, the Court's reasoning falters on its own terms. The Court asserts that Massachusetts is entitled to "special solicitude" due to its "quasi-sovereign interests," but then applies our Article III standing test to the asserted injury of the State's loss of coastal property. . . . In the context of *parens patriae* standing, however, we have characterized state ownership of land as a "nonsovereign interes[t]" because a State "is likely to have the same interests as other similarly situated proprietors." *Alfred L. Snapp & Son,* at 601.

On top of everything else, the Court overlooks the fact that our cases cast significant doubt on a State's standing to assert a quasi-sovereign interest— as opposed to a direct injury—against the Federal Government. As a general rule, we have held that while a State might assert a quasi-sovereign right as *parens patriae* "for the protection of its citizens, it is no part of its duty or power to enforce their rights in respect of their relations with the Federal Government. In that field it is the United States, and not the State, which represents them." *Massachusetts v. Mellon,* 262 U.S. 447, 485-486 (1923) (citation omitted); *see also Alfred L. Snapp & Son,* at 610, n.16. . . .

II

It is not at all clear how the Court's "special solicitude" for Massachusetts plays out in the standing analysis, except as an implicit concession that petitioners cannot establish standing on traditional terms. But the status of Massachusetts as a State cannot compensate for petitioners' failure to demonstrate injury in fact, causation, and redressability.

When the Court actually applies the three-part test, it focuses, as did the dissent below, *see* 415 F.3d 50, 64 (C.A.D.C. 2005) (opinion of Tatel, J.), on the State's asserted loss of coastal land as the injury in fact. If petitioners rely on loss of land as the Article III injury, however, they must ground the rest of the standing analysis in that specific injury. That alleged injury must be "concrete and particularized," *Defenders of Wildlife*, 504 U.S., at 560, and "distinct and palpable," *Allen*, 468 U.S., at 751 (internal quotation marks omitted). Central to this concept of "particularized" injury is the requirement that a plaintiff be affected in a "personal and individual way," *Defenders of Wildlife*, 504 U.S., at 560, n.1, and seek relief that "directly and tangibly benefits him" in a manner distinct from its impact on "the public at large," *id.*, at 573-574. Without "particularized injury, there can be no confidence of 'a real need to exercise the power of judicial review' or that relief can be framed 'no broader than required by the precise facts to which the court's ruling would be applied.'" *Warth v. Seldin*, 422 U.S. 490, 508 (1975) (quoting *Schlesinger v. Reservists Comm. to Stop the War*, 418 U.S. 208, 221-222 (1974)).

The very concept of global warming seems inconsistent with this particularization requirement. Global warming is a phenomenon "harmful to humanity at large," 415 F.3d, at 60 (Sentelle, J., dissenting in part and concurring in judgment), and the redress petitioners seek is focused no more on them than on the public generally—it is literally to change the atmosphere around the world.

If petitioners' particularized injury is loss of coastal land, it is also that injury that must be "actual or imminent, not conjectural or hypothetical," *Defenders of Wildlife*, at 560 (internal quotation marks omitted), "real and immediate," *Los Angeles v. Lyons*, 461 U.S. 95, 102 (1983) (internal quotation marks omitted), and "certainly impending," *Whitmore v. Arkansas*, 495 U.S. 149, 158 (1990) (internal quotation marks omitted).

As to "actual" injury, the Court observes that "global sea levels rose somewhere between 10 and 20 centimeters over the 20th century as a result of global warming" and that "[t]hese rising seas have already begun to swallow Massachusetts' coastal land." But none of petitioners' declarations supports that connection. One declaration states that "a rise in sea level due to climate change is occurring on the coast of Massachusetts, in the metropolitan Boston area," but there is no elaboration. And the declarant goes on to identify a "significan[t]" non-global-warming cause of Boston's rising sea level: land subsidence. Thus, aside from a single conclusory statement, there is nothing in petitioners' 43 standing declarations and accompanying exhibits to support an inference of actual loss of Massachusetts coastal land from 20th century global sea level increases. It is pure conjecture.

The Court's attempts to identify "imminent" or "certainly impending" loss of Massachusetts coastal land fares no better. One of petitioners' declarants predicts global warming will cause sea level to rise by 20 to 70 centimeters by the year 2100. Another uses a computer modeling program to map the Commonwealth's coastal land and its current elevation, and calculates that the high-end estimate of sea level rise would result in the loss of significant state-owned coastal land. But the computer modeling program has a conceded average error of about 30 centimeters and a maximum observed error of 70 centimeters. As an initial matter, if it is possible that the model underrepresents the elevation of coastal land to an extent equal to or in excess of the projected sea level rise, it is difficult to put much stock in the predicted loss of land. But even placing that problem to the side, accepting a century-long time horizon and a series of compounded estimates renders requirements of imminence and immediacy utterly toothless. *See Defenders of Wildlife*, at 565, n.2 (while the concept of " 'imminence' " in standing doctrine is "somewhat elastic," it can be "stretched beyond the breaking point"). "Allegations of possible future injury do not satisfy the requirements of Art. III. A threatened injury must be *certainly impending* to constitute injury in fact." *Whitmore*, at 158 (internal quotation marks omitted; emphasis added).

III

Petitioners' reliance on Massachusetts's loss of coastal land as their injury in fact for standing purposes creates insurmountable problems for them with respect to causation and redressability. To establish standing, petitioners must show a causal connection between that specific injury and the lack of new motor vehicle greenhouse gas emission standards, and that the promulgation of such standards would likely redress that injury. As is often the case, the questions of causation and redressability overlap. *See Allen*, 468 U.S., at 753, n.19 (observing that the two requirements were "initially articulated by this Court as two facets of a single causation requirement" (internal quotation marks omitted)). And importantly, when a party is challenging the Government's allegedly unlawful regulation, or lack of regulation, of a third party, satisfying the causation and redressability requirements becomes "substantially more difficult." *Defenders of Wildlife*, at 562 (internal quotation marks omitted); *see also Warth*, at 504-505. . . .

The Court ignores the complexities of global warming, and does so by now disregarding the "particularized" injury it relied on in step one, and using the dire nature of global warming itself as a bootstrap for finding causation and redressability. First, it is important to recognize the extent of the emissions at issue here. Because local greenhouse gas emissions disperse throughout the atmosphere and remain there for anywhere from 50 to 200 years, it is global emissions data that are relevant. According to one of petitioners' declarations, domestic motor vehicles contribute about 6 percent of global carbon dioxide emissions and 4 percent of global greenhouse gas emissions. The amount of global emissions at issue here is smaller still; §202(a)(1) of the Clean Air Act covers only new motor vehicles and new motor vehicle engines, so petitioners' desired emission standards might reduce only a fraction of 4 percent of global emissions.

This gets us only to the relevant greenhouse gas emissions; linking them to global warming and ultimately to petitioners' alleged injuries next requires consideration of further complexities. . . .

Petitioners are never able to trace their alleged injuries back through this complex web to the fractional amount of global emissions that might have been limited with EPA standards. In light of the bit-part domestic new motor vehicle greenhouse gas emissions have played in what petitioners describe as a 150-year global phenomenon, and the myriad additional factors bearing on petitioners' alleged injury—the loss of Massachusetts coastal land—the connection is far too speculative to establish causation.

IV

Redressability is even more problematic. To the tenuous link between petitioners' alleged injury and the indeterminate fractional domestic emissions at issue here, add the fact that petitioners cannot meaningfully predict what will come of the 80 percent of global greenhouse gas emissions that originate outside the United States. As the Court acknowledges, "developing countries such as China and India are poised to increase greenhouse gas emissions substantially over the next century," so the domestic emissions at issue here may become an increasingly marginal portion of global emissions, and any decreases produced by petitioners' desired standards are likely to be overwhelmed many times over by emissions increases elsewhere in the world. . . .

[T]he Court reasons, because any decrease in domestic emissions will "slow the pace of global emissions increases, no matter what happens elsewhere." Every little bit helps, so Massachusetts can sue over any little bit.

The Court's sleight-of-hand is in failing to link up the different elements of the three-part standing test. What must be likely to be redressed is the particular injury in fact. The injury the Court looks to is the asserted loss of land. The Court contends that regulating domestic motor vehicle emissions will reduce carbon dioxide in the atmosphere, and therefore redress Massachusetts's injury. But even if regulation does reduce emissions—to some indeterminate degree, given events elsewhere in the world—the Court never explains why that makes it likely that the injury in fact—the loss of land—will be redressed. Schoolchildren know that a kingdom might be lost "all for the want of a horseshoe nail," but "likely" redressability is a different matter. The realities make it pure conjecture to suppose that EPA regulation of new automobile emissions will likely prevent the loss of Massachusetts coastal land.

V

Petitioners' difficulty in demonstrating causation and redressability is not surprising given the evident mismatch between the source of their alleged injury—catastrophic global warming—and the narrow subject matter of the Clean Air Act provision at issue in this suit. The mismatch suggests that petitioners' true goal for this litigation may be more symbolic than anything else. The constitutional role of the courts, however, is to decide concrete cases—not to serve as a convenient forum for policy debates. *See Valley Forge*

Christian College v. Americans United for Separation of Church and State, Inc., 454 U.S. 464, 472 (1982) ("[Standing] tends to assure that the legal questions presented to the court will be resolved, not in the rarified atmosphere of a debating society, but in a concrete factual context conducive to a realistic appreciation of the consequences of judicial action"). . . .

I respectfully dissent.

[Justice SCALIA, with whom THE CHIEF JUSTICE, Justice THOMAS, and Justice ALITO join, dissenting, omitted.]

Notes and Questions

1. The Court found that "at least" Massachusetts has standing. This was significant because the environmental groups that commenced the lawsuit lacked standing. Set aside Massachusetts for a moment. Let's begin by considering why the environmental groups lacked standing. Congress clearly intended them to have standing because it enacted a "citizen suit provision" granting "any person" the right to invoke judicial review of EPA action. Why didn't this settle the issue, allowing the environmental groups to have their case heard? Why did the Court say that it cannot "entertain citizen suits to vindicate the public's nonconcrete interest in the proper administration of the laws"? Is that principle grounded in Article III? If not in Article III, can you think of another constitutional basis for refusing to hear cases filed by plaintiffs with only general complaints about how agencies implement their statutes? *See* Lujan v. Defenders of Wildlife, 504 U.S. 555, 573, 577 (1992) (refusing to allow courts to become "virtually continuing monitors of the wisdom and soundness of Executive action").

2. EPA thought that the widespread nature of the harm barred standing for any plaintiff, but the Court replied that, "the gist of the question of standing" is whether petitioners have "such a personal stake in the outcome of the controversy as to assure that concrete adverseness which sharpens the presentation of issues upon which the court so largely depends for illumination." Do you doubt that the environmental groups will serve as zealous advocates and avoid the atmosphere of a debating society?

3. The Court states that in addition to a personal stake or particularized harm, a plaintiff must show that the government caused her injury ("causation") and that the court can redress her injury ("redressability"). These overlapping constitutional requirements are obstacles when a third party is involved—such as individuals and factories contributing to greenhouse gas production. In light of the private sources of greenhouse gas emissions, did the government cause climate change by failing to regulate? Can the Court redress climate change by ordering EPA to take action? The Court did state that a plaintiff with a "procedural" injury can avoid these onerous requirements. If EPA was required to respond to a petition for rulemaking, then the Court could hear a case challenging that failure to act under

§706(1) of the APA. The agency's failure to respond in and of itself could create a procedural injury sufficient to grant standing. So why isn't that injury sufficient to grant standing to the environmental groups here?

4. Turning now to Massachusetts, the Court was persuaded that states have a special right of access to the federal courts in exchange for surrender of their sovereignty to the federal government. Is this persuasive? It is often said that the states can protect their interests through the political process. *See* JESSE CHOPER, JUDICIAL REVIEW AND THE NATIONAL POLITICAL PROCESS (1980); Herbert Wechsler, *The Political Safeguards of Federalism: The Role of the States in the Composition and Selection of the National Government*, 54 COLUM. L. REV. 543, 558-60 (1954). States are represented in Congress and have electoral ties to the President. Do they need protection in the courts?

5. The Court also determined that Massachusetts was losing coastline to the sea—as if Cape Cod were an arm or leg injured by EPA's conduct. Is this persuasive? If Massachusetts has suffered an actual injury to its coastline, why can't private property owners along that coastline obtain standing to challenge EPA's conduct?

6. What about the fact that most of the risk of climate change is in the future? The Court has long held that a plaintiff need not establish the full extent of the injury, such as the lung cancer that she may eventually develop as a result of breathing air polluted by a nearby factory. Rather, a plaintiff must demonstrate actual exposure to the triggering factor—the pollution from the factory. Has Massachusetts demonstrated sufficient exposure to the triggering factor, or is that exposure speculative, as Chief Justice Roberts contends? Does it matter whether we characterize the triggering factor as climate change or greenhouse gas emissions? Chief Justice Roberts finds in this distinction a true mismatch between the problem (climate change) and the lawsuit (to challenge the failure of EPA to regulate greenhouse gas emissions from new vehicles), which shows why standing is lacking.

7. What about the causation and redressability requirements? The Court acknowledged that new motor vehicles produced or sold in this country contribute a relatively small portion of greenhouse gas emissions, yet it was persuaded that some regulatory action concerning these vehicles would have a meaningful effect on climate change. Should redressability and causation be a high or low hurdle? Does this case mean they are no longer serious obstacles?

8. Chief Justice Roberts could not imagine how anyone had standing because he believed that the injury was so abstract and hypothetical, but also because he believed that this was a case for the executive not the courts. Is he right? Does this decision reflect the loosening of standing, thereby enabling courts to assert greater control of agency regulation (or under-regulation)?

9. How much of this decision can be explained in terms of the issue involved? Climate change is an issue like no other; it is potentially catastrophic and time-sensitive. Perhaps the majority felt that it could not afford to delay the issue by remitting it to the political process. Perhaps it felt that the President was exercising too much control. President Bush said that he preferred to address the issue incrementally and in consideration of foreign affairs. Does that make the Court's decision to hear the case more or less defensible as a normative matter?

b. Reviewability

Reviewability doctrine bars courts from hearing certain claims. Like standing, it functions as a limit on judicial review (and hence judicial control) of agency action. One difference is that reviewability focuses more narrowly; it prevents review of particular statutory claims, as opposed to barring review altogether. Note that reviewability operates against a general presumption of judicial review and must be viewed in that context. The APA creates a broad right to judicial review: "A person suffering a legal wrong because of agency action, or adversely affected or aggrieved by agency action within the meaning of a relevant statute, is entitled to judicial review thereof." APA, 5 U.S.C. §702. The Supreme Court has repeatedly emphasized that the APA "embodies a basic presumption that of judicial review." *See, e.g.*, Abbott Laboratories v. Gardner, 387 U.S. 136, 140 (1967); Lincoln v. Vigil, 508 U.S. 182, 190 (1993).

There are two primary statutory ways in which claims might still be unreviewable. First, Congress may preclude judicial review by statute. The APA provides that the right to review applies except to the extent that "statutes preclude judicial review." APA §701(a)(1). The Court has held that statutory preclusion applies both to statutes that expressly preclude review as well as to those that impliedly do so. *See* Block v. Community Nutrition Institute, 467 U.S. 340, 345-47 (1984) (holding that §701(a)(1) precluded claim despite lack of express preclusion provision). Second, the APA precludes review where the "agency action is committed to agency discretion by law." APA, 5 U.S.C. §701(a)(2). The basic idea is that some agency decisions will be so discretionary that courts simply have "no law to apply" in evaluating their validity. Citizens to Preserve Overton Park, Inc. v. Volpe, 401 U.S. 402, 410 (1971). In other words, there are no criteria with respect to which the court could judge the legal merits of the agency's decision; it was simply a choice Congress gave the agency to make.

A claim can be committed to agency discretion by law for a slightly different reason: it is the sort of claim that courts are reluctant to review for fear of micro-managing the executive branch. Does this reasoning remind you of anything in a case that you (just) read? Read the one below.

Heckler v. Chaney

470 U.S. 821 (1985)

Justice REHNQUIST delivered the opinion of the Court.

This case presents the question of the extent to which a decision of an administrative agency to exercise its "discretion" not to undertake certain enforcement actions is subject to judicial review under the Administrative

Procedure Act, 5 U.S.C. §501 et seq. (APA). Respondents are several prison inmates convicted of capital offenses and sentenced to death by lethal injection of drugs. They petitioned the Food and Drug Administration (FDA), alleging that under the circumstances the use of these drugs for capital punishment violated the Federal Food, Drug, and Cosmetic Act, 52 Stat. 1040, as amended, 21 U.S.C. §301 et seq. (FDCA), and requesting that the FDA take various enforcement actions to prevent these violations. The FDA refused their request. We review here a decision of the Court of Appeals for the District of Columbia Circuit, which held the FDA's refusal to take enforcement actions both reviewable and an abuse of discretion, and remanded the case with directions that the agency be required "to fulfill its statutory function."

I

Respondents have been sentenced to death by lethal injection of drugs under the laws of the States of Oklahoma and Texas. Those States, and several others, have recently adopted this method for carrying out the capital sentence. Respondents first petitioned the FDA, claiming that the drugs used by the States for this purpose, although approved by the FDA for the medical purposes stated on their labels, were not approved for use in human executions. They alleged that the drugs had not been tested for the purpose for which they were to be used, and that, given that the drugs would likely be administered by untrained personnel, it was also likely that the drugs would not induce the quick and painless death intended. They urged that use of these drugs for human execution was the "unapproved use of an approved drug" and constituted a violation of the Act's prohibitions against "misbranding."[1] They also suggested that the FDCA's requirements for approval of "new drugs" applied, since these drugs were now being used for a new purpose. Accordingly, respondents claimed that the FDA was required to approve the drugs as "safe and effective" for human execution before they could be distributed in interstate commerce. See 21 U.S.C. §355. They therefore requested the FDA to take various investigatory and enforcement actions to prevent these perceived violations; they requested the FDA to affix warnings to the labels of all the drugs stating that they were unapproved and unsafe for human execution, to send statements to the drug manufacturers and prison administrators stating that the drugs should not be so used, and to adopt procedures for seizing the drugs from state prisons and to recommend the prosecution of all those in the chain of distribution who knowingly distribute or purchase the drugs with intent to use them for human execution.

The FDA Commissioner responded, refusing to take the requested actions. The Commissioner first detailed his disagreement with respondents'

---

1. See 21 U.S.C. §352(f): "A drug or device shall be deemed to be misbranded . . . [u]nless its labeling bears (1) adequate directions for use. . . ."

understanding of the scope of FDA jurisdiction over the unapproved use of approved drugs for human execution, concluding that FDA jurisdiction in the area was generally unclear but in any event should not be exercised to interfere with this particular aspect of state criminal justice systems. He went on to state:

> "Were FDA clearly to have jurisdiction in the area, moreover, we believe we would be authorized to decline to exercise it under our inherent discretion to decline to pursue certain enforcement matters. The unapproved use of approved drugs is an area in which the case law is far from uniform. Generally, enforcement proceedings in this area are initiated only when there is a serious danger to the public health or a blatant scheme to defraud. We cannot conclude that those dangers are present under State lethal injection laws, which are duly authorized statutory enactments in furtherance of proper State functions. . . ."

Respondents then filed the instant suit in the United States District Court for the District of Columbia, claiming the same violations of the FDCA and asking that the FDA be required to take the same enforcement actions requested in the prior petition. . . .

[The district court granted summary judgment to petitioner, and a divided panel of the Court of Appeals reversed.] We reverse.

II

The Court of Appeals' decision addressed three questions: (1) whether the FDA had jurisdiction to undertake the enforcement actions requested, (2) whether if it did have jurisdiction its refusal to take those actions was subject to judicial review, and (3) whether if reviewable its refusal was arbitrary, capricious, or an abuse of discretion. In reaching our conclusion that the Court of Appeals was wrong, however, we need not and do not address the thorny question of the FDA's jurisdiction. For us, this case turns on the important question of the extent to which determinations by the FDA not to exercise its enforcement authority over the use of drugs in interstate commerce may be judicially reviewed. That decision in turn involves the construction of two separate but necessarily interrelated statutes, the APA and the FDCA.

The APA's comprehensive provisions for judicial review of "agency actions," are contained in 5 U.S.C. §§701-706. Any person "adversely affected or aggrieved" by agency action; *see* §702, including a "failure to act," is entitled to "judicial review thereof," as long as the action is a "final agency action for which there is no other adequate remedy in a court," *see* §704. The standards to be applied on review are governed by the provisions of §706. But before any review at all may be had, a party must first clear the hurdle of §701(a). That section provides that the chapter on judicial review "applies, according to the provisions thereof, except to the extent that—(1) statutes preclude judicial review; or (2) agency action is committed to agency discretion by law." Petitioner urges that the decision of the FDA to refuse enforcement is an action "committed to agency discretion by law" under §701(a)(2).

This Court has not had occasion to interpret this second exception in §701(a) in any great detail. On its face, the section does not obviously lend itself to any particular construction; indeed, one might wonder what difference exists between §(a)(1) and §(a)(2). The former section seems easy in application; it requires construction of the substantive statute involved to determine whether Congress intended to preclude judicial review of certain decisions. That is the approach taken with respect to §(a)(1) in cases such as *Southern R. Co. v. Seaboard Allied Milling Corp.*, 442 U.S. 444 (1979), and *Dunlop v. Bachowski*, 421 U.S., at 567. But one could read the language "committed to agency discretion by law" in §(a)(2) to require a similar inquiry. In addition, commentators have pointed out that construction of §(a)(2) is further complicated by the tension between a literal reading of §(a)(2), which exempts from judicial review those decisions committed to agency "discretion," and the primary scope of review prescribed by §706(2)(A) — whether the agency's action was "arbitrary, capricious, or an abuse of discretion." How is it, they ask, that an action committed to agency discretion can be unreviewable and yet courts still can review agency actions for abuse of that discretion? *See* 5 K. Davis, Administrative Law §28:6 (1984) (hereafter Davis); Berger, *Administrative Arbitrariness and Judicial Review*, 65 COLUM. L. REV. 55, 58 (1965). The APA's legislative history provides little help on this score. Mindful, however, of the common-sense principle of statutory construction that sections of a statute generally should be read "to give effect, if possible, to every clause . . . ," *see United States v. Menasche*, 348 U.S. 528, 538-539 (1955), we think there is a proper construction of §(a)(2) which satisfies each of these concerns.

This Court first discussed §(a)(2) in *Citizens to Preserve Overton Park v. Volpe*, 401 U.S. 402 (1971). That case dealt with the Secretary of Transportation's approval of the building of an interstate highway through a park in Memphis, Tennessee. The relevant federal statute provided that the Secretary "shall not approve" any program or project using public parkland unless the Secretary first determined that no feasible alternatives were available. *Id.*, at 411. Interested citizens challenged the Secretary's approval under the APA, arguing that he had not satisfied the substantive statute's requirements. This Court first addressed the "threshold question" of whether the agency's action was at all reviewable. After setting out the language of §701(a), the Court stated:

> "In this case, there is no indication that Congress sought to prohibit judicial review and there is most certainly no 'showing of "clear and convincing evidence" of a . . . legislative intent' to restrict access to judicial review. *Abbott Laboratories v. Gardner*, 387 U.S. 136, 141 (1967). . . .
>
> "Similarly, the Secretary's decision here does not fall within the exception for action 'committed to agency discretion.' This is a very narrow exception. . . . The legislative history of the Administrative Procedure Act indicates that it is applicable in those rare instances where 'statutes are drawn in such broad terms that in a given case there is no law to apply.' S. REP. No. 752, 79th Cong., 1st Sess., 26 (1945)." *Overton Park*, 401 U.S., at 410 (footnote omitted).

The above quote answers several of the questions raised by the language of §701(a), although it raises others. First, it clearly separates the exception provided by §(a)(1) from the §(a)(2) exception. The former applies when Congress has expressed an intent to preclude judicial review. The latter applies in different circumstances; even where Congress has not affirmatively precluded review, review is not to be had if the statute is drawn so that a court would have no meaningful standard against which to judge the agency's exercise of discretion. In such a case, the statute ("law") can be taken to have "committed" the decisionmaking to the agency's judgment absolutely. This construction avoids conflict with the "abuse of discretion" standard of review in §706—if no judicially manageable standards are available for judging how and when an agency should exercise its discretion, then it is impossible to evaluate agency action for "abuse of discretion." In addition, this construction satisfies the principle of statutory construction mentioned earlier, by identifying a separate class of cases to which §701(a)(2) applies.

To this point our analysis does not differ significantly from that of the Court of Appeals. That court purported to apply the "no law to apply" standard of *Overton Park.* We disagree, however, with that court's insistence that the "narrow construction" of §(a)(2) required application of a presumption of reviewability even to an agency's decision not to undertake certain enforcement actions. Here we think the Court of Appeals broke with tradition, case law, and sound reasoning.

Overton Park did not involve an agency's refusal to take requested enforcement action. It involved an affirmative act of approval under a statute that set clear guidelines for determining when such approval should be given. Refusals to take enforcement steps generally involve precisely the opposite situation, and in that situation we think the presumption is that judicial review is not available. This Court has recognized on several occasions over many years that an agency's decision not to prosecute or enforce, whether through civil or criminal process, is a decision generally committed to an agency's absolute discretion. . . . This recognition of the existence of discretion is attributable in no small part to the general unsuitability for judicial review of agency decisions to refuse enforcement.

The reasons for this general unsuitability are many. First, an agency decision not to enforce often involves a complicated balancing of a number of factors which are peculiarly within its expertise. Thus, the agency must not only assess whether a violation has occurred, but whether agency resources are best spent on this violation or another, whether the agency is likely to succeed if it acts, whether the particular enforcement action requested best fits the agency's overall policies, and, indeed, whether the agency has enough resources to undertake the action at all. An agency generally cannot act against each technical violation of the statute it is charged with enforcing. The agency is far better equipped than the courts to deal with the many variables involved in the proper ordering of its priorities. Similar concerns animate the principles of administrative law that courts generally will defer to an agency's construction of the statute it is charged with implementing, and to the procedures it adopts for implementing that statute. *See Vermont Yankee Nuclear Power Corp. v. Natural Resources Defense Council, Inc.*, 435 U.S. 519, 543 (1978). . . .

In addition to these administrative concerns, we note that when an agency refuses to act it generally does not exercise its coercive power over an individual's liberty or property rights, and thus does not infringe upon areas that courts often are called upon to protect. Similarly, when an agency does act to enforce, that action itself provides a focus for judicial review, inasmuch as the agency must have exercised its power in some manner. The action at least can be reviewed to determine whether the agency exceeded its statutory powers. . . . Finally, we recognize that an agency's refusal to institute proceedings shares to some extent the characteristics of the decision of a prosecutor in the Executive Branch not to indict—a decision which has long been regarded as the special province of the Executive Branch, inasmuch as it is the Executive who is charged by the Constitution to "take Care that the Laws be faithfully executed." U.S. CONST., Art. II, §3.

We of course only list the above concerns to facilitate understanding of our conclusion that an agency's decision not to take enforcement action should be presumed immune from judicial review under §701(a)(2). For good reasons, such a decision has traditionally been "committed to agency discretion," and we believe that the Congress enacting the APA did not intend to alter that tradition. Cf. 5 Davis §28:5 (APA did not significantly alter the "common law" of judicial review of agency action). In so stating, we emphasize that the decision is only presumptively unreviewable; the presumption may be rebutted where the substantive statute has provided guidelines for the agency to follow in exercising its enforcement powers.[2] Thus, in establishing this presumption in the APA, Congress did not set agencies free to disregard legislative direction in the statutory scheme that the agency administers. Congress may limit an agency's exercise of enforcement power if it wishes, either by setting substantive priorities, or by otherwise circumscribing an agency's power to discriminate among issues or cases it will pursue. How to determine when Congress has done so is the question left open by *Overton Park*. . . .

III

To enforce the various substantive prohibitions contained in the FDCA, the Act provides for injunctions, 21 U.S.C. §332, criminal sanctions, §§333 and

---

2. We do not have in this case a refusal by the agency to institute proceedings based solely on the belief that it lacks jurisdiction. Nor do we have a situation where it could justifiably be found that the agency has "consciously and expressly adopted a general policy" that is so extreme as to amount to an abdication of its statutory responsibilities. *See, e.g., Adams v. Richardson*, 480 F.2d 1159 (1973) (en banc). Although we express no opinion on whether such decisions would be unreviewable under §701(a)(2), we note that in those situations the statute conferring authority on the agency might indicate that such decisions were not "committed to agency discretion."

335, and seizure of any offending food, drug, or cosmetic article, §334. The Act's general provision for enforcement, §372, provides only that "[t]he Secretary is *authorized* to conduct examinations and investigations . . ." (emphasis added). [Section] 332 gives no indication of when an injunction should be sought, and §334, providing for seizures, is framed in the permissive—the offending food, drug, or cosmetic "shall be liable to be proceeded against." The section on criminal sanctions states baldly that any person who violates the Act's substantive prohibitions "shall be imprisoned . . . or fined." Respondents argue that this statement mandates criminal prosecution of every violator of the Act but they adduce no indication in case law or legislative history that such was Congress' intention in using this language, which is commonly found in the criminal provisions of Title 18 of the United States Code. *See, e.g.,* 18 U.S.C. §471 (counterfeiting); 18 U.S.C. §1001 (false statements to Government officials); 18 U.S.C. §1341 (mail fraud). We are unwilling to attribute such a sweeping meaning to this language, particularly since the Act charges the Secretary only with recommending prosecution; any criminal prosecutions must be instituted by the Attorney General. The Act's enforcement provisions thus commit complete discretion to the Secretary to decide how and when they should be exercised.

Respondents nevertheless present three separate authorities that they claim provide the courts with sufficient indicia of an intent to circumscribe enforcement discretion. Two of these may be dealt with summarily. First, we reject respondents' argument that the Act's substantive prohibitions of "misbranding" and the introduction of "new drugs" absent agency approval, *see* 21 U.S.C. §§352(f)(1), 355, supply us with "law to apply." These provisions are simply irrelevant to the agency's discretion to refuse to initiate proceedings. . . .

Respondents' third argument, based upon §306 of the FDCA, merits only slightly more consideration. That section provides:

> "Nothing in this chapter shall be construed as requiring the Secretary to report for prosecution, or for the institution of libel or injunction proceedings, minor violations of this chapter whenever he believes that the public interest will be adequately served by a suitable written notice or ruling." 21 U.S.C. §336.

Respondents seek to draw from this section the negative implication that the Secretary is required to report for prosecution all "major" violations of the Act, however those might be defined, and that it therefore supplies the needed indication of an intent to limit agency enforcement discretion. We think that this section simply does not give rise to the negative implication which respondents seek to draw from it. The section is not addressed to agency proceedings designed to discover the existence of violations, but applies only to a situation where a violation has already been established to the satisfaction of the agency. We do not believe the section speaks to the criteria which shall be used by the agency for investigating possible violations of the Act.

IV

We therefore conclude that the presumption that agency decisions not to institute proceedings are unreviewable under 5 U.S.C. §701(a)(2) is not overcome by the enforcement provisions of the FDCA. The FDA's decision not to take the enforcement actions requested by respondents is therefore not subject to judicial review under the APA. The general exception to reviewability provided by §701(a)(2) for action "committed to agency discretion" remains a narrow one, *see Citizens to Preserve Overton Park v. Volpe*, 401 U.S. 402 (1971), but within that exception are included agency refusals to institute investigative or enforcement proceedings, unless Congress has indicated otherwise. In so holding, we essentially leave to Congress, and not to the courts, the decision as to whether an agency's refusal to institute proceedings should be judicially reviewable. No colorable claim is made in this case that the agency's refusal to institute proceedings violated any constitutional rights of respondents, and we do not address the issue that would be raised in such a case. *Cf. Johnson v. Robison*, 415 U.S. 361, 366 (1974); *Yick Wo v. Hopkins*, 118 U.S. 356, 372-374 (1886). The fact that the drugs involved in this case are ultimately to be used in imposing the death penalty must not lead this Court or other courts to import profound differences of opinion over the meaning of the Eighth Amendment to the United States Constitution into the domain of administrative law.

The judgment of the Court of Appeals is
Reversed.

Justice BRENNAN, concurring.

Today the Court holds that individual decisions of the Food and Drug Administration not to take enforcement action in response to citizen requests are presumptively not reviewable under the Administrative Procedure Act, 5 U.S.C. §§701-706. I concur in this decision. This general presumption is based on the view that, in the normal course of events, Congress intends to allow broad discretion for its administrative agencies to make particular enforcement decisions, and there often may not exist readily discernible "law to apply" for courts to conduct judicial review of nonenforcement decisions. *See Citizens to Preserve Overton Park v. Volpe*, 401 U.S. 402, 410 (1971).

I also agree that, despite this general presumption, "Congress did not set agencies free to disregard legislative direction in the statutory scheme that the agency administers." Thus the Court properly does not decide today that nonenforcement decisions are unreviewable in cases where (1) an agency flatly claims that it has no statutory jurisdiction to reach certain conduct; (2) an agency engages in a pattern of nonenforcement of clear statutory language, as in *Adams v. Richardson*, 480 F.2d 1159 (1973) (en banc); (3) an agency has refused to enforce a regulation lawfully promulgated and still in effect;[1] or (4) a nonenforcement decision violates constitutional rights. It is possible to imagine other nonenforcement decisions made for entirely illegitimate reasons, for example, nonenforcement in return for a bribe, judicial review of which would not be foreclosed by the nonreviewability

---

1. Cf. *Motor Vehicle Manufacturers Assn. v. State Farm Mutual Ins. Co.*, 463 U.S. 29, 40-44, 103 S. Ct. 2856, 2865-2867 (1983) (failure to revoke lawfully a previously promulgated rule is reviewable under the APA).

presumption. It may be presumed that Congress does not intend administrative agencies, agents of Congress' own creation, to ignore clear jurisdictional, regulatory, statutory, or constitutional commands, and in some circumstances including those listed above the statutes or regulations at issue may well provide "law to apply" under 5 U.S.C. §701(a)(2). Individual, isolated nonenforcement decisions, however, must be made by hundreds of agencies each day. It is entirely permissible to presume that Congress has not intended courts to review such mundane matters, absent either some indication of congressional intent to the contrary or proof of circumstances such as those set out above.

On this understanding of the scope of today's decision, I join the Court's opinion.

Justice MARSHALL, concurring in the judgment.

Easy cases at times produce bad law, for in the rush to reach a clearly ordained result, courts may offer up principles, doctrines, and statements that calmer reflection, and a fuller understanding of their implications in concrete settings, would eschew. In my view, the "presumption of unreviewability" announced today is a product of that lack of discipline that easy cases make all too easy. The majority, eager to reverse what it goes out of its way to label as an "implausible result," not only does reverse, as I agree it should, but along the way creates out of whole cloth the notion that agency decisions not to take "enforcement action" are unreviewable unless Congress has rather specifically indicated otherwise. Because this "presumption of unreviewability" is fundamentally at odds with rule-of-law principles firmly embedded in our jurisprudence, because it seeks to truncate an emerging line of judicial authority subjecting enforcement discretion to rational and principled constraint, and because, in the end, the presumption may well be indecipherable, one can only hope that it will come to be understood as a relic of a particular factual setting in which the full implications of such a presumption were neither confronted nor understood.

I write separately to argue for a different basis of decision: that refusals to enforce, like other agency actions, are reviewable in the absence of a "clear and convincing" congressional intent to the contrary, but that such refusals warrant deference when, as in this case, there is nothing to suggest that an agency with enforcement discretion has abused that discretion. . . .

When a statute does not mandate full enforcement, I agree with the Court that an agency is generally "far better equipped than the courts to deal with the many variables involved in the proper ordering of its priorities." As long as the agency is choosing how to allocate finite enforcement resources, the agency's choice will be entitled to substantial deference, for the choice among valid alternative enforcement policies is precisely the sort of choice over which agencies generally have been left substantial discretion by their enabling statutes. On the merits, then, a decision not to enforce that is based on valid resource-allocation decisions will generally not be "arbitrary, capricious, an abuse of discretion, or otherwise not in accordance with law," 5 U.S.C. §706(2)(A). The decision in this case is no exception to this principle.

The Court, however, is not content to rest on this ground. Instead, the Court transforms the arguments for deferential review on the merits into the wholly different notion that "enforcement" decisions are presumptively unreviewable altogether—unreviewable whether the resource-allocation rationale is a sham, unreviewable whether enforcement is declined out of vindictive or personal motives, and unreviewable whether the agency has simply ignored the request for enforcement. . . . But surely it is a far cry from asserting that agencies must be given substantial leeway in allocating enforcement resources among valid alternatives to suggesting that agency enforcement decisions are presumptively unreviewable no matter what factor caused the agency to stay its hand. . . .

Moreover, for at least two reasons it is inappropriate to rely on notions of prosecutorial discretion to hold agency inaction unreviewable. First, since the dictum in Nixon, the Court has made clear that prosecutorial discretion is not as unfettered or unreviewable as the half-sentence in Nixon suggests. As one of the leading commentators in this area has noted, "the case law since 1974 is strongly on the side of reviewability." 2 K. Davis, Administrative Law §9:6, p. 240 (1979). In *Blackledge v. Perry*, 417 U.S. 21, 28 (1974), instead of invoking notions of "absolute" prosecutorial discretion, we held that certain potentially vindictive exercises of prosecutorial discretion were both reviewable and impermissible. The "retaliatory use" of prosecutorial power is no longer tolerated. . . . And in rejecting on the merits a claim of improper prosecutorial conduct in *Bordenkircher v. Hayes*, 434 U.S. 357 (1978), we clearly laid to rest any notion that prosecutorial discretion is unreviewable no matter what the basis is upon which it is exercised:

> "There is no doubt that the breadth of discretion that our country's legal system vests in prosecuting attorneys carries with it the potential for both individual and institutional abuse. And broad though that discretion may be, there are undoubtedly constitutional limits upon its exercise." *Id.*, at 365.

. . . If a plaintiff makes a sufficient threshold showing that a prosecutor's discretion has been exercised for impermissible reasons, judicial review is available.

Second, arguments about prosecutorial discretion do not necessarily translate into the context of agency refusals to act. . . . Criminal prosecutorial decisions vindicate only intangible interests, common to society as a whole, in the enforcement of the criminal law. The conduct at issue has already occurred; all that remains is society's general interest in assuring that the guilty are punished. . . . In contrast, requests for administrative enforcement typically seek to prevent concrete and future injuries that Congress has made cognizable—injuries that result, for example, from misbranded drugs, such as alleged in this case, or unsafe nuclear power plants, *see, e.g., Florida Power & Light Co. v. Lorion*, 470 U.S. 729 (1985)—or to obtain palpable benefits that Congress has intended to bestow—such as labor union elections free of corruption, *see Dunlop v. Bachowski*, 421 U.S. 560 (1975). Entitlements to receive these benefits or to be free of these injuries often run to specific classes of individuals whom Congress has singled out as statutory beneficiaries. The interests at stake in review of administrative enforcement decisions are thus more focused and in many circumstances more pressing than those at stake in criminal prosecutorial decisions. A request that a nuclear plant be operated safely or that protection be provided against unsafe drugs is quite different from a request that an individual be put in jail or his property confiscated as punishment for past violations of the criminal law. Unlike traditional exercises of prosecutorial discretion, "the decision to enforce—or not to enforce—may itself result in significant burdens on a . . . statutory beneficiary." *Marshall v. Jerrico, Inc.*, 446 U.S., at 249.

Perhaps most important, the sine qua non of the APA was to alter inherited judicial reluctance to constrain the exercise of discretionary administrative power—to rationalize and make fairer the exercise of such discretion. Since passage of the APA, the sustained effort of administrative law has been to "continuously narro[w] the category of actions considered to be so discretionary as to be exempted from review." Shapiro, *Administrative Discretion: The Next Stage*, 92 YALE L.J. 1487, 1489, n.11 (1983). Discretion may well be necessary to carry out a variety of important administrative functions, but discretion can be a veil for laziness, corruption, incompetency, lack of will, or other motives, and for that reason "the presence of discretion should not bar a court from considering a claim of illegal or arbitrary use of discretion." L. Jaffe, Judicial Control of Administrative Action 375 (1965). Judicial review is available under the APA in the absence of a clear and convincing demonstration that Congress intended to preclude it precisely so that agencies, whether in rulemaking, adjudicating, acting or failing to act, do not become stagnant backwaters of caprice and lawlessness. . . .

For these and other reasons, reliance on prosecutorial discretion, itself a fading talisman, to justify the unreviewability of agency inaction is inappropriate. . . . To the extent arguments about traditional notions of prosecutorial discretion have any force at all in this context, they ought to apply only to an agency's decision to decline to seek penalties against an individual for past conduct, not to a decision to refuse to investigate or take action on a public health, safety, or welfare problem.

II

The "tradition" of unreviewability upon which the majority relies is refuted most powerfully by a firmly entrenched body of lower court case law that holds reviewable various agency refusals to act. This case law recognizes that attempting to draw a line for purposes of judicial review between affirmative exercises of coercive agency power and negative agency refusals to act, is simply untenable; one of the very purposes fueling the birth of administrative agencies was the reality that governmental refusal to act could have just as devastating an effect upon life, liberty, and the pursuit of happiness as coercive governmental action. . . .

III

The problem of agency refusal to act is one of the pressing problems of the modern administrative state, given the enormous powers, for both good and ill, that agency inaction, like agency action, holds over citizens. As *Dunlop v. Bachowski*, 421 U.S. 560 (1975), recognized, the problems and dangers of agency inaction are too important, too prevalent, and too multifaceted to admit of a single facile solution under which "enforcement" decisions are "presumptively unreviewable." Over time, I believe the approach announced today will come to be understood, not as mandating that courts cover their eyes and their reasoning power when asked to review an agency's failure to act, but as recognizing that courts must approach the substantive task of reviewing such failures with appropriate deference to an agency's legitimate need to set policy through the allocation of scarce budgetary and enforcement resources. Because the Court's approach, if taken literally, would take the courts out of the role of reviewing agency inaction in far too many cases, I join only the judgment today.

Notes and Questions

1. This case, with its jarring facts, raises a difficult issue: to what extent should private parties and courts prioritize the actions that agencies take? Isn't that function quintessentially executive in nature? Think about prosecutorial discretion. What would happen if the victim of a crime could compel judicial review of a prosecutor's refusal to pursue the alleged perpetrator?

2. At the same time, why would it be problematic for courts to ask agencies like the FDA to explain their refusal to address certain issues, as Justice Marshall suggests? What if the refusal were premised on political or ideological biases, like disregard for the rights of death row inmates?

c. Timing

Timing encompasses several distinct doctrines, but most notable for our purpose are ripeness and finality. These doctrines also have the potential to block courts from asserting control of agency action—at least temporarily. They have different effects for the various forms of agency action that we have seen.

Ripeness has roots in the Article III "Case" or "Controversy" requirement: a claim brought too soon is not the subject of a live case or controversy. Why should the court intervene if a case might never materialize? The Court evaluates ripeness by "evaluat[ing] both the fitness of the issues for judicial decision and the hardship of the parties of withholding court consideration." Abbott Laboratories v. Gardner, 387 U.S. 136, 149 (1967). If the question depends on facts that enforcement might bring to light, then it is likely not fit for judicial decision. If the question is purely legal, such as a question of statutory interpretation, it is likely fit for judicial decision. If the parties have no choice but to incur compliance costs now for fear of facing noncompliance penalties later, they have likely demonstrated hardship. With respect to final rules, pre-enforcement review is the now the norm. Parties file their suits immediately rather than awaiting an enforcement proceeding.

Finality concerns the question of whether the agency's action is determinative rather than preliminary or advisory. It has a statutory basis. APA §704 provides that only "final agency action" is subject to judicial review. The Court has said final agency action "must mark the 'consummation' of the agency's decisionmaking process [and] not be of a merely tentative or interlocutory character" and "the action must be one by which 'rights or obligations have been determined,' or from which 'legal consequences will flow.'" Bennett v. Spear, 520 U.S. 154, 177-78 (1997). It should be clear from this description that a final rule issued through the notice-and-comment rulemaking process is final agency action, but a notice of proposed rulemaking is not. An order issued by the board of the agency after formal adjudication is also final agency action, but an ALJ's earlier ruling is not.

What about guidance? In general, agency guidance documents will not meet the two prongs of the finality requirement because such documents are neither legally binding nor the consummation of the agency's decision-making process. But there are exceptions. Guidance documents can constitute the consummation of the agency's decision-making process. *See* Appalachian Power Co. v. EPA, 208 F.3d 1015, 1022 (D.C. Cir. 2002). Moreover, as we saw in Chapter 5, sometimes agencies treat guidance as binding. *See id.* at 1022-28. If a court finds that a guidance document is final, watch out on the merits—a court can hold that document procedurally invalid for not having been issued through the notice-and-comment rulemaking process. *See id.*; *see also* 5 U.S.C. §553(d)(2). Is it right to link review of guidance documents to their validity in this way? Why not allow review whenever the guidance document appears to be the consummation of the agency's decision making? *See* National Automatic Laundry & Cleaning Council v. Shultz, 443 F.2d 689, 702-03 (D.C. Cir. 1971). What is the right balance between allowing judicial review and micro-managing agency action?

The regulatory state is the collection of laws and institutions that determine many aspects of social and economic policy. But you know that now. You have acquired a set of skills and tools for approaching problems that involve these laws and institutions. In addition, you have acquired a jumping-off point for evaluating modern government. We remind you that no set of skills or tools can relieve lawyers of the obligation to read actual statutes and regulations. Knowledge of the actual personnel involved is also indispensable if the goal is shaping agency regulations. Litigators are often interested in which court or judge will hear their case because that might provide a window on what sorts of arguments to make. Lawyers in the regulatory state are no different, although they are interested in more players—agency officials, White House officials, members of Congress, as well as courts. You may be one of those lawyers.

Appendix A

Selected Provisions of the Constitution of the United States of America

We the People of the United States, in Order to form a more perfect Union, establish Justice, insure domestic Tranquility, provide for the common defense, promote the general Welfare, and secure the Blessings of Liberty to ourselves and our Posterity, do ordain and establish this Constitution for the United States of America.

ARTICLE I

Section 1.

All legislative Powers herein granted shall be vested in a Congress of the United States, which shall consist of a Senate and House of Representatives.

Section 2.

[1]   The House of Representatives shall be composed of Members chosen every second Year by the People of the several States, and the Electors in each State shall have the Qualifications requisite for Electors of the most numerous Branch of the State Legislature.

[2]   No Person shall be a Representative who shall not have attained to the Age of twenty five Years, and been seven Years a Citizen of the United States, and who shall not, when elected, be an Inhabitant of that State in which he shall be chosen.

[3]   *Representatives and direct Taxes shall be apportioned among the several States which may be included within this Union, according to their respective Numbers, which shall be determined by adding to the whole Number of free Persons, including those bound to Service for a Term of Years, and excluding Indians not taxed, three fifths of all other Persons* [the previous sentence in italics was superseded by Amendment XIV]. The actual Enumeration shall be made within three Years after the first Meeting of the Congress of the United States, and

within every subsequent Term of ten Years, in such Manner as they shall by Law direct. The Number of Representatives shall not exceed one for every thirty Thousand, but each State shall have at Least one Representative; and until such enumeration shall be made, the State of New Hampshire shall be entitled to chuse three, Massachusetts eight, Rhode-Island and Providence Plantations one, Connecticut five, New-York six, New Jersey four, Pennsylvania eight, Delaware one, Maryland six, Virginia ten, North Carolina five, South Carolina five, and Georgia three.

[4]   When vacancies happen in the Representation from any State, the Executive Authority thereof shall issue Writs of Election to fill such Vacancies.

[5]   The House of Representatives shall chuse their Speaker and other Officers; and shall have the sole Power of Impeachment.

Section 3.

[1]   The Senate of the United States shall be composed of two Senators from each State, *chosen by the Legislature* [the preceding five words were superseded by Amendment XVII] thereof for six Years; and each Senator shall have one Vote.

[2]   Immediately after they shall be assembled in Consequence of the first Election, they shall be divided as equally as may be into three Classes. The Seats of the Senators of the first Class shall be vacated at the Expiration of the second Year, of the second Class at the Expiration of the fourth Year, and of the third Class at the Expiration of the sixth Year, so that one third may be chosen every second Year; *and if Vacancies happen by Resignation, or otherwise, during the Recess of the Legislature of any State, the Executive thereof may make temporary Appointments until the next Meeting of the Legislature, which shall then fill such Vacancies.* [The preceding words in italics were superseded by Amendment XVII.]

[3]   No Person shall be a Senator who shall not have attained to the Age of thirty Years, and been nine Years a Citizen of the United States, and who shall not, when elected, be an Inhabitant of that State for which he shall be chosen.

[4]   The Vice President of the United States shall be President of the Senate, but shall have no Vote, unless they be equally divided.

[5]   The Senate shall chuse their other Officers, and also a President pro tempore, in the Absence of the Vice President, or when he shall exercise the Office of President of the United States.

[6]   The Senate shall have the sole Power to try all Impeachments. When sitting for that Purpose, they shall be on Oath or Affirmation. When the President of the United States is tried, the Chief Justice shall preside: And no Person shall be convicted without the Concurrence of two thirds of the Members present.

[7]   Judgment in Cases of Impeachment shall not extend further than to removal from Office, and disqualification to hold and enjoy any Office of honor, Trust or Profit under the United States: but the Party convicted shall nevertheless be liable and subject to Indictment, Trial, Judgment and Punishment, according to Law.

Section 4.

[1]   The Times, Places and Manner of holding Elections for Senators and Representatives, shall be prescribed in each State by the Legislature thereof; but the Congress may at any time by Law make or alter such Regulations, except as to the Places of chusing Senators.

[2]   The Congress shall assemble at least once in every Year, and such Meeting *shall be on the first Monday in December* [the preceding seven words in italics were superseded by Amendment XX], unless they shall by Law appoint a different Day.

Section 5.

[1]   Each House shall be the Judge of the Elections, Returns and Qualifications of its own Members, and a Majority of each shall constitute a Quorum to do Business; but a smaller Number may adjourn from day to day, and may be authorized to compel the Attendance of absent Members, in such Manner, and under such Penalties as each House may provide.

[2]   Each House may determine the Rules of its Proceedings, punish its Members for disorderly Behaviour, and, with the Concurrence of two thirds, expel a Member.

[3]   Each House shall keep a Journal of its Proceedings, and from time to time publish the same, excepting such Parts as may in their Judgment require Secrecy; and the Yeas and Nays of the Members of either House on any question shall, at the Desire of one fifth of those Present, be entered on the Journal.

[4]   Neither House, during the Session of Congress, shall, without the Consent of the other, adjourn for more than three days, nor to any other Place than that in which the two Houses shall be sitting.

Section 6.

[1]   The Senators and Representatives shall receive a Compensation for their Services, to be ascertained by Law, and paid out of the Treasury of the United States. They shall in all Cases, except Treason, Felony and Breach of the Peace, be privileged from Arrest during their Attendance at the Session of their respective Houses, and in going to and returning from the same; and for any Speech or Debate in either House, they shall not be questioned in any other Place.

[2]   No Senator or Representative shall, during the Time for which he was elected, be appointed to any civil Office under the Authority of the United States, which shall have been created, or the Emoluments whereof shall have been encreased during such time; and no Person holding any Office under the United States, shall be a Member of either House during his Continuance in Office.

Section 7.

[1]   All Bills for raising Revenue shall originate in the House of Representatives; but the Senate may propose or concur with Amendments as on other Bills.

[2]   Every Bill which shall have passed the House of Representatives and the Senate, shall, before it become a Law, be presented to the President of the United States: If he approve he shall sign it, but if not he shall return it, with his Objections to that House in which it shall have originated, who shall enter the Objections at large on their Journal, and proceed to reconsider it. If after such Reconsideration two thirds of that House shall agree to pass the Bill, it shall be sent, together with the Objections, to the other House, by which it shall likewise be reconsidered, and if approved by two thirds of that House, it shall become a Law. But in all such Cases the Votes of both Houses shall be determined by yeas and Nays, and the Names of the Persons voting for and against the Bill shall be entered on the Journal of each House respectively. If any Bill shall not be returned by the President within ten Days (Sundays excepted) after it shall have been presented to him, the Same shall be a Law, in like Manner as if he had signed it, unless the Congress by their Adjournment prevent its Return, in which Case it shall not be a Law.

[3]   Every Order, Resolution, or Vote to which the Concurrence of the Senate and House of Representatives may be necessary (except on a question of Adjournment) shall be presented to the President of the United States; and before the Same shall take Effect, shall be approved by him, or being disapproved by him, shall be repassed by two thirds of the Senate and House of Representatives, according to the Rules and Limitations prescribed in the Case of a Bill.

Section 8.

[1]   The Congress shall have Power To lay and collect Taxes, Duties, Imposts and Excises, to pay the Debts and provide for the common Defence and general Welfare of the United States; but all Duties, Imposts and Excises shall be uniform throughout the United States;

[2]   To borrow Money on the credit of the United States;

[3]   To regulate Commerce with foreign Nations, and among the several States, and with the Indian Tribes;

[4]   To establish an uniform Rule of Naturalization, and uniform Laws on the subject of Bankruptcies throughout the United States;

[5]   To coin Money, regulate the Value thereof, and of foreign Coin, and fix the Standard of Weights and Measures;

[6]   To provide for the Punishment of counterfeiting the Securities and current Coin of the United States;

[7]   To establish Post Offices and post Roads;

[8]   To promote the Progress of Science and useful Arts, by securing for limited Times to Authors and Inventors the exclusive Right to their respective Writings and Discoveries;

[9]   To constitute Tribunals inferior to the supreme Court;

[10]   To define and punish Piracies and Felonies committed on the high Seas, and Offences against the Law of Nations;

[11]   To declare War, grant Letters of Marque and Reprisal, and make Rules concerning Captures on Land and Water;

[12]   To raise and support Armies, but no Appropriation of Money to that Use shall be for a longer Term than two Years;

[13]   To provide and maintain a Navy;

[14]   To make Rules for the Government and Regulation of the land and naval Forces;

[15]   To provide for calling forth the Militia to execute the Laws of the Union, suppress Insurrections and repel Invasions;

[16]   To provide for organizing, arming, and disciplining, the Militia, and for governing such Part of them as may be employed in the Service of the United States, reserving to the States respectively, the Appointment of the Officers, and the Authority of training the Militia according to the discipline prescribed by Congress;

[17]   To exercise exclusive Legislation in all Cases whatsoever, over such District (not exceeding ten Miles square) as may, by Cession of particular States, and the Acceptance of Congress, become the Seat of the Government of the United States, and to exercise like Authority over all Places purchased by the Consent of the Legislature of the State in which the Same shall be, for the Erection of Forts, Magazines, Arsenals, dock-Yards, and other needful Buildings;—And

[18]   To make all Laws which shall be necessary and proper for carrying into Execution the foregoing Powers, and all other Powers vested by this

Constitution in the Government of the United States, or in any Department or Officer thereof.

Section 9.

[1]   The Migration or Importation of such Persons as any of the States now existing shall think proper to admit, shall not be prohibited by the Congress prior to the Year one thousand eight hundred and eight, but a Tax or duty may be imposed on such Importation, not exceeding ten dollars for each Person.

[2]   The Privilege of the Writ of Habeas Corpus shall not be suspended, unless when in Cases of Rebellion or Invasion the public Safety may require it.

[3]   No Bill of Attainder or ex post facto Law shall be passed.

[4]   No Capitation, or other direct, Tax shall be laid, *unless in Proportion to the Census or enumeration herein before directed to be taken.* [The previous phrase in italics was modified by Amendment XVI.]

[5]   No Tax or Duty shall be laid on Articles exported from any State.

[6]   No Preference shall be given by any Regulation of Commerce or Revenue to the Ports of one State over those of another; nor shall Vessels bound to, or from, one State, be obliged to enter, clear, or pay Duties in another.

[7]   No Money shall be drawn from the Treasury, but in Consequence of Appropriations made by Law; and a regular Statement and Account of the Receipts and Expenditures of all public Money shall be published from time to time.

[8]   No Title of Nobility shall be granted by the United States: And no Person holding any Office of Profit or Trust under them, shall, without the Consent of the Congress, accept of any present, Emolument, Office, or Title, of any kind whatever, from any King, Prince, or foreign State.

Section 10.

[1]   No State shall enter into any Treaty, Alliance, or Confederation; grant Letters of Marque and Reprisal; coin Money; emit Bills of Credit; make any Thing but gold and silver Coin a Tender in Payment of Debts; pass any Bill of Attainder, ex post facto Law, or Law impairing the Obligation of Contracts, or grant any Title of Nobility.

[2]   No State shall, without the Consent of the Congress, lay any Imposts or Duties on Imports or Exports, except what may be absolutely necessary for executing it's inspection Laws: and the net Produce of all Duties and Imposts, laid by any State on Imports or Exports, shall be for the Use of the Treasury of the United States; and all such Laws shall be subject to the Revision and Controul of the Congress.

[3]   No State shall, without the Consent of Congress, lay any Duty of Tonnage, keep Troops, or Ships of War in time of Peace, enter into any Agreement or Compact with another State, or with a foreign Power, or engage in War, unless actually invaded, or in such imminent Danger as will not admit of delay.

ARTICLE II

Section 1.

[1]   The executive Power shall be vested in a President of the United States of America. He shall hold his Office during the Term of four Years, and, together with the Vice President, chosen for the same Term, be elected, as follows:

[2]   Each State shall appoint, in such Manner as the Legislature thereof may direct, a Number of Electors, equal to the whole Number of Senators and Representatives to which the State may be entitled in the Congress: but no Senator or Representative, or Person holding an Office of Trust or Profit under the United States, shall be appointed an Elector.

[3]   *The Electors shall meet in their respective States, and vote by Ballot for two Persons, of whom one at least shall not be an Inhabitant of the same State with themselves. And they shall make a List of all the Persons voted for, and of the Number of Votes for each; which List they shall sign and certify, and transmit sealed to the Seat of the Government of the United States, directed to the President of the Senate. The President of the Senate shall, in the Presence of the Senate and House of Representatives, open all the Certificates, and the Votes shall then be counted. The Person having the greatest Number of Votes shall be the President, if such Number be a Majority of the whole Number of Electors appointed; and if there be more than one who have such Majority, and have an equal Number of Votes, then the House of Representatives shall immediately chuse by Ballot one of them for President; and if no Person have a Majority, then from the five highest on the List the said House shall in like Manner chuse the President. But in chusing the President, the Votes shall be taken by States, the Representation from each State having one Vote; A quorum for this purpose shall consist of a Member or Members from two thirds of the States, and a Majority of all the States shall be necessary to a Choice. In every Case, after the Choice of the President, the Person having the greatest Number of Votes of the Electors shall be the Vice President. But if there should remain two or more who have equal Votes, the Senate shall chuse from them by Ballot the Vice President.* [The preceding paragraph in italics was superseded in part by Amendments XII and XX.]

[4]   The Congress may determine the Time of chusing the Electors, and the Day on which they shall give their Votes; which Day shall be the same throughout the United States.

[5]   No Person except a natural born Citizen, or a Citizen of the United States, at the time of the Adoption of this Constitution, shall be eligible to

the Office of President; neither shall any Person be eligible to that Office who shall not have attained to the Age of thirty five Years, and been fourteen Years a Resident within the United States.

[6] *In Case of the Removal of the President from Office, or of his Death, Resignation, or Inability to discharge the Powers and Duties of the said Office, the Same shall devolve on the Vice President, and the Congress may by Law provide for the Case of Removal, Death, Resignation or Inability, both of the President and Vice President, declaring what Officer shall then act as President, and such Officer shall act accordingly, until the Disability be removed, or a President shall be elected.* [The preceding clause in italics was modified by Amendments XX and XXV.]

[7] The President shall, at stated Times, receive for his Services, a Compensation, which shall neither be increased nor diminished during the Period for which he shall have been elected, and he shall not receive within that Period any other Emolument from the United States, or any of them.

[8] Before he enter on the Execution of his Office, he shall take the following Oath or Affirmation: — "I do solemnly swear (or affirm) that I will faithfully execute the Office of President of the United States, and will to the best of my Ability, preserve, protect and defend the Constitution of the United States."

Section 2.

[1] The President shall be Commander in Chief of the Army and Navy of the United States, and of the Militia of the several States, when called into the actual Service of the United States; he may require the Opinion, in writing, of the principal Officer in each of the executive Departments, upon any Subject relating to the Duties of their respective Offices, and he shall have Power to grant Reprieves and Pardons for Offences against the United States, except in Cases of Impeachment.

[2] He shall have Power, by and with the Advice and Consent of the Senate, to make Treaties, provided two thirds of the Senators present concur; and he shall nominate, and by and with the Advice and Consent of the Senate, shall appoint Ambassadors, other public Ministers and Consuls, Judges of the supreme Court, and all other Officers of the United States, whose Appointments are not herein otherwise provided for, and which shall be established by Law: but the Congress may by Law vest the Appointment of such inferior Officers, as they think proper, in the President alone, in the Courts of Law, or in the Heads of Departments.

[3] The President shall have Power to fill up all Vacancies that may happen during the Recess of the Senate, by granting Commissions which shall expire at the End of their next Session.

Section 3.

He shall from time to time give to the Congress Information of the State of the Union, and recommend to their Consideration such Measures as he shall judge necessary and expedient; he may, on extraordinary Occasions, convene both Houses, or either of them, and in Case of Disagreement between them, with Respect to the Time of Adjournment, he may adjourn them to such Time as he shall think proper; he shall receive Ambassadors and other public Ministers; he shall take Care that the Laws be faithfully executed, and shall Commission all the Officers of the United States.

Section 4.

The President, Vice President and all civil Officers of the United States, shall be removed from Office on Impeachment for, and Conviction of, Treason, Bribery, or other high Crimes and Misdemeanors.

ARTICLE III

Section 1.

The judicial Power of the United States shall be vested in one supreme Court, and in such inferior Courts as the Congress may from time to time ordain and establish. The Judges, both of the supreme and inferior Courts, shall hold their Offices during good Behaviour, and shall, at stated Times, receive for their Services a Compensation, which shall not be diminished during their Continuance in Office.

Section 2.

[1]   The judicial Power shall extend to all Cases, in Law and Equity, arising under this Constitution, the Laws of the United States, and Treaties made, or which shall be made, under their Authority;—to all Cases affecting Ambassadors, other public Ministers and Consuls;—to all Cases of admiralty and maritime Jurisdiction;—to Controversies to which the United States shall be a Party;—to Controversies between two or more States;—*between a State and Citizens of another State* [the preceding eight words in italics were modified by Amendment XI],—between Citizens of different States,—between Citizens of the same State claiming Lands under Grants of different States, and between a State, or the Citizens thereof, and foreign States, Citizens or Subjects.

[2]   In all Cases affecting Ambassadors, other public Ministers and Consuls, and those in which a State shall be Party, the supreme Court shall have original Jurisdiction. In all the other Cases before mentioned,

the supreme Court shall have appellate Jurisdiction, both as to Law and Fact, with such Exceptions, and under such Regulations as the Congress shall make.

[3]   The Trial of all Crimes, except in Cases of Impeachment, shall be by Jury; and such Trial shall be held in the State where the said Crimes shall have been committed; but when not committed within any State, the Trial shall be at such Place or Places as the Congress may by Law have directed.

Section 3.

[1]   Treason against the United States, shall consist only in levying War against them, or in adhering to their Enemies, giving them Aid and Comfort. No Person shall be convicted of Treason unless on the Testimony of two Witnesses to the same overt Act, or on Confession in open Court.

[2]   The Congress shall have Power to declare the Punishment of Treason, but no Attainder of Treason shall work Corruption of Blood, or Forfeiture except during the Life of the Person attainted.

ARTICLE IV

Section 1.

Full Faith and Credit shall be given in each State to the public Acts, Records, and judicial Proceedings of every other State. And the Congress may by general Laws prescribe the Manner in which such Acts, Records and Proceedings shall be proved, and the Effect thereof.

Section 2.

The Citizens of each State shall be entitled to all Privileges and Immunities of Citizens in the several States.

A Person charged in any State with Treason, Felony, or other Crime, who shall flee from Justice, and be found in another State, shall on Demand of the executive Authority of the State from which he fled, be delivered up, to be removed to the State having Jurisdiction of the Crime.

No Person held to Service or Labour in one State, under the Laws thereof, escaping into another, shall, in Consequence of any Law or Regulation therein, be discharged from such Service or Labour, but shall be delivered up on Claim of the Party to whom such Service or Labour may be due. [The preceding section was superseded in part by the Amendment XII.]

Section 3.

New States may be admitted by the Congress into this Union; but no new State shall be formed or erected within the Jurisdiction of any other State; nor any State be formed by the Junction of two or more States, or Parts of States, without the Consent of the Legislatures of the States concerned as well as of the Congress.

The Congress shall have Power to dispose of and make all needful Rules and Regulations respecting the Territory or other Property belonging to the United States; and nothing in this Constitution shall be so construed as to Prejudice any Claims of the United States, or of any particular State.

Section 4.

The United States shall guarantee to every State in this Union a Republican Form of Government, and shall protect each of them against Invasion; and on Application of the Legislature, or of the Executive (when the Legislature cannot be convened), against domestic Violence.

ARTICLE V

The Congress, whenever two thirds of both Houses shall deem it necessary, shall propose Amendments to this Constitution, or, on the Application of the Legislatures of two thirds of the several States, shall call a Convention for proposing Amendments, which, in either Case, shall be valid to all Intents and Purposes, as Part of this Constitution, when ratified by the Legislatures of three fourths of the several States, or by Conventions in three fourths thereof, as the one or the other Mode of Ratification may be proposed by the Congress; Provided that no Amendment which may be made prior to the Year One thousand eight hundred and eight shall in any Manner affect the first and fourth Clauses in the Ninth Section of the first Article; and that no State, without its Consent, shall be deprived of its equal Suffrage in the Senate.

ARTICLE VI

[1] All Debts contracted and Engagements entered into, before the Adoption of this Constitution, shall be as valid against the United States under this Constitution, as under the Confederation.

[2] This Constitution, and the Laws of the United States which shall be made in Pursuance thereof; and all Treaties made, or which shall be made, under the Authority of the United States, shall be the supreme Law of the

Land; and the Judges in every State shall be bound thereby, any Thing in the Constitution or Laws of any State to the Contrary notwithstanding.

[3] The Senators and Representatives before mentioned, and the Members of the several State Legislatures, and all executive and judicial Officers, both of the United States and of the several States, shall be bound by Oath or Affirmation, to support this Constitution; but no religious Test shall ever be required as a Qualification to any Office or public Trust under the United States.

ARTICLE VII

The Ratification of the Conventions of nine States, shall be sufficient for the Establishment of this Constitution between the States so ratifying the Same.

Done in Convention by the Unanimous Consent of the States present the Seventeenth Day of September in the Year of our Lord one thousand seven hundred and Eighty seven and of the Independence of the United States of America the Twelfth.

AMENDMENTS

AMENDMENT I

Congress shall make no law respecting an establishment of religion, or prohibiting the free exercise thereof; or abridging the freedom of speech, or of the press; or the right of the people peaceably to assemble, and to petition the Government for a redress of grievances.

AMENDMENT II

A well regulated Militia, being necessary to the security of a free State, the right of the people to keep and bear Arms, shall not be infringed.

AMENDMENT III

No Soldier shall, in time of peace be quartered in any house, without the consent of the Owner, nor in time of war, but in a manner to be prescribed by law.

AMENDMENT IV

The right of the people to be secure in their persons, houses, papers, and effects, against unreasonable searches and seizures, shall not be violated, and no Warrants shall issue, but upon probable cause, supported by Oath or affirmation, and particularly describing the place to be searched, and the persons or things to be seized.

AMENDMENT V

No person shall be held to answer for a capital, or otherwise infamous crime, unless on a presentment or indictment of a Grand Jury, except in cases arising in the land or naval forces, or in the Militia, when in actual service in time of War or public danger; nor shall any person be subject for the same offense to be twice put in jeopardy of life or limb; nor shall be compelled in any criminal case to be a witness against himself, nor be deprived of life, liberty, or property, without due process of law; nor shall private property be taken for public use, without just compensation.

AMENDMENT VI

In all criminal prosecutions, the accused shall enjoy the right to a speedy and public trial, by an impartial jury of the State and district wherein the crime shall have been committed, which district shall have been previously ascertained by law, and to be informed of the nature and cause of the accusation; to be confronted with the witnesses against him; to have compulsory process for obtaining witnesses in his favor, and to have the Assistance of Counsel for his defense.

AMENDMENT VII

In Suits at common law, where the value in controversy shall exceed twenty dollars, the right of trial by jury shall be preserved, and no fact tried by a jury, shall be otherwise re-examined in any Court of the United States, than according to the rules of the common law.

AMENDMENT VIII

Excessive bail shall not be required, nor excessive fines imposed, nor cruel and unusual punishments inflicted.

AMENDMENT IX

The enumeration in the Constitution, of certain rights, shall not be construed to deny or disparage others retained by the people.

AMENDMENT X

The powers not delegated to the United States by the Constitution, nor prohibited by it to the States, are reserved to the States respectively, or to the people.

AMENDMENT XI

The Judicial power of the United States shall not be construed to extend to any suit in law or equity, commenced or prosecuted against one of the

United States by Citizens of another State, or by Citizens or Subjects of any Foreign State.

AMENDMENT XII

The Electors shall meet in their respective states, and vote by ballot for President and Vice-President, one of whom, at least, shall not be an inhabitant of the same state with themselves; they shall name in their ballots the person voted for as President, and in distinct ballots the person voted for as Vice-President, and they shall make distinct lists of all persons voted for as President, and of all persons voted for as Vice-President and of the number of votes for each, which lists they shall sign and certify, and transmit sealed to the seat of the government of the United States, directed to the President of the Senate;

The President of the Senate shall, in the presence of the Senate and House of Representatives, open all the certificates and the votes shall then be counted;

The person having the greatest Number of votes for President, shall be the President, if such number be a majority of the whole number of Electors appointed; and if no person have such majority, then from the persons having the highest numbers not exceeding three on the list of those voted for as President, the House of Representatives shall choose immediately, by ballot, the President. But in choosing the President, the votes shall be taken by states, the representation from each state having one vote; a quorum for this purpose shall consist of a member or members from two-thirds of the states, and a majority of all the states shall be necessary to a choice. And if the House of Representatives shall not choose a President whenever the right of choice shall devolve upon them, before the fourth day of March next following, then the Vice-President shall act as President, as in the case of the death or other constitutional disability of the President.

The person having the greatest number of votes as Vice-President, shall be the Vice-President, if such number be a majority of the whole number of Electors appointed, and if no person have a majority, then from the two highest numbers on the list, the Senate shall choose the Vice-President; a quorum for the purpose shall consist of two-thirds of the whole number of Senators, and a majority of the whole number shall be necessary to a choice. But no person constitutionally ineligible to the office of President shall be eligible to that of Vice-President of the United States.

AMENDMENT XIII

Section 1.

Neither slavery nor involuntary servitude, except as a punishment for crime whereof the party shall have been duly convicted, shall exist within the United States, or any place subject to their jurisdiction.

Section 2.

Congress shall have power to enforce this article by appropriate legislation.

AMENDMENT XIV

Section 1.

All persons born or naturalized in the United States, and subject to the jurisdiction thereof, are citizens of the United States and of the State wherein they reside. No State shall make or enforce any law which shall abridge the privileges or immunities of citizens of the United States; nor shall any State deprive any person of life, liberty, or property, without due process of law; nor deny to any person within its jurisdiction the equal protection of the laws.

Section 2.

Representatives shall be apportioned among the several States according to their respective numbers, counting the whole number of persons in each State, excluding Indians not taxed. But when the right to vote at any election for the choice of electors for President and Vice-President of the United States, Representatives in Congress, the Executive and Judicial officers of a State, or the members of the Legislature thereof, is denied to any of the male inhabitants of such State, being twenty-one years of age, and citizens of the United States, or in any way abridged, except for participation in rebellion, or other crime, the basis of representation therein shall be reduced in the proportion which the number of such male citizens shall bear to the whole number of male citizens twenty-one years of age in such State.

Section 3.

No person shall be a Senator or Representative in Congress, or elector of President and Vice-President, or hold any office, civil or military, under the United States, or under any State, who, having previously taken an oath, as a member of Congress, or as an officer of the United States, or as a member of any State legislature, or as an executive or judicial officer of any State, to support the Constitution of the United States, shall have engaged in insurrection or rebellion against the same, or given aid or comfort to the enemies thereof. But Congress may by a vote of two-thirds of each House, remove such disability.

Section 4.

The validity of the public debt of the United States, authorized by law, including debts incurred for payment of pensions and bounties for services in suppressing insurrection or rebellion, shall not be questioned. But neither the United States nor any State shall assume or pay any debt or obligation incurred in aid of insurrection or rebellion against the United States, or any claim for the loss or emancipation of any slave; but all such debts, obligations and claims shall be held illegal and void.

Section 5.

The Congress shall have power to enforce, by appropriate legislation, the provisions of this article.

AMENDMENT XV

Section 1.

The right of citizens of the United States to vote shall not be denied or abridged by the United States or by any State on account of race, color, or previous condition of servitude.

Section 2.

The Congress shall have power to enforce this article by appropriate legislation.

AMENDMENT XVI

The Congress shall have power to lay and collect taxes on incomes, from whatever source derived, without apportionment among the several States, and without regard to any census or enumeration.

AMENDMENT XVII

The Senate of the United States shall be composed of two Senators from each State, elected by the people thereof, for six years; and each Senator shall have one vote. The electors in each State shall have the qualifications requisite for electors of the most numerous branch of the State legislatures.

When vacancies happen in the representation of any State in the Senate, the executive authority of such State shall issue writs of election to fill such vacancies: Provided, That the legislature of any State may empower the executive thereof to make temporary appointments until the people fill the vacancies by election as the legislature may direct.

This amendment shall not be so construed as to affect the election or term of any Senator chosen before it becomes valid as part of the Constitution.

AMENDMENT XVIII

Section 1.

After one year from the ratification of this article the manufacture, sale, or transportation of intoxicating liquors within, the importation thereof into, or the exportation thereof from the United States and all territory subject to the jurisdiction thereof for beverage purposes is hereby prohibited.

Section 2.

The Congress and the several States shall have concurrent power to enforce this article by appropriate legislation.

Section 3.

This article shall be inoperative unless it shall have been ratified as an amendment to the Constitution by the legislatures of the several States, as provided in the Constitution, within seven years from the date of the submission hereof to the States by the Congress.

AMENDMENT XIX

The right of citizens of the United States to vote shall not be denied or abridged by the United States or by any State on account of sex.

Congress shall have power to enforce this article by appropriate legislation.

AMENDMENT XX

Section 1.

The terms of the President and Vice President shall end at noon on the 20th day of January, and the terms of Senators and Representatives at noon on the 3d day of January, of the years in which such terms would have ended if this article had not been ratified; and the terms of their successors shall then begin.

Section 2.

The Congress shall assemble at least once in every year, and such meeting shall begin at noon on the 3d day of January, unless they shall by law appoint a different day.

Section 3.

If, at the time fixed for the beginning of the term of the President, the President elect shall have died, the Vice President elect shall become President. If a President shall not have been chosen before the time fixed for the beginning of his term, or if the President elect shall have failed to qualify, then the Vice President elect shall act as President until a President shall have qualified; and the Congress may by law provide for the case wherein neither a President elect nor a Vice President elect shall have qualified, declaring who shall then act as President, or the manner in which one who is to act shall be selected, and such person shall act accordingly until a President or Vice President shall have qualified.

Section 4.

The Congress may by law provide for the case of the death of any of the persons from whom the House of Representatives may choose a President whenever the right of choice shall have devolved upon them, and for the case of the death of any of the persons from whom the Senate may choose a Vice President whenever the right of choice shall have devolved upon them.

Section 5.

Sections 1 and 2 shall take effect on the 15th day of October following the ratification of this article.

Section 6.

This article shall be inoperative unless it shall have been ratified as an amendment to the Constitution by the legislatures of three-fourths of the several States within seven years from the date of its submission.

AMENDMENT XXI

Section 1.

The eighteenth article of amendment to the Constitution of the United States is hereby repealed.

Section 2.

The transportation or importation into any State, Territory, or possession of the United States for delivery or use therein of intoxicating liquors, in violation of the laws thereof, is hereby prohibited.

Section 3.

The article shall be inoperative unless it shall have been ratified as an amendment to the Constitution by conventions in the several States, as provided in the Constitution, within seven years from the date of the submission hereof to the States by the Congress.

AMENDMENT XXII

Section 1.

No person shall be elected to the office of the President more than twice, and no person who has held the office of President, or acted as President, for more than two years of a term to which some other person was elected President shall be elected to the office of the President more than once. But this Article shall not apply to any person holding the office of President, when this Article was proposed by the Congress, and shall not prevent any person who may be holding the office of President, or acting as President, during the term within which this Article becomes operative from holding the office of President or acting as President during the remainder of such term.

Section 2.

This article shall be inoperative unless it shall have been ratified as an amendment to the Constitution by the legislatures of three-fourths of the several States within seven years from the date of its submission to the States by the Congress.

AMENDMENT XXIII

Section 1.

The District constituting the seat of Government of the United States shall appoint in such manner as the Congress may direct: A number of electors of President and Vice President equal to the whole number of Senators and Representatives in Congress to which the District would be entitled if it were a State, but in no event more than the least populous State; they shall be in addition to those appointed by the States, but they shall be considered, for the purposes of the election of President and Vice President, to be electors appointed by a State; and they shall meet in the District and perform such duties as provided by the twelfth article of amendment.

Section 2.

The Congress shall have power to enforce this article by appropriate legislation.

AMENDMENT XXIV

Section 1.

The right of citizens of the United States to vote in any primary or other election for President or Vice President, for electors for President or Vice President, or for Senator or Representative in Congress, shall not be denied or abridged by the United States or any State by reason of failure to pay any poll tax or other tax.

Section 2.

The Congress shall have power to enforce this article by appropriate legislation.

AMENDMENT XXV

Section 1.

In case of the removal of the President from office or of his death or resignation, the Vice President shall become President.

Section 2.

Whenever there is a vacancy in the office of the Vice President, the President shall nominate a Vice President who shall take office upon confirmation by a majority vote of both Houses of Congress.

Section 3.

Whenever the President transmits to the President pro tempore of the Senate and the Speaker of the House of Representatives his written declaration that he is unable to discharge the powers and duties of his office, and until he transmits to them a written declaration to the contrary, such powers and duties shall be discharged by the Vice President as Acting President.

Section 4.

Whenever the Vice President and a majority of either the principal officers of the executive departments or of such other body as Congress may by law provide, transmit to the President pro tempore of the Senate and the Speaker of the House of Representatives their written declaration that the President is unable to discharge the powers and duties of his office, the Vice President shall immediately assume the powers and duties of the office as Acting President.

Thereafter, when the President transmits to the President pro tempore of the Senate and the Speaker of the House of Representatives his written declaration that no inability exists, he shall resume the powers and duties of his office unless the Vice President and a majority of either the principal officers of the executive department or of such other body as Congress may by law provide, transmit within four days to the President pro tempore of the Senate and the Speaker of the House of Representatives their written declaration that the President is unable to discharge the powers and duties of his office. Thereupon Congress shall decide the issue, assembling within forty eight hours for that purpose if not in session. If the Congress, within twenty one days after receipt of the latter written declaration, or, if Congress is not in session, within twenty one days after Congress is required to assemble, determines by two thirds vote of both Houses that the President is unable to discharge the powers and duties of his office, the Vice President shall continue to discharge the same as Acting President; otherwise, the President shall resume the powers and duties of his office.

AMENDMENT XXVI

Section 1.

The right of citizens of the United States, who are eighteen years of age or older, to vote shall not be denied or abridged by the United States or by any State on account of age.

Section 2.

The Congress shall have power to enforce this article by appropriate legislation.

AMENDMENT XXVII

No law, varying the compensation for the services of the Senators and Representatives, shall take effect, until an election of Representatives shall have intervened.

Appendix B

Selected Provisions of the Administrative Procedure Act

Public Law 404-79th Congress, 60 Stat. 237 (1946) (codified as amended in scattered sections of 5 U.S.C.)

Title 5. GOVERNMENT ORGANIZATION AND EMPLOYEES

CHAPTER 5. ADMINISTRATIVE PROCEDURE

SUBCHAPTER II—ADMINISTRATIVE PROCEDURE

Sec.

§551   Definitions
§552   Public information; agency rules, opinions, orders, records, and proceedings
§552a   Records maintained on individuals [omitted]
§552b   Open meetings [omitted]
§553   Rule making
§554   Adjudications
§555   Ancillary matters
§556   Hearings; presiding employees; powers and duties; burden of proof; evidence; record as basis of decision
§557   Initial decisions; conclusiveness; review by agency; submissions by parties; contents of decisions; record
§558   Imposition of sanctions; determination of applications for licenses; suspension, revocation, and expiration of licenses
§559   Effect on other laws; effect of subsequent statute

§551. Definitions

For the purpose of this subchapter—

(1) "agency" means each authority of the Government of the United States, whether or not it is within or subject to review by another agency, but does not include—

(A) the Congress;

(B) the courts of the United States;

(C) the governments of the territories or possessions of the United States;

(D) the government of the District of Columbia; or except as to the requirements of section 552 of this title—

(E) agencies composed of representatives of the parties or of representatives of organizations of the parties to the disputes determined by them;

(F) courts martial and military commissions;

(G) military authority exercised in the field in time of war or in occupied territory; or

(H) functions conferred by sections 1738, 1739, 1743, and 1744 of title 2of title 41; or sections 1622, 1884, 1891-1902, and former section 1641(b)(2), of title 50, appendix;

(2) "person" includes an individual, partnership, corporation, association, or public or private organization other than an agency;

(3) "party" includes a person or agency named or admitted as a party, or properly seeking and entitled as of right to be admitted as a party, in an agency proceeding, and a person or agency admitted by an agency as a party for limited purposes;

(4) "rule" means the whole or a part of an agency statement of general or particular applicability and future effect designed to implement, interpret, or prescribe law or policy or describing the organization, procedure, or practice requirements of an agency and includes the approval or prescription for the future of rates, wages, corporate or financial structures or reorganizations thereof, prices, facilities, appliances, services or allowances therefore or of valuations, costs, or accounting, or practices bearing on any of the foregoing;

(5) "rule making" means agency process for formulating, amending, or repealing a rule;

(6) "order" means the whole or a part of a final disposition, whether affirmative, negative, injunctive, or declaratory in form, of an agency in a matter other than rule making but including licensing;

(7) "adjudication" means agency process for the formulation of an order;

(8) "license" includes the whole or a part of an agency permit, certificate, approval, registration, charter, membership, statutory exemption or other form of permission;

(9) "licensing" includes agency process respecting the grant, renewal, denial, revocation, suspension, annulment, withdrawal, limitation, amendment, modification, or conditioning of a license;

(10) "sanction" includes the whole or a part of an agency—

(A) prohibition, requirement, limitation, or other condition affecting the freedom of a person;

(B) withholding of relief;

(C) imposition of penalty or fine;

(D) destruction, taking, seizure, or withholding of property;

(E) assessment of damages, reimbursement, restitution, compensation, costs, charges, or fees;

(F) requirement, revocation, or suspension of a license; or

(G) taking other compulsory or restrictive action;

(11) "relief" includes the whole or a part of an agency—

(A) grant of money, assistance, license, authority, exemption, exception, privilege, or remedy;

(B) recognition of a claim, right, immunity, privilege, exemption, or exception; or

(C) taking of other action on the application or petition of, and beneficial to, a person;

(12) "agency proceeding" means an agency process as defined by paragraphs (5), (7), and (9) of this section;

(13) "agency action" includes the whole or a part of an agency rule, order, license, sanction, relief, or the equivalent or denial thereof, or failure to act; and

(14) "ex parte communication" means an oral or written communication not on the public record with respect to which reasonable prior notice to all parties is not given, but it shall not include requests for status reports on any matter or proceeding covered by this subchapter.

§552. Public information; agency rules, opinions, orders, records, and proceedings

(a) Each agency shall make available to the public information as follows:

(1) Each agency shall separately state and currently publish in the Federal Register for the guidance of the public—

(A) descriptions of its central and field organization and the established places at which, the employees (and in the case of a uniformed service, the members) from whom, and the methods whereby, the public may obtain information, make submittals or requests, or obtain decisions;

(B) statements of the general course and method by which its functions are channeled and determined, including the nature and requirements of all formal and informal procedures available;

(C) rules of procedure, descriptions of forms available or the places at which forms may be obtained, and instructions as to the scope and contents of all papers, reports, or examinations;

(D) substantive rules of general applicability adopted as authorized by law, and statements of general policy or interpretations of general applicability formulated and adopted by the agency; and

(E) each amendment, revision, or repeal of the foregoing.

Except to the extent that a person has actual and timely notice of the terms thereof, a person may not in any manner be required to resort to, or be adversely affected by, a matter required to be published in the Federal Register and not so published. For the purpose of this paragraph, matter reasonably available to the class of persons affected thereby is deemed published in the Federal Register when incorporated by reference therein with the approval of the Director of the Federal Register.

(2) Each agency, in accordance with published rules, shall make available for public inspection and copying—

(A) final opinions, including concurring and dissenting opinions, as well as orders, made in the adjudication of cases;

(B) those statements of policy and interpretations which have been adopted by the agency and are not published in the Federal Register;

(C) administrative staff manuals and instructions to staff that affect a member of the public;

(D) copies of all records, regardless of form or format, which have been released to any person under paragraph (3) and which, because of the nature of their subject matter, the agency determines have become or are likely to become the subject of subsequent requests for substantially the same records; and

(E) a general index of the records referred to under subparagraph (D); unless the materials are promptly published and copies offered for sale. For records created on or after November 1, 1996, within one year after such date, each agency shall make such records available, including by computer telecommunications or, if computer telecommunications means have not been established by the agency, by other electronic means. To the extent required to prevent a clearly unwarranted invasion of personal privacy, an agency may delete identifying details when it makes available or publishes an opinion, statement of policy, interpretation, staff manual, instruction, or copies of records referred to in subparagraph (D). However, in each case the justification for the deletion shall be explained fully in writing, and the extent of such deletion shall be indicated on the portion of the record which is made available or published, unless including that indication would harm an interest protected by the exemption in subsection (b) under which the deletion is made. If technically feasible, the extent of the deletion shall be indicated at the place in the record where the deletion was made. Each agency shall also maintain and make available for public inspection and copying current indexes providing identifying information for the public as to any matter issued, adopted, or promulgated after July 4, 1967, and required by this paragraph to be made available or published. Each agency shall promptly publish, quarterly or more frequently, and distribute (by sale or otherwise) copies of each index or supplements thereto unless it determines by order published in the Federal Register that the publication would be unnecessary and impracticable, in which case the agency shall nonetheless provide copies of such index on request at a cost not to exceed the direct cost of duplication. Each agency shall make the index referred to in subparagraph (E) available by computer telecommunications by December 31, 1999. A final order, opinion, statement of policy, interpretation, or staff manual or instruction that affects a member of the public may be relied on, used, or cited as precedent by an agency against a party other than an agency only if—

(i) it has been indexed and either made available or published as provided by this paragraph; or

(ii) the party has actual and timely notice of the terms thereof.

(3)(A) Except with respect to the records made available under paragraphs (1) and (2) of this subsection, each agency, upon any request for records which (i) reasonably describes such records and (ii) is made in accordance with published rules stating the time, place, fees (if any), and procedures to be followed, shall make the records promptly available to any person.

(B) In making any record available to a person under this paragraph, an agency shall provide the record in any form or format requested by the person if the record is readily reproducible by the agency in that form or format. Each agency shall make reasonable efforts to maintain its records in forms or formats that are reproducible for purposes of this section.

(C) In responding under this paragraph to a request for records, an agency shall make reasonable efforts to search for the records in electronic form or format, except when such efforts would significantly interfere with the operation of the agency's automated information system.

(D) For purposes of this paragraph, the term "search" means to review, manually or by automated means, agency records for the purpose of locating those records which are responsive to a request.

(4)(A)(i) In order to carry out the provisions of this section, each agency shall promulgate regulations, pursuant to notice and receipt of public comment, specifying the schedule of fees applicable to the processing of requests under this section and establishing procedures and guidelines for determining when such fees should be waived or reduced. Such schedule shall conform to the guidelines which shall be promulgated, pursuant to notice and receipt of public comment, by the Director of the Office of Management and Budget and which shall provide for a uniform schedule of fees for all agencies.

(ii) Such agency regulations shall provide that—

(I) fees shall be limited to reasonable standard charges for document search, duplication, and review, when records are requested for commercial use;

(II) fees shall be limited to reasonable standard charges for document duplication when records are not sought for commercial use and the request is made by an educational or noncommercial scientific institution, whose purpose is scholarly or scientific research; or a representative of the news media; and

(III) for any request not described in (I) or (II), fees shall be limited to reasonable standard charges for document search and duplication.

(iii) Documents shall be furnished without any charge or at a charge reduced below the fees established under clause (ii) if disclosure of the information is in the public interest because it is likely to contribute significantly to public understanding of the operations or activities of the government and is not primarily in the commercial interest of the requester.

(iv) Fee schedules shall provide for the recovery of only the direct costs of search, duplication, or review. Review costs shall include only the direct costs incurred during the initial examination of a document for the purposes of determining whether the documents must be disclosed under this section and for the purposes of withholding any portions exempt from disclosure under this section. Review costs may not include any costs incurred in resolving issues of law or policy that may be raised in the course of processing a request under this section. No fee may be charged by any agency under this section—

(I) if the costs of routine collection and processing of the fee are likely to equal or exceed the amount of the fee; or

(II) for any request described in clause (ii)(II) or (III) of this subparagraph for the first two hours of search time or for the first one hundred pages of duplication.

(v) No agency may require advance payment of any fee unless the requester has previously failed to pay fees in a timely fashion, or the agency has determined that the fee will exceed $250.

(vi) Nothing in this subparagraph shall supersede fees chargeable under a statute specifically providing for setting the level of fees for particular types of records.

(vii) In any action by a requester regarding the waiver of fees under this section, the court shall determine the matter de novo: Provided, That the court's review of the matter shall be limited to the record before the agency.

(B) On complaint, the district court of the United States in the district in which the complainant resides, or has his principal place of business, or in which the agency records are situated, or in the District of Columbia, has jurisdiction to enjoin the agency from withholding agency records and to order the production of any agency records improperly withheld from the complainant. In such a case the court shall determine the matter de novo, and may examine the contents of such agency records in camera to determine whether such records or any part thereof shall be withheld under any of the exemptions set forth in subsection (b) of this section, and the burden is on the agency to sustain its action. In addition to any other matters to which a court accords substantial weight, a court shall accord substantial weight to an affidavit of an agency concerning the agency's determination as to technical feasibility under paragraph (2)(C) and subsection (b) and reproducibility under paragraph (3)(B).

(C) Notwithstanding any other provision of law, the defendant shall serve an answer or otherwise plead to any complaint made under this subsection within thirty days after service upon the defendant of the pleading in which such complaint is made, unless the court otherwise directs for good cause shown.

[(D) Repealed. Pub. L. 98-620, Title IV, §402(2), Nov. 8, 1984, 98 Stat. 3357]

(E) The court may assess against the United States reasonable attorney fees and other litigation costs reasonably incurred in any case under this section in which the complainant has substantially prevailed.

(F) Whenever the court orders the production of any agency records improperly withheld from the complainant and assesses against the United States reasonable attorney fees and other litigation costs, and the court additionally issues a written finding that the circumstances surrounding the withholding raise questions whether agency personnel acted arbitrarily or capriciously with respect to the withholding, the Special Counsel shall promptly initiate a proceeding to determine whether disciplinary action is warranted against the officer or employee who was primarily responsible for the withholding. The Special Counsel, after investigation and consideration of the evidence submitted, shall submit his findings and recommendations to the administrative authority of the agency concerned and shall send copies of the findings and recommendations to the officer or employee or his representative. The administrative authority shall take the corrective action that the Special Counsel recommends.

(G) In the event of noncompliance with the order of the court, the district court may punish for contempt the responsible employee, and in the case of a uniformed service, the responsible member.

(5) Each agency having more than one member shall maintain and make available for public inspection a record of the final votes of each member in every agency proceeding.

(6)(A) Each agency, upon any request for records made under paragraph (1), (2), or (3) of this subsection, shall—

(i) determine within 20 days (excepting Saturdays, Sundays, and legal public holidays) after the receipt of any such request whether to comply with such request and shall immediately notify the person making such request of such determination and the reasons therefor, and of the right of such person to appeal to the head of the agency any adverse determination; and

(ii) make a determination with respect to any appeal within twenty days (excepting Saturdays, Sundays, and legal public holidays) after the receipt of such appeal. If on appeal the denial of the request for records is in whole or in part upheld, the agency shall notify the person making such request of the provisions for judicial review of that determination under paragraph (4) of this subsection.

(B)(i) In unusual circumstances as specified in this subparagraph, the time limits prescribed in either clause (i) or clause (ii) of subparagraph (A) may be extended by written notice to the person making such request setting forth the unusual circumstances for such extension and the date on which a determination is expected to be dispatched. No such notice shall specify a date that would result in an extension for more than ten working days, except as provided in clause (ii) of this subparagraph.

(ii) With respect to a request for which a written notice under clause (i) extends the time limits prescribed under clause (i) of subparagraph (A), the agency shall notify the person making the request if the request cannot be processed within the time limit specified in that clause and shall provide the person an opportunity to limit the scope of the request so that it may be processed within that time limit or an opportunity to arrange with the agency an alternative time frame for processing the request or a modified request. Refusal by the person to reasonably modify the request or arrange such an alternative time frame shall be considered as a factor in determining whether exceptional circumstances exist for purposes of subparagraph (C).

(iii) As used in this subparagraph, "unusual circumstances" means, but only to the extent reasonably necessary to the proper processing of the particular requests—

(I) the need to search for and collect the requested records from field facilities or other establishments that are separate from the office processing the request;

(II) the need to search for, collect, and appropriately examine a voluminous amount of separate and distinct records which are demanded in a single request; or

(III) the need for consultation, which shall be conducted with all practicable speed, with another agency having a substantial interest in the determination of the request or among two or more components of the agency having substantial subject-matter interest therein.

(iv) Each agency may promulgate regulations, pursuant to notice and receipt of public comment, providing for the aggregation of certain requests by the same requestor, or by a group of requestors acting in concert, if the agency reasonably believes that such requests actually constitute a single request, which would otherwise satisfy the unusual circumstances specified in this subparagraph, and the requests involve clearly related matters. Multiple requests involving unrelated matters shall not be aggregated.

(C) (i) Any person making a request to any agency for records under paragraph (1), (2), or (3) of this subsection shall be deemed to have exhausted his administrative remedies with respect to such request if the agency fails to comply with the applicable time limit provisions of this paragraph. If the Government can show exceptional circumstances exist and that the agency is exercising due diligence in responding to the request, the court may retain jurisdiction and allow the agency additional time to complete its review of the records. Upon any determination by an agency to comply with a request for records, the records shall be made promptly available to such person making such request. Any notification of denial of any request for records under this subsection shall set forth the names and titles or positions of each person responsible for the denial of such request.

(ii) For purposes of this subparagraph, the term "exceptional circumstances" does not include a delay that results from a predictable agency workload of requests under this section, unless the agency demonstrates reasonable progress in reducing its backlog of pending requests.

(iii) Refusal by a person to reasonably modify the scope of a request or arrange an alternative time frame for processing a request (or a modified request) under clause (ii) after being given an opportunity to do so by the agency to whom the person made the request shall be considered as a factor in determining whether exceptional circumstances exist for purposes of this subparagraph.

(D) (i) Each agency may promulgate regulations, pursuant to notice and receipt of public comment, providing for multitrack processing of requests for records based on the amount of work or time (or both) involved in processing requests.

(ii) Regulations under this subparagraph may provide a person making a request that does not qualify for the fastest multitrack processing an opportunity to limit the scope of the request in order to qualify for faster processing.

(iii) This subparagraph shall not be considered to affect the requirement under subparagraph (C) to exercise due diligence.

(E)(i) Each agency shall promulgate regulations, pursuant to notice and receipt of public comment, providing for expedited processing of requests for records—

(I) in cases in which the person requesting the records demonstrates a compelling need; and

(II) in other cases determined by the agency.

(ii) Notwithstanding clause (i), regulations under this subparagraph must ensure—

(I) that a determination of whether to provide expedited processing shall be made, and notice of the determination shall be provided to the person making the request, within 10 days after the date of the request; and

(II) expeditious consideration of administrative appeals of such determinations of whether to provide expedited processing.

(iii) An agency shall process as soon as practicable any request for records to which the agency has granted expedited processing under this subparagraph. Agency action to deny or affirm denial of a request for expedited processing pursuant to this subparagraph, and failure by an agency to respond in a timely manner to such a request shall be subject to judicial review under paragraph (4), except that the judicial review shall be based on the record before the agency at the time of the determination.

(iv) A district court of the United States shall not have jurisdiction to review an agency denial of expedited processing of a request for records after the agency has provided a complete response to the request.

(v) For purposes of this subparagraph, the term "compelling need" means—

(I) that a failure to obtain requested records on an expedited basis under this paragraph could reasonably be expected to pose an imminent threat to the life or physical safety of an individual; or

(II) with respect to a request made by a person primarily engaged in disseminating information, urgency to inform the public concerning actual or alleged Federal Government activity.

(vi) A demonstration of a compelling need by a person making a request for expedited processing shall be made by a statement certified by such person to be true and correct to the best of such person's knowledge and belief.

(F) In denying a request for records, in whole or in part, an agency shall make a reasonable effort to estimate the volume of any requested matter the provision of which is denied, and shall provide any such estimate to the person making the request, unless providing such estimate would harm an interest protected by the exemption in subsection (b) pursuant to which the denial is made.

(b) This section does not apply to matters that are—

(1)(A) specifically authorized under criteria established by an Executive order to be kept secret in the interest of national defense or foreign policy and (B) are in fact properly classified pursuant to such Executive order;

(2) related solely to the internal personnel rules and practices of an agency;

(3) specifically exempted from disclosure by statute (other than section 552b of this title), provided that such statute (A) requires that the matters be withheld from the public in such a manner as to leave no discretion on the issue, or (B) establishes particular criteria for withholding or refers to particular types of matters to be withheld;

(4) trade secrets and commercial or financial information obtained from a person and privileged or confidential;

(5) inter-agency or intra-agency memorandums or letters which would not be available by law to a party other than an agency in litigation with the agency;

(6) personnel and medical files and similar files the disclosure of which would constitute a clearly unwarranted invasion of personal privacy;

(7) records or information compiled for law enforcement purposes, but only to the extent that the production of such law enforcement records or information (A) could reasonably be expected to interfere with enforcement proceedings, (B) would deprive a person of a right to a fair trial or an impartial adjudication, (C) could reasonably be expected to constitute an unwarranted invasion of personal privacy, (D) could reasonably be expected to disclose the identity of a confidential source, including a State, local, or foreign agency or authority or any private institution which furnished information on a confidential basis, and, in the case of a record or information compiled by criminal law enforcement authority in the course of a criminal investigation or by an agency conducting a lawful national security intelligence investigation, information furnished by a confidential source, (E) would disclose techniques and procedures for law enforcement investigations or prosecutions, or would disclose guidelines for law enforcement investigations or prosecutions if such disclosure could reasonably be expected to risk circumvention of the law, or (F) could reasonably be expected to endanger the life or physical safety of any individual;

(8) contained in or related to examination, operating, or condition reports prepared by, on behalf of, or for the use of an agency responsible for the regulation or supervision of financial institutions; or

(9) geological and geophysical information and data, including maps, concerning wells.

Any reasonably segregable portion of a record shall be provided to any person requesting such record after deletion of the portions which are exempt under this subsection. The amount of information deleted shall be indicated on the released portion of the record, unless including that indication would harm an interest protected by the exemption in this subsection under which the deletion is made. If technically feasible, the amount of the information shall be indicated at the place in the record where such deletion is made.

(c)(1) Whenever a request is made which involves access to records described in subsection (b)(7)(A) and—

(A) the investigation or proceeding involves a possible violation of criminal law; and

(B) there is reason to believe that (i) the subject of the investigation or proceeding is not aware of its pendency, and (ii) disclosure of the existence of the records could reasonably be expected to interfere with enforcement proceedings, the agency may, during only such time as that circumstance continues, treat the records as not subject to the requirements of this section.

(2) Whenever informant records maintained by a criminal law enforcement agency under an informant's name or personal identifier are requested by a third party according to the informant's name or personal identifier, the agency may treat the records as not subject to the requirements of this section unless the informant's status as an informant has been officially confirmed.

(3) Whenever a request is made which involves access to records maintained by the Federal Bureau of Investigation pertaining to foreign intelligence or counterintelligence, or international terrorism, and the existence of the records is classified information as provided in subsection (b)(1), the Bureau may, as long as the existence of the records remains classified information, treat the records as not subject to the requirements of this section.

(d) This section does not authorize withholding of information or limit the availability of records to the public, except as specifically stated in this section. This section is not authority to withhold information from Congress.

(e)(1) On or before February 1 of each year, each agency shall submit to the Attorney General of the United States a report which shall cover the preceding fiscal year and which shall include—

(A) the number of determinations made by the agency not to comply with requests for records made to such agency under subsection (a) and the reasons for each such determination;

(B)(i) the number of appeals made by persons under subsection (a)(6), the result of such appeals, and the reason for the action upon each appeal that results in a denial of information; and

(ii) a complete list of all statutes that the agency relies upon to authorize the agency to withhold information under subsection (b)(3), a description of whether a court has upheld the decision of the agency to withhold information under each such statute, and a concise description of the scope of any information withheld;

(C) the number of requests for records pending before the agency as of September 30 of the preceding year, and the median number of days that such requests had been pending before the agency as of that date;

(D) the number of requests for records received by the agency and the number of requests which the agency processed;

(E) the median number of days taken by the agency to process different types of requests;

(F) the total amount of fees collected by the agency for processing requests; and

(G) the number of full-time staff of the agency devoted to processing requests for records under this section, and the total amount expended by the agency for processing such requests.

(2) Each agency shall make each such report available to the public including by computer telecommunications, or if computer telecommunications means have not been established by the agency, by other electronic means.

(3) The Attorney General of the United States shall make each report which has been made available by electronic means available at a single electronic access point. The Attorney General of the United States shall notify the Chairman and ranking minority member of the Committee on Government Reform and Oversight of the House of Representatives and the Chairman and ranking minority member of the Committees on Governmental Affairs and the Judiciary of the Senate, no later than April 1 of the year in which each such report is issued, that such reports are available by electronic means.

(4) The Attorney General of the United States, in consultation with the Director of the Office of Management and Budget, shall develop reporting and performance guidelines in connection with reports required by this subsection by October 1, 1997, and may establish additional requirements for such reports as the Attorney General determines may be useful.

(5) The Attorney General of the United States shall submit an annual report on or before April 1 of each calendar year which shall include for the prior calendar year a listing of the number of cases arising under this section, the exemption involved in each case, the disposition of such case, and the cost, fees, and penalties assessed under subparagraphs (E), (F), and (G) of subsection (a)(4). Such report shall also

include a description of the efforts undertaken by the Department of Justice to encourage agency compliance with this section.

(f) For purposes of this section, the term—

(1) "agency" as defined in section 551(1) of this title includes any executive department, military department, Government corporation, Government controlled corporation, or other establishment in the executive branch of the Government (including the Executive Office of the President), or any independent regulatory agency; and

(2) "record" and any other term used in this section in reference to information includes any information that would be an agency record subject to the requirements of this section when maintained by an agency in any format, including an electronic format.

(g) The head of each agency shall prepare and make publicly available upon request, reference material or a guide for requesting records or information from the agency, subject to the exemptions in subsection (b), including—

(1) an index of all major information systems of the agency;

(2) a description of major information and record locator systems maintained by the agency; and

(3) a handbook for obtaining various types and categories of public information from the agency pursuant to chapter 35 of title 44, and under this section.

§552a Records maintained on individuals

[This section, sometimes referred to as the Privacy Act, is omitted.]

§553. Rule making

(a) This section applies, according to the provisions thereof, except to the extent that there is involved—

(1) a military or foreign affairs function of the United States; or

(2) a matter relating to agency management or personnel or to public property, loans, grants, benefits, or contracts.

(b) General notice of proposed rulemaking shall be published in the Federal Register, unless persons subject thereto are named and either personally served or otherwise have actual notice thereof in accordance with law. The notice shall include—

(1) a statement of the time, place, and nature of public rule making proceedings;

(2) reference to the legal authority under which the rule is proposed; and

(3) either the terms or substance of the proposed rule or a description of the subjects and issues involved.

Except when notice or hearing is required by statute, this subsection does not apply—

(A) to interpretative rules, general statements of policy, or rules of agency organization, procedure, or practice; or

(B) when the agency for good cause finds (and incorporates the finding and a brief statement of reasons therefore in the rules issued) that notice and public procedure thereon are impracticable, unnecessary, or contrary to the public interest.

(c) After notice required by this section, the agency shall give interested persons an opportunity to participate in the rule making through submission of written data, views, or arguments with or without opportunity for oral presentation. After consideration of the relevant matter presented, the agency shall incorporate in the rules adopted a concise general statement of their basis and purpose. When rules are required by statute to be made on the record after opportunity for an agency hearing, sections 556 and 557 of this title apply instead of this subsection.

(d) The required publication or service of a substantive rule shall be made not less than 30 days before its effective date, except—

(1) a substantive rule which grants or recognizes an exemption or relieves a restriction;

(2) interpretative rules and statements of policy; or

(3) as otherwise provided by the agency for good cause found and published with the rule.

(e) Each agency shall give an interested person the right to petition for the issuance, amendment, or repeal of a rule.

§554. Adjudications

(a) This section applies, according to the provisions thereof, in every case of adjudication required by statute to be determined on the record after opportunity for an agency hearing, except to the extent that there is involved—

(1) a matter subject to a subsequent trial of the law and the facts de novo in a court;

(2) the selection or tenure of an employee, except an administrative law judge appointed under section 3105 of this title;

(3) proceedings in which decisions rest solely on inspections, tests, or elections;

(4) the conduct of military or foreign affairs functions;

(5) cases in which an agency is acting as an agent for a court; or

(6) the certification of worker representatives.

(b) Persons entitled to notice of an agency hearing shall be timely informed of—

(1) the time, place, and nature of the hearing;

(2) the legal authority and jurisdiction under which the hearing is to be held; and

(3) the matters of fact and law asserted.

When private persons are the moving parties, other parties to the proceeding shall give prompt notice of issues controverted in fact or law;

and in other instances agencies may by rule require responsive pleading. In fixing the time and place for hearings, due regard shall be had for the convenience and necessity of the parties or their representatives.

(c) The agency shall give all interested parties opportunity for—

(1) the submission and consideration of facts, arguments, offers of settlement, or proposals of adjustment when time, the nature of the proceeding, and the public interest permit; and

(2) to the extent that the parties are unable so to determine a controversy by consent, hearing and decision on notice and in accordance with sections 556 and 557 of this title.

(d) The employee who presides at the reception of evidence pursuant to section 556 of this title shall make the recommended decision or initial decision required by section 557 of this title, unless he becomes unavailable to the agency. Except to the extent required for the disposition of ex parte matters as authorized by law, such an employee may not—

(1) consult a person or party on a fact in issue, unless on notice and opportunity for all parties to participate; or

(2) be responsible to or subject to the supervision or direction of an employee or agent engaged in the performance of investigative or prosecuting functions for an agency.

An employee or agent engaged in the performance of investigative or prosecuting functions for an agency in a case may not, in that or a factually related case, participate or advise in the decision, recommended decision, or agency review pursuant to section 557 of this title, except as witness or counsel in public proceedings. This subsection does not apply—

(A) in determining applications for initial licenses;

(B) to proceedings involving the validity or application of rates, facilities, or practices of public utilities or carriers; or

(C) to the agency or a member or members of the body comprising the agency.

(e) The agency, with like effect as in the case of other orders, and in its sound discretion, may issue a declaratory order to terminate a controversy or remove uncertainty.

§555. Ancillary matters

(a) This section applies, according to the provisions thereof, except as otherwise provided by this subchapter.

(b) A person compelled to appear in person before an agency or representative thereof is entitled to be accompanied, represented, and advised by counsel or, if permitted by the agency, by other qualified representative. A party is entitled to appear in person or by or with counsel or other duly qualified representative in an agency proceeding. So far as the orderly conduct of public business permits, an interested person may appear before an agency or its responsible employees for the presentation, adjustment, or determination of an issue, request, or controversy in a proceeding, whether interlocutory, summary, or otherwise, or in connection with an agency function. With due regard for the convenience and necessity of the parties or their representatives and within a reasonable time, each agency shall proceed to conclude a matter presented to it. This subsection does not grant or deny a person who is not a lawyer the right to appear for or represent others before an agency or in an agency proceeding.

(c) Process, requirement of a report, inspection, or other investigative act or demand may not be issued, made, or enforced except as authorized by law. A person compelled to submit data or evidence is entitled to retain or, on payment of lawfully prescribed costs, procure a copy or transcript thereof, except that in a nonpublic investigatory proceeding the witness may for good cause be limited to inspection of the official transcript of his testimony.

(d) Agency subpoenas authorized by law shall be issued to a party on request and, when required by rules of procedure, on a statement or showing of general relevance and reasonable scope of the evidence sought. On contest, the court shall sustain the subpoena or similar process or demand to the extent that it is found to be in accordance with law. In a proceeding for enforcement, the court shall issue an order requiring the appearance of the witness or the production of the evidence or data within a reasonable time under penalty of punishment for contempt in case of contumacious failure to comply.

(e) Prompt notice shall be given of the denial in whole or in part of a written application, petition, or other request of an interested person made in connection with any agency proceeding. Except in affirming a prior denial or when the denial is self-explanatory, the notice shall be accompanied by a brief statement of the grounds for denial.

§556. Hearings; presiding employees; powers and duties; burden of proof; evidence; record as basis of decision

(a) This section applies, according to the provisions thereof, to hearings required by section 553 or 554 of this title to be conducted in accordance with this section.

(b) There shall preside at the taking of evidence —

      (1) the agency;

      (2) one or more members of the body which comprises the agency; or

      (3) one or more administrative law judges appointed under section 3105 of this title.

This subchapter does not supersede the conduct of specified classes of proceedings, in whole or in part, by or before boards or other employees specially provided for by or designated under statute. The functions of presiding employees and of employees participating in decisions in accordance with section 557 of this title shall be conducted in an impartial manner. A presiding or participating employee may at any time disqualify himself. On the filing in good faith of a timely and sufficient affidavit of personal bias or other disqualification of a presiding or participating employee, the agency shall determine the matter as a part of the record and decision in the case.

(c) Subject to published rules of the agency and within its powers, employees presiding at hearings may—

> (1) administer oaths and affirmations;
>
> (2) issue subpoenas authorized by law;
>
> (3) rule on offers of proof and receive relevant evidence;
>
> (4) take depositions or have depositions taken when the ends of justice would be served;
>
> (5) regulate the course of the hearing;
>
> (6) hold conferences for the settlement or simplification of the issues by consent of the parties or by the use of alternative means of dispute resolution as provided in subchapter IV of this chapter;
>
> (7) inform the parties as to the availability of one or more alternative means of dispute resolution, and encourage use of such methods;
>
> (8) require the attendance at any conference held pursuant to paragraph (6) of at least one representative of each party who has authority to negotiate concerning resolution of issues in controversy;
>
> (9) dispose of procedural requests or similar matters;
>
> (10) make or recommend decisions in accordance with section 557 of this title; and
>
> (11) take other action authorized by agency rule consistent with this subchapter.

(d) Except as otherwise provided by statute, the proponent of a rule or order has the burden of proof. Any oral or documentary evidence may be received, but the agency as a matter of policy shall provide for the exclusion of irrelevant, immaterial, or unduly repetitious evidence. A sanction may not be imposed or rule or order issued except on consideration of the whole record or those parts thereof cited by a party and supported by and in accordance with the reliable, probative, and substantial evidence. The agency may, to the extent consistent with the interests of justice and the policy of the underlying statutes administered by the agency, consider a violation of section 557(d) of this title sufficient grounds for a decision adverse to a party who has knowingly committed such violation or knowingly caused such violation to occur. A party is entitled to present his case or defense by oral or documentary evidence, to submit rebuttal evidence, and to conduct such cross-examination as may be required for a full and true disclosure of the facts. In rule making or determining claims for money or benefits or applications for initial licenses an agency may, when a party will not be prejudiced thereby, adopt procedures for the submission of all or part of the evidence in written form.

(e) The transcript of testimony and exhibits, together with all papers and requests filed in the proceeding, constitutes the exclusive record for decision in accordance with section 557 of this title and, on payment of lawfully prescribed costs, shall be made available to the parties. When an agency decision rests on official notice of a material fact not appearing in the evidence in the record, a party is entitled, on timely request, to an opportunity to show the contrary.

§557. Initial decisions; conclusiveness; review by agency; submissions by parties; contents of decisions; record

(a) This section applies, according to the provisions thereof, when a hearing is required to be conducted in accordance with section 556 of this title.

(b) When the agency did not preside at the reception of the evidence, the presiding employee or, in cases not subject to section 554(d) of this title, an employee qualified to preside at hearings pursuant to section 556 of this title, shall initially decide the case unless the agency requires, either in specific cases or by general rule, the entire record to be certified to it for decision. When the presiding employee makes an initial decision, that decision then becomes the decision of the agency without further proceedings unless there is an appeal to, or review on motion of, the agency within time provided by rule. On appeal from or review of the initial decision, the agency has all the powers which it would have in making the initial decision except as it may limit the issues on notice or by rule. When the agency makes the decision without having presided at the reception of the evidence, the presiding employee or an employee qualified to preside at hearings pursuant to section 556 of this title shall first recommend a decision, except that in rule making or determining applications for initial licenses—

> (1) instead thereof the agency may issue a tentative decision or one of its responsible employees may recommend a decision; or

> (2) this procedure may be omitted in a case in which the agency finds on the record that due and timely execution of its functions imperatively and unavoidably so requires.

(c) Before a recommended, initial, or tentative decision, or a decision on agency review of the decision of subordinate employees, the parties are entitled to a reasonable opportunity to submit for the consideration of the employees participating in the decisions—

> (1) proposed findings and conclusions; or

> (2) exceptions to the decisions or recommended decisions of subordinate employees or to tentative agency decisions; and

> (3) supporting reasons for the exceptions or proposed findings or conclusions.

The record shall show the ruling on each finding, conclusion, or exception presented. All decisions, including initial, recommended, and tentative decisions, are a part of the record and shall include a statement of—

(A) findings and conclusions, and the reasons or basis therefore, on all the material issues of fact, law, or discretion presented on the record; and

(B) the appropriate rule, order, sanction, relief, or denial thereof.

(d)(1) In any agency proceeding which is subject to subsection (a) of this section, except to the extent required for the disposition of ex parte matters as authorized by law—

(A) no interested person outside the agency shall make or knowingly cause to be made to any member of the body comprising the agency, administrative law judge, or other employee who is or may reasonably be expected to be involved in the decisional process of the proceeding, an ex parte communication relevant to the merits of the proceeding;

(B) no member of the body comprising the agency, administrative law judge, or other employee who is or may reasonably be expected to be involved in the decisional process of the proceeding, shall make or knowingly cause to be made to any interested person outside the agency an ex parte communication relevant to the merits of the proceeding;

(C) a member of the body comprising the agency, administrative law judge, or other employee who is or may reasonably be expected to be involved in the decisional process of such proceeding who receives, or who makes or knowingly causes to be made, a communication prohibited by this subsection shall place on the public record of the proceeding:

(i) all such written communications;

(ii) memoranda stating the substance of all such oral communications; and

(iii) all written responses, and memoranda stating the substance of all oral responses, to the materials described in clauses (i) and (ii) of this subparagraph;

(D) upon receipt of a communication knowingly made or knowingly caused to be made by a party in violation of this subsection, the agency, administrative law judge, or other employee presiding at the hearing may, to the extent consistent with the interests of justice and the policy of the underlying statutes, require the party to show cause why his claim or interest in the proceeding should not be dismissed, denied, disregarded, or otherwise adversely affected on account of such violation; and

(E) the prohibitions of this subsection shall apply beginning at such time as the agency may designate, but in no case shall they begin to apply later than the time at which a proceeding is noticed for hearing unless the person responsible for the communication has knowledge that it will be noticed, in which case the prohibitions shall apply beginning at the time of his acquisition of such knowledge.

(2) This subsection does not constitute authority to withhold information from Congress.

§558. Imposition of sanctions; determination of applications for licenses; suspension, revocation, and expiration of licenses

(a) This section applies, according to the provisions thereof, to the exercise of a power or authority.

(b) A sanction may not be imposed or a substantive rule or order issued except within jurisdiction delegated to the agency and as authorized by law.

(c) When application is made for a license required by law, the agency, with due regard for the rights and privileges of all the interested parties or adversely affected persons and within a reasonable time, shall set and complete proceedings required to be conducted in accordance with sections 556 and 557 of this title or other proceedings required by law and shall make its decision. Except in cases of willfulness or those in which public health, interest, or safety requires otherwise, the withdrawal, suspension, revocation, or annulment of a license is lawful only if, before the institution of agency proceedings therefore, the licensee has been given—

(1) notice by the agency in writing of the facts or conduct which may warrant the action; and

(2) opportunity to demonstrate or achieve compliance with all lawful requirements.

When the licensee has made timely and sufficient application for a renewal or a new license in accordance with agency rules, a license with reference to an activity of a continuing nature does not expire until the application has been finally determined by the agency.

§559. Effect on other laws; effect of subsequent statute

This subchapter, chapter 7, and sections 1305, 3105, 3344, 4301(2)(E), 5372, and 7521 of this title, and the provisions of section 5335(a)(B) of this title that relate to administrative law judges, do not limit or repeal additional requirements imposed by statute or otherwise recognized by law. Except as otherwise required by law, requirements or privileges relating to evidence or procedure apply equally to agencies and persons. Each agency is granted the authority necessary to comply with the requirements of this subchapter through the issuance of rules or otherwise. Subsequent statute may not be held to supersede or modify this subchapter, chapter 7, sections 1305, 3105, 3344, 4301(2)(E), 5372, or 7521 of this title, or the provisions of section 5335(a)(B) of this title that relate to administrative law judges, except to the extent that it does so expressly.

. . .

[§§561-584, including provisions of the Negotiated Rulemaking Act and the Administrative Dispute Resolution Act, both of which were added to title 5, are omitted.]

CHAPTER 7. JUDICIAL REVIEW

Sec.

§701   Application; definitions.
§702   Right of review.
§703   Form and venue of proceeding.
§704   Actions reviewable.
§705   Relief pending review
§706   Scope of review.

§701. Application; definitions

(a) This chapter applies, according to the provisions thereof, except to the extent that—

(1) statutes preclude judicial review; or

(2) agency action is committed to agency discretion by law.

(b) For the purpose of this chapter—

(1) ["agency" is defined in the same terms as it §551(1)(A) through (H) above]; and

(2) "person", "rule", "order", "license", "sanction", "relief", and "agency action" have the meanings given them by section 551 of this title.

§702. Right of review

A person suffering legal wrong because of agency action, or adversely affected or aggrieved by agency action within the meaning of a relevant statute, is entitled to judicial review thereof. An action in a court of the United States seeking relief other than money damages and stating a claim that an agency or an officer or employee thereof acted or failed to act in an official capacity or under color of legal authority shall not be dismissed nor relief therein be denied on the ground that it is against the United States or that the United States is an indispensable party. The United States may be named as a defendant in any such action, and a judgment or decree may be entered against the United States: *Provided*, That any mandatory or injunctive decree shall specify the Federal officer or officers (by name or by title), and their successors in office, personally responsible for compliance. Nothing herein (1) affects other limitations on judicial review or the power or duty of the court to dismiss any action or deny relief on any other appropriate legal or equitable ground; or (2) confers authority to grant relief if any other statute that grants consent to suit expressly or impliedly forbids the relief which is sought.

§703. Form and venue of proceeding

The form of proceeding for judicial review is the special statutory review proceeding relevant to the subject matter in a court specified by statute or, in the absence or inadequacy thereof, any applicable form of legal action, including actions for declaratory judgments or writs of prohibitory or mandatory injunction or habeas corpus, in a court of competent jurisdiction. If no special statutory review proceeding is applicable, the action for judicial review may be brought against the United States, the agency by its official title, or the appropriate officer. Except to the extent that prior, adequate, and exclusive opportunity for judicial review is provided by law, agency action is subject to judicial review in civil or criminal proceedings for judicial enforcement.

§704. Actions reviewable

Agency action made reviewable by statute and final agency action for which there is no other adequate remedy in a court are subject to judicial review. A preliminary, procedural, or intermediate agency action or ruling not directly reviewable is subject to review on the review of the final agency action. Except as otherwise expressly required by statute, agency action otherwise final is final for the purposes of this section whether or not there has been presented or determined an application for a declaratory order, for any form of reconsideration, or, unless the agency otherwise requires by rule and provides that the action meanwhile is inoperative, for an appeal to superior agency authority.

§705. Relief pending review

When an agency finds that justice so requires, it may postpone the effective date of action taken by it, pending judicial review. On such conditions as may be required and to the extent necessary to prevent irreparable injury, the reviewing court, including the court to which a case may be taken on appeal from or on application for certiorari or other writ to a reviewing court, may issue all necessary and appropriate process to postpone the effective date of an agency action or to preserve status or rights pending conclusion of the review proceedings.

§706. Scope of review

To the extent necessary to decision and when presented, the reviewing court shall decide all relevant questions of law, interpret constitutional and statutory provisions, and determine the meaning or applicability of the terms of an agency action. The reviewing court shall—

(1) compel agency action unlawfully withheld or unreasonably delayed; and

(2) hold unlawful and set aside agency action, findings, and conclusions found to be—

(A) arbitrary, capricious, an abuse of discretion, or otherwise not in accordance with law;

(B) contrary to constitutional right, power, privilege, or immunity;

(C) in excess of statutory jurisdiction, authority, or limitations, or short of statutory right;

(D) without observance of procedure required by law;

(E) unsupported by substantial evidence in a case subject to sections 556 and 557 of this title or otherwise reviewed on the record of an agency hearing provided by statute; or

(F) unwarranted by the facts to the extent that the facts are subject to trial de novo by the reviewing court.

In making the foregoing determinations, the court shall review the whole record or those parts of it cited by a party, and due account shall be taken of the rule of prejudicial error.

[Selected Provisions Relating to Administrative Law Judges]

§3105. Appointment of administrative law judges

Each agency shall appoint as many administrative law judges as are necessary for proceedings required to be conducted in accordance with sections 556 and 557 of this title. Administrative law judges shall be assigned to cases in rotation so far as practicable, and may not perform duties inconsistent with their duties and responsibilities as administrative law judges.

§7521. Actions against administrative law judges

(a) An action may be taken against an administrative law judge appointed under section 3105 of this title by the agency in which the administrative law judge is employed only for good cause established and determined by the Merit Systems Protection Board on the record after opportunity for hearing before the Board.

(b) The actions covered by this section are—

(1) a removal;

(2) a suspension;

(3) a reduction in grade;

(4) a reduction in pay; and

(5) a furlough of 30 days or less; but do not include—

(A) a suspension or removal under section 7532 of this title;

(B) a reduction-in-force action under section 3502 of this title; or

(C) any action initiated under section 1215 of this title.

Appendix C

Presidential Administrations and Secretaries of Department of Transportation, 1967-87

President	Secretary of Transportation	Dates in Office	Biography of Secretary
Lyndon Johnson (D)	Alan Boyd (D)	1/16/67– 1/20/69	Appointed to Civil Aeronautics Board by Eisenhower; in 1959, promoted to President of the CAB by Kennedy. Worked to improve profits of airline industry; 1965, appointed by Johnson as Undersecretary of commerce for transportation; headed task force to study maritime industry; appointed the first Secretary of Transportation. In 1967, after leaving office became President of Illinois Central Railroad; then became President of Amtrak
Richard Nixon (R)	John Volpe (R)	1/22/69– 2/1/73	Appointed by Eisenhower as first Federal Highway Administrator in 1956; Governor of MA (1961-1963, 1965-1969) who, during his tenure as governor, reformed birth control laws and increased public housing; as Secretary, created NHTSA; Amtrak created while he was Secretary. After serving as Secretary, became U.S. Ambassador to Italy (1973-1977)
	Claude Brinegar (R)	2/2/73– 2/1/75	Worked in oil industry before his tenure as Secretary; after serving as Secretary, maintained executive position at Union Oil Co. (later Unocal)
	John Barnum (acting) (R)	2/2/75– 3/6/75	

President	Secretary of Transportation	Dates in Office	Biography of Secretary
Gerald Ford (R)	William Coleman (R)	3/7/75– 1/20/77	Second African-American Cabinet member; first African-American Supreme Court law clerk; co-author of NAACP's legal brief in *Brown v. Board of Education*; former President of NAACP Legal Defense and Educational Fund; member of U.S. delegation to 24th session of UN General Assembly; served on Warren Commission which investigated Kennedy's assassination; during his tenure as Secretary, NHTSA's automobile test facility in OH opened; joined O'Melveny and Myers after tenure as Secretary; awarded Presidential Medal of Freedom by Clinton in 1995; by invitation of U.S. Supreme Court, argued as amicus curiae in *Bob Jones U. v. U.S.*
Jimmy Carter (D)	Brock Adams (D)	1/23/77– 7/20/79	Served 6 terms (beginning 1965) in House of Representatives (D-WA); first Chairman of House Budget Committee; resigned from House to become Secretary; as Secretary, resisted airline deregulation and worked to improve airport security/screening; resigned as Secretary in 1979, practiced law and became lobbyist for railroad carriers; 1986, elected as U.S. Senator from WA (served only 1 term; did not seek re-election due to allegations of sexual misconduct, which he denied) then retired in 1992; as Senator, fought against turning nuclear reservation in WA into waste dump; involved in securing funding for Ryan White Act
	W. Graham Claytor, Jr. (acting) (D)	7/21/79– 8/14/79	President of Southern Railway 1967-1977; from 1977-1979, Secretary of the Navy– led U.S. Navy to allow women to serve on ships and allow gays to leave service without criminal record; Deputy Secretary of Defense (1979-1981) (his military assistant was Gen. Colin Powell); 1982-1993 was head of Amtrak
	Neil Goldschmidt (D)	8/15/79– 1/20/81	1973-1979, Mayor of Portland, OR; as Secretary, known for helping revive auto industry and deregulating airline, railroad, and trucking industries; Governor of OR 1986-1990; 2003, nominated to OR State Board of Higher Education–story in May 2004 *Williamette Week* exposed his affair with 14-year old girl while he was Mayor in the 1970s–he resigned from his positions with Texas Pacific Group and Board of Higher Ed, resigned from the OR State Bar. The author of the article, Nigel Jaquiss, won 2005 Pulitzer Prize.

President	Secretary of Transportation	Dates in Office	Biography of Secretary
Ronald Reagan (R)	Drew Lewis (Andrew L. Lewis) (R)	1/23/81– 2/1/83	Corporate executive; unsuccessful Republican candidate for Governor of Pennsylvania in 1974. Secretary during 1981 air traffic controllers' strike. After serving hired as Chairman and CEO of Warner-Amex Cable Communications; left Warner in 1986 to become Chairman and CEO of Union Pacific Railroad; 1986-1997, President and COO of Union Pacific Corporation. Since 1994, reported history of alcohol abuse, DUI arrests
	Elizabeth Dole (R)	2/7/83– 9/30/87	1969-1973, Deputy Assistant for Consumer Affairs; 1973-1979, FTC Commissioner; as Secretary, implemented third rear brake light requirement, worked with MADD to deny federal funding for highways to states with drinking age lower than 21, implemented random drug testing program in Dept. of Transportation; 1989-1990, Secretary of Labor; 1991-1999, President of American Red Cross; 2002-2008, U.S. Senator from NC (won seat vacated by Jesse Helms). Defeated in 2008 by Kay Hagan after running an ad accusing Hagan of atheism.

Table of Cases

Name and page number of principal cases in italics. Only the initial page is given unless there is an extended discussion in the text.

A.L.A Schechter Poultry Corp. v. United States, 123, 124, 126, 139-41
AT&T Corp. v. Iowa Utils. Bd., 804
Abbott Labs. V. Gardner, 934, 937, 945
Action for Children's Television v. FCC, 902
Adamo Wrecking v. United States, 173, 174
ADAPSO v. Board of Governors, 846
Alaska v. United States, 208
Alaska Prof'l Hunters Ass'n v. FAA, 888
Allentown Mack Sales & Service, Inc. v. NLRB, 909
Almendarez-Torres v. United States, 244, *248*, 254, 255
Andrus v. Glover Constr. Co., 194
Appalachian Power Co. v. EPA, 946
Atchinson, T & SFR Co. v. Wichita Bd. of Trade, 406, 410
Auer v. Robbins, 490, 818, *825*, 841, 845

Babbitt v. Sweet Home Chapter of Communities, 175, 206, 778
Bailey v. United States, 171-74
Barber v. Gonzalez, 163
Barnhart v. Peabody Coal Co., 194
Barnhart v. Thomas, 196-97
Barnhart v. Walton, 805, 817
Bates v. Dow Agrosciences LLC, 265
Baxter v. Ford Motor Co., 14
Bennett v. Spear, 946
Bifulco v. United States, 231
Bi-Metallic Inv. Co. v. State Bd. of Equalization, 881-82
Block v. Community Nutrition Inst., 934
Bloggett v. Holden, 242
Bob Jones University v. United States, 310, 408, italics, 417, 746
Boston Medical Center Corp. & House Officers' Association, 579
Boutilier v. INS, 351, 357
Bowen v. Georgetown Univ. Hosp., 476, 808, 815, 827, 832
Bowles v. Seminole Rock & Sand Co., 490, 823-25
Bowsher v. Synar, 660, 673, 750

Brown v. Gardner, 790
Buckley v. Valeo, 674, 732-36, 738-39, 742, 759
Burlington Truck Lines v. U.S. 406, 410, 411

Cabell Huntington Hosp., Inc. v. Shalala, 196
Carter, In re, 242
Chapman v. United States, 271
Chevron U.S.A. Inc. v. Echazabal, 194
Chevron U.S.A. Inc. v. NRDC, 479, 767 passim (*See* Index, Chevron doctrine)
Chicasaw Nation v. United States, 196
Chisom v. Roemer, 264
Christensen v. Harris Cnty., 194, 804, 809, 810, 811, 815, 819
Chrysler Corp. v. Department of Transportation, 381, 394, 410, 443, 503-04
Church of the Holy Trinity v. United States, 147, 152-58, 305, 328
Cipollone v. Liggett Group, Inc., 194
Circuit City Stores, Inc. v. Adams, 206-07
Citizens to Preserve Overton Parks, Inc. v. Volpe, 405, 407, 439, 576, *847,* 886, 894, 898, 901-02, 934, 937-41
City of Arlington v. FCC, 471, 822
Clean Air Act Council v. Pruitt, 371, 439
Clinton v. City of New York, 681
Commissioner of Intern al Revenue v. Lundy, 204
Crandon v. United States, 204
CSX Transp., Inc. v. Surface Transp. Bd., 190, 439

Dada v. Mukasey, 203-04
De Sylva v. Ballentine, 199
Dean v. United States, 174
Decker v. Nw. Envtl. Def. Ctr., 827, 828-29, 845
Dickinson v. Zurko, 846
Dolan v. United States Postal Serv., 191
Dudley v. Hannaford Bros. Co., 242
Dunlap v. Bachowski, 945

EEOC v. Arabian Am. Oil Co., 268, 809
Edward J. DeBartolo Corp. v. Florida Gulf Coast Bldg. & Constr. Trades Council, 252, 860

Environmental Def. v. Duke Energy
    Corp., 204
Erlenbaugh v. United States, 210-11

FCC v. Fox Television Stations, Inc., 855,
    889, 890
FCC v. Pacifica Found., 628, 631,
    637, 855-72
FCC v. Schreiber, 877, 882
Federal Crop Ins. Corp. v. Merrill, 643
Federal Trade Comm. v. Ruberoid
    Co., 741
Florida Lime & Avocado Growers, Inc. v.
    Paul, 112, 266
Foley Bros., Inc. v. Filardo, 268
*Food & Drug Administration v. Brown &
    Williamson Tobacco Corp.,* 219, 220, 288,
    715, 787
*Free Enterprise Fund v. Public Co. Accounting
    Oversight Board,* 665, *669,* 833
Freightliner Corp. v. Myrick, 112, 266
Freytag v. Commissioner, 868

Geier v. American Honda Motor Co., 98,
    106, 112
General Dynamics Land Sys., Inc. v.
    Cline, 205
General Motors Corp. v. National Highway
    Traffic & Safety Admin., 476, 483
Goldberg v. Kelly, 577, 598
Gozlon-Peretz v. United States, 204
Graham v. Goodcell, 207
Greater Boston Television Corp. v.
    FCC, 414
Green v. Bock Laundry Mach. Co., 342
Gregory v. Ashcroft, 255, 301-02
Grimshaw v. Ford Motor Corp., 18
Gundy v. U.S., 130
Gustafson v. Alloyd Co., 184, 192, 791
Gutierrez-Brizuela v. Lynch, 822

Hall St. Assocs., L.L.C. v. Mattel,
    Inc., 189
Hawaii v. Office of Hawaiian Affairs, 214
Heckler v. Chaney, 833, *934*
Holy Trinity Church v. United States.
    See Church of the Holy Trinity v.
    United States
Home Box Office v. FCC, 897
Hooper v. California, 242
Huddleston v. United States, 231
Humphrey's Executor v. United States, 647,
    652, 661, 664-78, 735, 752, 759

Industrial Union Dep't, AFL-CIO v.
    American Petroleum Inst., 126, 129-30
*Immigration & Naturalization Service v.
    Chadha,* 398, 417, 681, *730,* 744,
    752-59, 761
INS v. St. Cyr, 208
Inyo Cnty., Cal. v. Paiute-Shoshone
    Indians, 200

J.W. Hampton, Jr. & Co. v. United States,
    124, 125, 128, 734, 738
Jama v. Immigration & Customs
    Enforcement, 200
Jarecki v. G.D. Searle & Co., 179, 191, 192
Jones v. Rath Packing Co., 265

Kerlin's Lessee v. Bull, 199
King v. Burwell, 215, *802*
Kisor v. Wilkie, 829

Lagos v. U.S., 192
Lamie v. U.S. Trustee, 206, 222, 227
Landgraf v. USI Film Prods., 266-67
Lawrence v. Texas, 357
Leavitt v. Jane L., 254
Lexecon Inc. v. Milberg Weiss Bershad
    Hynes & Lerach, 199
Lincoln v. Vigil, 934
Lindh v. Murphy, 267
Lopez v. Davis, 199, 200
Loving v. United States, 125, 127
Lujan v. Defenders of Wildlife,
    922-24, 927-32

MacPherson v. Buick Motor Co., 6, 12-15, 25
Marbury v. Madison, 225, 226, 242, 820
Martin v. Occupational Safety and Health
    Rev. Comm., 811, 831-36
Massachusetts v. EPA, 921
Mathews v. Eldridge, 527, 591, 598,
    599, 601
McBoyle v. United States, 231-233
*MCI Telecommunications Corp. v. American
    Telephone & Telegraph Co.,* 779, 791,
    796-97, 800, 801
McLean v. Goodyear Tire & Rubber Co., 14
Merrill Lynch, Pierce, Fenner & Smith Inc.
    v. Dabit, 212
Michigan v. EPA, 820-21
Milner v. Department of Navy, 872
Mistretta v. United States, 126, 127, 129
Moore v. Harris, 289
Morrison v. Olson, 657, 668, 671

Morton v. Ruiz, 480, 768, 814, 819
Motor Vehicle Manufacturers Association v. State Farm Mutual Automobile Ins. Co., *403*, 420-21, 468, 570-71, *852*, 859-60, 869, 872, 891
Muscarello v. United States, 166, 174
Myers v. United States, 648, 654-56, 660-61, 666, 671, 675, 733, 752-53

Nader v. General Motors Corp., 82
National Ass'n of Home Builders v. Defenders of Wildlife, 200, 213-14
National Automatic Laundry & Cleaning Council v. Shultz, 946
National Cable & Telecomms, Ass'n v. Brand X Internet Servs., 816
National Fed'n of Fed. Employees, Local 1309 v. Department of Interior, 212
NationsBank of N.C. v. Variable Annuity Life Ins. Co., 809, 819
New York v. U.S., 410
Nix v. Hedden, 161
NLRB v. Bell Aerospace, 295, 590, 812, 813, 832-33

Pacific Legal Found, v. Department of Transp., 444
Panama Ref. Co. v. Ryan, 123
Paralyzed Veterans of Am. v. D.C. Arena, 886-91
Pennsylvania Dep't of Corr. v. Yeskey, 208
Perez v. Mortgage Bankers Ass'n, 820, 835, 827, *886*
Powerex Corp. v. Reliant Energy Servs., 204
Public Citizen, Inc. v. Minetta, 543
Public Citizen v. U.S. Dep't of Justice, 271, 303-04

Radzanower v. Touche Ross & Co., 212, 213
Raleigh & Gaston R. Co. v. Reid, 194
Reiter v. Sonotone Corp., 198
Rice v. Santa Fe Elevator Corp., 258, 265
Riegel v. Medtronic, Inc., 111, 266
Rotche v. Buick Motor Co., 10
Rowland v. California Men's Colony, Unit II Men's Advisory Council, 200
Rust v. Sullivan, 242, 251, 252, 790
Rybacheck v. EPA, 896

S.D. Warren Co. v. Maine Bd. Of Envtl. Prot., 342
SEC v. Chenery Corp. (1943), 143, 468, 813, 884

SEC v. Chenery Corp. (1947), 407, 590, 812, 813, 829-30, 882, 925
Sangamon Valley Television Corp. v. U.S, 897
Sinclair, In re, 348
Skidmore v. Swift & Co., 278, 490, *763*, 783, 804-17, 834, 837, 841-45
Smiley v. Citibank, 809, 814, 818, 828, 860
Smith v. City of Jackson, 212
Smith v. United States, 169, 170, 268

Tcherepnin v. Knight, 241
Touby v. United States, 126-27
Train v. NRDC, 769
Trainmen v. Baltimore & Ohio R. Co., 208-50
TRW Inc. v. Andrews, 206
TVA v. Hill, 177, 179, 308, 481, 766

United States v. Alpers, 190, 836
United States v. Atlantic Research Corp., 206
United States v. Bass, 173, 231, 233, 258
United States v. Fisk, 199
United States v. Florida East Coast R. Co., 577, 877, 881, 963
United States v. Gradwell, 231, 233
United States v. Hayes, 197, 198, 231
United States v. Jin Fuey Moy, 241, 251, 253
United States v. Locke, 252, *269*
United States v. Mead Corp., 278, 490, *805*, 834, 885
United States v. Morton, 807, 818
United States v. Nixon, 726, 742
United States v. Nova Scotia Food Products, Inc., 716, *891*
United States v. Perkins, 650, 666, 669
United States v. Santos, 231
United States v. Shabani, 231
United States v. Shimer, 769, 779
United States v. Stewart, 209
United States v. Villanueva-Sotelo, 208
United States v. Wells, 165, 170, 249
United States v. Williams, 191
United States v. Wilson, 268
United States v. X-Citement Video, Inc., 195, 244, 247, 271
United States v. Nat'l Bank of Oregon v. Independent Ins. Agents., 194, 268
Universal Camera v. National Labor Relations Board, 903, 911, 916

Vermont Yankee Nuclear Power Corp. v.
   National Resources Defense Council, Inc.,
   366, 423, 591-92, 874-76, *877,* 938-39

Wachovia Bank v. Schmidt, 209
Washington State Dep't of Soc. & Health
   Servs. v. Guardianship Estate of
   Keffeler, 190
Watson v. United States, 206
Watt v. Alaska, 160
West Va. Univ. Hosps., Inc. v. Casey, 212,
   299, 300-01
Whitman v. American Trucking Ass'ns, 124,
   787, 801
Wiener v. United States, 665, 676

Will v. Michigan Dept. of State
   Police, 257-58
Williams v. Taylor, 342
Williamson v. Lee Optical, 925
Winterbottom v. Wright, 3-4
Wyeth v. Levine, 112, 266

Yakus v. United States, 126, 736
Yates v. U.S., 190, 193
Youngstown Sheet & Tube Co. v. Sawyer,
   736, 738, 752, 757

Zadvydas v. Davis, 243, 254
Zuni Pub. Sch. Dist. No. 89 v. Department
   of Educ., 153, 165, 338

Index

1966 Motor Vehicle Safety Act. *See* Motor Vehicle Safety Act

Accountability
of Agencies, 402, 432-33, 436, 625-26, 646, 682-84, 710-16, 739-40, 820
Chevron doctrine and, 776, 777, 804, 816, 820-23
Common law and, 26
of Courts, 26, 804, 816
Delegation and, 135-43
of President, 682-84, 710-12, 750
Adams, Brock, 400, 443, 996
Adjudication (by agency) (*See also* Guidance)
Generally, 576-618
Administrative Procedure Act, 371, 576-78, 903-20
Complaint handling, 601-18
Formal adjudication, 371, 577, 578-90, 903-20
Immigration issues, 163-65, 243-48
Informal adjudication (incl. specific cases), 163-65, 243-48, 577, 590-91, 591-618, 779-87, 847-52, 855-72, 877-85
Motor vehicle safety (*See also* Recalls) 418, 601-18
Nuclear power plant licensing, 423, 591-92, 877-85, 938-39
Policy formation regarding, 578-79
Administrative Law Judges (ALJ), 418, 909-20, 946
Administrative Procedure Act (APA) (*See also* Adjudication, Judicial review, Rulemaking)
Generally, 360, 750, 944
Adjudication, 371, 576-78, 903-20
Arbitrary and capricious standard, 372, 403-19, 420-21, 468-69, 590, 600, 803-04, 846-91, 920
Ex parte contacts and, 698-99, 897-903
Finality, 427, 946
Formal adjudication under, 371, 577, 578-90, 903-20
Guidance (rules for) 618-19, 624-26
Informal adjudication, 590-91
Judicial review, 398, 845-920, 934-46
Procedures (required or not), 845-903
Reviewability, 846-52, 934-45
Rulemaking (requirements) (*See also* Rulemaking, separate heading) 366-67, 372, 403-18, 438-40, 468, 526-27
Substantial evidence standard, 903-20
Affordable Care Act, 56, 215-30, 801-03

Agency (*See also* Adjudication, Implementation, Statutory interpretation, Rulemaking)
Generally, 40-43, 435-36
Accountability of 402, 432-33, 436, 625-26, 646, 682-84, 710-16, 739-40, 820
Adjudication (*See also* Adjudication, separate heading), 576-618
Congressional control of (*See also* Congress, Statutory interpretation), 574-76, 717-62
Delegation to. *See* Delegation, separate heading.
Enforcement, 476-78, 483
Expertise, 131-33, 373, 410-12, 435, 480-81, 498-511, 611-12, 689, 775-76, 803-04, 866-67, 893-96, 917-18, 938-39
Failure to act, 406, 571-76, 859-60, 921-32, 934-45
Federal agencies, list, 42-43
Guidance (*See also* separate heading), 618-43
Independent (*See also* President, Congress), 478, 578, 647-79, 686, 690-91, 728, 740-41, 863-64, 868
Interpretation
of Rules (*See also* Auer doctrine), 824-41
of Statutes (*See also* Chevron doctrine, Guidance), 219, 478-84, 494, 618-44, 762-823, 837-40
Judicial control of. *See* Judicial Review
Notice and comment rulemaking. *See* Rulemaking, this heading and separate heading
Obligation to act, 361-67
Petitions to (generally), 371, 472-76, 571-73
Presidential control of (*See* Office of Information and Reg. Aff., President)
Refusal to act. *See* Failure to act, this heading
Rulemaking. *See* Rulemaking, separate heading
Size of, 41-43
Statutory interpretation. *See* Interpretation, this heading, and Statutory interpretation, separate heading)
Airbags. *See* Motor vehicle safety
Ambiguity (of Legislation) (*See also* Chevron doctrine, separate heading, Statutory interpretation)
Chevron doctrine, 478-84, 762-823
Delegation and, 122-23, 130-35, 478-84, 762-823
Drafting and, 72-76, 108, 122-23
Lenity, rule of, 166-74, 230-42
Politics and, 130-35

Appointments
   Generally, 43, 645-46, 679-80
   Constitutional rules, 647-79
   Inferior officers, 650-51, 657-67
   Removal of, 647-56, 668-79
   Senate, consent, 737
Appropriations, 54-55, 307-08, 720-23
Arbitrary and capricious standard. *See*
   Judicial review
Arrow's Theorem, 58-59
Auer doctrine, 823-41
Automobile safety. *See* Motor vehicle safety
Availability of review. *See* Judicial review

Base Realignment and Closure Commissions, 56
Bill. *See* Legislation
Borges, Jorge Luis, 193
Branches of government. *See* Constitution,
   Separation of powers
Budget control. *See* Congress
Bush, George W., 572, 576, 626, 682, 685, 933-34

CAFE standard. *See* Fuel economy.
Canons of construction. *See* Statutory
   interpretation
Cardozo, Benjamin, 6-10, 263
Carlin, George, 637
Carter, Jimmy, 400, 443
Casement, Roger, 195-96
Chevrolet Corvair, 436
Chevron doctrine (*See also* Ambiguity, Chevron,
   U.S.A. v. NRDC in Table of Cases)
   Generally, 219, 481, 478-84, 494,
      762-823, 841-45
   Accountability and, 776, 777, 804,
      816, 820-23
   and APA, 482, 829-38
   Applicability (*See also* Skidmore doctrine, this
      heading), 482, 787-820
   and Auer doctrine, 828-38
   Criticisms of, 815-17, 820-23
   Delegation and, 480-83, 768, 777, 787, 796,
      805-17, 820-23
   Empirical evidence regarding, 278,
      485-490, 493, 841-45
   Major questions exception, 787-803
   Rationale, 123, 265, 479-84, 487, 492, 763, 777,
      820-23, 852
   Separation of Powers Restoration Act, 823
   Skidmore test, 278, 490, 763-66, 804-17,
      838, 841-45
   Step One, 776-801
   Step Two, 777, 803-04
   Step Zero (*See* Applicability, this heading)
Chevron oil refinery, 479
Christian nation (Holy Trinity Case),
   151-52, 156
Citizens suits (*See also* Standing), 212-13, 728
Claybrook, Joan, 400, 423, 443, 536

Clean Air Act (CAA) (*See also* Environmental
   Protection Agency), 113-14, 124-30, 138,
   506-08, 767-75, 801, 925-38
Clean Water Act (*See also* Environmental
   Protection Agency), 214, 374
Climate Change (*See also* Environmental
   Protection Agency), 359, 571-76, 921-34
Clinton, William, 419, 685, 714, 853-54
Coleman, William, 400, 443, 451, 457,
   458, 995
Committee Reports, (generally) (*See also*
   Congress, Statutory interpretation), 50,
   99-106, 158-59, 286-87, 344-45
Committees. *See* Congress
Common law
   Accountability and, 26
   Competence of courts, 1, 25-27
   Motor vehicle safety, 1-30
      Contract law, 1-2, 27-30
      Tort law, 1-24
   Origin, 24
   Precaution, 2-27
   Precedent, 9-10
   Privity doctrine, 4-16
   Regulation and, 24-27
Congress (*See also* Legislation, House of
   Representatives, Senate)
   Appropriations, 54-55, 307-08, 720-23
   Canons, use of. *See* Drafting, this heading and
      separate heading
   Committees (generally), 48-50, 54-56
   Committee Reports (generally) (*See also*
      Legislation), 50, 153, 285-87, 305, 309,
      344-46, 347, 841
   Comptroller General, 750-61
   Concurrent resolution (*See also* Legislative
      veto), 395, 398, 407, 443
   Conference Committees
      Generally, 47, 53-54, 69-72, 285-86, 302-04,
         306, 349, 721
      Specific cases, 80, 55, 187, 293-94, 297,
         475, 906
   Congressional Review Act, 718-19, 745-50
   Contempt citations, 726
   Control of agencies
      Generally, 574-76, 717-62
      Appropriations, 720-23
      Congressional Review Act, 718-19, 745-50
      Delegation. *See* Delegation by, this heading
         and separate heading
      "Fire Alarms," 727-28
      Hearings, 140, 491-92, 602-05, 723-27,
         729, 863
      Independent agencies (*See also* President),
         740-41, 647-79
      Inspector General, 605-18
      Legislation (new), 719
      Legislative veto (*See also* Congressional
         Review Act), 394-96, 398, 728-45

Motor Vehicle Safety Act. *See* Motor Vehicle Safety Act, separate heading
Oversight, 140, 491-92, 602-05, 626, 723-27, 729, 863
Removal of agency officials, 647-52, 660, 750-62
Reporting requirements, 718-19
Veto (legislative). *See* Legislative veto, this heading and separate heading
Counsel. *See* Legislative counsel, this heading
Delegation by. *See* Delegation, separate heading
Drafting (generally) (*See also* Drafting, separate heading), 47-50, 61-76, 303-08
Executive Privilege, response to, 726-27
"Fire Alarms." *See* Control of Agencies, this heading
Filibuster, 52, 222, 306-08
Floor scheduling and debate, 50-53, 71
Hearings (generally) (*See also*, Control of Agencies, this heading, Oversight subheading), 49
Ignition interlock (response), 394-99
Joint resolution, 56, 88, 398, 718-19, 721, 745, 750, 758-761
Legislative counsel (*See also* Legislation), 60, 68-69, 70, 75-76, 285, 349
Legislative process, 45-50, 303-08, 328-33
Legislative veto, 394-96, 398, 728-45
Markup, 50
Motor Vehicle Safety Act. *See* separate heading
Oversight (of agencies). *See* Control of Agencies, this heading
Removal (of officials), 648-52, 660, 750-62
Staff, 67-71
Statutory interpretation. *See* Statutory interpretation, separate heading
Veto (legislative). *See* Legislative veto, this heading and separate heading
Vetogates, 56-57
Congressional Review Act, 718-19, 745-50
Constitution
Agency and, 647-81
Appointments, 657-668
Branches of government. *See* Separation of powers, separate heading
Broadcast regulation and, 865, 870
Case or controversy, 945
Chevron doctrine, 822
Constitutional avoidance canon, 230-31, 242-55, 264, 278, 488-89, 860, 871-72
Delegation (by Congress). *See* Delegation, separate heading
Due Process, 357, 436, 577, 591-92, 598-601, 821, 853, 881-82, 889-900, 902
Federalism (*See also* Federalism, separate heading), 111-12, 135, 256-57, 433, 749, 925-38

Independent agencies and, 647-81
Legislation (rules governing), 46
Legislative veto, 398, 728-45
Removal (of agency officials), 647-81
Separation of powers. *See* Separation of powers, separate heading
Standing, 920-34
Consumers (*See also* Market failure, Motor vehicle safety)
Complaints, 528-29, 602-03, 607-11, 613-14, 635
Discount rate, 553-55
Information, 14, 27-30, 33-34, 119-20, 548, 618
Motor vehicle safety, 14, 23, 27-30, 103, 405, 414, 445-47, 456-59, 363, 422, 462-63, 528, 589, 603, 607-11, 635, 713
Preferences, 2, 23, 27, 35, 103, 363, 548-49, 554, 789-90
Privity, 4-16
Contract (common law), 1-2, 27-30
Cost-benefit analysis
Generally, 15-24, 544-53, 555-57, 566-70
Congressional Review Act and, 748-49
Criticisms of (*See also* Limitations of, this heading), 23-24, 557-66, 711-12
Discount rate, 550-55
Executive order, 686-701
Legislation and, 566-70
Life, valuation of, 544-48
Limitations of (*See also* Criticisms of, this heading), 546-52
Methodology, 544-57
Motor vehicle safety, 15-24, 526-44
National Highway Traffic and Safety Admin. (NHTSA) (*See also* separate heading), 526-44, 549
Office of Information and Regulatory Affairs (OIRA) (*See also* separate heading), 685-714
Office of Management and Budget (OMB) (*See also* separate heading), 31-35, 550-58, 565
Pinto case, 15-24
Presidential control and, 685-714
Prompt letters, 703-10, 712-14
Regulatory review, 685-714
Return letters, 527-36, 702-03
Specific cases, 17-18, 527-44, 706-08, 748-49, 879-80
Counsel
Independent, 657-67, 668, 671
Legislative, 60, 68-69, 70, 75-76, 285, 349
National Highway Traffic and Safety Admin (NHTSA), 591-600, 638-43, 648
President's (and Office of Legal Counsel), 43, 327, 374, 423, 686, 716

Courts (as institutions) (*See also* Judicial review,
        Statutory interpretation)
    Accountability, 481, 776
    Institutional competence, 24-27
    Common law and, 3-30
Crash tests, 368-73, 386-93
Crash test dummies, 373
Cycling (in decision theory), 58-59

Definitions (*See also* Legislation, Statutory
        interpretation)
    Dictionary, (in statutory interpretation)
        Generally, 63, 146, 160-74, 188, 200-03, 240,
            280-81, 781
        Specific cases, 128, 158, 161, 167-69, 171,
            177, 181-82, 192, 205, 219, 232, 237,
            263, 582, 780-82, 785-86, 826
    Drafting, 62, 64, 69, 107-08, 188
    Executive Order 12,866 (cost-benefit), 689-91
    Motor Vehicle Safety Act, 82-83, 102, 386-94, 641
    Statutory interpretation of, 160-74, 176-88,
        220-22, 232-38, 258-59, 289-96, 301-02,
        579-87, 770-75, 780-86, 788-91, 797-99,
        817-19, 856-58
Delegation (by Congress)
    Generally, 54
    Accountability, 135-43
    Canons of construction, 203, 277-78
    Chevron doctrine, 480-83, 768, 777, 787, 796,
        805-17, 820-23
    Constitution, 123-30
    Democracy, 123-43
    Legislative veto, 738, 741
    Non-delegation doctrine, 123-30
    Omnibus bill, 55
    Politics of, 130-35
    Specificity of statutes, 122-43, 480-83, 506, 777,
        801, 816, 822
    Subdelegation (by agency), 669-79, 805-17
    Textualism and, 348-49
Democracy. *See* Accountability, Delegation, Politics
Department of Transportation (DOT). *See*
        Motor vehicle safety, Motor Vehicle Safety
        Act, National Highway Traffic and Safety
        Administration
Dictionary. *See* Definition, Statutory
        interpretation
Dictionary Act, 200-03
Dodd-Frank Wall Street Reform Act, 115-22
Dole, Elizabeth, 419-28, 429, 997
Drafting (*See also* Legislation)
    by Agency, 361, 436-40, 485-97
    in Congress, 47-50, 65-76, 203
    on Floor (of legislative chamber), 71-72
    Interest groups and 47-50, 67-68, 73-76, 81
    Lobbyists' role, 47-50, 67-68, 73-76
    Markup, 50
    Rules for, 61-65

Due Process, 357, 436, 577, 591-92,
        598-601, 821, 853, 881-82, 889-900, 902
Dynamic Interpretation (*See* Statutory
        interpretation)

Economic Analysis (*See also* Cost-benefit
        analysis, Implementation, Regulation)
    by Agencies, 525-70
    and Common law, 15-24
    Market failure, 27-30
    as Rationale for regulation, 31-39, 416
Endangered Species Act (*See also* Environmental
        Protection Agency), 37-38, 108, 175-89,
        212, 214, 308, 470-74, 778
Ehrlichman, John, 377-81
Ejusdem generis. *See* Statutory
        interpretation
Environmental Protection Agency (EPA)
    Automobile emissions, 568, 571-76,
        770-71, 921-34
    Bubble concept. *See* Chevron doctrine, Clean
        Air Act
    Clean Air Act, 113-14, 124-30, 138,
        506-08, 767-75, 801, 925-38
    Clean Water Act, 214, 374
    Control of, 767-75
    Cost-benefit analysis and, 703-06
    Delegation to, 137-38, 506, 801
    Endangered Species Act, 37-38, 108,
        175-89, 212, 214, 308, 470-74, 778
    as Executive Branch agency, 214
    Expertise of, 504-08, 523
    Fuel economy, 568, 571-74
    Political analysis (use of), 571-73
    Prompt letters (from OIRA), 703-10,
        712-14
    Risk assessment by, 523
    Rulemaking by (specific cases), 124-30, 175-87,
        504-08, 571-75, 767-76, 921-32
    Scientific analysis by, 504-08
Ex Parte Contacts, 698-99, 897-903
Executive Orders
    Generally, 467, 686
    Cost-benefit analysis, 694-97
    Executive Order 12,866 (regulatory review),
        686-701
    Memoranda, 524-25
    Rationale for regulation, 31-35, 687-88
Executive Privilege (*See also* Agency, Congress,
        President), 726-27
Expertise. *See* Agency
Expletives, 627-38
Expressio Unius. *See* Statutory interpretation
Externalities. *See* Market Failure

Failure to Act (by agency) (*See also* Agency,
        Rulemaking), 406, 571-76, 859-60,
        921-32, 934-45

Federal Communications Commission (FCC)
    627-38, 779-87, 794, 855-72, 897-900, 903
Federal Register (generally) (*See also*
    Implementation, Regulation, Rulemaking),
    366, 438, 526-27
Federal Trade Commission(FTC), 135, 652-56,
    660, 671, 794
Federalism
    Generally, 111-12, 753
    as Canon of construction, 111-12, 231, 255-66,
        278, 282-83
    Preemption, 105-06, 109-10, 111-12
    Standing, 921-32
Filibuster (U.S. Senate), 52, 222, 306-08
Finality, 427, 946
Floor. *See* Congress, Legislation
Food and Drug Administration (FDA),
    787-801, 934-45
Ford, Gerald, 396-99, 400
Ford Motor Company, 15-24, 374-77, 429
Ford II, Henry, 362, 374-77, 380-81
Ford Pinto, 15-24, 374
Formal adjudication. *See* Adjudication
Fourth branch of government. *See* Agency,
    Constitution
Fuel economy
    CAFE standard, 472-76, 553-56, 571-74
    Environmental Protection Agency and,
        568, 571-74
    General Motors Corp. and, 428-31
    NHSTA, 447, 456, 460, 472-76, 503, 549,
        553-56, 743-44
    Tire pressure and, 530, 535, 539, 543

General Accounting Office. *See* Government
    Accountability Office
General Motors Corp., 79-82, 388, 411,
    428-31, 472-76, 602-03, 639-43
Good cause (as grounds for removal of
    officials), 657-79
Government Accountability Office (GAO), 724,
    746-47, 755
Guidance (*See also* Agency, Implementation)
    Generally, 618, 19, 625-27, 823
    Administrative Procedure Act,
        618-19, 624-25
    Auer doctrine, 824-41
    Circular A-4, 31-35, 554, 555-57
    Congressional Review Act, 745-46
    Criticisms, 624-25
    Dodd-Frank Act, 120
    Estoppel, 643
    by FCC, 627-39
    FDA rules for, 620-24
    Finality, 946
    by NHTSA, 638-43
    NHTSA rules for, 619-20
    by OMB, 554, 555-57, 685
    OMB rules for, 624

Regulatory review of, 685
Specific cases, 627-39, 638-43

Haddon, William, 361-64, 367-68, 415, 423, 503
Hart, H.L.A., 111, 160
Hearings (Administrative). *See* Agency
    (Adjudication), Implementation
    (Adjudication)
Hearings (Legislative). *See* Congress (Oversight)
Henry II, King of England, 24
House of Representatives. *See* Congress, Legislation
Hybrid rulemaking, 875, 884-85

Iacocca, Lee, 374-77
Imaginative reconstruction. *See* Statutory
    interpretation
Implementation (of statutes)
    Generally, 435-36, 466-71
    Adjudication, 576-618
    Failure to act, 406, 859-60, 921-32, 934-45
    Guidance, 618-43
    Obligation to act, 361-67
    Petition (for review of agency action), 362,
        371, 471-76
    Rulemaking (generally) (*See also* Rulemaking,
        separate heading), 41-42, 359-60,
        399-400, 436-40, 466-69
    Sanctions. *See* Agency (Enforcement),
        National Highway Traffic and Safety
        Admin. (Enforcement), Recalls
    Tools (techniques)
        Economic analysis (*See also* Cost-benefit
            analysis, Risk), 525-70
        Political analysis (*See also* Politics, Statutory
            interpretation), 570-76
        Scientific analysis (*See also* Risk assessment),
            497-525
        Statutory analysis (*See also* Legislation,
            Statutory interpretation), 471-97
In pari materia. *See* Statutory interpretation
Independent Agency. *See* Agency
Independent counsel, 657-67, 668, 671
Informal adjudication. *See* Administrative
        Procedure Act
Informal rulemaking. *See* Rulemaking
Information Asymmetry. *See* Market Failure
Institutional competence (comparative), 26
Intentionalism. *See* Statutory interpretation
Interest groups (*See also* Ex parte contacts, Politics)
    Common law and, 26-27
    Drafting, role in, 48-50, 69-75
    Legislation, 40, 48-50, 57-58, 69-75, 81, 132,
        134, 140, 157, 230, 333, 336, 339
    Legislative veto, 743-44
    Oversight, 140
    Presidential control and, 683
    Regulation, 462-65, 505, 561-62, 570, 727,
        879-80, 902
    Standing, 932-33

Interpretation. *See* Chevron doctrine, Statutory interpretation.
Introduction of legislation. *See* Legislation.

Judicial behavior, 872-74
Judicial review (of agency action) (*See also* Administrative Procedure Act)
    Arbitrary and capricious standard, 372, 403-19, 420-21, 468-69, 590, 600, 803-04, 846-91, 920
    Availability of, 920-46
    Chevron doctrine (*See also* separate heading), 762-823
    Ex parte contacts, 698-99, 897-903
    Fact-finding (by agency), 903-20
    Finality, 946
    Logical outgrowth test, 439, 891-96
    of Motor vehicle safety standards, 362, 381-94, 403-18
    Notice requirement, 891-96
    Petition for, 362, 371, 472-76
    of Procedures (by agency), 874-903
    Reviewability, 846-52, 934-45
    Rescission (of rules or precedent), 405-07, 416, 855-72
    Ripeness, 945
    of Rulemaking procedures, 874-96
    Standing, 920-34
    Substantial evidence standard, 903-20
    of Statutory interpretation by agency. *See* Chevron doctrine
    Timing, 945-46

Lakoff, George, 193-94
Last Antecedent. *See* Statutory interpretation
Law. *See* Common Law, Constitution, Legislation, Regulation
Legal Process School, 155, 277, 323, 328-36, 496-97, 500-01, 838-41
Legal Realism, 276-77
Legislation (*See also* Regulation)
    Generally, 45-53, 359, 466
    Ambiguity of, 72-76, 108, 122-23, 254-55
    Automatic, 56
    Clarity. *See* Ambiguity, this heading and separate heading
    Committees (in Congress, generally), 48-56
    Common law (contrasted), 24-27
    Committee Reports,
        Generally, 50, 153, 285-87, 305, 309, 344-46, 347, 841
        Specific examples, 99-106, 150, 158-59, 179-80, 185, 187, 293-94, 297, 300, 317, 334, 392, 585, 772, 906
    Conference Committees, 53, 71-72, 304
    Constitutional rules for, 46
    Control of agencies by. *See* Congress
    Counsel. *See* Legislative counsel, this heading

Creation of agencies. *See* Organic statutes, this heading
Cycling and, 58-59
Defined terms (*See also* Definition, separate heading), 62, 107-08
Delegation by. *See* Delegation, separate heading
Drafting, 45-50, 60-76, 106-110, 203, 227-28, 254-55, 265, 266, 268, 277-78, 282-84, 288, 304, 349, 393, 801, 883
Emergency, 55-56
Floor procedures, 50-53, 71-72
Implementation provisions, 109-11, 359-60
Interest groups (*See also* Interest groups, separate heading), 40, 48-50, 57-60, 69-75, 81, 132, 134, 140, 157, 230, 333, 336, 339
Introduction of (in Congress), 46-48
Joint resolution, 56, 83, 214-15, 398, 718-19, 721, 745, 754-56, 758-60, 761
Legislative counsel (*See also* Drafting, this heading), 60, 68-69, 70, 75-76, 285, 349
Legislative Process, 45-53
Lenity, rule of, 166-74, 230-42
Lobbyists. *See* Interest groups, this heading and separate heading
Omnibus, 54-55, 75, 139, 721
Operative provisions (generally), 108-09, 110-11
Organic,
    Generally, 24, 493, 567, 700, 846, 885
    Motor Vehicle Safety Act, 82-106
Origin of, 46-48
Positive political theory and, 56-57, 59-60, 130-35, 306
Preemption by, 98, 109-12, 265-66
President, role in, 47-49
Process (in Congress), 45-53
Reports. *See* Committee Reports
Structure, generally, 106-113
Subsequent legislation (effects of), 297, 309-22, 350-57, 586, 780-81, 791-806, 995
Title, 106-07
Theories, 57-60
Transitive vs. intransitive, 123, 141-42
Unorthodox, 53-57, 135
Legislative Control. *See* Agency, Congress
Legislative History (*See also* Ambiguity, Legislation, Statutory interpretation)
    Generally, 179-80, 185-87, 285-309
    Committee Reports, 158-59, 286-87, 344-35
    Conference Committees (*See also* Congress), 47, 53-54, 69-72, 285-86, 302-04, 306, 349, 721
    Floor statements, 288
    Hearings, 287-88

Motor Vehicle Safety Act. *See* separate heading
Sponsor Statements, 286-87
Statutory interpretation
    by Agencies, 99-106, 175-89
    by Courts, 158-59, 285-309, 342-50
Legislative Process. *See* Congress, Legislation
Legislative veto, 394-96, 398, 728-45
Lobbyists. *See* Congress, Interest groups, Legislation

Mandatory use laws, 424-28
Market Failure
    Generally, 32-35
    Airbags and, 27-30
    Collective action and, 34-37
    Discrimination and, 37-38
    Externalities, 32, 34
    Free riders, 34-35
    Future generations, 38-39
    Information asymmetry, 32-33, 34
    Monopoly, 33-34
    Natural monopoly, 33-34
    Public goods, 32, 34-35
    as Rationale for regulation, 27-30, 31-35
    Rents, 30
    Spillovers. *See* Externalities, this heading
Mass marketing, 4-10
Motor vehicle fuel economy. *See* Fuel Economy
Motor vehicle safety (*See also* Motor Vehicle
    Safety Act, National Highway Traffic and
    Safety Admin.)
    Generally, 1-3, 14-15, 39, 99-102, 367, 372,
        403-04, 428-31, 442-44
    Airbags
        History, 368, 442-44
        Information asymmetry, 27-30
        Passive restraint standard, 368, 382-86,
            400-02, 403-18, 419-28, 445-46,
            498-504, 854-55
    Common law, 1-3, 6-24
    Congress, role of, 77-82, 394-400
    Consumer attitudes, 14, 23, 27-30, 103, 405,
        414, 445-47, 456-59, 363, 422, 462-63,
        528, 589, 603, 607-11, 635, 713
    Cost-benefit analysis of, 15-24, 526-44
    Crash tests, 368-73, 386-93, 498-500, 501-03
    Executive procurement standards, 77-78
    Ford Motor Co., 15-24, 374-77
    General Motors Corp., 79-82, 388, 411, 428-31,
        471-76, 602-03, 639-43
    Ignition interlock, 394-400, 407-14, 420,
        442-43, 445, 457
    Mandatory use laws, 424-28
    Nader, Ralph, and, 30, 78-82, 366, 369, 375-78,
        366, 381, 423, 453-54, 536
    Passive restraints. *See* Airbags, Seat Belts, this
        heading and separate headings
    President, role in, 79, 373-81, 396-99, 423-24
    Public attitudes toward, 394-400, 397,
        411-14, 456-58

Recalls, 90-94, 103-04, 418, 577, 601-18, 712,
    723-24, 855
Seat belts
    History, 361-63, 368, 442-44
    Passive restraint standard, 368-71,
        382-86, 394-402, 403-18, 419-28,
        444-65, 498-504
    Release from, 458
    Standard 208. *See* Motor Vehicle Safety Act
Motor Vehicle Safety Act (*See also* Motor vehicle
    safety, National Highway Traffic and Safety
    Admin.)
    Background, 76-82
    Committee Report, 99-106, 158-59,
        371, 384-85
    Consumer attitudes, 14, 23, 27-30, 103, 405,
        414, 445-47, 456-59, 363, 422, 462-63,
        528, 589, 603, 607-11, 635, 713
    Implementation of, 104-05, 359-433, 440-65
    Interpretation of, 106, 158-59, 381-94
    Legislative history, 99-106, 158-59, 384-88
    Passive restraint standard, 361-428, 444-65
    Politics of, 77-82, 394-99, 415, 417-19,
        423-24, 853-54
    Preemption by, 84, 105
    Rabbit/Chevette study, 412, 452-56, 459,
        509, 523
    Recalls, 90-94, 103-04, 418, 577, 601-18, 712,
        723-24, 855
    Regulations enforcing
        Generally, 361-64, 366-69, 371-73,
            422-24, 427-28
        Specific cases, 364-66, 368-71, 399,
            400-02, 403, 419-22, 424-27,
            444-65, 476-77, 498-500, 501-03, 536-43
    Specificity of, 102, 122
    Standard 208. *See* Regulations enforcing, this
        heading
    Technology forcing, 102-03, 145-46, 159,
        384-86, 393, 410, 458-60
    Text, 82-98, 441-42
    Tires and tire pressure, 96-97, 527-44, 530,
        535, 539, 543

Nader, Ralph, 30, 78-82, 366, 369, 375-78, 366,
    381, 423, 536
National Environmental Policy Act, 448, 449,
    467, 727
National Highway Traffic and Safety
    Administration (NHTSA) (*See also* Motor
    vehicle safety, Motor Vehicle Safety Act)
    Complaint handling, 601-14
    Counsel (for litigation and enforcement)
        591-600, 638-43, 648
    Crash tests, 373
    Enforcement (*See also* Recalls, this heading),
        476-78, 483, 591-601
    Fuel economy standards, 447, 456, 460,
        472-76, 503, 549, 553-56, 743-44

NHTSA (*cont.*)
    Guidance, 619-20, 629-43
    Interpretation, 638-43
    Office of Information and Regulatory Aff.
        and, 527-44
    ODI, 601-18
    Passive restraint standard, 361-428, 444-65
    Recalls, 90-94, 103-04, 418, 577, 601-18, 712,
        723-24, 855
    Reporting requirement, 95, 718
    Rulemaking by, 360-433, 444-65, 472-75,
        476-77, 498-500, 501-03, 536-43,
        553-55
    Standard 208. *See* Passive restraint standard
    Statutory authority, 94
    Structure (of agency), 617
    Tire pressure standard, 96-97, 527-44, 530,
        535, 539, 543
National Labor Relations Board (NLRB), 25,
    578-90, 872-74
National Traffic and Motor Vehicle Safety Act.
    See Motor Vehicle Safety Act
Nautical interpretation. *See* Statutory
    interpretation
New Deal, 31
Nixon, Richard, 368, 373-81
Nondelegation doctrine. *See* Delegation
Noscitur a Sociis. *See* Statutory interpretation
Notice and comment rulemaking. *See* Rulemaking
Notice of Proposed Rulemaking (NPRM). *See*
    Rulemaking

Obama, Barack, 624, 685
Obligation to act (*See also* Agency), 361-67
Occupational Health and Safety Administration
    (OSHA), 111, 559, 564-65, 619, 706-10
Office of Information and Regulatory Affairs
    (OIRA) (*See also* Cost-benefit analysis)
    Controversy regarding, 564-66, 710-12, 714
    Cost-benefit analysis, use of, 694-97, 714
    Ex parte contacts, 698-99
    Executive Order 12,866 (regulatory review),
        686-701
    Motor vehicle safety, 527-44
    Planning, 691-93
    President and, 686-701, 714-16
    Prompt letters, 437-38, 703-10, 712-14
    Regulatory review, 437-38, 526-36, 685-714
    Return letters, 527-36, 543, 702-03
Office of Management and Budget (OMB)
    (*See also* Office of Information and
    Regulatory Aff.)
    Budget control, 681-86, 751-52
    Circular A-4, 31-35, 554, 555-57
    Cost-benefit guideline, 31-35, 550-58, 565
    Environmental policy (assessment), 559
    Guidance practices guideline, 624-26
    Motor vehicle safety, 536
    Regulatory review, 31-35, 550-52, 565

Resource Management Offices (RMO),
    682-84
Risk assessment guidelines, 516
Orders. *See* Adjudication, Agency
Oversight (*See also* Congress), 140, 491-92,
    602-05, 626, 723-27, 729, 863
Overton Park, 846

Paperwork Reduction Act, 467, 695
Passive restraint standard (*See also* Motor
    vehicle safety, Motor Vehicle Safety Act,
    National Highway and Traffic Safety Adm.),
    361-428, 444-65
Paternalism (*See also* Regulation), 28-29,
    38-39, 397-98
Patient Protection and Affordable Care Act,
    215-30, 806-07
People. *See* Consumers, Interest Groups
Petition (for review of agency action,
    generally) (*See also* Judicial review), 371,
    472-76, 571-73
Pinto (car), 15-24, 375
Plain meaning rule. *See* Statutory interpretation
Politics (*See also* Accountability, Interest groups,
    Political Appointees)
    Agencies and, 570-76
    Common law, 26-27
    Delegation, 130-35
    Drafting (of statutes), 48-50
    of Motor Vehicle Safety Act, 76-82
    of Motor vehicle safety regulation,
        359-433, 440-65
    of Regulation generally, 39-40, 415, 417,
        418-19, 570-76, 853-54
Porter, Cole, 5
Powers. *See* Agencies, Congress, Constitution,
    President
Practical reasoning. *See* Statutory interpretation
Precedent
    Agency adjudication, 855-72
    Agency regulations, 818-20, 855-72
    Common law, 9-10, 23
    Guidance, 643
    in Judicial review of agency regulations,
        738-43, 817-20, 834-36
    Statutory interpretation, 643
Preemption (of state law) (*See also* Federalism,
    Statutory interpretation), 98,
    109-12, 265-66
President (*See also* Executive branch, Executive
    control, Office of Information and
    Regulatory Aff., Office of Management and
    Budget, Politics)
    Generally, 645-47, 666
    Accountability of, 682-84, 710-12, 750
    Appointments by. 679-81
    Appropriations and, 681-85
    Control of administrative agencies, 478,
        571-73, 645-716

Counsel (and Office of Legal Counsel), 43, 327, 374, 423, 686, 716
Directives, 714-16
Executive orders
Generally, 31, 417, 686-88
Executive order 12,866 (cost benefit), 478, 578, 647-83, 685-701
Executive privilege, 726-27
Independent Agencies (control), 690-91, 761
Legislation, role in, 47-49
Legislative veto and, 398, 728-45
Motor vehicle safety, role in, 79, 373-81, 396-99, 423-24
Office of Management and Budget (OMB), 31-35, 516, 550-54, 565, 624-36, 681-86, 751-52
Regulatory review, 437-34, 527-36, 543, 564-66, 685-714
Resource Management Offices, 682-84
Removal (of agency officials), 647-81
Signing statements, 288, 396-99
Presidential control (of agencies). *See* Agency, President
Privity, 4-16
Public choice theory, 57-59, 81, 135, 327
Purposivism. *See* Statutory interpretation

Rabbit/Chevette study (*See also* Motor Vehicle Safety Act), 412, 452-56, 459, 509, 523
Rationale for regulation. *See* Regulation
Reagan, Ronald, 402, 417, 444, 465, 571
Recalls (*See also* Adjudication, National Highway Traffic and Safety Adm.), 90-94, 103-04, 418, 577, 601-18, 712, 723-24, 855
Refusal to act (by agency), 406, 571-76, 859-60, 921-32, 934-45
Regulation (*See also* Regulatory Analysis, Rulemaking, Statutes)
Common law, compared to, 24-27
Cost-benefit analysis of. *See* Cost benefit analysis, separate heading
Judicial review of. *See* Judicial review, separate heading
Planning, 432-33
Rationale for
Generally, 31-39, 416
Collective desires, 35-37
Common law, limitations of, 1-30
Discrimination, 37-39
Equality, 37-39
Future generations, 38-39
Market failure, 27-30, 32-35
Paternalism, 28-29, 38-39, 397-98
Public goods, 34-35
Redistribution (*See also* equality, this heading
Social equality. *See* equality, this heading

Review of (*See also* Judicial review, separate heading)
Rulemaking. *See* Rulemaking, separate heading
Regulatory Accountability Act, 823
Regulatory Flexibility Act, 448-49, 467, 695, 702-03, 748
Regulatory review (*See also* Cost-benefit analysis, Office of Information and Regulatory Aff.)
Generally, 685-86
Background of, 685
Cost-benefit analysis (*See also* Cost-benefit, separate heading), 554-570, 693-700
Executive order 12,866, 686-701
Office of Information and Regulatory Aff. (*See also* separate heading), 689-91
Planning, 691-93
President (*See also* separate heading), 685-86, 689, 700-01, 710-11
Prompt letters, 703-10, 712-14
Rationale, 687-88
Return letters, 527-36, 702-03
Removal (of agency officials) (*See also* Agency, Civil service, President)
by Agency, 669-79
by Congress, 647-52, 660, 750-62
by Judges, 657-67
by President, 647-56, 669-81
Rents. *See* Market Failure
Representation. *See* Accountability
Rescission (of regulation), 402-19, 420-21, 444-65, 852-55, 859-60
Resource Management Offices (RMO), 682-84
Ripeness, 945
Risk assessment, 29, 458-60, 498-501, 506-23, 546-49, 557, 565-69, 603-05, 687, 692-93, 711
Rulemaking (*See also* Implementation, Regulation)
Generally, 41-42, 360, 399-400, 466-69
Cost-benefit analysis. *See* separate heading
Ex parte contacts, 698-99, 897-903
Failure to act (by agency), 406, 859-60, 921-32, 934-45
Fuel Economy standards. *See* Fuel economy, National Highway Traffic and Safety Adm., separate headings
Good cause exception, 399
Hearings, 423, 877-85
Interim final rule, 440, 498-301, 591
Judicial review of. *See* Judicial review, separate heading
Motor vehicle safety standards. *See* Motor Vehicle Safety Act, National Highway and Traffic Safety Adm., separate headings
National Environmental Policy Act, 448, 449, 467, 727

Rulemaking (*cont.*)
  Notice and comment procedure, 372, 399, 436-440
  Notice of proposed rulemaking (NPRM)
    Generally, 360, 366, 371, 438-39, 449, 465
    Specific examples of, 403, 419-22, 444-49
  Obligation to act (by agency), 361-67
  Passive restraint standard (*See also* Motor Vehicle Safety Act, separate heading), 361-428, 444-65
  Regulatory Flexibility Act, 448, 449, 467, 695, 702-03, 727, 748
  Rescission, 405-06, 439
  Rules, specific examples of, 364-66, 368-71, 399, 400-02, 403, 424-27, 449-64, 498-500, 501-03, 536-44, 553-55
  Statement of basis and purpose
    Generally, 366-67, 427, 439, 468-69
    Specific examples of, 364-66, 368-70, 399, 400-02, 424-27, 444-64
  Supplemental notice of proposed rulemaking, 424, 439, 469, 473, 703
  Unfunded Mandates Act, 467, 529, 749
Rules. *See* Rulemaking

Scientific analysis (by agency)
  Generally, 497-525
  Charade. *See* Misuse, this heading
  Epidemiology, 512-13
  Limitations of, 511-19
  Misuse, 516-25
  Obama memo, 524-25
  in Passive restraint rule, 412, 452-56, 458-60, 498-501, 459, 509-10, 523
  Risk assessment, 29, 458-60, 498-501, 506-23, 546-49, 557, 565-69, 603-05, 687, 692-93, 711
  Toxicology, 511-12
  Trans-science, 517, 523
Schoolhouse Rock, 45-46, 53
Scrivener's error. *See* Statutory interpretation
Securities Exchange Comm. (SEC), 241-42, 638, 669-79
Senate. *See* Congress, Legislation
Separation of powers (*See also* Constitution)
  Agency interpretation of regulations, 824-41
  Appointment and removal, 647-79, 750-62
  Auer doctrine, 824-41
  Delegation (*See also* Delegation, separate heading), 122-43
  Legislative veto, 398, 728-45
  Separation of Powers Restoration Act. *See* Chevron doctrine
  Statutory interpretation and, 328, 346
Separation of Powers Restoration Act, 823
Sherman Antitrust Act, 112-13
Skidmore doctrine. *See* Chevron doctrine
Social Choice Theory, 58-59
South Park, 638

Spillover. *See* Market Failure
Standard 208. *See* Motor Vehicle Safety Act, National Highway and Traffic Safety Adm.
Standards of review. *See* Judicial review
Standing (*See also* Judicial review), 920-34
State law
  Common law, 1-27
  Federalism, 11-12, 230-31, 255-66, 278, 282-83
  Motor Vehicle Safety Act and, 84, 98, 105-06, 424-28
  Preemption of, 98, 109-12, 265-66
Statement of basis and purpose. *See* Rulemaking
Statutes. *See* Legislation
Statutory implementation. *See* Implementation
Statutory interpretation (*See also* Implementation)
  Generally, 145-59, 322-57
  by Agency (*See also* Chevron doctrine) 175-89, 471-97
  Ambiguity, 122-23, 229-30, 254-55
  Appropriations bills, 308
  Committee Reports (*See also* Committee Reports, separate heading), 158-59, 286-87, 344-45
  Canons of construction (linguistic) (*See also* Substantive canons, this heading)
    Generally, 174-89, 215-30, 272-84
    Chevron doctrine (*See also* separate heading), 776
    Conjunctive vs. disjunctive, 198-99, 302
    Disjunctive, 198-99, 302
    Ejusdem generis, 183, 189-91, 193-94, 196, 203, 206-07, 278, 282, 494
    Expressio unius, 194, 203, 282-83, 278, 494
    Identical words, 204-06, 209-13, 312
    Inferences across statutes, 211-13, 288
    In pari materia, 209-13, 278, 312, 494
    Last antecedent, 196-98
    May vs. Shall, 199-200
    Noscitur a sociis, 183, 188, 190, 191-94, 203
    Ordinary meaning, 108, 148-49, 160-74, 334
    Plain meaning. *See* ordinary meaning
    Repeals by implication (presumption against), 213-14
    Scrivener's error, 174-75, 268-72, 341-42
    Surplusage, 62, 177, 188, 190, 199, 206-07, 222, 230, 282-83, 307
    Technical meaning, 160-74, 337-38, 839
    Text (as basis for interpretation), 152, 159-60, 289
    Title, 152-53, 207-08
    Whole act, 188-89, 203-08, 215-30
    Whole code, 208-15
  Changed circumstances, 309-22, 322-23, 350-57, 780-81, 873
  Congressional behavior and, 277-78, 303-08
  Clear statement rule. *See* Substantive canons, this heading
  Definitions (generally) (*See also* Definitions, separate heading), 63, 146, 160-74, 188, 200-03, 240, 280-81, 781

Dictionary Act, 200-03
Legislative history, 153-54, 189, 285-309,
    342-50, 475, 490-93
Legislation, subsequent, 309-22, 350-57,
    407-08, 586, 780-81, 791-806, 995
Linguistic canons. *See* Canons of construction,
    this heading
Ordinary meaning. *See* Canons of
    construction, this heading
Provisos, 208
Punctuation, 194-96
Scrivener's error, 174-75, 268-72, 341-42
Subsequent legislation. *See* Legislation,
    subsequent, this heading
Substantive canons (*See also* Canons of
    construction, this heading)
    Constitutional avoidance, 230-31,
        242-55, 264, 278, 488-89, 860, 871-72
    Extraterritorial application, 268
    Federalism, 111-12, 230-31, 255-66,
        278, 282-83
    Lenity, 166-74, 230-42
    Preemption (presumption against), 265-66
    Remedial purposes, 241-42, 267, 292-93
    Repeals by implication (presumption
        against), 213-15, 308, 799
    Retroactivity (presumption against), 266-67
Theories of interpretation
    Generally, 146, 322-23
    Dynamic, 157, 350-57
    Imaginative reconstruction, 156, 333-37
    Intentionalism, 153-54, 155, 324-33

Nautical, 350-57
Ordinary meaning, 108, 146, 149, 490,
    160-74, 177, 182-84, 226, 232-34, 271,
    337, 341, 582, 773
Plain meaning. *See* Ordinary meaning
Purposivism, 153, 155-56, 306-07,
    328-33, 337, 341, 493-97
Textualism, 156-57, 337-50
Title, 152-53

Technical meaning. *See* Statutory interpretation,
    Canons of construction, subheading
Telephone Consumer Protection Act, 114-15
Textualism. *See* Statutory interpretation
Titles (of statutes) (*See also* Statutory
    interpretation), 152-53
Tort (common law), 1-24
Transportation, Department of. *See* National
    Highway Traffic and Safety Adm.
Tradeoffs. *See* Cost-benefit analysis
Transitive statutes, 123, 141-42
Trump, Donald, 371, 416, 680, 685-86
Truth in Lending Act, 113

Uneeda biscuits, 5
Unfunded Mandates Act, 467, 529, 749
Unitary executive theory, 647-51, 666

Vermont Yankee Nuclear Power Plant, 876
Veto, Legislative. *See* Legislative veto
Vetogates, 56-57
Volpe, John, 374, 377-81, 423, 852, 995